D A

MAINE

MINN.

Lake Superior

Duluth

Sault Ste. Marie

VT. Montpelier · Augusta

· Portland

Burlington

Concord

WIS.

L. Huron

MICH.

N.Y.

· Boston

MASS.

Boston

eapolis · St. Paul

St. Paul

L. Michigan

Lansing

Detroit

L. Ontario

Rochester Albany

Buffalo

Ho

R.I.

N.H.

IOWA Madison

Sioux Falls

Milwaukee

L. Erie

PA. Scranton

N. New York

T. N.J.

Chicago

Cleve-land

Pittsburgh

Philadelphia

Sioux City

ILL.

Gary

IND.

OHIO

Harrisburg

W.

Atlantic City

Des Moines

Indianapolis

Columbus

MD. B.

Dover

MO.

Springfield

Cincinnati

W. VA.

A.

Washington

Lincoln

Kansas City

E. St. Louis

KY.

VA.

Norfolk

A.-Annapolis

eka

St. Louis

Louisville

Frankfort Charleston

Richmond

N.C.

B.-Baltimore

W.-Wilmington

Cairo

Knoxville

Charlotte

Raleigh

T.-Trenton

N.-Newark

TENN.

N.H.-New Haven

Tulsa

ARK.

Nashville

S.C.

H.-Hartford

Memphis

Chattanooga

Columbia

S.-Springfield

P.-Providence

KLA.

Little Rock

Huntsville

MISS. ALA.

Atlanta

Charleston

Atlantic

Birmingham

GA.

Dallas

Jackson

Montgomery

Savannah

LA.

Selma

Ocean

Jacksonville

Tallahassee

FLA.

New Orleans

Gulf of Mexico

Cape Kennedy

Houston

Tampa

Miami

KAUAI

sville

NIIHAU

OAHU

MOLOKAI

Honolulu

MAUI

Pacific

HAWAII

HAWAII

Ocean

Hilo

N

MILES

0   50   100   200

THE
MEGASTATES
OF AMERICA

By Neal R. Peirce
The People's President

THE

MEGASTATES

OF AMERICA

People, Politics, and Power

in the Ten Great States

NEAL R. PEIRCE

W · W · NORTON & COMPANY · INC ·
NEW YORK

FIRST EDITION

Library of Congress Cataloging in Publication Data

Peirce, Neal R
    The megastates of America.

    CONTENTS. New York; still the seat of Empire.—
Massachusetts; a golden age?—New Jersey; in the shadows
of Megalopolis. [etc.]
    1. State governments. 2. U. S.—Economic condi-
tions—1961– 3. U. S.—Social conditions—1960–
I. Title.
JK2408.P43   917.3'03'92   70–163375
ISBN 0–393–05458–6

1 2 3 4 5 6 7 8 9 0

CONTENTS

FOREWORD

THIS IS A BOOK ABOUT AMERICA, its 10 greatest states where more than half the people live. It is written to let Americans (and foreigners too) know something of the profound diversity of peoples and life styles and geographic habitat and political behavior that make this the most fascinating nation on earth.

Only one book like this has been written before, and it inspired this one: John Gunther's *Inside U.S.A.*, researched during World War II and published in 1947. Gunther was the first man in U.S. history to visit each of the states and then to give a good and true account of the American condition as he found it. But his book is a quarter of a century old; it was written before the fantastic economic and population growth of the postwar era, growth that has transformed the face of this land and altered the life of its people and lifted us to heights of glory and depths of national despair beyond our wildest past dreams. Before he died, I consulted John Gunther about a new book. He recognized its need, and gave me, as he put it, his "good luck signal."

But why this volume about the megastates? The first reason is that I found America today simply too vast, too complex to fit in a single volume. So I decided to concentrate first on the 10 most heavily populated states—California through Massachusetts—where so much of the essential action is in the U.S.A. today. This volume will be followed by publication of regional volumes completing the story of all 50 states.

A second reason is that the megastates make sense, seen as an entity. Indeed, the United States is dividing into new sections, 10 states versus 40. The 10, and especially the great metropolitan areas within them, dominate every aspect of American life. Fifty-five percent of the American people—111,422,366 in the 1970 Census—live in these 10 states. Scattered from one seacoast to the other, they are nonetheless tied together by bonds of economics, culture, and attitude as strong as any geographic area. They account for 62 percent of the manufacturing, 60 percent of the bank assets, 59 percent of the personal income, and 60 percent of state and local government spending. They are the home of the vast majority of powerful corporations, prestigious universities, centers of advanced thinking, capitals of the arts. Here are the great cities, which with their suburban hinterlands symbolize both the glories and abominations of the U.S.A. today: the troubled megacity of New York, the ultimate sprawl in Los Angeles, muscular Chicago, mellow Philadelphia, dying Detroit, swinging San Francisco, revived Boston, frenetically growing Houston and Dallas. For better or for worse, the future of these cities and their states is the future of America.

In immediate political terms, the megastates are important too. In 1968, they cast 56 percent of the popular vote for President. When they have been unified, they have never failed to decide a Presidential election; in fact, their combined electoral strength is only 11 votes short of an electoral college majority. Almost all of them are marginal politically, fiercely contested in each election. They showed their metropolitan-urban bias by giving Hubert Humphrey a plurality of 783,672 votes in 1968, while the smaller 40 states (preponderantly Southern, Plains, and Rocky Mountain states) registered a plurality for Richard Nixon of 1,293,987.* But the Republicans could scarcely overlook the megastates: they gave Nixon 57 percent of the popular vote he received nationally, and 123 electoral votes. The loss of just one megastate— California—would have deprived Nixon of his electoral vote majority.

Now a word about method. Like John Gunther, I traveled to each state of the Union (now 50 as opposed to the 48 that confronted him). I talked with about 1,000 men and women—governors, Senators, Congressmen, mayors, state and local officials, editors and reporters, business and labor leaders, public opinion analysts, clergymen, university presidents and professors, leaders of the Indian, black, and Spanish-speaking communities, and just plain people. Some of the people I talked with were famous, others obscure, almost all helpful.

My travel plan proceeded fairly systematically by region—the South first (because it was winter when I started), then the West, Midwest, and finally Eastern America. I went by plane, then rented cars, made a personal inspection of almost every great city, and must have walked several hundred miles in the process too, insanely lugging a briefcase full of notes and a tape recorder into the unlikeliest places. Perhaps the most difficult part of all was the logistics. Usually, I got names of suggested interviewees from my newspaper friends and other contacts in new states and cities and sent letters ahead saying I would like to see the people. Then the first half day or more in a new city would be a wild confusion of telephone calls, trying to fit in the maximum feasible number of interviews, getting everything set up for as many as six interviews in a day, and then suddenly having the governor's press secretary phone back and change an appointment time, so that the whole schedule juggling process would have to start over again. Rare were the interviews that

---

* The figures break down this way:

	NIXON VOTE	HUMPHREY VOTE	WALLACE VOTE
Megastates	18,109,025 (44.1%)	18,892,697 (46.1%)	3,972,915 (9.6%)
Smaller 40 + D.C.	13,676,455 (42.7%)	12,382,468 (38.7%)	5,933,558 (18.5%)
Total U.S.	31,785,480 (43.6%)	31,275,165 (42.9%)	9,906,473 (13.6%)

The megastates that gave Nixon their electoral votes were California, Florida, Illinois, Ohio, and New Jersey. Humphrey carried Massachusetts, Michigan, New York, Pennsylvania, and Texas.

didn't turn out to be fascinating in their own way; the best ones were dinner appointments, where the good talk might stretch into the late evening hours. Then it would be back to the hotel room for one to three hours of checking tapes for sections of interviews where my notes weren't clear enough. The interviewing period ranged from two days in some of the smallest states to a full month in California.

Altogether, the travel to 50 states took about a year and a half, starting in 1969; the writing of this particular volume took 12 months of 15-hour days. Always there would be unanswered questions, and I am looking forward to a post-book life when the monthly long distance telephone bill won't be $100 or more. The writing was complicated by the need to review hundreds of books and thousands of articles and newspaper clippings I had assembled over time; sometimes the floor of the study in my Washington home looked as if a paper blizzard had hit. And then each state manuscript, after it had been read and commented upon by experts on the state (often senior political reporters), and after last-minute developments in each state had been noted, had to be revised in part to make it ready for final typing.

Amid the confusion I tried to keep my eye on the enduring, vital questions about each state and its great cities:

What sets it (the state or city) apart from the rest of America?
What is its essential character?
What kind of a place is it to live in?
What does it look like, how clean or polluted is it, what are the interesting communities?
Who holds the power?
Which are the great corporations, unions, universities, and newspapers, and what role do they play in their city and state?
Which are the major ethnic groups, and what is their influence?
How did the politics evolve to where they are today, and what is the outlook for the 1970s?
How creatively have the governments and power structures served the people?
Who are the great leaders of today—and perhaps tomorrow?

For whom, then, is this book written? I mean the individual chapters to be of interest to people who live in the various states and cities, to help them see their home area in a national context. I write for businessmen, students, and tourists planning to visit or move into a state, and who are interested in what makes it tick—the kind of things no guidebook will tell them. I write for politicians planning national campaigns, for academicians, for all those curious about the American condition in our time. From the start, I knew it was presumptuous for any one person to try to encompass such a broad canvass. But a unity of view, to make true comparisons between cities and states, is essential. And since no one else had tried the task for a quarter of a century, I decided to try—keeping in mind the same goal Gunther set for *Inside U.S.A.*—a book whose "central spine and substance is an effort—in all diffidence—to show this most fabulous and least known of countries, the United States of America, to itself."

A word of caution: many books about the present-day American condition are preoccupied with illustrating fundamental sickness in our society, while others are paeans of praise. This book is neither. It states many of the deep-seated problems, from perils to the environment to the abuse of power by selfish groups. But the account of the state and city civilizations also includes hundreds of instances of greatness, of noble and disinterested public service. The primary job of this book is descriptive, to show the multitudinous strands of life in our times, admitting their frequently contradictory directions, and tying them together analytically only where the evidence is clear. The ultimate "verdict" on these great states and cities must rest with the reader himself.

We start with the metropolitan East and its heart in New York where, despite every crisis of recent years, the economic heart of America still beats, and where Nelson Rockefeller, the most remarkable and innovative of the postwar governors, still reigns. Then there is Massachusetts, throwing off the vestiges of century-old ethnic conflict and enjoying a remarkable scientific-intellectual-economic renaissance in our times. New Jersey we find obscured in the megalapolitan shadows, bereft of image, ultimate suburbia, shaking off the shackles of official corruption. Next-door Pennsylvania shows a rebirth of cities but the quandaries of an outmoded, heavy industry economy in a techno-electronic age.

From there, it is out across the Midwest: Ohio, still personification of middle-class America; Illinois, the economic capital of the heartland and home of America's most enduring big-city political machine; and Michigan, home of the auto behemoths and the remarkable United Auto Workers, the country's most activist labor union.

We then drop down to Florida, the sunshine state only recently risen to the first population ranks (it was only 20th in 1950), a remarkable mixture of tourism, old folks' culture, and rambunctious growth. Half a continent to the west is Texas, the state of oil and petrochemicals, of Lyndon Johnson and the equally remarkable John Connally, that state in all the 50 where economic power is most closely equated with the political, and where struggling Mexican-American and black minorities may pose deep challenges to the establishment in the 1970s. Finally, there is California, the great nation-state, the new state of ultimate political power in America because it now has more people than any other, the state of the slurb and aerospace, Berkeley and new life styles, Ronald Reagan and César Chávez. And there, looking to the Pacific and the world of our future, the book will end.

THE

MEGASTATES

OF AMERICA

NEW YORK

STILL THE "SEAT OF EMPIRE"

I. THE STATEWIDE SCENE

BEFITTING ITS SOBRIQUET OF EMPIRE STATE, New York is a place of many civilizations.

It is New York City, that perpetually fascinating, pain-plagued Colossus on the Hudson, one of the greatest cities of earth, our continent's center of finance, arts, crime, and municipal paralysis.

It is the state of bustling but obscure upstate cities—Buffalo, Rochester, Syracuse, Albany, Schenectady, et al.

It is a state of natural grandeur: the beautiful valley of the Hudson, Adirondack and Catskill mountains, of millions of acres of placid farmland, and woods and lakes.

It is the home of Westchester, America's senior suburb, and of Long Island, where a slapdash suburban civilization has been superimposed upon an ancient vacation retreat and farming-fishing economy.

It is the state of America's senior and most distinguished governor, Nel-

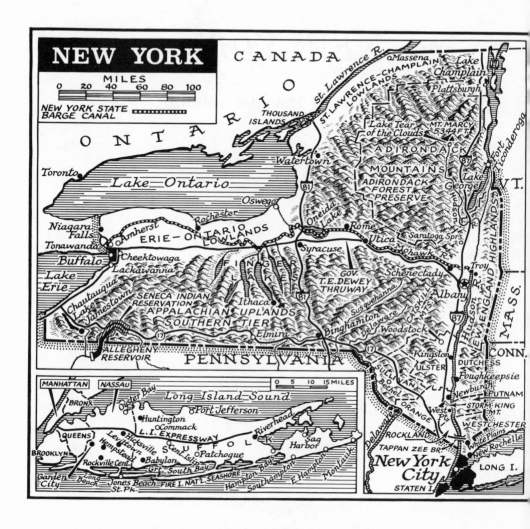

son A. Rockefeller, now in his fourth four-year term, who for all his false starts and foibles must be considered one of the most creative chief executives any state of America has ever had.

It is a state that has pioneered, in area after area, in innovative methods of government, a shining example of federalism in action.

It is a state now spending and living beyond its means.

It is the state where greed and selfishness of self-centered groups threaten to undermine the community of consent by which free peoples live.

It is a state now strangely in the shadows, doubted and mistrusted by the rest of the nation.

But still, it is the state of financial power and cultural distinction beyond all others.

Geography almost ordained that it would be so. Fifty million years ago the Hudson gnawed its way from the Great Lakes across the highlands of upper New York State to the sea. Forty million years later it carved a gigantic gorge and its waters cascaded for 36 miles down off the coastal plain into the great valley of the Atlantic basin. (From the air on a clear day, it is still possible to see that old gorge of the Hudson as the river streams out into the ocean and disappears, finally, into the depths off the Continental Shelf.) The ice came some 20,000 to 25,000 years ago, shaping and smoothing the hills of Manhattan, making it the island we know today. And the ice, as it melted, filled and flattened the land and the great gorge of the river. It made the Hudson an estuary, subject to tidal action, as far as Albany, 150 miles upstream. Man could hardly have planned a more superb harbor than the one at the Hudson's mouth. And as European explorers came on the scene, they found an excellent means of access to the hinterland along the Hudson Valley, on its line northward past Albany and into the Adirondacks, and the connection near Albany to the Mohawk River Valley and then the flatlands of the Lake Ontario Plain all the way out to Buffalo and Lake Erie—the chief natural highway into the interior of the continent. This incomparable "water level route" was exploited first by boat and barge, then by rail and highway connections, to capitalize on New York's unique status as the only American state that faces both the Atlantic Ocean and the Great Lakes.

From the time of Henry Hudson's first exploration in 1609, down through the development of the Dutch West India Company's Colony of New Netherland, Great Britain's arbitrary seizure in 1664 and up to the American Revolution more than a century later, New York developed slowly. But New York's strategic position made it an important battleground of the Revolutionary War, the scene of 92 of the 308 engagements in that conflict. In 1784, after a tour of the state's harbors, waterways, and fertile countryside, George Washington ventured the prediction that it would become the "seat of empire." Just at that time, changes were taking place to make his prediction come true. The back of Indian power was broken by a military campaign in 1779, making it possible to penetrate the wilderness in peace. Thousands of sturdy farm folk, despairing of ever making a good living on the thin, rocky soil of New England, were pouring into New York. The manorial system of colonial times was beginning to crack with sale of land to the new immigrants, a process accelerated by state laws restricting rights of inheritance in family-held land. The Yankee influx also had a profound political impact, transforming New York, as writer Seymour Freegood has noted, from "the most aristocratic of states [into] a mercantile-agrarian democracy."

New York City began to boom in the wake of the Revolution. Before, it had always been held back by the sparse population of its hinterland, the conservative ways of the Dutch merchants, and restrictive English trade laws. (It had, though, grown rich through government contracts and privateering during the French and Indian Wars, and while it lacked the population, trade, or culture of Philadelphia, it was the gayest of the colonial cities, number one in taverns, bawdyhouses, and the incidence of crime—a seeming constant in all subsequent development.) The War of 1812 slowed down development, but afterward the British dumped a large stock of textiles on the American market through the port of New York, and aggressive Yankee merchants closed in to make New York what it has been ever since, the textile center of the United States.

To become truly dominant, however, New York needed inexpensive access to the farm products and raw materials of interior New York and the Great Lakes. The obvious answer was water transportation, but the Mohawk was a largely unnavigable river. For 15 years, Gov. De Witt Clinton struggled against loud opposition and public derision to have the Erie Canal built to make possible barge transportation from the Hudson River to Lake Erie. Major engineering innovations and a then unprecedented $7 million investment went into the building of the 363-mile canal, but in 1825 the feat was completed and Clinton boarded a barge in Buffalo and traveled all the way to New York City by water, emptying a barrel of fresh water from Lake Erie into the Atlantic Ocean in a symbolic joining of the waters. Instantly, the cost of shipping a ton of freight from Buffalo to Albany dropped from $100 to $10. Within a few years, the little villages along the canal's route—Buffalo, Rochester, Syracuse, Rome, and Utica—had become important cities. To this day, the population of New York State remains thickly clustered along the Hudson Valley up to Albany, and then the Mohawk Valley westward toward Buffalo. Railroads took to the same route, and in the present generation, when the decision was made to build the New York State Thruway (since renamed the Gov. Thomas E. Dewey Thruway) from New York City to Buffalo, touching the major population centers of the state, it was no accident that a route was chosen which in large part parallels the Erie Canal.*

* Many feeder canals were built along the Erie, linking it with the centers of farm and industrial production and assuring New York City's destiny as a great port. With the coming of the railways, part of the canal fell into disuse, but early in this century the Barge Canal, following generally the old Erie route, was constructed. There are 36 locks on the canal between Buffalo and Albany, a distance in which the water level drops a total of 546 feet.

The People Story

When the first Census was taken in 1790, New York had 340,120 people and occupied a humble fifth ranking among the 13 states—behind Virginia (which then led with 691,737), Pennsylvania, North Carolina, and Massachusetts. A decade later, New York's population had almost doubled and it was third largest; by 1810 the state had almost three times as many people as it had had in 1790 and was first. For a century and a half, the state remained unchallenged as the nation's most heavily populated state. By 1840, it had 2.4 million people; by 1900, 7.3 million; by the eve of Pearl Harbor, 13.5 million. Sometime late in 1963, according to Census estimates, California overtook New York in population. The 1970 Census found 18,190,740 people in New York State, well below California's 19,953,134. But no other state seems likely to dislodge New York from second place—not in this century, anyway.

The traditional way of looking at New York population (and politics) has been in terms of New York City versus upstate—the latter a conglomerate of everything north of the Westchester County line, plus Long Island. The first half of this century was clearly the era of New York City dominance by this test. From less than 30 percent in 1830, the city's share of the state population rose to 52 percent in 1910. It peaked at 55 percent in 1930. By 1970, the figure was down to 43 percent, and it seems likely to continue dropping as the city's population (7,867,760 in 1970) remains about static (as it has since 1950) while the state as a whole continues to grow. The political consequences are even greater, since New York has a lower voting turnout than upstate. In 1946, the city still cast 51.5 percent of the statewide vote; by 1968, its vote was only 38.5 percent of the state total.

The postwar years, however, have introduced the new factor of heavy population in the suburbs. If one counts its entire metropolitan area, New York still represents 63 percent of the statewide total. But it is the breakdown between city, suburb, upstate, and then between metropolitan areas and small city-rural areas upstate, that tells the difference:

	1950 *Population*	1970 *Population*	% *Change*
New York City (5-borough total)	7,891,957	7,867,760	− 0.3
Suburbs (Nassau, Suffolk, Westchester, Rockland counties)	1,664,207	3,660,889	+120.0
Upstate Total	5,274,028	6,662,091	+ 26.3
Metropolitan areas	3,100,295	4,197,415	+ 35.4
Nonmetropolitan areas	2,173,733	2,464,676	+ 13.4
State Total	14,830,192	18,190,740	+ 22.6
As a percent of the U.S.A.	9.8%	9.0%	—

Up to 1820, most of New York's population was of English or Dutch extraction stock. Then began the great floods of European immigration, bringing five million immigrants into America, most of them by way of New York, between 1820 and 1860. The dominant groups were Irish, fleeing famine in their homeland, and Germans, seeking escape from political upheaval at home, or religious freedom, or both. A majority of the immigrants passed through, but many remained. Later in the century, the flood of Germans and Irish continued, complemented by many English, Scots, and Welsh. Millions of Italian peasants, uprooted from the land, joined the immigrant flow starting in the 1880s; by 1917, there were over 700,000 first- and second-generation Italian immigrants in New York City alone. Hundreds of thousands of Jews were driven out of Russia and Eastern Europe by persecution; collectively, they made New York the most Jewish state of the Union, which it remains today. (By one count in the late 1960s, New York State had 2.5 million Jews, constituting 14 percent of the total population—several times the totals, both in raw numbers and percentages, of the runner-up states of California and New Jersey. New York was also one of the nation's most heavily Roman Catholic states, with 6.6 million Catholic residents—36 percent of the state population.)

The figures from the 1950 Census, when many of the turn-of-the-century immigrants were still living, provide a good measure of the modern-day foreign-stock composition of New York. Counting both foreign born and their children, the count was about 1.5 million from Italy, 800,000 from Russia, 700,000 from Germany, 650,000 each from Poland and Ireland, 400,- from Great Britain, and 35,000 from Austria. Altogether, New York then had 4.7 million first- and second-generation immigrants, and almost one in four of all foreign-born people in the United States. Upstate as well as in New York City, Italians continue to be the largest single foreign-stock group. The exception is Buffalo, where Poles are predominant.

Since 1940, there has been a net inmigration of blacks into New York State of 917,000 persons.* In 1970, the Census takers found that New York City had 1.7 million Negroes in all, New York State as a whole 2.2 million. No other city or state in America even approaches those totals. A major portion of the racial and economic problems of the South, and of the overpopulation and economic problems of Puerto Rico, have simply been transferred to the banks of the Hudson—without New York ever having asked for the favor.

Paying the bill for support of the down-and-out ethnic groups, in terms of welfare and other social services, is the single factor that threatens to cripple both New York City and New York State today. Congress, Governor Rockefeller told me in an interview, could have taken over all welfare payments in the country—but couldn't do so politically because New York, California, and Massachusetts would have gotten 51 percent of all the money.

---

* The 1940–70 period also showed a net outmigration of 716,000 whites, almost 90 percent of the exodus occurring in the 1960s.

The industrial states, he pointed out, now have higher welfare-assistance standards:

So we're getting the poor from other parts of the country. And because we pay higher taxes to pay for the services, other states are getting our businesses and industries and people who want to avoid high taxes. This can Balkanize America and really destroy a lot of the strength of the country.

State Government: The Grand Tradition

The state government of New York has so long set the pace for all other states, and has so frequently been the incubator of inventive ideas later adopted for the nation as a whole, that a writer on the subject approaches it with something of the timidity he might feel in describing the development of the federal government.

The model was not so enviable in the decades of the Gilded Age following the Civil War. "In the state and its leading cities," David Ellis and his coauthors wrote in their *History of New York State,* "this was largely an era of boss domination, corruption, and favors for special interests." The infamous Tammany Hall leader in New York City, William Marcy Tweed, known to his contemporaries and history simply as "Boss Tweed," capitalized on the naiveté of the unlettered Irish to build an invincible political machine. The Tweed Ring pilfered as much as $75 million from the city government and with the help of blatant vote stealing even placed an ally in the governor's chair in Albany. It was smashed in the early 1870s by Samuel J. Tilden, who in turn became a respectable reform governor of the state. But neither Tilden nor Grover Cleveland, the other prominent Democratic governor of the late 19th century, undertook any fundamental changes in the weak and generally ineffective format of state government. Tammany Hall Democrats and Republican bosses like Roscoe Conkling and Thomas C. Platt remained powerful, often dominant, manipulating political office for private gain.

It was only in the Progressive Era, begun with Theodore Roosevelt's inauguration as governor in 1899 and climaxed in the administration of Charles Evans Hughes a few years later, that the tables were turned and New York government began to place public interest ahead of selfish private interests. The outstanding legislation of that era included laws to curb the excesses of utilities, regulate public service corporations, unify and improve the civil service system, guarantee certain basic rights to industrial workers, and create the nation's first workmen's compensation law. But still, state government was notoriously ill-organized and ill-equipped to guide the fortunes of a state that already had nine million inhabitants. A constitutional convention, held in 1915 and presided over by Elihu S. Root, recommended sweeping changes to make the governor chief executive in fact as well as in name. The amendments were opposed by various vested political interests and defeated in a popular referendum; nevertheless, in the succeeding years all the individual suggestions would be approved individually by the people.

In 1918, Alfred E. Smith, a native son of Manhattan's Lower East Side, a product of a close-knit Irish neighborhood, the Roman Catholic Church, and Tammany Hall, was elected governor of New York. Except for a brief interregnum in 1921–23, New York State has since been governed in a continuous stream, for a period now exceeding more than a half a century, by men of the highest character and ability—a record that no other American state has even begun to match:

Alfred E. Smith (Democrat)	1919–20; 1923–28
Franklin D. Roosevelt (Democrat)	1929–32
Herbert H. Lehman (Democrat)	1933–42
Thomas E. Dewey (Republican)	1943–54
Averell Harriman (Democrat)	1955–58
Nelson A. Rockefeller (Republican)	1959–

The vicissitudes of national politics have barred all but one of these—Roosevelt—from becoming President of the United States. But one could argue, with some plausibility, that at least three others—Smith, Dewey, and Rockefeller—would have been as good or better chief executives than the men sent to the White House in their stead.

Al Smith set the pattern for what was to follow. Through years of service in the state legislature, he had been molded into what the Republican New York *Herald Tribune* called "a true leader, a genuine compeller of men, a man of wit and force with an instinctive grasp of legislative practice." He was a leader of the constitutional convention of 1915. His political acumen was demonstrated by the fact that he never broke with Tammany Hall, but was able to demand and get increased independence from it. Yet as a good government reformer, he picked up backing from independent voters. His success in accommodating such disparate supporters, William Allen White once said, was due to the fact that he retained his old friends with his heart while winning new ones with his head. Smith's accomplishments as governor, Davis Ellis writes, "made New York a model for every other state in the Union."

In the administrative realm, Smith first got the legislature to approve and then the people to ratify the consolidation of 187 boards and commissions into 19 departments, the executive of each appointed by the governor and serving at his pleasure. Fifty years later, many states have still to take this fundamental step toward effective gubernatorial control. The second major reform was institution of the executive budget system, another step first recommended by the 1915 constitutional convention. The executive budget places on the governor responsibility for reviewing the needs of all branches of state government and then preparing an overall state budget, listing expenditures and tax sources, for submission to the legislature. The reform vastly increases the power of the governor, and reduces the legislature's power proportionately. The federal government adopted the system long ago, but amazingly, a majority of the states have yet to do so. Dr. T. Norman Hurd, New York's budget director for close to a quarter century under Dewey and Rockefeller, told me that the executive budget "was the start of responsible state government in New York. Since the 1920s, New York has not changed its constitutional language on the executive budget, and there have been only moderate changes in implementing legislation. There was not a week in the budget office when I didn't need to check back to those constitutional or legislative provisions." *

Throughout Smith's regime of the 1920s, New York stood out as a liberal island in a conservative nation. Under goading from Smith, the legislature vastly increased state aid to local schools and through an accompanying equalization program, which is still considered the best in the nation, saw to it that poor districts got commensurately greater aid. Consolidation of rural school districts was begun, the 48-hour maximum work week adopted for labor, many park and other public works projects initiated, and an income tax approved that would eventually become the mainstay of state government financing. State income was shared with local governments, so that property taxes could be cut. Smith's theory was that people were willing to pay more taxes if they were convinced they were getting sound value in return. In New York, he proved the case, creating perhaps the most alert and progressive citizenry in the U. S.

In 1928, Al Smith went off to make his unsuccessful bid for the Presidency, unfortunately 30 years ahead of the time that the country was willing to accept a Roman Catholic as its leader. Franklin D. Roosevelt, scion of an aristocratic Dutch-descended family from Dutchess County, ran in his place and was elected. FDR was not as distinguished a governor as he would prove to be a President—perhaps because he viewed Albany chiefly as a stepping-stone to Washington, and was not forceful about taking stands on controversial issues. He proposed many reform measures, based on suggestions of gubernatorial commissions, which the legislature rejected. Reluctantly and belatedly, Roosevelt cracked down on the extraordinary corruption then being revealed in New York City. But as the Depression deepened, he moved decisively to prevent bankruptcy of municipalities and starvation among New Yorkers by providing imaginative measures for public relief, including establishment of a temporary emergency relief administration. Thus the formula was developed in New York for the New Deal programs that would effect America's recovery from the severest depression it had ever known.

Herbert Lehman, the son of an immigrant Jewish family from Germany and founder of the successful banking firm of Lehman Brothers, was favored both by Smith and FDR to become governor in 1932, and won despite initial opposition from Tammany Hall. He was totally lacking in the charisma of his political mentors, and let the headlines go to President Roosevelt and Mayor Fiorello La Guardia, who were in office at the same time. But his record as governor was astounding. Not only did he push forward myriad Depression relief measures, but he managed to convert an inherited budget deficit into a surplus. He was one of the greatest champions the civil service system ever

* Hurd is presently director of state operations in the Rockefeller administration.

had, and he single-handedly pushed to approval a series of labor laws more progressive than either the federal or any other state's at the time.

For sheer administrative talent, it is difficult to think of a 20th-century governor who has excelled Thomas E. Dewey. A native of the little city of Owosso, Michigan, he went to New York City in 1923 to study music and law, became the fabulously successful prosecutor of mobster Lucky Luciano and countless other racketeers in the trucking, restaurant, poultry, and baking businesses, and after a first unsuccessful try in 1938, was elected governor in 1942 and served 12 years in the job. Dewey is the father of the tradition of progressive Republicanism which has thrived in New York State to the present day. He did it through forward-looking programs and hard-headed political maneuver. As Warren Moscow noted some 20 years ago in *Politics in the Empire State,* Dewey as governor "assumed complete control of his party. County leaders who opposed him were broken by cold, hard-bitten use of the patronage powers of the governor's office. Legislators suffered a similar fate. He brooked no interference."

Confident enough of his own abilities to surround himself with the best men, Dewey professionalized the governor's staff, the civil service department, and state purchasing arm, and brought in more professionally qualified department heads than any of his predecessors in Albany. Like his contemporary (and 1948 Vice Presidential running mate), Earl Warren in California, he refused to lower tax rates while the state experienced wartime budget surpluses. The result was a $450 million fund that could be expended for delayed public works projects after the war. Hundreds of thousands of New York youngsters owe him thanks for his leadership in creating a state university—which New York had lacked up to that time. A vigorous health department program virtually eradicated tuberculosis in New York, highway building was pushed forward, and the state's mental hygiene program was thoroughly reorganized. And in response to Dewey's initiative, the legislature in 1945 passed a proclamation of economic emancipation for New York's minority groups—the nation's first fair employment practices law. The legislation boldly stated that "the opportunity to obtain employment without discrimination because of race, creed, color or national origin is hereby recognized as and declared to be a civil right." A commission was established to enforce the law. It would be another 19 years before the federal government took the same step.

Fiscally, Dewey believed in "pay as you go" and could be called a straightforward Republican conservative; it was his political acumen that set him apart. A typical Dewey technique was to let the Democrats arouse the public's interest in some new social legislation. But just when the Democrats felt they had an appealing public issue, Dewey would step in with legislation, tailored to suit his party's needs, and take credit for the accomplishment. "This was a technique that had been perfected long ago by Britain's Tories," David Ellis notes, "but it was perennially new to New York's Democrats, and they never learned to cope with it."

Dewey's loss of the 1944 Presidential campaign against FDR, a popular wartime President, was no surprise or particular disappointment to him. His 1948 defeat at the hands of Harry Truman was another story. All that summer and up to and including the early edition of the Chicago *Tribune,* Dewey was elected President; sadly for him, his term ended late in the evening of the actual election day, November 2, 1948. Dewey's reserved public manner (belying real inner warmth), his somewhat platitudinous calls for national unity, some say even his mustache, had something to do with the surprise defeat. But pocketbook issues were chiefly responsible, as pollster Sam Lubell reported: "People voted for Truman because they thought he would protect their bread and butter interests. Labor rolled up the traditional Democratic majorities; farmers worried by the 80th Congress' refusal to extend grain storage, were seeking down to earth promises which they didn't find in Dewey speeches."

A man of lesser stature than Dewey might have taken to sulking and recriminations after the 1948 election, but instead he effected a graceful retreat from the front rank of national politics, winning a final term as governor in 1950 and then "retiring" to a Wall Street law practice in which he became a multimillionaire. It is difficult now to appreciate Dewey's youth when he first became a national figure. He was only in his mid-thirties when his racket-busting made his name nationally known, 40 when he was first elected governor, 46 when he lost the Presidency for the second time. Twenty years later, President Nixon offered to appoint him Chief Justice of the United States. But Dewey declined, saying it was too late for him. At last, he was too old for the job.*

In retrospect, Dewey's 1948 defeat may be viewed as the crucial failure in developing responsible American party democracy in the postwar era. Had Dewey been elected, he would in all probability have brought to the Presidency the same distinction he brought to the New York governorship—and might well have established the national Republican party as a broadly based organ of moderate progressivism, at least the equal of the Democrats in national politics. But instead, the Democrats remained the country's majority party, and the frustrated Republicans felt obliged to turn to a war hero to win the White House in the 1950s, and in 1964 to a likable but ideologically rigid man, Barry Goldwater, as their nominee. The Republican party's continuing negative image in the country, its turn to name-calling politicians all the way from Joe McCarthy to Spiro Agnew, and its appalling lack of appeal to youth today, all stem in a way from the party's failure to win with a responsible qualified candidate at the right time.

But Dewey's influence, behind the scenes, was not to be discounted. In 1952, he played a crucial role in getting Eisenhower the Republican nomination over Robert A. Taft. He helped Richard Nixon win the 1952 Vice Presidential nomination, and then keep his place on the ticket after the private-

* New York has been a breeding ground of great jurists, including the likes of Charles Evans Hughes, Benjamin Cardozo, Harlan Fiske Stone, John Marshall Harlan, Harold Medina, and Learned Hand. Dewey, with his logical mind, would probably have made a fine judge, too. But a man he appointed to the New York court of appeals 25 years ago, now that court's chief judge, Stanley Fuld, is one of the nation's most outstanding jurists. Fuld has often had the pleasure of seeing his dissents on issues such as free speech, obscenity, and literacy tests become law through decisions of the U. S. Supreme Court.

fund uproar that climaxed in the "Checkers" speech. Six years later, Dewey's circle of friends played an important role in getting Nelson Rockefeller his first gubernatorial nomination. Even in 1970, it was Dewey's law partner and associate of 33 years, R. Burdell Bixby, who managed Rockefeller's fourth-term campaign for governor.

Dewey's successor, Averell Harriman, the only Democrat to have broken the solid 30-year wall of Republican control in Albany, was a real disappointment in the job—a man of great renown in foreign affairs, but unfortunately preoccupied with the possibility that he might run for President in 1960. He did set up the nation's first office of consumer affairs, headed by Dr. Persia Campbell, but was frequently blocked by the Republican-controlled legislature. Withal, Harriman would probably have been elected to a second term in 1958 without an opponent of Rockefeller's stature.

Nelson Rockefeller and His Works

Thomas Dewey gave New York State government its finishing gloss of professionalism; Nelson Rockefeller took the instrument, experimented with it and reshaped it, added on appendages (some of dubious constitutionality) to make the money available to accomplish what he willed, and in the process built the most complex, fascinating, and socially advanced state government in U. S. history. To the job of being governor, Rockefeller brought (1) years of business-philanthropic-government experience; (2) the expansive world of knowledge, contacts, and staff support that comes with being a Rockefeller; and (3) the personality of an absolutely irrepressible builder-manager-operator. Despite his reputation as a liberal Republican, Rockefeller is essentially nonideologic, a *doer* rather than a *thinker*, a total pragmatist. Perhaps for that very reason (plus some lucky political breaks), he won four successive four-year terms in office, becoming the senior governor of the United States.

Nelson Aldrich Rockefeller was born in July 1908 in the fashionable summer resort of Bar Harbor, Maine. He was named for his maternal grandfather, Nelson Aldrich, a Senator from Rhode Island and a power in Republican politics. But the vital antecedent name was Rockefeller; Nelson was born, in fact, on the 69th birthday of his paternal grandfather, John D. Rockefeller, who in the best robber-baron tradition had manipulated his Standard Oil empire into monopolistic control of the U. S. oil industry—and then, just as industriously, began to give away part of his fortune. The story of the Rockefeller Foundation, Rockefeller University, and other philanthropies begun by Rockefeller with the encouragement of his son, John D., Jr., is beyond our scope here. But mention must be made of the remarkable generation of Rockefellers of whom Nelson is but one: John D., III, head of the Rockefeller Foundation and the Lincoln Center; Laurance, manager of the family's business interests and founder of the American Conservation Association; Winthrop, Arkansas cattle breeder and twice governor of that state; and David, president of the Chase Manhattan Bank, a leading promoter of the physical rebuilding of Manhattan, chairman of the board of Rockefeller University and of the Museum of Modern Art. With the exception of Winthrop, all are still New York based, clearly the premier family of their city and state. Now a fourth generation of 23 members is standing on the threshold, ready to take over stewardship of one of the world's greatest fortunes. But the fourth generation is active in more varied professions, and lives further afield; the best known, to date, is John D. Rockefeller, IV, or "Jay" as he is popularly known, the present secretary of state and prospective next governor of West Virginia.

Nelson graduated from Dartmouth College, Phi Beta Kappa, in 1930, married a childhood friend, Mary Todhunter Clark, "apprenticed" for a period in the family-owned Chase Manhattan Bank, and in 1937 traveled through South America on family (oil) business, thus beginning a lifetime interest in Latin American affairs. In 1940, he helped formulate President Roosevelt's Good Neighbor Policy and was a major architect of U. S.-Latin American policy in the State Department through 1945.

President Eisenhower in 1953 appointed Rockefeller Undersecretary of of the new Department of Health, Education and Welfare, and later his Special Assistant for Foreign Affairs. At one point, Eisenhower was reportedly ready to make Rockefeller Undersecretary of Defense, with the plan of making him Secretary when Charles Wilson retired. But Treasury Secretary George Humphrey opposed the nomination, because Rockefeller was "a spender." That was the last straw impelling Rockefeller to go into elective politics, where he would have his own base. (It may also have been George Humphrey's most substantive contribution to American government.) In 1958, Rockefeller waged an astounding, high-impact campaign as the New York Republican gubernatorial candidate. He mingled with the masses, gulped down blintzes and bagels and pizza, kissed babies, and assailed Democratic "bossism." The public responded, and he beat a thoroughly outclassed Averell Harriman by more than half a million votes.

Rockefeller has been hot news ever since 1958. There was, for instance, all the news coverage about his abortive bids for the 1960, 1964, and 1968 Republican Presidential nominations—Presidential politics apparently being the one area in which the fabled Rockefeller expertise comes to naught. The whole country watched with fascination, sometimes with opprobrium, as he divorced his wife of 32 years and in 1963 married Mrs. Margaretta Fitler Murphy, the just-divorced mother of four. Early in Rockefeller's governorship, much public attention, and ridicule, surrounded his proposal that New York should prepare for nuclear war by installing a fallout shelter in every building, theater, school, and home. Appropriately, the press rode him hard for preaching frugal "pay-as-you-go" fiscal policies in his first years in office and later incurring fantastic debts through questionable bonding practices, and for promising "no new taxes" in his 1962 reelection campaign, and then promptly proceeding to enact them. In more recent times, much of the public attention has revolved around his bitter and continuing feud with his onetime political ally, Mayor John V. Lindsay of New York City.

Often eclipsed in the public debate are the vast programs of Nelson Rockefeller, the planner and doer, which have, in the words of one writer, "changed the physical face of New York more than any governor since De-Witt Clinton built the Erie Canal." Universities, highways, mass transit, water-pollution control facilities, vastly increased state aid of every type to localities—they are all the work of Nelson Rockefeller, and he knows them all inside out. One of my reporter friends, Richard Dougherty, comments: "You can't go around New York State with Nelson, his slides and his twang, without being impressed." The programs are best viewed one by one:

UNIVERSITIES. When Rockefeller took office, the decade-old State University of New York had only 38,000 students and was, in the words of Ford Foundation president McGeorge Bundy, "an empty holding company." But projections by the state board of regents, and by a special commission which Rockefeller appointed, indicated that without vastly expanded facilities, thousands of qualified students would be denied a college education in New York State by 1975. With that, an expansion program of unique proportions ensued. "Others have built state universities over long periods of years. We did it over eight to ten years," Rockefeller says, adding (typically): "and we'll come out the largest." The State University's total full-time enrollment reached 220,000 in 1971, and is projected to reach 316,000 or more by 1975. California has a more extensive system but it has separate boards of regents or trustees for the University of California, state colleges, and community colleges. In New York, a single board of trustees now supervises four university centers (at Albany, Binghamton, Buffalo, and Stony Brook) as well as the 12 four-year colleges of arts and sciences and 38 community colleges. The state's annual appropriations for higher education have risen from $95 million in 1959–60 to $591 million in 1970–71, a rise of 520 percent.

All this growth would have been impossible, however, without an unprecedented program of capital construction costing upward of $1 *billion* since Rockefeller became governor, and eventually expected to reach $4 billion. The state constitution provides that approval of the people in a popular vote must be obtained to issue new bonds, but Rockefeller was anxious to begin construction on a broad scale, rapidly, and on a self-liquidating basis. He demanded that his legal counsel and budget office find a way around the barrier of submissions of a bond issue to the people (where there was always a risk of rejection). The idea that emerged and was then implemented was to set up a semi-independent agency, the State University Construction Fund, which could issue bonds without popular approval. The construction fund receives all tuition and other fees and income from the university, and uses that income to pay the debt service on the construction bonds. The real legal brain that perfected this system was that of John Mitchell, later Nixon's campaign manager and Attorney General of the U. S., who at the time was a member of a prestigious New York law firm that did a great deal of work in the municipal bond field. The "backdoor financing" bonding method has plenty of critics—as we will note later—but it has made possible a much more rapid expansion of state facilities than would otherwise have been possible.

Within a few years, the four university centers, offering both graduate and undergraduate degrees, have become not just diploma mills but distinguished centers of learning, actually luring (through high salaries and other devices) topnotch faculty from major institutions in other states. The State University at Buffalo has drawn the most national attention by its bold, pioneering educational patterns—and criticism for turbulence (which hit a peak in spring 1970). In 1960, Buffalo was a private university, primarily a streetcar college for the city. By 1970, it had doubled its enrollment to about 23,000 students, had an English department marvelously innovative and creative by national reputation, a school of pharmacology regarded as among the country's best, and pioneer graduate programs in fields like computer sciences and policy sciences. The State University at Albany has eight professional and graduate schools, offers undergraduates flexibility in their study patterns (including an opportunity to study abroad for a semester or a year), offers the country's first doctoral program in criminal justice, and is noted for its Atmospheric Sciences Research Center, one of the country's top centers for the study of pollution. The State University at Binghamton is especially well known for its programs in history, mathematics, and economics, and is building a fourth major collegiate structure, called "the College in the Woods," set in a 400-year stand of hardwoods. The State University at Stony Brook, on Long Island, has already won recognition as a national leader in a number of scientific fields, including ecology and evolution, urban engineering, petrology, and marine sciences. In addition, enrollment is growing rapidly at medical schools in Syracuse, Brooklyn, Buffalo, and the new medical center at Stony Brook.

As Rockefeller poured ever greater amounts of money into the state university system, private groups—mainly Roman Catholic—muttered about the unfair competition. The answer was the so-called Scholar Incentive Program, under which the state supplements tuitions of students attending colleges in New York State by several hundred dollars. In effect, it is a subsidy to the colleges, which promptly raised their tuitions to match the amount paid by the state. By the late 1960s, some quarter million New York students were receiving some form of state financial assistance.

HOUSING AND NEW TOWNS. New York had begun state-subsidized low-inome housing projects before Rockefeller took office, but the total inventory of new units produced was not satisfactory. Rockefeller wanted a vehicle to stimulate low-income and medium-income housing and on John Mitchell's advice created the Housing Finance Agency, which is able through local-property-tax abatement and the mortgage bonds it issues to facilitate participation of limited dividend groups in moderate-income housing projects. Since the HFA's creation in 1960, it has made $1 billion available for new housing; presently there is $4 billion in the fund for mental-hygiene facilities, for nursing homes, day-care centers, hospitals, youth facilities, and senior-citizens centers, all of which the state is financing for local government and private groups through the device of self-liquidating bonds.

But as Rockefeller explains the problem, New York found that even with low-interest government money, housing projects, complicated by zoning and code regulations, soon became too difficult for all but a limited group of sponsors. Thus the decision was made in 1968 to create the Urban Development Corporation, which as a single entity would have the power to do whatever might be required—condemn property, raze old structures, override local zoning and building code requirements, and use mortgage loans or just about any other conceivable form of financing, develop entire projects either on its own or in conjunction with private enterprise, and then operate or sell or lease back properties when completed. To head the UDC, Rockefeller selected Edward J. Logue, former redevelopment chief of New Haven and then Boston. Logue seemed happy to have the opportunity, claiming that the UDC represents "the most versatile and the most all-inclusive development legislation on the books in any of the 50 states." * He brought an unusual sense of urgency and push to the new agency and then staffed it with a highly competent group of people from outside the civil service system. (The result is a much freer, less constrained staff, with those on a professional level—architects, lawyers, planners, and the like—showing much more initiative and energy than in a typical state department.)

Nothing less than a gargantuan effort by the UDC and private industry will be required to solve New York State's housing problem. As of 1970, an estimated 1.4 million people lived in dilapidated or deteriorated housing that needed replacement. Together with a projected population increase of 26 percent by 1990, that would mean the necessity for new or rehabilitated housing for 6 million people by then. Yet housing starts in the state actually declined precipitously from 1959, when 105,000 units were built, to 1969, when only 67,000 units were constructed. The UDC, with its several-hundred-million-dollar bonding authority and expectation of being repaid out of its project revenues, should be the vehicle to do an important part of the job. One question is whether the UDC will really have the nerve to use its unique zoning-override power to put low-income and presumably racially integrated projects into suburban areas. To date, it has not done so, instead going the route of careful negotiation with communities, entering an area only when it has a specific invitation. But the UDC staffers find that despite their offer to build low-density, garden style, landscaped units in the suburbs, the only acceptance it gets is in suburban *cities* that already have a low-income population. The step to zoning override in those suburbs could obviously have a politically explosive effect. The decision of whether to use the power would ultimately rest with Logue's boss, Rockefeller, and the governor is reluctant to say what he might ultimately do. When I queried Rockefeller on the point, he first stressed the need for maximum possible cooperation with local governments. He agreed that "intelligent planning" would not leave all the

---

* At the time of this writing, California and several other states were considering adoption of similar legislation.

low income units in a suburban county in its cities alone. But he said: "We have to exercise power in such a way we don't lose it." * (The state assembly has passed laws in successive sessions to strip the UDC of its zoning-override power, but the proposal has—so far—been killed in the senate.)

The 1971 legislative session voted approval of a community-development article for the state constitution which will permit the UDC to "write down" values on land in order to provide, in effect, a subsidy to certain private enterprises to get them to locate their industries or shopping centers at places UDC chooses, so that housing and jobs can be developed in the same areas. But the voters rejected the article in November 1971 balloting. The result will be a serious slowdown in the more innovative types of UDC projects, a serious rebuff to Rockefeller's plans. But he is a stubborn man, and will in all likelihood try again in the coming years. This long-term evolution of policy, making it possible to plan over time and even live with delays like the 1971 referendum, is clearly out of the reach of governors with more normal years of incumbency than Rockefeller. "I'm lucky to have been governor so long," he said. "I've been able to take these steps one by one. We have developed the tools step by step, so that now we have a very flexible kit of tools to solve some of these problems, one that no other state has."

The standard run of UDC projects so far has been a chunk of city housing, anywhere from 100 to 2,000 units. The projects in New York City are usually high-rise, those in upstate mixed. But there are some dramatic exceptions. The most interesting effort is underway on Welfare Island, a thin strip of mostly vacant land in the East River opposite midtown Manhattan. Mayor Lindsay set up a committee to study the island's future, and on the basis of its recommendations an exciting master plan for the island emerged, designed by Philip Johnson and John Burgee. The UDC then went to the city and offered to be the developer. A 99-year lease was agreed on (after long negotiations). The new Welfare Island, when it is completed in the mid-1970s, will have thousands of units of housing for everyone from the poor to the rich.

The UDC has another controversial and extremely complex project underway in the town of Amherst, where the new campus of the State University at Buffalo is under construction. By 1985, according to the plan, 25,000 people should live on some 2,400 acres of now largely vacant land north of the campus—a site selected to avert disruption of the existing town of Amherst, where feeling against the new project has been strong. Some third of the people to be settled there will be low- and moderate-income, a blow to what is now a privileged high-income enclave. The Amherst project to date has been plagued by conflicts on the hiring of minority workers, and by confusion arising from its sheer size and complexity.

TRANSPORTATION. Rockefeller has been a big highway builder, and in fact capitalized on his record with a famed television commercial in his 1966

---

* When I tried to press Rockefeller further on the suburban-housing point, he said: "I'm not about to say something to you that's going to blow my plans out of the water on one side or another." Then, to soften the rebuke, he added this splendid platitude: "We have to show we can plan for the future in a way that doesn't destroy present values but does account for emerging needs." Then Rockefeller laughed at himself and added: "There's a pretty good sentence for you."

campaign, in which the viewer was taken down the central white strip of a seemingly endless highway as a voice pointed out that one can take all the roads Governor Rockefeller has built "and they'd stretch all the way to Hawaii—and back." Among the major projects have been the Long Island Expressway, the Southern Tier (Route 17) Expressway, the Adirondack Northway, and the North-South Expressway (Interstate Route 81).

But lots of governors have built highways; Rockefeller's uniqueness resides in the absolutely unprecedented way he has inserted a state government into the field of urban mass transit. Again, Rockefeller turned to a special authority to do the job—developing a way to avoid the slow bureaucracy of old-line agencies, a technique pioneered by Al Smith. The story is best told in Rockefeller's own words:

Our problem was that the Port of New York Authority didn't want to stretch out into mass transit. It just stuck to airports, bridges, tunnels, and seaport facilities, and did a good job on those. But the Port Authority has two weaknesses: it's bistate [with New Jersey], so that neither state really controls it, and it's too independent of elected officials. Also, its usefulness is restricted by its unwillingness to go into the money-losing proposition of buses and railroads.

I started out trying to help the private companies stay in the field of mass transit by cutting their taxes in half, setting up a commuter-car construction fund to finance new equipment, and similar steps. But it didn't work. They started to go into bankruptcy. We took over control of the Long Island Railroad —if it had gone out of business, it would have meant $1.5 billion in new highways.

Then we set up the Metropolitan Transportation Authority with very wide powers. And it has ended up taking over not only the Long Island Railroad, but all New York City subways, all New York City buses, the Triborough and other bridges, and now the New York share of the New Haven Railroad, and the Penn Central line running through Westchester.

The system moves 7 to 8 million people a day. We're re-equipping facilities. We've already put 640 modern new cars on the Long Island. And we're about to sign a contract now to develop a turbo-jet self-propelled electric engine to modernize mass transit for the New York area.

The MTA does a fantastic job. There are about 44,000 employees just in this one authority. The federal government talks about doing these things. But the state is doing it, as the *effective, active agent*.

The man Rockefeller chose to head the MTA system was William J. Ronan, so trusted a confidant that he had served eight years as the governor's personal secretary and a man variously described as brilliant, cool, resilient, brusque, and arrogant. Ronan presides over an 11-man board appointed for eight-year terms by the governor. (The mayor of New York proposed three members to the governor for appointment.) But it is generally agreed, writer Fred C. Shapiro has reported, that "it's Ronan's board. So total is his control, in fact, that the MTA is usually described as a 'Wholly Ronan Empire.'" The power is extraordinary for a man who, as dean of the New York University Graduate School of Public Administration and Social Services a few years ago, was known as a severe critic of authorities and advocate of decentralized government. Inevitably, Ronan and his board are a lightning rod for protest from all quarters about service, equipment, and ideology. Jack Newfield wrote in *New York* in 1970 that "the MTA includes no commuter, no poor person, no woman, no student, no black or Puerto Rican, no union representative. [A black has since been added.] It consists exclusively of affluent people who rarely use the dirty, unreliable, overcrowded, cold, dangerous New York City subways." New York City people point to the fare increase to 30 cents in 1970, and feared additional increases to as much as 50 cents, as evidence of MTA's cold-heartedness, especially to young and old people for whom the high fares constitute a real hardship, and sometimes a terrible burden on an already strained family budget. (Until 1948, the fare was only five cents.) From Long Island, there have been heated complaints about higher fares and slow progress in making up for 70 years of neglect by the previous owners. State Controller Arthur Levitt has been upset about unconscionable concessions to the unionized workers of the Long Island Railroad, who have been aptly described as "some of the nation's highest-paid and least-burdened railroad workers." And the unions themselves complained bitterly about indignities inflicted on trainmen by passengers in retaliation for delayed, inefficient (and of course rude) service.

The complaints about the MTA, however well justified, should not obscure what it *is* doing. It is beginning a $2 billion modernization and expansion of a vast transportation system which had simply been allowed to depreciate, without any major improvements, since well before World War II. Not only has the Long Island Railroad gotten modern new equipment, but 800 high-acceleration, stainless-steel cars, 600 of them air-conditioned, were ordered for New York City's straphangers. Under the East River, a massive four-track tunnel has been under construction for use by Long Island Railroad trains and as the keystone of a 52-mile addition to the subway system with new lines in Manhattan, Queens, the Bronx, and Brooklyn. Even long-forgotten Staten Island's transit line has undergone a $25 million face lifting. Most of these improvements are financed under part of a $2.5 billion general transportation bond issue approved in 1965. An additional $1.25 billion for mass transit was part of a bond issue rejected by the people in 1971, a blow to system modernization and chances of holding down the New York City transit fare. Yet in the long run, even direct subsidy of day-to-day operating expenses will have to come from public coffers. As Ronan has said:

> I don't take the approach that we can pay for either . . . capital construction or transit operations . . . out of the fare box any longer. What's happened in America today is that we've subsidized air and highway and water—particularly water—transport, and we've let rail go to pot, and now we realize it's impossible to operate a nonsubsidized system in competition with subsidized ones.

PURE WATERS. In 1965, at least four years ahead of the real wave of environmental concern in the U. S., Rockefeller requested and the legislature and people approved an unprecedented $1 billion bond issue to assist municipalities in building modern sewage-disposal plants. The idea was something of a gamble, since it was predicated on the idea of matching federal funds, a program that was not yet approved in Washington. But the federal government the next year did indeed approve a large matching grant program, and Rockefeller confidently predicted that the state program would result, by 1972, in "the elimination of water pollution in New York's lakes, streams and rivers." The prediction would not come true for a number of reasons—because the immensity of the problem was underestimated, because sewage plant efficiency standards were raised by the federal government, because it was decided to design plants for 1990 rather than 1970 population, and because construction costs escalated about 1 percent a month. Another factor was that by 1971, New York had received only 7 percent of the promised federal money. Eventual costs of the New York program seemed likely to go over $4 billion.

Rockefeller, however, was not discouraged. In fact, when I asked him to name his most strikingly successful programs, he started with the pure-water program, which he claimed would not only stop existing pollution in the rivers, lakes, and streams, but "clean up the material already deposited." The New York program was uniquely successful, Rockefeller claimed, because "we stayed afloat" with constant prefinancing, from regular state funds, of the federal pledge. "No other state is keeping up," he boasted.

On the environmental front, it might be mentioned that at Rockefeller's urging, New York in 1970 became one of the states consolidating all its anti-pollution offices under one superagency, the Department of Environmental Conservation. The acquisition of land for outdoor recreation, including parks and forest recreation areas, has also been pushed forward vigorously with bond issues of $75 million in 1960 and another $200 million in 1966.

THE ARTS. In 1960, Rockefeller acted to create the nation's first state-sponsored Council on the Arts. Its highly successful programs, based on suggestions by Senator Javits that even predated Rockefeller's interest, have centered on bringing symphony and theater into small cities that would never have been able to attract them otherwise.

NARCOTICS. Rockefeller acknowledges that narcotics control is the least successful effort of his administration. "We've spent over half a billion dollars so far and experimented with every possible approach and we still haven't found the answers," he told me. A state Narcotic Addiction Control Commission was started in 1966, after Rockefeller had made control of drugs an issue in the 1966 campaign, and in 1970 its budgetary appropriations, including capital construction, were $345 million. The commission, after some false starts, has learned to make wise use of its power to commit addicts. (Before 1966, addicts who did not want treatment could refuse it, and most, out of hedonism, immaturity, narcissism, or a desire for short-range kicks, took that option.) The commission's programs cover a wide range—from prison incarceration for addicts who are violent and dangerous to special treatment for the emotionally disturbed to the drug maintenance approach (methadone) for a large number of heroin addicts. In addition, the state subsidizes Daytop, which is a New York equivalent of California's Synanon, plus a whole host of private agencies, Odyssey houses, Exodus House, and Quaker rehabilitation programs. Millions of dollars are passed on to localities for narcotics guidance councils and similar programs.

Nevertheless, by 1971 only some 25,000 addicts had received direct state treatment—a small pass at the narcotics problem which some have likened to the "bubonic plague of the 1970s." A 1970–71 survey commissioned by the Narcotic Addiction Control Commission, in which a cross section of 7,378 New Yorkers were interviewed, resulted in these shocking estimates of the numbers of persons who were actually using the specified drugs *six* times a month or more in New York State:

Minor tranquilizers	525,000
Marijuana	487,000
Barbiturates	361,000
Diet pills (e.g., Dexedrine)	222,000
Sedatives-hypnotics (e.g., Doriden)	187,000
Heroin	157,000
Pep pills (e.g., Dexedrine)	110,000
Major tranquilizers (e.g., Thorazine)	71,000
LSD	45,000
Antidepressants	39,000
Speed (Methedrine)	35,000

ALBANY MALL. Nelson Rockefeller once said, "I always wanted to be an architect," and his critics are fond of accusing him of having an "edifice complex." He has been building things for most of his adult life, having played a hand in Rockefeller Center, Colonial Williamsburg, the United Nations headquarters, Lincoln Center, the World Trade Center, and the building of 17 new university and college campuses in New York State. Where many a critic thinks he has really gone overboard is the grandiose Albany South Mall project, which Rockefeller conceived in 1959 to make the decaying old city of Albany into "the most spectacularly beautiful seat of government in the world." The idea was to return the center of state offices, which Dewey and other predecessors had permitted to go suburban, back into the center of Albany, thus creating a nucleus for the city's renewal.

William K. Harrison, a lifetime Rockefeller friend, coarchitect of Rockefeller Center, and designer of many other notable structures, was asked to do the overall Mall design. *Fortune*, which has done the definitive coverage on the Mall, describes the Rockefeller-Harrison concept this way:

What the two master builders dreamed up was a modern imperial enclave, rising on a hill overlooking the Hudson River. A half mile long and almost a quarter mile wide, the site lies between the executive mansion and the nineteenth-century capitol building, and by this connection creates one great government complex.

The Mall itself will contain a forty-four-story office tower, four identical twenty-three-story agency buildings, a legislative building, a justice building, a headquarters for the motor-vehicles department, a cultural center (including museum and library), a meeting center, and a laboratory for the department of health. The heart of this complex of concrete and marble is a huge platform,

1,440 feet long and 600 feet wide, with a 500-foot reflecting pool flanked by two smaller pools as well as lawns, trees, fountains, and promenades.

One may dispute Rockefeller's assertion that the Mall "is going to turn out to be the greatest thing that has happened in this country in 100 years," but there is no questioning that it will be the most expensive project ever undertaken by a state government. Informal early estimates of the Mall's cost were $250 million, the first formal state estimate in 1964 was $400 million, and a state estimate late in 1970 was $850 million. State Controller Levitt has maintained for some time that the construction cost will be at least $1 billion and that bond financing will cost another $500 million. The bonding arrangement, Levitt says, is "beyond the control or even the comprehension of the electorate." Under it, the county of Albany floats the bonds to build the Mall and then leases the whole to the state on a schedule designed to amortize the bonds by the year 2004. This idea was conceived by Albany Mayor Erastus Corning II, who told *Fortune* that Rockefeller went for the idea "like a trout for a fly," since it was commonly assumed the state's voters would never approve a bond issue for a big mall in Albany. But as Levitt pointed out in an interview with this writer, using the credit of Albany County (single-A) as against that of the State of New York (double-A) is a difference of a half percentage point in interest—"a helluvalot of money over 30 years."

Sometime in the mid-1970s, probably after Rockefeller has retired as governor, the South Mall will be completed and New York will have its empire-scale state capital. Rockefeller obviously wants to be remembered by it, but the problem is that the Mall may be viewed primarily as a memorial to a man's extravagance. Together with the bloody outcome of the 1971 Attica prison uprising, which has been called "Rockefeller's Bay of Pigs," the Mall may go far to eclipse the legacy of innovative and humane programs by which Rockefeller has advanced New York State government beyond all others.

The Fiscal Quandary

One day in January 1971, the New York *Times* editorialized on Governor Rockefeller's annual message to the legislature:

Governor Rockefeller buried a dream yesterday. It was the dream that state government, if it but had the will, could do almost anything to meet its own emerging needs. He began his fourth, four-year term in Albany by failing to call for the enactment of any boldly new, innovative programs. He confessed instead the state's approaching fiscal bankruptcy, its utter dependence now on additional forms of federal assitance. . . .

The state lacks money for new programs; it even lacks money to continue all the present programs at their mandated or obligated levels. . . .

The essence of Governor Rockefeller's message is a requiem. The state's freedom to act, to impose taxes and to experiment, is all but gone now. . . .

This later-day fiscal squeeze in New York is not unique among the states, but it is made all the more severe by the progressive nature of state programs, developed by many governors but perfected under Rockefeller, and the high percentage of the state budget (62 cents of every dollar) that Albany sends back to the counties, cities, towns, and school districts in direct subsidies for their operations. New York is hard-pressed to increase taxes further, since it already has the highest state and local per-capita tax burden in the United States ($576 per year, compared to $540 in second-place California.) * New York's state budget is actually $1 billion greater than California's, even though California has 1.8 million more people. New York not only has high sales and local property taxes, but an income tax which brings in $2.5 billion a year and rises on a progressive scale to a 14 percent rate for the richest individuals. If any state has reached the maximum feasible rate at which it can tax its people, it would seem to be New York. Lt. Gov. Malcolm Wilson echoes Rockefeller's sentiments when he says New York "has gone as far as it can without destroying its competitive position with other states."

Rockefeller's hope for several years has been that some form of federal revenue sharing would alleviate the fiscal plight of his state. New York, he says, sends $23.5 billion in tax revenues to Washington each year, but gets back only $2.5 billion in return. At meetings of the National Governors Conference and before congressional committees, he has fought tenaciously for revenue sharing, warning of a possible "disaster" and "breakdown of confidence in local government" if federal aid fails to materialize. "The 16th Amendment to the Constitution," Rockefeller says, "made possible the federal income tax. The result now is that the federal government gets two-thirds of the tax dollars, but two-thirds of the problems are at the state and local level. The problem is: How do we get the money back to where the problems are?" But even if some revenue sharing or welfare subsidy to the states eventually emerges from Congress, Rockefeller feels that "we've reached a point where the hopes and aspirations of the people of this country cannot be expanded and realized at the pace at which we've been going. Now we have to slow down on the rate at which we render new and additional services."

That attitude on Rockefeller's part has led some to criticize him for an unconscionable desertion of his own liberal principles. Rockefeller disputes the point. "It doesn't make you a liberal," he says, "to spend money you don't have. It just makes you a damn fool."

Rockefeller also points out that the $8.4 billion budget which he submitted to the legislature in 1971—even after the rebellious lawmakers cut $760 million from it—included the second largest tax increase in the history of New York. But Rockefeller that year saw the previously docile Republican-controlled legislature, conservative in mood and dominated by the politically ambitious assembly speaker, Perry B. Duryea from Montauk on Long Island, take the initiative from him on issue after issue. Welfare allowances were cut 10 percent, even though Rockefeller had originally recommended a 7.5 percent increase; medicaid eligibility was reduced; and a state commitment to

---

* These figures, based on the 1968–69 fiscal year, also represent the country's highest tax burdens calculated as a percent of personal income—13 percent in New York, 12.6 percent in California.

share revenue with local governments was trimmed back. In addition, a power-plant-site bill Rockefeller considered a major priority was killed, as were proposals for reduction of marijuana-possession penalties he had endorsed, compulsory health insurance, a proposed state department of justice, gun-control legislation, and a no-fault insurance bill. "An unknowing observer," the New York *Times*'s Albany correspondent, Frank Lynn, noted, "might have thought the governor was a Democrat dealing with a Republican-controlled legislature."

And in the wake of the legislature's budget-cutting spree, Rockefeller felt obliged to dismiss over 7,000 state employees, with the worst cuts in such public services as health, higher education, and recreation. Soon the newspapers were running poignant stories about disheartened personnel and callous cutbacks in the schools and mental hospitals. For a state long dedicated to liberal big-government spending traditions, it was a dramatic reversal of form.

A comparison of the New York State budgets in Rockefeller's first year in office (the 1959–60 budget) and the most recently approved year (1971–72) illustrates the near-geometric growth rate that has thrown the state into what Rockefeller now calls a financial "maelstrom."

	Fiscal Year 1959–60	Fiscal Year 1971–72
	(Figures in millions)	
Assistance to local school districts, community colleges, and private schools	$ 631	$2,559
Higher education (University of New York, state colleges, City University of New York, scholarships)	95	591
Assistance to localities for public assistance (aid to the aged, blind, needy children, etc.) and state welfare activities	176	1,100
Highway Department	308	893
Total budget	$1,900	$7,700

Short of some form of revenue sharing, New York State and City seem doomed to remain forever shortchanged in federal aid programs. Federal grants to various levels of New York government went well over $1 billion a year in the late 1960s, but the dollar figure was 40 percent below California's. As a share of state and local revenues, federal aid represented 12 percent in New York—compared to 16 percent in California and 17.5 percent in the country as a whole. New York ranks 48th among the 50 states in the percentage of its government budgets paid by Washington.

The major reason for New York's shortchanging is that federal aid formulas favor low-income and lightly populated states—a kind of residual congressional attitude, as Senator Javits has put it, "that the greatest virtues are the rural or small town virtues." Geographic formula discrimination harms New York on airport aid (despite the fantastic amount of national air travel that passes through the state), and waste treatment facilities and hospital construction are parceled out on a formula that favors states with low per capita incomes—of which New York is most definitely not one. (The per capita income of the state is 20 percent over the national average, but in the metropolitan New York area, the cost of living is almost that much above the country as a whole—not to mention the extra vacation budget New Yorkers deserve "to get away from it all.") None of the federal aid formulas seem to take into account the problems of population density and higher cost of land and services in congested urban areas.

To top it all off, New York finds itself penalized by virtue of the very pioneering nature of its governmental programs. In water pollution, air pollution, and freeway programs, for instance, New York was years ahead of the rest of the country, and its constant battle in Congress often focuses not so much on new programs as getting reimbursement for refinancing of what it has already done. The state has never been reimbursed for the Thomas E. Dewey Thruway, for instance. "It's a shocking thing," Javits says. "Every other state got a 90 percent ride. We've never been brought up to par on probably the greatest road in the United States."

The grim fiscal picture raises the legitimate question of whether New York is not just living beyond its means. The state comptroller, Arthur Levitt, says he has grave concerns about the state's financial future. He is a man who speaks with some authority, since he antedates even Rockefeller in Albany (he was elected to the first of five four-year terms in 1954) and has built up a popular reputation as a kind of fearless nonpartisan fiduciary—"the people's Comptroller," he calls himself.*

Levitt is especially critical of the method of bond financing adopted by Rockefeller on John Mitchell's recommendation—the use of quasi-independent sponsoring agencies, which can offer the state's "moral pledge" of repayment but not the "full faith and credit" of New York State which stands behind bonds that are approved by the people in popular referenda. (To date, none of the sponsoring agencies have had a deficit which required them to turn to the legislature for supplementary funds. But if they did, and the legislature refused, the bond holders could end up in the cold.) Levitt's objection to "backdoor financing," as he calls it, is based on two grounds:

First, it circumvents a constitutional restraint which I believe is more needed today, because of inflation and high taxes, than ever before in the history of the state.

Also, it is much more costly than the constitutional method of borrowing. . . .

You have to remember that some of the bonds, like those for housing, run up to 50 years. I doubt if they will be able to maintain the debt service through rentals. Now the State Housing Agency is financing the State University, housing for the elderly, child day care centers and mental hygiene institutions—hardly things one would expect to make money, especially in light of the inflationary thrust of our economy. . . .

* Levitt is a Democrat, but has managed to survive all the Republican sweeps of the state. In 1970, he won with a 1,332,441-vote plurality when no other Democrat won statewide.

The only reason Rockefeller has failed to go to the people for financing of the new bonds, Levitt claims, is that the people would have rejected many of them:

What we really need now is to take stock of where we are and decide on priorities. What this state (like others) has done is to proceed on the assumption it can do everything it wants—that it can take the aggregate of public wants and satisfy them right away. . . . . What the people have to decide now is what comes first—What is so compelling, so vital, that it needs to be done right now. The people are the best judges of that.

The bonded indebtedness of New York State, Levitt says, is now several times over what it was 10 years ago. Direct debt, to which the state has pledged its full faith and credit by popular vote, reached $3 billion in spring 1971, triple the amount of a decade before. Indirect debt (like the Albany Mall) reached $1.8 billion in 1971, up from $24 million a decade before. Contingent debt—based on a "moral guarantee" of the state, and issued through special authorities—rose to $2.1 billion, where there had been none at all a decade before. "By any measurement," Levitt contends, "the state of New York is mortgaging its future to a point which approaches the capacity of public burden."

The present fiscal crisis of New York can only get worse in the next years as a result of costs mandated by already approved programs, inflation, and the constant pressure from militant government employees' unions for increased wages and pension benefits. Even Rockefeller acknowledges that federal revenue sharing "would only be a stop-gap for two or three years while we have a chance to rethink the whole problem of state and federal revenue potential." But neither he nor his staff appear, up to now, to have developed the conceptual outline of a long-term solution. The one man I met in New York (and one of the very few in the nation) who seems to be thinking deeply about fiscal solutions for the rest of the 1970s and the 1980s is Howard Samuels, present head of the New York City Offtrack Betting Corporation, former head of the federal Small Business Administration, and unsuccessful candidate for governor in the 1970 Democratic gubernatorial primary. Samuels' ideas are no panacea, and as he talks one constantly senses Samuels, the future public candidate, arguing on his own behalf. But the seeds of the kind of radical change necessary to revamp public institutions and make them workable, are in his concepts:

There is a lack of proper management organization at all levels of government. . . . State lines are obviously outdated. State government lines don't correspond to logical regions. Constitutions of the states are a disaster, and so are their legislative systems. State governments should have five-year budgets, but despite the fact that Comptroller Arthur Levitt has long urged such a budget, Rockefeller has failed to come forth with it. The New York budget bureau operates better than most, but it is still functioning as it did when the dollar figures were only a fraction of what they are now.

Our democracy makes mediators of our leaders. We need financial planning, city planning, welfare law reform, but you get the impression the country can't make any major decisions of change. There's not a single political institution in this country that doesn't have to be completely revitalized—whether it's our courts, our prisons, our welfare system, our higher education system, our primary education system or our transportation system. Every single one of these is desperately in need of tough, strong decision making, and right now the process doesn't allow it. . . .

But the public is much more ready for tough, strong leadership than political leaders think they are. Every day the crisis of the country becomes more and more evident, and more people become concerned about what's happening to our democracy, there will be more and more willingness to accept political candidates who talk about fundamental changes in America.

Samuels also insists—and in this he is joined by a man on the other end of the political spectrum, Lt. Gov. Malcolm Wilson—that the state and its cities "cannot dodge the key question of the need for greater productivity in the public sector." New York State, and New York City in particular, have been the breeding grounds in the last few years of a new militancy among public employees. It began with school teachers, has spread to numerous other categories of government workers, and is already beginning to move across the country. As Dean Alan K. Campbell of the Maxwell Graduate School of Citizenship and Public Affairs at Syracuse University points out, "This has great implications for public sector costs, because we haven't figured out how you get—simultaneously—increases in productivity to match wage increases. In some areas, public employee salaries are now 20 percent ahead of private sector salaries for similar work." In New York City, the high government wages are inducing workers to desert taxpaying private industry jobs, and forcing some companies to flee the city. Municipal workers in the city presently put in a 35-hour work week, and if one counts "sick leave" and holidays, they get 45 days vacation in their first year—a privilege unheard of in private industry. Unions move into an actual management role by such devices as teachers' contracts specifying pupil-teacher ratios and specifying that teachers can't stay overtime. In the summertime, the much-put-upon bureaucrats also get to go home at 4 P.M.—a privilege granted by Mayor Wagner, which Lindsay has not had the temerity to repeal.

Even more than basic pay or work privileges, the controversial element in public sector employment is now pensions. The problem is centered in New York City, but applies statewide, and it is not new; for years, mayors have been negotiating higher and higher pension benefits with unions, often as a substitute for some immediate wage gains. Such settlements often let a mayor off the hook politically on the short run, but the long-term effect on city budgets—as New York City has been discovering—can be disastrous. All pension agreements have to be approved by the state legislature, and in fact the public employee unions have been exceptionally influential there. Once approved, the agreements are irreversible because under the state constitution, membership in a public pension system is a contractual right that may not be diminished or impaired. But in 1971, the legislature finally balked when New York City negotiated a pension agreement with the 90,000-member District 37 Council of the American Federation of State, County, and

Municipal Employees that gave the workers half pay after 20 years of service and full pay after 40 years at age 55. Wilson said that the agreement meant, in effect, that a man could retire after 40 years at 190 *percent* of his last pay, because he would also be receiving Social Security (not considered a part of New York's pension agreements), a total tax exemption from the state and city income tax, and an exemption from federal income tax until he gets back as much as he paid into the pension fund. In protest against the legislature's refusal to approve their pact with the Lindsay administration, the workers called a wildcat strike that tied up all the drawbridges coming into the city and caused the most monstrous traffic jam in New York City's history.

The political potential in this issue is not hard to divine, since the taxpayers are not only being inconvenienced by public-be-damned strikes, but must sooner or later get the message that they are being asked to pay for pensions far beyond those they get themselves. (In fact, private industry pension plans in the U. S. are something of a scandal, since workers' rights are generally terminated when they shift jobs, and plans often fail to pay anticipated dividends by all varieties of actuarial legerdemain.) Dean Campbell suggests New York may soon witness the unusual sight of "politicians, instead of running with appeals to the public sector employee, running against him." But there is the problem, he adds, that "the public sector is now so large, if you take each employee and his family members, that if you take them on you have a helluva political fight on your hands."

New York has had more than its share of public employee strikes, and they have become more and more frequent in recent years. The history goes back to the immediate postwar era, when school teachers at Buffalo struck and the legislature responded with the very tough Condon-Wadlin Law outlawing all strikes, requiring immediate discharge of all strikers—with permission to rehire them on a probationary basis for five years but without a penny additional compensation for three years after a worker was engaged in a job action. The law kept labor peace in New York for many years, but was inherently unfair because it had no provision for negotiated settlements. But when Lindsay became mayor of New York City in 1966, he was hit immediately by a transit strike. Lindsay at first stood up to the union—"his finest hour," Samuels says—but then he caved in and made an immensely expensive settlement and triggered a series of leapfrogging demands by municipal unions that have brought the city immense fiscal woes. As part of the transit workers' settlement, Lindsay agreed to ask the legislature to provide amnesty for the strikers, thus spelling the beginning of the end of the Condon-Wadlin Law.

In 1967, the legislature passed the so-called Taylor Law, allowing public employees to organize and engage in collective negotiation but still forbidding strikes. The law has a provision permitting heads of unions who strike to be fined and sent to jail. It has effectively averted strikes by state employees. But it has not been well enforced in New York City—critics say because Lindsay "has tried to buy them [the unions] off." Thus the city has been hit by strike after strike, diminishing the quality of life for all its people.* One solution to the problem would be to elect a mayor, as Samuels puts it, who is "a tough s.o.b." and would simply not tolerate strikes, or ask for amnesty for strikers. (Samuels may well be thinking of himself.) Another device, proposed by Wilson, would be to reenact some of the tougher penalties of the old Condon-Wadlin Law, including the provision that let any taxpayer go to court to block additional salary for a public employee for three years after a strike.

Norman Hurd, Rockefeller's director of state operations, argues that there is little evidence of waste or irresponsibility at the state level. The number of state employees, 71,500 in 1950, has risen to 156,000—but at least half of that increase is in mental hygiene and the state university. State income tax returns, he says, are processed at a quite economical six dollars each. But Hurd says he "is not so impressed with New York City or some other cities around the state."

At the upper rungs of government, both the state and city have some exceptionally able executives. Comparing the state government with other states, Dean Campbell says only California, and to some degree Michigan, can compare to the quality of men at the upper and middle levels of the bureaucracy. Improved salaries under Rockefeller, he says, have helped in this area, and New York State can now compete effectively with the federal government, and in many areas the private sector, in the pay scales offered for junior executive entering jobs. Over the years, this could make a tremendous difference in the quality of state government.

Government and People

New Yorkers are constantly affected by their activist state government. In welfare, for instance, the rolls have shot up from 420,000 recipients in 1955 to 1.7 million in 1971, triggering controversial cutbacks in aid levels. New York enacted a pioneering and extremely expensive Medicaid program in 1966 but had to reduce it substantially. The state's mental health hospitals now contain a third less people than they did in 1960, a result of better community facilities; of the hospitals that remain, one national expert told me, "They're probably the best in the country—and that's bad enough." One exceedingly restrictive statute went off the books in 1966—the 179-year-old law that had forbidden divorce on any grounds except adultery. The law had forced thousands of New Yorkers to stage scenes in which a private detective would find one of the partners in intimate association with a third party; no other state had a law so regressive or foolish. Now several other grounds are permissible for divorce in the state.

One of the most fascinating modern stories surrounded the effort, finally successful in 1970, to repeal an 1830-vintage statute that forbade all

* On the question of responsibility for the excessive concessions to municipal unions, Lindsay and Rockefeller can both be faulted.

abortions in New York, except to save a woman's life. The new law, most liberal in the nation, permitted any woman to have an abortion, on her doctor's counsel, up to the 24th week of pregnancy (and after that to save her life). Nor are there the restrictions of new abortion laws in some other states: Hawaii's 90-day residence requirement, for instance; or Maryland's insistence that all abortions be performed in an accredited hospital. In New York, abortions can be (and now are) performed in clinics, and there is a big out-of-state business from women whose states are more conservative. (More than half the 70,000 abortions performed in New York City in the first year were for out-of-state women.)

What made abortion reform possible in New York? The New York *Times*'s Bill Kovach put it this way: "Population pressures, limited resources, illegal abortion butchery and the demand of women for more control of their own lives demanded change." In the end, only the Roman Catholic Church fought the new law, and in legislative debate there was much talk of the "murder" of unborn fetuses. The senate Republican leader, Earl W. Brydges of Niagara Falls, played a key role in letting the bill come to a vote, though he had blocked it in the past; yet as the legislation was approved, Brydges, a Roman Catholic, wept openly. In the assembly, the bill was a single vote shy of the required minimum of 76 "yeas" when an obscure upstate Democrat, George M. Michaels of Auburn, rose to stop the voting. His hands trembling and tears welling in his eyes, he said: "I realize, Mr. Speaker, that I am terminating my political career, but I cannot in good conscience sit here and allow my vote to be the one that defeats this bill—I ask that my vote be changed to 'yes.'" (Michaels was, indeed, defeated in his own party's primary in the next election.) Even after final passage, Terence Cardinal Cooke, speaking for the state's Roman Catholic bishops, appealed to Governor Rockefeller to veto the bill. But the governor signed it. The outcome marked a nadir in Catholic influence on modern state government—in large part, because so many laymen refused to support their own Church's position.

In the troublesome area of penology, New York has a reasonably progressive history, going back to 1876 when the Elmira Reformatory was opened in order to separate young first offenders from hardened criminals. In the early years of this century, wardens at Sing Sing—the legendary "big house" up the Hudson 30 miles from New York—introduced a new degree of understanding into the treatment of convicts.* Over the years, more and more constructive vocational training programs were introduced into the prisons, and in 1965 the legislature abolished the death penalty, except for murders of policemen and peace officers. But the general attitude of prison officials has been that security comes before rehabilitation, a position opposed only by small numbers of psychiatrists, counselors, and chaplains. Starting in the late 1960s, the base of protest widened, among both civil rights organizations and the prisoners themselves. The objections were against the worst abuses of

---

* Sing Sing, the place where the electric chair was introduced in 1891 (and took 614 lives until it was last used in 1963), celebrated its 145th birthday in 1970 by being converted into an adult reception center for transfer of prisoners to other and more modern penal facilities around the state. The costs of renovating Sing Sing, and its vulnerability to escape, were the basic reasons for the change in status.

solitary confinement, the "strip cells" in which prisoners are forced to remain naked in empty cells, and the arbitrary rights of prison officials to cancel "good time" which convicts try to build up so that they can win early release.

As black and other minority prisoners became increasingly politicized, seeing themselves as political prisoners of the state, trouble began to mount around 1970. A serious sign of trouble was the major disturbances that hit New York City's detention houses in summer 1970. Later that year, a one-day riot occurred at the Auburn Correctional Facility, touched off by a black solidarity day sitdown. Six months later the press carried harrowing reports of 72 black and Puerto Rican inmates at Auburn still kept in special disciplinary areas. The isolated men smuggled out letters (some written in blood) telling of repeated beatings, gassings, and allegedly unprovoked assaults by guards.

Several of the worst troublemakers at Auburn, however, were quietly transferred to the Attica Correctional Facility (about 30 miles east of Buffalo), thereby laying the groundwork for the bloodiest prison uprising in American history in September 1971. The all-white guard force at Attica was already ill-equipped to deal sensitively with a prison population 70 percent black and about 15 percent Puerto Rican, and even less prepared to cope with the radical, desperate prisoners it received from Auburn. (Of this new breed of prisoner, New York State Corrections Commissioner Russell Oswald has said: "They have the idea that they are victims of a racist society, repressed by racist pigs and racist institutions.") In the uprising at Attica, 32 guards were taken as hostages and the convicts then issued a long list of demands—more religious freedom, the right to communicate with anyone at their own expense, "realistic rehabilitation," less pork (which Black Muslims do not eat), more fresh fruit, "competent" doctors, and the like. The state agreed to meet all these demands but refused to grant amnesty to all participants in the uprising (in which a guard had been killed), or to guarantee the prisoners "free passage" to a "nonimperialistic country."

The stalemate between the rebellious prisoners and state authorities lasted four days, and finally state police and National Guard troops stormed the prison. When the smoke had cleared, 32 prisoners and nine hostage guards were dead from the bullets of the attackers. Rockefeller, who had refused the prisoners' request that he come personally to Attica to negotiate with them, was subsequently blamed by some for precipitous action that cost so many lives. (Activist civil rights lawyer William M. Kunstler called him a "murderer.") Rockefeller, in turn, took full responsibility for the decision to storm the prison (a decision he said was the toughest of his career as governor), but insisted he had had no alternative. At a meeting with Commissioner Oswald, Rockefeller said, the rebellious convicts "just lined up eight of the prisoners [hostages], bound, blindfolded, with an executioner with a knife at his throat. At that point the decision was made. There was no alternative but to go in."

The irony of the situation, the *Wall Street Journal* noted some days later, was that "American prisons probably have never before done as effective a job in caring for and rehabilitating convicted criminals as they are now doing—and probably never before has there been a greater potential for more prison violence like the Attica revolt." The prison population of the U. S., both in absolute numbers and as a percentage of the population, has dropped sharply since 1960; for one thing, fewer petty burglars or bad-check passers are being imprisoned. But that means that the actual inmate population includes more men serving time for rape, homicide, robbery, or other violent crime. The "old-time cons" who stoically accepted the criminal justice system have faded away, replaced by the new breed of activists who see themselves as political prisoners.

Legislators and Lobbyists

On the level of technical competence and depth of resources, the New York legislature ranks high among the states. The Citizens Conference on State Legislatures ranks it second only to California, and lists these strengths:

Annual unlimited sessions; control over its own resources: time, staff and funds, and the ability to set legislative salaries by statute; a wide range of staff services, including fiscal research, committee staffing, leadership staffing and a full array of technical support; uniform, published rules of committee procedure, the jurisdiction of committees spelled out in the rules, and committee roll-call votes regularly taken, recorded and published.

The Citizens Conference faults New York on only a few points—long night sessions, crowded calendars, "the circus atmosphere which attends the ending of annual sessions," passage of many bills without extensive public hearings, and a lack of rules barring legislators from practicing before state regulatory agencies.

With a few brief interludes, including the period immediately after the Goldwater debacle of 1964, the legislature has been under firm Republican control. The extraordinary prestige and use of patronage power by Governors Dewey and Rockefeller have generally made the legislature, even though its Republican majorities consist primarily of upstate legislators, responsive to demands for innovative new programs. The worst crunch has come in what the upstate legislators, inheritors of a long tradition of paranoia about New York City, are willing to do to help out the big city down the Hudson.

Within the New York system, the elected leaders—the senate temporary president and assembly speaker—wield vast power. They name the committee chairmen and memberships, control a legislative budget of more than $22 million, appoint all legislative employees, and largely determine which key bills can go to the floor, and when. Today those leaders are Perry B. Duryea and Earl W. Brydges.

Assembly Speaker Duryea, 50 years old in 1972, from the town of Montauk, Long Island, 110 miles out in the Atlantic Ocean from New York City, is head of a successful lobster wholesale firm which his father founded. Ideologically, he puts himself "a little to the right" of Rockefeller. He is a tall, silvery haired, and quite formal man who is more fascinated by the work-ings of politics and legislative procedure than ideology. Intellectually, he is more than a match for most of the city legislators, who are his most frequent adversaries. In 1971, Duryea was the man who spearheaded the successful move to cut an unprecedented $760 million from Rockefeller's budget; after the session, he said the legislature's greatest achievement was that "we recog-nized the limitations of our society."

Senate President Brydges, 67 years old in 1972, from Niagara Falls on the Canadian border, is a practicing attorney and has been a state senator for 24 years. He is noted for his interest in education. In contrast to Duryea, Brydges is, in the words of one New York journalist, "sentimental, emo-tional and outgoing." He has worked for bills that benefit the banks and utilities that provide a major share of Republican financing north of the Westchester County line, and it might be said that his Republicanism is more akin to the Midwestern Taft variety than the New York Dewey-Rockefeller brand. Niagara Falls is, after all, 120 miles closer to Cleveland than it is to New York City.

Yet Brydges, like Duryea, has widened his intellectual horizons far be-yond his native area, and has taken part in some of the pioneering legislative efforts of recent years. The problem with both men, as seen by one observer, is that "they are able to view the big city only as a constant thorn in the side of their tidy upstate world—not as the heart and soul of the Empire State." By the same token, they may be the ideal legislators for the rest of New York State.

The budget and powers of New York State government are so colossal that Albany draws lobbyists as flowers attract bees. The lobbyists are now a highly sophisticated group, representing virtually every interest in the state, and a far cry from the old stereotype of the cigar-chomping, vote-buying influence peddler.

By general consensus, the education lobby is the biggest, and many be-lieve the most powerful, on the Albany scene. Numerous organizations are included, not the least of which is the state board of regents, which has vast powers over the $2 billion-plus in aid to schools which the legislature doles out each year. The more direct pressure for teachers' salaries is exerted by the upstate-centered New York State Teachers Association and the newly formed New York State Federation of Teachers (the competitive, statewide extension of Albert Shanker's city-based United Federation of Teachers). Practically all the major universities, public and private, lobby in Albany.

Industry is very powerful, especially on the "little bills" that no one no-tices. Some major companies hire lobbyists to represent them during legisla-tive sessions, but there are also umbrella groups like the Associated Industries of New York (the state's NAM) and the Empire State Chamber of Com-merce. Banks are quite likely to send their own representatives to Albany, but they hardly need to: according to one report in 1971, nine of the 22 members of the Senate Banks Committee and five of the 22 members of the same committee on the assembly side were shareholders, officers, or directors of banks or savings and loan associations. However, there is a running feud between the savings and commercial banks.

While business interests swing the most weight with upstate Republicans, organized labor is especially influential with New York City Democrats. The AFL-CIO carries the burden for most labor lobbying, but the Teamsters have their own man in Albany too. Other important lobbies represent organized medicine and the Roman Catholic Church, although the Church's power, as we have noted, has recently been on the decline.

Not to be overlooked is the very active New York City lobby. It is headed by Richard A. Brown, a veteran of 12 years work in Albany, first as a staff counsel to legislative leaders and then as Lindsay's man on the scene. Brown has a large staff which does hundreds of favors for legislators, and in turn hopes to get a favorable ear from them on the multitudinous bills of each session that relate to the city. Most of the city bills get handled on their merits in the legislature, except for the controversial city aid measures that are perennially mired in the tug-of-war between the city, governor, and legislative leadership. (New York City—and also New York State—maintain their own lobby operations in Washington, too.)

"Good government" interests are represented by groups like the Citizens Union and League of Women Voters. But Assemblyman Stephen J. Solarz, a 31-year-old political science teacher at Brooklyn College, suggests that there are "significant interests in the society that go underrepresented"—including "the poor, the consumer, the non-union wage-earner, and the young."

Politics I: The GOP

As the weight of population and power in America has shifted westward, New York has lost its unique status as *the* preeminent source of Presidential candidates. In the course of American history, five Presidents have come from New York (Van Buren, Fillmore, Cleveland, both Roosevelts), and a sixth man (Tilden) won in the popular vote but lost in the electoral college. Between 1900 and 1948, 11 of the 26 Republican and Democratic party nominations for President went to New Yorkers. But in the five Presidential elections since 1952, only one New Yorker—William E. Miller, Goldwater's running mate—has appeared on a national ticket, and even his candidacy was taken seriously by few people (least of all himself). From this count one may exclude Eisenhower and Nixon, who though they had resided in New York for a few years just before their Presidential nominations, belonged spiritually to the open plains and Southern California respectively.

More than demographic change has reduced New York's Presidential role. With the exception of Robert Kennedy, who became a legal resident of the state to run for the Senate, not a single New York Democrat has mounted a major Presidential campaign in recent years—simply because the New York Republicans have monopolized virtually all the major offices in the state. And while local Republicans have been winning statewide elections in New York, their brand of Republicanism has been too liberal for national GOP tastes. In fact, it might be said that for countless Republicans who live south of the Mason-Dixon Line and west of the Appalachians, New York Republicans have been pariahs ever since 1952 when Dewey and the New York GOP got Eisenhower nominated over Taft. (New York-based communications media—especially *Time*—were used to publicize the alleged delegate "steal" by Taft forces in the South.) An essential part of the Goldwater movement was an emotional reaction against the monied Eastern liberal "establishment" within the GOP. But Republican anti-Easternism may turn out to have been a temporary phenomenon of the 1950s and '60s, easily overcome in the next few years if the ideological center of the national Republican party drifts more to the left, or if, as many believe is now occurring, the Republicans of New York become more conservative.

From the 1890s to the start of the New Deal, New York was strongly Republican in its Presidential voting. Then it turned Democratic, and it has really remained that way ever since, except for a narrow plurality for Dewey in 1948 and Eisenhower majorities in the 1950s. In 1960, Nixon lost the state to Kennedy by 383,666 votes; in 1968, he lost it to Humphrey by 370,538. Few people expect Nixon, or a Republican of like ideology, to win it in the near future. One could cite many reasons for New York's liberal-Democratic orientation in Presidential campaigns, starting with its heavy urban-minorities population. Perhaps the most convincing explanation is the activist-progressive model of executive which New York has had since the days of Al Smith, reinforced by the state's strong civil rights tradition.

For 10 of 11 successive gubernatorial elections, from 1918 through 1938, New Yorkers chose Democratic governors, and in almost every election the Democrats won by piling up huge New York City pluralities that overwhelmed the normal GOP upstate majorities. In those days, one old hand in New York campaigns told me, "the Republican party was a patsy for the Democratic governors—Smith, Roosevelt, and Lehman." The governors made a whipping boy out of the almost constantly Republican legislature, suggesting that the GOP was a regressive force controlled by Old Guard upstate utility interests and banks. Each succeeding Republican gubernatorial candidate would get tarred and feathered with the same brush, and go down to defeat.

It took a city man, Tom Dewey, to turn the personalities and historical pattern upside down. Dewey had an aura of glamor and courage from his success in driving the racketeers out of the city, and he exploited his advantage to get the votes of upstaters (always suspicious of the city's venality) *and* New York City people (who considered him one of their own). When Dewey took office, he quickly exercised his patronage powers to change the Republican party from a group of provincial baronies into a coordinated instrument under his own direction. By the same methods, he dominated the legislature, so that it began to lose its reactionary reputation. And he preempted the strong executive image of his Democratic predecessors and backed progressive programs that sometimes shocked the old GOP chieftans, but had wide voter appeal.

Under Dewey, the Democratic majorities in New York City (which had averaged well over 500,000 in the 1920s and '30s) were cut down to less than 200,000—though it was all done, as his longtime confidant, R. Burdell Bixby puts it, by personal appeal rather than any strong grass-roots Republican organizing drive in the city. At the same time, the upstate Republican majorities almost doubled, from a prior average of about 400,000 votes to a new average close to 800,000. Under Rockefeller, essentially the same pattern has continued. There has been some slackening in Republican majorities in the upstate cities, but it has been offset by the rapidly growing Republican suburban vote, and even more importantly, by Rockefeller's improved position in New York City. In 1958, Rockefeller lost the city by 309,814 votes, but in each succeeding election he narrowed the margin until in his fourth-term race in 1970, he was behind in the city by a minuscule 16,541 votes. In that election, Rockefeller carried upstate by 746,547 votes and emerged with a statewide plurality of 730,006, a margin unmatched by any gubernatorial candidate since Lehman in the depths of the Depression.

A lot of the credit for Rockefeller's amazing four-term winning streak goes to the dull, awkward campaigns of his Democratic opponents. Averell Harriman (1958) and Arthur Goldberg (1970) were men of national renown, but seemed more interested in debating international than state issues. Robert Morgenthau (1962), picked because of his famous family name and because he was Jewish, was a totally colorless candidate (but later turned out to be a crackerjack U. S. attorney in New York City). Frank O'Connor (1966) bore the marks of a big-city machine candidate and was a weaker choice than any of several candidates rejected by the party leaders. Rockefeller has also been winning because people think he is sincere and tries hard. Finally, and some say foremost, there have been the lavish, incredibly sophisticated Rockefeller campaigns. No state candidate in American history has ever mounted a comparable effort. James M. Perry wrote in the *National Observer* in October 1970:

> Four years ago, I suggested that Nelson A. Rockefeller's winning campaign for governor was the most astute, the most professional, the most imaginative, and perhaps the most ruthless this nation has ever seen.
> And I further suggested that we probably would never see another one like it. Wrong. Wrong. Wrong.
> Rockefeller is running for governor once more this year—and this campaign is the most professional, the most astute, and the most carefully organized. . . .

Only on the scores of imaginativeness and ruthlessness, Perry suggested, did the 1970 Rockefeller campaign fall somewhat short of the 1966 effort. The 1966 television advertising blitz was a classic, first creating a favorable image for a candidate who started an incredible 26 percentage points behind in the polls, and then moving to slashing attack on the opposition in the final stages. It began with a variety of amusing, sometimes animated commercials that plugged Rockefeller's record on issue after issue—roads, narcotics pre-

vention, consumer protection, "Rockefeller's Medicaid," the state's first minimum wage, increased aid for police protection, help for the retarded—without ever introducing the governor himself. The "goodness" and "caring" of
the man came across powerfully. But then, in the last stages, Rockefeller
himself came on the commercials, grimly attacking his opponent, Frank
O'Connor. For upstate audiences, for instance, there were commercials
blatantly appealing to their prejudices, calling O'Connor "a New York City
politician," suggesting New York State "will be run by the New York City
clubhouse crowd" if O'Connor won.

The 1970 commercials, though the same agency, Jack Tinker, handled
them, were more restrained, concentrating continuously on the single theme:
"Rockefeller: he's done a lot. He'll do a lot more." Most of the attacking was
left to defecting Democrats. But a series of questions, designed to question
Goldberg's credibility, were flashed on the screens. And in the last week of
the election, as the Rockefeller team began to worry about overconfidence
and a possibly low turnout in their areas of strength, 400,000 simulated tele-
grams were cranked out by a computer and sent to upstate voters with the
message: "I NEED YOUR HELP. UNLESS YOU VOTE THIS TUESDAY THE ORGANIZED
DEMOCRAT PARTY OF NEW YORK CITY COULD TAKE OVER YOUR STATE GOVERN-
MENT. . . . I NEED YOUR SUPPORT FOR GOOD GOVERNMENT. NELSON A. ROCKE-
FELLER."

In 1966, the Republican organization reported spending $5.2 million to
reelect Rockefeller, while the O'Connor campaign cost one-eighth as much
($576,000). By 1970, the Rockefeller outlay was up to $6.8 million, of which
$4.4 million came from Rockefeller and his family. But the reporting laws
under which the sums are reported are filled with loopholes, and a more reasonable estimate of the total cost, according to Fred Powledge in *New York*,
would be $12 to $15 million. The Goldberg campaign reported spending
$1.7 million. The unpaid organizational help of some labor unions (princi-
pally the municipal workers and International Ladies Garment Workers Union) doubtless added considerable value to the Goldberg effort. But Rockefeller, too, had labor support, and in fact on an unprecedented scale for a
Republican candidate. Victor Borella, Rockefeller's Dartmouth classmate and
longtime associate, had been nurturing union support for the governor over
many years. In 1970, he was instrumental in getting Rockefeller endorsements from unions representing over one million members, including 400,000
members of the Building Trades Unions ("the cornerstone of Rockefeller's
labor support," Borella says), the Teamsters, and in a disputed but unambiguous vote at its state convention, the New York State AFL-CIO. Aside from
personal cultivation of leaders, labor seemed to like Rockefeller because of
New York's $1.85-an-hour minimum wage (highest in the country) and a
remembrance of how well Rockefeller treats unions that endorse him. In
1963, just after he won reelection with first-time support from the Patrolmen's Benevolent Association and Uniformed Firefighters Association of New
York City, Rockefeller asked the legislature to pass a bill establishing the
principle that firemen's and patrolmen's pensions after 20 years on the job

would be computed on the basis of the individual's salary during his last year. The legislation was passed in 1967 and the principle later spread to transit police, sanitationmen, housing police, and correction officers. Rockefeller's action, the New York *Daily News* reported, was "the principal spur behind the rocketing costs of pensions" in the city ($290 million a year in 1962–63, $618 million in fiscal year 1970–71). Nor has Rockefeller ever sought repeal of New York's law granting unemployment compensation to strikers when they have been off the job seven weeks. (Only one other state, Rhode Island, has similar legislation.) The building trades unions, of course, have reason to be delighted with Rockefeller's vast construction programs, which have caused labor shortages and driven up wages across the state.*

The 1970 Rockefeller campaign got officially underway in February when 27,000 square feet of space was leased on Madison Avenue at costs that ran up to $27,000 a month. The Rockefeller organization eventually built up to 380 paid employees, including 35 on leave without pay from state jobs. Many had worked for the governor in several earlier campaigns and were among the top professionals in American campaigning. (Goldberg, by comparison, had 35 paid employees.) Rockefeller and his entourage traveled about the state in his private air fleet—a Grumman Gulfstream 2 jet worth $3.5 million, a helicopter, and a two-engine Fairchild. (Goldberg usually traveled by commercial airline, but occasionally chartered flights.) But it was particularly in the area of polling and direct mail, Richard Reeves reported in the New York *Times*, that Rockefeller was "expanding the frontiers of political technology."

On the direct-mail front, the Los Angeles firm of Decision Making Information (reviewed in our California chapter) was brought in for consultation. Based on information from polls, commercial mailing lists, and state records, the Rockefeller organization had worked for years to accummulate and then computerize details on the lives of as many as 75 percent of the state's voters. Thus letters with specially tailored messages could be "targeted" to a variety of professional and ethnic groups, families who had sought hospital care for a mental-health program, or people who were known (through extensive telephone canvassing) to be pro-Rockefeller. Some 30 million pieces of printed matter were prepared, including special brochures treating individually the Rockefeller record and promises on labor, education, the mentally retarded, health, higher education, recreation, environment, and the arts. There was even a "Rockefeller Mini Kit," designed especially for women, with brochures highlighting Rockefeller's appointment of women to public posts, a litter bag, and an index card with a recipe for Happy Rockefeller's Coffee Cake. There were also handsome little brochures to say especially what Rockefeller had done for the Lower Hudson Valley area, the Niagara frontier, the capital district, and the Central New York-Mohawk Valley area (but not New York City).

---

* The building trades, with their intransigence on letting in blacks—on the Albany Mall job, workers have been brought in from Canada while local blacks try in vain to get construction jobs—are *enfants terribles* in the eyes of New York liberals. New York *Post* columnist Murray Kempton once said of the building trades leadership: "They would build gas ovens if it was steady work."

Behind this vast outpouring of effort lay a carefully planned strategy based on a series of statewide polls coordinated by Lloyd Free, a Rockefeller friend of 30-years standing. Free is a noted lecturer, writer, and consultant in the public-opinion research field. (The actual polling is done by Political Surveys and Analysis Inc. of Princeton, N. J., which uses an affiliate of the Gallup organization for its field work.) The polls which Free commissioned showed that Rockefeller was 12 percentage points behind Goldberg in the spring, running neck and neck during the summer and up to mid-September, and then forged ahead by 12 percentage points in October. Free's final prediction, as the polls closed on election day, was that Rockefeller would win with 53 percent of the vote; the official tally eventually gave him an uncannily close 52.4 percent. But as with all good polling, the major contribution was to show the ethnic-religious-economic-educational differentiations of support for the candidates and to identify the pivotal groups on which the campaign should concentrate. These "pivotals" were people who ranked Rockefeller fairly high on Free's ladderlike attitudinal scale, but were not planning to vote for him for one reason or another. Half of the pivotals lived in New York City and tended to have lower educational levels and income levels than their upstate counterparts; a key problem, finally resolved satisfactorily by pinpointed messages and careful orchestration of what the candidate said, was to gain the support of both groups, despite their differing backgrounds. Also, the campaign was managed to magnify Rockefeller's lasting strength in the polls—the feeling of people that Rockefeller was a hard-working, sincere governor—and to neutralize the chief reason for opposition to him—his high-tax record. There is no question that the polls dictated a major part of campaign strategy. Campaign director R. Burdell Bixby said, "The polls tell us better than our instincts what it is the people are concerned about." (The Rockefeller people are so "poll happy" that they may have a number of separate operations underway simultaneously. In 1970, for instance, the Independents for Rockefeller organization sponsored a whole separate series of surveys by Decision Making Information of Los Angeles.)

According to Free's postelection analysis, Rockefeller retained his traditional bases of support from earlier years—upper- and middle-income people, older people, well-educated people, professional, business, and clerical-sales groups. But he extended his support much further down the socioeconomic pyramid than most Republicans, running even with Goldberg in the group of people earning $5,000 a year or less, losing by only 5 percent among those with a grade-school education or less, winning by 10 percentage points among skilled laborers, and getting half the vote of people in labor-union households. Among ethnic groups, Rockefeller won big in families of German, British, Italian, or Irish ancestry. He was far ahead among Protestants, 16 percentage points in front among Catholics, and lost badly only among Jews (who obviously identified with Goldberg).

Free believes that for all the talk of a swing to the right in New York State and elsewhere, the electorate remains what he has called "ideological conservatives" in terms of what they think government should generally be concerned with, but "operational liberals" when it comes to specific proposals to solve specific problems. On air- and water-pollution control, he says, the public was ahead of the politicians—an unusual case. But even on most programs of a social nature, a majority of the public is for continuing government programs and sometimes for increasing expenditures. Their big hang-up, Free says, is on welfare, where the Puritan ethnic—"it's a sin to be poor, the relief rolls are loaded with chiselers"—still holds on.

The polls also suggest that while suburbanites are not as inclined to favor large-scale urban aid programs by government, they are much more liberal on the subject than upstaters.

The Rockefeller-Republican success record of the last several years may be credited in varying degrees to Rockefeller's appeal beyond party lines, his wallet, and the professional cadre he built up on and off the state payroll. How much Republican strength will remain after Rockefeller leaves the scene—and few believe he will try for a *fifth* term in 1974—is conjectural. R. Burdell Bixby takes a mild view, seeing a "necessary vacuum" in leadership. Others see the party splitting into many camps, emulating the rival Democrats. It seems almost inevitable that the party will turn more to the right. Both Assembly Speaker Duryea and Lieutenant Governor Wilson, the leading GOP gubernatorial possibilities, stand to the right of Rockefeller. Duryea, as we noted earlier, represents a district far out on the tip of Long Island, beyond suburbia. Wilson comes from Yonkers in Westchester County, was educated in Catholic schools, has a superb grasp of state issues but no strong impulse for reform. "Our role in state government will be to the extent of our fiscal capacity to keep doing the things we're doing," he told me in an interview. (Wilson has been lieutenant governor since 1959 and likes to crack, "I've been No. 2 longer than Avis.")

Significantly missing from the future leadership equation is any progressive-type city or suburban Republican. Many see Lindsay's defection to the Democrats as a death blow to moderate New York Republicanism. It has been on the skids in its traditional stronghold, Manhattan Island, ever since Lindsay resigned his U. S. House seat to run for mayor. Presently, the only elected Republican from Manhattan is a state senator who would lose without Liberal party support. The liberal Republicans have few alternative leaders right now, especially if they would like to put one of their number into the governor's chair after Rockefeller. Sen. Jacob K. Javits and Attorney General Louis Lefkowitz are both popular officeholders of the GOP's liberal wing, but too old now to run for governor.

The alternative scenario is for the GOP simply to turn to the right, centering its appeal to upstate and the suburbs and toward the heavily ethnic blue-collar vote in the outer boroughs of New York. Two Republicans have done well there—Rockefeller in 1970, and James Marchi, the state senator who took the 1969 GOP mayoralty nomination away from Lindsay. But it is hard to imagine a charismaless Republican conservative, alienated from the financial and media support of Manhattan, winning election as governor. Rockefeller's own polls in 1970 showed that in terms of basic party loyalty, 44.6 percent of New Yorkers considered themselves Democrats and only 33.6 percent Republicans. (Another 14.5 percent were independents, and the rest adherents of the minor parties.)

Politics II: The Democrats ...

New York's Democrats have always been as quarrelsome a group as one can find in American politics, though they had an era of relative unity during the "Golden Age" of Smith, Roosevelt, and Lehman. In the early 1940s, as Lehman left the governorship, the Democratic coalition forged by the governors—a coalition essentially analagous to the national New Deal coalition, for which it was the prototype—began to break up. Ethnic rivalries were boiling to the top, and in 1949 the Italians, led by Carmine De Sapio of New York City, finally wrested control of Tammany Hall (the regular Democratic Manhattan organization) from the Irish. De Sapio looked mildly reformist when he came to power, and succeeded in electing Robert Wagner mayor in 1953, Harriman in 1954, and getting himself appointed secretary of state in the Harriman administration. Only time would tell how totally power doth corrupt. (In 1968, De Sapio was indicted for conspiring to bribe Lindsay's water commissioner, James L. Marcus, and for extorting contracts from the Consolidated Edison Company. He was convicted and went to prison.)

In 1949, the first glimmerings of the modern reform movement in New York Democratic politics emerged on Manhattan Island. Suspicious of the old Tammany way of doing things, the reformers responded naturally to a leader like Adlai Stevenson; in fact, his race for President in 1952 drew many of them into politics for the first time. Numerous reform clubs came into being during the 1950s, peopled by young professionals, especially from the publishing and communications industries. The movement made a quantum leap forward in strength after the 1958 Democratic state convention in Buffalo where De Sapio crudely dictated, in public view, the nomination of New York District Attorney Frank Hogan for the U. S. Senate. Hogan was an honorable and able man, but Harriman and many other delegates had wanted a "more liberal" candidate. Republicans promptly raised a cry of "bossism" and Harriman and Hogan went down to defeat the following November—while Democrats were sweeping elections in most other states.

The debacle at Buffalo gave the reformers the *cause célèbre* they needed to attract thousands of new supporters. An umbrella reform organization, the Committee for Democratic Voters, was established in 1959, and three prestigious Democrats—Mrs. Eleanor Roosevelt, Herbert Lehman, and Thomas Finletter—headed up a powerful drive to change the operation of the party, especially in New York City. Mayor Wagner, who had been De Sapio's candidate in his first two runs for office, decided that support was now more detriment than help and ran in 1961 as an "antiboss" candidate, trouncing De Sapio's candidate in the primary.

The reform element built strength steadily through the 1960s. One reformer, William Fitts Ryan, had been elected to Congress in 1960 from West Side Manhattan (a center of reform strength); that victory was followed up by two congressional victories in the Bronx in 1964, one of them the immensely symbolic defeat of one of the toughest old-line bosses, Charles A. Buckley, by reformer Jonathan B. Bingham. De Sapio was ousted from control of Tammany Hall in 1961. In 1965, Wagner and Robert Kennedy effected the election of John Burns, a man basically friendly to the reform cause, as state chairman. The Kennedy and McCarthy Presidential campaigns of 1968 invigorated the reform movement, and that was the year Paul O'Dwyer, an irascible liberal and one of the reform movement's founders, won nomination to the U. S. Senate in the first statewide primary after the old convention system had been abolished. The contrast between 1958, when De Sapio forced Hogan down the throat of the party, and 1968, when O'Dwyer was nominated, could scarcely have been more striking. The 1968 elections also saw new reform strength in Congress through the election of Edwin I. Koch from John Lindsay's old "silk stocking" 17th District on Manhattan's East Side, the victory of Shirley Chisholm, the first black Congresswoman, in Brooklyn, and the election of Allard K. Lowenstein, architect of the "dump Johnson" movement and one of the country's most articulate liberals, from Long Island. In 1970, redistricting cost Lowenstein his seat but the reformers gained a colorful new Washington voice through election of Bella S. Abzug from the lower end of Manhattan and other friends in Congress through the success of Charles Rangle in upsetting Harlem's Adam Clayton Powell and the election of Herman Badillo, former Bronx borough president and a prominent reformer, as the country's first Representative of Puerto Rican descent. Most of the new reformers replaced unimaginative machine stalwarts, a change that unquestionably improved the quality of New York's often dismal congressional delegation. A similar reform bridgehead, with general improvement of the Democratic membership, has been noted in the state legislature.

There has been a big change within the Democratic state committee. In short, it is being fairly run. John Shea, a longtime reform leader and head of the reform caucus in the committee, recalls that in the early '60s, "you'd show up at a state committee meeting and no matter what you said, you knew you'd lost, because the chairman would have more than 150 proxies (out of a total of 300 votes) in his pocket." As a result of the reformers' pressure, there is now a limit of five proxies per person, and general party procedures are much fairer. With chairman Burns's leadership, and under prodding from the national party, the Presidential primary rules have also been changed to have all delegates popularly elected. Previously, a third were chosen by the state committee, which meant a small group of men controlled a major part of New York's national convention delegates. (The democratic effectiveness of the Presidential primary is still vitiated, however, by state legislation which does not permit delegates to show on the ballot whom they prefer for the party's Presidential nomination.)

In 1967, the reformers achieved a long-term goal with repeal of New

York's noisy convention system of nominating statewide candidates. Conventions, they charged, were prone to boss control and essentially undemocratic. The campaign for a direct primary system also had strong backing from good government groups like the Citizens Union and League of Women Voters, and important newspaper support. But instead of shifting to a simple primary, New York opted for a hybrid system patterned after recommendations of the National Municipal League and American Political Science Association and actually used, in varying forms, by Colorado, Massachusetts, Connecticut, Utah, and Rhode Island. Under the New York version, the state committee of each party meets in the spring and designates its preferred candidate for each office. His name automatically goes onto the primary ballot. A losing candidate for the state committee endorsement, providing he has received 25 percent of the committee vote, can also get on the ballot without petitions. And other candidates can get on the primary ballot by collecting 10,000 signatures of party members, with at least 50 signatures from each of 47 of the state's 62 counties. The nomination is then finally decided in the primary. A like system had actually been in effect in New York a half century earlier, from 1913 to 1921, championed by Charles Evans Hughes who said the preprimary conference was a feasible way to curb the arbitrary powers of party organizations while leaving them a significant voice in the selection of candidates.

As ideal as it looks on paper, the hybrid committee-primary system was a disaster when New York tried it 50 years ago, and it is proving to be a disaster now. Regardless of a candidate's history, his merits, or his position on issues, chairman Burns points out, as soon as he gets the endorsement of the convention he is attacked as "the politicians' choice." (This upset Arthur Goldberg so much in 1970 that he announced, even in accepting the committee's endorsement, that he would circulate petitions among the voters to show he was not the candidate of the "bosses.") Nor does the preprimary endorsement procedure really help a man win in the primary or reduce the number of candidates. In 1970, Goldberg was challenged by and almost beaten by Howard Samuels in the primary. (Republicans privately acknowledge that if Samuels had been the candidate, Rockefeller would have had a much more difficult time winning his fourth term.) In that year's Democratic Senate primary, the endorsed candidate, former White House aide Theodore Sorensen, emerged with a feeble 16.5 percent of the vote in a four-man field. The unendorsed winner, Rep. Richard L. Ottinger, won with only 39.3 percent of the vote. The principal reason for Ottinger's victory was his lavish media campaign, estimated to cost as much as $50,000 to $60,000 a week over a three-month period; altogether, Ottinger spent $1.9 million, *nine* times as much as his three opponents combined. His campaign manager earned a cool $1,500 a week. Ottinger is a multimillionaire and could afford the expense (his mother kindly lent him $1.8 million), but the open primary system in New York may indeed evolve into a game for rich men only. Under the old convention system, a candidate could seek a statewide Democratic nomination by spending a few thousand dollars in trips around the state to talk with leaders of the various delegations. Today, it appears, he may as well stay at home unless he has several hundreds of thousands of dollars to spend.

The Democrats have still more problems with the primary system. The voter turnout has been appallingly low—about 20 percent of registered Democrats. Jews, endowed with a strong sense of civic duty, vote in relatively strong numbers and have a disproportionate voice; in 1970, for instance, the Democrats ended up with a ticket of four Jews and one black—hardly a representative cross section of New York. And with 75 percent of the Democratic vote concentrated in metropolitan New York (the city, Nassau and Westchester counties), the candidates make little effort to gain upstate support.

It may be that New York's Democrats are such an unstable conglomerate of conflicting factions that practically any nominating system will bring them woe. But there is general agreement that adopting the present hybrid system was a bad mistake, and that it would be far preferable to drop all endorsement procedures and simply have a wide-open primary. Burns would like to couple that step with a "tremendous registration and get-out-the-vote effort" to get rank-and-file Democrats participating in the nomination process.

The Republicans, though, are in no hurry to take Democrats off the hook. The same nominating laws apply to them, but Rockefeller's say over GOP nominees is so complete that the whole process turns into something of a charade.* Members of the Republican state committee who do the nominating, for instance, include a high percentage of middle-level leaders who support their families on direct or indirect state patronage. Opposing the governor's wishes, Richard Reeves noted, would be equated with "financial suicide." In 1970, despite the broad opposition within the GOP to the nomination of interim Sen. Charles E. Goodell for a full Senate term, at least one of Goodell's potential opponents could not find a single delegate willing to nominate him at the party meeting. Goodell, a former upstate Congressman who had been Rockefeller's appointee to the Senate seat vacated by Robert Kennedy's death, had swung so far to the left on the Vietnam war and other issues that huge numbers of Republicans opposed his election. But Goodell was Rocky's man, at least through the nominating season, so that he escaped without a single primary opponent. In the general election, he was defeated by Conservative party nominee James L. Buckley, who got the votes of hundreds of thousands of Republicans. By that time Rockefeller, sensing the elective disaster that awaited Goodell, had managed to align himself to a degree with Buckley while maintaining his *pro forma* support of Goodell.

But more about the troubled Democrats. With De Sapio gone, the reader may ask, where are the legendary "bosses" and "machine men"? The answer is that county party leaders are still to be found—men like Joseph Crangle in Buffalo, Meade Esposito in Brooklyn, Matthew Troy in Queens, Patrick Cunningham in the Bronx, and Frank Rossetti in Manhattan. But

---

* The Republican endorsing meetings will certainly get livelier when Rockefeller retires. But the Republicans have a propensity for decorum that may save them the worst effects of a preprimary endorsing system.

none has a fraction of the power De Sapio once exercised: now there is not enough patronage, and there are no longer the hordes of blindly faithful ethnic followers that a good machine requires. Several of the "regular" leaders are younger men, and try hard to keep passably good relations with the reformers in their midst.

The principal interest of most regular leaders is to rule for the sake of ruling, and the material rewards of office. The reformers are idealistic about issues, party reform, and party procedures. The present-day umbrella organization of reform groups is the New Democratic Coalition, formed after the 1968 campaign. It is the first really statewide reform organization. While its principal strength is in New York City, and in turn particularly in Manhattan, the reformers do control about a quarter of the votes in the Democratic state committee—an all-time high. Since Mrs. Roosevelt and Lehman died, the reformers have lacked a single, strong spokesman. Among their more effective leaders is Paul O'Dwyer—an appealing but stubborn man who refused to endorse Humphrey until just before the 1968 election.

The constant complaint of party leaders is that the reformers need to realize that to win in politics, one has to compromise occasionally. Reform ranks include a younger set of leftist-oriented zealots who take a cataclysmic view of politics—you must say "yes" to their 10-question set or you don't get a passing grade. Some of the more seasoned reformers tend to be more flexible, and discover that the regulars, though more conventional in outlook, are not all standpatters, thieves, and rogues, and that there are ways to work with them. Among the more seasoned and effective reformers are Jack Shea, to whom we referred previously, and Russell Hemenway, who was executive director of the Committee for Democratic Voters (a forerunner of the New Democratic Coalition) and went on to head the National Committee for an Effective Congress. The NCEC has for several years been a major conduit of liberal New York money to like-minded Democratic Senate candidates around the country, and Hemenway has lobbied hard for campaign spending reform legislation in Congress.

It is hard not to sympathize with Democratic State Chairman Burns when he reflects on how difficult it is to get the uncompromising elements of his party together to win an election. In 1969, he points out, after City Comptroller Mario Procaccino had beaten several liberals and reformers to get the Democratic mayoralty nomination in New York City, "hundreds of thousands of liberal voters and all the reformers left the party line and supported Lindsay." In 1970, although the reformers favored Samuels over Goldberg in the primary, Goldberg was acceptable to them and they supported him in the general election. "But the right wing of our party—particularly the Irish, Italian and Polish Catholics—they left the party and voted for Rocky." The voters, Burns notes, are becoming more and more concerned about issues and candidates. "It's healthy in a way, but certainly makes it hard for the party."

By joining the Democratic party in August 1971, John Lindsay became—instantly—the most powerful Democrat in the state. Even if Presidential politics prove frustrating to Lindsay, he would be in a strong position to run for governor in 1974.

. . . and a Note on Congress

For years the New York City delegation was packed with unimaginative machine stalwarts who generally viewed election to Congress as a way station to that juiciest of all patronage rewards, a judgeship. They refused to move their families to Washington, belonging instead to a "Tuesday to Thursday" club of commuting Congressmen who spent the majority of their time back home. Then-Republican John Lindsay was the first New York City Congressman to move his family to Washington, believing he became a better Congressman, husband, and father by so doing. In 1964, Democrat Benjamin Rosenthal of Queens took the same step and had time to become a House leader in consumer affairs. (One of Rosenthal's consumer bills had 162 co-sponsors in 1971.) Manhattan's William Fitts Ryan, Jonathan Bingham, and his fellow Bronx reformer, James Scheuer, also made the move of domicile to the Capital. So did Brooklyn's Hugh Carey, a close friend of organized labor, who has won a seat on the House Ways and Means Committee and become *de facto* leader of the New York delegation. The *de jure* leader has for years been Emanuel Celler, a distinguished octogenarian and New York law-firm partner who is chairman of the House Judiciary Committee and "dean" of the city and state delegation. (Celler's intelligence and skill have permitted him to stand above and beyond the conflict of regulars and reformers.)

There are still some exemplars of the old order on the New York delegation. One is Democrat James Delaney of Queens, a member of the House Rules Committee whom the Boston *Globe*'s Martin Nolan has vividly described as "newest icon of the Conservative party, superhawk and stalwart of the status quo." Delaney's district abuts Rosenthal's, but the two men have such distaste for each other that they don't even speak. Another symbol of the old order is John J. Rooney, a tough, bald little Brooklyn Irishman who heads the Appropriations subcommittee controlling funds for the State, Justice, and Commerce departments, and is the terror of the "striped pants" U. S. diplomats from one end of the world to the other. Reformers have almost upset Rooney in primary elections, and redistricting might well finish him off in 1972. Upstate, the most powerful congressional Democrat is Thaddeus J. Dulski of Buffalo, chairman of the House Committee on Post Office and Civil Service, whose campaign financing successes were exposed by the *Wall Street Journal*. Upstate's Sam Stratton and Long Island's Otis Pike both have high seniority on the Armed Services Committee. Both represent a kind of midpoint, ideologically and in terms of their approach to politics, between the hyperliberal city reformers and the old-time organization types.

Despite the Republicans' best gerrymandering efforts, Democrats controlled the New York State delegation throughout the 1960s and ended up with 24 seats to the GOP's 17 in 1971–72. (There will be two less seats on the delegation, starting in 1973, because of the reapportionment based on the 1970 Census. Redistricting will hurt the Democrats, with one of the four Democratic seats on Manhattan eliminated because of the island's static population figures.) For the most part, the Republican delegation has not been distinguished, though some of its members have important committee assignments, including Howard Robison from the Binghamton area (Appropriations) and Barber B. Conable from western New York (Ways and Means). Ogden Reid of Westchester County ranks high on the Government Operations Committee and is a leading liberal on the Republican delegation. The GOP delegation has moderated its traditional conservative upstate Republicanism with the times, and has been very responsive to Rockefeller. A symbol of the change over a generation is the difference in the Hudson Valley district that includes Franklin Roosevelt's Hyde Park. Back in the 1930s, the seat was held by Hamilton Fish, the conservative-isolationist who became the famed anchorman of FDR's "Martin, Barton, and Fish." Today Fish's son, Hamilton Fish, Jr., holds the seat. He is a moderate-to-liberal, interested in civil rights and environmental issues. A solid-waste disposal plan that he developed, in fact, earned him the endorsement (one of 12 so honored) of the Sierra Club's political arm.

An even more phenomenal vote-getter than Rockefeller is Sen. Jacob K. Javits, the son of immigrant parents on New York's Lower East Side who has been in the Senate since an initial victory over Robert Wagner in 1956. A symbol and articulate spokesman for liberal Republicanism in the Senate, Javits has added legislative substance to the public image over the years and is ranking Republican on the Labor and Public Welfare Committee and the ranking Republican Senator on the Joint Economic Committee. Among the major bills for which Javits can take major share of the credit are the student college loan program, major civil rights programs between 1957 and 1965, the medicare law, and all major housing legislation of the past two decades. In 1962 and again in 1968, Javits accomplished an unheard of feat for a present-day Republican—carrying New York City. But he also has a broad and substantial base of support upstate, proof that the gap between a liberal New York Jew and the native stock people of the small towns and cities may not be as great as one would imagine.

Politics III: Liberals and Conservatives

New York State has a history of significant "third" (and later fourth) parties that goes all the way back to 1829, when disgruntled laborers in New York City formed their own Working Men's party and upset the powers-that-were by electing several candidates to office. The minor-party tradition has been carried a lot further in this century, aided and abetted by New York laws which permit a candidate to run on the ticket of more than one party. This has opened the way for highly ideological minor parties that sometimes endorse major-party candidates, sometimes run their own, and frequently succeed in whipsawing the big parties into compliance with their policies.

In 1936, the American Labor party was founded in New York by a group of socialist-type union leaders, including David Dubinsky of the International Ladies Garment Workers Union and Sidney Hillman of the Amalgamated Clothing Workers. Initially, they had only one important purpose: to give New Deal supporters, who were unwilling to vote Democratic because of their opposition to Tammany Hall, a line on the ballot on which they could vote for Franklin D. Roosevelt. They did produce more than 275,000 votes for FDR that year, and in 1937 they stayed in business to provide the margin of victory for La Guardia as mayor and Dewey as district attorney.

The ALP eventually fell under Communist domination, and in 1944 Dubinsky and Alex Rose, chief of the United Hatters, Cap and Millinery Workers, broke away to form the Liberal party.* One of its important goals was to keep the Democratic party in the city and state left of center. The organizational core of the Liberals were first-generation central European Jews who worked in the needle trades and belonged to the sponsoring unions. But on election day, the Liberal party line was a favorite haven of independent voters who were Democratic at heart but fervently anti-Tammany. The Liberal vote was the margin of victory for Lehman when he ran for the Senate in 1950, for Harriman for governor in 1954, for Kennedy for President in 1960, and for Lindsay for mayor in 1965. Four years later, when Lindsay lost the Republican primary, the Liberal party represented the only organized support for his reelection. Nelson Rockefeller may well have owed his 1966 reelection to the Liberals, because they decided that year to boycott Frank O'Connor, the regular Democratic nominee, and nominate Franklin D. Roosevelt, Jr. The Roosevelt vote was more than Rockefeller's winning plurality.

The Liberal party is criticized by some who say that instead of being a lofty, crusading force, it is really an encrusted organization of elderly Jews, almost totally subservient to leader Alex Rose (now in his early 70s), a prime example of a wheeling-and-dealing political machine. Under Rose, for instance, the Liberals have shown scarcely more sympathy for reform Democrats than they have for Tammany regulars. Rose claims the party has no interest in patronage, but many of its leaders have been awarded prominent posts in the Lindsay administration, and the mayor frequently turns to Rose for counsel. One hesitates to repeat the premature funeral rites for the Liberal party which political writers have been making over the years, but the fact is that without youth, with leadership both aged and tied to the dying garment industry, its future is not bright.

In March 1962, the New York *Times*'s late and great political reporter, Leo Egan, wrote some prophetic lines:

The emergence of a militant conservative movement in New York State is raising serious political problems for Governor Rockefeller and other Republican

---

* The ALP gave up the ghost in 1952.

leaders. Depending on how these problems are resolved, they could have a major impact on elections and government in the state for many years to come.

Egan was writing just after formal announcement of the creation of the New York Conservative party—an idea hatched one day at lunch by two young Manhattan lawyers who happened to be brothers-in-law—Kieran O'Doherty and J. Daniel Mahoney. The Conservative party was founded to shift the spectrum of New York politics to the right by providing a pressure on the Republicans to balance the pressure of the Liberals on the Democrats. With some variations, the tactic has been essentially that of the Liberals—whose operations the Conservatives studied carefully before they got underway. The effort has been a smashing success. From 141,877 votes in the 1962 governorship campaign, the Conservatives advanced to 510,023 in 1966, even though their 1966 nominee, Paul L. Adams, was an obscure college professor. "That was the first and best tip-off," as my friend Jack Germond of the Gannett papers puts it, "that it was a movement and not a candidate." The 1966 election also shattered the simplistic old idea of "liberal" New York City and "conservative" upstate. Roosevelt, the Liberal party nominee, ran ahead of Adams in upstate New York. But Adams outpolled FDR Jr. by such a substantial margin in New York City that the statewide Conservative vote total was higher than the Liberal. (Adams ran especially strong in Queens and Staten Island, places packed with white, Catholic, middle-class home-owners worried about taxes and school integration—the very constituency the regular parties had been ignoring.) By edging the Liberals in 1966, the Conservatives got the coveted third line on the New York voting machines. In 1970, their gubernatorial vote was off slightly (but still ahead of the Liberal), but by then, they had already forced Rockefeller a few degrees to the right, thus achieving one of their fundamental objectives. And 1970 was the year that the Conservative party nominee, James L. Buckley, was elected to the U. S. Senate over Democrat Richard Ottinger, and (still sweeter for the hard-hitting Conservatives), over Charles Goodell, the Republican-Liberal nominee. The vote was 2,288,190 (37.2 percent) for Buckley; 2,171,232 (35.3 percent) for Ottinger; and 1,434,472 (23.3 percent) for Goodell—an amazing feat for a minor party in America.

F. Clifton White, Buckley's engaging and extraordinarily able campaign manager, claims that if Buckley had been the GOP candidate in a two-way race, he would have defeated Ottinger with at least 54 percent of the popular vote.* Many New York analysts dispute that judgment, saying that the over-all political complexion of the state is still too liberal for a right-wing Republican to win, except in a split field. But they agree that Buckley, a genial and articulate man, has special appeal, and that running for reelection as a Republican in 1976, he might win handily. Buckley took his seat in the U.S. Senate as a "Conservative-Republican." Governor Rockefeller claims that Buckley's election had "no major significance. It was a three-way race and he

---

* White will be remembered for his successful management of Goldwater's 1964 national delegate drive and his later representation of Ronald Reagan's Presidential interests. But he got his start in politics, interestingly, as an assistant commissioner of motor vehicles in the Dewey administration. When not running campaigns, White is a public affairs consultant for major corporations.

walked in between."

The Conservative surge that began in the 1960s depended on good leadership, but the fundamental reason for success was that a political vacuum existed in New York. Both Republicans and Democrats were for big government, civil rights, and by their deeds if not their words, high taxes. Practically, there was no difference between the major parties. The Conservatives provided an alternative on spending issues, opposed school busing, took the side of the police in the civilian review board controversy in New York City, and provided the only political voice continuing to call for victory in Vietnam.

The Conservative record is not without blemishes. In 1965, William Buckley, publisher of the *National Review* and brother of James, ran for mayor of New York and drew enough conservative votes from the middle-of-the-road Democratic candidate, Abraham Beame, to throw the election to John Lindsay, a particular bête noire of the Conservatives. In 1969, the Conservatives did not run a mayoralty candidate but split their votes between the more conservative Republican and Democratic candidates, helping Lindsay win a second term. (They promise a conservative fusion candidacy in 1973.) And in 1968, they were powerless to prevent Javits from winning re-election with a thundering 1,119,077-vote plurality. But in the present state legislature, 61 of the Republican members ran with Conservative endorsement. Nine members of the assembly—where the Republican margin is only four votes—would not have been elected without the support they got on the Conservative line.

Predictably, there is great uneasiness among Republicans about what the Conservatives might do to their party. According to Rockefeller, "There's a strong reaction against the Conservatives—a feeling that the Liberal party has destroyed the Democratic party, and that we don't want to let the Conservative party do the same thing to the Republicans." In 1971, the Republican organizations of Nassau, Suffolk, and Rockland Counties voted resolutions to require that candidates who want their support must sign a statement that they will not run on the line of any other party. The Democratic parties of those counties simultaneously adopted similar resolutions for *their* candidates. There is a practical necessity for the parties to act simultaneously on the issue, as explained by Gus Tyler, political director of the ILGWU: "The left-facing Democrats have their Liberal 'tail'; the right-facing Republicans have their Conservative 'tail.' If either party acted alone to prohibit dual endorsement, the other party could win by a tail. So they got together to announce that they are tired of having the tails wag the dogs."

There is some doubt whether the "drop-dead resolutions" aimed against the minor parties, for various legal and practical reasons, will work. They are probably just the first step toward state legislation prohibiting dual endorsements, a movement to isolate Conservatives and Liberals *by law* in the state. The idea comes up periodically, but both Republicans and Democrats shy away from leading the fight for such legislation, fearing reprisals if it fails to win passage. If the step is taken, however, and the Conservatives and Liberals lose their principal weapon of bargaining for their endorsements, then these minor parties will begin to wither away. Their more practical members would probably join the major parties, trying to get a foothold as important factions therein; the ideologues would probably stick with the vastly weakened Conservative and Liberal party shells, but cease to be a major factor in New York politics.

Geographic New York

New York's land area is the greatest of any northeastern state. It is a Great Lakes and Canadian border state along its northern reaches, a New England state on the east, a Pennsylvania-Appalachian state along its Southern Tier, an Atlantic state around New York Harbor and out along Long Island.

Any geographic division of the state raises some conceptual problems, but if the reader will keep his eye on the map, he may be able to keep his bearings as we move around the state in a clockwise direction, starting with the Catskills and leaving for last the New York City metropolitan region.

The Catskills and the Southern Tier

THE CATSKILLS. These gently rounded hills emerge from the Hudson's wooded west banks where Rip Van Winkle once slept and include the famous borscht belt in Sullivan and Ulster counties, where New Yorkers have headed for a bucolic interlude and sometimes gaudy entertainment since the turn of the century.

The Catskill town of Woodstock, long a haven for painters, musicians, sculptors, writers, and craftsmen, acquired a not-altogether-welcome notoriety when some of its residents promoted the gigantic Woodstock rock festival in 1969. The affair was actually held, though, at Max Tasgur's farm in another Catskill town, Bethel, 50 miles away. For three days, hundreds of thousands of 14- to 24-year-olds created a commune large enough to be New York's third largest city, an Event of their generation immortalized in the movie *Woodstock*.

THE SOUTHERN TIER. This section of deeply wooded hills and valleys, part of the Appalachian Highlands shared with Pennsylvania, runs along two thirds of the state's width and is cut by strong rivers like the Delaware, the Susquehanna, and the Allegheny. It is sparsely populated by eastern standards, the only cities of appreciable size being Binghamton (64,123), Elmira (39,945), Jamestown (39,795), and Ithaca (26,226).* All have been losing population in recent years. One of Governor Rockefeller's pet projects is making a four-lane, limited-access road out of Route 17, the east-west connector along the Southern Tier. As noted in our Pennsylvania chapter, Route 17 parallels the newly completed Keystone Shortway some distance to the

* All population figures are based on the 1970 census.

south, and the two roads encompass an immense, still unspoiled section of remote wildlands close to the eastern megalopolis.

Binghamton has suffered from the loss of many jobs in the tanning and shoe manufacturing business, its historic main support, but the main plant of International Business Machines is in adjacent Endicott, providing thousands of well-paid jobs. IBM, begun as a small tabulating-machine enterprise, later became, under the leadership of Thomas J. Watson, a great national and international corporation. Its computers and electric typewriters dominate their fields, and sales in 1970 totaled $7.5 billion. IBM's corporate headquarters are presently at Armonk, in Westchester County, and the Binghamton plant has only a small percentage of the company's total employment.

The Southern Tier also has some oil wells and refineries, famous factories for furniture and voting machines at Jamestown, and the Corning Glass Company, which produces the world-famous Steuben glassware and gigantic telescope mirrors. Both tourism and agriculture are mainstays of the local economy, and one finds here one of the nation's leading grape-producing areas. A big Indian reservation is home for the last of the proud Senecas. Near Lake Erie is Chautauqua Lake, center of the famed Chautauqua Circuit that once brought culture, with a small "c" and a loud voice, to crossroads and hamlets of the nation. William Jennings Bryan was one of its great orators.

The FINGER LAKES. Set between the Southern and Northern Tiers are the slender Finger Lakes, cradled in long, narrow basins cut out by the Ice Age. Now these lovely streaks of blue water—Lakes Canandaigua, Keuka, Seneca, Cayuga, Owasco, and Skaneateles—are a favorite summertime refuge for New Yorkers. Between and around them lies fertile agricultural country.

The social tensions of our time have not left the placid rural stretches of western New York untouched. A prime example is Cornell University, situated "high above Cayuga's waters" at Ithaca, where tension between black students and a university community not without vestiges of white racism led in spring 1969 to the shocking picture of protesting black students brandishing shotguns and rifles.

The Upstate Urban Corridor

Now our focus shifts to the urban corridor that stretches along the Great Lakes coastal plains, and then the Mohawk Valley, from Buffalo to Albany.

BUFFALO (462,768) AND ITS METROPOLITAN AREA (1,349,211). This is New York's second largest city—a place, as Gunther noted, perennially "overshadowed by Manhattan, though the latter is 398 miles away." The city has a superb location—the eastern terminus of the Great Lakes shipping lanes, the western terminus of New York's low-level water route from the east. Millard Browne of the Buffalo *Evening News* writes: "It is where the lakes meet the rails, where Dakota grains are milled into flour for eastern markets; where the water-borne ore from Minnesota and Labrador meets coal from

Ohio and Pennsylvania to form steel for New York and New England."
The building of the Erie Canal opened up Buffalo, then the railroads made
it second only to Chicago as a railhead. It is a sinewy city, a place a labor
leader once called a "toll-gate town with a toll-gate mentality." Great grain
elevators along the lake front remind one that this city mills more grain into
flour than any other city in the world; to the south, one sees the smoke
billowing out of the great Lackawanna plant of Bethlehem Steel, third largest
steel factory in America. The city has big foundries, too, a Westinghouse
plant, and Chevrolet and Ford plants inside and outside the city boundaries.
Many of the early auto companies first started operations in Buffalo, but in
time those that survived switched their base of operations to Detroit, leaving Buffalo, as it is in most of its enterprises, a branch town. The same
thing happened with aircraft, and today that industry is all but gone (except
for the Bell Aerospace Division of Textron).

Downtown Buffalo and its industrial suburbs are grim, gray, and outmoded. A grandiose street plan with radial avenues, laid out in the early
19th century, has been faithfully retained, but most downtown streets are
either seedy or strangely deserted. At night, Buffalo is like a ghost town. New
center city buildings have been few and far between for a city of Buffalo's
size. But now there is some action, including the 40-story Marine-Bank building, set audaciously astride Main Street.

Overall, the condition and appearance of Buffalo has deteriorated since
World War II. Total assessed valuation actually declined during the inflationary era of the 1960s.

Buffalo has a celebrated inferiority complex. George Wyatt, a spirited
young city budget officer who really seems to love his city, complains:

Our national image since the days of the completion of the Erie Canal has
been a bawdy, raffish, frontier town without class. And as a kid, I recall we only
made the national newsreels when there was a big snow or windstorm. Ask people
what they know about Buffalo and they'll reply, "a snow-covered Pittsburgh."
But we're no dirtier than other cities, and cleaner than many. The unfair treatment we get from the national press reinforces the old dirty image. Some outsider reporters come to town with their stories already written. People outside
are unaware of many very beautiful parts of this city—the big stretches of pleasant middle-class frame dwellings, and the clean neighborhoods.

But after talking with Wyatt, I went to have lunch with his friend, Ray
Herman of the Buffalo *Courier-Express*, who said there was a "germ of truth"
in a *Sports Illustrated* article that talked of Buffalo as the "armpit of the
East." Buffalo gets its basic character from steel and milling, Herman said,
and so "people are more attuned to sports than the arts." They give gung-ho
backing to their teams—major league in football, hockey, and basketball.

Winter comes early and stays late in Buffalo; on April 30, I was amazed
to see ice still clogging the harbor. Wind and snow storms sweep in from Lake
Erie, where there is nothing to stop them for 240 miles until they hit Buffalo
and other parts of the New York shore. Sometimes wind storms are so fierce

that ropes are strung along downtown streets to help pedestrians stay on their feet.

Buffalo is a premier American town for raw, muscular ethnic politics. The city divides into rather homogeneous nationality pockets: Italians on the West Side; Poles, Hungarians, and Czechs on the northwest; Irish in south Buffalo; blacks on the Near East Side, and Poles on the Far East Side; Jews and Wasps in the northern and northeastern sections; a last cluster of Germans in the farthest northeast; American Indians on the Lower West Side; a Puerto Rican community that rings the black community and comes up into the Lower West Side. The Poles, who came to work in the steel mills, are the largest single group, about 25 percent of the city's population—in fact, only Chicago has more Poles; Italians are about 20 percent; Irish 10 percent. Mayor Frank Sedita and Congressman Thaddeus Dulski reflect the Italian and Polish strength respectively. Negroes were 6 percent of the population in 1960 but over 20 percent in 1970. Sedita has appointed blacks to some prominent city jobs, including the post of fire commissioner. In his 1969 reelection race, he faced a Polish Louise Day Hicks named Alfreda W. Slominski; with little difficulty he defeated her and Ambrose L. Lane, a black candidate.

Buffalo the city is forever Democratic; Erie County is generally so in state and national elections, although it has elected a Republican county executive since 1960. The area became upset with Rockefeller's early tax programs and has turned out a majority against him in each of his three reelection races.

For a century now, the center city has been rigidly contained within its boundaries. Many of the factories are actually in the suburbs, and as George Wyatt puts it, this anomalous situation has developed: "The lower group of income earners go outside the city to work in factories and then come back to the city to spend their meager earnings. The big earners—the white collar people and professionals—come into the city from the suburbs to work in the office center, and then they get on the expressways to get out of the city and spend their money somewhere else."

Buffalo has been able to escape the ultimate fiscal crisis of New York City because the Erie County government has been transforming itself into a kind of metropolitan-area government, taking over one basic function after another from the city—welfare, hospitals and psychiatric facilities, sewer districts, and air- and water-pollution control. The decision to adopt a "strong executive" charter in 1960 was crucial to the county's expanded role.

Talking to people in Buffalo, one would think that organized crime is a negligible phenomenon there. The crime rate (the way the FBI estimates it, anyway) is quite low for a city of Buffalo's size, and I heard flat denials of any Mafia influence in political life. *But* officials of the Justice Department's criminal division consider Buffalo an important smaller pocket of organized crime in the U. S.; eight Buffalo mobsters were at the famous Appalachin meeting in 1967; and from officers of the General Services Administration,

I heard that it took nine extra months to put up a new federal building in Buffalo because of harassment by mob-connected unions against an outside construction firm which was the successful bidder for the job.

Buffalo's most famous suburb is Niagara Falls (85,615), where the world-famous cataract draws some three million visitors a year to a sight that hasn't changed much since Father Louis Hennepin first saw the falls in 1678. (Erosion on the American side of the falls has caused increasing concern since massive rock falls in 1931 and 1954, however.)

We end our visit to Buffalo with a glimpse of the new State University at Buffalo. For more than a century, the old University of Buffalo existed quietly as a peaceful streetcar college to turn out the local doctors and dentists and judges. Then came 1962 and the designation to become the primary center of graduate education of the state university system. Martin Meyerson, former acting chancellor at Berkeley, was brought in to head the startling new program, and did a highly creditable job until he left in September 1969. The quality of students escalated unbelievably; by the end of the decade the university actually found it necessary to reject some holders of Regents scholarships (the top 6 percent of high school graduates in New York State). But a tremendously impersonal institution evolved and it came to the point that when some students wanted recommendations, they couldn't find a professor who knew their name. Spring 1970 brought convulsions rarely seen on an American campus: $300,000 property damage, more than 125 students and police injured, 45 faculty members arrested and booked on various charges, more than 50 students charged on criminal counts.

A few years from now, the new state university campus may be finished at Amherst, a process long delayed by construction-union resistance to hiring black workmen. But there is no guarantee that the students' sense of isolation and alienation, or the creaky machinery of a huge and evolving university controlled in its every bureaucratic detail from Albany, will be solved. Millard Browne told me:

> A lot of people think that if Buffalo can get through the growing pains of a major new university, it will be redeemed. There is a sense of pioneering at the State University—that's why the good faculty and students come—to be in on the floor of a good thing. Already, there are many prominent new faculty. But the whole development has attracted a lot of frontier-radical-type faculty. Setting all of this down in an ethnic, blue-collar town has dangerous potential. Lots of our kids from New York City ooze contempt for Buffalo from every pore—a bad scene!
>
> But we must shepherd it through to the stature of a Berkeley or a Madison.

ROCHESTER (296,233) AND ITS METROPOLITAN AREA (882,667). Writer Seymour Freedgood, in *The Gateway States,* quotes a Rochester citizen who depicts his city's image as "quiet, conservative, contented and Kodak." The city was an old flour-milling town that grew and flourished with the opening of the Erie Canal. The first breakthroughs toward a modern scientific economy came in the 1850s when Joseph Bausch opened the optical business that would eventually become the world-famous Bausch & Lomb Co. Thirty years later, a young bank clerk named George Eastman became interested in photography and effected a major breakthrough by developing a practical and economic "dry plate" photographic process in place of the incredibly cumbersome "wet plate" method in use until then. He opened a factory, discovered the economic uses of nitrocellulose film, and evolved his great invention, the Kodak camera.

Today, of course, Eastman Kodak is a great national corporation (27th largest in the U. S.), dominating the amateur photography market (with nervous glances over its shoulder at Polaroid) and providing photographic devices that give it a stake in such glamor industries as education, medicine, and dentistry. Kodak is a leader in microfilming technology and does half a billion dollars a year in its chemicals, fibers, and plastics operations. In 1970, total sales were $2.8 billion, and the company had 110,700 employees.

In the three quarters of a century since Eastman made Rochester a company town, only one new company of importance has emerged. Its name used to be Haloid and it managed to exist "in the shadow of Eastman" by turning out photo supplies—tolerated, perhaps, because it was formed before Eastman Kodak became so dominant. Right after World War II, Haloid began to buy up the rights, held by other companies, to photocopying techniques. The Xerox 914 Copier went on the market in 1960; pushed by a well-trained and aggressive sales force, it (and successor models) rapidly gained entry to corporate, bank, publishing, law, school, and university offices. The company (itself renamed Xerox) grew at a spectacular rate, becoming the country's 60th largest industrial corporation with sales of $1.7 billion in 1970.

Rochester has been described as an orderly town with methodical, hardworking citizens—natural products of a technological work milieu. Important ethnic groups, outside of native Wasp stock, have been German, Italian, and Polish. In the late 1940s, a significant number of poorly educated Southern blacks began to arrive. It frequently turned out they were unqualified for the better jobs in the highly technical local job market—at the same time that firms were importing skilled labor from outside. Summer 1964 brought a nasty riot—a major urban disturbance for its time. This prompted local clergy to bring in Saul Alinsky on a two-year, $100,000 contract to organize the poor. Under Alinsky's tutelage, a group named FIGHT (acronym for Freedom-Independence-God-Honor-Today) was formed, and a powerful community organizer, the Reverend Franklin Lawrence, took over its leadership. The FIGHT group picked Eastman Kodak—'the plantation," they called it—as their principal target in the demand for more jobs for blacks. The riots and the FIGHT program came as a profound shock for Rochester's leaders, including Kodak, and much serious soul-searching ensued. Many new jobs and programs for the minority community have resulted, and Rochester is also one of the few cities today making provision for low-income housing, open to minorities, in its suburbs.

The Rochester *Times-Union* and the *Democrat and Chronicle* are flagships of the Gannett Newspaper chain, which controls newspapers in six other upstate cities as well as those in Westchester County. The Gannett papers provide continuous, high-grade Albany coverage and their influence is second only to the New York *Times* in the state. The editorial voice of the Rochester papers is one of moderate conservatism; many of the papers in the chain follow Rochester's editorial lead, although all have local autonomy and some (like the excellent Binghamton *Press*) are very independent. A quick review of the upstate press should also include the Buffalo *News* (full news staffs, comprehensive coverage, distinctly Republican but less so in news columns than it once was); the Buffalo *Courier-Express*; the Syracuse *Herald-Journal* and *Post-Standard* (both Newhouse papers, tough and hard-core conservative in their views, stridently opposed to Rockefeller and his tax programs); the Albany *Times-Union* and *Knickerbocker-News* (Hearst-owned, good coverage of state government); and the Watertown *Times* (a power in the Northern Tier).

SYRACUSE (197,208) AND ITS METROPOLITAN AREA (635,946). Politically, Syracuse and its environs are regarded as the real capital of upstate conservatism, a phenomenon for which the Syracuse newspapers are given major credit. A few years ago, when a prominent Republican legislative leader from Syracuse backed Rockefeller's tax proposals in Albany, he was damned and literally hounded out of office by the *Herald-Journal* and *Post-Standard*.

But Syracuse is not a closed, narrow-minded community. My friend Charles Willie, a professor of sociology at the Maxwell School at Syracuse University, says one finds a real sense of community in the city, a feeling on the people's part that they have some control over their environment and institutions, that they can get a hearing at City Hall regardless of which party (it has usually been the Republican) is in power. There have, however, been eruptions in the black community and Negroes are underrepresented in government and on the police force. The white community, Willie comments, accepts successful blacks, "but they appear to have no compassion for the disadvantaged."

One can point to several factors that make Syracuse an "open city." It has always been a crossroads: first, Indian trails passed through from every compass point; then came the Erie Canal, the Barge Canal, and the railroads; and today, two great superroads—the Thomas E. Dewey Thruway and the North-South Expressway (Interstate 81)—pass through. (The city has 80 truck terminals and massive rail-marshaling yards.) Syracuse makes everything from soda ash to electrical goods, from special steel to pharmaceuticals, in some 500 manufacturing plants. No single industry dominates, as Eastman Kodak does in Rochester; people need not be concerned that the gut decisions are all made in the back rooms of some corporation.

Ethnic diversity is another factor. Syracuse has quantities of Yankees, Irish, German, Italians, Poles, East European Jews, Negroes, and Puerto Ricans, all living in clearly defined neighborhoods. But no ethnic group has disproportionate strength; in fact, market research firms like to use the city to test new products, just because of its broad mix.

Finally, there is the influence exerted by Syracuse University, the country's third largest private university (22,700 students, 1,136 faculty members

—the two largest universities are NYU and Northeastern). Local people still speak of the university as something of a place set apart—"the university and the *host* community"—but the fact is that it is the largest single employer in the city, its faculty participates in local politics on all sides of the political fence, and its contacts with Washington help keep Syracuse in touch with the world.

Local government is fairly honest and competent, although sometimes indifferent to the city's poor people. Downtown Syracuse has an impressive new Clinton Square Redevelopment Project, but Rochester's core development is far superior. Inner-city decay and poverty plague it as they do so many other cities, in sharp contrast to the economic vigor seen in the outlying areas.

What is Syracuse's chief drawback? It may be the snow—an average of 108 inches a year, more than any other major American city. Not-so-old-timers remember with little fondness the blizzard of '66—January 1966, that is—when 42 inches fell in three days, accompanied by winds of up to 40 mph that created drifts as high as 20 feet.

THE MOHAWK VALLEY. We now pass into mountainous territory, cut by the handsome, historic Mohawk Valley. All the significant settlement is crammed into the rather narrow river valley; the two principal cities are Utica (91,611) and Rome (50,148). Industrially, this is tired, aged territory with little dynamism; not only did the cities lose population in the 1960s, but the entire metropolitan region (340,477) barely averted a net loss.

Utica's ethnic mix is heavily Italian, Irish, and Polish, but it also has the distinction of supporting the only Welsh-language newspaper in the U. S., *U Drych*, founded in 1851. Rome is big in various kinds of metal manufacture and is thankful for the payroll from nearby Griffiss Air Force Base.

As for politics, color the whole area true-blue Republican.

THE CAPITAL DISTRICT. The 1970 Census counted 720,786 residents in the Albany-Schenectady-Troy metropolitan area. The area is heavy with state offices, federal regional offices, and factories; if one's interest runs to history, the story is of Indian massacres, Dutch patroons, and colonial and Revolutionary War heroes and governors waiting for a chance to become President.

Albany (114,873) was once described as "one of the most resolutely backward communities in the state," a reputation it tries to live up to. The city is old and decayed, and aside from the fantastic rush of state-government building—the South Mall, discussed earlier, and the strikingly beautiful new State University of New York at Albany—the city per se shows little life. City taxes are low, but so is the level of services; as an embittered out-of-town reporter noted a couple of years ago, "the snow and ice are still taken away by the same methods the city fathers used in centuries past—solar heat."

Another thing about Albany that never seems to change is the political boss in charge. It has been the same *for half a century* now—Daniel P. O'Connell, 87 years old, who runs a smooth organization that has sustained remarkably few losses since it came to power in 1921. The O'Connell machine has been investigated repeatedly for corruption and tax favoritism to the boss's cronies, but even Governor Dewey, after a highly publicized investigation, could not lay a hand on "Uncle Dan." Albany is heavily Irish and overwhelmingly Catholic, but O'Connell has preference for mayoralty candidates from well-born Protestant families. The incumbent mayor, Erastus Corning II, is the epitome of the established upstate gentry and has been in office since 1942. Uncle Dan, reputed to have a personal worth of some $500,000, is rarely seen these days. In fact, Governor Rockefeller has never cast eyes on him, and when John Kennedy came through Albany campaigning for President in 1960, he had to be satisfied with a telephone call.

Schenectady (77,859), a grimy industrial city on the Mohawk, is home of General Electric's original and oldest plant, which turns out heavy electrical equipment and provides jobs for 12,500 workers. Close by on the Hudson lies Troy (62,918), the town where Uncle Sam was reputedly "born," a city really behind the times with an economy still tied primarily to the textile and apparel industries.

The illustrious old resort town of Saratoga Springs (18,845), just north of the capital district, leads a double life. During most of the year, it is like most other upstate towns, quiet and uncrowded under its old shade trees. But when summer comes, the Saratoga Performing Arts Center begins its season in its sylvan-set modern theater (the New York City Ballet, the Philadelphia Orchestra), and the social elite, millionaires, and gamblers descend on the town for the races at America's most beautiful thoroughbred track.

The North Country and the Hudson River

THE NORTH COUNTRY AND THE ADIRONDACK MOUNTAINS. Here is distant and truly "uncivilized" New York State, known to comparatively few Americans. In the northwest is Lake Ontario and the region of the Thousand Islands (there are actually some 1,700) and then a long stretch of the St. Lawrence River. At Massena (14,042) one finds the third largest electricity generating complex of the continent, and the largest one on the St. Lawrence Seaway. Yet as remote as the location is, one can still watch the commerce of the world on its way through the great locks, moving to or from the Great Lakes and the Midwest. Then, on the state's northernmost extremity, are 60 miles of border with Quebec. On the east, one comes upon the beautiful Champlain Valley, centered on 107-mile-long Lake Champlain (across from Vermont), which connects with Lake George to form the great north-south waterway that was the path of empire through several wars.

Making a living is an acute problem for the sturdy, independent people of this region; aside from some dairy farming, the chief industries are tourism, mining for iron ores, lead, and zinc, lumbering, and paper mills—all characterized by seasonal job opportunities. Thousands of families live in abject poverty in tarpaper houses, their plight unrecognized until welfare and services of the federal antipoverty program became available to them in the last few years.

The Adirondack Mountains fill the great land bulk of the North Country; for mile after mile, the uplands and mountains roll on, their slopes shaded by thick evergreens, bordering literally thousands of lakes and ponds and miles of streams and rivers. The terrain is too rough for much farming and too distant to attract industry. The Adirondack Park, decreed by the New York legislature in 1892, covers most of this territory. Within the park are more than two million acres of the New York Forest Preserve, guaranteed by an 1895 amendment to the state constitution to be "forever kept as wild forest lands." But 3.7 million acres of land in the park are in the hands of towns, businesses, and individuals, and now there is fear that the region's untamed character may be imperiled by uncontrolled summer-home and recreation-facilities growth.

THE HUDSON RIVER. Among the great rivers of America, the Hudson is one of the shortest. From its point of birth—jewellike Lake Tear of the Clouds, a two-acre pond below the summit of Mt. Marcy in the high Adirondacks—it flows only 315 miles until it enters the Atlantic at New York Harbor. Yet its role in the story of New York State—geologic, economic, aesthetic, ecologic—is a major one.

Three hundred years ago, Dutch explorers rhapsodized about the handsome forests and mountains that line the Hudson's banks, the abundance of game, and the fish teeming in its waters. In time, roads and railways crowded into the valley and old colonial settlements turned into dirty industrial towns. Now, a great suspense story of the late 20th century is whether the state and federal pure-waters programs will be sufficient to restore the Hudson to something approaching its cleanliness of times past, thus fulfilling the river's rightful role as a thing of beauty and a place of recreation for millions.

The upper Hudson is a fast-flowing trout stream, in springtime wild and often turbulent as it cuts down through the Adirondacks past such famous spots as Blue Ledge, where Winslow Homer did some of his finest paintings. But after the Adirondack Forest Preserve, paper company and other wastes intrude. The Mohawk, joining the Hudson near Troy, adds volume but not cleanliness. The accumulated municipal sewage and industrial wastes (acids, oil, dyes, and chemicals) of the capital district are so great that sanitary engineers speak of "the Albany Pool"—or sometimes "the Albany Cesspool." Massive fish kills have been recorded there in recent years.

About 25 miles south of Albany, the natural cleansing action of the river reduces the pollution to less egregious levels, and the river will be relatively clean until it reaches New York. After it has passed the Catskills and the cities of Kingston, Poughkeepsie, and Newburgh, the Hudson suddenly enters a narrow gorge. Naturalist Robert Boyle writes:

> The Hudson Highlands is perhaps the most magnificent stretch of the river. For 15 miles, forested mountain ramparts rise along both shores from Newburgh south to Peekskill, and there is vista after vista of incredible beauty. They have

a common theme—a sort of fairybook magic that lingers in the mind from childhood, the notion that this is the way the world is supposed to look.

Storm King is where New York City's Consolidated Edison Company has been seeking for several years to build a massive pumped-storage hydroelectric project that would provide two million kilowatts of electricity for peak or emergency periods. A group of conservationists formed the Scenic Hudson Preservation Conference, which persuaded the federal courts —at least temporarily—to block the Federal Power Commission order permitting the Storm King Project.

After Peekskill, the Hudson widens abruptly to its broadest areas— Haverstraw Bay and Tappan Zee, more than three miles across. This is the location of Indian Point, where Con Ed has operated a nuclear power plant since 1962, and has several other nuclear plants in the process of construction. The conservationists have been highly critical of these installations on the basis of the immense fish kills already caused by thermal pollution, but the work has proceeded without interruption.

The Hudson narrows again a few miles north of New York City, flowing past the dramatic 500-foot banks of the New Jersey Palisades on its west bank. Civilization thickens, the majestic sweep of the George Washington Bridge comes into view, and Manhattan's towers. Centuries ago, the world's greatest oyster beds were in New York Harbor and up the Hudson for several miles. Boyle writes:

Today, the oyster grounds are no more, and the Hudson is a mess as it flows into New York Harbor. Every day, without cease, the West Side of Manhattan alone empties 175 million gallons of absolutely raw sewage into the river. The sewage emanates from every variety of human activity and habitation. It pours down pipes from skyscrapers, gushes from apartment houses, issues from hospitals, gas stations, restaurants, laboratories, theaters, public rest rooms, tenements, factories, stores, and the streets themselves. All this washes down the drains that gird the streets and vomits directly into the river, where the tides rock it back and forth.

There are similar contributions from the New Jersey shore, and it is the considered opinion of one marine biologist that if Manhattan were not surrounded by salt water, which is inhibiting to pathogenic bacteria, the island would be a ghost town.

THE MID-HUDSON AND ITS ENVIRONS. The mid-Hudson Valley—from the capital district southward to the Westchester County line—is still relatively undeveloped. The biggest population concentrations are in the ramshackle, rundown river towns, but even the two largest of these, Poughkeepsie and Newburgh, have populations of only 32,029 and 26,219 respectively. There is only one really large employer—IBM—and it skims off the best of the local labor pool. Yet it takes little imagination to see that the population wave from New York City will continue to press inexorably northward in the next years. A major task of state and local planners is to find ways to cluster the housing developments and leave broad expanses of open space—so that, as Stephen Lefkowitz of the Urban Development Corporation told me, "it doesn't all come out looking like Queens when it's finished."

The U. S. Military Academy at West Point has long added luster to the mid-Hudson region, incidentally adding a stimulus to the local economy. Now the Point is under some attack, not from the solid valley burghers but from some centers of America where intellectual trends and new life styles emerge. It is said that the academy's martinetlike rules for plebes are anachronistic, and more seriously, that the heavy emphasis on math, engineering, and science, taught mostly by regular Army officers, fails to prepare young officers for the taxing political and social tasks involved in a war like that in Vietnam. But some quiet reforms are now underway: more civilian instructors, a broader curriculum, and recruitment of enlisted Army men to attend.

Agriculture—especially apple-growing and dairy-farming—is strong in the mid-Hudson area. (Overall, New York farms produce goods valued at about $1 billion a year, three-quarters of the total from livestock, poultry, and their products.) Lovely Dutchess County remains a leading dairy county and has a special niche in American history as the location of Hyde Park, FDR's ancestral home and the site of his Presidential library. The growth of light industries and population expansion from the metropolis were clear in the 1970 Census figures, which showed Dutchess County population up 26 percent in a decade (to 222,295), Orange County up 20 percent (to 220,558), and little Putnam County up 79 percent (to 56,696).

In sheer numbers, however, no growth compares to that of Rockland County. It encompasses 173 square miles of flatlands and rolling hills opposite Westchester County on the widest part of the Hudson, flanked by New Jersey's Bergen County on the south. Rockland had 89,276 people in 1950; 229,903 in 1970; and is projected to have 350,000 by 1985. The New York State Thruway and the Tappan Zee Bridge were the keys to opening up the country. Today bulldozers rip up the earth to build even more housing developments, shopping centers, schools, and offices where all was quiet and rural a few years past. And so now we come on the suburbs of New York City, in themselves a civilization of more people, more prosperity, and certainly more growth than the mother city herself.

Classic Suburbia: Westchester and Long Island

WESTCHESTER COUNTY (891,409). "Westchester County," the New York *Times* commented in 1971, "is the ultimate suburban myth":

> The myth is Scarsdale, symbol of a nation of self-satisfied suburban affluence. Surely all Westchester must be one big Scarsdale, the myth goes, one chain of fine Colonial homes and Tudor-style grocery stores stretching from the Hudson to [Long Island] Sound. . . .
> Westchester is no more one big Scarsdale than Manhattan is one big Fifth Avenue, or one big Times Square. . . .

In reality, Westchester is many worlds. It does have some of the choicest suburbs of the continent—clipped, groomed, and lovely places like Larchmont, Rye, Bronxville, Mount Kisco, Pound Ridge, Bedford, Irvington, and Scarsdale itself. Within their confines one finds America's greatest concentration of highly paid corporation executives. But Westchester also has 50,-000 people on the welfare rolls, with the number growing by 1,400 a month. It is not lily white; in fact, 85,020, or 9.5 percent of the county's people, are Negroes, and there are a few thousand Puerto Ricans too. In northern Westchester, the scene is still an idyllic one of rolling farmland, lush forests, and pristine villages; by contrast, the city of Yonkers (204,370) is really just an extension of the Bronx.

An important change of the postwar era has been the decision of several major corporations to abandon Manhattan and set up headquarters in parklike settings in Westchester—IBM in Armonk, General Foods in White Plains, Pepsico in Purchase, and others. Many smaller industries began or expanded operations in the county, so that by latest count, there were almost as many people commuting *into* Westchester as out to jobs in New York City and elsewhere.

The county seat of White Plains (50,220) used to be a quiet little town of neighborhood stores where one parked his car in front of his home or office, but blight struck in the late 1950s and early 1960s. Urban renewal arrived, with acres of brick-strewn sites awaiting new construction. Now the demolition era is beginning to end as high-rise parking garages and new office towers go up. Mount Vernon (72,778) got its share of underworld activity, including a police commissioner who ran a bookie joint in the middle of town. New Rochelle (75,386), a classic bedroom suburb, has a rapidly growing black community (14 percent in 1970) that runs the gamut from low-income people to substantial middle-class commuters.

But for all its difficulties, there is much to say for Westchester as a model for evolving suburbs. Back in the late 1930s, it went to a county-executive form of government—a model still followed by less than two dozen American suburbs. The county government has suffered from a lack of imagination or ability to impose its will in zoning or other matters on the fiercely independent towns and municipalities. But there has been no reversion to bitter right-wingism. Edwin G. Michaelian, the Republican county executive now in his fourth four-year term, is an extraordinarily able man who has been cautious in his administration. But he has begun to take initiatives in such fields as housing and narcotics. This county, because it had already functioning communities with zoning and planning regulations, was able to avert some of the worst effects of rapid postwar suburban growth noted in counties like Nassau. Nor is Westchester all affluence or all poverty. Congressman Ogden Reid has pointed out that "industry is bringing in a lot of creative young people who are aware of the issues. This is really a national district, with a real cross section of points of view."

LONG ISLAND. If Nassau and Suffolk counties were a city rather than a melange of townships, villages, and unincorporated areas on New York

State's Long Island, they would rank fourth among the cities of the U. S. A., trailing only New York City, Chicago, and Los Angeles. Nassau alone, with 1,422,905 people in the latest Census, would be America's sixth largest city, and Suffolk, with 1,116,672, would be the seventh largest. The history of European man's civilization on the island dates back to the 17th century, but 76 percent of the population growth there has occurred in the brief three decades since Pearl Harbor. It is a story of a fantastic, largely unordered boom in people, houses, and industrial plants that only modern California can match. Many, indeed, are the parallels to California's growth and problems, and fittingly enough Long Island is now experiencing a slump in aerospace to match California's, while its premier newspaper, *Newsday*, founded by the late Harry F. Guggenheim in 1940, has been sold to the Los Angeles *Times.*

In 1940 Long Island was still a series of quiet little villages, each with a Main Street, some shops, a movie house, and a soda parlor, with the land of the farmer at the back doorstep. Commuting in those days was almost entirely by the Long Island Railroad, and most workers headed daily for the city. The aviation industry had opened up plants on the island before the crash of 1929, however, and after Pearl Harbor the factories suddenly received multimillion-dollar government contracts and a great job boom ensued. After the war, New York's returning GI's were desperate for new housing and in 1947 entrepreneur-builder William Levitt and his brother began building the first of thousands of inexpensive Cape Cod-style homes on a potato field in the center of Nassau County. The result was the first Levittown—17,544 homes in all. There were many predictions that the Levitts' basementless houses, with their inexpensive construction, would be the "slums of the future." It did not prove to be so. The homes were kept up, expanded, and improved upon, vegetation improved their stark early appearance, and today they sell for an average price of $18,000, compared to their original selling price of $6,990. But Long Island's Levittown set the pattern for postwar suburbia: look-alike houses, row upon row, mile after mile.

As Nassau County filled up, the population pressure shifted to Suffolk County, and one need only check the latest home-builders' ads in the newspapers to see how far east the movement has progressed at any moment in time. At the present writing in 1971, the line is around Port Jefferson and Terryville in Brookhaven Township, 38 miles from the Queens line and 51 miles from Manhattan.

Long Island is no longer preeminently a bedroom area for New York City. A study in the late 1960s showed that only 30 percent of the Nassau-Suffolk work force actually commuted to jobs in New York City—some 90,000 by the Long Island Railroad, and 100,000 in their own automobiles (generally with no one else in the car). The auto commuters often head for jobs in the outer New York boroughs, but 25,000 of them—in what must surely be the grimmest commuting routine of the megalopolis—insist on driving their autos all the way into Manhattan, there to pay an exorbitant parking fee, each working day. In return, New York City sends about

100,000 commuters a day to jobs in Nassau and Suffolk Counties.

The 70 percent of the Nassau-Suffolk labor pool that now works on the island depends first and foremost on the military-industrial complex. The biggest contractor is Grumman Aircraft, which employed 37,100 workers in 1969 (but only 26,000 by 1971, as a result of the aerospace depression). Service industries are major employers, and the construction industry is a huge one on the island. Agriculture is still a vital factor in Suffolk County. The three big crops are potatoes, cauliflower, and ducks, in that order. Farm income was $67 million in the late 1960s, the most of any county in New York State. But farming's days on Long Island may be numbered. Rising real-estate taxes, low prices on farm goods, and difficulties in recruiting migrant farm workers from the South are encouraging more farmers to quit each year.

Tourism is also vital to Long Island, and increasingly so as more and more New Yorkers come out not just for the hottest summer weeks, but often for the whole season from May through October. Vacation resorts are scattered all about the island's shores, with some of the most beautiful near the tip of Suffolk, including the illustrious Hamptons (South-, East-, and West-) so popular with high society. For the masses, there is Jones Beach on the south shore, where 2,500 acres of beaches and woods can accommodate 100,000 bathers and, of course, their cars (23,000 at a time). As a result of a major conservationist victory in the early 1960s, the beautiful and unspoiled barrier beach, Fire Island, has been made into a National Seashore, without roads and with its entire shorefront in the public domain.

There is a temptation to identify Long Island's conservative brand of politics with Orange County, California, both places of scientific-age workers mostly anxious to protect their own turf against outsiders. But for all its conservatism, Long Island sometimes pulls surprises. Even if it was for just a single term, Nassau County voters did elect Allard Lowenstein to Congress, a man who relates to and expresses youth's questioning of American values on war and economic policy. In 1968, George Wallace could pick up only 4.8 percent of the vote in Nassau, 8.4 percent in Suffolk. And for three successive three-year terms in the 1960s, Nassau elected a Democratic county executive, Eugene Nickerson, who established the county's first human rights commission, its first governmental code of ethics (badly needed in the developer-wheeler-dealer-zoning-variance atmosphere of modern-day Long Island), the first narcotics commission, job development center, and departments of labor and commerce. Nickerson was a man who made no bones about Nassau's problems in areas like drug abuse and pollution of the air and water, which he said were "reaching disaster proportions."

Nickerson's election in Nassau was exceptional in that he was a Democrat in one of the nation's banner Republican counties, and a county that has contributed major GOP leaders in recent decades. Like Nassau, Suffolk also elected a Democratic executive during the 1960s. But Republicans control practically every township and village government in both counties, plus the county legislatures. (Nassau was the first New York county to adopt the executive county government form with a separate legislature, back in the 1930s. Suffolk followed suit 20 years later. Both counties are regarded as being among the most professionally run in the state.)

The Negro population of both Nassau and Suffolk is about 5 percent, but it is heavily ghettoized. Further movement of blacks onto Long Island is now impeded by zoning practices that exclude low-income people; thereby hangs one of the crucial social and political issues of the 1970s. The National Association for the Advancement of Colored People selected the township of Oyster Bay in Nassau County for a major class action. Of Oyster Bay's 329,142 residents, only 2 percent are black; Grumman Aircraft actually employs 1,248 minority group members at its big plant in the township, but only 50 of them have been able to find housing locally. Yet the same township, anxious to improve its local tax base, has been wooing "clean" industries with special zoning variances and offers of 100 percent site and plant financing. In 1969, the NAACP asked Oyster Bay to "downzone" 750 acres —then about half the residentially zoned vacant land in its unincorporated areas—to permit construction of 5,400 units of single-family and multi-family biracial housing on many scattered sites. The township refused, and the NAACP in 1971 instituted its class action, saying that existing zoning unconstitutionally excluded blacks and low-income workers from local housing, and thus from jobs in new local industry. "We don't believe," NAACP executive director Roy Wilkins said, "that America can shift from urban centers to the suburbs, take industry along with it, and then say, 'Bye-bye, blackbird.' "

Even outside its relatively small black communities, Long Island has many people living in poverty, or close to it. And there are social problems aplenty. As former *Newsday* correspondent Stan Hinden writes me:

One of the key things about suburbia is mood. It's deceptive. The tree-shaded streets and neat houses with their trimmed lawns and bushes look peaceful and serene enough. They don't look like the places you'd find drug addicts or alcoholics, car thieves and embezzlers, people who can't afford shoes for their kids or three squares a day, welfare cases and school dropouts, and race antagonisms, if not actual warfare.

You're not surprised to find all this in the slums—it's just bad environment. But when you find it in the green grass atmosphere of suburbia, what is it then?

Perhaps people take with them the problems of their time, no matter where they live. Perhaps it is as shattering to a man's well-being to have to come up with a big mortgage payment to the bank each month and to get caught in a rising tax squeeze as it is for him to live in a crummy city apartment house where he can hear the mice rattling in the walls.

Perhaps, too, in the homogeneous society, there are no city and county lines to problems, to social ills. Suburbia is in many ways a grand illusion. For many people in Nassau and Suffolk, the facts of life (soaring taxes, high crime rates, inadequate transportation) have helped shatter the illusion about suburbia.

But still they come. Of all the possible worlds, suburbia still seems to be the best one available.

II: THE CITY: NEW YORK, NEW YORK

ON THE DAY OF Thomas Dewey's funeral in 1971, President Nixon flew into New York City for the services, accompanied by New York's Senator Javits. As the two looked down, viewing the soaring towers of Manhattan and the rest of that premier city of America, where almost eight million people make their home Javits turned to the President and said:

It's fantastic. It could all go by the boards.

Nixon's response is unrecorded, but there is an element of pathos in Javits' afterthoughts:

The city is in such trouble. It's a terrible thing for me, because I was born there and lived there all my life, and I adore the city. But it needs massive assistance—a lot from without, *but a lot more from within.*

Certainly the interior resources are there, if they could be mobilized. For all its pains and sorrows, New York is the world's most brilliant and creative city. Name practically any human endeavor outside of government, and New York is the capital of America. What happens within it, in terms of finance, communications, art, theater, fashion, or intellect, sets the pace for the nation and sways the world. California is beginning to offer serious competition in several fields, and now seems to lead in that amorphous area known as life styles. But the *power* is still New York's. It is not as dominant as it was in past times, because the nation is so much larger and more diverse. But a society, no matter how immense, has its controlling and creative center, and New York is it. Javits offers an observation on this score:

Notice how anyone who's running for President beats a path immediately to New York to raise a little dough. It's not just because there's money in New York—there's money in Dallas, too. It's because New York is an open market for ideas, and courageous enough to back new things. And this has been its role for a century or more.

If New York were to "die," one suspects, we would quickly recreate it.

Yet for all its eminence, New York is an easy place to be frightened of. Across the country, in hundreds of interviews, I found confirmed what Richard Reeves, then the metropolitan correspondent for the New York *Times*, had told me: "The people of America are scared of New York City. They see it as a big, tough, vicious place."

It is true that turmoil, brashness, and a feeling of loneliness amid the millions have always marked life in the city. Walk down the streets and look into people's eyes, and you see the emptiness, the shell of desperate self-defense built up around each cell of the urban organism. The wellsprings of hostility seem to be closer to the surface in the last few years. Pushy subway riders, predatory motorists, abusive cab drivers, arrogant city workers, surly sales clerks and waiters, argumentative customers—they all fairly crackle with hostility. Philip G. Zimbardo, a Stanford psychologist but long-time New Yorker, says (in a New York *Times* interview) that the city's uncivil behavior stems from a feeling of anonymity, or as he puts it, deindividualism. "If no one knows who I am, what difference does it make what I do?" In the present day, as the city's traditional homogeneous ethnic neighborhoods begin to break up, no one is known as a person any more, so that the incivility (and, incidentally, the crime rate) gets worse and worse.

The same phenomenon exists in politics and government. Everybody has to have his piece *now*. Confrontation, not compromise and reconciliation, is the model. Inexorably, New Yorkers peck away at the very fabric of the society that holds them together and makes life viable. "John hates the word *demand*," Mayor Lindsay's wife Mary noted in an interview. I asked the mayor about it and he reacted philosophically: "You learn to roll with those things. Legitimate pressures are often involved." Perhaps so, but it must be nerve-wracking. Former Deputy Mayor Richard Aurelio notes: "You make a decision at 9 A.M., and they're out picketing at 11."

Yet in the strangest places in America you find as much sympathy as scorn for New Yorkers. J. Bracken Lee, the right-wing mayor of Salt Lake City, had this to say:

> People are friendlier when they're not jammed together too closely. If you moved everybody from Salt Lake City to New York, it wouldn't be six months until we'd be acting like New York people. And if you moved New York people to Salt Lake, it wouldn't be six months until they got a little more friendly.

Lee's point is underscored by the fact that New York has half again as many people per square mile as any other American city, and Manhattan alone has four times as many.

One reason New Yorkers are so uptight is the roster of afflictions in everyday life. These are just a few of them:

- A daily barrage of ear-shattering noise from air compressors, pneumatic drills, emergency sirens, garbage trucks, jet aircraft, commuter railroads, motorcycles, and honking traffic that must exceed any other place on the continent.

■   Traffic jams of such horrendous proportions that there are recurring proposals to ban all private autos from the streets of Manhattan, or charge high bounties. In 1907, the average speed of horse-drawn vehicles on the city's streets was 11.5 miles per hour; in the 1960s, motor vehicles in the central business district averaged only 8.5 miles an hour (and less during the noontime crushes).

■   The subways, described by John Burby in *The Great American Motion Sickness* as "236 miles of gloomy, grimy, gamy caves filled with steel beasts that scream and scrape around curves in mechanical agony." They do move as many as 61,000 people an hour per line of track during rush hour, 40 times the number that can travel a lane of highway by auto. But the system is plagued by breakdowns, delayed trains, begrimed stations, bands of hyperkinetic youths roving the cars after school, robberies, and molestations. The ranks of armed subway patrolmen had to be increased from 1,019 in 1965 to 3,200 in 1970 to deter felonies against passengers and station attendants, and still scores of incidents take place each month.

■   Streets left filthy from belching incinerators and the careless litter of an indifferent populace. A "small' but significant item: some 500,000 New Yorkers insist on having pet dogs. Each day the canines leave behind a reminder of their presence—110,000 pounds of excrement on New York's sidewalks, streets, and parks (not to mention 2,000 gallons of urine).

■   Selective blackouts and voltage reductions from an overtaxed Consolidated Edison Company. (Everyone remembers the massive power failure that plunged the metropolis into darkness one late November afternoon in 1965. Thousands of people were stranded in subway tunnels, trapped in elevators, or caught in rush-hour traffic without benefit of signal lights. But to everyone's credit, the crime rate was exceptionally low that night.)

■   One of the highest air-pollution rates in the whole world (although Con Ed has reduced the rate significantly in the last several years through the burning of low-sulphur fuels). On Thanksgiving Day 1966, an inversion layer settled on the city, trapping fumes laden with sulphur dioxide and other gases; 168 people died. (Similar inversions in 1953 and 1963 killed 220 and 300 respectively.) In July 1970, a thick blanket of smog again settled on the city, combined with a 90° heat wave, power brownouts, subway slowdowns, wrecks, and fires.

■   The highest crime rate (except for San Francisco) of any city of America perpetrated both by mobsters and petty—but often brutal—street criminals.

■   A housing shortage of near disaster proportions.

■   Crowded, inefficient hospitals (although New York has the most extensive free public health system in the country).

■   Schools of declining quality.

■   The nation's most breakdown-prone telephone system.

■   Fear of a repetition of the 1966 drought when there were grave fears about the future of the city's water supply.*

Then there is the roster of strikes. Consider just the major ones since Lindsay took office in 1966:

- January 1966. The very day Lindsay was inaugurated, New York was hit by a 12-day strike of transit workers, tying up every subway and bus in the city of America most dependent on mass transit to convey millions of workers to their jobs.

- February 1968. The city's 10,000 sanitation workers went on strike and close to 100,000 tons of refuse accumulated on the sidewalks of New York before a settlement was finally reached nine days later. Luckily, the weather was freezing and the stench—if not the litter—held to manageable proportions.

- Autumn 1968. A school strike kept a million children out of class for 36 school days as Albert Shanker's United Federation of Teachers (AFL-CIO) used the pretext of some teacher transfers to protest (and try to kill) an experiment with a locally controlled school board in the Ocean Hill-Brownsville section of Brooklyn. The confrontation turned quickly into a conflict between the heavily Jewish teacher's union membership and the black-controlled Ocean Hill-Brownsville school administration, thus severing old political understandings between blacks, Jews, and unions which had kept social peace in New York for generations.

- January 1971. Thousands of policemen, angry about a court ruling on their demand for back pay in a "parity" dispute, refused to patrol their beats for six days—thus escalating the climate of fear in the crime-infested city.

- June 1971. Victor Gotbaum's municipal workers and their AFL-CIO and Teamster Union allies tried to fulfill his wish for "the biggest, nastiest, sloppiest strike ever." The bridge tenders made 27 of the city's 29 drawbridges unusable by stripping gears, blowing fuses, and rendering the bridge mechanisms inoperable; other strikers drove road maintenance trucks to strategic positions on principal roads leading into the city, flattened the tires, took the ignition keys, and disappeared. The most monstrous traffic jam in New York's history occurred as three quarters of a million Manhattan-bound autos, trucks, and buses backed up for miles into New Jersey, Westchester County, and Long Island. Drivers who deliver school lunches were called off the job, forcing some 3,000 children onto emergency rations; attendants for garbage incinerators deserted their posts, leaving tens of thousands of tons of garbage to rot in 93° heat. Then Gotbaum called out his workers from the sewage-treatment plants, and a billion gallons of raw sewage poured into the Hudson and East Rivers and New York Harbor. The strike lasted only two days, but Gotbaum had made his point: "There is no such thing as a kosher strike. Either they kill you, or you kill them."

Our strike list has not even included the scores of other work stoppages over the past few years, including firemen, postmen, taxi drivers (at the

---

* New York actually has a splendid water reservoir system, constructed in Putnam County on the Hudson's east bank and in the Catskill Mountains on the other side, connected to New York by a tunnel underneath the polluted river.

height of the Christmas shopping season), plumbers, construction workers, parking-garage attendants, and various categories of municipal and service industry workers. Almost at will, it would seem, practically any small group can plunge this vast, incredibly complex and interdependent metropolis into chaos.

An Historic Perspective

When one looks back in history, some of the traumas of today seem, in comparison, not so bad after all.

From its earliest times, New York was a place of remarkable ethnic, cultural, and racial differences. Most of the colonial population was Dutch, but there were many Englishmen as well as Brazilians, French, Finns, Portuguese, and Swedes. There were blacks, most of them from Brazil, and there were slaves. There were Protestants, and then came Catholics and Jews. Quakers were persecuted, tortured, and banished.

In 1712, 23 black slaves rebelled and killed nine white householders. The rebels were cornered; one slave was suspended alive in chains without food or water until he died several days later. Two (one owned by a Roosevelt) were burned alive. In all, 21 were executed by various ghastly devices. In 1741, authorities arrested more than 150 blacks on a series of wildly false charges. By summer's end, 14 blacks had been burned alive, 18 hanged, and 71 banished to the West Indies. Four whites were also executed. Edward R. Ellis, in his *Epic of New York City*, called this the "ugliest orgy of Negro persecutions occurring anywhere in America during the colonial period."

In the early 19th century, as New York made its rise to prominence, displacing Philadelphia as the population center of America and Boston as the cultural center, immigrants began to pour in from Europe. Ethnic hatreds were pronounced and men gathered into gangs to protect themselves, their neighborhoods, and their property from other gangs. The Irish were particularly despised, except by Tammany Hall, by then an arm of the Democratic party. The working classes lived in squalor while the wealthy languished in comfort.

During the Civil War, the draft was deeply resented, and in July 1863 riots broke out on a scale that make 20th century disturbances seem pale by comparison. Between 50,000 and 70,000 Irish Catholics, who blamed blacks for the war and the draft, rampaged through the city and left a wake of death and destruction. They tortured and hanged blacks and burned and looted houses. Before order was restored, at least 1,000 people had been killed, hundreds of buildings burned, and millions of dollars of damage done. By contrast, in the worst racial disturbances of recent years, there was a week of rioting in July 1964 in Harlem and the Bedford-Stuyvesant section of Brooklyn. Some 140 persons were injured, but only one killed.

In the half a century following the Civil War, New York was the fulcrum of fantastic growth generated by freewheeling capital and the industrial revolution. Lords of finance like Cornelius Vanderbilt, Jay Gould, John D. Rockefeller, and J. P. Morgan masterminded the building of great empires of rail, steel, and oil and built their gaudy mansions along Fifth Avenue.

Yet in this same era politics was dominated first by the infamous Tweed Ring, and then by a succession of lesser Tammany Hall thieves. In 1898, a new city charter effected the consolidation of Manhattan with Brooklyn, Queens, the Bronx, and Staten Island, making a city of 3.3 million people, covering 320 square miles of territory. But as this vast metropolis entered the 20th century, it was crowded with the great waves of immigration (especially Jews and Italians) who had been pouring in in ever increasing numbers since 1880. Working conditions for the average man and woman were abysmal, more than a third of the populace was foreign born, thousands were illiterate or unable to speak English; ethnic and racial intolerance was rampant. Some 1.5 million poor people were jammed into hovels and rat-infested buildings on the lower East Side; Ellis contends that they "lived under worse conditions and paid more rent than the inhabitants of any other big city on earth."

As the U. S. entered World War I, New York—though it was a city with a huge German population—was torn by anti-German sentiment. Germanic sculpture was chipped off public buildings, names of foods changed, German operas canceled at the Met. After the war, New York was torn by the infamous campaign of U. S. Attorney General A. Mitchell Palmer against anything and anyone he could label Red or Bolshevik. There was the bombing of Wall Street in 1920, when 35 persons were killed, 130 injured, and the House of Morgan seriously damaged. The Weathermen's depredations of recent years have never come close to that destruction.

New York was a hyperactive, swinging town in the 1920s as its investment bankers increasingly took over world financing. The Stock Exchange boomed, the entertainment world blossomed with 60 theaters on or off Broadway, and thousands of speakeasies flourished. It all came to a roaring end on October 24, 1929, when the stock market crashed. The Depression saw New Yorkers by the thousands standing in bread lines or queuing up at the soup kitchens. Professional men slept in subways or on park benches. The city government almost went bankrupt, amassing a public debt nearly equal to that of the 48 states combined. Despite "recovery," 23 percent of the city's population was still on relief in 1934. And the Negroes, as writer Seymour Freedgood notes, were "scarcely better off than they had been during the Civil War." It really took World War II to revive New York again, but no sooner had peace come than the flight of the stable middle-class citizenry to the suburbs began.

In our time, it is fashionable to say that New York is dying. In a fiscal sense, that may be right. But every prophet of doom should recall what the city has faced in the past and has surmounted. And for all of today's problems, life is better than it once was. Fires no longer ravage great stretches of the urban landscape. The muddy streets and the worst municipal thievery are gone. Street urchins no longer starve or freeze to death. Poor women no longer die in childbirth without medical attention. Racial murders are a pale shadow of what they were in the past. Everyone gets a chance to have an education (however mediocre), now even through college, free of cost. Why, then, is New York said to be in such dire straits? "The city of New York is in trouble because it has set itself standards it's unwilling to pay for," according to Roger Starr, executive director of Citizens Housing and Planning Council. "It's like a person living beyond his moral means."

Mayors and Their Problems

New York is so huge, so complex, so diverse that it has been in vogue in the last few years to speak of it as simply "ungovernable." If the city were Manhattan alone, one might stretch his imagination and see a way to control the mass. But Manhattan contains only 19 percent of New York's population. "You move through the teeming areas of the Bronx and Brooklyn," Senator Javits notes, "and it's just beyond belief as to the problems and the seeming inability to solve them."

New York City's budget is larger than that of New York State or any government except the federal. In 1965–66, it was $3.5 billion a year; in 1971–72, it had shot up to $8.7 billion. The city has 415,000 employees, also a record among all governments except the federal; the municipal workers and their families could fill a city the size of Houston. There are 65,000 school teachers, 12,000 sanitationmen, 25,000 welfare caseworkers, and the ranks of the New York police have swollen to 32,000, more than the standing army of Australia. No other big city requires workers in like proportions in any of these categories. Overall, New York has 49 public employees per 1,000 population, compared to 35 in Los Angeles and only 30 in Chicago, where Mayor Daley's patronage minions are said to swell the public payroll. Why does New York need so many more? City budget director Edward K. Hamilton explained it this way to the New York *Daily News*:

> Because it is so big, because it is so dense, because it has a tradition of high levels of public service along with high expectations, because it has rigidities in its laws governing work load and work rules, and because it has unions, which tend to push very hard, much harder than unions in other cities.

A complementary explanation is offered by Edward N. Costikyan, a former Tammany leader. He claims that in the process of insulating its departments from political influence, the city has in effect succeeded in leaving all the major institutions of government—police protection, education, health and hospitals, sanitation, housing, and welfare—free of any significant exterior political or executive control. Who rules now? The bureaucrats, Costikyan suggests. And what is their primary interest? High pay, security, and building their own administrative empires. What is the result? Bloated, mediocre government.

The mayors of New York and Chicago are the most powerful in the

U. S. in terms of the power given to them under their city charters; they do not, for instance, have to submit appointments to the city councils for confirmation, and they are not limited by boards supervising various areas of municipal services. (New York has a city council and a board of estimate with powers to change the mayor's budget, but since charter changes in 1961, they have not had substantial impact on any mayor's administration.)

The mayor of New York faces an incredibly difficult job—some say second only in difficulty to that of President. Nevertheless, election as mayor of New York remains the ultimate prize in Municipal Politics, U. S. A. Whoever wins the office is the biggest man in the biggest town, surrounded by trappings of power: a beautiful City Hall from which to reign, an historic private residence (Gracie Mansion), a high salary, private limousine always available with chauffeurs, aides, and police bodyguards. He is the representative of urban America, sought out by the great from America and abroad—though the quality of men elected has rarely matched the governors of New York State. Some of the mayors remembered from earlier years are:

JIMMY WALKER (1926–32). A symbol of old Tammanyism but also a man of immense charm and wit. Walker neglected city business outrageously and brought back fraud and favor reminiscent of the Boss Tweed days. He kept a rather steady string of mistresses, to the distress of the Catholic hierarchy. The first citywide sanitation system, the first hospitals department, and tunnels for many subways came during the Walker regime, but the corruption in the city eventually got so bad that Governor Roosevelt appointed a commission, headed by anti-Tammany Democrat Samuel Seabury, to inquire into city government. Walker wisecracked his way through the sordid disclosures of the probe, but one step ahead of removal from office by FDR, he resigned in autumn 1932. The next day he sailed for Europe and oblivion.

FIORELLO H. LA GUARDIA (1934–45). La Guardia is still widely regarded as the best mayor New York ever had. Taking office in the depths of the Depression, he gave New York honest and effective government, instilled its citizens with a sense of hope, and added humor and personal charm to City Hall. (What hired PR man would ever have thought up an idea like reading the comics to children over the radio on Sunday mornings?) La Guardia ran for office at various times as a Republican, a Socialist, and a Progressive, and it was with independent Democratic backing, plus the official Republican nomination, that he first won election as mayor—thus inventing the "Fusion" model Lindsay would use 30 years later.

La Guardia made superb appointments to office, cracked down on crime and police corruption, brought in Robert Moses to rebuild the parks and start bridges, got new housing started, brought aviation to the city, obtained a new city charter, and reformed civil service. In 1947, only two years after leaving office, he died of cancer at 65.

WILLIAM O'DWYER (1946–50). A Tammany Hall regular who appointed some good men to high posts and rushed postwar school- and housing-construction programs. But O'Dwyer was reputed to have underworld connections even before his election. In 1949, after the *Brooklyn Eagle* ran a series on how bookmakers were buying police protection, President Truman was prevailed upon to appoint O'Dwyer ambassador to Mexico. (O'Dwyer later returned home, just to prove, it seemed, that he was not afraid of being indicted. He never was.)

ROBERT F. WAGNER, JR. (1954–65). Son of the distinguished New Deal era Senator who authored the Wagner Labor Relations Act in the 1930s. Wagner, Warren Moscow has written, inherited from his father a social consciousness, a keen ability to negotiate conflicting interests, and a tendency to delay decisions. The result was a bad press image, although when Wagner stepped in to settle a long newspaper strike in the winter of 1962–63, publishers were amazed at his capacity, sagacity, and endurance. Wagner was as honest in money affairs as La Guardia had been, and went much further in fields like education, housing, hospitals, health, traffic, and civil rights. His middle-income housing program, Moscow says, was the nation's best, but he let two obscure state legislators take credit for it. Wagner ended up covering city deficits through bonding, a fairly inglorious end to an able administration. But in many of the bitter labor conflicts of the last few years, his conciliating talents might have brought much happier results.

And Now Lindsay

Nature endowed John Lindsay with a fine, chiseled face, curly hair, and a frame almost as long as Abraham Lincoln's; when you watch him in any group of people, he naturally stands out, and he is tailor-made for television. (London's *Daily Sketch* has ranked Lindsay as the sexiest man in the world, an obviously unscientific finding that nonetheless says something about his political appeal.)

Lindsay's credentials are Wasp, Eastern prep school (St. Paul's), Yale University, and Yale Law School. Naturally he started as a Republican, and by winning election in 1958 from New York City's East Side, so-called "silk stocking" congressional district, he became a prominent symbol of liberal Republicanism. Storefront headquarters helped spread his name and message to the outer boroughs when he ran for mayor in 1965, but he might well have been defeated by the lackluster Democrat, Abraham Beame, if William Buckley, the *National Review* publisher, had not entered the race. Buckley provided a handy target for Lindsay's anti-right-wing oratory, and drew off some old-fashioned ethnic Democratic votes from Beame.

Similar luck rode with Lindsay in 1969, when he actually lost the Republican primary to a moderately conservative state senator, James Marchi, and had only the Liberal party line to run on. But Marchi and the rather colorless Democratic contender, Mario Procaccino, split the middle-income and blue-collar vote, leaving Lindsay to ride in on a tide of high-income, black and Puerto Rican votes, an amazing coalition of the two ends of the economic spectrum. At least in three-candidate fields, the revival of La Guardia's old Fusion principle seemed to be working wonders. But Lindsay won by only

45 percent of the total vote in 1965, and 42 percent in 1969. How he will fare in the future as a Democrat, which he became in August 1971, only time will tell. Now he deals increasingly with regular Democratic borough leaders, to the dismay of some of his earlier reform backers. (Martin and Susan Tolchin make an interesting point about Lindsay in their book, *To the Victor . . . Political Patronage from the Clubhouse to the White House*. Lindsay rode into office, they recall, pledging to "expel [the] sordid compound of privilege and patronage" in city government. But he ended up building his personal organization around patronage in matters over which he had control: judgeships, high-level jobs, zoning variances, and the antipoverty campaign. With his conversion to the Democratic party, Lindsay came close to identification with the very forces that he excoriated to win office.)

Beneath all the glitter and image, Lindsay is a human being with real strengths and weaknesses. One of the greatest strengths is his legitimate concern for the most down-and-out people of the city. As the great ghettos seethed with racial tension in the 1960s, Lindsay personally strode the streets, bringing—by his very presence—a message of concern and respect unknown before. New York might well have experienced a holocaust in the days following Martin Luther King's assassination if Lindsay's sympathetic figure had not been there, moving among the mourners in the black neighborhoods.

A second strength is his desire to make the city human and livable—summed up in his phrase "fun city," so often derided in the midst of New York's crises. When Lindsay took office, Central Park and its counterparts in other boroughs were often left in disuse, especially in the evenings. Now, concerts, plays, music festivals, and movies have been brought into the parks. They are frequently closed to traffic, and bicycling has soared in popularity (with Lindsay himself often cycling—and being photographed as he does). The critical present-day problem is park maintenance; the parks are often so overused that it takes three days after a weekend to get them back in shape. Concurrent with all this, the first stabs have been made at giving the streets back to the people. Fifth and Madison avenues have been made into pedestrian promenades on selected days, and the arrangement may be made permanent on Madison. Similar plans are afoot in the other boroughs.

Such projects of a dashing, urbane mayor may be no substitute for clean air or safe streets or a decent transit system, but they do make life a bit more livable while one waits for the other amenities to arrive. They point to Lindsay's greatest strength: the symbol of America's cities as places of style and class that *are* worth saving. Lindsay, in December 1969, took the lead in forming an alliance of the mayors of New York's six largest cities to lobby with the legislature for more urban aid. With Lindsay's glamor and platform, the other mayors (those of Buffalo, Albany, Rochester, Syracuse, and Yonkers) found the press—and legislature—paying more attention to their common needs. In the autumn of 1970, Lindsay took the process a step further by marshaling the mayors of 17 major cities into a legislative action committee under the U. S. Conference of Mayors. On a monthly basis, the full committee lobbies in Washington and visits a major American city for tours and press conferences, a kind of "Paul Revere" action to warn America about its urban crisis. Both the congressional lobbying and "road shows" appear to be playing a role in shifting public and federal attitudes on the needs of America's great cities.

When I asked Lindsay what he considered his most important accomplishment as mayor, he named the reshaping and modernization of city government. Lindsay created 10 "superagencies" or umbrella agencies, replacing 50 old city departments, and, in a fascinating administrative balancing act, tried simultaneously to decentralize power to the city's multitudinous small communities. The "superagencies" did make it possible to rationalize and coordinate many city functions as well as for Lindsay to recruit some of the finest young executives in America to head them. (Lindsay points with pride to "the caliber of the cabinet I could attract—they'll be heard from again, in business and political administration in the country." Many knowledgeable observers agree with him.) The superagencies have also been faulted, however, for just adding a new level of bureaucracy, contributing to a surge of thousands of new municipal jobs noted during Lindsay's term in office (including a trebling of public relations costs, to $3.6 million a year). The city administration remains snarled in red tape; for the Model Cities program, for instance, five agencies have to process pieces of paper through 56 steps before a person can be hired. Intricate checks and balances are kept in city administration to guard against thievery, but the price is that often nothing gets done.

The road to decentralization has proven long and arduous. When he took office, Lindsay tried to set up "little city halls" (paralleling his storefront campaign headquarters), a way to bring government closer to the people. The Democratic-controlled city council quickly identified the little city halls as competition to the local Democratic clubhouses, and turned down the proposal. Later, Lindsay converted the idea into 40 urban action task forces, operating all over the city; one of their major functions was to channel citizen complaints and suggestions (about 400,000 a year) to City Hall or appropriate departments, another to try and improve conditions in the local communities. Lindsay actually assigned several of his very top aides, including Deputy Mayor Aurelio, to act as coordinators with individual urban action task forces. The communities began to get a feeling of direct access to City Hall on a scale they had never enjoyed before, and the task forces that were well and sensitively administered had some extraordinary successes. Sadly, the budget crisis of 1971 forced elimination of all funding for the task forces. They went ahead as a largely volunteer effort after that, and some even managed to borrow space in churches and other places to keep headquarters open.

Substantial decentralization has also been effected, after fantastic pain and travail, in the school system and the hospitals. Acting in the wake of the convulsive autumn 1968 teachers' strike, the legislature in 1969 directed that substantial but not total operating control over the city's elementary and junior high schools (but not the high schools) be transferred from central city headquarters to 31 newly established districts. But the school bureaucracy remains so entrenched, within each school and in the central administration, that little real change seems to have occurred. According to a 1971 report of the City Club of New York, "the entire bureaucratic level above that of the principal is possibly redundant." Between 1965 and 1970, the school budget went up from $1 billion to $1.6 billion a year and the total number of teachers rose by 6,000. But the reading scores plummeted to well below national norms, the high school dropout rate rose to 32,000 per year, and crime and violence became an ever more serious problem in schools. The flight of middle-class families from the schools has accelerated; from 38.9 percent in 1961, the black-Puerto Rican share of the city school population rose to 57.2 percent. Yet paradoxically, this same school system produces more Westinghouse Scholarship winners, by raw numbers and on a percentage basis, than any other in the country. Throughout the city are students who excel in art, science, music, and academic disciplines, and who are frequent winners of Regents and National Merit Scholarships.

"The Health Department," Lindsay found, "was producing precious little real health care. They wanted a pristine system, and seemed to have a purist worry about pure medicine. We said—'What if you're really not delivering?'" The old bureaucracy was shaken to its roots by the creation, in 1970, of a public-private health corporation which actually runs all 18 municipal hospitals on contract for the city. Lindsay claims the corporation is working. "You feel it in the hospital structure. Things are happening faster —the sponges are moving, the bed sheets are moving, the window screens are getting in. They're getting performance."

The theme of more and better services for disadvantaged people follows over into higher education, where the City University of New York (CUNY) has undergone rapid enrollment, maintained its tradition of total city payment of tuition, and in 1970 became the first free U.S. university to proclaim a policy of open admissions. The program promises a place to any city high school graduate, regardless of his academic record; if he needs it, he gets massive doses of remedial training and counseling. Its announcement drew howls of protest from those who said CUNY would lose its academic distinction (traditionally a training ground for fiercely competitive, bright young Jewish students). Vice President Agnew said the plan was a giveaway of "100,000 devalued diplomas." But the commitment of any student willing to face CUNY's cold environment, where one can walk for days through the crowds of students (195,000 in all) without seeing a familiar face, must be great. "Through open admissions," M. Ann Petrie wrote in *New York*, "City College has renewed its great tradition and special mission—the business of changing lives." Lindsay administration officials see the new program as a chance for education to families—Irish, Italian, Puerto Rican, or black —who could not afford to send their kids to college anywhere before. (Two-thirds of the white families of New York still make $9,000 or less a year; the average Puerto Rican family makes only $6,000.)

Many observers of Lindsay feel that he often shows brilliance and understanding of individual problems, but tends to work on them one at a time, without the across-the-board follow-up or attention to detail required. Faced with a city of selfishly and bitterly competing groups, Lindsay instinctively understood that the old Wagner method of patch-up-and-compromise was just a sure ticket to eventual deterioration. A strong executive hand was needed. But in labor relations, a prime city problem, Lindsay has failed to get the backing, either from the city's people or from the governor, to force a real showdown in the broad public interest. And his own demeanor, in which he seemed to speak from a high moral plateau, has not helped. In the big 1966 transit strike that greeted him as he entered office, he disdained the traditional mediating services offered by attorney Theodore W. Kheel, a smooth labor lawyer, and Harry Van Arsdale, Jr., president of the city's Central Labor Council. Lindsay refused to deal through what he called "power brokers." The strike dragged on for 12 days, at the end of which Lindsay agreed to much greater wage increases than he might have been able to negotiate by more intelligent bargaining earlier in the process. One of the concessions granted in the negotiations was a $500-a-year pension bonus for transit workers. The Transit Authority had opposed that proposal for years, but Robert Price, Lindsay's deputy mayor at that time, made the concession without consulting the Transit Authority's own seasoned negotiators. The $500 pension upped the cost of the settlement by 54 percent, created a precedent which has later been applied in negotiations with other city workers, and *in toto* may cost New York tens of millions of dollars within the next few years.

In the 1968 garbage strike, Lindsay took an extraordinarily hard line against any concession to John DeLury's sanitation workers. The stand appealed, at least to the upper-class part of his constituency, but not among the city's Italians (who dominate the sanitation union). But again, Lindsay's tough public stance did nothing to achieve a favorable settlement. When the state intervened, the sanitation men emerged with a handsome pay increase —but a figure no higher than what Lindsay could have negotiated peacefully before the strike started. There are many people in New York who feel the municipal unions should be curbed. But the growing attitude is that Lindsay should make sure he has the strength and support to control or break a strike, before he makes the public endure one.

Yet on several occasions, Lindsay has submitted rather meekly to the unions' demands. The criticism centers not so much around increasing wages —it is acknowledged that with living costs being what they are in New York, many wages were substandard. But the pension privileges being granted are close to scandal. Not only was there the original $500 annual bonus in transit workers' pension, but the full-pay-at-40-years deal worked out with Victor Gotbaum's municipal workers, and in 1969 an agreement with the United Federation of Teachers that may have a cumulative cost, according to union offiials, of $400 million. Deputy Mayor Aurelio says that in the future, the Lindsay administration will insist on productivity gains and concessions from the unions in return for higher wages. But the city's ability to get such concessions has yet to be demonstrated, and even if it does, the built-in pension costs, now irrevocable, may be the single factor driving the city to the point of bankruptcy in the 1970s and '80s.

Lindsay can be seriously faulted for his on-again, off-again efforts to assert civilian control over the police, purge corruption in the police department, and clean up the hideous conditions in the city jails. Nor has the administration been able to do anything about the soaring welfare bill. When Lindsay took office in 1966, there were about 500,000 people on welfare in the city; by mid-1971, there were 1.2 million, or one out of every seven residents of the city. In 1965, the total welfare bill for the city was $487 million, in 1970 it was $1.9 billion of which the city's direct share was $549 million. The sheer numbers on welfare are only tangentially Lindsay's fault; the blame instead rests primarily on the fantastic migration of poor people into the city and federally mandated standards. But as the New York *Daily News* reported in 1971, "from national authorities on welfare to caseworkers in the slums, there is general agreement that millions of tax dollars that could be saved are being needlessly lost in tangles of red tape, archaic procedures, administrative bungling and even outright fraud." Just to administrate its welfare department, New York spends $300 million a year.

Finally, note must be taken of the polarization of New York's groups that has taken place under Lindsay. His humanitarian impulses have won him easy rapport with youth, intellectuals, blacks, Puerto Ricans, Jews, and many women. But there is a corresponding lack of rapport, and often real hostility, in his dealings with "middle Americans." As Robert T. Connor, the conservative Republican borough president of Richmond, said in 1969: "Lindsay may be great at Lincoln Center and in Bedford-Stuyvesant, but right now the Boston Strangler could beat him on Staten Island." Obviously, Connor reflects the feelings of Staten Islanders upset about high taxes, blacks on welfare, and all the rest. Some degree of resentment against any liberal mayor would be registered there.

But Lindsay has shown a proclivity for seeking out conflicts he might avoid—for example, the 1966 fight over a police civilian review board (a device of dubious merit, even if one sympathizes with its objectives), or the 1967 Blaine Amendment controversy over parochial schools, in which Lindsay became a vocal champion of strict state-church separation, thus offending many Catholics. Every year since Lindsay became mayor, New York has been gripped by some type of crisis that polarizes its people. Not all of it is his fault, but there is a grain of truth in the politically oriented criticism of Congressman Herman Badillo, himself an unsuccessful 1969 candidate for mayor, who claims that as a result of Lindsay's administration:

New York is ripped apart to the point where everyone's nerves are shot. Everyone now is so afraid of another controversy that might blow up the city. The tremendous convulsions of the city have left everyone so exhausted that nobody even makes any recommendations for moving along. We're just glad that the city doesn't blow up. Nobody has any creative ideas now because everything comes against the potential wall of ethnic-racial confrontation.

A National City—or Albany's Vassal?

The mayor of New York finds his job immensely complicated by a state legislature in Albany that can and often does restrict his every movement. The city is legally a creature of the state, and subject to its complete control. Mayors have perennially pleaded with Albany for more home rule, but they still have precious little of it. In one recent year, for example, the city had to go to Albany to get authorization to reassign its policemen to a platoon covering high-crime hours, and to raise the price of dog licenses. Then there is the annual budget trauma, since any new city tax must be authorized by the state. Each year, the mayor goes hat in hand to the state legislature to plead for new tax authorization and new types of state aid which sometimes, but never in the measure requested, are granted. "It's a horrendous system," Deputy Mayor Richard Aurelio says. "Instead of the city having control of its own destiny, it becomes a slave to the state and people who really don't understand it."

The city's perennial complaint has been that it is egregiously shortchanged by the state, that its people feed in much more in state taxes than they ever receive back in state aid. During the 1920s and up to the late 1950s, New York was indeed shortchanged, but in recent years the city has been paying in only about 43 percent of all taxes paid in the state, while it gets back 47 percent of the money allocated to localities from Albany. (In dollars per capita of state aid, New York City got $32 in 1950–51 compared to $218 in 1970–71; the gross dollar-aid figure in that period rose from $255 million to $1.7 billion.) Of course, state taxes were soaring in those same years. But the city can argue, and quite convincingly, that on the basis of where the need is—to solve crushing problems like the education of ghetto kids or solving drug problems—it should get an even greater preponderance of aid.

The relations between city and state have been exacerbated in the last few years by the unseemly, roaring feud between those two patricians, Nelson Rockefeller and John Lindsay. Back in 1965, Rockefeller played a hand in getting Lindsay to run for mayor and greased the way with $500,000 of family money. Almost immediately, he was miffed when the Lindsay people, intent on proving Lindsay was his own man, virtually denied the money even existed. On the surface, relations were calm enough in the first few years. Writing his annual plea to Rockefeller for state aid in 1967, Lindsay said: "We of the city not only acknowledge your sensitive and sympathetic understanding of the city's problems but also the significant enlargement of state financial aid to the city by your administration."

The first open break came with the garbage strike of 1968, which hit while Rockefeller was making one of his bids for the Republican Presidential nomination. Lindsay asked Rockefeller to send in the National Guard to pick up the litter; Rockefeller refused and settled the strike against Lindsay's will. For a week, Lindsay raged on camera and off about Rockefeller's "cowardice, . . . capitulation to extortionist demands, . . . giving in to blackmail." Rockefeller believes Lindsay's stand sabotaged his quest for the nomination, and has never forgiven.

In 1969, Rockefeller refused to endorse Lindsay for reelection after the mayor lost the Republican primary, and in 1970 the final blow (as if one were needed) came when Lindsay endorsed Goldberg over Rockefeller in the gubernatorial campaign. By the time of the 1971 budget battle, it was all-out warfare. Galled by his exclusion from conferences between Rockefeller and Republican legislative leaders to decide on the city's tax package, Lindsay charged he was being "locked out." Rockefeller then joined GOP legislative leaders Brydges and Duryea in a charge that the mayor was responsible for "declining city services due to inept and extravagant administration of the city government." Both the city and state budgets had to be cut heavily that year, but the city was not allowed to increase commuter taxes that would have helped to cover its yawning deficit. Lindsay's charge: "We've been raped, but we're being charged with prostitution." Rockefeller's retort: 'He's not responsible for what he's saying. He's emotionally upset. The poor man has been under a lot of pressure."

Then, as the legislature wound up action on its tax authorization bill for the city ($525 million—$370 million less than Lindsay had requested, but higher than had seemed likely in the heat of the debate), both Rockefeller and Lindsay announced formation of special commissions to study the operations of each other's governments.

As Rockefeller explains the developing city-state relationship:

> In the past, New York City was a very progressive center. It achieved standards in social awareness and competence long before the state did. But the state now has the efficiency and competence and is under less local political pressure than the city. So now we've reversed 100 years of tradition and the state will bring New York City under state regulation and supervision. This is a little traumatic.

The city's books will be audited, Rockefeller says, and more action taken "to reestablish confidence and trust in the city and to preserve it as the financial, business, and industrial center of the country." As examples of the city's inability to meet problems, Rockefeller names water pollution caused by the city's own lack of sewage-treatment plants, and deterioration of the West Side Highway which the governor says will be condemned in five years because of lack of maintenance. The legislature acted to lift rent control on vacated apartments, he said, to stem the deterioration of 40,000 apartments a year. Others note that the various state bodies cutting into city jurisdiction, like the Metropolitan Transit Authority and the Urban Development Corporation, all fit the pattern of the governor becoming a kind of supermayor of the city.

Lindsay's interest is to reverse that entire process. At times he has talked of the possibility of New York City breaking away completely from the state and becoming the 51st state of the Union, with each of the five boroughs a separate city within it. Everyone recognizes the improbability of that happening, not only because the state would never stand for it, but because New York City would thus cut itself off from its rich suburbs—the very place from which funding can and should be drawn to relieve inner-city problems. In 1971, when 90 percent of the readers responding to a *New York* magazine poll said they favored statehood for the city, author Michael Harrington wrote an effective rejoinder:

The city of New York is not economically or socially independent. It is part of a gigantic megalopolitan system which reaches into New Jersey, Connecticut, Pennsylvania and other parts of New York State, most notably Long Island. It is this area, and not the five boroughs or New York State, which constitutes a labor market, a transportation system, a unified—and deteriorating—environment and other crucial determinants of modern life. To create a new political jurisdiction standing on no functional relationships to the problems in these areas is to guarantee that they will not be solved.

The clear solution would be a scrapping of state boundaries to form new entities which combine the metropolises and their natural hinterlands. Again, so many existing political forces would oppose the idea that it probably has little viability in the foreseeable future. But Lindsay is very serious about his idea of New York and other cities of more than 500,000 population becoming "national cities," with a federal charter and grant of special powers from Washington. "Under their charter," Lindsay says, " 'national cities' could deal directly with Washington on matters of trade, finance and social welfare. They could receive broader financial support in order to insure functions of national responsibility." The idea would presumably free the biggest cities from their dependence, at least fiscal, on hostile state legislatures, and formalize the federal responsibility for large-scale urban development. At a minimum, it should facilitate a transfer of wealth from affluent suburbs to needy center cities, through the device of the federal income tax.

The Lindsay proposal moves in a sensible direction because its really crucial financial problem lies not with Albany, which is strapped itself for money, but with the federal government. Each year New York City residents pay a staggering $12 billion in income taxes to Washington, of which only 13¢ on the dollar returns. "New York," Richard Reeves notes, "is the wealthiest city in the world and its name is synonomous with international power, but its government can mobilize only a fraction of the city's resources to deal with the problems of the people who live here."

The Lindsay national-city idea, however, will doubtless face tough opposition in a Congress that is now more suburban than ever, and one where key positions of power are still held by many rural Congressmen for whom the big cities are anathema. Rockefeller, by contrast, presides over a state government that has the power, and perhaps the will, to make New York City its complete vassal. This presents a nightmare sort of prospect for New York City: the state government extending its powers under Rockefeller— a man who *does* care about the city—and then exercising those powers in an oppressive manner under some less understanding man who might succeed him.

What Makes New York Tick

New York appears to have achieved its historic destiny as a global nerve center. As Robert Alden writes:

> Its office towers are magnificent and can be counted among the greatest achievements of man. They are more than a miraculous kaleidoscope of massive shapes and soaring spires and myriad lights. They provide the interplay and excitement that breeds invention and inspiration.
> New York has become the cockpit of cultural and commercial interchange. It is a glorious vehicle for the exchange of ideas, for the cross-fertilization of minds, for the propagation of ideas, for the inspiration that drives man to achieve.

Several major "industries" make New York what it is:

CORPORATE HEADQUARTERS TOWN. New York has the headquarters offices of 118 of the nation's 500 largest industrial corporations, 20 of the 58 largest nonindustrial corporations, four of the five largest airlines, and four of the 10 largest utilities of the United States. Why so many in one place? First, because the others are there. They are constantly making deals with each other, financing each other's projects, exchanging ideas, stealing each other's personnel. Second, because of the incredible array of financing and support services so easily accessible.

CENTER OF FINANCE. Six of the seven largest commercial banks of the nation—First National City Bank, Chase Manhattan Bank, Manufacturers Hanover Trust, Morgan Guaranty Trust, Chemical Bank, and Bankers Trust —are located in the city. Among them, they have assets of $73 *billion* dollars. Bank clearings reached $3.2 *trillion* dollars in 1969, *eight times* what they were in 1950 and 19 *times* the volume of second-ranking Los Angeles. The New York Stock Exchange and its junior partner, the American Stock Exchange, are in the city. The New York Stock Exchange alone handles about 70 percent of the shares traded in the United States; though in dollar terms it now does a majority of its business with such big institutions as mutual funds, insurance firms, and banks, the number of owners of corporate stocks has ballooned from 6.5 million in 1952 to 30.8 million in 1970. New York is the insurance capital of America, accommodating three of the five largest life insurance companies of the nation—Metropolitan Life, Equitable Life, and New York Life. Those three have combined assets of $53 billion; add Prudential in nearby Newark and the total is $82 billion, a fantastic source of financing. The city is also the chief bond market of the nation, whose decisions can make or break thousands of governments and school districts in search of long-term capital financing.

COMMODITY EXCHANGES. Again, one finds a concentration unparalleled elsewhere: the Produce Exchange (wheat and other grains), Cotton Exchange (cotton and wool), Coffee and Sugar Exchange, Commodity Exchange (hides, silk, rubber, metals), Cocoa Exchange, and Mercantile Exchange (butter, eggs, and many other farm products). Each of the exchanges is a world unto itself, composed of men who know their particular markets in minutest detail; their face-to-face communication on the floors of the exchanges reaches an almost psychic level—the phenomenon of personal interaction which is New York's secret but perhaps greatest asset.

RETAILING. Thirteen of the 50 largest retailing companies of America have their headquarters in New York, led by such multibillion-dollar giants as A & P, J. C. Penney, and F. W. Woolworth. The nation's most illustrious group of department stores is in New York City—Macy's, Gimbels, Lord & Taylor, Bloomingdale's, Abraham & Straus, Saks, Bergdorf Goodman, and others. In all the world, there is no shopping town like New York. There are thousands of smaller stores of every imaginable variety; New York, as John Gunther noted, is the town where "you can buy anything from Malabar spices to Shakespeare folios."

SERVICES. Every conceivable type of service industry, from the mundane to the incredibly sophisticated, is located in New York. Firms specializing in market research, advertising, public relations, management consultation, engineering, custom brokerage—the biggest and best are all in New York. They are a major inducement to great corporations to make their headquarters in the city. The same, of course, is true of New York's multitudinous law firms, packed with experts on taxes, corporate law, bonds, or virtually any other specialty.

WHOLESALING. New York State accounts for about a fifth of the nation's wholesale trade, and five sixths of that total is in New York City. The wholesaling is national and international in scope, but also intensely local because the New York-N.E. New Jersey urbanized area, with 16.2 million people, is the largest market area of the hemisphere. Second-place Los Angeles, with 8.3 million people, is barely half as large.

PORT. The port that made New York still sustains it. The harbor is the best in North America and one of the largest and best in the world. It is virtually fog and ice free; it is calm and protected; its shores are easily accessible. The port has an astounding 833 miles of direct water frontage, 578 of which are in New York City, the remainder in New Jersey. There are 400 berths for ocean-going vessels, the world's greatest docking capacity, and each year some 26,000 ships come and go. The dollar volume of goods handled is about one quarter that of all the ports of the nation. Kennedy International Airport handles more than half the country's overseas air travel and is the largest import-export air-cargo center of the nation.

MANUFACTURING AND CONSTRUCTION. New York State leads the nation in value added by manufacture—$25.3 billion in 1969—and New York City accounts for almost half the employment and half the value of goods. The city's greatest employers are the garment trade and allied textile products, accounting for about a quarter of a million jobs. Printing and publishing come second with 125,000 jobs. Food products account for 60,000 jobs; one finds the workers in hundreds of bakeries, breweries, distilleries, cold-storage warehouses, packing houses, and confectionaries. Tens of thousands of people work in factories turning out fabricated metals, machinery, paper products, chemicals, leather goods, and furniture. The construction industry employs over 100,000—and with good reason; in the last 20 years, Manhattan alone has added twice as much office space as the next nine cities combined.

Thus New York, despite the alarms raised about its future, certainly appears to have a sound economic base. Most other cities would be delighted to have a fraction of its assets.

Nevertheless, there are areas of gnawing doubt, and some problems that the city will ignore at its peril. The loss of corporate headquarters is a case in point. Between 1967 and 1971, 22 large firms pulled out of the city, a high proportion going to Connecticut, several to New Jersey, and several out of the metropolitan region altogether.* Among the largest were American Can, Olin, Continental Oil, and General Telephone & Electronics, all moving to Connecticut; Pepsico and IBM to Westchester County; and CPC (Corn Products), Nabisco, and Union Camp to New Jersey. Why did they leave? Partly, it would seem, because of the frustrations of doing business in New York, and partly for the lower taxes and the personal convenience of executives (in a suspiciously high number of cases, the corporation moved out to the suburbs near the chief's personal home). In the late 1960s, there was an extremely tight labor market in New York, and many Puerto Rican and black employees had to be hired to fill clerical ranks—a psychic shock for many white executives and managers. Executives looked around them and noted an appalling lack of housing for their middle-income executives, the snarled transit system, bottlenecks in transportation of goods, higher personal income taxes in the city, strife-ridden public schools, unsafe streets, faltering public utilities, and high office-space prices. They found middle-level executives balking at coming to New York, not only because of its physical hardships, but a cost of living 16 percent more than in Los Angeles, 28 percent more than in Dallas. Thus a wave of pull-out decisions began. By 1971, even as overbuilding caused a surplus of office space (and lower rentals), the outflow seemed to continue at a steady (but not accelerating) clip.

New York officials are not as upset as one might expect. They point out that there have been some companies moving into Manhattan at the same time as others have been pulling out (Atlantic Richfield, Avon, and big conglomerates like Norton Simon and UMC Industries). Because it is the seat of international commerce, New York automatically draws U. S. companies going "multinational" and has increasing numbers of U. S. headquarters of major foreign firms (like Japan's Toyota, Sony, and Mitsubishi). IBM, which departed for Armonk in Westchester, now leases "considerably more" space in the city than when it left in 1964. In 1971, David Rockefeller said he believed the trend out of the city might soon reverse:

* One big company—Shell Oil—moved lock, stock, and barrel to Houston, 1,700 miles away.

As more and more firms move out, they'll discover that the suburbs are not as ideal as they first thought. The labor market will grow tighter. The open spaces will be eliminated by virtue of what they're building. Company presidents will find that they are leading a much more insulated and isolated life. They will come to miss the contact with their peers and the excitement of the cultural and intellectual life of the city.

And eventually, companies will find it difficult to attract bright, young people to work in isolated suburban locations. There is also the question of what suburbanization does to a company's "soul." D. Kenneth Patton, the city's economic development administrator, calls going suburban "a form of semi-retirement." He attacks companies for imbedding office development in areas restricted to big-lot zoning (meaning most employees can't live nearby), and for using auto-oriented campus sites that move back to the transportation technology of the 1950s. The result, he warns: "We will Los Angelize our land, Balkanize our region's finances and South Africanize our economy."

Assuming New York City's living conditions get no worse and no better over the next few years, the likelihood seems to be that many more firms will leave, but that others will move in, banks and advertising agencies and brokerage houses will stay put, and the work force will expand rapidly enough to keep downtown office employment rising. One expert (David L. Bitch, a Harvard Business School professor) told *Forbes:* "Actually, cities are becoming more popular as elite management centers. . . . More and more medium sized and small managements find they must rely on the interaction of the city."

But what if conditions are allowed to deteriorate in the city as badly in the 1970s as they did in the 1960s? What if strikes and lawlessness reach an intolerable point, the ultimate blackout occurs, and the ultimate traffic jam? Could the great companies simply *desert* Manhattan, turning it over to the National Park Service for guided tours through the deserted skyscraper canyons? Senator Javits comments: "The assessed valuation of real estate in New York's central business district is over $20 billion, but the business interests haven't begun to protect their investment from the decay which is lapping at the threshold of every one of these buildings—the physical condition of the city, and people's increasing unwillingness to live there." Javits believes the business interests should form a group like Pittsburgh's Allegheny Conference or the Greater Philadelphia Movement. Incredibly, these gigantic corporations, with power in New York *and* Washington that can scarcely be overestimated, have yet to coalesce to save their city.

There was talk in the 1960s that the entire New York Stock Exchange might pull up its roots and depart, perhaps for New Jersey. But the city was able, with state help, to bargain successfully to keep the Exchange, granting a reduction in the stock-transfer tax in the process. The Exchange's problems have been immense but internal—its inability to handle the fantastic paper work with stock certificates, the 1969–70 market crash in which a staggering total of 129 member firms failed or merged, and protection of individual investors when brokers go under. Numerous reforms were begun at the start of the 1970s, however, and plans developed for a brand new, expanded Stock Exchange in Lower Manhattan.

The problems of big corporations in doing business in New York are probably milder than those of retailers, distributors, and others doing business directly "on the street" in the city. For them, the problems of crimes against persons, burglary, high taxation, and arbitrary urban-renewal decisions are likely to be much more immediate. There are countless stories of the smaller companies, even those who have done business in New York for years and years, being forced out of the city.

On the other hand, the city has been moving imaginatively to set up sub-centers for offices, services, medical facilities, and some light manufacturing in several boroughs, with the aim of providing opportunities close to people's homes. Some 1,000 acres of land have been developed industrially with city help, as against none in the mid-1960s.

Thousands of new low- and middle-income jobs will be needed in the 1970s to offset the loss in manufacturing jobs the city has suffered in recent years. The most troublesome story is that of the garment trade. One would not expect it to be so, since New York remains the undisputed center of fashion in America, home of the most creative designers, the trend-setting place where the buyers from across the country congregate, the receiving port for the choicest hides and skins, and the home of America's best fashion libraries and textile and costume collections. The garment district on the Lower West Side has much the aura of decades past, with boys pushing racks loaded with dresses through incredibly snarled traffic in the narrow side streets. But actual production of standard-type garments has been drifting away from Manhattan since the 1920s; manufacturers figure, with good reason, that designs originating in New York can as well be executed in abandoned old New England textile plants or cheap new buildings put up in rural Pennsylvania or the South—especially since labor is often cheaper there. Within the decade of the 1960s, the garment industry lost 54,000 jobs in New York City (from 279,-000 down to 225,000), and the trend is expected to continue, especially in the face of stiff foreign competition.

Sad to say, the garment industry may not "belong" in New York at all. Some of the skilled pressers and cutters earn more than $10,000 a year, but unskilled employees like cleaners, pushboys, and shipping clerks usually make $4,000—much less than a living wage in the city today.* The venerable old ILGWU (International Ladies Garment Workers Union), which organized early in the century to drive the sweatshops out of the city and now has 460,000 members across the U. S. A., has been faulted by some for fighting for high pay for its older, Jewish craftsmen, while letting much lower wages prevail for the unskilled, black, and Puerto Rican workers. (The union has a minority membership of 30 to 50 percent, depending on various estimates, but only one minority member on its governing board—a fairly content 64-

---

* Average garment workers' pay in the city is $107 a week, including substantial overtime. In the country as a whole, garment workers make an average $83 a week, compared to $130 for the average American factory worker.

year old Puerto Rican. Its membership is 80 percent female, but it has only one woman on the board.) But even if the ILGWU could instill young blood into its veins, fighting for youth and minorities, the limits of what it could do would be strictly circumscribed by the import flood from Japan, Hong Kong, Taiwan, Korea, and Italy.

The port of New York presents a wholly different set of problems. The modern-day move to big prepacked containers caught the city asleep as it continued to put its port investments into obsolete piers on the Hudson River, even while the Port of New York Authority was building special containership piers at Newark and Elizabeth. The Manhattan waterfront lacks enough backup space for containership freight, but it can and should be developed for cruise-ship piers. (Jet aircraft finally swept the last American ships out of the North Atlantic run in 1969, but the cruise business is still a healthy one.) The city now hopes to get Brooklyn, and later Staten Island, converted to containership piers. The whole process is complicated by burgeoning dockside and airport pilferage (sometimes whole truckfuls of goods), the relationship among the feuding longshoremen's unions (Irish locals in Manhattan, Italian locals in Brooklyn), and the guaranteed wage which the shippers granted the longshoremen in return for being able to shift to containerization. The men get paid, in effect, whether they work or not. There have been a great many workless days in Brooklyn, despite the big work force of skilled longshoremen there, and the city has now dedicated all the landfill from its new subways to produce the technical equivalent of Port Newark in Brooklyn—with a much better disciplined and experienced work force than Newark's.

Severe overcrowding at Kennedy International Airport (which now accommodates 20 million passengers a year) has created demands for yet another area jetport, in addition to JFK, Newark, and La Guardia. One has the feeling that even with another airport, it would not be long until the same fantastic delays—on the ground and in the holding patterns aloft—would return. More rational approaches would include more emphasis on rapid rail connections to other Eastern cities (beyond the promising but still primitive Metroliner experiment), and shifting a substantial amount of the transatlantic business to less crowded East Coast airports (Logan at Boston, Dulles near Washington, and Philadelphia).

Communications and Culture

New York television, radio, newspapers, magazines, books, and fashions mold and influence American thought year-in, year-out, as no other force in the land. Sometimes the country reacts *with* New York, sometimes *against* it, but always *to* New York. The major networks (CBS, NBC, ABC) all have their headquarters in the city and determine the news and entertainment diet of a nation. The evening network news programs have replaced the daily newspaper for a formidable proportion of the American people and have played a major role in the history of our times (i.e., bringing the horrors of the Vietnam war into the nation's living rooms, making race riots and student demonstrations an almost personal experience for millions of Americans, and making household faces and names of many more politicians and public figures than Spiro Agnew). An almost equally powerful role is played within New York City by the local evening news programs of the network's wholly owned subsidiaries in the city, plus Metromedia. In all, New York has 46 television and radio stations, including the country's only municipal broadcasting system, which operates a UHF television station and broadcasts on AM and FM radio.

The New York *Times*, despite growing competition from the Los Angeles *Times* and Washington *Post*, is the country's only national newspaper, in that it is read by government, business, and other opinion leaders from one coast to the other and influences millions of other readers through syndication of its news service. In quality and comprehensiveness, the *Times* may be the finest newspaper in the world today. The tabloid New York *Daily News*, a property of the Chicago *Tribune*, speaks with a more conservative voice and caters to the less sophisticated and affluent New Yorkers. It is far ahead of the *Times* in circulation—2,129,909 to the *Times*'s 846,132 on weekdays, and 2,948,786 to the *Times*'s 1,407,549 on Sundays. But it is little read outside the city. The *Wall Street Journal* and *Women's Wear Daily* (the latter's midi-length debacle of 1970 notwithstanding) are the national opinion leaders in business and fashion respectively, although the *Journal* (circulation 1,215,750, in several regional editions) also provides excellent feature coverage on almost any subject under the sun. The New York *Herald Tribune* was an important voice of liberal Republicanism until its demise in the labor and price-squeeze wars of the 1960s, one of the saddest occurrences in modern American journalism. Dorothy Schiff's stridently liberal evening *Post*, published on a tight budget, suffers from often mediocre news coverage, although it runs some excellent columns. But with the demise of all the other significant afternoon dailies it stands alone in the P.M. market.*

The two leading national news weeklies—*Time* and *Newsweek*—emanate from the city, as does *Life* for the general market; *McCall's* and *Ladies' Home Journal* for the distaff side; *Fortune*, *Forbes*, and *Business Week* for executives; *Vogue* for the fashion consumer; *New Yorker* for the literary and cultured; and *Harper's Magazine* for the literati and politically sophisticated alike. There are several magazines of quite differing tastes and approaches for the book world—*Saturday Review* (which also takes a lively interest in environment), the *New York Review of Books*, *Publisher's Weekly*, and *Printer's Ink*. Scores of specialized trade publications are published in the city.

* Big trouble for New York's newspapers was presaged by the union-forced collapse of the *Brooklyn Eagle* in 1955. In 1962–63, there was a disastrous strike that resulted in all the city's big dailies being closed down for 114 days. Rising costs and fear of another long strike prompted the *World Telegram and Sun* and *Journal American* to merge with the *Herald Tribune* in 1966, but the combined paper was immediately hit by a disastrous strike by the printer's union demanding security for its workers. The newspaper published for a few months but then expired, causing *all* the workers to lose their jobs and irreparable loss to the city.

In a hostile era for new magazines, one has emerged since 1968—*New York*, a spunky weekly that focuses on the city's foibles and glories, suggests to a sophisticated audience how to survive in modern Manhattan (title of one column: "The Urban Strategist"), and has included lively political commentary by fine personal journalists like Gloria Steinem, Tom Wolfe, Pete Hamill, and Jimmy Breslin. *New York* almost went under in its first year, but by 1970 had a quarter of a million subscribers—well beyond the Upper East Side influentials to whom the magazine first seemed geared. In fact, it was telling about parts of New York life few of the elite appreciate; in 1971, for instance, there was one story on how all the best fashion buys are in Brooklyn (yes, Brooklyn!), and another on the more than 50 neighborhood weeklies around the great city, all the way from *Brooklyn's Home Reporter* and *Sunset News* and *Flatbush Life* to the *Bronx Press-Review*. (In addition to all these, of course, New York has dozens of foreign language newspapers.)

And New York remains, as it has been since the early 19th century, the book publishing center of America—some 35,000 titles a year by latest count.

Like every other part of the New York economy, the communications industry faces rafts of problems (but will doubtless survive). The networks were thrown off balance by Vice President Agnew's celebrated attacks on the Eastern Establishment's control of television news, and critical public scrutiny is likely to be a permanent (and to a degree, quite healthy) phenomenon. The networks may be past their prime, at least economically, as an increasingly sophisticated national audience opts for the wide range of programs, many filmed or locally originated, made possible through multichannel cable television and video cassettes. Insistence of the FCC on more locally produced programs on network affiliates may also harm New York, and as the networks lose or level off in revenue growth, the city's big advertising agencies may be hurt (or fail to expand).

Foundations and charities abound on the island of Manhattan, making it the center of America's "Philanthropic Industrial Complex." National and international philanthropies there raise well over $1 billion each year, not to mention the distribution of grants from the multimillion- and multibillion-dollar foundations. The Ford Foundation has received the most notice in recent years, a direct result of president McGeorge Bundy's bold and controversial contributions in the social field (including money to start up the decentralization experiment in the Ocean Hill-Brownsville school district). But Ford's chief activities have been in education on a national and international scale.* Its assets are about $3 billion, nearly four times those of the Rockefeller Foundation, the next wealthiest trust. Some of the other illustrious New York-based foundations are the Carnegie, Guggenheim, Hartford, Commonwealth, Twentieth Century, Field, Stern, Taconic, and Vera. The

* The Ford Foundation's headquarters building on Manhattan's East Side is a sight to behold: a stunning 12-story gallery of offices that surrounds a giant roofed courtyard with great plants, and birds flying about.

city even has a Council on Foundations, set up to aid community foundations like those in Cleveland and Kansas City.

Some of the inventiveness and daring of the country's foundations was doubtless sapped by the Tax Reform Act of 1969, which circumscribes their activities. (Part of the impetus for the act was real abuse by foundations of their tax-exempt status; part was also due to opposition in Congress to some daring social projects, especially Ford's.) The foundations flock to New York for many of the same reasons corporations do—for communication among themselves and rapid access to the financial and intellectual communities. New York is also filled with nonprofit institutions of every stripe, from the businessmen's Committee for Economic Development to the National Association for the Advancement of Colored People, from the Council on Foreign Relations to the Urban League.

New ideas and movements come spilling out of New York with startling rapidity. One example, from 1971. Three hundred women met in Washington to proclaim formation of the National Women's Political Caucus. And who were the four prominent leaders? Two New York City Congresswomen —Bella Abzug from Manhattan and Shirley Chisholm from Brooklyn; New York writer Gloria Steinem (whom *Newsweek* calls "a liberated woman despite beauty, chic and success"); and Betty Friedan of New York, author of *The Feminine Mystique* and founder of the National Organization for Women.

In the performing arts, New York seems ever to have been the premier city of the land. Despite the growth of a strong regional theater in America since World War II, no play is considered a true success until it has undergone baptism by fire of the critics and audiences of Manhattan. A classical concert artist may receive warm receptions in Los Angeles or Cleveland, but not be counted a full success until New York joins in the accolades. New York remains the cultural center of the nation because it has the huge, sophisticated audiences concentrated in one great metropolitan center, and because the required money—lots of it—is there to launch productions.

New York's overall number of legitimate theaters—30 or 31 in the last few years—has held fairly steady, but there have been low seasons like 1969–70, when at one point half of Broadway's legitimate theaters were "dark"— without plays. Due in large part to extremely high labor costs (and no small amount of featherbedding), it can cost $400,000 to $800,000 to launch a musical comedy, or $150,000 to $200,000 for a straight play. Off-Broadway theater, which was conceived as an opportunity for actors to make their mark, has taken on many of the characteristics of its parent—frequent money-losing plays and ticket prices that are seemingly astronomical. There is also Off-Off-Broadway, which critic Clive Barnes describes as "a kind of inspired amateur theater of professional standards," but one where "the actors are not paid nor is anyone else."

By the mid-1960s, expansion of the midtown office area had reached the heart of the traditional "great White Way" and legitimate theaters were threatened. Mayor Lindsay created a consultative group known as the Urban

Design Group which pressed hard for a new zoning regulation covering a specified Theater District from 40th Street to 57th, and from Eighth Avenue to the Avenue of the Americas. Within it, developers of new office buildings may increase the size of their structures by 20 percent if they will include a theater in their new structure. As a result of this so-called "incentive zoning," more than $20 million in theater construction has occurred, including five new theaters.

Until World War II, the symphony, opera, and ballet in New York were frequented almost exclusively by society elite. Since then, these serious forms of culture, both in live performances and through records and tapes, have become the province of millions. The physical embodiment of this is New York's massive Lincoln Center for the Performing Arts, which covers no less than 14 acres, a block to the west of Central Park between 62nd and 66th streets. The concept was born in the mid-1950s when the Metropolitan Opera decided it would have to abandon its romantic but decrepit old quarters and the New York Philharmonic feared that Carnegie Hall might be torn down. The idea of a federation of cultural institutions emerged; the Julliard School of Music, the Music Theatre, the New York City Ballet, and the New York City Opera decided to join in; and a gap was filled by creation of the Lincoln Center Repertory Company. The construction funds —over $160 million—were raised from foundations, wealthy individuals, the city and state governments.

The Lincoln Center building complex has become one of the city's prime tourist attractions; behind the monumental walls of the New Metropolitan Opera House, Philharmonic Hall, New York State Theater, and the other structures, the nation's greatest concentration of the lively arts thrives—albeit with grim financial crises like those that plague so much high culture in the U. S. A. today. Some of the constituent parts of the Lincoln Center might find their match in other American cities, but not so the New York City Ballet or the Metropolitan Opera. The gala opening of the new opera house in 1966 was one of the most glittering events in New York's history.

New York is also the art nexus of the continent, and one of global importance; as American artists operating largely out of New York made their mark internationally in the years after World War II, the English critic Lawrence Alloway said that "New York is to mid-century what Paris was to the early 20th Century: it is the center of Western art." The abstract expressionism of our time, photography, sculpture, applied graphic arts—they are all centered in the city. There are hundreds of distinguished private galleries, and then the great public museums: the Metropolitan Museum of Art (largest museum of the Western Hemisphere, now presided over by the youthful "art to the people" enthusiast and Lindsay's first parks commissioner, Thomas Hoving); the Museum of Modern Art (founded in 1929 by Mrs. John D. Rockefeller); the striking Whitney and Guggenheim museums opened in the postwar era; the Cloisters; the Brooklyn, Riverside, and Jewish museums; the Frick Collection; the Museum of Primitive Art—and more.

Who Runs New York?

The question is not simply answered, and perhaps unanswerable. The power balance, Richard Reeves said when I asked him the question, is constantly shifting, depending on which group is interested in a particular problem, and all the more complicated by the fact that many of the power groups have national and international as well as New York interests.

New York magazine has made a noble stab at the power question each year since 1968; Dick Schaap, who did the study at the end of 1970, observed: "The simple, terrifying fact is that the city . . . is out of control, not just out of control of its citizens, but out of control of its power bloc, too." The last man who clearly determined the quality of life, Schaap observed, was the man who pulled the wrong switch in Ontario back in 1965 and triggered the great power blackout. The closest contenders, he suggested, would be the New York Mets, Jets, and Knicks, on the days each won a world championship and gave New York a brief, bright glow; of these, the Mets rank first because the champagne dousing they gave John Lindsay in 1969 helped determine who got elected mayor that autumn.

Labor leaders appear quite frequently on *New York*'s list of the most powerful, and when Schaap polled 14 well-known New Yorkers for suggested names, the man most frequently mentioned was Harry Van Arsdale, president of the city's Central Labor Council. Van Arsdale, Schaap noted, rated because he "force-fed the state AFL-CIO the brilliant idea of supporting a millionaire [Rockefeller] against a former labor lawyer [Goldberg] for the governorship" and because he helped ease the traffic crisis by calling a cab strike. Two Rockefellers qualified for Schaap's list—Nelson for obvious reasons, and David because, "if nothing else, he has survived." Austin Tobin, chairman of the Port of New York Authority, was considered to have great power because the Authority, under him, had favored automobiles over mass transit. Edward Costikyan, compiler of the *New York* list for 1968 and 1969, notes that Tobin's Port Authority "has killed the commercial construction industry, not on purpose but by colossal inadvertence—by building the World Trade Center, thus absorbing the demand for commercial space for the foreseeable future."

Earl Brydges and Perry Duryea made *New York*'s list in 1970 because they control the city's taxes. A. M. Rosenthal, managing editor of the New York *Times*, was included because "anyone in his right mind knows that a news story in the *Times* carries far more weight than an editorial." Frank Hogan, the impeccably honest Manhattan district attorney, was included, as were Theodore Kheel, the labor lawyer and mediator, and Joe Colombo, the Italo-Mafia leader whose star was then rising.

Schaap noted with interest that not a single black or Puerto Rican or woman or young person qualified for the top ten; "that gives you some hint of what's wrong with the city," he said.

Some interesting names appear on the list of those nominated by some members of *New York's* panel but not chosen for the top 10. A selective list includes these: Terence Cardinal Cooke, the church moderate who succeeded the beloved and fearsome Francis Cardinal Spellman in 1968; William Ronan, chairman of the MTA; William Paley, chairman of CBS; Albert Shanker, president of the United Federation of Teachers; President Nixon; McGeorge Bundy; Robert Sarnoff, chairman of RCA; Stephen Smith, leader of the Kennedy Democrats in New York; Vincent Albano, the Manhattan Republican leader; Sen. James Buckley and his brother William, the editor and political columnist; Carlo Gambino, long-reigning Mafia boss in the city; Bess Meyerson Grant, the former Miss America who is Lindsay's commissioner of consumer affairs; Louis Harris, the pollster; Andrew Heiskell, chairman of Time Inc.; Hulan Jack, assemblyman from Harlem; Gustave Levy, chairman of the board of governors of the New York Stock Exchange; Robert Moses, planning czar emeritus; Police Commissioner Patrick Murphy; Alex Rose of the Liberal party; Daniel Mahoney, chairman of the Conservative party; Anthony Scotto, Brooklyn waterfront leader; and Harvey Scribner, chancellor of the city school system. One unusual choice was Leonid Brezhnev, head of the Soviet Communist party, who was named in all seriousness by Walter Cronkite, who pointed out: "He has the power to launch a nuclear attack on the city."

Crime in Fun City

Of the monstrous problems facing New York, none is more frightening than crime. New Yorkers—rich, poor, white, black—are preoccupied by it. Fear of crime molds election campaigns, shapes judgments at government and business levels, dictates the life style of a city's people. A fortresslike mentality develops in which people resort to incredibly complex locks and security alarm devices, are afraid to walk the streets at night, and close their stores earlier every year.

And with good reason. In 1970, there were 471,819 reported crimes, including 98,482 crimes against persons (1,028 murders, 1,975 rapes, 66,585 robberies, and 28,894 aggravated assaults). Department of Justice officials estimate that 80 percent of the organized crime in the U. S. is centered in New York City and neighboring northern New Jersey. The city is the heroin and numbers-racket capital of America. And then there is the problem of corruption within the 32,000-man New York police department. In a major exposé printed in 1970, the New York *Times* reported:

Narcotics dealers, gamblers and businessmen make illicit payments of millions of dollars a year to the policemen of New York, according to policemen, law enforcement experts and New Yorkers who make such payments themselves.

Despite such widespread corruptions, officials in both the Lindsay administration and the Police Department have failed to investigate a number of cases of corruption brought to their attention.

Catching wind of that upcoming exposé by reporter David Burnham, Lindsay had appointed a blue-ribbon citizens' commission to investigate police corruption, headed by Wall Street lawyer Whitman Knapp. The commission did not, as defenders of the police expected, turn up a picture of a few bad apples in a basically honest and effective police department. Instead, it reported in 1971 that the whole barrel had become so rotten that corruption had become the rule rather than the exception. For example, members of the narcotics squad were found to be engaged in extortion and bribery and some even in the sale of hard drugs themselves. Police officers were being paid off regularly, it was reported, by gamblers, pimps, illegal liquor distributors, construction bosses, and restaurants. And the mayor himself, Knapp said, "cannot escape responsibility" for the corruption.

Up to the 1960s, the police department functioned as a semiautonomous duchy, effectively isolated from control of mayors from the early Tammany times up to Wagner's era. Lindsay tried to change that, refuting in his inaugural address the idea that the department could be a law unto itself. But his first move, to create a civilian review board to hear complaints of police brutality, backfired badly when the powerful Patrolmen's Benevolent Association (PBA) led a successful campaign to have the board abolished in a 1966 popular referendum.* Howard R. Leary, whom Lindsay recruited from Philadelphia to be police commissioner, instituted a number of promising innovations, including the country's first emergency dialing number, a computerized dispatch and control system which keeps track of all men on the street at any moment, neighborhood patrols of black and Puerto Rican policemen who live in communities like Harlem and can speak the ghetto language, and recruitment of college graduates to be members of the force. But the police bureaucracy grew under Leary, without his very full control, and he proved powerless to stem the tide of corruption in the ranks or to stop such outrages as the police failure to intervene when hundreds of construction workers set upon and roughed up antiwar demonstrators. In 1970, as revelations of police corruption were aired, Leary resigned (telling friends one of his chief frustrations was interference in running the department by Lindsay's young and inexperienced personal aides).

The police commissioner picked to succeed Leary was Patrick Murphy, former police chief of Syracuse, and public safety director in Washington and police commissioner in Detroit, a certified member of the New York Irish ascendancy that has dominated the department for almost 100 years. (Murphy's father and two brothers were New York policemen, and he started himself on the beat in the Red Hook section of Brooklyn.) But Lindsay's choice seemed inspired, because Murphy had won the reputation in his prior posts of being a shrewd and innovative reformer, and also a liberal on racial matters. Murphy faces a near impossible job in New York, with charges of broad police corruption coinciding with swelling police resentment

* A paper organization when it began in 1894, the PBA is a little empire in its own right, taking in $10 million in dues and pension contributions each year. As powerful as it is, the PBA found some of its more militant young members hard to handle during the New York police strike in January 1971.

about being the targets of the hostilities of blacks, Puerto Ricans, and angry demonstrators. But Murphy began with a sweeping shake-up of the police department, the most thorough-going in 20 years, which augured well for the future.

Organized crime is so extensive and deeply ingrained in the city that the New York *Times* occasionally prints stories on the five leading Mafia "families" as detailed as its reportage on political organizations and major industrial concerns. The coordinated federal attack on the Mafia, made possible by new legislation in recent years, is taking its toll among top syndicate leaders, however. A new twist in Mafia affairs emerged when the oft indicted Joseph Colombo, heir to the Joseph Profaci family of Mafia in Brooklyn, organized his Italian-American Civil Rights League and got more than 50,-000 hard-working men and women to join. (It was an amazing story, one city official told me, of the Mafia founding an organization to convince the world that the Mafia didn't exist.) Inevitably, Colombo's bid for citywide Mafia mastery marked him as a man for extinction by rival syndicate warlords. The police believe that was the reason for the almost fatal attempt on his life during a 1971 rally in the city.

Every conceivable problem seems to land in the hands of New York's cops, from keeping peace in the seething ghettos to protecting United Nations personnel from terrorist groups to restraining the surge of blatant prostitution and pornography houses that have infested Manhattan. Vast quantities of heroin flow into the New York syndicate-controlled heroin factories, by ship, car, and plane. The number of addicts in the city increases by 7,000 or more a year. Eight hundred New Yorkers died of heroin poisoning in 1969. Anyone at a city high school, one of the universities, or in the slum neighborhoods knows where to pick up his "smack," pot, or pills. Heroin begets still more crimes, and the police have yet to show they can deal with the problem.

Directly related to New York's police dilemma is the shocking condition of its clogged courts and antiquated, overcrowded prisons. Lindsay has been criticized in some quarters for responding to citizen complaints about crime by increasing the number of men on the police force while failing to follow the advice of penologists who say more police will never cut crime, that the courts must be improved and massive rehabilitational services provided for inmates. But the problems of the correctional system go back over decades, and are not easily corrected. The criminal court of the city of New York is a fractured, uncoordinated complex of 96 judges and six courthouses, which open their doors every morning to some 15,000 shackled prisoners, victims, witnesses, and police and detectives diverted from street duty. The courts begin each year with a backlog of hundreds of thousands of cases; and even if no new arrests were made, it would take the judges two and a half years to clear the calendars. Despite the staggering backlog of work facing them, many judges fail to work a full day. Corruption has always attended the selection of judges in the city, and to this day payoffs of one or two years' salary must be made to appropriate party leaders to get a place on the bench, according to Martin and Susan Tolchin.* Judges of the notorious surrogate court are able to dole out immense patronage through receiverships, guardianships, and trusteeships.

For the prisoners languishing in New York's jails, it must often seem that justice is unobtainable. (Convictions are hard to get, too; if you commit a felony in New York City, the chances of your being arrested, indicted, found guilty, and sent to prison are less than one in 200.) The prisons have an official capacity of 8,000, but many weeks there are almost double that number of men locked into crowded cells. About half of them have never been convicted, but they may wait almost a year for their first court appearance.†

The city's most infamous jail, the Tombs (Manhattan House of Detention), is a dank fortress that holds twice the 932 inmates it was designed for. They are crushed in a world of fear, violence, filth, and degradation. In August 1970, the situation erupted into window-smashing, bed-burning violence. (One rioter threw a dead rat from a window, with a note saying "Help" tied to its tail.) Even some persons held hostage by the rioters agreed that complaints of brutality, racial prejudice, and overcrowding were well founded. The city negotiated, promising reforms, but little change will come until the confusion in the courts is resolved. Men like David Ross, new administrative judge of the criminal court, have sparked a strong movement to reduce the backlog of cases, but much remains to be done.

Even better courts and jails and an honest police department would not be enough to purge New York of its rising tide of lawlessness. Eventually, the tap roots of organized crime in the city must be attacked. And many believe illegal gambling is central to the whole system.

The numbers racket began in Harlem as a money-sucking wrinkle invented by a beer baron named Arthur Flegenheimer (Dutch Schultz). He ran the numbers racket so well it developed into crime's major money producer after Prohibition ended. It was so good that it was taken over (in a hail of bullets and blood) by Charles ("Lucky") Luciano. That empire eventually broke into smaller duchies, but the numbers racket has since continued to be the financial foundation from which the organized mob has invaded other enterprises—loansharking, bookmaking, labor racketeering, narcotics, industrial extortion, and corruption of government.‡

Here is how the regressive cycle of growing horror operates today. From desperate people in Bedford-Stuyvesant, Harlem, and the South Bronx, the numbers racket takes about $105 million a year (perhaps as much as $250 million citywide). The money is used to finance the importation of heroin,

* The Tolchins quote an anonymous state judge describing how he got his judgeship: "The county leader told me to pay the district leaders in cash . . . untraceable."

† An imaginative program to free some suspects without bail pending trial, initiated by the Vera Institute of Justice, a private foundation, has helped some, but the magnitude of the problem is beyond easy solution.

‡ A typical form of the numbers game in New York is the "Brooklyn" number, in which the player picks any number he likes from 000 to 999; the winning "number" will then be the last three digits of the total mutuel handle for the day at one of the local race tracks (Belmont or Aqueduct) or Saratoga during the month of August.

which is sold retail for about $180 million in a year. The narcotics addicts have to maraud in the communities in order to get money to buy the heroin. Since from resale they get on the average only 20 percent of the value of the property they steal, the average amount of money that must be stolen may be close to $1 billion a year. The organized mob takes its percentages out every step of the way. According to the New York State Joint Legislative Committee on Crime: "At the same time that this lecherous cartel is siphoning off millions of dollars from the ghetto as a result of its policy, loansharking and other illicit operations, it is spewing back into the same ghetto a reign of misery and death in the form of traffic in Heroin!"

These days, the mob princes do not come even close to the street action. From lofty positions they "cream" wealth out of the ghettos through the percentage they get from the numbers racket. They still control (through the capital they provide) the importation of heroin, even while they allow increasing control of the wholesale drug market by Negro and Spanish-speaking manpower that they have developed or tolerated—and to which they may be obliged to cede a large part of their operations in the next few years.

The numbers game has become such an integral part of ghetto life that in the opinion of black leaders like Basil Patterson, Charles Rangel, and Hulan Jack, it could not be routed even if the U. S. Army came in to help and placed men with fixed bayonets at every corner. The obvious solution would be for government to step in and take over the numbers, and that is precisely what New York City's new Off-Track Betting Corporation (OTB) would like to do. OTB officials estimate that they could run the system at a 10 percent overhead; even if they turned in 15 percent of the take to the local and state governments, they could still return to the people of the community 75 percent of every dollar bet. That would compare to the meager substantially lower 25 to 50 percent which is reportedly returned to the public under the present illegal numbers games.

The OTB sprang into being in 1970 after the state legislature voted to let cities with 125,000 or more people have off-track betting to raise revenues for local government. (The city has been asking this authority for some 20 years, but had been rebuffed by leaders like Governor Dewey, who called the idea "shocking, immoral and indecent," saying that "corruption and poverty" followed gambling wherever it had been legalized.) The legislature's purpose in approving off-track betting was to give some relief to the city's financial squeeze, but Howard ("Howie the Horse") Samuels, whom Lindsay appointed to head up the OTB, says his primary purpose is a social one—to undercut organized crime. The OTB started up in spring 1971 with a brisk volume of business in horse betting that, Samuels expects, can mean $50 million to $75 million a year in profits for the city. But his real design is to go further:

> If they give me sports betting and numbers, which I'm asking the legislature for, we can do to organized crime's gambling business what repeal of Prohibition did to the bootleggers. Right now, we give organized crime an exclusive franchise on gambling by the hypocrisy of our laws. Take it away from the

gambler and let me run this thing as a business and I'll take his God-damned business away from him." *

The revenue, Samuels says, could be $200 million a year. He dismisses the idea of effective law enforcement stopping betting: "People want to bet. Maybe its part of the dream of the majority of Americans who are frustrated economically. If we don't make it available, and it's happened since the history of man began, they'll just go to organized crime to do it."

The Housing Mess

When I asked Congressman Herman Badillo for an evaluation of the Lindsay administration, he said it had been "a disaster" and named one key reason: since 1965, the number of slums has multiplied by three in the city. "All else is irrelevant," Badillo said. "Once an area becomes a slum, it takes 50 to 100 years to recapture it. This damage is irreparable—although it may have been, in large measure, inevitable."

The grim facts about housing are these:

■ By conservative estimates, 400,000, or 14 percent of the city's 2.9 million housing units are substandard (other estimates run as high as 800,000). Hundreds of thousands more are on the brink of disintegration. The entire population of Arizona could fit into New York's substandard housing. Yet in most cases, the abandoned buildings are structurally sound; their problem is tenant abuse and landlord desertion.

■ The private housing market is at a virtual standstill. Large quantities of luxury apartments were constructed in the city from the 1950s through the mid-1960s. But then inflation and a tight money market hit, halting all new construction except a trickle of ultra-ultra-posh apartments. Construction and mortage-loan interest rates have soared from 6 percent a few years ago to a near prohibitive 10 to 15 percent. And they are not available at all in huge swaths of the city where deterioration is advanced, or even threatened—most of the Bronx, much of Brooklyn, parts of Manhattan and Queens.

■ At least 200,000 apartments and houses have been abandoned in New York City in the past six years. "When Lindsay came in," Badillo comments, "he used to boast he was getting after the slumlords" to make repairs; "now he's thankful when he can find a slumlord." Landlords face the quandary of high repair costs, expensive fuel oil, high real estate taxes, high mortgage interest costs, and tenants slow in paying rent. Many are in real financial straits— yet tenants still harbor unmitigated hostility toward them, seeing the landlords as rank exploiters, ready and anxious to collect rent but never available when repairs are needed to rotting walls, broken windows, or leaking pipes. In an hostility-packed city, the landlord-tenant hostility may be the deepest and most enduring. Robert Alden of the New York *Times* tells the story

---

* Samuels is not interested in extending state operations to legalized casino-type gambling because (1) casinos are not part of organized crime's major income, and (2) casino gambling has a more debilitating effect on people.

of a small entrepreneur who bought an apartment house 15 to 20 years ago as a hedge against inflation:

> Now his age of decline has arrived and he stands on a littered Bronx street before the rundown six-story apartment house, once his dream, now his nightmare. From some open window above, an angry, derisive call is heard: "The Jew landlord is here to collect his bloody money!"

Sooner or later, as such a man's costs run beyond his rental incomes, he will look for a buyer—and probably find none. The next logical step is simply to abandon the property.* Then the electricity is turned off, there is no heating, tenants begin to flee, derelicts and dope addicts break in, garbage piles up, rats begin to infest the property, and the cancer begins to spread up and down the street and may soon engulf a whole community.

Many housing experts believe this discouraging downward spiral cannot be reversed as long as such huge sociological and attitudinal differences exist between landlords and tenants. In an atmosphere of all-out warfare between the two sides, the prospect for satisfactory housing is almost nonexistent. So more must be done to foster new forms of ownership, often cooperatives, in which tenants have a real stake in keeping their apartment houses in good condition. That happens frequently in better-off Manhattan neighborhoods, but extremely rarely in the deteriorating communities that need it most.

The need for some kind of a radical breakthrough in the city's housing quandary can hardly be overstated. The citywide rental vacancy rate is under 1 percent, less than a fourth of the national rate. Poor and middle-income people alike are affected. The waiting list for public housing is well over 100,000, and at the present rate of construction of publicly subsidized units, a family at the bottom of the list could wait half a century to get in. Many poor families break into condemned buildings just to have a roof over their heads.

On the upper end of the income scale, the prices demanded and received for apartments in Manhattan are beyond belief. In a desirable neighborhood like the East 70s, small, cramped two-bedroom apartments may cost $600 a month, and a commodious three bedroom apartment near Fifth and Park Avenues as much as $1,500 to $2,000 a month. Some of the highest prices are paid for cooperative apartments, which do provide buyers (if they can afford the price) with security, equity, and pride of ownership. But 85 percent of available co-ops sell for over $60,000, with monthly maintenance fees of hundreds if not thousands of dollars.

So it is that quality housing soars beyond the price range of even the upper-middle class. Robert Alden notes: "People are driven to the suburbs and, as land values increase, to the far suburbs. The breadwinner finds himself spending more and more of his life aboard crowded, uncomfortable, tardy commuter trains [or] backed up bumper to bumper each day on the West Side Drive, the Long Island Expressway or the approaches to the Lincoln Tunnel." And corporations encounter increasing reluctance of middle manage-

---

* A black leader in the city offered me a more cynical interpretation: "Guys buy tenements, put them in dummy corporations, and when they get too bad, the owner just runs away."

ment executives to transfer to New York and bear the city's hardships.

There are, of course, hundreds of thousands of apartment units in the city with more reasonable sounding rental levels. About 1.3 million of the 2.1 million apartment units are under rent control, which New York (alone among major U. S. cities) has clung to since World War II. In many cases, it has been the artificially low payments for rental apartments that has forced owners to abandon their properties. In 1971, the state legislature directed that when rent-control apartments changed hands in the future, they could seek their own open market price. The immediate result was an approximate doubling of rents in those apartments leased by new tenants.

The housing story is doubly tragic because no city in America has tried so hard over the years to fill the housing needs of its people. New York got a huge infusion of postwar public housing, enough to hold more than half a million people. Designed with barrackslike monotony, the projects dot the horizon in several boroughs. And the effort was not only federal; since the days of Al Smith, New York has made a strong effort in city- and state-sponsored low-income housing, and has more housing put up with that kind of backing than the rest of the country put together.

But in the 1960s, federally assisted public housing came to a dead standstill because Washington objected to the high unit costs of construction in the city. The flow of federally assisted housing opened again around 1969–70, but it is filling only a tiny percentage of need. Several big state-assisted projects (including Welfare Island) are underway, but not on the massive citywide scale needed to really save the situation.

There might be more new housing in New York, both public and private, if it were not for the modern-day sensitivity of government and private developers to community objections about proposed development sites. Some vocal residents will almost invariably have an objection to building new housing in *their* community. Always, they say developments should go elsewhere. So high-income projects get blocked, middle- and low-income projects stymied, new public facilities are stopped in their tracks, and the entire city of New York suffers.

One gargantuan state-aided project, begun in the mid 1960s, has now opened its doors. Its name is Co-op City, it is located in the northeast Bronx between some parkways on 300 acres of land, and it is the world's largest housing cooperative and the nation's largest single apartment complex. Sponsored by the United Housing Foundation and financed primarily by a $261 million mortgage loan from the New York State Housing Finance Agency, Co-op City has 35 high-rise apartment buildings that range between 24 and 33 stories. It houses more than 50,000 people—enough to make it, if it were built outside an already existing city, a metropolitan area on its own right. To get a Co-op City apartment, one must make less than $12,000 a year; the down payment is $450 a room with a carrying charge that averages a very reasonable $32 a room each month. The population is roughly 75 percent Jewish, 15 percent Negro and Puerto Rican, and 5 to 10 percent Irish and Italian. No one can doubt the excruciating need New York has for projects on the massive scale of Co-op City, and the people who live there are delighted with the opportunity. But the sight of that army of massive buildings, rising to the sky at such a height that each man's apartment looks like a fly speck on the face of a vast and monolithic structure, is one of the most frightening I have seen on the American continent. If this is how the multimillions of the future must be housed, one fears for the spirit of man.

The Worlds of New York

And now for a view of the fantastic city in its constituent parts, though we will be obliged, for reasons of space, to omit many interesting communities. The raw statistics are these:

Boroughs	Population (1970)	% Population Shift (1960–70)	Negro Percent	People Per Square Mile
Manhattan	1,524,541	−10.2	24.9	67,458
Brooklyn	2,601,852	− 1.0	25.2	33,144
Queens	1,973,708	+ 9.1	13.1	17,208
Bronx	1,472,216	+ 3.3	24.3	34,158
Richmond (Staten Island)	295,443	+33.1	5.3	4,851
Total	7,867,760		21.2	24,602

MANHATTAN

Everyone knows the story of how the crafty Dutch managed to buy Manhattan Island from the Manhattoes Indians in 1626 for $24 worth of doodads. The Indians did not realize what a fine deal they had. Sidney Homer of Salomon Bros., author of *The History of Interest Rates*, has calculated that if the Indians had taken a boat to Holland, invested the $24 in Dutch securities returning 6 percent a year and kept the money invested at 6 percent, they would now have $13 billion. That would be enough to buy back all the land on the island, and still have $4 billion left for trinkets.

What kind of a place is Manhattan today? Along with all its woes, it is a romantic vision unequaled on earth and one seen best, like a beautiful woman, at night. As Le Corbusier has written:

Beneath the immaculate office on the 57th floor the vast nocturnal festival of New York spreads out. No one can imagine it who has not seen it. It is a titanic mineral display, prismatic stratification shot through with an infinite number of lights, from top to bottom, in depth, in a violent silhouette like a fever chart beside a sick bed. A diamond, incalculable diamonds.

Is the load of people and activity on Manhattan simply too much? The New York City Planning Commission argues that it is not:

Concentration is the genius of the city, its reason for being, the source of its vitality and its excitement. We believe the center should be strengthened, not weakened, and we are not afraid of the bogey of high density.

The planning commission also argues that New York has "more of everything that makes a city jump and hum with life" and that "at the very time critics have been most energetic in prophesying imminent doom, the center has been going through its most vigorous period of growth."

Growth, status quo, and decay, we view in some of Manhattan's chief districts and neighborhoods, moving south to north:

LOWER MANHATTAN. Here is Battery Park, and within a handful of blocks north and west of the park, the greatest concentration of financial power in the world: the canyons of Wall Street, the Stock Exchange, great banks and insurance combines, offices of such colossal firms as American Telephone & Telegraph, the huge law firms including President Nixon's own Mudge, Rose, Guthrie & Alexander.

In the summer of 1970, Anthony Lewis, the New York *Times'* London bureau chief, returned by ship on home leave. As his vessel steamed into New York Harbor one morning, Lewis expected to glimpse first the Statue of Liberty. But instead, his eye was caught by

twin massive towers, the tallest building in the world, rectangular blocks, thrusting gracelessly into the sky, dark and hulking, beyond human scale. It was a sight that cried out: money! power! technology! It spoke of the America that has relentlessly sought profit, and "progress," at the expense of human values. It seemed to me a brutal symbol of what has gone wrong in our society.

A lot of New Yorkers agree with Lewis' assessment of the World Trade Center, the 110-story, 1,350-foot towers being put up by the Port of New York Authority with tax-exempt dollars. The Center will contain 10 million square feet of floor space—seven times that of the Empire State Building and 80 more acres of office space than the Pentagon. At 2:15 P.M., October 19, 1970, the north tower rose above the height of the Empire State Building, ending that illustrious structure's 40-year reign as the world's tallest. But work was already underway in Chicago on a building that will top the World Trade Center.

Each day, 50,000 workers will crowd into the World Trade Center, adding to the already unbelievable congestion of downtown Manhattan. Scores of other great buildings have risen in Lower Manhattan since World War II, several over 50 stories, the square footage of office space numbering in the tens of millions.

In 1971, construction began on Battery Park City, a $1 billion self-contained community of apartments, offices, schools, shops, and parks located off a one-mile section of previously decaying waterfront. City officials see a bright future for Lower Manhattan, its development anchored by the World Trade Center on its west flank and the new Stock Exchange building on the east and Battery Park City adding the first residences of this century.

New York still has its legendary Lower East Side of bustling streets filled with shops and street vendors and fruit carts, the port of entry of multitudinous ethnic groups (Irish, Italians, and Jews especially), the boyhood neighborhood of men like Al Smith and Jacob Javits. The Lower East Side was always poor; today it is desperate. Conditions are perhaps half tolerable in the huge public housing developments along F. D. Roosevelt Drive (Baruch Houses, Alfred E. Smith Houses, etc.), but consider the staid New York *Times*' description of the rest: "A grimy string of tenements, murky storefronts and nondescript industrial establishments" that is populated by "motorcycle gangs, hippies, drug users and thieves," a world where "rape, assault, gang warfare and even murder are almost commonplace."

THE VILLAGES. Chic, bohemian Greenwich Village is the home of artsy millionaires, musicians, entertainers, hipsters, students, and dope fiends. It is probably the most individualistic neighborhood on Manhattan, possibly because it is still a stronghold of small homeowners and has maintained its traditions and look. The population remains overwhelmingly white.

There is the West Village, a quiet neighborhood of residences. There is the East Village, now a major East Coast hangout for hippies and runaways. There is Washington Square, at the foot of Fifth Avenue, one of the more urbane places in New York, where New York University students lounge illegally on the grass and old men play chess on summer afternoons.

Greenwich Village's traditional *laissez-faire* attitude toward deviationist life styles is now being put to the test as crime rises alarmingly. Villagers are demanding more police protection, are helping police catch dope peddlers (hard drugs seems to have lost their chic), and are cooperating to blunt an onrush of robberies.

The Bowery, traditional hangout of drunks and derelicts on the east edge of Greenwich Village, remains the mixture of commercial activity and human squalor it has been for a century. But an interesting sociological phenomenon is taking place; the Bowery is being depopulated as its older denizens die off, and younger men (perhaps because of the prosperity of our times) fail to replace them. The population was 14,000 in 1949, but fell below 5,000 in the late 1960s and continues to decline by about 5 percent a year. The Depression produced as many as one million of the rootless Skid Row dropouts, who abjured marrying, voting, or close friendship for a drifting life, seeking only hermetic shelter. Now there are probably no more than 100,000 in all the U.S.A.

MIDTOWN—EAST. In 1946, six city blocks of slaughterhouses along the East River were razed to make way for the United Nations headquarters. The city agreed to plow First Avenue underground, John D. Rockefeller donated $8.5 million for acquiring the site, and an international team of architects designed the structures. The 544-foot-high slab of the Secretariat dominates the group, with a library to the south and the striking General Assembly building to the north. The U. N. is a major national tourist attraction (10,000 visitors a day). This whole area of the city, known as Turtle Bay, has been rejuvenated. A number of swank apartment complexes now surround the U. N., including Sutton Place South and the United Nations Plaza. The latter, with twin 32-story towers, is perhaps *the* ultimate apartment house of the world, filled with corporate and society leaders beyond compare. There are 27,000 U. N. personnel in New York, including families of delegates and 5,000 staff members. Their consulates add an exotic touch, underscoring New York's status as *the* world city.

MIDTOWN. Here is the glittering heart of Manhattan, 234 square blocks throbbing with people, packed with soaring skyscrapers. Midtown has experienced the most extensive growth of its history in the past 25 years; more than ever it deserves to be called the business-entertainment center of the nation and the world. The street and place names alone are evocative: Fifth Avenue, Park Avenue, Madison Avenue, Broadway, 42nd Street, Grand Central, Times Square, Empire State Building, Rockefeller Center.

No "economic development" plan is needed here, but some controls are; and Lindsay set up an Office of Midtown Planning and Development, headed by an imaginative young urban designer, Jaquelin Robertson, to try and see to it that Midtown does not become a monolith of steel and glass slabs that repels people. That fate has already overtaken the upper stretches of the Avenue of the Americas (Sixth Avenue) and has been threatening Fifth Avenue, the nation's choicest and most exciting shopping street. So Robertson led the way to set up a special Fifth Avenue zoning district that permits developers to put more square feet of floor space on a parcel of land *if* they will follow the city's recommendations to include ground-level arcades lined with stores.

Times Square, at 42nd Street and Broadway, continues to jump 24 hours a day, but these days the jumping may be to avoid a marauding prostitute. (The brazen hookers, run by what must be small armies of pimps, seem to survive every big clean-up the city orders.) Amidst the porno shops and dirty movies, Times Square still has numbers of top-flight movie houses, legitimate theaters, actors' hangouts like the Lambs Club and Sardi's, and the national New Year's Eve celebration every year.

So much is concentrated in Midtown that a mere cataloguing could take pages. The major television networks are centered here, the splendid New York Public Library, airline and travel bureaus beyond count, the art-gallery concentrate near 57th Street, the nation's jewelry center (with almost 2,000 people working on diamonds alone), hotels swank and not so swank (51,000 rooms within a mile's radius of Times Square), and restaurants without peer on the continent. Just on the Avenue of the Americas, more than 25 million square feet of office space were under construction in the late 1960s; the avenue has received such giants as the CBS and Sperry-Rand headquarters, and the New York Hilton and Americana Hotels. Rockefeller Center, begun in 1931, remains the largest and by far the most successful effort at urban-office-building clustering in the city and its Christmas tree competes with the one on the Ellipse in Washington as the nation's favorite. By 1973, work is to be completed on a $300 million addition to Rockefeller Center.

The power and elegance of New York is at its most complete in the one-mile stretch of Park Avenue north of Grand Central—the stunning new glass buildings of giant corporations and banks, the elegant apartment houses of the socially prominent. Some of the distinguished buildings are Lever House (built in 1952 as the first glass-walled building in the city), the Seagram Building (with its formal plaza of granite, trees, and pools, and wonderfully luxurious Four Seasons Restaurant), and the Union Carbide Building (53 stories of stainless steel and gray glass). Unfortunately, there are also many unimaginative office towers where greed for maximum allowable floor space dictated every design decision. But good or bad, note again, the postwar development is the determinative.

CENTRAL PARK. Now, and one hopes forever, this is one of America's grandest municipal parks, 840 sylvan acres, filled with sunken roads (revolutionary when the park was laid out in the 1850s), miles of paths, bridges, gates, lakes, lawns, statues, the Zoo, and skating rinks. The Lindsay parks program has made the park a safer place to be, although dangers remain; in 1971, for instance, there was a wave of attacks on unsuspecting bicyclists, who fell victim to knife- and bottle-wielding assailants who lurked along bike paths waiting to knock riders off their cycles and steal their bikes.

WEST SIDE. From the Lincoln Square and Columbus Circle area all the way up to the Upper West Side, this portion of land between Central Park and the Hudson River has been improving rapidly from the condition of deteriorated slumhood that characterized it at the end of World War II. The congested tenements around Lincoln Square have been replaced by the impressive travertine marble Lincoln Center complex and two middle- and upper-income housing developments. New boutiques and theaters are springing up, and the rents are going up, too. In the 70s, 80s and 90s, young people are moving into and remodeling brownstones and paying for private guards to watch their streets—with a substantial reduction in crime rate. The massive West Side Urban Renewal Plan is creating thousands of new units of low- and middle-income housing.

UPPER EAST SIDE. This choicest of all areas in the city begins at the southern end of Central Park and extends up the East River to the border with East Harlem. It has New York's greatest concentration of wealth, culture, and treasures. This is the New York of elegant apartment houses, exclusive clubs of the rich, art galleries, museums, cultural and scientific academies, expensive cafés and restaurants, townhouses, and great hospitals.

HARLEM. Harlem dominates Manhattan above Central Park (110th Street). The image is one generated by the flamboyant politicians such as Marcus Garvey early in this century and Adam Clayton Powell, Jr., in recent years, by the great black nightspots now gone by (the Sugar Cane, the Savoy, the Cotton Club), and by modern-day riots and crime.

Reality differs from that image in that Harlem really is many places and large parts of it are now undergoing substantial change. At the northwest corner of Central Park, for example, at 110th Street and Eighth Avenue, is one of the bleakest sections in New York, row after row of dilapidated but inhabited walkups, garbage-strewn streets and sidewalks, broken windows, and burned-out apartments, people lounging around on the stoops and street corners (almost half of Harlem's 240,000 people are on welfare). Harlem also has Lenox Terrace, which boasts 25 doormen, four gardeners, carpeted halls, and occupants who are making it big—judges, entertainers, politicians (including Manhattan Borough President Percy E. Sutton). Harlem is an area with numerous churches, including Powell's Abyssinian Baptist Church, the largest (12,000) Protestant congregation in the country,* and St. Phillip's Protestant Episcopal Church, once reputedly the wealthiest black congregation in the nation. There are other churches, some huge and modernistic and some tiny and makeshift. One block is said to contain 11 churches.

A large number of antipoverty and other projects have started in Harlem in the past few years. The big antipoverty push has been administered by HarYou Act, using federal antipoverty funds; its accounting procedures were challenged, however, and its days may be numbered. The Harlem Urban Corporation, formed in 1971 as a subsidiary of the state Urban Development Corporation and made up of 30 business and professional people, is seeking public and private financing for redevelopment on a scale never attempted before.

Who are the leaders of Harlem today? One, of course, is its Congressman, Charles B. Rangel, the young Harlem native and lawyer (now in his early forties) who defeated the once mighty Adam Clayton Powell in 1970. Black leaders view Rangel as an able, flexible man, still growing in his job. Another Harlem leader is Livingston Wingate, executive director of the New York City Urban League who was the first executive director of HarYou Act. He is now chairman of the Council of Harlem Organizations, which runs the whole gamut from extreme militants to moderates.

But what shall we say of Adam Clayton Powell, before the music fades? His defenders insist that as chairman of the House Education and Labor Committee, Powell exerted strong influence over approval of 60 pieces of legislation, much of it (like the 1964 Poverty Act) of real importance to the nation's blacks. Let us hear, though, the assessment of a black man—Julius Lester, author of *Search for the New Land:* †

We remember him from the days when there was no other Black man like him in America. Before Martin Luther King Jr., Malcolm X, and Stokely Carmichael, Adam Clayton Powell Jr. was.

He was elected to Congress from Harlem in 1942 and needed do nothing more than stand for reelection every two years to assure his Congressional seat for life. . . . He gave Blacks a national voice when they didn't have one.

Powell reached his pinnacle in the mid-50s. He was a militant before any of us knew the word and time after time he stood on the floor of the House of Representatives and delivered blistering speeches against proposed legislation, particularly in the field of education, which did not even take cognizance of the needs (or even the existence) of Black America. . . .

Most important, however, was Powell himself. In his person he represented what we wanted to be (or thought we did). He was incredibly good looking, tall, immaculate, and yet, his heart was with us. He could talk our language and make it sound like his own. And he lived well. He had it and he flaunted it—his expensive tastes, his love of a good time and beautiful women. . . . His very person was an act of defiance toward white America and they hated him for it. . . .

In the early 60s, however, history caught up with and passed Adam Clay-

---

* Powell resigned as pastor in 1971; a sick man, he rarely leaves Bimini now.
† "Homage to Adam Clayton Powell," *The Black Politician,* July 1971 (reprinted from the New York Times).

ton Powell. Out of the South came Martin Luther King Jr., and from the North, Malcolm X. Powell found his leadership challenged by new ideas and new methods. . . . Before he realized it, we had replaced him as the embodiment of our dreams and the Establishment sacrificed him to the wolves of the white backlash.

He went to Bimini, but vowed to return to Harlem. Harlem waited. It waited and waited. But Powell did not return to do battle and when he didn't, he was finished. Eventually, he came back (when he no longer had to risk arrest), and his rhetoric was more militant than ever. But it was empty. . . .

Too, he no longer looked like the Adam of old. His face showed the adumbrations of a Dorian Gray transformation. His handsomeness had become fleshy and flaccid. . . . And the expensive clothes which had made him look as if he owned the world, now made him look little better than a hustler. . . .

It is sad to see a great figure decline. But, many of us will never forget the man who walked with pride and refused to let any white person regard him as inferior. He was not a man for all seasons, but getting through the long, cold winter would have been infinitely more difficult without him.

MORNINGSIDE HEIGHTS. This section of Harlem, along the Hudson River, is the site of Columbia University, where a scenario of how a university should not treat its neighbors, and the excesses of both militant students and police, was played out with tragic consequences in 1968.

In 1971, when the American Council on Education issued its report on graduate programs around the country, Columbia was found to have slipped in a number of areas between 1964 and 1969. The soundings had been taken so soon after the campus disorders, however, that no one could be sure whether the temporary disruptions were responsible, or whether a great university had received a lasting setback.

THE BRONX

Asked what sets the Bronx aside from the rest of New York, former Bronx Borough President Herman Badillo replied: "Nothing." The answer seems facetious, but it is not. In greater or lesser degree, the same general groupings of people appear in almost every borough:

AFFLUENT AND ALMOST AFFLUENT NEW YORK. An echo of the East Side. The Bronx has precious little of this, but the community of Riverdale, just above Manhattan, is an example: a white suburbia within the city, people living in gracious colonial, Tudor, and Georgian homes in rustic elegance. Many public, political, and professional people live in Riverdale, including well-known names like Robert Morgenthau, Theodore Kheel, Louis Harris, and Herman Badillo himself. Sociologically, there is not much difference between these people and younger professionals like those restoring brownstones in Brooklyn today. Politics: reform Democrat.

MIDDLE-CLASS NEW YORK. Heavily Irish, German, Italian, and Jewish, these people live in quite stable neighborhoods and are preoccupied with keeping their neighborhoods the way they are. They are office workers, teachers, minor bureaucrats, and the elite of the blue-collar class. In the Bronx, you will find them living north of the Cross Bronx Expressway (the safe, or Westchester side). Politics: regular Democrat, and many (especially the Irish and Italian) now turning Republican.

LOWER-MIDDLE-CLASS NEW YORK. Again, an Irish-Italian-German-Jewish polyglot, but older and poorer. In the Bronx, they are heavily Jewish and may be discovered along the Grand Concourse, living on small pensions or Social Security, their income stagnant and decreasing in buying power. Their children have often gone to college, becoming accountants and attorneys, and have moved to better parts of the city or to Nassau, Suffolk, Westchester, or New Jersey. But the old folks are stuck where they started. Politics: a mixture of regular and reform Democrat.

POOR NEW YORK. With limited exceptions, this means simply Negro and Puerto Rican. In the Bronx, it means the South Bronx, a seething ghetto. The South Bronx is part of a black-Hispanic poverty belt of the city which runs from New York Bay up the west sides of Brooklyn and Queens to the Bronx, with counterparts on Manhattan's Lower East Side and Harlem. Today 40 percent of the Bronx population and two thirds of the school enrollment is black or Puerto Rican. Politics: Democratic, usually reform.

Roughly speaking, 33 percent of New York City is black and Puerto Rican now. Another 15 percent consists of the older lower-middle class. Thus well over 45 percent of the city is poor, and that percentage increases steadily. Thereby hangs the city's problem.

The Bronx has lots of heavy industry, especially along its southern flanks, and it is a place of many neighborhoods, not all as simple as our income-ethnic groupings may suggest. In the north section of the borough, for instance, is Baychester—a community of middle-class whites (two thirds) and blacks (one third) who have both risen above their childhood circumstances and now share the pressure of mortgage payments, rising property taxes, and fear of slipping back into tenement life.

Along the Harlem River facing Manhattan's Washington Heights is the community of Highbridge, determined not to become a slum. The community is integrated, even to the same block of brownstones or the same apartment building. The population is one-third black, one-third Puerto Rican, and one-third white (Irish, Italian, Jewish).

The Bronx has its extremes, however. Consider the South Bronx. Photojournalist Herb Goro spent one year getting to know the people and rooftops and back alleys of a block on 174th Street near Washington Avenue in the South Bronx. He wrote a book about what he found there—the indifferent landlords, the broken buildings with their broken windows and doors and broken plumbing, the rats, the garbage-strewn alleys used as playgrounds, the cold, the job discrimination, the filth and noise of the El, the drugs. This is one of the most densely inhabited areas of the nation; it has some 50,000 people living in a 55-block area, 48 percent black, 48 percent Puerto Rican, and 4 percent elderly white.

Perhaps the most interesting political fact about the Bronx is not that it has gone reform (good-by Charles Buckley and the Edward J. Flynn tradition), but that it has become the first seedbed of political growth by New

York's latest immigrant group, the Puerto Ricans. New York today has about one million Puerto Ricans (more than San Juan). There have been Puerto Ricans in the city since early in the century, but in significant numbers only since 1940. The influx went first to East Harlem, then shifted to the South Bronx, and later to Brooklyn (the borough with the most Puerto Ricans today). But only in the Bronx have the Puerto Ricans taken hold politically, starting with Badillo's 1965 election as borough president. Badillo himself, a six-foot, one-inch package of cool articulation and self-confidence, has become a major political factor in New York. In 1969 he ran in the Democratic mayoral primary and came within 38,000 votes of winning.

The Puerto Rican crisis—in the homeland, and in major American cities —is one most Americans know little of, but one that will force increasing national attention in the 1970s. The island's population density of 546 persons per square mile is one of the world's highest, the unemployment rate over 12 percent, per-capita income only half of Mississippi's. At the same time that agricultural mechanization has reduced farm-labor needs on the island, a combination of better health care and Roman Catholicism has caused a population explosion of awesome proportions. The safety valve has been immigration to the U. S. mainland, which is unlimited due to Puerto Rico's commonwealth status. The immigrants are only the poor and desperate people of the island. Once they arrive in the U. S., they cannot hope for much more than menial, low-paying jobs in factories and restaurants. Compared to blacks, Puerto Ricans have a higher unemployment rate, a lower median income, a greater percentage of school dropouts, and are four times as likely to be on welfare.

Most alarming of all, only the young and the poor Puerto Ricans remain in the U. S. Those with initiative, who save up money or manage to get a good education or technical training, almost invariably return to their native island where their skills will permit them to live better than they can in the U. S. How does one build stability and leadership in this revolving-door community? It is a tough job, Badillo responds, and made no easier by the fact that the median age of the Puerto Ricans in the U. S. is only 19 years.

The Southeast Bronx today illustrates the worst side of the Puerto Rican problem: thousands of kids on each block, open narcotics trade, derelict cars, shootings on the street, conflicts with the police, and the language barrier most cops face in trying to deal with the young Puerto Ricans.

QUEENS

Queens is the wealthiest, whitest, most spacious, and fastest growing of New York's four major boroughs, and in the next few years it hopes to become a significant office center to complement its present mix of factories and homes, homes, homes. It is a borough of distinct communities; instead of saying they are from 'Queens," people say they are from "Flushing," "Jamaica," or "Astoria," reflecting often intense community pride. The borough has an astounding 16,397 acres of parks, almost as much as the other four boroughs combined. Until 20 years ago, there were endless jokes about Queens being "the borough of cemeteries," and, indeed, those prime wasters of space still form the bulk of the borough's open urban areas. But the jokes vanished in the wake of a postwar apartment-house explosion that terminated Queens' rurality and brought with it the familiar suburban headaches of sewers, schools, and even urban renewal. Often, Queens feels slighted and neglected by the city government. Mayor Lindsay had to make a kind of penitential trip in 1969 when Queens disappeared temporarily in a blizzard and the city was found woefully short of the equipment to dig it out.

Highway congestion and inadequate public transportation are key problems. The borough lies between Nassau County and Manhattan, feeds 40 percent of its own work force into Manhattan every day, and has to accommodate the vast flow of people to and from the New York City airports—La Guardia and John F. Kennedy—both of which lie within its borders.

Quiet stability characterizes many parts of Queens. In towns like Flushing, the scene is often one of two- and three-story white clapboard Victorian houses on tree-lined streets. In Hollis Hills, a Jewish and Catholic community near the Nassau border, the only break from single-family homes and garden apartments are a few high-rise apartment houses, and they are for the wealthy. All of northeast Queens is filled with stable communities, including many strong Irish areas.

Queens has formidable numbers of blacks—more than a quarter of a million, in fact. The largest concentrations are in southwest and southeast Queens. There are middle-class black enclaves where the biggest problem is sewers; but also places like South Jamaica, a massive slum where the shanties on South Street are reminiscent of Tobacco Road.

The Rockaways, an 11-mile-long peninsula that encloses Jamaica Bay, began as an exclusive summer resort in the last century and still have many posh sections, and of course the magnificent beaches. But one section, filled with flimsy summer bungalows, was taken over by blacks as year-round residences; the city demolished many of these tinderboxes.

An ambitious plan, endorsed by President Nixon in 1971, is to form a Gateway National Recreation Area (at the extremity of the Rockaways), including Breezy Point, Jamaica Bay, and Sandy Hook (across the mouth of the Hudson in New Jersey). With 10 miles of ocean beach and 23,000 acres of land and water preserve, the area will be a closed-in recreation point for the millions of the metropolitan area.

BROOKLYN

Brooklyn is first of all a massive fact: 2.6 million people, enough to make it, if it were independent, the fourth largest city in the United States. It has 225,000 manufacturing or wholesale jobs with an annual payroll of $2.8 billion. The downtown Brooklyn retail district does a business of over $3 billion a year and attracts 200,000 visitors on a typical day. The Brooklyn waterfront receives half the general cargo coming into the port of New York.

The borough has great cultural and educational institutions: the Brooklyn Museum, the Academy of Music, the Botanic Garden, Brooklyn College, Pratt Institute, Long Island University.

Second, Brooklyn is a legend. Do you remember when the Dodgers came from Brooklyn; when Coney Island, massed throngs and all, still stood for summertime fun; and when all America thought warmly of *A Tree Grows in Brooklyn?* Why, the place even had its own patois and a fierce local nationalism practically no other American community could match.

Third, Brooklyn is a place in trouble—deep trouble. It harbors two of the largest, worst ghettos in the world—Brownsville and Bedford-Stuyvesant. Writer Peter Hamill sums up Brownsville as a "bombed-out shell of a community"; when Boston's Mayor Kevin White made a 1971 tour of Brownsville, he saw it as "the first tangible sign of the collapse of our civilization." *

Fourth, Brooklyn has islands of growth and renewal. The most vivid examples are Brooklyn Heights (directly opposite Lower Manhattan) and nearby Park Slope, both of which began as suburbs of Manhattan's well-to-do in the past century, declined during the Depression years, but then were revived after the war by young adults who restored or remodeled old homes and created one of New York City's most pleasant and desirable neighborhoods. In addition, there are stable, attractive middle-income communities in Brooklyn, of which Bay Ridge (across from Staten Island) is perhaps the most distinguished example.

The great bulk of Brooklyn, however, is a case study of what happens when a city begins to decay, its more stable citizens leave and only the old and weak and poor are left. Most of the broad belt of northern Brooklyn, running from the East River to Jamaica Bay, is like that. So are parts of southern Brooklyn, including Coney Island.

Consider the problems: neighbors who speak different languages and have differing religious customs; communities bitterly divided over whether land should be used for housing or schools; absentee landlords and a steady downward slide in services; real-estate blockbusters playing on the fears of homeowners; and, overriding all other considerations, racial conflict.

Consider the blighted area at the Brooklyn end of the Williamsburg Bridge. (It seems that the shaded areas under bridges and elevated railroads everywhere in New York are blighted.) Here, in the Williamsburg section, there are few community services, no community center; streets deadend at the Brooklyn-Queens Expressway; buildings are boarded up. This section is entirely Puerto Rican.

Moving to the east, out to Nostrand Avenue, the neighborhoods of Williamsburg change abruptly from Puerto Rican to ultraorthodox Jewish. A large group of Jews, the Chassidim, are led by a Grand Rabbi and observe the traditional customs: the men wear long sideburns and long black coats; the women shave their heads and wear wigs. On Friday night and Saturday,

---

* In 1950, Brooklyn was 90 percent white; today it is about 60 percent white, 25 percent Negro, 15 percent Puerto Rican. Brownsville was predominantly Jewish at the end of Word War II; now it is more than 90 percent Negro and Puerto Rican. Bedford-Stuyvesant was 50 percent black in 1950, 90 percent by the late '60s.

everything in these neighborhoods shuts down. Custom prohibits the Jews from operating anything, such as a car or an elevator. Less orthodox Jews can use an elevator if they don't punch the floor button. Thus, in city housing for these people, there are elevators programmed to stop at every floor on Friday night and Saturday—they are known as "Sabbath elevators." The Jews speak Yiddish and the Puerto Ricans speak Spanish, and the two groups cannot even talk with each other, much less resolve differences.

Farther east, one comes on the six square miles of Bedford-Stuyvesant, the second largest black ghetto (after Southside Chicago) in America. The population is between 400,000 and 450,000. There are really two communities in one. On tree-shaded streets of sturdy brownstones, many freshly restored, live members of a settled old West Indian community. Many are leaders in law, medicine, government, and politics, and they include Congresswoman Shirley Chisholm, Bed-Stuy's most prominent political figure today.* The rest of Bed-Stuy is the fruit of recent years' immigration from the South. It is of these people and their world that Jack Newfield writes when he describes his boyhood community today:

Diseased debris rotting under a halo of mosquitoes in a vacant lot. Teen-age girls ducking and punching with the fluent fury of grown men. Rorschach tests of vomit staining the gutter. Burned-out houses with families living behind the boarded-up windows. . . .

There is the sour stench of urine that pollutes the Myrtle-Willoughby IND subway station. . . . The visor of suffocated hatred that comes down across every black youth before his 13th birthday. . . .

Then, the statistics: Eighty percent of the teen-agers high school dropouts. Thirty-six percent of the families headed by women. Twenty-seven percent with annual incomes under $3,000. The highest infant mortality rate in the country. One of the highest homicide rates in the country. And no one has ever counted the rats.

On a February day of 1966, the late Sen. Robert Kennedy made a walking tour of Bedford-Stuyvesant; several months later he announced a comprehensive rehabilitation plan, which still functions largely as he envisaged it. There are two corporations. One is black, community-based, and highly visible. It was named the Bedford-Stuyvesant Restoration Corporation, and Franklin A. Thomas, a black former police commissioner and lifetime Brooklyn resident, became its president. The second corporation was named Development and Services Corporation; it is primarily white and works behind the scenes to attract private finance. Its president is John Doar, former head of the Justice Department's civil rights division.

There have been concrete results from the effort Kennedy inspired. The Superblock, a new recreational area, was completed early in the game. Some 1,800 brownstones have had at least their exteriors renovated. IBM opened a plant with more then 400 employees—though no major corporations fol-

---

* Black political leaders across the country, anxious to promote a single candidate who would give them strength and unity at the 1972 Democratic National Convention, found to their astonishment as the primary season approached that Mrs. Chisholm—capitalizing on her unique position as the country's most prominent *black, woman* elected official—was gaining wide support in her audacious bid to be the standard bearer of the black cause.

lowed it into the area. The Restoration Corporation has channeled loans to several dozen small businessmen. And a community center was created in an abandoned dairy, using mostly indigenous workers.

At the same time, the Bed-Stuy community has learned to press more effectively for the things it wants. In July 1971, I watched Mayor Lindsay and Congresswoman Chisholm dedicate a handsome swimming-pool complex that covers an entire block (the main pool large enough to hold 1,000 kids at once!). The community had not only been consulted on every planning phase of the pool, but there was general agreement that without the community's insistence, the pool would never have materialized.

Brownsville has only a quarter of Bed-Stuy's population, but it is a more hopeless place, and always has been. In recent years, there has been the hopeful experiment with the Ocean Hill-Brownsville school district, but also outcroppings of nihilist black and Puerto Rican militancy. In 1971, when the state legislature cut back on the programs that provide practically the only significant income for Brownsville—Aid for Dependent Children, Medicaid, drug-addiction centers, and school aid—hundreds of Brownsville teenagers, along with derelicts and addicts, staged a medium-level riot in which dozens of stores were looted and 15 major fires started. The Associated Press released a frightening photograph of three teenagers lounging contentedly along a mesh wire fence while flames licked from every window of the tenement building in front of them.

People fear and hate Coney Island now, once the fun center of the city. Blacks and Puerto Ricans go there on the subway for a little relaxation, but the whites largely keep away. Nobody dares go there at night. The place and the beaches are dirty and depressing. The boardwalk needs new boards. The water is so polluted that it may not be swimmable much longer.

STATEN ISLAND

Staten Island (the borough of Richmond) is the most un-New Yorkish of the five city boroughs. It is only now emerging from a leisurely, rural history. Its hills still offer splendid vistas of the city and the ocean; it still has a few dirt roads and marvelous old buildings; it still has beaches with room to walk and sunbathe and—water pollution levels permitting—to swim. The borough has 20 percent of New York City's land area but only 3.8 percent of its population (295,433 in 1970).

A rush of land speculation and building came to Staten Island, however, with completion of the lovely, soaring Verrazano Bridge in 1964. The bridge provides easy vehicular access to Brooklyn, and thence to Manhattan; previously the only bridges had been to New Jersey. The developers are coming in with their blueprints and bulldozers, and the future is assured only in terms of numbers of people—by estimate of the New York City Planning Commission, 550,000 by 1985. What exists now is a rather untidy assemblage of two-story houses, crowded row upon row onto treeless 40 by 100-

foot lots, interspersed with lovely old mansions that recall the island's days as a fashionable summer retreat for wealthy New Yorkers.

The new Verrazano Narrows Bridge is neither the cheapest nor the most pleasant way to get to Staten Island. Since 1712, there has been some form of ferry service from Manhattan, and you can still take the famed Staten Island Ferry, one of the great short water voyages of the world. The price—five cents—has not changed since 1898, and *nothing* else in New York costs that little.

The view of New York Harbor is stupendous, but two sights are food for thought: the Statue of Liberty and Ellis Island. In a way, they speak to a time past—when the floodgates of immigration were open and Ellis Island accepted 20 million new Americans, when America really meant what Emma Lazarus wrote for the statue's pedestal, those romantic lines: "Give me your tired your poor, / Your huddled masses yearning to breathe free . . . / Send these, the homeless, tempest-tost, to me, / I lift my lamp beside the golden door!" The closing of Ellis Island in 1954 underscored the end of all that. But did it? The great city continues, really, to be the port of entry and point of sojourn for the tired and poor. The only difference is that they come now from the American Southland and Puerto Rico instead of Europe. New York never had an easy time with its immigrants, and does not today. But as the city's economic development administrator, Kenneth Patton, told me:

Urban economies are the only places that do what America is supposed to care about—the resurrection of people who've been left out, and newcomers who have yet to get in, and are not admitted to other places. Cities are successful in their ability to take people from some point of entry and elevate them to some higher level in the economic order of things. Suburbs look successful, but they are not. They just preserve and contain a certain measure of achieved success. They are not creative. Cities look unsuccessful, but by definition they are not. . . . It's an outrage that the country looks at New York and other cities as down and out. They are the only thing that holds the country together.

MASSACHUSETTS

A GOLDEN AGE?

As AMERICA EMERGED from World War II, Massachusetts seemed headed into a long decline. Its cities and its industries were obsolescent, its politics ethnic-oriented and patronage-ridden, its leadership tired and unimaginative. Only its universities continued to show some of the vitality that had made Boston the Athens of America in the 18th and 19th centuries, and now they seemed oddly cut off from the political and governmental life of the state. A patina of historic preciousness, of proper Bostonianism contraposed to Irish sentimentality, lay over Massachusetts. The state would have been anyone's last candidate for a center of American growth and thought in the postwar period.

But while the nation was looking westward and away, some remarkable things occurred in the old Commonwealth:

■ Its people began to discard the ancient enmities between Protestant and Catholic, Yankee, and Irish, that had corroded public life for a century.

■ Old Boston began to rebuild itself, becoming one of America's most handsome and livable cities.

■ The universities in Cambridge became vital and advanced intellectual centers, not only on the national scene but in the political life of the state.

■ The economy emerged from the trough of despair created by the flight of textiles to the South. Massachusetts evolved into a preeminent state in electronics and industry based on imaginative scientific research.

■   A new class of highly educated and progressive-minded people was drawn by the science-based industries, and Massachusetts became perhaps the most liberal state, politically, in the Union.

■   The tradition-encrusted Massachusetts legislature began to pioneer in field after field of creative social legislation.

■   Great strides were made in purging corruption from government.

■   And Massachusetts furnished a President who could fire the ideals of a nation.

Now it must be acknowledged that not every progressive change took place rapidly or is completely effected as Massachusetts heads into the 1970s. And there are still grave drawbacks to life in Massachusetts. Its center cities have been deserted by their natural elite and by their middle class. Many old mill towns have yet to recover from the loss of their great factories, and the slowdown of the space race and research in new weaponry has raised serious questions about the future of Massachusetts' scientifically based industries. Since 1969, unemployment has been a grim specter, for both mill hands and scientists. Though the 1970 Census found that of Massachusetts' 5,689,170 people,* only 3.1 percent (175,817) were Negroes, and despite remarkably progressive state legislation written to enhance the opportunities of minorities in schooling and housing, racial discord is growing. The various forms of campus dissent threaten to sever the tenuous ties between faculties and public life.

Yet some future historian, reviewing the history of Massachusetts from the days of the Pilgrims onwards, may well decide that the present era—starting, perhaps, in the late 1950s, and proceeding well into the decade of the 1970s or beyond—was a golden age of the Commonwealth.

Overcoming Ethnicity

"The modern history of politics in Massachusetts," political scientist Murray B. Levin wrote a few years ago, "begins with the great Irish potato famine of 1845." In five years, an estimated million Irish died of starvation and another 1.6 million left their native land, a high percentage of them to settle in New England and especially the state of Massachusetts. By 1860, 61 percent of the population of Boston was foreign born, and the percentage was not far different in cities like Lowell, Lawrence, and Fall River. Starting in the 1880s, large numbers of Italians, Poles, Lithuanians, Portuguese, Scandinavians, and Germans began to follow the Irish. By 1920, more than two-thirds of the people of Massachusetts were either foreign born or of foreign parents. Boston elected its first Irish-born mayor in 1885, Massachusetts its first Irish Catholic governor in 1918.

The Irish and their fellow immigrants did not enter a political vacuum. For more than 200 years, a homogeneous Yankee Protestant population had held sway on the shores of Massachusetts Bay. The story of that civilization,

* The population has grown by 1.4 million, or 32 percent, since 1940.

begun on the November day of 1620 when the hardy Pilgrims first touched the bleak shore at Provincetown and "fell upon their knees & blessed ye God of heaven, who had brought them over ye vast & furious ocean," is so classically American as to barely require retelling here. In those two centuries Massachusetts had grown from one of the strictest theocracies the world has ever known to a seedbed of sedition in the days of John Adams, John Hancock, and Paul Revere. It had been the site of the Boston Tea Party, the Boston Massacre, and the shots from Lexington and Concord "heard 'round the world." From a colony of hardscrabble farming and modest cottage industries, it had grown in eminence as an Atlantic fishing center, as the home port of prosperous seaborne commerce in the West Indian trade (including rum and slaves), then even greater profits in the China and East India trade and the brief, colorful era of the Yankee clippers racing at full sail across the world's oceans. The great New England insurance industry had arisen from a pooling of maritime shipping risks in the late 18th century, and the textile industry from a pirating of secret English mill techniques around 1800. Transcendentalism, America's first major intellectual movement, had begun to flower in Massachusetts, expounded by writers like Bronson Alcott, Ralph Waldo Emerson, and Henry David Thoreau. And this was the leading American state in the move to abolish slavery under the American flag. In every part of life, Massachusetts deserved the region's title of "New England"; as Yale President Timothy Dwight wrote of the Bostonians in 1796: "They are all descendants of Englishmen and, of course, are united by all the great bonds of society—language, religion, government, manners and interest."

The clash between old Yankee and Catholic immigrant was predictable, bitter, and lasting. Both sides abhorred the other's religion. The Puritan settlers of early New England had gained their name because their sect wanted to "purify" the Anglican Church of all vestiges of popery, and they had persecuted and driven from Massachusetts nonconformers to their narrow way, including Baptists and Quakers. The Roman Catholic Irish viewed all Protestantism as apostasy; writer Joe McCarthy quotes one of their spokesmen as saying that "a *Christian* Protestant . . . is a contradiction in terms." The Yankees were proud of their British ancestry; the Irish, remembering centuries of English exploitation of their homeland, despised everything British. The Yankees were reform-minded, fond of causes like abolition, women's rights, and improving conditions in the prisons; their philosophy was one of the perfectability of man. The Irish Catholics viewed true salvation as an occurrence of life after death; they feared job competition from Negroes and were proslavery; they believed in hierarchy and authority and rigid class lines and a politics based on personal loyalties rather than abstract philosophies.

The old Yankees stopped at nothing to subjugate the Irish immigrants. An unskilled workman would earn a mere $4.50 to $5.50 a week, a woman working as a domestic as little as $1.75 a week, of which 75 cents was taken for board. The Irish were crowded into the mudflats of the cities and waterfront slums. Five to 15 might live in a single basement; as James MacGregor

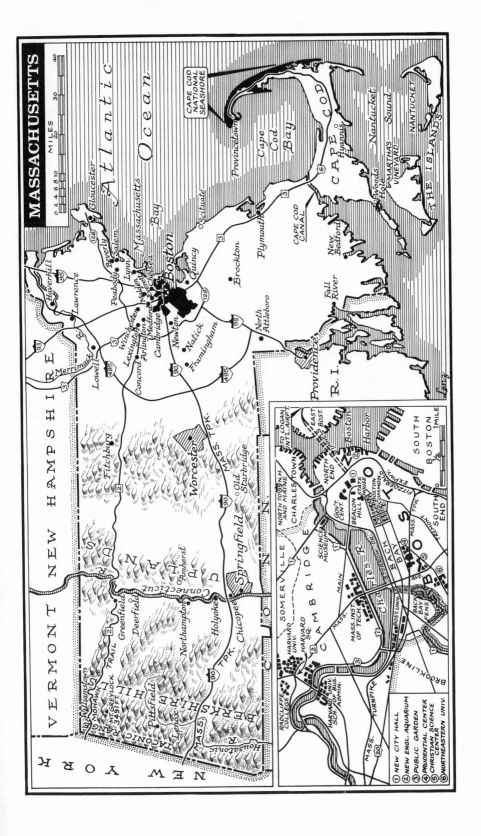

Burns writes of the time that John Kennedy's grandfather came to Boston, "One sink might serve a house, one privy a neighborhood. Filth spread through courts and alleys, and with it tuberculosis, cholera, and smallpox, which thrived in the poorest sections, where the Irish lived." Election laws were purposely rewritten to delay the day that the immigrants might vote.

But with the professions and economic advancement closed to them, the Irish turned to their favorite avocation—politics—and made a grand success of it. Because the Yankees were Republicans after the Civil War, the Irish were automatically Democrats. As the Irish and their fellow immigrants began to outnumber the Yankees, they gained offices. The ward political organizations provided loyal voters with jobs, licenses, street lights, emergency welfare aid. The system flourished right up through two World Wars and into the 1950s. James Michael Curley was a symbol of it all, a kind of Robin Hood whose stealing from the rich was tolerated because he "took care" of his own. Robert C. Wood (now president of the University of Massachusetts) said in 1961 of the Democratic party in Boston: "The 'in' group in politics here is still playing 19th-century politics. They see the problem as dividing the spoils, not how to manage society."

The cleavage between Irish and Yankees plagued Massachusetts life for more than a century. Up to World War I, the Boston newspapers segregated social items about Yankees and Irish Catholics in different pages. Yankees looked down on Irish as a kind of social scum. Irish detested Harvard because, as John Gunther observed, "Harvard is the great rival of the archbishopric for intellectual control of the community." It was at a Holy Cross alumni dinner in 1910 that Irishman John Collins Bossidy first recited the satiric jingle:

> And this is good old Boston
> The home of the bean and the cod
> Where the Lowells talk to the Cabots
> And the Cabots talk only to God.

A few years later Boston experienced its famous police strike, pitting the two groups against each other. (My own Boston grandfather was one of the citizen strikebreakers, and proud of it to his life's end. But my friend Robert Healy of the Boston *Globe* reminds me *his* grandfather was one of the leaders of the strike.)

Between the world wars, the Irish became so strong that they controlled both Boston politics and much of the state's politics. After voting Republican in every Presidential election from the Civil War (except the three-way race of 1912), Massachusetts cast a final sentimental vote for its own Calvin Coolidge in 1924 and then switched to Al Smith and the Democrats in 1928, to remain in the Democratic column (except for the Eisenhower elections) ever since. Curley served not only four terms as mayor of Boston, but one as governor of the state of Massachusetts (1935–37). Yet the success of the Irish, outside of politics, was limited. After visiting Boston in 1944, John Gunther reported:

Only one small Boston bank is Irish owned, and only four out of 30 directors of the chamber of commerce are of Irish descent. There are few dominating Irish figures in law, medicine, or finance, and none of the big department stores is Irish controlled; not a single Irishman is an officer, a committee chairman, or a member of the executive committee of the New England Council.

The first Irishman to make a strong breakthrough into the Yankee-held State Street banking and financing community was Joseph P. Kennedy, father of President John F. Kennedy, son of Patrick J. Kennedy (an East Boston Democratic leader, owner of three saloons and a wholesale liquor business), and grandson of Patrick Kennedy (native of County Wexford, Ireland, who had arrived penniless in Boston in 1848). Joseph Kennedy was the first of his clan to attend once-hated Harvard, graduating in 1912. Two years later, he was a bank president; five years later he penetrated the Yankee stronghold of the board of trustees of the Massachusetts Electric Company; in the 1920s, he became phenomenally successful in the stock market and moving pictures and acquired the famous Kennedy fortune; in the 1930s President Roosevelt made him first chairman of the Securities and Exchange Commission, and later Ambassador to Great Britain.

The rise of the Kennedy family as Green Brahmins and the climactic election in 1960 of John Kennedy to the Presidency, the first Roman Catholic ever to hold that post, were grand symbols of what was happening more quietly and more importantly for the civilization of Massachusetts. Thousands of young Irishmen took advantage of the GI Bill after World War II; they emerged as talented professionals, pragmatists, able to communicate and work with the Yankee aristocracy as equals. Their interest in petty political patronage was minimal. The "new" Irish, one might say, won out by co-opting the Yankees' value system. "The old Yankee," Robert Wood told me, "won out in terms of attitudes. The desires for probity, for effective government won out in the mind of most of the voting population. . . . With Kennedy and other Massachusetts figures of national stature, you see the rational, problem-solving, consensual politician."

The vital turn from old ethnic to new pragmatic politics seems to have occurred in Boston city government with the election of John Collins as mayor in 1959 (a story we will return to later). On the state level it emerged through a series of political scraps, Irish versus Yankee, Yankee versus Italian, and Irish versus Italian, in the late 1950s and early 1960s. It should be remembered that when the Irish became dominant in the 19th century, they turned as cold a shoulder on the Italians and Poles and other ethnic groups as the chilly Yankees had turned on them. The fierce inter-ethnic rivalries have remained strong, especially in Democratic party conventions and primaries. In 1960, the Democrats nominated an "All-Green" statewide ticket that offended Italian, Jewish, Polish, and other voters and opened the way for the election that year of a Republican governor, John A. Volpe, the first Italian and Catholic ever to be nominated for that office by his party. In 1962, the Kennedys intervened indirectly to secure the Democratic gubernatorial nomination for a Yankee Democrat, Endicott Peabody, just so there would be no "All-Green" ticket in the election when Edward M. Kennedy was first running for the U. S. Senate. Peabody, Wood points out, was a symbol of "the nonethnic probity." But Peabody failed to perform effectively as governor and was upset two years later for renomination by his own party in a primary charged with ethnic animosity. The man who beat Peabody, Lt. Gov. Francis X. Bellotti, seemed to have no discernible qualifications save his desire for higher office—and being Italian. That was enough to beat Peabody in the primary. But Volpe (just as Italian and ambitious as Bellotti, but a lot more capable) recaptured the governorship in that year's general election. Massachusetts has not had a Democratic governor since, and everyone seems to agree that a lot of the juice has been drained out of the old ethnic issue.

But not all. As Robert Wood points out:

> The successful practitioner of politics, operating on old ethnic/personal principles he knew, continues to play an outmoded game. Publicly, there is much talk of ethnic tickets—while the public has gone on beyond them. The result is a gap, much greater than in most states, between voter expectations and actual performance. It increases the disillusionment, cynicism, and skepticism with politics. . . .
> The guys who want to do the right thing will get more support than they expect to get. But they are always trapping themselves by falling back into ethnic politics more than they really have to. It is still a factor in primaries, but not so much in general elections.

An overnight transformation from ethnic to issue-based politics is more than one could reasonably expect in a state with 54 percent Roman Catholic population (highest of any state except Rhode Island), a 5 percent Jewish population (third highest in the country), and a 1960 "foreign stock" population figure of 40 percent (highest of all the states). Of the two million Massachusetts citizens in 1960 who were immigrants or children of immigrants, the largest single group was Canadian (largely French-Canadian), numbering 537,236. The French-Canadians lack the political effectiveness of other ethnic groups, however. The Census also counted 311,053 Italian first- and second-generation Bay Staters, 276,166 Irish, 193,137 British, and 136,-942 Polish. It should be remembered that these figures reflect immigration of much later times than the original Irish influx of the 1840s and 1850s.

The days when rivalries between these ethnic groups could be exploited for political purpose are beginning to wane. A key factor was the high amount of intermarriage, following World War II, between Irish and Italians. Congressman Silvio O. Conte, himself a son of Italian immigrants and a war veteran who broke the old ethnic lines by marrying a girl named Corinne Duval, recalls: "The guys came back from the war with a completely different attitude. Irish parents could no longer tell Irish boys and girls just to marry Irish. Hell, the guys had been all over the world and seen every kind. They weren't about to let their parents tell them whom they could marry. This had a great effect in breaking down the barriers among the nationalities."

As the intermarrying got underway, so did the postwar suburban housing boom. Today, the settled, generations-old ethnic communities still exist in Boston and other cities, but more and more of the descendents of immigrants live in a homogenized suburbia where ethnic loyalties, like straight ticket voting, are out of style. Yet on occasion, old-style ethnic politics bubble up in an ugly way. In 1971, house speaker David Michael Bartley was willing to tell a Boston *Globe* reporter, for attribution, how he had "learned to dislike Yankees" as a golf course caddy in his youth (they didn't tip well) and accuse the Holyoke *Transcript-Telegram* of being "viciously anti-Irish Catholic" (an exaggerated if not utterly false charge). One close observer of the Boston political scene told me that on election day, "an Italian can't do well in an Irish district, but an Irishman can do well in an Italian district." But the Boston city council, once an Irish stronghold, was neatly split up in 1970–71: four Irish, three Italians, one black, one Wasp.

The overall Protestant-Catholic animosities of Massachusetts were tremendously lightened by the changes within the Roman Catholic Church in Massachusetts, especially the Archdiocese of Boston. William Cardinal O'-Connell, leader of the Boston flock until his death in 1944, has been described by John H. Fenton as a "haughty, aloof figure . . . who could freeze a dissenter at 50 paces with a baleful glare. . . . One of his primary aims was strengthening the Catholic parochial school system. His acknowledged intent was to protect the children of the archdiocese from the heretical influence of Protestantism." Richard Cushing, O'Connell's successor, was an open, warmhearted man of quite another temperament. Born in 1895 in a third-floor flat of a cold-water South Boston tenement, he had made his mark in church work as an indefatigable and amazingly successful fund raiser, an activity he continued as Archbishop and later as Cardinal (raising, by some estimates, $300 million over his lifetime). But what Cushing will longest be remembered for is his tireless work to build bridges of understanding between Catholics, Protestants, and Jews. "We are told there is no salvation outside the church—nonsense!" he once said. "Nobody can tell me Christ died on Calvary for any select group." Cushing candidly admitted he was "no scholar," but at the Second Vatican Council his impassioned plea for religious liberty and condemnation of the doctrine that the Jews, as a people, are responsible for the crucifixion of Christ, led the assembled bishops to break the rules of silence and applaud the crusty, warmhearted man from Boston.

The potential power in heavily Catholic Massachusetts of the leader of the Boston See is immense, though it is easy to exaggerate the extent to which church influence is actually exerted. Cardinal O'Connell had a registered lobbyist and other emissaries to the legislature who carried his messages concerning birth control bills, a proposed state lottery, and child labor. Under Cushing, the influence was much less direct, perhaps because he had much less interest in pushing traditional church doctrines in politics. Cushing did, however, once pronounce in a pastoral letter that "When a Catholic fails to take a stand against race intolerance or prejudice he is a slacker in the army of the church militant." He was a lifetime member of the NAACP but by the same token endorsed the John Birch Society for its outspoken anticommunism. The Catholic hierarchy was a major defender of the 1879 law forbidding dissemination of birth control information in the Commonwealth, and helped defeat proposed abolition in two referenda (1942 and 1948).* Despite his ecumenicism, Cushing opposed the rise in the late 1960s of the "underground church" in which Catholics and Protestants join together for holy communion in their homes.

Through the Kennedys, with whom he had a close association over many decades, Cushing became something of a national figure. Few will forget his raspy voice (which was likened to the sound of "coal rattling down a chute in a South Boston basement") delivering a seemingly interminable invocation at President Kennedy's inauguration in 1961 (while white smoke poured from the lectern from a small fire). But then there was the private Cushing, weeping alone in his private chapel the day he received word of John Kennedy's assassination, and his prayer cracking with grief at the funeral, as he called on the angels to carry his "dear Jack" to Paradise.

Cushing's 26-year leadership of the 1.9 million Roman Catholics of the Boston area came to an end with his resignation, at age 75, in 1970. Two months later, he was dead. Rome's choice for a new archbishop was a surprise—Humberto Sousa Medeiros, a 55-year-old native of the Portuguese Azores who had for five years been bishop of Brownsville, Texas. For the first time in 124 years, Boston had a non-Irish archbishop. But Medeiros was no stranger to Massachusetts; he had grown up in Fall River, where he once swept floors at 62 cents a day and gave up a promising career as an artist to become a priest. In Texas, he had become a sturdy friend of the impoverished Mexican-Americans, and was a close friend of César Chávez. His selection was a sign of the changing times, since Boston has experienced in recent years a heavy influx of Spanish-speaking Puerto Ricans and Cubans.

While a friend of the poor, Medeiros is no flaming liberal on other church issues. Soon after assuming his new job, he attacked efforts to liberalize abortion laws as "a step backward" and "a new barbarism."

While the Roman Catholics get the most public attention, other religious groups continue to prosper in Massachusetts. The Mother Church of the Christian Scientists is there, and that group's newspaper, the *Christian Science Monitor*, is one of the finest in America and distributed nationally (217,000 copies daily)—an organ with more influence outside of Boston than within it. Editor-in-chief Erwin D. Canham is highly regarded nationally and has served as president of the Chamber of Commerce of the U. S. In the prestigious 125,000-member Episcopal Diocese of Massachusetts, a change as momentous as the Catholics' shift to a non-Irish bishop took place in 1970. To succeed retiring Bishop Anson Phelps Stokes, Jr., the Episcopalians chose the Rt. Rev. John M. Burgess, son of a dining-car porter and the first black man to head an Episcopal diocese in the United States.

* The law was finally declared unconstitutional by a federal court in 1970. The court found that the statute "conflicts with fundamental human rights." A similar Connecticut statute had been nullified earlier, leaving no state with anti-birth control legislation.

The Political Cultures

The confusing cross-currents of modern Massachusetts politics are easier to fathom if one keeps in mind the four principal political strata of the state, defined by Edgar Litt in his valuable book, *The Political Cultures of Massachusetts:*

THE PATRICIAN ELITE. These are the Lodges, Herters, Saltonstalls, Websters, and Elliotts of Massachusetts, born to wealth and high social status, members of the elite religious groups (often Episcopal or Congregational), educated at the best private schools and usually Harvard University, residents of high-grade Boston suburbs like Lincoln, Bedford, or Weston. In fiscal matters, they have traditionally been conservatives who, "like their Puritan forefathers, strive to carry out the handiwork of God with a modest profit [and] a balanced budget." They are also conservatives on many educational issues. Their political interests rarely conflict with those of State Street and the First National Bank, but first and foremost, they are interested in honest, decent government. On questions of civil liberties, they have been liberals since the days of the abolitionist movement. This Yankee community, Robert Healy of the *Globe* told me, is "the main force of the liberal stream" in the state today. "The kids of Yankees are furthest to the left," he said. "The highly politicized campuses are products of New England prep schools." Their parents, of course, are more cautious. Litt describes them as "brokers of a changing economic society [who] mediate between the larger world of Washington and the confines of the town and the ward. Their links with the past and their confidence in mastering the future provide experience with which to meet the impact of international cartels, common markets, and automation on the home, the family, and the job." I have never seen a better definition of what a modern-day aristocracy ought to be.

THE YEOMEN. Once the numerical majority in Massachusetts and now a fast-declining minority, these are the rural and small-town businessmen and workers of old Protestant stock. They are to be found in the small towns and villages of nonmetropolitan Massachusetts, which contain only 15 percent of the population. Litt describes their prevailing ethos as that of 19th-century America "with its emphasis on individual initiative, its distrust of bigness in government, corporations, labor unions, . . . and a personalized, informal attitude toward friends and neighbors." Here we catch a glimpse of old town meeting New England, even, as Litt suggests, *Saturday Evening Post* New England. It is staunchly Republican and conservative on social welfare, civil liberties, and governmental reform; its representatives have frequently held leadership positions in the legislature, reflecting those attitudes. Litt observes: "Replaced by a young managerial stratum, bypassed by the industries, turnpikes and shopping developments of a consumption-oriented society, the yeomen have lost their sense of usefulness, their participation in the mainstream of American society." Yet, he might have added, they feel they preserve some quintessence of Old America in their little towns and villages, quiet and pastoral, which have a peace and dignity no suburb or city has ever approached.

THE WORKERS. This is Ethnic Massachusetts, the urban-based Irish Catholic and their sometime friends, the Italians, Poles, and assorted other European arrivals of the past century and a quarter, as they are still embodied in ethnic neighborhoods. "They are localists," Litt observes, "with a deep resistance to governmental, social, and economic change because they perceive, often correctly, that the strategies of constitutional reform and urban renewal threaten their entrenched positions in the neighborhood [and] the legislature." The story is told of the city of Boston's proposal a few years ago to put an urban renewal project into Charlestown. At a public meeting to discuss the idea, a man stood up and told the Boston Redevelopment Authority: "I have an unalienable right to be a slob." What he was saying, in effect, was that he was part of an Irish or Italian immigration movement, that by the sweat of his brow he'd acquired his place in the sun, and that whether some elitists thought his community an eyesore or not, he liked it and wanted to keep it as it was. Where resistance to Negro encroachment is strongest in Massachusetts, it is presumably centered in these neighborhoods. They are parochial, resistant to change of any kind, conservative on civil liberties, liberal only on social welfare (as long as their communities are not disturbed). Unions are their champions, and their party (especially among the Irish) has been, is, and most probably will remain the Democratic.

THE MANAGERS. Here is the new postwar society: highly educated and professional—the administrators, teachers, lawyers, clergymen, scientists, technicians, advertising and communications specialists. Here the lines of ethnicity disappear: they may be Yankee, Irish, Italian, Jewish, or whatever. They earn well but they have yet to acquire the social status, reserves of wealth, or corporate power of the patricians. While their heritage, Litt observes, is "Democratic, urban, immigrant, blue collar," they are highly independent in politics, the proverbial ticket splitters. They were attracted to John Kennedy, but often vote Republican in contests for statewide office in Massachusetts. Many are attracted to the peace movement, a small minority to political conservatism in the model of Orange County, California. But they see themselves as rational men, and believe in social and economic welfare measures to improve society.

The long hegemony of the Massachusetts Republicans—from the Civil War to the late 1920s—was attributable to the power and prestige of the patricians and the then-still-strong numbers of the yeomen. The Democratic era that began with Al Smith's victory in Massachusetts and continues to this day has been due (1) to the emergence of the Democratic workers as Massachusetts' majority group, and (2) to the general inclination of the new managerial class, all other things being equal, to vote Democratic. Beguiled by the presence in the highest Massachusetts offices of men like Leverett

Saltonstall, Christian Herter, Edward Brooke, John Volpe, Elliot Richardson, and Francis Sargent (the present governor), outsiders have been prone to think of the Bay State as a two-party state. In some ways, the thesis is correct. While the Democrats have a 2–1 registration lead, the number of independents, when added to the Republicans, forms a majority:

	Registration (1970)	
Democratic	1,135,103	43.2%
Republican	547,393	20.8%
Independent	946,085	36.0%

Without that independent vote, Republicans would long since have been closed out entirely from effective participation in Massachusetts political life. It gives them the potentiality of winning, but only with candidates who represent the liberal wing of the party and have strong personal appeal, or when the Democratic opponents are exceptionally weak. When one looks behind the façade of the GOP glamor candidates, one finds a dry rot has infected every part of the GOP organization. The grass roots party, still strongly yeoman-oriented, is old and tired. The Republican state committee has begun only in the last few years to add ethnics to its heavily Yankee Protestant ranks. The party's yeoman-oriented legislative leaders are as likely to block as to support the progressive programs of Republican governors, fearing more taxes. And the patricians, as Litt notes, are caught up in the changing economy as establishment forces like the John Hancock Insurance Company and the First National Bank of Boston cooperate with Harvard and MIT. The party's successful statewide candidates are obliged to create their own highly personal organizations. But the loyalty—as with the many Italians whom Volpe brought into Republican activity—is to the man, not the party, and the result is highly divisive. The Democrats' factionalism, dividing into camps of rival warlords, is similar, but the Democrats have the vote cushion and think they can afford the luxury (though they often end up losing elections for statewide office as a result).

The lack of true Republican party government in Massachusetts is illustrated by the fact that no GOP governor since the late 1950s has had a plurality of both houses of the legislature and among the statewide elective offices. In the space of one decade, 1954 to 1964, the Republican strength in the legislature declined from 53 percent to a mere 29 percent of the seats. The Republicans were even worse off after the 1970 election, with only 10 of 40 seats in the state senate and 62 of 240 seats in the house. In the same election, the Democrats won all eight seats on the governor's council. The outcome was largely foreordained by the Republicans' appalling failure to recruit candidates.* Only one of the eight Democratic candidates for the governor's council was opposed, and there were Republican candidates for only 113 of the 240 house seats and 19 of the 40 senate seats. The Boston *Globe* quoted an anonymous but loyal State House Democrat as hoping the Republicans

---

* Another factor was the past action of the Democrats in the legislature to redistrict many Republican seats out of existence. In the Boston area, for instance, there are wedge-shaped senate districts with a safe minority of suburban voters, deliberately designed to keep Democrats in office.

would show more spunk. "It would be better, not only for the two-party system but for Democratic party discipline, if the Democrats got cut back to say, 150 [house] seats," he said. "You can't appeal for a party-line vote now; they say, 'Hell, there are 169 others. You don't need me.'"

But now, Republicans are far short of the legislative strength needed to sustain a veto by GOP Governor Sargent. Sargent and his running mate for the lieutenant governorship, Holyoke newspaper publisher Donald Dwight (the two offices having been joined together for election by a single ballot in the 1960s), were the only Republican statewide winners in 1970. Their victory was due in large part to the political adeptness of Sargent, who wisely and firmly "invited" Vice President Spiro Agnew to stay out of Massachusetts during the campaign and managed to put the Democrats in a bad light by leaving them with the blame for the less savory shenanigans in the legislature while taking credit himself for some of the outstanding progressive legislation authored and approved by the same legislators. (Sargent is also a strong environmentalist, which puts him well in tune with the times, and has a pleasant personality the Democrats find difficult to attack.)

Even the occasional statewide victories for the Republicans might not occur, however, if it were not for the "Massachusetts Ballot," adopted years ago and now a model for several other states. Under it, there is no single party column or voting machine lever, and the voter is obliged to make an individual choice for each office. In the top two or three offices, where the candidates are familiar as individuals to the voters, Republicans have a chance of winning; in voting for most other posts, however, many have a tendency just to seek out the candidate with the word "Democratic" written beside his name and vote for him.

Things may get even worse for the Massachusetts GOP in the next few years. In March 1971, a new Conservative party of Massachusetts was announced to fight the "rush to liberalism" in the state's Republican party. The new party, headed by John J. McCarthy, an Irish Catholic conservative who served in the Volpe administration, is frankly modeled after the New York Conservative party which played a spoiler role in Empire State politics until it finally elected James Buckley to the U. S. Senate in 1970. McCarthy claimed a new party was necessary to give Massachusetts a real two-party system. "All we have now is party A and party A prime," he said. The Conservatives' first target is Republican Senator Brooke, up for reelection in 1972. It is also hoped, by threatening opposition, to frighten liberal Massachusetts GOP congressmen into giving greater support to the conservative stands of the Nixon administration. But the chances of the Massachusetts Conservatives to make a true breakthrough, like the Buckley election in New York, are probably minimal. Among its present Republicans, Massachusetts lacks a broad conservative constituency comparable to upstate New York, some of the New York boroughs, or parts of Long Island. Enticing working-class Democrats to join a conservative movement may be especially difficult because of the strong emotional ties which the Irish and other ethnic groups have to the Massachusetts Democratic party. In the last election that gave

Bay State voters a clear liberal-conservative choice, the 1968 Presidential election, Humphrey the liberal swamped Nixon the conservative by a margin of 702,373 votes (63 percent). It was Humphrey's biggest numerical majority in any state of the Union. Nixon got only 33 percent of the Massachusetts vote, and Wallace less than 4 percent.

Where do the Democrats pick up these huge majorities? First and foremost, it is from the cities and urban-type suburbs of eastern Massachusetts. Of Humphrey's 702,373-vote plurality, 402,157 votes came from Boston and its suburbs, many of which (like Cambridge, Somerville, etc.) are very urban in character. But once-Republican suburbs have also turned Democratic in Presidential races. Wellesley, which went 79 percent for Dewey in 1948, was only 57 percent for Nixon in 1968. Between the same two elections, Concord dropped from 71 to 48 percent Republican, Brookline from 56 to 26 percent Republican, and Belmont (home of the John Birch Society!) from 67 to 42 percent Republican. And the western Massachusetts cities of Springfield and Pittsfield, which had given Dewey just over 45 percent of their vote in 1948, barely mustered 30 percent for Nixon in 1968. The situation would be even worse for the Republicans if Boston were not declining in population and relative vote weight in the state (19 percent of the statewide vote in 1952, just under 10 percent in 1968). Still, Boston could muster 171,250 votes for Humphrey—75 percent of the total cast in the city.

The Democrats' problem is that only the old, settled, ethnic worker cities like Boston will stick with them when they put up a lackluster candidate for governor and U. S. Senator. But when the hard-line Democrat leaves the city, he tends to leave his straight-ticket voting habits behind. "The suburbanite," Democratic state chairman David Harrison told me in 1970, "loses party and ethnic identity. The South Boston guy goes to Sharon or Quincy or Braintree, and he's making more money than Dad did, and sees himself in a new class. Thus we have to have appealing candidates." And the only two appealing enough since 1960, he acknowledged, had been Ted Kennedy and "Chubb" Peabody—"and Peabody botched as governor."

The strange inability of Democrats to capitalize on their basic strength and sweep the governorship and both Senate seats may be traced to (1) the inchoate nature of the party, where personal loyalties, animosities, and maneuverings dominate, (2) lack of party discipline in the legislature, because of their swollen majorities, and (3) the preprimary convention endorsing system, which dramatizes and exaggerates the splits.

The Republicans, a decorous lot, have generally had well behaved conventions whose endorsees have been approved by the voters in the primary. But the Democratic conclaves have been raucous, emotion-packed affairs whose handiwork—especially in nominations for governor and U. S. Senator—have frequently been reversed. Hoping to avoid the stigma of "booze, broads, and boodle" surrounding earlier Democratic conventions, party chairman David Harrison scheduled the 1970 affair in the sylvan setting of the University of Massachusetts campus at Amherst. He might as well have put the meeting in South Boston. A single ballot for governor took more than six hours, at least two major fistfights broke out on the convention floor, and there were scuffles, dead microphones, and a woman who fainted as her delegation was called to vote.

"The delegates," R. W. Apple, Jr., reported in the New York *Times*, "were overwhelmingly Irish-American, overwhelmingly insiders, overwhelmingly middle-aged." He spotted one of them, an oldtimer in a black suit with a two-day growth of beard, who shrugged his shoulders during a shouting match and said of the candidates for the nomination: "Kevin's my cousin, I play handball with Frank Bellotti, and I went to school with Maurice Donahue. I gotta make a connection with Kenny O'Donnell." The candidates referred to were Mayor Kevin White of Boston (who was short on delegates but longest on popular support), state senate president Maurice Donahue (favored with the delegates but disadvantaged with the voters because of his boss role in the widely scorned legislature), former Lt. Gov. Francis X. Bellotti (who ran in the vain hope that a split in the Irish vote would permit him to slip through to a minority vote victory in the primary), and former White House aide Kenneth P. O'Donnell (still trying to cash in on his association with the Kennedy family). Donahue turned out to be the convention winner, but one of his backers predicted: "We know Mossie will lose in September and Kevin will lose in November. That's the way it always is." He was right.

The only man who wins in the convention charade is named Edward M. Kennedy. Up for reelection in 1970, he showed up at Amherst long enough to deliver a brief speech of high moral tone accepting renomination. Then he got out of town. Kennedy, and his brother John before him, have never sought to bring chaos out of the tribal warfare of the Massachusetts Democrats. When party chairman Harrison asked him to take a strong stand in 1970, Ted Kennedy replied: "How can I? Maurice Donahue is a friend of mine, Kenny O'Donnell was a friend of my brother, and Kevin White's a good Democrat."

And so the mayhem continues. Many Democrats would like to discontinue the preprimary conventions altogether. The fierce inter- and intraethnic battles might continue, but at least they would not get the publicity the conventions afford. But the Republicans are not too interested in removing the albatross from their opponents' necks.

Some miscellanea on Massachusetts politics:
- The state has a Presidential primary that used to be a fairly meaningless nonbinding write-in preference poll but since the mid-1960s has been strengthened to require that names of leading candidates be placed on the ballot. In 1968, Senator Eugene McCarthy won the Democratic primary, a real shock to the practitioners of the Old Politics who then had to go to Chicago pledged to a man many of them disliked. Nelson Rockefeller won on the Republican side in a write-in vote over favorite son John Volpe.
- The Ripon Society of independent and progressive-minded younger Republicans was founded in Cambridge early in the 1960s and still exercises an influence substantially beyond its numbers—a thorn in the side of the

conservative, contented national Republican establishment and the nemesis, of course, of groups like Young Americans for Freedom, which are also strong in Massachusetts.

▪   The peace movement has blossomed in the Bay State, starting on a very modest scale in 1962 when independent candidate H. Stuart Hughes polled 2.4 percent of the vote for the U. S. Senate against Ted Kennedy and George Cabot Lodge. Now Massachusetts sends to Congress two men who personify a new, freewheeling, antimilitary liberalism—Michael Harrington, first elected in 1969, and a Jesuit priest, the Rev. Robert F. Drinan, first elected in 1970. Both men are Democrats and owe their elections to the small armies of students from eastern Massachusetts' activist universities who poured in to help, plus the support of the new managerial class in sophisticated, liberally oriented suburban towns. Father Drinan, however, barely won with a 3,367-vote plurality and only 35.4 percent of the 169,800 ballots cast in a three-way general election race. In addition to a Republican opponent, he had to cope with the write-in opposition of the 14-term congressional incumbent, Philip J. Philbin, the second-ranking member of the House Armed Services Committee, whom he had upset in the Democratic primary. (Drinan's victory was entirely due to a big vote he got in wealthy Boston suburbs like Newton; he lost heavily in working-class and lower-middle-class towns further to the west.) The Vietnam war was the central issue Drinan used to win; the issue that almost defeated him, despite a distinguished record as an educator and lawyer (including several years as dean of Boston College Law School), was the fact that he was also a priest. Roman Catholics especially appeared to resent his entry into the active political arena. Whether Drinan survives in politics or not, he has helped to set precedents: the first election of a Catholic priest to Congress since the Rev. Gabriel Richard served as a territorial delegate from Michigan in 1882; the second person in a whole century to defeat an incumbent Massachusetts congressman in a primary.*

▪   The way Drinan was nominated also made history, and perhaps points to new directions in the politics of the 1970s. The groups of McCarthyites, Bobby Kennedyites, "peace" partisans, as well as people grouped within a new statewide organization called Citizens for Participation Politics, convened a citizens caucus to nominate a candidate for Congress against Philbin. There were 852 delegates—Democrats, Independents, and Republicans, middle-aged and teenagers. All participated as equals, and by a complicated vote allocation by town (according to the numbers of registered voters), votes in the caucus were tallied on a computer and made available to delegates and observers on closed circuit television. "A sense of openness and fair play marked the proceedings," Boston *Globe* columnist John Saloma reported of the caucus, which picked Drinan over two other would-be candidates. The organization of Citizens for Participation Politics remains active in Massachusetts under the leadership of the Rev. John Elder of Harvard Divinity

---

* The only other Bay State primary upset was in 1966 when Mrs. Margaret Heckler upset an aging Joseph W. Martin, Jr., in the Republican primary in Martin's southeastern Massachusetts district.

School. It retains its liberal and issue-oriented stance as it organizes independent voters but refuses to affiliate with partisan groups like the New Democratic Coalition.

Does all the evidence point to Massachusetts being the most liberal state, politically, in the U.S.A.? The answer, based on all the evidence we have reviewed, may well be "yes," and the most important reasons may be the strong intellectual influence of Massachusetts' many universities, whose faculties are often direct participants in public life, the liberality of the Yankee elite, and the progressive attitudes on race and programmatic policies of leading Democratic state legislators like Maurice Donahue, or another former legislator, Michael Dukakis of Brookline. (Retired from public office by his 1970 defeat for governor, Donahue taught university courses in practical politics and organized an institute of government services.)

But there is another side, symbolized in recent years by a woman named Louise Day Hicks. A dowdy attorney in her early fifties, Mrs. Hicks rose to power in Boston on a single issue: ethnic white Bostonians' concern about the incursion into their neighborhoods of Negroes, whose numbers increased from 9.8 to 18.2 percent of the city population in the decade of the 1960s alone. Mrs. Hicks's first and most loyal supporters were the blue-collar Irish of South Boston—"my people," as she calls them. But she gained national prominence by her fight against school busing to achieve racial balance while she served on the Boston school committee. "You know where I stand," was her rallying cry. In 1967, she lost a bitter mayoralty campaign to Kevin White by a vote of 102,706 to 90,154; two years later she led the pack to win election to the Boston city council; in 1970 she was elected to Congress from the Boston congressional district that John W. McCormack had represented for 40 years. In 1971, she ran for mayor as the candidate of those who want to preserve white neighborhoods and stop crime on the streets—"the fact that people don't dare walk out of their own doorway." But Mrs. Hicks's performance in Congress had been lackluster, and Mayor White defeated her the second time around by a resounding 112,875–70,214 vote. She also faced a doubtful political future in a redistricted House seat that included suburban towns not at all attuned to her way of thinking.

State Government: Glory and Travail

Being the old and tradition-bound state it is, Massachusetts has had to struggle through most of the 20th century to bring its archaic structures of state government into line with the needs of the times. Finally, substantial success is in sight.

As a legacy from colonial times, Massachusetts entered the century with a form of government deliberately designed to restrict the governor's authority. The system had originally been intended to prevent executive abuse, a remembrance of the conflicts with the Crown before the Revolution. The 20th-century results were less desirable. The governor had to work with an independently elected governor's council that could reject any appointment he made and pass on *every* state contract—an invitation to partisan maneuver or graft, with no commensurate policy responsibility to the public. Secondly, there was a large, domineering legislature that controlled the executive departments by overlapping appointments to commissions, which in turn had to return to the legislature for their money and could easily bypass the governor.

The system was palatable enough to the Republicans who dominated state government up to the late 1920s, since divided authority mitigated against any strong governmental programs that might mean more taxes or an impingement on private capital. Then, when the Democrats took control of the governorship and the governor's council in the 1930s, they used those offices to circumvent the rural-dominated legislature, increase the power of labor, and enhance the interests of a patronage-oriented, ethnic coalition at the expense of the Republican patricians. During World War II, there was something of a hiatus in politics and state government, and that truest of bluebloods, Leverett Saltonstall, was governor. As the postwar era opened, the patricians of the business and financial community became preoccupied with national and even international economic issues and felt some despair in controlling state government because of the preponderant numbers of the Democratic-ethnic coalition. They did, however, furnish one distinguished governor—Christian A. Herter (who was later U. S. Secretary of State). And in time, the patrician-managerial strata discovered they needed, in Edgar Litt's words, "integrated centers of political power within the state to which they [could] relate national policies and economic developments. . . . They [found] that the governorship and the party systems are vital instruments for bringing about rational, managerial changes." As it turned out, their principal opponents were the very groups most entrenched in the legislature—the yeomen and core-city politicians, both intent on protecting their particularistic economic and social interests. And the managers and patricians faced another problem: the harm to Massachusetts' national image that stemmed from corruption in government. There was a distinct danger that without corrective action, Massachusetts' prospects for business deals, new industries, and government contracts might be seriously impaired.

Official skulduggery had been a problem in Massachusetts since the 1920s, occasionally among Republicans but mostly among Democrats. By the end of World War II, political corruption—payroll padding, kickbacks on contracts, payments for jobs—was taken for granted. In 1945, Curley was elected mayor of Boston even while under federal indictment for mail fraud (a charge on which he was later convicted and sent to prison). In 1956, Congressman Thomas J. Lane, a Democrat from Lawrence, was convicted of income tax evasion, served four months in federal prison, and then returned home to be reelected by his understanding constituents. In 1960, Democratic state representative Charles Iannello's Boston South End district reelected him by a 2–1 margin after he had been tried, convicted, and sentenced for a year to the house of correction on charges of larceny from the state by his family-owned firm.

The revelations of widespread public malfeasance began in 1958 when the Boston *Herald* uncovered a broad pattern of corruption in the rental of equipment by the state department of public works from private contractors. William F. Callahan, then chairman of the Massachusetts Turnpike Authority and a man who exercised vast power in the legislature and through job patronage, became a leading target of investigators and newspaper writers. Democrat Foster Furcolo, governor from 1957 to 1960, was eventually indicted on charges of conspiracy to arrange a bribe. The case was thrown out of court for lack of evidence, but several persons who had served in Furcolo's administration were convicted and went to jail. In 1960, following the income tax evasion conviction of a consulting engineer named Thomas Worcester, who agreed to tell what he knew in exchange for a lighter sentence, federal Judge Charles E. Wyzansky issued a report scoring what he called a "sordid racket of extortion, bribery, and corruption." He suggested that the same unsavory practices might have affected broad areas of the Massachusetts body politic.* The corruption issue was a key factor in the election of John A. Volpe as governor. Once elected, he proceeded to establish a state crime commission that eventually reported: "Corruption permeates the state, from town governments to the State House and involves politicians, businessmen, lawyers and ordinary citizens."

Today official corruption is less of a problem than it was in Massachusetts, but by no means expunged. Some people in Massachusetts claim that the corruption issue was blown up far beyond its true proportions; as state representative William Bulger of South Boston told me in reference to the crime commission and its $589,000 budget, "When you have a Manhattan Project, you have to explode the bomb." Some decent men found their public lives ruined just by being mentioned in the reports of the time, he says, and Callahan was even named in one indictment after he was dead. Nevertheless, public morals had declined so far in the late 1950s that ordinary citizens had to make political payoffs to get such minimal services from government as licenses to be hairdressers, electricians, or plumbers. I worked myself as a salesman for political printing in 1958, visiting many politicians in the state house in Boston, and the place reeked of corruption. Members of the governor's council sat at their desks between sessions bargaining over the telephone for jobs for favored constituents and mentioning suspicious cash sums. (Four former councilors were among those later indicted and convicted on charges of bribery, based on evidence the crime commission gathered.) This was the same era during which a bookie operation was found to be flourishing within the very corridors of the State House.

The crime commission findings have borne important fruit. While Republicans benefited most from them politically, it was Democratic Governor

---

* An apparent end to the whole bizarre era was reached in 1969 when FBI agents in Atlantic City arrested a six-year fugitive from justice, George L. Brady, ex-head of the Massachusetts Parking Authority and a man under indictment on charges of larceny in the disappearance of $784,480 in construction of an underground garage beneath Boston Common. According to an account by John Fenton in the New York *Times*, Brady had been trudging forlornly back to a dreary rooming house with a bundle of groceries when his captors accosted him. *Sic transit gloria.*

Endicott Peabody who capitalized on them to have the governor's council stripped of all its powers except approval of pardons and ratifying judicial appointments. At the same time, state officers were switched from the archaic two-year terms to four-year terms, starting in 1966. These proposals were approved by a referendum vote of the people in 1964 by a vote of 1,-133,624 "yes" to 589,219 "no" votes. Peabody later told ex-Governor Terry Sanford of North Carolina (as quoted in Sanford's *Storm Over the States*):

These amendments to the constitution have considerably overhauled the executive in Massachusetts and given him real authority to match his responsibility. I think that the outlook for the long run—in giving Massachusetts effective government, in restoring the confidence of the alienated voter, in eliminating corruption—is tremendous. Ten years from now constitutional reforms will be looked upon as doing more to clean up corruption in the state than 10 crime commissions put end to end.

The next logical step would be the total abolition of the governor's council. But, like that other dangerous anachronism, the electoral college feature of the federal Constitution, it seems to hang on, and on, and on.

Massachusetts has, however, just completed the first major overhaul of its executive branch in half a century. Ten cabinet-level departments have been created, each with its own secretary appointed by the governor and serving at his pleasure. They are absorbing 300 previously independent agencies of state government, 170 of which reported directly to the governor. The new structure will eliminate numerous examples of duplication and fragmentation. For instance, there were 21 separate agencies handling youth services, 30 dealing with environmental problems, and 17 responsible for aid to needy families. The reorganizational proposal was first put forward by Governor Volpe and brought to fruition under Governor Sargent. "We surprised even ourselves by being able to get it through the legislature," Sargent said. (Later, the legislators renewed their image of obstinacy by slowing down the funds needed to implement the new structure.) Sargent put his lieutenant governor, Donald Dwight, to work on a broad-scale talent hunt for candidates for the new cabinet secretary slots. Some of those finally named were top-drawer talent, including Prof. Alan Altshuler, an outstanding MIT political scientist, to be secretary of transportation and construction, and Mary B. Newman, one of the best state legislators of recent years, to be secretary for manpower affairs. (Among the other new cabinet-level departments are ones responsible for human services, consumer affairs, administration, and finance and environmental affairs.)

Change is coming a lot slower to the legislature, familiarly known by the bombastic name of the Great and General Court of Massachusetts. Big city ethnics and Yankee yeomen still combine to defeat the will of reform-minded governors who reflect a broader and more modern constituency. The house has 240 members, second only to the New Hampshire house (with 400 members) among all state legislative bodies. It has fought obdurately against the efforts of the strong, reform-minded Massachusetts League of Women Voters to cut its size down to 160. The League even went to the trouble of getting 150,000 signatures on an initiative proposal to force a vote of the people on the issue, but in the legislature, where only 70 votes were required to authorize a referendum vote, the leadership pressured some legislators to make last-moment switches against ballot authorization, and the proposal lost by a 191–69 negative vote in 1970. The League president, Mrs. Norma Jacobsen, called it a "naked abuse of power." The voters seemed to agree, toppling several of the anti-cut legislators in the ensuing elections. By 1971 the public pressure had built up so much that the legislature approved house reductions on its own accord; final ratification, however, is dependent on approval by still another legislature and then a vote of the people.

The legislative membership says a lot about Massachusetts life and politics. The Democratic leadership is all Irish-American; the Republican, Wasp. With its size, the membership reflects every age, color, profession, ethnic, and professional group imaginable, though there are some imbalances: only five women out of 280 house and senate members, but heavy numbers of lawyers, and, oddly enough, funeral directors. When I looked around the house floor one day in 1970, I saw five gaunt snowy-haired Irishmen who were spitting images of the then aged and ready-to-retire House Speaker, John W. McCormack. But the legislature is moving fast to incorporate youth. By 1971 it had a dozen legislators under 25, and 38 who were under 31 years of age. The state constitution sets no minimum age for officeholders, and perhaps the hoary old Commonwealth will be first with teenage legislators.

The General Court is characterized by an unusual constitutional right of free petition by all citizens, together with the custom of giving all the petitions a hearing before a legislative committee. But the "democracy" in the system tends to end there. Party discipline is strong, the speaker and senate president exert often heavy-handed leadership, and the public and even the press are barred from the crucial executive sessions of joint legislative committees where many of the gut decisions are made. There are so many bills (over 7,000 a session) that most legislators rubber-stamp committee recommendations. The legislature has some modern features, like annual unlimited sessions (which now tend to run most of the year until they are "prorogued"), and a legislative reference bureau of exceptional quality. But the Council on State Legislatures in 1971 gave it a rather mediocre rating of 29th in the U.S.A. in terms of its overall effectiveness. One drawback is terribly limited office space. As Representative Martin F. Linsky of Brookline wrote in 1969 (before his 1971 election as assistant Republican leader in the house):

Being a Republican, I have no legislative office. I am privileged to share a five-girl secretarial pool with my 239 colleagues, I answer my phone calls in one of a row of telephone booths lining one side of the House Lobby and discuss personal matters with constituents in a large waiting room which doubles as a corridor between the phones and the chamber. And so in an atmosphere of privacy comparable to Boston Common during the lunch hour, I discuss welfare checks, jobs, getting speakers recruited, retrieving suspended driving licenses [a favor much demanded of legislators], and conduct a bit of informal psychiatry. Such are the perquisites of power.

Now each legislator is guaranteed at least a desk and a place to park his briefcase, an achievement for which the youthful house speaker, David M. Bartley of Holyoke, takes some credit. Sometimes Bartley knocks heads in a manner some have likened to the late speaker John Thompson of Ludlow. But the resemblance stops there. Thompson was a big, burly personification of the Irish boss, a tough, partisan figure who never forgot to collect a political debt. He called himself a "delightful rogue," an apparent excuse for his heavy-drinking ways and wicked temper. (In 1963, Governor Peabody tried to purge Thompson—and failed.) But Bartley, by contrast, is extremely concerned about his own image and that of the entire General Court. He travels about the state giving speeches on how the legislature is being modernized —in rules, staff help, computerization, and office space—so that it can be one of the advanced ones in America. Bartley was also a guiding spirit behind channeling money from the legislative budget to print a three-color glossy brochure on the accomplishments of the legislature. And the record, in fact, is a remarkable one. Some examples:

- An "anti-snob" zoning law, passed in 1969, designed to break down suburban resistance to low-income housing, and a $515 million bond issue to encourage construction of low-income housing units.
- A 1970 "bill of rights" for the protection of consumers, a consumer protection unit-pricing law, and a generic drug law. Earlier, Massachusetts passed a truth-in-lending act that served as a basis for subsequent congressional legislation.
- An "environmental bill of rights," numerous antipollution laws, and a $300 million bond issue for environmental protection.
- The toughest campaign spending reporting law, after Florida and Kentucky, in the U.S.A.
- The 1970 Vietnam bill, which said Massachusetts inhabitants need not fight abroad unless Congress declared war, and instructed the state attorney general to file a complaint in the Supreme Court. (The court, by a 6–3 vote, refused to hear the case, but Massachusetts had made its symbolic point.)
- A pioneering public-school racial imbalance law, passed in 1965, which gives communities a 15 percent bonus in state school-construction aid if they place new schools in locations that will relieve or eliminate imbalanced classroom enrollments. (The law remains a major point of contention in the state. Its backers, like State Education Commissioner Neil V. Sullivan, claim it has been "very successful" in bringing hundreds of nonwhite students into predominantly white schools in Boston, Cambridge, Springfield, and New Bedford. But the number of blacks in Boston schools has risen from 25 percent in 1965 to 32 percent in 1971, and the number of city schools with a black majority from 46 to 63. Some of the imbalance law's opponents are blue-collar ethnics whose leaders claim it was imposed on their inner-city communities by suburban and rural legislators. Nor is it especially popular with some blacks, who are more interested in having more black teachers and principals and additional "black studies.")
- America's first "no fault" insurance law, passed in 1970 in an attempt to

cut down on Massachusetts' highest-in-the-nation auto insurance rates. The law applies only to bodily (not property) injury claims, but it was a major defeat for the trial lawyers. (In its first months of operation, the law resulted in an immense reduction of bodily injury claims and the prospect of lower premiums and an early extension to property claims.)

▪ What is claimed to be the strongest firearms control law in the nation.

▪ A 1970 mental health treatment and commitment reform act—an attempt to build on Massachusetts' reputation of having one of the best mental health treatment systems in the U. S. (Its penal system, however, lags far behind other states.)

All of this is not to suggest that Massachusetts has become a Utopia of progressive legislation. Many of the bills cited have serious defects. And the lobbies have not lost their teeth. As Martin Linsky observed in 1969:

> To the benefit of a thriving illegal abortion industry, moralists in the wrong area continue to keep unjust birth control laws on the books at the expense of the increasing number of out-of-wedlock and unwanted children who spend their youth in a foster home.* The road builders and their friends keep the Massachusetts highway fund inviolate long after the public demand for reallocation of resources in favor of mass transportation has been made clear. Interest groups like the cemetery owners, Elks, and Moose fight for state-granted tax advantages which put increasing burdens on the financial structure of the cities and towns. Occupational groups, from chiropractors to auto mechanics, seek "protection" which more often than not gives them an unearned and unfair advantage over both the public and others legitimately seeking to compete with them.

Even that account, however, fails to cover some of the big, powerful statewide lobbies like the Associated Industries of Massachusetts, which has succeeded—even in a heavily Democratic legislature—in bending tax legislation to the benefit of business. Organized labor is also a factor to be reckoned with, though its power is considered less now than in the early 1950s, when it was a potent force in elections and got a substantial amount of pro-labor legislation passed. The state's union heritage is more one of conservative craft unionism of the AFL variety than militant industrial unionism of the CIO type; in fact, Massachusetts lacks any mass union like the UAW or ILGWU. The leadership is heavily "ethnic," involving many of the same factions as the Democratic party.

For all its liberality, Massachusetts has a tax structure in distinct need of reform. About half of all governmental revenue, counting state and local government together, comes from the local property tax, which is at the second highest per capita level in the U.S.A. Yields are vastly disparate, depending on the wealth of individual communities, and the rates are close to confiscatory in Boston and some other cities.† Not until 1971 did Massa-

---

* Birth control has since been made legal but legalized abortion is probably light years away in Massachusetts. "We can pass the Vietnam bill but we can get only 30 votes for abortion," one state legislator told me.

† The typical tax on a house and lot with a sale value of $25,000 in American cities was $595 in 1969; in Boston the rate was $1,130, the highest of any city in America. The rate for suburban Waltham—$1,085—was second highest.

chusetts move toward some type of direct state subsidy for cities—based on a so-called "equalized municipal grants" system, designed by the ever active League of Women Voters. Massachusetts' per capita tax collections of state and local governments reached $453 in 1968–69, the fifth highest in the U. S. As a percentage of personal income, the ranking was only 14th among the states because Massachusetts per capita income—$4,360 in 1970—ranks a high ninth among the 50 states.

Per capita income has been growing faster than the East Coast average over the past decade, reflecting the basic economic strength of the state. The problem is that the heavily relied upon property tax fails to reflect that income growth adequately. The state government does impose an income tax, but Massachusetts voters have twice refused in public referenda to make it a progressive income tax. There are exemptions which allow low-income voters to avoid most of the income tax, but the wealthy escape fairly lightly. Thus the heaviest burden falls on middle-income taxpayers, the same group which is hit most heavily by the property tax and quite heavily by the sales tax. The middle-income, ethnic Democrats so thoroughly in control of the legislature should be ashamed not to have done better for their own people.

The Massachusetts state budget has literally quadrupled since 1960, to $1.9 billion for fiscal 1972. The increase reflects higher costs for all phases of government, but especially education and welfare. The education increases were long overdue, but even with major increases during the 1960s, Massachusetts still ranked only 50th among the 50 states in per capita state government expenditures for all education in 1969. The Massachusetts state government in 1969 became the first in the Union to assume the full burden of welfare costs in the state, a vital point of relief for the sorely pressed municipalities which had borne much of the burden before then. But the lawmakers did not anticipate the fantastic increase in welfare benefits which would follow as more eligible people applied and recession-time unemployment hit the state. By early 1971, one out of every five persons in Boston (21.2 percent) was receiving some type of welfare, compared to 9.6 percent in 1966. Over $800 million—43 percent of the entire 1972 state budget—had to be set aside for welfare.

While the tax and welfare issues in Massachusetts have been getting the headlines, some believe that another issue—reform of the civil service system —ought to be next on the Commonwealth's agenda. The problem is that so many state and local jobs are frozen into protected civil service status that governors and mayors and their department heads lack flexibility to bring in their own people at the top, especially at the appropriate level for "bright young men." A self-perpetuating bureaucracy, Robert Wood told me, captures effective control of government. "It doesn't protect you from patronage abuses and at the same time it doesn't allow you the techniques of modern management." He adds:

In most state and local governments, we've been living off the capital of the people who came in the '30s. Now they're dying and retiring. Many of my students want to go abroad or to Washington. But my mind runneth not back to one who wanted to be water works commissioner of Boston. It's getting that kind of ability that's key.

In Massachusetts, the problem is all the more severe because—all "progressive" legislation notwithstanding—government is rife with excess jobs and incompetent people at the lower rungs. There is a kind of hangover of the ethnic era, in which government service is doled out to cronies or acquaintances on a preferential basis.

A Leadership Roundup

The names of some Massachusetts politicians, especially those named Kennedy, have been household words in America for more than a decade now. The name of Edward Brooke strikes a bell with Americans because he is the first Negro Senator of this century—though there is a lot more to Ed Brooke than that. The names of John Volpe, President Nixon's Secretary of Transportation, and Elliot Richardson, first Undersecretary of State and then Secretary of Health, Education and Welfare, have become increasingly familiar to the country. Volpe is an ex-contractor and onetime Federal Highway Administrator who surprised everyone in his Cabinet post by moving to curb indiscriminate freeway construction and foster mass transportation. Richardson, a former lieutenant governor and attorney general of Massachusetts, turned out to be one of the most competently cool and farsighted administrators of the entire Nixon Administration.

Massachusetts in recent decades has contributed two prominent leaders of the U. S. House of Representatives—John W. McCormack, who was Speaker from 1962 through 1970, and Joseph W. Martin, Jr., Speaker during the Republican 80th Congress (1947–48) and his party's spokesman as minority leader for many years. Both were able, honorable men, and in their prime skillful negotiators in the personalized world of the U. S. House. But neither will long be remembered for any substantive contribution to American government. Both lingered too long in public life—McCormack as Speaker into his 79th year of life, when the intellectual tides of national life had long since passed him by, Martin as a House member until he was 82, though he had been deposed as minority leader eight years previously.

There is little one can add now to the familiar record of John F. Kennedy, the President who enunciated so many goals but had a chance to implement so few. As a Senator for Massachusetts, his record was passing but not brilliant; before he had had a chance to build seniority, in fact, his sights were set on the Presidency. Kennedy's initial election to the Senate, in 1952, had the byproduct of retiring from elective office the Republicans' great white hope of the first postwar years and the Eisenhower preconvention campaign manager of that year, Henry Cabot Lodge, Jr., grandson and namesake of the famous Massachusetts Senator who had led the successful fight to prevent U. S. entrance into the League of Nations. The defeat did not end Lodge's career; he went on to be U. S. Ambassador to the United Nations, Richard Nixon's Vice Presidential running mate in 1960, Ambassador to Vietnam and Germany and U. S. negotiator at the Vietnam peace talks in Paris. Finally (in one of those superb ironies of history), President Nixon made Lodge his personal envoy to—the Vatican. The present-day vogue is to see Lodge as an outmoded Cold Warrior, and politicians belittle his 1960 campaign on the Nixon ticket. Lodge was an early and strong advocate of the liberal brand of Republicanism which has since triumphed in Massachusetts, however, and certainly an unselfish public servant.

Senator Edward M. Kennedy, youngest of the three famous Kennedy brothers, is by most standards a conscientious and able Senator, a stalwart liberal who has grown immensely in his grasp of national issues. It is easy to forget now that in 1962, when he first ran for the Senate at 30 years of age, his candidacy was seen by many as crude capitalizing on the family name by a very inexperienced young man. But he easily defeated his Democratic opponent of that year, Edward J. McCormack, nephew of the Speaker, and won the general election with a smashing 71.8 percent of the vote. Then came the years of tragedy: his brother John's assassination in 1963, his brother Robert's assassination in 1968, and the death of his auto companion and pretty secretary, Mary Jo Kopechne, at the bridge at Chappaquiddick Island in 1969. Before the latter incident, Kennedy had been the all-but-certain next Presidential candidate of his party; after it, he won a second Senate term in 1970 by 58.8 percent—13 percent less than six years before.* The effects of the triple tragedies on Kennedy himself pose troubling questions, for they may have produced a shell-shocked man, too fearful of his own safety; on the other hand, they may have made Kennedy a man of depth and compassion extraordinary in national leadership.

The Kennedy saga often recalls the extraordinary statement of John Kennedy, when he was a Senator in the 1960s—words that once sounded so arrogant, and now so strangely prophetic: "Just as I went into politics because Joe [the oldest brother] died, if anything happened to me tomorrow Bobby would run for my seat in the Senate. And if Bobby died our younger brother Ted would take over from him."

Edward Brooke is a calm, articulate legislator, carrying on in the liberal Republican tradition of Massachusetts, a clear reflector of thought in his state. The son of a bourgeois Negro family and a successful lawyer, he built his home-state reputation fighting corruption, first as chairman of the Boston Finance Commission (1961–63) and then as attorney general of the state (1963–66). President Nixon twice offered him a Cabinet position, which he declined; while his stands on the Vietnam war and social issues were well to the left of the President's, Brooke took care to keep the lines of communication open to the President and his party. "I do not intend to be a national leader of the Negro people. I intend to do my job as a Senator from Massachusetts," Brooke said in 1966, the year he ran for the Senate. He has kept

---

* The following January, Kennedy was deposed from the position of Senate Whip he had won just two years before.

that promise, but national black leaders nonetheless consider him an effective agent for their cause. A leader of the Black Caucus of Negroes in the House told me that "too many blacks stay hung up on the race issue, which is one reason we don't win more elections in districts without black majorities. This is the reason we don't put pressure on Brooke. He needs a Black Caucus like a hole in the head."

The man Brooke succeeded, veteran Senator Leverett Saltonstall, was a perfect model of Yankee probity and moderation. Saltonstall had been an able wartime governor of his state but never made a strong mark on the Washington scene. He did do a superb job of representing special Massachusetts interests, like fishing, electronics, and the military. Brooke's effort is not comparable on that score, nor does Ted Kennedy's staff—despite the campaign slogan of doing "more for Massachusetts"—take the initiative on state issues. That role has now switched to the House side.

The House delegation lacks a depth in quality, perhaps because its members are generally isolated from the political stepping-stone process of the state. Some members, however, have made a mark for themselves. Thomas P. O'Neill, Jr., a former Massachusetts house speaker and big, hulking legislator from the Boston area, surprised everyone when he suddenly rejected the Johnson Vietnam war policies in 1967 and became an avowed dove. His big Cambridge and Brookline constituencies, and pressures from his own teenaged children, had something to do with the decision. In a 1971 compromise choice acceptable to both Speaker Carl Albert and Democratic Majority Leader Hale Boggs, O'Neill was appointed whip of the House Democrats. Edward Boland of the Springfield area, a former House spokesman for the Kennedys, is on the Appropriations Committee. Representatives James A. Burke and Torbert Macdonald have advanced to very high positions on the Ways and Means and Interstate Commerce Committees respectively, and could be chairmen in a few years. Macdonald, whose first claim to fame was that he roomed with Jack Kennedy at college, compiled one of the worst attendance records in the House but has recently made a more substantive mark chairing a subcommittee on communications and energy resources.

Among the four Republicans on the 12-man delegation, the most articulate are Silvio O. Conte, who represents the western end of the state, and F. Bradford Morse from Lowell. Both are liberals with broad appeal beyond their own party; Conte, on at least one occasion, got the Democratic nomination on write-ins. Conte is a member of the Appropriations Committee, a scrappy fighter against big farm subsidies, foreign weapons sales, and federal oil import restrictions harmful to New England's economic interests. Every four years he shows up at the Republican national conventions to fight for a more liberal platform. Morse is active in the Wednesday Club of liberal Republican legislators, a member of the Foreign Affairs Committee, and an author of an "Amendment to End the War" in Vietnam. He shocked some of his liberal friends by endorsing Nixon early in 1968, but was not rewarded with an important government job or other favors.

Economy: From Mill Town to Route 128

*In the nineteenth century, saws and axes made in New England
cleared the forests of Ohio; New England ploughs broke the prairie sod;
New England scales weighed wheat and meat in Texas; New England
serge clothed businessmen in San Francisco; New England cutlery skinned
hides to be tanned in Milwaukee and sliced apples to be dried in Missouri; New England whale oil lit lamps across the continent; New England
blankets warmed children by night and New England textbooks preached
at them by day; New England guns armed the troops; and New England
dies, lathes, looms, forges, presses and screwdrivers outfitted factories far
and wide. But by the twentieth century, New England plants were closing
up and laying off workers. To most New Englanders the cause of the region's economic decline seemed obvious—loss of industry. They brooded
upon reasons for this loss: cheaper labor in the South, obsolescence of the
old brick factories along the rivers and beside the waterfalls, the decay of
Boston's docks, imports from Switzerland and Japan.*

—*Jane Jacobs, in* The Economy of Cities

The solutions to the economic ills of New England had to wait until
the years following World War II. Wisely, the region did not put its stock
in reviving its eclipsed industries. Massachusetts' textile employment, for instance, continued to decline precipitously—from 122,000 right after the war
to 27,000 in 1971. In the same period, the job rolls for shoes and other
leather products dropped from 74,000 to 32,000. Much of the old Massachusetts wealth, built up in the days of the China trade and textile-mill ventures along the rivers, remained tied up in restrictive "Boston trusts" that
limited heirs' ability to do much constructive with their fortunes.

But a solution was found, in utilizing the university-based scientific brain
power which was almost unique to Massachusetts in the nation. An early
pioneer was Ralph Flanders, who later became U. S. Senator from Vermont.
In 1946, Flanders persuaded a few Boston capitalists to experiment with a
new firm called American Research and Development, which was founded to
invest in (but not control) promising new enterprises. The initial customer
was Tracerlab, the first of Boston's postwar science-based industries. Tracerlab
was the creation of three young Harvard scientists, working out of a decrepit
old building in downtown Boston. They bought radioactive isotopes from
Oak Ridge, Tennessee, and packaged them for the numerous hospitals and
medical centers of Boston for use in diagnostic and treatment work. Boston
banks turned down Tracerlab's request for capital to grow to meet its market,
but American R & D quickly moved in with a $150,000 expansion loan that
put Tracerlab on the road to prosperity.

In the years that followed, hundreds of electronics and highly technical
research and development companies sprang up in Cambridge, drawing on the
scientific talents at Cambridge and MIT. In the early 1950s, a new circum-

ferential expressway—Route 128—was built to divert through traffic from Boston's streets. Critics said the road was an unnecessary extravagance and criticized the governor of the time, Paul Dever, for building it. They could not have been more wrong. Route 128 in a few years had become a foremost world center of space-missiles-electronics technology. It grew to have 30 industrial parks and over 700 firms.* The Air Force, which is the nation's largest purchaser of electronic equipment, placed its Electronics Systems Division at Hanscom Field in Bedford, near 128, and the Air Force's Cambridge Research Lab, Lincoln Lab, and MITRE Corporation, plus the Draper Lab at MIT, were all within easy reach. NASA's Electronic Research Center also went to Cambridge—some said as an act of political favoritism by President Kennedy to his brother, Senator Edward M. Kennedy, who had promised in his 1962 campaign to do "more for Massachusetts." By the late 1960s, nearly 50,000 professional engineers and scientists worked in the Cambridge– 128 area. Fed by military contracts (in which Massachusetts ranked seventh in the country) and the outpouring of funds for research in connection with the moon-landing program, eastern Massachusetts was enjoying the greatest economic boom of its history.

Then, in 1969, recession struck. The reasons were the same as for the great letdown that began at the same moment in California: NASA cutbacks with completion of research and equipment manufacture for the Apollo missions, and a rapid reduction in Defense Department orders. In Massachusetts, there was not the accompanying blow from cutbacks in air frame construction, but the state may have been harmed by what some saw as a deliberate Nixon administration policy of punishing Massachusetts Senators Kennedy and Edward M. Brooke for their lack of support on the ABM, Supreme Court nominations, and other key issues in Congress. Just before Christmas 1969, NASA announced closing of the Electronic Research Center at Cambridge that had been the political *cause célèbre* of the early 1960s.† In a year and a half, no less than 10,000 of the scientists and engineers in the Cambridge–128 area lost their jobs. By spring 1971, total Massachusetts employment in electrical equipment and supplies manufacture, which had peaked at 103,000 in 1967, was down to 80,800. Virtually every company in the electronics field laid off workers; some closed down entire branches; several small firms went bankrupt. Unemployment in Massachusetts soared to 8 percent, a 20-year high and 1.5 percentage points ahead of the level for the country as a whole.

But even while many engineers found themselves pressed into emergency work situations as auto mechanics or taxi drivers—a nasty blow to the pride and standard of living of many $15,000-a-year and over men—some firms survived the storm quite well. Foremost among these was the giant of New England electronics, the Raytheon Company. Founded in 1922 as a radio

* Some of the principal electronics and related scientific firms of the 128–Cambridge complex are RCA, Avco, Minneapolis-Honeywell, Raytheon, Polaroid, General Electric, Geodyne, Textronic, Thermo Electron. Actronics, Litton, Adcole, General Radio, Xerox, and Sylvania.
† ERC subsequently got a second life as Transportation Systems Center for the Department of Transportation—headed by former Massachusetts Governor Volpe.

tube manufacturer in Newton, Raytheon began its great era of prosperity in World War II when it cooperated with MIT to develop microwave tubes to be used to power radar systems. For 16 years, up to 1964, Raytheon was headed by Charles Adams, a great-great-great grandson of John Quincy Adams. He steered the firm ever deeper into defense work and toward its contracts of recent years to develop the Hawk and Sparrow missiles, the sonar system for Navy submarines, the SAM-D and Sidewinder missiles, and a subcontract for ground-based radar for the Safeguard system. But then Thomas S. Phillips, a Boston-born design engineer who joined Raytheon in 1958, became its president and proceeded to turn the company toward acquisition of marketing-oriented commercial firms like Amana Refrigeration, the textbook publishing firm of D. C. Heath, and Caloric Corporation, which makes dishwashers and kitchen equipment. Thus in 1970, even though it had to lay off 8,000 men, or 15 percent of its 55,000-man work force, Raytheon showed profits just short of its 1969 showing of $35 million.

Even as Massachusetts headed into the grim trough of recession in 1970, the Cambridge-based research firm of Arthur D. Little, Inc., predicted that development of three new industries could guarantee "a very bright future" for the state's economy. If the projections come true, Massachusetts might achieve the conversion to nonmilitary and nonspace projects which has been so elusive for aerospace and electronics companies. The three recommended industries for expansion were computer peripheral, biomedical, and pollution control. About a third of the nation's computer peripheral employment, centered in 100 firms, was already in Massachusetts, and the report suggested that with "a concerted effort" to lure International Business Machines (IBM) from New York, complementing the RCA and Honeywell-General Electric operations already there, Massachusetts "would become the world leader of the computer industry." In the biomedic instrumentation industry, the report suggested establishing a fully computerized diagnostic medical examination center and initiating vocation training courses in biomedical instrumentation at Massachusetts universities and community colleges. In pollution control, it was suggested that the state adopt strict pollution controls for its own area, support pollution control research, and press for location in the state of the National Environmental Research Institute.

Whether these wishes (and a 34,000-job addition by 1975) come true, it seems inevitable Massachusetts will remain a national leader in electronics —if for no other reason, because of its already-built facilities and the continuing input from the universities. (Massachusetts' relatively high labor costs could retard it, however, in a race with states like Texas for new scientific industries.) Massachusetts has already become, as Edgar Litt wrote in 1965, part "of a post-industrial society that emphasizes technical, clerical, and professional skills to man the burgeoning scientific, defense, educational, and administrative institutions."

And to its scientific skills, Massachusetts in modern times has added amazing entrepreneurial talents. The outstanding example of this is Dr. Edwin Land, inventor of the Polaroid camera. As founder, chief executive officer, and director of research of the Polaroid Corporation, Land has seen its assets rise past the half-billion dollar mark with annual sales over $400 million. The secret has not just been the ever improving technology of his cameras that develop their own pictures, but brilliant merchandising—like the $19.95 black and white "Swinger" camera, of which more than five million were sold within two years of their introduction on the market in 1965, and equally successful subsequent low-priced color models. Land also has more than 100 inventions in the field of optics to his name, and developed cameras (like those used in the U-2 espionage plane) that can capture ground detail from 70,000 feet altitude. He lives in a modest Cambridge home. As Frederick Lund noted in *The Rich And The Super-Rich*, "Like Pasteur, Edison and other creators, he lives mainly in order to work." He is also an advanced social thinker, anxious to find ways of humanizing machine society and solving the "problem of mass boredom and mental stagnation" in American life.

The soft underbelly of the Massachusetts economy is the long, depressing decline of its once mighty textile and shoe industries. The greatest exodus of textile companies came between the world wars, but textiles and shoes continue to decline, imperiled both by low-wage Southern plants and severe foreign competition. Just in 10 months of 1970, for instance, 14 New England shoe companies went out of business—seven in Massachusetts, four in New Hampshire, and three in Maine. By spring 1971, the downturn in these once great industries created some of the worst unemployment rates in America in certain Massachusetts cities—12.1 percent in New Bedford, 11.8 percent in Lowell, 8.8 percent in Springfield-Holyoke, 8.9 percent in Lawrence-Haverhill. By contrast, the Boston area's unemployment figure of 6 percent was even with or less than the national figure.

Like the miners of Appalachia, textile and shoe workers often have no realistic career alternatives. The Boston *Globe* reported the story of Mrs. Mary Scott, one of 300 workers to lose a job when the Bori Shoe Co. folded in Lynn in 1969. A 64-year-old widow, she had spent 12 years doing fancy stitching on women's shoes and was earning $77 a week when the plant closed. Running to the end of her period of unemployment compensation, Mrs. Scott despaired of finding work anywhere. She lived frugally, rarely venturing from her $18.50-a-week apartment. Some Social Security and old age as a ward of the state were all that seemed to await her.

For the engineers and scientists laid off work, the long-term outlook—no matter how dim the immediate prospects—is incredibly brighter. In fact, Massachusetts developers are so confident of the future that a firm like Cabot, Cabot & Forbes, one of the chief investors of Route 128 development, is busy with similar projects on Interstate Route 495, which roughly parallels 128 about 20 miles farther out. A spokesman for the Cabot firm said in 1970: "There are no more that 1.5 million square feet of vacant space on 128. If a company needs a large space, it will have to move elsewhere."

Other notes on the Massachusetts economy:

■   Important income is earned from out-of-state visitors—businessmen and tourists—who number about 8.5 million (one and a half times the resident population) and bring $1.25 billion into the state each year. One major tourist attraction to be added in the 1970s will be the John F. Kennedy Presidential Library at Cambridge, for which $20 million was raised shortly after the late President's death. The long-delayed structure, on the banks of the Charles River, will include both a central library-museum building and quarters for the John F. Kennedy School of Government and the Kennedy Institute.

■   Overall value added by manufacturing is $8.3 billion, putting Massachusetts 10th among the states, precisely where it stands on the population scale too. Some major industries, in addition to those already mentioned, are machinery, apparel (which has not declined like textile manufacture), printing and publishing, and rubber and plastic products.

■   Agricultural produce brings in a rather insignificant $170 million a year, 42nd in rank among the states. But Massachusetts does grow about half the cranberry crop of the entire world, and has small but thriving dairy, tobacco, fruit, and maple syrup industries.

■   Boston remains one of the great medical centers of the Western world, with institutions like the Harvard Medical School, Peter Bent Brigham Hospital, Boston City Hospital, and the Children's Hospital Medical Center. The struggle to modernize and meet rising budgets is a whole story in itself, especially acute in a municipal hospital that has become a famous national institution, like Boston City Hospital.

■   The port of Boston, its illustrious history notwithstanding, has limped from crisis to crisis in recent times and many of its dock facilities are in disrepair or disuse. Logan International Airport, by contrast, is the eighth busiest in the world and is rapidly increasing its position as an embarkation point for transatlantic passengers from the northeastern U. S. and the Midwest. The airport's physical expansion and noise pollution have blighted life in the heavily Italian North End of Boston; on the other hand, it is the transportation nexus that has helped to make Boston-Cambridge-128 an intellectual and economic national and world force. From Logan's easily reached runways, the area's academicians, scientists, businessmen, and government experts commute easily to Washington, New York, other U. S. cities, and abroad.

■   "The Massachusetts fishing industry," according to Frank Donovan of the Boston *Globe*, "is like a ship without a rudder, bobbing aimlessly on a stormy sea and in danger of sinking." In fact, the New England fishing fleet is in such poor condition that 119 vessels have been lost at sea in the past decade. Problems include foreign competition, especially in frozen fish; incursion of Russian and Canadian ships on the Georges Bank, which has contributed to overfishing that has dangerously depleted the stocks of haddock; trawling by Russian ships that cuts the lines laid by New England lobstermen; and the fragmented condition of the industry, which leaves each fisherman in competition with his neighbors and foreign fleets. The big ports are New Bedford, Gloucester, and Boston, with New Bedford the clear leader. But despite recent addition of some modern trawlers with huge nets, the total catch is valued at only $40 million a year. In an ironic twist, many jobs and substantial income for an historic old fishing town like Gloucester are provided by reprocessing of ground fish shipped to the city in 50-pound frozen blocks—from the very foreign fishing fleets that have put so many Gloucester fishermen out of work.

Collegia Massachusettensis

Massachusetts has education resources rivaled only by California's. It has 117 institutions of higher learning, including 15 which grant Ph.D. or equivalent degrees. Massachusetts attracts more students from out of state —80,000 at last count—than any other state.

Harvard and MIT stand at the apex of the pyramid. As Ford Foundation president McGeorge Bundy told me: "You can't get away from the Cambridge complex. There's no doubt that just for sheer first-class intellectual manpower, it's the most powerful single nexus in the country." Bundy's remarks have a lot more behind them than the sentimentality of an Ivy Leaguer. A survey appearing in *Science* magazine indicated that of the 41 major advances in the social sciences made in America between 1930 and 1965, nine occurred in Cambridge, compared to only five each in New York and Washington, the two runner-up cities. The electronics-technology boom of Route 128–Cambridge industries would have been inconceivable without the concentration of scientific talent at MIT and Harvard.

Concomitant with this has been the shift in the role of the intellectual in Massachusetts politics. The traditional town-gown antagonisms, part of an anti-intellectualism that was next to anti-British sentiment, were overcome by John F. Kennedy. His brain trust of 50 to 60 Cambridge academicians working on national problems has been copied within Massachusetts, with each major politician of subsequent years gathering his own brain trust of bright men and women. Massachusetts intellectuals have been active both in campaigns and in program policy development, a fruitful new relationship in the state's development that has been only partially disturbed by new tensions arising from the era of campus revolts.

First, a view of the major Boston area universities:

▪ Harvard (15,198 students in 1970). Many people view this oldest of all American universities as also the greatest, even if recent studies of the American Council on Education have given it slightly lower marks in its graduate department quality than its only serious competitor, the University of California at Berkeley. Harvard faculties were rated ahead of all others in the U. S. in classics, music, sociology, biochemistry, zoology, geology, and mathematics, and scored in the top rankings in almost every other discipline (engineering excepted). The university's law, medical, and business schools continue foremost in their fields, and now turn out a high complement of very socially conscious graduates. Listing the Harvard faculty who have achieved international reputations or contributed importantly to American government would take pages.

The postwar era has been one of rapid change for Harvard. Its student body has shifted from a preponderance of private prep school graduates to a broad cross-section of the U. S. A. Through association with Radcliffe College, the university has become fundamentally coeducational. While campuses of other prestige universities like Berkeley and Columbia exploded in the mid-1960s, Harvard remained calm; then came 1969, the occupation by radicals of University Hall, the early morning raid by 400 policemen, the subsequent shocked reaction by faculty and students, and a student strike. The next year featured a Weathermen's raid on the Center for International Studies and a tenants' protest that marred the Commencement. Leaving the Kennedy Institute of Politics after a year's sojourn in 1969–70, newsman David Broder described Harvard as "a place trembling with both promise and peril." He noted a politicization and intellectual line-hardening in the conflict-ridden milieu, but also beginnings of long overdue structural reform as faculty and students joined in a discussion of the future.

Harvard has had three postwar presidents, each in a way symbolic of his times. James B. Conant has been described by Harold Taylor, a reviewer of Conant's memoirs, *My Several Lives,* as "the first of the new breed of scientist-administrators produced by the Second World War, . . . a liberal-minded conservative, . . . a supporter, in some ways a leader, in cold-war doctrine" but also "one of the first to urge a liberal and long range policy for the control of atomic energy." His view of education was conservative, rooted in the European ideal of the university as "a collection of eminent scholars." Conant was succeeded in 1953 by Nathan M. Pusey, a former president of Lawrence College, who increased student enrollment by a third and doubled the faculty to 6,000, vigorously defended Harvard against the attacks of Senator Joseph McCarthy of Wisconsin, proved a phenomenally successful fund raiser, and succeeded in keeping Harvard from becoming too financially dependent on the federal government. But he proved aloof and ineffective in dealing with the student uprising of 1969 and took early retirement in 1971. Derek Bok, who succeeded Pusey, is a Stanford graduate who joined the Harvard faculty in 1958, built an innovative record as dean of its law school, but was only 40 years old when he became president—an outgoing, approachable man popular with both students and faculty, perhaps the right man to heal Harvard's internal divisions and confirm its historic position as the moral leader of higher education in America.

Bok will have his work cut out for him, not only on the human but on the financial front. As the Carnegie Commission on Higher Education reported in 1971:

[Harvard's] costs are increasingly relentless. During the 1960s operating costs rose at the average of $12 million a year, due much to inflation. Federal support is declining. Arts and Sciences is operating at a deficit. Cutbacks have severely weakened the School of Education, School of Design, and Divinity School. Other parts of the university—Public Health, Medical School, the Division of Engineering and Applied Physics, and several other departments—are being threatened. Federal fellowship and traineeship cutbacks are serious. Much more student aid will be needed. Computer and library costs are rising rapidly. Student and faculty aspirations are increasing, and unless the funding situation changes, they cannot be met.

■ Massachusetts Institute of Technology (8,024 students). In engineering, MIT remains preeminent in America. Its physical sciences departments are also outstanding; its economics department is rated best in the nation by the American Council on Education and is headed by Paul A. Samuelson, recipient of the 1970 Nobel Prize for his efforts to "raise the level of scientific analysis in economic theory." James R. Killian, who became the first White House science advisor, under President Eisenhower, was the primary figure in building MIT to its position of excellence in the postwar years, although the widening of its role from the physical sciences to humanities, creating a true university, had begun under his predecessor, Karl T. Compton. MIT has made distinct national contributions in a multitude of fields, including time-shared computers, automated libraries, and an imaginative program in secondary school physics instruction. Institute scientists have been at the forefront of science political activism, including the fight against the ABM.

One of MIT's excruciating problems of the past few years has been what to do about the vast amount of war-related research performed within its academic confines. For years, the Institute has received more Defense Department research funds than any other university in America. Most recently, some $50 million in U. S. research money has flowed to the MIT campus, where no classified work is done, and a total of $120 million to two defense-related research centers—the 20-year-old Lincoln Laboratory at nearby Lexington, which was first set up to develop U. S. continental air defense systems, and the Draper Laboratory in Cambridge, which has specialized in guidance for the Apollo lunar flights and the Poseidon multiple-warhead missile. In the face of strong protest by many students and radical faculty alike, MIT in 1970 began to cut its ties with Draper.

Another MIT problem is the neglect of undergraduates and even some graduate students by faculty perennially out of town on various types of outside consulting contracts. The Institute did avoid some of the worst student confrontations by the off-and-on-again retreats of president Howard Johnson in 1969. In 1971, Johnson was succeeded by Jerome B. Wiesner, former science adviser to President Kennedy who helped achieve Senate ratification of the 1963 nuclear test ban treaty and in 1969 was one of the leaders of a national campaign against the antiballistic missile.

■ Boston University (23,826 students). BU is the nation's fourth largest private univeristy but has one of the smallest endowments ($14 million compared to Harvard's $1 billion-plus).* It has a dynamic and controversial new president who seems likely either to make it into a distinguished university or lead it to disaster—John R. Silber, former dean of the college of

---

* Boston is also home of *the* largest private university in the world, Northeastern, with 42,149 students in 1970–71.

arts and sciences at the University of Texas. Silber took the job on the condition he would have a free hand to go out and hire dozens of outstanding teaching professors and actually speculate with BU's unrestricted $12 million endowment in the hope it might generate at least $5 million a year. Then he suggested the city or state governments should provide financial support for BU—a proposal promptly termed "absolutely outrageous" by an aide to the mayor. With Silber in town, the scenario is bound to remain lively.

▪   Boston College (10,214 students). This Jesuit institution, situated in Chestnut Hill to the west of Boston proper, is remarkable for its diverse and intensive efforts to improve the Boston community. Its citizen seminar program, begun in 1954 by the Rev. W. Seavy Joyce, S.J., then dean of business administration and now president of BC, was perhaps *the* most crucial single element in bringing together the differing religious, ethnic, political, and racial groups of Boston who simply were not talking with each other at that time. Joyce used the issue of ecomomic revival to get the Yankee businessmen and Irish businessmen communicating, and the citizen seminars have continued ever since, covering a myriad of problems that face the Boston area. As institutions, it is worth noting, neither Harvard nor MIT has become as substantively involved in their communities as BC. The main focus of the Joint MIT-Harvard Center for Urban Studies, for instance, was on federal-level projects and research into faraway cities (until a reversal of that policy was announced in 1971).

An example of BC's continuing deep involvement in state issues is the leadership role which the director of its bureau of public affairs, Robert J. N. O'Hare, has taken in investigation of possible routes to regional or metropolitan-wide government in Massachusetts. In 1971, he suggested abolishing the existing counties of the state, which tend to be perpetually short of funds and lacking in effective powers, and replacing them with seven new regions, each with its own popularly elected government having broad powers in areas such as water supply, sewage, and solid waste disposal, law enforcement, conservation and open space, mass transit, health services and public education.

▪   Brandeis University (2,171 students). This Jewish-sponsored but officially nonsectarian institution has been characterized by *Newsweek* as "a veritable *wunderkind*" among American colleges. Founded in 1948 on a tree-shaded campus in suburban Waltham, it received a Phi Beta Kappa chapter more rapidly than any other university in the past century and is widely respected for its academic excellence. But it has become, and remains, one of the most radical and agitated colleges in America. It was early in accepting substantial numbers of deprived black and white students, many of whom were party to a series of sometimes violent demonstrations that began early in 1969 and have shown few signs of abating. The scene has been marked by seizure of buildings, vandalism, disruption of classes, and intimidation of students and professors. In 1970 two students and a recent graduate were accused of perpetrating a bank robbery in Brighton and another in

Philadelphia; two of them disappeared and were placed on the FBI's "most wanted list." Whether justified or not, that incident and the names of some of Brandeis' graduates—Abbie Hoffman (class of 1958) and Angela Davis (class of 1965)—created the image of Brandeis as a seat of the worst kind of uncontrolled radicalism. Most of its students and faculty deny that is the case, but there are many faculty members with grave reservations about the university's course. They include John P. Roche, a professor of international relations and White House aide in the Johnson administration.

The Boston area picture is rounded out by Tufts University (4,810 students), known chiefly for its Fletcher School of Law and Diplomacy. Tufts also takes pride these days in an improved engineering school, headed by Dean Ernest Klema of atomic bomb discovery fame. Wellesley College (1,750 students) is a good quality women's residential college but is outshone by Radcliffe.

▪ Western Massachusetts has a set of distinguished small colleges where the emphasis is strictly on good teaching—Williams (1,260 students), Mount Holyoke (1,744), Amherst (1,212), and Smith (2,491). The ideal was summed up by President James Garfield, talking about Williams: "The ideal college is Mark Hopkins on one end of a log and a student on the other." All attract exceptionally well qualified students and have in small, unpublicized ways been drawing abreast of or even moving ahead of the times. Williams, for instance, was once a strong fraternity college, but the students lost interest in them and in effect disestablished the fraternities in the early 1960s. (And now Williams, like many others, is going coed.) Williams also instituted the first college-level environmental studies program in the mid-1960s. Mount Holyoke developed a strong women's rights orientation decades before the term "women's liberation" was invented, and has long had strong woman presidents. One of its political science faculty members, Victoria Schuck, exemplifies the combination of exceptional teaching skills, sound scholarship, and political activism. Williams' James MacGregor Burns, author of distinguished historical and political science works, is perhaps the best known academician of the western colleges.

A "four-college" plan, allowing students to interchange institutions in the courses they take, was begun a few years ago by the four colleges in close proximity in the rolling Connecticut River Valley—Amherst, Smith, Mount Holyoke, and the main campus of the University of Massachusetts at Amherst. In 1958 these four also conceived the idea of a completely unstructured college for gifted and highly motivated students. Called Hampshire College, it opened its doors in 1970 with 268 charter students. At Hampshire, faculty and students are intended to shape the curriculum together. Even though no faculty tenure will be granted, there were more than 1,000 applications for the first 50 faculty positions.

The University of Massachusetts was long the proverbial stepchild of higher education in Massachusetts, dedicated mainly to agriculture and completely overshadowed by the great private institutions. But in 1960, Dr. John W. Lederle was brought in from Michigan and began the difficult process of transforming UM into a university in the tradition of the great public institutions of the Midwest and West. The main campus at Amherst was expanded to an enrollment of 18,000 by 1970, and projected for an eventual 70,000 figure. It is intended to be detached, residential, academic, and excellent. A medical school was planned for Worcester, to evolve around the idea of providing instruction in total health service delivery. And in 1971, construction was begun on a $355 million Boston campus of UM, to be located at a former city dump point in Dorchester, 2.5 miles from center city. (It is the largest construction project ever undertaken in Massachusetts.) UM Boston will be a thoroughly urban-oriented institution—its business school working on local economic development, for instance, and its teachers involved with the big city schools. Eventually it will have 5,000 students.

Lederle resigned in 1970, to be succeeded as UM president by Robert C. Wood, a man we have quoted earlier in this chapter. Wood was director of the Joint Center for Urban Studies of MIT-Harvard, former board chairman of the Massachusetts Bay Transportation Authority, and had been under secretary of the federal Department of Housing and Urban Development in its development years—one of Massachusetts' outstanding scholar-administrators.

Massachusetts has 11 state colleges and the expanding network of community colleges, some of which are of exceptional quality. The state is considered a national leader in the field of vocational education. It was a pioneer in the development of public schools in America and recently has ranked fourth among the 50 states in its annual per capita expenditures for elementary and secondary school students. Appropriately with its high Catholic population, the state has been strong in parochial schools. The fame, however, has gone to the select college preparatory schools like Phillips Andover, Groton, Deerfield Academy, Milton Academy, and the Boston Latin School. Some of the less richly endowed private boarding schools are in serious financial straits these days, and one, the Northampton School for Girls, was simply closed and its campus put up for sale in 1971.

The New Boston

Boston, the tired old city where cowpaths became streets, "Last Hurrah" politics reigned, and municipal tax rates first turned astronomical, has suddenly become one of the two or three most livable and exciting cities of America. For one who once lived in the closed old Boston, and now returns to the new Boston, the experience is a continual wonder. With its neighbor Cambridge across the Charles River, Boston has opened up—physically, spiritually, ethnically, economically. It is no longer an historic relic, but a vital center of the U. S. A. in our times.

Yet the old charm lingers on. You will find it in the lovely old red brick homes of Beacon Hill, with cobblestoned Acorn Street and Louisburg Square, where a little green park is ringed by stately 19th-century houses and gas lampposts. Historic Boston can be seen in an hour or two along the mile-and-a-half Freedom Trail in this most walkable of all American cities: the State House with its 23-carat gold dome, begun from designs by Charles Bulfinch in 1795; the pleasant expanse of the Boston Common, which the town bought as a "trayning field" for the militia and for the "feeding of Cattell" back in the 17th century, and where pirates, witches, and Quakers were hung from an elm near Frog Pond; Park Street Church, where William Lloyd Garrison delivered his first antislavery speech in 1829; the Old Granary Burying Ground with the graves of John Hancock, Samuel Adams, and Paul Revere; the Boston Athenaeum, the literary *sanctum sanctorum* of old Boston; King's Chapel, which was the Episcopal place of worship of early British governors and later the first Unitarian church in America; the Old State House and scene of the Boston Massacre; the Old South Meeting House where Bostonians met to protest the British tea tax before staging their famous Tea Party; Faneuil Hall, where Sam Adams and James Otis delivered the fiery speeches that led to Revolution; the Paul Revere House, Boston's oldest wooden frame building (1677); and the Old North Church, immortalized by Longfellow's poem about Revere's midnight ride ("One if by land and two if by sea"). Add to all this Bunker Hill, the Charlestown Navy Yard where the old frigate *Constitution* rests, Back Bay, the Public Garden, and Lexington and Concord not far distant—well, there can only be one Boston, and America needs one.

Writing in the Boston *Globe* in 1970, Ian Menzies suggested that Boston and San Francisco—especially among young Americans today—are "the two most exciting cities in the nation." There are certainly strong similarities. Both have water on three sides, strikingly similar skylines, almost equal land areas (Boston's 45 square miles, San Francisco's 47), and similar populations (Boston's 641,071—16th largest in the U. S. A.—and San Francisco's 715,674—13th largest). And both, Menzies observes, "have that mix of academe, of history and of the arts. While one has a Puritan heritage, the other Spanish, both today are managed by a rambunctious Irish-Italian political culture sitting uneasily over new militant minorities while a Waspish establishment watches on the sidelines with the ultimate weapon of money." * Neither city, he points out, overawes one as a New York, Chicago, or Los Angeles may. "People know each other in San Francisco and Boston. They talk to each other, eat with each other, banker and cultural entrepreneur, student and newspaper editor, professor and legislator, architect and community leader. They are walkable cities, centralized, physically compact, friendly." Both have a big academic suburb—Boston's Cambridge, San Fran-

---

* The ethnic division of Boston, according to a 1970 study by the Harvard-MIT Joint Center for Urban Studies, is 22 percent Irish (with the heaviest concentration in South Boston—an area described by its state legislator William Bulger, as one of the "last remaining vestiges of American tribalism"), 18 percent black (principally in Roxbury and the South End), 11 percent Italian (the North End and East Boston), 13 percent white Protestants (generally scattered with special pockets in the Back Bay and Beacon Hill areas), and 6 percent Jewish (Back Bay, Brighton, Dorchester-Mattapan). The rest is a scattering of French-Canadians, Puerto Ricans (now a fast-growing contingent), Greeks, and Chinese (Boston has the country's fourth largest Chinatown). The proud, liberal old town of Brookline, which is geographically but not politically part of the city, has shifted to about 50 percent Jewish (Irish and Wasps splitting the other 50 percent).

cisco's Berkeley.

Of the two cities, of course, San Francisco is more raucous, given to the new no-matter-what, while Boston reveres tradition. Topless and bottomless could not have happened in Boston; they did in San Francisco. In Boston, even the Old Howard Burlesque has fallen before the renewers' iron ball; but gone too, happily, are the days of book burning, the Sacco-Vanzetti trial, and "banned in Boston." And there is a final difference: San Francisco is not a capital, Boston is. Boston is ultimately more important to its state than San Francisco is to California. "We are virtually alone among the states" Massachusetts' Martin Linsky notes, "in that our capital city is also our most significant city in terms of culture, sports, population, sin, food, and fun."

There is always danger in attributing too much of the change in a city or state to one man, but by almost universal consensus, the vital turnaround from the "old" to the "new" Boston occurred during the reign of John F. Collins, mayor of Boston from 1960 to 1967. I have heard more than one person refer to Collins as "the best mayor Boston ever had."

When Collins became mayor, Boston was in near-desperate straits. As long as James Michael Curley and his type had been mayor, there was no chance that the Brahmin-dominated business community would invest in downtown Boston. Curley left City Hall for the last time in 1950, but John Hynes, the mayor of the next decade, while a pleasant and well intentioned man, lacked the skill to bring even his good ideas to fruition. In Collins' own words, these were the conditions in 1960:

> In the prior 25 years, Boston had lost $500 million worth of assessed property. In terms of Manhattan, that may not be a staggering figure, but it was in fact 25 percent of the potentially accessible tax base. In the 10 years between 1950 and 1960, Boston had lost 100,000 people, so its population had dropped to less than 650,000. And they were the people whom we could least afford to lose—the better educated and more affluent. Beyond that, blight and decay had been given such a headstart that the place was simply dilapidated. The citizens of Boston had essentially lost faith in the government of their city—they simply felt hopeless about the whole thing. The postwar building boom had bypassed Boston entirely, and there had been only one major building built in 25 years —the John Hancock Life Insurance Company building. The tax rate had been going up at an average annual rate of $8 a year. Boston was heading for insolvency.

Collins' own election was a major upset in which he defeated John Powers, an influential, classic type of politician who had support from prominent clergymen in the Boston Archdiocese and was considered the all-but-sure winner in the contest. Collins, however, brought fresh approaches and thought to his campaign. Five years before, Boston was struck by a polio epidemic, and he and three of his children contracted the disease. "I was to have died, and didn't, and then I was not to have been able to get out of bed into a wheelchair, and never be able to walk, but thanks be to God, all of those things didn't happen," Collins told me. "I mention that only because during the period of enforced convalescence, I had an opportunity to read just about everything that had ever been written about Boston, urban problems, and Boston's history and contemporary situation. I was determined in 1959—though I was still confined to a wheelchair—that Boston was entitled to one last clear chance to see whether or not it could commence to modernize its structure, physically, sociologically, and fundamentally."

As soon as he took office, Collins instituted a number of new policies which helped to bridge the traditional walls of distrust between City Hall, State Street, and the Cambridge academia. To avert fiscal insolvency, he ordered a belt-tightening in city government, beginning with a no-fire, no-hire policy that made it possible to eliminate 1,250 permanent city jobs. This enabled him to win the support of Brahmin business leaders like Charles A. Coolidge, president of the Boston Chamber of Commerce and a former member of the Harvard Corporation. Unlike his predecessors, Collins had a crisp, businesslike way of doing things; at a crucial set of meetings with the business leaders, held "at the vault" (one of the Boston banks), he lined up their support for numerous reforms. Both business and academic talent were obtained to help reorganize several departments of city government. Boston's perennial shortchanging by the state legislature was righted to a degree, after some very acrimonious sessions, by enactment of a limited sales tax to be used for aid to education on a formula favoring the poorer, older cities. And an income tax was passed, which in turn permitted the state to take over the responsibility for the municipal share of welfare.

The most visible monuments to the Collins regime emerged in the area of physical reconstruction of the city. "The blight and decay had received such a headstart," he explains, "that we could not afford the traditional and comfortable manner of almost finishing one job before undertaking another in urban renewal. I determined we should commence eight to 10 projects simultaneously. So I needed the best man in the country to run the program, and I finally settled on Ed Logue." At the time, Edward Logue was urban renewal director for the nationally acclaimed effort in New Haven. (At the end of the Collins administration, Logue ran unsuccessfully for mayor of Boston and was then selected to head the New York State Urban Development Corporation.)

Logue's presence in Boston helped to stir up investors' interest and draw federal dollars. As a first step, he and Collins resolved the tax problems that had stalled, for five years, the plans of Prudential Insurance Company to erect a huge office building complex in the Back Bay area with plazas and arcades on the scale of New York's Rockefeller Plaza. The problem was that under Boston's existing tax rate, Prudential would have been obliged to pay an annual tax bill of $15 million or more—even after spending $150 to $175 million to build the center. Yet it was obvious that if national corporations of the dimension of Prudential could be induced to spend hundreds of millions of dollars in Boston, the economic multiplier effect in terms of jobs and other construction would accrue to the city's benefit. Under Mayor Hynes, the idea had already been developed of a "capitalization of income method" to tax the new Prudential Center. But the proposal was bogged down in economic infighting and legislative bickering. Collins and Logue helped persuade the legislature to enact it in the so-called "Prudential law," permitting a payment of 20 percent of gross rental income in lieu of taxes, with a guaranteed $3 million annual fee. The Prudential project then rose rapidly. Its 52-story tower, completed in 1965, became the highest building in New England or, in fact, in the entire U. S. outside of Chicago and New York. A "skywalk" on the 50th floor became an important tourist attraction in itself. The complex included a new Sheraton hotel, Boston's first big new hotel since 1927.

The new tax formula used for the Prudential Center was subsequently copied for numerous new buildings in Boston. As a result, Boston has suddenly become a highly attractive center for insurance companies, banks, professional services, and corporate headquarters. Some major new buildings have included the 34-story State Street Bank Building, the 40-story New England Merchants National Bank Building, Center Plaza (eight stories tall and 900 feet long), the 41-story Boston Company Building, and several other smaller office buildings. In 1970, the momentum still carried forward with these projects in progress: a $50 million First National Bank Building, the $85 million new home office of the John Hancock Life Insurance Company, the $20 million new Keystone building, and a $35 million Christian Science Center adjacent to the Prudential Center. (The Christian Science Church, to its credit, has also leased land to private developers to build $70 million worth of middle- and low-income apartments near its Back Bay headquarters.)

More than the Prudential Center, perhaps, Collins and Logue will be remembered for the massive and dramatic Government Center built on 60 acres of land in the heart of the city, where scabrous old Scollay Square once stood. Again, Hynes had had the idea of a government center, but Collins had the skill to implement it. The victory was won and I. M. Pei was commissioned to draw up the overall area plan, replacing 22 old streets with six new ones, two of them broad thoroughfares leading to a vast central plaza before the new City Hall.

The City Hall design was chosen by open architectural competition, thought to be the first such contest for a public building in America in this century. "This was the only area really of disagreement that Ed Logue and I ever had," Collins told me. "He didn't believe in architectural competitions. For one thing, they take too long, and they result in delays and acrimony and controversy. I thought, however, that we only build a city hall once in a hundred years, and that it was appropriate we build something of a monumental nature." The challenge stimulated an outpouring of preliminary designs from 256 architects. Of the 10 finalists, none was a major, established firm—and thus it can be assumed that none would have had a chance under normal selection procedures. The final award went to Architects Kallmann, McKinnell & Knowles, two of whose members were then professors of architecture at Columbia University and had never designed a major building.

The resulting structure, completed in 1969, is architecturally the most exciting city hall in America and certainly one of the most successful public buildings of our times—on a plateau, perhaps, with a few other modern achievements like the St. Louis Archway and the new Hawaii Capitol. The designers eschewed any kind of boxy, office-building-like creation that could be torn down without qualm in 30 or 40 years. Nine stories high, the structure has a free-form exterior and many interior elements of simple rough concrete, supplemented within by red New England brick. It is most reminiscent of the style of the French architect Le Corbusier, with asymmetrical façades and deep recesses. It is a hollow rectangle built around a court with a lobby which rises on two sides to skylights nine stories above. At a distance, the building seems terribly solid, but in fact the red brick of the great courtyard before it follows through the lobby, and city pedestrians are constantly running in and out of the building.

Interestingly, many Bostonians were highly skeptical of the building when it was completed, but seem to be liking it more and more as time wears on. Given a chance, it seems, people's taste may indeed rise to a higher common denominator. One thing is sure: the City Hall Plaza in front, while it may be windy and deserted on an icy winter day, turns into a mass of relaxed people, lolling in front of the large fountain and sunken pool, on a spring or summer day. It has quickly become a favorite place for demonstrations and big public gatherings. A truly civic place, one might say.

When completed, the Government Center will have 30 buildings worth $260 million (including $21.6 million for City Hall itself). The location is crucial, bordering the State Street financial center, Beacon Hill, and Faneuil Hall and the waterfront. When the entire area's development is complete around 1980, Bostonians will have a "walkway to the sea" from Government Center Plaza through the restored Faneuil Hall Market district, scheduled to have outdoor cafes, restaurants, and shops, to the new Boston waterfront with parks, marinas, three 40-story towers by I. M. Pei, hotels, a nautical museum, and a new aquarium. In extending the pedestrian link to the waterfront, however, Boston must cope with the massive barrier of the elevated Fitzgerald Expressway, which separates both the waterfront and the North End from downtown, an ugly reminder of the 1950s when the highway planners were rampant.

Many people looking at Boston, Collins claims, "see the Prudential, the new dramatic city hall and Government Center. But they fail to realize that we built more low-income, moderate-income housing in the 1960s than any city in America. . . . Take a ride through Roxbury, and through Washington Park, and you will discover nonprofit, neighborhood-oriented housing. Now Charlestown is underway, and the South End and a number of other neighborhoods." The city, however, continues to face a grim shortage of decent housing at reasonable rates for poor and lower-middle income people—a result, at least in part, of relocation forced by urban renewal.

Boston's problem, Boston Redevelopment Authority Director John Warner told me in 1970, is that "the work-save-reward ethic for low and middle income people isn't working any more. You simply can't buy a house on that kind of income." Between 1960 and 1970, the number of owner-occupied units in Boston valued at less than $20,000 dropped by almost 50 percent and the number of units available for rental at less than $100 a month by 46 percent. Yet a third of the families in Boston earn less than $5,000 a year. Over 200,000 middle-class people have left Boston in the past two decades, leaving behind two groups—those people who had enough money to enable them to ignore the unpleasantries of city living, and those with so little money that they just couldn't get out.

The only bright spot is the return to the city of middle-upper and upper income people, noted in apartments on Tremont Street, along the Charles River, and in the Back Bay.

Problems in City Government

The Collins era, focused on physical renewal and economic city administration, came to an end in 1967. Despite his stature, Collins had been defeated in a bid for the U. S. Senate in 1966, losing 21 of the city's 22 wards in that race—a reflection, some said, of a feeling in individual city neighborhoods that Collins had neglected their interests in favor of downtown renewal. Collins is now a professor of urban studies at MIT. His successor as mayor, Kevin White, beat out Louise Day Hicks to win election.

Once installed, White tried to turn the focus of the city toward the neighborhoods, concentrating on gestures like creation of a series of little city halls throughout the city and expanded housing. But problems beset him on every side. The police proved insubordinate, Boston's tax rate hit an all-time high of $174.70 per $1,000 of assessed valuation in 1971, and recession made it all the more difficult to make ends meet financially. White was also diverted from his job by an unsuccessful 1970 race for governor, in which he actually lost the city of Boston to Republican Governor Sargent by more than 16,000 votes. In 1971, White proved singularly unsuccessful in getting the legislature to enact bills to avert further tax increases. But politically, White demonstrated a new finesse. Making common cause with hard pressed ethnic communities, he built a unique alliance of blacks, Wasps, Italians, and even some South Boston Irish. He hired a promising 30-year-old former Detroiter, John Marttila, as his campaign director—the same man who had masterminded Drinan's 1970 campaign for Congress. Some 5,000 volunteers (a fifth of them City Hall employees) were put to work. An expensive computer operation was launched, and mass rallies and broadcast advertising were downgraded in favor of a steady flow of personalized literature to some 130,000 potential White supporters who had been identified by door-to-door canvassing. The payoff was a record-breaking 62 percent vote for White.

Some of Boston's problems are unique, at least in degree, to the city. Between universities, churches, libraries, hospitals, museums, and the like, 50 percent of the property in Boston is not on the tax rolls at all. The area universities have been expanding by leaps and bounds in the postwar era, appropriating huge chunks of commercial real estate for tax-exempt academic institutions. Bills proposing taxation of dormitories and faculty housing are introduced in the legislature each session, but have yet to pass. The Boston housing shortage is aggravated by the rapidly rising number—now 20,000—of area students who live off campus, driving up rents.

The problem is compounded, Thomas Moccia of the Boston Chamber of Commerce notes, because "we spend a lot of money policing this town for a population that doubles during the day. A helluva lot of our uncontrollable costs—police and fire protection, museums and libraries, for instance —are metropolitan or regional in nature." Boston is the classic case of 100 suburbs around a small center city. The city's population, in fact, is only 23.3 percent of the Boston metropolitan area count (2,753,700 in 1970), a smaller percentage than any other major U. S. cities except San Francisco and Newark. What keeps the parts from cooperating are traditional hostilities—between city and suburb, Catholics and Yankees, and now blacks and whites.

Yet oddly enough, in a rudimentary way, Boston began metropolitan planning before any other region of America. The start was 1889, when the Metropolitan Sewerage Commission was created as an independent state agency to serve Boston and nearby towns. Later, two more autonomous state agencies were set up, to handle water supplies and the preservation of publicly owned parklands. In 1919, all three services were than consolidated under the Metropolitan District Commission. MDC has survived for a half century, perennially the whipping boy of municipal officials who criticize its independence (commissioners appointed by the governor) and lack of initiative in improving its facilities. Governor Sargent has also been dissatisfied with MDC and put one of the state's most imaginative young Republicans, John Sears, in charge of it, hoping for proposals for long-term change. Any reform would also have to decide what to do with organizations like the Metropolitan Air Pollution Control District (another pioneer effort, dating from 1910), the Massachusetts Port Authority, the Metropolitan Area Planning Council (1963 vintage), and the Massachusetts Bay Transportation Authority.

What one discovers in urban politics today, Robert Wood says, is a similar demand in both suburban and ghetto neighborhoods. In one, the call is for governmental autonomy; in the other, for neighborhood participation and control. But the essential goal is identical.

The real issue in regional development these days, [Wood says], is not what we talked of in the 1950s—a single, consolidated government for a region —but the problem of how you decentralize some functions like police and welfare that touch people's lives so intimately and terrifyingly, and at the same time centralize and regionalize developmental programs like those in air, water, transportation, and pollution. What you really want is a simultaneous diffusion of power to the people—we'll never put the cork back in the bottle of citizen participation that was taken off in the mid-1960s—while at the same time we have some consolidated developmental programs.

An area where the problems seem out of hand, despite effective regionalization, is in Boston's mass transit system. Boston had the first subway in the U. S. (1897) and with its narrow streets and confined land area proved to be an ideal city for rapid transit. Between commuter rail lines, subways, and buses, the Boston region had an annual passenger load of 456 million passengers in 1942. But then, in the postwar period, new patterns of suburban settlement and work locale, plus more universal car ownership, made mass transit less and less desirable. Commuter rail lines began to go out of business and Boston's subway-bus system was in financial trouble. In 1964, the legislature created the Massachusetts Bay Transportation Authority to own and run all public transportation in a 78-town area that embraces the entire Boston metropolitan area. On the map, the MBTA seems to have lines going everywhere one might want to go; moreover, from a planning point of view, it looks like the perfect model of a single authority, transcending all jurisdictional lines, with power to tax the people of the serviced communities to make up any deficit.

Some farsighted planning has gone into MBTA, including work on lines extending its rapid rail connections to the north and south. The system's boosters say that with that improvement, MBTA will have more miles than San Francisco's BART and will be the country's most effective system in terms of service and cars and combinations of rail and bus.

Nevertheless, the problems are closing in. Much of the equipment is old—trolleys over 25 years old, for instance, and three major repair facilities over 40 years of age, some dating from the 1800s. MBTA chairman Henry S. Lodge (son of Ambassador Henry Cabot Lodge) said in 1971 that the situation "requires an enormous amount of ingenuity, dedication, and just plain hard work from our workers to keep the system together and running." The labor situation is incredibly complicated with 6,500 employees in 27 unions. The system has long been a dumping ground for political patronage, with the Irish heavily favored. It has the highest paid bus drivers in the world. When Robert Wood, Lodge's predecessor, took over as chairman in the 1960s, he asked where the equal opportunity office was. The reply: "Equal opportunity office? We don't even let the Italians in." (Wood then instituted a lottery system to pick new bus drivers.) A spokesman for the authority told a New York *Times* reporter of unusual work rules which often result in four or five men doing the same job:

To simply replace a broken windshield on a bus, and make a slight adjustment on an engine [the spokesman explained], this is what has to happen:
The bus is driven to a repair shop by an operator of the carmen's union. At the apron of the garage, a member of the machinists' union has to take over and drive it inside. A member of the pipefitters' union then removes the windshield wiper. The windshield is then removed and replaced by a member of the sheetmetal workers' union. Then a diesel mechanic would work on the engine after its doors have been opened by a sheetmetal worker.

The region's people, frustrated by irregular MBTA service and preferring their own autos, are now taking only 170 to 180 million rides a year on the system—less than 40 percent of the 1942 figure. The MBTA deficit has passed the $60 million-a-year level, passed on to the taxpayers in the form of a tax add-on of about $10 for a typical homeowner. Deteriorating service and the high taxes have prompted some communities to threaten to pull out of the MBTA system. U. S. Secretary of Transportation Volpe told *Business Week* in 1971 that Boston should be a shining example of what a transit system can accomplish, once it breaks free of the restrictions of financing itself through the fare box. "Instead," Volpe said, "Boston seems to be proving a distasteful corollary—that dependence on public funds and sensitivity to political control lead to runaway deficits."

Highway building is another area in which Boston is moving to regional cooperation, though this is a case of city and suburbs unifying to *stop* the growth of new facilities, not to foster them. As Bill Kovach of the New York *Times* tells the story, Boston area highway planning was controlled until the recent past in the typical American pattern of single-purpose technicians with a powerful construction industry lobby behind them, well insulated from public pressures. There were plans for a superhighway cutting the city from north to south, a loop encircling the city and another in its heart. The only protest came from small and uncoordinated community groups, without technical expertise. Then, in 1963, Frederick Salvucci, a planner for the Boston Redevelopment Authority, began to question the engineering analysis that led to the plan for an inner belt that would dump thousands of autos into the crowded, narrow streets of Boston. Help was enlisted from architects, sociologists, and graduate students and faculty at the local universities.

When the Department of Public Works began to move ahead with plans to build a highway through part of a wildlife sanctuary in the suburbs, the conservationists and environmentalists were drawn into the battle. This meant cooperation from middle- and upper-class suburbanites who had a powerful lobby in the State House. Thus a unique coalition emerged of inner-city blacks, ethnics, academics, suburban businessmen, housewives, and professionals. It could not be ignored by the politicians. In 1969 Governor Sargent, onetime hearty supporter of the inner-belt concept, privately told his highway administrator: "The old highway building game is over." The next year, he went on television to announce: "I have decided to reverse the transportation policy of the Commonwealth. . . . [Our] plan will be based on an answer to the question, . . . not where an expressway should be built, but whether an expressway should be built." The net result was to halt work on a major segment of the inner belt (I-95), on expressway construction through Cambridge, on a new two-mile-long runway at Logan International Airport, and half a dozen other major highway projects in the Boston area.

Bostonian Culture and Communications

The arts organizations of Boston, Bernard Taper has written, "live a life of exquisite misery"—superb in quality and variety but limping along with chronic deficits, low support from the city's people, and an almost invisible level of government support. In the late 1960s, when the San Francisco city government was expending $3.6 million to subsidize the arts, the figure in Boston was less than a tenth as much. In fact, even such cities as Buffalo, Rochester, Fort Worth, and Seattle do much better by way of supporting the arts than does Boston.

The city's two preeminent cultural institutions are the Boston Symphony Orchestra and the Boston Museum of Fine Arts. The orchestra was begun in 1881 by Henry Lee Higginson and personally supported by him for three decades thereafter, at a cost of some $1 million. Still regarded as one of the world's best orchestras, the symphony plays a long Boston season (33 weeks) and then eight weeks in the summer at Tanglewood in the Berkshires. Its celebrated pops concerts and free outdoor performances on the Esplanade beside the Charles River Basin make it an integral part of Boston's life. Between them, the symphony and the justly renowned Fine Arts Museum had a budget of over $7 million in the late 1960s, some 70 percent of the entire expenses for the fine arts in Boston. In 1970 the legislature was arguing over whether to give the Massachusetts Arts Council $160,-000 or $100,000 in what the Boston *Globe* described as "a tawdry display of philistinism and ignorance as, even from the point of commercialism, surveys have shown that history and culture draw more tourist dollars than any other attraction, including sports."

In the performing field, major contributions are made by the Opera Company of Boston, the Boston Ballet, and Charles Playhouse. And for those with less sophisticated tastes, there are two magnificent scientific-type museums—the Museum of Science, with its Charles Hayden Planetarium at Science Park, and the New England Aquarium, since 1970 in a splendid $6.5 million concrete-and-glass home on an abandoned Boston wharf, the blue-green lit interior evocative of undersea life.

Boston does have a lot of private art galleries (Back Bay, Cambridge), some of America's most delightful bookstores, shops to please the most discriminating and off-beat purchasers, and establishments like "The Restaurant at the Orson Welles" Theater in Cambridge with hippie waiters and waitresses and slide light shows; in all, one of America's most sophisticated urban mélanges. There is a thriving underground press (*Boston After Dark, The Phoenix*) and even a station (WBCN-FM) that broadcasts very sophisticated rock for the younger generation. WGBH-TV, the public television station, has had the guts to broadcast some imaginative programming, including shows oriented to black life and women's liberation; in fact, it is regarded as one of the country's outstanding public television stations. In sports, the city no longer has a National League team but it can boast the Red Sox (1967 American League pennant winners), the Bruins of the National Hockey League (1969–70 Stanley Cup winners), the Celtics (frequent world champions in basketball) and the Patriots in football. And what other city has anything like the annual Boston Marathon foot race? As many as 1,000 people enter, from some of the world's greatest long distance runners to pure amateurs from all over the United States. The 26-mile race is run every April 19, Patriot's Day, and attracts some quarter million people, one of the largest crowds to watch any athletic event anywhere.

For years, the quality of Boston's newspapers (the *Christian Science Monitor* excepted) was dismal indeed; by commonly accepted practice, a good third of every front page was covered with advertisements, and news coverage was rarely distinguished. The old Boston *Post* was perhaps the worst of the lot. Catering, apparently, to the market of people who could not afford eyeglasses, it ran most of each story in big heads and subheads, with a runty little story in small type beneath. What happened first to change all this was that Boston papers began to die off—the *Transcript* in 1941, after 111 years of publication, the *Post* in 1956 after 125 years. The *Daily Record* and *Evening American* merged in 1961 and the *Herald* and *Traveler* in 1967. The surviving *Record American* is an unspectacular tabloid, the *Herald-Traveler* an improved product (though it depends too much on New York Times Service articles, instead of sending its own reporters into the field, and is in shaky financial shape with imminent loss of its television station, WHDH-TV).

By any measure, the leading paper of Boston today is the *Globe* (circulation 438,000). Not only has it spurted ahead of all competition in circulation and advertising lineage, but the *Globe* has hired aggressive reporters willing to dig up scandals in government, write frank coverage about city problems, and even move into the national bigtime (through publication in 1971, for instance, of some of the disputed Pentagon Papers stories). Chief credit for the bright new era apparently goes in the first instance to editor Thomas Winship, who has put a heavy emphasis on youth in his hiring policies and then permitted the talent he hired to bloom. Robert Healy, who acts both as executive editor and political editor, shows amazing skill at remaining conversant with Massachusetts and national political developments despite his administrative duties. On public issues like the Vietnam war, race and community relations, the *Globe* has become as "sensitive" or "to the left" (the reader may choose his own word) as any major city daily in the U. S. today. Editor Winship believes the paper can exert strong weight for reform, its power second only to the Archbishop or Cardinal. The policy upsets some conservatives, who argue that the paper writes more for dilettantish suburban liberals than the hard-pressed low-income whites left in the center city, where the gut problems really are. And it may be that a young, highly educated writing staff and heavily suburban circulation influence the *Globe* in that direction. But the fact is that the paper is written with integrity and enthusiasm, and may in itself have something to do with Massachusetts' complexion as the country's most liberal state today.

The Other Worlds of Massachusetts

Massachusetts is a small state by national standards (it ranks only 45th in land area), but pleasing to the eye of man for all its recorded history. The eastern third of the state, including all of the Boston orbit, the North Shore, South Shore, New Bedford area, and Cape Cod, is part of a coastal lowland that was once submerged beneath the sea. Starting around Worcester, the land becomes hillier—an upland region which is actually a southerly extension of the White Mountains of New Hampshire. Still farther west, the Connecticut River courses from north to south across the state. The valley offers a rich harvest of tobacco, onions, and potatoes and is heavily settled in places like Springfield, Holyoke, and Greenfield. West of the valley rise the Berkshire Hills, a continuation of Vermont's Green Mountains. Long a barrier to commerce, the Berkshires are now favorite summer vacation places, interspersed with small upland farms. Still farther west, the land dips again into the pleasant Housatonic River Valley, where Pittsfield is the largest city. Finally, Massachusetts ends with the Taconic Range along the New York border.

Boston's multitudinous suburbs vary from industrial towns that are virtually undistinguishable from parts of the city proper to privileged sanctuaries of big-lot zoning to which the elite and semi-elite have migrated to guarantee themselves some greenery and keep the city at a safe, long distance. Immediately north and northwest of Boston is a belt of rather unattractive industrial-residential cities like Revere (43,159), Somerville (88,779), Medford (64,397), Malden (56,127), and Arlington (53,524). Like Boston, virtually all have heavy ethnic populations and have been losing population in recent years. The North Shore cities—Salem (40,556) and Beverly (38,-348), with their rich historical lore of witchcraft and the days of the West Indies trade, and Gloucester (27,941), still a fishing port and surrounded now by choice summer resorts—still have a special kind of magic about them. Farther north, in the Merrimack River Valley, are cities like Lowell (94,239), Lawrence (66,915), and Haverhill (46,120), all sooty children of the industrial revolution who are reaching for electronic employment to offset the loss of textiles and shoes. Many of the same problems are shared by cities like Lynn (90,294), and the depressed southeastern Massachusetts cities of New Bedford (101,777), Fall River (96,898), and Brockton (89,040).

Although Route 128 makes a full loop around Boston, the concentration of research, electronics, and weaponry plants is to the northwest and west, an immense boon for old cities like Waltham (61,582). Historic Lexington (31,886) and Concord (16,148), favorite residential spots for the engineers and highly skilled workers, have doubled and tripled their population in recent decades. Towns of affluence and high social consciousness lie west of Boston, including Newton (91,066) and Framingham (64,048).

The South Shore, stretching from Boston to Plymouth, has never had the social distinction of the North Shore, even though there are many attractive bayside communities like Cohasset, Scituate, and Duxbury. The biggest city directly on the South Shore is Quincy (87,966), one of New England's most progressive industrial cities. If one treasures history and tradition, it is hard to outpoint the town of Plymouth, where a visitor seeking directions may be told to "go down past the Mayflower until you come to Plymouth Rock, and then take a right." Along with its treasures of times past, Plymouth has a huge new nuclear plant, with a 300-ton reactor core, built by Boston Edison Company.

Massachusetts' foremost vacation resort is Cape Cod, that low-slung spit of sand and scrub pine that offers 300 miles of coastline, the magnificence of the new Cape Cod National Seashore, and quaint towns like Provincetown, Falmouth, Chatham, Orleans, and Hyannis Port (where the Kennedys repair in times of triumph and tragedy to their well-known compound of houses). Modern air connections have reduced the isolation of the picturesque off-shore islands of Nantucket and Martha's Vineyard, but the onslaughts of tourists have not altogether erased the early charm.

Out to the west, Massachusetts' second city of Worcester (176,572) continues to prosper with widely diversified industry and has forsaken its unsavory municipal ways under an exceedingly able city manager, Francis J. McGrath, in the past 20 years. Like most Massachusetts cities, Springfield (163,905) has been losing population and is encountering increased problems with its black minority. But Springfield still has many strong industries and the 24-town Connecticut Valley metropolitan area, of which it is the center, is experiencing growth in its prosperous suburbs and the academic communities centered around Northampton. Neighboring Holyoke (50,112) is a prototype of the deteriorating mill town, in contrast to Pittsfield (57,020), an attractive elm-shaded city set between the upper branches of the Housatonic, where the biggest payroll is from a big General Electric plant.

Western Massachusetts is filled with little towns of immense attraction —little Berkshire hamlets like Florida and Peru, known for their beauty and year-round weather; the charming old Berkshire summer resort of Lenox, where the Boston Symphony Orchestra plays each summer at Tanglewood; the pleasing college town of Williamstown. Perhaps the most fascinating of all is Deerfield, in the Connecticut River Valley. It really suffered through the French and Indian Wars, became an agricultural center in the 18th century, was a favorite spot of the literati in the 19th century, and still has Old Deerfield Street, set under an arch of 200-year old elms, where the preservation of colonial homes has been underway for a century. Past the houses, one has glimpses of open country and far hills. The visitor feels transported back over time, into the milieu that makes New England such a precious part of America.

NEW JERSEY

IN THE SHADOWS OF MEGALOPOLIS

NEW JERSEY HAS A PROBLEM WITH ITS IMAGE. Suspended between the massive urban centers of New York and Philadelphia, it still has some of the attributes James Madison ascribed to it—a cask tapped at both ends. There are places in America, like Oakland and East St. Louis, that suffer from what is known as a "second city" syndrome; only New Jersey could be said to have a second (or perhaps third) *state* syndrome. Even though it is, next to California, the most urbanized state of America, New Jersey lacks a single city of distinction. To recite the names of New Jersey's cities is depressing enough; the reader can test himself on the list of places like Newark, Jersey City, Paterson, Camden, Trenton, Elizabeth, Bayonne, Hoboken, and the rest. All have decayed alarmingly in the postwar years and have become cauldrons of racial discord. New Jersey is the most suburban state of America, the suburban towns ranging from handsome to drab and ugly.* Jersey's once glittering resort town, Atlantic City, has sunk into decrepitude.

New Jersey has the greatest population density of all the 50 states (953 people per square mile), but it lacks communications media of statewide

* The terms "suburban" and "urban," as used here, require some definition. "Suburban" refers to the percentage of the population which lives in metropolitan areas but outside of the central core cities of 50,000 or more population. It is in this category that New Jersey leads the nation. "Urban" may refer to the center core cities, in which category New Jersey ranks about midpoint among the states. But if one uses the Census Bureau's time-honored alternative definition of "urban," meaning any town or city of 2,500 population or more, then New Jersey at 88.9 percent is first in the U. S. except for California (with 90.9 percent).

scope. There is not a single commercial television station in all of New Jersey —a plight no other state shares. Somehow the New York-Philadelphia press steal the thunder of the big Jersey papers like the Newark *News* and *Star-Ledger.* On the other hand, there are strong local papers—the Bergen *Record,* Camden *Courier-Post,* Elizabeth *Journal,* Asbury Park *Press,* and others—which have their individual territories so well in hand that papers of statewide scope cannot penetrate.

A measure of low public consciousness in New Jersey is the fact that organized crime, here more than in any other state of the Union, has been able to take over whole city governments and even infiltrate to high levels in the state government. And as if this were not bad enough, the image most outsiders have of New Jersey is confined to the dreary view of belching factories, oil refineries, railroad sidings, and auto graveyards along the Philadelphia-New York transportation corridor (also known as "Pollution Alley"), the most heavily traveled highway and rail route in America. Life in the heart of megalopolis, it seems, has more than its share of drawbacks. Jersey's problems are made no easier by an archaic tax structure, based principally on the property tax, which has bankrupted its cities, and a lack of high-level talent in its public life.

But it is not enough to accentuate the negative, as true as all we have said may be. Jersey's Revolutionary-era cities are not likely to get a face-lifting for some time to come, but the state is making an heroic effort to clean up the infestation of organized crime—aided by federal prosecutors. One can only admire the comprehensive antipollution campaign being mounted by the new Department of Environmental Protection in Trenton. There is a good chance that the Republican state administration, elected in 1969, will take the bull by the horns and come up with an entirely new way of financing government that will tap the immense wealth within the state—probably a graduated state income tax, accompanied by drastic reductions of the local property taxes that are forcing businesses and homeowners alike out of the older urban areas and generating suburban sprawl.

The fact is that New Jersey has vast economic and human resources on which to live. The per capita income, $4,598 in 1970, ranks third in the nation. The percentage of people in the working age bracket (21 to 64) is second highest in the U. S. The state is seventh among the 50 in the value of its manufactures and is getting increasingly into sophisticated research-type industries. With its superb central location on the East Coast and proximity to the centers of national wealth, the state should have an unlimited economic future. Long a parasite on its neighbors in higher education, it has stopped exporting so many young people out of state for their college educations and has undertaken a massive university-building program. There is already the skill and knowledge in New Jersey's educated elite to effect fundamental changes, especially as the long entrenched and often corrupt county and city political machines wither away and make room for more effective citizen politics.

Frederick H. Sontag, a public affairs and research consultant based in

Montclair, sees a "major hope for the development of a vigorous New Jersey in the '70s in the emergence of some gutsy, young, experienced leader who can really inspire its people." The older generation of leaders in politics, labor, and business, he suggests, is retiring or dying, and there is a real opportunity for an imaginative new generation, perhaps mobilized by a well staffed and financed citizens movement, to look for solutions that "go beyond taxation and more spending." With an active statewide network of highly motivated citizens, he believes, "New Jersey could become a state to be respected and emulated and, at long last, one to be reckoned with."

The population figures attest to New Jersey's continuing viability. In 1970, the Census found 7,168,164 people in the state, 72 percent more than the 4,160,165 who were there in 1940. (The national population grew by 54 percent in the same 30-year period.) New Jersey's largest increase, both in actual numbers and percent, occurred in the 1950s, the biggest decade yet for filling up the suburbs. But the decade of the 1960s saw a growth of 18 percent, compared to a national growth of 13 percent. Of New Jersey's 1.1 million increase in the 1960s, 645,000 was due to natural increase (births over deaths) and 488,000 to net migration (the excess of people moving into the state over the number choosing to leave it). The net migration figure was actually the highest for any state except California.

Physically, New Jersey is vest pocket size—only 7,532 square miles, 46th among the 50 states. But there is a lot more to New Jersey than the congested cityscape and industrial wastelands one sees from a car on the New Jersey Turnpike, or from the window of a train on the Penn Central line. Despite the constant inroads of suburbia, almost three-quarters of the land remains in forest, farms, and small towns, populated by a scant 11 percent of the state's people.

There are two broad areas of natural beauty in New Jersey—the Appalachian foothills in the northwestern part of the state, and the Atlantic Coast. The northwestern section, divided from Pennsylvania by the upper (and still relatively clean) waters of the Delaware River, is crossed by the Appalachian Trail and offers many cabin- and resort-lined lakes between forest-covered hills. The dramatic Delaware Water Gap, where the river has cut a 1,200-foot gorge through the Kittatinny Mountains, is a great tourist attraction. Although the region is threatened by an ever growing tide of summertime and retirement homes of refugees from the big cities, one still finds dairy farms in the valleys, as well as old settlements like Chester and Mendham, with a New England flavor to their village greens and church spires. Here, too, are lovely rural suburban areas and the homes of some of New Jersey's fabled old families like the Frelinghuysens and Forbeses, living a genteel life with their horses and estates in counties like Morris, Hunterdon, and Somerset. As the Delaware moves southward toward Trenton, still through countryside of quiet charm, it passes historic old places like Lambertville and Washington's Crossing where the Continental Army crossed the ice-choked river on the Christmas night of 1776. A few miles to the east is Princeton, a university town of rare beauty.

The glistening white expanses of the Jersey Shore, stretching in more or less continuous form from Sandy Hook on New York's Lower Bay for 125 miles to Cape May at New Jersey's southernmost tip, offer the people of megalopolis some of the most magnificent natural beaches in America. Despite the affluence in old towns like Bay Head or Mantoloking, with their weather-silvered homes, the shore is not a chic resort area of modern America. But each spring winter's gray swells give way to a sunny blue Atlantic surf, and middle-class Jerseyites, Philadelphians, and New Yorkers pour in by the millions to claim their foot of beach. The shore communities have look-alike ways but differ greatly in character: honky-tonk Atlantic City and Asbury Park, puritanical Ocean City (a resort founded by Methodists in 1879 that still forbids public bars), sedate and quiet Cape May (where Lincoln and other Presidents vacationed in the last century, now a place of picturesque narrow streets, old shade trees, and historic homes). Only 12 miles from Atlantic City is the Brigantine Wildlife Refuge, where more than half a million birds gather during spring and autumn migrations. Surf fishermen and bird watchers predominate at Island Beach, a seven-mile-long state park. Sandy Hook, a government preserve for 200 years, is to become part of the ambitious National Gateway Recreation Area shared with New York. And the southern parts of the shore include long stretches of beach where development is not yet heavy.

Just inland from the shore in South Jersey lie the Pine Barrens, 3,000 square miles of sandy soils, swamplands, pine stands, and blueberry and cranberry tracts, one of the largest ecologically undisturbed areas along the Boston-Washington urban corridor. The concentration of plant life in this vast botanical museum is unappreciated by the millions who speed by on the turnpikes.

An Economic Scorecard

New Jersey's difficult role as an economic hinterland of New York, but separated governmentally from the metropolis, dates from 1664 when the English took over the New York area from the Dutch. It was in that year that the Duke of York, given a vast tract of land on the eastern seaboard, unwisely severed the territory between the Hudson and Delaware Rivers from the natural capital in New York and assigned it to two of his court favorites. Unfortunately, the duke failed to inform Richard Nicolls, whom he had dispatched to New York to run the entire new province. Nicolls had already made land grants in Jersey conflicting with those of the new Lords Proprietors, and a century of court wrangles ensued. A few years later, William Penn gained control of West Jersey, making that territory the first Quaker settlement in America, and in 1682 he got control of East Jersey —and thus the entire present state of New Jersey—as well. But Penn presumably became discouraged with the interminable disputes over land ownership, dating from the Duke of York's original error, and petitioned Charles II for a patent to what is now Pennsylvania. Philadelphia, the great Quaker city, rose on the west bank of the Delaware River, instead of in New Jersey. Thus New Jersey was left between the two great cities and came to regard itself, as an 18th century pamphlet expressed it, as a "poor, slavish dependent" of its neighbors.

Due to its strategic location, New Jersey was the scene of nearly 100 battles and skirmishes in the Revolutionary War, a conflict which set neighbor against neighbor and brother against brother in the state. The future role of New Jersey began to appear in 1791 when Alexander Hamilton founded the Society for Establishing Useful Manufactures and chose the falls of the Passaic River as a site for the industrial town of Paterson. The 19th century witnessed rapid growth of canals and railways and of cities like Jersey City, Newark, Paterson, and Camden as manufacturing centers. Ownership either began in, or inevitably gravitated toward, New York or Philadelphia. Likewise, the chief market for Jersey's farm goods was in the big cities on its borders. Politics took on an unsavory color when the Camden and Amboy Railroad was granted an exclusive charter for the Philadelphia–New York run, and from the 1840s to the 1870s the railroads dominated economic and political life in the state. Liberal incorporation laws passed in the 1870s would lead to a charge by Lincoln Steffens that New Jersey was the traitor state that let the big corporations fleece the poor.

New Jersey has always been a melting pot of nationalities. Dutch, British, Finns, and Swedes were all there in ample numbers before the Revolution. In addition to the Quakers, there were Baptists from Long Island and New England who came in search of religious freedom. The 1900s brought vast numbers of Irish to dig the canals and build the railways. Germans immigrated in vast numbers, later to be joined by Poles and Hungarians who worked in the factories. Many Russian Jews arrived early in the 20th century, and today the state has about 400,000 Jews, or 5.5 percent of its population. Only New York state has a higher percentage. (Jersey's Jews, however, have shown fewer leadership qualities than their counterparts across the Hudson.) And then there are the Italians, who arrived in such huge numbers toward the end of the 19th century and early in the present one that they represent today, by some estimates, as much as 35 percent of the population. (The overall Roman Catholic share of the population, which would include most but not all the Italians, is 41.7 percent—the fourth highest Catholic population share among the 50 states). Writer Adeline Pepper uses the fact that pizza is the most popular dish in the school cafeterias as proof of the "Italianization" of Jersey; others point to the high incidence of organized crime as another evidence, though one hopes that observation can be made without associating the vast bulk of honest, hard-working Italian-Americans with the depredations of a few who share their ancestry.

The population of New Jersey is so polyglot, Professor Richard McCormick of Rutgers University has noted, that "the native, third-generation Jerseyman is a rarity." About a quarter of the people moving into New Jersey in recent years have been Negroes, increasing the Negro share of the population from 5.5 percent in 1940 to 10.7 percent in the 1970 Census. Most have moved into the big cities, where they have been joined by growing numbers of Puerto Ricans and other Spanish-speaking peoples. But the new minorities' portion of Jersey's population is no greater than that of the U. S. as a whole, and it should be a manageable problem *if* more Negroes and Latins can be channeled into the suburbs.

New Jersey's modern economy rests on several pillars: manufacturing, research, corporate headquarters, farming, commuting, and transportation. The $12 billion-plus output of the state's factories springs from a fantastic array of manufactures, perhaps the broadest of any state. Of the country's 75 largest industrial firms, 62 operate in the state; 90 percent of all types of manufacturing are represented. New Jersey is the national leader in chemical production, with big pharmaceutical, basic chemical, and paint plants. Among the states, it ranks third in apparel, sixth in food products, electrical machinery, and instruments, seventh in fabricated metal products, paper, printing, and publishing, eighth in petroleum, ninth in textiles. In 1969, there were 897,100 workers in manufacturing—almost 40 percent of the nonfarm employment. The biggest single payroll—117,000—was in chemicals.

New Jersey has long been a state of discoveries, starting with Thomas Edison's electric light bulb and continuing with Lee De Forrest's basic vacuum tube, Allen Du Mont's cathode ray tube, Edwin Armstrong's development of FM radio, and the transistor for which scientists Walter H. Brattain, John Bardeen, and William Schockley received the Nobel Prize in 1956. The state is still a national leader in both pure and applied research and is said to have more scientists and engineers per capita than any other. There are more than 600 laboratories, including Bell Telephone at Murray Hill, Esso at Linden, and the James Forrestal Research Center at Princeton. Many of the laboratories are located in bucolic suburban or exurban locations, far away from the smoky industrial corridors.

Despite Jersey's heavy role in manufacturing, the white-collar share of the employment pool is higher than in all but six other states. A leader in the preferred office-job field is Prudential Life Insurance, located in Newark, the country's largest insurance company with $28 billion in assets. Insurance, real estate, retailing, service industries, and government all account for thousands of white-collar jobs, although government employment accounts for a significantly lower share of total jobs than the national average. Preeminently, New Jersey is a self-supporting state; its per capita grants-in-aid from the federal government rank only 49th among the 50 states. The state is the ninth biggest state in defense contracts (over $1 billion a year), but direct defense-generated employment accounts for only 3.1 percent of the labor force, less than the national average.

In the late 1960s, New Jersey revised its corporation laws to make them as liberal and flexible as any in the U. S., thus encouraging big firms to incorporate, and in some cases to actually set up headquarters staffs, in the state. Before that, the corporation laws, scandalously loose in earlier times, had become so encrusted that they actually discriminated against New Jersey-based corporations. The number of new industries coming into Jersey has been increasing rapidly, with giants like Corn Products (now CPC International), American Cyanamid, and Squibb Beech-Nut in recent years. The diversity of Jersey industry is illustrated by the names of the others on *Fortune*'s "top 500" list: Campbell Soup, Warner-Lambert Pharmaceutical, Johnson & Johnson, Walter Kidde, Merck, Union Camp, Curtiss-Wright, Fedders, Thomas J. Lipton, Jonathan Logan, General Instrument, Schering, Becton Dickinson, Interspace, Federal Pacific Electric, and Triangle Industries. Three Jersey-based retailers—Grand Union, Vornado, and Supermarkets General—are on the *Fortune* list of the biggest retailing firms. Few major firms have sought to leave Jersey. But significantly, not a single New Jersey bank is on the list of the 50 largest U. S. banks.

The Jersey business firm which has traditionally exercised the most influence in politics is Johnson & Johnson, first under the late General Robert W. Johnson and presently under his successor as board chairman, Philip Hofmann. Old General Johnson used to swing back and forth from left to right in politics, but Hofmann's role has been a steadier, straight Republican one. "He kept the lights on at Republican headquarters during the dark years," one of his fellow Republicans once remarked. Johnson & Johnson pushes its employees into public life; of 38,000, more than 500 hold some sort of elective or appointive office, most of them in New Jersey. Hofmann himself was appointed to the New York Port Authority board by Gov. Cahill.

Warner-Lambert Pharmaceuticals has connections at the highest places through its honorary board chairman, Elmer Bobst, so long a friend and helper of Richard M. Nixon that he is known as "Uncle Elmer" at the White House. (Bobst is a rich uncle; he gave $63,000 to the 1968 Republican campaign.) Former Governor Driscoll is an ex-president and board chairman of Warner-Lambert. Other Jersey companies with a say in the state's public life include Prudential Insurance, Campbell's Soup at Camden, and Becton Dickinson in Bergen County (a big instrument manufacturer). Among the individuals who play a strong role are W. Paul Stillman, president of the First National State Bank in Newark, Paul Troast, chairman of the New Jersey Manufacturers Association, Leon Hess of the Hess Oil Company and Gene Mori, who operates the Garden State Race Track and is closely aligned with Cahill and South Jersey business interests.

In the mid-1960s, the late Dr. V. D. Mattia, president of the pharmaceutical firm of Hoffmann-La Roche, helped a bright young slate of Essex County Republican reform candidates, headed by state senator James H. Wallwork, an ex-West Pointer, sweep to office. (The movement continues with leadership also from a GOP civic leader and attorney, Robert J. Citrino, now deputy chairman of the New Jersey Turnpike Authority.) Mattia's own story—from the Newark Italian slums to presidency of an internationally owned company—illustrated an upward mobility in Jersey that many states, especially in the eastern U. S., would not provide. Mattia was the same man who won some measure of national fame for refusing to cooperate with the Pharmaceutical Manufacturers Association's national advertising campaign to improve the industry's image and take the heat off customer complaints of high drug prices.

Tourism is a vitally important part of New Jersey's economy, bringing in some $2.7 billion a year from visitors to Jersey resorts, historic sites, and conventions. This business, plus heavy intra- and interstate commuting, helped to justify the vast superhighway net constructed within the state since World War II. New Jersey is fortunate it made the investment when it did, because even with the hundreds of miles of new roads, it still has the most densely traveled highways in the nation.

The New Jersey Turnpike, America's busiest toll road, now carries more than 90 million vehicles a year. When the turnpike opened in 1951, the projection had been for an eventual annual load of 30 million vehicles—in 1980! The turnpike stretches from the Delaware Memorial Bridge in the southern part of the state to the George Washington Bridge near New York, a distance of 118 miles, plus spurs to connect with the Pennsylvania Turnpike and Holland Tunnel. A multilane widening of the turnpike's "bread and butter" stretch in north Jersey was completed in 1970, and soon the same process will be completed to a point south of New Brunswick. Traffic has also soared beyond expectations on the 173-mile-long Garden State Parkway, opened in 1955, which runs along the entire length of the Jersey Coast and then through Newark to connect with the New York State Thruway. It is so overused that an entirely new turnpike is projected to run west of and parallel to it for almost 100 miles.

The stories of gargantuan traffic tie-ups on the big toll roads, and especially the monster smash-ups when fog hits the New Jersey Turnpike, are almost legendary. Driving along their congested stretches can be among the more dehumanizing experiences of travel anywhere in America today. But the New Jersey highway authorities took one offbeat step when they commissioned a Garden State Arts Center, designed by Edward Durell Stone, on the parkway 30 miles south of Newark. The center, which opened in 1968, has botanical gardens, an art exhibition mall, nature trails, and a large amphitheater. The cost of the center, $10.5 million, was just a tiny fraction of the cost of the superhighways. But it *was* a first step toward humanizing the great macadam and concrete octopus.

New Jersey still has important agriculture—large dairy herds raised in the Appalachian valleys of the northwest, truck farming for vegetables on the rich soil of central and southwestern Jersey, peaches and apples on the sandy coastal plain, cranberries in the marshy bogs, and poultry in the Pine Barrens. Other crops of note include tomatoes, corn, asparagus, spinach, blueberries, and strawberries. In recent years about $250 million has been realized in annual farm income—the most per acre of any state, but a small overall figure compared to the country's major farm states. The land for farming seems to be shrinking at an alarming rate as suburban subdivisions, factories, highways, and shopping centers gobble up more and more fertile farm territory. Dairy herds are moving toward extinction. In 1960, there were 1.8 million acres in farms in New Jersey; in 1969, the figure had shrunk to one million and was still diminishing. The number of actual farms has declined even more precipitously: from 25,000 in 1930 to less than 8,500 by latest count. One can almost envision the day when only two farm occupations will survive: raising race horses for the sportsmen and race tracks, and growing ornamental shrubs for suburbia's million yards.

In the meantime, however, there is the grim problem of 20,000-odd black and Puerto Rican migrant workers who come up the eastern seaboard, or are bused out daily on rickety buses from the Camden and Philadelphia slums, to harvest the vegetable crops each summer. They are herded along by black crew leaders who have a way of bartering men for profit that has been likened to the Angolan slave traders of centuries past. Despite numerous New Jersey laws and regulations designed to curtail the worst abuses in the migrant camps, they seem to persist through lax enforcement and the opposition of the New Jersey Farm Bureau Federation. Local officials are often in connivance with the farm owners and summarily arrest—and often hold for days—migrants they think may be stirring up any kind of trouble in their camps. In 1967, the New York *Times* reported:

At one camp in Vineland, Negroes have been crowded into chicken coops. In another, they cook, drink, and bathe from a foul water tap that has been grossly polluted by a nearby privy that has overflowed. In every camp, flies swarm over the garbage-strewn dust, the young children and the cooking grits and stolen vegetables that migrants usually live on.

At night in the camps as many as six or more children are stacked like cordwood into one roach-infested bed. . . . Many children have distended navels . . . and many also were ridden with lice and ticks. Worm-infested infants, left unattended in the camps for hours by their mothers in the fields, are sometimes bitten by rats.

Three years later, the *Times*'s Ronald Sullivan reported many of the same conditions prevalent in the South Jersey camps. He was assaulted by a local farmer and then arrested with two antipoverty workers when they ventured onto a farm at Bridgeton to investigate a migrant camp. The trespass law, critics said, was being used by farmers to perpetuate the squalor in their camps and also to isolate workers in various camps so that they could not compare notes on their working and pay conditions, or begin organization. In spring 1971, the state supreme court ruled that the state's farmers could no longer use the trespass law to keep qualified visitors from entering migrant worker camps, and Governor Cahill signed bills to guarantee a minimum wage for field hands and guarantee them toilet facilities and visitation rights.

Politics: Prototype Suburbia and the History of Hague

New Jersey has always had close, competitive two-party politics. Now, like the prototype suburban state it is, Jersey is developing prototype suburban politics. Angelo Baglivo has described it this way in the Newark *News*:

At this stage in New Jersey's political evolution, there is one dominant new force that is shattering traditional voting patterns. It is the independent voter who lives in his mortgaged home in the suburbs. On his middle-income salary, he frets about rising taxes—but demands more and better services from government.

He worries about the quality of education his children are receiving—but votes against increased school budgets and complains about teacher strikes and student activists.

He expresses sympathy with the plight of the disadvantaged in the city ghettos —but is frightened by black militancy and asks where it is all going to end.

When these voters lived by the thousands in the apartments and cold-water flats of Newark and Jersey City and Paterson, they formed the backbone of the Democratic machines. Jobs and favors from the local district leader were what politics and government were all about.

But they have migrated now to the sprawling housing developments of Manalapan Township in Monmouth and Madison Township in Middlesex and Jackson Township in Ocean County. They own homes, pay taxes and bills for utilities, have children in school and commute to work on congested roads and behind-schedule trains.

Government and the men who run it have direct impact now on the family budget and day-to-day life; there is a personal stake, an involvement in politics that was not there before. It has produced a voter who is neither Democrat, nor Republican; neither left-wing nor right-wing.

He seldom votes the straight party line. He votes his self-interest, or what he thinks it is. He can be attracted by the personal appeal of a candidate—that overworked word, "charisma." But most of all he is influenced by the times, the events of the day. . . . If there is any generalization that can be made about him in New Jersey, it is that he appears to prefer the middle ground of politics.

The elections of the past few years are dramatic proof of modern Jerseyites' scorn of party regularity. In 1965, Democratic Governor Richard J. Hughes won reelection with a sweeping 363,572-vote plurality (57.4 percent), the biggest vote lead of any governor in New Jersey history. On his coattails, Democrats won 2–1 majorities in the legislature. It was the first time Democrats had controlled the state senate in half a century. But just one year later, the state's popular liberal Republican U. S. Senator, Clifford Case, won another term by a massive 491,322-vote margin (60 percent). In 1967, in an astonishing reversal of political power on the state scene, the Republicans not only dislodged the Democrats from control of both houses of the legislature but took control by 3–1 margins. In 1968, Nixon beat Humphrey in Jersey by 61,261 votes (46.1 percent in the three-way race of that year), even while Democratic congressmen who were supposed to be in trouble easily won reelection. In 1969, Republican William Cahill won a landslide election for governor by 500,902 votes (59.7 percent) over his Democratic opponent; at the same time, the legislature stayed overwhelmingly Republican. But anyone who predicted a safe Republican era would have been mistaken. In the 1970 election for the U. S. Senate, Democratic incumbent Harrison A. Williams was returned with a plurality of 254,048 votes (54.0 percent) and the Republicans failed totally in dislodging the Democrats from their 9-6 edge on the U.S. House delegation. This was followed by the 1971 elections for both houses of the legislature, which were viewed partially as a referendum on the Cahill administration. The returns showed the Republicans had lost most of their majority in the state senate and were on the verge of losing control of the assembly to the Democrats.

Looking behind recent statewide figures, one finds some astonishing reversals of form in time-honored political patterns. Bergen County in northern New Jersey, middle-to-upper income and the GOP's banner county in the state, actually went Democratic by 41,100 votes in the 1965 election. The Democrats also took Atlantic County on the coast, long the domain of a Republican machine presided over by state Senator Frank S. Farley. But in 1969, both those counties were back to their old Republican ways (Bergen by a whopping 94,904-vote margin). Now it was the Republicans' turn to carry some counties that once voted as Democratic as surely as night follows day. Republican Cahill won Hudson (Jersey City and environs) by 30,687 votes and Essex (Newark and suburbs) by 15,709 votes.

Hudson might well have shown some Democratic edge in 1969 if the Republicans had not been handed their victory there on a silver platter by the old-style county political boss, John V. Kenny, who harbored a grudge against the Democratic nominee, former Governor Robert Meyner, dating from the early 1950s. But the fact is that the urban, city-dominated counties like Hudson and Essex have diminished so rapidly in political weight, while the counties with booming suburban housing developments have mushroomed in population and vote power, that the traditional voting patterns are being distorted beyond recognition. Between 1960 and 1968, Hudson lost 35,995 registered voters and Essex 19,372. (Registration actually dropped by 34,000 in Newark, with a partial offset in the Essex figure due to gains in the suburban parts of the county.) At the same time, Bergen gained 46,536 voters, so that it now has more than any other county in the state. Similarly dramatic gains were registered in predominantly suburban counties like Monmouth, Morris, Ocean, Burlington, and Middlesex.

It used to be said that a Democrat could carry New Jersey if he could build up a big enough lead in the party's six most reliable counties—Hudson, Essex, and Passaic in north Jersey, Middlesex and Mercer in the central portion of the state, and Camden, across the Delaware from Philadelphia. In 1960, Kennedy beat Nixon in New Jersey by a narrow margin of 22,091 votes, precisely because he registered an impressive plurality of 199,238 in the combined vote of those counties. In 1968, by contrast, Nixon gained his 61,261-vote victory in New Jersey because the same counties gave Humphrey a net advantage of only 107,944 votes, barely more than half the 1960 Democratic edge.

But the picture is not quite as bright for Republicans as the recent figures suggest. The actual Republican net plurality in the rural-suburban counties of the state declined from 180,979 to 169,187 votes between 1960 and 1968, even while suburban growth increased the total vote cast within them in a dramatic way. Two factors seem to be at work in the normally Republican areas: the fact that a voter does not automatically shift to the

GOP when he moves to the suburbs, and the weakening of the old-line Republican rural county organizations. Unless the Republicans nominate personally attractive and politically moderate candidates, the margins for them in suburban Jersey can switch to the Democrats in a twinkling. If Rockefeller had been the Republican candidate in 1968, he almost certainly would have taken New Jersey in a landslide. For the same reason, leading Republicans in the state warned after the party's 1970 debacle that unless the Nixon-Agnew Administration stopped its negative tack and assumed a more progressive image, the Democrats would be virtually guaranteed a victory in Jersey in the 1972 Presidential election.

Though their day seems finally to have passed, a word should be said about the county party bosses who made such an indelible mark on New Jersey. The entry into politics of the most illustrious Jerseyman of all time, Woodrow Wilson, was in fact sponsored by Democratic bosses such as James Smith, Jr., and James Nugent of Essex County and Robert Davis of Hudson County. (After Wilson's nomination for governor had been steamrollered by these worthies, who historians record "had auctioned off the state to the burgeoning railroads and utilities in return for juicy stock options and side deals," Wilson repudiated them, thus asserting his independence and beginning his climb to national fame.)

From 1917 to the late 1940s, the Democratic boss of Hudson County and mayor of Jersey City was Frank ("I Am The Law") Hague, a perfect example of his breed: born of immigrant parents and raised in the teeming Horseshoe slum of Jersey City, a devout and almost puritanical Roman Catholic who rose to power first on the issue of "reform," an intractable opponent whose enemies would often end up in jail—or the hospital—and an almost totally uneducated man with a taste for personal violence.* Yet Hague showed benevolence toward his constituents, who were rewarded for their support with Christmas food baskets, summertime boat rides and picnics, a great free medical center, and the highest city tax rates in America.

Hague himself earned only $7,500 a year as mayor, but by his own secret admission a few years before his death, he ended up worth at least $8 million. He said his wealth came from stocks and lucky investments; the more probable truth was that he got rich from the pound of flesh exacted from those who did business with Jersey City, and especially the gamblers who operated big off-track betting and numbers games there throughout his reign. (On the other hand, Hague drove out organized prostitution and was so intolerant of mobsters that his city detectives, disguised as bums, hung around the ferry slips and railroad stations, ready to ship any suspicious characters right back to New York.) Every Hudson County office-holder had to contribute 3 percent of his salary to Hague's organization, supposedly to finance election campaigns. "Jersey City Has Everything for Industry" was a slogan of those years, and a sweetheart contract was available for new

---

* A major source for much of the account which follows is an article, "I Am The Law," by Thomas J. Fleming, himself the son of a Jersey City ward leader, which appeared in *American Heritage* for June 1969.

factories since there was not a labor union in Hudson County which Hague had not reduced to docility.

Hague demanded extraordinary efficiency and breathtaking effort of his political machine. Not only did the Irish line up with him, but his ward and precinct captains found thousands of latter-day immigrants—Italians, Czechs, Poles, and Slovaks, many of them illiterates—who were cajoled into registering and then totally controlled. Republican poll watchers were bought out and made into "Hague Republicans." Thus it was that Hudson County could produce incredible pluralities, often in excess of 100,000 votes, at election time. Hague controlled the governorship for most of the 1920s and 1930s, since the Hudson County bloc vote was enough to control a Democratic primary and usually a general election. Hague delivered Hudson for the Democratic Presidential ticket by such huge margins in 1932, 1940, and 1944 that Republican pluralities in the rest of the state were overcome and Jersey turned to Franklin D. Roosevelt.* FDR openly embraced Hague in return, and Hague was chairman of both the Democratic Hudson County and New Jersey State Committees, as well as a member and vice chairman of the Democratic National Committee. He was one of the nation's great power brokers.

Hague's downfall came in the 1940s when he began to lose touch by spending inordinate amounts of time sojouring at the Plaza in New York or at his mansion on Biscayne Bay in Miami. A succession of Republican governors cut back on his power, and then rebellion arose within Jersey City itself, led by then ward boss John V. Kenny. In 1947, Hague resigned as mayor and had his nephew, Frank Hague Eggers, installed in his place; two years later, in a great wave of revulsion against Hagueism, the voters turned out Eggers in favor of Kenny.

The night of that election, Kenny's supporters snake-danced through the city streets and then stormed City Hall, hoping to find incriminating records. But the organization had known for hours that it was beaten, and nothing was found except charred paper in the furnace room. According to some witnesses, two suitcases full of money had been removed to a vault of the First National Bank earlier in the afternoon. Hague became a virtual exile from Jersey City, living in a Park Avenue apartment but fearing to enter Jersey because a subpoena was always waiting in connection with a $15 million suit filed against him by the three percenters trying to regain their tribute money of the past decades. Thus the last half of Hague's oft repeated statement—"In the Horseshoe I was born, in the Horseshoe I will die"—was proven false. He died in New York on January 1, 1956, and only then was his body returned to Jersey City for burial. A sparse crowd of Jersey Cityites turned out to watch the funeral, one of them an elderly woman standing in the street holding an American flag and a hand-lettered sign. The sign read: "God have mercy on his sinful, greedy soul."

---

* Only in one FDR election—1936—did the rest of New Jersey register a plurality for Roosevelt. Those who now romanticize the Roosevelt era should not forget that an important part of his electoral strength rested on the likes of Frank Hague.

Hague's removal from the Jersey scene did not end bossism. John V. Kenny, as it turned out, remained the power upon or behind the throne in Hudson County into the early 1970s, presiding over a system rife with graft, vote-roll padding, nepotism in government, and outright thievery. There was scarcely a let-up, for instance, in the ancient 3 percent for the Democratic organization that all city hall employees felt obliged to pay. The tribute always had to be paid in cash—no checks accepted; the income reportedly amounted to millions of dollars that the organization could use secretly or to finance campaigns. The political kickbacks were augmented by a 3 percent kickback demand on all contracts done with the city or county. Kenny retired as mayor in 1953 to concentrate on running the organization, or as the United States Attorney later put it, to oversee the "plunder" of public money.

Late in 1970, Kenny and his satrap, Jersey City Mayor Thomas J. Whelan, were among nine persons indicted by a federal grand jury on counts of extortion, conspiracy, and falsifying income tax returns. Kenny's case was severed from the others because of illness, but the other eight defendants were convicted following a 1971 trial in which the government estimated they had netted $3.3 million in kickbacks. "Anyone who wanted to do business with Hudson County or Jersey City was required to pay tribute, to kick back," U.S. Attorney Herbert Stern said in his summation. He said the trial would last a year if every contractor forced to make kickbacks were to testify.

During the trial, one witness said that Bernard G. Murphy, the Jersey City purchasing agent and alleged "bag man" in the conspiracy, climbed aboard a private jet at Newark Airport to tell a contractor that a $3 million kickback in cash would be required if he wanted to be the successful bidder on a $40 million reservoir project. That particular offer was rejected, but other evidence indicated that Mayor Whelan and City Council President Thomas Flaherty, another defendant, had stashed away $1.2 million in cash and bonds in a Miami Beach bank.

The 1971 trial, revealing a depth of corruption almost unprecedented in American history, would most probably never have taken place if the opposition political party, the Republicans, had not held national power at the time. Old Frank Hague was protected from prosecution by a Democratic administration in Washington during his last years in power.

After his conviction, Whelan was removed from office and a special autumn 1971 election held to fill the remaining eighteen months of his term. The Kenny organization at first decided to endorse no candidate for the seat, but then came out for a contender who ended up third in the balloting. The winner was a 30-year-old public health physician, Dr. Paul Jordan, candidate of the reformist Community Action Council. "Free at last!" Jordan exulted at a victory celebration. "We're free at last. Boss politics is dead in Jersey City, after 22 years of political corruption." And indeed, for the first time in living memory, Jersey City appeared to have elected a *truly* honest mayor.

Outside of Hudson County, the late Dennis F. Carey of Essex has probably been the most powerful Democratic boss of the last several years. Frank S. ("Hap") Farley was the best known equivalent on the Republican side. The power of the county chairmen is ingrained in the basic structure of New Jersey government and politics. Down to the legislative reapportionment of 1967, for instance, virtually all public officials—senators, assemblymen (lower house members), freeholders, and sheriffs—were elected in each county at large. The county leader who controlled his party's machinery controlled the nominating process and thus the access to power. Inevitably, all patronage began to flow through his hands, and if his party controlled the governorship, it would be to the governor's interest to clear all local appointments with the county chairman first. Thus the state party organization was relatively weak, while the county chairmen operated like arrogant feudal barons.

Often a county chairman could tell the members of his county's legislative delegation to Trenton just how they should vote. When Democratic Governor Richard Hughes proposed a graduated state income tax in the mid-1960s, for instance, the bill was scuttled by the Hudson and Essex County Democratic leaders who forbade their delegations to vote for it. (When I asked a high-ranking Democratic official of that era why the leaders had bucked Hughes on the tax, a revenue idea which accords with general Democratic party philosophy and state platforms, he replied that they had done so to protect their "personal" incomes!) The state then had to turn to the general sales tax, which hits the masses of low- and middle-class people in counties like Hudson and Essex much harder than the affluent suburban population. Even though Meyner and Hughes, both highly regarded Democratic governors, presided over Jersey government from 1954 to 1970, it might almost be said that five big county Democratic leaders actually controlled New Jersey in that time. In 1961, for instance, scarcely anyone in New Jersey had ever heard of Richard J. Hughes until a small conference, dominated by the big county bosses, met and chose him as what they thought would be the sacrificial lamb for the gubernatorial race against the prestigious former U. S. Secretary of Labor, Republican James P. Mitchell. At the time, Hughes's sole distinction had been as a lower court judge. But as it turned out, the bosses had hit on a jewel—a warm, gregarious, and totally honorable man, who turned out to be the greatest New Jersey campaigner of modern times and in the autumn eked out a narrow victory over Mitchell.* But today in New Jersey even Hughes closest friends will tell one that his major fault was in trusting people too much—especially the bosses. He went along with their recommendations of men to be county prosecutors, for instance, thus failing to avert the penetration of organized crime that would spring to view at the end of his term and tarnish his image.

Hughes himself became one of the first to warn his party to mend its ways through democratization—an end to the day of the closed, back-room direction by a handful of leaders—and finding a role for youth and people like the 1968 backers of McCarthy and Kennedy. In 1970, Hughes endorsed the controversial proposals of a Democratic party reform commission, headed

---

* Mitchell helped Hughes out by showing little sensitivity to New Jersey issues and then, after a few drinks one day, falling in a bathtub and breaking his leg, so that he couldn't campaign.

by one of the state's most prominent congressmen, Frank Thompson, Jr. The Thompson committee proposed reapportioning of various party committees to eliminate vastly differing population bases of the members, and also direct election in primaries of county chairmen. Not surprisingly, the ideas encountered stiff resistance by party regulars, grown indolent and self-satisfied after 16 years of patronage support by Democratic governors. Hughes has gone so far as to call the Democrats a party "searching for its soul," the present status akin to "lying on our backs, clawing the air like a dying cockroach . . . but not quite that bad."

Part of the Democrats' problem is the disorganization of the youthful and dissident members it might like to incorporate. The New Democratic Coalition, formed in the late 1960s to undertake that very task, fell apart in warring factions. New Jersey also lacks a strong, activist labor movement that could act as a catalyst of reform. The state AFL-CIO is dominated by quite conservative building trade unions, which withhold support from outspokenly liberal Democrats and tend to be hung up on the race problem. Some of the old CIO unions broke away in 1964 to form a more aggressive and politically liberal state Industrial Union Council, which was headed initially by Joel Jacobson, the UAW's most prominent leader in New Jersey. The IUC and UAW (the latter with about 50,000 workers in Jersey) do the most of any unions to define issues, promote voter registration, and the like. New Jersey has 737,000 union members, who make up 31 percent of the work force, the 15th highest percentage in the U. S.; if unified, they could be a potent political voice in the state.

Another ticklish problem for the Democrats is how to retain the overwhelming support they have been receiving from Negroes in the cities, especially as the blacks gain in political sophistication and know-how and challenge the old white power structures in the urban counties—the process presently taking place, for instance, in Essex County, where Newark has elected a black mayor. The black population would justify a Negro congressman, but none has been elected to date. A number of aggressive younger black leaders claim they have been excluded from the important decision-making processes in the Democratic party.

Ethnic rivalries may also plague the Democrats. Many of their top leaders are now Irish in a state with many more Italians, who will be clamoring for a gubernatorial candidate of their own kind soon.

The Republicans' problems are both like and unlike the Democrats'. The party does have patronage-oriented county chairmen like Atlantic's Farley, but they have been neither as numerous or as powerful as their Democratic counterparts. The Republican governors—Alfred E. Driscoll in the immediate postwar years and Cahill since 1970—have been strong men intent on running their own shows, largely immune to county influence. However, there is a clear ideological split between the Republican moderate-liberals, including Cahill, Case, many of the congressmen and state legislative leaders, and the more conservative factions which have run strong if losing statewide primary races in recent years. The power of the GOP's conservative bloc was substantially undercut by reapportionment in the 1960s, which ended the old system in which each county had a single state senator, regardless of population. The result of the old system had been that for 40 of 69 years, New Jersey had Democratic governors, yet the Republicans held senate control for all but four years.

With the old rural GOP organizations in eclipse and a Republican governor in office from south Jersey (an area lacking the political weight for long-term control), it is hard to see the likely source of the next generation of Republican leadership. But it might well come from Bergen County, the only area where the GOP has the money and vote muscle to exert lasting statewide influence. A leadership role for Bergen would probably be good, for that county has the income and educational levels to produce younger, brighter, more socially conscious leaders for the party. Bergen also has one of the nation's most astute younger Republican politicians, Nelson Gross, a man who lost overwhelmingly when he ran himself for the Senate in 1970 but shines in party managerial work and strategy planning for others.

Another problem for present-day Republicans is how much direct appeal they want to make for the growing black vote in the urban areas. In 1968, typical urban black precincts gave the Nixon-Agnew ticket only 12 percent of their vote. But Senator Case got 33 percent of the vote in the same areas in 1966, and Cahill 30 percent in the 1969 governorship election.

Amid all these confusing cross-currents, it may also be noted that regardless of ideology, New Jersey likes to reelect incumbents. The last three governors have all won second terms with ease.* New Jersey political reporters have difficulty recalling the last time a sitting U. S. Senator was defeated for reelection. Congressmen, once elected, tend to hold on regardless of the political complexion of their districts. Strangely, New Jersey has propelled few important leaders onto the national stage since the days of Woodrow Wilson (a born Virginian). The two Senators of recent years, Republican Clifford Case and Democrat Harrison A. Williams, Jr., are able men but are not regarded as heavies on the Washington scene. Case's voice is one of quiet, responsible liberalism among Senate Republicans. He is a bit of a loner, a man of high intellectual ability and moral stature with strong commitment in the civil rights area but easily faulted as a press-release do-gooder. Williams, a liberal who became chairman of the Senate Labor Committee in 1971, undercut his own effectiveness for years by heavy drinking and partying ways until he finally went on the wagon around the end of 1968. (Earlier that year, the New Jersey chapter of the NAACP publicly censured Williams for behavior unbecoming a Senator after an appearance he made at the group's state convention.) Williams is best known for his work on migrant worker and urban mass transit problems but is regarded by many as somewhat of a lightweight.

On the House side, Rep. Frank Thompson, Jr., of Trenton has built a record as one of the more articulate liberal Democrats and has a high-ranking

---

* Governors are elected for four-year terms with elections in odd-numbered years, coinciding neither with Presidential nor congressional elections. Only three other states—Kentucky, Louisiana, and Mississippi—have an analogous pattern of "off-season" gubernatorial elections.

slot on the Education and Labor Committee. Two younger progressive Democrats from North Jersey, James J. Howard and Henry Helstoski, have entrenched themselves in basically Republican districts since their first election in 1964. Republican Rep. Florence P. Dwyer, an eight-term veteran who always runs far ahead of her party's ticket in a Union-Essex County district, remains a spunky advocate of liberal Republicanism as she approaches her 70th birthday. She is senior Republican on the Government Operations Committee. Rep. William B. Widnall from Bergen County is the highly regarded ranking Republican on the House Banking and Currency Committee, where he has taken a leading position on housing legislation, and Rep. Peter H. B. Frelinghuysen of Morris County, scion of a family prominent in New Jersey public life for more than 200 years, is second-ranking Republican on the House Foreign Affairs Committee and a leading House spokesmen for his party on international relations.

Among other Jersey congressmen who made a mark in the postwar years were Republican Fred Hartley, coauthor of the Taft-Hartley Labor Relations Act, and J. Parnell Thomas, who was at the center of the Alger Hiss controversy as chairman of the House Un-American Activities Committee in 1947–48 but later went to prison for padding his congressional payroll. *Life* magazine in 1968 accused Congressman Cornelius E. Gallagher from Hudson County of being associated with top Mafia racketeer Joseph Zicarelli, but the voters have tolerantly returned him to office anyway. Gallagher is one of several New Jersey incumbents with thin records but safe seats.

Only state legislators, more faceless and thus nameless to the general public, tend to get shunted in and out of office rapidly in Jersey. It may be that those fickle suburban voters, once they get the name of an officeholder in their heads, simply vote the familiar until some cataclysmic event propels them to change their habits.

Two items of unfinished business should be on New Jersey's political agenda for the 1970s: reform of the campaign spending laws, and a change in the Presidential primary system. Election spending can be a special problem in New Jersey because of the very high cost of television appeals over New York and Philadelphia stations, which naturally charge candidates several times what the fair rate would be for reaching New Jersey alone. Candidates and political committees at all levels are required to file reports of their spending. But while these statutes have been on the books for several years, a 1969 report of the Citizens Research Foundation, a Princeton-based group which specializes in study of campaign finance all over the U. S., found that virtually no municipal committee reports and only half the required county reports had been filed.

New Jersey has had a Presidential primary since 1912, but the elected slates of delegates are often just the creations of the state party organizations, and therefore few serious Presidential candidates find it worthwhile to enter the nonbinding preference poll held the same day. Thus, with a semblance of democratic primaries, the state has in effect left it to the professional politicians to decide on its role in national conventions.

Under New Jersey law, it is almost ludicrously easy for minor-party candidates to qualify for the ballot. But the power of the major parties, and perhaps the lack of strong ideological movements, has suppressed third- and fourth-partyism on the model of neighboring New York. The last minor party which got any measure of public notice was the one-man effort of Henry Krajewski, a pig farmer from Secaucus. Krajewski ran for President in 1952, 1956, and 1960 on the Poor Man's Party and American Third Party tickets, trying to prove to the world that a poor man could become Chief Executive. George Thayer in *The Farther Shores of Politics* describes Krajewski as a Runyonesque character from an earlier age, soft-hearted with a vivid wit. He spoke with a Jersey City accent, scorned the regular parties as "boids of a feather," and pulled stunts like taking a baby pig mascot with him when he filed for President. (The proceedings were disrupted somewhat when the little fellow defecated on some of the more vital documents.) Reporters had a field day covering Krajewski, one of the last men to mock the absurdities of American politics. He died in the 1960s, and Jersey is a poorer place for his departure.

Life Under a New Constitution and the Tax Dilemma

New Jersey state government deserves an "A" for its constitution and organizational simplicity, a "C" for its ill-staffed but much-improved legislature, and an "F" for its antediluvian tax structure.

First the constitution. The state labored until 1947 under an incredibly outmoded constitution of 1844 vintage which gave the governor a three-year term with a prohibition on succeeding himself, let his veto be overridden by simple majorities in the legislature, provided one-year terms for assemblymen (facilitating county boss control of them), and in general fostered wasteful and inefficient government. For instance, the legislature created more than 100 independent or semi-independent agencies which the governor could not control. Some department heads were selected by the legislature, and the terms of officials the governor could pick generally did not coincide with his term, so that he might be stuck for the better part of his time in office with men not in sympathy with him. To top it all off, the court system was complex and cumbersome in the extreme.

Pressure for constitutional reform mounted rapidly in the 1930s, especially as government improvement groups recognized how the old document played into the hands of both Mayor Hague and the rural interests. After several false starts, an entirely new constitution was written in 1947 and approved by the voters the same year. It was practically the opposite of its predecessor. Instead of one of the weakest governors in America, New Jersey suddenly had the strongest. His term was extended to four years, and he could run a second time, he became the only official to be elected statewide, and he received sweeping powers of appointment—the normal "constitutional offices" like attorney general, treasurer, and secretary of state, the heads of all departments, some county administrative officials, members of policy-forming and advisory boards, commissions, agencies, and members of interstate and intrastate authorities. The legislature was given power to create departments, but they could not number more than 20, with no commissions, boards, or agencies independent of them. (Eventually 17 departments emerged, and there has been a proposal in later years to cut the number to six.) The new constitution also strengthened the governor's veto power and gave him authority to convene the legislature at will. In effect, he emerged with power in his state comparable to the President on the federal level.

At the same time, the new constitution took another leaf from the federal document by placing few specific restrictions on the power of the legislature to make laws for the welfare of the state. (One especially annoying provision was included, however: a requirement for voter approval of any state debt beyond a minuscule level. Governmental improvements, especially in the higher education field, have been seriously delayed by this provision.) The new charter extended assemblymen's terms to two years and set senate terms at four years. But it did not change the one-county, one-senator reapportionment rule—a change that only the federal courts were able to effect, two decades later. The 1947 constitution also decreed a simplified and more unified court system, under the clear control and direction of the chief justice of the state supreme court.

So admired was New Jersey's 1947 constitution that when Alaska joined the Union in 1959, the first new state in almost half a century, it copied its basic charter quite closely from the New Jersey model.

In large measure, the New Jersey constitution has lived up to its authors' fondest expectations. Alfred E. Driscoll, the man who was governor when it was passed, is thought by some to have been the finest chief executive in New Jersey's history. A true patrician and intellectual, he is given credit both for guiding the constitution to passage and for implementing it skillfully in the seven additional years he was governor. (Driscoll was also father of the New Jersey Turnpike and Garden State Parkway. His politics were progressive and honest, and he suggested the idea of federal revenue sharing years before its time. Actually, the past tense is ill used, since Driscoll has remained active in New Jersey life and at this writing serves as chairman of the Turnpike Authority.)

Driscoll's successors have all been men of stature too: Robert Meyner, amazingly prudent and frugal for a Democratic governor, the man who brought his party back to respectability in the post-Hague era; Richard Hughes, a warmhearted liberal who made a manly effort to get Jersey to face up to its fiscal follies by enacting a broad-based tax; and finally incumbent William Cahill, a tough, no-nonsense Irishman, whose public image on the issues he has tackled (standing up for Jersey's interests in the New York Port Authority, holding budgets in line, fighting for a major league sports complex in Northern New Jersey) has been a popular one. The appointments of most of these men have been excellent, though Hughes was faulted for heeding big-county bosses in some of his selections and Cahill for packing the state house with many of his South Jersey Irish cronies.*

The legislature was strengthened by the constitution but remained hung up for a number of years thereafter on the dual spikes of malapportionment and the caucus system. Equally populated districts were decreed for assemblymen, but senators were still elected on the old one-a-county basis, creating districts so grossly unequal that less than a fifth of the voters could elect a majority of the senate. Then the Republican caucus (sometimes just 11 of the 21 senators) would meet behind closed doors to scrutinize all bills and decide whether they should go to the senate floor for action. Thousands of meritorious bills—and probably some bad ones—met their death in the caucus.† By tradition, the Republican senators voted en bloc, despite their personal positions, in support of any action taken by the caucus. Thus an old wheeler-dealer like Atlantic County's Hap Farley could control the entire senate by getting just five other senators (a majority of the Republican caucus) to vote with him.

For years, Democrats made a chief campaign plank out of the encrusted caucus system, which endured until the courts forced equally populated districts in the mid-1960s and the senate fell to the Democrats. When the Republicans returned to power in 1968, they reestablished their old caucus, but without malapportionment it seemed to lack its most Mephistophelean attributes. In the assembly, the caucus principle continues but in the new, somewhat bipartisan format of a conference committee which regulates the flow of bills to the floor and has the power to expedite or kill controversial measures. One of the unhappy results of the caucus or conference system is that it undermines the authority of the existing legislative committees, which sometimes lapse into nearly total inactivity. Only one or two of the committees have viable, full-time staffing, and the office of the legislative counsel, though expanded in recent years, is tremendously overworked. In short, the Jersey legislature is lacking in substantive work done by more than a select few legislators. Part of the problem is the weird scheduling practice, in which the legislature keeps meeting almost year-round, but only one or two days in each week. Members are expected to commute on chosen days (presently Monday and Thursday) from their homes to Trenton. When they arrive, they have no offices to work in, and they just mill around the assembly and senate chambers. Sometimes, before they have time for any serious debate or work, it is time to commute home again. The State House building is incredibly crowded, but although a new legislative building was authorized in the late 1960s, work has not gone forward. All these impediments led the national Citizens Conference on State Legislatures, in its 1971 report evaluating legislative bodies across the coun-

---

* To be really "in" with Cahill, according to one of his protagonists in Trenton, "you got to be not only Irish, Catholic, Republican, and from South Jersey, but then you got to come from a triangle defined by the Garden State Racetrack, Mt. Holly, and Cherry Hill." Some Italians, members of a group who voted strongly for Cahill in 1969, claim he has slighted their group in appointments, either because of ethnic tunnel vision or because he sees a Mafioso behind every Italian name.

† The Rules Committee of the U. S. House has traditionally functioned in the same manner. A good Jersey example of the practice came in 1971, when the more level-headed legislators feared a bill to legalize casino gambling might well pass if brought to an open vote. So they had it quietly killed in the caucus.

try, to rank New Jersey only 32nd in terms of its decision-making capabilities.

These impediments notwithstanding, the Jersey legislature has produced some highly regarded leaders in the past few years, especially in its senate. (The assembly, by contrast, is encumbered with an archaic rule limiting the presiding officer to a single two-year term.) Senate president Raymond H. Bateman claims that the quality of legislators in Trenton has risen sharply since the late 1950s. "Then," he said, "the senate was small [21 members compared to the present 40], dominant, and very conservative. Today the senate, through reapportionment, is the more liberal body. The assembly, where members have smaller districts and more parochial attitudes, is where the new ideas break down. But this legislature [1970–71] is the best I've ever served in, and it's also the most city-oriented." But how, I asked him, can a heavily suburban, Republican legislature really be expected to care about Democratic center cities? He replied: "The urban-suburban lines begin to fade. We're the most urbanized of all states. You just drive from one city into another, and it's hard to know where the line is, and they all have the same kind of problems." Bateman said that the pace of business in the legislature had picked up so rapidly since the late 1960s that about a third of the ablest members were retiring because of the press of their businesses; the only long-term solution, he said, would be a smaller legislature, working full time for high pay. (Jersey legislators currently receive $10,-000 a year.)

The record shows that the New Jersey legislature has made forward steps in correcting the sins of omission and commission of past decades but still has a long way to go. The depth of problems was highlighted in this 1968 report of the Governor's Commission to Evaluate the Capital Needs of New Jersey, which seemed to suggest a number of Armageddons might be on the agenda for the 1970s:

Everywhere that this commission looked, it saw the tragic results of years of neglect. Passenger rolling stock is on the verge of collapse. Railroad stations are dark and dilapidated. Highways are choked. A severe drought brought us to the brink of real peril. Prisons and mental health institutions are patched and worn, with many positively inhumane facilities. Secondary and elementary schools are overcrowded and many of the older ones are sadly in need of repair or replacement. Our colleges and universities can accommodate only a fraction of our applicants, forcing most of them to go out of state. Our rivers are polluted and our cities are pockmarked with crumbling ghettos.

Comparative state statistics bear out the dreary assessment of New Jersey's performance. State tax revenue as a percentage of personal income ranks only 48th among the 50 states; this is offset to a degree by an exceptionally high local property tax (the third highest in the U. S. A.), but even when one counts all state and local levies, the tax burden in New Jersey, related to personal income, is only 31st among the 50 states.

The excessive reliance on local taxation goes back to the 18th century, when the primary wealth of Jersey was in land for agriculture and the colonial assembly delegated part of its taxing power to the counties, thus beginning a tradition of unfettered "home rule" which endures to this day. With its perennial inferiority complex vis-à-vis its neighbors, New Jersey seemed to feel through its history that (1) it lacked the financial resources for major universities or other facilities, and (2) in any case out-of-staters could be taxed to make up any shortage that property taxes failed to produce. In the 19th century, the Camden and Amboy Railroad, in return for the monopoly given it by the legislature, charged "transit duties" on all passengers and freight passing through (but not originating in) New Jersey. The yield was enough to finance the entire state government for many years, at the expense of citizens of other states. Along the same lines, a proposal was made in 1963 to float a $750 million bond issue for both current and capital needs. The bonds would have been amortized by toll receipts on the New Jersey Turnpike, again fleecing out-of-staters for Jersey's own expenses. Strangely, the voters turned down this idea, but in Trenton one still hears dark forebodings about the angry citizen reaction that will await any politician who raises taxes.*

Only by the greatest wrench with instinct and tradition did the legislature bring itself to enact a sales tax in 1966. (Up to that year, Jersey had been one of only three states in the entire country without some form of broadbased tax, either on sales or income.) In 1970, the sales tax was increased from 3 to 5 percent to meet an impending budget crisis, but anyone with a rudimentary knowledge of state finances knew it was only a matter of time until Jersey joined its neighbors with an income tax. Local property taxes were raising about $2 billion a year, some $200,000 more than *all* other state and local taxes in New Jersey, including the sales tax. The property tax is an oppressive burden for everyone in the state, but has reached disaster proportions in big urban counties like Essex and Hudson, where low-income blacks have flooded into the center cities and the burdens of sharply increased public employee salaries and welfare are almost intolerable. Urban tax rates, in fact, are threatening the extinction of Jersey's cities as viable economic entities. By 1972, a report was due from a blue-ribbon citizens tax reform committee, headed by retiring state senate majority leader Harry L. Sears and containing prominent leaders of both parties; the expectation was that the committee would recommend New Jersey's first income tax, tied to general property tax relief. But then there was the eternal question: would the governor or leaders in the legislature have the courage to associate themselves with such a radical reform and see it through to passage?

When the tax battle is finished, New Jersey will face an issue just as delicate and controversial: Governor Cahill's proposal that the state be given power to override local zoning regulations and enforce a statewide building

---

* New Jersey is trying one "painless" way of raising money, a state lottery that went into operation in December 1970 after an overwhelming referendum approval of the people. Designed to outclass and outperform the more disappointing experiments in New York and New Hampshire, the New Jersey version has weekly drawings (instead of every month, as in New York, or New Hampshire's seven times a year), the tickets are less expensive, and they are freely available in supermarkets, liquor stores, drugstores, newsstands, luncheonettes. Within a few months, the lottery had proven itself a smashing success—and probably helped to cut the ground out from under illegal numbers games in the state.

code. The idea is an explosive one in Jersey, because of the long and passionate history of strong home rule for municipalities. But state control will doubtless be required if New Jersey is to succeed in preserving adequate amounts of open spaces, chiefly parklands, before development gobbles up all the prime land in the state. Land is presently being wasted by some suburban zoning codes that require a minimum of one or two acres for single-family houses and totally forbid multi-unit buildings. The same stratagem, of course, effectively excludes low-income families—meaning most blacks—from the suburbs. Many municipalities fear that statewide building codes and zoning power would be a forerunner of some form of metropolitan government—an idea whose day must come but has yet even to dawn in New Jersey.

Education, Transportation, and the Environment

Limited resources have predictably meant limited government in New Jersey. Per capita spending of state and local governments ranks 43rd in the U. S. in public welfare, 28th in highways, a quite respectable 18th for public schools (with one of the highest teacher salary scales in the country), but only 49th in support of colleges and universities. The dismal record in higher education is a holdover from the days when New Jersey simply sloughed off its responsibilities in the field to private universities, with Princeton the centerpiece. The legislature designated Rutgers College at New Brunswick as the land-grant college for New Jersey in 1864 but did not favor the college with its first dollar of state aid for 38 more years. In 1945, still primarily a private college in character, Rutgers belatedly got the title of "state university," but it was more than a decade more until commensurate financial assistance appeared. "Meanwhile," Richard McCormick has written, "most of the children of New Jersey who sought higher education had to go to colleges out of state. And why not? If other state universities would accept and educate our children, why should we burden our own taxpayers with such costs?"

In the late 1960s, New Jersey was still the biggest "debtor" state in higher education in the U. S. The 1968 figures, for instance, showed Jersey was "exporting" 98,710 more students to out-of-state universities than it was accepting from other states. But starting under a master plan for education drawn up in the 1960s, plus much more generous state financing, major improvements have started and are progressing. Rutgers has been able to boost its enrollment to over 30,000 at 18 colleges and schools in five campus locations. The state moved from having no publicly supported medical schools to two by the late 1960s. Starting from ground zero, the state opened 13 community colleges with 35,000 students and anticipated three more and a total enrollment of 85,000 by 1975. Six old single-purpose teachers colleges were expanded into full-fledged state colleges, and two were on their way to university status in the early 1970s.

There has even been room for some experimentation. In 1969, Rutgers' new Livingston College opened, with a curriculum oriented to urban problems and an enrollment 25 percent black and Hispanic. Rutgers also inaugurated a special program, available at its New Brunswick, Newark, and Camden campuses, which seeks out blacks and Puerto Ricans from slum communities, starts them with remedial courses, and then moves them on to regular university courses, with the hope they can earn a bachelor's degree within six years. Interestingly, the new students turned out to be more conservative and industrious, and less given to political activity, than their middle-class colleagues. Joel Jacobson, a Rutgers trustee, told me the program's result up to 1971 had shown a mixture of brilliant breakthroughs by some students and the inevitable disappointments in other cases.

In the aggregate, however, New Jersey has leagues to come before it can even be mildly competitive with other states in higher education. But there are fields where it has been doing a lot better: court administration, social legislation, transportation planning, and protection of the environment.

Acting in 1948 under the new constitution, the Driscoll administration effected a reorganization of the courts that many considered a national model, and to this day impartial observers like the Institute of Judicial Administration in New York call the Jersey judiciary "one of the very best administered in the country." But this may be a case where the best is not good enough. After a 1970 survey, the New York *Times* reported that New Jersey courts had congested calendars, inadequate representation of the poor, erratic treatment of traffic and minor criminal cases. The reasons were familiar enough: too few judges, prosecutors, lawyers, and court personnel, a sharp increase in crime over the past several years, and the rulings of the U. S. Supreme Court which make possible a plethora of pretrial motions with great delaying effects. Chief Justice Joseph Weintraub of New Jersey suggests the criminals themselves are somewhat responsible for court delays. "Realistically," he says, "most of them are guilty, and they're in no hurry to go on trial."

New Jersey has taken some interesting steps in social legislation. In 1971, it passed one of the country's first divorce laws permitting "no-fault" decrees for couples living apart with no hope of reconciliation. The year before, it led the entire nation in passing a drug law which defined a "small amount" of marijuana, established reduced penalties for anyone caught with lesser amounts,* but sharply increased penalties for convicted pushers of hard drugs like barbiturates and amphetamines. There was real personal drama in the drug bill for Governor Cahill, whose 19-year-old son had been arrested twice on charges of possessing marijuana. And senator Fairleigh S. Dickinson, Jr., of Bergen County, a multimillionaire philanthropist and chief author of the legislation, had even more reason to be personally involved. His

---

* A lesser amount was defined as 25 grams of marijuana, or enough for about 70 marijuana cigarettes. Previously, possession of any quantity of the drug had made a person liable to a prison sentence of two to 15 years; under the new legislation the figure was reduced to six months for the lesser amounts, and not long after that the state supreme court effectively eliminated any jail for a person (on a first offense) possessing marijuana for his personal use only. Prison sentences, the court said, could have a "particularly devastating" effect on many young persons.

only son and heir, Fairleigh S. Dickinson, III, had died the year before at age
19 from an apparent overdose of opium in his room at Columbia College.

But in programs that cost more money, New Jersey often falls down. One
example, not unique to this state but still serious in the extreme: there is a
need for 50,000 subsidized, low-cost housing units in New Jersey each year.
But only 1,500 are being built. In 1966, Hughes recommended and the
legislature created a new state department of community affairs; to head it,
Paul Ylvisaker, one of the nation's most brilliant urbanologists and a former
Ford Foundation official, was selected. Ylvisaker's department handled federal poverty grants for New Jersey practically as a block grant, and administered low-income housing efforts. Ylvisaker demanded of Hughes and got
the right to appoint his staff of about 85 professionals without regard to political connections; given that freedom, he picked a young, bushy-tailed
group (average age: late 20s) with a sensitivity to race and urban problems.
With its job ill defined, Ylvisaker's staff acted as a kind of mobile striking
force. It moved into Newark during the 1967 riots to help in food distribution, bringing in medicine under fire and conducting peace-making missions.
But the financing of the new department, while it was enough "to keep our
bureaucrats occupied," as Ylvisaker put it, was not great enough to make a
fundamental attack on urban problems as they exist in the state. He would
have liked to inaugurate an experimental income maintenance (or "negative
income tax") program for low income families, for instance, but never got the
chance. Ylvisaker left the job after the 1969 Republican gubernatorial victory to take a seat on the faculty at Princeton, departing state government
with a conviction that fundamental "flow changes" in the way public dollars are channeled would be necessary to a solution of the country's urban
ills—putting all education costs on the state governments, for instance, and
health and welfare expenditures on the federal government.

In transportation, New Jersey faces the excruciating problem of getting
almost 300,000 workers across the Hudson into New York every day and
back home at night with relative ease and comfort. Compared to this task,
the building of the great New Jersey Turnpike and Garden State Freeway
was a straight-forward, uncomplicated task. The *interstate* nature of the problem complicates it to begin with. New Jersey in 1921 joined in the Port of
New York Authority with New York State but for years let the authority concentrate on New York City-oriented construction projects. A first break in
Jersey's complacent attitude came in 1962 when it demanded that the authority take over, rehabilitate, and operate the old Hudson and Manhattan
Railroad (the Hudson "tubes") as a *quid pro quo* for New Jersey's agreement to the authority's construction of the World Trade Center on Manhattan. Modernized and improved, the old tubes (now called PATH—Port
Authority Trans-Hudson system) carry over 100,000 passengers a day, albeit
with an annual deficit the authority must cover out of other revenues. In
southwestern Jersey, the Delaware River Port Authority was formed with
Pennsylvania in 1951; it took over major bridges across the Delaware and
also constructed a new high-speed transit line linking Philadelphia with the

greater Camden area, one of the country's most successful rail mass transit experiments of recent decades.

These advances have only slowed the trend toward obsolescence and bankruptcy in the road, rail, and air transit systems of the heavily traveled New York-Jersey-Philadelphia corridor. Massive traffic jams and commuter-line breakdowns have become especially prevalent on the approaches to New York City, all the railroads have demanded subsidies to continue in operation, and New Jersey has feuded with the Port Authority over its effort to build a fourth New York area jetport somewhere in northern New Jersey. (Cahill became so frustrated with the Port Authority's nonessential undertakings that he issued an ultimatum saying he would henceforth exercise his veto power unless New Jersey got "dollar for dollar" parity on new construction projects. He insists that a network of STOL—short take-off and landing—airports in New Jersey and neighboring states could eliminate the need for a fourth jetport.)

In 1966, at Hughes' instigation, a New Jersey department of transportation was created, starting overall planning in the transit area but often running afoul of the existing turnpike and highway authorities. The department issued a $2 billion, 10-year expansion program in 1968, which got underway with approval of a $640 million transportation bond issue that year (a third for rails, two-thirds for highways).* But Cahill, after one year in office, pronounced transportation the most difficult problem he had had to deal with and started to campaign for a fantastic array of programs, including the parallel roads and extensions to the New Jersey Turnpike and Garden State Parkway systems, a vastly expanded rapid-transit system radiating from Newark, big parking facilities beside the turnpikes and rail commuter lines of north Jersey, and consideration of ideas like mass transit lines along the turnpikes and restricted highway lanes for commuter buses. His get-tough stand with the Port Authority produced agreement in 1971 to build a $200 million rapid transit network linking Newark Airport with downtown Newark, Manhattan, and parts of Union County.

Environmental control is an area of special difficulty for New Jersey, but one in which it is making significant progress. Richard J. Sullivan, the talented young civil servant selected to head the new department of environmental protection, states the problem this way: "Bad things that happen to the environment happen in New Jersey first. We have more of the things per square mile that make the air and water dirty than any other state—we are the most densely populated, we have the most cars per square mile, and we have the biggest chemical industry. For decades, we've let the growth of New Jersey greatly outdistance the methods of waste disposal needed to accommodate that growth." Predictably, pollution problems are severest in the grimy industrial areas adjacent to New York and Philadelphia, but the problems spread throughout the state. New Jersey is practically an island, except for its 48-mile northern border with New York State, and

---

* New Jersey is one of a small handful of states which finance their highways from general fund appropriations rather than earmarked or dedicated funds. One result is a climate much friendlier to mass transit alternatives than one finds in other states.

makes intensive use of its waterways for water supply, industrial applications, seafood, recreation—and as effluent carriers. Obviously, the various uses conflict. Virtually all the major waterways are polluted, but the worst are the Passaic River in north Jersey * and the lower Delaware. As far as air pollution is concerned, one needs only to take a ride along the northern stretches of the New Jersey Turnpike, past putrid-smelling refineries and chemical plants, caught in an air pocket laden with the sulphur dioxide, carbon monoxide, and other noxious vehicle emissions, to know what the problem is all about.

Comparatively, Jersey has made its biggest strides fighting air pollution, and all in the limited period since 1967, when the legislature gave state authorities the strictest enforceable regulations in all the states. Since then, hundreds of cases have been taken to court, and the state has won every one. A celebrated battle was with the airlines to make them modify their jet engines to create less smoke while using Newark Airport; another was with the fuel and power industry on the sulphur content of coal and oil. New Jersey also became the first state to require inspection of all automobiles as sources of pollution—a brave step, Sullivan claims, since it is *voters'* cars which are inspected.

Progress in water pollution control has been slower, because the most persistent offenders turn out to be municipalities and their inadequate sewage treatment plants. The local governments involved are often broke and can try to exert political pressure to avoid orders to upgrade their water treatment plants.

Under a strong 1970 bill, the state is also stepping in to protect some 300,000 acres of wetlands along the Jersey Coast—salt marshes, estuaries, and inlet flats that are essential to the ecological life chain but endangered by uncontrolled growth. "We don't want to end up," Sullivan says, "with houses, marinas, lagoons, and waterfront restaurants lining our coast, elbow-to-elbow, from Sandy Hook to Cape May." Unsound sanitary and land-use methods are the worst danger. Some coastal communities have been poisoning themselves on their own waste, generally through a superfluity of septic systems which result in sewage rising in ground water on front lawns, spewing into bayside lagoons, and poisoning coastal tributaries. Under the new legislation, Sullivan is using his power to intervene in critical areas where he has the power to suspend all septic tank construction. New Jersey also passed a tough 1971 bill requiring that sewage sludges and industrial wastes be dumped 100 miles out in the Atlantic, or at least beyond the continental shelf, rather than the existing 12-mile limit. In signing the bill, Governor Cahill said: "Ocean dumping of sewage and polluted dredge-spoil a scant 12 miles from our coastline and beaches is a primitive, insensitive, and completely unacceptable method of waste disposal." It was hoped the new measure might save Jersey beaches from an annual "red tide" of tiny organisms

* In 1969, Murray Stein, assistant commissioner of the Federal Water Pollution Control Administration, called the Passaic a "disgrace to the United States, . . . a fetid, polluted stream that offends human sensibilities and is a danger to health and welfare." The river flows past Paterson, Clifton, Passaic, and Newark.

that redden the sea, give swimmers rashes, and threaten the shore's ecology.

But in the area of solid waste disposal, Sullivan admits, New Jersey has "yet to move into a program we could dignify with the term management." It's not enough anymore, he says, to take garbage to the end of town and dump it—"because most of our towns don't have edges anymore."

With federal regional standards for air and water pollution in effect, a tough enforcement authority like New Jersey's no longer need be concerned with industries fleeing to avoid pollution control. Sullivan regards the whole "runaway industry" concept (traditionally used by big factories to scare off pollution crackdowns) as "a bugaboo" under present-day conditions. Clean air and water devices, he suggests, are now regarded by industry—along with taxes, water supply, availability of skilled labor, proximity to markets, and transportation costs—as "just another element of the cost of doing business." Sullivan also takes issue with what he calls the "calamity merchants"—those who suggest that all the environmental protection efforts underway are pale shadows of the effort that would really have to be made to save the continent's air and waters from an ecological disaster soon. The rapid, almost total shifts of public, government, and industry attitudes on the environment have built a momentum for enforcement, he suggests, that is likely to strengthen rather than slacken in the coming years.

The bill creating New Jersey's department of environmental protection was signed by Governor Cahill on Earth Day 1970—a pulling together of many related agencies on the theory that if the environment is indeed an interdependent entity, there should be a department of state government responsible for all its areas. Only time will tell whether the bureaucrats of all the separate parts—air and water pollution control, fish and game, beach protection, water supply, solid waste management, state parks and forests —will work together well on a day-by-day basis, though Sullivan claimed good progress in that direction during the first year. Sullivan's own start in environmental control had been in the last three years of the Hughes administration; then Cahill continued him in office and elevated him to the new departmental directorship. I asked whether there was a difference working for the two political parties on environmental control. No, Sullivan replied, he had not encountered problems with either party and would not characterize Cahill's as a business-oriented Republican administration. The stakes were much too large for that; he insisted: "The climate here is that people know the environment is closing in on them. The hard enforcement line is popular with everyone." His own ability to survive a change in administrations was due in part to a group of dedicated environmentalists in the private sector and the legislature.

A Criminal Encounter

Up through the late 1960s, organized crime was able to bore within to take control of the city of Newark, infest other northern Jersey governments, and even influence New Jersey's state government to a degree never before documented and perhaps never achieved in one of the 50 states. Then the federal Justice Department stepped in with a concerted campaign to break the back of Jersey's Mafia. There followed a blizzard of indictments and convictions which, in the words of Fred J. Cook, author of *The Secret Rulers*, "outlined the most complete network of crime and official corruption that has yet to be brought to trial in an American courtroom. There has been nothing remotely comparable to this since the Murder, Inc., trials of 1940; and by comparison even Murder, Inc., was pallid stuff." Now many of Jersey's hoodlum chiefs sit behind bars, former Mayor Hugh Addonizio of Newark stands convicted of 64 counts of conspiracy and extortion, state law enforcement has been fundamentally reformed under the new Republican administration, and organized crime in Jersey has apparently subsided significantly. But Jersey's bitter experience is one the other states might well take to heart.

But why, one asks, did it all happen in New Jersey? There seem to be two answers: first, Jersey's peculiar governmental-political system, and secondly, the accident of geography. Voters turn out in such low numbers for primary elections that the county political bosses could hold almost unlimited power for decades. The governor technically appoints county prosecutors and judges, but the county political bosses in effect dictated the choices. Thus law enforcement officials became answerable to the county bosses, not Trenton. Under law, the county prosecutors had almost autonomous control over county law enforcement, and the state attorney general's office could do little to interfere.

New Jersey's strategic location was a major factor. Organized crime first took hold in the state during Prohibition. Newark's Abner ("Longie") Zwillman, a suave businessman of crime, organized a bootlegging ring that reaped some $50 million in profits between 1926 and 1931. The state's extensive, cove-dotted coastline offered a nearly endless supply of hiding places for the swift boats of the rumrunners, and it was thought that 40 percent of the nation's bootlegging operations took place there. Zwillman became the effective Democratic boss of Newark's Third Ward, and his money financed several Democratic gubernatorial and legislative campaigns.

During the 1930s, when Thomas E. Dewey made New York too uncomfortable a place for racketeers, many of them moved across the Hudson to New Jersey—tough practitioners of the art like Frank Erickson, Joe Adonis, Anthony ("Tony Bender") Strollo, Albert Anastasia, and Vito Genovese. Genovese was to head the New Jersey Mafia until he went to federal prison in 1960 on a narcotics charge and later died. His successor was said to be Gerardo ("Jerry") Catena, a man with a police record of eight convictions ranging from truck hijacking to bribery of a federal juror. Using the proceeds of his gambling, extortion, and loan-sharking rackets, Catena built up several legitimate businesses in trucking, restaurants, and vending machines and exercised heavy political influence in the Newark city government and, some said, in the state legislature. The New York *Times* reported that

Catena's ties with Meyer Lansky and Zwillman helped strengthen the bonds between the Italian mob and their Jewish gangster associates.

Gradually the tentacles of organized crime spread across New Jersey. A police chief was bought here, a mayor there. Selectmen, sheriffs, and county political leaders were also cajoled, threatened, or greased. The money rolled in, from gambling, narcotics, loan-sharking, and labor racketeering. By the late 1960s, organized crime was estimated to gross up to $1 billion annually in northern New Jersey. Up to that time, the public only rarely got a glimpse of what was happening. A major exception came in the wake of the Kefauver Committee's investigation and tandem state probes in the early 1950s, which flushed out Mafia infiltration of the state Republican party, centered in Bergen County. There were indictments, trials, and convictions, which played a role in the 1953 Democratic takeover of state government.

Then came more years of silent prosperity for the Mafia. The range of activities was incredibly broad. Gambling, for instance, took the nickels and dimes of poor Negroes playing the numbers and also the big bills of heavy gamblers who dealt with the syndicate bookmakers in betting on horse races and football and basketball pools. One of the biggest gambling operations was run out of Newark by Ruggiero ("Richie the Boot") Boiardo, a veteran mobster who had once been saved from death in an assassination attempt by Zwillman's boys when his $5,000 diamond belt buckle stopped a bullet. Zwillman and Boiardo later made peace and divided the Newark territory between them. Zwillman committed suicide in 1959, but Boiardo carried on until 1968 when, at age 78, he was convicted of running a numbers operation and packed off to jail. Boiardo's son Anthony ("Tony Boy") took over the gambling operation in his dad's place. (Back in 1950, when Tony Boy was married, more than 2,000 guests turned out for the wedding, including then Mayor Ralph Villani of Newark, then Congressman Addonizio, and Peter W. Rodino, who is still a Congressman from New Jersey's 10th District and next in seniority to become chairman of the House Judiciary Committee.)

The really big action, though, seemed reserved for Catena. He controlled Port Newark through minions who were officers of the International Long-shoremen's Association, and it was reported that the syndicate was heisting tens of millions of dollars worth of goods each year at the docks. (More than two dozen New Jersey unions were said to be under mob influence, ranging from Teamsters to restaurant workers' locals, with many a sweetheart contract that lined the pockets of the gangsters but deprived workers of a fair wage or job security.)

The traditional wall of secrecy about Mafia activity and infiltration of government began to crumble in the wake of the 1967 Newark riots. The commission appointed by Governor Hughes to investigate the disorders reported that an important underlying cause was "a pervasive feeling of corruption" in Newark. The commission said several knowledgeable officials had used an identical phrase: "There is a price on everything at City Hall." In subsequent state legislative hearings, Prof. Henry S. Ruth, who had been deputy staff director of the President's Commission on Law Enforcement and the Administration of Justice, touched sensitive political nerves by saying: "Official corruption in New Jersey is so bad that organized crime can get almost anything it desires." (Apparently it had been that way for a long time. A former high official in the Meyner administration told me that a man one day walked into his office at the state house in Trenton asking to be a judge. In his hand, the visitor had a bag with $15,000 in cash—apparently the going price. In that case, the offer was rejected, but it is not hard to imagine that many similar offers were accepted.) In December 1968, William J. Brennan, III, a young state prosecutor and son of the Supreme Court Justice, caused a great uproar when he remarked that a number of legislators were "entirely too comfortable with members of organized crime." Initially, there was a strong effort to characterize Brennan's charges as groundless and irresponsible. But, in the end, he was vindicated. Two of the state legislators he named were censured and a third, Democratic assembly leader David J. Friedland, was found after a disciplinary hearing by the state supreme court to have improperly tried to have a criminal case dropped against a reputed Mafia loan shark. The court suspended Friedland from the practice of law.

Not long after the Newark report and Brennan's charges, a new Republican administration—unencumbered by political debts to Democratic-held New Jersey—took office in Washington. On the recommendation of Senator Clifford Case, Frederick Lacey, a highly successful 48-year-old lawyer and member of an old Essex County family, was appointed U. S. Attorney for New Jersey. Lacey took the job only after winning Attorney General John Mitchell's assurance that he and his independently chosen staff would have a free hand to develop cases on their own, rather than simply waiting for leads from federal investigative agencies.

To back up Lacey, Mitchell also ordered a Justice Department anticrime strike force into New Jersey. An invention of Mitchell's predecessor, Ramsey Clark, strike forces team up agents from various federal law-enforcement agencies including the FBI, Internal Revenue Service, and Narcotics Bureau, thus effecting interagency cooperation often lacking in normal operations. Strike forces are also able to get testimony from nervous informants by offering them not only immunity from prosecution but also, in sensitive cases, relocation in different parts of the country under new names with new jobs, thus alleviating their fear of Mafia retaliation. The technique has been used especially effectively in northern Jersey, leading for example to the conviction on a numbers racket case of Sam ("the Plumber") De Cavalcante, the boss of a New Jersey Cosa Nostra family with operations in New York and Connecticut as well. Two one-time agents for De Cavalcante's rackets were the people who gave the crucial testimony against him, and have since been whisked off by the task force to new and secret lives elsewhere in the U. S. A.

In a little over two years, Lacey and the task force racked up a record virtually unprecedented in U. S. law enforcement: 37 indictments involving 179 defendants, and 53 convictions with many cases still pending. Law enforcement by the state government, stepped up in Hughes's last months in office, moved into high gear when Cahill took office in January 1970 (inevitably disturbing many of the cozy relationships that had formed during the 16 years of the Meyner-Hughes Democratic administrations). De Cavalcante and nine members of his Mafia "family" got substantial prison terms. Catena was jailed for the first time since 1934 and held indefinitely on civil contempt charges after refusing to testify before a state investigating committee. Addonizio and four other persons were convicted for taking part in a scheme to squeeze payoffs from contractors doing business with the Newark city government; Tony Boy Boiardo, who had been indicted with Addonizio, suffered a heart attack, but the government said it would try him if he recovered. Other indictments hit the Newark magistrate's court, IRS officials in Newark (some of whom were said to be bought off by the mob), and members of the Newark police department, accused of tolerating gambling in return for payoffs.

In 1971, all this was followed up when Lacey's successor, Herbert Stern, successfully prosecuted the sensational extortion conspiracy trial against eight key Hudson County government and political figures. Jersey City Mayor Whelan and a former city council president were sentenced to 15 years in jail, and Stern obtained a brand new indictment of Kenny on charges that he and three other men extorted a $20 million subcontract at a big new automated post office in Kearny. Indictments began to pour forth in quantity against some of New Jersey's leading political figures—former secretary of state Robert Burkhardt, who was the chief Democratic political operative in the state under both the Meyner and Hughes administrations; Walter H. Jones, a Port of New York Authority commissioner and former Republican state senator who once ran for his party's gubernatorial nomination; and Willard B. Knowlton of Bergen County, a prominent Republican state senator. Burkhardt and Knowlton were charged separately with bribery and extortion against a New York construction firm, while Jones was accused of covering up a $2.4 million bank fraud that forced stockholders to raise millions to prevent a collapse. The accused quickly protested their innocence, including Burkhardt, who said: "I categorically deny and completely refute the charges in the indictment. I have never taken a bribe in my life and I was never in any position to grant contracts on any construction job in New Jersey." (I had personally interviewed Burkhardt a few months earlier, at which time he had expressed deep concern about the pattern of corruption in the state's public life.) Neither the Hudson County trial nor the indictments of public officials indicated any direct connection with the criminal syndicate, it might be added.

With many of New Jersey's known Mafia leaders now behind bars, the worst of the crime nightmare seems to be past. Cahill's election on an anticrime platform in 1969 also helped to change the climate in the state, encouraging many witnesses to come forth with testimony incriminating to Mafia figures and their cohorts. Cahill stopped taking the word of county party leaders in picking prosecutors, who now have to be full time in big counties and stop the private practice of law. The legislature also helped out by creating a new state investigating commission, which has power to put a man in jail if he won't talk. New legislation also made the New Jersey attorney general one of the most powerful law enforcement officers in the U. S., with unilateral power to initiate or take over control of criminal investigations anywhere in the state. A division of criminal justice was set up in his office and state antitrust legislation written in an effort to thwart the penetration of legitimate businesses by organized crime. The attorney general and governor were given the power to step in and supersede any county prosecutor for cause—a power actually exercised by Cahill in 1971 against his own appointee, Robert Dilts, in the state's top GOP county, Bergen. Dilts was under investigation for downgrading charges in a hijacking and extortion case involving mob figures, and was subsequently indicted by a state grand jury on related charges.

The fascinating test of the 1970s will be whether the new laws and attitudes turn out to be mere palliatives, or whether New Jersey has really turned over a new leaf and can finally purge the remaining vestiges of the cancer of organized crime from its public life.

North Jersey: Sad Cities into Suburbia

Just over five million people, or 70 percent of the entire population of New Jersey, live in a ring of eight counties that extend 40 to 50 miles north, west, and south of Manhattan Island. They divide rather neatly into three groups.

First comes the part of New Jersey which is really part of the New York City core area—namely, that urban disaster at the other end of the Lincoln and Holland Tunnels which is called Hudson County. The population, as of the 1970 Census: 609,266, holding virtually steady since 1920.

Next comes an inner ring of counties generally suburban in character but also the site of aging industrial cities like Newark, Paterson, and Elizabeth. The inner ring cities blend into more purely bedroom communities in one vast urban-suburban complex where it is hard to know when one has left one municipality and entered the next. With some exceptions, like northern Bergen County, this is tired old suburbia. The big tracts of land were filled with houses years ago, and the process of the recent past has been to fill in empty strips with garden apartments and high-rise apartment buildings. Five counties are included: Bergen, Passaic, Essex. Union, and Middlesex. The total population in 1970 was 3,415,709, an increase of 12 percent since 1960 and 63 percent since 1950.

Finally there is the "exurban" territory of the outer ring, once the sole province of farmers and business moguls with their big estates, now fast developing with light industries and thousands of acres of colonial and ranch-style homes and even some garden apartments. The outer ring has three counties: Morris, Somerset, and Monmouth. In 1970, they had 1,041,205 people, up 41 percent since 1960 and 188 percent since 1950.

In physical terms, the thought of Hudson County conjures up images of endless miles of low, dingy slums, crumbling waterfront, grime-caked bridges, oil tanks, and fetid marshlands. Practically alone among the urban counties of America, Hudson has virtually no sections one could call even faintly suburban. It is just one city after another: Jersey City, Hoboken, Union City, Bayonne, West New York, and the rest. Negroes make up about 10 percent of the county, joined in the last few years by a heavy flow of Puerto Ricans, Cubans, and other Spanish-speaking peoples. But for the most part, Hudson County remains the Irish-Italian-Slavic ethnic stew it has been for decades.

Jersey City (260,545) dominates Hudson County as it always has, the life of its people still centered around the church and political clubhouse, the political corruption flourishing like the weeds in the empty lots.

In the nearby Hackensack Meadowlands, a giant swamp 18,000 acres in size that stretches from Hackensack to Harrison, plans are now underway to build a great new urban complex with homes for 200,000 people and huge office buildings and shopping and cultural centers. In 1971, Governor Cahill got agreement from the New York Giants football team to leave Yankee Stadium in the Bronx and play in a projected new 75,000-seat stadium in the Meadowlands. North Jerseyans, nursing their long-felt inferiority complex in relation to New York, were jubilant that they had enticed a big league sports team from the big city—"especially," as one told me, "with New York City fighting like hell to keep it."

Bergen (population 898,012) is Jersey's most prosperous big suburban county and also provides some of the most dramatic illustrations in the U. S. A. of how local governments use their zoning powers to bolster their own fiscal position in a way that fosters racial and economic ghettos. The ultimate example of zoning abuse may be the town of Teterboro, heavily industrialized with more than $75 million in assessed property but a total population of only 14 people. Its tax rate, 68¢ per $100 of assessed valuation, compares to rates as high as $4.84 in some less fortunate townships in the county (and more than $9.00 in not-distant Newark).

Passaic County (460,782) is a mixture of close-in, older cities like Paterson (144,824) and Passaic (55,124), dingy and polluted and wracked with problems of sharply increasing black and Puerto Rican populations, and in the upcounty area, burgeoning bedroom communities like Wayne (49,141). Essex County (929,986) is split between its great and problematic city of Newark (382,417), to which we will return shortly, and a suburban hinterland that ranges from affluent towns like Montclair (44,034) and Orange (43,715), to middle-class (and heavily Italian) cities like Bloomfield (52,029) and Nutley (32,099), to East Orange (75,471), which is 53 percent black. Union County (543,116) is a Jersey bellwether in many elections and also runs the gamut in types of cities, from Elizabeth (112,654), certainly one of the most bleak, rundown, depressing cities in America, to Plainfield (46,-862), a comfortable old bedroom town with tree-lined streets and many handsome old houses. Middlesex County (583,813) has been growing by leaps and bounds and now has more than twice as many people as it did two decades ago. Many of the migrants are from old north Jersey cities like Newark, and they have made of Middlesex a classic ethnic melting pot— Italians, Slavs, Poles, Hungarians, and many others. Kevin Phillips identified Middlesex as epitomizing his "emerging Republican majority" of ethnic blue-collarites, but the combined Nixon-Wallace vote in 1968 was only 53.5 percent. Middlesex's most interesting city is New Brunswick (41,885), a Revolutionary-era town ringed by heavy (and odoriferous) factories but also home of Rutgers University and a large, liberally-oriented academic community. The town has been fortunate in the last few years to have a good, honest government headed by a woman mayor, Mrs. Patricia Sheehan, an employee of Johnson & Johnson. She is a sensitive but no-nonsense type of leader who has shown great skill in working with every element from the ethnics to the blacks and academics.

The outer ring counties have received a massive influx of people in the last quarter of a century but nonetheless retain large strips of undeveloped, rural territory. Today they are a curious mixture of open fields, industrial parks, fast-growing tract housing—most of it in the middle-upper income range—and the remaining estates of the landed gentry.

The counties of Morris (383,454) and Somerset (198,372), west of the metropolitan core, evoke images of lush, rolling hills where the affluent ride to their hounds.

The affluent-only pattern does not apply everywhere, however. In sprawling Parsippany-Troy Hills (55,112) in Morris County, where the population more than doubled in the 1960s, many garden-style apartments have risen, and much of the development took place so rapidly that it was *fait accompli* before adequate building codes and controls could be imposed.

A great conservation victory was won in Morris County in 1965 when Jerseyans rallied to fight and defeat the proposal of the Port of New York Authority to drain the Great Swamp, a preserve of natural fauna and flora unmatched anywhere in the northeastern U. S., and build in its place a monstrous jetport big enough to accommodate supersonic planes. Aroused conservationists raised $1.5 million to purchase 3,000 acres of the 13,500-acre swamp and contribute the land to the federal government for a wildlife preserve.

Finally, the outer ring includes the southern (but lightly populated) section of Middlesex County, and Monmouth County on the coast. The resort industry, centered in towns like Asbury Park (16,533) and Long Branch (31,744), has traditionally been the economically dominant force in Monmouth, but in recent years bedroom communities have been filling up with people at an amazing rate.

Newark's Plight

The name of Newark is fast becoming a generic term for the pauperized, ghetto-ridden American city, deserted by its upper and middle classes, filled with poorly educated Negroes from the South, afflicted with horrendous crime rates, faced with social problems far beyond its own capacity to solve, on the verge of bankruptcy.

One tells the story with sadness, because of what Newark was, and what it might be. Settled in 1666, it postdates only Boston and New York among the major cities of America. The city's heart is still the "Four Corners" intersection selected by the first Connecticut Puritan settlers. Its ethnic history is a microcosm of America—from the time of the Yankee Protestants through German and Irish eras, times when Jews set the tone of public life, then Italian ascendancy, and now the black man's turn. An engaging and well-meaning man, Kenneth Gibson, now sits in City Hall as Newark's first Negro mayor.

There are good reasons why Newark should *not* be a dying city. It has always been, and remains today, New Jersey's most heavily populated city and its business and financial center. Newark banks have assets of $2.5 billion, and the city is second only to New York in life insurance sales. Newark is both a corporate headquarters and a factory town. Its port ranks among the largest in the U. S. A. (first in auto imports, with advanced containerization facilities) and is undergoing expansion which will make it dominant in the New York area. Newark Airport, one of the nation's busiest and safest, is also undergoing major expansion. The Penn Central main route goes straight through town, and America's greatest superhighway (the Jersey Turnpike) goes by the front door. All told, the city must be considered a natural transportation point unmatched in eastern America. And then there is the fact of Newark's physical rebuilding: $1 billion worth of new construction since 1957, including a quota of gleaming downtown office buildings and the ambitious Gateway Plaza urban renewal area beside Penn Central Railroad Terminal, over $100 million worth of private apartment houses, the fourth highest number of public housing and other federally assisted low-income housing units among all American cities, and the impressive new academic facilities—Rutgers' new $60 million Newark campus (which will soon have 25,000 students), a new medical and dental school on a $90 million campus, and a vast expansion of the Newark College of Engineering.

A driving tour of Newark reveals no garden city, but at least a much better looking place, on the whole, than most outsiders would expect. The city is divided into five wards. The most depressing, predictably, is the Central Ward, predominantly black, containing riot-scarred Springfield Avenue, which has been described as "a cobblestoned horror of abandoned, filthy buildings, derelicts, and palpable disrepair."

The East Ward includes downtown and is the clanging industrial district known as the Ironbound, where factories are interspersed with blocks of very plain row houses that would quickly become slum were is not for the tidy ways of the area's multitudinous ethnic groups—Italians, Poles, Germans, Brazilians, Dominicans, Puerto Ricans, Ukrainians, and the country's biggest Portuguese colony.

Also of interest is the Italian stronghold in the North Ward, which includes some handsome middle-class residential neighborhoods like Forest Hills and has succeeded better than any other Newark community—not always in the most delicate way—in keeping the oncoming Negroes at bay.

One need not search far to discover that the city labors under a set of frightening disabilities. Mayor Gibson acknowledges that Newark "may be the most decayed and financially crippled city in the nation." The evidence is clear enough:

▪ Crowded land area (24 square miles) of which a full third (eight square miles) is occupied by Newark Airport (whose owner, the New York Port Authority, makes no payment in lieu of taxes). Sixty percent of the land is tax-exempt.

▪ The highest crime rate in the United States.

▪ The highest per capita incidence of venereal disease and infant mortality in the nation.

▪ Unemployment (in spring 1971) of 13.0 percent. Manufacturing, long the source of training for the unskilled, has declined almost 25 percent in the past two decades; while the expansion of bank and insurance company headquarters has added many new jobs, the vast bulk of them have gone to suburbanites, not ghetto dwellers. One out of every two residents of Newark interested in work cannot find adequate employment. Thirty percent of the un- or underemployed group consists of youths aged 16 to 22; among them unemployment runs at 34 percent.

▪ A third of the entire population is on welfare. In 1966, the city's welfare bill was $42 million; by 1970, it had gone up by 107 percent, to $87 million.

▪ Real estate tax rate of $9.21 per $100 of assessed valuation, either the highest or close to the highest in the entire U. S. A. This means that the owner of a Newark house valued at $25,000 has to pay about $2,300 in taxes, $500 more than he would have to pay for a $50,000 house in the fashionable suburb of Short Hills. Gibson has one word for the Newark tax rate: confiscatory. It is an inducement, if not a compelling reason, for homeowners and businesses to leave the city.

▪ Deteriorated housing. Only 10 percent of Newark's dwelling units are owner-occupied, compared to 66.8 percent in nearby Bergen County; the common pattern is for absentee slumlords, many traceable only by a post office box in the suburbs, to run their properties into the ground, and then abandon them. Thirty percent of the housing units are so dilapidated they are beyond hope of rehabilitation. And in 1970, only $165,000 in new residential construction took place—a minuscule 4 percent of what had been built as recently as one year before.

▪ Deteriorated municipal facilities. Of Newark's 84 public schools, almost half predate the First World War; there is one all-black elementary school that was built in 1851. Mayor Hugh Addonizio ended a long quietus in school construction by starting 26 buildings in the 1960s, but an estimated $1 billion investment would be needed to bring the Newark school plant up to par. Underground, Newark is rotting too. There are miles of 125-year-old sewers; the cost of replacing them and repairing the pothole-studded streets could run to $2 billion. But Newark has reached the end of its bonding power.

■ A population 60 percent black, 11 percent Puerto Rican and Cuban, 29 percent white (largely ethnic). The black population rise began with World War I but has taken on its incredibly rapid pace in the last two decades. Negroes represented 17 percent of Newark in 1950, 34 percent in 1960, 54.5 percent in 1970; the expectation is that the figure will pass 75 percent around 1975.* Newark could well become the first major all-black city of the U. S. A. And it will not be a socially diverse black city, but one composed almost exclusively of the economically disadvantaged. The black middle class has been moving out to suburban towns like East Orange and, from there, further into suburbia.

These were precisely the social ingredients that led to the 1967 Newark riots, in which 23 persons—one white fireman, one white detective, and 21 Negroes—lost their lives. Most of the fatalities were attributable to the inept reaction of white police and National Guard to the scattered rioting and looting led by young blacks; many of those killed were clearly innocent bystanders. One was a 73-year-old woman, and two were children. Property damage was about $10 million, three-quarters of which was stock loss from looting, the rest damage to buildings.

Two immediate causes are often cited for the Newark riot—the refusal of Mayor Hugh Addonizio, who had been elected by an Italian-Negro coalition in 1962, to appoint an able black contender to the post of secretary to the city board of education, and a dispute over the massive displacement of low-income black housing for the new state College of Medicine in the Central Ward. But another, largely unspoken factor was the feeling in the black community that the Addonizio administration and its police were "on the take" for illicit profits, a standard of official conduct hardly conducive to docile obedience among those who felt themselves oppressed.

Three years later, Newark was treated to the unusual spectacle of its incumbent mayor spending his days in Trenton, where he was being tried before a federal court on charges of plotting with others to extort more than $1.4 million from contractors doing business with the city, and having succeeded in extorting $253,000 over a five-year period.† Then Addonizio would return in the evening to Newark and campaign for reelection until the early morning hours. "Hughie," one of his admiring supporters said, "is a wounded bull who simply won't go down." His career had all the earmarks of an American tragicomedy: born of Italian immigrant parents in 1914 on Newark's Bergen Street, World War II service in which he enlisted as a private and was discharged as a captain with a variety of medals for bravery in action, 14 years of service in Congress (1948–62) when he voted a straight

---

* Whites have been leaving Newark faster than Negroes replace them. Almost 100,000 whites left Newark in the 1950s, and a similar amount in the 1960s. Even with Negro arrivals and a high black birth rate, the overall population slipped from 438,776 in 1950 to 405,220 in 1960 and 382,417 in 1970. A half-century ago, one out of every eight New Jerseyans came from Newark; today the figure is one in 20.

† There are many in Newark today who believe that Addonizio's actual take may have approached $1 million a year.

liberal line. In 1962, when he announced for mayor, big, affable Hugh Addonizio had said: "I want to come home. I want my home to be in a decent city, a place my wife, my children, and myself can be proud of." Eight years later, when he stood accused in federal court, U. S. Attorney Lacey would accuse Addonizio of running for mayor "because, in his [Addonizio's] own words, there was no money in being a Congressman, whereas *you could make a million as mayor of the city of Newark.*" [Emphasis supplied.] Addonizio, as previously noted, was convicted along with two City Hall associates and two Mafia figures, and given a 10-year prison sentence.

In the 1970 mayoralty election, blacks were in a slight minority among the 133,502 registered voters. In the first voting (the election is nonpartisan), Kenneth Gibson outpolled Addonizio by a 2–1 margin but failed to get an absolute majority because of the vote received by four minor candidates—including 15.3 percent (13,978) for white militant Councilman Anthony Imperiale, the gun-toting, bull-necked chief of the vigilante-like North Ward Citizens' Committee. In the runoff campaign, Addonizio's supporters suggested that if Gibson were elected, the power behind the throne would be that of black nationalist LeRoi Jones, the playwright-poet. They said that a repeat of the 1967 disorders could be expected if Gibson won. Jones did indeed play a significant although behind-the-scenes role in Gibson's campaign. Gibson ran as a moderate and got outside liberal money (especially from New York). In the runoff, he combined solid support from blacks with a significant white minority vote, some of it from older Italians who deeply resented the dishonor Addonizio had brought on their ethnic group, to win election by a margin of 12,011 votes (56 percent). Newark's Negroes were ecstatic. But in the elections for nine city council seats, whites loyal to the old Democratic machine captured six seats and Negroes only three.

Kenneth Gibson is a sturdy, seemingly imperturbable man of palpable good will. Born in Alabama, he grew up in Newark's Central Ward as the son of a hard-working butcher and an aggressive, Bible-teaching mother. He was a successful structural engineer before entering politics in the early 1960s. As mayor, he has helped restore confidence in Newark city government as an honest, viable institution, and given business the feeling that there is a hopeful future in the city. But Gibson has never made any bones about the depth of Newark's problems; indeed his most noticeable achievement has been to convince both the national press and many prominent officials in Trenton and Washington that Newark's crisis is worse than that of any other American city—thus coaxing out some amount of extra state and federal funds for his city. His favorite saying is: "Wherever America's cities are going, Newark will get there first."

Gibson is not without faults. Some suggest that he fails to move with the vigor and dedication required to make a dent on Newark's ills. "He's a one-term mayor," one observer of black elected officials around the country told me. "People try to help him grow, but he doesn't. He's incredibly naive, and seemingly unable to boss his police or school system."

Gibson is the opposite of the modern "hero mayor." "I can't decree changes—only work toward them," he says. "My worst limitation is finances, because Newark is broke. The second limitation is the city council; in most cases I have not been able to get my programs through." Gibson is hampered by a weak personal staff (though some selections of department heads have been excellent) and more particularly by his refusal or inability to consult closely with the council—or, as some say, to wheel and deal with the councilmen for patronage in the age-old way. As an example, the council blocked Gibson's attempt to hire a new accounting firm, which had worked on a grand jury probe of crime in Newark, to conduct a special audit and examination of the city's finances. Instead, the council insisted on sticking with a firm that had audited the city's books for 24 years—and never discovered a single irregularity. When I asked Louis Turco, the tough, glib young man who is council president, why Newark had not selected a new auditor to restore confidence in the wake of the Addonizio conviction, he offered three interesting reasons: (1) the council had voted 9–0 to stick with the old accounting firm; (2) all an auditor does is check and routinely approve vouchers (all would-be embezzlers please take note!), and (3) the auditing job "is one of the most important pieces of patronage" the council has to give out.

Less than three months after taking office, Gibson and his aides discovered that the government they had inherited was even more corrupt than they had imagined. Virtually every contract signed by the city in recent years, they found, had been inflated 10 percent to allow for kickbacks. Gibson said he could personally have received $31,000 "under the table" in exchange for appointing certain persons to four city posts, including police director and tax assessor.

Newark is discovering that election of a black mayor of integrity and good will has only limited effect toward solution of its problems. Faced with an appalling $70 million 1971 budget deficit, a reflection of rapidly escalating pay levels for city workers and stagnant tax receipts, Gibson appealed, on a direct, one-human-being-to-another basis, to Governor Cahill. One of his requests was for a tax on commuters, who pour into Newark in immense numbers each day, using its roads and public safety facilities but paying nothing in return. The suburban-dominated legislature turned that request down cold. Despite Cahill's best efforts to help, all Gibson got was a modest package of state aid in a takeover of hospital costs, some operating and urban aide subsidies, and permission to put a temporary 1 percent tax on payrolls—to be paid by employers, not the commuters. "In the final analysis," one observer told me, "Ken got the privilege to go back and tax his people. If you call that political victory, you're being somewhat naive."

Race-related problems continue to plague the Newark city government. Despite the black majority in the city, 70 percent of city workers are white, including 85 percent of the police. Partly to relieve white fears, Gibson included a number of whites in his major appointments. One of these was John L. Redden, a courageous career Newark police officer so honest that the Addonizio-Spina regime had stuck him in a meaningless slot. The Redden appointment solidified middle-class black and white support for Gibson, but it infuriated LeRoi Jones to the point of calling Redden a "racist turkey" who has "trained his zombies to eat black flesh." Gibson spurned Jones's demand that he fire Redden, but there were still allegations that Jones was a behind-the-scenes power in the new administration.

Tensions came to a head during a crippling 11-week teacher strike in spring 1971. The teacher union, 70 percent of whose members are whites who live outside the ghetto, demanded relief from such nonclassroom duties as monitoring the hallways, play periods, and cafeterias. (Vandalism and racial clashes have been frequent in the Newark schools, which are now 85 percent black or Spanish-speaking.) The school board, with a black-Puerto Rican majority, rejected the union demands, in effect backing up the claims of militant, separatist blacks like LeRoi Jones that the union was trying to frustrate community control of the schools, and that the teachers were showing a "racist" disregard for black children. Long, angry meetings of the school board practically erupted into guerrilla warfare, and a gang of blacks using clubs and bicycle chains brutally attacked a group of picketing teachers, including some who were black. (Ironically, the head of the teachers' union is a black woman, Carole Graves. But in membership, the union has many Jews, some of whom are past middle age, have taught in Newark all their lives, and have their sights set on retirement benefits. Anti-Semitism, aimed at Jewish teachers, shop owners, landlords, and others, many of them people of quite moderate means, is practiced by the black militants with few qualms.) At one school-board meeting, reporter Fox Butterfield of the New York *Times* was grabbed by the neck and punched by three blacks who took his notebooks and wallet and refused to return them. The assailants were urged on by a black former school-board member, Dr. E. Wyman Garrett, who said: "We're going to kiss you off, honky, and you better believe it." A nearby policeman, seeing the incident begin, simply turned his back.

Gibson could have used such incidents to condemn black racism, but he failed to do so, simply warning each side in the strike of the dangers of open racial confrontation. Finally, he proposed a compromise settlement that kept teachers assigned to nonclassroom duties on a "voluntary" basis. But everyone seemed to agree he should have intervened, much more decisively, before an exacerbation of race tensions which Newark might long remember.

In some respects, Newark seems well advanced toward the ultimate confrontation which Jones (who now prefers to be called by the Swahili name of Imamu Amiri Baraka) and other black separatists would like to force. Their goal is to make Newark the microcosm of a black nation—an issue which overrides all others in the city.

Gibson scoffs at the idea of a "black nation" in Newark. "The real power through history," he says, "is economic power. . . . How can you have a black nation when you don't even control the economics of the city? There are no black banks in this city at all. This is the banking and financial capital of the state of New Jersey, and we [blacks] don't control any of that. We could have the mayor and nine city councilmen and all 7,000 city employees and still no real power. It's important for black people to go through the political process and get better government services, as all other ethnic groups have done—but not to assume that's utopia, or the real route to power."

The Philadelphia Orbit, Trenton, Atlantic City, Princeton

Close to a million more Jerseyans—exactly 952,104, according to the 1970 Census—live in the three-county ring of Camden, Burlington, and Gloucester across the Delaware from Philadelphia. All three counties are much poorer than the Jersey-wide average, and in fact it is difficult to think of a suburban grouping of such minimal distinction.

The core city is Camden (102,551), separated from Philadelphia by the 1.81 miles of the Benjamin Franklin Bridge.

Camden is physically repulsive, an unordered *mélange* of ancient box-like factories like those of RCA and Campbell Soup, dingy row houses (average value $8,300), a blighted waterfront, and barren, empty fields. Among Jersey cities, Camden is closest to Newark and in some respects worse, because it lacks Newark's big insurance industry or education complex. Race tensions are high, with both black and Puerto Rican contingents at odds with the white establishment and its police.

The 1970s may be a decade of real hope for Camden and the surrounding Jersey waterfront, however. After the city of Philadelphia failed to develop a feasible in-city site for the 1976 Bicentennial Exposition, the decision was made to locate most of the major expositions on Pettys Island, a 362-acre tract on the Jersey side of the Delaware near Camden. New Jersey officials feel the exposition will bring $3 billion in regional industrial, commercial, and residential development; just one feature, for instance, may be a new community of 45,000 persons on Pettys Island. Some historic exhibits will be on the Philadelphia side, at Penn's Landing, but the greatest benefit will inure to New Jersey —an historic reversal of roles.

New Jersey has a capital city. Its name is Trenton. Trenton has a grand Revolutionary era history, the State House, some gleaming new government buildings, and acres of dreary row houses and vacant land awaiting renewal. The population (104,638 in 1970) has been declining, off 18 percent in 20 years. In a competition for America's least attractive capital, Trenton would be a strong contender. It is a working class city, dominated by Italians and Negroes; there have been some ugly racial incidents, but good poverty and Model Cities programs may relieve some animosities. The state government provides many jobs but doesn't make payments it ought to in lieu of taxes, so that Trenton, like so many other Jersey cities, is broke.

New Jersey also *had* a vibrant, exciting resort city. Its name was Atlantic City, the first sizable U. S. city devoted exclusively to amusement. It was the birthplace of the boardwalk, saltwater taffy, the rolling chair, and the picture postcard. Up to the early decades of this century, Philadelphia and New York aristocracy loved to check into the Byzantine hotels along the ocean front, and the memory of that era lingers on in grand old hostelries like the Chalfonte-Haddon, the Claridge, and the Marlborough-Blenheim. During the 1930s and '40s, the bluebloods began to lose interest and were replaced by the stolid middle class of the big Eastern cities. The course since then has been steadily downhill.

Today, there is a place called Atlantic City, complete with boardwalk, steel pier, big hotels, and all the rest. But in style, it is nothing like the old. The clientele now is lower and lower-middle class: ethnic working families from megalopolis and the Appalachian coal regions, poor blacks coming in busloads from New York, Philadelphia, and Wilmington, millions of conventioneers each year (the likes of the Lions and Shriners—big income producers for Atlantic City), and old people (for whom it seems too late in life to find a new place). Atlantic City had one of the blackest and oldest populations among American cities: 44 percent Negro (out of a city total of 47,-859 permanent residents in 1970), and among the whites 45 percent 65 years of age or older, a geriatric quotient I believe is excelled only by Miami Beach. The old élan is gone: now one finds constant gouging (starting with exorbitant parking fees), plenteous slums, brazenly visible prostitution, a crime rate that rivals the big cities, and a deterioration of boardwalk stores into little more than souvenir and junk shops, second-class restaurants, and hot dog stands.

For almost 30 years, Atlantic County and the city have been in the iron grasp of the old-style political machine of state senator Frank S. (Hap) Farley. Farley's predecessor, Enoch (Nucky) Johnson, went to jail for tax evasion. The ingrained corruption has continued, a matter of public knowledge in the state. Finally, in 1971, U. S. Attorney Herbert Stern and Internal Revenue Service officers began a thorough investigation. In a stunning 1971 election upset, Farley was ousted from the state senate seat he had occupied for 31 years.

Finally, we conclude with New Jersey's preeminent university town: Princeton (25,962), which F. Scott Fitzgerald once described as "rising, a green Phoenix, out of the ugliest country in the world." Princeton harbors not only the university, but the Institute for Advanced Study, a number of industrial plants (mostly research-oriented), and one of the most sophisticated groups of commuters in the world. Many of them are high-ranking officers of investment and publishing houses, advertising agencies, banks, and insurance companies, who ride the train to New York each day but then return to a town that is uniquely cosmopolitan and cultured.

Despite its relatively small size (about 5,000 students), Princeton remains one of America's finest universities in two respects: a faculty-student ratio which is exceptionally high among undergraduate schools, and a graduate school which ranks among the top five in the U. S. for 16 departments (including number one rank in philosophy and mathematics). Princeton's strength is that its faculty members, even men of national repute, are expected to teach both graduate and undergraduate courses in addition to their research.

Princeton was conspicuously absent from the group of universities which degenerated into patterns of overt violence, including burning and looting, in the wave of student protests about the Vietnam war and university policies in the late 1960s and early 1970s. But the Princeton community was alarmed and angered by President Nixon's April 30, 1970 speech announcing the U. S. incursion into Cambodia. A mass student-faculty-administration meeting decided the university would allow a strike in protest of the escalating war. (The strike did not, however, involve closing down the university because classes had already ended and the pre-exam period begun.) The university community opted for channeling its energies into a New Congress Movement, designed to elect candidates pledged to peace at home and abroad, on the suggestion of Cary Orfield, a 28-year-old assistant professor of politics. A decision to arrange the school calendar so that students would have a two-week period free to work in election campaigns before the November election was adopted on the suggestion of Luther Townsend Munford, a junior from Jackson, Mississippi, who was chairman of the *Daily Princetonian*.

The New Congress Movement rapidly became a national phenomenon, coordinated from Princeton. As it turned out, the percentage of students actually willing to work in election campaigns was lower than expectations in the emotion-packed weeks of the Cambodian operation. Ironically, NCM and the fall recess period also spurred some conservative students to work for candidates like James Buckley, the victorious Conservative candidate for the Senate in New York. But NCM workers did provide the extra measure of support needed for several liberal House candidates and for U. S. Senator Vance Hartke of Indiana. The movement is expected to resurface for the 1972 Presidential and congressional campaign.

The town of Princeton is home of the Institute for Advanced Study, the nation's ultimate ivory tower, directed by J. Robert Oppenheimer for many years, and the place where Albert Einstein worked for the last years of his life. (The institute is not related to the university, but Einstein was a familiar figure on the campus, rambling along to some errand wearing an old sweater and knit woolen hat.) The institute's tradition of pure, unharried research is being carried on under director Carl Kaysen, a former Harvard economist and national security adviser to President Kennedy, who associates say is as close to the universal man as anyone in our time. To foster a fusion between study of natural sciences and humanities at the institute, Kaysen opened a new school of social sciences at the institute in 1970. But the basic character of the institute, as described by one of its faculty, former ambassador George Kennan, is not likely to change. "The institute," he said, "fills the place of a monastery in the Middle Ages. It's a refuge for the highest order of scholarship."

In the same state with Newark and Camden, teeming suburbia and gaudy Atlantic City, the Mafia and Pollution Alley, the Institute for Advanced Study is . . . well, a striking contrast.

PENNSYLVANIA

TWILIGHT TIME?

It's Twilight Time in Pennsylvania and the Bills Are Coming Due. That 1970 line in the *National Observer,* in the midst of one of Pennsylvania's bitter budget and tax crises, has a lot to say about public life in what a Harrisburg reporter friend of mine calls "this tired old state in a tax vise."

Of all the megastates, Pennsylvania has the most stagnant population: a growth of only 4.2 percent in the 1960s, for instance—only half New York's growth, a quarter of New Jersey's, a sixth of California's. (The national growth rate was 13.3 percent.) Any increase is attributable only to births exceeding deaths; since 1940, there has been a net outmigration of 1,422,-000 whites from Pennsylvania, offset in part by a net inmigration of 207,000 Negroes. Due to its standstill population levels, Pennsylvania has lost 13 U. S. House seats since 1910; its current apportionment of 25 seats is down two from the 1960s and five from the 1950s, with corresponding losses in national political power.

Yet the fact remains: Pennsylvania is still the third most populous state of the Union, with 11,793,909 people in the 1970 Census count. Any national politician or business planner ignores it at his peril.

Pennsylvania underwent an entire generation of depression, starting in 1928–29 and ending in 1965. During that entire period, its rate of unemployment was second highest in America—better only than West Virginia's. The reasons are fairly clear. It had been the banner industrial state of the 19th century, but its manufacturing plant had aged. Too much of the economy was geared to steel and coal and rails, even as those industries headed into a long decline in employment. There was too little investment in modern, intelligence-oriented industries. And even when the state's economy, along with that of the country, perked up in the 1960s, the rate of new capital expenditures by industries in Pennsylvania lagged behind the other major industrial states. Now, with the completion of big, technologically advanced steel plants in the Midwest, Gov. Milton Shapp predicts "a westward trek of production" that will cost Pennsylvania thousands of jobs in its most basic industry.

But it is too soon to write off the old commonwealth as an economic disaster area. True to its old nickname of Keystone State, Pennsylvania is still dead astride the great transportation routes that connect the Great Lakes and the Midwest with the major markets and seaports of the East. Its rail service is suffering badly today, but at the same time a network of east-west and north-south interstate roads has opened up previously inaccessible parts of Pennsylvania and put most of the state within quick, easy trucking range of both the East Coast and Great Lakes megalopolises. Still occupying first place in the U. S. A. in steel production, Pennsylvania can sell to the growing and vital Eastern steel markets. With some $19 billion worth of manufactures each year (fifth highest among all states), Pennsylvania leads the country in television picture tubes, cigars, shoes, plastic materials, transformers, flat glass, and several other product lines. It added jobs during the 1960s in industries like machinery manufacturing, electrical equipment and supplies, printing and publishing, and to some degree transportation equipment. There are still close to 60,000 Pennsylvania farms, sending produce worth close to $1 billion to market each year. Some kinds of payrolls (especially retailing, services, real estate, and banking) are increasing dramatically, all evidence of a more diversified economy.

The bright spots in the economic situation are not altogether accidental. In the late 1950s, a concerted effort was begun in industrial recruitment through the Pennsylvania Industrial Development Authority (PIDA), the first of its kind in the country. PIDA arranges low-cost loans for new and expanding industries. Part of its success has been in low-paying industries, especially apparel plants, which hire mostly women at an average wage of $81 a week (as of 1969). Apparel plants account for 182,000 jobs and are second only to steel as an employer in the state. But PIDA loans have gone to increasingly sophisticated industries in the last few years, and even some of Pennsylvania's giants (RCA, PPG Industries, etc.) have taken advantage of its financing.

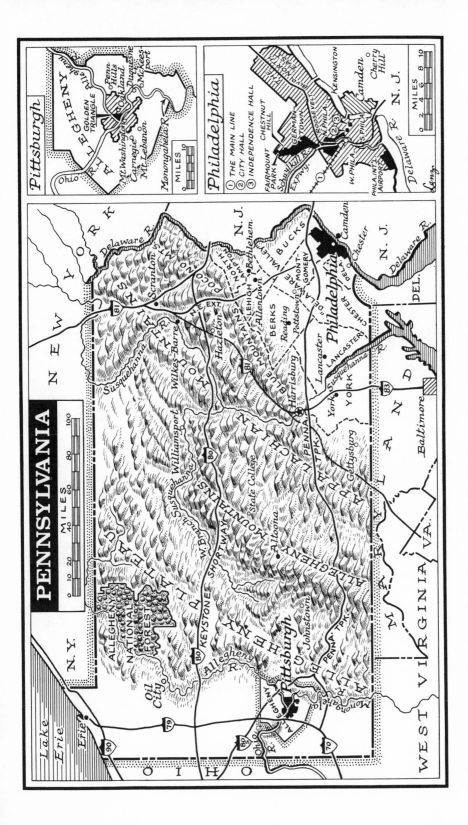

William W. Scranton recalls that in the 1962 gubernatorial campaign, both he and his Democratic opponent, Richardson Dilworth, were struck by the alarm of parents because their children couldn't get good jobs in the state and were moving away. After his election, Scranton made it his chief goal "to turn Pennsylvania around economically and morale-wise." He set up a council of business and industry and another on science and technology, both of which made quite specific recommendations, many of which were implemented. Then he launched a task force called "100,000 Pennsylvanians for the Promotion of Economic Growth." "All the press pooh-poohed it," he recalls, "but more than 100,000 did join, the effort was entirely with private money, and we promoted the economic and tourist attractions of Pennsylvania with a grand tour of the United States." Slowly, Pennsylvania's national image did seem to improve. Scranton claims that the outflow of young people was stemmed by the mid-1960s, and though the Census figures fail to bear out that assertion,* it may well be that the efforts at the state level restored enough confidence to let Pennsylvania share in the general economic boom of the 1960s and to hold, for instance, the central operations of some of its great corporations.

The fruits of the various revival efforts can be seen in the growth of electronic firms (especially in the Philadelphia orbit), a heavy inflow of food and other distribution facilities, industrial parks sprouting up along the major arteries, and economic upturn in once dead-and-out places like Scranton and Wilkes-Barre. In the 1958–61 recession, unemployment in Pennsylvania had zipped up to a catastrophic 9.4 percent, a third greater than the national average; in the later recession year of 1970, Pennsylvania's unemployment was only 4.0 percent, almost a whole percentage point *less* than the national average. Some skeptics said the net migration outflow was responsible for the better showing in 1970, but the fact that unemployment in the state failed to rise rapidly as the recession hit basic industries suggested that there must be increased diversity and resilience in the economy.

Scranton believes that the slow postwar growth may have a silver lining. With the exception of some areas in southeastern Pennsylvania, the state failed to get the huge suburban influxes that gobbled up the land in a reckless way in places like Southern California, northern New Jersey, or Long Island. "We do not have the problems of reckless suburban growth, and due to our conservation and public land policies, which are almost unique in the East, we have a chance to keep a good deal of the state for recreational purposes, and also to do a much better planning job for better living conditions around towns and cities," Scranton said in an interview.

Pennsylvanians are prone to grouse about their skyrocketing state taxes, which are now *three and a half times* greater than they were a decade ago. The state has a sky-high sales tax (6 percent) and the highest cigarette tax

* The 1970 Census figures showed a drop of 108,000 in the key 25–44 age group during the 1960s; presently the percentage of the population in the prime working years lags slightly behind the national average. Census year-to-year population estimates are not broken down by age group, but they did indicate that the state population growth was more sluggish in the last half of the 1960s (when the state population rose 170,000) than the first half (when the figure increased by 300,000).

(18¢ a pack). Asked in a 1970 poll to name the single most important problem facing the state, 50 percent of the people named taxes and budget problems, seven times as many as named the second-ranking category (crime and gang wars). But up through 1970, Pennsylvanians still paid out a smaller percentage of their income in state and local taxes (9.3 percent) than the people of 34 other states. Then, in 1971, the state adopted its first tax on personal incomes, which will cost the people almost $1 billion a year and put Pennsylvania among the high-tax states of the Union.

But for all their tax money, Pennsylvanians can hope for a better future. Under the administrations of three governors—Scranton, Raymond P. Shafer, and Milton J. Shapp—the state has finally abandoned its derelict ways in the field of higher education and begun to spend heavily for state-supported universities and technical schools. So there is hope that in the next decades Pennsylvania will have a much better-trained work force and be able to compete more effectively with California, Texas, *et al.* for sophisticated industries.

In national politics, it has long been fashionable to belittle Pennsylvania's contribution and point out that its first and last President was James Buchanan. Part of the reason for the paucity of great leaders emanating from Pennsylvania was the oppressive century-long control of its politics by narrow-minded business interests which were allied with often corrupt Republican bosses like Boies Penrose and Joseph Grundy. In the first years after World War II, Scranton told me, "Pennsylvania remained stagnant in its politics just as its economy remained stagnant. The Republican party was owned and operated by business, especially big business—the railroads, steel, and the like. The Democratic party was owned by the AFL-CIO. And there was little in between." But in the 1960s, the conservative big business clique was reduced to near impotency in Republican circles, and the Democratic bosses were challenged successfully in their own bailiwicks. We will return to those stories later, but the essential point is that the upper echelon of Pennsylvania officeholders no longer need be the marionettes of political bosses or vested interests. They can stand as proud and independent as did those Pennsylvanians who helped write and champion the Declaration of Independence and the Constitution.

Aside from prostituting the political process, Pennsylvania's old industrial barons did their state a second disservice: for private profit, they raped the natural landscape of Penn's Woods and spawned scabrous slum housing for their workers. Today, much of the blight endures: the anthracite fields of northeastern Pennsylvania, where fires and cave-ins of the earth go on for decades after abandonment of mine sites and monstrous smoking culm dumps mar the countryside; the soft-coal fields of the west, with thousands of acres churned up by reckless strip mining; the wretched little mill towns in the river valleys. Add that to the decay of many of the urban cores, and Pennsylvania seems to be in a sorry state indeed.

Yet here again, the picture is changing. Reclamation efforts are underway in the coal fields. Many of the mill towns seem beyond hope, and so do some of the slums of the two great Pennsylvania cities, Philadelphia and Pittsburgh. But the downtown areas of those two cities have experienced exciting physical renewal since World War II, in both instances the work of high-minded politicians and financiers. Now the alliances that effected the great urban renaissances (beginning more than 20 years ago) are falling to pieces and the cities seem engulfed in self-doubt, racial tension, and bitter struggles for power. But new and creative forces are at work, too, even in the seething ghettos. Some of America's most promising black self-help projects are emanating from Philadelphia. Pittsburgh is in a trough of uncertainty following the death of its great billionaire mentor, Richard King Mellon, but there too, new direction is likely to emerge in the next years.

Finally, Pennsylvanians are rediscovering the charm and beauty of the Pennsylvania countryside. Great mountain chains, lakes and meadows, forests and quiet farmland still cover most of the state, and they are there for Pennsylvanians and the other people of the crowded Eastern Seaboard to enjoy. Then there are the man-made reminders of Pennsylvania's early history: Independence Hall and the other colonial landmarks of Philadelphia, Valley Forge, the battlefield at Gettysburg, the Pennsylvania Dutch country, the great meeting place of the rivers at Pittsburgh. All of this has spawned a great wave of tourism, stimulating the sluggish Pennsylvania economy by some $5 billion a year (a fivefold increase in a decade). But the importance is ultimately not economic, but of the spirit. Urban people need quiet and solace in nature; Pennsylvania now provides it to millions each year, in the heart of megalopolis. All Americans need to know more of their magnificent revolutionary era history and Pennsylvania, "cradle of a nation," offers that, and with scarcely a touch of tinseled Disneyism. Past the era of industrial pillage and cruel political bossism, still aching with problems, Pennsylvania is probably closer now than it has been for a century (and certainly closer than in 1890, when he wrote it) to the romantic vision of Rudyard Kipling:

> The things that truly last, when men and time have passed.
> They are all in Pennsylvania this morning.

Noble Beginnings

An extraordinary spirit of thoughtfulness, tolerance, and care runs through all the writings of William Penn, that remarkable Quaker who founded Pennsylvania and proved to be the noblest of the colonial proprietors. The Great Law which he worked out with his colonists, starting with his arrival in America in 1682, was so progressive as to be radical in its time. It included broad guarantees of religious freedom and of suffrage to males who could meet modest property requirements, an assurance of education for all young children, and stipulation that all laws would be made "with the Consent and Approbation of the Freemen in General Assembly met." "This clear mandate for a permissive, popular government," writer Ezra Bowen has noted, "was one of the pillars upon which, in time, the U. S.

Constitution would rest."

Penn later regretted his loss of power, and it should be remembered that real power in colonial Pennsylvania rested with an oligarchy of Quaker leaders, not a broad popular mass. But Penn's promises of religious and political freedom were enough to draw great numbers of colonists. Welsh Quakers came first, then Scottish-Irish Presbyterians, Lutherans, Pietist Germans, Swedes, French Huguenots, and others. Numerically, the Germans were most noticeable, concentrating in inland counties like Lancaster where their mark is heavy to this day.

With a Quaker's penchant for wise business, Penn located Philadelphia at the tidewater confluence of two great rivers—the Delaware and the Schuylkill. Along their banks, back into the interior, lay tens of millions of acres of forest with a seemingly endless supply of prime white oak. And in the river openings, and under the forests lay prime farmland, which would make Pennsylvania the foremost food producer among the colonies.

By the time of the Revolution, Pennsylvania was the third largest colony with 275,000 people, and Philadelphia had forged ahead of Boston to become the metropolis of colonial America and in many respects its culturally most prominent city. The colony's most illustrious citizen was Boston-born Benjamin Franklin, that author, publisher, scientist, politician, diplomat, and inventor of world repute. While Boston was an earlier scene of revolutionary agitation, it was in Philadelphia that the first two Continental Congresses met and adopted the Declaration of Independence, chose George Washington as commander in chief, and first unfurled the American flag. In the Revolutionary War, Pennsylvania was a major scene of action, including the battles of Brandywine, Paoli, and Germantown. It was at Valley Forge that Washington and his troops spent the cruel winter of 1777–78. In the war, Pennsylvania's fledgling ironworks turned out weapons and its rich farmlands supplied grain, fodder, cattle, sheep, and hogs to feed the army. And it was a decade later, in 1787, that the Constitutional Convention met—again, in Philadelphia. Pennsylvania sent the largest delegation, which fought hard for a strong national government. Then Philadelphia became, for 10 years, the first capital of the United States.

The Age of Steel and Coal, and Its Decline

In the six decades stretching from the end of the Civil War and the advent of the Gilded Age through to the Great Depression, the life of Pennsylvania was characterized not by high idealism but rather by an incredible forward surge of great industry. Pennsylvania was amply endowed with the raw materials for industrial greatness. Western Pennsylvania was underlaid with vast fields of bituminous coal, low in sulphur content and thus easy to convert into coke for steel production. (By one estimate, there were 200 billion tons in and around Pittsburgh alone.) Iron ore was also present in substantial quantity, and later could be imported easily across the Great

Lakes from locations such as the Mesabi Range in Minnesota. Limestone was plenteous. So were the tycoons who would build the great empires of iron and steel: Henry Clay Frick, who became the largest producer of coal and coke in the world; Andrew Carnegie, who arrived in Pittsburgh at age 13 to start work for $1.20 a week, brought the Bessemer steelmaking process to America, and eventually became the world's richest man by selling out his massive steelworks for $492 million; J. P. Morgan, the great financier who dared to create U. S. Steel (that gigantic corporation that had 149 plants, capitalization of more than $1.4 billion, and 65 percent of U. S. steelmaking potential the day of its birth in 1901); and Charles M. Schwab, sometimes called "the world's greatest salesman," who was midwife in the negotiations between Morgan and Carnegie that led to creation of U. S. Steel, served as its first president, and then went off to build the rival Bethlehem Steel Company into a giant producer of steel and ships.

Then there were the remarkable Mellons—Thomas, son of a poor Scottish-Irish farming family who arrived in Pittsburgh at the age of five, later became that city's greatest financier and real-estate dealer, and set the foundations of the great banking and coal combine that would prosper under his sons, Andrew and Richard B., and his grandson, Richard King Mellon.

Pennsylvania had oil; in fact the world's first spouting oil well was driven in 1859 near Titusville in the western part of the state. For a half century, oil contributed to Pennsylvania's prosperity, giving birth to the Standard Oil trust and eventually to the Gulf, Sun, and Atlantic oil companies. While the state's petroleum reserves were eventually eclipsed by those of the Southwest, Pennsylvania's Joseph N. Pew did build Sun Oil into one of the largest producers and refiners of oil.

But as varied as Pennsylvania industries might be, the big muscle remained with big steel, and after 1901, with U. S. Steel—The Corporation, as it was familiarly called. Closely allied were, of course, the coal-mining interests, and also the railroads, which themselves ran on steel rails with great steel locomotives and earned much of their money by carrying supplies for the mills and finished steel as freight. In the 1920s, The Corporation controlled as much as 46 percent of all U. S. steel production and had a work force averaging 240,000 men—larger than the U. S. Army. To assure itself of an adequate supply of bituminous coal, The Corporation was probably the largest U. S. coal operator—in an era when three-quarters of a million men worked in the mines. As for the railroads, there was none greater than the Philadelphia-based Pennsylvania Railroad, which employed more than 250,000 men and whose trackage carried an eighth of all passengers in the U.S.A.

Starting around 1890, reformist elements began an outcry about the power of big steel and the big rail interests, but to little avail. In much the same way that strategically placed Texans have been able to defend oil tax privileges in recent decades, strategically placed Pennsylvanians in the late 19th and early 20th centuries stopped antitrust, freight regulation, or child labor legislation which might harm The Corporation and its friends. The year U. S. Steel was formed, the Attorney General of the U. S. was Phil-ander C. Knox, a close friend of Frick and Mellon. Elihu Root, a member of both the McKinley and Theodore Roosevelt cabinets, had been an attorney for the old Carnegie Steel Company. The list is a long one and perhaps is best capped off with the ultimate example: Andrew Mellon's position as Secretary of the Treasury during the Harding, Coolidge, and Hoover ad-ministrations. The massive mergers in the birth of The Corporation some-how got the approval of government antitrust lawyers. Obvious price-fixing agreements among the big steel producers went unpunished, nor did govern-ment do anything to curb the steel and coal companies' inhumane labor practices.

In historic perspective, it is clear enough that World War I marked the apogee of Pennsylvania's role as America's great energy and metals producer. The succeeding years have been a half century of steady decline, one of cata-strophic proportions in the Depression, artificially relieved by World War II and to some degree by the Korean and Vietnam wars, but nevertheless of deterioration throughout.

The problems and terrors of Pennsylvania industry can be catalogued easily. Both big steel and big coal, in a frantic race to meet any demand of any peak year, built production facilities far beyond the needs of normal times and failed to diversify their operations so that they could withstand the shock of economic reverses. The prime steel customer of all time—the railroads—reached the full extent of their routes in the 1920s; after that, steel rails were no longer in great demand, and the need for rolling stock de-clined sharply. At that same moment of time, the Pennsylvania financiers made the fundamental error of failing to get in on the ground floor of the great *new* industry of 20th-century America—automobile and truck produc-tion. That business went to Michigan instead, and Midwestern steel mills supplied most of the automakers' needs. And to this day, Pennsylvania is the only major state without an automobile assembly plant.

The steadily increasing national demand for steel in the past two dec-ades (from 75 million tons in 1950 to 132 million in 1970) has kept many Pennsylvania mills busy. But the state is still producing only 50 percent more steel (about 30 million tons a year) than it did in 1918—hardly an impressive growth rate in a rapidly expanding national economy. A half cen-tury ago, about half of America's steel production came from Pennsylvania mills; in 1970, the figure was only 22.9 percent. Pennsylvania employs less people in its primary metals industry (253,000 in 1969) than it did 20 years ago. The decline, slowed a bit by the Vietnam war, is continuing and likely to get worse. The steel industry has been making its primary new plant in-vestments in the Midwest in recent years, and sophisticated new factories that require only a fraction of the labor force needed in Pennsylvania mills have recently gone on line in Hennepin, Illinois (Jones & Laughlin), and Burns Harbor, Indiana (Bethlehem). A high percentage of Pennsylvania's mills are technologically old and may soon be obsolete. The average age of steelworkers in the state is over 50 years; the younger people are now being hired in the Midwest.

To top it all off, the entire U. S. steel industry faces difficult times with low profits and bruising competition from foreign producers, who have seized 17 percent of the U. S. market. In 1970, U. S. Steel and Bethlehem (the two largest) showed a net income of only 3.1 percent on sales of $4.8 billion and $2.9 billion respectively. Inflationary wage settlements with the United Steel workers have been one factor harming the competitive position of U. S. steel producers, but another has been the pressure of Japanese import competition. The import situation had become so severe by 1971 that Nixon administration economic advisers were suggesting that some of the 10 top steel companies, operating at a thin profit margin, should be allowed to merge to help them defend their markets against the Japanese.

Related to the woes of big steel are those of the railroads, traditionally the lifeline of commerce in Pennsylvania. Freight service—not to mention passenger service—has been declining in terms of area serviced and reliability over most of the postwar period, making it commensurately more difficult to maintain profitable industry in the state. In 1968, when the mighty Pennsylvania Railroad merged with the New York Central to form Penn Central, the number of lines was cut back, plus many service connection points for smaller railways. Pennsylvania was also hurt because the merged line began to upgrade its water level route over the former New York Central tracks, which is cheaper to ship over than the mountainous route of· the Penn Central through Pennsylvania. This undercut the competitive position of the Port of Philadelphia and cost railway jobs in the Keystone state.

The great financial crash of the Penn Central in 1970 was the biggest commercial bankruptcy in American history, a blow to the pride and prosperity of Philadelphia, and an evil omen for the 50,000 Pennsylvanians still working on the railroads. (Back in 1947, there had still been more than 150,-000 railroad jobs in the state.) What was it that led the Penn Central to the abyss? To the railroad's customers, it seemed like the outgrowth of years of deferred maintenance, deteriorated roadbeds, outmoded equipment, chronic jam-ups at terminals and connecting points with other railways, misdirected freight cars, and archaic work practices forced by the unions. What was even more shocking than poor management was the revelation some months after the bankruptcy that some directors and key officers had neglected the railroad and saved themselves thousands of dollars by dumping personal stock before the Penn Central's troubles became public knowledge. The railroad kept on paying dividends on its stock even when its cash position had become desperate, and deceptive bookkeeping was used to hide the true state of affairs. And according to congressional staff reports and the suits of aggrieved stockholders, the company had been bled dry by a series of questionable acquisitions in nonrailroad businesses throughout the 1960s. A private investor's club made up of Pennsylvania Railroad officers, directors, friends, and relatives had been set up in 1962 and invested heavily in companies that the railroad later either invested in or acquired control of; in several cases the stock value of the companies soared when they were acquired and the investors could sell out at big profits to themselves. The Associated Press reported in January 1971 that even as the Penn Central was rolling toward bankruptcy court, its directors voted to buy a $10 million Lloyd's of London insurance policy to protect themselves, the company, and key officers financially against charges of wrongdoing. The three-year policy carried a $305,000 price tag and the full cost was placed on the teetering Penn Central, rather than on the officers themselves, by a timely new state law actually written by a Philadelphia lawyer whose firm represented the railroad. It was a move worthy of the most rapacious policies of the earlier Robber Barons.

Despite herculean efforts by the newly appointed trustees and president William H. Moore to revamp operating procedures and upgrade the Penn Central's equipment, the prospects seemed dim indeed at the end of 1971 for a return to solvency. Continued injections of government aid would probably be necessary for years to come.

Less than 29,000 men work in the coal mines of Pennsylvania today—a catastrophic decline from the 210,000 who worked there in 1940, and the 387,000 in 1910. Production in the great anthracite fields of northeastern Pennsylvania has declined to a mere trickle. The story is different in the western Pennsylvania fields, where there are still many deep-pit mines. They are almost exclusively the captives of the big steel companies—U. S. Steel, Bethlehem, Jones & Laughlin, and Republic—who continue to prize low-sulphur, metallurgical-quality bituminous for making coke in the steel process. But on the eastern edge of the bituminous field, around Johnstown and Altoona, there are beds of medium-sulphur coal and some huge mine-mouth electric generating plants where the coal comes up on a conveyor belt and is immediately fed into the power station. The expanding part of the western Pennsylvania coal industry is in strip mining, where it is now possible with huge earth-moving and coal-cutting machinery to get at deep seams of coal that previously seemed inaccessible or too costly to recover.

The human costs of the dramatic reduction in coal-mining jobs can still be seen in Pennsylvania's old mining towns, where unemployed miners, unprepared for any other profession, live out their sad and unfulfilled lives. The problem is not a new one—it has been there since the 1920s. Life in the mines especially the deep-pit ones, is still a dangerous affair for miners lucky enough to have work. Pennsylvania has had its share of hair-raising mine disasters. Underground miners still live in constant danger of being crushed, gassed, burned, or electrocuted and must reckon with the clear possibility of getting "black lung" disease from the coal dust they inhale through a lifetime.

If there is a bright spot in the modern-day coal story in Pennsylvania, it must be in the good efforts being made to reclaim the natural landscape when the strip miners are through. My friend Ben Franklin of the New York *Times*, who has made a specialty of coal problems, says the Pennsylvania strip-mining law, first passed under the Scranton administration, is the best in the U. S. by far. One unique provision requires that after contour mining, the high wall—referring to the sheer rock face, sometimes as high as 120 feet, that's left after a bench has been cut to dig out coal from the side of a mountain—must be blasted away and filled in, so that no slope greater than 45° results. Another provision obliges strip-mining firms to post a very high bond which is not released by the state until the area is not only graded, but seeded, *and* the vegetation has begun to grow. (Other states generally release most or all of the bond when the seed is put down. But often the ground is "hot"—chemically toxic—so that nothing grows.) But as Franklin points out, the word *reclaimed* is something of a travesty as it is generally used. To get a strip-mined area back to its essential prior condition, with full vegetation and humus and a nitrogen base in its soil, is a century-long proposition. It also takes that long for rocks churned up in the earth-moving process to break down by freezing and thawing so that the land can be plowed again for crops.

Labor in Pennsylvania

The century preceding World War I witnessed the great "peopling" of Pennsylvania. The population rose from 810,091 (1810) to 7,665,111 (1910). Attracted by Pennsylvania's job opportunities, many settlers came from New York and New England. From the South came the first Negroes, attracted by Pennsylvania's strong abolitionist views. Starting in 1840, Ireland's potato famine brought a flood of immigrants from that country. As the wave of industrialization gathered steam after the Civil War, vast numbers of Germans, Irish, Italians, Poles, and other Slavs poured in, and then there were Jews from Eastern Europe and Russia. As recently as 1960, 22 percent of Pennsylvania's people were immigrants or the sons and daughters of immigrants —half a million Italians and large numbers of Germans, Austrians, Poles, British, Irish, Czechs, and Russians; if the count had included the third and fourth generations, it would doubtless have been well over 50 percent. The religious heritage of the immigration is revealed in modern-day figures showing that 31 percent of Pennsylvania's people are Roman Catholic and 4 percent Jewish, well above the national averages.

The conditions in the early factory towns are one of the darkest chapters in American history. Men were obliged to work 12 hours a day, seven days a week, for wages as small as $350 a year—and often that pittance came in company-issued scrip which could only be spent at inflated prices in the company store or for rent of the shacks or tiny wooden frame houses owned by the company. In the coal fields, child labor was used extensively; only in 1909, in fact, did the state adopt a law against the practice. Tiny boys, sometimes only eight years of age, were put to work separating slate from coal and at other tasks deep in the mine shafts, at wages of 25 cents a day. The toll in miners' lives was appalling: 43,000 Pennsylvania miners lost their lives between 1880 and 1936. Thousands died in the steel mills, too; there, one of the greatest dangers was white-hot metal gushing out of giant ladles that frequently slipped off overhead cranes.

In the Pennsylvania mill and mining villages, Ezra Bowen recounts, living conditions—especially for the new immigrants—were sordid and disease-ridden. Backyards were often a filthy jumble of privies, open sewage ditches, and rubbish, and in one ward of Homestead occupied primarily by recent immigrants, one child out of two died before it reached two years of age.

The social ethos of the time allowed for little criticism of all this; indeed a prevailing feeling seemed to be that the poor were poor because they were lazy and need only apply themselves to become Horatio Algers.

Labor unions to press for higher wages and safety precautions for the workers were fought ferociously by the same owners who championed the sacred rights of property and the ideal of survival of the fittest. Indeed, the struggle of the workers for a more decent life was every bit as bitter, intense—and violent—as that of the modern American Negro. The universal reaction to strikes was to beat them down with troops and bullets, and the owners would not even consider talking to a union representative. In 1877, in Pittsburgh, a great general strike broke out after the Pennsylvania Railroad cut back weekly paychecks by 10 percent and 650 militiamen moved into the city to battle with mobs which surged through the city streets and rail yards, looting and wrecking railroad equipment, for two days. Finally federal troops had to be called in to restore order and the final toll was 26 dead, $5 million in damage, and bitter class hatred such as America had never known before.

Slowly, tentatively, with many setbacks, labor unions began to form—the American Federation of Labor (succeeding the old Knights of Labor) in 1881, the United Mine Workers in 1890, the Amalgamated Association of Iron, Steel and Tin Workers in 1878, and finally the Congress of Industrial Organizations in 1935 and the United Steelworkers that same year. The steel industry proved the most obdurate of all, its workers thoroughly cowed by experiences like the strike at Carnegie's Homestead Works in 1892 over the issue of the 12-hour day, seven-day week, low pay, and manager Henry Clay Frick's cold refusal to recognize any kind of union. For five months the workers stayed off their jobs and at one point engaged in a bloody fight with 300 Pinkertons dispatched by the company, a struggle marked by the use of cannon and pistol fire, dynamite and burning oil and gas. Finally the obliging governor acceded to Frick's request to send in 8,000 militia, who took over the plants, arrested many strike leaders, and started up the furnaces with scab labor. Their strike totally broken, the crestfallen workers went back to work without a single concession from management.

Part of the steelworkers' problem was that their union, the Amalgamated Association of Iron, Steel and Tin Workers, recruited only skilled workers and spoke only for their aims. The coal miners, by contrast, had by necessity learned teamwork in their dangerous underground work and showed much more solidarity. The United Mine Workers also developed shrewd, able leaders like ex-miner John Mitchell, who led successful strikes in 1900 and 1902 which led to an eight-to-nine-hour working day and a 10 percent pay increase. By the 1920s, the powerful and often dictatorial figure of John L.

Lewis was leading the UMW. He scored some early successes, saw his union decimated by the aftermath of the 1929 crash, but came into his own with the arrival of the New Deal and passage of the National Industrial Recovery Act in 1933. That law guaranteed workers the right to organize and bargain collectively through "representatives of their own choosing"—a provision Lewis was instrumental in getting into the act, and which he proudly called Labor's Magna Charta. Soon 300,000 workers were signed up with the UMW and the major coal operators agreed to recognition of the union, a seven-hour day with time and a half for overtime.

Still, there were coal companies that resisted, and they might have succeeded in bucking the union if there had not been a new state adminis-tration at Harrisburg, headed by an illustrious liberal, Republican Gifford Pinchot. He pledged that the National Guard would be impartial to all citi-zens and revoked the commissions of all the private company police. By 1942, every commercial coal mine in America was operating as a closed union shop under the United Mine Workers' banner.

In the meantime, Lewis had broadened his sights to great industries like autos and steel and in 1935 broke with the AFL to form the CIO, putting his old friend Phillip Murray in charge of organizing the steelworkers. A great strategic victory was won with General Motors' capitulation to the CIO in Detroit in 1937. Soon after that, The Corporation (U. S. Steel) quietly succumbed to union organization.

The years since World War II have been sunny ones for the Steelworkers but grim ones for the UMW—the result in large part of the general health of the steel industry and declining days for coal, but also of the strikingly differ-ent ways in which the two unions have been run. Thriving under basically sound leadership and democratic operating procedures, the Steelworkers have constantly expanded until they now represent 1.5 million workers in the U.S. and Canada, the largest of all industrial unions (and second only to the Teamsters, which have two million, in overall membership).

Founder Phil Murray headed the Steelworkers until his death in 1952 and still shines in the memory of most union members as the finest leader they ever had. He was succeeded by David J. McDonald, the union's original secretary-treasurer, but in 1965 McDonald was ousted in unionwide ballot-ing by I. W. Abel, the union's president today. Abel, who began life as a blacksmith's son in Magnolia, Ohio, was able to capitalize on McDonald's loss of contact with his district directors and the notion that McDonald had become too popular as a golfing and nightclub companion of the steel execu-tives he was supposed to fight.

There has been a marked change in the Steelworkers' way of operating under Abel. Formerly, the union's top officers decided before any negotia-tions on a clear-cut set of demands and bargaining strategy and took it to the union's wage-policy committee where it would usually be accepted without major change; the wage-policy committee then had full authority to make or reject agreements and to order strikes. Under Abel, the wage-policy com-mittee was retained but individual industry committees—for basic steel, aluminum, nonferrous metals, cans, and others—were set up and given authority and responsibility to implement the wage-policy program and modify it to the needs of their respective industries, and also to make agreements and recommend strike action. "Thus we have a broader base—much greater participation," Abel told me. Howard Hague, the Steelworkers' vice president under McDonald, says that the strength of central leadership has gone under Abel and that by failing to set a clear line of policy, Abel encourages too many voices, too much confusion, and in the end impairs the union's strength and ability to deliver for its membership. He predicts Abel will have difficulty getting reelected when his term is up in 1973. There have indeed been grumblings in the ranks that Abel is often as inaccessible as McDonald was accused of being. How the internal politics of the union will stand in the coming decade may be beyond prediction of outsiders, but it does seem that any challenger will have to plan his strategy well to unseat Abel, a thoroughly delightful man with a weatherbeaten face and granite handshake who has already proven he knows how to play intraunion politics with gusto and success.

In fact, Abel was strengthened by the three-year contract signed with the major producers in 1971, which boosted wages by a total of 30 percent over the life of the contract and reinstated a cost-of-living escalator that had been watered down in 1959 negotiations. But the agreement was palpably inflationary: within 12 hours of its signing, U. S. Steel, followed by the others, raised its prices 8 percent; combined with a 6.5 percent increase earlier in 1971, that meant a 14 percent increase *in a single year*. (These alarming increases in wages and prices were a major factor in the wage-price freeze ordered by President Nixon in August 1971.)

Working in steel mills has always been a particularly hazardous occupation, with men exposed to great extremes of temperature and—especially in older mills—high levels of air pollution. The younger and more militant union members are pressing aggressively on the safety issue. They are less willing to accept union or company discipline than the older workers, many of whom are immigrants. In a 1971 survey of working conditions in industry, the New York *Times* quoted Ronald Koontz, a 22-year-old steelworker at the Bethlehem plant in Johnstown, as saying that younger workers were often refusing to do hazardous jobs like sealing the coke ovens. "You wear two to three shirts a day it's so hot," he said. "There's lots of gas, smoke, dirt. Some guys just tell the foreman 'No' and then rely on the union to protect their jobs."

By appearances, the political activity of the Steelworkers is more limited, and they are much less willing to take an advanced stand on social issues, than the United Auto Workers (who trail the Steelworkers slightly in membership). In 1968, Steelworkers worked hard, especially in Presidential primary states like Indiana, to defend Hubert Humphrey's interests over those of Eugene McCarthy. Abel told me his union would continue its centrist Democratic course. "No possible change there—the Steelworkers never go off one end or the other," he said. But Abel's personal feelings may have divisive effects on his union's ability to act single-mindedly and effectively in politics. He was so infuriated with Milton Shapp for backing McCarthy in 1968 that in the 1970 election he refused to endorse Shapp, leaving it to his union's local leaders in Pennsylvania to decide on their own what they should do. (Most were for Shapp.) That situation lent some credence to the assertion of a critic like Hague, who accuses his old union of having a "hodgepodge policy" or "no policy at all as a national body" in the political arena.*

Whatever the problems of the Steelworkers may be, they are minor compared to those of the United Mine Workers. John L. Lewis began the postwar era with walkouts in violation of injunctions barring strikes, bringing down heavy fines on the union and himself. But the turbulence ended quickly in the late 1940s. Coal at that point found itself in an unfavorably competitive market as the railroads switched to diesel engines and homes to oil and gas heating. Coal's only real hope seemed to lie in large-scale automation that could hold coal prices down and make it the principal source of fuel for rapidly growing power-generating plants. Lewis agreed to the automation —despite the fact that it would throw thousands of miners out of work. But for the remaining miners, Lewis got a major concession: agreement by the owners to finance, by means of a royalty on every ton of coal produced (40 cents since 1952), a welfare and retirement fund that made UMW workers among the first in American industry eligible for job pensions and free medical care. At the same time, wages advanced handsomely. The perennial conflicts between the UMW and the mine owners ceased, and peace seemed to reign in the coal fields for the first time in decades.†

Lewis retired in 1960 and soon afterward the presidency of the UMW was taken over by W. A. (Tony) Boyle, Lewis' hand-picked, $50,000-a-year successor. "Boyle carefully patterned his image after the master," writer Ward Sinclair has noted. "The self-righteousness, the roll of the tongue, the combative rejection of outsiders, the thundering responses to criticism all are pages from the Lewis book." Boyle also continued to run the UMW as a personal fiefdom, as Lewis had done. Years before, Lewis had placed 19 of the UMW's 23 districts under trusteeship (alleging that the districts were in financial straits, or that some "irregularities" had taken place). This permitted Lewis, and then Boyle, to appoint all the district presidents, secretary-treasurers, and members of the UMW executive board—in effect, a self-perpetuating oligarchy. The Landrum-Griffin Act, passed in 1959, limited all trusteeships to 18 months, but for years the government did nothing to clean up the practice in the UMW. Boyle's own concern with the fate of the ordinary miner was next to impossible to discern; in fact, as time wore on and the UMW benefited from every ton of coal dug, the relationship with the mine operators seemed to get cozier and cozier. Until the

---

* Abel claims the Steelworkers are major political factors in Pennsylvania, Illinois, Indiana, New York, and several other states. In Illinois, he said, "our fellows have always worked well with Daley." Potentially, the Steelworkers could be a major factor in U. S. politics. They have the largest staff (985) of any union in the U. S., concentrated in the big, electorally pivotal states.

† There was no peace, though, for independent mine owners and nonunion operators who felt they could not afford to pay royalties to the pension fund. Union organizers used terroristic methods to make them join up.

Farmington, West Virginia, disaster of 1968, the UMW failed to support a single piece of mine safety legislation. The union does not defend members of local safety committees from reprisals by mine owners. Boyle in 1969 said the UMW "will not abridge the rights of mine operators in running the mines. We follow the judgment of the coal operators, right or wrong."

In 1969, Boyle had to stand for reelection as president and suddenly an opponent emerged—Joseph A. (Jock) Yablonski, former president of District 5 in the Pittsburgh area and supposedly a stalwart of the Boyle regime. For years, Yablonski had silently balked at what he considered misrule of the union and neglect of rank-and-file miners. A key figure in persuading him to run for the presidency was Ralph Nader, and a key part of the package was Nader's assurance that Joseph Rauh, a brilliant Washington attorney and Democratic leader, would be his campaign manager and legal brains. The Yablonski campaign had an electrifying effect on thousands of miners who had never thought anyone would have the courage to oppose Boyle's iron regime. Yablonski was a volatile, colorful personality who relished his rebel's role. He was for union democracy, for tough safety legislation, for a fair pension system (many miners had been denied pension or disability rights on flimsy technicalities), and for an end to "sweetheart ties" between the UMW and the coal industry.

The Yablonski-Boyle campaign was marked by appalling bribery, intimidation, fraud—and violence. At a campaign appearance in Illinois, Yablonski was knocked unconscious by a karate chop to the neck. He regarded the incident as a calculated attempt on his life. Rauh lodged repeated complaints with the U. S. Labor Department—which discounted them all and said, in a tortured interpretation of the Landrum-Griffin Act, that it had a policy of never investigating a union election until it was all over and the result certified. The result of that, Rauh and Yablonski said, would be to give Boyle and his cohorts three to four months to cover up before any investigation—time to destroy records, including those of the hundreds of thousands of dollars of union money allegedly misappropriated to finance Boyle's campaign. Early in the campaign, Boyle had himself appointed to the welfare and retirement fund's trustee board to replace Lewis, who died that year. Within a day, Boyle raised pensions from $115 a month to $150 a month for 70,000 retirees—thus garnering nearly 90 percent of the retiree vote (which is eligible in union elections). Boyle got just a bare majority of the reported active miners' vote in that December 1969 election. Yablonski immediately challenged the result, charging a stolen election. Twenty-two days later, the bodies of Yablonski, his wife, and his young daughter were found in his Clarksville, Pennsylvania home—each shot to death. Only then did the Labor Department prepare to enter the case.

In death, Yablonski became a near-legendary figure to rebels within the UMW. He had never been the world's most saintly man, but now he was lionized. A movement called Miners for Democracy sprang up in western Pennsylvania; its official head was Mike Trbovich, a flamboyant, uneducated miner from Clarksville (given to arm-waving, purple shirts, and yellow ties);

the real leader, however, was Yablonski's son, Joseph, an attorney in Washington, D. C., who took on the cause as a near-holy one. Miners for Democracy makes Pennsylvania the cockpit of a major revolt against UMW leadership; the other principal base lies in the West Virginia Disabled Miners and Widows Association, which filed the sensational suit that resulted in having Boyle thrown off the board of trustees of the welfare and retirement fund. (The fund is likely to go broke by 1975 because of the 1969 election-year raises in pensions ordered by Boyle, according to a report of the U. S. Comptroller General.) The problem afflicting all the insurgent groups is that they lack the high-quality leadership needed for a major assault on Boyle's fortress. The Yablonski murders—especially since they included his wife and daughter—had a chilling effect on any insurgent activity within the UMW. And through trusteeships and other devices, Boyle in 1971 still had power great enough to cut off most opposition at the sapling stage.

Nevertheless, the judicial process was slowly closing in on the *ancien régime*. A belated suit by the Labor Department, to overturn Boyle's election on the grounds of fraud, intimidation, and irregularity, was finally coming to trial. If sustained, it would force brand-new elections. In retrospect, the Labor Department's refusal to intervene early and decisively in the UMW election, despite its clear mandate and responsibility under the Landrum-Griffin Act to protect rights of trade unionists, stands out as a clear dereliction of duty by a government agency. Ultimate responsibility lay with the then Secretary of Labor, George P. Shultz, who later became director of the President's Office of Management and Budget. Apparently Labor Department officials thought Yablonski was of the same caliber as Boyle & Company—the attitude reflected in George Meany's comment that "Yablonski was just one of the boys in the kitchen trying to move into the living room." By that reasoning, of course, government protection of individuals' rights would only be available for well-dressed "good guys" already in the dining room. Even after Yablonski's murder, Shultz at first suggested it was unconnected with the UMW election. Now the government believes quite differently. It indicted five persons for murder and in November 1971 obtained a conviction of one of them, Aubran W. Martin of Cleveland, Ohio. One of the accused killers, Claude E. Vealey, had pleaded guilty and named Martin as the triggerman. Vealey said an otherwise unidentified man named "Tony" had paid $5,200 for the killings. Federal agents now say the killers' payoff came from union funds; Boyle denies any knowledge of the murders.

In another action, Boyle was indicted by a federal grand jury for embezzlement, conspiracy, and illegal use of union money for political purposes. The government charged the UMW with spending almost $11 million in 1967–69 in violation of Landrum-Griffin reporting requirements; there were 3,000 expenditures totaling $7.6 million, for everything from fancy expense-paid trips for UMW officials to suspicious multithousand-dollar "loans" to UMW districts during the 1969 election period, for which proper documentation or justification was unavailable. Boyle's daughter was revealed to be drawing $40,000 a year as a union attorney in a moribund Montana district.

And Ralph Nader revealed the existence of a previously secret special pension fund which will permit Boyle and two other high UMW officials to retire at full salary for life, with more than $1.5 million of miners' money as a nest egg.

Finally, after interminable and unexplained delays, a Justice Department suit was finally coming to trial in 1971 to force the union to abandon its palpably illegal trusteeship system. The suit had originally been filed in 1965, but was never prosecuted during the Johnson-Humphrey administration—for apparently political reasons.* When the trusteeships are dissolved, elections will be obligatory throughout the UMW districts and the fresh breeze of democracy may finally come rushing through the crumbling old house of labor that John L. Lewis built.

Keystone Politics

The Republican party got a hammer lock on Pennsylvania's body politic in the Civil War years and was not forced to let go until the New Deal came on the scene 70 years later. One reason was the protective tariff, which helped turn the state for Lincoln in 1860. Pennsylvania was the Union's preeminent manufacturing, rather than commercial or trading, state; thus the tariff, together with other policies to benefit big business, made the Grand Old Party the natural ally of steel, coal, oil, and textile interests—interests which in turn repaid the favor with ample campaign financing. Secondly, there was the memory of the Civil War. Pennsylvania *had* been invaded, Gettysburg had given the people a great fright, and the bloody shirt could be waved for a generation afterward. Third, no ethnic grouping rose up to fight the ruling classes as the Irish did in Boston. Protestant, Catholic, Jewish, German, Irish, Negro—everyone was Republican. Finally, a succession of Republican bosses, men of shrewdness and power rarely seen in America, sprang from Pennsylvania soil. They ruled over an Organization whose power extended from the sooty mill towns to the dogwooded suburbs of Philadelphia and Pittsburgh, from the ward clubhouse to the U. S. Senate—and was rarely thwarted. The Republicans scored an astounding chain of Presidential victories, unbroken from 1860 through 1932, except for 1912, when the state voted for Progressive party candidate Teddy Roosevelt. In the same seven decades, Pennsylvania elected 15 Republican governors and only two Democrats, though one of those Republican governors—Gifford Pinchot—was the renowned conservationist and progressive and an implacable enemy of the Organization.

Nathaniel Burt in *The Perennial Philadelphians* has given a colorful account of the trilogy of great Republican bosses—Simon Cameron (1865–87), Matthew S. Quay (1887–1904), and Boies Penrose (1904–21). Cameron

---

* The UMW has been just as chummy with the national Democratic party as it has been with some of the mine owners. Boyle is accused of making an illegal $30,000 contribution from union funds to the Humphrey-Muskie Presidential campaign in 1968.

was a somewhat unsavory character from western Pennsylvania who began his career by defrauding the Winnebago Indians of their lands and moneys and landed in Lincoln's cabinet as Secretary of War through a political deal. He used that position to benefit himself and his contracting friends and the only way Lincoln could get rid of him was to appoint him minister to faraway Russia. In 1867 the Republican legislature made him U. S. Senator and he continued as absolute boss of the state until his retirement a decade later.

Quay, the Latin-reading son of a clergyman, is depicted by Burt as "a sinister personage whom Kipling considered the best-read man in America, and who kept a file, known as 'Quay's Coffin,' which furnished him with items for blackmail, at need, on anyone of political consequence in Pennsylvania." He became the Republican state and national chairman and a U. S. Senator.

About Penrose, whom Gunther described in *Inside U. S. A.* as a man "who ate himself to death," Burt offers fine detail:

He was an Old Philadelphian of the most unquestionable sort; but there was also no question about the ungentlemanliness of his politics. . . . As absolute ruler of Pennsylvania after the death of Quay in 1904, and therefore dominant figure in the Republican party nationally, Penrose was in the early years of the 20th century one of the most powerful men in the country. . . . It was he who by choosing T.R. as V.P. "kicked him upstairs." [He] collected and distributed all major contributions to the party, dominated all important Senate committees and hence all legislation, and kept the Pennsylvania Organization he inherited from the Camerons and Quay in prosperous and working order. . . .

He disdained the People, the democratic process and other politicians. . . . He respected only power and force and the clever use of force to maintain power. . . . Graft disgusted him. No money scandals ever dented his own hide. [But] he had clients and he served them well [including] Frick and Carnegie, lords of Pittsburgh and steel, for whom he supported tariffs and emasculated antitrust and labor laws. . . . He was the Old Philadelphia figure of the Iron Age in politics. . . .

He swore, he drank, he whored and he didn't care who knew it. . . . He was a giant in size and strength, six feet four and powerful. . . . He grew immensely fat, almost 300 pounds, but till the very end never lost his dignity, presence or appetite. . . . There are awed accounts of his breakfasts—a dozen fried eggs, a half-inch slice of ham, a dozen rolls, a quart of coffee. . . .

Penrose could absorb immense quantities of liquor without showing it, but made no pretense of hiding either his occasional drunkenness or continued lecheries. "I do what I damn please," said Big Grizzly. "The masses like that."

One of Penrose's last acts, according to legend, was to order the nomination of Warren Harding for President from his deathbed in 1920. In the years that followed, the GOP splintered and a powerful right-wing faction rallied around Joseph P. Grundy, president of the Pennsylvania Manufacturers' Association and a perfect symbol of old-style exploitative capitalism. Grundy continued as president of the PMA, a pervasive influence in the legislative halls at Harrisburg, and was a factor in state politics until he died in 1961, at 98 years of age.

The Democrats' anemia through the 1920s was illustrated by the vote for their Presidential candidate in 1924—a skimpy 19 percent of the statewide vote. But the Depression changed all that. The Republicans were still able to carry the state for Hoover in 1932, but in 1934 the first Democratic governor and U. S. Senator of the 20th century, George E. Earle and Joseph F. Guffey, were elected to office.

With the waning of New Deal fervor, the Republicans returned to power in 1938, due in part to John L. Lewis' attempt to name the Democratic candidate that year. FDR carried Pennsylvania in 1936, 1940, and 1944, however, and even though the Republicans reestablished the legislature control they had lost in the mid-1930s and held the governorship and both the state senate and house from 1943 to 1955, politics were fought on much more even terms than in the earlier times. In 1948, Pennsylvania gave Dewey the biggest plurality he received in any state, and it was predictably for Eisenhower in both his races; in 1960, however, John F. Kennedy rode to a narrow Pennsylvania victory (116,326-vote plurality) due entirely to the gigantic margin (331,544 votes) he received in Philadelphia. In 1968, Humphrey carried Pennsylvania by 169,388 votes, the Philadelphia margin (271,-615 votes) again accounting for his entire plurality.

In one of those "rules" of politics more honored in legend than fact, it has been said in recent years that if the Democrats can be held to less than a 200,000-vote plurality in Philadelphia, the GOP can win statewide. But as Philadelphia GOP chief William Meehan told me dolefully, "In 1970 I held it under 200,000, but our ticket wasn't home—in fact it got licked by a half million." One reason for the extraordinary reversal in form was the success of the 1970 Democratic gubernatorial candidate, Milton Shapp, in carrying wealthy Republican Montgomery County in the Philadelphia suburbs.

Other Republican strongholds are Dauphin County (Harrisburg), Lancaster and York Counties in the prosperous Pennsylvania Dutch country of southeastern Pennsylvania, the Allentown and Williamsport areas, and virtually all the rural counties along the northern tier. The Democrats' base, outside of Philadelphia and Pittsburgh, has been in the depressed northeastern coal counties like Lackawanna (Scranton) and Luzerne (Wilkes-Barre) Northampton (Bethlehem and Easton), and virtually all of western Pennsylvania, from Erie down to the southwestern corner of the state (territory that includes all the tired steel and coal counties around Pittsburgh).

The Republican party might have slipped into perennial minority status in the postwar years if it had not been for a succession of moderate-liberals who took on the conservative Old Guard faction allied with the Pennsylvania Manufacturers' Association. The first of these was the late James H. Duff—a charming, practical political operator who made his start as a Theodore Roosevelt Progressive Republican in 1912. In 1943, Gov. Edward Martin brought "Big Red" Jim Duff in from Carnegie to be his attorney general. All Republican factions, including the PMA, then anointed Duff for governor in 1946, and he won handily. Once in office, however, Duff decided that business wasn't paying its fair share of taxes and broke decisively with the PMA faction headed by Grundy.

Duff turned out to be a remarkably progressive governor, putting across a tougher clean streams law, cleaning up the Schuylkill River to provide water for Philadelphia and Reading (so that it was no longer necessary, as Gunther reported, for Philadelphia to "drink its own sewage"), and passing an effective "tax anything" law that let hard-pressed local governments and school boards tax anything, including wages, not taxed by the state. In 1950, Duff won a decisive victory over the PMA faction—the "high-buttoned-shoes reactionaries," as he called them—by putting over his candidate for governor, John S. Fine, and winning election himself to the U. S. Senate. In the following two years, he won national stature by the part he played in persuading Gen. Dwight D. Eisenhower to seek the Republican Presidential nomination and helping to manage his primary campaign.

Duff and his allies gradually lost power and influence and Duff found himself less suited to life in the Senate than as a hard-hitting administrator in Harrisburg. In 1956, cut by many GOP stalwarts who resented his independence, he was defeated for reelection by the reform mayor of Philadelphia, Democrat Joseph S. Clark. But the PMA was never again to elect a governor. The Democrats, in fact, were able to elect their first two governors in succession since the 1850s—George M. Leader, a remarkably aggressive campaigner from rural York County who was only 37 at the time of his election in 1954, and David Lawrence from Pittsburgh, who became Pennsylvania's first Roman Catholic governor at the mellow age of 73. (Latent anti-Catholicism almost beat Lawrence, despite the strong Democratic tide in 1958. In office, as *Time* later reported, he was "one of those rare bosses capable of combining a strong party organization with a progressive, relatively scandal-free administration.") But Lawrence made no contribution to state government comparable to what he had done earlier in the postwar revival of Pittsburgh; it can safely be said he came to the office too late in life.

The 1958 election also saw the first election to the Senate of Hugh Scott, bucking the Democratic tide to defeat George Leader. The Old Guard had hoped to run Congressman James Van Zandt, a tried and trusted "regular" from Altoona, but Scott simply outmaneuvered the conservatives to win the nomination. It turned out to be a costly loss for the conservatives because Scott, reelected in 1964 and 1970, would turn out to be the most enduring and effective leader of the party's progressive faction. Scott's most brilliant maneuver came in 1962, when the PMA and the party's conservative legislative wing wanted to run a colorless old party wheelhorse, Judge Robert Woodside, for governor. Scott feared a conservative turn in the Pennsylvania GOP that would make his own reelection chances in 1964 practically nil. Scott went to visit retired President Eisenhower at his Gettysburg farm and emerged quoting Ike as saying the proposed slate of Woodside for governor and Van Zandt for U.S. Senator (to oppose Clark) would be a "miserable" ticket. Scott even threatened to run for governor himself. The man Scott really wanted, however, was the liberal young Congressman from Scranton and squire of that community, William W. Scranton. Scranton coolly insisted he would not run unless all the party factions backed him. Finally, a compromise was reached with Scranton slated for governor and Van Zandt for the Senate. That autumn, Van Zandt was beaten but Scranton scored a smashing 486,291-vote victory (55.4 percent) over Democrat Richardson Dilworth. (For all of Scott's coolness in the nomination maneuvering, "he literally turned white when he thought he might really have to run for governor," Scranton recalls.)

Scranton's fight against Goldwater for the Republican Presidential nomination put Pennsylvania into the Presidential sweepstakes, however briefly, for the first time in living memory. And in dealing with legislators and politicians at home, he demonstrated an extraordinary charm and an ability to get people to work with him and to move programs forward. But the Scranton meteor was a brief one: ineligible under state law to run to succeed himself as governor, under pressure from wife and family to abjure elective office, he said: "I am not going to run, ever again, for any office, under any circumstances." He has remained active in public life, however: as leading spirit of a convention which drafted a new Pennsylvania state constitution, as president of the National Municipal League, and in 1970 as chairman of the President's Commission on Campus Unrest, which was set up in the wake of the Kent State and Jackson State killings. The report criticized excesses among some student groups and law enforcement officers. And it also criticized President Nixon himself (to the administration's chagrin and anger) for failing to exercise stronger and more unifying national leadership.

To succeed Scranton as governor, the Republicans picked then Lt. Gov. Raymond P. Shafer, a craggy-jawed, plodding, well-intentioned former state senator from western Pennsylvania with important backing from the Mellon interests in Pittsburgh. Shafer won election with ease, but after his inauguration proceeded to press for the right things in such a maladroit way that his relations with the legislature and his public image declined disastrously. (History will probably be kinder to Shafer than immediate political commentary. He did give higher education a strong push forward, obtain meaningful constitutional reform, and had the courage to speak up for the state income tax which his successor, Milton Shapp, quickly enacted into law.)

By 1970, it seemed that the verve and direction of the progressive Republican era begun by Scott and Scranton had been badly blunted. The nomination went to Raymond J. Broderick, the lieutenant governor and favored candidate of the GOP organization in his home town of Philadelphia. Broderick is a man of intelligence and integrity, but he turned out to be the most abysmal candidate to get a major party nomination in the state in many years. Under pressure from Philadelphia GOP boss William Meehan, he came out openly against the income tax backed by Shafer, claiming that economies could balance the spiraling state budget—a notion shared by hardly anyone with a rudimentary knowledge of Pennsylvania's near-bankrupt condition. Broderick also injected religion into the campaign by vociferously opposing any shift in the state's rigid law against abortions, and particularly Shapp's proposal that a panel of women be appointed to recommend what changes should be made in the law. But these positions failed to gain Broderick many Democratic votes; to the contrary, they contributed to a sharp decline in the normal Republican vote in rural Protestant counties. The election produced the largest Democratic gubernatorial victory (a margin of 500,175 votes) in Pennsylvania's history.

Scott reached his 70th birthday a few days after winning a third term in 1970, and the question I asked of many Pennsylvania Republicans—without hearing a single convincing answer—was who will be the moderate Republicans' leader when he is gone from the scene. The junior Republican Senator, Richard Schweiker, is a personally attractive and hard-working fellow, but his policy stands are so liberal that many GOP organization types might find it hard to work with him. Right now he has the disadvantage of working in the Scott shadow. Several of the younger Republican Congressmen show promise, however, and Philadelphia District Attorney Arlen Specter, a former Democrat, now a moderate Republican, would like to run for governor in 1974 and become his party's leader. A return to the moss-backed Republicanism of earlier times is not likely, because the PMA and its allies have virtually no power left in Republican circles. There is a core of Goldwater-type conservatives centered in Allegheny County, but their numbers and influence are minimal.

Pennsylvania's Democrats have been split into two groupings in recent years. On the one side, there has been the camp of regular organization politicians who rose to the top through the precincts and wards—men like David Lawrence, Joseph Barr (who succeeded Lawrence as mayor of Pittsburgh and Democratic national committeeman), the late Congressman and city Democratic boss William J. Green, Jr., of Philadelphia, and James Tate (mayor of Philadelphia from 1962 through 1971). The other camp, consisting of insurgent reformers, began with the two men who upset the encrusted Republican machine in Philadelphia two decades ago—Richardson Dilworth and Joseph S. Clark. Their modern-day successors are few and far between— but include, significantly, Governor Shapp and Pittsburgh Mayor Peter Flaherty.

Relative peace reigned between the Democratic factions until the early 1960s, due in large measure to the immense personal power of Lawrence in the Pittsburgh area and Green in Philadelphia. (Both men also wielded national power and played key roles in getting the 1960 Presidential nomination for John F. Kennedy.) Lawrence and Green dominated the organizational slate-making sessions in which the Democratic statewide ticket was selected. In several elections, the slatemakers—sometimes to avoid a bloody open primary fight—gave major nominations to Clark and Dilworth. Dilworth was nominated for governor in 1950 and 1962, but lost both times; Clark ran for the Senate in 1956, 1962, and 1968, winning the first two times.*

Before the 1964 elections, Green died unexpectedly and his successor, a singularly insensitive old-line politico named Francis R. Smith, put the

---

* There was, however, tension between Green and the Clark-Dilworth alliance and Green did blackball Dilworth's nomination for governor in the year he might have had the best chance to win —1958.

weight of the Philadelphia organization behind Michael A. Musmanno—a state supreme court justice who was depicted by his enemies as a "Last Hurrah" type of politician—for the U.S. Senate nomination to oppose Hugh Scott. Fearing an open primary, Lawrence and other party leaders went along with Musmanno despite their personal preference for the candidate generally favored before the slating session—state secretary of internal affairs Genevieve Blatt, a "Stevenson Democrat" with sterling liberal credentials. But they got a primary anyway when Miss Blatt, with Senator Clark's backing challenged Musmanno and upset him by the thin margin of 491 votes out of more than a million cast. In the autumn, she lost narrowly to Senator Scott, but the power of the Democratic slatemakers had received a severe body blow. In 1966 (and again in 1970) they picked a youthful Scranton lawyer, Robert P. Casey, as their candidate for governor. Each time, Milton Shapp ran in the primary against Casey. And each time, Casey was defeated.

Shapp is just the kind of candidate organization regulars abhor. First of all, he is openly contemptuous of old-line party structures and alliances. Second, he was initially a risky choice as a candidate because he is Jewish and Pennsylvania had never before elected a Jew as its chief executive. And third, Shapp has money and brains beyond the organization's own resources. A self-made millionaire businessman who had founded the first cable television company in the U. S. in 1958, he was worth, by his own estimation, $12 million by 1965. He immersed himself in study of state government, believing, as he said, that "state government is where an executive can make a contribution." Through his privately financed foundation, Shapp made in-depth analyses of Pennsylvania's economy, governmental structure, and transportation problems—documents of outstanding quality, and all going far beyond any other privately commissioned studies of state government I am aware of, with the possible exception of what the Rockefeller brothers have initiated from time to time.

Shapp's 1966 campaign was an early test of whether unlimited campaign funds, saturation television, and the accompanying services of a professional, outside campaign-management firm can take a state by storm. Shapp hired Joseph Napolitan and gave him authority over most phases of media and campaign organization. Shapp's name was made a household word through heavy mailings and a skillful mixture of convincing 30-minute documentaries on Shapp the man, followed up by saturation short commercials in the final stretch. The technique worked in the primary (to the regulars' dismay), but it backfired in the general election when there was much talk of Shapp "buying" the election. His overall campaign expenses were $4 million.

Instead of disappearing from the scene after his defeat by Shafer, Shapp remained active, speaking out frequently on Pennsylvania issues. In 1970, he openly scorned the Democratic slate-making process, and instead of rehiring Napolitan, virtually ran his own campaign. With his name already well known, he could order much less television time and concentrate on strategically timed announcements, letting the press do some of his campaigning for him. This time, he spent only $3 million. He beat Casey again for the nomination and then proceeded to swamp Broderick in a campaign in which he minced no words about the probable need for an income tax.

Even though Shapp's coattails swept Democrats to control of both houses of the legislature in the 1970 election, little love developed between the party troops and their new governor. In fact, Shapp had been governor less than four hours when the Democratic majority in the state senate rejected all 10 of his cabinet appointments. The reason? Because he had ignored the job recommendations of county chairmen—and even refused to listen to their suggestions, the senators said. The action was soon rescinded, but continuing conflict between the new Democratic governor and his party was as sure a prediction as one could make for Shapp's four years in office. And by a change in the state constitution effected under Shafer, Shapp will be the first Pennsylvania governor eligible to run for election to a second four-year term. The election will be in 1974.

Since the old masters like Lawrence and William Green the Elder passed from the scene, the Democrats' city machines have fallen into disrepair. Now an upstart reformer named Peter Flaherty presides at City Hall in Pittsburgh, and the Philadelphia organization has atrophied under row house politicians and law-and-order politicos. The Democratic city pluralities have declined, not precipitously but still enough to cause concern for the party. A governor like Shapp does nothing to provide the sustenance in patronage that once nourished the party, and old-style politicking is proving more and more repugnant to younger Democrats and Negroes.

A sure sign of trouble to come was the bitter dispute that erupted in the party before and at the 1968 Democratic national convention, when the old-line regulars went solidly for Humphrey and employed the most autocratic methods to suppress dissent in the delegation—even though Eugene McCarthy had won the state's Presidential preference primary. Shapp had used the Chicago convention to underscore his differences with the traditional leaders. He endorsed McCarthy for the Presidential nomination and marched in the streets with delegates protesting tactics of the police and Mayor Richard J. Daley in handling the convention. A youthful 55 when he made that protest, Shapp was symbolizing a sentiment sure to increase its voice in Pennsylvania politics as 18-year-olds register to vote and fundamental party reforms, like those mandated by the McGovern Commission, are put into effect. A first step, taken before the 1972 Presidential primary season at Shapp's urging, transformed the Pennsylvania primary from a purely advisory poll to a system in which most delegates, pledged to specific Presidential candidates, are directly elected by party voters.

Pennsylvanians' vocabulary contains a peculiar word for which the reader will search in vain in his dictionary—*macing*. Broadly, it refers to shakedowns of government employees for political contributions, and despite a law prohibiting it, macing continues unabated to this day. Not only are there suspect dinner "invitations," but government workers who fail to give a percentage of salary must fear for their jobs. In 1970, the Harrisburg area Republican party went about it quite systematically, asking state employees for .5

percent of their salary for the primary election and 1 percent for the general election. Perhaps 100,000 public employees in the state of Pennsylvania are subject to such pressures. But macing may soon be in its death throes as a result of the threat to the old patronage system that has been posed by a public employees' bargaining law passed in 1970—a story to which we will turn later.

Pennsylvania Democrats have been much more systematic about macing than the Republicans. But particularly when they are in office, the Democrats turn up their share of substantial gifts from businessmen. They do receive a goodly share of liberal "conscience" money. And they have the great crutch of organized labor, which has in most elections been a working partner of the Democratic party. Pennsylvania has been lacking in recent years, however, in socially conscious, aggressive unions. The liberal, independent-minded Democratic candidate who hopes for important labor support may find himself out in the cold.

Business interests remain the mainstay of GOP financing, but the most overt supergifts designed to undermine politicians' independence have been declining. The most massive political givers of the right-wing variety have been the Philadelphia Pews, who control 42 percent of the Sun Oil Company and have a collective family fortune estimated at almost $1 billion. The Pews have given millions to favored political candidates since the turn of the century, and the family patriarch, J. Howard Pew, also favored the John Birch Society with indirect if not direct aid. He died in 1971 at the age of 89.

One great Republican contributor throughout his life was Pittsburgh's Richard King Mellon. I was told by Arthur B. Van Buskirk, Mellon's attorney, confidant, and chief agent in political campaigns, that Mellon "liked warm-hearted and honest people," and "Ike was his all-time favorite." When Eisenhower asked Mellon to open his checkbook for a candidate, in fact, Mellon invariably responded. In 1960, the Mellon family contributed an officially reported $40,000 to Republican causes, and in 1968 $118,000. It was later reported that Mellon was never personally enthusiastic about Nixon. On one occasion, Mellon gave $30,000 to a Republican governor, ostensibly for political purposes, but later was hounded by doubts of whether the money had gone further than the governor's personal safe box.

Moderate Republican givers became quite prominent in the 1960s, including Thomas McCabe of Scott Paper, the state's Republican national committeeman. McCabe helped bankroll the Scranton campaigns, both from his own wealth and by approaching friends in business and banking. Another important liberal GOP contributor is Mrs. Elsie Hillman of Pittsburgh, whose husband Henry is the head of Hillman Industries.

Pennsylvanians on the Potomac

The circumscribed role of Pennsylvania in national circles is illustrated by the fact that Hugh Scott, by winning election as Republican leader of the

Senate in 1969, became the first man from his state to hold a major leadership role in Congress since Frederick Augustus Muhlenberg was Speaker of the House in the First and Third Congresses. Joseph S. Clark, serving in the Senate from 1957 to 1969, gained distinction as a battler for liberal social causes and congressional reform but often seemed like a Don Quixote charging the seniority system, the filibuster, and other impregnable bastions of senatorial privilege. As *Philadelphia Magazine* wrote of Clark after his defeat for reelection in 1968, "His lofty conception of the role of the United States Senate and his persistent championing of high standards of personal ethics for members of the Congress established a moral tone which in our judgment easily compensated for whatever shortcomings he may have demonstrated as a political diplomat."

After Scott and Clark, one looks long and hard for Pennsylvanians who have made an important contribution in Washington in our time. Rep. Thomas E. Morgan, a county doctor from rural Fredericktown in western Pennsylvania, became chairman of the House Foreign Affairs Committee in 1959. But he failed (until some reforms were instituted in 1971) to advance that body far beyond the status of a detail-checker of the foreign policies espoused by the executive branch. On the Republican side, John P. Saylor of Johnstown is ranking Republican on the Interior and Insular Affairs Committee and has occasionally been mentioned as a possible Secretary of the Interior.

But when one thinks of real Pennsylvania power on the Potomac, the subject returns quickly to Hugh Scott. Since the departure of Kentucky's Thruston B. Morton he has been the only really effective political operator among Republican moderates in the Senate. Scott's old friend but political antagonist, former Senator Clark, has said of him: "His ear is closer to the ground than the ear of any other politician I know. . . . He knows where all the bodies are buried, and he can cut your throat with the most charming smile. He wants to know what the people of Pennsylvania want him to do, and then he does it." *

Scott was born in Fredericksburg, Virginia, and still carries traces of Virginia in his speech. After graduating from the University of Virginia Law School, he moved to Philadelphia and got his political start as an assistant district attorney bringing in indictments against corrupt magistrates, and in 1940 won election in a Germantown congressional district in Philadelphia. In 1948, he served as Republican national chairman during the Presidential campaign of Thomas E. Dewey, exhibiting a slashing partisan oratory which has softened over the years. He has always enjoyed a tolerably good working relationship with Richard Nixon, but in 1968 backed Rockefeller for the GOP Presidential nomination (as he had Pennsylvania's own William Scranton in 1964).

Since he became Republican leader, Scott has also been obliged to listen

---

* Quoted in "The Politician—Starring Hugh Scott," by Julius Duscha, *Washingtonian*, October 1970. While Clark was still in the Senate, he and Scott had a unique weekly television show, aired across the state, in which they argued public policy between themselves and with guests with gusto and humor.

carefully to White House signals, going along with the administration most, but definitely not all, of the time. One of his problems is that bucking Nixon's conservative policies too often would expose him to overthrow by the right wing in GOP Senate ranks. He did oppose Nixon on the nomination of Clement Haynsworth for the Supreme Court and on a proposed watering-down of the Voting Rights Act of 1965. Civil rights is one subject Scott feels deeply about. "You'd be surprised how many Southern Senators feel the way I do, but feel they can't do anything about it because of Southern politics."

Like his politics, Scott's view of a Senate leader's role is centrist: "I don't favor the Johnson technique of the eyeball and lapel, the favor and reprisal. Nor do I share Mike Mansfield's concept that he is the servant of the Senate. I feel my job is a sort of a mixture. You use strength, measured strength, when you have it, which means when you have the votes. But the job is also that of a conciliator among my own Republican colleagues."

Yet it would be a mistake to think that Scott is exclusively a political animal. The visitor to his office is quickly impressed by the exquisite pieces of ancient Chinese art standing about, and Scott is quick to tell of the interest in collecting 1,000-year-old pieces, which he and his wife Marian have been engaged in for more than 35 years. In fact, Scott is accomplished enough in Chinese art to have written a book during the 1960s—*The Golden Age of Chinese Art: The Lively T'ang Dynasty*. The story is told of the day Kentucky's Sen. Marlow Cook came to discuss a touchy issue with Scott. As Scott developed an argument trying to win Cook over, the visitor picked up a beautifully shaped white T'ang bowl from the coffee table and swung it between his fingers. After he had won Cook over, Scott relaxed and said as Cook was about to leave: "I just want to let you know, Marlow, that breaking a bowl like that would be the equivalent of pushing a Cadillac over a cliff."

Scorecard on State Government

Seldom an innovator among the states, Pennsylvania government is now rushing belatedly into the 20th century, rapidly expanding its services, trying some unique approaches, and suffering some severe fiscal headaches. Some salient items:

BUDGET. Pennsylvania's general fund budget was $990 million in 1961–62; by the start of the 1970s it had zoomed to $3.3 billion. Oddly enough, the last governor to hold expenditures fairly well in line was the Democrat David Lawrence. Then came the Scranton and Shafer administrations, determined to pull Pennsylvania out of its slough of unemployment and stagnation. They picked education as the key to progress, and now Pennsylvania spends $1.7 billion a year for education, almost twice the size of its entire budget during the Lawrence years. But other, less welcome items have escalated the budget as well. A prime example is welfare, $220 million a decade ago, now over $600 million a year.

TAXES. As noted earlier, Pennsylvanians so abhorred the income tax that they permitted their sales tax to become what was then the nation's highest—6 percent—before they accepted the income tax. When Shapp took office in 1971, the state faced an immediate deficit of hundreds of millions of dollars and payless paydays for government workers. Even then, it took weeks of cajoling and arm-twisting of his own Democratic-controlled legislature to get an income tax passed. Then the state supreme court struck down the new tax because it granted exemptions to low-income families, which the jurists (mostly conservative Republicans) interpreted as violating the state constitution's prohibition against a graduated tax. (Governor Rockefeller of New York scornfully told me this indicated Shapp's "inexperience.") After more protracted negotiations, the legislature finally approved a flat-rate 2.3 percent income tax.

Pennsylvania has one of the highest corporate income taxes in the U.S.A. and business, through various levies, pays about $1 billion a year in taxes to the state—compared to $2.5 billion for individuals. Many big corporations think they are taxed far beyond reasonable rates by the state, and in 1971 a group located around Philadelphia (including the likes of General Electric, Scott Paper, Sun Oil, and Smith, Kline & French) took out full-page newspaper ads threatening to leave Pennsylvania unless they got a better tax break.

CONSTITUTIONAL REFORM. The anachronistic state constitution of 1873 was substantially revised by amendments in the 1960s and a state constitutional convention that met in 1967. Although the legislature restricted the scope of the convention and tailored the delegate-election mechanics to provide for partisan elections, some important changes emerged. The one-term limitation on the governor was removed, a splendid local government article written, and lines of responsibility among the three branches of state government made clearer. The convention also worked out a major reorganization of the judiciary, with all state courts placed under the state supreme court in a unified administration.

Scranton, a leader of the convention, says it was a landmark in reducing the hyperpartisanship of Pennsylvania politics. Though Republicans had won a slight majority in the delegate elections, he and others staged a successful first-day fight to have it organized on a nonpartisan basis with a Republican president, Democratic vice president, cochairmen of both parties, and equally balanced party memberships on each committee. Scranton acknowledges that Pennsylvania is still one of the country's most partisan states. *Every* public officer—from governor and judges down to mayors and school boards —is elected on a partisan basis. Rarely will a member of the opposition party vote for a governor's budget. But men like Scranton, who was the first Republican governor to appoint a Democrat to his cabinet, have been pressing with some success for less partisanship, and gradually the idea is catching on.

PATRONAGE. Despite an expansion of civil service under Scranton, 45,000 of Pennsylvania's state workers are still appointed through a political patronage system—easily the highest percentage of any state of the Union. "Your only qualification," says Duke Kaminski of the Philadelphia *Bulletin's* Harrisburg bureau, "is endorsement by the party chairman, or the current administration, the blessing of the governor or a ranking staff member."

The days of the patronage system are numbered, however. In 1970, Pennsylvania suddenly took an innovative step by enacting a public employees' collective-bargaining act which actually guarantees to all government workers—state, county, and municipal—the right to strike. Pennsylvania was second only to Hawaii in enacting legislation of this type. Provisions are established for unions to win certification as bargaining agents. Strikes may then be called if (1) they are preceded by mediation and a report from a fact-finding panel, and (2) they do not imperil the "public health and safety" —a definition that was left to the courts to interpret. The practical effects will be that workers can only be dismissed with cause and that workers need only turn to their unions for protection when a new administration comes to power and tries to dislodge them. The parties' only chance to designate workers will be in high positions where union organizing will not reach, or when normal attrition creates vacancies.

The politicians may not, in fact, be as sad about the end of wide-scale patronage as one might expect. Except for the 10 to 15 percent of jobs which pay good money, most are sought after only in hard times when unemployment is high. And the politicians' experience is that they may lose a couple of votes for every one they gain in handing out the desirable jobs.

CONSUMER PROTECTION. Pennsylvania's regulatory commissions—especially the public utility commission, which regulates electric, gas, and water rates and franchises intrastate truckers, and the milk marketing board, which sets milk prices—are frequently accused by critics (including Milton Shapp) of protecting the vested interests of those they are to regulate, rather than the public. A favorite *bête noire* of the critics is PUC chairman George Bloom, 74, a canny lawyer from Washington County, delightful in conversation and highly conservative in his views. He is a former Republican state chairman. Scranton appointed Bloom to a 10-year term as PUC chairman in 1965, which means he will serve throughout Shapp's term. Shapp would like to have a new department of consumer affairs established, merging the PUC, the milk marketing board, the banking department, and insurance department and thus obliterating Bloom's power, but few believe Shapp's clout, even with a Democratic legislature, will ever match Bloom's and that of the utilities. Thus the status quo is likely to endure.

The milk marketing board, set up in the Depression era to relieve farm poverty by setting minimum wholesale and retail milk prices, is the perfect example of a good idea turned sour by the course of time. Presently, Pennsylvania consumers pay about 20 cents more a gallon or 5 cents more a quart for their milk than people in neighboring states. The system supports inefficient small dairies and fosters illegal trade practices like rebates and interest-free loans by dairies to stores in return for handling their milk. (Pennsylvania is not alone: 13 other states also continue milk price-fixing by state fiat.)

One important breakthrough for consumers has been scored—thanks to Shapp's appointment of Herbert S. Denenberg, a professor at the University of Pennsylvania and friend of consumer advocate Ralph Nader, as state insurance commissioner. Shapp asked Denenberg to "transform the insurance department of Pennsylvania into an insurance-consumer protection agency," and Denenberg began to do so with a vengeance, starting with orders and requests to the Philadelphia Blue Cross. Denenberg argued that since some 60 percent of the area population has Blue Cross coverage and since hospitals depend on Blue Cross as a major source of revenue, Blue Cross should demand efficient operating and cost accounting procedures in the hospitals rather than meekly accepting higher charges and passing them on to subscribers.

In quick order, Denenberg ordered Blue Cross to (1) reorganize its board of directors to eliminate seats for physicians and hospital representatives and add slots for more consumers and employers who pay its premiums; (2) renegotiate its contracts with all hospitals to make sure that costs of research and medical education of little direct benefit to patients are not passed along in the form of increased hospital costs; (3) try to have doctors, rather than patients, pay the salaries of interns and residents, since their work is directed by the physicians, not the hospitals; (4) pay doctors' bills for visits to patients in nursing and recuperative facilities, instead of restricting payments to visits in overcrowded (and more expensive) hospitals; (5) consider allowing hospital pharmacists to fill prescriptions with less costly generic equivalents of trademarked brand-name drugs. Each of the proposals was likely to generate physician opposition, and Pennsylvania's big drug firms (like Merck and Smith, Kline & French) could hardly be pleased with the suggestion to restrict use of their brand-name drugs. But with hospital costs, as elsewhere in the U.S., escalating beyond sight, Pennsylvania's regulatory effort was one of the first countermeasures sighted anywhere in America in a long time. Naturally, it fit into Shapp's avowed role for his administration: "To be the People's Advocate."

ENVIRONMENT. As an old industrial state with many outmoded sewage systems and ancient factories, Pennsylvania is extremely vulnerable to environmental dangers. Occasionally ecological disasters occur. At Donora, a steel-mill town of 12,000 people south of Pittsburgh, a heavy mixture of smoke and fog settled during the last days of October 1948 as a result of a temperature inversion. People's lungs became clogged with smoke from locomotives and factories, auto exhausts and floating solid particles. Five women and 17 men met their death as a result. Rivers are constantly threatened by acid mine water from abandoned coal mines. In summer 1970, a flow of up to five million gallons a day of acid water high in iron oxides and mineral salts was released from a mine in Cambria County into the Susquehanna River, killing all aquatic life for miles downstream.

Despite the Duff-era clean-streams laws, an investigative reporter for the Philadelphia *Bulletin* in autumn 1970 reported scores of violations along the Schuylkill River after he and a colleague bravely canoed from Pottsville down to Philadelphia. One morning they discovered a dense wall of white steam stretching from bank to bank; behind it there was a Philadelphia Electric Company generating station pumping 98° water into the river, despite the limitation of 87° in state law. "Our steam bath," reporter Gary Brooten wrote, "was a mind-boggling opener for a day in which we also saw milky papermill wastes; foamy, smelly, brown half-treated sewage; rust red steel plant wastes; and black gritty washings from an air pollution control device being dumped into the Schuylkill. On the same day we encountered eye-smarting coke gases and watched immense black clouds of coke plant air pollution." Along the banks of the Schuylkill at Philadelphia, Brooten found —on a day without rain—storm sewers emptying raw sewage into the river —a stinking gray mass, containing quantities of partially dissolved toilet paper which settled out of sight as the sewage mixed with the murky green of the river. The Schuylkill is also lined with lagoons holding hundreds of millions of gallons of oil, chemical, and sewage wastes, and in November 1970 a lagoon at a Berks County factory spilled three million gallons of oil sludge into the river.

The most one can say of all this is that now, late in time, a serious anti-pollution effort does seem underway in state government. In the last year of the Shafer administration, a new state department of environmental resources was set up to assume the duties of 14 existing and often competing and ill-coordinated agencies. Dr. Maurice K. Goddard, a respected former professor of forestry at Penn State who had been secretary of forests and waters for 16 years, was appointed to head the new agency. About the same time, Shafer created—and Shapp later continued—an extraordinary strike force of six young attorneys (most from Philadelphia law firms, the oldest man 31 years old) to stop pollution in its tracks by heavy use of injunctions rather than going the route of criminal prosecutions and fines. Early reports indicated the strike force was extraordinarily successful.

It will doubtless be a long time until Pennsylvania's air and water are really clean. When I discussed the subject with the *Bulletin*'s Duke Kaminski in a 1971 telephone conversation, he said:

I'm looking out the Capitol window here and I can see three smoke stacks belching out poisonous gases—two of them belong to Pennsylvania Power and Light Co. Down the road at Bethlehem there's one of the worst oxygen furnaces you ever saw in your life. The poisonous pink cloud is something to behold. Shapp's best estimate is that unless you want to wipe out current industry, it might take 15 years to get it under control. My reply to that was: "Fifteen years?! Why, I'll be dead!"

UNIVERSITIES. Pennsylvania is just now emerging from the Dark Ages in respect to public support of higher education. Its investment in public colleges and universities is now six times greater, in relation to per capita income, than was the case in the early 1950s, but the state's financial effort in higher education still ranks only 48th in the U.S.A.

For more than a century, Pennsylvania has had a public land-grant university—Penn State, located at remote State College (now called University Park) in the Allegheny Mountains some distance north of Harrisburg. By 1955, Penn State already had 14,000 students; today the figure at the central campus and 20 satellite campuses is over 50,000. But Pennsylvanians have never thought of Penn State as *their* college in the way that people from the South, Midwest, and West view their state university. Penn State's main feature has been a very good football team, plus good agricultural and engineering departments. These days its chief innovation is broad-scale use of television to let one professor cover many classrooms.

The great expansion in higher education started with Scranton, who more than doubled appropriations for higher education (to $134 million), and continued at a fast clip under Shafer to a total of $325 million in his last budget. A whole new string of community colleges has come into existence in the past decade. But perhaps the most interesting innovation was the marriage of convenience between the state and the previously private University of Pittsburgh and Temple University.* The state needed to increase its enrollment capacity to match the needs of its population; Pittsburgh and Temple were in a desperate way for money. So in return for an adjustment of their tuition fees and some minor changes on their boards of trustees, Pittsburgh and Temple suddenly became "state-related" institutions. The aid is not minimal: about $130 million a year between them at last count (covering about half their basic budgets). The University of Pennsylvania, on the other hand, continues as a "state-aided" school, which means the state pays less than a quarter of its budget. In addition, Pennsylvania youngsters from families with less than $16,000-a-year income are eligible for scholarships to study wherever they please, a program now costing over $65 million a year. A decade ago, the only comparable state-financed activity was a quite limited competitive scholarship program. It cost only $\frac{1}{325}$ as much.

In the meantime, state aid to public schools has gone from under $400 million to more than $1 billion a year in the past decade. Per pupil expenditures reached $892 a year in 1970–71, a very respectable 10th rank among the states (and quite a contrast to the years just before World War II, when the figure was an incredibly low $20.56 per pupil per year). In 1968, Pennsylvania broke with tradition on the subject of state aid to private (prin-

---

* Before it became state-related, the University of Pittsburgh went through a fascinating period of trying to be a national institution with prestigious graduate programs. The bubble burst in the mid-1960s when Chancellor Everett Litchfield was ousted and it was discovered, much to the surprise of its own board of trustees, that the university was $30 million in debt. Now Pitt is an institution of mass education, even though it retains some distinguished departments—most notably philosophy—and excellent schools of law and medicine. Outside of its public institutions, Pennsylvania has many private colleges and universities of high stature. Among these are Swarthmore and Haverford (Quaker-founded institutions in the Philadelphia suburbs), Villanova (Catholic and Philadelphia suburban), Lehigh (Bethlehem), Lafayette (Easton), Chatham (a small, prestige college with advanced and free-form courses, located in Pittsburgh), and Carnegie-Mellon University, a recent merger of the old Carnegie Institute of Technology and Mellon Institute in Pittsburgh. Carnegie-Mellon has a rather ugly campus but academic standards that make it a good substitute for Cal Tech or MIT for engineering students.

cipally parochial) schools. A new law permitted state assistance to the private schools for the "actual cost" of teachers' salaries, textbooks, and teaching aids in secular fields. Opponents of the law, saying it constituted a breach of the First Amendment–mandated separation of church and state, took the matter into the federal courts and in 1971 the U. S. Supreme Court declared it unconstitutional. Friends of the parochial schools in the legislature then began to demand a program of flat payments to children attending nonpublic schools (up to $150 a year for high school students).

"The House of Ill Repute" Mends Its Ways

It may be a little rough to call Pennsylvania's legislature "The House of Ill Repute" as *Philadelphia Magazine* did in a 1969 review of shenanigans in the ornate halls of the Italian Renaissance–style capitol building at Harrisburg. The quality of legislative work, the ethics, and also the qualifications of legislators today are certainly a dramatic improvement over the days when Penrose and Grundy, working in tandem with the special interests, manipulated representatives and senators at will. Things are even a cut above a decade ago when the leader of the Philadelphia Democratic organization used to sit on the floor with a phone at his ear waiting for Bill Green's machine to flash the word on how he and his colleagues should vote.

But in no way does Pennsylvania compare to New York or California in the quality of its legislative output, or in its decision-making capabilities. The 1971 rankings of the Citizens Conference on State Legislators put Pennsylvania fifth in the U.S. in terms of independence—a fact to which governors bloodied in their efforts to put through an income tax can well testify. But Pennsylvania ranked only 23rd in its information sources, 23rd in accountability, 36th in representative character, and 37th in functional capability. "Not too impressive," one newsman commented, "for a state which has four college basketball teams among the country's top 20."

One problem of the Pennsylvania legislature is the inordinately large size of its house—203 members. This leads to vast confusion during sessions, difficulties in organizing majorities to move legislation, and a distinct lack of decorum. (A number of proposals to reduce the house size were made at the 1967–68 constitutional convention, but all were voted down. Republicans from thinly populated rural areas join ranks with big-city Democrats, who want to retain every nuance of urban minority strength, to prevent a sensible reduction.) A second problem is the lack of staff professionalism; the legislature hires over 600 people, but the number includes sergeants at arms, messengers, secretaries, and janitors in addition to a limited number of professionals, and an estimated 5 to 10 percent "phantom" employees, who are on somebody's patronage and never show up for work. Without expert staffs, legislators more easily fall prey to lobbyist enticements on complex and/or innocuous-appearing bills that favor private groups at the public's expense.

Like many legislatures, Pennsylvania's has an inordinately high proportion of white, married, middle-aged men within its ranks. Even after reapportionment on a one-man, one-vote basis was effected in 1966, the new house had only 10 blacks and eight women among its 203 members. The new 50-seat senate had only one black and one woman. (By 1971, there were two blacks.) Average age in the new house was 48, in the new senate 52.

Before the courts forced one-man reapportionment in the mid-1960s, rural (generally meaning Republican) and big-business control of the legislature usually coincided neatly. For several years, it was said that the late Harry Davis, Sun Oil's lobbyist, and William A. Reiter (the Pennsylvania Railroad's and then Penn Central's man) were the 51st and 52nd senators respectively. It was their responsibility to see to it that the senate always had one more Republican than Democratic vote, and the appropriate dollars were invested to make sure that happy condition continued. In 1970, the senate fell to the Democrats for the first time in many years. "It was no accident," one Pennsylvania observer said, "that the senate fell to the Democrats in the year that the Penn Central Railroad went bankrupt."

Today there are still important business lobbies in Harrisburg—the steel companies, oil firms, public utilities—but a lot of the power has shifted to service-type industry lobbies (retailers and the like), who see things differently from the old industrial moguls. And for sheer power, one must look to entirely different types of lobbies—the Pennsylvania State Teachers Association (now considered by some the single most influential lobby), the Pennsylvania branch of the national Welfare Rights Organization, and the AFL-CIO (though labor usually involves itself only with labor legislation). The teacher and welfare organizations, of course, are responsible for much of the huge budget increases of the time, and a taxpayer revolt may not be long in coming.

Philadelphia: Renewal and Decay

The city of Philadelphia, as its social historian, Nathaniel Burt, has written, is "a fine vintage, warm, rich, flavorful; but there's a drop of bitterness in the bottom of the glass." It has had three great flowerings, each followed by an era of decay. The first flowering was its birth as William Penn's City of Brotherly Love, building for a century to the crescendo of the Golden Age of Revolution, the Age of Franklin, when in government, finance, commerce, and letters, Philadelphia was the preeminent city of the New World. Then, early in the 19th century, the federal government went to Washington, the state government was transferred to Harrisburg, supremacy in commerce went to the great deep-water port of New York, and financial power—the *coup de grâce* administered by President Jackson's abolition of the National Bank—was transferred to New York, too. Cultural dominance shifted to Gotham as well, and Philadelphia has lived ever since in the shadow of the great world city to its north. It became (and largely remains) a private city, a place for living.*

A second flowering, industrial in nature, rose through the Civil War and was signaled by the Centennial Exposition of 1876, attended by 10 million visitors and one of the grandest shows of technology the world had ever seen. The peak of the boom came in the 10 years before 1900. Burt writes: "Then boomed Iron and Railroads and Coal, Cramp and Baldwin. The fox hunting and . . . Cricket and coach-and-four flourished together. Then began the Orchestra and the Curtis Publishing Company."

For the prosperity of its Iron Age, Philadelphia had to pay the same kind of price all of Pennsylvania was paying: ugly political corruption (this was the era of the sinister bosses, culminating in Penrose) and physical blight. The almighty Pennsylvania Railroad decided it needed a station at the city's very heart, opposite city hall, and put up a great brick castle called Broad Street Station. To connect with its main lines, the railroad erected a massive stone causeway out to West Philadelphia, a block wide (so it could hold 16 parallel tracks) and appropriately called the Chinese Wall. It was penetrated only by gloomy dripping tunnels for cross streets and effectively blighted development in a large part of the city's heart. Simultaneously, the railroad built up sumptuous suburbs—which would become some of the most beautiful in all America—along its commuting routes, one westward along the Main Line, another northwesterly to Germantown and Chestnut Hill. Thus began the process of suburbanization of Philadelphia's aristocracy which would ruin center city.

Down from the Gilded Age, straight through the New Deal and World War II, Philadelphia's politics were unflinchingly Republican, in the grip of one of the most corrupt and unsavory political machines the country has ever known.

Since the 1880s, there had been sporadic reform efforts by good government types, but the Organization had quickly beaten them all back. But in 1939, the so-called "Young Turks"—a group of bright young Depression-era graduates of Ivy League colleges who had been inspired by the New Deal and La Guardia's achievements in New York, formed to work for charter revision and, later, physical renewal of the city and political change. By the start of the postwar era, the elements of a broad-based reform coalition had begun to coalesce—the Young Turks, Old Philadelphians, ideological liberals in the Americans for Democratic Action, ethnic minority leaders like Jack Kelly and Matthew McCloskey, and Democratic ward heelers.

But the whole reform movement might have collapsed, like so many in the past, had it not been for two bright, aggressive Democratic attorneys from old Republican families who emerged to assume leadership. The first was Richardson Dilworth, a colorful trial lawyer, who ran for mayor in 1947 citing chapter and verse on the pervasive municipal corruption he had learned about as lawyer for the Philadelphia Transit Company. He lost to the medi-

---

* The 1970 Census takers found 1,948,609 people in Philadelphia, 2.7 percent less than a decade before but still enough to make it America's fourth largest city (after New York, Chicago, and Los Angeles).

ocre old GOP war-horse, Mayor Bernard Samuels, by about 90,000 votes. But revelations of wholesale corruption followed in the next two years, and in 1949 Dilworth was elected city treasurer and in 1951 his close associate in the reform movement, Joseph S. Clark, won election as mayor. The Augean stables at City Hall were cleansed and Philadelphia embarked upon a decade of remarkable physical and political renaissance. Dilworth, in turn, became mayor in 1956, finally leaving office to run for governor in 1962. Despite its shortcomings, the Clark-Dilworth era must be called Philadelphia's modern Golden Age.

Clark and Dilworth were not obliged to start the city's renewal from ground zero because the reform elements which elected them had already begun. A citizens' committee in 1947 had staged a spectacular "Better Philadelphia Exhibit" to show citizens, quite graphically, what good planning and renewal could do to revive their decayed city. The exhibit, viewed by 400,000 at a downtown department store, was most Philadelphians' introduction to the exciting ideas that would transform the city's inner core in the following years: a park and a great mall around Independence Hall, bright new buildings where the Chinese Wall still stood, a promenade along the Delaware River as William Penn had originally planned. Not all the plans have been implemented as foreseen that day, but many have, and more may be in the next years. The Independence Hall and neighboring Society Hill renewal efforts are among the finest in the nation and have given the city a new sense of its history and urban elegance. The ugly old Broad Street Station was finally torn down in 1952 (the Philadelphia Orchestra playing "Auld Lang Syne" as the last train pulled out), and where the Chinese Wall stood, there are now the massive buildings and walkways of the Penn Center, centerpiece of the downtown renewal put through under a skilled and strong-headed master of urban renewal, Edmund Bacon. Penn's Landing along the Delaware, already scheduled to be developed in the 1970s into one of the most exciting recreation areas in any American city, will play an even more central role as a result of the decision to make it a focal point for the 1976 Bicentennial Exposition. (Most of the exposition halls, however, will be on Pettys Island, actually on the New Jersey side of the Delaware River—the end result of incredible bungling of Bicentennial planning by Philadelphia leaders.) The same city fathers would also have permitted a blight on Penn's Landing, which the highway builders planned to separate from adjoining Society Hill by means of a broad, open trench for the Delaware Expressway. But private citizens fought a long, arduous, and ultimately successful battle to have the expressway covered. A young lawyer, Stanhope Browne, was a catalyst in getting the expressway covered in what *Philadelphia Magazine* editor Alan Halpern calls a glowing example of what "one determined individual" can do.

Finally, note should be made of the plans to construct Franklin Town, a splendidly conceived private inner-city renewal project, during the 1970s. Franklin Town will be in the vicinity of Philadelphia's grand achievement of the 1920s, the Benjamin Franklin Parkway, which runs from ostentatious old City Hall to the magnificent Philadelphia Museum of Art on its hilltop location several blocks to the northeast of center city.

The postwar years have witnessed successful development in West Philadelphia, where the University of Pennsylvania has been enjoying sound academic and physical growth. In Philadelphia's immense Northeast area, east and west of tree-lined Roosevelt Boulevard, great quantities of decent if not inspiring housing has been constructed for the middle-income Jewish and Catholic families who were once concentrated in the urban core. And while Philadelphia has its share of ghettos—the seemingly endless blocks of North Philadelphia and the broad reaches of West Philadelphia for blacks, throbbing Little Italy in South Philadelphia, and a grim blue-collar ethnic factory enclave called Kensington—there are places of great charm: the broad reaches of Fairmount Park, so colorful and urbane Rittenhouse Square (one of the most pleasant city places on the continent), the posh boutiques and specialty stores along Chestnut Street. If one wants to find the symbols of old establishment Philadelphia, they are still there along Broad Street south of City Hall: the big banks, offices of those famous Philadelphia lawyers, the Bellevue-Stratford (Philadelphia's foremost old hotel), the redoubtable Union League (where Democrats still need not apply), and the Academy of Music (home of the incomparable Philadelphia Orchestra, directed since 1938 by Eugene Ormandy). For all its failings, Philadelphia is a human and personal city, a city with a vivid past and vibrant possibilities, a city eminently worth saving.

The Greater Philadelphia Movement was launched in 1948 on the model of Pittsburgh's Allegheny Conference, its board composed principally of "movers and shakers"—presidents of home-owned corporations who can make decisions for them—along with a share of minority-group and labor spokesmen. The GPM made reform of Philadelphia's outmoded form of government its first order of business, and a new charter strengthening the mayor's executive role, upgrading civil service, and putting city planning on a long-range basis, was approved by the voters in 1951 and went into effect as Clark became mayor.

As time went on, Philadelphia developed an inventive structure of public interest corporations close to, but independent of, the government and political structure, performing vital tasks for the city rapidly and effectively. In 1957, for instance, the Old Philadelphia Development Corporation was formed at Dilworth's request with its top priority the renewal of center-city Philadelphia, starting with the Independence Hall area. The OPDC's board includes government officials but is also heavy on presidents and board chairmen of major banks, insurance companies, utilities, department stores, and hotels and the senior partners of prestigious law firms—the kind of a group that can give investors confidence that they are working with a responsible and nonpolitical type of effort.

While the thrust of many of these groups was elitist and business-oriented, real efforts were made to obtain extensive participation of interested citizen groups. If there is one unique element in the Philadelphia story, it must be the broad and diverse assortment of organizations and individuals who contributed to rebuilding. Philadelphia not only has its prestige organizations, but a multitude of thriving civic groups in its neighborhoods, and the lines of communication have usually been kept open. In a sense, this had to be so, because the economic power of the city lies in so many hands; Philadelphia lacks the single, dominant economic power, capable of making almost unilateral decisions, which the Mellons at least until recently have been in Pittsburgh. Thus progress has sometimes been slower, but more firmly based on citizen consent, than in the companion city to the west. There has been another dividend in the Philadelphia system: many believe that the interlocking network of community organizations, rather than the publicized tough tactics of the city police department, can be thanked for the fact that Philadelphia's ghettos have not exploded in major riots.

The greatest contribution of Clark and Dilworth was the high sense of dedication and belief in Philadelphia's future which they brought to City Hall. Dilworth, the utterly courageous man, warm and extroverted, and Clark, more the thinker, reflective, idealistic—they brought a quality to city government that old Philadelphia had not experienced in a century, and they encouraged a generation of bright and idealistic young leaders. But that old goblin, rawly partisan politics, still lurked in the shadows, ready to restore the old order. The regular organization types in the Democratic party did not take to it kindly when Clark started out by appointing young reformers and talented Old Philadelphians to key posts in his administration, spurning the clamor for Democratic patronage after the long famine of the Republican century. Clark lacked enough power to prevent replacement of his own reform-minded city chairman by William Green, a cultivator of precinct- and patronage-based power of the old school. The conflict endured through the Clark-Dilworth era.

James H. J. Tate, the man who succeeded Dilworth in 1962, had made his way upward as a plodding member of the Democratic organization, demonstrating, as he would in the mayor's job, excellent instincts for political survival. "His great strength," one local observer told me, "was that he was always interested in the exercise of power. He discovered everyone else was interested in money. He wasn't. This gave him great power over others." From the start of his term, Tate seemed to assume that the business elite of Philadelphia which supported Clark and Dilworth and the reform era were against him. Or perhaps it was the other way around—in any event, the relationship led to an emotional counterreaction in a very proud man. Tate actually kept many of Dilworth's best department heads in office and tried for a while to keep the reform era alive. After Bill Green's death in 1963, Tate fought tooth and nail against the old party hack Francis Smith, who succeeded Green as Democratic party chairman in the city. In 1967, when the Democratic city committee decided Tate could not be reelected and tried to defeat him in the primary, Tate appealed to the business leaders for help. They turned him down cold. Tate turned to his friends in organized labor—especially James J. O'Neill, the ruthless boss of Plumbers Local 690, then president of the powerful building and construction trades council in the city. O'Neill, one local trade unionist told me, "forced Tate down the throat of the labor movement." But the labor support was decisive in Tate's easy primary win and then general election victory by only 11,000 votes over the popular young Republican district attorney, Arlen Specter. (In turn, Tate gave labor in the city practically anything it wanted.)

When I spoke with business establishment leaders during Tate's last year in office, they were uniformly disdainful of him—in fact, they almost seemed to make a scapegoat of Tate, blaming him for every urban ill and using him as a handy excuse for their own lack of strong civic initiative. But a man who had attended some of the uneasy confrontations between the businessmen and Tate told me: "All the establishment guys cower in Tate's presence. He's tall, big, *important*, a born leader of men—and a terrible bully. He cuts people down in public and has a terrible persecution complex. But he has a great ability to blunder into the right solution to difficult problems."

Overall, the signals were not positive for Philadelphia as the 1970s began. During the Tate decade, the city's once-vaunted urban renewal effort had slowed down alarmingly. A grand jury, convened by Republican District Attorney Arlen Specter in 1969, uncovered reeking corruption in area after area of the housing-redevelopment program, resulting in scores of indictments including a number against high-ranking officials and civic leaders. City government itself was badly in need of administrative reform, but Tate made only scattered changes, and they were of the kind that fragmented responsibility rather than coordinating it.* Increasingly, Philadelphia found itself in the midst of an impossible tax bind. The reasons were apparent enough: a large low-income population, dilapidated physical plant, languidly increasing property taxes, the heavy financial burden for poverty, slums and crime, rampant inflation, and wages for government workers that constantly outstripped those paid by private businesses in the city. In 1971, the Federal Reserve Bank of Philadelphia conducted an in-depth study of the city's financial outlook and proceeded to issue a report so gloomy in tone that it was dubbed "the doom report." The report projected a cumulative city budget deficit of $1.3 *billion* by 1975 (starting at $60 million in 1970–71 and reaching $520 million in 1974–75).

A surge in local taxes to fill the income gap is hardly likely. The city already imposes a 3.31 percent payroll tax, which, added to the new state income tax, a high sales tax, and high property taxes, scarcely leaves much room for new or higher levies. Nor is local business likely to grow to fill the void with its tax dollars. The fact is that Philadelphia's employment rolls, despite a strong effort by the Philadelphia Industrial Development Corporation, have been essentially static in the postwar period. Now a flight of companies to the suburbs, where the tax climate and working conditions are said to be more amenable, poses a deadly threat to Philadelphia's economy.

In contrast to the stagnant conditions in Philadelphia, the economy of

---

* As an example of zero coordination, no one in city government knew how much money was coming from the range of federal assistance programs, nor which sections of the government were receiving it.

southeastern Pennsylvania as a whole has been moving forward briskly, with an increasingly diversified "mix," in the postwar era. The area continues to have heavy manufacturing—some steel mills (including the huge Fairless Works built by U. S. Steel in Bucks County after the war), heavy equipment and electrical machinery manufacture by companies like GE and Westinghouse, and transportation equipment by Budd (railway cars) and Boeing Veritol division (helicopters). The apparel, chemical, publishing, and drug industries employ many thousands. The area also has the biggest concentration of oil refineries in the East and a port which ranks among the top in the world in total tonnage. (It does less well in general cargo, having failed to adapt early to containerization. *Philadelphia Magazine* charges that "neglect, sheer incompetence and political dealing have badly mauled Philadelphia's port" in the last few years.) Service industries have grown rapidly in recent years and accounted for the lion's share of growth.

Ward Politics and the Story of Frank Rizzo

Philadelphia ward politics are strictly a page out of yesteryear. For the ward and precinct committeemen, the reward is usually patronage—a number of city jobs still available (though most jobs went under civil service during the Dilworth-Clark era) and an even juicier prize, the 2,500 to 3,000 jobs that a state administration can make available within Philadelphia for friends of the party in power.* The archetypal party leader these days, oddly enough, is not a Democrat but rather the leader of the beleagured Republicans, William A. Meehan. Meehan is one of the most thoroughly delightful city politicians I have met in America—a firm-jawed Irishman of compact build in his late forties with a sunny personality who long ago learned to roll with the punches. His father was Sheriff Austin Meehan, a bald, barrel-chested man who was Republican monarch in the city for two decades.

"We were brought up not to depend on politics for a living—always to keep yourself in a position where you can tell 'em to go where you want 'em to," Bill Meehan told me in the office from which he conducts a highly successful law practice. "When people are totally dependent on politics," he said, "it's pathetic. Involvement in politics is like a weakness for betting the horses or the numbers. It's a fun thing, but it's hard to break away once you're into it." Then, with a twinkle in his eye, Meehan added: "Dad said there were two reasons to be in politics—to do something nice for people who've helped you, or to get even with some guy you want to get even with."

I have heard Meehan described as a man with "incredible power in the city," and it is easy to see how he accumulated it: through meticulous attention to organizational detail. "I know more Democratic committeemen than

* Typical state patronage jobs are in the revenue and highway departments, plus the turnpike and bridge authorities. In a sharp break with precedent, Governor Shapp began filling these positions *without* prior consultation of the city Democratic committee.

the Democratic city chairman. Whenever they need anything, they call on me. I try to help 'em out. Maybe they have more confidence in me and I'm more available—my name is in the phone book, and they know I'll serve them if I can." As for his own committeemen, Meehan expects them to stay active year-round, visiting people and trying to do favors for them, even though he admits that government's broadened activity in welfare, unemployment compensation, housing, and medicare has cut back on a committeeman's area of usefulness to constituents. "But still we can operate," Meehan insists. "We play for a small percentage of the vote—the 20 percent that shift from election to election are our goal."

One reason Philadelphia still turns out a strong Republican vote, Meehan says, is that many people were "born Republican—people whose fathers and grandfathers were Republican," so that there is some residue of loyalty that good precinct work can keep cultivated. The large Italian vote is usually split evenly between the parties, and the GOP is cutting in some to the generally Democratic Polish vote. The Democrats, by contrast, have a lot more to draw on: 80,000 federal, 32,000 city, and 14,000 to 18,000 state employees, all generally Democratic in voting habits, plus 150,000 Jewish voters and 250,000 Negro voters.

Meehan says the Republicans usually spend $800,000 to $900,000 on a mayoralty campaign and insists the Democrats spend more. The GOP spends about $200,000 on election day, money which the 67 ward leaders hand out to their committeemen in each of the city's 1,800 divisions (precincts) to hire workers at $10 or $15 a day. In Bill Meehan, it is not hard to detect a streak of dislike for big-business interests; he even claims that Democrats in the city get more business money than the Republicans (a point others dispute).

For their efforts since the Democratic era began two decades ago, the Republicans had two good years: 1965 and 1969, when they elected citywide candidates. But they have yet to elect a mayor.

Final notes on Meehan: His title is general counsel of the party in Philadelphia. Someone else always "fronts" as chairman. No one is fooled. And when the campaign money starts rolling in before an election, Meehan happily collects checks and cash alike. But there is a difference from his confreres in the business of politics. For any gift conveyed in green bills, there must be a *cash receipt*.

As the majority party in Philadelphia, the Democrats have become quite content and show a lot less imagination than Meehan. In national elections, they do turn out massive Democratic pluralities, but in local contests they are now constantly threatened by Meehan's Republicans. After the 1967 election, the city organization was basically just an extension of Tate and his political cronies. Younger, more imaginative Democrats found themselves shouldered aside for nominations to most important offices by the older hacks.

And then there was the matter of Frank Lazzaro Rizzo.

One of the ways Tate paved the way for his difficult 1967 reelection contest was to appoint that volatile, controversial career cop as police commissioner. The selection was doubly brilliant: Rizzo, whose immigrant father was a policeman before him, became the first police commissioner of Italian ancestry in Philadelphia's history—a plus for Irishman Tate with the Italian vote. Secondly, Rizzo had a reputation as a fearless and colorful policeman whose technique of knocking heads first and asking questions later had already endeared him to Philadelphia's fearful middle-class home owners.

Rizzo ran a highly efficient police department which claimed it brought 42 percent of its cases to solution, double the national average. He increased the number of police from 6,000 to 7,200, put dog patrols in the subways, expanded the narcotics squad, equipped his men with walkie-talkies, and expanded the police budget from $60 million to $92 million. Confidential dossiers were kept on thousands of political dissidents and black activists. Rizzo's tactics with Black Panthers and other dissenters were tough—and well publicized—in the extreme. All this delighted his natural constituency—the people he describes as the "guys with lunchboxes and the oil-stained shirts." It horrified liberals, of course. Police services became the largest item in the city budget, at the same time that city outlays for health, recreation, and sanitation services held constant or declined. Wherever trouble erupted in Philadelphia, the big, muscular form of Frank Rizzo (six feet, two inches, close to 240 pounds) would appear to direct police operations, once with a billy club stuck in his cummerbund when he was called away from a formal evening affair.

Barred by the city charter from seeking a third consecutive term as mayor, Tate decided on the man he wanted to succeed him: Frank Rizzo. The Philadelphia Democratic city committee obsequiously went along. In the spring 1971 primary, Rizzo was opposed by U.S. Rep. William Green—son of the late boss Bill Green, but a liberal reformist—and Hardy Williams, a freshman state legislator and street-wise product of the ghetto, who counted on the black vote. Rizzo ran principally on his image and record; his campaign biography drove home the oft-repeated point: "He made Philadelphia the safest of the nation's 10 largest cities." (The statistic is based on once-sacrosanct FBI crime statistics, which are the only comparative figures of their type available in the country but may not be totally accurate because of uneven crime-reporting techniques.) When the votes were counted, Rizzo had 176,621 (49.9 percent), Green 127,902 (36.2 percent), Williams 45,026 (12.7 percent), and David Cohen, a former city councilman who had withdrawn in Green's favor, 4,176. The blacks gave half their vote to Green, 38 percent to their fellow Negro, Williams, and an interesting 12 percent to Rizzo (the residue of middle-class Negroes who are as concerned as many whites about law and order).

The Republican choice was Thatcher Longstreth, who had already run for mayor once, back in 1955, and lost to Richardson Dilworth. But Longstreth, an urbane and elegant man of the Philadelphia establishment, had maintained excellent credentials as a business and civic leader over the years, serving as executive vice president of the chamber of commerce and a city councilman. One reporter wrote of Longstreth: "Six feet, six inches, he looks like the Princeton end he was; the husky Rizzo [a high school dropout] comes on as a sandlot fullback." Longstreth campaigned tirelessly. Rizzo's appearances were infrequent (generally to friendly groups), but everyone knew where he stood and Billy Meehan was probably right when he said: "This whole election is a referendum on Rizzo." When he did take stands, Rizzo spoke of firing the school superintendent, said he would cut business taxes to keep or attract industries, and promised no new income taxes (the city's rising deficits notwithstanding). Many prominent liberals and black leaders endorsed Longstreth, but Tate saw to it that the unions and Democratic machine stuck with Rizzo. Election day saw a reversal of old political patterns. A heavy majority of blacks voted for the Republican Longstreth. But the heavily Italian communities, long a base of Republican strength, went heavily for Rizzo. The vote was 53 percent for Rizzo, 47 percent for Longstreth. And so it was that the City of Brotherly Love elected the "toughest cop" as its mayor.

The Philadelphia Negro

The first Negroes were brought to the banks of the Delaware as slaves of the Dutch even before Penn and the Quakers arrived in 1682, and they have been a significant factor in Philadelphia history ever since. As W. E. B. Du Bois, the great Negro sociologist, told the story in his 1899 book, *The Philadelphia Negro,** the first expression against the slave trade occurred in Philadelphia, as did the first abolitionist organization, the first legislation to end slavery, the first attempt at Negro education, and the first Negro convention. The Du Bois book, read even 70 years after its first publication, is a compelling social documentary on the burden of being black in Philadelphia. Two themes appeared early and have endured to the present day. The first involves Philadelphia's location as a natural gateway from the South; as each generation of Philadelphia Negroes has begun to establish itself socially and economically in the city, a new wave of less educated blacks has arrived from the South, causing social tensions and vicious new discrimination by the white community, not aimed just at the newcomers but at *all* Philadelphia Negroes. The second recurrent theme has been the fierce and often losing competition for jobs that blacks have found themselves immersed in as successive waves of immigrants arrived from Europe.

In the 1890s, Negroes were scattered throughout the city, a high proportion working as domestic servants close to (if not in the homes of) their white employers. Today, the vast majority of Negroes live in clearly defined ghettos. The day-to-day social interaction of whites and blacks that marked earlier times is greatly reduced. Another change is that Philadelphia's middle- and upper-income Negroes—now a growing and prospering

* This seminal work in the sociology of American Negroes, long out of print, was reprinted in 1967 (New York: Schocken Books) with an illuminating introduction by Prof. E. Digby Baltzell of the University of Pennsylvania.

group—do not live in the ghetto; instead they have migrated to desirable communities like Germantown and Mt. Airy, or all the way out to the suburbs. Many wealthy Negroes in the mid-city luxury high-rises pay $400 or more a month in rent. (A measure of the change of things is that 35 years ago, *no* Philadelphia Negro moved into a new home—only old houses abandoned by whites.) The absence of the Negro business and professional people in the ghettos means that underprivileged children growing up there have few success models they can look to.

The second dramatic change from Du Bois' day is simply in terms of numbers. In 1890, Philadelphia had 39,371 blacks (3.8 percent of the total city population). According to the 1970 Census, there were 653,791 blacks in Philadelphia—33.5 percent of the city total. The figure continues to rise, and the day of a black majority may not be too distant—by one projection, as early as 1977.

Summing up the change of conditions for Philadelphia's Negroes between 1960 and 1970, the *Evening Bulletin* reported: "The poorest parts of the city are probably worse off now. . . . There is more vandalism, more narcotics, more gang fighting, more filth in the streets, more dangers of all kinds." Indeed, a series of facts and statistics can be rolled out to support the projection of a violent explosion in the city:

■ For reasons unclear, Philadelphia is a gang-fight center of the U. S. A. From 1962 through 1969, gangs accounted for 374 shootings, 314 stabbings, and 245 major rumbles; from 1962 to the end of 1970, there were 153 gang murders.

■ There are as many as 15,000 heroin addicts in the city, and three times that number hooked on amphetamine drugs—according to the city's own health commissioner.

■ The black unemployment rate is twice that of whites and unlikely to improve much as more and more heavy industries—the kind that can offer blacks the most numerous job opportunities—desert the high-tax, crime-plagued city for the suburbs. Despite the federal government's widely promoted Philadelphia Plan to get blacks accepted in significant numbers in the construction trade unions, the effort in its first year (1969-70) produced no more than 50 new places for blacks among the 9,400 white members of the iron workers, steamfitters, electrical workers, plumbers, sheet-metal workers, and elevator construction unions in metropolitan Philadelphia. The new total was 147, a mere 1.54 percent, and at the rate of progress indicated, it would take a century to meet the Philadelphia Plan goals.

■ Despite scores of ambitious projects, the amount of new housing for low-income blacks is but a drop in the bucket compared to need. There are 13,000 people on the waiting list for public housing—but only 12,000 units were added through all federally subsidized housing programs during the *entire decade* of the 1960s. The picture was somewhat brighter in terms of individual housing-unit rehabilitation in the slums, a program in which Tate took a special interest; nevertheless, so hopeless are conditions in the ghettos that slumlords have abandoned an estimated 20,000 buildings.

- In Philadelphia's schools, which now have a black enrollment of over 60 percent, an estimated 40 percent (80 percent in some inner-city schools) perform below the "minimum functioning level." (Students so ranked may be able to read a little and do sums, but not well; they place below 85 percent of the pupils in the U. S. A. in their age groups.) Basic educational attainment does not seem to have improved despite a brilliant reform effort led by Richardson Dilworth as school-board president (until his retirement in 1971) and Dr. Mark R. Shedd as superintendent.*

Every discouraging fact notwithstanding, there are those who see hope in the Philadelphia black man's situation—perhaps more hope than in any other great city of America. Home ownership among blacks is rising rapidly, and the white noose around the ghettos is beginning to loosen, if ever so slightly. Since World War II in Philadelphia, the proportion of blacks who have finished high school has tripled, the proportion of college graduates has tripled. Where an educated black might be reduced to waiting on table in Du Bois' day, or even the 1930s, today the problem is to find qualified black applicants for the jobs that are available. Where in the 1920s none of the great Philadelphia law firms had black attorneys on their staffs—and a Negro could not even rent professional office space downtown—today the big firms hire blacks enthusiastically and some Negroes sit on the local bench. Negro business opportunities have multiplied, and black men sit on the boards of some of the great financial institutions. Philadelphia's universities actively recruit blacks for their faculties. Job opportunities for blacks in local government have expanded dramatically, starting in the Clark-Dilworth era. The Philadelphia police force is about 19 percent black (a figure topped only by Washington, D.C., and Atlanta), and despite Rizzo's outside reputation, relations between blacks and whites on the force appear to be among the best in the country.

Then there is the question of real leaders in the black community. Philadelphia not only has them, but it has them in amazing numbers. A brief assortment:

- Judge Raymond Pace Alexander of the Philadelphia court of common pleas, who was coldly rejected for his color when he applied to a major downtown law firm after passing the Pennsylvania bar exams in 1923. Alexander then went into practice for himself, successfully fought a lonely battle to upset an attempt at forced segregation of suburban schools in the early 1930s, got an open accommodations law passed by the state legislature in 1939, helped in the Dilworth-Clark political upheaval, served on the city council, and eventually won appointment to the bench.

- Federal Judge A. Leon Higgenbotham, Jr., who was named an assistant district attorney under Dilworth in the early 1950s and became the first

---

* An example of the imaginative effort the school administration has made is the remarkable Parkway "school without walls" that uses the city and its resources instead of classrooms and has proven an exciting educational experience for the few hundred students who (by random drawing from thousands of applicants) have been able to attend it. But the effort seems so small, compared to need. As Dilworth said: "We have to deal with children many of whom never met a decent man, a kind man or even a responsible man in their lives. We have to deal with children at least a quarter of whose homes can't be called homes. These kids come to school and their vocabulary consists mainly of four-letter words."

Negro of that rank to argue cases before the state supreme court. He became president of the local NAACP and was appointed to the federal bench by President Kennedy in 1962; he is also a trustee of Yale University.

■   Charles Bowser, a former deputy mayor, a product of the Philadelphia public schools, who has learned to deal on equal terms with the monied elite of Philadelphia and runs an $8-million-a-year program as head of the Philadelphia Urban Coalition.

■   Cecil Moore, the flamboyant, brash former head of the Philadelphia NAACP who was "Mr. Civil Rights" in Philadelphia for a few years in the 1960s. Moore bombed out with a tiny percentage of the vote when he ran for mayor, but he left a lasting imprint by initiating and doggedly pursuing to victory a court case challenging the provision of Stephen Girard's will which restricted to white males only the right of admittance to Girard College, a private school and home for orphan boys in the midst of the North Philadelphia ghetto.

■   Walter Palmer, who runs street-corner colleges teaching black power and black pride and has been identified by the Philadelphia *Bulletin*'s Negro columnist, Claude Lewis, as "perhaps the most articulate spokesman" among Philadelphia blacks.

■   Mattie Humphrey, a highly articulate social agitator who has stimulated many other black women to action for their communities and is forever ready to pounce on any black leader who makes a male-chauvinist statement.

■   Roxanne Jones of the Welfare Rights Organization—one of those "social workers without portfolios" leading the welfare masses and confounding the budgetmakers in Harrisburg.

There are many others, both in and out of politics, but two—Leon Sullivan and Herman Wrice—require our special attention.

Sullivan was born in 1922 in a little, unpainted clapboard house in an unpaved slum alley of Charleston, West Virginia. For the past 22 years, he has been pastor of the Zion Baptist Church in the heart of North Philadelphia, a position which represents his sole source of support. He is also the founder and guiding spirit of the Industrial Opportunities Center and its many offshoots, an enterprise which employs 3,000 people and is the largest program, in dollar terms, ever organized by Afro-Americans in the history of the United States. Since spring 1971, he has been a member of the board of directors of General Motors, a breakthrough of historic proportions for blacks in the American business world.

Sullivan is an amazing and multifaceted man, propelled forward in life by the memory of a visit back home as a young man to the alley home in Charleston where his grandmother, the matriarch of the family, lay dying of consumption:

As I looked about her room that night, I saw the misery of poverty. I noticed the wallpaper that had been plastered up layer over layer, thick and ragged, torn and spotted and damp, I noticed the pictures on the wall that were covering holes, trying to decorate the place. I saw the room's one small table, antiquated and brown, a little tilted, with an empty Pepsi-Cola bottle on it, and an empty water glass, and all kinds of drugstore prescriptions lying about. The mattress of Mama's bed sagged in the middle beneath her weight. And as I sat there in the faint light of the oil lamp, amidst the dreariness and the smell of death, Mama looked up at me and said: "Leonie, help your people. And don't let this kind of thing happen to anybody else."

A few days later Sullivan decided to become "a minister of God, to work for Him, to help people who were poor—people who were in the kind of condition Mama was in." In 1943, he met Adam Clayton Powell and on his invitation went to New York, a gangling youth six feet, five inches tall, studied at Union Theological Seminary, and learned the arts of community organization from A. Phillip Randolph of the Brotherhood of Sleeping Car Porters. He advised Mayor La Guardia on Harlem, became an assistant pastor at Adam Clayton Powell's Abyssinian Baptist Church. Then in 1945, Sullivan decided he was "losing touch with God" and took a pastorate in South Orange, New Jersey, for five years.

In 1950, Sullivan moved to North Philadelphia, a fetid slum that "beat Harlem in housing decay." But his major interests turned to juvenile delinquency, and then to a youth employment service he began in his church. The job referral system, he discovered, was to be frustrated at every turn by the city's continuing wall of segregation against hiring blacks in any but menial work categories. Only a handful of blacks held jobs as bank tellers, clerks, or secretaries. The major soft drink companies, big sellers to the black community, had absolutely no black salesmen-drivers for their trucks. In a Sunday sermon to the 2,000 regular attendees at his church, Sullivan preached on the theme "The Walls of Jericho Must Come Down!" With that, he launched his "selective patronage" campaign—a polite term for economic boycott. It was organized through 400 Negro preachers in the city, who picked target firms based on the experience of black applicants and inside tips and then visited the companies with specific demands for increases in black employment. Where firms refused to make the requested hirings, a boycott would be called through that best communications line to the black community, the church pulpits.

Not for three years, and not until selective patronage had won agreement from two dozen companies and opened up some 2,000 jobs, did a single news story about the effort appear in Philadelphia's daily newspapers or its radio or television stations. The campaign was well known to the local media chiefs (indeed the *Bulletin* itself was boycotted), but they apparently concluded that any piece of publicity would simply spread the idea. It took an out-of-town newspaper, the New York *Times*, in a front-page story in June 1962, to bring the campaign to national attention. By then, selective patronage had already wrung concessions from giant firms like Gulf Oil, Sun Oil, Coca-Cola, and Esso and spread to several other cities. Sullivan may also take credit for the much-publicized Operation Breadbasket of the Southern Christian Leadership Conference, an idea which only took form after he went to Atlanta in 1962 to explain the boycott idea to black ministers and lay leaders at the request of Martin Luther King, Jr.

Soon Sullivan discovered that he simply could not produce enough qualified black applicants for all the opening-up jobs "that the white man had always kept to himself"—stenographic and secretarial, sheet metal and machinist, computer keypunch, merchandising, teletype, and manufacturing jobs. A massive training program was needed, and thus the idea of Opportunities Industrialization Center (OIC) developed. An abandoned old jailhouse in North Philadelphia was rented from the city government and training began in January 1964—but only after Sullivan, in what would prove to be one of the great keys to his success, had lined up the support of the chamber of commerce plus firms like Bell Telephone, General Electric, Philco, the Budd Company, and IBM, and among the unions, the restaurant and garment workers. The companies donated training equipment and the courses covered everything from sheet-metal work to electronics assembly. Financing was short and tenuous, but a grant of $200,000 from the Ford Foundation, arranged by Paul Ylvisaker, helped at an early, critical point.

But even as OIC got off the ground, Sullivan and his associates encountered the now-familiar bugaboo of all manpower programs for ghetto people and other underprivileged: slovenly work habits (or no work habits at all) and frequent illiteracy. The solution was a "feeder program." In brightly painted rooms (as unlike ghetto schools and daily life as possible) students were taught "cleanliness—time—think—work—togetherness." The three R's were taught, and minority-group history (principally black history, but also that of European minorities, Jews, and Appalachian whites). The feeder program became a prerequisite for *anyone* planning to enter an OIC technical course. The approach had sure-fire appeal to businesses, foundations, and government, and soon huge amounts of support were flowing in.

The program began to spread to other cities, and Sullivan saw the necessity to involve industry on a national scale to provide the OIC centers with technical assistance on a continuing basis. By this point, Sullivan really had the gold chips on his side with an advisory board which the press in 1968 called "the most formidable and influential group of business leaders assembled in the recent history of Philadelphia, at one place at one time." But there was more to come. President Johnson flew into Philadelphia to view OIC operations at first hand, Richard Nixon visited during his 1968 campaign. For the black preacher born in the Charleston slum, it was quite an achievement.

Leon Sullivan likes to talk in superlatives, and when I interviewed him in 1971, he could point to quite a few. The OIC, he said, had spread to 100 U.S. cities, enrolling 40,000 people a year, thus becoming "the largest nonprofit manpower training program in the country." It had also expanded to several foreign countries, especially in Africa. "Something internationally important has emerged out of Philadelphia and a Philadelphia Afro program. And it's the first program that serves the total American community—blacks, poor whites, Chicanos, and Indians," he said. From other sources, however, I heard that the OIC programs in other locations have yet to equal the quality of the effort in Philadelphia, where remarkably high levels of enrollee attendance and subsequent retention of jobs have been attained.

More has emerged from Sullivan's Zion Church than OIC and the boy-cotts (now long-since discontinued). Starting with his parishioners in 1962, Sullivan organized a collective mutual fund in which each member con-tributes $10 a month for 36 months. The best-known result of this has been the Progress Plaza shopping center on North Broad Street, where all the stores are owned or managed by blacks. The collective mutual fund also fi-nanced some large housing developments and made it possible, with GE's help, for Sullivan to start Progress Aerospace Enterprises in 1968. Now that company has annual sales of $2 million.

Sullivan's personal stature seemed to reach a hard-to-repeat zenith in 1971 when General Motors board chairman James Roche traveled personally to Philadelphia to ask him to join the GM board.

The story of Leon Sullivan can be dismissed as a fluke of black penetra-tion of white-establishment America that is unlikely to be duplicated. But Philadelphia has also produced Herman Wrice, a dynamic young black who has captivated the business elite with his work and may prove to be one of the most amazing personalities to rise out of the ghetto in our time.

Back in 1965, as Wrice tells his own story, he was enrolled at graduate school at the University of Pennsylvania but still living in the West Philadel-phia black community of Mantua. "The gangs were completely out of hand then—I was a former gang member myself. I'd gotten married, and I was headed toward business, to be the good nigger, to get out of the ghetto soon with a good house and two cars, maybe even play golf some day with some white guys." But one night Wrice's wife went to the local grocery store and was almost hit by a shotgun blast as the gangs pursued one of their victims through the store. Wrice heard the police sirens wailing, went to investigate and found his wife there shaking and the boy shot by the gang bleeding on the floor. "I was so mad I said, 'I'm gonna kill those guys.' I went back to my apartment, stuck a little piece in my pocket, and went out to teach the little bastards a lesson." But when he found them, Wrice decided "they needed someone to help them, not kick them." Within a few days, he had adopted several gangs, mediated dangerous disputes, organized baseball games, gotten personal T-shirts and equipment for the gang teams, and become a hero in his community. But he was also broke.

"Then one day," Wrice recalls "a white kid suddenly showed up and wanted to play baseball with us. He did better than the gang members. The second day he showed up with 25 baseball gloves—said his father had sent them." The father, it turned out, was named Clayton Hewett, an Episcopal clergyman who had been given a freely defined "urban mission"—to roam the black community and see how he could be relevant and helpful. Hewett helped write up a $25,000 foundation grant proposal; with the money Wrice could buy baseball uniforms for dozens of gang members, get transportation to drive the teams out of the neighborhood, rent a storefront (where 100 gang members would show up every night), and thus begin serious organiza-tion. Hewett introduced Wrice to Episcopal Bishop Robert L. DeWitt, the man who had dispatched Hewett on his urban ministry. DeWitt hired Wrice at $100 a week as an urban missioner, so that he could keep up his work. Wrice's organization became known as the Young Great Society, and the projects it undertook multiplied like OIC centers—recreation programs, counseling and employment referral for youths, hundreds of appearances in court for young people in trouble, a self-help clinic, two day-care centers, a narcotics rehabilitation office, its own schools, and an "urban university." Wrice also scrounged in dozens of imaginative ways to find money he could parlay into renovated slum housing—taking shells of buildings and redoing them completely inside, in the process developing training programs for carpenters and other craftsmen. DeWitt characterizes what was done as "a beautiful illustration of blacks trying to lift themselves by their own bootstraps."

By 1971, the Young Great Society was operating on an annual budget of $860,000, financed by the Ford Foundation, the Episcopal and Presbyterian churches, the Philadelphia Foundation, and federal programs like those of the Economic Development Administration. Herman Wrice presided over a staff of 263 paid employees and had shown such a sensitive political touch that he was on good terms with everyone from the black militants to Frank Rizzo. One secret to Wrice's success seems to be his determination to steer clear of partisan politics (though it is hard not to imagine him as a future mayor); a second is his avoidance of black-white confrontation. "My whole organization is 30 percent white. You bring up racism, I fire you," he told me. The day I talked with him, he was ecstatic over his appointment by Governor Shapp to be state chairman for youth programs in Pennsylvania and set up programs for young people in communities across the state.

Wrice's schedule is an incredible one that keeps him running 18 to 20 hours a day, seven days a week—without a vacation since 1965. In addition to all his formal local and state programs, he finds time to teach at the University of Pennsylvania and has been ordained as an Episcopal priest. He and his wife have 15 children—11 of them adopted. And they still live in Mantua.

The establishment loves Wrice, as it loves Sullivan. It abhors a local firebrand named Muhammad Kenyatta, who has been demanding gigantic reparations payments from Philadelphia's churches to compensate for generations of repression of the black man.* But there is a unity in the black effort hard for outsiders to believe. In 1970, a letter was written to Bishop DeWitt to be read at that year's Episcopal Diocese convention. "There appear to be mounting efforts to bring division among some of us," the letter said. "We want it to be clearly known that we are working toward the same goal, which is the freeing of black people from racial oppression in America. Our methods may not always be the same, but our aims are certainly similar." The signers of the letter were Sullivan, Wrice—and Kenyatta.

* Paul Washington, an Episcopal priest who has cooperated with Kenyatta in the black reparations movement, states the case as well as I have heard it put anywhere: "It has nothing to do with a white's personal responsibility. The fact is, in America the system favors you as a white. It's almost as if you're receiving stolen goods. Since the whites have amassed so much wealth, they should as a moral matter see that something is returned to those who are deprived."

Bishop DeWitt is perhaps more admired and trusted by Philadelphia's black leaders than any other white leader in the city. Wrice and Sullivan, he says "know that they get some of the support they do from the white community because of people turning away from Kenyatta. This I can document. Kenyatta has stabbed people's consciousness awake but they can't tolerate the wave length he's on. 'Now why can't he be like some of these good people like Leon Sullivan and Herman Wrice?' they say. O good heavens! What they were saying about Sullivan and Wrice a few years ago!"

The extent of black leaders' optimism in the face of phenomena like Frank Rizzo is amazing to behold. Talk is even turning to the possibility of a black mayor by 1975 or 1979, with several of the names we have mentioned here openly discussed. "Whoever it is," says the Urban Coalition's Charles Bowser, "he won't get a dying city like Newark or Cleveland. Philadelphia will be the first live, growing city with a black mayor."

The Establishment Now

Philadelphia, John Gunther observed in *Inside U. S. A.*, has "an oligarchy more compact and more complacently entrenched than any in the United States."

Is it still so today? In some ways, the answer is surely yes. An aristocracy born to wealth and position lives on, maintaining and fostering its customs and institutions. First, there are the clubs, very exclusive and central to all Philadelphia Society. The most famous are the Philadelphia (a men's city social club considered the *crème de la crème*), the Rittenhouse (almost as prestigious), the Union League, the Racquet (excellently appointed and a favorite of eligible young men), the Acorn (tops for women); fox hunting, cricket, lawn tennis, and barge clubs (Nathaniel Burt calls the latter, centered in their quaint Victorian clubhouses, "the Schuylkill Navy"); and even eating clubs—the Fish House and the Rabbit.

The families that have adhered to Old Philadelphian codes over time include Biddles, Ingersolls, Morrises, Cadwaladers, Robertses, Wisters, Scotts, Cassatts, Lippincotts, Woods, Peppers, Pews, and the like; one can find them all in the *Philadelphia Social Register*, a black-and-orange-bound annual book one might mistake for a Princeton course catalogue. The *Register* has become progressively less exclusive over time (up from 135 families in 1890 to 5,150 in 1940 and about 7,500 today), but still it includes only a minuscule percentage of the people of Philadelphia and its suburbs.

Old Philadelphia Society, of course, cannot put itself in a time capsule and resist every tide of social change. Its daughters are increasingly rejecting the formal debut, which was *de rigueur* just a few years ago, in favor of trips to Europe or other fun. Sons are less likely to accept the appointed university and career courses. And the ideas of Maintenance, and especially a code which excludes all but old-family White Anglo-Saxon Protestants (WASPs) from positions of Privilege, become more anachronistic with every passing year in these United States. But in large measure, Old Philadelphia Society has withdrawn from a central role in Philadelphia's life by its own decision. Old Philadelphians started to suburbanize themselves almost a century ago, and only a few hundred of them live in the center city today. This disengagement as a class is underscored by the cautious way that the aristocracy has invested its wealth. Its risks were dispersed, with much less of a financial stake in Philadelphia-related enterprises than one might expect—nothing even faintly resembling the Mellons' stake in Pittsburgh, for instance.

Yet another factor has been the rapid pace at which Philadelphia has been losing corporate headquarters and turning into a branch-office town. Between 1956 and 1965, according to a study by the Federal Reserve Bank of Philadelphia, the city lost major corporate headquarters at a faster rate than any of the nation's other large metropolitan areas. Since then, only Pittsburgh has been losing ground more rapidly. To a degree, corporate mergers and acquisitions exact a toll of corporate headquarters in any area, but Philadelphia's problem has been its lack of dynamic growth-oriented business leadership—the kind of settled contentedness that Old Philadelphia Society itself embodies.

Banker John Bunting, who was later to become president of the First Pennsylvania Bank, put his finger on the problem in a 1964 book, *Hidden Face of Free Enterprise:*

Philadelphia and New York were similarly endowed with natural blessings making for great cities. Neither had a real strategic advantage. After a while, however, Philadelphia society closed itself at the upper end. To receive full social acceptance family money had to be old and substantial, with emphasis on the "old." But in New York, if you had *enough* money, you didn't have to wait in line very long. As a consequence, ambitious, talented people gravitated toward New York and away from Philadelphia.

No self-respecting Old Philadelphian would ever write such a thing, and of course John Bunting is not. He comes from Philadelphia, but he grew up in Tacony, a distinctly other-side-of-the-tracks community. And his own mercurial rise within the nation's oldest and Philadelphia's largest financial institution, in which he outclassed three of the Main Line's finest to become president and chief executive officer in 1968, is a sort of living refutation of the old order. He pushed the First Pennsy into an aggressive campaign for savings accounts, thus voiding comfortable noncompetitive relationships that had been worked out by the banks and savings-and-loan institutions over the years. Then he started down the conglomerate road by making the bank a subsidiary of a holding company and beginning to buy up small loan companies all over the U. S. and some abroad. He began to tear down the barricades against hiring Jews and Negroes at all levels and advanced more than $5 million in loans to budding black enterprises, more than all the other Philadelphia banks combined. And to the consternation of New York bankers, he began the reversal of the sky-high interest rates of the late 1960s by making First Pennsylvania the *first* bank to lower the prime lending rate, then lowering it again, and forcing the haughty New York banks to follow his lead. And he laid plans to put a woman, a black, and a consumer advocate on his bank's board.

Amidst the constant grumbles of Philadelphia Establishmentarians, Bunting—who was only 46 in 1971—has suddenly become the city's prime mover and shaker. He helped Governor Shapp get through the state's first income tax, hitting the Old Philadelphians where it hurts the most, and he stepped in to bolster support for the faltering 1976 Bicentennial plans. His antagonists, who consider him a publicity-seeker and distastefully on the make, frequently block his efforts. But the fact is that Philadelphia now has a remarkably aggressive young business leader in a position of power where he should be able to effect many changes over the years. The death or retirement of many of the prestigious older leaders in the past several years has helped to clear the track for him.

A special word should be said about Philadelphia's Jews, since they have played an important role in the city's life since colonial days when the then Quaker establishment welcomed them with open arms. That early generation was welcomed in the choicest Philadelphia clubs through the past century and tended to conform by becoming Episcopalian. Gradually their blood stream merged with Old Philadelphia's. It was a later wave of Jews, coming from Germany in the mid-19th century, which had more difficulty being accepted by the Christian community. In recent times, Philadelphia's Jews have really come into their own. For many years, the late Albert Greenfield was the largest and richest real estate operator in Philadelphia, and he was actually a member of the third—or East European wave. Today his protegé, Gus Amsterdam, is a member of the GPM board and owns fantastic amounts of real estate in the city. The Philadelphia metropolitan area has 350,000 or more Jews now, second only to New York City. They have separated out into two distinct groups: the lower-middle class, consisting of shopkeepers, teachers, and the like, who live in the city and may vote for a Frank Rizzo; and an upper-middle class that lives in the suburbs and is very civil libertarian. The two groups have practically nothing to do with each other.

Quakers, Episcopalians, Roman Catholics

The Quakers settled Philadelphia as a place of refuge against religious oppression for themselves and others, and though their day of numerical dominance is now a matter of distant history, their character has set a mark on the city that endures to this day. "Caution" and "calm," Burt observes, are the Quakers' and Philadelphians' middle names. And even though many of the famous Quaker families long ago converted to Episcopalianism, he points out, "the façade that Philadelphia still presents to the world is a Quaker façade —subdued, careful, moderate, puritanical but never ascetic, honest but shrewd, modest but firm." But along with these virtues come their defects—"conform-ism, anti-intellectualism, materialism and lack of enthusiasm." Anyone whc has ever attended Quaker meetings, as I did for several years, remembers the amazing sense of community, the search for "the sense of the meeting." Questioning and going against the grain of the body is discordant, unwelcome behavior.

Philadelphia is still the national headquarters of the Society of Friends and of its very effective adjuncts, the American Friends Service Committee and National Friends Legislative Committee. And in their activities, the Quaker conscience, vivid to America since they became foes of slavery two centuries ago, lives on. One hears that though the Quakers have quietism and don't assert themselves, they are able to accomplish a great deal in their own low-keyed way. This is true in some city issues, but especially international ones. They have consistently opposed the Vietnam war, like all before it, and taken such steps as sending ships to Hanoi with medical supplies, furnishing surgical equipment to both the North and South Vietnamese, and drawing up a novel Jewish-Arab peace plan in 1971.

Little public contention arises within Quaker circles, perhaps few members question the society's agreed-upon liberal aims. Not so with the Episcopalians. The Episcopal Church was founded in Philadelphia and the Philadelphia diocese is the oldest in the country. For generations its face to the world was that of the church of the Best People, a handmaiden of Privilege. That element remains strong within Philadelphia Episcopalianism. But the quiet-spoken New Englander chosen as the bishop in 1964, Robert L. DeWitt, has shattered the old tranquillity. DeWitt ringed himself with articulate and controversial churchmen imported from all over the country. He started program after program to deal with ghetto conditions, brought activist youth into the powerful diocesan council, and began to explore the meaning of women's liberation for the church. ("I hope we solve the black problem in order to be able to solve the youth problem in order to be able to face the women's liberation problem," he said in an interview.) DeWitt's course prompted a fierce counterattack from traditionalists within his own diocese and a severe decline in the diocese's financial support. But he persevered, generating fierce loyalty (especially among young people) and making the diocese, in the opinion of many people I spoke with, a vital cutting edge in the struggle for social change in Philadelphia.

The Roman Catholic Diocese of Philadelphia could hardly be more different. First of all, it has many times the communicants of the Episcopalians or any other denomination—1.3 million, with about 1,000 priests. It has the largest percentage of Catholic children attending parochial schools of any U. S. city, a program for which local Catholics give some $40 million a year. And the leadership exercised by its leader, John Cardinal Krol, qualifies as perhaps the most conservative and authoritarian of any Catholic diocese in the U. S. today.

Krol was born in Cleveland in 1910 as the fourth of eight children of Polish immigrant parents. He was a fairly obscure auxiliary bishop in 1959 when Pope John singled him out to help with organization of the Second Vatican Council and then to speed John's far-reaching reforms over conservative opposition on the council floor. Krol's skills, according to a church theologian quoted in the Philadelphia *Bulletin,* are those of "a good administrator and perhaps the most brilliant canon lawyer in the church, . . . [but] he is not a theologian and not a philosopher." He assumed direction of the Philadelphia diocese in 1961 and seemed to exercise fairly noncontroversial leadership until 1965, the bright hopeful years of the Vatican Council. Since then, he has been in the position of resisting any steps toward reform or change which go beyond the letter of Vatican II documents. He rarely speaks out on problems of race relations.

In 1971, a significant exodus of priests seemed to be underway; among those leaving for secular jobs was Msgr. Terrence F. Monihan, the 38-year-old chancellor of the diocese and the very man who had been assigned by Cardinal Krol to deal with priests on matters of discipline and leaving the priesthood. Monihan started the job with enthusiasm, but found himself broken inside by its pressures.

Philadelphia Journalism: A Tumultuous Time

The last decade has been a tumultuous one for Philadelphia journalism. The Curtis Publishing Company floundered, permitting the venerable *Saturday Evening Post* to die after 148 years of publication that dated back to Benjamin Franklin. The Philadelphia *Inquirer,* which had degenerated into a vehicle for the personal whims and vendettas of owner Walter Annenberg, was sold in 1969 to the Knight Newspapers and is now enjoying an illustrious rebirth. The ever-prospering *Evening Bulletin,* cautious and provincial, reacted to the *Inquirer's* renaissance by becoming a lot livelier itself. And a sleeper, *Philadelphia Magazine,* emerged from its cocoon as a "magazine for executives" to become a lively, fearless journal that outstrips the entire new breed of city monthlies in quality and profits.

Curtis Publishing once dominated magazine publishing in America the way its brick-and-marble headquarters (now sold) dominate Independence Square. In 1960, Curtis looked healthy enough to the outside world. It had revenues of $248 million, published the *Post* (circulation six million plus), *Ladies' Home Journal,* and *Holiday,* and owned several big paper mills. But over the course of the 1960s, Curtis suffered an operating loss of over $80 million.

In 1968, when the *Post* was on the ropes, a young conglomerate builder named Martin S. Ackerman took over Curtis, slashed the *Post's* circulation back to three million in an effort to make it profitable, sold *Ladies' Home Journal,* engaged in refinancing, and when all else failed, killed the *Post* and was in turn purged himself.* Ackerman's record is easily faulted, but he was doubtless right when he later wrote: "Since the early '30s the com-

---

* Ackerman has been immortalized as the man who said to his new employees: "I am Marty Ackerman, I am 36 years old, and I am very rich. I hope to make the Curtis Publishing Company rich again."

pany had been run according to an outmoded Main Line Philadelphia philosophy, with the president, directors, officers, and most of the top executives hailing from the old school of management." There would seem to be at least some parallels in that story to that of the Penn Central.

In 1971, the heirs of Cyrus Curtis—those who had been chiefly responsible for the company's problems—sold their debt-ridden property to an Indianapolis industrialist named Beurt SerVaas. SerVaas revived the *Post* as a quarterly, heavily laden with reprints of its golden past and devoid of all controversy.

Moses Annenberg was a Jewish immigrant from East Europe who made a fortune through racing papers that supplied information to bettors, and through a string of wire services to illegal "horse parlors." In 1936, he acquired the *Inquirer*. Three years later, "Moe" Annenberg, his son Walter, and others were accused of massive income tax evasion. "Moe" pleaded guilty and agreed to pay $9.5 million in back taxes, fines, and interest, the largest income tax settlement ever recorded. He was also sent to jail but paroled shortly before his death in 1942. As part of the court settlement, the charges against Walter and nine lesser defendants had been dropped. Walter Annenberg proceeded to build a fantastically successful communications empire, including the *Inquirer, Seventeen,* radio and television stations, and *TV Guide,* with more circulation than any other weekly magazine in America. He struggled, with only partial success, for social acceptance in Philadelphia and gave tens of millions of dollars to various philanthropies. By 1969, Annenberg had a personal fortune of more than $150 million and happily accepted the offer of his friend President Nixon to become U. S. Ambassador to the Court of St. James.

Under Annenberg, according to Philadelphia attorney and reform leader Henry Sawyer, the *Inquirer* was "the greatest institutional force for evil in the city." Annenberg abused his position by ordering total blackouts on news about persons or institutions he disliked—Annenberg's "shit list," as it was called in the *Inquirer* newsroom. Those honored by placement on the list included such diverse figures as University of Pennsylvania president Gaylord Harnwell, Dinah Shore, Ralph Nader, the American Civil Liberties Union, and Philadelphia's professional basketball team, the 76ers. In 1966, the *Inquirer* campaigned savagely against Milton Shapp's gubernatorial candidacy.* But favored politicians could easily influence news coverage. Tate and Rizzo, for instance, never had any difficulty in calling Annenberg and getting him to kill stories not to their liking.

The spiritual sickness of the *Inquirer* came to light in 1967 when Gaeton Fonzi revealed in *Philadelphia Magazine* that Harry Karafin, the paper's star investigative reporter for almost 30 years and the best-known and most feared newspaperman in the city, had been engaged in wholesale blackmailing, shaking down shoddy characters and even prestigious corporations

---

* Shapp's campaign was geared to fighting the proposed Pennsylvania Railroad–New York Central merger. Five months after the election, Annenberg was elected a director of the Pennsy and revealed to be the owner of $8.5 million of the company's stock.

and banks to keep unfavorable stories about them out of the paper. His take from this illegal operation apparently went as high as $100,000 a year.

So it was that few tears were shed in Philadelphia when Annenberg in 1969 decided to sell the *Inquirer* and its afternoon tabloid companion, the *Daily News*, to the highly respected Knight chain. John McMullan, an aggressive newsman in his mid-forties who had been executive editor of the Knight-owned Miami *Herald*, took over the same position at the *Inquirer* and the change in the paper was soon apparent. There was a substantial house-cleaning at the reporting level that included replacement of the *entire* city hall bureau. The paper deemphasized routine news in favor of depth reports and analyses written by specialists in several fields. Political hatchet jobs, like the one practiced on Shapp in 1966, were eliminated, and the editorial page took on a moderate-to-liberal stance.

The *Evening Bulletin*, owned by the local McLean family, has always been a voice of moderation and decency in Philadelphia, but terribly non-combative. Until veteran political reporter John McCullough took it over in the mid-1960s, the editorial page was tops in the country for landing squarely on both sides of any crucial issue. There were exceptions to the run-of-the-mill news coverage, especially the investigative stories of 20 years ago that exposed scandals in the old GOP regime and paved the way for the Clark-Dilworth era. But rejuvenation was needed in the late 1960s, and even before the stiffer competition from the new *Inquirer* developed, first steps were underway. In 1969, managing editor William Dickinson picked as his successor George R. Packard 3rd, the son of a wealthy Main Line family who had earned a doctorate and become chief diplomatic correspondent for *Newsweek*. Only 37 when he took over his job, Packard soon enlivened urban affairs coverage, made room for a local black columnist, and started several other new features. But conservative forces in the *Bulletin* newsroom were able to thwart some of Packard's plans and cast a shadow over the paper's climb to real excellence.

The blueprint for a successful city magazine was not written in 1948 when the chamber of commerce sold *Greater Philadelphia*, as it was then called, to Arthur Lipson. Under Lipson's son Herbert, who is now publisher, and Alan Halpern, editor since 1951, the way has been found by trial, error, and some fine investigative reporting. The real blossoming of the magazine came in the 1960s as it hired some top writers and let them cover controversial Philadelphia stories which the comfortable big dailies were ignoring. These included the exposé of Harry Karafin, a story discrediting the nationally prestigious Pearl S. Buck Foundation, stories on rat infestation and air, water, and trash pollution (long before they became national issues), the plight of unwed black mothers, the impact of black influx destroying an ethnic neighborhood, and the real life of the Black Panthers. It was hard to see an ideological line in the story choice or orientation, though in 1971 the magazine disappointed many of its sophisticated readers by slanting its stories in favor of Rizzo over Longstreth in the mayoralty election. (The *Inquirer* and

Bulletin both endorsed Longstreth.) But with a dash of sex thrown into its coverage, *Philadelphia* had a 1971 circulation of 85,000, enthusiastic advertisers, and a healthy profit margin. In a move Ben Franklin would have approved, *Philadelphia* also bought out *Boston* and laid plans to introduce some of the same aggressive reporting and packaging on Massachusetts Bay.

A word about mass transit. Philadelphia pioneered, starting under Dilworth, with public subsidies to keep commuter lines operating. The Southeastern Pennsylvania Transportation Authority (SEPTA) was set up in the early 1960s to take over most local transit operations; beset by strikes and poor service since its inception, it has been accused of being a quasi-public body unresponsive to the people. But at least, no transit lines have died under its aegis.

Surprisingly enough, the nation's first really automated, electronic-controlled suburban commuter system now serves Philadelphia on a 14-mile run from Lindenwold, New Jersey. The system was opened by the Delaware River Port Authority with Budd-built cars on seamless welded rails and a crew of just one man on a train. The trains, which cross from Camden into Philadelphia over the Ben Franklin Bridge, draw more than 40 percent of their customers from people who used to drive to work. A clever way was found to finance the $94 million system—doubling of the tolls to 50¢ on the Ben Franklin and Walt Whitman bridges between Philadelphia and Jersey. Thus those who insist on driving still not only have to fight the traffic jams, but are obliged to help finance the ride of the rail commuters.

Beyond Philadelphia

The growth of Pennsylvania has been well described by James Reichley as one of concentric arcs ranging outward from Philadelphia. In the first arc are four suburban counties, heavily populated with Philadelphia commuters. Except for some pockets of heavy industry and poor-quality tract housing—and the Philadelphia suburbs have less of these than any other major East Coast city—this is still an area of rich, rolling countryside, endowed with both present charm and colonial history. Bucks County (415,056) has a pleasant exurbia of gentle hills, early stone houses, and colorful barns that make it one of eastern America's most beautiful areas (and a favorite second-home place for New York writers), together with a lower end near Philadelphia that has ugly old Bristol (67,498) and the mighty Fairless U. S. Steel Works that went on line in 1952. Montgomery County (623,799) is Pennsylvania's wealthiest and most sophisticated county, suburban and especially rich close to Philadelphia, German farm territory further out. Delaware County (600,-035) has an eastern end that is overbuilt, close to Philadelphia's industrial underbelly and the site of grimy, unlovable Chester (56,331); the western end, by contrast, is more rural and lovely and has a few miles of Main Line wealth in Bryn Mawr and Wayne. The county is the home of the infamous

Republican "War Board" political machine, the creation of the late boss John McClure which continues to flourish well past his death in 1965. Chester County (278,311) is where the Main Line ends at Paoli.* Here one finds Valley Forge, the ultra-ultra Radnor Hunt and Devon Horse Show, no large cities, a handful of industries, and lots of rolling peaceful farmland.

The second arc out from Philadelphia swings from the Maryland border near Gettysburg to the industrial Lehigh Valley cities near the Delaware opposite New Jersey. The arc contains a high proportion of those remarkable people, the Pennsylvania Dutch, who with pride and simplicity have preserved so many aspects of their 17th-century culture clear into the cybernetic age. The principal cities are York (50,335), filled with Revolutionary-era history and troubled by racial discord; Harrisburg (68,061), the state capital set dramatically on the banks of the Susquehanna; the prospering farm center and industrial city of Lancaster (57,690); the city of Reading (87,643), which gained some national notoriety in 1967 when a federal agency selected it as a case study in how local officials can tolerate and personally profit from illegal gambling and other illegal activities; Allentown (109,527), one of Pennsylvania's most handsome and prosperous cities; and Bethlehem (72,686), home of the great Bethlehem Steel Corporation, Moravian culture in America, and Lehigh University.

The early Pennsylvania Dutch stopped their penetration of Pennsylvania where the farmlands give out—namely, at the Blue Mountains, the front of the Appalachian Highlands. North of the Blue, the first settlers found a densely wooded region of high open hills and mountains running up to the New York State border. Much of the region is still sylvan and charming today. But at an early point, some of the world's greatest beds of anthracite coal were found. Thousands of sturdy Welsh, Irish, Italian, and Slavic miners were brought in to mine the black gold; today the anthracite industry is dead, but it has left behind a hideous legacy of smoldering culm heaps, collapsing land surfaces, and rivers polluted by mining acids. The cities of Scranton (103,564) and Wilkes-Barre (58,856) and their neighbors have begun major economic redevelopment programs, bringing in thousands of apparel and electronics jobs, but the area is still losing population. In 1971, the Mitre Corporation revealed a visionary plan to spend $1 billion over the next years in restoring the landscape, with plans for new towns, new lakes for recreation, and new industries.

Stretching westward from the anthracite region, out to western Pennsylvania, is the Appalachian "T-Zone," a far-flung region of forests and streams and endless mountains. "This whole area," former Governor Scranton told me, "is completely undeveloped in regard to any postwar boom—there just wasn't any." He predicts a great tourist boom in these northern counties, but a controlled boom because the state has bought up vast chunks of property to prevent undesirable development. A brand-new road, the Keystone Short-

* The other concentration of residences for Philadelphia's wealthy is in the city's Chestnut Hill neighborhood.

way (Interstate 80), runs through the region (far superior in quality to the now-aging Pennsylvania Turnpike to the south) and will help to develop this still-pristine portion of the eastern U. S. A.

Pittsburgh: Alliance, Renaissance, Decay

Pittsburgh is one of just three places in America—New York and San Francisco are the other two—where geography demanded a city. Here, the Ohio River, America's historic water life line to the West, is born at the place that the Allegheny River, flowing southward from New York, meets the Monongahela, flowing northward from West Virginia. A 21-year-old major named George Washington observed the site in 1753 and described it as "extremely well situated for a Fort, as it has the absolute Command of both Rivers." In 1754 Virginian troops started fortifications but were quickly driven out by the French who constructed Fort Duquesne; the French, in turn, were vanquished by British troops in 1758 and Fort Pitt (named after William Pitt, the English prime minister) rose at the juncture of the rivers. Since then, some form of Anglo-Saxon occupation has been continuous.

Before I visited Pittsburgh, I had heard of a superb view of the city from the heights of Mount Washington, just to the south across the Monongahela. My host, Robert Pease, executive director of the Allegheny Conference, was kind enough to drive me up to one of the restaurants there for a late evening drink, and I discovered one of the most stunning views of a city anywhere in America. Down in the valley, the city of Pittsburgh on its thin trowel of land lies sparkling with a million lights like a little Manhattan. Off to the left (or west) one can see the spot where the rivers meet, with the new Three Rivers Stadium, home of the Pittsburgh Pirates (1971 World Series winners) and Steelers football team, glowing white on the Allegheny's far bank. Then, at the tip of the "Golden Triangle," lies 36-acre Point State Park. A dreary mélange of warehouses and railroad tracks was cleared away there in the late 1940s, and finally in 1970 two old bridges at the apex were demolished to give Pittsburgh a grassy front lawn centered on the still-standing Fort Pitt blockhouse. Immediately east of the park stand the jewels of Pittsburgh's postwar renaissance, the Gateway Center with towering office and apartment high-rises, the Pittsburgh Hilton Hotel, and buildings of the state government, Bell Telephone, Westinghouse, and IBM. Further to the east, one sees a grouping of great canyonlike buildings where the corporate behemoths of Pittsburgh have their seat of power: U. S. Steel, Gulf Oil, Koppers, Alcoa, and others. Towering above them all is the new U. S. Steel Building completed in 1971, 64 stories high, rust-colored, and each floor an acre in size. Then there is the Chatham Center (an office-apartment-hotel complex completed under urban renewal in the 1950s), Pittsburgh's Civic Arena with its sliding domed roof; the black ghetto called the Hill District (there is also Polish Hill, which is white, depressed, and hopeless like Philadelphia's Kensington); the Oakland area which includes the University of

Pittsburgh, Carnegie Mellon University, and the city's medical center; the nearby Shadyside neighborhood, Pittsburgh's answer to Georgetown with an architectual style dubbed "Gilded Age High-Ceilinged"; the big Schenley and Frick parks; and Squirrel Hill and East End, the Jewish neighborhoods.

As World War II ended, Pittsburgh lived as it had for a century under a thick pall of coal smoke. John Gunther, visiting the city then, described it as "one of the most shockingly ugly and filthy in the world." If ever there was a great American city that represented the exploitive excesses of the industrial revolution, it was Pittsburgh. As Jeanne Lowe has written of the era from the Civil War to World War II: *

> The huge steel works sprawled along the flatlands of the river banks, pouring industrial sewage into their waters, slag into the green valleys and heavy coal smoke into the air. . . . Docile, unlettered blue-collar immigrants [from Eastern Europe] became the main body of Pittsburgh's and Allegheny County's population. Their lives were mean and drab. . . . The poverty and insecurity of their lives were intensified by the violent cyclical ups and downs of the heavy industry and mines. . . .
>
> No sooner had the 40 new "Carnegie millionaires" [created by the formation of U. S. Steel] turned their shares into convertible securities than most of them took themselves and their stocks away from the source of their wealth. They built showy palaces in New York and Newport, and flaunted in Europe and Florida the wealth they continued to siphon off from the region. . . .
>
> As it "prospered," Pittsburgh continued to grow without plan or community-mindedness. Its steep slopes were covered helter-skelter with cheap frame houses that were reachable only by a long climb up rickety wooden staircases from the streets below. Factories expanded into attractive residential neighborhoods and drove the residents to the suburbs. Choking coal smog was pervasive, and the decaying wreckage from the late railroad wars cluttered up the city's gateway at the Point.

By the early 1940s, it was clear to many Pittsburgh business and civic leaders that unless something was done to improve the city, it would gradually be abandoned. And in one of those odd quirks of history, two men came on the scene whose alliance to rebuild Pittsburgh would create the now-legendary postwar renaissance of the city.

The first was Richard King Mellon, a shy and retiring man who in 1934 became the active head of the celebrated family of bankers which had built its wealth by lending money to promising ventures and taking ownership interests in return. As governor and president of T. Mellon & Sons, he managed the interests that controlled Gulf Oil, Koppers, and Alcoa and had a major influence in a number of other major corporations including Westinghouse Air Brake, Pittsburgh Plate Glass, Pittsburgh Consolidation Coal, and the Pennsylvania Railroad. Under his direction, the First Boston Corporation and General Reinsurance Corporation were added to the group. In addition, the Mellons have a controlling interest of about $250 million in the Mellon National Bank and Trust, which in 1971 had $5.7 billion in assets and ranked as the largest bank in Pennsylvania and 16th largest in the U. S. The value of the Mellon interests was estimated in 1971 to be be-

* In *Cities in a Race with Time* (New York: Random House, 1968).

tween $3 billion and $5 billion, an American family fortune second only to the DuPonts.

Mellon was deeply influenced by his father, Richard B., who counseled him to "live where you work, work where you live and stay behind your home town." In 1941, Mellon went off to war, and like many Pittsburghers, when he returned home on leave, he found the city he had accepted before choked with smoke from the war-busy mills and unbelievably drab and depressing. Not long after, in June 1943, associates of Mellon took a leading role in organizing the Allegheny Conference on Post-War Community Planning (subsequently renamed Allegheny Conference on Community Development). It would be the moving force to mobilize Pittsburgh's business elite to back smoke abatement, downtown renewal, and virtually every other major civic program in the succeeding years. Other figures like the late city planner Wallace Richards and now-retired lawyer Arthur Van Buskirk, who was Mellon's close adviser and anchor man in civic activities, played crucial roles. But everyone knew the powerful, determinative influence was that of Richard King Mellon. Mellon could, for instance, commandeer the top official of almost any of Pittsburgh's leading 20 corporations—in half of which he had a controlling or large ownership—to do any job he wanted done within the Conference.

As the nascent Allegheny Conference began to lay its plans, it became clear that businessmen's wealth alone would not do the trick. Before the New Deal, local Republican bosses, tied in with the corporate-oriented statewide GOP, had run Pittsburgh. But the local Democrats were able to use the Mellons and the PMA as their whipping boys and seize complete control of the city and county government by 1936. They would be able to block the Allegheny Conference, made up almost entirely of Republicans, at any turn.

Enter now the second key figure of the Pittsburgh renaissance, David Lawrence. By delivering Pittsburgh and then Pennsylvania to the Democrats in the 1930s, Lawrence had become a major power broker in national Democratic politics. But he had always been a political manager, never a candidate. In 1945, the Democrats seemed headed for a divisive mayoralty primary, and Lawrence solved the problem by agreeing to run himself. And though he had grown in the "hate-Mellon" tradition, Lawrence astounded the city by pledging he would work with the Republican-dominated Conference to improve Pittsburgh. He took another political risk by announcing in his campaign that he would enforce a strong smoke abatement ordinance, passed by the city council in 1941, which had been shelved for the war.

Lawrence was narrowly elected, and before long his remarkable alliance with Mellon began to take shape. For example, coal interests threatened to boycott Pittsburgh industry if the smoke ordinance went into effect; Mellon used his power as a director and substantial owner of Consolidation Coal to get the threat withdrawn. Then the problem arose of the railroads firing up their old coal-burning locomotives outside the city limits and still throwing quantities of coal smog into the air. A state law was needed to ban the practice but ran into strong opposition from the redoubtable barriers of the Pennsylvania Railroad in the state senate. Mellon, a director of the Pennsy, let its management know that if the line failed to comply with the ordinance or blocked the new law, he would have the companies he controlled switch their business to competing railroads. Thus the smoke law quickly passed the legislature, and the railroads' change to diesels played an important role in the rapid, almost miraculous cleansing of the Pittsburgh air in the late 1940s.*

The monuments of the Pittsburgh renaissance may be seen all over the city today. The $150 million Gateway Center, for which the government people cleared legal hurdles and the business contingent arranged financing from the Equitable Life Assurance Society, is the most dramatic but only part of the strong boom in office building for the city's many corporations. In the very center of downtown, Mellon Square, an exquisite oasis of stone deck, lush with fountains and shrubbery, has been built on top of a subterranean garage to replace a blighted block of old buildings and parking lots.† Point Park was built, and so was the civic auditorium, giving Pittsburgh a chance to get major conventions and also a place for open-air concerts of the Civic Light Opera by use of the retractable roof. The auditorium and surrounding civic center buildings went into the Lower Hill district, which had been a festering slum right beside downtown. Finally, much work was done on highway improvement in and around Pittsburgh, and dams were built to prevent a recurrence of floods like the disastrous one of 1936, which had inundated much of the city.

The renaissance had its limits, however. By the mid-1950s, it was obvious that the city faced an alarming shortage of decent lower- and middle-class housing to replace deteriorated units and those demolished for urban renewal. The Allegheny Conference tackled the job with an offshoot called ACTION-Housing that concentrated on new buildings, and starting in 1967 with "Ahrco" (Allegheny Housing Rehabilitation Corp.), an organization that rehabilitated old structures. The cumulative effort has been called the best-conceived and most comprehensive attack on slum housing in America, producing the positive result of almost 5,000 new or rehabilitated units. But the new low-income-housing supply is still only a fraction of what is needed.

A second drawback to the renaissance was the problematic Pittsburgh economy, muscle-bound by its century-long dependence on coal and steel. While the national economy boomed in the 1950s and '60s, Pittsburgh and environs lost 13 percent of their steel industry jobs (the remaining total:

* Even when it lost the title of "smoky city," Pittsburgh had air pollution. With emissions from coke ovens and power plants posing an increasingly serious problem, irate citizens in 1969 forced passage of a new ordinance regarded as a model for industrial cities. Enforcement was placed in the hands of a board of appeals and variances which can fine industries, imprison company officials, or even close down a plant entirely.

† Mellon got the idea for a city park atop a garage from San Francisco's Union Square, which he had seen while on duty with the army in California in World War II. To build Mellon Square, which has miraculously created a little bit of San Francisco's human warmth in the midst of old Pittsburgh, Mellon arranged a $4 million gift from his family-controlled foundations. Lawrence used the city's powers of eminent domain to acquire the land.

122,000). The area's boosters point to an increase of white-collar jobs as evidence of Pittsburgh's growth as a service and distribution center. But the number of Pittsburgh-headquartered corporations on *Fortune*'s top 500 list dropped from 23 in 1965 to 14 in 1970, a sobering fact for a city whose jewels are its big companies.* There was some movement of new and diversified industries into industrial parks in the area, together with a growth in scientific laboratories, but not nearly enough to offset the loss in basic metals. If the population figures are any indication, there is a distinct loss of faith in Pittsburgh's future, especially among younger people. One study in the late 1960s showed that more than 220,000 persons, most of them 20 to 24 years old, had left the area since the start of the decade, while only 110,000 had moved in. The population figures for the city of Pittsburgh proper show a decrease of 23 percent between 1950 and 1970, to a new total of 520,117 (25th in rank among the country's cities). Not until the late 1960s was there any sign of a reversal in the population outflow. And the 1970 Census report for the entire Pittsburgh metropolitan area (2,401,245 people) showed a 1 percent drop since 1960, a failure of suburban growth to compensate for core-city decline that makes Pittsburgh unhappily unique among the 50 large population centers of America.

Why, one asks, should the Pittsburgh metropolitan area lose population when St. Louis and Cleveland, which have experienced an even more severe center-city drop, show an areawide increase? In a 1970 survey, the New York *Times*'s Douglas Kneeland identified four reasons: Pittsburgh's location off the route of the Negro migrations from the South; steel industry recessions; the topography of the region, with steep hills and narrow river valleys that limit development of vast suburban tracts or new industrial sites; and finally the lingering image of Pittsburgh as a grimy steel town, spitting fire and smoke. When one adds to that equation the possibility of still more steel employment loss as production shifts to more automated Midwestern plants in the 1970s, the future economy of Pittsburgh has to be considered just as uncertain as it was a quarter century ago when the renaissance began.

Even at its height, the renaissance never did much to change Pittsburgh's picture as the ultimate company town. "What gives Pittsburgh its own unique juice and flavor is not how it plays but how it works," according to writer Jack Markowitz.† "This is what underlies the joyless, grimy image people have of the place: all work and no play." Even "socially and physically," he observes, "business holds the dominant role in town—its massed skyscrapers resembling nothing so much as the superstructure of a vast ship plowing relentlessly forward." Within that milieu, the arts have not been strong, though there are glowing exceptions: the Pittsburgh Symphony, the Annual International Arts Show, and especially in the earlier postwar years, the Pitts-

---

* The 14 remaining were Gulf Oil, Westinghouse Electric, Alcoa, National Steel, PPG Industries, H. J. Heinz, Koppers, Wheeling-Pittsburgh Steel, Allegheny Ludlum Industries, Rockwell Manufacturing, H. K. Porter, Joy Manufacturing, Cyclops, and H. H. Robertson. Some of these might leave were it not for the Mellons' ownership interests and influence. The list does not include U. S. Steel, which technically has its headquarters in New York but in fact has most of its executive and office staff in Pittsburgh.

† "Pittsburgh—Is It Pennsylvania's Second City . . . or Its First?" in *Philadelphia Magazine*, September 1969.

burgh Playhouse's repertory company. Both newspapers—the evening *Press* and morning *Post-Gazette*—are rather provincial, though each has some fine writers. WQED sprang up in Pittsburgh as the nation's first educational television station and its provocative nightly "Newsroom" hour of news often outshines the papers and strong television competitors like Westinghouse's KDKA.

Pittsburgh's main attraction, however, is for those who treasure an industrial rather than a cultural climate. A successful Pittsburgh businessman can have a real feeling of *belonging*. His day, as Markowitz puts it, is "a progress of conferences that *do* reach decisions, of meetings in paneled rooms guarded by worshipful receptionists, . . . and of a noon-day ritual enjoyed by the top brass, the stately processions to the Duquesne Club, where chauffeured Cadillacs line up as they do after Friday afternoon concerts at Philadelphia's Academy of Music." (The Duquesne Club is a grim old fortress of blackened stone, sitting directly opposite two equally blackened old and prestigious churches, one Episcopalian and the other Presbyterian. Pleasantly decorated within, the club is literally packed with private meeting rooms where many a business deal and corporate merger has been effected. Ethnically, the membership holds few surprises, but present-day doers rather than grand old families are dominant. The cuisine is superb.)

Pittsburgh: New Politics?

In retrospect, it is clear that the Pittsburgh renaissance, for all its accomplishments, was an elitist phenomenon in which the wealthy business and strong government leaders made rather unilateral decisions on what would be best for Pittsburgh. If the planning was at the expense of the well-being and self-esteem of a lot of communities in Pittsburgh, that was simply the price that had to be paid. The renaissance shone in solving physical problems, and it flourished in the 1940s and '50s, before emergence of the human collision of disparate economic, race, and generation groups typical of the '60s and '70s.

The deceleration began in 1959, when Lawrence left to become governor of Pennsylvania. Joseph M. Barr, his successor as mayor, was a standard big-city liberal Democrat and organization man. As Van Buskirk puts it, "He did his best to be loyal to Lawrence's ideas and ideals. But he was no Dave Lawrence." For one thing, Lawrence had always maintained a complete separation between his coterie of Irish Catholic political workers from the wards and precincts and the bright young men he hired to work with the Allegheny Conference. Barr, who would remain in office until 1969, made the mistake of allowing confrontation between the two camps.

A measure of the change of Pittsburgh's mood and temper in the 1960s was provided by the unhappy fate of an ambitious "Great High Schools" plan unveiled in 1966 by the city's distinguished superintendent of schools, Sidney P. Marland, Jr. (now U. S. Commissioner of Education). Marland noted the deterioration of the city's 17 obsolescent academic and vocational high schools, the last of which was built more than 40 years ago. At the same time, he was alarmed by the patterns of *de facto* segregation in the schools and increasing flight of white families to the suburbs. As an answer, he proposed building five superhigh schools on 40-acre campuses, each to accommodate 5,000 to 6,000 students. These Great High Schools would be located at places that would draw students from across the natural boundaries (rivers, steep slopes, and valleys) that have traditionally chopped Pittsburgh into isolated ethnic communities. The price tag for the new schools would be $120 million, the largest single investment of money in Pittsburgh's history. Assembling the money out of federal, state, and local funds was precisely the kind of challenge that the men of the old Pittsburgh renaissance would have relished tackling. If the idea had come forward in the 1950s, it might well have been implemented.

But it was too late. The crucial problem was one of attitudes, especially in the black community, toward the school board, whose members are appointed to six-year terms by the judges of the common pleas court. In a 1969 report on social planning in Pittsburgh, the Institute for Community Studies of Kansas City, Missouri, observed: "The school board is generally regarded as an elitist board, representing the affluent, well educated, civic leadership of Pittsburgh but out of tune with public sentiment. Along with the school administration, the board has guided a school system that has operated for some 50 years in considerable isolation not only from the political life of Pittsburgh but from all other public and private agencies and the general public as well."

Many white citizens had hostile attitudes toward the school board and Pittsburgh establishment, and there was a widespread fear of social problems in big schools. Finally, inflationary pressures almost doubled the original estimate of cost for constructing the schools. With what was probably great relief to escape the hostilities directed toward him in Pittsburgh, Marland left in 1968. With his departure, the Great Schools idea was dead.

The Great High Schools demise was used by the Institute for Community Studies to underscore its basic conclusions about the effectiveness of the city's social planning machinery to solve education, wealth, and welfare problems. The Institute decided the fundamental new reality is that *"process is policy"*:

This simple statement means that the manner in which we seek to reconcile people and groups in our cities now alienated from each other transcends in importance the solutions we arrive at from time to time on particular questions at issue. . . . We are impressed with the need for creating wholly new organizations to serve the social needs of Pittsburgh. . . . *The process adopted for bringing about change is crucial*. It is necessary to give all groups a place at the table.

No entrenched group is very interested in inviting others to a place at the table. But the reaction of the heirs of Lawrence and Mellon to the pressures for change in the past few years has been instructive. First, we may consider the Democratic organization. Lawrence, for all his fame as a city rebuilder, was no reformer when it came to the old clubhouse way of practicing politics. Richard Thornburg, the U. S. Attorney in Pittsburgh and an ambitious young Republican who would one day like to be mayor, offers a rarely heard critique of Lawrence:

The mystique of Lawrence as a Second Coming is just not true. He and Barr gave free reign to Mellon and the Allegheny Conference just as long as they were left free to hold on to their own political power, clout and patronage. Syndicate operators in Allegheny County established their foothold in the '40s and '50s through the cooperation of the Democratic administration here at the time. . . . Lawrence was very tight with the guys in the rackets in the city. He never put a nickel in his own pocket in the corrupt sense. But these guys [the criminal element] were financing the Democratic party all this time. And he was tolerant of police corruption. . . .
Under Lawrence and Barr, the favored politicians held four or five jobs. They'd be the alderman, the police magistrate, the Democratic ward chairman and probably be on the city payroll. We have 32 wards in this city. The Dave Lawrence claque held sway there, tolerating illegal operations in every ward. No one can tell me Lawrence didn't know about it. That legacy is part of the problem we have today.

During the Barr era of the '60s, little was done to clean house within the Democratic organization. On the city council, Democrats were expected to go along with Barr—or else. When allegations were made of widespread corruption in the police department, Barr made no move to fire the police superintendent, James Slusser. The Democratic machine, however, suffered a dramatic loss in 1969 when the voters turned down its hand-picked man to succeed retiring Mayor Barr and elected instead a dashing 44-year-old embodiment of the "new politics," Peter F. Flaherty. A product of Pittsburgh's tattered North Side, Flaherty had been a docile ally of the Barr regime on the city council but then broke with the organization in 1969 to run as a "man against the machine." He promised to be a mayor without strong ties or debts to big business, big labor, or the old political alliances—"nobody's boy," as he repeatedly boasted. After trouncing the organization in the primary, he spurned its offer of general election help, saying, 'My severance with the Democratic machine in Pittsburgh is not a separation, it is a divorce." He then scored a landslide victory over Republican John Tabor, an attractive young lawyer and state official who was able to outspend Flaherty $400,000 to $80,000 by virtue of massive big-business giving.
Once installed in office, Flaherty replaced Barr's division chiefs with his own cadre of politically untried lawyers, architects, engineers, and business experts, most of them younger than himself. Along with the hacks, he fired John T. Mauro, the city's skillful planning director and Barr's liaison man with the Mellon Patch. The planning staff was decimated, apparently part of Flaherty's effort to deemphasize big downtown projects and turn attention (in ways rather ill-defined) to neighborhood development. By refusing to go along on patronage-based appointments and the familiar cozy deals, Flaherty was immersed in almost continuous bickering with the city council. He fired hundreds of city employees hired by past administrations for make-

work patronage jobs and broke a jurisdictional strike by the Teamsters-controlled city garbage collectors (whose average pay is $11,000). "Flaherty," Ralph Hallow of the Pittsburgh *Post-Gazette* wrote, "was left the undisputed champion of the people and slayer of the ancient dragon of labor-political bossism."

Flaherty's reforms were not standard "liberalism," nor were his critics limited to those who lost their place at the public trough. Faced with a budget deficit, he devoted much of his time to slashing expenses, thus averting a tax increase. While proceeding to decimate the old Democratic machine, member by member (by cutting off patronage), he also became distant from many of his own original supporters. Some business-supported social programs began to languish because of Flaherty's determination to stay independent of the Allegheny Conference crowd.

And if the old politics is out of style in Pittsburgh proper, it continues to prosper in the Allegheny County government where figures with connections to the rackets are in key positions. Richard Thornburg says he has a strong suspicion of kickbacks in county business and suspects that a major portion of the money that goes into county elections comes from racketeering interests. "But Allegheny County," he adds, "is so fragmented and the county is so ineffective on a regional basis that it really doesn't matter much as far as government goes." (The county government, we should note, has been Democratic for years, and Thornburg is a Republican. But his view is widely shared. The GOP's own organization is pathetically weak, and few Pittsburgh Republicans winced when I quoted the words of an eastern Pennsylvania Republican politician: "I wouldn't trade you one Philadelphia ward leader for the whole Allegheny County Republican organization.")

Meanwhile, back at the Mellon Patch, the Allegheny Conference in 1968 debated its future course and decided to turn its focus from physical to human problems. Two leaders spearheaded the Conference's shift toward social renewal. The first was Henry Hillman, a financier active in coal, mining equipment, and airlines, whose family ranks second (albeit a distant second) to the Mellons. He became chairman of the board of the Conference. And Robert B. Pease, the cream of the crop of young technocrats assembled to effect the Conference's renaissance-era programs, became its executive director. The Conference chartered an employment committee which worked with the Pittsburgh National Alliance of Businessmen, finding more than 9,000 jobs for the disadvantaged between 1967 and 1970. (The retention rate was reported at a high 58 percent.)* Black capitalists got a helping hand through a minority enterprise loan program coordinated by the Conference; by the end of 1970 local banks had lent $5.2 million. In the wake of Martin Luther King's assassination, discussions between black leaders and the Allegheny Conference leaders led to establishment of a broad, entirely black-directed social welfare fund ("Program to Aid Citizen Enterprise") which

---

* There are some skeptics on this score. Wendell G. Freeland, a prominent local Negro attorney, told me regarding the NAB effort: "If I could believe all the statistics I read, every black guy in this town would have three jobs. Unemployment among blacks is still very high."

was continuing in 1971 with an annual budget of about $700,000. But could the renaissance really be recycled in the nonmaterial, social sense? "There is an emotional tithe to some very pressing problems, but not the total commitment that was present in the physical rebuilding of the '40s and '50s," one local observer told me.

In June 1970, Richard King Mellon died, and Pittsburgh wondered if any leader of his vision and his *power* would again emerge. Mellon left two adopted sons, both around 30 years of age. Richard Prosser Mellon began to concentrate on the Mellon family's charitable interests—which include three family foundations with assets of $975 million. (One of these, the Andrew W. Mellon Foundation, made grants of $29.9 million in 1970. Only the Ford and Rockefeller Foundations dispense more.) The other son, Seward Prosser, took charge of the family's multibillion-dollar investments. Both showed some promise, but it was obvious that the vitality and wisdom had been drained away with Richard King Mellon's demise. Leland Hazard, attorney, author, and one of the leaders of the renaissance, told me:

No one exists in Pittsburgh now with the convictions of Mellon and Lawrence. We have lost the faith. While Richard King Mellon lived, the conceptions generally, though not invariably, came to him, and then emerged in the Allegheny Conference. . . .

What we don't know is whether Mellon was so dominant no one else was brave enough to think for himself—or if in truth and fact the heads of the 20 other great corporations were not community conscious individuals. An ill wind blows, and we'll learn now . . . whether the yearnings and hopes and ambitions and unselfish aspirations of the community will show up from sources which during Mellon's lifetime did not make bold to speak.

In Pittsburgh, we now have a complete loss of that rapport and mutuality of understanding, that joint dedication of wealth and politics, which made the renaissance. Our community is disorganized, disrupted, unled, and the forces of anarchy are uninhibited. Our mayor is a reflection of this. It's a distemper. But it will pass.

Hazard, who has gained the reputation of a "Mr. Transit" in Pittsburgh, has campaigned assiduously for federal funding for an 11-mile skybus track running from South Hills to the city. That would cost more than $200 million, and an eventual 60-mile system serving the entire county would cost $1 billion or more. He acknowledges that transit was an "orphan" in the heyday of the Allegheny Conference, when repeated studies were made but killed by Mellon, who "was misled by close advisers." As a result, Hazard says, Pittsburgh has had to "wait to approach that universal traffic jam in which some prophets of doom say the 20th century will end." Hazard sees only two possible alternatives to mass transit—outlying shopping centers reached by automobile, or totally new cities:

I've rejected those alternatives out of hand. Why? The cities of the world are the centers of excellence. There's little excellence anywhere outside of cities. How are you going to put a Titan in every shopping center? The great architecture is in the city—the cathedrals, the churches, the spires, the domes, the towers—those beauties of architecture which lift men's souls out of the muck of dreary, drab, routine existence. They can't be in "new cities." Unless the United States is to become a cultural waste, unless suburbia is to become a cultural slum—and it *is* a cultural slum, full of the banal—then there must be mobility, then there must be access: frequent, cheap, and maybe free, from the periphery (however wide it spreads) to those centers of excellence. . . .

In selecting a technology, there are fundamentals which can't be compromised. Public transit must have its own right of way, with utter separation from all other traffic. (A bus is no faster than the flat-tired car in front of it and express lanes for buses are only temporary expedients because they depend on the internal combustion engine which is now as anachronistic as the caveman's club, and because they require men to drive them, and that is one thing technology cannot tolerate.) Mass transit vehicles must be unmanned, operating on a planned, computerized system like horizontal elevators. And we must avoid subways; they are a product of the iron, coal, and steel age when the humanistically insensitive engineer was in charge of our society. As a man moves, he should be able to look, smell, feel color. A modern transit system won't make a smell in the environment. It won't make a sound in the environment. It will be as quiet as an Indian path in Penn's woods.

Beyond Pittsburgh, western Pennsylvania has few major cities. Up in the far northwestern corner there is Erie (129,231), which shares economy, outlook, and icy weather with its Great Lakes neighbors rather than the rest of Pennsylvania. (Even the local Mafia is controlled out of Buffalo). Tourism and remnants of America's first oil industry are the only elements of the western Pennsylvania economy that distinguish the region from Pittsburgh. Indeed, the region really is one of little Pittsburghs.

Starting in Allegheny County and then covering the whole face of southwestern Pennsylvania, there are the blue-shirted steel-mill towns crowded into their narrow valleys. Along the Monongahela south of Pittsburgh, there is a practically unbroken chain of them—places like Homestead, Braddock, Duquesne, McKeesport, Clairton, and Donora. Ambridge and Aliquippa on the Ohio are in the same category. Here are the massive blast furnaces and coke ovens, rolling mills, and coal breakers of Big Steel, belching out their fumes over the landscape. The story is much the same in outlying cities like Sharon, New Castle, Washington, and Jeannette. None of these cities has more people than McKeesport (37,977), and all are dying cities, losing population and business at a rapid clip. Most of them are in the grip of small-time racketeering tied closely to the political structure, McKeesport being perhaps the most notorious of all. "Some people," Richard Thornburg says, "are critical of the military-industrial complex. But in these cities, they have what I call the 'politico-racket complex.' " For the families of the hardy ethnics who serve the steel mills—Poles, Irish, Italian, and others —the future could hardly be more bleak.

OHIO

THE MIDDLE-CLASS SOCIETY

OHIO, MOTHER OF SECOND-RATE PRESIDENTS, hung up about its own identity (East to Westerners, West to Easterners), the personification of the middle class society, is the least distinctive of the great industrial states of the U.S.A. New York has its stimulating world city, Pennsylvania its Quaker and "Keystone" traditions, Illinois has brawny Chicago and colorful "clout" politics, Michigan the auto empires and advanced unionism, Texas is its own unique world, California a nation in itself.

But Ohio? What is a "Buckeye"? He may embody, as one writer records, "dedication to the homely virtues of honesty, thrift, steadiness, caution, and a distrust of government." Perhaps the homely virtues could bear reassertion in a modern world all too rife with materialism and a flashy culture. My editor for this book, Evan Thomas, recalls that his father, the illustrious Norman Thomas (often Socialist candidate for the Presidency) told many "tales of the essential decency of his childhood neighbors" in Ohio. "They were hipped on the fundamentalist religions, but they were thoroughly human. In fact, it was mainly because Dad had spent his childhood in Marion that he went through Princeton a Republican, of all things."

But the "wonderful world of Ohio," as the hucksterish governor of the 1960s, James Rhodes, called his state, has in recent times cared less for the homely virtues. (In Ohio, Rhodes said again and again and again, "profit is not a dirty word.") In the measure of what a state does for its people—in education, health, welfare, mental care, environmental control—Ohio remained near the bottom of the 50-state rankings and in the absolute cellar among the great industrial states throughout the 1960s. And there was little color, verve, or great culture to relieve the monotony. Ohio just plowed through history, turning out immense amounts of manufactured goods, shortchanging its own people, practicing a politics of indifference. In 1970, Ohio was the scene of the killing by the National Guard of four Kent State students—the first such casualties of the modern student revolution. The following autumn, after a great scandal that wracked the ruling Republicans, Ohio elected John J. Gilligan, a vigorous young Irishman and liberal-intellectual Democrat from Cincinnati, as governor. Ohio may be ready to turn a new leaf, but it is still too early to say for sure.

All along, of course, Ohio has had its redeeming graces, its imaginative and dedicated men and women, some innovative institutions. Doughty Cincinnati, decades past her prime, still has a certain old world charm and is in the midst of a graceful renewal; Dayton is one of the cleaner and more progressive of Midwestern cities; there are numerous small colleges of exemplary quality (Antioch, Oberlin, Kenyon, Ohio Wesleyan, and the like). A dedicated Citizens League tries to keep state and city government headed in a sane direction; Cleveland may be "the mistake on the lake" that some have called it, but it had the courage to become the first predominantly white town among America's big cities to elect a black mayor.

As John Gunther correctly recorded, "basically, Ohio is nothing more or less than a giant carpet of agriculture studded by great cities." The state has no less than eight cities with more than 100,000 people, 16 metropolitan areas which house 78 percent of the state's 10,652,017 people, and 153 cities with 10,000 or more inhabitants.* One can't be on a highway headed in any direction in Ohio for an hour and not hit a medium-sized city—a Steubenville, a Warren, Niles, Sandusky or Fremont; "our state is really microscopic," one Ohioan told me. Of the major cities, ranging from Cleveland (population 876,000) to Springfield (85,907), we will have more to report later; suffice it here to note that none has the weight of a Chicago in Illinois, a Detroit in Michigan or a New York City in New York; which has not a little to say about the fragmented nature of urban politics in a basically metropolitan state.

Most of Ohio's borders are wet—Lake Erie (color it dirty) to the north and the Ohio River stretching 436 miles along the east and south; there are, however, some arbitrary cartographer's lines along the Pennsylvania, Michigan, and Indiana borders, so that the overall impression is more or less square.

The geographers say there are three regions of Ohio. About a quarter of the land area, mainly in the southeast quadrant, is the Appalachian Allegheny

---

* The total population has risen by 3.1 million, or 48 percent, since 1946—compared to a national growth of 45 percent. Now sixth among the states in population, Ohio was third from 1840 until the 1880s, fell behind California in the 1940s and behind Texas in the 1960s.

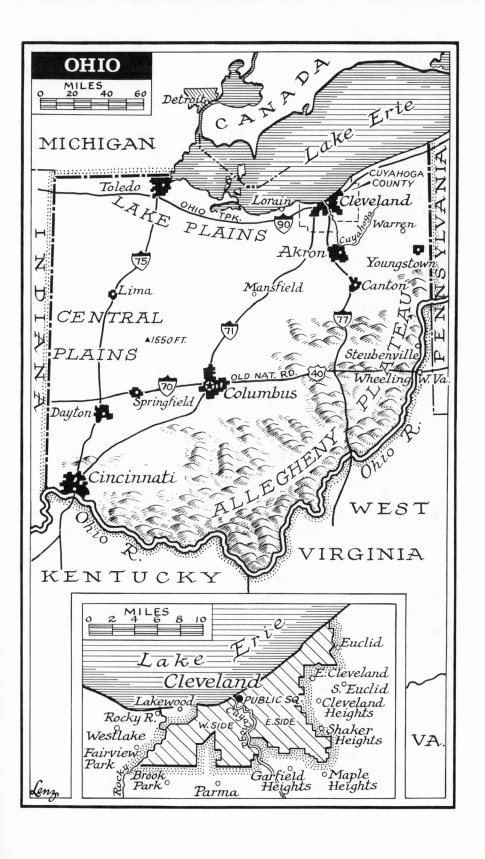

Plateau, remnants of the Allegheny Mountains spilling over from Pennsylvania and West Virginia, becoming more gentle as they move westward. Along the shores of Lake Erie from Cleveland to the northwest corner of Ohio is a strip known as the Lake Plains, or the onetime Black Swamp that thwarted early settlers until they found a way to drain it. All the rest of Ohio—the great land bulk, moving out to the Indiana border—is a Central Plains area, gently rolling land similar to the plains of the more westerly states except that the first settlers found practically the entire region covered by forest, not grass.

The rugged, hilly country of the southeastern Allegheny Plateau, a mixture of sylvan wood and land ravaged by strip coal mining, harbors few cities of any note and much rural poverty; along the Ohio River are some heavy industries including steel companies run out of Wheeling and Pittsburgh. Many of these counties are poor in the extreme, with subquality schools and poor public facilities. The original settlers were mostly Virginia and Kentucky woodsmen. On the political scale, this region votes predominantly Republican but is likely to switch to the Democrats in hard times.

Northeastern Ohio is highly industrialized and heavily populated, a smokestack-studded industrial complex of befouled air and great productivity including the cities of Youngstown, Warren, Canton, Akron, Cleveland, and, somewhat farther west, Toledo. These cities are actually part of the growing megalopolis called Chi-Pitts, anchored by Pittsburgh on the east, Chicago (or possibly Milwaukee) on the west. John Steinbeck in *Travels With Charley* wrote of passing through these "great hives of production" and "my eyes and mind were battered by the fantastic hugeness and energy of production, a complication that resembles chaos and cannot be." And then Steinbeck added: "What was wonderful was that I could come again to a quiet country road, tree-bordered, with fenced fields and cows, could pull up . . . beside a lake of clear, clean water and see high overhead the arrows of southing ducks and geese." How long those countryside charms can remain, as suburbia gobbles up the farms and industrial pollution exacts an ever increasing toll, is open to question. Once a haven of New England settlers, this region is now heavily peopled by the children and grandchildren of European workers—Italians, Slovenians, Hungarians, Poles—who were imported to man the heavy steel and rubber industries earlier in this century. And there are ever increasing numbers of American Negroes. The political coloration (except for some farm counties and suburbia) is overwhelmingly Democratic.

Finally, occupying roughly half the land and representing half of the state's population, is central and western Ohio, the easterly terminus of the great Midwestern farm belt but also strong manufacturing territory and site of cities great and small, among them Columbus at center state, Dayton and Cincinnati at the southwesterly corner. Here are the descendants of the Scots, Irish, Pennsylvania German, and assorted Civil War veterans. The German flavor is especially strong in southern Ohio and equals conservatism. Many of the overwhelmingly Republican counties of the U.S.A. are in these central and western regions, but interestingly there are still a handful of counties that have been voting Democratic ever since the Civil War. (The political scientist John Fenton has shown an amazing correspondence between the counties that voted for the Copperhead Democratic Clement L. Vallandigham in 1863 and were still voting Democratic in the 1960s.) But these old Democratic counties are but a small fraction of the population, and the salient political factors are generally rural and especially small city Republicanism, and the fact that metropolises like Columbus and Cincinnati—despite great industries, labor unions, and black population—have been so dominated by the thought patterns of their conservative establishments that they register Republican majorities in virtually every election.

An Economy of Heavy Industry

Heavy manufacturing dominates the Ohio economy, the natural result of her strategic location between the iron ore deposits of Minnesota and the coal mines of Appalachia, between the St. Lawrence Seaway to the north and the Ohio River to the south, and within 500 miles of two-thirds of the nation's population and three-quarters of its wealth. Her manufacturing output of more than $20 billion a year ranks third among the states; her coke ovens, blast furnaces, and finishing mills place her second among the 50 in primary and fabricated metals production. Ohio is first in the U.S.A. in rubber as a result of the output of Akron's factories, and also ranks high in machinery, automobile assembly, and automobile parts manufacture. But the product lines are a picture of diversity; Ohio is first, according to the promotional literature that pours out of Columbus, in products ranging from business machines to coffins, buckets and pails to Chinese food and Liederkranz cheese, roadbuilding and earthmoving equipment to playing cards and Bibles. Other major factors are coal, lime, and some oil and gas mining, the growing service industries, plus trucking and lumbering. Ohio has a healthy and diversified agriculture (chiefly dairy products, cattle, corn, and hogs) with a total farm income of $1.2 billion a year—12th among the states. Hardly a tourist mecca, Ohio nonetheless picks up $3.3 billion a year from travelers passing through.

In a real sense, however, Ohio is musclebound by the dominance of heavy industry, a portion of the economy most susceptible to automation. Announcing proudly that jobs are the answer to every social ill, Governor Rhodes set out in the 1960s to draw thousands of new industries to Ohio. Rhodes' industrial "Raiders" undertook scores of industry-hunting tours around the U.S.A. and several foreign trade missions. A national advertising campaign stressed the already-cited theme, "Profit is not a dirty word in Ohio," as well as the pitch, "In Ohio, government is run as a business." Prospective advertisers were reminded that Ohio had the lowest state and local tax rates in the country and also the lowest proportion of government employees.

By the end of the decade, the success of the industrial recruitment drive was obvious. Aided by an expanding national economy, the state had attracted 2,500 new manufacturing firms, 10,000 industrial expansions had occurred, and business had spent over $8 billion in new capital investment. Ohio had shot ahead of all other major industrial states in her annual rate of capital investment by manufacturers (well over $2 billion annually).

But there were serious deficiencies in the growth. With automation making its impact ever more obvious, actual manufacturing jobs registered only modest gains and never went far beyond a peak hit in 1953, during the Korean War. The overall job growth of Ohio in the years from 1961 through 1968 was 23.3 percent, a respectable enough showing in its own terms but behind the job growth rate in 31 other states. The new jobs in Ohio were one-sided, concentrated in heavy manufacturing such as rolling mills, assembly plants, and rubber factories, but very light in the more exotic, electronic age industries which pay comparatively higher wages. Thus, despite its industrial wealth, the state ranked 37 among the states in per capita income growth over the decade.

Though he began to press more for expanded vocational educational facilities toward the end of his term, Rhodes seemed basically unconcerned with the quality of the jobs being created in Ohio. Quantity, not quality, was his chief concern, and he could point out with justification that Ohio unemployment sank to an exceptionally low level among all the states. But the tax structure was not adjusted to encourage "think tanks" or advanced industries. The hallmarks of the Rhodes approach were to keep taxes low, to move ahead of all other states in completion of interstate roads, to get state financing for industrial bonds to save businesses first investment costs, and to promote the Ohio State Fair until it became the nation's most successful. Rhodes was fond of passing out homilies such as this one (referring to tomato juice production, in which Ohio leads the U.S.): "If every Ohioan drank one quart of tomato juice a year, it would mean 5,000 more jobs in Ohio." Left to future years were the problems of modifying the structure of an old-line economy, heavy industry state so that the people could share more fully in the benefits of the electronic age.

Neglectful State Government: From Lausche to Rhodes

When Frank J. Lausche was first elected governor of Ohio in 1944, he bore all the marks of a true American folk hero: son of a Slovenian-born steel worker, self-made lawyer and outstanding city judge, respected mayor of his home city of Cleveland, disdainer of old-line machine politics, a Democratic candidate who could appeal across all party lines. Gunther devoted the first six pages of his Ohio chapter to an enthusiastic review of the Lausche personality and record, calling him a man of "charm, vitality," of absolute honesty and "sympathy for the underdog" whose only major defects stemmed from "a lack of an academic education and a disinclination to think abstractly." An honored slot in history seemed to be in store for Lausche when he finally left the governorship in 1956.

But in Ohio today, it is hard to find a knowledgeable observer with a kind word for Frank Lausche. For this frugal and conservative Slovenian imposed such a parsimonious, strict pay-as-you-go philosophy in Ohio, akin to the low-spending Byrd regime in Virginia, that the state has yet to regain the position among the states in services to people—in education, welfare, criminology, or mental care—which it held before he took office. Benefiting first from a wartime-generated surplus in the state treasury, and later refusing adamantly to increase taxes, Lausche failed to inaugurate needed capital investments or adequately finance basic state services except in one area—highway construction. Highways of course provided a major political payoff in jobs, campaign money from contractors, and visible achievement. All the time, the children of Ohio were being deprived of educational investment equal to the other states of the Union, especially the large and wealthy states comparable to Ohio. As John H. Fenton points out in *Midwest Politics*,

In 1956, at the close of Lausche's period in office, some 1,000 boys were in residence at the Boys' Industrial School, which admitted to a rated capacity of about 600. In the sleeping quarters of the school there were as many as 70 beds jammed one against the other so that the only access to beds beyond the outer row was to step from bed to bed. According to Lausche's critics, the reason for spending so little on children's services was that they did not vote.

As for the electoral base that made all this possible, Fenton observed that Lausche was able to attract votes from conservative Republicans. "These votes, when superimposed on the Democratic votes cast by ill-informed low-income voters in the cities, provided him with comfortable majorities in the general elections." Lausche's electoral downfall in fact came not in a general election but in a Democratic primary. He served two terms in the U. S. Senate after leaving Columbus but was finally turned out in 1968 when the liberal leadership of the state Democratic party decided it had had enough of a Senator who usually voted with the Republicans, and it backed John J. Gilligan of Cincinnati in a successful primary race against Lausche.*

The first postwar Ohio Governor to make a serious effort to make Ohio government responsive to growing education, mental health, and welfare needs was Michael V. DiSalle, the genial, roly-poly former mayor of Toledo and wartime chief of the Office of Price Administration elected in the 1958 Democratic sweep. But to achieve just a few modest reforms and meet rising state costs, DiSalle had to raise taxes—for the first time in 20 years. (State government had limped along through the Lausche years with status-quo taxes and a couple of bond issues, passed by the legislature over Lausche's opposition.) DiSalle lacked political finesse, the taxes backfired against him seriously, and in 1962 he was defeated by Republican James A. Rhodes, who rode into office on a promise of "no new taxes."

* Lausche's Senate service was without major distinction. In 1959, Democratic Majority Leader Lyndon Johnson arranged for Lausche to go on the Foreign Relations Committee. He would have done well to read Gunther's admonition: "(Lausche) is little more than a child as regards foreign policy; his views on world affairs are parochial in the extreme."

Rhodes shares with Lausche the distinction of having been one of the two most influential men in postwar Ohio history; he was governor from 1963 to 1971, and his mark will be felt on the state for years to come. A sturdily built man whose personal manner ranges from hearty back-slapping to cold discourtesy, Rhodes was born into rather poor circumstances, his father a coal miner. As governor, he avoided press conferences and confrontations with opponents and delegated the details of administration to a highly competent but nonintellectual staff. In more than three decades of office-holding, Rhodes revealed himself as a robust type, a man's man, fond of golf and poker, given to ribald jokes,* and for the most part, a superbly successful politician. His plurality in winning a second governorship term in 1964 was 703,233 votes—an all-time Ohio high.

What the public wanted, Rhodes decided, was no new taxes, and he promised, "There'll be no new or additional taxes as long as I'm governor of Ohio." In his second term, Rhodes finally was obliged to force some tax and fee adjustments through the state legislature. But overall, Ohio had to limp through the 1960s on a regressive sales tax base for state government and ever increasing local property taxes, much to the distress of hard-pressed homeowners and marginal businesses.

The net impact of the Rhodes regime, in fact, was to continue the Lauschian politics of fiscal status quo in the very years when most American state governments were taking long forward steps. In constant dollar terms, state government expenditures (per capita) rose 133 percent in the U. S. as a whole between 1950 and 1967, but only 91.5 percent in Ohio. Ohio's tax effort (as a percent of personal income) ranked 41st in the nation in 1950, 42nd when Lausche left office, but only 47th by the end of Rhodes' term (and as low as 50th in some studies). Whether compared to other Great Lakes states, or the five poorest states of the Union, or the overall national average, Ohio was slipping farther and farther behind. But for the industrial promoters in Columbus, this was a plus, not a minus. They took out full page ads in the *Wall Street Journal* to proclaim: "OHIO'S STATE AND LOCAL TAXES ARE THE LOWEST IN THE NATION! . . . Ohio makes dollars go farther without loss in essential services. . . . Profit is *not* a dirty word in Ohio."

But in the words of David Hess, a reporter for the Akron *Beacon-Journal*, "While the administration fiddles a happy tune, Ohio's education, mental health, welfare and corrections programs sink steadily into indifference and neglect." Measured against its ability to pay, Ohio by the late 1960s stood 48th among the states in its support of education, 43rd in health and hospitals, and 38th in public welfare. In 1969, Ohio was reported to rank 46th among the states in per capita support of mental health programs.

State aid for public schools provides perhaps the best example of the gap between promise and publicity and actual performance during the Rhodes

---

* At one governors' conference, while Michigan's George Romney was rambling at the speaker's stand, Rhodes slipped a note to fellow Governor Roger Branigin of Indiana. It read: "This guy couldn't sell pussy on a troopship."

years. State aid to local schools did rise dramatically, but so did teacher salaries, all costs compounded by inflation. Despite an early Rhodes promise
that his administration would fund 50 percent of school costs, the figure was
still under 30 percent by the time he left office (compared to a national level
of about 40 percent). Thus Ohio had the dubious distinction of leading the
nation in school closings when local property taxes (up more than a third
during the 1960s) became so onerous that rebelling taxpayers in locality after
locality refused to approve additional increases.* In the fall of 1969, more
than 19,000 children in 40 Ohio schools were locked out of their classrooms
for days or weeks when their school districts were forced to close down for
want of operating funds. "A less dramatic but chronic deprivation," according to reporter Hess, "is the effect that bare-bones budgets have on thousands
of other youngsters whose schools get by from year to year by employing
untrained teachers, using outdated textbooks, and operating on curtailed
schedules."

Where Rhodes made his strongest mark on Ohio—and differentiated
himself clearly from the old Lausche approach—was in selling the people on
massive bond issues (totaling some $2 billion in all) for highways, higher
education facilities, and other physical improvements. For years under
Rhodes, the bonds in effect substituted for new taxes. Half of them went for
highways. "We get the most political credit for another mile of superhighway. And don't worry—maintenance won't be a problem; our voters will vote
anything for highways," Rhodes's finance director, Howard L. Collier, told
me. The statistics showed that Ohio under Rhodes was spending more on
highways than any other state service.

But Rhodes's breakthrough in education facilities was not to be gainsaid.
A total of $665 million in bond money was provided for bricks and mortar to
expand the Ohio educational system from five universities and a college to
12 state universities, a new medical school, and dozens of permanent branch
facilities (including the equivalents of junior colleges.)† The bulk of these
facilities were not completed until he left office, leaving to his successor the
task of raising millions of new money to staff and operate the new educational facilities.

The Rhodes political formula was simple: hold down taxes, do nothing
in regulatory or tax policy to offend business, and reap the publicity windfall for capital construction which future generations will have to pay for. An
extremely harsh but not wholly inaccurate summation of the dynamics of
this situation was provided by David Hess in a 1970 article for *The Nation:*

For the past 75 years, starting with the long reign of kingmaker Mark Hanna,
the state's politics have reeked of intrigue and manipulation. Voters have come

---

* Who were the people voting against property tax boosts for schools? CBS News reporters
discovered that they included homeowners on static pensions, businessmen (especially those dependent
on agriculture) with their backs up against the wall, the Ohio Farm Bureau seeking to force an income
tax, and people like a filling station operator who told a reporter that lots of folks are overeducated
anyway and think they're too good to work, so a little less education might not be such a bad thing
anyway.

† In the entire 160-year period preceding Rhodes' terms, only $200 million had been spent by
Ohio for higher education facilities.

to expect a certain dissembling, sometimes even mild corruption, from their political leaders. Candor and intellectual integrity are seldom rewarded; more often than not, they are greeted with suspicion and hostility.

The state's most successful politicians—men like Hanna, John Bricker, Frank Lausche, James Rhodes—are those able to move most skillfully among the state's power blocks, wheeling and dealing for favors and concessions while deftly creating a public image of rectitude and incorruptibility. Such men are pragmatic, alert to opportunity, and only superficially committed to any ideology or grand design of government. (The late Sen. Robert A. Taft may have been an exception to the rule.) Such men accommodate themselves to the interests of big business, since great power resides in the directorates of Ohio's giant mills, banks and insurance companies.

They also know that the conservative tone of the urban establishment is endorsed in rural Ohio by the stolid and prosperous farmers. . . .

All of this, along with the rising conservatism of Ohio's trade and industrial unionists, produces a milieu in which human progressivism can hardly flourish. Materialism, social indifference, racial intolerance and economic discrimination are traits shared by both the working and the managerial classes.

Reporter Hess went on to charge that Ohio's major newspapers reinforce the beliefs and myths of the reigning establishment. "In Columbus and Cincinnati, the major papers have for years operated largely as extensions of the banking-industrial elite," Hess wrote, and he went on to characterize Cleveland newspaper management as "uncertain and effete" and to criticize even the generally respected newspapers of Toledo, Dayton, and Akron for hesitating to define social goals, even if they do engage in sporadic criticism of state policy. "There is a tradition, too, of chummy relationships between politicians and newspaper executives," Hess wrote, confirming a judgment I heard from many others in Ohio.

All the good press in the world may not elect a man, however, if his personal integrity comes into question. In 1969, *Life* magazine alleged that Governor Rhodes had converted political funds to his personal use, had run afoul of the Internal Revenue Service, and had also acted questionably in commuting the life sentence of Mafia leader Thomas Licavoli when money was reportedly available to buy that convict's way out of prison. No illegal conduct on Rhodes's part was ever revealed, but the faint aroma of suspected corruption was probably the decisive factor in his very narrow loss to Robert Taft, Jr., in the 1970 Republican primary for the U.S. Senate.

An unrelated statehouse loan scandal then paved the way for the election as governor of John J. Gilligan, a 49-year-old graduate of Notre Dame and one-time teacher of literature at Xavier University in Cincinnati, a man about as unlike Rhodes as one could imagine. In his campaign, Gilligan not only refused to dodge the tax issue, but actually insisted on repeating again and again that Ohio would need new taxes to solve its fiscal crunch and provide adequate services in the 1970s. "The people in this country don't resent taxes so much," Gilligan told an interviewer later. "They resent the fact that the taxes are unfair and that they don't get anything for them."

So it was that in March 1971, Gilligan recommended a $9.1 billion biennial budget for 1971–73, about 50 percent more than Rhodes's last $6.2

billion budget for 1969–71. And to finance it all, Gilligan proposed crossing the financial Rubicon: enactment of the first income tax in Ohio's history, applicable to both corporations and individuals. The rate would be steeply graduated and tied to property tax relief. Rounding up support for such a daring program was difficult in a legislature still under solid Republican control (54–45 in the house, 20–13 in the senate). But ironically, it was opposition from organized labor, dead set on tax reform that would put practically all the additional burden on businesses, that blocked a majority for the Gilligan tax package through most of 1971. Finally, labor relaxed its opposition, brightening the chances for passage.

The danger for Gilligan is that he may be stuck with the "big spender" tag that sank DiSalle a decade before. But Gilligan had a lot on his side, too: a compelling personality and persuasive manner, the dire financial straits of local schools and state services, and the populist aura of his tax recommendations.

Gilligan also showed no little political courage in proposing a quite radical plan to make virtually all of Ohio's 182,000 students in state colleges and universities pay back, over their working careers, the entire cost of their education. The Ohio Plan, as it quickly became known, emerged at the same time that many private colleges were considering pay-as-you-earn plans. But Gilligan's was the first such proposal for a state system. Specifically, it would require every student entering a state university to agree to repay the state subsidy for his education—about $3,200 for four years—in interest-free annual payments starting as soon after graduation as his income reached at least $7,000 a year. (The charge would be in addition to the $660-a-year annual fees Ohio students already have to pay.) Graduate students would also have to agree to repay the subsidized portion of their educational costs. Repayments would be graduated according to income, from $50 a year at the $7,000 minimum income for repayment to $1,000 a year for a man making $100,000. A husband and wife who both attended the state universities would only have to pay back for one.

"My plan," Gilligan told an interviewer, "simultaneously provides a new source of income for higher education (estimated at $5 billion within 30 years), and lowers the economic barrier keeping many out of school. It will enable any kid, even off of welfare, to get the same break as a millionaire's son and to go as far as he wants in education as long as he's willing to pay it back in the future." To relieve the admissions pressure on the four-year colleges, the plan specifically exempts students at Ohio's community colleges from deferred tuition responsibility.

Predictably, Gilligan's "Ohio Plan" stirred up a hornet's nest of opposition among university officials, students, and their families. About the only group strongly for it were the "hard hats." Thus chances of early passage were slim, but as on the income tax issue, Gilligan had some powerful forces working on his side: the huge costs of running state universities in a time of financial strain, the public policy issue of how much taxpayers—especially the poorer ones—should be obliged to pay the educational costs of a college elite, and the feeling in many circles that the United States has been putting altogether too much emphasis on the sanctity of a four-year college education for many students whose intellectual capacities and actual career prospects make it quite unnecessary.

One thing seems certain: if Jack Gilligan leaves office with both the income tax and some form of the "Ohio Plan" firmly entrenched in state law, he will go down in history as a watershed figure in the development of modern Ohio.

Issueless Politics: the Bliss Phenomenon

Packed with cities, heavily industrialized and unionized, harboring large populations of East and South Europeans and Negroes, Ohio has every reason to be a liberal Democratic state. Polls of basic party preference almost invariably show more Ohioans identifying with the Democrats than with the Republicans. Yet a Republican aristocracy of industrialists and small-city conservatives has dominated Ohio through most of the past century. Democratic Presidential victories (as in three of FDR's four elections, or 1948 and 1964) are exceptions to the rule; with rare exceptions (like 1958 and 1970), Republicans win the governorship unless the Democratic candidate is equally conservative; the legislature since 1941 has been under Republican control three times as often as the Democrats have controlled. What are the reasons for this startling dichotomy between demography and electoral performance?

Geography is perhaps the most important. Ohio has no single dominating city akin to Detroit in Michigan, Chicago in Illinois, or New York City in New York. Cleveland, Ohio's largest city, casts only 7 percent of the statewide vote. Split asunder into many camps, the normally Democratic groups —labor unions, ethnic coalitions, Negroes, intellectuals—lack a single population center in which they can coalesce and begin a bid for statewide dominance. Of the large cities, only Cleveland is dependably Democratic; the Republican business-elite monopolizes the press and public forums of second- and third-ranking Columbus and Cincinnati. All but a handful of the smaller cities are Republican bastions under similar conservative domination and form the backbone of GOP voting strength in Ohio. Generalizing about the smaller population centers, John Fenton observes:

The small towns tended to be rather monolithic, with the business community holding sway. The Chamber of Commerce, Rotary Club and other business organizations were virtually the only groups that met and discussed issues. . . . The vice president of the bank was not a faceless, bloated plutocrat to workers in the small corn belt town that he was in the big city. On the contrary, he drank his morning cup of coffee in the same restaurant and often at the same table as the shoe clerk and the mechanic. In these face-to-face situations he presented the business point of view concerning issues, and his word was accepted by the listeners as akin to law. After all, he was informed and articulate and a "good guy."

History is a second factor. The Republican party emerged from the Civil War years as the party of patriotism and the establishment; virtually the only Democratic counties for many decades were those that had voted for the Copperhead Democrat, Clement Vallandigham, in 1863. The people of these counties often found themselves labeled as "promoters of sedition" and "traitors," but they did hold together a semblance of a statewide party in years when the Democratic party almost disappeared as a functioning unit in states like Michigan, Minnesota and Wisconsin. Thus when the liberal-labor coalition of the New Deal and post-New Deal days appeared on the scene, the Democratic party was not an empty shell that it could seize with ease. Under the banner of a candidate like FDR, the disinherited of two generations—the descendants of Vallandigham's supporters and the foreign born, Catholic, and Negro population that suffered so much in the Depression—could be drawn together in effective majority coalition. But thereafter their ideological differences surfaced and division ensued; when the statewide Democratic party in 1968 finally summoned up its courage to back liberal John Gilligan against Frank Lausche in the party's Senate primary, the move was more resented by conservative rural Democrats than by ethnic party leaders of Lausche's own heritage.

Another factor in Democratic weakness over many years was the Balkanization of the party leadership into separate urban enclaves across the state. Entrenched urban county organizations, especially the one headed for many years by Ray Miller in Cleveland, went their own way with little regard for the perennially anemic statewide Democratic organization; Miller in fact explicitly maintained that his organization had neither legal nor moral ties to a state Democratic party.

The fragmented condition of organized labor has also led to Democratic weakness. Unlike Michigan's UAW, Ohio has no single dominant union; there are scores of unions across the state whose leaders prefer to make their own arrangements with political candidates, rather than working in concert. Nor are Ohio's labor leaders "issue oriented" like those in Michigan; they have been described as a "bread-and-butter" lot for whom politics is a secondary consideration. Only when the interests of all of organized labor seem in peril—as in 1958, when "right to work" was on the ballot, or in the Goldwater race of 1964—does organized labor pull together in a concerted campaign. (It won on both occasions.) Late in the 1960s, the state AFL-CIO did begin publication of a carefully researched, well designed monthly issues and politics pamphlet for all AFL-CIO members in the state; it was the best of its kind I saw anywhere in the country and is helping build more labor unity and effectiveness in the political arena. Ohio's most powerful unions include the Teamsters and Machinists (both spread out across the state), the United Auto Workers (most numerous in Toledo, Cleveland, Cincinnati, and Columbus), the Steelworkers (in Youngstown, Canton, Cleveland, Lorain, and other towns), and the Rubber Workers (almighty in Akron). Coordinated and activated in politics, they would be a powerful force; up to this time, they have failed to bulid staffs of liberal intellectuals who could act as the party's advance thinkers and election agents. Like all big state unions, they now face the problem of internal division between blue-collar ethnics and blacks.

If the Ohio Democrats have traditionally been a faulty alliance of the have-nots in society, exactly the opposite can be said of the Republicans. John Fenton has shown that a substantial number of the people voting Republican in Ohio today are the descendants of the first settlers of the ancient and all-but-forgotten boundaries of the Virginia Military District and Western Reserve areas, settled early in the past century by Whigs who became Republicans and never thereafter altered their partisan preference. When modern industry came to northeast Ohio in the late 19th century—especially steel and oil refining, the latter in Cleveland under John D. Rockefeller's Standard Oil Company—it was Republicans who owned and managed the new enterprises. That colorful era was well depicted in *The Ohio Guide* prepared by the WPA Writers' Program:

> With industrialism, there arose a new type of politician, whose dealings gave rise to abuse, scandal and corruption. In the 1880s "boss government" flourished, and for a quarter of a century two men, Mark Hanna of Cleveland and George B. Cox of Cincinnati, each boss of his own city, despotically controlled the government of the state. Hanna was an ironmaster who went into politics to protect his business interests, and then made it his life work. Cox was a saloonkeeper. Both were millionaires. At first they quarreled, but later compromised, Hanna taking over the northern part of the state as his domain, and Cox the southern. They named Ohio's national representatives and officials.
>
> Their day was one of almost unchecked abuse, not only in politics but also in all fields of business. Exploitation was ruthless. . . . Hanna's spectacular career reached a climax in 1896 when his protege, William McKinley of Canton, was elected President of the United States. . . . At that time Hanna approached more closely than any other man in history to being "boss" of the United States.*

It is true that there were reform elements in Ohio. Democratic Senator George H. Pendleton, an associate of the prewar reformers of Cincinnati, wrote the Civil Service Act in 1882, and Republican Senator John Sherman, brother of the Civil War general, fathered the Sherman Antitrust Act in 1890. In the early 1900s a group of great reformers took control of Cleveland, Cincinnati, and Toledo from the corrupt bosses. The state government in the 1910–15 era enacted a number of significant reforms. Yet throughout, it was the Republicans who represented Ohio's privileged—and in 1920 nominated and elected one of their own, Warren G. Harding, as President.

The Republicans of recent years—businessmen small and large, suburbanites, small townsmen, well-to-do corn belt farmers, members of old families, and relative newcomers—have shared one thing in common between themselves and their historic predecessors: they are "on top" and they want to remain there. Since they are a numerical minority, they have recognized the need to coalesce and indeed have formed a superb statewide organization. At least until recently, there was a single county—Hamilton (Cincinnati)

---

* John Gunther's wonderfully quotable remark about Hanna: he "wore a President like McKinley practically as a watchfob."

—which had the wealth and votes to control most Republican primaries, thus giving a focal point of political control and leadership. And finally, the Republicans have succeeded because of the handsome bankrolling arranged for them by the Ohio business community.

The chief architect of postwar Republican organizational strength in Ohio was Ray C. Bliss, a man whose modest demeanor (that of a small-town banker, or the Akron insurance broker which he is) belies unusual intensity when it comes to matters political. Bliss was called on to head the state GOP after a surprise Democratic sweep in 1948, coming into office as the party's first fulltime and salaried chairman. He had one condition for taking the job—that all fund raising be conducted by the party's independent finance committee, which operates like a political community chest. On only two occasions while Bliss was chairman did the big contributors interfere with party policy—in 1958, when they insisted (over what Bliss later claimed were his vehement opposition and warnings of defeat) on putting a "right-to-work" proposition on the Ohio ballot, and in 1964, when many of them supported the right-wing crusade to nominate Goldwater for the Presidency. (Bliss feared an election day disaster if Goldwater were the nominee and was furious with Governor Rhodes for throwing the delegation to the Arizonan before the convention opened.) Both 1958 and 1964 brought sweeping Republican defeats in Ohio.

As state chairman, Bliss built the prototype of the successful modern state party organization (a model since copied in many states). A permanent fulltime staff of about 16 people (and more at election times) was hired. Field representatives worked to foster party organizations in counties throughout the state. A well-oiled public relations department turned out releases favorable to Republicans and negative on Democrats and published the weekly *Ohio Republican News* to warm up the party faithful and propagandize others. Professional polls were ordered to gauge public opinion on issues and candidates. Widespread voter registration drives were undertaken. A speakers' bureau arranged for big-name GOP speakers at party affairs. Special attention was given to state legislative and congressional races, with major emphasis on candidate recruitment and behind-the-scenes work to avoid bloodletting primaries. A full research division kept newspaper morgue-type files. Other divisions took care of Young Republican, women's, and veterans' affairs. Bliss himself worked closely with Republican members of the legislature to develop party positions (especially when there was a Democratic governor.)

The one thing Bliss never, never did as a party chairman was to talk in public about issues. He was essentially a technician, to whom issues were a propaganda tool, not an end. His ideological neutrality assured him longevity on the job in Columbus and made him the natural choice (especially with behind-the-scenes backing from former President Eisenhower and former Treasury Secretary George Humphrey) to be chosen Republican National Chairman after the Goldwater debacle of 1964. Bliss performed fairly creditably in Washington, pouring oil on the troubled Republican waters, running a tight ship at GOP headquarters, but failing—perhaps because national issues were beyond his ken, perhaps because of the independent nature of the state party organs under him—to register the same measure of increased Republican vote he had been able to accomplish in the smaller world of Ohio. President Nixon ungratefully fired him shortly after the 1968 election.

Only time will tell whether the Gilligan election of 1970 represents a fundamental turn to more issue-oriented politics, or just a temporary deviation from the norm. Gilligan's hard-won victory over Lausche in the 1968 Senate primary did constitute an historic repudiation of the conservative rural bloc in the Democratic party. After its consummation, Gilligan seized control of the state party apparatus and turned it into a far more aggressive, youth-oriented, socially conscious organ. Nixon carried Ohio in 1968 by only 90,428 votes, a startling decline from his 1960 margin of 273,363, and Gilligan himself lost the Senate election by only 114,812 votes to a very popular Republican, William Saxbe. While Gilligan's 1968 primary victory had been fashioned in the big urban counties, almost all the others going to Lausche, by 1970 he had strengthened his hold on the party so thoroughly that he won 87 of Ohio's 88 counties in the primary, the biggest vote ever for a Democratic gubernatorial primary candidate, opposed or unopposed. "That means," he told me in 1971, "that I just don't have any opposition in the Democratic party." Others dispute that judgment, saying there is still strong conflict between the big-city Democratic machines and the party's rural, downstate base. But all agree the Democrats are more unified now than at any time in recent history.

The Democratic resurgence was eased by fierce internecine conflict in the vaunted Republican state organization, first as a result of the bitter Taft-Rhodes Senate primary fight, and even more particularly the reeking scandal that erupted in May 1970. It was revealed that several leading Republicans —including Rhodes himself, Auditor Roger Cloud, State Treasurer John D. Herbert, and state Sen. Robin Turner—had received thousands of dollars in campaign contributions from Crofters, Inc., a year-old Columbus firm that arranged for private companies to receive hundreds of thousands of dollars in loans from the state treasury. Crofters was headed by former state tax commissioner Gerald A. Donahue, a prominent Republican operative and confidant of Rhodes. The loans, which included $4 million to the Four Seasons Nursing Home Centers of Oklahoma City and $8 million to Denver's King Enterprises (a firm which was seeking to shore up Bernard Cornfeld's International Mutual Fund empire), were determined by a subsequent state investigation to have been illegal because they exceeded the state's statutory limit for commercial investments and did not satisfy state risk requirements.

In the imbroglio which ensued, the Republican State Committee publicly repudiated Herbert's 1970 candidacy for attorney general and Turner's candidacy for state treasurer. Both men, however, refused to withdraw from the already nominated state ticket. The state committee gave a vote of confidence to Cloud, the party's nominee for governor, who claimed his contribution from Crofters had been given to an aide and returned when he learned of it. In the autumn campaign, Cloud, a generally soft-spoken and rather colorless man, tried to shift voters' attention to Gilligan's ADA membership, left-wing academic following, and rhetoric that "inflames student revolutionaries." In a normal year, Gilligan might have been harmed, but the scandal was just too much for the GOP to overcome. (Commenting on the feuds within the state GOP, Gilligan's campaign manager, Mark Shields, could gleefully joke about "civil war in the leper colony.")

On election day, Gilligan won with a plurality of 342,811 votes. All of the Republican statewide nominees went down to defeat save the party's nominees for lieutenant governor and secretary of state, and Robert Taft, Jr., in the Senate contest. Taft eked out a 70,420-vote victory over wealthy Cleveland industrialist Howard M. Metzenbaum, who had made some political history earlier in the year by upsetting the famed astronaut, John H. Glenn, in the Democratic primary.

The Republican debacle, however, by no means assured a continuing GOP decline in the state, or a Nixon loss in 1972. The Republican state organization, under chairman John S. Andrews, an able professional in the Bliss mode, continues to be strongly financed and may demonstrate the recuperative powers the GOP demonstrated after its debacles of 1958 and 1964.

Profile of a Legislature

An inveterate reader of state newspapers is struck again and again by the superficial and uninformative nature of reporting on the state legislatures which make so many vital decisions about the rules of American society, the services people will receive, the taxes they will pay. In many states one discovers that the local press had never stepped back to review the major power bases in the state legislature, the changing nature of membership, the real impact of the reapportionment decisions of the 1960s. An exception was a fine series of articles on "How the Ohio Legislature Really Works," written in 1969 by Richard Zimmerman and Robert Burdock of the Cleveland *Plain-Dealer*, from which some key paragraphs are quoted:*

The General Assembly is made up of four houses—the Senate, House, the lobbyists and the press corps.

The most important work of the General Assembly is done in the Maramor and the Top of the Center restaurant, behind the closed doors of the Neil House, in the bar of the Columbus Sheraton, in closed meetings of the majority party leadership, in the governor's office—and only sometimes in the open committee rooms.

In fairness, it would be said that the Ohio General Assembly is probably one

* An interesting commentary on the press corps itself is the fact that Zimmerman and Burdock were two of only three Statehouse reporters who had been on the job for more than two legislative sessions in Columbus in 1969. If the American press would only pay legislative and political reporters —perhaps three or four on a typical big city daily—salaries commensurate with their delicate and vital job in reporting on the intricacies and shifting patterns in public life, the newspaper managements would be able to retain more good men on the beat and do more for the quality of government and public life than thousands of high-minded editorials. I know scores of fine, promising reporters who have felt obliged to leave daily reporting for newspaper management jobs, public relations, or government positions—just to make a decent living for themselves and put their children through college.

of the better state legislatures. The leaders of both parties are, within a framework that existed long before they came to Columbus, responsible and honorable men. The members, for the most part, believe themselves to be serving the public good, insofar as practical politics permit.

Gone are the days when lobbyists openly paid off legislators in cash in the halls of the Statehouse after they had cast a "right" vote. Gone are the days when "Boss" Hanna arrogantly sat in his Neil House suite and pulled the strings of power, perverting the legislative process as drunken legislators reeled among brass spittoons.

But not gone is the tremendous power of the special interest lobbyists who lurk in the legislative halls. Not gone are the log-rolling and the pork-barreling which waste millions of dollars of tax money in the home districts of particularly powerful committee chairmen. Not gone is a governor who will buy votes with promises of public works projects.

Many if not most of the more complex omnibus bills come directly from Columbus-based lobbyists representing trade, business and professional associations. The insurance industry, for example, practically dictates the laws that are supposed to control that industry. The same can be said of the banking industry, the utilities, savings and loan organizations.

The 33 members of the Senate include 13 lawyers, four educators, two insurance agents, two union representatives, a couple of "public relations" men on payrolls of companies with vested interests in legislative actions, a strip mine operator, plus a variety of assorted businessmen. Most legislators have other sources of income which at one time or another will put them in a conflict of interest with their elected positions. . . .

When Democrats are at the helm, labor sups well at the captain's table. (But) as a constantly potent force in Ohio politics, organized labor is only a myth.

The coalition of Republican legislators and business-oriented trade associations is a formidable power structure. As a result, social reforms and needed tax revisions in Ohio are not forthcoming.

In all the wheeling and dealing, one wonders who speaks for the people. Perhaps the most consistently sane and influential voice for the common man is the Citizens League of Greater Cleveland, a 75-year-old group ably represented in key legislative battles at Columbus by Blair R. Kost, executive assistant to its director, Estal E. Sparlin. Early in its history the League wrote the municipal home rule amendment at the 1912 state constitutional convention. Its many interests of the recent past have included establishment of a constitutional revision committee to work over the state's basic charter, section by section, for submission to the people. The League also pushed conflict-of-interest legislation, won approval of legislation permitting any county to set up a strong mayor-council form of government, and persuaded the state to contribute $175 extra to school districts for each ADC child.

Reapportionment of the legislature, Kost told me, had contributed to the general movement toward younger, more intelligent, and more ambitious representatives, and especially to increased suburban representation. "The suburbs are now the most powerful bloc, dealing with either the center cities or the cornstalk brigade from the rural areas to form a majority on specific issues," Kost said. While rural and conservative voices are still strong, moderation is more the order of the day. The first session of the reapportioned legislature, Kost said, hired more staff, set up additional work space for legislators and secretaries, voted annual sessions, and instituted centralized bill drafting and a regular research position for each standing committee—all steps recommended by the League.

The Congressional Contingent

No Ohioan of recent times has enjoyed national prominence akin to that of Senator Robert A. Taft; but for the sudden emergence of Dwight D. Eisenhower on the political scene in the early 1950s, Taft would most probably have won the Republican Presidential nomination in 1952 and possibly the Presidency. Taft would have been the eighth Ohio President, following in the footsteps of Grant, Harrison, Hayes, Garfield, McKinley, his own father William Howard Taft, and Warren G. Harding. Despite his general conservatism, Taft had a progressive record on such issues as aid to education and housing, and no one ever doubted the honesty and integrity of this scion of the aristocratic Cincinnati family. Few legislators of our time have had a more supreme grasp of American law and done their legislative homework more thoroughly. Taft's most brilliant legislative contribution was doubtless the Taft-Hartley Labor Management Relations Act of 1947, the basic labor law of the postwar years. (In retrospect, it is amusing to recall the fury with which the unions fought Taft-Hartley, calling it the "slave labor act" and every other evil name. In reality, American labor has done quite well under the legislation.)

Taft's judgment in other fields, however, is dimmed by the perspective of history. He was fiercely isolationist before World War II, voting against the draft and lend-lease; he was also a bitter enemy of public power development. After the war, he voted against the Marshall Plan and favored a "Fortress America" in the early 1950s. Taft's sobriquet of "Mr. Republican" is really a reference to the pre-New Deal and pre-Wendell Willkie Republicanism that lingered on in the Midwest after the rest of America had accepted its passing. Perhaps the official demise came with Taft's own death in 1953.

In 1970, at the age of 53, Robert Taft, Jr., finally won election to the U. S. Senate, following the grand family tradition. A warmer and more outgoing man than his father, but lacking his brilliance, the younger Taft rose at a deliberate pace in Ohio politics, first spending several years in the legislature, then running for Congress in 1962. In 1964, he tried for the Senate and was barely beaten. The statistics tell the story: Goldwater lost Ohio that day by 1,027,466 votes; Taft lost by a slim 16,827. Without Goldwater on the ticket, Taft would almost surely have won. But he took his defeat in good grace, ran two years later for Congress from Cincinnati (upsetting Jack Gilligan), and in 1970 defied the Rhodes machine by running for the Senate and defeating the governor himself in the primary. In the general election, he defeated Democrat Howard Metzenbaum by 70,420 votes. A thoughtful, somewhat phlegmatic man, little given to extreme ideology, Taft seems likely to build a record of moderate conservatism in the Senate—but not to set any worlds on fire.

Snowy-haired Senator (and onetime Governor) John Bricker of Ohio was once considered a major national figure and actually was selected by Thomas E. Dewey as his Vice Presidential running mate in 1944. But compared to Taft, Bricker was the shallowest of politicians. Bricker left no other legacy on the national scene than the now all-but-forgotten Bricker Amendment to restrict the President's treaty-making powers. (Interestingly, some suggest that if the Bricker Amendment had passed, the President would have lacked authority to negotiate the SEATO treaty and the Vietnam war might well have been averted.)

Bricker was beaten in 1958 by the irascible, unpredictable Stephen Young, an aging Populist-style Democrat who won some renown during his two Senate terms by refusing to endure abusive letters from constituents, firing back salvos in kind.* In his initial campaign, Young attacked Bricker for remaining head of a Columbus law firm that represented the Pennsylvania Railroad and other rail interests, and then as a Senator breaking with the rest of the Ohio delegation to vote against the St. Lawrence Seaway, which the railroads feared as unduly competitive. Young promised that if he were elected, he would give up his own profitable law practice and make annual public disclosures of his financial holdings and status. He held true to the promise, in 1959 becoming the first member of Congress publicly to reveal his outside income and securities.

Senator William Saxbe, the Republican who succeeded Lausche, is an even more startling switch from the old industry-satrap style of Ohio Senator. A shrewd country "squire" from a one-stoplight country crossroad called Mechanicsburg, Saxbe has such a rustic air about him—chewing tobacco from a red-and-white striped package of Union Workman and spicing his conversation with barnyard expletives and down-home metaphors—that many assumed in his 1968 general election race against John Gilligan that he was a run-of-the-mill conservative. But when he arrived in Washington, Saxbe made peace issues his overriding concern, taking a leading role in the fight against the Nixon Administration's antiballistic missile program. He called Vice President Agnew a "witch hunter" and fought President Nixon's nomination of Clement Haynsworth to the Supreme Court. And Saxbe insisted—in a heresy of heresies for an Ohio Republican—that America's middle class is "wallowing in materialism." When conservative Ohio Republicans questioned his voting record, Saxbe replied: "If they wanted me to vote like Bricker, they would have elected him."

Through wily redistricting and able candidate recruitment, Ohio Republicans maintained overwhelming control—usually by a 3-1 margin—of Ohio's 23 or 24 House seats in the postwar period. The delegation has har-

---

* To a Cleveland resident who wrote that he looked in the obituary page every day hoping to find the Senator's name, Young, then in his late seventies, wrote: "I am feeling better than you would look if you were to take me on."

bored its share of mediocrities, but several from each party have risen above the mass. Some have been skilled power brokers, like conservative Clarence J. Brown of rural west central Ohio, who led Republicans on the House Rules Committee, or Michael J. Kirwan, the blunt old Irishman from Youngstown who parlayed his two positions—as chairman of the House Appropriations Subcommittee on Public Works, which dispenses rivers, harbors, and other public works projects for virtually every district of the country, and the Democratic Congressional Campaign Committee, which apportions election funds for Democratic Congressmen—into a position of influence almost unparalleled on Capitol Hill up to his death in 1970. "Kirwan is almost a dictator when it comes to dispensing favors and funds for Congressmen's pet projects," the Cleveland *Plain-Dealer* once commented; others in the press nicknamed him the "Prince of Pork." Kirwan bulldozed the House into accepting two pet projects of dubious merit—an aquarium for Washington, D.C. (nicknamed Kirwan's "fish hotel"), and a 125-mile canal to link Lake Erie and the Ohio River, a project that made little economic sense and promised to work untold ecological harm by lowering the level of Lake Erie and flooding some 90,000 acres of land, including some of America's finest dairy farms. Later, clearer heads prevailed and both the canal and aquarium projects were killed.*

Another Ohio Democrat, Wayne Hays, high ranking on the Foreign Affairs Committee, has been aptly described by the Chicago *Tribune* as "one of the most petulant, unpredictable members of the House" whose floor speeches are "not infrequently somewhat crude and tinged with sarcasm." A harsh critic of foreign aid, Hays is nonetheless one of Congress' most widely traveled junketeers. Republican John M. Ashbrook, chairman of the American Conservative Union, is a national spokesman for right-wing groups, a zealot in the cause of unseating moderate or liberal Republicans, a defender of regimes like the Greek dictatorship or Ian Smith's white government in Rhodesia. Until 1970, another Ohio district sent to Congress a hard-driving young conservative named Donald E. Lukens, who first won fame when he won the chairmanship of the national Young Republicans on the rising Goldwater tide of the early 1960s. One of the most skilled grass-roots organizers of modern American politics, especially among the conservative young, Lukens first won nomination to Congress in 1966 by upsetting the hand-picked candidate of Ray Bliss's regular GOP organization. In 1970, he ran in the Republican gubernatorial primary but lost; later he was awarded a vacated state senate seat and may well be heard of again.

Other Ohio Congressmen of note include two Cleveland Democrats— Charles A. Vanik, member of the powerful Ways and Means Committee and a leading fighter for antipollution programs to save Lake Erie, and Louis Stokes, hard-working brother of former Mayor Carl Stokes and a rising power among blacks in the House. Democrat Thomas L. Ashley of Toledo has been

---

* An amusing and thorough account of Kirwan and his works appears in *The Case Against Congress*, by Drew Pearson and Jack Anderson, pages 284–288. To Kirwan's credit, it should be recorded that he usually left operation of the Democratic Congressional Committee to its executive director, Kenneth Harding, one of the most fair-minded and honorable political professionals in the U. S. today.

a leading advocate of social welfare legislation. On the Republican side, Charles W. Whalen of Dayton, a former economics professor, became an anti-military maverick on the Armed Services Committee and one of his party's most outspoken and articulate opponents of American involvement in the Vietnam war.

Of all the men Ohio has sent to Congress in recent times, none has exercised such vital leadership as soft-spoken, diminutive William M. Mc-Culloch, ranking Republican on the House Judiciary Committee. McCulloch is a product of the flat, rich farmlands of western Ohio, some of the most conservative territory in the U.S.A., and for most of his career he was an obscure Congressman whose voting record reflected the cautious conservatism of his constituents. But in the 1960s, McCulloch became an articulate and obstinate fighter to win for American Negroes the basic rights he saw as theirs under the Constitution. McCulloch's role in conciliating various proposals for reform, in drafting and then winning the essential Republican support for the civil rights acts of 1964, 1965, and 1968, was essential to their passage. Fighting for extension of the 1965 voting rights act over opposition of his own party's administration in 1969, McCulloch said that the legislation provided "for the thrust of black power in the best tradition of America—at the polling place." Ironically, few of the millions of American Negroes to benefit from the legislation McCulloch made possible will have ever heard of the unassuming figure from the Ohio farmlands for whom constitutional and human rights were more important than normal political advantage. Because of ill health, McCulloch announced he would retire from Congress in January 1973.

Cleveland, Now

Cleveland . . . is the ethnic family trapped in a flat and going to the dogs. . . . It is neighborhood after neighborhood after neighborhood. It is more suburbia than a bulldozer could love. Cleveland is industry: huge complexes that create steel and a Central Avenue that shouts. Cleveland is young, old, middle-aged, and everything else. Cleveland is Lake Erie and those who, from one year to the next, never see the lake at all. Cleveland is the Catholic nun, the train station bum, a thousand housewives, and on that corner the man dressed as a woman. Cleveland is Euclid Avenue, a neighbor named Krtchmareck, and the Shaker trolley. Cleveland is expressways and narrow alleys. . . .

Yet somewhere in this—between the Cleveland Tower and the melancholy neighborhoods and the pleasing suburbs decked out in early American Formica and the factories and all the people these items feast upon —exists the dream, the beauty, and the anger that is Cleveland. Because Cleveland is much more than an empty terminal lobby, where on days the wind blows cold, old men assemble, waiting to die. Cleveland is not waiting to die.

—Dick Perry, Ohio: A Personal Portrait of the 17th State

Cleveland has about as much charm as an automobile cemetery or the inside of a dynamo.

—*John Gunther*, Inside U. S. A.

Two million Americans—one out of every 100 residents of the nation —live today in what is called the Cleveland metropolitan area,* a megalapolitan mix of factories, warehouses, docks, high rises, freeways, tenements, bungalows, ramblers, shopping centers, schools and universities, churches, parks, and turgid rivers that stretches some 45 miles along the shores of Lake Erie and for an average of 10 miles inland. Cleveland's first reason for being was as a modest port city, spurred to growth from 1832 onward when it began to receive goods shipped on the Erie Canal, that great man-made transportation invention of the 19th century. Then, after the Civil War, big industry came: steelmaking after the first iron ore shipment arrived from the Lake Superior region in 1852, oil refining dating from 1862 when John D. Rockefeller began the operations that would lead to that monopoly to end all monopolies, the Standard Oil Company.

Today, according to its promoters, Cleveland is "a major iron and steel producer, research center, transportation center, and world port." It makes machine tools, industrial equipment, and motor vehicles; it still refines vast quantities of oil and is deep into petrochemicals; it is a global leader in iron ore management and supply; the printing and publishing industries furnish income, and it is even alleged that the area leads the world in hothouse tomatoes. Cleveland is a potent headquarters city for great industries; in fact 16 of the top 500 U.S. industrial corporations, among them such heavies as TRW, Republic Steel, Eaton Yale & Towne, White Motor, Standard Oil (Ohio), Addressograph Multigraph, and Hanna Mining (George Humphrey's old firm) are Cleveland-based.

But while the production of goods is the main thing that Cleveland is all about, it does offer other amenities: an "emerald necklace" of fine parks that ring the city, one of the nation's finest art galleries, the superb Cleveland Symphony Orchestra, directed until his death in 1970 by George Szell, a public library system more heavily used than almost any other in America, American League baseball (the Indians) and National League football (the celebrated Browns). And it has a prestige university, Case Western Reserve, which resulted from the merger of Case (known for its scientific disciplines) and Western Reserve (liberal arts, medicine, engineering, and law).

First to settle the city were New Englanders, then Irish to dig the canal and build the railroads, then more Easterners, and from the 1870s onward, a flood of Germans, Irish, Welsh, French, Scots, Bohemians, Jews, Poles, Slovenes, Lithuanians, Hungarians, Rumanians, Italians, Czechs, and Russians to man the hearths, refine the oil, and build, build, build the city. At one time three-quarters of Cleveland's people were foreign born; the descendants of these people, called the "cosmos," still fill almost every block of Cleve-

* Cuyahoga County (1970 population 1,721,300), containing Cleveland itself, represents the lion's share of the metropolitan area population, but sometime in the 1950s suburban Cuyahoga surged ahead of the city proper in population, a trend not likely to be reversed in the lifespan of anyone alive today.

land's West Side with well-defined little ghettos, each preserving its own customs, languages, religions, foods, and costumes. Cleveland offers, for instance, the only Rumanian folk art museum this side of Rumania; the ethnic festival days are too numerous to count. No less than 63 separate ethnic groups have been identified on the West Side; often their children move out to Parma or other working class suburbs while the old folks stay on in the city to protect their hard-earned homes and vote against new taxes. Except for a couple of black enclaves of many decades' standing, the West Side is all white (and determined to stay that way); block after block the old wood frame houses and narrow yards march on in dreary procession, the residential monotony relieved only by corner stores and markets, churches of a hundred faiths, and a few dismal old fortress-like structures called schools. The only variation to the "cosmo" flavor is offered by pockets of impoverished Appalachian whites up from the hills of Kentucky, West Virginia, and Tennessee.

Cleveland's East Side is as black (except for the central business district, which it encompasses) as the West Side is white. Between the two there is the natural barrier of the Cuyahoga River, twisting filthily through center city and lined by warehouses, terminals, and railroad tracks. Negroes have lived in Cleveland since early in the 19th century, but the great black influx began with World War I and continued until the late 1960s. Gradually the blacks forced the cosmos out of old neighborhoods like Hough (scene of a cataclysmic riot in 1966) and Glenville (where black militants and police staged a celebrated shoot-out in 1968). The visitor to Hough today sees hundreds of deserted buildings, refuse-strewn lawns, streetfront churches, metal grills on store windows, and evidence of the revival in the wake of the 1966 upheaval: community development centers, headquarters for militant groups, black capitalism (like Jet Foods, a spiffy black-run supermarket), and the impressive but struggling new Martin Luther King Plaza, with stores and apartments.

The fundamental change in Cleveland's population which led to the racial outbreaks of the 1960s (and coincidentally to a black mayor) emerges from a glance at the population figures. Between 1950 and 1970, the population of Cleveland proper declined from 914,808 to 750,903, a loss of more than 150,000. But what is most fascinating about the net loss of population is that more than 300,000 whites fled the city during the 20-year period, while at the same time the Negro population rose about 100 percent (to 287,841). Population projections to the year 1990 suggest there will be 480,000 black people in Cuyahoga County, of whom 408,000 will be in Cleveland. The city will be 60 to 65 percent black. But by virtue of continued white population growth in the suburbs, blacks will not represent more than a sixth of the total county population. Ironically, the swank Cleveland suburbs—of which Shaker Heights is without question the most famous *—lie to the east of the city; the well-to-do white commuters to center Cleveland must pass through

---

* Shaker Heights' exclusiveness has actually been diluted by a trickle of Jews and blacks, integrated into this bastion of wealth with remarkable success. The really exclusive, posh suburbs now lie further east of the city: Pepper Pike, Hunting Valley, Gates Mills, and the like.

the black population belt on their way to downtown and back home each day.

Cleveland's center remains its Public Square, dominated by the grim old 52-story Terminal Tower. The square harbors a ghastly war memorial and is the hub from which the great avenues—Euclid, Superior, and Ontario—spoke out to all directions save north, a course which would soon land one in Lake Erie. For more than a generation, center city atrophied; then in the 1960s came the $250 million Erieview urban renewal project which will eventually mean more than 40 new buildings over a 200-acre area. But Erieview was developed as a business office and political center, not for retailing or entertainment; in fact the space between its clean, soaring new towers is antiseptic and all too often devoid of people and life. The streets are often dead after the 150,000 commuter bankers, lawyers, merchants, and secretaries desert downtown at the close of business each day.

Yet Cleveland is now experiencing a surge of private office building, and not too far distant from downtown is the campus of the new Cleveland State University, which one day may be drawn closer by revival along Euclid Avenue. (The other city area of principal growth in recent years has been University Circle, home of Case Western Reserve, many cultural institutions, and modern industrial expansion.) While a number of older factories are closing down their Cleveland locations to shift to the suburbs, no one suggests that the Terminal Tower, the stock exchange, the big oil refineries or steel mills are about to desert center Cleveland. On a scale of urban viability, Cleveland would seem to fall somewhere between lusty, vigorous Chicago and decadent Detroit.

Few world cities have so despoiled their natural environment, or moved so close to choking on their own pollutants, as Cleveland. The symbol of this is the slimy, chocolate-brown Cuyahoga River, bubbling with subsurface gases, filled with phenols, oils, and acids from the steel mills and refineries along its banks. (Among the denizens of the Cuyahoga's downtown "flats" area are Republic Steel, U. S. Steel, Sherwin-Williams Paint, Standard Oil, and National Sugar Refining.) The Cuyahoga, indeed, is the only river of the U.S.A. to be officially declared a fire hazard; on one June day of 1969, its oil-slicked waters burst into flames and burned with such intensity that two railroad bridges that span it were nearly destroyed. Now Cleveland's two fireboats cruise the river periodically, hosing off docks and pilings so that the inflammable materials will be freed to move downstream and into Lake Erie. According to the Federal Water Pollution Control Administration, "The lower Cuyahoga has no visible life, not even low forms such as leeches and sludge worms that usually thrive on wastes."

All of this leaves untold the air pollution problem Cleveland faces; according to the Center for Air Pollution Control of the U. S. Public Health Service, the city ranks fifth in the nation for filthy air—behind New York, Chicago, Philadelphia, and Los Angeles. The situation is especially serious on days when there is a cloud cover and little wind off Lake Erie; then the smoke from Cleveland's steel mills, power plants, building furnaces, and automobiles casts a sickening smog over the city.

Should the day ever come when Cleveland's air and water are once more clean and wholesome, one wonders if the city can ever reverse the planning errors which separate it so sadly from the view of the lake which first gave it birth. In sharp contrast to Chicago, which preserved inviolate the view to Lake Michigan across open parkland, Cleveland allowed its access to Lake Erie to be cluttered by the nation's first lakeside expressway and by a wide swatch of industrial no man's land dotted with power plants and junk-strewn empty lots. Few American cities have shown such a callous disregard for their greatest natural asset.

A brief word on rapid transit, perhaps the only area in which Cleveland of late can be said to have made more progress than its sister cities. Cleveland introduced the country's first new postwar rapid transit service in 1955, part of a line that has now stretched to 19 miles—an S-shaped route that runs from East Cleveland, through downtown, and out to the Hopkins International Airport. The airport extension, completed in 1968, made Cleveland the first—and to date the only—city to provide a direct rapid transit line for its airport travelers.

Metropolitan-scale government reorganization seems likely to occupy the Cleveland area in the 1970s, with proposals abroad to bolster the county government and give it a strong executive and power to contract with cities and towns for a wide array of services. But Cleveland is somewhat unique among the major cities in that the existing financial arrangements do not seem to result in the suburbs milking the center city; the city is permitted to retain, for instance, three-quarters of the 1 percent payroll tax it imposes on suburbanites working in town. This does not mean that Cleveland has incorruptible government with adequate schools, streets, police and fire protection, garbage collection, or snow removal (in fact all are deficient, and some corrupt). And it is now beginning to face an incredible budget squeeze (tax collections down, wages of city employees way up).

Power in Cleveland

Over Cleveland's history, corrupt political machines and waves of reform have come one after the other. The major political parties have switched places in ascendancy. Mayors and city governments have come and gone. But one thing has remained constant for a century: the steady hand of self-interested control by the powerful moneyed and industrial forces. Under Mark Hanna's rapacious regime, the control was blatant and direct. But business control remained firm behind the scenes during the reform movement that gave Cleveland one of America's most progressive governments early in the century, and later during the cosmo period of control from the early 1930s to recent times. In 1967, it was the decision of the business elite that made the black man Carl Stokes mayor of Cleveland, a decision which cynics said was based less on a belief in equal rights than a desire to buy peace and protect Cleveland against racial riot and the destruction of property. To this date, the doughty old Union Club at 13th and Euclid, home of the power structure (the club of men like George Humphrey or Republic Steel's Thomas Patton), has yet to admit a single member who is black or Jewish.

Perhaps the most powerful single individual in Cleveland is a man who says, "I've always wanted to stay in the background": John W. ("Jack") Reavis, senior law partner of the 100-man law firm of Jones, Day, Cockley and Reavis. Reavis' power stems from the firm's close ties with the major industries and banks it represents; the client list reads like a *Who's Who* of firms headquartered or operating in Cleveland, ranging from Hanna Mining, Republic Steel, Cleveland Trust, and Sherwin-Williams to General Motors, Chrysler, and Firestone Tire and Rubber. Reavis himself is a director of Jones and Laughlin Steel, National City Bank, Westinghouse Electric, and several other behemoths of the industrial and financial world; other partners in his firm represent still more powerful industries. H. Chapman Rose, a partner in Reavis' firm, helped George Humphrey set up the million-dollar iron ore development project of Iron Ore Company of Canada, a firm in which Hanna Mining and Republic Steel each own a quarter interest. Rose served as U. S. Assistant Secretary of the Treasury under Humphrey and has close ties to the Nixon administration.

Reavis' political identification is safely Republican; he has been a member, for instance, of the $1,000-a-head Republican Booster Club to elect new Republican members of Congress. But in Cleveland, he was a major political backer of Democrat Carl Stokes—even though a member of his own firm, Seth Taft, was the Republican mayoralty candidate defeated by Stokes in 1967. Reavis' civic interests have included chairmanship of the Businessmen's Interracial Committee, a group of leading white industrialists and bankers and black businessmen who work in the fields of housing, education, and employment. He was named by Stokes as a member of the six-man expenditures committee to apportion funds under Stokes's highly publicized "Cleveland Now" program, and it was his intervention, at Stokes' request, that many thought responsible for state passage of an open housing law. He is a member of the Inner City Action Committee, set up in the wake of the Hough riots, and also a member of the board of trustees of Case Western University. So extensive are Reavis' activities in race relations that the Cleveland NAACP bestowed on him its Human Rights award. In perhaps overdrawn fashion, left-wing critics of Reavis suggest that all his civil rights and urban interests are designed, like the election of Stokes, to keep the lid on race tensions in order to protect the investments of big industry. Even if one rejects that interpretation, it seems hard to believe that Reavis would carry his support of black advancement to the point where uncomfortable confrontation would emerge between the city's dispossessed and its great wealthy industries.

Cleveland's industrial firms and utilities (power, gas, telephone) tend to exercise greater weight than its banks, even though the latter, as we have seen in the Reavis example, are closely tied to the ruling circle. One of the most powerful utility executives is Ralph Besse, chairman of the board of Cleveland Electric Illuminating Corporation, his firm's most progressive leader in many decades. Special spheres of power also belong to City Hall, the board of education, private welfare organizations, and especially the Cleveland *Plain-Dealer*. Quiescent in earlier years, the *P-D* was sold to the Newhouse chain in the 1960s but nevertheless moved to more vigorous leadership under editor Thomas Vail. In 1967, for instance, it ran a page one editorial urging Stokes's nomination for mayor. *P-D* news coverage is often first rate, although some of its aggressive young reporters complain that stories in controversial areas (especially if they would be to the disadvantage of the business establishment) are quashed.

Concurrently, the Cleveland *Press* has become more timid in its news coverage and editorial stands, perhaps as a result of the retirement in the mid-1960s of veteran editor Louis Seltzer, a strong-willed little bantam rooster of a man who delighted in playing the role of the king-maker in Cleveland and statewide politics. Every Cleveland mayor from Frank Lausche to Ralph Locher (Stokes' predecessor) was picked by Seltzer, and the Seltzer blessing had not a little to do with Rhodes' rise to power. The *Press*, a Scripps-Howard paper, is locked in a spirited and losing circulation war with the *Plain-Dealer*; *Press* circulation is mostly among Cleveland's sturdy working classes, while the *P-D* is read more by the intelligentsia and throughout much of northern Ohio.

No review of the Cleveland scene should omit the powerful, progressive-minded twins of its philanthropic world, the Cleveland Foundation and the Greater Cleveland Associated Foundation (GCAF). The Cleveland Foundation was the pioneer community foundation of the U.S.A., founded in 1914, and currently uses the proceeds from its $130 million capitalization (largest of any comparable foundation in the country) to fund a wide variety of programs in fields such as health, family planning, care of children and the aged, scholarships, university development, recreation, and family services. Some 1,700 Clevelanders have made gifts or left bequests to the foundation since its founding, most with no instructions save an admonition to use the funds for the Cleveland community. Determined to be more of a cutting edge in solving concrete urban problems, the foundation a decade ago spawned the GCAF. This group functions almost as a surrogate for timid municipal and county government, concentrating on experimental solutions to some of the toughest urban problems.

A common staff and the same director, Dr. James A. Norton, serve both the Cleveland Foundation and GCAF. Norton is a quiet, scholarly native of rural Louisiana who has shown remarkable skill in managing millions of dollars in foundation funds and dealing with Cleveland's power elite, many of whom (including Reavis and his law firm) have been closely connected with various foundation programs. The GCAF has been accused of an amount of "self-dealing"—making grants to organizations represented by individuals who were trustees or former employees of GCAF. GCAF funds have not gone into controversial areas which might upset the local business establishment, such as air and water pollution control. But the foundation has moved courageously in many other areas where normal political pressures might have forestalled official government action for years or permanently; even if the foundation, as some of its critics charge, is an "elitist" tool, it has doubtless moved further than many of its original benefactors ever dreamed in creating a more open and responsive society in Cleveland.

The Stokes Saga

Out of the red-clay country of northern Georgia, a restless young woman named Louise Stone came to Cleveland in the mid-1920s looking for a better way of life. Soon she married a quiet, strong, low-wage worker named Charles Stokes and bore him two sons. While the boys were still infants—Louis, 2½, and Carl, one year old—Charles Stokes died, and Louise Stokes went to work for wealthy ladies in the suburbs to earn some $15 a week, often resorting to welfare payments when work was unavailable.

Louis, the elder son, was a serious student, on his way to law school by the mid-1940s. But Carl grew up as an extroverted talker, no stranger to the East Side streets and poolrooms, a high school dropout at the age of 17. Then he went off to World War II, matured a lot, got his high school diploma and used the GI Bill to make his way through college and law school. Along the way he worked at a series of temporary jobs, including that of a dining-car waiter on the Rock Island Railroad. In 1947 he got his first patronage job—as a liquor inspector; after law school, there was private law practice with his brother, appointment as an assistant city prosecutor, then several terms in the state legislature. By the mid-1960s, it was clear that Carl Stokes would indeed be somebody. An articulate man of immense personal charm, he could deal on equal terms with the people of the ghetto out of which he had risen and the business-political elite alike. Those who knew his work in the legislature were impressed with his depth. And thus it was that Carl Stokes in 1967 became the first Negro mayor of a major city in American history. A year later his brother Louis was elected to the Congress.

Why did a city still 63 percent white elect a black mayor? The first relevant fact is that it barely did so—by a margin of only 2,501 votes in 1967, or 3,678 votes for reelection two years later, and with disputed vote tallies in each election. The second reason is the sorry state to which Cleveland had sunk by the mid-'60s; as the Cleveland *Press* wrote, it was "a city on dead center—shut off from federal funds, slum-ridden, air and water polluted, streets grimy and unsafe, crime rising, funds short, taxes high, schools inadequate, racially tense, saddled with a costly yet inadequate public transportation system." For a quarter century, the town had been afflicted with a series of caretaker mayors, the last of them, Ralph Locher, so incompetent that the Federal Department of Housing and Urban Development felt obliged early in 1967 to cut off several millions of dollars for already-approved urban renewal projects. Not long afterwards, the Moody Bond Survey reduced the city's credit rating.

Race relations had been deteriorating steadily since 1964 when a young white minister threw himself before a bulldozer at a protest at a school site and was crushed to death. Hough had erupted in the summer of 1966 in a five-day battle of firearms and firebombs, followed by more violence in April 1967. Locher's police chief was photographed in Hough during the riots wearing sports slacks, carrying a hunting rifle, and promising to get him one. Thus the blacks were totally unified, the business establishment appalled about what might happen next, and there was the candidate—Carl Stokes—a black man everyone found hard to dislike, his candidacy made respectable by the *Plain-Dealer* endorsement. To pick up the white support he needed, Stokes crossed over to the West Side and radiated the image of the sincere young man, fair-minded on race and aware of issues, at countless small gatherings. A Ford Foundation grant to the Cleveland chapter of CORE helped get blacks registered. On primary day, Stokes picked up better than 95 percent of the black vote and 15 percent of the white vote. Because blacks voted in far greater numbers, he won. In the general election, essentially the same pattern was repeated to give Stokes his victory over his moderate Republican opponent, Seth Taft, nephew of the late Senator; in 1969 the pattern worked again to win Stokes reelection, this time over a "cosmo" type opponent.

Stokes's candidacy had a cathartic effect on the black people of Cleveland; their attitude after the Stokes election was exultant and possessive: "He's *our* mayor," or as one of Stokes's campaign workers put it, "Where there was no hope at all for black people, now they got hope."

The primary effect of Stokes' first years was psychological, reversing the pessimism and despair of the Locher years. "In just 12 months we had begun turning Cleveland completely around and started the city to moving again," Stokes boasted with some justification after a year in office. The federal spigot for every type of aid was turned on again, the city's credit rating was restored, a port authority necessary for future economic growth was voted, as was the $100 million sewage bond issue. Within two years, 5,000 units of low-cost housing were going up—more than in the entire previous two decades. In the wake of Martin Luther King's assassination, Stokes walked the ghetto streets for five days urging the black community to stay cool, and it did. A multimillion dollar program called "Cleveland: Now!" was announced, encompassing every possible federal aid for the city along with renewal aids by the business community; the program was mostly a public relations gimmick, but it had its intended psychological lift for the city.

But like every "hero mayor," Stokes began to encounter problems. Some he inherited—including a blatantly racist police force hostile to the idea of a black mayor. But many problems stemmed from Stokes' unwillingness to deal with members of the powerful city council—an unwieldy 33-man body that reflects Cleveland's multiple ethnic nuances—or with others on a basis of mutual respect. Stokes' major legislative proposals were presented on a take-it-or-leave-it basis as emergency legislation, offending natural allies. Even black councilmen were treated in a cavalier fashion. Critics noted that while

Stokes' only visible source of income was his $25,000 city salary, he was living in a large house, sending a child to private school, wearing modish suits and monogrammed shirts, and carrying expensive cigars.

For a long time the newspapers and establishment forces in the city remained friendly to Stokes, seeing him as the one man who could keep peace in the city. But eventually they became disillusioned with the lack of concrete performance and Stokes' abrasive ways. By 1971, federal aid has slowed down and the city was headed for a deficit of as much as $10 million. With thoughts in mind of becoming a potent national black political leader, freed of the burdens of the mayoralty, Stokes announced his retirement. In the Democratic primary, he gave a last-minute endorsement to wealthy lawyer-developer James Carney, not because he wanted Carney elected but in order to humiliate his arch foe on the city council and Democratic organization favorite, Anthony Garafoli. The so-called 21st District Congressional District Caucus put together by Stokes and his brother Louis mounted a last-minute telephone blitz in the black wards and defeated Garafoli. But immediately, Stokes endorsed a black man, Cleveland School Board president Arnold Pinkney, who was running as an independent in the general election.

Stokes' objective was clear: to make Cleveland a kind of pilot city to show black political "clout," manipulating Negro voters in a way that would impress the national Democratic party and its 1972 national convention. The strategy backfired disastrously. Instead of electing Pinkney—or Carney—the voters elected Republican Ralph Perk, the Cuyahoga County auditor, a scrappy five-foot, seven-inch favorite of the ethnic communities. (As one correspondent reported, "Perk can speak Czech, dance Slovak, sing Polish and pray Bohemian—not to mention that he married an Italian girl.) Perk had promised in his campaign to "unshackle" the police department and restore financial integrity to City Hall. His election was the first Republican mayoralty victory in Cleveland in 30 years. (He got 38.7 percent, Pinkney 31.8 percent and Carney 28.7 percent.) But the main significance was what the election had to say about the black vote. As Horace Busby, a Washington-based consultant to state and local governments and onetime special assistant to President Johnson, said in a *National Journal* interview:

It would suggest to me that you're not going to get the black monolithic vote that Stokes and his group had been dreaming about. You're past the cohesive "It's Us Against Whitey" stage in the metropolitan areas. Cleveland indicates that black politicians . . . just can't get [their votes] by talking up racial issues or simply by being black. The novelty is gone among their own people.

Columbus: The City the Wolfes Run

Well-scrubbed, provincial, and complacent, Columbus is a spacious plains city whose spirit is entirely Midwestern and logical: set almost dead center in Ohio because it is the state capital, laid out on an orderly grid system, with the inevitable central square at its very center, and in the middle of that square, the State House.

It is hard to believe that Columbus now has more than half a million people (officially 539,677 in 1970) within its borders; somehow the old rural flavor lingers on and on. The people have a lot of lebensraum; the city's land area, vastly expanded by postwar annexations, is the largest in Ohio, complete with inner belt, outer belt, split-level suburbs, and industrial parks. German was the dominant gene of Columbus' early history, but the strains are now well mixed with pockets of West Virginians, Kentuckians, and Negroes, and a tiny share of foreign born. No American city of Columbus' size seems so homogeneous and middle class in every way. In 1968, continuing its long-standing conservative voting habit, Columbus gave the Nixon-Agnew ticket one of its strongest majorities in the nation's cities.

Maynard E. Sensenbrenner, the man who has been Columbus' mayor most of the past decade, is a Democrat, a conservative, and a deep believer in brotherhood. In 1965, he was given the Fiorello LaGuardia Award for being the best mayor in the nation. In his lapel, Sensenbrenner wears an inch-square rhinestone-encrusted American flag. He likes to quote the Bible and is active in the Boy Scouts. And he is fond of telling visitors that the key to the success of his All-American city is not just "planning and doing and letting everybody have his say. No siree," Sensenbrenner insists, "you need a lot more than that—a dynamic faith in God and a dynamic faith in the United States and a dynamic faith that you can be anything that you want to be. And that old spizzerinktum. Now that's 1000 percent better than enthusiasm. If you've got it, you've got everything."

In 1969, however, Columbus' carefully nurtured image as a "clean city" was tarnished a bit when Justice Department officials charged that "almost every member of the vice squad" had been paid off by gamblers and that the Columbus police had obstructed efforts at a federal crackdown. A series of indictments was lodged against eight members of the force and a reputed numbers kingpin. Justice Department officials also disclosed that they were looking into the mayor's $100 Club, an organization of political donors never publicly disclosed, as well as salary kickbacks by political appointees to their employers. By 1971, Columbus voters had tired of Mayor Sensenbrenner and defeated him for reelection in favor of Republican Tom Moody. But even then, Sensenbrenner lost by only 1,000 votes out of 155,000 cast.

The Columbus *Dispatch* building, facing onto the city's central square a few yards from the State House, is topped by a great red neon sign proclaiming the *Dispatch* "Ohio's Greatest Home Newspaper." Inside the foyer, one discovers two of the grimmest portraits of modern *homo sapiens* I have ever seen: the cold, arrogant, calculating faces of Robert Frederick Wolfe and Harry Preston Wolfe, founders of what may well be the most powerful and ruthless single-city based communications and economic establishment of the United States. Laughed and sneered at (though usually in private), the Wolfe empire still has an iron grip on Columbus, even though the founders have long since gone on to their reward.

The Wolfe brothers made their first fortune by founding the Wolfe Wear-U-Well Shoe Corporation, which turned out to be a fabulously successful manufacturing and retail operation. Then, early in this century, they got control of the *Dispatch*. Next came bank acquisitions leading to formation of Banc-Ohio, a far-flung holding firm which by the 1960s controlled 22 central Ohio banks, including the largest in Columbus, with deposits of some $700 million. The present-day Wolfes also control the Ohio Company, a large securities underwriting firm with about 26 offices in Ohio. They own hundreds of acres of choice Ohio farmlands and include in their portfolio Columbus radio and television stations WBNS. (The call letters stand for Wolfe Banks Newspapers & Shoes.) The Wolfes also own the Neil House, Columbus' leading hotel, plus extensive other downtown real estate.

"The Wolfe clan is involved in all that transpires. You bank with them, you may rent from them, you hire your employees through their newspapers, you advertise your goods in their papers, you get your view of the world from the news they carry in their papers and on their television stations," a local businessman told me. Even after death, a man's estate may well fall under Wolfe control, for it is reported that for decades the Wolfes have had absolute control of the county probate court, which often assigns estates to the Wolfe-owned Ohio National Bank. Frustrated in earlier decades in their desire to take control of Ohio State University, the Wolfes now have a close ally in president Novice Fawcett. Often they control the county sheriff and the chief of police as well. For decades, the Wolfes have had close connections to politicians, especially Republicans; at their summer place, called the Wigwam, they have been entertaining GOP bigwigs ever since the days of Hoover and Landon. John Gunther reported that at the Wigwam the Wolfes kept pet wolves.

The *Dispatch* is a pedestrian newspaper that reportedly makes little money for the Wolfes (radio and television are far more profitable). But of course control of the news is a key to economic and political control.

Of the two founders, Robert Wolfe, who had once served a term in the penitentiary for jailbreaking after being incarcerated for assault in a barroom brawl, met his end by falling off the top of the *Dispatch* building; Harry, who got his start as a lamplighter, died in his bed in 1946. Robert's son Edgar is now dead too, but his grandson John runs the bank. Harry's son Preston, now in his sixties, is a small, plump man with a cold stare who for decades has been the real ruler of the clan. Preston is president of the Dispatch Company, while his brother Robert, said to be something of a playboy, is board chairman and publisher.

About the only significant counterforce to the Wolfe group in Columbus is the prestigious Lazarus family, owner of Columbus' leading department store (and the Federated Department Stores chain). The Lazarus family tends to support liberal, usually non-organization Democratic candidates locally, but has shown little taste for an open power struggle with the Wolfes.

Columbus' industrial development has been on a strong upswing ever since 1940, when the federal government erected a large aircraft plant later taken over by private interests. Initially low wages, especially compared to northern Ohio, attracted many industrial plants, which could draw on an ample labor supply in neighboring rural Ohio and the Appalachian belt; eventually many highly trained technical and professional personnel were hired as well. Today, Columbus' largest industrial payrolls are those of firms like Western Electric, Westinghouse, General Electric, North American Rockwell, and GM-Fisher Body. And contributing not a little to Columbus' enduring rural flavor is the Ohio State Fair, a piece of country Americana reminding one that there is something besides industry in Ohio.

Ohio State University, located out a dreary stretch of road northeast of center city with 38,000 students and 12,000 employees, has itself been a major factor in Columbus' economic growth. Considering its parsimonious financing by the state government, the university has advanced quite respectably in academic quality. It was said to have one of the more docile U.S. student bodies until 1970, when the campus erupted in a series of demonstrations in which 26 persons were wounded by shotgun blasts and scores were injured, and Governor Rhodes ordered 1,200 National Guardsmen onto the campus. The OSU disturbances rivaled—except for the casualties—those at Kent State, 120 miles to the northeast of Columbus.

But it was the Kent State incident—with demonstrators' vandalizing of downtown stores, the burning of an ROTC building, and then the death of the four students—which aroused the entire nation. The President's Commission on Campus Disorders later reported that the deaths were "unnecessary, unwarranted, and inexcusable," but when a special state grand jury handed down indictments, it was 25 students and sympathizers—and no National Guardsmen—who were indicted. Governor Rhodes was quick to call out the National Guard while he was in office and in fact sent it onto the Kent State campus without giving the university advance notification. A more restrained use of Guardsmen seems likely in the Gilligan administration; while he refrained from making an open political issue of Kent State, Gilligan did say the Guard troops should not have been permitted to load their weapons without specific approval of a superior officer. All the OSU and Kent State post-mortems, however, leave troublesomely unanswered the questions of how such a terrifying chasm in attitudes and standards could have opened between the staid burghers of the middle-class society and their children on the campuses.

The autumn after Ohio State and Kent State erupted, there was another great mob scene in Columbus as thousands of students surged along High Street, lighting bonfires, drinking, and smashing bottles. But now the police were all smiles, for the occasion was a different one: celebrating Ohio State's defeat of its undefeated archrival, Michigan, thus assuring the home team a berth in the Rose Bowl. "The [police] condone football because this is how things were 30 years ago," a coed senior from Toledo told a reporter. "But if we demonstrated against the war or on local issues, they'd come down hard on us."

Cincinnati: Soft Charm in a Heartland City

> And this song of the Vine,
> This greeting of mine,
> The Winds and the birds shall deliver
> to the Queen of the West
> In her garlands dressed
> By the banks of the Beautiful River.
>
> —Henry Wadsworth Longfellow

Before Chicago was, and while Cleveland struggled to be more than a village, Cincinnati was one of America's great cities. Set fortuitously on America's early mainline to the West, the Ohio River, Cincinnati prospered as a port city, an early industrial center, a place of culture in the early 19th century, winning the sobriquet of Queen City from Longfellow and others before him. For decades, she was the largest American city west of the Alleghenies and north of New Orleans; in 1860, she was one of three American cities with a population of more than 100,000 people.

After the Civil War, the Ohio River was eclipsed as a main route to the West and Cincinnati began a long decline in relative population and importance; today her population (452,524 in 1970) places her 29th among American cities. But her charm and grace, what Gunther called "a certain stately and also sleepy quality, a flavor of detachment, soundness," lingers on in this most untypical of all heartland cities.

Geography and ethnic strains combine to give Cincinnati its unique flavor. The setting is not unlike a giant amphitheatre, with the legendary seven hills surrounding a lower central Basin along the grand curving sweep of the Ohio River. Some of the hills are steep in the extreme; many were vineyards in earlier times. Heights and water combine to give drama and excitement to the scene; one of the grandest urban vistas I have seen in America was from the blufftop home of Governor Gilligan just east of the city, seeing the twisting golden cord of the river in the late afternoon sun, the constant commerce of boat and barge along the great waterway, the riverside city enveloped in the haze of a dying day.

While middle and upper class people pushed first out to the hilltops, and then into outlying suburbia, the Basin has been the receptacle for the city's poor: Negroes over many decades (now 135,000 strong) and, especially in recent years, poor Southern Baptist white folks from Appalachia. On the eastern outskirts are the wealthiest suburbs, places like Hyde Park and Indian Hill, home of the aristocratic Tafts (who have been in Cincinnati since 1839) and other families of privilege like the Gambles, Guyers, Pogues, or Lazarus clan.

Cincinnati has long been said to have the most honest and efficient government of any large American city, and it is the largest governed by a city manager. It was not always so. From the 1880s until 1925, the city was in the grasp of a corrupt, conscienceless Republican machine. The leader for almost 30 years was a former saloonkeeper named George B. Cox, who became a bank president and millionaire but never lost his touch for predatory politics, keeping a card file on the personal lives and arrests of citizens, dispensing city jobs to ward heelers and many incompetents (including some illiterates). Occasional reformers tried to clean out the Augean stables of city government, but lacked staying power; permanent change did not come until the 1920s when influential and dedicated rebels, mainly Republicans, persuaded the long-abused citizens of the city to approve a new home-rule charter. To keep the city government honest and efficient, the city manager for many years was paid one of the highest public salaries in the United States.

The Charter party early made the basic decision to continue as a party on its own, competing with the Democrats and the conventional Hamilton County Republicans. For years the Charterites were either a majority of the city council or—because of the unique system of proportional representation which Cincinnati kept for many decades—a potent and influential minority. The early Charter base was primarily in the silk-stocking hilltop areas, but during the New Deal the blacks and other underprivileged of the Basin joined as well. Trouble began to appear in the postwar era, when increased city reliance on federal aid led Republican and Democratic Charterites to split more and more frequently; since 1960 the regular Republicans have won all council elections, but the Charterites have formed an alliance with the Democrats and are an important minority still. The ethical standards of city government are still of the highest; since this was the first Charter goal, one must conclude that the movement was one of the most successful citizen reform efforts of modern urban history.

A Charterite from the start and doubtless the most distinguished Cincinnati citizen of the past half century has been Charles P. Taft, a warm-hearted and public-spirited man with enduring interest in liberal Republicanism, philanthropies, and national church work. "Charles Taft's loyalty and enthusiasm for bipartisan innovation," political scientist William H. Hessler wrote a few years ago, "have never wavered, despite the fact that his defiance of the regular Republican organization at the local level has surely cost him a distinguished career in national politics." Taft was elected a Charter council member in election after election, and also served as mayor in the 1950s. Yet his brother Robert stuck with regular GOP organization for life and never lost a chance to disparage or oppose the reform program in his home town.

As a result of the postwar suburban push, Cincinnati now has little more than a third of the population of the metropolitan area and a half of Hamilton County; a future generation of reform may lie in unification of the city and county governments, a proposal backed both by the mayor of the city and the president of the county commissioners.

Power in Cincinnati evolves predictably into the hands of a business-industrial elite, some of whom are Social Register types, some self-made men. Unlike Columbus, no single family dominates—there are too many powerful home-owned industries for that. And unlike Cleveland, there is no establishment of Democratic office-holders with which the normally Republican business elite must deal. The interests of the business elite and the Republican party seem close to identical; if it were not for the fact that both act in a relatively enlightened (though somewhat paternalistic) way, the result could be disastrous. Members of the elite are found to be on the interlocking boards of the great corporations, as chief supporters of the United Appeal campaigns, as powerful fund-raisers on their own, and as the finance and organizational backbone of the Hamilton County Republican organization.

When Gunther visited Cincinnati a quarter century ago, he found the slums in the Basin "among the most insufferable in the nation." A businessmen's group formed in the late '40s spearheaded the first step of renewal, clearing a monotonous square mile of grimy slums in the West End for a modern industrial-commercial complex with ready access to rail sidings and loading docks. In 1962, again at the businessmen's urging, Cincinnati voted $150 million toward partial or complete demolition and replacement of eight major downtown blocks. A $10 million convention exhibition hall rose, along with new high-rise office buildings, overhead pedestrian walkways, an underground garage beneath Fountain Square, a new Contemporary Arts Center, and a $40 million sports stadium for the Cincinnati Reds baseball team and an American League football team. Downtown emerged elegantly refurbished, a place of shape and character.

Cincinnati has never aspired to be a city of heavy industry like Akron or Cleveland, but she is no slouch in producing goods for a nation. Procter and Gamble, which started in 1837 with two brothers making and peddling tallow candles, lard oil, and German soap, is now the 30th largest industrial corporation of the U.S.A. (annual sales $2.5 billion).* The city has many medium-sized specialized industries that employ skilled workmen; many of these firms turn out machine tools; indeed Cincinnati bills herself as the machine tool capital of the world. She also produces the most playing cards of any city, and is big in everything from tin cans, chemicals, mattresses, and shoes to anchovy pizzas, jet engines, and pianos. (The pianos I am constrained to mention since my great-grandfather made his fortune producing them.) Cincinnati's economy today is so diversified that she seems almost depression-proof; the city is one of the last to feel a slump in the economy. In addition to P & G, her largest employers include Cincinnati Milling Machine, General Electric, and Monsanto. The city is also a banking and financial center and headquarters town of the Lazarus-owned Federated Department Stores and the Kroger Company.

And still there is the river, the lusty, busy Ohio coursing 981 miles from Pittsburgh (where the Allegheny and Monongahela Rivers meet) to Cairo, Illinois (where the mighty Mississippi awaits). The river made Cincinnati, and she is still its chief port city, even as the day of the side-wheelers and stern-wheelers recedes further into history. Today the Ohio carries twice the

---

* P & G could be a driving civic force but is so slow and cautious, both in business and public affairs, that its bright young men tend to leave. But its Washington lobbyist, Bryce Harlow, did indeed become Nixon's chief legislative strategist for two years.

freight tonnage of the Panama Canal and three times the design capacity of
the St. Lawrence Seaway, and it is practically all great bulk stuff in huge
tows of as many as 20 steel barges loaded with 20,000 pounds each—coal, iron
ore, oil, chemicals, metals, salt, sand, gravel. The Ohio River Valley has been
called the Ruhr of America, but it is a classic case of the son outgrowing the
father: since World War II, there has been the development of four Ruhr
Valleys in the stretch from Pittsburgh to Cairo. Coal is the greatest freight
item, much of it from West Virginia and Indiana fields destined for huge
steam generating plants along the river which furnish the needs of industries
(especially aluminum) with great electricity demands. Other coal barges will
be destined for Ohio towns like Steubenville, a place that breathes smoke
and fire and exhales great slabs of hot searing steel for the industrial machine
of the heartland.* Cincinnati watches the industrial flotilla pass her doorstep
but prefers for herself, if you please, a less gross way to make money.

Down the Population Ladder: Toledo—Akron— Dayton—Youngstown—Canton—Springfield

Brawny, thriving industry . . . downtown decay and the glimpse of renewal . . . ring on ring of suburbia . . . shopping centers with their parking
lots eating up the green earth . . . the world of the interstate road . . . and
somehow, an incessant insularity, even in the age of instant communications
—these are the hallmarks of Ohio's middle-ranked cities, down the population ladder from Toledo (383,818) to Springfield (81,926). Here is a quick
tour:

Set at the westernmost point of Lake Erie, not far from Detroit, Toledo
is a port of no mean proportions that receives 5,000 ships each year, many
from distant points of the globe—but the city has about as much international flavor as Omaha or Kansas City. As writer Dick Perry points out, "Few
youngsters running away to sea head to Toledo."

A multiplicity of ethnic groups make their home in Toledo, and the city
comes complete with a substantial black segment and its own Black Panthers
chapter, in bitter conflict with the established order. The Democratic party
is all-powerful and traditionally liberal in its outlook. Downtown Toledo is in
transformation from down-at-the-heels to modern steel-and-glass renewal, the
east side of town is well described as grimy and melancholy, close-in old neighborhoods harbor thousands of the lower middle class, and the forever growing suburbs show a new if dull face.

Rubber center of the universe, Akron (pop. 275,425) was made by, is
sustained by, and is totally dominated by the single product. Four of the five
great rubber makers have their home in Akron. Two of them, Firestone and
Goodyear, gross more than $2 billion a year; the other two, General Tire

---

* Steubenville, which has a population of 30,771, is apparently America's dirtiest city. It topped
the list of cities in visible particulate emissions—such as dirt, smoke and soot—in a 1970 study for the
National Pollution Control Administration. Enterprising reporters found the air so dirty that the grass
turned blue, houses turned black overnight, and cows' teeth fell out.

and Goodrich, are not far behind at more than $1 billion each. The great rubber names are everywhere—on schools, banks, country clubs, and residential sections. When the winds are unfavorable, the piercing smell of concentrated rubber chemicals pervades the town—but it is a sweet smell for the Akron businessman, for rubber means money.

Predictably, the 30,000-member United Rubber Workers union is important to Democratic politics (and by virtue of numbers, usually victorious); the rubber companies give backstage support to Republicans. Akron politics emphasizes reason and shuns extremism, a reflection in part of the moderate-to liberal editorial position and excellent news coverage of the Akron *Beacon-Journal*, perhaps the best newspaper in Ohio. (The *Journal* is the original newspaper in the Knight chain, which now includes the prosperous Miami *Herald*, the Detroit *Free Press*, the Charlotte *Observer*, the Philadelphia *Inquirer* and others—all papers that are a distinct credit to their communities, which is more than one can say of many newspaper chains in America.)

Set in a rich agricultural valley of southwestern Ohio, Dayton (pop. 243,-601) is a clean, well-governed town with a great deal of civic pride—although in 1971, it barely averted having to close down its public schools as the result of the voters' refusal to approve proposals for higher school taxes. The good government tradition of Dayton dates back to 1913, when it became the first major American city to adopt the commissioner-manager form of government, an indication of the early hope of reformers to "remove politics from government." Dayton used to be a safe Democratic area and was the home city of Governor James M. Cox, the 1920 Democratic Presidential nominee. But with the suburbs, conservatism has grown, and the overall area is now marginal politically. Cox's old paper, the Dayton *Daily News*, is the most liberal daily newspaper in Ohio today, counterbalanced in its home town by the moderately Republican *Journal-Herald*.

Passing through Dayton, I found it in the midst of a major building boom, with a number of buildings of distinction rising on a large urban renewal site.

Dayton has the ingredients of racial conflict—a large population of Kentucky and West Virginia hillbillies on its East Side, thousands of blacks (some 30 percent of the city population) on the poverty-stricken West Side. A major racial disturbance did break out in the summer of 1966, but at least an honest effort was made to improve the lot of blacks in the aftermath, with self-help centers, job training, and one of the country's pioneer model cities programs.

Dayton has been scoring other points on the race relations front. In 1970, Negro lawyer James H. McGee, long considered a civil rights militant, was chosen by his fellow city commissioners as mayor following the resignation of the incumbent. Dayton emerged as one of the country's outstanding law-enforcement cities, aided by imaginative programs funded in part under the 1968 Safe Streets Act.

Dayton has well diversified industry including a number of plants that require skilled labor, resulting in the highest average wages in Ohio. Over 30,000 workers are employed by five General Motors divisions, led by Frigidaire and

Delco. Dayton is remembered as the city where James Ritty's "mechanical drawer" began the cash register industry, and to this day National Cash Register employs well over 12,000.

Youngstown (pop. 139,788) and Canton (pop. 110,053) form with Akron a smoky, clanging triangle of heavy-industry towns southeast of Cleveland. Steel and gangsters are the two commodities for which Youngstown is most famous. The big steel mills are those of U. S. Steel, Republic Steel, and Youngstown Sheet and Tube, their hearths and rolling mills manned by Germans, Poles, Slovakians, Hungarians, and Italians. The gangsters are both of the home-grown and professional Mafia type, and bombings were a way of life until the quite recent past. Youngstown also has the distinction of being the first American city whose schools had to close down because the voters refused to approve taxes to pay for them. (Six times in two years, Youngstown voters voted down an increase in school taxes, not relenting until Dan Rowan and Dick Martin made them a national laughingstock on a nationally televised "Laugh-In" program in 1969.)

Labor strife, including killings, plus all sorts of vice and crooked dealings in city government, were the order of the day in Youngstown for decades. The city is a strong contender for the title of ugliest in the U.S.A. Labor dominates Democratic politics and in turn is dominated by the Steelworkers Union and the United Auto Workers; in a major surprise, the Republicans took over city hall in 1969, an occasion of unusual joy for the ultraconservative Youngstown *Vindicator.*

Canton is a workingman's town one would expect to vote solidly Democratic on the basis of its strong unions, heavy Catholic element (Polish, Rumanian, Italian, and Spanish-speaking), plus a Negro bloc. But it is actually a swing area, has had a Republican mayor for several years, and sends ultraconservative Republicans to the state legislature.

Finally, there is Springfield (pop. 81,926), a town in sad eclipse. Located some miles west of Columbus on the old National Road (now U. S. 40) that first opened up the heartland to surface travel, Springfield has a rich cultural history—home of Wittenberg University (founded in 1845), the place where hybrid corn began, birthplace of the 4-H Clubs, and a literary-publishing center through the Crowell-Collier Publishing Company (founded in the 1880s). But today, Springfield is an aging town of old frame houses and dingy brick buildings at its core. Many of the old family-owned businesses hold on, and the city still has its distinctively German-Lutheran-conservative flavor. But Crowell-Collier folded in the 1950s, the tax structure is deteriorating, public transportation is sick, and the population is static.

Mansfield, Ohio

The heart of Ohio, and its typicality, may well lie not in the great cities which we have, perforce, been discussing, but in the vast numbers of smaller cities that account for so much of its population and so much of its conservatism—places like Lima, Middletown, Marion, Zanesville, Lancaster, Portsmouth, Kent, Athens, Alliance, Chillicothe, Ashtabula. Before departing the Buckeye state we will pause in one of these—Mansfield, a manufacturing and supply center set about halfway between Columbus and Cleveland.

Mansfield sometimes votes Democratic for local offices but almost always Republican in state and national elections. The perceptive local newspaper editor, D. K. Woodman, summed up the present-day feelings of his city in these words: "Mansfield wants to conserve and protect what it has. We're part of the Nixon-Agnew silent majority. We have a deep resentment about violence on the campuses, and we abhor what is happening with black revolts in cities like Cleveland."

The town of Mansfield got its start as a county seat and service center for surrounding farm areas, a role it still plays. Today it is also a ski center, with two ski runs and lodges nearby; there are also three man-made lakes which make the area a boating and fishing center in the summer. Industry began to arrive in Mansfield with Tappan Stove in 1889, followed by Ohio Brass early in this century, then a Westinghouse plant, a local rubber factory and steel mill, and Fisher Body in the 1950s. The diversity protected Mansfield from the worst effects of the Great Depression and makes it relatively recession-proof today. More than 12,000 are employed in the major plants, labor unions have won their recognition battles with the large employers (though a few small plants still resist), and Mansfield's population has grown steadily from 37,154 in 1940 to 55,047 in 1970.

Power shifted early in the century from the farmers to the industrialists, and has remained with them ever since; they are a conservative and cautious lot who meet to make (or fail to make) the essential decisions for Mansfield at places like their exclusive Fifty-One Club in an old downtown building. Negroes and Jews are excluded from the elite country club, but it is liberal, intelligent Jews who have taken a leading role on the mayor's human relations committee and pressed the big employers to hire more blacks.

Where the establishment has clearly failed Mansfield is in saving its downtown area, a dreary mixture of old brick buildings and some old Victorian wood homes. With suburban shopping centers sprouting and parking an ever-greater problem, the downtown began to decline in the 1960s, and before long all but one of the major stores had fled; for ten years Mansfield has talked about urban renewal but has done nothing about it, and today there are scores of abandoned and empty stores.

Mansfield feels that its race relations are fairly good; blacks who came first via the Underground Railway, later for industrial jobs, account for 15 percent of the population and are small enough in numbers so that none of the city schools (integrated some 30 years ago) is predominantly black. The Negro leadership is split between an older preacher-teacher conservative faction and more militant younger blacks led by men like a local minister who is the nephew of Martin Luther King, Jr. The Negro standard of living is predictably far below the white average, not to mention any admission to the power structure. But the worst slums are occupied by Kentucky and Tennessee hillbillies who came to work for Tappan and proudly reject all offers of help.

Like virtually every American city, Mansfield has its pollution problems; a huge yellow cloud rises from the Empire Steel plant, fortuitously blown away from the city most of the time by the prevailing winds. But soot from the tire company and air-borne particles from the brass company are still a problem. Slowly, under pressure, the industrialists begin to take clean-up measures.

Radical change in Mansfield hardly seems in store, even as it heads into the late 20th century. A generally conservative and Republican tone is set by the Mansfield *News-Journal,* part of a chain owned by Harry Horvitz, a man whose home is in Shaker Heights near Cleveland. It is this same alliance of business-industrial interests with the organs of public opinion that seems to keep so much of Ohio on a steady, conservative course—avoiding, at all costs, open social conflict.

A touch of glamor has long applied to Mansfield, perhaps separating it from many other smaller Ohio cities. More than a century ago, railroad financiers used to meet in Mansfield, and Abraham Lincoln's name was first mentioned in regard to the Presidency at such a Mansfield gathering. Senator John Sherman of Antitrust Act fame was from Mansfield, and it was the birthplace of the late Pulitzer-prize winning author, Louis Bromfield, who turned his famed Malabar Farm outside the city into a conservation showcase and gathering place for writers and entertainers. Kay Francis, movie star of the '30s, used to come and dance with her shoes off; another visitor was John Gunther, traveling the country to write *Inside U.S.A.* But nothing more famous ever happened at Malabar than the 1945 marriage of Humphrey Bogart and Lauren Bacall; as if nothing were holy, their nuptial bed can still be viewed on daily tours of the home.

ILLINOIS

AND THE MIGHTY LAKESIDE CITY: WHERE

CLOUT COUNTS

I. CHICAGOLAND

CHICAGO—CHICAGO—how can one adequately describe it? The heart of the heartland, or as a visiting Sarah Bernhardt said some 70 years ago, "the pulse of America," this lusty, masculine, beauty and terror-filled metropolis remains the archetype of all our cities. It throbs with life and energy, it worships Mammon without qualm, it attracts and repels, it is perennially young yet perennially decaying. It is the one place on the continent where the exercise of power—raw, unfettered, physical, economic, and political power—has been brought to its apex. Chicago is the glory and damnation of America all rolled up into one. Not to know Chicago is not to know America.

Thus our story of Illinois must begin with this mighty lake city, for in its shadow every other aspect of Lincoln's prairie state slides toward afterthought. A native son, John Gunther, sets the stage:

Being a Chicagoan born and bred I can recall much. . . . The icy wind
screaming down snow-clogged boulevards; the sunny haunch of Lincoln Park near
the yacht moorings in torrid summers; the angry whistles of angry traffic cops and
the automobilelike horns of the Illinois Central suburban trains; the steady lift of
bridges, bridges, bridges; holes, bumps and yawning pits in the streets; the marvelous
smooth lift of the Palmolive Building and how the automobiles seem to butt each
other forward like long streams of beetles; the tremendous heavy trains of the
North Shore slipping like iron snakes through the quivering wooden suburban
stations; the acrid smell from the stockyards when the wind blew that way, and the
red flush of the steel mills in black skies—all this is easy to remember.

The feel of Chicago remains true to the Guntherian image; some of the
specifics are transformed. The stockyards, victims of decentralization of the
packing house business, lie quiet like a deserted battlefield, no longer filled
with thousands of animals awaiting their moment of terror and dissection.
The Palmolive Building stands, but now overwhelmed in a great crush of
higher buildings and its name, indignity of indignities, actually changed to
Playboy Building, symbol of the first (now almost passé) sex breakthrough of
the postwar era. The North Shore Line is gone, and one's eyes are easily diverted to the screaming jets landing and taking off in an incessant stream from
O'Hare. Chicago's raw interchange of man and machine remains; so does the
jewel of the city, her beautiful and unspoiled shoreline off which white sails
sparkle on a summer day.

People Count and Economic Clout

Chicagoland—to borrow the descriptive if somewhat nauseous term pop-
ularized by the Chicago *Tribune*—is the home and workshop for well over
half the 11 million people of Illinois. The reader can take his pick of three
levels of population analysis: the city of Chicago alone, Cook County (which
embraces Chicago and a multiplicity of close-in suburbs), or the six-county
Chicago metropolitan area (including Lake County in Indiana). The population of Chicago alone, since 1890 second only to New York's, was 3,366,957
according to the 1970 Census and had been static for 30 years, declining in
fact by 7 percent between 1950 and 1970. Cook County, on the other hand,
has grown 35.2 percent to 5,492,369 in the past 30 years. The population of
the entire metropolitan region reached 6,978,947 in 1970, but the area ranks
third, not second, in the U.S.A., because the burgeoning Los Angeles area
overtook it about a dozen years ago.

What raw population counts fail to reflect adequately is the remarkable
economic resilience of the "Chicagoland" economy, which has grown more
rapidly than the country at large for most of the postwar years and has a
substantially lower unemployment rate. Except for its 800,000 or so poor
(those living under established "poverty line" definitions), the Chicago area
is a great place to make money, and a lot of people are making a lot of it.

What gives Chicago its economic dynamism? The basic fact is an amazingly well diversified economy, with finance, manufacturing, and transporta-

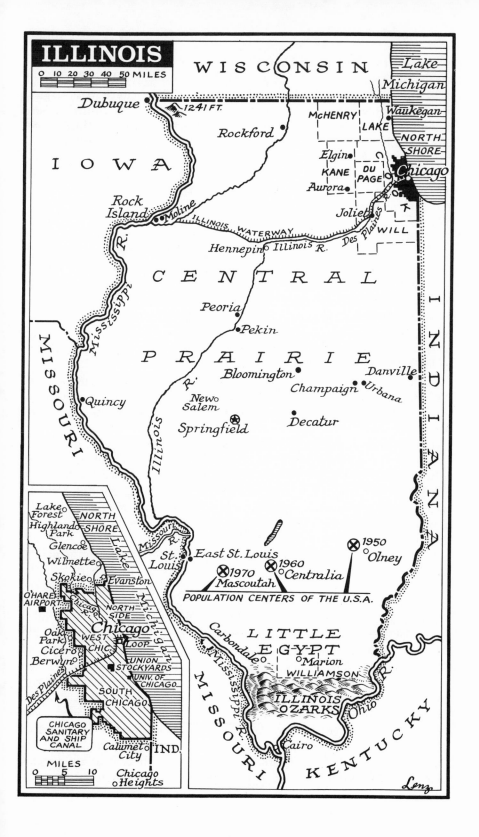

tion its great mainstays—and virtually no defense industries. By one estimate, the Chicago area contributed 5.1 percent of the gross national product though it has only 3.4 percent of the U. S. population. The city is both a great headquarters town (with home offices of 44 of the 500 largest industrials listed by *Fortune*) and a great branch office town. The long list of man-made items of which Chicago makes the most includes such disparate items as household appliances, radios, candy, athletic goods, television sets, plastics, railroad equipment, diesel engines, telephone equipment, and soap. More steel and machinery are fabricated in the Chicago area than anywhere else in the world, and food processing remains a $5 billion-a-year business. Chicago is also the nation's biggest wholesaling center, its traditional mail order headquarters (Sears and Montgomery Ward), and through its Board of Trade and Mercantile Exchange, the world's busiest commodity market and trader in livestock futures. Amazingly successful businesses include the switched-on world of consumer electronics (Zenith, Admiral, Motorola, etc.), printing and publishing (R. R. Donnelly & Sons Co. is the world's largest commercial printing company), and conventions (grossing a third of a billion dollars a year, 20 percent ahead of New York). Chicago is one of the three largest financial centers of the U.S.A. with bank clearings of more than $100 billion annually; of course it has the Federal Reserve Bank for its region.

The recital of these superlatives has not even touched on transportation. Chicago has long been the world's greatest railhead, and railroad payrolls are over half a billion dollars a year. O'Hare Airport is the busiest commercial field in the world and in 1969 handled 31 million people in 650,000 scheduled plane movements, an average of more than two flights a minute, day-in and day-out. By 1975, the passenger load is expected to reach 60 million, by 1980 between 80 and 90 million. O'Hare is being expanded, and there has been talk of a huge new airport some eight miles out in Lake Michigan, connected by special access road to the Loop. (Environmentalists are hotly opposed to the airport-on-the-lake idea.) Chicago also boasts of having a "Fourth Seacoast" because of its capacity for global freight shipments through the St. Lawrence Seaway; the city is the busiest Great Lakes port and fifth largest in the nation, even though the business on the Seaway has not lived up to early expectations. The port has been damaged as a handler of general merchandise by massive looting and terrorism on the docks.

Chicago has been at the center of the new atomic age; it was on a snowy day in 1942 that Dr. Enrico Fermi and his colleagues, working under the plank board seats of the abandoned football stadium at the University of Chicago, succeeded in accomplishing the first sustained controlled production of atomic energy in human history. The Atomic Energy Commission's important Argonne National Laboratory for research and development is at suburban Lemont. In 1969, ground was broken at Weston, a little town 30 miles southwest of Chicago, for the Atomic Energy Commission's $250 million atom smasher, which will be the world's highest-energy proton accelerator (and will create 5,000 jobs for the area). Weston, a hamlet of 350 persons when the AEC finally selected it in 1966—rejecting applications from 44 other states which had been equally hopeful of landing the $60 million annual payroll—almost lost out when Congressional hearings brought charges that it discriminated against Negroes and had no open housing law. Rising above principle, Weston quickly passed a fair-housing ordinance. As a final nuclear note, it should be recorded that Chicago's Commonwealth Edison Co. built one of the earliest nuclear energy plants at nearby Dresden and is planning a second soon at Zion, just north of the city. The utility is immersed in a big battle with environmentalists who insist on cooling towers to prevent thermal pollution.

The Architectural Lodestone of Chicago

Power, we have said, is the essence of Chicago; many who know it well refer to it as "clout"—a peculiarly brutal, raw kind of power. It must be examined in its many faces: economic, political, criminal, religious, racial, even architectural. Since the architecture is what first meets the eye, we will start there.

Chicago, city of the Big Shoulders, regards itself with good reason as the world capital of modern architecture. Indeed, the gigantic structures of steel and glass and concrete which thrust at the sky along the lakefront and around the Loop * are a symphony of might and mass—and excellence—that few world cities can compete with.

There have been two great eras of Chicago architecture. The first began a century ago, when Chicago rebounded from its disastrous Great Fire of 1871 to give birth to the first skyscrapers of the world. Many still stand, making the Loop a kind of outdoor architectural museum. Here architect William Jenney shifted from the 5,000-year old tradition of buildings with weight-bearing walls to designing the first steel skeleton building of history. Here the masters of the Chicago School built classic high buildings that rejected Victorian gingerbreadism in favor of a simplicity in which "form follows function."

In the early years of this century, little of distinction was built. A second golden era of Chicago architecture was inaugurated in the mid-1950s and continues unabated to this day; its dominant figure until his death in 1969 was Ludwig Mies van der Rohe, a stonemason's son from Germany who never took an architectural degree but by his later years was widely regarded as the dean of world architecture. The new Chicago classicism which Mies fathered is true to the spirit of the first golden age: simple, direct expression using modern techniques in which newer kinds of steel span vast distances. Mies designed modern classics of structural clarity, stripped of adornment; one of the finest examples is his four "glass house" apartment towers on Lake Shore Drive, their black-coated metal and shimmering glass mirroring the clouds and the lakefront. Mies' building at the Federal Center, according to Chicago *Daily News* architectural critic W. M. Newman, "fills its great envelope of

* The Loop, Chicago's mercantile and financial center, gains its name from the elevated tracks which encircle it.

space with mysterious rightness, daring to hurl its regimental rhythms along an entire block. This is the best new federal building in any city."

Another prime example of the Miesian "skin and bones" principle is the 1966 Chicago Civic Center, in which the steel skeleton is close to being one and the same with the outside of the building. Chief designer of the Civic Center was Jacques Brownson, a pupil of Mies who became a master himself. He directed that the building be finished in an alloy that weathers to a deep bronze; to grace the noble plaza before the center, the city commissioned Pablo Picasso to design a great five-story-high steel sculpture which has been executed in a steel alloy that oxidizes to a russet color akin to that of the center. (The abstract Picasso design triggered great controversy among those who saw in it everything from Picasso's dog to a baboon to a great dragon fly; Picasso settled the dispute by saying it was a woman's head. To this writer —as to many—it is a threatening, brooding, fascinating structure of a thousand faces, not at all unconsonant with the Chicago political machine that rules from across the street in City Hall.)

There are dozens of other modern Chicago buildings by Mies or his school, structures which have literally transformed the city in a few short years. Some prime examples are the Time-Life Building with tinted mirrored glass that reflects a bright orange to the outside world; the twin tube-like towers of Marina City on the Chicago River front; and the First National Bank Building, soaring 850 feet over the Loop, sheathed in glistening white granite and shaped like a long, thin stick of butter that has begun to melt at the bottom. Perhaps the most negative note of the present-day building boom is that many of the historic structures of the late 1800s are falling before the wrecker's ball; among these have been 66 of the 92 buildings of Louis Sullivan, whose superb designs, combining ornamentation with functional austerity, influenced great architects like Frank Lloyd Wright. The last Sullivan office building in the Loop, the 13-story Old Stock Exchange, built in 1894, was demolished in 1971.

As one drives along Lake Shore Drive and glances inland, a single quarter-mile-high structure arrests the eye—the tapered design of the John Hancock Building, a structure of such mass and height that every building near it is dwarfed—and the words of William Butler Yeats' *The Second Coming* spill through the mind:

> And what rough beast, its hour come round at last,
> Slouches toward Bethlehem to be born?

Indeed, Newman of the *Daily News* aptly describes the Hancock Building, as seen from afar, as "some large horned animal, gazing serenely along the rim of the world." He also describes the building as a symbol of the dangers of "giantism"—"the hard, impersonal power of overwhelming technology, the dwarfing of man, the dehumanizing of the city." (Yet, good Chicagoan that he is, Newman quickly adds: "It took boldness and guts to put it up that way, it is very impressive, very Chicagoan.")

There are advantages in the Hancock design for humans. The upper stories of the building are for apartments, the lower ones for offices; an apartment dweller can "commute" to his office in 90 seconds by high-speed elevator; the views from the upper stories are nothing short of breathtaking (though residents are sometimes disconcerted by looking *down* on the clouds, and many have taken to phoning the doorman to see how the weather is downstairs).

Now the race for the ultimate skyscraper is on in earnest. In 1970, Standard Oil (Indiana) unfurled plans for a Chicago headquarters that will top the Hancock Building by nine feet. Then Sears, Roebuck & Co. went a step further with the announcement of a headquarters building in the city which will be *the* highest building in the world—1,450 feet and 110 stories high (surpassing the twin towers of New York's World Trade Center by 100 feet and the Empire State Building by 200 feet). Sears will spend more than $100 million on the structure, financing the *entire* cost out of accumulated earnings.*

The Machine and The Leader

"Organization, not machine. Get that. Organization, not machine," Mayor Richard J. Daley insists when the subject comes to the Cook County Democratic organization. But this "antique and high-powered juggernaut," as one observer has described it, is a political machine if the term has any meaning—and the best functioning machine in America.

"Chicago," says Leon M. Despres, one of the city's few reform aldermen, "is governed by a firmly run, businesslike organization of about 35,000 persons who live off politics. . . . Indeed, it is really a business. It controls the mayoralty, 38 of the 50 members of the city council, the school board, the park board, the library board, the housing authority, the transit authority, two-thirds of the county board, nearly all the county offices, many suburban governments, the judiciary." Until 1969, the governor and attorney general of Illinois were also organization men and the machine had a decisive voice in the designation of federal judges and other local federal officials through its close ties with the Kennedy and Johnson Administrations. It still controls the state auditor and treasurer, a chunk of the state legislature, and almost all of the Chicago congressmen.

Under this authoritarian, hierarchical organization, some 500 patronage jobs are allotted to each ward. Virtually every precinct committeeman has a city job; the public, in effect, subsidizes the system by salaries paid to patronage workers. Many ward committeemen own insurance agencies and do a land-office business with retailers and real estate owners who see an obvious way to get access to City Hall. But the ward and precinct committeemen, in turn, are under tremendous pressures to contribute and work on election day, or they can expect to be thrown out on the street. The machine knows what they are doing, and it brooks no election day inefficiency—or dissent. Adlai Stevenson

* Sears can well afford to spend $100 million for a building. In 1969, it had net sales of nearly $8.9 billion and a net income of $441 million. It has 355,000 employees, 31,200 in the Chicago area alone—the magnitude of a small country, and a pretty wealthy one too.

III has called it "a feudal system that rewards mediocrity or worse, with jobs for the blind party faithful, special favors for business, and ineffectual civil service." But its power is so great that he, like his father before him and that otherwise fearless United States Senator, Paul H. Douglas, has made his peace with it.

According to their own particular "clout," Chicago's varied ethnic groups are allowed to queue up for the rewards of power. Irish get the top jobs like mayor, president of the county board, county assessor, and state's attorney, plus the major local patronage slots beneath them; the Poles get jobs like city clerk or a couple of seats in Congress; Jews get some judgeships but are generally dealt the lesser cards. Other ethnic groups, assuming they are part of the coalition, pick up the scraps from the table; among these are Italians, including some who have influence from participation in organized crime. Negroes, the most faithful election-time supporters, are shortchanged worst of all, except in menial jobs.

The election-day pluralities which the mighty Democratic machine can produce are sometimes nothing less than phenomenal: in 1948, 558,111 for Harry Truman for President; in 1960, 456,312 for John F. Kennedy for President; in 1967, 516,208 for Richard Daley for mayor; in 1968, 421,199 for Hubert Humphrey for President; in 1970, 521,353 for Adlai Stevenson III for U.S. Senator. It is on the basis of such one-sided votes that Daley wields the power he does in national Democratic politics.

Chicago emerged from World War II under the tight control of a city-wide Democratic machine controlled by Mayor Edward J. Kelly, a master of private profiteering in public office, and Patrick Nash, sewer contractor and Democratic boss since the 1930s. In the Kelly-Nash era, everything could be bought or sold, organized crime prospered, and the center city was dying rapidly. But the machine's gross inefficiencies in public services, together with severe school administration problems, weakened Kelly so much that the Democratic machine ousted him in 1947 in favor of a reform-flavored candidate, Martin Kennelly. A clean and handsome millionaire warehouseman who had previously fought the local machine as director of the Chicago Crime Commission, Kennelly was sponsored by one of the cleverest politicians of modern Chicago, Col. Jacob M. Arvey. (Arvey, a diminutive, bald attorney who mixed idealism with a background in corrupt ward politics, is still Illinois' Democratic National Committeeman but no longer a major power.)

In office, Kennelly turned out to be too naive (and vain) for tough Chicago, and the hoodlums and political machine carried on as before. In 1955, he was defeated in a primary fight by none other than Richard J. Daley, prototype of the good Irish ward politician. Many viewed Daley as little more than a hack politician, the machine's last gasp. Daley's reply: "I would not unleash the forces of evil. It's a lie. I will follow the training my good Irish mother gave me—and Dad. If I am elected, I will embrace mercy, love, charity, and walk humbly with my God." *

* This was one of Daley's more grammatical statements; in his early years as mayor he was still doing violence to the English language in everyday speech, referring, for instance, to Chicago's "Nort'

Today, by general agreement, Daley represents far more than an average ward politician, even if his heavy-set look and jowls, and a sometimes awesome temper, set the image of a strong-armed boss from the smoke-filled rooms. He has a thorough grasp of the details of Chicago government; he is a master of finance and has introduced cost accounting in city administration; he is a keen judge of the level of performance and influence of thousands of Chicagoans in and out of government. When new power bases arise in the city, Daley finds ways to incorporate them—or if their holders decline his muscular embrace, to freeze them out. His working alliance with Chicago's big business and labor unions, as we shall see later, is extremely close, and it was under his administration that Chicago began its great postwar central building boom. Daley is extremely hard working and strong willed, a man whose personal honesty has never been questioned. He has succeeded in curbing the bolder thieves in his organization, even though ward and precinct bosses are allowed to carry on "clean graft" of a type that will not embarrass the regime.

Yet, despite all, this master of political weight-balancing remains a product of the simple, Irish neighborhood of Bridgeport (2,262), where he was born the son of a sheet-metal worker; he still lives in a modest bungalow on a street of inexpensive but creditably well painted and tended homes. Like many Chicago neighborhoods, Bridgeport retains clear-cut community and ethnic identity. Some 40 percent are immigrants or the children of immigrants; the typical resident has a ninth-grade education and lives in a house worth about $12,000; Negroes are not permitted to buy homes here and indeed are said to be afraid to walk its streets at night. A good family man, Daley still returns here almost every evening for dinner at home with wife and children. Every day he attends Mass, though, as writer David Halberstam points out, his religion is pre-Ecumenical, pre-John XXIII, where there is individual sin but little social sin. He can tolerate small and petty graft, excuse an occasional roaring drunk or failing of business virtue, but he cannot excuse adultery and cannot understand or tolerate a man who fathers a family and then deserts it.

Next to mother church, Bridgeport's first loyalty is to the Democratic party, a lesson Daley learned well as a boy from the age of 12 when he started doing small political chores. The last three mayors of Chicago have all come from the 11th Ward, of which Bridgeport is the heart. "All this political clout," Chicago *Daily News* columnist Mike Royko comments, "means nearly every family has got somebody on a government payroll. In the East, some

---

Side" and Sout' Side." Today most rough corners have been rubbed off His Honor's speech, though the press has duly recorded such Daley gems as these:

"I resent the insinuendos."—Chicago *Daily News,* May 15, 1965.

"Together we must rise to ever higher and higher platitudes."—*Newsweek,* March 13, 1967.

"It is amazing what they will be able to do once they get the atom harassed."—*Life,* February 8, 1960.

". . . for the enlightenment and edification and hallucination of the alderman from the 50th ward."—*Life,* February 8, 1960.

"They have vilified me, they have crucified me, yes they have even criticized me."—*Harper's,* August 1968.

An entire volume of Daleyana, *Quotations from Mayor Daley,* compiled by Peter Yessne, was published in 1966 by G. P. Putnam's Sons.

families register a newborn son at Harvard or Yale. In Bridgeport, they sign him on with the city water department."

Daley got his law degree from De Paul, climbed steadily though unspectacularly through the Cook County Democratic organization in his early career days, served a period as state director of public revenue under Governor Stevenson in the late 1940s, and in 1955 won election as mayor with a bloc vote in many ethnic wards plus vital backing from the black ghettos presided over by Congressman Bill Dawson. Since then, the center of Daley's support has moved "right and white" through his success with the business community and as spokesman for the hard-working, much-put-upon whites in the years of black agitation. In his fifth-term race in 1971, Daley beat Richard Friedman, a liberal Democrat-turned-Republican, by more than 400,000 votes. In the midst of the campaign, Federal Judge Richard Austin ordered publication of a list of Chicago Housing Authority sites. Austin ruled that the CHA was promoting segregation and therefore public housing had to be built in white areas. The CHA produced the sites and Daley said the order would be ignored. That did the trick for Daley, and the backlash areas went for him.

For the patronage favors Daley does offer black neighborhoods, he expects gratitude, and he is all the more shocked when bitterness and rioting are the answer. For a native of Bridgeport, it is indeed difficult to understand the desperate plight of Negroes in ghettos like the raw, tough West Side. When Daley enters such areas, his coming and going are rapid in his Cadillac limosine; he would never think of walking the streets of an explosive black neighborhood as Lindsay of New York has done. His information on the black communities comes instead from a police intelligence network and Negro politicians often beholden to him. David Halberstam has reported in *Harper's* that when a militant civil-rights activist nun working on the West Side went to Daley and pleaded with him to come out and witness the deplorable condition of the children and their schools, he replied, "Look, Sister, you and I come from the same background. We know how tough it was. But we picked ourselves up by our bootstraps."

One key to Daley's success has been his dual roles: mayor of Chicago and chairman of the Cook County Democratic Central Committee. Holding these two jobs is a bit like being Premier of the U.S.S.R. and First Secretary of the Communist Party at the same time. The vast power of the two offices has permitted Daley, with his well developed political skills, to become an authoritarian ruler of his city, a Buddha-like figure whose slightest word is law. As each election approaches, for instance, Daley appoints a Democratic slatemaking committee, usually with himself as chairman. The sessions are secret, and potential candidates are asked to come; they never, if really serious, invite themselves. One by one, hat in hand, the office-seekers are allowed to appear and make a brief review (rarely for more than three minutes or so) outlining their qualifications, their potential financial and group support. Then they are expected to show their unqualified fealty to the party by offering to run for *any office* that the party might stipulate. The slatemaking sessions are a mysterious affair; the public has no idea of what goes on behind the closed doors. They are also scheduled so close to the primary filing dead-line that it is hard for any independent candidacy to get organized after-ward.

In 1968, Adlai Stevenson, III, offended the statewide slatemaking session by stating that he might not be able to support President Johnson's Vietnam policies. By that implied disloyalty, he hoped to be slated for governor. But it turned out to be a poor ploy. Though Daley still wanted him for Senator, his statement had put a loaded gun in the hands of his enemies, many of whom were enemies of his father. They jumped all over him, and Daley apparently decided it wasn't worth a fight despite Stevenson's obviously popular name. At the 1970 slatemaking session, Daley was still for Stevenson, and a number of his opponents were now up for election themselves and wanted Stevenson at the top of the ticket. They had no stomach for a primary fight, and feared Stevenson (who had already taken menacing steps like ordering bill-board space) might stage one. But though they knew they would slate him, Stevenson's opponents subjected him to a brutal half-hour grilling. One city committeeman got up and, to prove Stevenson wasn't one of them, asked Stevenson to identify him. Stevenson couldn't.

An open primary is virtually assured over the 1972 Democratic guberna-torial nomination, thanks to the candidacy of Daniel Walker, former chair-man of the Chicago Crime Commission and author of the controversial "Walker Report" that condemned police activities at the 1968 Democratic National Convention. Walker said he would disdain the slatemaking pro-cedure altogether. With his candidacy, Illinois Democrats were assured their first contested gubernatorial primary since 1960 and only the fourth (the others were in 1936 and 1952) in 40 years. Borrowing a page from the success-ful campaign book of Florida Sen. Lawton Chiles, Walker in 1971 made a walking tour of more than 100 days and 1,000 miles throughout Illinois, gar-nering much television publicity and trying—in his own words—to counteract "the ordinary guy's sense of remoteness from elected officials, his sense of powerlessness and lack of faith." Using computerized election returns of re-cent years, Walker concentrated on precincts that vote heavily Democratic in general elections but have failed to turn out big primary votes in the past. His to-the-people campaign aroused much favorable comment, especially when people learned that this lean 49-year-old could have chosen to remain in his comfortable position as a $118,000-a-year vice president of Montgomery Ward.

Especially within Chicago, Walker will face a rocky, uphill race. The only dissenters to the Daley regime have been some militant black politicians, plus a number of reform minded whites like Despres who have seized from Daley's grasp a handful of aldermanic districts around Hyde Park and in a row along Lake Michigan north of the Loop, an area populated by many Jews and young professional people.

Up to this point, the most serious problems for Daley and his machine have come not within their own party, but rather from the growing Repub-lican vote in the suburban sections of Cook County. In 1946, the city of Chi-cago accounted for 82 percent of the total cast in Cook County, but by 1970 it was only 62 percent. During the 1960s, the Republicans began to gnaw away at the Democrats' countywide superiority, winning the offices of county board president, treasurer, sheriff, seats on the sanitary district board and other posts. All of these positions are vital to the Daley patronage machine. In 1970, with Adlai Stevenson on top of the ticket, the Democrats swept the county offices, including recapture of the sheriff's office that had been in Republican hands for eight years. Stevenson actually carried the Cook suburbs with an 11,393-vote plurality. But his liberal and independent image, with strong appeal even in Republican suburbs, is the antithesis of the machine's normal patronage-ethnic appeal.

Daley has been unsuccessful in building a firm Democratic party base in the suburbs. In the long run, this spells trouble for the machine, because unless Democrats can carry Cook County by a substantial margin in statewide races, it almost surely means, because of the normal GOP downstate majority, that they will lose the entire state of Illinois *—costing the machine dearly in patronage jobs that a friendly regime in Springfield can channel to it. It is one thing to slate a liberal Paul Douglas or Adlai Stevenson for the U.S. Senate, a job with nil patronage power. It would be another thing to slate such a man for governor. That might produce what political columnists Rowland Evans and Robert Novak describe as "that most dreaded monster— a Democratic governor making decisions independent of City Hall on state legislative and national political matters."

An interesting new challenge to the organization was posed by the 1971 court suit, filed by Michael L. Shakman, chairman of the Independent Voters of Illinois, which charged that the prevailing patronage system, under which government employees must contribute time or money to the Democratic party as a condition of employment or promotion, gives Democratic-endorsed candidates unfair advantages and deprives taxpayers of the service of the patronage employees. Federal Judge Abraham L. Marovitz, a close Daley ally, first dismissed the suit, but the U.S. Appeals Court instructed him to conduct further hearings. The county Democratic organization then made a novel pledge—that it would refrain from the disputed patronage practices if Republicans in 18 northern Illinois counties, including Cook, would do the same. The Republicans consented, and while they admitted no guilt, their agreement underscored the fact that Illinois Republicans act quite like their Democratic brethren when the power falls to them. What will be the long-term effect of the court order? John Dreiske of the *Sun-Times* suggested to me that the parties would continue their old patronage policies, but "they will be more subtle and less flagrant."

A small cloud on the Chicago Democrats' horizon is the prospect of the retirement in this decade of Richard Daley, who was approaching 69 when he won his fifth term as mayor in 1971. One line of speculation is that he might run for a sixth term in 1975, if his health permitted, but turn over the Democratic county chairmanship to his trusted lieutenant, George W. Dunne, president of the Cook County board of commissioners. Dunne is a poor

* See chart, page 386.

speaker and campaigner and lacks Daley's toughness, but seasoned observers depict him as "1,000 percent honest" and admire his careful bookkeeper's approach to the affairs of government. His selection as party chief would leave open the choice for mayor when Daley finally retires.

But whatever its future problems may be, the truth is that the Chicago Democratic machine has endured, robust and healthy, years after the atrophy or even death of big city machines like those in New York and Philadelphia, Kansas City and Jersey City. The same reasons given for the decline of the others—increasingly sophisticated electorates and the substitution of government aid, often federal, for breadbaskets—should apply equally in Chicago. Why have they not? Strong leadership and able management of the Chicago machine are certainly major reasons. In the 1971 mayoralty election, for instance, Republican candidate Friedman struggled, unsuccessfully, to combat the notion that if Daley's kind of one-man control were removed, the city would fall apart. This has been defined as the "Lindsay problem," namely Chicagoans' knowledge of the strikes, shutdowns, and repeated fiscal crises that have attended the administration of John V. Lindsay in New York. All around them, Chicagoans can see the seething tensions, and the safe choice does indeed seem to be to stick with the heavy-handed father figure. Yet even that kind of a formula is not sufficient to all seasons; we must look further to the powerful allies the Chicago machine has made and kept—big and little business, organized labor, and organized crime—and to that most time-honored of all methods of maintaining power, plain old vote stealing.

Machine Allies: State Street, Captive Unions

In Chicago one can find widespread agreement with this assessment of the Democratic machine's ties to big business, offered by Alderman Despres:*

Chicago's most pampered neighborhood is the central business area, comprising downtown and the near North Side along Lake Michigan. When visitors speak of Chicago's "dynamic, modern progress," they usually refer to the central business area. There you see bold new buildings, daytime vigor, and excellent city maintenance. New projects are always in the works. Speedy public transit converges on the area. Hundreds of millions of dollars in expressways pour people into the area by day and back to the suburbs at night. Get off the subway anywhere in the central business area and you won't find a broken city sidewalk. Get off the subway almost anywhere else, and you will. Between the central business area and the outskirts lie large, almost uninterrupted gray areas of urban dry rot. This is where most Chicagoans live.

The pampered central business area evidences the basis of Chicago politics, the unwritten compact between Chicago's Democratic political machine and the business and financial interests. Under this tacit agreement the business and financial interests receive luxurious support for the central business area, subsidies of valuable public works, indulgent business-oriented drafting and enforcement of ordinances regulating business, and, for the rest of Chicago, a firm hand on the

* From "The Chicago the Delegates Won't See," *The Progressive*, August 1968.

city's tiller and on the till. In exchange, the business and financial interests provide the machine what it needs in money and Republican backing, and deliver nearly full support of all parts of the public opinion media.

Evidence to support this view is not difficult to find. Whenever Daley runs for reelection, he is backed by a blue-ribbon bipartisan committee with suburban as well as city membership. Nor does the assistance stop with Daley's personal campaigns. In 1967, the campaign to elect Daley's candidate to the presidency of the Cook County Board was headed by Donald Graham, who later succeeded David Kennedy as chairman of the board of the Continental Illinois National Bank Trust Co., Chicago's largest with over $7 billion in assets. Kennedy, who became Secretary of the Treasury in the Nixon Cabinet, had been chairman of Daley's committee on cultural and economic improvement and once said: "I don't think there is a mayor anywhere who is doing more for his city in an intelligent, forthright, objective way than Mayor Daley." C. Virgil Martin, now chairman of Carson Pirie Scott & Co. (which is second only to Marshall Field as a State Street retailer) was co-chairman of Daley's own campaign fund in 1967. In 1971, business again lined up behind Daley as he sought a fifth term. Robert S. Ingersoll, chairman of Borg-Warner Corp. and president of the prestigious Commercial Club, said: "Daley realizes what makes an economy tick. Those who criticize him are people who have no responsibility for maintaining a viable economy." Principal Daley backers include Ben Heineman, chairman of Northwest Industries, and Joel Goldblatt of Goldblatts, another large State Street retailer. Charles Kellstadt, former president of Sears, Roebuck, and Ernest Marsh, president of the Santa Fe Railroad, were appointed to the Illinois Racing Commission by former Gov. Otto Kerner, a Daley protegé.

In the words of Emmett Dedmon, vice president of the Chicago *Sun-Times* and *Daily News*, "Chicago, far from being run by its ethnic groups, has been run by its puritanical, white Anglo-Saxon Protestant minority from years ago. There is a business establishment which functions pretty much as an extra government within the city—and that's what has given it its continuity." This business community, Dedmon told me, "has been free to develop its own interests as long as it does not interfere in the political sphere" in a way hostile to the controlling party of the moment. "The system endures in Chicago," Dedmon said, "because of the traditional alliance between politics, business, and labor."

Just how effective that alliance is can be illustrated by the excellent police protection of the Loop, the extremely efficient snow removal provided for downtown, and low tax assessments imposed by P. J. (Parky) Cullerton, the Daley-controlled county tax assessor. In 1971, investigative reporters discovered that Cullerton had granted millions of dollars in tax breaks to real estate developers who were big Democratic contributors and members of the committee for Cullerton's reelection as assessor. Later a story broke about underassessment of five of the largest Chicago banks. One of the banks was Continental Illinois Bank, which had saved $1.8 million by the preferential treatment. The chairman of the board of Continental Illinois is Donald M.

Graham, co-chairman of the 1971 businessmen's Nonpartisan Committee to Re-elect Mayor Daley.

The mutual aid flows in hundreds of ways. In recent years, for instance, Daley has strongly supported the creation of a special tax district to finance construction of a subway in the Loop and get rid of its ugly, rumbling overhead rapid transit—thus hopefully drawing even more customers into what is still a thriving, vigorous State Street retail core.* In 1968, there was scarcely a murmur of protest to Daley's strong-arm tactics in controlling demostrations at the Democratic National Convention—even when the daughter of one business leader was arrested and roughed up by the police.

Organized labor has a similarly close relationship with the machine; in fact the ties are sometimes so close that one could well say that in Chicago the Democratic party is not in the hip pocket of labor, but rather that labor is in the hip pocket of the Democratic party. No major Chicago union has opposed Daley, nor has there been a major public strike of significant duration in the city—in vivid contrast to now bossless New York City. In some unions, Daley can even dictate who will be elected to leadership positions. In 1971, labor staged a gigantic dinner in Daley's honor, attended by 10,158 in cavernous McCormick Place. Sitting on the dais flanked by a praetorian guard of the labor elite and sitting under a Mao-sized portrait of himself, Daley could gaze out on 1,100 tables—275 occupied by Teamsters, 190 by building trades, 50 by Steelworkers, etc. At election time, it is not unusual to see the head of a small local union presenting Daley with a $10,000 campaign check—with a picture of it all in the paper. In return for this subservience, labor gets special breaks and privileges. Joseph Germano, the district Steelworkers director and powerful man in the national union, has been given a voice in party slatemaking. The building trades, Teamsters, and janitors' unions are especially close to Daley; gross featherbedding has been reported in city jobs, and a janitor in Chicago City Hall is reputed to be the highest paid janitor in the world. Elevators are automated, but there are more elevator operators than ever. Many union people are on the mayor's policy advisory commissions.

The close relationship, however, does not mean that Daley regards the unions as equals. During the 1965 session of the legislature, some Democrats sponsored a bill to extend collective bargaining rights to public employees. But the word came through Governor Kerner that Daley was opposed and the bill would be killed. Why, asked some of the Democrats. Isn't labor our friend? The reply (roughly) was as follows: "We're not going to give them anything. We don't want them across the table as equals. We want them to come to us, so we can get something from them." In another episode of the 1960s, the news director of WCFL, the radio station owned by the Chicago Federation of Labor, was fired because he balked at orders to give only positive news about the city of Chicago and Mayor Daley.

---

* State Street is still the largest *concentrated* shopping center in the world—all within about five blocks. Potter Palmer, the real founder of State Street, and Marshall Field believed that if you put your competitor next to you, maximum traffic would be pulled into the area. The formula worked in the 19th century and still works, even while many center city retail centers are losing their viability. State Street's annual gross is close to $400 million.

Vote Theft and Ties to the Mafia

Unadulterated vote stealing is another underpinning of the Democratic machine; in any given election, by reliable estimates, between 50,000 and 150,-000 unlawful votes are registered for the straight Democratic ticket. Nowhere in America is vote theft practiced on so grandiose a scale. The importance of this was graphically demonstrated in the 1960 Presidential election, when John Kennedy squeaked through in Illinois by a plurality of 8,858 votes in a close national contest. Just two more votes in each of Cook County's 5,199 precincts would have given Nixon Illinois' 27 electoral votes, and after checking only 699 paper-ballot precincts, Republicans charged that Nixon was entitled to at least 4,539 more votes than the Democratic-controlled election board credited him with in those precincts alone. Contempt charges were brought against 677 election officials and precinct workers, but a special judge disposed of all the cases without requiring the persons cited to respond and explain what had happened in their precincts on election day. Charging a "whitewash," the Chicago *Tribune* editorialized: "The net result of this judicial mummery is that election officials have received further assurance that stealing votes is no crime in Chicago."

Illegal registrations, coercion of voters by Democratic precinct captains, and intimidation of Republican poll watchers (who in many wards sell out to the Democrats and collaborate in vote theft) are all part of the Chicago pattern. Since 1960, reformers have been able to cut back some in the degree of vote stealing, but the pattern remains. Chicago's highly respected Better Government Association in 1968 dispatched an investigator to register in skid-row hotels under fictitious names—at the McCoy Hotel (owned by Charles Swibel, chairman of the Chicago Housing Authority) under the name of James Joyce, at Workingmen's Palace as Jay Gatsby, at the Legion Hotel as Henry Locke. Sure enough, when the registration sheets for the November election were inspected later, the fictitious names were miraculously registered to vote. On precinct registration day, BGA investigators saw highly paid city employees paying derelicts $2 each to register. One $12,000-a-year sewer inspector, they discovered, registered from the Starr Hotel at 610 West Madison (the same flophouse murderer Richard Speck once lived at), even though the official was also registered at another address in the city and somehow was able to afford a $70,000 Chicago home and a $100,000 Wisconsin summer home. Among other BGA findings:

> Chicago police officers double as precinct captains.
> Thousands of persons were registered to vote from empty lots and burned-out buildings, or from expressway cloverleafs, city parks, and many parking lots.
> Numerous persons who had died years before were carried on the voter rolls.

As a result of the BGA's investigations, seven election officials resigned before the election. The Democrats' election day chicanery was also hampered by "Operation Eagle Eye," a Republican-sponsored vote-security operation in which thousands of junior corporate executives and other volunteers fanned out across the city to monitor suspect precincts. Despite these precautions, it still seemed likely that tens of thousands of illegal votes had been cast. As a result of the BGA investigations, two Democratic precinct captains were convicted of vote fraud in 1969.

Precisely the same kind of skulduggery has been reported in elections since 1968. In 1970, the Republican candidate for sheriff lost a narrow race when a number of precincts were held out for more than a day. In 1971, investigators dispatched by the Republican attorney general of the state were refused admission to polling places, as were poll watchers for the Republican candidate for mayor. Reporters said they saw machine-controlled election judges repeatedly enter the voting machines and draw the curtains before the polls opened. In one precinct, reporters with binoculars watched voters receiving yellow slips at the polling place, which were then taken around the corner and exchanged for money.

The Better Government Association is the only one of its kind in the country—a privately sponsored, unofficial watchdog agency to ferret out malfeasance in government. (A $175,000-a-year budget is contributed by business and professional leaders.) BGA's six-man investigative staff, headed by George Bliss, a former Pulitzer Prize-winning labor reporter for the Chicago *Tribune*, has no subpoena power or shred of legal authority. Nevertheless, it has worked effectively to reveal scores of scandals in city, suburban, and state government and save Illinois taxpayers millions of dollars. BGA's standard operating method is to select one of Chicago's fiercely competitive newspapers or television stations to work with it on an investigation, or to cooperate with reporters from one of the papers when they turn up first leads on a potential scandal.

One BGA investigation revealed that some of Chicago's worst slum buildings were owned by officials of the city building department, and that lackadaisical or compromised code enforcement was causing thousands of Chicagoans to live in indescribable filth in dangerously unsafe tenements.

A BGA investigation into crime syndicate political alliances in the Veterans Park District, which administers local parks in five western suburbs, led to the indictment of six men on charges ranging from grand theft to forgery, conspiracy, and official misconduct; five were subsequently convicted. The Oak Forest police chief was fired after BGA men photographed him lounging at the race track with Mafia hoods. In 1969, the BGA was able to document lucrative graft and corruption at the Illinois State Fair. Its allegations of rampant waste, inefficiency, and loafing by employees of Chicago's vast Park District and the Cook County Forest Preserve roused the ire of Mayor Daley, who accused the BGA of being an arm of the Republican party. But other BGA probes have embarrassed Republicans just as much.

In substantial measure, I was told by Bliss of the BGA, Chicago has put behind it the days when the Syndicate mobsters terrorized and virtually ruled the city, the era of wide-open red light districts, Prohibition bootleg profiteering, Al Capone, and raw murders in the streets. But the mob—variously referred to as the Syndicate, Cosa Nostra, Mafia, and other titles—still has a Chicago branch that Ovid Demaris in his 1969 book *Captive City* describes as "the most politically insulated and police-pampered 'family' this side of Sicily." Unlike the many-headed Mafia structure of the New York-New Jersey area, the Chicago syndicate is a single system. The first postwar leader was Tony Accardo, onetime bodyguard to Al Capone; when he got embroiled in an income tax evasion case in 1956, Accardo turned the reigns over to Sam Giancana, the prime suspect in countless murder investigations and a man who has been described by one police official as "a snarling, sarcastic, ill-mannered, ill-tempered, sadistic psychopath." In the late 1960s, Giancana in turn had a scrape with the law and stepped down in favor of William (Willie Potatoes) Daddano, alleged assassin, torturer, gambling and pinball machine czar and convicted burglar.

While Dan Walker was president of the Chicago Crime Commission, he published reports listing the names of more than 100 firms and 200 individuals with crime syndicate connections. The notoriety forced many companies out of business. One firm, with an American Stock Exchange listing, was forced to reorganize. Demaris charges that tens of thousands of Chicagoans are involved in organized crime, a vast army of "burglars, hijackers, fences, counterfeiters, moonshiners, panderers, prostitutes, B-girls, cab-drivers, bartenders, extortioners, narcotics peddlers, juicemen, collectors, torturers, assassins, (corrupt) cops, venal judges and politicians, union and business fronts, plus an array of gamblers including bookies, steerers and policy runners."

A measure of the Chicago syndicate's efficiency is that while there have been more than a thousand mob slayings in the city since Capone arrived there in 1919, only two have been solved. By contrast, the police are able to solve 62 percent of all run-of-the-mill killings—those committed by average men and women in the passion of a moment.

And there is a seemingly endless web of interconnection between the Chicago mob and Chicago politicians, amply documented over the years by the BGA, the Chicago Crime Commission, the Chicago newspapers, and writers like Demaris. The prime example is the First Ward, a downtown area including the Loop, the banks, City Hall, museums and luxury hotels, slum homes of derelicts, newly arrived immigrants, and the dispossessed. Up to the mid-1960s, this was a strongly Italian area; in 1962 it was estimated to hold 30,000 Italians, 15,000 Negroes, 14,000 Mexicans and Puerto Ricans, 10,000 Poles and Bohemians, and smaller assortments of Chinese, Jews, Irish, and Greeks. (Since then urban renewal has shifted the population focus and poor blacks now dominate.) For years, the First was the heart of Chicago gangsterism and corrupt politics; here flourished such figures as "Bathhouse" John Coughlin and Hinky Dink Kenna, the diminutive 5-foot, 100-pound ward committeeman for 50 years (1895–1944) who ran a flourishing red-light district and fostered countless hoods, including the infamous Al Capone himself. As Demaris tells the story,

Kenna and Coughlin collected votes and tribute for every racket and vice operation in their bailiwick. . . . They had their own policemen, prosecutors, judges, state legislators and always at least one United States Congressman for speechifying on patriotic occasions. . . . Some precinct captains were gamblers, bootleggers and male madams. Whatever their origin, precinct captains had a slice of the rackets, especially bookmaking . . .

Back in his Blackstone Hotel suite, the Dink was guarded by city policemen and Syndicate gunmen. . . . Finally, in 1946, at the age of 86, he died. He left $1,100,000 in cash to relatives who proved to be just as greedy as he was—they ignored his request for a $30,000 mausoleum for his wife and himself; instead, their graves were marked by $85 headstones.

An illustrious First Ward leader for several decades was Roland ("Libby") Libonati, who defended accused murderers in some 200 trials and looked the picture of a mob member himself. Asked about his friendship with Al Capone in 1947, Libonati told a reporter: "Mr. Capone showed me great respect as a person of Italian extraction who represented one of the pioneer families of Chicago, and naturally I . . . ah . . . returned . . . I returned . . . I treated him in accordance with . . . I treated him with respect as I would do any American. . . . You know, politically that man was not a politician. If people treat me nice, I treat them nice." On other occasions Libonati delighted listeners with such pronouncements as: "Nobody can speak asunder of the governor's reputation. . . . Not by any creeping of the imagination. . . . I am trying not to make any honest mistakes. . . . The moss is on the pumpkin. . . ."

Libonati served in the legislature for 22 years, where he was an able member of the "West Side bloc," a bipartisan group that strove to kill all anti-crime legislation. In 1957, the mob chose Libonati to go to the U. S. Congress, where two interesting things happened to him: he was immediately placed on the House Judiciary Committee (to the horror of some of his more scrupulous colleagues), and he found it wise to take on as a Congressional aide a young attorney named Anthony P. Tisci—the son-in-law of none other than the man who had decided Libonati would be Congressman, syndicate boss Sam Giancana.

In 1963, Libonati suddenly announced a desire to retire; as widely assumed at the time and proven by a secret federal report printed by Demaris, this was at Giancana's orders.* Giancana picked Frank Annunzio, an above-average First Ward product who had indeed been Governor Adlai Stevenson's labor director, to succeed Libonati, and the party and voters in customary fashion ratified his choice with 85.9 percent of the vote. Although Annunzio has taken a Congressional interest in consumer fraud and veterans affairs that make him more than a mere Mafia figurehead, he would surely retire if the syndicate told him to.

The most charitable view one can take of Mayor Daley's attitude toward

---

* Why did Giancana force Libonati to retire? According to one report, Libonati backed a weakening amendment to the 1963 civil rights bill at a crucial point in committee deliberations. Robert F. Kennedy, then attorney general, called Daley to protest and by some accounts said that if Libonati returned to Congress, Kennedy would see to it that he went to jail. Daley apparently got the word to Giancana and Libonati was axed. Libonati told my reporter friend Andrew Glass that he "was caught in the switches" and "given a Mickey Finn." Now Libonati is a sad figure who stands around LaSalle Street talking to the City Hall types. He has nothing to do.

the mob-infested First Ward and the Libonati-Annunzio Congressional district is that he deliberately ignores the brazen control of criminal elements. In the mid-1960s, the FBI was able to establish clear connections between four leading First Ward politicians and the syndicate's shakedowns, payoffs to police, and vice and gambling networks in the area. The U. S. Attorney, Edward Hanrahan, was given specific information about two payoffs totaling $30,000 from Giancana to First Ward politicians. Yet Hanrahan, loyal son of the city Democratic machine, refused to press for indictments. (U. S. Attorneys are Presidential appointees who serve four-year terms.) When press agitation mounted for Hanrahan's resignation, Mayor Daley leaped to his defense, saying, "Hanrahan's reputation for integrity, intelligence, and courage is unequaled."

Yet when questioned at press conferences about the corrupt leadership of the First Ward, Daley became general, evasive, the master of platitude. His most specific answer to reporters' questions about the skulduggery: "The leadership of the First Ward is selected by the people of the ward. . . . I am proud of the leadership I have exerted in this entire community." Daley's reasons for professed ignorance of pervasive and frequently documented corruption is not hard to divine: the First Ward turns in four- and five-to-one margins for Democratic candidates on election day; clear pluralities for Democratic candidates from Annunzio's House district range over 100,000, a major asset to the Cook County Democratic organization and, as 1960 showed, perhaps even vital in electing a President of the United States.

The Police, the Syndicate, and the Democratic Convention

Corruption is as endemic to the Chicago police force as patronage to its political system. For decades, there have been policemen on the take—accepting penny-ante payoffs for minor infractions * or, at the highest levels of the department, senior commanders accepting bribes to let the Mob carry on its work of numbers games, prostitution, and extortion, unmolested by honest cops. Up to 1960, according to Sandy Smith, *Time-Life's* former investigative reporter in Chicago, "Commanders in police headquarters were on the Mob's payroll. The graft system, or the Fix, worked almost openly in most station houses where the payoff distributor—the bagman—was easily identifiable. Gangsters who operated rackets in a district sometimes held enough political power to dictate the choice of a district captain."

In 1960 came perhaps the worst scandal ever to rock the Chicago Police Department, as eight policemen were arrested and sent to jail for burglary. Daley fired the police superintendent of the moment and appointed in his stead the highly respected Orlando Wilson, dean of the school of criminology at the University of California. Wilson cleaned up the most blatant corruption, built new police stations, installed a $2 million highly computerized

* Mort Sahl once said Chicago's Outer Drive was "the last outpost of collective bargaining."

communications system considered one of the finest in the world. But the system of ingrained corruption was more than even a man of Wilson's stature could deal with adequately. A secret FBI report, prepared in 1963 under orders from Attorney General Robert Kennedy, named 43 Chicago policemen allegedly working in collusion with the underworld. One of those specifically named was Lt. Paul Quinn, one of Wilson's chief aides (and still a top deputy to Wilson's successor, Superintendent James B. Conlisk, Jr.). Quinn has liaison duties with City Hall and is known as "the mayor's man" at police headquarters. The FBI alleged that Quinn had received $200 monthly from the mob "in compensation for his activity as a tipoff man for North Side hoodlums." Another man named in the federal report, Captain James Riordan, commander of the Central Police District, was alleged to be protecting strip-tease honky-tonks and to have "sanctioned" the distribution of payoffs.

Mayor Daley said he had not read the FBI report but nonetheless attacked it as a "vicious document." Wilson also brushed aside the FBI's allegations. But when he retired in 1967, Wilson acknowledged that the Cosa Nostra was so entrenched in Chicago that he had barely scratched its surface. And he said he had not been able to eradicate corruption on the police force.

Much of business as usual returned to police headquarters with the accession of Conlisk, a man close to Daley and member of an old Chicago police family (his father had been one of the nine "old men" who resigned from the force when the 1960 scandal broke). Indeed, Conlisk had been in office less than a year when he sacked the courageous chief of the department's anti-mobster Intelligence Unit, Captain William Duffy. Duffy had just led a raid, in conjunction with federal authorities, on a North Side headquarters for "bolita," the Cuban numbers game. The raid turned up "ice lists"—the mob's list of protection payoffs it had made to police, including members of the Vice Control Division, which is supposed to be responsible for suppressing gambling in the city. The monthly graft payroll to the Chicago police paid by this single operation had been $8,020, or nearly $100,000 a year. In the wake of the raid, one of the mob's gambling bosses reportedly boasted: "We got a promise that Duffy will go." And shortly, on Conlisk's orders, Duffy did go —to a 4 P.M. to midnight job as watch commander in the quiet, Jewish district of Albany Park.

As Sandy Smith of *Time-Life* sums up the situation, "There is a climate around Chicago police in which organized crime thrives like jungle shrubbery. There are good cops in Chicago—but not enough of them."

In calmer times, a compromised Chicago police force might have presented no clear and present dangers. Before the 1960s, the Chicago police had been even more corrupt and the people of Chicago seemed to accept it. But the late 1960s were also the time of black revolt, and a huge majority of the force was made up of men from white ethnic communities that had the least natural empathy for militant blacks. During the explosive protest marches led by Martin Luther King, Jr., in 1967, the police handled themselves well. In the spring of 1968, when the tumultuous West Side ghetto erupted into a major riot in the wake of King's assassination—leading to arson that destroyed blocks of buildings, widespread looting, sniper battles, and the calling up of 12,000 National Guard and federal troops—Daley assigned the elite police units to guard the Loop and let the ghetto streets go undermanned; nevertheless, the police on the West Side acted with general restraint, despite some question-able deaths. But then Mayor Richard Daley let the genie of police violence out of the bottle. Provoked, confused, angered by the rioting in his beloved city, Daley said he had told Conlisk "very emphatically and very definitely that an order be issued immediately and under his signature to shoot to kill any arsonist or anyone with a Molotov cocktail in his hand in Chicago because they're potential murderers, and to issue a police order to shoot to maim or cripple anyone looting any stores in the city." It mattered little that the next day Daley said that the police would use only "minimum force" in carrying out orders, and blandly asserted, "There wasn't any shoot-to-kill order. That was a fabrication." As D. J. R. Bruckner, the Los Angeles *Times'* Midwestern correspondent pointed out, "The mayor's repentence will always be sus-pect. . . . The revelation of his inner anger has set loose evil spirits which may never be laid to rest again."

Only four months later, the Democratic National Convention of 1968 opened in Chicago, and with it came thousands of youthful demonstrators bent on protest against the Vietnam war and discrediting the old-line polit-ical system that was about to nominate the Johnson Administration's candi-date, Hubert Humphrey, for the Presidency. Raw intelligence from FBI files raised the specter of widespread street violence, of disruption of convention proceedings, of LSD in the water system or uprisings in the black ghettos. The reports frightened Daley and his colleagues and put them in a frame of mind to use whatever force might be necessary to maintain order.

Into the city streamed a motley band of hippies, yippies, SDS'ers in search of a confrontation—but also thousands of McCarthy-style liberals who abhorred any kind of violence, and thousands of innocent bystanders swept up in it. No repetition is needed here of the agonizing story of repeated and esca-lated street clashes between protestors and police, of tear-gassing and the senseless nighttime curfew at Lincoln Park and the bludgeoning of the curfew-breakers by police in the dark, of the cruel violence perpetrated before television cameras, of obscene provocation on the one side and brutal police attacks on the other. "It left a scar on the city of Chicago," *Newsweek* com-mented, "that may become as indelible a part of its violent history as the Hay-market Riot and the St. Valentine's Day Massacre." *

At the request of the National Commission on the Causes and Preven-tion of Violence, a 212-man staff under Chicago attorney Daniel Walker inter-viewed thousands of witnesses to prepare a report on just what had happened at the convention. Some highlights from its report:

> The Chicago police were the targets of mounting provocation by both word and act. It took the form of obscene epithets, and of rocks, sticks, bathroom tiles and even human feces hurled at police by demonstrators. That was the nature of

---

* *Newsweek* might have added that Chicago's violent history also included the Pullman strike of 1893, in which federal troops were called in to quiet rioters; the race riot of 1919 which took the lives of 38; the Republic Steel strike of 1937 in which 10 died.

the provocation. The nature of the response was unrestrained and indiscriminate police violence on many occasions, particularly at night. That violence was made all the more shocking by the fact that it was often inflicted upon persons who had broken no law, disobeyed no order, made no threat. . . .

On the part of the police there was enough wild club-swinging, enough cries of hatred, enough gratuitous beating to make the conclusion inescapable that individual policemen, and lots of them, committed violent acts far in excess of the requisite force for crowd dispersal or arrest. To read dispassionately the hundreds of statements describing at first hand the events of Sunday and Monday nights is to become convinced of the presence of what can only be called a police riot.

One incident within the 343-page Walker report bears special relevance to the story of Chicago's police over the years. A deputy commissioner of police, distraught by the attacks of individual policemen on demonstrators, started to pull his men away, crying, "Stop, damn it, stop. For Christ's sake, stop it." But these police were not to be controlled, even by their officers. In a police force honeycombed with payoffs and favors from the syndicate, involving officers and their men alike, and in a city where a mayor talks of shooting to kill, it is not surprising to hear that police discipline evaporates in a moment of stress.

The Church: Catholic and Ecumenical

For many decades, the Roman Catholic Archdiocese of Chicago and the Cook County Democratic organization have been closely allied—if for no other reason than the fact that they share the same heavily Irish, Polish, and Italian constituencies. George Cardinal Mundelein, who gained world renown for his public denunciation of Hitler in the early 1930s, was a personal friend of President Roosevelt; in Chicago, he cooperated extensively with the mayor and party boss of the era, Ed Kelly. John Cardinal Cody, leader of the flock since 1966, is an authoritarian figure similar to Mayor Daley, and in fact the two men have a close working relationship.

But just as reform movements and black militancy threaten the Democratic machine, so the winds of change symbolized by the Vatican Council and Pope John's leadership are threatening the authoritarian regime of the church. Under Cody's two direct predecessors, Samuel Cardinal Stritch and Albert Cardinal Meyer, many new and creative ideas were introduced: a Catholic Interracial Council, work with the Catholic workers movement, cooperation with Chicago's pioneer community organizations such as the Woodlawn Organization, and an Interreligious Council on Urban Affairs which led to deep involvement of Catholics, Protestants, and Jews together on inner-city problems.

Cardinal Cody, while outspoken for the record on equal rights in race matters,* has attempted to cork the bottle of change and ecumenism

---

* Theory and practice in church race policies may not always go together. The Rev. Rollins Lambert, who in 1949 became the first Negro priest in the Chicago Archdiocese, has described Cody and "the whole white church" as "unconsciously racist."

among both the clergy and laity. One of his first moves was to remove from his key diocesan urban affairs post a foremost spokesman for racial amity and inner-city social work, Monsignor John Egan. Egan had also been the first outspoken critic within the church of Daley and the Democratic machine. The atmosphere within the church has shifted from one of openness and innovation under Cardinal Meyer to a stifling of initiative and creativity under Cody.

Dozens of Chicago area priests have found the situation intolerable and have left the priesthood in the last several years. Another form of response, begun in 1965, has been the Association of Chicago Priests, a forerunner of various priests' organizations across the country. About 900 of the 2,400 priests in the archdiocese have joined. The group has pressed for a strong church social action program (including work in the ghettos), lifting the requirement of celibacy, permitting men to be worker priests, and consideration of team ministries which would eliminate the pastor as an authority figure and include priests, laity, and sisters working together as a "pastoral team." In spring 1971, charging that the Chicago hierarchy had failed to represent the views of Chicago priests at the National Conference of Catholic Bishops, the Association met and took the drastic step—unprecedented in Chicago, and perhaps in the world—of censuring Archbishop Cody and his five auxiliary bishops. "We want the Catholic world to know," one of the leaders of the Association said, "that we will no longer be content with the paternalism of the past."

Cody must face this turbulence in his own ranks at the same time that many parishes face financial crises and the parochial schools are being threatened by a shortage of funds and the challenge to improve radically their quality of instruction. The traditional fountainhead of parochial teachers, the sisters of the church, is drying up as fewer and fewer young women enter orders and many leave for the greater freedom of the noncloistered life. A reservoir remains of dedicated nuns and lay teachers in the church's inner-city schools, where they see a real challenge. But recruitment of nuns to teach in middle-class and suburban neighborhoods is becoming difficult in the extreme. In apparent tune with the times, the once-heavy emphasis on religious instruction and proselytizing in the parochial schools has all but disappeared. In 1971, a special commission of the city's Catholic school board proposed sweeping changes in the financially troubled archdiocesan schools, including a transfer of control to independent local school boards and possible cooperation with some Protestant parochial systems.

As internal problems and dissent start to sap the institutional strength of the Chicago archdiocese, it begins to slip perceptibly in its political influence. Yet in less heralded ways, new Christian thought and direction develop in the city. There are so many programs, so many new approaches, under so many denominational banners, that the mere cataloguing of them for Chicago or other great cities would be beyond the scope of this book. Selectively, I have chosen one program, actually national in scope, which is centered in Chicago: the Urban Training Center for Christian Mission, with its headquarters in a time-ravaged old Congregational seminary building in the

West Side slums. UTC was begun in the early 1960s as a way that clergy from the Catholic Church and numerous Protestant denominations could learn more about the life of the shoddy, deprived inner city, and how their churches might serve it. Trainees, either clergy or seminarians (and some nuns), undergo the cultural shock of a "rock bottom plunge" into the community as soon as they arrive to start their course. Given $6 in pocket money, they are sent out to forage for themselves in a Skid Row area for four days. Some line up for day labor, others seek help from other derelicts, some just pound the pavement to experience, however briefly, the despair of the unemployable.

The result of such exposure is major cultural shock, especially for many ministers from established parish backgrounds. But like the worker priests of past decades in Europe, they have a taste of the poverty, the degradation to which others are subjected, and then are ready to immerse themselves in workshops on major issues (ranging from housing to city politics), on the role of "prophetic" words and "servant" deeds in Biblical settings, on radical new approaches to liturgy. They also spend a great deal of time working with community organizations or social action agencies. The confrontations involved in these experiences, in the words of the Rev. James P. Morton, director of UTC, lead participants "to look at the city with joy and hope, instead of running away defeated."

Morton is a breathless, forceful, fast-thinking man in his early forties who had served in a team ministry along the Jersey City waterfront and headed urban programs for the Episcopal Church before taking on the UTC assignment. It had been his sad experience, Morton notes, that rather than expecting the church to play a role in community action, "our civic assemblies called upon the clergy to perform a very different role—common to the medicine man and magicians of all ages—which principally involved the blessing of the status quo, ringing the curtain up and down on the day's program (whatever it is); and then to collect one's fees and go home. Clergy so often tend to be necessary ornaments." He sees the rightful role of the church as prophetic, spelling out man's creative relationship to man under God, condemning sick institutions, serving as the servant of society. "But she is always a servant with a song," he insists. "The church is present in any place to witness to the truth of the Gospel in that situation. Out of ten agencies at work on some problem, one should be in there with a certain levity, a sense of abandon. That would be the group of Christians."

By the early 1970s, the Urban Training Center had spawned some 19 copies in other cities from Washington to Los Angeles, and in Chicago UTC was narrowing its focus to such problems as employment for the unschooled and underschooled, the problem of "colonialistic" exploitation of dependent and powerless ghetto residents, and institutional racism. It had already furnished the manpower and talent to start The Westside Organization, which was growing into a black community agency not unlike The Woodlawn Organization in South Chicago. UTC was also accusing the Chicago YMCA and other social welfare groups of racist policies and attitudes. As its role became more controversial, UTC's emphasis on social action seemed likely to incur more and more criticism from the very standard denominations—from Baptist to Roman Catholic, from Greek and Russian Orthodox to Mennonite—which were supporting it.

Social Work in the Melting Pot; Back of the Yards and Saul Alinsky

One of America's most complex and colorful melting pots, Chicago has been making a major effort to ease conditions for its polyglot immigrants ever since Jane Addams started Hull House to help newly arrived Greeks, Lithuanians, Italians, Jews, Irish, Germans, and Poles more than 75 years ago. The very first settlers, the American Indians, numbered only 400 in Chicago in 1940 but have since risen to 11,000 in population, necessitating their own Indian Center in the city with a salaried director. One of the newest ports of entry is the "Uptown" area on the North Side, a polyglot of impoverished Appalachian whites, Cubans, Mexicans, and Chinese set down among the more indigenous alcoholics and addicts; one form of help for this community is being provided by the Rev. Tom Millea, an activist Catholic priest who is trying to reform the exploitive practices of the day-labor agencies who arrange a day's work for desperate derelicts and winos and then sometimes pay them just half what the employer actually pays the agency.

Chicago deserves to be remembered as the city that gave birth to the modern community organization techniques of confrontation, sit-downs, boycotts, and militancy that have become a vogue in recent years. The man probably most responsible for this is Chicagoan Saul Alinsky, a sharp-witted nonconformist, now in his early seventies, who enjoys the sobriquet *Harper's Magazine* gave him in 1965: "The Professional Radical."

The test tube for Alinsky's method was the sprawling steeple-and-smoke-stack neighborhood of stockyards workers living in the late 1930s in the area in back (to the west) of the famous Chicago Stockyards, close to Daley's Bridgeport. The area was afflicted with severe problems of poverty, juvenile delinquency, health, housing, unemployment, but perhaps most serious of all, deep-seated hostilities among its 24 various nationality groups. Joseph B. Meegan, who worked with Alinsky in founding the Back of the Yards Council and is still its active head, recalls that "the Poles didn't speak to the Lithuanians or the Slovaks to the Bohemians or the Slovenians to the Ukrainians, and the Irish called them all foreigners." Stockyards workers were earning 39¢ an hour but were so hostile to each other that the Packinghouse Workers were experiencing great difficulties in organizing them. One of the first things the Back of the Yards Council did was to arrange a unity meeting of some 16,000 packinghouse workers; under threat of a strike, an immediate increase of 17¢ an hour was obtained; later on, strikes were actually called and in some, clergy joined the picket line.

The principal groups which threw in their lot with the Back of the Yards

Council were the workers, the churches (virtually all Roman Catholic, but split up into Polish, Lithuanian, Mexican, Irish parishes, etc.), and the small merchants of the area. The plan succeeded spectacularly in drawing the community together, and major accomplishments were ticked off year by year: first labor organization to get living wages for the packinghouse workers and to make sure men from the neighborhood got the available stockyards jobs, then a broad school lunch program, an infant care clinic, water fluoridation, employment counseling for workers (especially necessary as the stockyards later declined and gave way to light industry *), and sustained efforts to control street gangs and help out youngsters as soon as they are arrested for a first juvenile offense. The Council has sustained a painstaking record-keeping program to track the ownership and condition of every house and piece of land in the area, in order to encourage maximum property maintenance. I have seen no other American community in which so many low-cost homes have been so well tended; one may question the tastefulness of stucco applique or aluminum siding, but the tenant's love of hearth and home is there for all the world to see. No less than 80 percent of the homes are owner occupied.

Joe Meegan, who has run the Back of the Yards Council ever since Alinsky left it to its own devices in the early 1940s, is a locally born man, soft spoken, florid faced, the father of nine children, and as he puts it, "one of the few Irish" of the neighborhood. Meegan has made some interesting friends. In Washington, to lobby for the school lunch program in the first years of the Council's life, he met John McCormack of Massachusetts. The two men struck up a friendship, and whenever the House Speaker went to Chicago, he and his wife had dinner with Meegan virtually every night. Another friend was Everett M. Dirksen, who called Meegan "a live saint." Meegan and his organization are extremely close to Mayor Daley. None of these are the kind of Establishment friends an Alinsky would be likely to attract, and indeed there is much grumbling among integrationist leaders in Chicago that the Back of the Yards has become an island of racist exclusion and something of an anachronism. Meegan told me that a few Negroes would be welcome to live in the neighborhood, but a foremost housing expert in Chicago commented that "a Negro would be scared to death to walk the streets after dark in Meegan's area."

Alinsky, who has had no ties with the Back of the Yards for almost 30 years, has traveled all over the U.S.A. helping numerous other community organizations get their start: The Woodlawn Organization in South Chicago, the FIGHT organization to mobilize blacks to deal with Eastman Kodak in Rochester, and helping César Chávez start the organization of California grape pickers.

---

* The century-old Union Stockyards, which inspired Carl Sandburg to call Chicago "Hog Butcher for the world" and Upton Sinclair to write *The Jungle*, culminated a long decline by dropping handling of the last farm animals in February 1971. The decline began in the 1950s when the big packers like Swift, Wilson, and Armour shifted their slaughtering to more efficient, one-story plants at locations near the farms and feed lots where cattle and hogs are born and fattened. Rapid truck transport of the already slaughtered animals made the decentralization feasible. Now the stockyards are rapidly turning into an industrial park, and the hardy ethnics whose fathers and grandfathers once sweated to earn 15¢ an hour in the steaming slaughter rooms are employed in small factories or on Chicago's many construction projects.

The Black Nation in Chicago

For half a century now, and most spectacularly in the years since World War II began, the cars of the Illinois Central Railroad have been transporting vast numbers of Negroes up the Mississippi River Valley, from Louisiana and Mississippi, Arkansas and Tennessee, into the city of Chicago. According to the 1970 Census figures, there are at least 1,102,620 blacks in Chicago, 33 percent of the city's population.* I say "at least" because after 1960, when the Census takers counted 837,656 Negroes in Chicago, reliable studies suggested that about 157,000 had been missed in the official count.

In all America, only one other city—New York—has more blacks than Chicago. The city's Negro population is twice again as large as the black count in Washington, D.C., and a third higher than the figure for Los Angeles, Philadelphia, or Detroit. The black civilization of Chicago is so multifaceted —from the great daily Negro press, *The Defender*, an institution of great pride and vigor, to the longtime headquarters of the Black Muslims—that we can only sample some aspects of its life in this chapter.

With the possible exception of Cleveland, no city is as rigidly segregated in its housing patterns; when blacks begin to move into a Chicago community, the whites flee like locusts. In 1968, 5.2 blocks a week in Chicago shifted from white to black. By 1984, according to some projections, Chicago will have a black majority. Sometimes whites organize to stem the black expansion; in the white communities on the western side of Ashland Avenue, a great Chinese Wall of segregation that stretches through the city's southwest section, a Catholic priest, the Rev. Francis X. Lawlor, has organized block clubs to keep the neighborhoods white. But it is probably a losing battle, for there are only so many square miles of territory in the city, and as long as the almost totally white suburbs can find ways to exclude blacks while the black population continues to rise, simple mathematics dictate more black communities and more white flight to the suburbs. (In 1971, Lawlor defeated the Daley machine candidate to win election as a city alderman.)

There are two great black population concentrations in Chicago. The first, and by far and away the largest, is the South Side. Many of its neighborhoods—Woodlawn, Kenwood, Grand Boulevard, and the like—have been black for decades now; many others, clear down to the city border, are more recently black or turning black. Only a handful, most notably Hyde Park, North Kenwood, and the South Commons area,† have witnessed successful and durable integration. Especially in its southern sections, the South Side has some prosperous, middle-class black neighborhoods; the more desperate slums are in its more northern sections. One South Side area, Woodlawn, is

* The Negro percentage is up from only 8 percent in 1940, 14 percent in 1950, 23 percent in 1960.
† South Commons, a completely new area with 4,000 residents, has succeeded as an integrated community because the entrepreneur who built it had the guts to build in a quarter-million-dollar school, which he then succeeded in leasing to the city. With a quality, integrated school, many young white families have been kept who might otherwise have fled to the suburbs.

the home of the first and most effective community organization in any American ghetto. In all, the South Side has about as settled a feeling about it as any large Negro section of a U.S. city.

The new, raw, volatile ghetto is in Lawndale and other sections of the West Side. These were Jewish communities little more than a decade ago but then experienced a lightning transformation into all-black islands. The West Side is the modern-day port of entry for Southern blacks, and it has all the social instability associated with an immigrant center. When West Siders begin to make some money, they quickly escape to better-to-do sections of the South Side. Community organization is much newer but gaining strength.

Victor de Grazia, who started and for several years ran the Kate Maremount Foundation, which does extensive rehabilitation work in Chicago's slums, says that the South Side is the easiest area in which to get community participation and follow-through on maintenance of redone housing. The West Side is substantially more difficult, though possible in spots. The most hopeless area is not black at all, but the totally disorganized, violent community of poor Appalachian whites in the uptown section.

The sociologist Pierre De Vise reports in his book, *Chicago's Widening Color Gap*, that compared to the white Chicagoan, the average Negro of the city is younger by ten years, only half as likely to hold a craft job, three times as likely to be a laborer, eight times as likely to be a domestic. He (or she) has only a third as great a chance to be a salesperson or manager and is three times as likely to be without any job at all. Black families are one-fifth larger, have only two-thirds of the income, and occupy housing units which are one-fifth smaller and five times more dilapidated, but cost just about as much, as the superior homes and apartments occupied by whites.

Chicago Negroes are failing to make the strides of blacks in other cities. Between 1959 and 1967, for instance, the number of Chicago area Negro families living below the poverty line increased from 55,000 (30 percent of the total) to 71,000 (33 percent of the total).* In the same period, New York City's percentage of black families living in poverty went down from 26 to 24 percent, and the Los Angeles percentage was reduced from 24 to 20.

Part of these grim statistics for Chicago, of course, reflect the continuing immigration of Southern blacks, even if the influx is slackening to some degree. Yet at the same time, thousands of blacks have been able to move into middle-class status. Francis Fischer, until recently regional director for HUD in Chicago, told me that "the number of white-collar blacks working on Michigan Avenue today as opposed to just four years ago is simply striking. So are the number of casual interracial groupings you see—secretaries sitting together at lunch, or young guys looking at stock reports on their way to lunch. Innumerable whites are being exposed to intelligent, articulate blacks for the first time in their lives, and the eventual impact on our society will be great. The contacts are highly destructive of the old notion that blacks are inferior." He points out that in 1952, the Yellow Cabs in Chicago had not a

* The figures apply to the entire Chicago metropolitan area within Illinois, but the figure is essentially a Chicago one, since 95 percent of the area's blacks live in the city. Only 6 percent of the Chicago area white families live on incomes below the poverty line.

single black driver, only one State Street store had black sales people, and only one or two Loop restaurants served Negroes. "The bright, educated person in Chicago today knows he or she can get a good job—in contrast to the discouragement and desperation of a few years back."

This is not a solution, Fischer acknowledges, for the 16-to-18-year-old school drop-outs with police records or for families mired in the worst slums. The high count of black Chicagoans living in poverty is likely to continue into the future, barring massive private or government efforts to reverse the trend. Despite their inadequate incomes, Chicago Negroes have a fertility rate 45 percent greater than that of whites; the rate is even higher among the poorest groups, where illegitimate births are on the rise. Slum Negroes are failing to get the education to prepare them for advanced jobs; deep segregation continues in the public schools, with 85 percent of Negro students in schools that are 95 to 100 percent black. The black school districts are uniformly lower in both reading skills and the percentage of certified teachers. On the lower end of the job scale, white construction workers have staged brawling demonstrations to protest efforts of blacks to get more building trades jobs.

There is ample evidence to show that the segregated housing patterns of Chicago, which in turn are the major cause of school segregation, are fostered by government itself. In 1968, a federal district court ruled that the Chicago Housing Authority, a creature of the city government which uses federal funds to put up public housing, was guilty of racial discrimination in choosing building sites and assigning tenants. Of 54 public housing projects in Chicago, containing some 30,000 units, all but four had been constructed in black neighborhoods and had black tenant rates of 99 percent. By contrast, there were four projects in white sections of the city; these had a Negro occupancy rate of only 1 to 7 percent (set by quota), and the most lily-white of all was located just nine blocks from Mayor Daley's Bridgeport home.

The real villain in this scenario is probably not the housing authority, but the city council. Aldermen from white districts invariably veto any proposed public housing in their areas, and thus it is not built. Federal Judge Richard B. Austin took note in the 1968 decision of a "desperately intensifying division of whites and Negroes in Chicago." Despite objections from Daley and the aldermen, his court orders to put more projects in white areas seem likely to effect a change—but not until the mid- or late 1970s.

Perhaps the most deplorable housing project of Chicago is a string of 28 high-rise buildings along the railroad tracks near South State Street, known as the Robert Taylor Homes. Of the 28,000 people in the project, 20,000 are under 21. The residents, according to a Chicago *Daily News* reporter, are "all poor, grappling with violence and vandalism, fear and suspicion, teen-age terror and adult chaos, rage, resentment, official regimenting. They're second-class citizens living in a second-class world, and they know it, and hate it." One wonders how this misuse of federal money came to be, and hears the story that Col. McCormick's wife, riding on the 20th Century Limited from the East, would wake up early in the morning as the train entered Chicago and see the terrible slums. So she asked the Colonel if something couldn't be done about the eyesore, and that led to Chicago *Tribune* support and construction of a project which may be even worse than what preceded it.

The subjugation of Chicago's black population is made all the more complete by the success of the Democratic machine in neutralizing effective political opposition in the ghettos and indeed making the black vote a mainstay of its own power. For almost 30 years, the principal agent of machine power in the black wards was Georgia-born Congressman William L. Dawson, who had failed in politics as a Republican but then succeeded brilliantly after Mayor Kelly picked him as his black plantation chief. Elected in 1942 as the second black Congressman of the century, Dawson rose to become the first Negro Congressional committee chairman in U.S. history (the Government Operations Committee), but he never introduced major legislation and showed scant interest in the Negro rights drive of the 1960s. Though a member of the House District of Columbia Committee, presiding over heavily black Washington, Dawson often skipped committee sessions and left his proxy with none other than that nemesis of Washington Negroes, Committee Chairman John L. McMillan of Florence, South Carolina. At 84 years of age, Dawson died in 1970.

Dawson's base of power was his position as Second Ward Democratic committeeman; from it he built, in the words of former Chicago *Defender* editor Chuck Stone, "a black political machine that was as efficient and vicious as the city-wide Democratic machine." Ill-educated blacks were often led to believe that if they defied him, they might lose welfare benefits or be turned out of public housing. For the South Side Negro in search of a job or a favor or a bailbondsman, Dawson's organization was the place to go. As a lawyer before his election to Congress, Dawson had specialized in defense of Negro gamblers; as boss, he permitted the numbers racket, organized prostitution, and illegal bookmaking to flourish in exchange for support of his organization.

In 1964, Dawson was challenged by a vigorous reform Democrat, A. A. (Sammy) Rayner. In that campaign (which Dawson won with ease) his Second Ward secretary and 26th Precinct Captain, Lawrence C. Woods, signed a mimeographed letter to voters urging Dawson's reelection. The letter, in part, read as follows:

I am very proud of you, and I always try to show my appreciation by thinking about you and your family at Christmas, Easter, and at the closing of school. After every election victory, a dinner basket is placed in your home. You understand how I feel about you and your families. Let no man come between us. . . . When I bless my table on April 15, I shall bless the table of 582 REGULAR DEMOCRATIC VOTERS of the Twenty-sixth Precinct.

At one point, it appeared that Alderman Rayner, unabashed in his open criticisms of Mayor Daley, might replace Dawson in Congress. Rayner seemed to have all the attributes of a relevant "new" black politician—he was smart and articulate, he related to (and even helped) youth in street gangs and the Panthers, he was a flamboyant campaigner, he had "soul." Perhaps too much "soul," one might say. In 1970, with Dawson retiring, Rayner ran again for Congress but made the mistake of defending the gangs. He was overwhelmingly defeated by the machine's choice, Alderman Ralph H. Metcalfe, an Olympic sprinter of many years past. Later Rayner also lost his job as alderman, and with his political demise Chicago's blacks lost a remarkably free-spirited leader.

In the same primary, a second Chicago black was nominated for Congress, George W. Collins from the West Side. He, too, is a machine man. Despite breakthroughs of reform elements in a few aldermanic elections, recent Chicago elections suggest that the "new politics" and "reform," for all their popularity in the press and among intellectuals, will be a long day coming into real power in the Chicago of Richard Daley and his machine stalwarts. But the reform movement has forced the machine to dump some inept office-holders and slate better men.

Despite the inability of the reformers to make broad advances through elective politics, two powerful and innovative organizations of and for blacks in Chicago—The Woodlawn Organization and Operation Breadbasket—have sprung into being in recent years and may become models for new forms of Negro self-assertion in the United States.

Located just south of the University of Chicago on the city's South Side, Woodlawn is one of Chicago's most densely populated areas (some 60,000 in a square mile), a neighborhood of absentee landlords, decaying buildings, boarded up shops, and, in the words of one local clergyman, "spray-paint graffiti on buildings and fences to remind everyone of the explosive mixture of hope and suppressed rage to be found in every young person who roams the streets." Here in 1959, in a unique ecumenical effort, one Roman Catholic and three Protestant pastors combined forces to start a strong umbrella-type community organization. After prolonged controversy, they decided to invite the colorful Saul Alinsky, of Back of the Yards fame, to advise and consult with the newly forming group, The Woodlawn Organization (TWO).

In succeeding years, with more than 100 community organizations participating, TWO mounted an Alinsky-style program of issue confrontation and action on an amazingly broad scale. Early undertakings included an attack on unscrupulous businessmen for sales tactics that antagonized local residents, the first rent strike in the U.S.A. to force absentee white landlords to make necessary repairs to buildings, and a crucial battle with the gigantic University of Chicago to make it compromise on its monstrous urban renewal plans, which in their first forms would have consumed a major portion of the Woodlawn area. Through a sit-in in Mayor Daley's office, TWO finally got an agreement that no urban renewal demolition would begin until construction could actually begin on a large (502-unit) low-cost housing project on Cottage Grove Avenue to house potential displacees; it was the first agreement of that kind any community organization in the country had evoked from government. TWO went to Victor de Grazia of the Kate Maremount Foundation for consultation and seed money to plan the federally financed housing. And, in another unique move, the residents were called in to say what the new housing should be like before it was even designed. Their almost unanimous judgment: build no high rises; we want a dense, low-rise community with no buildings over five stories. What they wanted to avoid, de Grazia says, was the kind of high-rise vertical ghetto horror symbolized by the Robert Taylor Homes. So the promotional folders for the Cottage Grove literally and truthfully claim: "Designed by the residents of Woodlawn." Sociologically, de Grazia points out, "when you're dealing with people who are the least sophisticated about urban living, you don't require them to live in the most sophisticated kind of housing—high rise apartments. The more the housing can be like single houses, the better it will be in terms of people's own ability to cope with their physical environment."

TWO took the lead in closing up the infamous "Sin Corner" in Woodlawn, a fountainhead of dope traffic and prostitution, by means of a localized prohibition ordinance. And TWO was able to get an experimental decentralized school board established in which community residents, in conjunction with the University of Chicago and the Board of Education, actually run a local high school and several feeder grade and junior high schools. Local people have the major say in hiring of the administrator, teacher assignment, and curriculum—the same type of effort which would cause such pandemonium and a citywide teachers strike in New York two years later. The local board has had some severe personnel problems and is periodically threatened with a cutoff in funds, however.

Alinsky glows with pleasure when he thinks of some of the unconventional tactics TWO has occasionally improvised. Examples: "TWO got Mayor Daley to deal with them after they threatened to tie up all the rest rooms at O'Hare—keeping all the booths occupied. O'Hare is one of Daley's sacred cows. Another time TWO people piled rats on the steps of City Hall. Daley got that message too."

One of the most controversial projects TWO ever became involved with was a national poverty program grant of $975,000 to set up a special kind of youth project in its area, an admittedly "high-risk venture" that would utilize the existing structures of street gangs such as the Blackstone Rangers and the Devil's Disciples. Gangs are nothing new to Chicago; back in the 1920s the Moran, O'Banion, and Capone gangs ruled the streets and murdered at will; there are still violence-prone gangs in many lower class white areas. In the postwar era it was almost inevitable that a new and virulent form of gangism would emerge among the desperate youths of the black ghettos. Individual members of gangs like the Rangers (now called the Black P. Stone Nation) have been charged with all manner of crimes—including robbery, murder, rapings, knifings, extortion, and traffic in narcotics*—especially in connection with their ongoing feud against the Disciples, who have refused to join with them. (Many lesser South Side gangs, ranging from the Maniacs to the Pharaohs, have found it advisable to join the Rangers, so that total membership apparently ranges between 3,500 and 8,000 boys and men.) But at the same time, the Ranger Nation has been credited with keeping the

* The worst violence is perpetrated by "gang-bangers"—boys in their early teens who like to fight with firearms; older Rangers disdain the youngsters but cannot control them. By their mid-twenties, a friend of the Rangers told me, "they're either in jail, dead, or they've changed their sinful ways."

South Side "cool" when West Side ghettos erupted in the wake of King's assassination, and have reportedly used their persuasion to keep alcoholics, prostitutes, and drug peddlers out of their neighborhood.

Predictably, the TWO program with the gangs involved the organization in semi-scandals and the intense conflict between the police and gang members. Some of the worst alleged abuses were aired in June 1968 hearings before Senator McClellan's Senate Investigations Subcommittee. The program became a liability for the national Office of Economic Opportunity and was discontinued.

The counterpart to the Rangers on the West Side of Chicago is the Vice Lords, a group that held its neighborhood in terror in the early 1960s but tried to go "legitimate" with a restaurant, shops, and a teaching center at the heart of its "turf" on West 16th Street later in the decade. The Vice Lords, however, were afflicted by both internal conflicts (including killings) and police harassment.

It was also on the West Side, in December of 1969, that police staged a 4:45 A.M. raid on Black Panther headquarters, ostensibly in search of illegally held weapons. But it was the police who ended up doing virtually all of the shooting, including killing state Panther chairman Fred Hampton in his bed. The director of the raid was state's attorney Edward Hanrahan, who was said to be making a name for himself in the suburbs as a youth-gang and Panther buster. Hanrahan is the same man we met earlier as U. S. Attorney under the Johnson Administration, reluctant to press for indictments against Mafia-connected Democratic politicians in the infamous First Ward. A bright attorney, dutiful precinct captain, and favorite of the ruling Irish Catholic clique in the Daley machine, Hanrahan had been considered a leading choice of the machine for the governorship in 1972. But a special grand jury went to work on the Panthers case and in August 1971 indicted Hanrahan and 13 other law officers for conspiring to obstruct justice in the investigation which followed the raid. The indictments were delayed two months while the chief judge of the criminal court, Joseph Powers, moved heaven and earth to squash them. Powers is a friend, neighbor, and former law partner of Mayor Daley. He opened the indictments only when the state supreme court ordered him to do so.

As the chief of its amazingly successful Operation Breadbasket, the black community of Chicago has harbored a veritable folk hero and emerging national leader of his race: 29-year-old Jesse Louis Jackson, Baptist preacher, son of South Carolinian poverty, organizer of economic boycotts, fiery battler for black rights, politician and prophet. In the spring of 1968, Jackson was talking with Martin Luther King, Jr., on the balcony of the Lorraine Motel in Memphis when the sniper's bullets cracked across the void. Jackson cradled the dying man in his arms; less than a day later, standing in a sweater stained with King's blood in the City Hall chambers in Chicago, he responded to a platitudinous testimonial by Mayor Daley with a shout to the Chicago political establishment assembled: "His blood is on the hands of you who would not have welcomed him here yesterday!"

"That gesture demonstrated both the militant indignation and the dramatic flair that mark Jackson's charismatic style," writer Arthur Kretchmer has noted in *Playboy*. The New York *Times* has written that Jackson "sounds a little like the Rev. Dr. Martin Luther King, Jr., and a little like a Black Panther."

Technically, Jackson's sole position has been that of economic director of King's Southern Christian Leadership Conference; in fact, the Operation Breadbasket which he has developed in Chicago since 1966 is (with the Rev. Leon Sullivan's activities in Philadelphia, which helped inspire it), one of the most impressive demonstrations in America today of black economic power and self-determination. Through use or threat of boycott, great corporations doing business in the ghettos have been led to sign far-reaching agreements with Operation Breadbasket—to hire stipulated numbers of blacks, to stock their shelves with products produced by black-owned companies, to use black construction firms to build their ghetto stores, to bank with black-owned banks, even to use black-owned janitorial and exterminating services for their ghetto installations. Late in 1969, Operation Breadbasket sponsored a three-day Black Expo in Chicago, described by *Ebony* as "undoubtedly the largest, most successful black trade fair ever held;" the attendance was a scarcely believable 900,000. By 1971, the Black Expo had grown to 500 commercial booths (90 percent sponsored by black concerns) and even Richard Daley was impressed enough to pay a personal visit. The cohesiveness among Chicago black concerns grew so much that in the four years following Breadbasket's first businessmen's seminar in 1966, the capital of the city's two black banks grew from $6 million to $55 million. Even in the face of disappointments for Chicago Negroes—a reported annual failure rate of 31 percent among black-owned Chicago businesses, and the complete failure of the Labor Department's "Chicago Plan" to foster black employment in the building crafts—Operation Breadbasket was spelling out a unique story of black progress in America.

An understanding of the wellsprings of Jackson's power must begin with a visit to the weekly Saturday morning Operation Breadbasket sessions—a mixture of religious revival, indignation meeting, strategy session, and joyous soul music celebration—attended by some 4,000 persons, first in churches, then in a big old theatre the organization bought for about $250,000. No old folks' church atmosphere here; indeed the preponderance is young black adults. One sees a smattering of white visitors; Jackson is one of very few younger black leaders still interested in a coalition with whites. ("When we change the race problem into a class fight between the haves and the have-nots, then we are going to have a new ball game," he declares.)

On the stage as the Breadbasket program begins are several dozen SCLC troops in blue denim jackets, many bearded with African hairdos. A full band, its star performer a gifted trombone player, belts out slow, religious music, and then makes a breathtakingly rapid transition to fast, hand-clapping jazz with the thousands present joining in the clapping in a great outpouring of exuberance. "We are resurrecting the spirit of black people, and in turn the spirit of this dead city—with the music that lifts our dry bones," proclaims a speaker.

The high point, of course, is Jackson's own appearance; no matter where he may be in the country, he will fly back to Chicago each Saturday morning. The victim of a chronic blood disease, Jackson has sometimes risen from his hospital bed for the sessions. His introduction—as "the country preacher" and "the man who lives on the edge of danger and opportunity"—is followed by minutes of standing, clapping ovation. The figure is young, fragile, proud; the head leonine, with black mustache and sideburns; he wears a grey turtle-neck sweater with a pendant around his neck.

The sermon is concentrated, passionate; it ranges from pure religion to assertive black pride to calls for practical economic action:

> We are a beautiful people. . . . When your brothers and sisters are in anguish, hear their cry. . . . We are one third of the city, 95 percent in the jails, and only five percent in the universities. I wonder why? . . . In America, it is always assumed that when you say Senator or President or anything good, it means white. You worship in a white church, you even go to heaven in a white robe! But everything that's black is mean—"Black stay back." Some of us heard it so often we even believed it. But the night is black and it's beautiful because God called it into existence. The stars and moon come out in black. Coal and iron are black. People from the East who formed the Christian religion were black. . . . Black is the way God chose to make me—and I'm glad.

And then Jackson starts a chant and the ecstatic audience shouts the words back: "I am somebody. . . . Maybe I'm poor, but I am somebody. . . . Maybe been on drugs, but I am somebody. . . . Maybe on welfare, but I am somebody. . . . Maybe unemployed, but I am somebody."

Inevitably, Jackson comes to the subject of King:

> But it's a trauma to me. It's not easy when you go to sleep at night, when you close your eyes and pray—to see the prophet, lying on his back, with his throat shot out and his chest exploded. It's not easy to open my closet and see the shirt—with his blood stains on that shirt. . . . When most of us were talking church, he was doing church. When we were saying we weren't afraid to die, he proved it. This world will never be the same because of that man.

And then there is a call to support the boycott or cause of the week, and it is finished, and a trombone rises again in a searching, yearning sound— of what might be.

But the power lies not just in the emotion, but in practical results, economic and political. Evidence of the latter was Jackson's 1969 success in leading a "hunger march" of 3,000 on the state capitol in Springfield and getting Gov. Ogilvie and then-House Speaker Ralph T. Smith to withdraw their proposal for cutting some $25 million in welfare aid. In 1968, Jackson supported Humphrey for President but backed Ogilvie, the Republican, over Daley's choice for governor; a few months later Jackson was collecting his bills from Ogilvie on the welfare issue; a year later he was supporting certain Daley candidates in primary elections, opposing others.

There is, however, a mercurial aspect to Jackson's approach that leaves many confused about his real goals and reduces his effectiveness. In 1971 he seriously considered running for mayor, and some backers reportedly gathered $300,000 in pledges. Then Jackson suddenly reversed course and said he would endorse Daley in return for a pledge of appointment to key positions of a number of blacks. Daley ignored him. On the eve of the election, Jackson endorsed Friedman, the Republican candidate, but it was too late and Daley swept the black areas. After that, Jackson said he would work for a third-party black Presidential candidate in 1972; two days later that was modified to a 'third force," not necessarily a party. In mid-1971, he was on leave of absence from Operation Breadbasket and SCLC chief Ralph Abernathy wanted him to go back to Atlanta—whether to cut a potential rival down to size, or for reasons of consolidation, no one was quite sure.

Still, if Jackson plays his cards right, he could be a major national black leader: young, disciple of King, militant, commanding natural respect, and, through his window to the white world, able to deal effectively in the marketplace and, potentially, in practical politics as well.

Suburban People and Politics and an
Exception to the Transit Blues

Chicago has a bewildering variety of suburbs, some in Cook County, some without, most Republican but many Democratic. In rough terms, they may be divided into four groups.

Oldest and most settled in their ways are the North Shore "establishment" suburbs—cities and villages like Evanston (population 79,808), Wilmette (32,134), Glencoe (10,542), Highland Park (32,263), and Lake Forest (15,642), many of them places of stately high trees lining streets of gracious older homes. In the more outlying areas there are also quantities of high-grade postwar residential developments; more recently, apartment buildings for young singles have been sprouting up. Census figures show these areas ranking at the very top of national surveys of income and educational levels. They are overwhelmingly white and Protestant, though in recent years some have received immigration of Jews, and in Evanston there is a substantial black community. The voting pattern of the North Shore has been predictably Republican, but there are many more independents now, and Evanston has gone Democratic.

At the opposite geographic and ethnic pole are the industrialized, middle and lower income suburbs to the south of Chicago. They are peopled with white laboring folk who have "made it" through diligent saving and are mainly concerned with escaping the problems of the inner city. The population is mostly ethnic: Polish, Italian, Slavic. Some of the larger towns are Oak Lawn (60,305), Calumet City (32,956), and Chicago Heights (40,900). The area has many cheap postwar tract housing developments that are literally coming apart at the seams with normal use. In general, the resistance to integration remains the fiercest in the areas with the lowest education and income levels.

To the west and southwest of Cook County, subdivisions each year consume thousands of acres of prairie in the fast-growing suburban counties of Will (249,498) and DuPage (491,882). With the exception of a few towns like Joliet (80,378), a decaying industrial center, these counties are almost completely residential and peopled by young professionals on their way up who either commute to Chicago or indirectly make their living off the big city. The political complexion is strongly Republican.

Finally, there are the two close-in west side suburbs of Cicero (67,058) and Berwyn (52,502), aging bastions of the middle and lower class ethnic—Bohemian, Polish, and other Slavic. Business streets are dreary, but the home-owners keep immaculate lawns. Cicero has a rich heritage as hangout of Al Capone and the crime syndicate and still harbors some vice and gambling despite periodic raids.

Chicago's suburbanites are superbly served, at least in comparison to any other American metropolis, in one area: public transportation for commuters. With some justification, city leaders boast of having "the finest commuter railroad service in the world." No less than five excellent rail commuter services are in operation: the Chicago and North Western (C&NW) and Milwaukee lines radiating out to the north and northwest, the Burlington and Rock Island lines serving the west and southwest, and the Illinois Central going south along the lake and out into the suburbs. The most outstanding service is provided by the C&NW, with excellent equipment, frequent schedules, and amenities like bar service to soothe the nerves of home-bound commuters. Credit for C&NW's success goes largely to corporate lawyer Ben W. Heineman, whose management team took over the line in 1956 when it was losing $2.5 million a year on commuters and by the late 1960s was registering an annual commuter service profit of $2.2 million. Then it was sold off to a conglomerate and was subsequently acquired by its employees.

In the 1950s, when the city was planning major expressways to the north and south, farsighted planners saw that even on the day the new freeways would open they would be overcrowded in the self-defeating way that center-city expressways are known for. So provision was made, despite no little grumbling by the highway-only bureaucrats of the federal Bureau of Public Roads, to acquire sufficient extra right-of-way for two-way rails down the medians of the new freeways.* So now the Eisenhower, Dan Ryan, and John F. Kennedy Expressways have miles of rapid transit line substantially expanding the city's commuter services. The Kennedy line reaches two-thirds of the way to O'Hare Field, and median right-of-way has been reserved to go all the way to the field and around its parking lot.

* The men chiefly responsible for this imaginative move were George De Ment, then Chicago Commissioner of Public Works and now director of the Chicago Transportation Authority, and his chief engineer at the time, Ralph Bertelsmeier, now director of the U. S. Bureau of Public Roads.

Chicago Miscellany: The Media,
the Universities, the Environment

Illinois has traditionally been regarded as two distinct entities—Chicago and "downstate." By Chicago, people also meant Cook County; by downstate, every other place in Illinois from the Wisconsin border to where the Ohio River meets the Mississippi at Cairo. But Gov. Richard B. Ogilvie, as shrewd a political observer as one could hope to meet, told me that the dominant region of Illinois today is "the Chicago viewing area"—the territory within the 65-mile viewing radius of the Chicago television stations, with 70 percent of Illinois' population.* Television makes Chicago news and personalities preeminent in Illinois, Ogilvie said. By general agreement, the most influential person in television is Len O'Connor, who comments editorially for WMAQ-TV, the NBC outlet; with a whiff of understatement, Ogilvie says of O'Connor: "I'd rather have him as friend than as enemy."

This introduction is clearly intended to make the reader ask whatever happened to the Chicago *Tribune*, described by John Gunther as "more than a mere newspaper, more than even the 'World's Greatest Newspaper,' as it fondly calls itself, a domain, a kind of principality." The *Tribune* is still there, and doing very nicely, thank you, with circulation of some 770,000 weekdays and 1,015,000 Sundays; its conservative, Republican way of looking at the world doubtless continues to influence millions of Midwesterners. But the winds of change have enveloped the Tribune Tower, and the mighty clout is gone. Fewer and fewer people read the *Tribune*, even as the population rises. Television gives *Tribune* readers a new view of reality. Colonel Robert R. McCormick, the grand, domineering, ferocious ruler of the *Tribune* empire for 45 years, went to his grave in 1955. The days of rampaging anti-New Deal, anti-British, anti-Russian editorials are past, though the familiar front-page editorials of yore still appear, excoriating Communists, Democrats, or unions. The paper remains staunchly Republican, with one regular exception: along with the other Chicago dailies, it backs Daley's reelection bids; some see a connection in the fact that the tax assessment of the Tribune Tower building is suspiciously low. But a new Sunday section, *Perspective*, occasionally features the world of blacks, the young, and women as the old *Tribune* would never have done. In 1971, a new "op-ed" page was inaugurated; it includes cartoonists and columnists of moderate to liberal opinions, including Nick Thimmesch, Clayton Fritchey, and the Los Angeles *Times'* Paul Conrad. The paper has its own Negro columnist, Vernon Jarrett, and five black reporters. The changes can be attributed to a post-McCormick generation of editors now coming to power; they are no flaming liberals, but less erratic, far more responsible than their predecessors.

Chicago is one of the few remaining truly competitive newspaper towns

* Ogilvie got the idea from my friend Norton Kay, former political correspondent for *Chicago Today*.

in the U.S.A. The Marshall Field newspapers—the morning *Sun-Times* and evening *Daily News*—range from moderate to liberal in their editorial views, and offer lively, issue-oriented news coverage prepared by staffs that include experts in many specialized fields. The *Sun-Times'* cartoonist, Bill Mauldin, is one of America's greatest, and the *Daily News'* Mike Royko is an authentic and influential voice of Chicago. The *Tribune* owns an afternoon paper, *Chicago Today*, a lively and liberal tabloid that rivals the *Daily News* in circulation. (*Chicago Today* is permitted to have a Democratic editorial policy, reportedly on the theory there are so many Democrats in town.)

In influence, the Chicago newspapers far outshine any others in the state.* They are also monitored these days by the *Chicago Journalism Review*, begun in 1968 by Chicago reporters who provide telling critique of the failures and foibles of the newspapers they work for. The *Review* has since been copied in several cities across the country.

Chicago is also a center of the black press in America. John H. Johnson publishes *Ebony*, modeled after *Life*, which has a circulation of 1.2 million, as well as the newsweekly *Jet* (circulation 394,134) and the polemical *Negro Digest* (circulation 50,000). A daily tabloid, the *Chicago Defender*, is the flagship of a chain of 10 papers which are owned by publisher John H. Sengstacke. One of Sengstacke's chief executives is Louis Martin, former deputy chairman for minority affairs of the Democratic National Committee and a thoroughly charming man who continues to exercise great unseen power in national black politics. The *Defender's* circulation is only 21,000, small potatoes compared to the 400,000 claimed by another Chicago-based publication, *Muhammad Speaks*, the propaganda organ of the Black Muslims. But *Muhammad Speaks* is sold on a pushy, shakedown basis, so that its influence is easily overrated.

In broadcasting, Chicago has never provided serious competition to Manhattan or even Los Angeles. But it is (by his insistence) the point of origin for the daily news-and-opinion broadcasts of Paul Harvey, self-styled "voice of the silent majority" who provides listeners on 407 ABC affiliate stations with a kind of political fundamentalism loyal to all the old American values and suspicious of all the new.

Chicago harbors 31 colleges and universities and with its five medical schools trains one of five of America's physicians. One of the nation's outstanding inner-city university branches is the magnificently designed Chicago Circle campus of the University of Illinois which opened its doors in 1965 (after 20 years at a temporary site on the Navy Pier). Other outstanding institutions include Northwestern University at Evanston and the Catholic institutions of Loyola and DePaul.

But the University of Chicago, founded in 1891 through the largesse of

---

* The papers outside Chicago taken most seriously by the politicians include the Rockford *Morning Star* and *Register Republic*, the Peoria *Journal Star*, the Bloomington *Pantagraph*, the Lindsay-Schaub newspapers in Decatur, East St. Louis, and other cities, and the two interlopers from across the Mississippi—The St. Louis *Globe-Democrat* and *Post-Dispatch*, both heavily read downstate. The *Post-Dispatch* is especially influential.

John D. Rockefeller, remains the greatest of all. Since its founding, the institution has had no less than 31 Nobel Prize winners on its faculty. The university established the first sociology department in the United States in 1893, and its commitment to urban problems and studies has remained strong over the years. Pioneer work on planned parenthood was done at Chicago, and the faculty today includes Hans Morgenthau, a leading foreign policy expert and pioneer Vietnam war critic, and Milton Friedman, the renowned economist.

Despite its prominence in social science, Chicago is not as prominent as it once was. *Science* in 1971 issued a report identifying Chicago as the city where seven of the 12 major advances in social science in the United States were made in the years from 1900 to 1929, but only three of 41 major advances from 1930 to 1965. (Cambridge has been the major leader in recent years.) Nevertheless, the report on graduate schools of the American Council on Education, also issued in 1971, placed Chicago in the top handful of American universities in virtually all the social sciences (anthropology, economics, history, political science, and sociology).

One of the most fascinating case studies of a large inner-city university's relationships with its community is provided by the University of Chicago. In contrast to the turmoils Columbia experienced at Morningside Heights, it is largely a success story. The fate of the university in its Hyde Park-Kenwood neighborhood hung in the balance, however, for some years following World War II. Low-income blacks began to inundate the neighborhood, slum landlords chopped up apartments into units to house five times as many residents as originally planned for, and real estate owners engaged in unscrupulous "block busting." The undergraduate enrollment declined from 3,200 to 1,300 and recruiting faculty became increasingly difficult. The university trustees seriously considered moving the campus lock, stock, and barrel to a suburban location or even to another city.

In the early '50s, however, the university decided to stay put and to throw its full power and prestige behind a fight against neighborhood blight. The university formed a private citizens' organization, the Southeast Chicago Corporation (SECC), to lead the battle by court action against housing code offenders and by pressing for widescale urban renewal in the area. Julian Levi, a professor of urban affairs with good City Hall connections and a talent for wheeling and dealing, became SECC's head and showed no compunctions about forcing out low-income Negroes. But eventually he and SECC came to accept stable, middle-income blacks, and after 1956 a neighborhood population balance of 38 percent Negro, still present today, was achieved. As comedian Mike Nichols explained it: "This is Hyde Park, whites and blacks, shoulder to shoulder against the lower classes."

Today the renewal of Hyde Park-Kenwood must be judged a major success. Hundreds of new townhouses and high-rise apartment buildings have gone up and many old ones have been renovated; there are restaurants of wide gastronomic variety, coffee houses, and theatres. The crime rate is one of the city's lowest, due in part to the $400,000 the university spends each year on a security force to augment Chicago police in the area. Adding to all this, the spacious Midway strip is a little architectural showplace all on its own, with buildings by Wright, van der Rohe, Saarinen, and Edward Durrell Stone.

Despite its traditionally radical student body, the University of Chicago has demonstrated unusual skill in dealing with protests, even while great institutions like California, Harvard, and Cornell—and even the rurally set Champaign-Urbana campus of the University of Illinois—were in the throes of violent demonstrations. This has not been because of an absence of agitators; the Students for a Democratic Society, in fact, led a 16-day-and-night takeover of the administration building in 1969, demanding tenure for a radical sociology department instructor and a permanent 50-percent say in faculty hiring. The issue stiffened the back of Chicago's proud faculty; Professor Morris Janowitz, one of the university's outstanding urbanists, told the students it was all right with him if they had a 50-percent say on hiring, "so long as you'll give me a 50-50 say on who you can marry and sleep with." The university administration met the crisis by avoiding what Dean Wayne Booth calls the twin traps of "calling in the cops, which is disastrous, and amnesty, which only brings more and more sit-ins." Plagued by increasing ennui and internal divisions as their sit-in dragged on, the protestors quit without a single concession from the university. Then president Edward H. Levi gave the job of disciplining the offenders to the faculty senate—which proved firm and tough, expelling 42 students and suspending 81 others. The punishments stuck and the university remained calm. Now the university's crucial problems may not be so much its activist students as its constraining budget.

One resident of the university community who has made a unique contribution to the neighborhood is Mrs. Laura Fermi, widow of the late great physicist. She relates that in 1959 she noticed that during the winter months, everything in her Hyde Park apartment was covered with grime from the coal burning furnaces of the area. Aroused by the nuisance, Mrs. Fermi and a group of other women, mostly faculty wives, set up a committee to fight the local smog wave. She delights in telling the story of how her little band of smog battlers "undertook the education of the University of Chicago," which is the greatest real-estate holder in Hyde Park, persuading it to agree to a schedule for conversion to non-coal heating.

Bit by bit, government agencies, aided and often prompted by private conservationist groups, are making a little progress in reducing the amount of Chicago's air and water pollution. Even the Chicago Sanitary District, a big "wholesaler" of sewage disposal for Chicago and 115 other municipalities in Cook County, has taken an interest.* U. S. Steel, one of the most

* The Sanitary District is a favorite target of downstaters, who say it sends Chicago's effluent their way in the waters of the Chicago River. The District reversed the flow of the Chicago River in 1910 to prevent the epidemics of cholera and typhoid Chicago had suffered when open sewage dumped into the river entered the lake and thus returned in the city's water supply. In later years, the agency acquired a sordid history of great and petty graft. But its general counsel today, Allen S. Lavin, seems

egregious polluters of Lake Michigan and the Chicago area's air, in 1971 bowed to pressure from the Sanitary District and a state attorney general's suit and agreed to a plan to end by 1975 the daily dump of 36,000 pounds of chemicals and suspended solids into the lake from its enormous South Works plant, built in the 1880s. Environmental groups have also persuaded the U. S. Environmental Protection Agency to heed a little-known 1910 law and withhold permission for seven heavy-industry companies, including U. S. Steel, to discharge waste into the southern end of Lake Michigan. Suits have also been filed against 27 airlines serving Chicago for pollution from their jet engines, and against many municipal dumps.

But a fantastic amount remains to be done. During his first year in office, I asked Governor Richard B. Ogilvie what he thought of the progress Illinois had made up to that time in fighting air and water pollution and got a one-word answer: "lousy." Some impressive progress has been made under his regime. A muscular new Environmental Protection Agency (EPA), embracing the pollution control functions previously performed by several agencies, was created by the legislature in 1970, along with a rule-making Pollution Control Board and research-oriented Institute for Environmental Quality. The new Illinois system is considered unique because it avoids the device of a single environmental superagency now being adopted by many states and deliberately separates the jobs of environmental research, prosecution, and adjudication of cases. The idea is to introduce an element of tension into the process, so that more violations are in fact tracked down and stopped. One way this is accomplished is by giving not only the EPA, but also the attorney general and any interested citizen, the right to bring action against an environmental offender.

A Last Chicago Note: Women

The little success story of Laura Fermi and her smog battlers is one of the very few where women have made a mark in Dick Daley's Chicago. Ultimately masculine, the home city of *Playboy* and thus capital of the sexual putdown, Chicago has—according to writer Jean Komaiko in *Chicago Magazine*—probably fewer women in top-flight jobs today than it did 25 years ago. She identifies a mere handful: one in merchandising, one who is the first female member of the Board of Trade, one professor of law, one psychoanalyst, one columnist, a few in public relations and advertising, a sprinkling in medicine and social work, "and you've had it." None of the top five banks has a woman on its board, nor does one of the 25 largest Chicago corpora-

---

more interested in the public than some of his predecessors. In his job, Lavin told me, "I have really become a conservationist. I never was before. . . . No one gives industry a right to use Lake Michigan to get rid of their garbage. . . . My philosophy now is: sue the bastards." Most of the suing, however, is being done by private groups and the state and federal governments. And the Chicago River, as Lavin acknowledges, is still an "open sewer." Mayor Daley throws some green dye into the river to celebrate St. Patrick's Day each year, but the gesture is fairly superfluous, since the river is green anyway.

tions have a woman director. After undergraduate pressures, the University of Chicago put one woman on its board of trustees, but only seven percent of its faculty consists of women, compared to an 18 percent national average for universities. In 1971, Chicago finally elected two lady aldermen (one a machine-backed white, one a reform black), the first two of their sex in 138 years of municipal history. Concludes Miss Komaiko:

If ever this city with the big chip on its "big shoulders" is to become humanized, to discard its frontier mentality, its predilection for crime, confrontation and conspiracy, one suspects it must begin by listening to and learning from its women.

II. STATEWIDE AND DOWNSTATE

Politics of Party, Patronage, and Corruption

Illinois presents the classic picture of the big Democratic city against the Republican countryside. But the modern equation must figure in the Chicago suburban vote, now more than half again as big as Chicago's, growing pockets of Democratic strength in cities like Peoria in the rich farmbelt of central Illinois, and "Little Egypt," the depressed southernmost counties where Democratic strength remains solid through vestiges of Civil War antagonisms fused with modern economic issues.

From the Civil War to the advent of the New Deal, Illinois had a political pattern practically the reverse of what we know today. Northern Illinois, which had sympathized with the Union, was staunchly Republican; Southern Illinois, with strong Southern ties, was comparatively more Democratic. The Republicans held the balance of power and won all but two Presidential and gubernatorial elections between 1860 and 1928.

But starting around the turn of the century, Bryan's silver policies began to eat away at Democratic loyalties in downstate. And by the middle of the New Deal, virtually all the rural counties and small towns, outside of Little Egypt, revolted against Franklin Roosevelt's free-spending policies. Today, rural Illinois is big Farm Bureau territory. The heart of Democratic strength is in the big industrial cities with high numbers of low-income ethnic group voters and Negroes in uneasy alliance—Chicago, Moline and Rock Island, East St. Louis. The big city coalition was large enough to give the Democrats victory in all but two Presidential elections between 1932 and 1964. But now the Chicago suburban vote is growing so steadily that some analysts believe Illinois may be turning into a normally Republican state. The arithmetic (indicating pluralities only) has worked out in some recent races as shown below. It should be noted that by 1970, Cook County represented 50.6 percent of the vote—31.3 percent in Chicago, 19.5 percent in the suburbs.

"Downstate," including some suburbs outside Chicago, accounted for the remaining 49.4 percent.

Race	Chicago	Suburban Cook	Downstate	Statewide
Senate—1966				
(Percy–R versus Douglas–D)	185,710–D	267,184–R	340,828–R	422,302–R
President—1968				
(Nixon–R versus Humphrey–D)	421,199–D	200,376–R	355,783–R	134,960–R
Governor—1968				
(Ogilvie–R versus Shapiro–D)	374,006–D	204,349–R	297,451–R	127,794–R
Senate—1970				
(Stevenson–D versus Smith–R)	521,353–D	11,393–D	12,408–D	545,336–D

"Under primary, under convention, under despotism or under a pure democracy, Illinois would be corrupt and crooked. . . . It is in the blood of the people," William Allen White opined some 45 years ago. The judgment was harsh and categorical, but there is ample evidence to show it is as true today as when it was made. Within this century, Adlai Stevenson III pointed out to me in a 1969 interview, there has been no true reform movement in Illinois state government. A primary reason, he said, is the division of Democratic big city politics and Republican downstate politics. Each produces its own disciplined, well structured party apparatus. Despite the growing political independence of the suburbs, he pointed out, much of the old system still prevails, including universal recognition of the Chicago Democratic leader as the statewide Democratic leader, and the "authoritarian party structure" in the big city. A high proportion of Illinois state offices and state legislators are in politics for profit or patronage and show minimal interest in issues of public service. In California, the governor has 120 patronage positions to fill, in Oregon 12, in Iowa 35, in Wisconsin 26. But in Illinois the governor and other cabinet officials have 15,000 patronage positions in their control, And there are at least twice that many patronage jobs in Cook County, and thousands more in county courthouses where Republican-sponsored venality is just as egregious as the venality of the big city Democrats. Some members of the Illinois legislature have close ties to the Chicago crime syndicate and some are under its absolute control.

Few Illinois politicians actually go to jail for corrupt practices, largely because prosecutors' offices and the courts are often compromised. An exception was Republican State Auditor Orville E. Hodge, who in 1956 was sentenced to 20 years in prison for embezzling at least $1,612,639 in state funds to pay for his own lush living.

The classic example of all time has to be that of Paul Powell, the self-styled "country boy" from impoverished southern Illinois who died in 1970 leaving an estate of about $3.1 million—even though his lifetime earnings, all in 36 years of public service, had come to less than $300,000. When Powell died in 1970, his body lay on the same catafalque that once bore Lincoln. A thousand officeholders and politicians crowded the crepe-draped rotunda of the State Capitol to honor the most powerful of all downstate Democrats.

Governor Ogilvie and Mayor Daley were on hand to eulogize Powell. Only two and a half months later was the public suddenly told that $750,000 in cold cash had been found crammed into an old shoe box, a bowling-ball bag, and other containers in the closet of Powell's modest hotel room in Springfield. Then all the sordid details of Powell's way of operating came spilling out, with a flurry of talk (fruitless, it later turned out) about stiff new financial disclosure requirements for public officials.

Of course the politicians had known all along what Powell was up to. The late Adlai Stevenson once said of Powell that he could have been one of the great political figures of American history "if only he didn't believe that the shortest distance between two points is a curve." Powell had close ties to Chicago's infamous syndicate-controlled West Side Bloc; in fact the Bloc made Powell speaker of the Illinois house in 1963 by instructing two Republican legislators it controlled, Republicans who held jobs on the Chicago Sanitary District, to vote for Powell instead of the Republican candidate. The house was so closely divided that the defection caused Powell's election as speaker. Later, as secretary of state, Powell had big contracts to award and was revealed to be receiving several thousands of dollars a year from a race track for consulting services.

Following Powell's death, even more details came out, especially in regard to the hundreds of thousands of dollars of race track stock Powell had acquired at a minimal price years ago and financed through a loan repaid out of dividends. His estate also included a substantial chunk of stock in Illinois-based small banks and insurance companies, whose interests Powell had assiduously defended in the legislature. Powell's effects turned up hundreds of thousands of dollars in negotiable securities made out to the Paul Powell Dinner Committee, although under Illinois law campaign contributions are not to be converted into personal wealth. Details of two girl friends to whom he left hundreds of thousands of dollars, an extra Springfield apartment known as "Powell's love nest," and his tight-fistedness to maids and doormen who had served him for many years, also came to light.

Others recalled that Powell had been a flamboyant stump speaker, inveighing mightily against "hippies, yippies, dippies, and all other long-haired animals," as well as Republicans and newspapers, and that he had always shown his patriotism by wearing an American flag in his lapel and insisting his employees do the same. The man's colorful quotes were recalled, especially the lines: "I can smell the meat a'cookin'. . . . My friends always eat at the first table. . . . The horses that do that pullin' in the field are the first ones to get the hay throwed to them." It all conjured up visions, newsman John Kifner observed, "of patronage, fat contracts, and other plunder awaiting the victors."

How did Powell's constituents react to his shenanigans? "He was always a hero to the downstate voter," John Gardner, editor of the *Southern Illinoisan* at Carbondale, was quoted as saying. "He was the guy who out-slicked the city slickers." The reaction is a little like Harlem's long-time toleration of Adam Clayton Powell as long as he was beating the white man at his own game. But now it is all over for Paul Powell, and while the Internal Revenue Service, state agencies, and legatees head into years of litigation, Powell lies under a gravestone with the words chiseled as he had directed in his will: "Here lies a life-long Democrat."

The important point about Powell was that he was no bizarre aberration, but simply a master practitioner of a familiar game. In 1964, state senator Paul Simon (now lieutenant governor) wrote an article for *Harper's* in which he estimated that about a third of Illinois legislators took payoffs—some in the form of payments for legal services, public relations work, or as campaign contributions, and a smaller number in the shape of outright bribes. In 1971, federal investigators discovered that former Gov. Otto Kerner, other leading Chicago Democrats, and some Republicans had realized large profits from racing stock transactions in the 1960s—transactions hidden at the time from the public. The transactions were made when Kerner controlled, through his appointive power, the membership of the Illinois Racing Board. Kerner reportedly reaped $125,000 from one transaction.

In 1965, former Republican Governor William G. Stratton (1953–61) came to trial on a federal income tax fraud indictment. Stratton did not dispute the government's charge that he had received $93,959 which he failed to report as income; his defense was that the money was in nontaxable gifts from prominent Republican politicians and others. Stratton was acquitted on the criminal charges, but the court testimony is fascinating reading. Stratton argued that expenses for vacations, formal clothes, and trips to the beauty parlor for his wife, or for the use of a luxurious lodge and houseboat, were all necessary political entertaining. Senate Republican Leader Everett M. Dirksen flew to Illinois to testify for Stratton, maintaining that the governor was justified in accepting "contributions that came to him from time to time." Dirksen said he had "clocked" his own expenses over six months and found that they "ran at the rate of a hundred dollars a day," so that he too was pleased to receive "contributions from those who recognize the difficulty that public service interposes for you." And in the summer of 1969, Governor Ogilvie charged that the state government had been "defrauded of half a million dollars a year" for several years through illicit operations at the Illinois State Fair.

When this many scandals come to light, one can just image what transpires in secret and is never revealed. Of course there have been and are men of great personal integrity in Illinois state government. But when I asked veteran state political reporters to name the high state officials of the postwar period they were convinced were absolutely honest, the list was embarrassingly short. It included former Governor Adlai Stevenson, II, and his son Adlai, III (former state treasurer and now a United States Senator); Joseph Lohman, Democratic state treasurer in the late 1950s (who was crushed by the organization when he tried to run for governor and left the state brokenhearted); Latham Castle, Republican attorney general who prosecuted Hodges; Elbert Smith, Republican state auditor in the 1950s; and the bipartisan team currently in office—Republican Governor Richard B. Ogilvie (though his designation for the list is tentative pending proof of actual conduct in office) and Lieutenant Governor Paul Simon, a crusader for higher ethics in government.

Men like U. S. Senator Charles H. Percy, and his predecessor, Paul H. Douglas, would have qualified for the integrity list, but neither ever held a position in state government. This may be no accident. Percy, a successful businessman who had made his fortune as head of Bell & Howell in Chicago, was obviously an alien force to the "system" and had less than full support from the downstate courthouse Republicans when he ran for governor in 1964. Douglas, a professor at the University of Chicago and pillar of integrity, would have liked to run for governor in 1948 but was slated for the U. S. Senate instead by Jake Arvey, then undisputed Cook County Democratic boss. Arvey did slate Stevenson for governor that year; he may have felt Stevenson would be more pliable than Douglas and in any event probably thought both men would lose in the anticipated Republican sweep of '48 that never materialized.

A story about Jake Arvey, related by John H. Fenton in *Midwest Politics*, may illustrate a reason why essentially corrupt party machines sometimes slate top men for statewide office. The story is borrowed from Boss Plunkett of Tammany Hall but is just as applicable for Illinois. It appears that a candidate for lesser office complained to Arvey that his name was never used on radio and television or on campaign posters, while Stevenson monopolized the publicity. "Look," said Arvey, "have you ever watched a boat dock along the lakefront?" "Yes," was the reply. "And did you notice the garbage and the trash that was drawn into the dock by the boat?" "Uh huh," said the candidate. "Well," Arvey concluded, "Stevenson is the boat and you are the garbage."

The inevitable results of a politics of patronage and payoff is a low level of service for the people. The state's per capita income was $4,502 in 1970, seventh highest in the United States. But Illinois spends less than the national per capita average for education, for highways, for public welfare, and for health and hospitals. In 1969, it ranked 43rd among the 50 states in state and local revenue as a percentage of personal income. Recent tax hikes are changing that picture, but over most of its history, Illinois has been a rich state that could do a lot more for its people but has not.

Illinois Governors: From Stevenson to Ogilvie

Two postwar Illinois Governors have served with unusual distinction. The first was Adlai Stevenson, II, elected in 1948 by a record-breaking plurality of 572,067 votes. Though he served just a single four-year term, Stevenson was able to double state aid to school districts, place the state police under a merit system, and effect a big increase in gasoline tax and truck license fees to expedite highway construction. But Stevenson's more important contribution was to bring a fresh breeze of integrity and a higher quality of official service into the musty corridors of the state capitol at Springfield; for many, he restored a belief in the viability and purpose of government. Even in defeat, he made a similar contribution to the nation through his eloquence and leadership in two unsuccessful campaigns for the Presidency. Stevenson's distinguished public service, running through the years he served as U. S. Ambassador to the United Nations before his death in 1965, has won him a secure place in history and requires no further recital here.

Business as usual returned to Springfield under Stevenson's two successors, Republican William Stratton (1953–61) and Democrat Otto Kerner (1961–68). Stratton was a capable technician and does deserve credit for pushing through the first reapportionment of the legislature in a half century. Kerner's major contribution was outside of Illinois government—in his chairmanship of the Civil Disorders Commission to study racial divisions in America following the great urban riots of 1967. In Springfield, Kerner was strictly Daley's man. His office issued an "idiot sheet" to Democratic legislators telling them how they should vote; on issues of importance, the line was invariably set by Daley, not Kerner himself.

Richard B. Ogilvie, the Governor of Illinois today, is a totally different commodity from any of his recent predecessors—and promises to outshine them all in performance. In demeanor, Ogilvie lacks the Stevensonian charisma or many politicians' physical glamor. He is stocky, stolid, speaks with a hoarse voice, and reminds many people of a small-town banker. As a tank commander in World War II, he was struck by a Nazi shell that ripped into the left side of his face; plastic surgery left him with a grim, set expression that is a special liability on television. But few contemporary American governors demonstrate natural executive skill equal to Ogilvie's. His approach to problems is totally pragmatic, businesslike, and low-keyed. And he is a gutsy man, willing to undergo stiff criticism if he thinks he is right. Every Ogilvien instinct is political, but he appears to believe sincerely that the best government is the best politics.

Ogilvie got his start in the tough world of Cook County politics, upsetting Mayor Daley's man to become county sheriff in 1962. In that post, he cracked down hard on the crime syndicate and won fame through a successful prosecution of mobster Tony Accardo. In 1966 he again upset the Democrats to be elected Cook County board president. Normally a Cook County politician would face stiff opposition from downstate Republicans in a gubernatorial primary, but Ogilvie's glowing reputation as an antagonist of the Daley machine helped him win the 1968 GOP gubernatorial nomination with ease and go on to win the general election with a 127,794-vote plurality.

But Illinois was hardly prepared for the flurry of creative activity that Ogilvie would unleash when he hit Springfield. Within a few months he had chalked up more concrete major accomplishments than any other governor of modern Illinois history. By executive order, he created a powerful management tool by establishing a bureau of the budget (modeled after the federal bureau), thus taking from the dawdling and often compromised legislature the right one of its committees had long enjoyed to pass on departmental budget requests before they even reached the governor's office. To staff the budget bureau, Ogilvie then installed a group of young "whiz kids," some direct out of federal service and all beholden to him rather than the old-line political structure of the state. State support for local schools was increased 75 percent, with special weighting provisions to give additional help to some urban school districts—though not enough to tackle the gut problems in ghetto schools. A full department of law enforcement, with an IBI modeled on the FBI, was created to wage war on organized crime in the state, though in practice it has tended to concentrate more on chasing students for drugs and peace demonstrations than pursuing the syndicate.

Finally, with Illinois government on the point of bankruptcy because of rising expenditures, Ogilvie forced through a reluctant legislature the first income tax in the state's history. "For 50 years," the Chicago *Sun-Times* commented when Ogilvie unveiled his tax program, "Illinois has talked about a state income tax, and for 50 years the politicians and the citizens have dodged the issue." But despite the howls of protest from timid legislators, Ogilvie got the tax approved in a single session. Ogilvie asked for a flat 4 percent rate, but the legislature modified it to 2½ percent for individuals, 4 percent for corporations. The personal tax was essentially progressive because a liberal $1,000 personal exemption was allowed each taxpayer and each of his dependents, meaning that poor families would pay little if any tax. But the tax was on total gross income after those exemptions, and thus not subject to the myriad deductions which plague many tax structures (including the federal). The income tax reduces the comparative burden of two highly regressive taxes: sales (5 percent in Illinois) and property. Finally, it actually results in a return of federal money to the state, since individuals can deduct the amount on their federal forms.

An important element of the Illinois income tax was that one-twelfth of the revenues were earmarked for direct, no-strings-attached sharing by city and county governments on a simple per capita basis. The provision not only had appeal as a precursor of President Nixon's national revenue-sharing plan, but sweetened the tax package for reluctant state legislators. It even helped Ogilvie get some Cook County votes he needed to pass the program.

Ogilvie uses not only carrots but sticks. Early in the legislative session, he had announced backing for an excellent statewide electoral reform measure and a bill to institute a complete civil service system in Cook County—the latter a reform which would gut the Daley patronage machine. At the crucial moment in the tax debate, Ogilvie agreed to drop the reform bills, in return for Daley's instruction to several of his men to vote for the income tax.

Can Ogilvie survive the severe backlash from the income tax and the perils of gubernatorial incumbency to win a second term in 1972 and perhaps be a viable Presidential or Vice Presidential candidate in 1976? When that year comes, he will be 53 years old. One statehouse politician was quoted as saying: "Dick will ride into 1976 like the white knight who slew the dragon —assuming, of course, that the dragon doesn't eat him first." Winning reelection, in fact, may turn out to be no mean task. The conservative Bourbon

Republicans of downstate Illinois were so furious with him over the income tax that they were talking of dumping him in the 1972 primary in favor of State Attorney General William Scott. That talk began to subside in 1971 as a result of laborious rebuilding of ties to the party regulars, arranged in large part by his political aide, James Mack, a onetime protegé of F. Clifton White. Another factor in Ogilvie's favor was that polls showed his support for school aid, mental health, and state governmental reform was gaining support from independent suburban voters. Ogilvie was reportedly planning to model his reelection campaign after that of Nelson A. Rockefeller, who also bore the brunt of furious resentment against tax increases but still won an amazing reelection victory in 1966. The two men were said to be in close contact.

Ogilvie of course lacks Rockefeller's glad-handing ways and effusive personality. But there is a buoyant self-confidence in the man; after an interview in which he recited the long list of knotty problems—taxes, education, pollution, ghettos—that he hoped to solve in office, I wished him luck as I left. Ogilvie's reply: "Oh, I'm an optimist. It'll work."

I have heard the Illinois legislature variously described as "very average," "thoroughly mediocre," and "very corrupt." The wheelings, dealings, and conflicts between Cook County machine Democrats, reformers in both parties, conservative downstate Republicans, suburban Republicans, the downstate Democratic contingent, and crime syndicate elements in both parties could fill volumes. Bipartisan collusion has long been a hallmark of the legislature, just as it is in some of the machine wards of Chicago and in some of the Republican county courthouses. However, the Citizens Conference on State Legislatures in 1971 said there had been a "rapid rate of improvement" in the operating capability of the Illinois legislature since reapportionment and gave it a high rating of third in the U.S. It was pointed out that Illinois has one of the stronger year-round staffing patterns among state legislatures, especially for major committees, with both majority and minority party staff represented. It also found Illinois exceptionally "open" in terms of uniform rules, easy media access, public committee roll call votes, and the like. The weakness of the study was that it failed to take into account the ethical standards of the legislators. (Even in the wake of the Paul Powell scandal, the legislature in 1971 killed an ethics bill that would have required public officials to disclose in detail their sources of income.)

Reapportionment had long been opposed by a bipartisan cabal of downstate Republicans and Democrats who both stood to lose if it were approved. The first house reapportionment since 1901 came in the early 1950s, but the senate was not reconstituted on a full population basis until federal court orders forced such a move in the 1960s. Reapportionment has had the greatest effect on the senate, where the old rural GOP oligarchy that long held sway has been dispersed, and the Democrats in 1970 were actually able to win control for the first time in 30 years. But the senate Republicans have changed too, with a shift away from downstate and toward Chicago suburban leadership. Cook County now has many more legislative seats than it used to, but it is not a unified force because of the split between Daley machine Democrats and suburban Republicans.

A reapportionment stalemate in the house in 1964 led to the ludicrous situation in which all 177 members had to be elected at large on one incredibly complicated statewide ballot. A "blue ribbon" legislature of many famous-named individuals was elected that year; in office it did enact major anticrime legislation, but it failed to do much to change the way that things are traditionally done in Springfield.

Reapportionment has cut down the once mighty clout of the Farm Bureau lobby. Lobbies of most influence include the Illinois Manufacturers Association (which helps finance many Republican campaigns), the Illinois Chamber of Commerce, coal operators, insurance companies like State Farm and Allstate, the Illinois Education Association, and the Illinois Medical Society (Chicago is AMA headquarters), AFL-CIO unions (especially the Steelworkers), retail merchants and the race tracks—the latter a key source of patronage with many legislators owning race track stock. Many special interests now exert influence in Springfield by getting their own employees or operatives elected to legislative seats. And the chambers are packed with lawyers, real estate, and insurance people who often find the special interests throwing business their way, making them more and more beholden. Thus the technique of direct bribery becomes passé, almost an anachronism.

The Chicago *Tribune* wields great influence in the legislature, especially through its veteran Springfield correspondent, George Tagge, who acts as a kind of father confessor to the Republican party. Pushing an idea of Colonel McCormick, Tagge lobbied successfully for legislation that would divert race track tax revenues to finance McCormick Place on the lakefront. The building's informal nickname: Tagge's Temple. Actually the first version, an architectural monstrosity, burned down, forcing the Democrats to hold their 1968 convention at the old International Amphitheatre beside the odoriferous Chicago stockyards. The new version of McCormick Place has a low, black silhouette. It is an invasion of the lakefront but not as offensive as its predecessor.

The newest thing in Illinois government is a fresh state constitution, written by 116 delegates over nine months in 1970 and approved by the voters in December of that year. The new document was not a terribly distinguished piece of work. It did purge anachronistic sections of the 1870-vintage constitution which Illinois had been living under, including provisions on cartways, drains and ditches, lotteries, and "World's Columbian Exposition." It changed the legislature from semiannual to annual sessions, included an innovative clause giving any citizen the right to sue polluters to secure his "right to a healthy environment," shifted primary responsibility for financing public schools to the state, gave local governments some more flexibility in reforming their own structures, and included a long Bill of Rights article with an explicit open-housing and fair employment provision.

But the new constitution actually made the revenue system more restrictive rather than more flexible, failed to reduce the vastly oversized state house of representatives (177 members), and did not effect the far-reaching structural reforms needed in state and local government. Fearful that the whole constitution might go down to defeat if encumbered with controversial provisions, the authors submitted four separate vote proposals to (1) abolish election of judges and have them appointed by the governor from nominees submitted by judicial nominating conventions; (2) abolish the death penalty; (3) lower the voting age to 18; and (4) abolish the confusing cumulative voting system for legislative candidates in three-man districts (a device which breeds lack of competition and cozy relationships between the parties).

Thanks in part to belated but clear support from Mayor Daley, the constitution itself was approved by a 1,122,452 to 838,168 vote. But all the controversial separate proposals went down to defeat. The most interesting test of "old" versus "new" politics was the vote on appointment of judges. Governor Ogilvie, three of the four Chicago dailies, civic organizations, many law school professors and other "good government" forces were for the provision with its so-called "merit selection plan" similar to existing provisions in Missouri and California. But Daley wanted to keep the elective system because judgeships and the jobs which go with them are big plums in the Democrats' patronage system. Downstate Republican organizations felt the same way about *their* own patronage. Only the suburbs were strongly in favor. So a blizzard of negative Chicago city and downstate votes stopped "merit selection" in its tracks.

The whole effort for constitutional change might never have begun had it not been for the 20-year campaign in behalf of reform launched by Chicago attorney Samuel Witwer. He was chosen president of the convention and helped to smooth over the fiery clashes that erupted among the delegates. If the speed of reform in Illinois seems glacial, it may be because the prevailing climate discourages all but a few civic-minded leaders with Witwer's determination.

Illinois in Washington

The outstanding legislators Illinois has sent to Washington in the postwar years have reflected the state's many images: the intellectual community represented by Senator Paul Douglas, rural and small-city Illinois symbolized by Senator Everett Dirksen, suburban and new industrial Illinois in Senator Charles Percy.

The outstanding members of the House delegation are even more of a microcosm: Daniel Rostenkowski, a keen big-city spokesman and Mayor Daley's man; Abner J. Mikva, brilliant but sole representative of the Democratic reform contingent on the Chicago delegation, whose congressional career may be cut short by hostile redistricting in 1972; Roman C. Pucinski, voluble one-time liberal turning to the right in tune with the fears and concerns of his ethnic Chicago district; Leslie C. Arends, aging Republican Whip of the House, military oriented and the epitome of stand-still rural conservatism; John B. Anderson from booming Rockford northwest of Chicago, chairman of the House Republican Conference and a self-described "onetime conservative who has been steadily jogging leftward" (apparently in tune with the increasing industrialization and cosmopolitan tone of his district);* and Paul Findley of the Springfield and West Congressional district, a Republican who started as a super conservative but became interested in issues like North Atlantic union, publishing Vietnam casualty lists, and expanding trade with the communists (pleasing incidentally the exporting farmers in his constituency). In 1969, the delegation lost one of its most promising members when the youthful North Shore Congressman, Donald Rumsfeld, resigned to become director of the federal Office of Economic Opportunity and later Counselor to President Nixon with Cabinet rank and director of operations for the Cost of Living Council. A progressive by inclination, Rumsfeld has subordinated his own ideologic preferences in service to the President but may well reemerge as a potent Illinois political figure in his own right.

Now senior Senator from Illinois is Charles H. Percy, a man who has been in the national eye since, at 29 years of age, he became president of the Bell & Howell camera firm. Then the youngest chief executive of any major U.S. corporation, Percy showed a business genius that carried Bell & Howell from $5 million to $160 million in annual sales during the 15 years he was in command. In the process, Percy earned all the money he would ever need: in 1967 he estimated his personal worth at "conservatively" $6 million.

After an abortive start in elected politics in 1964, when he ran for governor but lost in the Goldwater debacle, Percy shook some of the brashness which had characterized his first campaign (and been especially offensive to downstate Republican old-liners) and in 1966 won election to the Senate over incumbent Paul Douglas. The strongest margins for Percy came in the suburbs; it is this "new Illinois" which his image matches: the successful businessman, pragmatic, centrist in his political views. Percy has a proclivity for self-promotion which offends some, but also a facile mind, a grasp of national problems, and a capacity for hard work many politicians might emulate. In the Senate, he has made some creative suggestions (a home-ownership plan for the poor, an "All-Asian" peace conference to settle the Vietnam war) and also begun to cast extremely liberal votes for an Illinois Republican—including opposition to the Haynsworth and Carswell "Southern strategy" Supreme Court appointments. Illinois' Bourbon Republicans would dearly love to unseat Percy but will probably be unable to do so.

Tragedy crossed Percy's path in 1966 when his 21-year-old daughter Valerie was murdered in the family's lakeshore Kenilworth home. Five years later the $50,000 reward was still out for the killer, and Percy told of the life

---

* Anderson's shift from standard conservatism, including a strong dissent from the Nixon administration's ambiguity on civil rights, has hurt him in the House. A group of ultraconservative GOP House members in 1971 ran Rep. Sam Devine of Columbus, Ohio, an undistinguished model of conservative orthodoxy, against Anderson for the Conference chairmanship. Anderson barely survived on a vote of 89 to 81. Anderson has the intellectual credentials and public presence to be a strong candidate for higher office.

of dread he and his family had continued to live with the murderer at large. The joyous counterpart is the happy life his other daughter, Sharon, is leading as the wife of John D. Rockefeller, IV, secretary of state and prospective next governor of West Virginia. Percy has frequently been spoken of as a Presidential candidate, but there are those who think his daughter Sharon may be the family member who ends up living in the White House.

Adlai Stevenson, III, elected to Illinois' other Senate seat in 1970, lacks the grace and wit that made his father an illustrious national and international figure. But he seems to have about everything else going for him. His performance, first as a state legislator in the famous "blue ribbon" legislature of 1965–66, when he was named that body's outstanding member, and later as state treasurer, a job in which he opened account ledgers to the public and increased investment returns to the state by millions of dollars, helped Stevenson build on the inherent advantages of a famous name. By the end of the 1970 Senate campaign, it was also clear that he was an astute politician. His opponent, interim Senator Ralph Smith, was a glib statehouse politician who tried to "radicalize" Stevenson's image through a series of innuendo-packed commercials that depicted Stevenson as an enemy of the police cut from the same cloth as yippie agitator Jerry Rubin. "When I see Adlai, I see red," Smith said in one speech. The commercials backfired with ordinary voters, and Stevenson skillfully deflected the attack by putting an American flag in his lapel, saying he "detested" violence whether "by Black Panthers, white students, or state troopers," and then making Thomas Foran, prosecutor of the "Chicago Seven," a co-chairman of his campaign. (Dan Walker was his regular campaign chairman, however.) As noted earlier, Stevenson won in a veritable landslide, even carrying downstate Illinois. It is too early to judge his Senate performance, but he is a hard worker, deeply committed to fundamental government reform, and will doubtless be heard from.

An interesting postscript to the 1970 Senate campaign was provided by the Washington *Post*'s Bernard Nossiter, who got firm expenditure estimates from both the Smith and Stevenson camps. Smith was reported to have spent about $1.1 million and Stevenson about $950,000, with each man investing just over $300,000 in television and radio advertising. Even if Illinois had a reporting law—and it has none—it would not have shown the help Stevenson got from Daley's 5,000 precinct workers in Cook County, or the footwork done for him by union staff members. Nor would it have indicated Smith's dependence on Illinois' business elite for goods and services—computers, billboards, executive assistance, and other items. Smith's biggest individual donor was W. Clement Stone, the rags-to-riches Chicago insuranceman who puts his personal worth at $325 to $350 million and in 1970 said he was willing to back up Smith's campaign with loans and gifts of up to $1 million. Stone's actual cash outlays for the Smith campaign, however, seem to have come to less than $250,000—less than half the $500,000 he says he spent to get his friend Richard Nixon elected President in 1968. (Stone, a small and pudgy man with a thin, waxed mustache, hardly fits the role of a venal profiteer out to control politicians. More likely, he probably just basks in the glory of acquaintance with the great. He has said he is ready to go all-out with campaign money to reelect Nixon in 1972. "If a family has wealth in the neighborhood of $400 million," he asks, "what's a million" in gifts?)

Paul Douglas no longer sits in the United States Senate, a victim of age and the swirling new tides of suburban politics which propelled his onetime student, Charles Percy, into the seat in 1966. But Douglas merits a word of note before the tides of history obscure the contributions of a brave, proud man who, like many Quakers, never doubted the righteousness of what he stood for. Though a pacifist, Douglas was convinced of the justifiability of World War II; he entered the Marines at age 52 as a private and was twice wounded in combat. (Douglas was later a vigorous cold warrior and remained a "hawk" on Vietnam to the end.) In the Senate, he demonstrated both great intellectual skill and sharp partisan wit; he was at once an author of liberal measures like the landmark 1949 Housing Act and a prime opponent of "pork barrel" federal public works spending. (In 1962, Douglas credited himself with saving the taxpayers nearly $2 billion through economy amendments.) Douglas served as chairman of the Joint Economic Committee, pioneered in consumer protection legislation (especially "truth in lending") and was a long-time battler of the Congressional seniority system, which he claimed was a device to let Southern conservatives control committees in league with conservative Republicans. Such views precluded his ever becoming a member of the Senate "club."

Everett McKinley Dirksen, by contrast, was a personification of the Senate inner circle and perhaps the most powerful single Senator during the decade of the '60s. Apparently a conservative by natural inclination, he first won national attention when he pointed at Thomas E. Dewey from the rostrum of the 1952 Republican National Convention and intoned angrily: "We followed you before and you took us down the road to defeat." (Dewey was for Eisenhower for the nomination, Dirksen for Taft.) In his 33 years in Congress, Dirksen was variously regarded as an isolationist and an internationalist, a New Dealer and a conservative, a friend and foe of civil rights. Though opposed to Ike's nomination in 1952, he became his valued lieutenant when elected minority leader in 1959. "I am a man of principle, and one of my first principles is flexibility," he once said. It was Dirksen's personal change of position which shifted enough conservative Republican Senators to make possible passage of numerous Kennedy-Johnson measures, including the Nuclear Test Ban Treaty and the Civil Rights Act of 1964 ("an idea whose time has come," said Dirksen). Yet he was a defender of Senator Joseph McCarthy, nominated Barry Goldwater for President in 1964, and was the leading figure in a failing effort to turn back the clock on the Supreme Court's reapportionment and school prayer decisions.

In his excellent biography, *Dirksen: Portrait of a Public Man*, Neil Mac-Neil, *Time's* chief Congressional correspondent since 1958, says Dirksen was "committed to the idea of compromise as a good in itself" and was a man who "played the game of politics for the zest of the game itself, for its fascination, for its exhilaration." Toward the end of his career, *Newsweek* and other publications suggested an underlying theme of venality in Dirksen's activities, pointing to his extraordinary interest in legislation affecting certain industries (drugs, chemicals, gas pipelines, steel, and lending institutions), his placement of "Dirksen men" in federal regulatory agencies, and his bitter opposition to any requirement that members of Congress disclose their income or holdings. It seemed the suspicions were being borne out when the attorneys handling his estate were more than a year remiss in filing a full inventory, and when the inventory was finally made public it included $53,379.43 in unspent campaign funds in a Washington lock box at the time of his death. But Dirksen's total estate, even counting a valuation of $150,000 placed on 11 crates of personal papers, was only $302,235, certainly slim pickings in comparison to what Dirksen's *opportunities* for under-the-table money had been. MacNeil was probably correct when he said that Dirksen "sought power and influence, not money."

Robert Novak, reviewing MacNeil's book, provides a fitting epitaph:

> Everett Dirksen's place in history is as ambiguous as was his own ideology. His flexibility time and again prevented deadlock of the legislative process and produced legislation where, otherwise, there might have been none. But that same flexibility kept him from charting even a broad course for himself, his party, and his nation, and this may exclude him from the first order of American statesmen.

Downstate Illinois: Prairie, City, Farm, and Factory

For the past quarter century, the population center of the United States has been creeping westward across southern Illinois. In 1950 it was in the little town of Olney, not far from the Indiana border; in 1960 not far from a small city prophetically named Centralia; in 1970 in farmer Lawrence Friederich's fallow soybean field 5.3 miles east of Mascoutah—and 23 miles to the east of East St. Louis. But, as others have noted in the past, this is not the only sense in which Illinois is the "state in the middle" or "the most American." The naturalist-writer and Illinois native Donald Culross Peattie a few years ago proclaimed that "Illinois is the best state precisely because it is so American. More, it is heartland. As Castile is of Spain, as the plain of Beauce is the granary of France, or Tuscany of Italy, so Illinois is core America. . . ."

Outside of the Chicago metropolis, Illinois remains essentially rural; in the 400 miles of her length, the top north of Boston, the bottom south of Louisville, there are only a handful of significant cities. The largest of these is Rockford (1970 population 147,370—only a thirtieth of the Chicago figure), a healthy manufacturing center set in the forests and low hills of the Rock River valley of north central Illinois. The flavor is strongly Scandinavian and conservative with pockets of John Birchish sentiment; the city refused until recently to accept urban renewal funds it needed to rebuild its center. But with a growing black population, more factories, and more unions, the tone is moderating and Rockford has one of the most successful "scattered site" public housing projects in America.

Peoria (pop. 126,963), set in the midst of Central Illinois' endless corn-fields, used to be so renowned for municipal corruption, whiskey bootleg-ging, and unsolved murders that John Gunther called it "one of the toughest towns on earth." But just over a decade ago, reformers took over city hall and began a thoroughgoing renovation of the decaying central city. Indica-tive of the new spirit, Caterpillar Tractor, largest Peoria employer with a local payroll of some 27,000, moved its national headquarters into the city proper.

The major business of Springfield (pop. 91,753) is politics and state government, despite a scattering of industries. As a state capital with con-siderable tradition, Springfield has a social strata of sorts; there are still many names that were prominent in Lincoln's day. True to the Lincolnian heritage, this territory remains staunchly Republican.

Diversified industry and dull politics typify most of Illinois' other down-state cities in the 40,000 to 90,000 population bracket—Decatur (90,397; self-proclaimed "soybean capital of the world"); Moline (46,237; home of John Deere and "farm implement capital of America"), Rock Island (50,-166; site of the government's largest manufacturing arsenal), Champaign (56,532; which shares with neighboring Urbana the site of the main campus of the University of Illinois), Aurora (74,182), Alton (39,700), Danville (42,570), Elgin (55,691), and the old river town of Quincy (45,288) on the Mississippi.

For all of Illinois' industrial might, farming remains its biggest single in-dustry. Rich black glacial soil that goes as deep as 75 feet—called gumbo by early settlers, who had difficulty plowing it—covers all of Illinois except the southern counties, and no less than 84 percent of the state is in farmland. Most of central and northern Illinois is prime corn belt territory, and the state vies with Iowa for number one position among the states in corn harvestings and trails only Iowa in hog production. Illinois is also strong in beef production and second only to Iowa as a meat packer; throughout the state new, auto-mated packing plants are filling the gap created by the demise of the Chicago stockyards. In the north, there are also Wisconsin-like dairylands. Illinois ranks number one among the states in soybeans, the great (and versatile) crop of U.S. agriculture in the postwar period. Overall, Illinois farmers regis-ter $2.6 billion in receipts each year, ranking behind only California, Iowa, and Texas. There are 123,565 farms, averaging 242 acres in size.

Outside of Chicago, principal industrial growth is coming along the Illinois Waterway, a combination of the Cal-Sag Canal and the Des Plaines and Illinois rivers stretching 300 miles from Chicago to Joliet, Peoria, and then into the Mississippi River north of St. Louis.* A major industrial cor-ridor is developing along the Waterway, which can deliver coal, iron ore, chemicals, petroleum products, and construction materials by cheap barge transportation. On its banks at Hennepin, Jones & Laughlin Steel has re-cently built a fully integrated steel-making complex that will eventually em-

---

* The Waterway provides the direct link between the Great Lakes and the Gulf of Mexico.

ploy some 4,500 men. Little Hennepin (pop. 535) will never be the same.

Enough coal underlies Illinois to supply world needs for a century, and she is currently the fourth largest state in coal production (behind West Virginia, Pennsylvania, and Kentucky). A third of the 200 coal mines are of the land-despoiling strip variety, and the state has very weak laws dealing with strip mining.

Egypt and Its Cairo; East St. Louis

Far from booming "Chicagoland" and ranging southward from the rich glacier-tilled prairie of central Illinois lies a 31-county region of hilltop and bottom country wedged between the Ohio, Wabash, and Mississippi Rivers that looks like, thinks like, and acts like the American Southland. Perhaps because of its similarity to the deltalands of the Nile, the region has long been known as Egypt (or Little Egypt) and comes complete with towns named Cairo, Karnak, Thebes, and Dongola. It is not only a land of levees and overflowing rivers, but of the Illinois Ozarks with their valleys and hills where the first settlers hacked farmsteads out of the magnificent hardwood forests of walnut, oak, beech, sycamore, and poplar.

Egypt lies south of prosperity and indeed has been in a spiraling economic decline for several decades. Since the 1890s the major industry of the region has been coal mining. But while the market demand for coal remains high, overworked veins have been depleted, strip mining is ever more prevalent, and mechanization has erased thousands of jobs. Unemployment in Southern Illinois is about twice the national average, in some counties four times as high, and thousands are on welfare. Young people leave the region in droves, despite the efforts of such institutions as fast-growing Southern Illinois University at Carbondale to expand technical education in varied fields.

Those who know the region have written of Southern Illinois as "an intemperate land" of "great and bitter passions." It was in Williamson County (49,201) that one of the most gruesome episodes in American labor history took place in 1922, as 500 striking miners massacred 19 strikebreakers (a story graphically recounted in Paul Angle's *Bloody Williamson*).

And now new kinds of terror and trouble stalk across Southern Illinois, centered in the town of Cairo and the city of East St. Louis.

Cairo (actually pronounced Kerro), perhaps the only walled city in the U.S.A., is a squat, drab river town set behind 60-foot levees at the very point of confluence of the Ohio's gray waters and Mississippi's yellow tide.

In its heyday, Cairo was a great port of call for river crews, a trading and cotton production center, crossroads for seven railroads, and county seat where close to 20,000 people lived. It was also a wide open town, very wet during Prohibition, a place where riverboat crews could always find women and gambling. The economy began a long decline a generation ago, and the town now has just 6,277 people. For the past several years, it has been wracked by the bitterest conflicts between blacks and whites of almost any town in America. In 1969 alone, fires were reported to have destroyed over $1 million of business property in Cairo. The racial conflict became so intense that the mayor, in tears, resigned, quickly followed by the police chief, who said: "When the people of the community, black and white, say they are going to arm themselves and take the law into their own hands, I, as a professional policeman, cannot continue."

East St. Louis, a town of 69,996 people some 125 miles northwest of Cairo on the Mississippi opposite St. Louis, has a raucous and violent history that dates back to 1885 when the first mayor was assassinated by a disgruntled city employee. Up to World War I the town was largely white, but then the industries (railroads and big meat packers) imported Southern Negroes as strikebreakers; the result in 1917 was the worst race riot of the first half of the 20th century, in which 39 Negroes and nine whites were killed, more than 300 buildings and 44 railroad cars burned in three days of mob rule.

A big clean-up of organized vice and crime came under Mayor Alvin Fields in the 1950s, but most of the postwar years spelled a compounding of misery for East St. Louis. Three major employers—Swift, Armour, and Alcoa —pulled out of the city. Poorly educated northbound blacks from the South flooded in in ever increasing numbers, and by 1970 the city was 69 percent black.

As the poverty level rose and the tax base dwindled, the East St. Louis government for 15 years was obliged to resort to what is euphemistically called "judgment financing"—a ploy by which the city lets its cash balance go down to zero, creditors go to court and get a judgment against the city, and the city may then (under Illinois law) issue bonds to cover the indebtedness.

The hard-working East St. Louis Negroes thrown onto relief when the packing houses closed were not of the rioting type, but their sons and daughters turned militant by the mid-1960s. Most of the protesting youngsters refrained from violent protest, but there were disturbances in 1967 and 1968. Then a small element of black hoodlums, capitalizing on the black revolution, began a wave of terror that drove law-abiding blacks and whites alike behind locked doors at home each night. Murders and strong-armed robberies increased sharply, and between early 1968 and mid-1969 there was a wave of unexplained snipings that wounded dozens and killed several. On a midwestern swing in 1969, I was repeatedly warned not to enter East St. Louis.

Up to the late 1960s East St. Louis was ruled by an antique, patronage-based Democratic machine with a cadre of ill-educated white precinct committeemen who curried favor by paying occasional grocery or light bills for families in trouble, providing dinners for wakes, getting people out of jail after fights or drinking bouts, and paying up to $3 a vote on election day. But gradually blacks took over committeeman and leadership posts, the local antipoverty campaign, and the model cities program; everyone knew that the future of East St. Louis was as a black-run town. The question was what kind of black leadership—militant, reformist, or old-line political—would emerge. The answer came in 1971 when Fields retired voluntarily, and a "clean" reform slate of moderate blacks (with one white ally) took control of the mayoralty and a majority of the city council. The new mayor was James E. Williams, Sr., 49, a political novice who ran on a pledge not to be a puppet for a political machine. He scored an upset victory over another black, city commissioner Virgil E. Calvert, who had been the favorite because of his control of nearly all the Democratic committeemen in the city's 51 precincts. But Williams countered with a volunteer force that numbered in the hundreds by the day of the nonpartisan election. He also received help from Governor Ogilvie, who promised to build a state office building in East St. Louis, but only if Williams was elected. Williams, who had been executive director of the St. Clair Legal Aid Society before his election, is deeply religious, soft-spoken, and serious. His campaign not only rejected the old-school patronage way of doing business, but involved many whites, giving hope for better race relations in the future.

The school board, which had been a terrible source of corruption under the old regime, also got a thorough housecleaning in 1971. Its majority is now reformist, and the new school board president is Fred Kimbrought, a young black activist militant who believes in working through the system but may demand much more radical and rapid change in the city than Mayor Williams, a man trained in the law who favors proper procedure and rational approaches, may prefer.

Another example of the kind of black leader trying to pick up the pieces of the mess left by the old white power structure in East St. Louis is Fred Teer, head of the city's model cities program. Teer and his wife, Lila, who directs a neighborhood opportunity center for the poverty program, have deliberately kept their home in the bleak, impoverished south side slum area of East St. Louis, working to keep surging black militancy under control and to convince young black rebels to "cool it" both in their hatred of "Whitey" and in crosstown gang rumbles. But Teer, a man of frenetic energy, is no Uncle Tom; he fought tenaciously to get black control of the model cities program, he is scornful of many "regular" black Democratic politicians, and he can take credit for spearheading the successful effort to get the first meaningful low-income housing construction on the town's south side in half a century. Both Teers are accomplished professionals who were among the relatively few Negro graduates of the University of Illinois at Champaign-Urbana during the 1930s; both could doubtless get desirable jobs elsewhere but have chosen to stick it out in their difficult and dangerous community.

A new St. Louis regional airport, now projected for a location on the Illinois side of the Mississippi, may bring a new economic impetus for the East St. Louis area. But as for the city of East St. Louis itself, many despair of redeeming and rebuilding it in its current degenerated physical plant. Harold Gibbons, the area Teamsters leader, told me "the only thing they can do with it is to take a bulldozer, level it, rebuild it, and call it Stevenson, Illinois."

MICHIGAN

AUTO EMPIRES AND UNIONS

THE STATE OF MICHIGAN is the keystone of the Great Lakes. The waters of Lakes Michigan, Superior, Huron, and Erie wash up against her shores along a coastline 3,121 miles in length (greater than any other state save Alaska). And the Straits of Mackinac, separating Lake Huron from Lake Michigan, in fact divide Michigan into two separate geographic entities, also a distinction among the states.*

But it is not the division of Upper Peninsula and Lower Peninsula, so apparent from the map, which really divides Michigan. (In fact, the two since 1957 have been joined by the graceful five-mile span of the Mackinac Bridge.) Michigan is like Caesar's Gaul—really three parts:

Across the whole of the Upper Peninsula and the northern half of the Lower Peninsula is a vast expanse of wooded hills, lakes, and resorts, a territory shorn of its virgin forests by the lumber barons of yesteryear. This is a land of depleted mines, of poor soil, and few inhabitants (a mere 6 percent of the state's people).

* The sheer physical size of Michigan warrants notice; the distance from Ironwood on the Upper Peninsula to Detroit, for instance, is 595 miles—more than the distance from Detroit to New York City. Another oddity: Ironwood is west of St. Louis; Port Huron is east of Greenville, S. C.

Spread throughout the southern half of the Lower Peninsula are rich fruit and dairy farms and quiet towns and villages whose frame houses and steepled churches evoke the spirit of the New England and New York pioneers who first settled there. Here, too, there are few people.

Finally, there is industrial Michigan—bustling, materialistic, and seat of one of the greatest industrial and labor empires ever developed by man. It thrives in brawny Detroit and smaller carbon copies like Flint, Lansing, Grand Rapids, Saginaw, and Muskegon, all in southern Michigan. Three quarters of Michigan's 8,875,083 people live here. So do the wealth, the power, and the principal troubles of the state today. Industrial Michigan and its great hallmarks—the automotive behemoths, the sinewy and socially conscious United Auto Workers, and "programmatic," issue-oriented politics—are the essential Michigan story. First we will examine those phenomena, then state government, then the plight of the Michigan cities and suburbs.

The Auto World

The history of the auto industry is littered with the wrecks of the 2,000-odd makes once introduced but eventually doomed to extinction in one of the world's most fiercely competitive industries. Such illustrious makes as Duryea, Mercer, LaSalle, Pierce Arrow, and Stanley Steamer succumbed long before World War II, and later years have seen the demise of such once great stalwarts as Packard and Hudson. The only firms of any consequence surviving are General Motors, Ford, Chrysler, and American Motors. All have their headquarters in Detroit, although American Motors, a weak fourth in the industry with only 6 percent of GM's output, in fact has no actual Michigan production. Assembly plants have spread increasingly across the continent in the postwar period; now 35 percent of the automobiles produced roll off Michigan production lines, with Missouri, California, and Ohio among the other leading assembly locations.

General Motors is the most gigantic industrial corporation the world has ever seen. On its global payrolls are three quarters of a million men, half a million at 119 plants in 18 states and 70 cities of the United States. Its sales in 1969 were $24.3 billion; it paid $2.5 billion in taxes but still had a hefty $1.7 billion profit.* That General Motors benefited both from the prosperity of the postwar years and its own ingenuity is demonstrated by the percent of increase in sales in two decades: a staggering 425 percent. The firm's gross is three times larger than the budget of any of the states and in fact larger than the budgets of all the countries of the world save the United States and the Soviet Union. Aside from producing about half of the passenger autos of the United States (Chevrolet, Buick, Oldsmobile, Cadillac, Pontiac), GM has gigantic divisions producing trucks, buses, refrigeration equipment, diesel motors, marine engines, aircraft engines, earth-moving

---

* In 1970, with a long strike, GM's sales were down to $18.7 billion, the lowest in half a decade. But there were still profits of $609 million.

equipment, inertial navigation systems, and space components. The corporation is the tenth largest military contractor, but so large are its total operations that military and space work account for only 3 percent of its total sales. In 1970 the Bureau of Labor Statistics estimated that 1,766,700 U.S. and Canadian workers—in every field, from manufacturing (435,240) to business services (88,920), construction (21,060), and mining (18,720)—were either on the GM payroll, or dependent on it for their employment.

From a corporation with such immense national and international power, one can fairly demand innovative leadership not only in technological breakthroughs and advanced planning in its own field of vehicle manufacture, but in social and political fields as well—areas in which General Motors has been shockingly negligent over most of its history. Not only has it failed to lead, but it has often been a poor follower. Smugness and complacency were long the hallmarks of its executive leadership; critics were to be dismissed as unworthy of consideration, because GM knew what was right. The nation got a brief glimpse of this in the Senate Armed Forces Committee hearings on the nomination of GM president Charles E. Wilson to the post of Secretary of Defense in the Eisenhower cabinet, when Wilson uttered his famous line: "What is good for the country is good for General Motors, and what's good for General Motors is good for the country." The problem was that GM, neither then nor for many years afterward, had a single person among its 600,000 to 700,000 employees specifically assigned to looking far ahead and seeing what GM and the entire auto industry could and should be doing to meet conditions in a changing world—the safety, size, and ultimate disposal problems of automobiles, their impact on cities and the natural landscape, the potentiality of exerting a creative and positive impact on the development of governmental policies all the way from Detroit to the international scene.

The problems of auto safety, for example, were known long before Ralph Nader came on the scene. And, in fact, some inventive people in GM would develop new safety features and the styling staff might sell them to the engineers, but when they got to the car divisions, the general managers would veto the ideas, saying that "this safety stuff won't sell." Apparently the basic policy issues were never brought to their proper forum—the GM board of directors. Yet since GM so dominated the industry, it was incumbent on it to lead; the other companies, competitively, were simply in no position to take risky initiatives.

Indicative of GM's *modus operandi* is that it dispenses virtually no charitable contributions on a national scale, but rather contributes in the local communities where its plants are located—and local good will can be obtained. Instructions to plant managers have run along these lines: Don't initiate any movement to start something like a new hospital or YMCA building in your community. But if someone else initiates such an idea and comes to you for help, well, then give a nominal amount of assistance.

In partisan politics, GM traditionally placed pressure on its employees on the senior bonus roll (those eligible for bonuses in addition to salaries) to contribute to the Republican party of Michigan. They received cards on which to record their contributions (in some years with the name of the Michigan GOP actually printed thereon) and were expected to send them not to the party but the business manager of their departments at GM. David L. Lewis, a former GM public relations officer and now professor of business history at the University of Michigan, explains that "the checks were then presented to the party and GM—not the donors—got the thanks." According to Stuart Hertzberg, treasurer of the Michigan Democratic party, "GM had no bipartisan contribution program until 1968, when we talked them into it. We didn't get a dime out of GM until then." After that, Hertzberg told the *National Journal* in 1970, GM employees had given about $2,000 a year to the Michigan Democrats and, based on state filings, between $100,000 and $200,000 a year to the Michigan GOP.

Yet as unimaginative as many aspects of the GM record may be, the fact is that at least in areas of the most pressing social concern directly related to it—auto safety, pollution control, and minority hiring—GM has begun, just in the recent past, to move aggressively forward. And being the biggest, it has become the inevitable top target of reformers—an effort institutionalized in 1970 under the Nader-inspired Campaign to Make General Motors Responsible. This "Campaign GM" began by focusing on GM's accountability in the fields of safety, pollution, and minority employment. The odd coalition of forces working within "Campaign GM"—ranging from students to churches, foundations, and universities—seemed at first blush to be repulsed. But it was not long after that GM announced a new "public policy committee" and elected Philadelphia's the Reverend Leon Sullivan to the GM board, the first black man ever to sit on that august body.

Professor Lewis suggests that one result of the spotlight on GM's internal policies may be that it will bend over backward so far in an effort to neutralize criticism that serious errors may result—for example, hiring so many unqualified minority group workers that the company's competitive position could be impaired. "It's a brand new aspect of the bigness problem," he notes.

At this point in history, the average wage of GM workers is close to five dollars an hour, but for financial remuneration the great prizes go to its top executives. In the banner year of 1969, board chairman James M. Roche earned about $750,000, counting both salary and bonuses. President Edward N. Cole's earnings were about $500,000. The other gainers are 1,363,000 shareholders, who live in every U. S. state and Canadian province plus more than 80 foreign countries. The bulk of the stock, however, is held by a narrow group of U. S. banks (the National Bank of Detroit being foremost in the group), plus insurance companies, foundations, universities, and retirement funds.

Old Henry Ford, the brilliant titan of the automobile industry, inventor of the assembly line, and introducer of the then revolutionary five-dollars a-day wage in 1914, has been dead for close to a quarter century. But the Ford Motor Company, third largest U. S. industrial corporation with annual sales of $14 billion, retains intensely personal, family-flavored leadership through chairman of the board Henry Ford II. This grandson of the founder, a callow youth of 28 when he took command in 1945, has long since disproven the suspicion that he is a figurehead. In fact, as *Time* commented in 1970, he is "perhaps the most psychologically secure chief executive in the U.S.," possessed of immense wealth, bearing the family name with its aura of power, the man to which all major questions, suggestions, ideas, and issues in the Ford empire must be brought for final decision. When Ford took over in the 1940s, it was only by forcing his aged grandfather to give up control of a financially troubled company that was losing $10 million a month; through sound fiscal management and the building of good relations with the United Auto Workers, Ford guided the company to its phenomenal postwar success. Through the same years, quiet but significant influence has also been exerted by his mother, Mrs. Edsel Ford, who lives the life of a *grande dame* in Grosse Pointe Farms.

That Ford is really still a family-held corporation is obvious from examining the stock structure; through the wills of old Henry and his son Edsel, a major chunk of Ford stock went to the Ford Foundation (avoiding the punitive 91 percent inheritance tax). But the Ford Foundation stock was nonvoting, so that effective control remained with the family through its own stock holdings in the firm. Even today, despite the millions of shares owned by outside investors, the Ford family still has effective control through its 10 percent of the stock—which has 40 percent of the vote weight. The market value of the family's stock was about $546 million in 1970, but in reality was probably worth two or three times that sum—perhaps $1.5 billion—because of the value of holding effective control of the great corporation.*

The stories of the Motor City's triumphs and failures, of flashy fins (the foremost design abomination of recent decades), of Chrysler's ups and downs (though it still had annual sales of $7.1 billion in 1969), of scrappy little American Motors' Rambler, and George Romney's assault on the "gas-guzzling dinosaurs" of the Big Three, could well fill chapters, because for better or worse, what Detroit designs (and fails to design) is part of the warp and woof of American culture.

Yet it is perhaps best to forget the colorful specifics and say the obvious: that the endless stream of automobiles pouring out of Detroit and its satellite factories for the past half a century has had an impact on Americans' everyday life second to no other modern invention save electricity. The dividends in mobility and convenience are simply stupendous, and the industry has given birth to others which themselves are giants of the modern American economy: petroleum, tires, road and superhighway construction. Without the automobile, we might well have remained an essentially rural nation.

And then, quite suddenly in the late 1960s and early 1970s, the U.S.A.,

* For a more thorough analysis of the Ford family wealth and the basis on which the above figures are compiled, see Ferdinand Lundberg's *The Rich and the Super-Rich* (New York: Lyle Stuart, 1968), pp. 162–69.

as if in a great rush of horrified awakening, began to see the bane mixed with the blessing in what Detroit had wrought. The problems:

SAFETY. Between 1950 and 1970, some 900,000 Americans met their deaths in automobile accidents, a carnage far exceeding the battlefield casualties of all the wars the nation has ever fought (636,000 through Vietnam). Yet as recently as 1965, the official Detroit attitude had been that the culprit in all this was the driver behind the wheel, and that automobiles were as safe as they could be expected to be. "Safety doesn't sell," Ford executives used to say. But then, virtually singlehandedly, a young attorney named Ralph Nader changed the nation's mind on that subject. Nader's book, *Unsafe at Any Speed*, showed Detroit putting style, horsepower, comfort, and sales ahead of safety. Nader rejected the "driver at fault" theory, saying there would always be human error, but that proper engineering and design could work dramatic reductions in the death rate by reducing the chance the riders would be impaled, crushed, mangled, or decapitated within their cars or thrown out at high speeds.

General Motors then committed a monumentally foolish act of the kind usually reserved for great heads of state. It put private investigators on Nader's trail (a deed to which it confessed), and at the same time Nader was approached by questionable women, harrassed with late-night telephone calls, and questioned on his sex life, potential anti-Semitism, and professional competence by various private agencies. Called before a Senate committee, General Motors president James Roche was obliged to apologize to Nader before national television "to the extent that General Motors bears responsibility" for the harassment. (Later, Nader's invasion-of-privacy suit against GM was settled out of court for $425,000)

The GM episode gave instant national exposure to Nader and his views. The first automobile and highway safety acts of American history sailed through Congress in a few months with scarcely a murmur of opposition. As Daniel P. Moynihan wrote later, the legislation, passed "almost without notice," suddenly subjected "the largest manufacturing complex on earth, which in the sixth decade of the 20th Century had persisted as an utterly unregulated private enterprise, . . . to detailed and permanent government regulation."

Soon the federal government was requiring scores of safety modifications in new cars, ranging from seat belts and padded dashboards and windshield visors to collapsible steering columns. Tire standards were also put into effect, and by 1970 it was apparent that the highway death rate (both in absolute numbers and in relation to the number of vehicles on the road) was starting to decline. The 1970s promise even more innovations, including an air bag that blows up on impact and protects front-seat passengers in case of a collision.* Yet Detroit finds itself increasingly at bay as defects, serious

---

* By 1971, one impartial Michigan source suggested to me, the industry effected or programmed about 85 percent of the safety features that can probably be expected. If the U. S. is really serious about reducing highway injuries and fatalities, it will have to crack down next on perennially careless drivers and people driving under the influence of alcohol.

enough to require recalls for adjustments, are found in more and more of the 13 million new cars bought by Americans each year.

POLLUTION. Late in the 1960s, Americans for the first time became concerned about the growing pollution of their air. And it was discovered that at least 60 percent of the pollutants in the atmosphere come from the internal combustion engine. By one estimate, automobiles spew forth 8 percent of all particulates in the air (bits of solid matter, including lead), 42 percent of the nitrogen oxides (which give the air a brownish tinge and act as fertilizers, thus inducing harmful growth of algae in lakes and rivers when they settle from the atmosphere), 63 percent of the hydrocarbons (unburned fuel that helps cause smog), and 92 percent of the carbon monoxide (a lethal gas). In some cities' smog belts, auto emissions account for as much as 92 percent of the air pollution; each year American automobiles dump 90 million tons of pollutants into the air (and potentially the lungs). GM vehicle-generated pollution alone is said to account for 35 percent of the total air-pollution load of the United States.

As recently as 1958, auto spokesmen were blithely dismissing air pollution as the responsibility of car owners; for many of the postwar years, the industry regularly spent $1 million a year on pollution-control research, one tenth of one percent of what it spent each year to change over its models. A growing national cry of protest—and government pressure—made the industry change its mind. By 1970, the big four had in the test stage a total of 26 different cars powered by everything from steam, gas turbine, and electricity to the type of fuel cells used for moon spacecraft. President Nixon set a goal for production of a "virtually pollution-free" car in five years, but even he must have been surprised when Sen. Edmund Muskie's amendments were adopted to the 1970 Clean Air Act, requiring by statute a 90 percent reduction in exhaust pollutants by 1975 (with a possible one-year extension).

Ford and its competitors must also deal with the wretched outpouring of pollution from their own plants. Ford's gigantic River Rouge plant at Dearborn, for instance, not only assembles autos (spiffy, hard-to-get-in-and-out-of little Mustangs and Cougars) but also makes its own steel from raw iron ore and coal and produces its own glass. From the plant flows what *Newsweek* has called "a ribbon of bilge that has contributed measurably to the 'death' of nearby Lake Erie." Yet Ford officials assure a visitor that they are in the midst of an $80 million project to eliminate all significant air and water pollution from their plants by 1973.

To another form of pollution—the thousands of auto graveyards which scar the American landscape from Maine to Los Angeles—no clear answer was in sight, despite the obvious possibilities (with the right technology) of reducing the hulks to basic materials for recycling through the industrial machine.

PROLIFERATION. With the vehicle population well above 100 million and on its way to 200 million by the year 2000, there were increasingly difficult questions of where to put them all—especially in large cities, where the vehicle population growth is greater than the human population growth. Parking costs have skyrocketed into the billions; it costs, for instance, $3.50 to park an automobile in downtown Detroit for just a few hours, not to mention the astronomical rates in New York City and other major metropolises. The interstate highway system, built with government largesse to accommodate the automobile, will finally cover some 42,500 miles at a cost of $57 billion, devouring (with right of way) a territory equal to one and a half times the size of Rhode Island. Yet Detroit, despite its inventive genius, has taken a head-in-the-sand attitude toward mass transit or intercity rail transportation. It was taken by surprise in the late 1960s when more and more Americans (especially the young and better educated) began to reject all the preposterousness surrounding the Auto, U.S.A.—excess (and polluting) power, planned obsolescence, wasteful year-by-year style changes, the sex- and status-symbol advertising. Suddenly Detroit began to talk less of size and power in autos and more about safety, repairability, and economy.

RACE AND POVERTY. The automobile industry was one of the first in the United States to open wide-scale job opportunities for blacks, and high UAW-won wages have indeed created a stable class of homeowning Negroes in the $10,000-a-year bracket with a real stake in society. Some plants, like Ford's River Rouge complex, have 50 percent black employment. But Detroit has more than its share of destitute blacks, and in the wake of the 1967 riots the auto industry began a determined effort to find jobs for the once-thought-unemployable Negro. Of the Big Three, Chrysler developed sensitivity in the hiring of blacks much earlier and more comprehensively than General Motors, and somewhat ahead of Ford. (Some 35 percent of Chrysler's 150,000 employees and 10 percent of its foremen and high-ranking workers belong to minority groups, the best record in the industry. Chrysler can also take credit for the biggest single government contract for training the hard core, and it was the only auto company to adopt a ghetto school, donating a completely stocked auto-repair shop. All of this is of special importance in Detroit, where Chrysler production so far outweighs that of its competitors that it is considered the home-town auto.)

But it was Ford that got the most headlines and showed the most imaginative approach in the immediate post-riot era. Henry Ford threw his full personal prestige behind minority hiring and became the first national chief of the National Alliance of Businessmen to hire hard-core unemployables. In Detroit, Ford's company not only relaxed its old hiring criteria—a written examination and insistence that a new employee have no police record—but went into the ghetto to recruit new men, setting up special hiring locations to attract hard corers. Many potential workers had gone to plant gates in the past and been rejected; Ford decided the best way to overcome their fear of renewed rejection was to go directly to them. A fresh group of interviewers was instructed to adopt a policy that would screen "in" instead of screen "out"; specifically the interviewers were told to bridge the cultural gap by ignoring purple pants or natural hairdos. The only disqualifying points would be failure to pass a physical exam, a record of dope pushing, or of physical assault. The program was spectacularly successful; the day Ford opened its ghetto employment offices, more than 2,000 men showed up to apply. In two years Ford hired 5,800 of the 7,800 men it interviewed at its inner-city locations, as well as thousands more who appeared at the plant gates. While absenteeism was higher, the actual retention rate among the hard core was just a little higher than that of other employees.

Of the thousands of hard core it has employed, Ford's favorite story is still that of Harry Palmer, a stockily built, muscular man in his mid-thirties who hadn't held a job for 15 years—and, indeed, had served several years at the Jackson state penitentiary for an attempted break-in into a jewelry store when he was 20 years old—when Ford opened up its employment rolls. Both Ford and Chrysler had previously turned Palmer down because of his prison record, and the only income for him, his wife, and four children was his wife's occasional salary as a domestic worker or occasional jobs he picked up himself in small foundries for as little as $1.25 an hour. When Palmer heard of the new Ford policy, he at first hesitated about applying because of his parolee record. To his amazement, however, he was hired and quickly gained promotions at Ford's Dearborn Iron Foundry. His wife could stop working and stay at home with the children, he bought a color television and could lay plans for buying a home outside the ghetto.

The auto companies still have a long way to go in hiring a fair share of blacks in skilled trades or in management positions, but they are making a serious effort to go beyond mere tokenism. Ford is expected to appoint the first black plant managers in the industry's history soon, and its top black employees insist the company is "clean" in its minority hiring and promotion policies. Chrysler and GM are moving in this area, too, but resentment of old policies lingers on. I heard from a black associated with the UAW: "General Motors is an extremely racist company, in all employment and community programs. . . . I resent the hell out of any Negro who buys the Cadillac." But the cold figures show that the minority share of GM's labor force rose from 8.1 percent in 1961 to 15.3 percent (over 90,000) in 1970, making GM the nation's largest single employer of minority persons.

The dearth of black dealerships has been a second sore spot. In 1969, for instance, blacks held only .008 percent of the 30,000 auto dealerships in the country, even though American blacks spent $3.8 billion for new and used cars in that year alone. For many years, Ed Davis, a Chrysler-Plymouth dealer in Detroit, was the only Negro new-car dealer in the U.S.A. Up to 1967, there was not a single GM dealership owned by a black in the United States. But then everyone "got religion" and a spate of new black dealerships opened under auspices of all the big auto makers. Unfortunately, all the perils of doing business in the ghetto awaited—pilferage and theft, high insurance premiums, credit turndowns on about half the potential sales, lack of qualified black personnel as middle managers, and on top of it all, the recession that began in 1969. Several failed, including the lonely pioneer, Ed Davis. By 1971, there were still less than 30 Negro dealerships in the country.

The UAW: Powerful Engine of Change

Michigan has the most powerful labor movement of any state of the American Union. There are 1,135,000 union members—one of every 17 unionists in the U. S. A. Michigan factory workers have been so successful that their average weekly pay is 33 percent greater than the national average.

The Depression did a good job of turning auto workers to the left. In 1928, the booming industry turned out close to five million cars and there were 435,000 workers earning an average pay of $33 a week. Then came the massive layoffs. "These are really good times," Henry Ford said in March 1931, "but only a few know it." Five months later he shut down his plants, throwing 75,000 men out of work. The other manufacturers closed down as well, banks busted, and schoolmarms were paid in scrip. By 1933 the auto workers who still had jobs were earning an average of only $20 a week.

As the slow recovery began, so did the intensive organizing efforts of the unions, a chaotic process in which not a few Communist organizers were involved and the leading Detroit industrialists launched a campaign of murder, mayhem, and relentless intimidation of auto workers.

In 1935 the chaotic plethora of early unions began to solidify in the United Automobile Workers, whose steep climb has been described as the "greatest surge forward of the underpossessed" in the history of industry. The National Labor Relations Act of 1935 required employers to bargain collectively with unions, and after breakthroughs with a number of smaller firms, the UAW in 1937 staged its great sit-down strike against General Motors at Flint and won recognition. Later that year, a similar sit-down strike broke Chrysler's resistance, and by the end of 1937 the UAW had contracts with 400 companies. But old Henry Ford refused to give in; Walter Reuther, for instance, would earn fame in the annals of labor industry as one of the organizers severely beaten by Ford's hired thugs at a confrontation on an entrance overpass at the River Rouge plant in 1937. But in 1941 Ford was finally obliged, following a short strike, to recognize the UAW, and in fact granted it the first union shop and dues checkoff in the industry. After that, the UAW's power grew rapidly and it has since been total master of unionism in the automobile (and now farm implement) field.

Walter Reuther was the central figure of the UAW's history and the most influential single trade unionist of the postwar era in America. Son of an old Socialist German brewery worker, Reuther was an expert tool and die worker at Ford in his early years. Even while he worked a full day at the plant, he worked his way through college. After Ford fired him for union activity in 1933, he took a magnificently educative 33-month trip around the world with his brother Victor, observing trade union activity everywhere. Part of the trip was through the Soviet Union, and Reuther's right-wing enemies would claim for years that the stay there proved his Communist leanings. The fact is that Reuther was always a Socialist, never a Communist, and in fact won the

UAW presidency in 1946 after a decisive battle with Communist elements in the union.

Reuther was known as a pugnacious redhead in his younger years and never lost his superb organizing and tactical skills in dealing with the heavies of the auto industry. During his career, the UAW went from zero to 1.6 million members, replaced Henry Ford's prescribed five-dollars-a-day wages with more than five dollars an hour in average wages and benefits, and pioneered such innovations as profit sharing for workers, a cost-of-living escalator in contracts, a guaranteed annual wage for workers (in a formula including unemployment compensation benefits), management-paid pensions, and early retirement plans. There was a time in the 1940s and 1950s when Reuther was the most feared and hated of American labor leaders, called by George Romney "the most dangerous radical in America."

In resistance to Reuther, the big firms also sharpened their negotiating methods and, in fact, since 1958 have worked in perfect tandem in dealing with the UAW. Contract negotiations are now almost a matter of routine. After both sides have presented and discussed their demands, the Big Three finally present absolutely identical offers to the union at three locations— Chrysler at its Highland Park headquarters, General Motors at the GM building in Detroit, and Ford at Dearborn. One year the offers were so identical that they contained the same typographical errors. Union officials regret this industry solidarity, because, as one official relates, "in the old days the firms were fiercely independent and that was a great advantage for us because we could play one off against the other."

The auto industry is blessed with an absolute minimum of featherbedding and has traditionally registered high levels of productivity (although in the last half of the 1960s, auto officials complained that the productivity increase of some 3 percent a year was not keeping pace with average annual wage boosts of 6.5 percent). Pay and benefits aside, there is a limit to what the UAW can do to better the everyday working milieu for its membership. The man who spends his life at the monotonous, repetitive job of putting the left front wheel on 60 vehicles an hour can hardly be expected to value his job as a great privilege.*

Both union and company leaders acknowledge that with a work force younger, blacker, and better educated than just a decade ago, worker dissatisfaction with dead-end assembly-line jobs is increasing, as is the turnover on employment rolls. Younger workers think nothing of talking back to foremen, of turning down jobs they think might hurt their health or safety, or of staging wildcat strikes in defiance of their own union leaders. Absenteeism and the use of drugs are on the upgrade, and contribute to the soaring recall rate of new vehicles.

Reuther's unusual contribution went beyond solid bargaining-table successes to the unique way he led his massive union. He believed in internal

---

* Automation, which came some years ago to the stamping and matching plants, reduces some of the most monotonous jobs—though, of course, it threatens jobs, too. Some believe the industry may be on the threshold of a major breakthrough in automating the assembly lines with robot welding machines, the use of more plastic and molded parts to eliminate cut-and-sew operations, and the like.

trade-union democracy, and the UAW became the most democratically run major union in America with such devices as an outside grievance procedure to which members can resort when they feel the union is treating them unfairly. Reuther fought hard to get Negro representation on the UAW board, and later to get a woman on the board as well.

And Reuther's horizons extended beyond traditional union concerns to broad social issues and politics. Following his death in 1970 in an airplane accident, the Washington *Post* editorialized that Reuther "left his imprint upon the social and economic life of the United States more indelibly, perhaps, than any political figure in his time, Franklin Roosevelt excepted. He was part labor leader, part social reformer, part evangelist." During his lifetime Reuther was often faulted for aggressive moralizing, but the fact was that his mind produced an almost endless stream of romantic, imaginative ideas. Some were amazingly farsighted, like his 1945 proposal to convert war plants to mass production of housing and transportation rolling stock (advice the country would have done well to accept). Others were simply a matter of a burning conscience—a dedication to racial equality and nonviolence, to aid for the poor, nuclear disarmament, better medical care and housing, and a cleaner environment. In retrospect, the "radical" tag opponents so often pinned on Reuther simply lacks credibility. Three weeks before his death, he warned that "we have got to stop violence in America before it destroys our society," and that "we reject the voices of extremism in America, whether they be white or black." Never once did Reuther yield to the chic modernism that "integration is dead."

Reuther's leadership skills received national recognition in 1952 when the militant CIO (Congress of Industrial Organizations) chose him as its president. Only three years later, however, the CIO merged with the parent AFL (American Federation of Labor), the more conservative and craft-oriented organization from which it had split in the mid-1930s. Reuther became a vice president of the combined AFL-CIO and head of its seven-million-member Industrial Union Department. But he soon began to chafe at what he believed were a lack of devotion to social causes and an absence of the zeal and fervor of the earlier days of trade unionism on the part of the AFL-CIO president George Meany and the governing board of the combined unions. Over the years the role of Reuther as activist reformer and gadfly in the AFL-CIO posed mounting problems. Reuther attacked the AFL-CIO for its unstinting support of the nation's Vietnam policy, for its connections with the Central Intelligence Agency, for alleged failure to organize hard enough in new fields such as technical, professional, and farm workers, for failing to avoid disruptive public-service strikes, and for failing to press hard enough for liberal ideas such as national health insurance.

Much of the fight was one of personalities—Reuther, scrappy and uncompromising, faced by Meany, authoritarian and oriented to past policies as any man in his seventies is likely to be. In 1968 the final break came and the UAW was no longer part of the AFL-CIO.

Within Michigan, the UAW's splitoff splintered the labor movement's once unified political effort. August Scholle, veteran AFL-CIO chief for the state, lost 60 percent of his membership at one fell swoop. ("Gus got sawed off at the knees," one old labor reporter told me.) Of the million-plus union members in Michigan today, the UAW has 500,000, another 270,000 are associated with the regular state AFL-CIO, and the remainder are Teamsters or independent. "The split with the UAW would have never occurred on a Michigan basis alone," Scholle insists, and UAW officials tend to agree.

Following his split with the AFL-CIO, Reuther led the UAW into a new alliance with the International Brotherhood of Teamsters under the title of Alliance for Labor Action (ALA). The Teamsters, a classic, hard-bitten, bread-and-butter trade union, had begun to move toward issue-oriented politics after president James Hoffa went to jail in 1967 to serve an eight-year sentence for jury tampering.* Reuther hoped the ALA would pioneer in community union work among the working poor and the unemployed and prod AFL-CIO leaders "to get off their rusty bottoms." But it got off to a slow start in its first years and a financially pressed UAW suspended membership payments in 1971. Many suspected it might just be a matter of time until the UAW—and perhaps the Teamsters too—would rejoin the AFL-CIO. An early UAW return to the fold was unlikely for two reasons, however: a shortage of money to pay AFL-CIO per capita dues, and deference to Reuther's memory.

Reuther never groomed a single successor during his quarter of a century as UAW president. On his death, the presidency went not to the man some believe he might have preferred—Douglas Fraser, the personable and humane man who heads the union's Chrysler division—but rather to another 35-year veteran of organizational work within the UAW, GM division chief Leonard Woodcock. Some of the "liberals" in UAW leadership circles feared Woodcock might be too centrist for their taste, but Woodcock appeared to surprise them pleasantly, in his first year in office, by showing sensitivity in working with black, Mexican, and student committees, in strong opposition to the Vietnam war, and in working amicably with Fraser, whom he had defeated in the contest for the presidency. William Serrin of the Detroit *Free Press* reported that "there are those in Detroit labor circles who will say, privately, that [Woodcock] surpasses Reuther in several areas: intellect, ability to analyze problems, and ability to speak quickly and concisely." But clearly, he lacks Reuther's charisma, and it may be some years before the UAW's future role is clearly identified.

Woodcock's first year in office was rocky enough. The union suddenly found itself faced by a severe cash shortage, the result of a recession-time dip in membership and an overrun of several million dollars in the cost of Walter Reuther's "dream project" at Black Lake in northern Michigan—an educational center for union members and their families. (It was during a flight to Black Lake, going in person to check on construction progress, that Reuther had died.) To cover the shortage, the UAW pared its international representatives staff of 966 by about 125 men—inevitably causing some slowdown in

---

* The Teamsters were expelled from the AFL-CIO in 1957 after congressional investigations had disclosed ties with gangsters and misuse of union funds by its officers.

its ongoing organizational and political programs. Some of Reuther's old braintrust left, and Victor Reuther, head of the international division, let it be known he would retire early. The financial pinch also obliged the UAW to borrow $25 million. The Teamsters turned out to be willing lenders, but the UAW actually had to mortgage both Black Lake and Solidarity House to the heirs of Jimmy Hoffa. Then there was a strike by secretarial and maintenance personnel at Solidarity House and the undignified spectacle of UAW chieftains being called "scabs" and "finks" in front of their own building.

As fate would have it, the UAW was headed into contract negotiations at the very moment that Reuther died, and General Motors had already made it clear it would take a stiff stand against runaway labor costs and, if need be, endure a long and costly strike in 1970. As if to prove his manhood and leadership mettle, Woodcock decided to call the first strike against GM since a 119-day strike Reuther had led in 1945. (In the intervening years, Ford and Chrysler had been struck, but never the massive GM complex.) Had Reuther lived, there is no way of telling how the 1970 strike might have turned out. But as the scenario was finally played out in 1970, GM—perhaps anxious not to trigger a rank-and-file revolt in the UAW that might lead to prolonged turmoil in the industry—agreed to a very costly (and potentially inflationary) package including an immediate 51-cents-an-hour raise, improvements in the early retirement plan, and restoration of the landmark cost-of-living plan which had been partially bargained away in 1967. The benefits were more than triple what Reuther had been able to achieve in the historic showdown with GM right after World War II and represented what some called a "fantastic" victory for the union. But the UAW members might well have rejected it if two months of strike had not already drained their union strike fund. (The strike cost the UAW $160 million.)

The 1970 settlement all but guaranteed Woodcock's reelection as UAW president in 1972, but the big union's problems may be as much internal as external in the coming years, springing from two conflicts—younger, militant members demanding bigger settlements with management, and the related problems of race and the union's general political image. Eighty percent of the union's membership is white, often moving toward solid, middle-class respectability, and the union would doubtless have been pulled further to the right in recent years if it were not for the exceptionally large UAW staff whose sole job is political education of the membership. In 1968, some local UAW presidents actually supported Wallace, but their effort was offset by a frantic pro-Humphrey drive organized out of Solidarity House in which Reuther personally got on the telephone to opposition factions around the country to get them to line up for the regular Democratic ticket. (Wallace's campaign managers recall the incident with bitterness.)

The race situation may be even harder to resolve. High tension reigns in some of the plants around Detroit, where there has been real guerrilla warfare between white and black UAW members. One hears in the city that many blacks feel they are restricted to low-level assembly jobs and that members of their race have been shortchanged in important UAW positions, including international executive board slots. Detroit even has a determined coterie of black radicals, centered in the Chrysler division, who have staged unauthorized strikes and promised to free Negro workers from "the racist, tyrannical, and unrepresentative UAW, so that we can deal with our main adversary, the white racist owners of the means of production." The UAW has been obliged to reply that it "will not protect workers who resort to violence and intimidation for the conscious purpose of dividing our union along racial lines."

When one considers the fact that the UAW has gone further than any other to accommodate blacks and give them important responsibilities, and still faces such problems, the outlook for American industrial unions in general in the next years may be turbulent indeed. This is because, as the NAACP's labor director, Herbert Hill, has noted: "Black workers are becoming the basic blue-collar labor force throughout the economy. And if the present rate of increase continues, within five more years the black workers will be in a position to compete for real organizational power in the big industrial unions."

Twice Transformed Politics—Williams and Romney

Twice since World War II, the politics of Michigan have been transformed, and today they bear little resemblance to the condition that prevailed before 1948. For the better part of a century, the Republican party had ruled with scant opposition from an often scandal-ridden Democratic party that waited to pick up the crumbs of federal patronage. The GOP, dominated by rural conservatives and big manufacturers, had controlled the Michigan governorship for 80 of the previous 94 years and had an iron hold on the legislature and the congressional delegation. As the postwar era dawned, the prospect was for continued conservative Republican domination. In 1947, there were only five Democrats in the 100-member Michigan house and only four Democrats among the 32 senators.

But a series of events in the New Deal '30s and wartime years had created new conditions that would lead to fundamental change. The rise of the UAW, abetted by the Wagner Act, meant that Michigan for the first time in its history had a cohesive, militant trade-union movement with deep interest in politics. And in 1941, the state had passed a strict civil service law that erased the patronage potential which had drawn many old line Democrats as bees to flowers. The state's Democratic party was actually slipping into the control of James Hoffa, then an up-and-coming president of the local Teamsters and a man with little interest in issues or ideology.

In a series of conferences in 1947–48, the decision to bid for control of the Democratic party was made by a coalition of liberal labor leaders and intellectuals. On the labor side, the chief figures were Walter Reuther, his brother Roy, and August Scholle, president of the Michigan CIO. With Reuther's support, Scholle got the state CIO convention to approve labor's becoming an active participant in the Democratic party. But the movement was not labor's alone; also involved were a group of respected and respectable liberals. They included Neil Staebler, a wealthy Ann Arbor oil man and ex-Socialist who would serve as Democratic state chairman for many years,* and G. Mennen Williams, 37-year-old heir to the Mennen soap fortune who had become an ardent New Deal convert in the 1930s.

Williams, an effervescent politician in a perennial polka-dot green bow tie, was chosen as the Democrats' candidate for governor and proceeded to turn in one of the most spectacular performances in modern state politics. Archconservative Republicans helped Williams win his first election in 1948 by failing to support then Republican Gov. Kim Sigler, who had incurred their disfavor; the conservatives apparently figured they could let the boyish soap king be elected and then dispose of him two years later. But the Republicans had underestimated Williams' brains, shrewdness, and ambition and made an egregious tactical error. Reelected by narrow margins in 1950 and 1952, Williams won by landslide proportions in the following three elections and served a record 12 years as governor of the state. Reporters were fond of saying that "Soapy has been campaigning 365 days a year since 1948," and in fact he used to travel 75,000 miles a year throughout Michigan, attending any clambake, sports event, convention, Fourth of July picnic, or labor meeting he could find. An inveterate square-dance caller with a smattering of no less than 13 languages, he proved a naturally effective campaigner among the state's polyglot ethnic population.

Republicans constantly attacked Williams, either as a "phony" or as a CIO stooge and "a captive of Walter Reuther." But Williams was able to build stature on his own and sometimes made decisions against labor's will. In fact, he may have done as much for labor as labor did for him; John H. Fenton comments in *Midwest Politics*, "Soapy Williams and Neil Staebler proved to rural and small-town Michigan that the Democrat as a labor racketeer or 'drunken Irishman' was merely a stereotype." Power and influence within the Democratic party were truly shared between labor and the business and university liberals; in the early 1960s, when labor made the mistake of ramrodding its own choice for governor (John B. Swainson), the way was cleared for Republican resurgence.

In area after area—civil rights, compulsory health insurance, training programs for the unemployed, public recreation, education—Williams and Reuther sought to make Michigan a laboratory for social democracy. They took advanced stands, ahead of their time, and permanently altered the political complexion of the state.

Business and conservative circles rightly recognized Williams' governorship as the harbinger of vastly increased state taxes and services—of the kind which in fact would become commonplace in many states in the 1960s. In the

* Staebler turned out to be one of the most skilled practitioners of citizen politics in the U.S. and later served a term in Congress, only to be beaten by Romney for governor in 1964—the classic case of the political manager who should not have tried to change roles. He is a superb raconteur of politics and likes to recall that when he and his friends set out to revive the Democratic party in Michigan, "there were counties where any known Democrat could be fired from a public or private job —so we used to meet like early Christians in the catacombs."

Republican-controlled legislature, its senate still outrageously malapportioned to the benefit of rural areas, they were able to minimize Williams' achievements. (Williams returned the contempt; as James Reichley wrote in *States in Crisis*, "Williams dealt with the legislature as though setting out to whack the snout of a large and obstreperous hog.") Frustrated in Lansing, Williams often appealed to the people over the legislators' heads and had partial success in such fields as unemployment and workmen's compensation, mental-health reform, and higher teachers' salaries. But his greatest impact was in an area where the legislature could less easily thwart him—appointments to the bench and to regulatory boards and commissions. Here Williams effected a minor revolution by appointment of dedicated liberals, some of whose rulings drove businessmen up the walls.

As Williams' terms went on, the defenders of the status quo became increasingly alarmed about his impact. Opposition was not only rampant in rural areas and among businessmen, but in Detroit, where the mayor criticized Reuther's behind-the-scenes power and the newspapers constantly assailed Williams and his labor allies. "Everybody was trying to hang Soapy by his bow tie and make sure he never became a Presidential candidate," one reporter told me 10 years later. The conflict came to a head in 1959 when Williams couldn't get the legislature to approve his then-record budget or to enact the corporate profits tax he demanded to finance it. The corporate tax, with no effect on individuals, was of course a red flag to the Republicans. They took the opposite tack of demanding an increased sales tax instead—anathema to the liberals. Both sides fell back to increasingly intransigent positions, and Williams finally, as a tactic, let state employees go without their paychecks for a couple of paydays.

The tactic backfired. Michigan's government became a national laughing-stock (there was a joke that year about a drink called "Michigan on the rocks"), the state's industrialists compounded the problem by conjecturing on the possible loss of industry to Michigan, and the market fell out of the bottom of bonds with the Michigan name attached. Detroit and out-of-state papers had a heyday at Williams' expense, but the state's national image had suffered greatly. Williams switched to support of a corporate profits and graduated personal income tax, but the legislature bulled through a sales-tax increase instead. Ironically, the Republican businessman George Romney in the governor's chair during the 1960s would enact a flat-rate form of the income tax and boost state taxes to $1.4 billion by 1969—*three times* the magnitude of the 1959 Williams budget that had been labeled so irresponsibly extravagant.

The change in Michigan's Republican party since World War II was slower in coming and less radical, but perhaps of as much significance for Michigan as the Democratic shift. In past years, the Michigan Manufacturers' Association held inordinate power in Republican policy-making through its hold on Republican state legislators. Business tycoons like Arthur Summerfield, the General Motors dealer in Flint who became Eisenhower's Postmaster General, were extremely influential. The policy of the GOP, reflecting its twin pillars of support in big business and the rural hinterland, was in favor of low taxes, minimal government services, and the protection of private property—the diametric opposite of a Democratic party controlled by those who wanted to reallocate the power, goods, and opportunities of the society.

As Williams' years in the governorship wore on, the Michigan GOP became increasingly anemic. By 1957, the Democrats held all the elective statewide posts in Lansing and the Associated Press was able to report from Washington: "Republican campaign officials said today that for all practical purposes there is no GOP statewide organization in Michigan." The Democrats and labor had, in fact, succeeded in painting the GOP as the kept creature of big business. And the Republicans had succeeded in casting Williams and the Democrats as the handmaidens of big labor. Thus Michigan entered the 1960s with a stalemate in need of a resolution. The man who proved capable of doing that was George Romney, and his contribution looms as large in the Republican history as Williams' does in the Democratic.

Yet it was not originally as a Republican, but as a nonpartisan, civic-minded man above party that Romney first made his mark in politics. He rose to prominence in the 1950s as apostle and chief salesman of the compact Rambler of the American Motors Corporation he headed, arguing that Americans were tired of the "gas-guzzling dinosaurs" then being turned out by the Big Three. The Rambler campaign not only proved Romney's business prowess in one of the most startling corporate success stories of modern times, but it cast him in the role of a sort of David fighting the Goliaths of his industry in behalf of the Little Man. The precedent-shattering profit-sharing plan which Romney negotiated for American Motors with the UAW in 1961 enhanced his independent image. Thus when he finally did enter politics, the UAW and the Democrats had little success in labeling Romney a rubber stamp for big industry—or a typical Republican.

Romney's first major step into the public arena was in 1959 as head of the bipartisan Citizens for Michigan, a reaction to the "cash crisis" stalemate between Williams and the GOP legislature. Other participants in CFM included the League of Women Voters and Robert McNamara, then president of Ford. Romney viewed CFM as a kind of third force to break the impasse, and only in 1961, when he ran for the post of delegate to the constitutional convention which CFM had succeeded in creating, did Romney openly declare himself a Republican. Romney served creditably as an officer of the convention and then in 1962 challenged and beat for the governorship Williams' lackluster successor, John Swainson. The pitch of the Romney campaign was tailor-made to the mood of the times—he attacked the Democrats as dominated by labor, admitted the GOP had been dominated by business, and said that the state needed "a governor who recognizes that the common interests of all the people of Michigan are superior to the special interests of any special group or individual in the entire state." The depth of the Democratic loyalty built up since the war was reflected in Romney's narrow first-time margin: only 80,573 out of 2,764,618 votes cast.

Michigan made a quantum leap forward in the six years that Romney served as governor, a record in no way diminished by the fact that a booming national economy bolstered the auto industry and went a long way toward solving the budget crisis left behind by the Democrats. Romney restored confidence in the Michigan government, won approval of the excellent new constitution, set the state's finances in order through enactment of the first income tax in its history, and finally—despite all his earlier talk of citizen action over party action—revived and reinvigorated the Michigan Republican party and left it an even match for the still powerful Democratic-labor machine.

The new constitution, replacing a 1908 version that had been amended dozens of times, represented a major step forward for the state. State government was reorganized with a reduction of the former unwieldy 120 boards and commissions to 19 umbrella departments. A permanent state civil rights commission was established. The top-heavy ranks of state elected officials were thinned out, a powerful state board of education created, and the judicial system reorganized with a unique authority for the supreme court to control local courts. In what appeared to be a final resolution to the age-old arguments over legislative apportionment, the house was put on a strict population base and the senate on an 80-percent-population, 20-percent-geography basis (a provision later wiped out by Supreme Court reapportionment decrees). Perhaps the most controversial feature prohibited a graduated income tax; this feature particularly aroused the ire of Democrats and organized labor and prompted them to oppose the constitution. But it was approved by the voters, albeit narrowly, during Romney's first year in office.

In 1964, Romney said he would "accept but not endorse" Barry Goldwater as his party's Presidential nominee, an apostasy that offended the right wing of his party throughout the country. Finally, in 1966, Romney was ready to abandon his "lonesome George" campaigning style and go to the voters as a full-fledged Republican. The reason, of course, was his desire to win the 1968 Republican Presidential nomination as a party man with coattails broad enough to carry in other candidates of the party. After an exceptionally vigorous campaign, Romney won reelection with a 527,047-vote plurality—60.5 percent of the vote, a better showing than even Soapy Williams had been able to achieve in his salad days. And not only did Romney win himself, but he helped interim U. S. Sen. Robert P. Griffin win a six-year term (with a 94,416-vote edge) and guided the Republicans to victory in five marginal congressional districts the Democrats had held. The GOP also regained control of the legislature. Griffin and the new Republican congressmen were all of a progressive mode—virtually the antithesis of the stuck-in-the-mud, business indebted Republicans of just a few years before. Romney's lieutenant governor, William G. Milliken, who would succeed him in 1969, was the same type of modern Republican.

The 1966 Republican sweep was all the more amazing because the man Griffin beat for the Senate was none other than G. Mennen Williams, returned from service as Assistant Secretary of State for African Affairs to reenter the political wars. On the face of it, there should have been no contest:

Williams, the proven champion at the polls, favorite of the UAW and liberal wing, almost an institution in himself, opposed by Griffin, a rather modest, quiet veteran of 10 years in the U.S. House described by one writer as a man "with the presence of a certified public accountant."

The Williams-Griffin race suggested that labor and the Democrats would have to move beyond some of the old bromides of labor against capital if they hoped to win in the future in Michigan. As one veteran Michigan newsman described the race to me:

> Soapy was campaigning as the voice of the common man. Well, he'd been a Navy staff officer during the war; Bob Griffin had been an Infantryman. Soapy had gone to Princeton; Griffin went to Central Michigan. Soapy boasted of having a Juris doctor degree in law; so did Griffin except he did it on the GI Bill. Soapy was the son of a millionaire; Griffin was the son of a factory worker whose brother was a union steward. So Soapy had a helluva time making Griffin look like the voice of wealth. It just didn't work.

Romney's smashing 1966 victory made him, overnight, the leading contender for the Republican Presidential nomination. And some recalled the remark President John F. Kennedy is said once to have made about the man from Michigan:

> The fellow I don't want to run against is Romney. No vice whatsoever, no drinking, no smoking. Imagine someone we know going off for 24 or 48 hours to fast and meditate, awaiting a message from the Lord on whether to run or not. Does that sound like one of the old gang? *

But the Presidency is the Big Time, and George Romney, sincere, moral, the evangelistic Mormon, would prove within a little more than a year that he lacked the depth or staying power required in a campaign for the White House.

Which of the two men—Romney or Williams—left the most lasting mark on Michigan politics? In the wake of Romney's smashing reelection victory in 1966, it looked as if the Republican party were about to compete with the Democratic as a vigorous, issue-oriented, broad-based movement. There were still archconservatives in the Republican party, including even some Birch-oriented district leaders whom Romney tried unsuccessfully to purge. But the rural voice was diminished and the Arthur Summerfield types were gone; business was still a campaign contributor to the GOP but no longer controlled it as it once did.† Many middle-management men from the auto industry continued to work in the Republican party, but their politics were not extremist. Without Romney, it is difficult to believe that would have happened. And without the long rule of the liberal-labor wing of the Democratic party, which shifted the center of gravity of Michigan politics so clearly to the left, it is difficult to believe that the old Michigan GOP would ever have accepted George Romney at all. As Neil Staebler told me shortly after Romney

---

* Quoted by Paul B. Fay in *The Pleasure of His Company*.
† Henry Ford II became so disenchanted with the national GOP that he made big contributions to the Democratic Presidential campaigns of 1964 and 1968. But the GOP was not without big-business money. In 1968, Detroit oil man and industrialist Max M. Fisher gave a reported $105,000 to the Republicans.

left the state, "We made them (the Republicans) become a decent bunch."

Even before Romney's departure for Washington, however, there was evidence that the Republican revival might be paper-thin. In the 1968 elections, the Democrats demonstrated their continued vitality by turning in a 222,417-vote plurality for Humphrey over Nixon—the biggest Democratic Presidential margin in any state outside the Northeast. With Milliken installed in the governor's chair, the moderate Republicans lacked their flamboyant leader, and the conservative wing began to reassert itself. In 1970, Romney's wife, Lenore, sought the U.S. Senate seat of Democrat Philip A. Hart and barely won the primary over an archconservative millionaire-businessman, state Sen. Robert J. Huber. In the autumn election, Mrs. Romney was beaten by 886,234 votes; in fact, she got only 32.9 percent of the total cast and the conservative forces in the GOP claimed that the Romney era had come to a definite end in Michigan. Despite their well-financed campaign, the Michigan Republicans in 1970 showed a remarkable lack of good organization or good candidates. Democrat Richard H. Austin of Detroit was elected secretary of state, the first black man in the U.S. to told that office. Soapy Williams and John Swainson made a comeback by winning election to the state supreme court. Democrats kept control of the state house and almost won the state senate. The only Republican statewide winner was Governor Milliken, who virtually divorced himself from the state GOP and Mrs. Romney's campaign, appealed to independent Democrats, the blacks, and urban voters, and barely scraped through with a margin of 44,111 votes out of 2,656,-093 cast.

The Democratic factionalism many had expected in 1970 failed to develop in large degree, primarily because the party was among the first in the nation to reform its procedures and invite participation from all dissidents. As 1972 approached, it was the Democrats who appeared to have it all together —a small debt, growing party interest, and strong faith in prospects for victory. The Republicans faced a big debt, an organization in transition, and growing conservative distrust of Milliken.

The 1970 elections tended to blur some of the traditional regional loyalties in Michigan politics, but this is how the state has usually divided regionally in recent years. The Democrats receive a generally overwhelming vote in Wayne County, which includes Detroit and a number of its suburbs. The Wayne County vote as a percentage of the statewide total, however, has been dropping steadily—from 40 percent in 1948 to 31 percent in 1968. But UAW votes and the growing black population of Detroit help to buoy the actual Democratic plurality in Wayne, which was actually much greater for Humphrey in 1968 (383,519 votes) than it had been for Truman in 1948 (238,400 votes). The only other area the Democrats can be relatively sure of winning is a string of counties on the western end of the Upper Peninsula, a mining and lumber area where the unions are strong. The Republicans, on the other hand, have a hammer lock on most of the rural and small-city counties, constituting the great bulk of land mass of the Lower Peninsula. They usually win by huge margins in prosperous Oakland County (Detroit's northern suburbs) and have shown enduring strength in the counties that house Michigan's second-ranking cities—Flint, Grand Rapids, Lansing, Saginaw, Muskegon, and Kalamazoo.

Government Performance, Milliken,
Reapportionment in Retrospect

It would be a mistake to think that the Williams-UAW years or the Romney regime turned Michigan into an island of far-out socialistic experimentation. Applying the yardsticks of a state's relative tax effort or actual per capita dollar outlays for education, welfare, and health, Michigan is well ahead of her more regressive neighbors, Illinois, Ohio, and Indiana. (Judging by appearances, ethics in Michigan government are also superior to the other large Midwest states, the seemingly inevitable result when a state switches from patronage-based politics to issue-based politics.) But Michigan's taxes and expenditures, on a per capita basis, are far below those of the big-state spenders of modern times, like California and New York, and somewhat behind nearby Minnesota and Wisconsin.

The net result of the Williams years was to give respectability to socially activist government, pulling Michigan—despite all the screaming and yelling of the oxcart-era legislature—into the 20th century. During the Romney years, the state's administrative and financial house was put in order. And the courts finally forced legislative reapportionment. But what Romney had failed to do was to find any kind of solution for the escalating problems of the cities (especially crisis-plagued Detroit) or to initiate badly needed and fundamental reforms in education and environmental control. Those problems were left for his successors.

William G. Milliken, the man who stepped into George Romney's shoes when Romney left for Washington and a post in the Nixon cabinet in January 1969, scarcely fits the image of the dynamic, charismatic leader that central casting might pick to tackle Michigan's current-day problems. Roger Lane of the Detroit *Free Press* has aptly described him as "patient, courteous, always smiling, sincere, athletic, youthful-appearing for his 47 years, groomed as a Yaleman should be." Milliken in fact has an uncannily boyish demeanor for a man of his age, and his home town of Traverse City (population 18,048), set in an area of cherry orchards and summer resorts some 240 miles northwest of Detroit, is hardly in the fulcrum of the modern urban crisis. (There must be something special about Traverse City, since it has also produced another sleeper, the Republican Whip of the U.S. Senate, Robert Griffin.) Milliken served eight years as a state senator before election as Romney's lieutenant governor in 1964.

Once in the governor's chair, self-effacing William Milliken showed a mettle and imagination few anticipated. He started out by replacing most of Romney's top aides with his own staff of keen, young (average age 31) professionals, and a sharply increased number of Negroes were appointed to state posts (more, in fact, than all previous administrations combined). The new staff's greenness and Milliken's reticence in knocking heads impaired prompt approval of his program by the legislature. But the type of program Milliken suggested was clearly 1970s-oriented. Describing Michigan as "primarily urban," he urged the legislature to make a $5 million bloc grant to Detroit "as evidence of the state's commitment to urban Michigan . . . and a city with unique and awesome problems." An official governor's office was set up in Detroit, and Milliken visited the city frequently. In parceling out benefits of a $100 million bond issue, he fought for and got a substantial share for new recreation facilities in and near cities (battling ruralites and sportsmen who wanted all the money spent for distant parks, fisheries, and wildlife projects). A new environmental quality commission was set up and, with Milliken's encouragement, Michigan became the first state to ban the sale and use of "hard" pesticides. Environmental proposals contained several measures, including coastal zoning, to protect the Great Lakes. Milliken warned against letting Detroit's pride in the automobile "obscure the need for mass transit systems to supplement the car" and also pushed for stiff gun controls and a "little FBI" to fight organized crime in Michigan.

And just ten months after taking office, Milliken proposed the most radical restructuring of school financing ever officially backed on the U.S. mainland. He suggested virtual abolition of local property taxes for school operating purposes, replacing them with a statewide property tax and increased income taxes, plus a "value added tax," so that the schools would basically be financed through Lansing rather than locally. The proposal was designed to eliminate gross inequalities in per pupil expenditures between poor and wealthy areas (varying from $1,000 to $3,000 outlays per student). A second objective was to create some accountability in school systems, especially those in urban areas that often fail to provide meaningful education for poor children, most notably blacks.

Predictably, state takeover of school financing was fought covertly by much of the education establishment. But in the 1971 legislature, a Milliken-backed constitutional amendment to ban almost all local property tax use for schools, thus forcing state financing, actually passed one house. Milliken told me in spring 1971 that he was pleased by the national attention paid his school-financing proposals, and that several other state governors were giving it serious consideration. Then came a California court decision, banning use of local property taxes for schools in that state and creating a precedent of national implications. In Michigan, Milliken and Attorney General Frank J. Kelley, a Democrat, quickly joined in asking the state supreme court to make a decision like California's. Intertwined with the school financing issue in Michigan is the question of whether the income tax should be made graduated—a proposal Kelley and other Democrats are pressing for. The rate of the existing flat-rate tax was increased from 2.6 to 3.9 percent in 1971 but would have to go to close to 6 percent if the state were to cover all schooling costs.

When one-man, one-vote reapportionment finally came to Michigan in the mid-1960s, many had hailed it as the harbinger of a solid progressive new era in Michigan government. But reapportionment, as many in Michigan suggest, really came a decade too late. Instead of adding new city seats, it benefitted the suburbs—often as conservative as the old rural hinterland.

Michigan's contribution to the Supreme Court's one-man, one-vote decisions is not generally appreciated but, in fact, was extremely significant. Since the early 1940s, Michigan labor leader Gus Scholle had been fighting for equally populated legislative districts. He filed a landmark court suit for reapportionment in 1959, incurring the opposition even of Democrats who feared offending members of their own party from the Upper Peninsula, which was overrepresented. But Scholle noted the presence of the liberal Warren Court in Washington and felt it was time to press the issue, fearing the opportunity might be lost for decades if the Court later turned conservative. The AFL-CIO counsel, Theodore Sachs of Detroit, did the basic research and then as a courtesy passed it on to the plaintiffs in the famed Tennessee suit of *Baker v. Carr*. "Then they beat us into the Supreme Court and got the credit," Scholle laments.

Since the real reapportionment winners turned out to be the Republican suburbs, I asked Scholle in 1969 whether he regretted having made the fight. His answer: "I had never anticipated it would mean automatic victory for any one political party. My objective was simply that everybody should be equal at the polls. If one man's vote counts 15 times more than another's, in no way can you construe it to be a democratic society." Those who know Scholle may take his words with a grain of salt, since he was one of the most fiercely partisan Democrats of modern Michigan. But no one can gainsay the importance of the one-man, one-vote victory. It may not have made legislatures automatically more "liberal," and in some cases the precise mathematical equality of districts insisted on by the courts has bordered on the preposterous. But as Michigan's experience showed, even in the first term after reapportionment, the reform did clear out the rotten borough deadwood of the largely conservative hinterland and send a younger, more educated, flexible, and modern-thinking generation of men and women to the state capital. In northern states, the reform meant that the Democrats had at least a chance of winning legislature control—a fact that inevitably sharpened the Republicans' competitive instincts and responsiveness to public demand. And by tightening the partisan balance in legislatures, reapportionment has given Negroes a chance to bargain for their interests there. In Michigan, the blacks now represent about a fifth of the house Democratic caucus and a sixth of the Democrats in the senate. The 1969 legislature passed a $100 million bond issue for low-income housing which was a clear manifestation of black political power.

This is not to say that everyone in Michigan is pleased with the new legislature's performance. In 1971, after the legislators had raised their own salaries to $17,000 a year and voted themselves several other favors—while proving exceptionally sluggish in approving a budget and passing few new bills

—a movement was launched to create a unicameral legislature. The Michigan Jaycees got behind a movement to put a constitutional amendment for a single 96-member house on the 1972 ballot, and it had real prospect of approval.

A Leader in Public Education

Since 1837—and still today—the Michigan state constitution has declared: "Schools and the means of education shall forever be encouraged!" Michigan had the nation's first state superintendent of public instruction and was the first state to provide free high school education. Despite the gross inequalities between school districts and widespread failure to meet the problems of the environmentally handicapped, Michigan's elementary and secondary schools stand well above the national average in overall per pupil expenditures and third in the Union in teachers' salaries.

Michigan's system of public higher education, however, is its more distinctive achievement, and many regard her public university complex as second only to California's in quality. The state's huge and virtually autonomous major universities—Michigan State at East Lansing, the University of Michigan at Ann Arbor, and Wayne State University in Detroit—rank 11th, 14th, and 19th respectively in full-time enrollment in the U.S.A., with a total of 112,000 students. The University of Michigan has long been the intellectual leader of the group with an excellent arts and sciences faculty, as well as internationally known medical and law schools.* It draws a politically activist intelligentsia and the state's natural aristocracy in much the same mode as the University of Wisconsin at Madison. And some of the same problems that Berkeley and Madison face—loss of support among legislators, taxpayers, alumni, and the business community—are now haunting Ann Arbor. In 1970, a Black Action movement and white radicals, partly through physical intimidation, forced president Robben W. Fleming and the regents to agree to increase the Negro percentage of enrollment from an existing 3 percent to 10 percent of the university's 33,000 students by 1973–74. Since only 6 percent of Michigan high school graduates are Negroes, there soon ensued the spectacle of the university looking all over the U.S. for marginally qualified black applicants and then promising them an average $4,000-a-year support. Not only was the level of assistance discriminatory vis-à-vis qualified but economically deprived white students, but there were early reports of a dilution of the level of classroom teaching, declining faculty morale, and questions about the university's long-term academic standing.

Michigan State, founded in 1855 and the nation's first land-grant college, was still a sleepy agricultural school when John A. Hannah took over its presidency in 1942. Viewed by friends as a masterful builder of the modern univer-

---

* In 1971, the American Council on Education rated Michigan's graduate faculties among the top five in the U.S. in classics, philosophy, anthropology, geography, political science, sociology, botany, population biology, and electrical and mechanical engineering. The university is one of the major social-science research centers of the U. S. It has close ties to the economically independent Survey Research Center, which has pioneered in advanced polling techniques.

sity and by others as a ruthless academic entrepreneur, Hannah stayed in office so long (27 years in all) that some suggested he might be called "the Methuselah of university presidents." But in those years, Hannah transformed Michigan State from a cow college into a major engine of public training—a 5,000-acre "megaversity" with an enrollment of 42,541 and an annual budget of more than $100 million. There was a saying in the legislature: "The concrete never sets on Hannah's Empire." Purists criticized him for making MSU into a big "service station, filling its students with courses like Sewage Treatment or the Dynamics of Packaging." Hannah brushed off the criticism and took it as a compliment: "The object of the land-grant tradition," he said, "was not to de-emphasize scholarship but to emphasize its application." And under his tutelage, MSU also launched an extensive graduate program in virtually all nonprofessional areas. One interesting program was a College of Human Medicine, oriented more to producing general practitioners than specialists. And defying MSU's reputation as a party school, Hannah paid top salary for outstanding faculty. By 1969, MSU had more Merit Scholars on campus than any other U. S. university (684 compared with second-place Harvard's 503).

Not a small part of Hannah's success at MSU was his high-pitch salesmanship in getting money from the legislature; the MSU budget rose at a rate almost twice that of the University of Michigan. Sometimes Hannah's entrepreneurial talents brought embarrassment, as in 1966 when *Ramparts* magazine alleged that an MSU program for training South Vietnam policemen had provided a cover for CIA agents. But Ann Arbor was not free from all criticism either; there, some faculty (especially in scientific fields) made fortunes in spinoff technical companies that sprang up around Ann Arbor.

On the more positive side, it should be reported that University of Michigan students were in the forefront of the national environmental protection movement by the early 1970s, and that an amazing army of 9,500 Michigan State students were giving from three to 10 hours a week without pay to help people in need in ghetto areas, schools, and hospitals. Such "good news" about college youth fails to make the headlines of violent demonstrations but it is a heartening and vital part of the modern university scene. Most MSU students were also pleased in 1969 to learn that their trustees had named a highly competent black man, Dr. Clifton R. Wharton, Jr., as the university's new president. Wharton had once been something of a student activist himself, helping found the National Student Association while a student at Harvard in 1946. Before taking up his duties at MSU, he was vice president of the Agricultural Development Council in New York, a group founded by John D. Rockefeller, III, to support teaching and research on economic and human problems of agricultural development. Thus the appointment was in keeping with MSU's land-grant tradition, but also broke new ground because Wharton was the first Negro to head a major predominantly white American university.

More than half of all university students in the United States live at home and commute to college, among them the 34,000 students at Wayne State University in Detroit, the third of Michigan's "big three" universities.

Wayne State, which began in the 1890s-vintage Central High School building near center city, is a not untypical example of the potentialities and problems of the commuter college. Already of substantial size at the end of World War II, WSU grew rapidly in the GI Bill era and decided to continue in center city rather than move to the suburbs. And a few years later it was fortunate to have the state of Michigan take over its financial support from the hard-pressed city of Detroit.

Wayne State had 15 percent Negro enrollment by the start of the 1970s, the highest percentage of any predominantly white university in the U.S. The 1967 Detroit riots swirled through WSU's immediate neighborhood, and since then the institution has striven mightily to relate itself to the Detroit black community through such varied programs as community based extension centers, off-hours management and technology training, the Teacher Corps (actually begun at Wayne in 1966), social-work students interning in city agencies, legal-aid assistance, and the clinical staff provided to Detroit General Hospital through the medical school.

Americans who have never attended a commuter college have difficulty understanding the obstacles and problems of getting one's education in the hectic on-again, off-again type of schedule of a student who lives at home. Still the model for higher education is the English college system of "houses of scholars" living together in a relaxed, meditative environment designed to develop the "whole man" through concentration and contact with peer and professor. The commuting student's life is precisely the opposite. At Wayne State, more than 75 percent of the students are obliged to hold down full- or part-time outside jobs. Students often arrive exhausted at class from lack of sleep and long commuting trips, and frequently are obliged to skip courses they would like to take because of their complex work schedules or car-pool arrangements. Family pressures on the student living at home are an emotional drain for many. Making friends and social contacts on campus or finding an opportunity to talk informally with faculty are extremely difficult. At Wayne State, study areas and congenial eating places are at a minimum and students are frequently seen studying in their parked cars between classes. More lounges and informal eating places and even university-run bus service from outlying places are being considered as a partial solution to students' problems, but the problems for the commuting student will obviously continue to be formidable.

The Statewide Economy, Tourism,
the Upper Peninsula

There is an old saw to the effect that "when the U.S. economy catches a cold, Michigan gets pneumonia." Automobiles are one of the most easily postponed consumer purchases, and all the postwar recessions have hit with special vengeance in Michigan. Automobiles are, indeed, the big factor in the

Michigan economy. By the same token, when there is an auto strike, all of Michigan suffers; the 1970 walkout at General Motors, for instance, cost the state government $25 million in lost revenues and added $25 million in welfare costs.

But there is a lot of nonautomotive Michigan, too. The state leads in a wide variety of goods ranging from breakfast cereals to steel springs. The 16,000 manufacturers in the state represent 93 percent of all standard industrial classifications, and of the top 1,000 U. S. manufacturers, 265 have plants in Michigan and 47 have their headquarters there. Among the states, Michigan ranks sixth in its industrial output ($17.6 billion a year). A growing diversification of the state's economic base is reflected in employment figures that show that service industries have doubled their payrolls since the mid-1940s while manufacturing jobs slipped from more than half the total in 1947 to about one third today. Few states have such a small percentage of their work force in federal civilian or defense-generated employment.

Mineral production—chiefly of low-grade iron ore on the Upper Peninsula—brings $610 million a year into the Michigan economy. Salt mines (including some under the city of Detroit) are said to have deposits of 71 trillion tons, and the state is the nation's foremost salt supplier. Lumbering has passed the exploitive era of the state's early history but forest products still contribute about $1 billion to the state's economy each year. A diversified agriculture of dairy products, cattle, wheat, and fruits produces an annual income of about $900 million. The state boasts of being "the bean capital of the world." The Great Lakes—cooling the prevailing winds in summer and warming them in winter—make the lands along their shores ideal for fruit growing; Michigan ranks number one among the states in tart cherries and she is a leading producer of blueberries, apples, sweet cherries, spearmint, peaches, pears, strawberries (a juicy 34 million pounds a year), beets, and tomatoes. For those interested in odd facts, it may also be reported that Michigan has no peer in its output of hothouse rhubarb. For many who work the land, farming is a marginal occupation and there are many part-time or "retirement" farmers. On the other hand, large farming operations draw thousands of migrant workers, whose living conditions are a subject of increasing concern.

Woods, lakes and waterways, ski hills, snowmobile trails, and a handful of man-made attractions (like Henry Ford's unique museum and Greenfield Village at Dearborn) make Michigan an important tourist state. In all, Michigan is said to draw some 15 million visitors a year who leave $1.3 billion behind.

With some concern, one reads in a chamber of commerce report that "an estimated 500,000 outboard motors churn Michigan's waters" and claims that Michigan has more snowmobiles registered than any other state, a development one may see as asset or debit depending on his attitude toward nature. More reassuring is the revival of sport fishing in Lake Michigan. The St. Lawrence Seaway allowed sea lamprey to infiltrate the lakes; these parasites in turn almost wiped out lake trout before chemicals and electric screens at their spawning grounds stopped the destruction. Then, in 1966, some 800,000 coho salmon from salt waters along the West Coast were planted in streams along the Great Lakes and some had grown up to 22 pounds, providing a bonanza for the sport fisherman. Fear of killing off this new sporting opportunity contributed to Michigan's decision to ban the sale of DDT, traces of which were found in some salmon catches. Yet pollution problems in the lakes continued to threaten fishing; in 1970, for instance, all fishing in Lake St. Clair had to be banned because traces of deadly poisonous mercury, released from chemical plants, were found in lake fish.

Michigan's other tourist attractions include the Sleeping Bear Dune between Lake Michigan and Glen Lake and the magnificent old Grand Hotel on Mackinac Island, which claims it has "the longest porch on earth." The Grand Hotel is where Michigan's Republican elite, some thousand strong, gather every other year for what one party leader calls simply "the nicest political event in the country."

Michigan is so far-flung geographically and so cosmopolitan in its ethnic strains that it appears to lack a common personality. Before statehood was achieved in 1837, most of the settlers were from New York and New England. Then came Germans, populating Saginaw, Ann Arbor, and other parts of southern Michigan and continuing their influx well into the 20th century. Starting in 1846, there were substantial numbers of Dutch immigrants; they left their mark in the geography books with western Michigan cities such as Holland and Zeeland. Irish came in substantial numbers; but even more significant were Swedes, Norwegians, Finns, and Italians, many of whom worked in the north Michigan lumber industry that flourished in the past century. From 1910 on, substantial numbers of Poles and other East Europeans arrived, drawn to the factories of the Detroit area. Finally, there was the Negro population influx, starting 60 years ago; the black percentage of Michigan's population was then .6 percent (17,115 out of 2,810,173), today it is 11.2 percent (991,066 out of a statewide population of 8,875,083). Michigan still has a high percentage of poor Southern-born whites and their children; the largest club in Pontiac for instance, is said to be the Arkansas Club, made up of the families of people who came to work in the auto plants.

The Upper Peninsula requires a special word because it is so vast (equal to the combined areas of Connecticut, Delaware, Massachusetts, and Rhode Island), so distant, and so much a stepchild of modern Michigan. First populated by early French explorers, the area was once a great supplier of pelts. In the 1880s, its magnificent pine forests were razed; today some are growing back, but lumbering is not exactly a booming industry. Over the past century, the region yielded nearly 11 billion pounds of copper, but both that industry and iron ore mining are now in decline. Thus the region's economic reason for being seems to be largely behind it. About all that is left are widely scattered, thinly populated towns, trout-rich streams and woodlands, parks and wastelands, ugly slag heaps left by defunct mines, waterfalls, ski jumps, swamps, and tree stumps. Hunting, fishing, and other forms of tourism provide some sustenance, but not enough.

Detroit: A Dying City?

Detroit has every reason to be a great, prosperous city. With the fifth largest population of U.S. cities, it has a convergence of resources—financial, managerial, and transportation—which should make it an indispensable resource for Michigan and the region. The total investment in the core city probably approaches $15 billion. Yet a visitor to the mighty Motor City finds a metropolis in pain, uncertain about its future and viability. The population dropped by 158,662—to 1,511,482—between 1960 and 1970.

The depth of problems is suggested in a page-one story in the Detroit *News* by Robert Popa, under the headline: "Is Detroit Dying because No One Cares?" The article begins:

> What's wrong with Detroit?
> Well, to start with:
> Its school system isn't doing the job.
> Its downtown heart isn't too strong. Decay has set in.
> Its streets aren't very safe or well lighted.
> Valuable land sits vacant in the downtown area.
> And its civic and industrial leaders haven't been leading.

This searing assessment comes from a most unexpected direction. It was made this week by Dwight Havens, president of the Detroit Chamber of Commerce, an organization usually dedicated to boosterism or apologies rather than to criticism. . . .

Popa's story, appropriately illustrated by a weed-infested empty block in the downtown area, continues with a recitation of building booms sparked by strong civic leadership in Pittsburgh, Dallas, and other great industrial cities —but so obviously missing in Detroit, where everything seems to be moving to the suburbs or dying. Detroit, Havens points out, can boast of being the home of the Big Three auto companies, the Burroughs Corporation, and National Bank of Detroit, one of the nation's largest banks. "Per square foot, we've got more talented leadership in Detroit than any other city of the world," Havens is quoted as saying, "but nobody's doing anything."

A magnificent new $100 million Civic Center sits on a handsome 75-acre riverfront site, including Cobo Hall (the largest convention and recreation hall in the world) and Ford Auditorium (home of the Detroit Symphony Orchestra). But with one or two notable exceptions, the new hotel construction needed to permit the city to maximize its convention potential has been stymied and there is a shortage of hundreds of rooms.

Downtown Detroit's skyline is dominated by older, narrow-windowed, high brick office buildings of forbidding 1920s and 1930s architecture. Since World War II, not a single major new building has been constructed in downtown Detroit except for structures that by their nature have no choice other than to be there (banks, public facilities, and the like). Ford and Chrysler headquarters are outside the city borders, and GM's is removed from downtown.

In place of the booming retail center one would expect downtown, Detroit has just one quality department store—Hudson's—and the overwhelming majority of its clientele is so low-income that it could as well become a
discount outlet. Downtown and environs are filled with ugly strip commercial
development and secret fears linger in the hearts of Detroiters that even
Hudson's might one day abandon its still magnificent center-city store.
That unhappy eventuality was made less likely, however, by the November,
1971, announcement of Henry Ford II that his company would act as
catalyst for a $500 million complex of office towers, stores, apartments,
and a huge new hotel on the city's waterfront. Mayor Roman Gribbs
ventured a prediction that "Henry Ford II will become synonomous with
the rebirth of Detroit."

Especially at rush hours, downtown streets (set at disharmonious angles
to each other by an ill-conceived or badly executed plan by Pierre L'Enfant)
are clogged with automobiles. Parking is prohibitively expensive. But the
Motor City has never had a subway or elevated system and staunchly resists
the idea of starting one now.

Detroit is blessed with a fine location between Lake St. Clair to the north
and Lake Erie to the south; along the busy Detroit River at its very doorstep
pass a colorful panoply of great and small ships—grain-, ore-, limestone-, and
coal-carrying barges. But the aesthetic and recreational potential of the riverfront is thwarted by scores of obsolete industrial plants. Office, plant, street,
and home fill so much of Detroit that relatively little land is left for sports
and relaxation; the city's percentage of park and recreation land is much less
than New York's, Philadelphia's, Chicago's, or San Francisco's.

Looking west and southwest along the riverfront from center city, the
view is of forests of steel and chemical plant smoke stacks, throwing a dark
pall across the city and darkening the setting sun. Once or twice a week a cli-
matic inversion coats Detroit with air pollution, creating a thick haze while
the sun shines just a few miles away.

Where is the enlightened, strong civic leadership that men like chamber
of commerce president Havens would like to provoke into action? One place
from which it *could* emerge, if it had the will, is described thus by the
New York *Times*:

In a valley of the modern skyline here is an ivy-covered, brownstone anachronism called the Detroit Club. Its red, sun-faded canopy is a time tunnel
leading away from noisy downtown traffic into a quiet, unhurried 19th Century.

It is here that the decisions of the 20th Century and even the 21st Century
are made.

Each noon, men with enough status, power and/or riches to belong to this
exclusive womanless club take the canopied route to a variety of dining rooms to
discuss business progress in an atmosphere that progress vaguely touches.

"The members' lives within the club today are practically the same as was
lived by members nearly 70 years ago. That to me is the ineffable charm of our
club," wrote James Holden, who had been a member for 64 years at the time of
his death in 1968.

There is charm in the reception room where the floors creak, a grandfather
clock ticks off timelessness, . . . [in] massive, darkly, varnished furnishings with

red carpeting and that cliché of clichés of men's clubs—rows of wing-backed, brown leather chairs in the lounges. . . .

When one looks at the membership roster, with recurring names each generation—such as the McMullins (city transit), Bagleys (tobacco), Algers (lumber), Newberrys (ship builders), Kresges (dime stores), Walkers (distilleries), Strohs (breweries), Briggs (of Briggs Stadium), Wilson (of insurance and the Buffalo Bills) as well as Ketterings, Motts, Fords, Coles, Knudsens, Fishers and Wilsons (of the auto industry), one can see at a glance how important contacts have been and are now at the Detroit Club. . . .

Yet not until 1969 did the doughty club admit its first Jewish member (Joseph Wineman, third generation owner of People's Outfitting). The only blacks who cross the threshold, of course, are servants. It is probably fruitless to look to a place like the Detroit Club for leadership of a troubled city, since it never came from there in earlier times either.

Thus when I asked who exercises real power in Detroit today, the not infrequent answer was: "Nobody."

Blacks and Politics

The 1970 Census showed that Negroes represented 44 percent of the Detroit city population (up from 29 percent in 1960); in the view of some, Detroit went over the point of no return from white to black in the mid-1960s and it is just a matter of time until Negroes are both a numerical majority and the holders of governmental power in the city. A mere black majority of course, does not indicate what kind of city Detroit will be. However homogeneous the color and however freely blacks may rule in future years, the question will be whether they have a strong enough middle class to create a solid tax base so that Detroit can be fairly self-supporting, not a stepchild dependent on state and federal governments.

A second question will be the type of black leadership. Out of Detroit have come many of the most provocative black-nationalist types of movement —the Black Muslims, the Black Jesus theology, the extremist DRUM movement in the auto plants, and the separatists of the Republic of New Africa. Yet there is no indication those groups command real or potential broad-based political support among Negroes. In 1969, a black man—Wayne County Auditor Richard Austin—came within 7,000 votes of being elected mayor, receiving a monolithic 94 percent of the black vote and one out of every five white votes. A thoroughly competent contender, he had strong backing from the UAW, Teamsters, and the Detroit *Free Press*, and in 1970 (as noted before) was elected secretary of state. His strong vote for mayor indicated that an able black contender could look to election in Detroit in the near future (perhaps 1973). In the same 1969 election, black representation on the city council rose to three out of the nine seats.

The man elected mayor in 1969 was Roman S. Gribbs, son of Polish immigrant parents who served previously as county sheriff. Though an overwhelming white vote (about 80 percent) elected him, Gribbs proved to be no racist, starting with appointment of a number of blacks to important city posts. He faced the delicate task of being a transition leader in Detroit's white-to-black development, sure to be a painful and difficult process. The conventional wisdom is that Poles like Gribbs cannot get along with blacks. The Detroit *Free Press* in March 1969 printed a survey of population trends in the city, writing about the constant black push out from the narrow beach-heads of pre-World War II days to cover most of Detroit, with whites (of whom the Poles are a substantial segment) fretting and retreating in the process. "The whites who have traded city for suburbs are the more prosperous, the more enlightened and the more racially tolerant," the *Free Press* reported. "The whites who have stayed largely form an economic, ethnic and age group inclined to think harshly of Negroes."

Yet in 1969, a unique new ethnic coalition was formed in Detroit—of Poles and Negroes. The movement began with conferences of leaders, then expanded to social affairs where the press reported: "Fried chicken coalesced with sausage and sauerkraut; modish Afro hairdos made small talk with flat, square-jawed faces of Eastern Europe." The key assumptions of this Black-Polish Conference on Greater Detroit, which was still thriving two years after its launching, were simple enough: that blacks and Poles have much in common, that the tension between the groups has been artificially created, that cooperation will serve the interests of both, and (contrary to standard "liberal" thinking) that Poles are not essentially racist. One thought was to combine the Polish vote (about 20 percent) with the Negro vote (over 40 percent) to coalesce on common goals, but the general objectives were more social. The *Michigan Chronicle*, Detroit's Negro newspaper, editorialized: "If Detroit's two largest minority groups could cooperate, that would rescue Detroit from ever increasing chaos and might just turn this town around."

To anyone who has followed the bitter conflicts between Negroes and Detroit's ethnic white community in the 1960s—one of the most dreary and hateful episodes of race relations of recent times—the Polish-black coalition strains the bounds of credulity. This is a city where black and white high school students fight openly in classroom and corridor, where a Negro moving into an all-white housing area may face physical violence, where blacks and the lower-middle-class police (over 90 percent white) are constantly at each other's throats.

The Hero Mayor and the Great Riot of 1967

For a few Camelotlike years in the 1960s, Detroit seemed to be on its way to salvation under a witty and sophisticated hero-type mayor named Jerome P. Cavanagh. Cavanagh burst onto the political scene in 1961 when the tired old city was laboring under a $34.6 million deficit, auto production was down and unemployment at a high 10 percent, and industry and home-owners were accelerating their flight to the suburbs. Incumbent Mayor Louis Miriani, the builder of Cobo Hall, had the two newspapers and virtually the entire Detroit establishment behind him and was expected to win with ease. A virtually penniless attorney with no elective experience behind him, about all Cavanagh had was youth (he was then 33), a beautiful wife (she was a former campus beauty queen), many children to bolster his Catholic image in a heavily Catholic city, and a keen sense of the deep currents of discontent in the city. He put together what has been described as "a strange alliance of gadflies, young liberals, and crusty old pols" to pull a startling upset victory. A key factor was the Negro vote, about a third of the total. A few months before, in response to a wave of white murders and muggings, Miriani had ordered a police crackdown which hit the largely innocent black community the hardest. Negroes resented this and provided about 72 percent of Cavanagh's winning vote.

"Almost overnight," the Detroit *Free Press* noted a few years later, "Cavanagh became America's most glamorous mayor. He was smart, shrewd, committed to social change, surrounded by a brilliant brain trust, a man who seemed to draw vitality from the very city air." To put the city's financial house in order, he rammed through a 1 percent income tax on city workers (later reduced to .5 percent on nonresidents). For the first time, Negroes were given important city posts.

The young and vibrant mayor also discovered and perfected what was described as Cavanagh's Law for raiding the federal treasury: think up a program to benefit cities, lobby for its passage by Congress, and then be first in line, palms upward, when the dollar spigot is turned on. Within 12 hours after President Johnson enunciated the Great Society, the mayor's gifted young aides were at work on a way to tap it for millions. "We stand at the threshold," Cavanagh declared jauntily in 1965, "of being 'Demonstration City, U. S. A.'" Within a few short years Cavanagh had obtained $267 million in urban renewal, poverty, and related federal funds, a record exceeded only by New York and Chicago. Cavanagh became the first man in history to head both the National League of Cities and the U. S. Conference of Mayors simultaneously, and in this halcyon year national news magazines rushed to write laudatory articles on his performance. One of his aides liked to say: "On a clear day, Cavanagh can see the White House."

Then, as Cavanagh headed into his second term in 1966, Camelot vanished. It was as if neither man nor program was really big enough to cope with the spreading blight of the inner city, the tearing hatreds, white and black racism, black and white militancy. LBJ began to divert poverty money to Vietnam and it turned out that the city's housing program had succeeded in razing 11,000 slum dwelling units during the Cavanagh regime, but that only a fraction had been replaced—and mostly with middle- and upper-income housing.

Then came Cavanagh's personal problems. His worldly, swinging ways failed to sit well at home where Mary Helen Cavanagh, the typical Irish Catholic girl who wants her husband to stay home, was becoming increasingly estranged. Certainly not all the fault was on Cavanagh's side, but in 1967 she sued him for separate maintenance and messy divorce proceedings followed in which both fought for custody of the eight children; this was followed by a humiliating (though unsuccessful) law suit in which his sister-in-law accused Cavanagh of hitting her. Reports of Cavanagh's varied romantic involvements were so rampant that one aide felt compelled to say: "If all that talk was true, we'd have him stuffed and put on display at Harvard Medical School."

Five days after Cavanagh's break with his wife became public, the most destructive race riot in the history of the United States broke out in his Detroit. Within a week's time, vast blocks of the city were gutted by flames, 43 persons were killed (33 Negroes, 10 whites), 7,200 were arrested, and damage of close to $45 million was inflicted. The death and damage toll would exceed that of Watts or Newark or even of the Detroit race riot of 1943, when 34 died (25 Negroes, 9 whites). Yet this new Detroit riot would be of far different complexion from the conflagration of 1943, when gangs of whites and blacks clashed in open street warfare. Summer 1967 was the great season of racial convulsion across the entire U.S.A. One week before, Newark had blown—a spectacle instantly relayed to Detroit and the nation by television. The hallmarks of the 1967 riot were looting and arson, and a chance for hardpressed blacks to pick up a free case of whiskey or television set, and to get revenge on local stores which constantly gave them the short end. No racial gangs clashed; even at the height of the disturbances white reporters were rarely molested in the Negro areas.

Why, then, was the 1967 riot so terribly destructive of life and property? One reason was the relatively slow police response to the first day of rioting, touched off by a predawn police raid in a 12th Street blind pig (illegal after hours drinking and gambling spot). Cavanagh was later criticized for early morning orders that prevented the police from putting down the rioting and looting with quick, harsh efficiency—though no one knows if such orders would really have been effective. As it was, the rioting and subsequent arson had risen to massive proportions before the National Guard and regular federal troops were committed.

The Detroit riot was all the more tragic because it happened in the city where virtually everyone thought it "couldn't happen," where black-white dialogue was more advanced than in practically any other great American city, where the mayor was intensely sensitive to the Negro community, where a high proportion of blacks owned their own homes, where the auto industry had helped many earn substantial livelihoods. But as later investigation would show, the chief rioting was not mainly practiced by a "riffraff" of young dropouts, uneducated and jobless. Only 10 percent of those arrested, in fact, were juveniles. A high proportion of the rioters had at least a foothold in middle-class society—of the males, for instance, 83 percent were employed (40 percent by the auto companies), 45 percent were married (and four out of five of them living with their wives), two-thirds had no previous criminal convictions, and the average income, by some estimates, was around $6,000. Why did this group, then, take to the streets? Only tentative answers can be given. One reason may lie in televison and increased education: this generation realized what it was missing, was beginning to recognize the white racism built into "the system" for what it was. The repeated incidences of gross police brutality later documented by the Kerner Commission were but a reflection of what the Detroit Negro had been faced with for years. The white man's promises, the web of false expectations raised by President Johnson and Cavanagh and their poverty program, were recognized as a sham in large part. As Irving J. Rubin wrote for the *Reporter* a few months after the Detroit conflagration: "The riots were an outburst of frustration over unmet demands for dignity and for economic and political power. They were a tragic, violent, but understandable declaration of manhood and an insistence that Negroes be able to participate in and to control their own destinies and community affairs."

In the wake of the riot, Cavanagh and Romney took the leading hand in organizing a blue-ribbon committee, New Detroit, Inc., to guide the city's reconstruction. With $10 million from the United Auto Workers and the Ford Foundation, plus the active involvement of Detroit's top leadership, New Detroit plunged into employment, recreation, and black-capitalism projects and seemed to offer vital new hope for the city. Some 30,000 youths were given summer jobs and the state was persuaded to pass an open-housing law. But before too many months had passed, discouragement replaced euphoria about New Detroit's potential. Business participants were offended by continuing black-militant harangues, the UAW's follow-through proved seriously deficient, and finally it became apparent that the magnitude of Detroit's problems—from decaying schools to constant tension between blacks and police —might be beyond the reach of any one organization or power group to solve.

Cavanagh's own leadership deteriorated rapidly in his last two years in office. The city crime rate continued to soar, race relations polarized more and more as whites reacted in anger or flight from the riots. The financial cushion from the payroll tax disappeared and the city faced a $50 million deficit. (About the only happy development of 1968 was the Detroit Tigers' American League pennant win, its first in 23 years—followed by victory in the World Series. The hysteria and street-corner hugging that followed were utterly color-blind.) Early in 1969, Cavanagh announced his retirement, and by his last months in office he had, in the words of one Detroit newspaper editor, "virtually abdicated."

There are two daily newspapers—The *Free Press* (morning) and the *News* (evening). Of the two, the *News* is the more conservative, has the larger circulation (over 660,000 daily), and profits greatly from ownership of WWJ-TV in Detroit. The *Free Press*, somewhat more liberal, more dedicated to the preservation of the inner city, breezier in its writing style, has a circulation of about 100,000 less and belongs to the vigorous Knight Newspapers chain. Detroit has been the most strike-prone newspaper town in the U.S.A. since World War II, suffering a 134-day-long strike in 1964 and another 267 days in 1968–69—a record length in U.S. history. Reasons for the long strikes are complex, ranging from multiple unions with excessive demands to intransigence or poor negotiating tactics on the part of the newspapers (especially the *News*).

The 1967–68 newspaper strike broke out just three and a half months after the riot, tragically bad timing for Detroit. Postriot fears could sweep the city unchecked, citizens began to buy firearms in unprecedented quantities, rumors spread in the white suburbs of black invasion and in the ghetto of concentration camps being readied for blacks. "It's reached the point of insanity," Cavanagh said in desperation.

Equally destructive to good race relations was the poststrike effort of the papers—especially the *News*—to regain their previous circulation. The *News* began a well-displayed daily crime blotter—covering every kind of street crime —and started to identify the suspected criminals by race. Since Negroes commit most of the inner-city crime (and the blotter carefully omitted the suburbs), blacks naturally resented the blotter as a move to smear them all.* Thus the city's leading daily lost its credibility among the black community; in the words of one city leader, "the paper played a racist game while denying it." The *News*'s alienation from its downtown black neighbors seemed complete when it walled in some of its exterior ground floor windows, ostensibly to protect the building against vandalism in strikes. But the "old gray lady of Lafayette Bouevard," as the *News* is familiarly called, also instituted a tight internal security system with guards and special passes for visitors. (The *Free Press* had no comparable system.) In a sense, the *News* was just doing what the rest of white Detroit was doing; as William Serrin reported in the *Atlantic Monthly*, "Detroit inner-city business is now conducted behind solid walls of cement block, an architectural style that wags have dubbed 'riot renaissance.' Shop windows are covered at night with fencelike burglar guards, and vigilante patrols are in vogue."

Suburbia and Detroit Metro

Detroit's geography, from center city to suburb, runs roughly this way: first comes the decaying downtown center with its exceptions like Cobo Hall, of which we have spoken; forming a choke collar around this business district is the U-shaped black ghetto, closed off by the river; beyond the ghetto are industrialized and largely white-working-class areas, most experiencing constant black population pressure.

Two independent towns are actually encircled by Detroit—Hamtramck (population 27,245), a citadel of poor Polish and Ukrainian whites, however one quarter black; and Highland Park (35,444), home of huge Chrysler and Ford plants and a one-time ethnic bastion, now becoming black faster than Hamtramck. Highland Park, in fact, in 1968 elected the only full-time black Republican mayor in the U.S.A., Robert P. Blackwell, an articulate ex-UAW official. No sooner had Blackwell's fellow Republican, President Nixon, taken office in Washington than Highland Park began to receive an amazing flow of federal money, more in a few months than it had received in the previous

---

* As in other American cities, blacks are also the most frequent victims of crime by members of their own race. In 1967, 61 percent of Detroit's 315 murders were committed by Negroes against Negroes, as were 69 percent of the 733 rapes. Detroit also has one of the highest overall crime rates among major U.S. cities, especially in the category of crimes against person.

half a century of its existence. The town could use some help; it has, for instance, the highest suburban crime rate for a place its size in the nation. Hamtramck (pronounced *Ham-tram-ack*) has some interesting claims to fame: it is the headquarters of the Olsonite Company, the world's largest manufacturer of toilet seats; and it appears to be the most impoverished city in America. It has a nonbonded debt of $31.5 million and annual revenues of only $4.5 million—the sea of red ink attributable to an incredible amount of petty graft and freeloading on the city payroll. In 1971, the city was considering declaring bankruptcy.

A colorful variety of suburbs surround Detroit. Ranging southward along the Detroit River and a few miles inland are a group of factory-dominated, lower-middle-class white cities like Ecorse, Southgate, Wyandotte, and Dearborn. My friend Robert Pisor of the Detroit *News* conjectures that these cities may constitute "the most polluted congressional district in the nation: the air stinks, the waters are technicolor, and sky filled with smoke and debris."

An officeholder with extraordinary longevity is Dearborn Mayor Orville Hubbard, who has held office since the early 1940s, longer than any other U. S. mayor. Dearborn (population 104,199) is a tight white island of Poles, Syrians, and Italians, proud homeowners who can be seen of a summer evening watering their lawns, standing side by side in their undershirts. The 1970 Census found 13 Negroes in Dearborn, but their location is a well-kept secret. Tax money from the huge Ford River Rouge complex pays 57 percent of Dearborn's taxes, and with this largesse Hubbard has purchased hundreds of acres 35 miles from Dearborn around rural Milford, Michigan, as a summer camp for the town's residents and also provided retirement homesteads for older Dearbornites in Florida.

Just north of the Detroit line are a number of middle-class working suburbs like Warren, Royal Oak, and Oak Park in Oakland and Macomb counties. One of these, Warren, gained a measure of fame in 1970 when it became the fulcrum of an effort by the national Housing and Urban Development Department, headed by George Romney, to achieve some measure of racial integration in the white suburban noose around Detroit. Warren is entirely a creation of the postwar population movement of people bent on escaping the grime and crime—and some say, the Negroes—of the inner city. In 1950, 727 people lived in Warren, in 1970, 179,260.

Thirty percent of the workers in Warren's auto plants are Negroes, but the community has been so hostile to blacks moving in—in 1967, for instance, a mob attacked a house bought by a mixed couple—that Warren has only 28 black families in residence. This stark case of housing discrimination, necessitating a massive "reverse commute" for blacks working in Warren but forced to live in Detroit, led HUD officials to believe they could use Warren as a test case to force suburban integration in return for $3 million in urban-renewal funds the city needed badly for neighborhood development. But angry residents got up a referendum to repeal the city's entire urban renewal program and passed it in November 1970, thus cutting off millions in federal aid—and choking off any chance of integration.

After the close-in middle-class suburbs typified by Warren, the northern Detroit suburbs shift to wealthier enclaves like Troy, Bloomfield Hills, Birmingham, West Bloomfield, and Farmington. This is favorite territory of the new generation of young auto and advertising executives and many of Detroit's up-and-coming civic leaders.

Further to the north lies the troubled city of Pontiac (85,279 people), one of GM's principal outposts (home of the Pontiac division), a grimy city with anemic leadership, a dismal downtown where blocks of urban-renewal land sprout weeds, and a combustible mixture of Southern whites, blacks, and Mexican-Americans. In 1971 a controversial school busing plan was imposed on Pontiac, accompanied by violent demonstrations and the dynamiting of 10 empty buses—a crime the government blamed on six members of the Ku Klux Klan, including the former grand dragon of the state KKK. Pontiac is also the home town of the founders of the Republic of New Africa, an embittered band of blacks who demand that the black man be given five Southern states and $400 billion in reparations for three centuries of black suffering.

Pontiac's school busing disputes may prove mild harbingers of a real convulsion in the metropolitan-wide schools, stemming from a 1971 ruling by Federal Judge Stephen J. Roth that found the state of Michigan and city of Detroit guilty of deliberately maintaining segregated schools—one of the first findings of *de jure* (instead of mere *de facto*) segregation in northern schools. Roth, a former state attorney general associated with Soapy Williams in earlier years, was ruling on a suit filed by the NAACP. He blamed not only government, but also lending institutions, real estate associations, and brokerage firms for segregated living patterns. "For many years," he ruled, "federal housing administrators and the Veterans Administration openly advised and advocated maintenance of 'harmonious' neighborhoods, i.e., racially and economically harmonious."

The solution Roth was approaching was a busing plan for the three counties—Wayne, Oakland and Macomb—that would interchange many city and suburban pupils. The counties have a combined school attendance of about one million, of whom 208,000 are black—184,000 from Detroit. Integration is probably no longer possible in Detroit alone, since its school enrollment is already 65 percent Negro.

The move to city-suburban busing caused a political uproar of immense proportions. Grass roots suburban groups opposed to busing, many with determined women at their fore, sprang up everywhere. Many normally liberal politicians scurried for the cover of newly formed antibusing positions. The fears of suburban parents were partly on racial grounds—the fear of violence in the schools, or intermarriage; another concern was subjecting their children to the inferior quality of underfinanced Detroit schools. The moves of Milliken and others for equal statewide school financing might solve the funding problem—but not the racial fears.

One of the great breakthroughs in American mercantile history was made in the early 1950s just north of the Detroit line in Southfield Township, where Hudson's bought a huge tract of land and constructed the spectacular Northland shopping center. "One of the few uniquely American building types," according to architectural critic Wolf Von Eckardt, is "the new trading post in the exurban wilderness—the regional shopping center." Northland was not only a pioneer of the new breed of marketplaces, but one of the best. Designer-planner Victor Gruen not only consigned the omnipresent autos to the outer periphery but endowed the central shopping areas with trees, flowers, fountains, and quiet protected pedestrian areas.

Northland's success was so great, in fact, that it became in many ways the focal point of the entire Detroit area (though, significantly, it is not on the Detroit tax rolls). It threw the city center off base and drained downtown of its life blood. By the mid-1970s, according to some projections, there will be more retail floor space at Northland than in all of downtown Detroit. Even the city's Negroes stream out to Northland on weekend shopping expeditions, rather than face the parking problems and crime danger downtown.

Curving along the shore of Lake St. Clair just east of the city in a closed-in, compact strip of privilege and cool green shade is Grosse Pointe, dwelling place for *la crème de la crème* of Detroit's nuts-and-bolts society. The auto aristrocracy—Mrs. Edsel Ford and her three sons, the top executives of Chrysler, Ford, and General Motors—all make their home in the Grosse Pointes.

To this point in time, the Detroit metropolitan area has grown topsy-turvy with scarcely any coordination or planning between the parts. The Detroit Regional Transportation and Land Use Study (TALUS), set up in the mid-1960s as the first local effort at comprehensive regional analysis and planning, found that the seven-county area of Southeastern Michigan had only 2.6 million people in 1940, 4.8 million in 1970, and would likely grow to 5.7 million in 1980 and 6.9 million in 1990. The growth curve poses frightening problems in terms of land use, which has accelerated far more rapidly than the population, and in areas like transportation, where the number of automobiles on the already crowded streets and freeways is set to go from 1.5 million in 1965 to 4.1 million in 1990 (making, one would think, an alternative in sophisticated mass transportation an absolute necessity).

But the more his agency delved into physical problems, according to TALUS director Irving J. Rubin, the more it became convinced that the physical problems were only symptoms of much deeper and harder-to-solve social problems. "We became disturbed," Rubin told me, "by the tremendous gap between city and suburban household incomes, even independent of race." In some areas of the city in 1965, median family income was as low as $3,900 a year; in wealthier suburbs (like the Grosse Pointes and spots like Bloomfield Hills) it exceeded $20,000 a year. The overall median income in Oakland County was 50 percent again as great as that in the city of Detroit.* Great gaps also existed in educational levels and housing standards. Yet

---

* The startling index of poverty in Detroit in 1965: 38,000 Negro families living on less than $3,000 per year, but more than 64,000 white families in the same category.

when TALUS projected these indexes forward to the year 1990, it found the gap between the haves and have-nots *widening;* even though the lot of the poor might be expected to improve somewhat, the middle class and wealthy would leap forward to median family incomes of at least $15,000 with commensurate educational and municipal services in their communities. "And it's that kind of gap," Rubin points out, "that the riots were all about."

In the 1960s and the dawn of the 1970s, at least some elements of the Detroit community began to recognize the futility and danger in regarding Detroit and its suburbs as two separate entities. The first initiatives for metropolitanwide cooperation, significantly, came not from the government but from the private sector—namely, Detroit's Metropolitan Fund, one of a broadening group of areawide nonprofit corporations operating in the U.S. to pull together a broad power structure (business, labor, intellectual, philanthropic) in a concerted effort to approach problems that spill out over several cities and towns.

Michigan's Other Cityscape

There is another industrial Michigan outside of Detroit and its immediate suburbs, consisting of 11 Lower Peninsula cities with populations ranging roughly between 50,000 and 200,000 (in the aggregate, about two thirds of the Detroit total). A startling number of these medium-ranked cities turn out to harbor microcosms of Detroit's black-white dilemma, even maintaining well-defined ghettos in which impoverished and middle-class Negroes alike are confined.

At the center of the "outstate" complex is Lansing (population 131,-546), the state capital with a dependable government payroll. Lansing's first love and big dollar, however, comes from the auto industry; both the Oldsmobile division of GM and Fisher Body are on location. The city has a large contingent of motorcycle-type Southern whites, often in confrontation with blacks who are largely confined to the city's southwest side.

An hour's drive northwest of Lansing and just a county short of the Lake Michigan shore is Grand Rapids (population 197,649), once a placid city of white, blond-haired, Republican conservatives who all seemed to have some sort of Van in front of their surnames. But the high cost of skilled labor drove most of the once prospering furniture business to the South and the population changed with an influx of Poles and Negroes imported to man varied new industries.

Arthur Vandenberg was doubtless the most illustrious man ever to emerge from Grand Rapids (his birthplace in 1884); Americans remember him as the isolationist-turned-internationalist who helped write the United Nations charter at San Francisco in 1945 and chaired the Senate Foreign Relations Committee when many of the pioneer postwar international programs were being molded. Gerald R. Ford, Jr., moved to Grand Rapids at the age of one and was a Vandenberg protegé when he first won election to the House in 1948; since 1965 he has served unspectacularly as Republican Leader of the House of Representatives (and is a potential future Speaker).

Lying south of Lansing and Grand Rapids, pointed in almost a straight line from Detroit to Chicago, are four cities of somewhat lesser magnitude: Ann Arbor (population 99,797), Jackson (45,484), Battle Creek (38,931), and Kalamazoo (85,555). Ann Arbor is the most atypical of the lot; it does make some automobile parts and other industrial goods but is chiefly the campus town of the University of Michigan. The intellectual community competes for power with a wealthy old conservative Republican faction and the blacks and blue collars.

Northward, in the vicinity of Saginaw Bay, are two run-of-the-mill GM cities, Saginaw (population 91,849) and Bay City (49,449), the former with so many blacks and Mexican-Americans that a Negro was actually chosen mayor in the 1960s.

Finally we come to Flint (population 193,317), the epitome of the blue-collar lunch-bucket city and General Motors town *par excellence*. Sixty percent of the men in Flint work at the Chevrolet, Buick, and Fisher Body plants, a total GM payroll exceeding 60,000. No city in the U.S.A. has a higher average workingman's wage. Flint's problem, of course, is the lack of economic diversification; GM dominates so totally that the second largest employer in town is the Hamady Brothers Supermarket chain.

Flint has an ample supply both of Southern rednecks and blacks and a strangely contradictory race history. In October 1967, the Ku Klux Klan, headed by a pipefitter leading more than 100 Klansmen from "eight Flint units," boldly staged a march down the main street of town, complete with satin robes, hoods, sashes, and insignia. That same year, there were disturbances in the black community and Mayor Floyd McCree walked the streets to calm tensions. Amazingly, McCree was a black man—the first Negro mayor in the city's history, a salaried foreman for Buick with 23 years seniority and an extraordinarily able political figure. With its huge UAW membership, Flint should be a stronghold of issue-oriented strong Democratic leadership. But instead, most of the Democratic leadership—especially on the white side—is patronage and job oriented.

Lackluster Democratic leadership and organization led in 1966 to a major Republican coup in Flint: ouster of the run-of-the-mill, patronage oriented Democratic Congressman by a dynamic and attractive liberal Republican, 28-year-old Donald W. Riegle, Jr. Riegle contracted with the California professional campaign management firm of Spencer-Roberts to launch a sophisticated computer and poll-backed onslaught on the sleepy Democrats. Physically attractive, extremely hard-working, possessed of one of the best staffs on Capitol Hill, Riegle would one day like to take a run for the Presidency. Riegle's ambition has aroused no little enmity among state Republican leaders, who consider him arrogant and an upstart. He became a vocal opponent of the Vietnam war and in 1970 ran with UAW support.

Flint does have one priceless and unique asset: the Mott Foundation, creation of Charles Stewart Mott, the grand old patriarch of Flint and one of the richest men in America. Persuaded by General Motors pioneer W. C. Durant to bring his axle-producing plant from Utica, N.Y., in 1906, Mott became and remains Flint's leading industrialist. He has been a member of the General Motors board of directors since 1913 and has long been the largest single GM stockholder. Six decades ago Mott served as mayor of Flint and in 1920 even ran (though unsuccessfully) for governor. Then, in the mid-1920s, he established the Charles Stewart Mott Foundation, now the nation's fourth largest with about $430 million in General Motors stock and other assets. (Stewart Mott, C. S.'s 32-year-old son who lives in New York managing his own inheritance and dispensing hundreds of thousands of dollars in philanthropic and political contributions for liberal causes, estimates that the family fortune, including the assets of the foundation, add up to $800 million.)

Interviewing Mott in Flint in 1969, I discovered a still alert and compassionate old gentleman of 94 years who still evidenced a boyish enthusiasm for his town and for the work of his foundation. "Instead of scattering our shots," Mott said, "we have concentrated the foundation's efforts in Flint and tried to make the city a laboratory and proving ground of what can be done to improve education and recreational opportunities." The undertaking of which Mott seems the proudest—and which others in Flint consider the foundation's most vital contribution—is the 35-year-old program to open the schools after hours for adult education and community programs. If any 10 people in Flint want an adult education course, the foundation will finance it for them. The open schools program (recognized as early as the 1930s by Eleanor Roosevelt as a pioneer in its field) has increased the number of hours that all Flint schools are open each year from 1,400 to 3,800 hours. The theory is that the buildings belong to the taxpayers and they have a right to use them. "What a whale of an increase in the use of property, with adult education classes in these schools," Mott says. In the last few years, the foundation has begun to branch outside its own city by fostering similar programs in Washington, D.C., and Minneapolis, and training scores of community schools administrators from around the country in Flint each year.

Other major Mott Foundation undertakings include physical-fitness courses, medical and dental examinations for all children in the Flint schools ("Hell would freeze over before a city health department would do this," Mott insists), a "big brother" program to help young boys, summer camps, kindergarten programs for inner-city children, and vocational guidance for ex-convicts. "I gave 90 percent of my assets for the foundation. Why? What makes me tick?" Mott asks. His answer: "I get more pleasure out of the money spent for these activities than anything else I do. The reaction on me is terrific. I'm 94 years old and I work every day and night and Sunday on this thing."

C. S. Mott's wealth and resources would permit him, if he chose, to rule Flint with an iron hand from behind the scenes. But he uses his power very sparingly, is not a major political contributor, and has kept the foundation scrupulously clear of politics. About the best judgment one could make about Mott and his works is that every major American city could use one of the same.

Michigan's Men in Congress

Before we leave Michigan, brief note must be taken of the state's present-day U.S. Senators—Democrat Philip A. Hart and Republican Robert P. Griffin—who play a national role of greater significance than any Michigan representatives since the days of Arthur Vandenberg.

Hart, a product of the Williams era of Michigan politics, is a soft-spoken man who developed quietly in the 1960s into a highly effective spokesman for liberal Democratic Senators on civil rights and consumer issues. Hart became the acknowledged leader of the Democratic civil rights bloc, carrying the floor fight for the landmark Voting Rights Act of 1965 and the 1968 open-housing civil rights bill. And the Senate Judiciary Antitrust Subcommittee, the chairmanship of which Hart inherited from the late Estes Kefauver of Tennessee, has tackled controversial consumer-oriented issues such as auto repairs and insurance, drug prices, and oil import quotas. Hart has also been a leading sponsor of truth-in-lending and truth-in-packaging legislation and an articulate opponent of the antiballistic missile system. In an episode Hart would as soon forget, he carried the unsuccessful floor fight to nominate Abe Fortas as Chief Justice; after President Johnson was obliged to withdraw the nomination, he offered Hart a place on the Court. But the idea came to naught because it was too late in the 1968 session to hope for confirmation of an opponent.

Hart's growing influence as leader of the Democratic liberal bloc may be attributed to hard work, good staff, steadily reliable judgment, and as Spencer Rich of the Washington *Post* has pointed out, "considerable behind-the-scenes influence and capacity to get things done in the everyday committee work and floor action of the Senate." In this respect, Hart differs markedly from liberal spokesmen of earlier years like Illinois' Paul Douglas and Pennsylvania's Joseph Clark, men often so blunt in debate and intolerant of their opposition that their effectiveness was seriously undermined. Though he is a favorite of the UAW and the liberal wing of the Michigan Democratic party, Hart's genteel manner somehow even gives Republicans in his state the feeling he is one of them; somehow they can't believe that a man with a home on Mackinac Island can be such a dangerous liberal.

Most wives of Senators are rarely seen except at Washington parties and as smiling backdrops for campaign brochures, but Hart's wife Jane is a distinct exception. She became an outspoken dove on the Vietnam issue well before Hart himself, once fed her family for a week on a welfare budget to demonstrate the inadequacy of federal aid to the poor, and has even helped set up a home for dissenting priests. In 1969 she managed to get herself arrested (and later convicted) of disorderly conduct at a praying, singing, and hand-clapping antiwar demonstration inside the Pentagon.

We have already had a glimpse of Senator Griffin, the bespectacled giant killer from Traverse City who brought Soapy Williams to his knees. Griffin is an expert in seizing on seemingly impossible causes and turning them into victories. In 1959, as a House Member, he coauthored the Landrum-Griffin Labor Reform Law which was then passed by a House packed with union-backed Congressmen elected in the 1958 Democratic sweep. Six years later, Griffin was a key strategist in dumping Indiana's Charles Halleck as Republican House Leader, replacing him with fellow Michigander Gerald Ford. In 1968, only two years after entering the Senate, he started out with scarcely an ally to block President Johnson's appointment of Abe Fortas as Chief Justice, and eventually thwarted the nomination.

Again in 1969, Griffin's decision to oppose President Nixon's nomination of Clement Haynsworth to the Supreme Court was a key turning point in the South Carolinian's eventual defeat. And though he was a virtual greenhorn by Senate "club" standards, with only three years service behind him, Griffin in 1969 won election as Assistant Republican Leader (or Whip) of the Senate. Griffin's days, William Serrin reported for the Detroit *Free Press*, "run to 12 hours, his tastes to white shirts and dark blue suits, and his mind to tactics rather than theory. The tactics and the 12-hour work days paid off." Griffin's 1972 reelection prospects were not originally considered bright, but he improved his position substantially by sponsoring a constitutional amendment to bar all school busing on racial grounds.

U. S. Rep. James G. O'Hara, from sprawling blue-collar Macomb County outside Detroit, has not only contributed importantly to social legislation but has that unusual talent among liberals, a keen feeling for the intricacies of House parliamentary maneuverings. He has been a leader of the liberal House Democratic Study Group, and was chairman of the Democratic party commission to improve national convention rules and procedures in advance of the 1972 convention. His colleague John D. Dingell, whose district covers the southwestern part of Detroit and a number of adjacent suburbs, became a leading conservationist and environmentalist in Congress long before those issues gained the national popularity they have today.

Detroit's Rep. John Conyers, Jr., is viewed by some as inheritor of the mantle of House black leadership that slipped from the shoulders of Adam Clayton Powell. Conyers has taken a lead in building a black caucus in Congress and has demonstrated unusual skill and will in rising to the top of Negro leadership ranks. I have heard him variously described as "the Julian Bond of Congress," "a New Left Democrat who still thinks the system can be made to work," "a good bellwether on what blacks will do or not do," "a master of organization," "an extreme opportunist," and "grandstander." Anyone who evokes such reactions is sure to be heard from often in the future.

Another Detroit House member, Democrat Martha W. Griffiths, has the distinction of being the first and only woman to sit on the House Ways and Means Committee. A quiet and persuasive former trial lawyer, she won a measure of national fame in 1970 when she masterminded House passage (by a 346 to 15 vote) of a constitutional amendment to give women equal rights. (The measure was later killed in the Senate but reenacted by the House in 1971.) In 1960, the other nine women in the House suggested that Mrs. Griffiths be named to the U. S. Supreme Court.

A Michigan Postscript

When all is said and done with Michigan, the whole may be something less than the sum of the parts. The auto industry, with its incredible wealth and manpower resources, could and should have been a pacesetter for American business and life, brave enough to take the early plunges—into safer and less polluting cars, into mass transit and city planning, into advanced opportunities for blacks. Instead, it waited for Ralph Nader and the Detroit riots to spur it to action, and while it has improved greatly, it is still missing many opportunities. The UAW has, indeed, been an innovative force in American life, but inflationary wage increases over the years—especially that of 1970— suggest the union may not have counted the costs for the U.S.A. as a whole, just as the auto companies failed to count the deleterious national effects of the cars they built.

With its wealth and opportunities, Michigan should never have let Detroit "happen," or for that matter let Lansing or Flint happen quite the way they did. In race, housing, regional government, Michigan is a disappointment. For too long, men of much wealth but little breeding or culture held the ultimate power in Michigan, and even today one senses a lack of strong forces challenging the power system. How will Detroit ever be saved? Who really cares about fighting through Milliken's exciting school-tax reform ideas? Are the narrow-minded, selfish towns like Dearborn and Warren the wave of our future? What happens when the day of the automobile passes in America? Why aren't Michiganders fighting and dreaming and thinking more about their future? They are certainly more awake than they were a decade ago— events saw to that. But are they awake enough?

FLORIDA

THE MAN-MADE STATE

FLORIDA IS A Johnny-Come-Lately to the family of megastates. In 1950, it ranked only 20th in population among the states; today it is ninth. In 30 years, the state has had a cumulative growth rate of 175 percent, a figure rivaled only by states like Arizona and Nevada. In 1940, less than 2 million people lived in Florida; in 1970, the Census Bureau counted 6,789,443.

Why this phenomenal boom? A big part of the answer can be traced to Americans' increased longevity and the affluence that lets them buy a retirement bungalow or apartment under the warm Florida sun. Floridians wince at the notion, but the Census figures prove it: this is the old folks' state par excellence. Just between 1960 and 1970, while the numbers of Floridians under 65 rose 32 percent, the ranks 65 or over went up 78 percent (an increase of 435,000, up to 989,000). Overall, 14.5 percent of Florida's residents are presently 65 or older, compared to 9.9 percent nationally. No other state has a comparable percentage of senior citizens; in California, once thought of as a great retirement mecca, the figure is only 9.0 percent. In St. Petersburg, 30.6 percent of the people are 65 or older; of the permanent residents of Miami Beach, 48.7 percent match that description.

The retirees, of course, are only one part of the Florida boom. Tourism has been growing by leaps and bounds, and in a recent year 22.5 million visitors were counted, spending a tidy $6.2 billion. There are big, permanent military installations at Pensacola, Key West, Jacksonville, and many spots in the interior, the Space Center at Cape Kennedy has brought billions of dollars into Florida, manufacturing has made great strides, and a third of the world's entire citrus production still comes from Florida orchards.

Driving from Miami Beach along the Gold Coast to Fort Lauderdale, one sees a continuous, virtually unbroken wall of hotels and high apartment buildings that now face the Atlantic for 25 miles, a high proportion of them built within the past decade. And then going further north around 38 miles to Palm Beach, the concentration is almost as heavy; soon this area, too, will be 100 percent built up. Filling in the cracks and intruding into the hinterland are massive park- or village- type developments designed to hold tens of thousands of people when completed in the 1970s; the construction costs range as high as $800 million for a single project.

One is hard put to believe there could be enough wealth in the U. S. A. to pay for such gigantic playgrounds, but there they are, rising from the flat, sandy beaches before one's very eyes. In a way, they make sense. Given the fact that thousands upon thousands of Americans have the ready cash to pay hundreds or thousands of dollars for a winter vacation at a resort hotel (where a room for two in the high winter season easily runs $50 to $75 a day), they are often well advised to go ahead and buy a condominium. It is a hedge against future inflation, a good investment in its own right, it can be rented out when the owner is away, and it thus becomes depreciable-income-producing property for tax purposes. While one's there, of course, there is bright sun, a proximity to the Bahamas and Caribbean for quickie vacations, fishing, and all other manner of entertainment in the nearby resorts.

Neither luxury hotels nor condominiums are restricted to the Gold Coast, of course. One finds them scattered, in greater or lesser degree, all along the 1,200 miles of Florida coastline, from Jacksonville down to Key West and then up the Gulf Coast to Tampa–St. Petersburg and Pensacola. Florida has become—thanks to air conditioning, plus smart promotion—a year-round instead of a strictly winter vacation spot. One can now cross off as obsolete John Gunther's report on "a large proportion of the people living high for three months during the tourist season and then living low on fish and grits for the rest of the year." Amazingly, about a third of Florida's tourist volume occurs between June and August, months in which the north Florida resorts —Daytona Beach, Jacksonville Beach, Pensacola, and Panama City—do their biggest business. Yet even in those dog days of summer, incredible numbers of people, lured by cut rates and intensive advertising, still seem willing to shell out hundreds of dollars for vacations in the suffocating heat and humidity of places like Miami Beach.

Increasingly, the line between vacationer and retiree blurs, especially as jets make it possible to virtually commute in and out of Florida if one has the money, and people buy houses or apartments into which they gradually retire over time. But there are still the instant retirees—usually poorer—who suddenly descend on Florida with lifetime savings to try and soak up some post-retirement sunshine before the final line is drawn. In Sarasota, I visited one of their closest observers and sternest critics, the author MacKinley Kantor. Kantor's home is in a luxuriant subtropical junglelike piece of land along Siesta Key, where only a few hundred souls lived 30 years ago, and some 10,000 today. He is not a little resentful about all the new population; he would be happier if things would stay peaceful and quiet "so that we can live close to the mockingbirds and the raccoons." But Kantor (who himself crashed the 65-year barrier in 1969) adds: "Even a savage old square like myself must admit that the lives of so many are so much better." Of his fellow and less affluent senior citizen compatriots, he says:

> I feel so sorry for them. . . . So many just dissolve and die. A few have the head and the heart to adjust to their new existence. But many lack the built-in self-discipline system.
> The happiest ones are in trailer parks. Camp living is more like the little towns they knew in Ohio and Indiana and Michigan. You see them out playing shuffleboard together and they're having the time of their life. They're a core of elderly humanity who are already harmonized to each other. True small-town social life develops. New folks are easily accepted. It's like the simple openness of life in Agony, Oklahoma, or wherever they came from. They're with their own ethnic group—the same kind of people a man may have known when he had his own hardware store up north. And they all appreciate each other. . . .
> Those in the subdivision homes—they know less people. They are the unhappy faces you see in the supermarkets. You go into the Kwik-Chek, and they're all glowering at everybody else and each other. Their faces are gloom. "Well, it doesn't cost this much up in Akron, I can tell you that." They're rude, discourteous, unobliging, their attitude being "You Florida people better be glad you have us down here spending our hard-earned money. You don't treat us right—you raise our taxes—then there's always California, there's always Arizona."

More fortunate are the elderly with enough money to take up a hobby like boating; they are forever refurbishing their boats or joining yacht club or power-squadron activities, and there's the special camaraderie of the boat world to brighten their lives. A special danger, Kantor says, awaits the retirees "without enough gumption to start something new, but enough money to lie back on their cans. Then they get bored and start drinking in the morning. I used to do that and in that way lies madness—I know."

Geography and Ecology

Before the synthetic civilization came, there was only natural Florida— a remarkable peninsula, extending more than 300 miles south of the major continental land mass, a great green mat, often broken by lakes and swamps, floating in a deep blue sea. The further south one looked, the more remarkable it was. From north to south, this was the view: first, the low-rolling, pine-covered hills of the north and the panhandle, close kin to the red clay hills of neighboring Georgia and Alabama, a land of magnolias and the languid Suwannee River, live oaks and Spanish moss. Then came the central

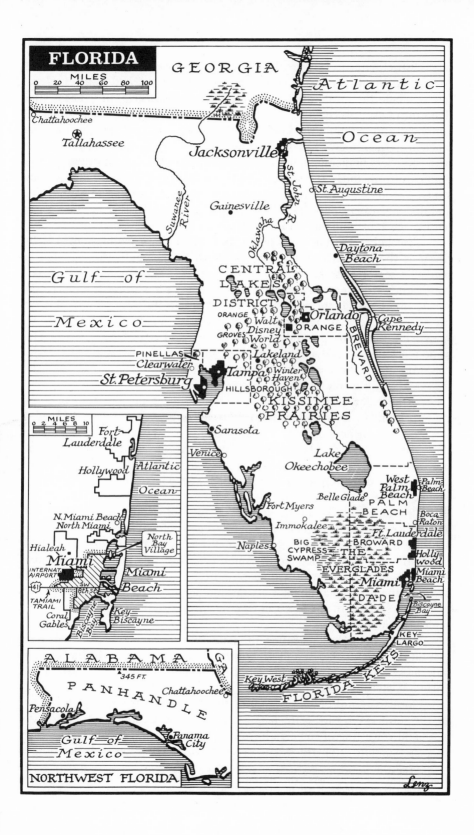

FLORIDA

MILES
0 20 40 60 80 100

GEORGIA

Atlantic

Ocean

Chattahoochee

Tallahassee

Jacksonville

Gainesville

St. Augustine

St. John R.

Suwanee River

Oklawaha

Daytona Beach

Gulf of

Mexico

CENTRAL
LAKES
DISTRICT

ORANGE
GROVES

Walt
Disney
World

Orlando
ORANGE

Cape Kennedy

BREVARD

PINELLAS
Clearwater
St. Petersburg

Lakeland

Winter Haven

Tampa

HILLSBOROUGH

KISSIMEE
PRAIRIES

Sarasota

Venice

Lake
Okeechobee

West
Palm
Beach

Palm
Beach

Fort Myers

Belle Glade

PALM
BEACH

Boca
Raton

Immokalee

Ft. Lauderdale

BROWARD

Naples

BIG
CYPRESS
SWAMP

THE

Hollywood

EVERGLADES

Miami
Beach

Miami

DADE

Biscayne
Bay

KEY
LARGO

Key West

FLORIDA KEYS

MILES
0 2 4 6 8 10

Fort
Lauderdale

Hollywood

Atlantic

Ocean

N. Miami Beach
North Miami

North
Bay
Village

Hialeah

Miami

INTERNAT.
AIRPORT

41

SW
8th ST

TAMIAMI
TRAIL

Coral
Gables

Biscayne Bay

Miami

Beach

Key
Biscayne

ALABAMA

GA

345 FT.

PANHANDLE

Chattahoochee

Pensacola

Gulf of

Mexico

Panama
City

NORTHWEST FLORIDA

Lenz

lakes district, later to become the heartland of Florida's great citrus industry. After this, the Kissimmee Prairies, covered with grass and patches of palmetto, where the great cattle ranges would later be developed.* These lands drain into Lake Okeechobee, one of the largest lakes on the North American continent and certainly the largest of the 30,000-odd that dot the Floridian landscape. In primeval times, Okeechobee was shaped like a shallow saucer with short legs branching out where muddy waters from the northern prairies drained into it; today the shape is more regular, since a levee has been constructed around the lake to prevent its waters from escaping in a hurricane, and drainage canals have been built around it to reclaim the rich soils for intensive vegetable and sugar cane cultivation.

Okeechobee has no single outlet, but rather flows southerly toward the ocean as the land tilts ever so slightly down to the south through that remarkable sea of grass known as the Everglades. (The dominant sawgrass is hardly grass at all, growing 10 feet tall with edges set with teeth.) Over 5,000 square miles stretch the Everglades, the muddy waters draining imperceptibly below, the level stretch broken only by occasional "hammocks" where the underlying limestone protrudes to the surface and trees have grown. (That same limestone, underlying almost all of southern Florida, also has a higher elevation along the coasts, saving stretches like the Atlantic beaches from degenerating into total swamp.)

As the ocean is reached, along some of the keys and the coast of southwestern Florida, the mangrove forests appear, constantly building land out of water until hurricanes occur to demolish their work. Nowhere else in America does one come on a plant like the mangrove, its gnarled roots reaching down into sea water which would be lethal to most land plants, forever spreading by dropping seedlings into the water which float off to find new homes.

Also unique geologically, across the face of North America, are the Florida Keys, a fantastic coral-built archipelago stretching 200 miles south and southwesterly from Miami. Naturalist Peter Farb points out that while corals are found on other North American shores, the conditions for reef-building—shallow seas with temperatures over 70° and currents strong enough to bring the little coral animals a constant supply of food—are present only at Florida's southern tip. Even now, a new living wall of coral is being built under the indigo waters.

Finally, one should mention the long, sandy buffer spits or islands lying just off the Atlantic Coast and part of the Gulf Coast. Not only did they provide most of the fabled Florida beach front, but behind their banks a safe Inland Waterway could be created.

Florida's record of stewardship of this land is mixed. The state has one of the most impressive state park systems in the nation, covering 177,000 acres and consisting of some 22 historical memorials and 61 parks. The effort to preserve state property began in 1915 when the Florida Federation of

---

* Florida is forever boasting about its huge, growing cattle industry. However, its cattle population (1.8 million in 1970) ranks only 23rd among the states, and its total livestock marketings only 26th ($374 million in 1699). It had no more cattle in 1969 than it did five years before.

Women's Clubs acquired an area that became the nucleus of the massive (1.5 million acres) Everglades National Park, established in 1947. The state first appropriated funds for parks in 1935 and it found a good investment: in Fort Lauderdale's oceanfront Hugh Taylor Birch State Park, for example, an acre is valued at $40,000. And the parks are popular; some 500,000 people visited the parks in 1949–50, and in 1970 the figure was 7.5 million.

But the drive to remake nature into a synthetic environment has been costly to the ecology, and now nature is handing in the bill. For some 80 years, men have been building drainage canals around Lake Okeechobee for land development and diverting fresh water for use in the coastal cities. In 1971, when a fierce drought hit southern Florida, the Everglades suffered massive fires, covering some 500,000 acres of scrub and fertile muckland—fires which the land, deprived of its own natural moisture, was unable to withstand. The Gold Coast was darkened by heavy clouds of ash and smoke, its first serious air pollution crisis. In the Everglades, many snakes, turtles, and alligators were trapped and destroyed by the flames. And as the natural water level dropped, there was a serious danger of salt water from the Atlantic seeping inland to contaminate Florida's fresh water supply. Arthur R. Marshall, a noted ecologist at the University of Miami, said: "It's unbelievable to me that while the fires burn at this moment across the parched Everglades, dredges are building more canals to drain away more water."

The Everglades fires, while the most spectacular, are only one of many dangers to Florida's environment. Tampa Bay's estuaries are so polluted that algae growth dies and produces massive amounts of hydrogen sulfide which bubbles to the surface and gives off the odor of rotten eggs. The bay also was hit by a serious oil spill (10,000 gallons) in 1970, a reminder of that constant threat to Florida's beaches. Like many freshwater lakes in Florida, lovely little Lake Thonotosassa near Tampa was virtually killed by wastes which rotted and choked off the oxygen necessary to sustain fish life. Lake Apoka (50 square miles of water), one of the nation's great freshwater fishing lakes, was so ravaged by sewer and industrial wastes that the Florida Air and Water Pollution Board drained the lake and cleansed its bottom in sunlight.

Escambia Bay near Pensacola became so polluted with wastes from factories, sewage from several cities, and pesticides from upstream farms in Alabama that its seafood industry was severely damaged: shrimp almost disappeared, oysters were declared off limits, blue crabs did disappear, and the shores were littered with millions of dead menhaden.

Pollution hit the Florida Keys, and the breathtaking beauty of Biscayne Bay remains in constant threat from the thermal pollution of the generators (conventional in operation, nuclear under construction) of the Florida Light and Power Company, the state's biggest utility. The Miami River is badly polluted, largely by industrial and sewage wastes from Miami International Airport and from boats docked in the river. Much the same condition prevails in the St. Johns River in Jacksonville. Indeed, one can say that most of the rivers and lakes in Florida, and much of its coastline, have been seriously damaged by the discharge of untreated industrial and municipal wastes.

Florida also has its own brand of strip mining—principally for phosphates, a prehistoric marine life laid down some 25 million years ago. This industry has left several hundred thousand acres open to the sky.

The early 1970s brought two important turnabouts on the environmental front. The first was the Presidential decision, in January 1970, halting construction of a 39-square-mile jetport in Big Cypress Swamp, just north of Everglades National Park. As President Nixon noted, the decision was a major victory for conservationists. One who could take special credit was Joe Browder, a young activist working with the National Audubon Society; another was Miami lawyer Daniel Paul. The decision against the airport was also pushed along by a damning report prepared by federal and state environmental experts under the direction of Dr. Luna B. Leopard, the noted ecologist in the Interior Department's Geological Survey.

The second major turnabout came a year later, in January 1971, when President Nixon stopped further construction on the Cross-Florida Barge Canal—for years a favorite pork-barrel project of the Florida congressional delegation. The canal, 107 miles long, would have run from Jacksonville on the Atlantic to the Gulf of Mexico near Yankeetown. It would have cost $200 million and benefited a handful of shipowners. It would also have destroyed the Oklawaha River and been one of the biggest boondoggles in the already mottled history of the Army Corps of Engineers (but brought vast profits to the construction industry and allied banks, which were its chief backers). Some 25 miles, costing $50 million, had already been built when the stop-work order came, but maverick Republican Congressman C. W. Young of the state spoke well when he said: "I'd a lot rather have a 25-mile ditch that isn't worth anything than a 100-mile ditch that isn't worth anything."

New environmental problems may be posed by the prospective development of Florida as a major oil-producing state in the 1970s. There are indications that enough oil reserves to make Florida a kind of "South Slope," corresponding to Alaska's North Slope, may be found in a geologic formation that begins about 60 miles northeast of Pensacola and runs offshore parallel to a spot just south of Sarasota, and then inland in a big curve to the Big Cypress Swamp. In June 1971, the Interior Department announced that the eastern Gulf of Mexico would be offered to oil companies for drilling in May 1973. Environmentalists are already up in arms about the possibility of oil drilling in the Big Cypress Swamp, which is responsible for 56 percent of the Everglades' water supply. They are sure to be just as upset about offshore oil drilling that could imperil Florida's beaches.

Discovery and Development

Except to the Seminole Indians, the land called Florida was unknown until the Spanish conquistador Don Juan Ponce de Leon came upon it in April of 1513 while following a commission from the king of Spain to "explore and colonize Bimini." The Spanish had no idea they had hit upon the

North American mainland, but they did learn quickly of some perils. Even before they could land, a tropical squall came up and almost wrecked their ships on a promontory that would later become known as Cape Canaveral, and still later, Cape Kennedy, departure place for the moon. But before all that could happen, the whole region had to be named, and Ponce de Leon did that on the evening of April 2, 1513, selecting the name *Florida* because —as the royal chronicler later wrote—"it has a very beautiful view of many cool woodlands, and it was level and uniform; and because, moreover, they discovered it in the time of the Feast of Flowers (Easter season)." A day later, Ponce and his men landed at what would become St. Augustine, looking for the fountain of youth (as so many after them); in 1565 there was indeed a permanent settlement at St. Augustine, and the serious peopling of the continent had begun.

Between Ponce's discovery and formal U.S. proprietorship, 308 years were to pass. But the Spanish were continually harassed by competing French and English colonists, and when they finally relinquished the land in 1821, there was little to show for all their efforts except the small towns of St. Augustine and Pensacola. Most of the Spanish flavor one finds in Florida today—Tampa, with its Ybor City and Spanish restaurants, Miami with the big Cuban colony—dates from comparatively modern times. And as for Florida's early years under U. S. rule—the winning of statehood in 1845, Indian wars, involvement on the Confederate side in the Civil War, Reconstruction—they have been well depicted as a "faint duplication" of life elsewhere in America in those times.

The real history of modern Florida awaited the 1880s and the arrival of the first big promoters—hotel and railmen Henry M. Flagler and Henry B. Plant. Shocked by the primitive hotel accommodations Florida had to offer, Flagler in 1885 began to build the fabulously opulent Hotel Ponce de Leon in St. Augustine. Stung by Flagler's success, his west Florida rival, Plant, spent more than $3 million building the Tampa Bay Hotel, opened in 1891. But Flagler, who had already made millions as a partner of John D. Rockefeller, was not to be outdone. Thousands of affluent East Coast residents began to travel down to Florida on the posh all-Pullman train he put into service. First St. Augustine was the southernmost point; then Flagler decided on a southerly extension to Palm Beach, which he literally "made" with its sumptuous new hotel, The Breakers. Soon the private railway cars of the ultrarich could be seen on the Palm Beach sidings, and large private homes called "cottages" were erected near the Breakers. "In the evenings," historian Marjory Douglas recorded, "the music from the hotel ballrooms mingled with the rustling of palm fronds, glittering in moonlight, and the winds from the sea."

In those days, Miami was just a frontier village with a few sand trails and makeshift wooden shacks, but one of its first genteel Northern settlers, a young widow named Julia Tuttle, had a vision of its future. After a savage frost in the winter of 1894–95, which destroyed the citrus crop of middle Florida, Mrs. Tuttle was able to send Flagler sprigs of unharmed orange blossom to prove that Miami was south of the frost line. Within a year's time, the railroad was extended to Miami, and out of the "tangled mass of vine, brush, trees and rocks" Mrs. Tuttle had once described to a friend, there began to grow a great city—starting, of course, with a Flagler hotel.

But this was the era of Manifest Destiny, and Flagler dreamed of an even greater city, at the very tip of the continent, Key West. And true enough, from 1904 to 1912, the work went on to construct the Overseas Railroad across the subtropical keys. Huge engineering obstacles, mosquitoes, blazing summers, and three hurricanes had to be endured, and 700 men were washed away by storms. But in 1912 an 82-year-old Flagler—only four months from his own death—could ride the first train, all the way down from Jacksonville, over the bridges and viaducts and the sea, and into Key West. Florida's eastern coast had been conquered, and the frontier was no more. (A raging hurricane in 1935 swept away key sections of the Key West line, and a whole train with its passengers, but Flagler's roadbed was used to extend U. S. 1 across the keys on the Overseas Highway of today.)

Just a few years after Flagler's death, the great Florida land boom of the '20s was on. Hundreds of thousands of land speculators poured into the state—2.5 million people in the year 1925 alone—and prices zoomed to many times real value. But in the spring of 1926, the bubble broke; banks began to fail; paper millionaires became paupers overnight. And in the autumn of that year, hundreds died in one of the worst hurricanes of recorded history. Marjory Douglas, an eyewitness, recorded that the hurricane, rushing in from the Atlantic without advance warning, struck exposed Miami, "vulnerable with flimsy boom-time buildings, real estate shacks, garages, with the explosive force of a vast bomb." And when the 125-mile-an-hour winds abated in the light of early morning and people began to pour out into the streets to view the wreckage, they were caught by the steely winds and rains of the opposite side of the storm center, and many more lost their lives. After that, Miami adopted a new building code, drafted with an eye to potential hurricane effects, and this code later became a model for all of Florida.

But Florida seems to prosper through all adversities. Half a million permanent new residents were noted in the 1920s, even though the Depression had arrived in Florida a few years early. Despite the crash of 1929 and national depression, another 430,000 people found their way to Florida by the eve of World War II. Tourism fell off abruptly with the war, but right afterward a little big boom ensued as people tried to spend their wartime savings, lots of ex-GIs decided to mix some sun with their GI Bill studies, and the Social Security generation began to hit its stride. But the great boom of all Florida history—the one which continues, little abated, to this day—began around 1950. Lavish hotels began to spring up everywhere; air travel made it easy for Northerners to spend quick vacations; the retirement communities boomed and air conditioning arrived in a serious way. From 2.8 million people in 1950, the population spiraled to 4.9 million in 1960, a 78.7 percent increase unequalled by any other state. In the 1960s, everything accelerated even more, with NASA's $2 billion expenditures enriching the economy as well. The decade brought another 1.8 million people, an increase of 37.1 percent unmatched among the larger states. There was some slackening with the recession around 1970, but no one expected the economic downturn to last long. Some of the reasons:

■ Tourism bolstered by a growing national population and increased personal income; earlier retirements with ever more generous pension and Social Security benefits (now reaching even to groups like trade unions that buy retirement communities for their members); Florida's ever hucksterish promoters, intent on squeezing maximum profits out of every market. Over 60,000 Floridians make their living in hotels (compared to 20,000 in 1950), and 387,000 are employed in all sorts of services, many of them tourist-related; then there are 165,000 working in the construction industry, closely tied to tourist and retirement-home construction. The only threat would seem to lie in foolhardy overbuilding that outpaces real hotel and residential demand.

■ Agriculture. The state's farm products sell for about $1.3 billion a year, produced on relatively few but huge farms. The leader is citrus; Florida boasts it sells even more grapefruit than California does oranges. Two-thirds of the crop is now processed into frozen concentrates, easily preserved and shipped all over the country. (The frozen orange juice craze has taken on so strongly it's hard to get a glass of fresh orange juice—in Florida!) To avoid dangerous freezes, more and more citrus planting is in south Florida, in a wide circle around Lake Okeechobee. There are now a million acres of citrus planted in the state—about three-quarters oranges, the rest grapefruit, tangerines, and limes. But the industry is nervous it may have overplanted and would like the federal government to bale it out by purchasing frozen orange juice for school lunch programs.

Florida also runs a respectable second to California in winter vegetables like tomatoes, white potatoes, celery, cabbage, sweet corn, cucumbers, watermelons, lettuce, and snap beans, with great concentrations from Dade County (Miami) up to Palm Beach and the Okeechobee area, as well as south of Tampa. On display in the winter markets, however, the displays of vegetables and fruits are of strictly mediocre quality, especially in comparison to what California offers at the same time of year. Sugar cane is also an important crop, and cattle as a result of successful crossbreeding of Angus and Hereford with India's Brahmin, more resistant to heat and pests. In a related field, Florida markets about $40 million worth of fish, oysters, and shrimp each year.

■ Manufacturing. Florida is just beginning to establish itself as an important manufacturing state, and its 330,000 manufacturing employees are still less than half the number in Massachusetts, which trails in overall population. But the highly diversified Florida industries have moved from a gross output valued at $116 million in 1940 to $2 billion in 1960 and close to $4 billion in recent years. Products range from food products, chemicals, paper and pulp to printing, metals, cigars, fashions, electronics, and aerospace—a base, it would seem, for continued healthy growth. And aside from its military bases, the state also does well in defense contract awards, which have been close to $1 billion a year of late.

▪   Mining. Some $300 million worth of minerals are taken out of the Florida earth each year, the biggest being phosphate (used for fertilizer and other products). The dual problems of pollution control and outside competition are starting to imperil this industry. But how serious the loss would be to the overall Florida economy is open to question. The phosphate industry employs only 5,000 men—in a work force of over 2 million. Compared to what Florida may rightfully hope for in even a single new field, like oceanography, such a loss would not be serious.

Even with cuts in space and defense work, however, an essential question of Florida's economy is whether it is too overheated—expanding too fast, gobbling up land too fast for the good of the people, or the natural Floridian environment. A step behind California, but entirely predictably, Florida has begun to consider the problem. In 1970, a University of Miami–sponsored conference came to the general conclusion that there may already be too many people living in south Florida. (One expert said the state should brace itself "for a coastal Main Street extending right down from Georgia and right on up again to Alabama.") The threats to Florida's vital "river of grass" were depicted as pollution, deadly pesticides, "exotic plant" imports, and ill-considered development plans. The best solution, everyone agreed, would be to stop overpopulation. How to do it was another question. "The human animal," Dade County Metro Commissioner Earl Starnes said, "is probably the most migratory animal on the face of the earth. . . . How we begin to reduce this migration, I don't know."

As a modest first step, efforts were mounting in the state legislature to cut down on appropriations for industrial recruitment. Participants at a water management parlay at Miami Beach in 1971 suggested a land-and-water use program, with the banning of additional drainage and reflooding of some areas already dried up for development. Another suggestion is statewide rationing of the limited fresh water supply, with each community obliged to zone in a way that would prohibit development beyond a certain level. Even the Greater Miami chamber of commerce was starting to think, according to a 1971 report, about an end to development in Dade County. One could almost hear old Henry Flagler turning over in his grave.

Old and New Politics in the Retirement State

The demographic profile of Florida has been so completely transformed by northern migration that there is little profit in reviewing old political patterns other than to note that the state was implacably Democratic from Reconstruction to the late 1940s. The flood of new postwar voters has created, in the words of University of Florida professor Manning J. Dauer, "a giant suburbia" where the people have little awareness of past politics and few local ties. On the map, one can identify a conservative urban belt that looks like a horseshoe and votes like a midwestern suburb. It runs from Fort Lauderdale and West Palm Beach on the east up the coast to Daytona Beach and the Cape Kennedy area, then across through Orlando in center-state to St. Petersburg on the west and down the Sun Coast to Fort Myers and Naples. The exception in the pattern is Tampa, with an industrialized-unionized economy fairly unusual in the state today. In the far southeast, there is Miami, which votes strongly Democratic for President, supports liberals in Democratic primaries, and can be characterized politically, as Dauer puts it, as "a piece of Manhattan Island which floated off 1,000 miles to the south and is warmed by the waters of the Gulf Stream." And up in the northern Florida, conservative-segregationist politics on the model of neighboring Deep South states are still practiced. Northern Florida also differs from metropolitan Florida as a place where one still hears people talk about "my [state] senator," "my representative," "my [county] commissioner."

Florida's political structure up to 20 years ago, as V. O. Key put it, was "an incredibly complex mélange of amorphous factions," virtually all centered in the one (Democratic) party. Anyone who got the itch and was willing to pay the filing fee could file for governor; the proof of political pulverization was offered in 1936 when 14 men entered in the first Democratic primary for governor and the winner had only 16 percent of the whole. Not until 1970 did Florida Democrats coalesce into a unified state organization —a reaction to stinging defeats the party had suffered in 1966 and 1968.

Ideologically, Florida's Democrats have been a mixture of conservatives and middle-of-the-roaders with an occasional maverick liberal enlivening the scene. A typical conservative was Sen. Spessard Holland, governor in the 1940s and Senator from 1947 to 1971. Holland was a states' righter, a citrus and big-business man, a chief sponsor of legislation giving the states title to tidelands. But he also led the fight against the poll tax, which he helped abolish in Florida in 1937 and for the U.S. through constitutional amendment in the 1960s. Claude Pepper, who held one of the state's Senate seats from 1937 to 1951, was a strong liberal—but by 1950, as it turned out, just a little too far left for the state. George Smathers challenged and defeated Pepper in the primary, accusing him of "softness" on communism and being an advocate of "treason." *

Florida's Democrats rarely engaged in the demagogic race-baiting typical of many Deep South states. But in the postwar era many of their candidates found ways to tap the strain of ultraconservatism evident in Florida life —a kind of mixture of fiscal conservatism, antigovernmentalism, opposition

* This was the same campaign in which Smathers reportedly told an audience of yokels: "Are you aware that Claude Pepper is known all over Washington as a shameless extrovert? Not only that, but this man is reliably reported to practice nepotism with his sister-in-law, and he has a sister, who was once a thespian in wicked New York. Worst of all, it is an established fact that Mr. Pepper, before his marriage, practiced celibacy." (Smathers now disputes authenticity of the speech, but not everyone is convinced.) Twelve years later Pepper made a comeback as a Congressman from Miami, a liberal stronghold where his strong social welfare stands are welcome. Smathers stayed in the Senate for three terms, working unremittingly for special economic interests and against migrants and other unfortunates, becoming a confidant and business partner of Bobby Baker and standing up for the likes of Dominican Republic dictator Rafael Trujillo—a record brilliantly and scathingly reviewed by Robert Sherrill in his *Gothic Politics in the Deep South* (Grossman Publishers, New York, 1968). The Long Island newspaper, *Newsday*, reported in 1971 that shortly after Smathers left the Senate in 1969, he paid $20,000 for $435,000 worth of stock in Aerodex, a Florida defense contractor frequently accused of "shoddy work, poor records, and fraud." Smathers reportedly "led a behind-the-scenes Congressional campaign" in 1967 to prevent cancellation of a big Air Force contract with Aerodex.

to any kind of welfare, nationalistic patriotism, and mild racism. Outside of the Miami and Tampa areas, the Democratic congressmen have been well to the right of center. Through the mid-1960s, most Democratic governors were in the same mold, the major exception being LeRoy Collins (1954–60), a native of Tallahassee who nevertheless made every effort to smooth the way to peaceful integration in the state and backed other progressive measures. (In 1968, when Collins ran for the U. S. Senate, he beat a more conservative opponent in the Democratic primary but was subsequently tagged as "liberal LeRoy" by his Republican opponent, Edward F. Gurney, and decisively defeated.)

Florida's governor from 1965 to 1967 was Haydon Burns, a former mayor of Jacksonville, who made the big time by campaigning against the Civil Rights Act of 1964 and defeating Miami's liberal mayor, Robert King High, in the 1964 primary. In office, Burns arrogantly channeled state purchases and insurance business to his campaign contributors, accepted a loan of an airplane from a grocery chain, and engaged in similar shenanigans. Even an avowedly racist line in the runoff primary failed to save Burns from defeat by High in 1966. But High lost the general election to Claude Kirk—the first Republican governor of the century.

For the Republicans, there has been little danger of an ideological split, since virtually all their supporters are avowed conservatives. Modern Florida Republicanism got its start in the 1940s under C. C. Spades, the first state chairman with interests broader than waiting for a Republican President to pick up local patronage. Major effort was put into the urban counties receiving the big migration from the North, with the first payoff in 1948 when Dewey carried Pinellas (St. Petersburg), Sarasota, Palm Beach, Broward (Fort Lauderdale) and Orange (Orlando). With Eisenhower leading the ticket, this urban base was expanded on for solid Republican victories in 1952 and 1956, and with Nixon heading the ticket, again in 1960 and later in 1968. Pinellas County was the seedbed of the Republican renaissance and the place which elected a young William Cramer to Congress in 1954, the first Republican Congressman from Florida since 1875. In 1962, a second Republican Congressman was added—Gurney, from the Orlando district—and in 1966, a third was added—J. Herbert Burke from Fort Lauderdale. Kirk's election as governor came the same year, Gurney's Senate election in 1968. At the same time, the Republicans had taken over local offices like county commissions, school boards, and sheriff's positions in several urban counties; in the wake of reapportionment, Republicans upped their membership in the Florida legislature from 8 percent to 35 percent between 1965 and 1967.

Between 1950 and 1970, Republican registration in Florida grew by a 12-times factor, from 60,665 to 711,090, while Democratic registration approximately doubled, from 1,006,580 to 2,024,387. The Democrats still represented 73 percent of the registered voter pool and outnumbered GOP registrants in all but two counties (Sarasota and Pinellas). But survey data showed that 40 percent of the voters really considered themselves independents and registered with either party in order to participate in the closed party primaries for local city and county elections.

One factor sustaining Democratic registrations was increased total Negro enrollment—up from 48,157 in 1946 to 295,229 in 1970. Incredibly, the Republicans had less black registrants in 1970 (11,961) than in 1946 (15,877).* Blacks represent only 1.7 percent of the Republican registration, but 14 percent of the Democratic, making them a factor to be reckoned with in the Democratic primary. Happily gone are the days of repression of would-be black voters. In 1951, the state NAACP chairman, Harry T. Moore, was killed by a dynamite explosion that destroyed his house, and as late as 1964, two of the 67 counties—Lafayette and Liberty, in north Florida—had not a single black registered. Now, black registration lags only 4 percentage points behind the percentage of the statewide voting age population that is Negro. The gap is attributable to cultural-educational factors rather than repression.

Another sign of political maturity is increased voter participation. The turnout in Presidential years hovered between 30 and 40 percent of eligible adults through the 1940s, but then rose rapidly to 50.0 percent by 1960 and 55.8 percent in 1968—still about 10 percentage points behind other big urban states, but the highest in the southeastern U. S. and a vast improvement over earlier years. Both the Negro vote and increased party competition have contributed to the change.

According to Professor Dauer's studies of recent voting patterns, the type of county most likely to go Republican is urban, high-income, with higher proportions of northern retirees in the over-65 age bracket. The exceptions are Dade County (Miami) and Hillsborough County (Tampa), where there is a heavy labor union vote. On the whole Democrats continue to do best in counties with low urbanism, low per capita income, low levels of education, and less retirees. In 1968, when Wallace picked up 28.5 percent of the statewide vote, he ran strongest in poor rural counties, whether in northern or southern Florida. Humphrey ran barely ahead of Wallace, with 30.9 cent of the vote, contrasted to Nixon's 40.5 percent. The Republican Presidential winning streak has been unbroken since 1952 except for 1964, and even then Goldwater got 48.9 percent of the vote and would probably have won if he had not upset many retirees on the Social Security issue.

Given their strong upward surge in the urban counties that now dominate Florida politics and their election of a governor in 1966 and a Senator in 1968, the Republicans had all right to face the 1970s in a spirit of high expectation, anticipating a total take-over of Florida government. But instead, they bombed out in the 1970 elections, losing the governorship, failing to win a U. S. Senate seat that seemed all but assured them early in the campaign, and slipping in the legislature. Part of the reversal had to do with the

* For this, the Republicans would seem to have no one to thank but themselves. No significant effort has been made to include Negroes in party activities, or to shape policies friendly to them. The 1964 GOP gubernatorial nominee, Charles R. Holley, campaigned on statements such as these: "Government's function should be limited to protecting the possessors of property against those who possess nothing." Governor Kirk, who long appeared to give at least tacit support to civil rights progress, in 1970 saw it to his political advantage to defy the federal courts and engage in a crude form of interposition to delay school integration in Manatee County. After a pseudocomical struggle with federal marshalls for physical control of the school-board offices, Kirk was slapped with a federal contempt of court order and threat of $10,000 a day fine and finally backed down.

Democrats' newborn unity and nomination of politically moderate nominees, fresh faces on the statewide scene who could not be tarred and feathered as "ultraliberals" like the losing statewide Democratic candidates in 1966 and 1968. But more than anything else, the Republican defeat was attributable to fierce internecine battles—a culmination of the pettiness and factionalism that had afflicted the Republican organization for several years—and the mercurial, buffoonish personality of Claude R. Kirk, Jr.

The Kirk story is a sad one, because of all he might have accomplished for his party and for Florida. He is a man of immense energy and native brilliance, who in fact opened the way for several innovative and promising new directions in state government—a story we will review later. But in the end, it would all be vitiated by the quixotic, flamboyant, and seemingly irresponsible way Kirk handled himself. Born in 1926 in California, educated in Illinois and Alabama, Kirk moved to Florida in the 1950s, made $500,000 exercising stock options for the American Heritage Insurance Company of Jacksonville (a firm he helped found), and in 1960 started in politics as state chairman of Democrats for Nixon. After that he switched parties, ran against Senator Holland in 1964, and lost badly, but bounced back to win the governorship in 1966 with virtually no program.

It did not take Floridians long to discover that their new governor was a master of surprise and showmanship. He appeared at his inaugural ball with a beauteous blonde whom he introduced only as "Madam X." She turned out to be Erika Mattfeld, 32, a German-born Brazilian divorcee, whom he married not long after and took off to Europe for a whirlwind honeymoon (as it later turned out, paid for out of state development funds). Within hours of taking office, Kirk announced he would launch his own private "war on crime" by hiring former FBI agent George Wackenhut and his detective agency; by the time this unique foray in private lawmanship was finished, there was an embarrassing debt of $550,000 Kirk had to cover from private contributions, although the episode helped persuade the legislature to set up a bureau of law enforcement and a number of Florida's worst local officials, including sheriffs, were forced out of office. In August 1967, when H. Rap Brown appeared at a Jacksonville "black power" rally, Kirk showed up unexpectedly, grabbed a microphone from Brown, and said, "Welcome to Florida. Are you here in good spirits? . . . I don't want any talk about guns." Brown's angry message was effectively defused and even the young blacks in the audience were captivated by the governor and his smile—which has been described as having "50,000 candlepower." Some likened Kirk to Florida's state bird —the gregarious flamingo, known for its scarlet wings and theatrical flair. Kirk's reputation as a ladies' man and drinker (with big bags below his eyes, bespeaking a life of dissipation) did nothing to detract from the image.

Kirk refused to let his life-style be limited by an official $36,000 state salary plus contingency funds of $13,000 and $159,000 to operate the governor's mansion. A rented Palm Beach house, Duck's Nest, cost him about $1,000 a month. Soon he was jetting all over the U.S. in chartered aircraft (generally Lear Jets) in a quest for the Republican Vice Presidential nomination. The Florida Development Commission placed a $90,000 contract with William Safire, a Madison Avenue public relations expert and political strategist, in a thinly disguised effort to get Kirk on the national ticket. And for a time, the Florida Republican party was intoxicated by Kirk and gladly paid his mounting bills for the Lear Jets, entertainment, hotel suites, and flowers for politicians' wives. Then the party cut Kirk off, and as the bills kept pouring in, the Miami *Herald* reported that money raising had become almost a full-time job for some of Kirk's staff and friends. A 1969 state audit of the governor's office disclosed controversial expenditures such as overpayment for travel and spending without statutory authority for flowers, credit cards, Christmas cards, and food. Some $1 million to $3 million "campaign funds" were collected by Kirk in his first three years in office, and even the official records of a $500-a-year "Governor's Club," which a court forced him to disclose publicly, showed receipts of $420,680 between April 1968 and January 1970. The 233 contributors to the fund included 47 who received Kirk appointments to state boards, committees, and commissions, 18 who were liquor licensees, 31 architect-engineers (most with state contracts), and 20 construction contractors eligible for state road projects.

The irony of it all, as Miami *Herald* writer Clarence Jones observed in late 1969, was that Kirk was the one politician who might have "beaten the system"—the commonplace Florida practice of governors turning to private contributors with a stake in state action, or a desire for contracts, in order to run their offices and political machines. Kirk had entered office with few commitments. His 1966 primary was a low-cost walkaway; in the general election the big-money people were eager and anxious to contribute to Kirk's cause just to make sure that Robert King High, who had defeated conservative incumbent Haydon Burns in the Democratic primary, wouldn't win. Just by upsetting High, Jones observed, Kirk had "paid off the mortgage, free and clear." Yet within two years he was struggling with huge debts and forced to accept money from special interests on a scale rarely paralleled among American governors.

The final denouement of the Drama Kirk came in 1970, when he became the would-be kingmaker in an attempt to make defeated U. S. Supreme Court nominee G. Harrold Carswell of Tallahassee the Republican nominee for the U. S. Senate. Already running was Rep. William C. Cramer, the eight-term St. Petersburg Congressman and virtually the founding father of the present-day Republican party in Florida. Kirk had long been jealous of Cramer's power and at one point attempted, unsuccessfully, to purge him as Republican national committeeman. U. S. Senator Edward Gurney also had good reason to resist the elevation of the more prestigious and more able Cramer to the Senate. So only a few days after the Senate rejected Carswell, Kirk and Gurney held long conversations with Carswell and put him into the Senate race. (White House political aide Harry Dent played a considerable role in the Carswell decision to run, though the official White House line was neutral; President Nixon had, in fact, earlier urged Cramer to run in the first instance.)

At first, Carswell's entry looked like a brilliant move, and many Florida Democrats and Republicans saw Carswell sweeping triumphantly to election on the wave of bitter Southern resentment about the Senate's rejection of his court nomination. But Carswell turned out to be a paper tiger, unskilled in the ways of politics, and ideologically, it was impossible to get to the right of Cramer.

So it came about that Cramer crushed Carswell 2–1 in the Senate primary. In the meantime, the Democrats did an unusual thing. They rejected several old party war-horses (like former governor Farris Bryant, running for the Senate, or former attorney general Earl Faircloth, running for governor) in favor of two bright young state legislators: gubernatorial candidate Reubin Askew, from Pensacola on the northern panhandle, and Senatorial candidate Lawton Chiles, from Lakeland in the citrus belt. Askew appealed to many voters by arguing that the tax laws favored corporations and special interests, at the expense of the little man, and should be changed. Chiles decided the voters had become frustrated by slick advertising campaigns and remote politicians. So he made a calculated decision to spurn large newspaper and television advertising; instead he undertook a walking tour, over 1,000 miles from one end of Florida to the other, meeting some 45,000 common citizens.* As he explained after his election: "The common theme of everyone I talked with—young and old, rural and city, black and white—was that 'no one listens to me, my vote doesn't count, no one cares any more, government is so big and far away.' My walk did say to these people that I cared." Chiles, of course, was no fool; he knew his walking tour would get him a lot of free time on television news programs, and it did. But the fact remains that in the year of the homogenized, prepackaged, standardized slick media campaign, a man who rejected it all could win.

Cramer ran an orthodox campaign based on heavy television advertising and importation of big Republican names to campaign for him, including Attorney General John and Martha Mitchell and President Nixon himself. But the tone of the Cramer campaign was strongly negative—asking voters to "join the fight to stop cop killers, bombers, burners and racial revolutionaries who would destroy America."

Chiles and Askew both won strong victories (53.9 and 56.0 percent respectively), built on an amazing combination of the rural cracker vote from northern Florida and the support of cosmopolitan Dade and several other urban counties. (Only two counties with any significant population—Orange and Sarasota—voted for both Kirk and Cramer.) The new-found Democratic unity was underscored by the fact that the first governor from the panhandle in living memory was elected, joining in a ticket with three successful nominees for cabinet posts from Miami. It was the first time Dade County had elected *anyone* to the cabinet, and two of its successful nominees were Jewish as well.

---

* The visitor to Chiles' Washington Senate office finds a memo of the celebrated walk—a pair of old hiking boots, with holes worn in the soles—adorning his mantle.

No one can say yet whether the 1970 elections represent just a momentary delay in Florida's evolution to Republicanism, or a lasting return to a middle-of-the-road kind of Democracy. But it does seem likely that the Republicans will have to produce some leaders of higher quality, and more positively oriented party platforms, if they hope to capitalize on the strong demographic trends running in their favor.

State Government: Demise of the
"Pork Choppers" and a New Constitution

Florida's state government, just a decade ago one of the most archaic and unrepresentative in the Union, has recently undergone fundamental reform in both the legislative and executive branches and can face the 1970s with renewed confidence in its capacity to deal with fundamental problems.

The malapportionment of the legislature, based on restrictive provisions of the state constitution, was so egregious that by the 1961 session, 12.3 percent of the state's people could theoretically elect a majority of the senate and 14.7 percent a majority of the house. The five most populated counties accounted for more than 50 percent of the population, but only 14 percent of the senate membership. In the house, every county was guaranteed at least one representative; this meant that to have equally populated districts, because some counties were so lightly populated, the house would have to have been expanded to 1,600 members.

The infamous Florida "Pork Chop Gang"—a name brilliantly conceived by Tampa *Tribune* editor James Clendinen—emerged in 1953 when 22 rural senators, enough to exercise control, banded together to fight any reapportionment which would imperil their seats. Their districts encompassed about half of Florida's land area but only 18 percent of the population; for the most part, they came from counties along the Georgia and Alabama borders and in central Florida. Not only did they succeed in blocking reapportionment efforts (which began in earnest under Governor Collins in 1955), but they put their mark on broad areas of state legislation. According to a 1962 estimate, Pork Chop counties with 18 percent of the population accounted for about 15 percent of state taxes but received 30 percent of state disbursements. State racetrack revenues were apportioned on an equal basis among the 67 counties, which in some small counties was enough to pay all county government expenses; big landowners, of course, were among the principal beneficiaries. Road funds and state institutions were both channeled in disproportionate amounts to thinly populated counties, and the Pork Choppers blocked legislation authorizing urban renewal and government reorganization.

In addition, the Pork Choppers were closely tied to special interests—banks, private utilities, truckers, the liquor industry, timber and paper mills, small loan companies, and the like—and were easy prey for the lobbyists, since they lacked sophisticated constituencies that could catch them in irregularities.* There was a glaring absence of effective lobby registration or conflict of interest legislation, and Senator Chiles (who was then in the state legislature) recalls that when such matters were first brought up in committee, they were just laughed at. When he proposed making a statewide district for clean air and water regulatory purposes, a pulpwood lobbyist told him exactly how many votes he would get in committee—three out of 11. Seven of the eight who voted against the bill had a pulpwood plant in their districts.

Between 1955 and the mid-1960s, nine special legislative sessions were devoted primarily to reapportionment. But rural control held solid until a court test was finally resolved by the U. S. Supreme Court. A three-judge federal court then ordered new elections, in 1967, under a one-man, one-vote reapportionment plan proposed by Professor Dauer of the University of Florida. Under the new formula, there was a maximum population variation of 5 percent in districts for 119 house members and 48 senators. In the special election, the share of Republican seats, centered in the urban areas, escalated instantaneously from 7.9 percent of the combined membership to 35.3 percent. As of 1971, the Republicans continued to hold 38 house and 16 senate seats, or 33.7 percent of the two-chamber total. Now urban legislators are frequently elected to the house speakership and senate presidency, both powerful officers with authority to appoint all committees. The first house speaker in Florida history from Dade County, Richard Pettigrew, a progressive in the Askew-Chiles mold, was elected in 1971.

It would be naive to think, of course, that the influence of special interest lobbies has withered away in the wake of reapportionment. Lobbying may be lower-keyed, and there has been some drying up of the supply of free drinks and meals and other forms of "entertainment" to legislators in Tallahassee. But there is increased contact by business and labor groups in members' home areas and campaign contributions are more important than before. On the conservative side, the most potent forces are Associated Industries, the big utilities (Florida Power Corporation, Florida Power and Light), the Farm Bureau, bankers, liquor interests, chain stores, the race tracks, and the phosphate council. Much weaker in influence, but still real factors, are the Florida Education Association, the AFL-CIO, and representatives of retired people. The new legislature, Professor Dauer reports, reflects the wishes of urban areas—but the suburban areas in the urban counties, far more than core-city liberal groups, which are a distinct minority on a statewide basis. There is no big urban state in America where organized labor is so weak as in Florida. Only in Miami, Tampa, and Jacksonville are there enough union members to have any appreciable political impact, and overall only 13.6 percent of the nonagricultural workers are organized, ranking Florida 46th among the 50 states on a scale of unionization. Florida in 1944 became the first state to enact a right-to-work law, and most of organized labor's legislative effort is to hold the line and if possible improve the

---

* Some urban legislators, notably from Jacksonville and Pensacola, anxious to get in on the gravy train, also felt themselves politically secure enough to join the Gang.

levels of workmen's compensation. Labor officials told me they were often headed off in the legislature by conservatives' threats to put more teeth into the right-to-work law, thus impeding the small level of unionization achieved to date. Union officials have little influence over their members in elections; in 1968 there were some industrial plants where 100 percent of the work force seemed to be for Wallace (sometimes, of course, with the approval of conservative local union leaders).

Reapportionment has, however, brought fundamental reform in state government that would have been inconceivable before 1967. Governor Kirk, to his lasting credit, called the legislature back into session three times until it finally approved a brand-new constitution for submission to the people in November 1968. The new charter, replacing an antiquated 1885 version amended more than 150 times, was approved and went into effect in January 1969. It created an office of lieutenant governor, permitted the governor to seek a second four-year term, gave official status to the elected state "cabinet" (of which more shortly), provided limited home rule for cities and counties, required the consolidation of almost 200 executive agencies and boards into no more than 25 departments, and made the legislature a continuing operation with annual sessions, the power to appoint standing committees, authorize special studies, and the like.

By 1969, the legislature was operating smoothly with regular presession meetings to deal with prefiled legislation; it had one of the most competent legislative staffs in the country (working both for a legislative service bureau and on permanent staffs of the standing committees), and a sophisticated computer tracking system on all current bills, cross-keyed to existing Florida statutes. In 1971, when the Citizens Conference on State Legislatures issued its index on the capacity of legislatures "to perform in a functional, accountable, informed, independent and representative manner," Florida actually scored fourth highest among 50 states—an unthinkable achievement a half decade before.

In 1969, with Kirk's encouragement, the new legislature enacted the most far-reaching reorganization of the executive branch since the Civil War. Acting under the mandate of the new constitution, the multitudinous state boards and commissions were consolidated under 22 departments. The powers of the governor were greatly increased by giving him executive authority over half the departments. In other states, that might have seemed a minor reform, but in Florida the elective cabinet has had extraordinary power, vis-à-vis the governor, because its members are not only elected directly, but have a right of succession (which the governor lacked until 1969) and also sit ex officio on many boards and commissions. Some called it the "seven governor" system, because the six others—the secretary of state, attorney general, comptroller, state treasurer, superintendent of public instruction, and commissioner of agriculture—could and did build their own independent political bases, served an average of 12 years, knew the bureaucracy and legislative maneuvering better than the average governor, and could oblige him to share responsibility with them as a collegial executive. Like the malapportioned legislature, the system was tailor-made for entrenchment of special interests. The comptroller, with wide regulatory power over banks, was often supported by them in campaigns and thus indebted to those he was elected to oversee. The same was true of the state treasurer in respect to the insurance industry, the attorney general in regard to the bar, the agriculture commissioner in regard to big farming interests, and the like.

The reorganization, enacted into law by a coalition of Republicans and urban Democrats, could not and did not abolish the cabinet, but it greatly enhanced the governor's powers by making several major departments and functions his sole or primary responsibility. Kirk used these powers to put outstanding people into key posts like pollution control; Askew, in turn, took the bold step of appointing a black woman, Mrs. Athalie Range, to head the new department of community affairs. Later, Askew startled the South by endorsing school busing as an undesirable expedient, but one perhaps necessary to reach the goal of a desegregated society. (In Florida, as in many Southern states, massive busing, forced by court decisions, took effect in 1971.) Kirk, despite his many shortcomings, can be credited with bringing fresh blood and fresh ideas into state government, often in ways not generally recognized. Political influence in road building was vastly curtailed by staggering the terms of highway commission members and putting a professional engineer in charge of day-to-day operations. Florida became the eighth state to set up a transportation department, and Kirk started "Operation Concern" to attack problems of the poor in the big cities. As Roger Williams observed in *The Nation* in 1970, Kirk turned out "ideas and programs as a pinwheel gives off sparks."

The Askew administration, in contrast, was left with the more difficult job of increasing the quality of state services and effecting a reform of the highly regressive Florida tax system. Askew was the first governor of modern times to run on a platform advocating new taxes (specifically on corporate income), an act of candor and courage which alone should win him a place in the history books. Once in office, Askew first got the legislature and then the people in a statewide vote to authorize a corporate income tax.* Even that reform, however, will be just a first step. Florida is prohibited by its own constitution from levying taxes on personal income, and it has a high sales tax. The sales tax is often advertised as a way to put the bite on tourists, but the fact is it also penalizes low-income families and relieves richer people of the major tax burden that even a flat-rate income tax would effect. Florida also lacks any state inheritance tax, and for those over 65, there is a homestead exemption (property that cannot be taxed) of $10,000. Not until 1971 did Florida place even a moderate severance tax on its phosphate industry or other minerals.

The net result of all this is (1) gross inequality and (2) inadequacy of tax base and services. A 1969 study showed that the share of various taxes paid by Florida families earning less than $3,000 a year was $10.3 million for higher education, but their children received only $6.4 million in benefits.

---

* The affirmative popular vote on the tax was an unprecedented 70 percent, leading knowledgeable observers to rate Askew the strongest governor of modern Florida history.

The tax share for education of families earning more than $10,000 was more
—$25.7 million—but received back $41.5 million, or 161 percent of what
they paid in, in benefits. When one thinks of the squalor in which many of
Florida's poor live, the appropriation of their meager incomes to educate
rich people's children is little short of criminal.

There is little doubt that Florida could raise its taxes, assuming they
were appropriately apportioned, without great pain. State and local tax collections as a percent of personal income in the late 1960s were only 3.2
percent, ranking 31st in the nation. The level of services delivered is accord-
ingly low: on a per capita basis, 45th in the U.S. for public welfare, 48th
for highways, 28th in support of local schools, 41st in support of higher education. Low teacher salaries triggered a statewide teachers' strike in 1968,
finally prompting Kirk to ask for and get an increase in the sales tax to 4
percent to increase public school spending. The state has done quite well in
the junior college field, providing 25 two-year institutions for college and
vocational education, located within commuting distance of practically every
home in the state. About 140,000 students are enrolled. But state university
expenditures have risen very slowly by national standards and the American
Association of University Professors reported that the University of Florida
has become "not a state-supported but a state-assisted" institution, which
depends on foundations and Washington for more than half its budget.

Florida was also one of the last states to commit itself to the Medicaid
program and, until 1969, funded it at the most minimal level. Effective regulation of public utilities has been hampered by lack of funds to investigate
rate structures. The state government has permitted innovations like metropolitan government for Jacksonville and on a more modest basis for the Miami area, but the state constitution puts very strict millage limitations on
real property taxes and the cities are desperate for more financial aid from
the state government—which is slow in coming. Not until 1969 was general
authority given for local governments to undertake urban renewal. But a progressive drift in Tallahassee was reflected in two innovative "no-fault" bills
passed in 1971—no-fault divorce and no-fault auto insurance.

The prison system is regarded by many as the most shockingly deficient
area of Florida government. Caught in a population boom that has placed
heavy demands on all levels of government, Florida found it easy to put
last priority on prison development and has begun to reap the whirlwind.
No new prison construction has taken place since 1960, despite a 35 percent
population increase and spiraling of the crime rate. (Florida ranks third
in the nation in per capita murders and other violent crimes, eighth in
crimes against property.) In 1967, a wooden barracks of World War II vintage
at the state prison farm in Jay caught fire, killing 38 inmates; the subsequent
state investigation, however, led to no new funds for prison construction. In
1971, the state prison at Raiford, designed to hold 2,400 prisoners, held
3,600. Many cells were packed with twice as many prisoners as their design
capacity. Hundreds of men slept on the floors and the problems of sexual
assaults and other violence reached crisis proportions. When a rebellious

group of 700 prisoners staged a sit-down on the prison recreation field, guards peppered the convicts with birdshot and some machine-gun bullets, wounding 63. Of this "Lincoln's Day massacre," as the inmates called it, Florida corrections director Louie L. Wainrights said: "I gave the order to shoot. . . . I did it to protect the inmates themselves." Now corrections officials are asking for two new 600-man state prisons, costing $21.5 million.

The state's new attorney general, Robert Shevin of Miami, has taken a special interest in the prisons since his days in the legislature and is pressing hard for new construction and reforms. His proposals include improved medical services, conjugal visits for inmates, overhaul of the restrictive parole system, abandonment of the old road-camp system, and state take-over of local jails. The latter proposal gained new supporters in January 1971 when a 17-year-old runaway was strangled to death at the vastly overcrowded Dade County Jail. A local judge declared that the jail was a "jungle . . . where living conditions are unsafe" and ordered local officials to move out a third of the prisoners within 10 days.

The Sunshine Laws

To wind up a review of Florida government, three bright spots may be noted. The first is nicknamed, quite literally, the Sunshine Law. Enacted in 1967, it stipulates that any meeting between Florida officials must be open to the press. Decisions made at secret meetings, either at the local or state level, are simply illegal. According to court interpretations, there are *no* exceptions to the law outside of limited "judicial deliberations." Some mayors and state officials even had the doors removed from their offices so that they could not be accused of holding secret meetings in violation of the law. There has been some thought that Florida may have gone overboard with its Sunshine Law, but it is certainly a fresh change from the secretive ways that continue in many parts of American government—generally to the disadvantage of the public.

Secondly, there is Florida's "Who Gave It?–Who Got It?" campaign finance law, first enacted in 1951 and a pioneer state statute in trying to get to the roots of money in politics. Interest in the law began when word spread that Smathers and Pepper, though they said they had spent only $100,000 each in the 1950 Senate primary, actually spent in the neighborhood of $1 million each. Then came the Kefauver Crime Committee hearings and a revelation that three men had met in a Jacksonville hotel room to split the $450,000 cost of the 1948 gubernatorial campaign of Fuller Warren. One was W. H. Johnston, a race-track operator with connections to the Al Capone mob; the second was C. V. Griffin, one of Florida's most prosperous citrus growers (an industry that seems always to receive favorable treatment at the hand of state government); the third was Miami Beach multimillionaire Louis Wolfson, who would later land in jail as a result of convictions for stock manipulations. The St. Petersburg *Times* took up the crusade for a full disclosure law and almost single-handedly embarrassed the legislature into passing the 1951 law.

Twenty years later, what is the law's record? Certainly, the voters have been given an impressive body of knowledge of where money comes from and goes to in campaigns. Candidates must designate exclusive campaign treasurers to receive and disburse all money in their behalf; campaign contributions must be put in a designated depository bank within 24 hours of receipt; frequent public disclosure of money received and spent must be made, and there is a prohibition against last-minute contributions to avoid publicity. Though the state government simply receives and files the reports, the press has open access to them and prints frequent stories on candidates' budgets and support. Enforcement, left somewhat in limbo when the law was first passed, later was tightened up when individual citizens were permitted to file complaints. The attorney general was obliged to decide in each case if prosecution of violators was warranted.

What the 1951 law did not do was set dollar limits on campaign expenditures, and as time went on, they climbed and climbed. In 1960, Farris Bryant won the governorship at a cost of $768,000, but in 1964, Haydon Burns's election expenses were $1.1 million. In the two 1966 primaries, Burns spent another $1.4 million in an unsuccessful effort to win renomination for a full four-year term. In 1970, Republican Jack Eckerd spent $1.1 million trying to upset Kirk in the primary. But by this time, the weight of expenditures was getting to be too much, even for the politicians. The secretary of state, Tom Adams, helped some to blow the whistle when he pulled out of the 1970 gubernatorial campaign, announcing that to raise the needed money to become governor, he would have needed to commit himself to so many privilege-seekers that his hands, as governor, would be tied.* And then Adams named the interest groups: road contractors who can profit from contracts and work-change orders, polluting industries anxious to avoid installing expensive control equipment, suppliers of automobiles and other major equipment to the state, land developers interested in having road interchanges or new roads built near their property, industries looking for tax breaks, liquor license applicants, engineers and other professionals anxious to snag state business.

Thus the way was paved for a 1970 law setting strict limits on expenditures: in gubernatorial and U. S. Senate races, $350,000 for any candidate in the primaries, and a like amount in the general election; for other statewide offices, $250,000 in each category; for the U. S. House, $75,000 in the primaries and the same in the general election; for legislative, county, and city offices, $25,000 in each category. The law was circumvented in 1970 by some candidates who spent big sums before its effective date, but it held down spending in the fall election and is likely to have a major dampening effect on escalating campaign costs in the future. Another important provision forbids any individual from contributing more than $1,000 for local, $2,000 for congressional, or $3,000 for statewide contests.

* Adams ran for and was elected lieutenant governor instead.

No one pretends that the Florida statutes tell all and control all in the campaign money field. More money than reported doubtless gets spent. Cash contributions and outlays are exceedingly difficult to trace. Contributors of record may simply be conduits for other people's money. Nevertheless, no state has yet enacted a better law than Florida, "the land of the fast buck and the quick deal."

Strangely, another long-time Florida institution—the Presidential primary, in effect since 1904 and updated in 1955—has failed to win the national attention that Florida's big state status would seem to merit. One reason may be that it has involved only election of delegate slates (often pledged to a favorite son); another has been the relatively late date in the primary season (late May). But the 1971 legislature session changed the law fundamentally. Under legislation sponsored by House Speaker Pettigrew, provision was made for a true preference poll, with the Florida secretary of state, subject to review by a bipartisan committee, placing the names of all potential Democratic and Republican Presidential nominees on the ballot. To stay off the ballot, a prospective candidate has to swear in an affidavit that he is not running and does not intend to run. Delegates, also elected in the primary, must vote for the preference poll winner in their own congressional district (or in the case of at-large delegates, the statewide winner). Favorite-son candidacies and uncommitted delegates are no longer possible, so that the state parties are drawn closer to their national counterparts.

Most interesting of all, the new Florida primary, set for March, puts the state in competition with New Hampshire for early attention in the Presidential election year. (The New Hampshire primary is only one week earlier.) A much larger and more representative state than New Hampshire, Florida could turn out to be a bellwether—not only for the Sunshine belt of states like Texas, Arizona, and California, which it typifies in many ways, but for the nation as a whole. And none of the candidates is likely to complain about the chance to spend part of the winter away from the snow of New Hampshire, under sunny Florida skies.

Lingering Poverty

Few states can match Florida's stark contrasts between wealth and poverty, opulence and squalor. It came home to me most clearly when I spent one morning touring the facilities at Cape Kennedy, where billions were being poured into the moon shots, and that same afternoon saw a sick farm laborer's child, flies swarming around its little body, lying on a bed at the Old Top Labor Camp near Winter Haven. From the glitter and ostentatious consumption of Miami Beach, one need not travel far to find thousands of retirees waiting in their drab, sun-drenched little towns for the next Social Security check. From select and sumptuous Palm Beach, it is but a few miles to some of the most wretched migrant labor camps in all America. Within the same state are places like Coral Gables, Boca Raton, and Naples, where the *average* home value is more than $30,000, and scrubby north Florida or Panhandle counties like Liberty or Holmes, where the average value is around $5,500.

Florida's net income has crept up steadily, from 74 percent of the national average in 1928 to 88 percent in 1960 and close to 100 percent today. But much of the rise can be attributed to the tremendous wealth of a narrow cross section of upper-income Floridians—a privileged 15 percent of the population. The average Florida worker gets substantially less pay than the national average, partly because over 50 percent of the work force is in three low-paying industries—agriculture, retailing, and services. And a quarter of the state's households have cash incomes of less than $3,000 a year—a higher incidence of poverty than 40 other states.

In a way, the poverty that lingers on from one end of Florida to the other is a kind of legacy or remembrance of the days when Florida was so much more a Southern state. But today, the worst ravages of poverty are to be found among a newer class: the migrant workers. Their life of deprivation was an almost secret one to most Americans until that Thanksgiving weekend of 1960 when Edward R. Murrow's familiar face appeared on CBS stations across the country, proclaiming a *Harvest of Shame* that in historical perspective seems like a kind of introduction to the poverty wars of the 1960s. With a dusty road and battered trucks and milling people behind him, Murrow intoned:

> This scene is not taking place in the Congo. It has nothing to do with Johannesburg or Capetown. This is a shape-up for migrant workers. The hawkers you hear are chanting the going piece rate at the various fields. This is Belle Glade, Florida. This is the way the humans who harvest the food for the best-fed people in the world get hired. One farmer looked at this and said, "We used to own our slaves, now we just rent them."

From Murrow that night, America learned that every ambitious plan of the New Deal and Fair Deal and all of America's postwar affluence notwithstanding, there were still in America "the forgotten people, the underprotected, the under-educated, the under-clothed, the underfed . . ."

Ten years later, in 1970, another television crew and commentator—this time from NBC—visited Belle Glade. For all the rhetoric of the 1960s, little seemed to have changed. There were heart-rending scenes of migrants telling how "we 'bout starved to death down here in Florida," of mothers without money to feed their children or buy them shoes to go to school, of the degradation and shame all felt in their poverty. And still, the raw statistics: average migrants' annual income of $891, or $2,700 for a family of four, $900 below the official poverty line; migrant worker camps, filled with decrepit shacks lacking running water or toilet facilities, many long since condemned but still in operation; illegal child labor in the fields, with half the migrant youngsters failing to get to seventh grade, 80 percent never seeing a high school classroom; a migrant farm worker's life expectancy of 49 years, compared to 70 for other Americans. Estimates of the number of Florida migrants who work the long eight-month growing harvest season of the state range from under 100,000 to 200,000; of these, NBC reported, 55 percent are Negroes driven there when machines replaced them in the cotton fields of the Old South, another 35 percent are Mexican-Americans migrated from Texas.

A few white Northerners are migrants, too, and a scattering of West Indians, the latter remnants of big importations of offshore workers which Florida resorted to between 1943 and the late 1960s. One of the most delightful characters I met in Florida was Ralston O'Connor, a genial, in-charge Jamaican who bossed a racially mixed migrant camp near Winter Garden, his personality obviously overcoming any resentments the Anglos and Mexican-Americans in his camp might have felt against him as a black man. O'Connor's camp was a thoroughly human place, with some showcase families like Felix Sanchez and his family from Nebraska, who make $500 a week during the height of the season and live in pleasant, middle-class surroundings in their $24-a-week rented house . . . or almost as well off, Mrs. Edna Thompson, a proud and dignified black woman with doilies and flowers on her color television set and pictures of Jesus, Martin Luther King, Jr., and Robert F. Kennedy on her walls.

For every happy story, there seem to be a dozen sad ones. Many of the worst have come out of Immokalee, Florida, a flat, sprawling town a few miles inland from Naples on the southwest coast. This self-proclaimed "watermelon capital of America" has been visited by congressional investigating committees and the Collier County officials are finally consenting to food stamp programs, seeking subsidized government housing and supporting a drive for a hospital. But no reforms were in sight as recently as 1969, when the New York *Times*'s Homer Bigart preceded the first Senate investigators and reported on Smith's Camp, "a dozen or more windowless plywood shacks, all without toilets or running water, all painted a dull green and facing a dark slough choked with bottles and trash." There were two privies, he reported, but "the latrines are unspeakably filthy, seats and floors smeared with dry defecation. So the people use the woods. . . . A spigot planted in the ground provides water [which] is foul smelling and foul tasting. The only apparent amenity is the naked electric light bulb hanging from the ceiling of each shack." In 1968, when outpatient examinations were given to a sample population of 23 migrant children in the Immokalee area, two were found to have pneumonia, one tuberculosis, 14 upper-respiratory infections, 11 ironic deficiency anemia, one otitis, three diarrhea, three impetigo, one ascariasis, one sickle cell trait, and one hydrocephaly.

One of the terrors of migrant life, one learns, are the crew leaders, who have power of life or death over each migrant's job, often misrepresent working conditions and pay a worker can expect, make big profits personally and have been assailed by a spokesman for migrants as "thieves, con men, fraud artists and alcoholics—any one or combination." Another weapon of enslavement is the company store, which extends credit to workers, sells groceries and other essentials at a markup, and in effect holds men in bondage to the end of each season.

The work of a citrus picker is no easy one; a man must be in top condition, able to go up a 30-foot ladder and handle a 90-pound bag on his shoulder. If he hurts himself, or becomes ill, he has none of the recourses—unemployment compensation, hospitalization, disability insurance—available to other workers. Work in the cane fields can be even tougher. There, some growers transport workers in large cage-type trucks normally used for sugar cane, with up to 120 men standing upright on a single load. A few years ago, one of these trucks turned over and 20 men died. Now legislation forbids the practice, but it reportedly continues in some areas.

Normally, there are plenty of jobs around January of each year for the migrants where the winter vegetables are maturing around the shores of Lake Okeechobee, south of Miami and in Collier County. But in 1971, the crops failed to mature at all—the result of a year-long drought that had lowered the water table in southern Florida, and even more serious, unusual hard freezes in the vegetable fields. Suddenly, 15,000 or more workers, recently arrived from Texas or the Deep South, where they had lived during the autumn months, found themselves without a hope of income. Then, three amazing events occurred. First, the state's new governor, Reubin Askew, appealed to President Nixon for assistance under the Diaster Relief Act—legislation earlier used only in the event of calamities like floods, hurricanes, and earthquakes. Second, a fledgling farm workers' organization—the Organized Migrants in Community Action (OMICA)—sent 500 migrants to Key Biscayne to demonstrate near President Nixon's winter White House, where he was relaxing for a weekend. The result was a spate of new coverage by the White House press corps, which could hardly miss the incongruity of starving farm workers assembling at gold-soaked Key Biscayne. Peaceably, the migrants knelt in prayer to ask "God and President Nixon" for help "because we are desperate," and then piled into their 10 old buses and 15 ancient cars and chugged back to their labor camps. The third amazing event was that President Nixon actually released several million dollars in disaster funds to tide the migrants over their emergency period.

Thus an immediate emergency was averted, and the Florida migrants began to learn the advantages of organization. OMICA is not technically a labor organization, but its leader, 33-year-old Rudy Juarez, has increasingly been referred to as "the César Chávez of the Florida migrant workers." It is probably just a matter of time until real labor organization starts in Florida, with the AFL-CIO—which took an interest a few years ago but decided the battle too tough—lending a helping hand. Friends of the migrants maintain that wages could be *doubled* for pickers and marketplace prices raised only a penny for a dozen fruit or for an average pound of vegetables. The trend also seems to be toward less and less annual migration of the field workers to the north; as this trend continues, it will be easier to school and organize the migrants, and easier for them to demand more in their permanent home communities. The 1971 legislature began some response to migrant needs by placing all agricultural workers under workmen's compensation and establishing mandatory standards for farm labor contractors.

Another hopeful straw in the wind is the newborn feeling of corporate responsibility on the part of some of the big companies who own thousands of acres of Florida groves and vegetables lands. The biggest of these is the Coca-Cola Company, which bought out Minute Maid orange juice in the early 1960s and owns or controls more than 30,000 acres of Florida citrus groves. Coca-Cola was mightily disturbed to find the slumlike conditions in some of its Florida worker camps revealed in the 1970 NBC News special. After complaining bitterly to the network, Coca-Cola quickly made public an ambitious program to put proper plumbing and other improvements in its housing, to establish permanent social-service centers for child care and pre-school training, and raise the wages of its 300 full-time grove workers to $2 an hour. Critics pointed out it should hardly have taken 10 years for Coca-Cola to learn about the problems of its own workers, but the fact was that the company was indeed finally taking action—and that it might well set a standard for the entire industry.

Metropolitan Florida

Florida's most explosive growth has come in four distinct sections: the Gold Coast, Jacksonville, Tampa–St. Petersburg and Orlando. These population figures tell the story:

Metropolitan Areas	1940 Population	1970 Population	Increase
Gold Coast			
Miami (Dade County)	267,739	1,267,792	+ 374%
City of Miami	172,172	334,859	+ 95
Fort Lauderdale–Hollywood			
(Broward County)	39,794	620,100	+1,458
Fort Lauderdale	17,996	172,196	+ 857
Hollywood	6,239	106,923	+1,614
West Palm Beach			
(Palm Beach County)	79,798	348,753	+ 337
West Palm Beach	33,693	57,375	+ 70
North			
Jacksonville metropolitan area	210,143	528,865	+ 151
Jacksonville	173,065	528,865	+ 206
Orlando			
(Orange, Seminole counties)	92,378	428,003	+ 353
Orlando	36,736	99,006	+ 170
West			
Tampa-St. Petersburg (Hillsborough, Pinellas counties)	272,000	1,012,594	+ 272
Tampa	108,391	277,767	+ 156
St. Petersburg	60,812	216,232	+ 256

Outside of these, smaller pockets of growth have occurred in Brevard County (home of Cape Kennedy), which rose 1,325 percent—from 16,142 to 230,006—between 1940 and 1970, more than half that growth in the 1960s alone; Escambia County (Pensacola), up 326 percent to 243,075 in 1970; Leon County (Tallahassee), up 227 percent to 103,047; and Alachua (Gainesville), up 171 percent to 104,764. But the most significant growth has been on the Gold Coast, which in 1940 accounted for 20 percent of the entire Florida population, in 1970 for 33 percent. Tampa–St. Petersburg held relatively stable around 15 percent of the state population over 30 years, and Jacksonville actually slipped from 11 to 8 percent. As of 1970, seven out of every 10 Floridians lived in a metropolitan area; in 1940, the figure had been four out of 10. The sunshine state, it turned out, was also a very urban state.

Miami Metro, the Beach, and Crime

The image of Miami and its satellite communities has been described as one of sun, sand, sex, and sin—depending on one's age and proclivities, possibly sin, sex, sand, and sun. Arnold Toynbee, in his *Cities of Destiny*, lumped Miami together with Los Angeles as a hive of "renters," a place without singleness of vision, an eruption that has yet to attain even "the rudiments of soul." It is certainly the newest of the great cities of America—only 40 years ago it was just coming out of its wild boom-and-bust days of real-estate speculation, and not many decades before that it had been a mere assemblance of tents and sun-warped wooden shacks on the bank of a muddy tropical river. The carnival atmosphere of the 1920s still holds on, especially across the bay in Miami Beach; there the chief huckster of recent years has been Hank Meyer, whose flamboyant promotion ideas culminated in the Miss Universe contest of the 1960s and in persuading Jackie Gleason to produce his shows at the Beach. Meyer is an engaging man with a quiet flash to his clothes who can perform that marvelous feat of talking on two telephones simultaneously; with my own eyes I saw him do it, and Gleason was on the end of one of the lines.

But the Hank Meyer of today has some surprising observations, chief of which is that Miami is about to receive a great infusion of creative talent in medicine, the law, and arts—"not the kind of razmatazz I've thrown out for 20 years." Some believe this is already happening, and point to the strong efforts of Miami University to build its reputation in marine science, law, medicine, and inter-American studies and cast off its image as "Sun Tan U."

Efforts at consolidation of government functions by the 27 separate municipalities of Dade County have led to more political participation and maturity. Acting under broad new home-rule powers granted by the state government, the county in 1959 enacted a form of metropolitan government —a sort of truce between those who wanted full consolidation and some local governments showing prickly independence. The metro government got wide powers over functions like sewers, water supply, transportation, and central planning, while the municipalities were allowed to keep their own departments like police, fire, garbage collection, parks, and that most delicate and important of all—zoning. Schools, hospitals, and airports had been put under countywide supervision more than a decade earlier. During the early years of metro, a coalition of municipalities tried to destroy the system. But it was saved by a coalition that included the areawide newspapers, the downtown chamber of commerce, the League of Women Voters, and even some members of the academic community. They not only turned back the attack but strengthened the metro charter in 1963. There are nine council members elected directly by the people (from separate districts); one of these serves as the metro mayor. A professional county manager runs the show on a day-to-day basis. In a 1969 report, the University of Miami faulted the metro government on inadequate water, sewer, and tax equalization policies, but praised it for having "transformed an obsolete and anachronous commission form of government into a first-rate, high-caliber administration" which had undertaken many valuable public projects.

Miami's very newness and lack of encrusted power structure may have made it possible for the area to embrace metro government. The mobility of population, the tourist atmosphere, the no-party system, the weak position of labor and minority groups, and the dominance of the big Miami papers all made possible an important step forward that older American cities were rejecting left and right in the same years.

Economically, Miami is much more mature now, too. Tourism remains king, bringing in hundreds of millions of dollars each year and supporting about a fifth of the population. Retirees, many people of substantial wealth, provide an important source of external income. Huge construction and service payrolls are associated with hundred-million-dollar apartment and shopping center complexes like Century 21, Fontainebleau Park, and Leisuretown. There are several *thousand* small manufacturing plants. The Miami International Airport, one of the busiest in the world, is the hub of travel with Latin America, the Bahamas and Caribbean. Miami benefits doubly from the airport because of the huge aircraft-maintenance facilities there; the airlines in fact qualify as Dade County's biggest employer. Latin-American visitors help swell Miami's $3 billion in annual retail sales, and amazingly, many of them also come for a visit at the Miami Beach hotels. With the new Oceanographic Laboratory of the Environmental Sciences Administration, combined with the U. S. Bureau of Commercial Fisheries' Tropical Atlantic Laboratory and the University of Miami's Institute of Marine Sciences, Miami sees itself as the world's leading center of undersea study. To all of this one can add huge incomes from horse and dog racing, the business generated by the Orange Bowl game each winter, Dade's standing as the fourth-richest agricultural county of Florida, and one has the picture of one of the luckiest metropolitan areas, in terms of economic growth, anywhere in the U.S.

Befitting its newness, Miami lacks an entrenched power structure. Of the 17 leading white community figures the University of Miami identified in its 1969 report on "Psycho-Social Dynamics in Miami," only four had been raised in Florida. The rest came from assorted places from the northeast as far west as Minnesota. They identified the Miami Club—the city's only club with a limited membership—as the place where the most significant "behind the scenes" decisions were made. Everyone agrees that the Knight-owned and -run Miami *Herald* is one of the most influential papers in any U. S. city (and one of the best, too).* Other influential organizations in Miami include Florida Power and Light, Southern Bell Telephone Company, and the wealthy independent operators like Mitchell Wolfson, whose business holdings range from television stations to bottling plants.

With all these things going in their home town, Miamians are prone to complain when outsiders dismiss the entire city as a tinseled tourist haven or old folks' home. But that appurtenance across the bay, Miami Beach, still fits the old billing. Since 1915, the Beach has grown from a sand bar and clotted mangrove swamp, two-thirds inundated at high tide, into a Babylon on the sea such as the world has never seen—362 hotels, 29,627 rooms, a permanent population of 87,027, a peak winter population of close to 1,000,000. Now the first hotels, built by Carl Fisher and the other early developers, have been torn down to make place for new hotels lined up along the ever receding beach.

Driving across Biscayne Bay toward Miami Beach of a summer afternoon, seeing the huge cumulus clouds and thunderheads blown in by the trade wind and the line of gleaming white hotels below, there is a feeling of pristine beauty about the Beach. Closer up, one has to be pleased with the hundreds of thousands of flowering plants that border every street, the lovely lagoons and waterways, the snipped perfection of everything. But then comes the realization: this is no longer a beach, it is a teeming city. The great hotels are packed together so closely the Atlantic is not to be seen beyond them. Collins Avenue, the main drag, becomes a traffic-snarled nightmare, and on some stretches, neon is everywhere. And inside the big hotels, there is the grotesque lobby decor, the very worst our civilization has produced in ostentation and bad taste; one needs only to think of the Fontainebleau, too haughty to put up a sign outside with its name, announcing in its blurbs that it is "in all the world . . . in any season . . . the most beautiful resort hotel . . . anywhere!"

For many years after the war, each season would bring the grand opening of a new hotel extravaganza . . . the Deauville, Eden Roc, Doral, Americana, Carillon, Casablanca . . . the list goes on and on. Then, in the mid-1960s, the applications for new hotel building permits suddenly fell to zero. The building that did take place was in condominium apartments. The recession starting in 1969 began to cut back on business. People began to worry about the South Shore slum where—as the Miami *Herald* wrote "aged Jews have come for many years to die in the sun, where Cuban immigrants are now settling, and where governments park buses and garbage trucks along the bay." The constant erosion of the beach—by sand washed away by the tides, and by hotels greedily building out to the water line and beyond—became a hot political issue, with the mayor of Miami Beach, Jay Dermer, openly fighting

---

* The morning *Herald* and evening *News* share joint production facilities in a handsome bayside building informally dubbed "the Taj Mahal of U.S. journalism." The *News*, a Cox-owned paper, has only a fraction of the *Herald* circulation (almost 400,000 daily, covering the entire Gold Coast and Florida down to the Keys).

for public access to all beaches and for a $35 million beachfront reclamation project by the Corps of Engineers (with at least part of the cost paid by local bonds). The hotels finally backed down and agreed to permit public beach access in return for the Engineers' reclamation project.

And then there was the worry about competition. Neighboring island resorts like the Bahamas and Jamaica could offer American tourists a touch of the truly exotic, uncrowded beaches and casino gambling.

In a super resort city like this, the question inevitably arises of hotel owners' manipulation and control of politics. Observers find it passing strange that councilmen often spend $50,000 to win offices that pay only $7,000 a year, and that so many zoning variances are made for high-rises to go up without the legally required parking spaces. Hank Meyer, long close to the hotel interests, claims that their owners often live elsewhere and have but a shadow of the political clout of the Beach's retiree class. "Anyway," he says, "the hotels are so affluent and have such big egos that they end up fighting with each other" instead of putting up a strong common front. Mayor Dermer saw it differently, calling himself "the first mayor not controlled by the hotels." Dermer retired voluntarily in 1971 and was succeeded by former Dade County Mayor Chuck Hall, a man less likely to tangle with the hotel interests.

A new chapter opened for Miami Beach when the Republicans decided to hold their 1968 National Convention there. There was without question a numbing effect from the indulgent world of sun bathing and pool loafing and girl watching and rich eating at the Beach that made it not difficult for the Republicans to bypass the burning issues and choose a bland new Richard Nixon as their candidate. But what looked like a bizarre convention city choice in 1968 became commonplace when the Democrats decided to hold their 1972 convention at the Beach. The reasons were dual: some of the nation's best hotel accommodations (outside of Chicago, to which the Democrats obviously could not return), and Miami Beach's superb setup in terms of physical security. (It would be feasible, for instance, to screen *all* traffic at the causeways to the mainland.)

A Republican official who spent months in Miami Beach planning for the 1968 convention told me that the political establishment of Miami Beach met in the back room of Mendelsohn's kosher meat market to make its decisions, like determining that Elliott Roosevelt would be mayor of Miami Beach, and then a few years later, that Elliott Roosevelt would no longer be mayor. The Fontainebleau, he said, was the scene of some very fancy gambling where thousands of dollars changed hands—but it was all in private, not house games. (Condoned gambling has largely disappeared from the Beach since the Kefauver investigations two decades ago.) The prostitutes, my source said, were certainly in evidence, but as far as could be determined, on their own. The Miami Beach owners and managers, Jewish in background like 80 percent of the Beach's population, were out to make all they could off the convention but acted honorably, kept their commitments, and did not engage in gouging. The real offender was organized labor, which did all service work on double time and got its pound of flesh from everyone. Electricians, for instance, insisted on charging $18 an hour for overtime—just on standby! One had only to talk a few minutes with one of these privileged workmen to find he was a rabid Wallaceite, railing against "them niggers" and all their sins.

Just north of the Beach is the gaudy, unincorporated strip known as North Bay Village, a glaring example of the kind of vice and corruption that has long existed through the presence of Mafia hoodlums living and operating openly in Florida. Illegal activities centered around the 18 motels of North Bay Village's "Motel Row" were the subject of a 1968 state legislative investigation and subsequent suits filed by the state's attorney general. The legislative investigation found that North Bay Village had become nationally known as a place for prostitutes to operate with virtual impunity, that underworld figures could live or meet there safely, and that the police department was so corrupt that it should either be overhauled from top to bottom or abolished altogether, with the police function turned over to the Miami metropolitan public safety department.

But to hear the story told by Florida law enforcement officers, North Bay Village is but a small part of the Mafia story in southern Florida. Miami has become the home, vacation spa, meeting place, and retirement goal of a large assortment of top underworld figures. Some are the lesser lights: the two-bit hoodlums sent south while things cool off in Boston or Baltimore, the Mafiosi rank and file being rewarded with a brief vacation. But the distinctive figures in Miami criminal circles are the major leaders of syndicated organized crime in America—practitioners of the kind of crime that involves a large organization, top accountants and lawyers, national- and international-scale operations. They have not selected Miami as a place for an especially great amount of overt criminal activity, but rather as their rest and retirement center, and as a place to invest in quite legitimate business ventures. A favorite investment property is Miami hotels.

This is not to say that Miami is devoid of serious crime. The city is a major point of distribution of stolen goods (gems, watches, etc.) from the whole East Coast. A large amount of narcotics is said to enter the U.S. through Miami—including, recently, cocaine from Latin America, often brought in by young American students who are paid $1,000 to make one flight with packets of the drug concealed on their bodies. Across the Florida peninsula, Tampa's Mafiosi are reportedly linked with those in New Orleans, controlling illegal gambling along much of the Gulf Coast.

Florida's top hoodlum for many years has been Meyer Lansky, the Bernard Baruch of syndicated crime in the U.S.A. Born Maier Suchowljansky in Russia in 1902 and brought to this country by his parents in 1911, Lansky is not a member of the Mafia establishment at all because of his Jewish birth. But he has amassed a personal fortune estimated at between $100 million and $300 million; as Nicholas Gage wrote in *Atlantic* in 1970, Lansky in his chosen field of work "is as much a visionary and innovator as Andrew Carnegie, Henry Ford and John D. Rockefeller were in theirs." Until a 1971 departure—possibly permanent—for Israel, Lansky lived unobtrusively in a Miami beachfront apartment near the Fontainebleau, constantly watched by the FBI (on whom he actually depended for protection). One reason for the sudden move abroad, it seemed, was Lansky's anticipation of a federal grand jury indictment in March 1971 accusing him and three others, including Morris Lansburg, Miami Beach's biggest hotel operator, of illegal gambling in connection with the Flamingo Hotel in Las Vegas.

Miami: City Proper and the Cuban Story

The habitable area of Miami and its surrounding cities is confined to a narrow strip of high-lying land bordered by the Everglades on the west and Biscayne Bay on the east. Aside from Miami Beach, the big attractions of Biscayne Bay are beautiful Virginia Key and the self-proclaimed island paradise of Key Biscayne, the latter made famous in recent years by the aforementioned Richard M. Nixon. (Nixon's home there, purchased from his old Capitol Hill friend, former Democratic Senator George Smathers, is next door to that of his discreet and loyal companion, Miami businessman Charles Gregory [Bebe] Rebozo.) Biscayne Bay literally swarms with pleasure craft of every description and also has man-made Dodge Island, where the big cruising ships, increasing sharply in number in recent years, tie up after their runs to Nassau, San Juan, and St. Thomas.

Right beside the docks is Miami's verdant Bayfront Park, remembered as the spot where Franklin Roosevelt barely escaped assassination in 1933. Behind that, one sees the high white buildings, old and new, which constitute "downtown Miami"—a rather disappointing center, now aging and almost incongruous in a region where everything else is so new and filled with exciting modern architecture (like the startling buildings of the University of Miami campus). Downtown Miami, like parts of the Beach, recalls the culture of the first waves of retirees, a generation ago now.

Back from downtown and the bay, the city of Miami proper stretches toward the Everglades in a monotony of white stucco checkerboard blocks. Through the heart of this, headed due west on its way toward Tampa, is the Tamiami Trail, Route 41; within the city limits it is S.W. 8th Street, which with nearby West Flagler Street forms Little Havana, the heart of the Cuban exile colony in the United States. Miami's Cuban population has risen from 22,000 to substantially more than 300,000 since 1959, when Fidel Castro stepped off the Sierra Maestra and into power. One out of every four residents of Miami is a Cuban today. "Cuba has been relocated here," some say. The immigration has also had a profound impact on the city. Before the Cubans came, the downtown area was in financial decline, much property vacant, landlords and businessmen retrenching. Quickly, all that changed, as tens of thousands of Cubans poured in, renting and beginning to restore old buildings, starting their own shops and little businesses, adding a new vibrancy to Miami's life.

One reason for the Cubans' success has been the $300 million and more that the federal government has poured into relocation assistance.* But the more important reason has been the Cubans themselves. Literally, they are the cream of Cuban society. Of those who worked in Cuba before the revolution, the average annual income was four times the average on that island. Over 12 percent had been to college, almost two-thirds lived in Havana rather than small towns and villages, and they included a disproportionately high percentage of doctors, lawyers, teachers, and other professional people. Among these educated Cubans, the period of menial labor in Miami—lawyers washing dishes, engineers tending gardens, physicians working as lowly helpers in hospitals—was short-lived indeed. And then the entrepreneureal middle-class Cubans went to work, and by 1971 there were some 4,500 Cuban businesses scattered along Miami's palm-lined streets, ranging from cigar factories, boat yards, restaurants, gas stations, and repair shops to markets, bakers, undertakers, cinemas, night clubs, auto dealers, and chemists. The Cuban labor pool suddenly propelled Miami to third place in the U.S. (after New York and California) in garment manufacturing. A special Census report released in 1971 showed a stunningly low Cuban unemployment rate of 2.0 percent—compared, for instance, to rates three times as high for Mexican-Americans and Puerto Ricans.

Miami's gain from the Cuban influx has been more than economic; one might say the Cubans have brought spirit to a pretty soulless city. A new center for Cuban studies prospers at the University of Miami. Music conservatories, ballet schools, and exile theater groups teach culture with a Latin accent to Cuban and American youngsters alike. And then there is the gastronomic input. What other city, Frank Soler of the Miami *Herald* asks, boasts over 70 restaurants that serve *congri, paella,* and *frijoles negros con arroz?*

Gone now are the days when the Miami Cuban colony seethed with plots and vainglorious schemes to reconquer the homeland and drive Castro from power. The Bay of Pigs, in matter of fact, settled that, and despite their bitter disappointment, the Cubans know it, and more and more are readjusting to a new and probably permanent life in the United States. Hope of a return to Cuba delayed Cubans' entry into the mainstreams of American politics, but now, as more and more pass the five years' residency requirement and obtain their American citizenship—and thus the right to vote—this is changing. At first it had been assumed Cubans would simply vote for all anti-Communist candidates—one reason Richard Nixon won a clear majority among them in 1968. But in the 1970 elections, they cast about 60 percent of their votes for the Democratic candidates for Senator and governor, indicating a strong ingredient of social liberalism.

*Without condemning the aid for Cubans, some ask why the U. S. government has never been willing to provide similar relocation assistance for its own great class of displacees, the nine million Negroes forced out of the South in this century. As a group, their economic and cultural deprivation far exceeds that of the Cubans. "You say you're anti-Communist and you get the best of everything," Ohio's Gov. John Gilligan told me. "The Negroes should be treated as political refugees." The cost of the refugee program has been spiraling to a Nixon administration budget request of $144 million for fiscal 1972. Americans on welfare get less than Cuban refugees requiring assistance. The Miami *Herald* editorialized in 1971: "We think that there should not be a separate welfare program for Cubans, but one program under which they and all other needy of this country receive the same concern and care."

Miami is flanked on the south by the exclusive, independent city of Coral Gables (42,494) and the once-independent town of Coconut Grove, a Bohemian-flavored enclave of winding streets and estate homes. The metropolitan area has 189,763 Negroes, largely confined to three areas including the Liberty City-Brownsville district where rioting broke out during the 1968 Republican Convention. The city's record on race relations is a strangely mixed one of token integration and heavy community-police tensions, perhaps fitting to Miami's character as a half-Southern, half-Northern city.

Up the Gold Coast, and Beyond

The major landmarks as one moves up the Gold Coast are Fort Lauderdale, now one of the great yachting centers of the Western world and growing in affluent splendor, and that exclusive island, Palm Beach, where the cream of Eastern society still winters.

North of the neon-lined Gold Coast, Florida's flank to the Atlantic begins to take on much of the untouched air of pre-Flagler days. Only occasional seaside villages and small cities disturb the sight of ocean pounding onto uncluttered sandy shores. But there are exceptions: Cape Kennedy (with its urbanized spinoff around Cocoa Beach), Daytona Beach (striving for metropolitan status, but still offering a magnificent 23-mile arc of beach that rates among the hemisphere's best), St. Augustine (steeped in Spanish history), and finally the new metropolis of Jacksonville (not far south of the Georgia border).

Out at the tip of Cape Kennedy, which juts like a sharp elbow into the Atlantic, stands the delightful old Cape Canaveral Light House, flashing its warnings to ships at sea as it has for more than a century. But the placid scene began to change in 1948 when the government decided to use the Cape area as a base for launching long-range guided missiles. A long series of experimental launchings began in 1950. On December 6, 1957, while millions watched and listened, a Navy Vanguard missile, carrying America's hopes of regaining some world prestige after the surprise of Sputnik, misfired on its launching pad and exploded in a burst of flame. But seven weeks later, on January 31, 1958, the first American earth satellite, Explorer I, was launched from the Cape.

That same year, the National Aeronautics and Space Administration was created and a massive program of expansion and construction got underway at the Cape. Unmanned satellites and space probes, bearing such names as Echo, Tiros, Telstar, Early Bird, and Explorer, were launched. In 1961, President John F. Kennedy proclaimed the national goal of landing a man on the face of the moon before the end of the decade, and manned space flight progressed through Projects Mercury and Gemini to Project Apollo. The guided missiles came to be called launch vehicles. And they got bigger and bigger, starting with Redstone, which developed 78,000 pounds of thrust at liftoff, and growing into the awesome Saturn V, which developed 7.5 million pounds of thrust at liftoff. A Redstone launched Alan B. Shepard, Jr., America's first man in space, on his May 1961 suborbital flight. A Saturn V launched Neil A. Armstrong, Edwin E. Aldrin, Jr., and Michael Collins for the July 30, 1969, lunar landing by Armstrong and Aldrin, who thus became the first human beings to walk on the moon.

The impact of the Space Age on the Cape was tremendous. A local newspaper began to carry a daily banner line: "Fastest Growing County in the U.S.A.," and, indeed, it was. Brevard County's population soared from 23,653 in 1950 to 111,435 in 1960; by 1970, it had more than doubled again, to 230,006. In 1950, there were 9,500 housing units, in 1970, 77,700. But even at that some workers were commuting from as far away as Daytona, Vero Beach, and Orlando with round-trip travel each day of up to 150 miles. Schools had to resort to double, even triple sessions as enrollment rocketed from 4,163 to 59,000.

The burgeoning Brevard population was due not only to NASA's own personnel, but workers for the multitude of contractors working on various stages of the rockets—companies like Boeing, North American Rockwell, Bendix, RCA, McDonnell Douglas, IBM, General Electric, the Martin Company—plus TWA and Pan American for base maintenance. Riding up and down the elevators inside the huge Vehicle Assembly Building,* one has the feeling of viewing America's whole aerospace industry, working on the Saturn stages in layer-cake fashion.

In a national paroxysm of memorialitis after the assassination of President Kennedy, Cape Canaveral was summarily renamed Cape Kennedy, thus expunging from the maps a name dating from the earliest Spanish explorations. And the Cape gradually found itself forced to share the glory of the space age with NASA's Manned Spacecraft Center in Houston, which directed the design, development, and testing of manned spacecraft, plus selection and training of astronauts and earth control of manned flight. The Cape was reduced to playing the role of a glorious launching pad. According to one scarcely credible story long in vogue at the Cape, Houston's selection for manned space flight control was part of the arrangement under which Lyndon Johnson, of Texas, agreed to become John Kennedy's running mate in 1960. The least expensive alternative might well have been to locate the manned flight control at the Goddard Space Flight Center in Maryland, which was already laden with sophisticated satellite control equipment.

As the U.S. entered the decade of the '70s, there were rapidly mounting doubts about the need for post-Apollo manned space flight, the appropriateness of vast expenditures for a space program in the face of great unmet human needs on earth, and the future role of the Cape, where the government, by now, had invested some $1.5 billion in facilities. The result was a long, slow letdown in the national space program. NASA and its contractors, which had a peak employment of 26,500 working at the Cape in 1967–68 (the height of Apollo flight preparation), slipped to 15,000 by early 1971. And

---

* With 125 million cubic feet of space, the building is the second largest enclosed space in the world, trailing Boeing's 747 plant at Everett, Washington.

the totals seemed headed even further downward. As early as 1969, the first dry rot showed up in the Brevard County economy. Houses went on the market at sales prices well below their previous values, and off the palm-lined highway between Cape Canaveral, Cocoa Beach, and Satellite Beach, boarded up motels, empty parking lots, and half-filled office buildings told a story of woe.

Meanwhile, Florida politicians and Cape-area boosters began in 1970 to lobby hard for the space program's next big project: the space shuttle. It will be a two-stage reusable rocket resembling a huge jet plane in some respects. Launched vertically like a rocket to loft men and equipment into orbit, it is to be piloted back to earth and will land horizontally like an airplane. Despite the Cape's hunger to share in some of the $9 to $12 billion which will be spent on the shuttle, other areas were bidding for it with equal ferocity— White Sands in New Mexico, Edwards Air Force Base and Vandenberg Air Force Base in California—and the issue remained in doubt in 1971.

Whatever happens to the spaceport, residents of all political persuasions have made clear one desire: they would like the Cape's old name back. Florida Congressmen are sympathetic and have been sponsoring legislation, so far unsuccessful in a Democratically controlled Congress, to restore that name assigned four centuries ago by the first Spanish explorers, Cape Canaveral.

Jacksonville (World's Largest City), *North Florida, and Panhandle*

The largest city in the world, in terms of area, is Jacksonville (1970 population 528,865), once the famed "Gateway" to Florida in the heyday of the passenger railroads, now desperately seeking a new identity and a new future.

Jacksonville is an oddity. It is isolated in the northeast corner of the state; tourists fly over it on the way south instead of passing through it in train or car. It serves the back country of northern Florida and not much more. It is dominated by the conservative attitude of nearby southern Georgia. Yet the city embarked on a daring experiment in consolidated metropolitan government with a strong mayor-council form of government. What Jacksonville has already done, many other cities are likely to copy in the 1970s. Few American cities have had such a renewal of spirit in recent times.

It was not always so. After World War II, Jacksonville experienced a steady decline, with urban white population moving to the suburbs and abandoning a deteriorating center city to low-income blacks. The governments of Jacksonville and surrounding Duval County were so fouled up that the area had the reputation of being one of the worst governed in the nation. All Jacksonville high schools were disaccredited in 1964 for lack of financial support. Property was assessed for tax purposes at only 20 percent of fair market value. And then, in 1966, came the final blow to Jacksonville's self-esteem: television station WJXT investigated city insurance dealings and disclosed practices which led to the indictments of two of the five city commissioners, four of the nine city councilmen, the city auditor, and the recreation department chief. The city tax assessor discreetly resigned.

With that, the public rebelled. Citizen leadership brought about establishment of a local government study commission, which proposed merging Jacksonville (pop. 200,000) with surrounding Duval County (pop. 325,000) in a consolidated metropolitan government. A group called Citizens for Better Government recruited 1,000 workers to push doorbells for the proposal, and it carried on Aug. 8, 1967, by a 2–1 margin. In a twinkling, Jacksonville grew from 30 to 827 square miles.

Under Mayor Hans Tanzler, a raw-boned, six-foot, five-inch dynamo, the city moved on race relations (once among the worst in the state), tax relief, improved fire and police protection, ambulance service, and cleaning up the horribly polluted St. Johns River, which bisects the city. Rebuilding of the moldering downtown, which had actually begun a few years before, proceeded apace, and now both banks of the river gleam with new buildings.

A television station polled citizens in March 1969 and found that 64.1 percent accepted the new government. In March 1970, the figure had risen to an astounding 78.8 percent.

There had been fears in the black community that its political power would be severely diminished by consolidation; blacks constituted 44 percent of the city before the metro plan and only 23 percent after. Yet a majority of blacks supported consolidation. In the old city council, there were two blacks. In the new city council, consisting of 19 members (14 elected from districts, five at large), there were four blacks, including one elected at large. Two of the blacks were women, the first ever to serve.

The success of blacks in elective politics is all the more amazing in light of Jacksonville's long history of racial violence. The Ku Klux Klan, its membership fed by rural migrants from south Georgia and north Florida, was strong in the city and sent shock troops to St. Augustine, 35 miles to the south, when Martin Luther King, Jr., was demonstrating there for open accommodations legislation. Jacksonville synagogues were frequent targets of terrorists in the early 1960s. And in 1971, Panther-type organizations of young blacks were involved in ugly clashes with local police accused of brutal tactics by both blacks and some responsible white leaders. A breadth of antiblack sentiment was evident in George Wallace's winning 36.3 percent of the Jacksonville vote in the 1968 Presidential election.

The most powerful man in Jacksonville and arguably in Florida is Edward W. Ball, head of the billion-dollar Alfred I. DuPont estate, long an archconservative and potent force in Florida politics. Juanita Green, the Miami *Herald*'s outstanding urban affairs editor, once described Ball as "arch conservative, segregationist, antilabor, antibureaucrat, anti-big government." He is also against the income tax and all forms of government regulation, both of which have caused him no little trouble.

"Mr. Ball," as even longtime friends call the octogenarian, had the good fortune to be the brother of a schoolteacher who married Alfred I. DuPont. Things were never the same again. DuPont feuded with his brothers in Wilmington and left to do good works with some $30 million in Florida in the late 1920s. DuPont died in 1935 and Ball took over as dominant trustee of an estate that came to own vast holdings of timber land throughout the state, the Florida East Coast Railway, a telephone company, and 30 banks in the Florida National group. The late Mayor Robert King High of Miami once testified: "You can hardly drive 50 miles in Florida—in any direction—without encountering some facet of the DuPont estate."

Ball guided the estate with a heavy hand and saw it increase in value to well past the billion-dollar mark, perhaps twice that. He was the key figure behind George Smathers' defeat of Claude Pepper in 1950, close to Governors Farris Bryant and Haydon Burns, and helped Edward Gurney beat Leroy Collins for the Senate in 1968. Ball was also a leading figure in getting Florida to adopt a sales tax instead of any kind of income tax, and thus can be given important credit for the state's regressive tax structure.

His intractability finally caught up with him in the late 1960s. During a long strike by railway workers, unions complained to Congress of the feudal character of the DuPont estate which, among other things, held 30 banks under an exemption to the Bank Holding Company Act of 1956. The act forbids companies owning two or more banks from simultaneously holding nonbanking businesses, and it defines ownership as having an interest of 25 percent or more. In 1966, following a bruising battle behind the scenes on Capitol Hill, Congress closed the loophole and Ed Ball lost his biggest fight for the estate.

Or did he? Ball worked out a plan for a DuPont holding company to take over an interest of 24.9 percent in each of the 30 banks, then spread out the remaining interest to small stockholders. He won an initial favorable ruling from the Federal Reserve Board on this plan. But under continuing federal pressure, he resigned in 1971 as an official of the holding company and seemed about to sell off his controlling interest.

A feeling of the Old South, in the look of the land, in race attitudes and politics, pervades northern Florida from Jacksonville west and, in large measure, out across the panhandle as well. Here are miles and miles of Dixie-style piney woods and a great pulp farming industry, tobacco and peanut farms, and still those languorous rivers of yore. But like the rest of the South, this region is changing. In Gainesville (1970 population 64,510), home of the University of Florida, Thurmond's Dixiecrat party won in 1948 but Humphrey led the field 20 years later. The charming old capital city of Tallahassee (71,897), guided by a very conservative and dignified power structure, has mellowed perceptibly on the race issue. Out on the panhandle, the old South flavor is leavened with cosmopolitanism, perhaps because of the tourist trade drawn by the miles and miles of magnificent white beaches, perhaps in part by the heavy military component in places like Pensacola, which has a large Naval airbase.

Central Florida: Orlando, Disney World, et al.

Central Florida is preeminently citrus Florida, mile after mile of orange and sometimes tangerine and grapefruit orchards, the greatest concentration of citrus in the world. The largest city is Orlando, grown from a trading post on a cow range in the late 19th century to a booming metropolis of some 100,000 people with 330,000 more in its immediate hinterland. Citrus and the prosperity of a well-to-do retirement center gave Orlando its initial thrust; military bases, electronics, aerospace, and the proximity to Cape Kennedy 65 miles distant have propelled it forward in the past two decades; all these advantages plus the prospect of immense profits from the new Disney World have led to projections of a metropolitan population of a million by the end of the 1980s. Some see a second Florida megalopolis, rivaling the Gold Coast, coming into being on the axis of Orlando to Tampa–St. Petersburg and then down the coast to Sarasota and Fort Meyers; already some 2½ million people live in this region.

In a pattern akin to San Diego, California, the combination at Orlando of affluent retirees, the military, and a staunchly conservative newspaper all add up to a strongly Republican voting pattern. In 1970, Orange was Florida's only metropolitan county to go Republican for governor—and did so with a whopping 65.3 percent vote.

Sixteen miles west of Orlando, on a huge drained swamp, rises the latest and perhaps the greatest American monument ever to the gods of fun and escape: Walt Disney World. The great Disney himself, before his death in 1966, had personally set in motion the plans for Disney World and announced the idea.

In some respects, Walt Disney World is simply in the genre of the original California Disneyland, complete with fairyland castles (Cinderella's castle is 18 stories high with gold turrets), the plaster mountains (Space Mountain is 30 stories high), the animated animals, the monorails, the boat rides. But Walt Disney World (27,400 acres) is vastly larger than Disneyland (230 acres) and it is far more than an amusement park. It has several hotels (American, Asian, Polynesian, Venetian), three golf courses, bridle trails, picnic grounds, lagoons and a big lake, beaches and campgrounds on a 2,500-acre Vacation Kingdom, a 100-acre Magic Kingdom with six fantasy-lands ranging from Frontierland to Tomorrowland—and, eventually, a planned community with 20,000 or more persons living, as Disney decreed, "a life they can't find anywhere else in the world today."

Land-buying for the project began in secret in 1964, a year before Disney announced his plans. Disney did not repeat the mistake he had made at Disneyland, where the small amusement park is surrounded by non-Disney enterprises which are parasitic on the tourists and their dollars. Frontmen bought up thousands of acres on all sides to protect the main project. (Nonetheless, land speculation around Disney World was rampant virtually from the beginning; the Marathon Oil Co. paid $155,000 for a single acre of land for a service station at the main gate.)

If Disney World is the ultimate in calculated and programmed amusement for the millions, Cypress Gardens—at Winter Haven, some 60 miles southwest on the way to Tampa—is Florida's best indigenous specimen of how one uses publicity, cheesecake, and pure nerve to make something worth millions out of virtually nothing. In this case, the nothing was a tangled muck swamp that the engineers had given up on draining in the 1930s; the something is Cypress Gardens, one of the most fabulously successful tourist attractions in the U.S.A. and the creation of a single master promoter, Dick Pope. Pope and his imitators are the type who make it possible to state seriously: *Florida is the state man made*. God may have supplied the sun and sand and rains and swamps, but more than in any other state, the hand of man was needed to make a place (1) habitable, and (2) an attraction for millions.

Down the Sun Coast, on to Key West

The big population center on Florida's western flank is around Tampa and St. Petersburg, the northern anchor of the so-called Sun Coast which covers some 120 miles on the Gulf of Mexico, down through Bradenton and Sarasota to Fort Myers. In spots, the Sun Coast is sprouting forth with tall seafront condominum apartments. But it will be years before this becomes another tightly packed Gold Coast; on the stretch from Sarasota south to Fort Myers, for instance, there are beautiful beaches where one can still walk for miles and not see a soul.

Tampa, western Florida's biggest town, "does its share of pickin' Yankees," as an old Florida saying goes, but essentially it is an industrial and distributing center, quite unlike most Florida cities. There are big, masculine industries like beer brewing (Schlitz, Budweiser), steel, and cigar-making. The port of Tampa is one of the most important in the southeastern U.S. and the world's largest export point for phosphate, which is mined only 40 miles away.

Tampa became Florida's first urban renewal city, leading to a great face-lifting for the old waterfront, where railroad lines and old warehouses were torn out to make room for a $4.5 million convention center, a splendid new library, and a hotel. The central business district has been rejuvenated with new high-rise office buildings and hotels. Ybor City, which still has the country's largest cigar factory, has been revived as a center of Spanish culture. First came demolition of old slumlike buildings, then construction of 400 low-income family apartments in a Spanish design, and finally, to lure tourists, a four-acre Spanish walled city. Despite a heavy Negro influx, Ybor City has been able to sustain its Spanish atmosphere through the architecture and, more particularly, some of the world's finest Spanish restaurants. The proprietor of the Columbia Restaurant, an engaging Latin bon vivant named Cesar Gonzmart, deserves major credit for inspiring the renewal of Ybor City. The Columbia got its start around the turn of the century when Cuban immigrants working in the cigar factories would pay $5 a month for lunch and supper. To this day, the original old room is in operation, supplemented by more opulent dining halls. Gonzmart likes to boast of his great mix of clientele —local workers, kids from the universities, and "the high-class, diamond perfume trade"—a unique brand of gastronomic egalitarianism.

Basking in the sun on the seaward side of Tampa Bay lies St. Petersburg, removed from Tampa by just a few miles of open water but its diametric opposite by almost any standard you can think of.

Tampa is a rich ethnic stew; St. Petersburg has people from everywhere in the U.S.A., but predominantly it is white, middle-class America.

Tampa has 3 percent less old folks than the Florida average; St. Petersburg has twice as many (30.6 percent) and sometimes thinks it succeeded too well in its early slogan—"St. Pete, the Perfect Retirement Center."

Tampa lives off its port and old-style factories; St. Petersburg lives off the pension checks of its retirees and a sprinkling of electronic-aerospace companies which have filtered in since the 1950s.

Tampa is Democratic; St. Petersburg pioneered with present-day Republicanism in Florida.

Tampa is a leading antipoverty city; St. Petersburg has little patience for such programs and in the late 1960s angrily drove a girls' Job Corps Center out of town on the basis that the federal government was running a "disorderly house."

Tampa seems to be trying to build bridges between its white and black communities; St. Petersburg rather callously broke a 1968 strike by Negro sanitation workers who had the temerity to suggest that salaries as low as $3,890 a year were not enough to support a worker and his family in the modern U.S.A.

But when it comes to newspapers, the pattern suddenly reverses:

The Tampa *Tribune*, property of the Richmond, Virginia, papers, is generally conservative; The St. Petersburg *Times*, owned by local publisher Nelson Poynter, is liberal and sometimes downright crusading. Ideologies aside, both are outstanding in their circulation league.

Depending on their economic status, St. Pete's elderly are to be found in stately old hotels, $50,000 retirement homes in posh sections, dingy downtown rooming houses, or in infinite rows of little white cottages surrounded by palm trees and tropical flowers. The big middle-class elderly vote was an early foundation of the Republican revival which brought GOP control of most local government positions and, starting with the 1954 election, Florida's first Republican Congressman of the 20th century. But the St. Petersburg–Pinellas area is not irrevocably Republican. In 1964, when Goldwater ran and many of Florida's redneck areas turned Republican for the first time in living memory, Pinellas rebelled and gave Lyndon Johnson 55 percent of its vote. The implied Goldwaterian threat to the Social Security card was just too much to contemplate. In 1970, in a wave of revulsion against the swashbuckling Claude Kirk, the county gave 54.7 percent of its vote to Democrat Reubin Askew for governor.

One activity in which the Tampa Bay area seems to have an edge on the rest of Florida is baseball winter training. St. Petersburg has the St. Louis Cardinals and New York Mets, Tampa the Cincinnati Reds, Clearwater the Phillies, Bradenton the Kansas City Athletics and nearby Sarasota the Chicago White Sox. Florida cities bid anxiously to get these teams, since the exhibition games can be a great boon to late winter tourism.

Sarasota used to have another form of winter training: the circus. Now the great Ringling Bros. and Barnum & Bailey has migrated a few miles south to the town of Venice, where animals, trainers, clowns, acrobats, and all the rest go through their paces each winter before heading north in March. In matters of arts and the intellect Sarasota seems to lead all Florida. MacKinlay Kantor is only one of several well known authors and cartoonists in residence, and the area has a plethora of art schools and shows, little theater and concert groups. Some renowned architects have designed local schools, homes, and churches.

Several miles farther south, at Fort Myers, two huge communities designed to attract retirees have been erected on pine and palmetto flats beside the Caloosahatchee River. Lee County, where this development is located, grew from 54,539 people in 1960 to 105,216 in 1970.

By contrast, Collier County, directly to the south, has only 38,040 (a third of them in the city of Naples with its posh retirement community). After that, all that remains of the southwest coast are swamplands including the Ten Thousand Islands (of mangrove) and Everglades National Park.

Then, across Florida Bay, lie the Keys, dotted with resort areas of every stripe. At the Keys' southern tip is the old city of Key West, where the Census takers found 27,563 people in 1970. In recent decades, the navy has been key to the city's life, and Key West suffers intermittent pangs of fear of a pullout of the military installations.

A big factor in putting Key West back on the map after World War II— outside of the Overseas Highway, a precondition to meaningful tourism—was all the publicity stemming from President Harry Truman's frequent visits to his "little White House" there. But then, in 1960, came Castro's revolution in Cuba and an end to the bustling ferry and air service to Havana that had been a major reason many tourists chose to come all the way to Key West at all. During the 1960s, the city's population dropped a full 18 percent, while the rest of Florida boomed. Distant, isolated, so totally exposed to the sea, with its own distinctive mix of nationalities and ways of making a living, Key West has always been a place set apart from greater Florida. It doubtless always will be.

TEXAS

LAND OF THE MONIED "ESTABLISHMENT"

BIG, BRAWLING TEXAS, always the braggart in the family of American states, has been obliged in recent years to take a long, hard look inward. Simultaneously, Texas' image to the world has been transformed. A change of character and complexion that would normally take generations seems to have occurred in a twinkling of time.

To appreciate the change, one needs only to think back to a decade ago. Remembering that we speak as much of image as reality, recall what Texas stood for. Its global image was of a vainglorious, blustering, illiberal kind of place where money was worshipped without shame. Its man in the Senate, Lyndon Baines Johnson, was the most consummate wielder of power that chamber had seen in years and years. Money and power—the two words seemed to add up to Texas. Non-Texans remembered perhaps a glimmering of the Alamo, of the tradition of fiercely independent Americans who had migrated to a huge land north of the Rio Grande and built themselves a "civilization." But Texans themselves permitted and abetted a distortion of the Texas tradition, a bigger-and-bestest-of-everything braggadocio that evinced sometimes wonder, sometimes scorn from afar.

Writes historian Joe B. Frantz, a Texan:

Whether you . . . thought that Texans were pleasant buffoons, a bit tiresome but still good for some extravagant yaks, or petted Texans the way you might a cavorting Eskimo husky; whether you were impressed with the private airplanes, Olympic-sized swimming pools, 40-foot fireplaces, or ranch females built with all the reassuring solidity of an Anheuser-Busch draft horse, or whether, like my thrifty Illinois father, you always felt a bit superior to those Scripture-quoting Texans who spouted waste-not, want-not slogans while cotton wore out their black land, rivers carried their farms to the Gulf, their farm machinery rusted and ruined for want of simple upkeep, their Negroes rusted and ruined on a diet of cornbread, syrup, and grease, their Mexicans' insides exploded on corn, hot chilis, and amoebic dysentery, and their bankers refused credit to rehabilitate acres that cried for comeback—regardless of how the non-Texan viewed the Texan, he gloried in some aspects to him, commercialized and exploited him where he could, and steadily built the myth. . . .

It is easy to say it all changed that sad November day in 1963 in Dallas, and that single event should not be underestimated. But there was more. There was the little pinprick of the Texas balloon the day that Alaska joined the Union, and suddenly Texas suffered the indignity of being but the *second* largest state. There was the important shift of national attitudes in the 1960s, when the United States began to wonder if values like biggest and richest counted for so much, and the country began to look to the deprived in its midst, and Texas' blacks and downtrodden Mexican-Americans were suddenly no longer mute about their own fate. Who, as the more sensitive value system of the 1960s began to take form, could still be impressed by the boasts of Dallas that it had the biggest churches anywhere in Protestantism, when government statistics showed the lowest per capita income anywhere in America in the counties along the Rio Grande? How could one remain open-mouthed in amazement over Houston's phenomenal economic growth, when the price for it (especially in petrochemicals) was some of the vilest air and water pollution anywhere in the world?

Finally, there was the Presidency of Lyndon Johnson. First he helped Texas regain its self-confidence after Dallas, when the state went through a time of sadness and perplexity such as Texans had never before experienced. But then Johnson, through his own excess of promise and unhappy ending as President, ruined the Texan image even more. Now, writes Texas novelist Larry McMurtry, "we aren't thought of as quaintly vulgar anymore. . . . The majority just find us boring. . . . Having yielded Mr. Johnson, it is hardly to be expected that the state will yield anything funny in the next few years, much less anything aesthetically interesting."

As for bragging, McMurtry aptly sums it up: "Texans have finally learned that bragging is a form of discourse they can no longer afford. The old, loud, vulgar, groin-scratching Texan is rapidly giving way to a quieter sort of citizen, one who knows how to live with his itch." Not all do, of course. In Dallas, I was regaled with the story of the Texan who went to New York and encountered a young lady of the town with whom he then went to bed. The next day a furtive little man accosted the Texan, showed him pictures of himself in various compromising positions from the night before, and said the photos would cost him $1,000 each. The Texan replied: "OK, I'll take

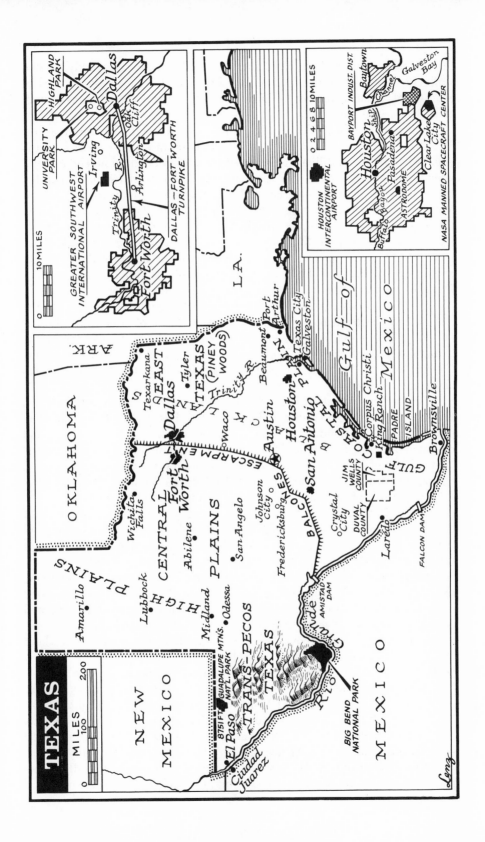

TEXAS

MILES
0   100   200

NEW MEXICO

OKLAHOMA

ARK

LA.

MEXICO

HIGH PLAINS

CENTRAL PLAINS

TRANS-PECOS TEXAS

BALCONES ESCARPMENT

EAST TEXAS (PINEY WOODS)

GULF PLAIN

Gulf of Mexico

Amarillo

Lubbock

Wichita Falls

Midland
Odessa

San Angelo

Abilene

Fort Worth

Dallas

Texarkana

Tyler

Waco

Austin

Johnson City

Fredericksburg

San Antonio

Houston

Beaumont
Port Arthur
Texas City
Galveston

Corpus Christi
King Ranch

PADRE ISLAND

Brownsville

Crystal City

Duval County

Jim Wells County

Laredo

Falcon Dam

Amistad Dam

Big Bend National Park

Rio Grande

Trinity R.

8751 FT. GUADALUPE MTNS. NAT'L. PARK

El Paso

Ciudad Juarez

Lenz

Dallas–Fort Worth inset:

10 MILES

HIGHLAND PARK

UNIVERSITY PARK

Dallas
Oak Cliff

Irving

GREATER SOUTHWEST INTERNATIONAL AIRPORT

Trinity R.

Arlington

DALLAS–FORT WORTH TURNPIKE

Fort Worth

Houston inset:

0 2 4 6 8 10 MILES

BAYPORT INDUST. DIST.

Baytown
Ship Channel

Galveston Bay

HOUSTON INTERCONTINENTAL AIRPORT

Houston

Buffalo Bayou

Ship Channel

Pasadena

ASTRODOME

Clear Lake City

NASA MANNED SPACECRAFT CENTER

three of those, four of these, six of these. . . ." There are still stoutly attested stories of wives who run up bills of over $200,000 at Neiman-Marcus, and of the rush of Texan males to buy their own ranches and run cattle as a proof of their place in the world.

Some of the richest Texans of all time—men like Sid Richardson of Fort Worth, Clint Murchison of Dallas, and H. L. Hunt of Dallas—never went the road of flamboyance. Billionaire Hunt, of course, has financed no end of right-wing propaganda activities, but the man himself has stayed somewhat in the background in his great mansion, a bigger-than-life reproduction of Mount Vernon. Most of the latest generation of Texas millionaires—bankers, petrochemical magnates, computer wizards, financiers, insurance men, with names like H. Ross Perot, John Mecom, Jr., Lamar Hunt, and Joe Albritton—have tended to be quieter and less eccentric men than the millionaires of the '30s and '40s. Perot has said he is willing to use half his vast fortune from the Dallas-based computer software company he founded to right social ills in America; among other projects, he has made highly publicized journeys to the Far East in chartered planes to try to get the release of American prisoners of war in Vietnam. In 1971, he was making headlines by coming to the financial rescue of the New York brokerage house of F. I. DuPont, Glore, Forgan, William R. Staats. This may be flamboyance, but of a kind Texas never knew before.

Now almost forgotten in Texas is a man who was briefly a millionaire, fertilizer tycoon and swindler Billie Sol Estes. His multimillion-dollar empire was based on fraudulent credit, including fertilizer, grain elevators, and cotton allotments; for a while Estes was much admired as the Bible-quoting "boy wonder of West Texas agriculture," but it all came crashing down when he was arrested in 1962 and sent to federal prison for mail fraud and conspiracy. (In 1971, Estes was paroled to work on his brother's farm.)

And now there is a conscious effort on Texans' part to deflate some of the old swashbuckling image that surrounded the state's cattle barons and rich oilmen. Congressman Bob Eckhardt of Houston reminds a visitor of the rather unprepossessing surroundings of the ordinary Texas cattleman. His ranch house "may ramble all over the place," but it's one-story and very utilitarian. The only plantation houses in Texas, Eckhardt points out, were built in the river-bottom areas of East Texas by men rich through cane and cotton, not cattle. "The cattleman," he says, "tends to wear hat and boots worth in the aggregate about $100, and everything else in between about $11.50 at J. C. Penney. Fancy boots have developed only in the last few years. It's a lobbyist's flair and probably borrowed from the movies."

There is also the renewed suggestion that the Texas tradition belongs to many more than the privileged Wasp elite who occupy the heights of the Texas power structure and have monopolized attention for so many decades. The historic essence of Texas, Joe Frantz suggests, is not any narrow corral but "its universalism and its diversity." A lion's share of the early settlers came from the nearby Southern states, "for reasons of propinquity. But other participants came from Indiana, New York, Massachusetts, and from beyond

—England, Ireland, Denmark, France, German states, and Africa. Truly they were a United Nations' force dedicated to building a social and political climate in which men could go their separate, non-conforming ways without fear." The real Texas tradition, in this view, runs from old Sam Houston bravely warning against joining the Confederacy (and being removed from the governorship for his apostasy) to Stanley Marcus urging modern-day Dallas to face up to its slums and discard its spirit of absolutism, to Mexican-American farm workers in a long, dusty march to demand a share of their birthright.

Are such events simply quixotic assaults on an entrenched establishment of wealth and power that is not about to be dislodged or even threatened? The weight of evidence is in that direction. The essential power in Texas remains in the hands of an immense oil-insurance-banking-construction axis which is so closely identified with the ruling political circles that the two are virtually indistinguishable—a remarkable story to which we will return shortly.

But things have happened in Texas that make one wonder. In the 1960s, the Texas legislature passed the first minimum wage law in the state's history, and made it—wonder of wonders—apply to *farm workers* as well as those in industry. The state elected its first Mexican-American Congressmen, and may soon send its first Negro to the U. S. House. Closed, conservative Dallas chose as mayor a man worth $100 million (no surprise) but then he launched perhaps the United States' most advanced program to involve ordinary citizens in long-term planning of their city (a fantastic surprise). Radical protest by young Chicanos about the feudal white control of Rio Grande counties, while outside the political mainstream, has contributed to new ferment among a long quiescent people and the probability of great change in the years to come.

So one can detect the stirrings of a new era. No one expects the citadels of wealth and power to topple. But there will be renewed competition for influence. As oil, the exploitive product, declines in relative importance, petrochemicals and other industries involving more unionized labor, and also a more independently minded management and technician class, will continue to rise. While Texas universities are scarcely hotbeds of radical thought, they do create a current of opinion to the left of establishmentarian thinking. Texas' dispossessed millions will increasingly demand a say about their lives and their society, and will be heard more. Within a few years there will be a state income tax and, with it, at least a partial redistribution of the wealth. The breakdown in old-line Democratic "regularity," triggered by Republicans who are just as conservative as the old Democrats, will bring in its wake more and more citizen political participation, from the little counties up to the statewide level. In short, Texas will have a more open society than at any time since the days of her infancy. Perhaps there will be a rounding of the circle, a return to the spirit of those early years when the early Anglos and indigenous Mexicans made successful common cause against the oppressors from Mexico City. In victory, it will be remembered, they established their own republic (1836–45), a boisterous experiment in frontier democracy without parallel in the settlement of the continent.

The Economy: Good Times Come to Texas

Forty years ago, Texas was drifting along as a rural, agrarian, poor state. Almost 60 percent of its 5.8 million people lived on farms or in little towns, making their living principally from cattle and cotton. Then, in the 1930s, the great East Texas oil field came in, to be followed a few years later by major discoveries on the West Texas plains. Thousands of Texans became proficient in the skills of exploration and drilling for oil, hundreds became millionaires in their own right, the great pools of petroleum generated equally great pools of risk capital, a gigantic petrochemical industry formed and Texas became one of the great manufacturing states of the Union in chemicals, electronics, aircraft, and metals. Military bases sprouted in World War II, and in the postwar years Texas became the country's second largest defense contractor (after California). Dallas and Houston, the big financial, legal, and headquarters cities, grew into great American metropolises, continuing their growth through the 1960s and into the 1970s at a stunning rate.

By 1970, 11,196,730 people lived in Texas. Only 20 percent of them lived on farms and in little villages, which had fallen from 3.4 million people in 1930 to 2.3 million in 1970. Virtually all the growth had occurred in 24 metropolitan areas (more than any other state), scattered from Texarkana in the northeast to El Paso in the west, from Amarillo in the north to Brownsville in the south. The aggregate metropolitan population was 8.2 million, about 74 percent of the total Texas population. At the same time, the per capita income of Texans had risen from $478 in 1929 (then 68 percent of the national level) to $3,531 in 1970 (up to 83.3 percent of the U. S. average).

Texas remains the preeminent oil and gas producing state of the nation. In 1970, more than a billion barrels of oil were produced at a value of over $4 billion; gas production of 8.5 billion cubic feet was valued at $1.2 billion. The petrochemical industry born during World War II continues to grow, up 25 percent even since 1960. It is centered in Houston, Beaumont, and along the whole Gulf Coast in a complex informally called the "spaghetti bowl"—a reference to the thousands of miles of pipelines running from one factory to the next.

Texas oil production is still increasing and seems sure to remain Texas' dominant industry through the end of this century. But the great boom period has ended, and no one expects any more major discoveries. There are now less than a fifth as many exploratory rigs in Texas as there were 15 years ago. Secondary recovery techniques (such as the pumping of water underground to force pockets of oil toward the wells) have actually doubled Texas' reserves, but even at that, some wells are no longer able to produce their "allowables" under state oil conservation regulations. M. A. Wright, chairman of the board of Humble Oil (the largest Texas producer) pointed out in an interview that U. S. petroleum demand is increasing at about four percent a year, "but our reserves are not developing that fast." Thus Humble and the other majors continue aggressive global searches for new oil sources and are heavily involved in the Alaskan North Slope development. They are also looking down the road toward eventual conversion to synthetic crudes. Major sources are expected to be the oil shale fields of Colorado, Utah, and Wyoming, and U. S. coal deposits that can be converted to gas. On the latter score, Humble has invested about $20 million in coal lands in the Illinois Basin and Rocky Mountains, and practically all the majors now see themselves as total energy producing firms, not oil companies alone. Nevertheless, they are sure to go slow on development of synthetics until they have depleted their existing resources in regular crude oil.

The technology of oil development has made it impossible for most of the old-style "shirttail" operators and wildcatters to remain viable. The reasons are fairly simple—drilling and pumping costs have gone up faster than crude oil prices, and virgin territory for drilling is becoming rarer and rarer. Wildcat drilling has fallen off about 40 percent in the last 15 years, and the day of the high-rolling wheeler-dealer with his big tan Stetson and gleaming cream Cadillac is on its way into history. The "independents" who do prosper, and indeed still drill the holes to discover most new oil, work in close cooperation with the majors who do the advanced geophysical and analysis work.*

A brief review of federal-state oil policy is necessary because it lies at the heart of Texas' drive for national political influence. A conservative economist, Milton Friedman, has written: "Few industries sing the praises of free enterprise more loudly than the oil industry. Yet few industries rely so heavily on special government favors." The special privileges started back in 1926 with enactment of the oil depletion allowance, which exempted from taxation 27-½ percent of the gross income from oil wells. That figure held inviolate until 1969, when it was reduced to 22 percent on the crest of a taxpayer revolt. Even if all costs have been covered, the depletion allowance can be taken throughout the life of an oil well. State limits on production, begun in the name of conservation but continued (many believe) for the purpose of propping up prices, were begun in the 1930s. Allegedly to ward off heavy foreign oil imports that would discourage domestic oil exploration, a national oil import quota system was instituted in 1959 and is still in effect.

Critics claim that the oil import quotas result in $5 billion higher prices paid by U. S. consumers each year. The depletion allowance, they say, costs the federal government about $1.3 billion a year in taxes not paid. Major oil companies pay a laughably low percentage of federal tax on their net income. Some examples from 1968: Standard Oil of New Jersey paid 12.8 percent on $2.1 billion net income, Texaco 0.8 percent on $953 million, Gulf 0.4 percent on $992 million, Mobil 5.7 percent on $729 million, Tenneco zero percent on

---

* In Dallas, I hoped to interview Jake L. Hamon, an "independent" of the old school who has prospered just as well in the latter-day oil world. This is the reply I received to my letter of inquiry:
Dear Mr. Peirce:
I regret that I will be out of the country on the days you plan to be in Dallas.
I am not leaving because you plan to be in Dallas; I had already planned to go.
Yours very sincerely,
/s/ Jake L. Hamon

$89 million, etc.

Oil companies reply that they pay billions of dollars each year in various other forms of taxes, including local levies. "The whole case for the . . . depletion allowance," according to Houston oilman J. R. Parten, "rests upon national security. We have fueled two world wars, largely out of our oil and gas resources, and in my opinion this would not have been possible without the tax incentives." The same rationale is used to justify oil import quotas. "If we took off the import controls," Humble's Wright says, prices would fall so far that "U. S. oil exploration would fall off rapidly and much of our oil —maybe half—would come from abroad.* Do we want the U.S. to be, like Europe, dependent on foreign sources of energy, to accommodate its needs?" In a national emergency, oilmen argue, the country would want to have ample domestic reserves. That argument is somewhat vitiated, however, by the fact that America generally has a 10-year reserve in already tapped wells from which it could draw, and there is some doubt that a national emergency would last that long. Also, new energy sources like oil shale could be exploited more rapidly in such a situation.

Whatever the merits, one indisputable fact is that Texans and their Southwestern neighbors have held crucial seats of national power which have enabled them to protect the industry's tax advantage and import quotas. For years, Lyndon Johnson of Texas was Senate Majority Leader and later President. His colleague, Speaker Sam Rayburn, was a zealous guardian of the gates to the tax-writing House Ways and Means Committee for two decades. Oklahoma's Senator Robert S. Kerr, a wealthy oilman himself, was the powerful number-two man on the Senate Finance Committee for several years; since 1966 the chairman of that committee has been Louisiana's Senator Russell Long, who is reported to have made $1.2 million on oil leases since 1964. Texas' Robert B. Anderson became Secretary of the Treasury in the Eisenhower Administration; another Texan, John B. Connally, was appointed to the same post by President Nixon.

Even today, Texas' power in Congress remains formidable. In addition to its two Senators, the state has 23 Representatives (rising to 24 with the 1970 Census reapportionment), a not insignificant bloc of seats. Rep. George H. Mahon reigns over the House Appropriations Committee, the foremost holder of the national pursestrings. The chairman of the House Banking and Currency Committee, Rep. Wright Patman, is now in his late seventies but still a vigorous scourge of big banks, high interest rates, and the foundations (but no enemy of big oil). Rep. Olin E. Teague is both chairman of the Democratic Caucus in the House and chairman of the House Veterans Committee. Even liberal Senator Ralph Yarborough, before his 1970 defeat, defended the oil depletion allowance. An influential spokesman for the same cause in Republican circles is Senator John G. Tower, a staunch conservative, who has risen to high seniority on the Armed Services and Banking and Currency Committees.

* Since my interview with Wright, however, the cost differential between U. S. and foreign oil prices has shrunk substantially.

The same congressional bloc makes it its business to defend Texas' big aerospace and defense industry, military and NASA installations, and also Texas farm interests. The state is the nation's No. 1 producer of cotton, an industry heavily dependent on federal farm subsidies, and in fact Rep. W. R. Poage of Texas is chairman of the House Agriculture Committee. Texas also grows some three million acres of wheat a year, another subsidy-dependent crop.

The other big Texas farm products are less tied to government largesse. Texas has traditionally been the nation's foremost breeder of cattle, shipping the animals to the Midwest for feeding and eventual slaughter ever since the days of the first great cattle drives. Today there are still more head of cattle being raised in Texas than any other state—over 12 million. But fewer cattle are being shipped away for fattening, and in 1971 the Agriculture Department found that Texas, for the first time in history, had surpassed Iowa in feedlot cattle counts. Most of the feedlots are in the Panhandle, an operation computerized and mechanized on a scale unparalleled in the Midwest. Slaughtering is increasingly done in-state, too. Together with Oklahoma, Texas in 1970 was marketing an estimated 3.2 million head of feed cattle in a year, compared with only 345,000 in 1955.

This is not to say that old style cattle raising has disappeared in Texas. Real cowboys still drive cattle in West Texas, and the huge cattle ranches still exist, each now complete with its own planes and airstrip.

Texas farm marketings reached $2.8 billion in the late 1960s, second only to California and Iowa. Livestock sales accounted for about 60 percent of the total. In addition to cattle, the state ranks first in the U.S. in sheep (three million to five million, depending on the year), and it is second in turkeys, eighth in chickens. Its rice, pecan, and peanut crops are among the country's largest, and it is first or nearly so in spinach, onions, carrots, cabbage, and watermelons. There are significant citrus crops in the Rio Grande Valley. The big growers there think they could make more money if they could produce more grapefruit, but there is simply not enough water to permit expansion of the industry. Even darker clouds over Texas agriculture are droughts and the prospect of exhaustion of the aquifers that have been tapped to irrigate great stretches of West Texas—a story to which we will return later.

The Establishment: Connally, LBJ—and Barnes?

The political life of Texas is directed by a single monied establishment. There is no other state of the Union where the control is so direct, unambiguous, and commonly accepted. The establishment has its roots in the banks and law firms of Dallas and Houston and, to a lesser degree, those of Austin. Its untold billions of wealth are in oil, insurance, high finance, construction, broadcasting, real estate, electronics, and the manufacture of weaponry. Its spokesmen are the great metropolitan dailies of Texas—papers like the Dallas *Morning News,* the Houston *Chronicle,* and the Fort Worth *Star-Telegram*—and, in turn, the great bulk of the state's television stations. Lyndon Johnson is very much part of this establishment; John B. Connally is the epitome of it.

A strong case can be made that Connally, not Johnson, is the pivotal figure of postwar Texas history. He grew up in a small farm town near San Antonio, one of seven children of a dirt-poor butcher, farmer, and later bus driver. But no one would dream today that Connally came to town on a load of cobs; in all America, there are few politicians who can compete with him for cool, suave manners, good looks, and height, a man never ill at ease. San Antonio lawyer John Peace, who met Connally at the University of Texas (*de rigeur* training ground for aspiring Texas politicians), recalls even then a quality about the man that made others "want him to be chairman of the board," without resenting his position at all. Predictably, Connally was elected UT student body president and was on his way politically.

"Connally did more to make Johnson than anyone else in the U.S.," Peace insists, recalling that most of the Johnson forces were originally Connally people whose "first loyalty and tie was to Connally." The group included Jake Pickle and Frank Ikard (both of whom later became Congressmen, and Ikard later the chief oil lobbyist in Washington), John Singleton and Al Woodward (now federal judges in Texas), and many others. "From the juices of youth and loyalty [to Connally] we helped, all the way back to LBJ's first race for Congress, then his Senate elections." LBJ, Peace admitted, would regard this interpretation "as heresy," and of course it would be foolish to discount the contributions made to Johnson's rise by men like Franklin Roosevelt and Sam Rayburn.

Finishing law school in 1938, Connally started almost immediately as an aide to freshman Congressman Johnson in Washington, and though he was to take countless other jobs in the succeeding years, he never really left Johnson. He served four and a half years in the Navy during the war, rising to the rank of lieutenant commander and winning decorations for combat duty on the Carrier *Essex;* then he went back to Austin and used his mustering out pay to open a radio station. In 1948, he was the ramrod of the initial election of Lyndon Johnson for the U. S. Senate, operating in the thick of the events which led to the appearance of a miraculous uncounted vote box from Jim Wells County that suddenly turned a narrow Johnson loss into an 87-vote victory.

In 1951, Connally moved to Fort Worth to become an attorney for Sid Richardson, who had amassed a fortune of some $2 billion in oil, making him one of the richest men on earth. Now the skein of corporate directorships began to form as Connally served as director (or officer) of the Richardson Oil Co., Richardson Carbon Co., the Richardson Foundation, the New York Central Railroad, and four broadcasting companies. Testifying before a Senate committee in 1961 (during confirmation hearings for his appointment as Secretary of the Navy in the Kennedy Administration), Connally revealed a

Texas-sized list of duties he had been assigned by his friend and employer Richardson, including "problems concerning the production of oil and gas, and the running of two radio stations, the running of a television station, and operating cattle ranches of approximately 4,000 head on 70,000 acres of land, running five drugstores in Fort Worth, various mining interests, housing development corporations, a carbon black plant, a gasoline extraction plant," etc., etc. In 1956 Connally had been sent to Washington to lobby for a "fair market price" natural gas bill that would have profited the gas industry between $2 billion and $12 billion over time; as it turned out, the bill passed, but President Eisenhower vetoed it because of the taint of scandal following the charge of Sen. Francis Case of South Dakota that an oil company lawyer (whom he did not identify) had offered him an improper campaign contribution in exchange for his vote. In that year, Johnson urged Connally to register as a lobbyist, but he refused to do so. (Connally would later be criticized for his close ties to the gas lobby, but no one ever suggested he was personally involved in unethical practices.)

When Connally went to work for Richardson, the old man had promised: "I'll pay you enough so Nellie and the kids won't go hungry, and I'll put you in the way to make some money." He kept his promise. Connally steadily built his fortune during the Fort Worth years, and in 1959, when Richardson died, he became one of the executors of his estate, work for which he eventually received compensation of $750,000. In 1965, he purchased the 14,500-acre Tortuga Ranch in South Texas for about $300,000. By 1970, he owned several other substantial pieces of property, and by his own admission it was all done with borrowed money.

Stephen D. Berkowitz, in a muckraking account of the Connally record in 1971, wrote:

> While much of the impetus behind his meteoric rise can be traced to the New Deal and its aftermath, like Johnson, Connally has been embraced by ultra-conservative cattle barons, bankers and oil magnates as one of their own. . . .
>
> Connally's earliest ties were with the Austin-based grouping which grew up in the hothouse atmosphere of cost-plus contracting and political pork-barreling during and immediately after World War II. Spearheaded by political power in Congress—especially in the important House and Senate military appropriations committees—this grouping began to expand and develop strong interests in a number of areas; banking and land; large-scale construction; oil drilling and exploration; broadcasting; and insurance. Directly or indirectly each of these was dependent on federal largesse: *construction* on funds for building military bases, dams, and pipelines; *broadcasting* on federal licenses; and *oil drilling*, in many cases, on leases and direct subsidies. . . .

Throughout the Connally career, one hears of his business and political contacts growing wider, year by year. His work for Richardson brought him into contact with the Murchison clan, which has major interests in railroads, steel, insurance, and oil. Among his close contacts were Ed Clark, a lobbyist, bank executive, and later Ambassador to Australia; J. C. Kellam, a business executive with broad contacts, president of the LBJ Corporation and former chairman of the Texas State Colleges Board of Regents; Robert Phinney, destined to become director of the Internal Revenue Service; Willard Deason, who became a member of the Interstate Commerce Commission. . . . The list goes on and on. At the same time, Connally remained a chief political operative for Johnson, lining up financial backing among his oil industry friends, serving as LBJ liaison man with local Democratic leaders, and working for Johnson's unsuccessful bids for the Presidential nomination in 1956 and 1960.

When Johnson became Vice President, Connally was appointed Secretary of the Navy—not, Connally told one biographer, as a result of LBJ's intervention, but rather on the direct suggestion to President Kennedy of House Speaker Sam Rayburn. Connally was to stay with that job less than a year, however, before returning home to run for governor. The rather false issue used against Connally in that 1962 campaign was that he was running as "Lyndon's Boy." Actually, Johnson has always had a great disdain for state government and tried to dissuade Connally, telling him he already had a more important job in Washington (where, as LBJ saw it, the real action was). But there were strong reasons for Connally to run. He and some of his old political-business colleagues, then in their mid-40s, detected what they thought was drifting in the Texas economy, a failure to be really competitive with the East and California in education or business growth. They were determined to make Texas a Class A state, not to go, as one told me, "the route of Mississippi, Alabama, and Louisiana." The Connally group saw Price Daniel, then the governor, as a drifter and do-nothing figure, or even worse, a man developing dangerous populist ideas through his opposition to a business-backed sales tax. Finally, Connally and his friends were determined to prevent decisive change in Texas' one-party system, to freeze out the Republicans (who had won Johnson's old Senate seat in 1961) and keep out of the statehouse the left wing of the Democratic party (militant unionists, liberals, and minority group leaders).

So Connally came home, took the air-strip set away from Daniel, and ran well ahead in the first primary. But he failed to make 50 percent and was forced into a runoff with an aggressive young liberal named Don Yarborough (no relation to Senator Ralph Yarborough). The runoff vote was a perilously close 565,174 for Connally, 538,924 for Yarborough. As it was, Connally succeeded only through all-time record spending made possible by contributions of his oil industry friends and associates, plus the monolithic backing of the state press. According to writer Robert Sherrill, only one of the 114 daily newspapers of Texas endorsed Yarborough, who had "the entire financial and industrial community arrayed against him." A victory by Yarborough would probably have accelerated by a decade some of the liberalizing changes in state government now likely to take place in the 1970s; unlike many Texas liberals, Yarborough had a tough pragmatic streak and ability to deal effectively with a broad range of the political spectrum. (He ran again for governor in 1964 and 1968 and lost both times.)

Connally took office in January 1963, and in November of that year President Kennedy scheduled his ill-starred trip to the state to try and calm the fierce internecine war between the liberal wing, led by Senator Ralph Yarborough, and the conservative wing, already becoming known as the Connally wing. In the Presidential motorcade going into Dallas, Connally had a coveted seat in the Presidential limousine and was almost killed by a bullet; he has told friends his doctor said he survived only because he slumped forward and staunched the flow of blood from wounds in his chest.

After Dallas, Connally was politically invincible and coasted to easy second- and third-term victories in 1964 and 1966. He proved a master of articulation of Texas' long-term needs in fields ranging from constitutional revision to higher education, public school reform and water supply. (As Dallas newsman Jim Lehrer suggested to me, "he could see further than the next bridge on the Trinity River.") But Connally proved to be an aloof figure in Austin, lacking determination to follow through on many of his own proposals. Part of Connally's problem may have been his very conservative friends; when he appointed them to a constitutional revision commission, for instance, few of the needed structural reforms, including annual legislative sessions, better pay for legislators, or a cabinet system, emerged in the final product.

Labor and the minorities got the back of Connally's hand. He boasted of voluntary integration in Texas but opposed the Kennedy-Johnson Administration's public accommodations law as striking at "one of our most cherished freedoms—the right to own and manage private property." He showed contempt for Mexican-American farm workers marching to Austin and refused to support the state minimum wage law they asked for. This was balanced by more appointments for Mexicans—at least politically "acceptable" ones—than any prior governor had made. But the sales tax was doubled under Connally, without corresponding increases in taxes that affect the wealthy. Connally became a superhawk on the Vietnam war and assailed "peace" demonstrators as "bearded and unwashed prophets of doubt and despair" for whom, as he put it, "liberty is merely a license to preach and practice individual and ideological perversions of their responsibilities as free men." Connally specifically included the late Martin Luther King, Jr., in that group. At Chicago in 1968, he led the fight for a platform plank backing up the Administration on the war, and threatened Johnson's reentry into the Presidential race if his conditions were not met.*

By the time Connally left the governorship, a national image of Texas as an aggressive, space-age-oriented state was well established—a far cry from the Old South syndrome of a few years before. The Houston and Dallas areas were in the midst of spectacular booms. The gap between Texas and national per capita income (an area in which Texas has always lagged) had

---

* Connally was outraged with Hubert Humphrey for permitting the convention to drop the unit rule for delegate voting, a traditional source of power for the state's conservative Democratic establishment, and was also upset that Humphrey would not even consider him for the Vice Presidency. But Connally has stoutly denied the report in Jules Witcover's book, *The Resurrection of Richard Nixon*, that he actually worked secretly through most of the campaign to raise money for Nixon while publicly ignoring Humphrey. According to Witcover, Connally decided with less than a week to go to election day that Humphrey would carry Texas, so he finally leaped on the bandwagon and bestowed blessings on Humphrey at a huge rally in Houston. Humphrey ended up carrying the state with a plurality of 38,960 votes out of 3,079,216 cast.

been significantly narrowed. Almost 1,500 new plants were settled in Texas and 150,000 new industrial jobs were added; tourism doubled to about $1 billion a year, with 140,000 new jobs. Unemployment levels were among the lowest in the nation. Some of Connally's conservative friends might object to the increase in the state budget (up from $1.3 billion to $2.5 billion during the Connally years), but there was little arguing about the general prosperity. A significant share of the budget increase went to higher education.

Texas also enjoyed a great military-industrial boom in the 1960s. During World War II and Korea, pressure from Johnson and other members of the congressional delegation had helped—along with the Texan climate—to make the state a center for military training and manufacturing. By the mid-1950s, there was scarcely a Texas city of significant size without one or more major military facilities nearby. In Congress in the 1950s, Johnson used his role as Senate majority leader to fight for higher military appropriations than the Eisenhower Administration wanted. But with Johnson installed as President and the Vietnam war build-up underway, the spigot could be turned on in deadly earnest. From a 1963 level of $1.2 billion in defense prime contract awards (representing just 4.3 percent of the national total), Texas' gross receipts climbed 242 percent to $4.1 billion in 1968 (10 percent of the national total). And these figures do not even include the NASA Manned Spacecraft Center, which was located at Houston as a result of Texas' political muscle under the Kennedy Administration.

When 1969 came, Lyndon Johnson retired to his ranch to nurse his investments and write his memoirs. John Connally, still a vigorous 52, did nothing of the sort. Instead, he moved his center of operations to Houston and became a partner in Vinson, Elkins, Weems and Searls—the biggest law firm in Texas, and one long regarded as the state's most powerful lobbying group. (The firm's senior partner, James Elkins, Sr., is believed to be the most influential man in Texas in deciding who actually gets the money to run for governor.) Connally was also invited to sit on the board of directors of the huge First City National Bank of Houston, twice the size of its closest Houston competitor. The senior chairman of the board of First City National is James Elkins, Sr. Another member of the board is George Brown of the huge Texas construction firm, Brown & Root, which does about $1.5 billion business a year (second largest in the U. S.).* Brown & Root has played a powerful role in Texas politics over several decades, and George Brown was perhaps Johnson's first major financial backer. Brown's participation in First City National links the company with oil drilling (Halliburton) and land companies, steel (Armco), pipelines (Texas Eastern Transmission), airlines (TWA) and a major conglomerate (ITT). Connally brought some of his own connections, since he sat on the boards of directors of the

---

* Brown & Root was one of four companies that did a billion dollars' worth of business in Vietnam. It has operated since the late 1960s as a quasi-independent but wholly owned subsidiary of Halliburton Co., which provides oilfield services and owns a research subsidiary that makes explosives and pyrotechnic ordnance in Arlington, Texas. Connally became a member of the Halliburton board of directors in 1969.

Gibraltar Savings Association (Houston) and the U. S. Trust Co. (New York).

Then, in 1971, the Texas political world was shocked by Connally's decision to become Secretary of the Treasury in the Nixon cabinet—a decision Lyndon Johnson learned of only after it had been made. With consummate skill, Connally moved rapidly to become the leading architect of U. S. economic policy, the crucial figure behind the administration's new programs of controls on wages and prices. In a few months, the *National Journal* reported, Connally had become a "Presidential adviser and confidant with influence reaching far beyond his official jurisdiction." Few figures on the national scene were so clearly of Presidential timber.

The endless chains of inter- and intra-city, family and club, formal and informal relationships which characterize the Texas monied establishment would no doubt delight a man whom some regard as the godfather of it all—Jesse Jones, the great financier-builder of Houston and owner of a good chunk of other Texas cities as well. Jones topped off his career by going off to Washington to use his marvelous skills as head of the Reconstruction Finance Corporation and later as Secretary of Commerce. The foundation he left behind in Houston still exerts a major influence in the city. Among its holdings is its voice to the world, the Houston *Chronicle*. But in Jones's day, things were essentially simpler. The Texas of the 1930s was still a largely unformed place as the initial fortunes were just being made out of the East Texas oil fields. Today the monied structure is many times as large as it was, has expanded into highly innovative fields (universities, computer companies), and under Johnson and Connally has extended its power into the very heart of national decision-making.

Texas' monied establishment has its Achilles heel—ethics. There is not even in theory a line between private interest and public responsibility, as the establishment sees it. For instance, if an establishment politician appears on the scene without prior wealth, steps are taken to see that he stays a poor boy no longer, apparently with little concern that his independence might be undermined in the process. A favorite way to do this is to sell a man stock in an up-and-coming local corporation. One of the establishment's banks is lined up to lend the man money to buy the stock, with the securities themselves the sole collateral.

In 1971, a sordid scandal broke into the open with revelation that a single bill passed by the Texas legislature the previous year had profited several leading Texas politicians, including Gov. Preston Smith, speaker of the house Gus Mutscher, and state Democratic party chairman Elmer Baum, by a total of $359,150. The federal Securities and Exchange Commission began a full-scale investigation of what it called a multimillion-dollar case of stock fraud and influence peddling. The scandal also involved the collapse of a Houston bank and one of the largest FDIC payoffs of insured deposits in the national history of bank failures. At the center of the whole mess was an admitted swindler, Houston banker and real-estate promoter Frank W. Sharp.

After the SEC built an impressive case against him on fraud charges, Sharp pleaded guilty and received a light $5,000 fine and a three-year probation sentence—part of a deal in which he then became a federal witness and proceeded to implicate many Texas political figures, especially Democrats. Indictments followed, including one of Mutscher for bribery. He resigned as speaker, and Baum as party chairman, and in Washington, no less a figure than Will R. Wilson, chief of the Justice Department's Criminal Division, was asked to resign. Wilson had once been Sharp's personal attorney. The Sharp case was more shocking to the outside world than in Texas. The truth was that if a federal agency had not intervened, it would probably have never been brought into the open in Texas. Manipulation of government for direct personal gain is simply not regarded as very immoral.

Campaign contributions, as in so many states, are the primary vehicle for the transfer of private money to politicians. In 1970, reporter Morton Mintz of the Washington *Post* undertook a study of the identity of contributors to that year's election in Texas. (No Texas paper chose to do the same research). Mintz found that oilmen accounted for almost 46 percent of the individual contributors of $5,000 or more in his half-million dollar sampling, while bankers, mutual fund managers, and others in the financial world accounted for another 19 percent. Then there were major gifts from contractors, insurance men, realtors, and doctors. Liberal Senator Ralph Yarborough reported $247,652 in gifts that year, of which only a paltry $8,300 came from labor union sources.* Instead, Yarborough had a scattering of larger gifts from business and liberal leaders. "But," Mintz reported, "businessmen's contributions of $5,000 or more seemed to fall like confetti" into the coffers of Lloyd M. Bentsen, Jr., the banking, insurance, and mutual funds multimillionaire from Houston who defeated Yarborough in the primary, and Republican Representative George Bush, who lost the general election to Bentsen. Both Bentsen and Bush ended up receiving and spending about $1 million. How a man with that kind of support can defy the monied establishment, even if the notion should cross his mind, is hard to imagine.

The 1970s, however, promise a new, perhaps unique era in Texas establishment politics. The man everyone agrees should be watched is an aggressive, brilliant young politician named Ben Barnes. Barnes was born in 1938 as the son of a hard-pressed Texas peanut farmer and spent his youth in the little hamlet of De Leon, where from the age of six or so everyone considered him a natural-born politician and leader. In 1960, at the age of 22, he ran for the legislature from his home area and won. No one took much notice of him, and his voting record was like an old mossback's except on civil rights. But Barnes came to the notice of the Connally crowd and was invited to a 1961 meeting of about a dozen men at a South Texas ranch to decide whether Connally should run for governor the next year. At about 3 o'clock in the morning, Connally's close friend Robert Strauss (later Democratic national committeeman and treasurer of the Democratic National Committee) took

---

* The low labor total for Yarborough is hard to believe, since his reelection was a prime goal of the Texas AFL-CIO. Certainly if political organizing services were counted, he received immense labor assistance.

Connally aside and told him: "John, that dumb-looking red-headed boy was the astutest politician in this room."

Soon, good things started happening to Ben Barnes. In 1963, he became chief liaison man between Connally and Byron Tunnell, then speaker of the Texas house. He also became a close friend of Austin attorney Frank Erwin, Jr., one of the key members of the Texas establishment. (Erwin had been one of the first to urge Connally to run for governor and later received the prestigious post of chairman of the board of regents of the University of Texas). In a surprise move early in 1965, Connally appointed Tunnell to a state agency, and Barnes, who had been acting as Tunnell's campaign manager for reelection as speaker, waged a blitz campaign and turned the Tunnell pledges into Barnes pledges, thus becoming speaker at the age of 26.

Soon it became apparent that Barnes was getting some financial breaks that might not have come his way back on the peanut farm at De Leon. As Bo Byers, veteran Houston *Chronicle* capital correspondent, reported in 1969:

> For a man whose only jobs prior to election to the legislature in 1960 were relatively menial and whose legislative pay is $400 monthly, Barnes has done quite well financially. The combination of his rapid political rise and outward signs of affluence—expensive suits and shoes, quickness to pick up the tab for dinner parties and social outings, and heavy travel expense—has made Barnes the target of much inquiry.
>
> The common question is "how did Barnes happen to get where he is so fast?" There is no clearcut answer.

Soon afterwards, there were reports that with little personal financial risk, Barnes had acquired various degrees of interest in construction, broadcasting, apartment, hotel, and shopping center ventures. No improprieties were evident, but the holdings did make Barnes suspect in the eyes of some liberals who had seen many establishment politicians get rich in office.

In 1968, Barnes ran for lieutenant governor and was elected. The lieutenant governor exercises almost dictatorial control over the Texas senate, just as the speaker does in the house. Barnes began to use his power more and more for liberal causes, and was the key figure in getting a minimum wage bill passed covering farm workers. If the states are to remain viable, he told me in a 1969 interview, "you have to be very liberal and progressive at the state level" or Congress will take over. "And if this makes me a liberal, I guess I'm liberal. Like bilingual education, or minimum wage, or more money for vocational education—in the area of human rights, I suppose I'm very liberal."

If he had become a real liberal, why did some liberals distrust him so much? "What they find wrong with me is that I'm just a part of the Johnson-Connally establishment that they like to speak of." Could he take liberal stands and not be in trouble with the conservatives? "This is a real problem, beyond any question. [But] I think my rural background helps me overcome a lot of rural opposition. . . . The newspapers have been very kind to me—the publishers. I think I can count on the newspaper support, and this helps keep the other part of the conservative establishment in line. . . .

I've never apologized for my friendship with Lyndon Johnson or John Connally—never one time." (Barnes also said, however, that he was interested in rebuilding the Democratic party nationally, in bringing in new faces and giving them a say, adding: "I think Johnson really destroyed the national Democratic party committee and the national party to some extent because he dominated it as one man.")

As the 1970s began, Barnes continued his liberal direction on state issues while trying to keep his close ties with the Johnson-Connally establishment. It was a balancing act no one had ever really tried before in Texas politics, and inevitably there were grumbles in the board rooms and among some hard-core liberals. With the mass of voters, all signs were that Barnes was succeeding brilliantly and would be a formidable candidate in 1972 for governor, a 1970 divorce (and subsequent remarriage) notwithstanding. Suave, articulate, a handsome blue-eyed young man with wavy hair and an intense manner, he seems likely to go far unless some side-issue—like the apparently unsuccessful 1971 effort to link him with the Sharp bank loan scandal—trips him on his way.

In fact, there is a possibility that Barnes might turn out to be uncomfortably liberal and innovative for the establishment crowd. It was hard to believe a status-quo establishment politician was talking when Barnes said:

> Texas is the fourth largest state in the U. S. in population, second largest in land area, first in natural resources and high in human resources, but our state per capita tax of $208 a year ranks 44th in the nation. We're growing by nearly 300,-000 people a year and 82 percent of our people live in urban areas. We're fortunate our cities are still young, and we can avoid some of the mistakes of places like Philadelphia and New York. We need to do something to solve our air and water pollution problems, to save our streams and lakes, and we can develop mass transit. . . . But we can't operate the fourth largest state in the U. S. on a tax per capita that's 44th and really solve our problems. It just can't be done.

In 1971, when Connally decamped for Washington to be Treasury Secretary, some fresh doubts were raised about Barnes's base of support. But at an autumn 1970 "Ben Barnes appreciation dinner" at Austin, it had looked like an official passing of the torch as Lyndon Johnson said: "Ben Barnes is the future. At 32 years of age, he's the youngest lieutenant governor Texas has ever produced." Johnson then pointed out that Presidents Jefferson, Jackson, Theodore and Franklin Roosevelt, and John Kennedy had all held important positions by the time they were 32. "Each of them wound up leading this country," Johnson said. "You and I know that Ben Barnes is going to lead it too."

Politics, Texas Style

The Democratic party has been dominant in Texas since before the Civil War, its rule interrupted only briefly by a few years of Reconstruction in the 1860s and 1870s. There has not been a Republican governor since

1874. But a basic conservative-liberal split has existed and bobbed up periodically in Texas for the better part of a century. Farm depressions hit the state in the 1880s and 1890s, and Populists and Greenbacks exploited the discontent by turning the farmer's ire on the railroads which transported his crops, on the financial houses which held his mortgages, trusts which fixed prices on his supplies, and businesses and realtors who benefited from depressed farm values. In 1890, Texas elected an exceptional governor, James Stephen Hogg, who ran on a platform attacking business abuses and asking for trust and railroad regulation. In 1906, Governor Thomas Campbell, endorsed by Hogg, continued the fight by strengthening antitrust legislation, instituting control of lobbies, and setting a maximum-hour law for railroad workers. Interspersed between progressive governors of this type were men more pliable to the various special business interests.

Around the turn of the century, Texas' Republican party and other political splinters faded into insignificance. A poll tax law, adopted at this point, discouraged Negroes and old Populists from voting. Only the Democrats held a primary, and all the interest centered on it (Negroes were effectively excluded). Enough colorful personalities arose to entertain Texans for decades, while their state government largely marked time. The dominant figure from 1915, when he was first elected governor, until the 1930s, was James or "Farmer Jim" Ferguson, a stemwinder and self-professed champion of the rural voter. Ferguson opposed both Prohibition and the Ku Klux Klan, rather popular causes in those days. The state legislature caught Ferguson with his hand in the till, impeached him in 1917, and said he could never again run for office in Texas. Ferguson then hit on the strategem (then an original idea) of running his wife instead. The slogan was: "Two Governors for the Price of One." "Ma" Ferguson ran five times and was elected twice, in 1924 and 1932. (Then as now, Texas limited its governors to frustratingly short two-year terms, though they may run to succeed themselves). Generally speaking, the Fergusons were the liberals of their time.

A similar appeal to the rustics launched Wilbert Lee (or "Pappy") O'Daniel on his political career in 1938. O'Daniel had become known through his hillbilly band, which he directed on a daily radio program advertising "Hillbilly" flour and dispensing homilies to a statewide audience. Promising to give everyone over 65 a $30-a-month pension, abolish the poll tax, and defend the Ten Commandments, O'Daniel jumped into the 1938 gubernatorial primary and won without a runoff. He won again in 1940 and in 1941 ran for the U. S. Senate in a special election, defeating a young New Dealing Congressman, Lyndon Johnson, by only 1,311 votes. Sent back to Washington for a full term in 1942, O'Daniel continued to talk the language of the country people but voted like a Chicago *Tribune* Republican.

By 1948, it was clear enough to Pappy O'Daniel that his support had slipped, and he voluntarily retired. It was a crucial year: retirement of the last of the rustics, and the election of Lyndon Johnson to the Senate. It was also the last year that the Democrats would elect their Presidential ticket virtually by default in Texas.

The Republican party, long a hopeless minority with little interest save patronage, began to assert itself in these years. In 1952, many independents and former Democrats moved into the Texas Republican party and tried to get delegates favoring General Eisenhower elected to that year's GOP National Convention. It was the last thing that the party Old Guard, strongly in favor of Senator Robert A. Taft, wanted to see happen. (Texas Old Guard chieftain Henry Zweifel was quoted as saying, "I'd rather lose with Taft than win with Eisenhower.") The Eisenhower forces elected many delegates, but the party regulars succeeded in disqualifying many of them. This created a cause which the Eisenhower Republicans could use and publicize. National magazines helped dramatize the delegate "steal" issue, and the pro-Eisenhower delegates were seated at Chicago, giving "Ike" a psychological advantage that helped him win the nomination four days later.

The disillusionment of vast numbers of conservative Texas Democrats with their national party became nationally significant in 1952, when Governor Allan Shivers endorsed Eisenhower for President over Adlai Stevenson. With Shivers' help and the revitalized GOP effort, Eisenhower carried Texas that autumn and again in 1956. The form of present-day Democratic politics in Texas actually took shape in these years. On the right wing there is a group like Shivers who disagree so fundamentally with national party nominees that they frequently bolt to the Republicans in a Presidential election, although they remain officially Democrats and vote for conservatives in state and local primaries. To the left of these are the regular Democrats, who were led by Lyndon Johnson and Sam Rayburn in the 1950s and then came under John Connally's tutelage in the 1960s. The monied Texas establishment of which we have spoken embraces both the right-wing and the moderate Democrats. But it obviously excludes the left-wing of the Democratic party: organized labor, Negroes, Mexican-Americans, and assorted white liberal allies. The only statewide officeholder this group has ever elected was Senator Ralph Yarborough. He won in a special election in 1957, in 1958, and 1964—and lost to a conservative opponent in the 1970 primary.

The liberal Democrats continually hope, without quite succeeding, to become a majority force in their own party. In 1960, they tried to take over the state party convention, but Johnson and Rayburn easily beat them back. Often, they resort to the expedient of "going fishing" on election day, or actually voting Republican, when a very conservative Democrat has won their party's nomination. Eventually, they keep hoping, the conservative Democrats will be driven into the Republican party, at which point the liberals—or "real Democrats," as they put it—can take over the Democratic party.

The liberals first tried their strategy in 1961. The year before, Johnson had been elected Vice President on the ticket with Kennedy, carrying Texas by a narrow 46,257-vote plurality. Taking no chances, LBJ had also run for and been reelected to the Senate. When he resigned his seat, a conservative "brass-collar" Democrat, William Blakley, was appointed to fill it pending a special election. After an initial election eliminated other contenders, a run-off was held between Blakley and Republican John G. Tower. Members of the left-wing coalition decided Blakley would be worse than Tower. Tower won, becoming Texas' first Republican Senator of the century, with a bare 50.6 percent of the vote—thanks, in no doubt, to the liberal coalition.

Again in 1966, liberal defections from the conservative Democratic nominee (Attorney General Waggoner Carr) led to the reelection of Tower, this time by an impressive majority. It seemed that the strategy was working, at least to the extent of driving some ideological right-wingers out of the Democratic party and into the Republican or, in years like 1968, into the Wallace movement. But the liberals continued to suffer from two imposing disabilities: lack of money and lack of a voice. In a statewide or Congressional campaign, they are simply incapable of raising funds anywhere comparable to what the business-oil establishment can and does make available to more conservative opponents. And with scarcely a major newspaper or major television station friendly to their cause, the liberals have great difficulty getting their message across. The biweekly *Texas Observer*, published in Austin, probes fearlessly into areas often ignored by the establishment press, ranging from statehouse scandals and the plight of the minorities to the establishment itself. Ronnie Dugger, editor or major contributor over many years, has molded the *Observer* into a sheet of liberal thought read by opinion leaders of every stripe. But its overall circulation is only 8,000.*

The 1970 defeat of Senator Yarborough came as a bitter blow to the Texas liberals. A man of mercurial temperament, disdainful of the monied establishment, Yarborough has been the liberals' acknowledged leader and hero since 1952. Lyndon Johnson, an old enemy, arranged mediocre committee assignments for Yarborough in Washington, but he eventually shifted onto the Labor and Public Welfare Committee (of which he became chairman in 1969) and onto Appropriations. Yarborough was able to deliver on the kind of issues liberals believe in: achieving Senate passage of the broad minimum wage expansion bill of 1966, chief sponsorship of the landmark Occupational Safety and Health Act of 1970, passage of a GI Bill for post-Korea veterans, and federal funding for bilingual education programs to ease the transition into English of youngsters with alien mother tongues (a boon for Texas, where one child in six entering the first grade speaks Spanish). He also won approval of the new Padre Island National Seashore (on the Gulf Coast) and Guadalupe Mountain National Park (in West Texas).

Yarborough made an occasional bow to Texas regularity, like supporting the oil depletion allowance, but on almost every other issue he was against the establishment. He knew it and they knew it. The only question was when the opportune moment to defeat him would come; it arrived in the "law-and-order" atmosphere of 1970 and in the person of Lloyd Bentsen. Bentsen's previous public service was limited to six years in Congress from South Texas between 1949 and 1955, after which he returned home to concentrate on private business. But he had the advantages of ample finances,

* Some clear-eyed reporting out of Austin is also provided by the Long News Service, perhaps the most sophisticated of its kind in a U. S. state capital. Stuart Long and his colleagues service some 18 newspapers daily and also have accumulated expertise in specific fields like insurance and water problems, which are the subject of individual newsletters the service publishes.

well connected campaign advisers like George Christian (former White House press secretary under President Johnson), and an advertising firm (Rives Dyke of Houston) with years of experience in political campaigns. Extensive polls were taken to gauge issues worrying the people—which turned out to be in the category of "youth rebellion," "social unrest," and "crime in the streets." A series of 30- and 60-second campaign films were then prepared to show that Yarborough was "ultraliberal" and out of touch with his people. The most controversial of these began with 15 seconds of the sounds of violence—people screaming and running at night along city streets. Bentsen's voice said: "That was the violence in Chicago spawned by supporters of Eugene McCarthy during the Democratic Convention. Sen. Ralph Yarborough endorsed McCarthy for President. Did he represent your views when he backed McCarthy?" Then there were sounds of sirens and people yelling as the film showed flames shooting out of buildings, and Bentsen continued: "That was violence in Washington during the moratorium last fall. Senator Yarborough endorsed the moratorium. Did he represent your views on these demonstrations? I don't think his actions represent the viewpoint of the people of Texas. That's why I'm running for the United States Senate against him."

Numerous other commercials along the same line were produced, including one accusing Yarborough of ducking out on a Senate vote on school busing. (He was clearly announced against the idea of busing.) Yarborough was thrown off balance, always replying a few days late to charges, and without the finances to regain the initiative. After Yarborough's defeat, Maury Maverick, Jr., of San Antonio, a well known liberal leader, summed up his camp's reaction in words the *Texas Observer* chose to make into a headline: "It was anti-nigger, anti-Mexican, anti-youth, and sock-it-to-'em in Vietnam."

One reason Yarborough lost was a sharp decline in support for him among his natural allies, white working-class people. Many of them reacted positively to Bentsen's law and order appeal. Also, Yarborough suffered from a pitifully low turnout in Negro and Mexican-American areas, the product of overconfidence and poor organization of his campaign. (Yarborough was defeated by about 90,000 votes as less than 1.6 million of the 4.1 million registered Democrats bothered to vote). A strong minorities vote is indispensable to Democratic victory in Texas. In 1968, for instance, minorities were responsible for Humphrey carrying the state. I heard one estimate that Humphrey's vote came one-third from Mexican-Americans, one-third from Negroes and one-third from Anglos.

Organized labor has difficulty making a major impact on state politics, despite the politically attuned leadership of the state AFL-CIO. One reason is that Texas has about as many laws restricting unions as one can imagine, including right-to-work, anti-picketing, and prohibitions against collective bargaining by public agencies. Until 1969, Texas had the lowest rate of workmen's compensation of any state, and no minimum wage law at all. Of Texas' total work force of about 4 million, just over 10 percent are organized (one of the lowest unionization rates in the entire U. S.). Unions also have difficulty influencing their members in elections because the membership they do have is concentrated in eastern Texas, where racial antagonisms are the worst. Another problem has been schisms among the top leaders of the AFL-CIO, though this may be relieved by the 1971 retirement of president Hank Brown, a George Meany-style regular, and his replacement by his arch rival, Roy Evans, the first United Auto Worker to head a state AFL-CIO. Detecting a need to educate Texans on issues like honesty in government, the environment, and minority rights, Texas liberals in 1971 formed the Action Coalition of Texas with white, Negro, and Mexican-American leadership. Under Evans' leadership, the state AFL-CIO promptly endorsed the ACT effort.

Another group with reason to be discouraged, despite all brave hopes and efforts of recent years, are the Texas Republicans. In 1952, the party succeeded in shaking off the image of a back-room patronage operation, but the young professionals, oilmen, and assorted business types who moved in to man the party still had something of a country club image 18 years later. And they were hard put to outpromise the entrenched monied establishment on the Democratic side. Only a perfectly arranged disarray on the Democratic side—as in the 1961 and 1966 Tower elections—permitted a Republican breakthrough. Otherwise, even exceptionally attractive candidates like George Bush of Houston and Paul Eggers of Wichita Falls went down to defeat (Bush for the Senate in 1964 and 1970, Eggers for governor in 1968 and 1970).

Under professional party leaders like state chairman and later national committeeman Peter O'Donnell of Dallas, the Republicans invested millions of dollars to build their position in Texas. But after Eisenhower's victories, they failed to carry Texas once for a Republican Presidential candidate. They elected Tower two times but won not a single other statewide victory. Foolishly, they climbed first and most enthusiastically on the Goldwater bandwagon in 1963–64, an exercise that almost obliterated the party in Texas. But six years of rebuilding from that debacle yielded the Republicans only three of the 23 Texas seats in the U. S. House, 10 of the 150 seats in the Texas House, 2 of 29 seats in the Texas Senate, and so few county and municipal offices as to be laughable.

Every Texas analyst can give you a theory for the Republicans' failure. One is the very fact that Democrats so dominate local and state offices that all the real talent goes into that party's primary, leaving the Republicans empty-handed. Another is that "me-tooism" in serving the monied establishment will cut little ice when the majority Democrats operate so effectively for Texas in Washington. (In 1968, the Republicans made much of their support for the 27½ percent oil depletion allowance, apparently to no avail. "Could it be," the San Antonio *Express/News* asked after the election, that "the average Texas voter suddenly realized he did not own an oil well?") Another criticism is that the GOP has been indifferent to or at least hostile to Latins and Negroes, in line with the Southern strategy born in the Gold-water days and carried on under the Nixon-Agnew Administration.* As long as the minorities represent about a third of the vote in Texas, and all their vote goes Democratic, the Republicans will have to win more than 75 percent of the remaining two-thirds to win elections. In a state packed still with brass-collar Democrats, many of them just as conservative as the Republicans, that task is almost impossible. (I am obliged to recall a *Texas Observer* comment: "The Bush/Bentsen contest just goes to show you that there are more Democrats than Republicans in this state. Given a choice be-tween Pillie Winkle and Winkie Pop, Texans'll take the dude with the Democratic label.")

The Republican bastions of modern Texas are Dallas and Houston, which are significantly also the centers of dynamic economic and population growth. Cities like Amarillo, Lubbock, Midland, Odessa, and sometimes Austin are also Republican, but San Antonio and El Paso, both with large populations, are made safely Democratic by the Mexican-American vote. Fort Worth is classically a swing town. When one reaches the smaller cities and towns, Republican strength is submerged in a sea of brass-collar Demo-cratic voters casting ballots like their fathers and grandfathers. One reason the Republicans lost in 1970, for instance, was an outpouring of country voters, mostly Democrats, intent on defeating a constitutional amendment to permit liquor by the drink (on a local option basis). A thirsty city vote de-feated the rural types on this issue, but only narrowly, and a lot of politically disinterested Democrats had gotten to the polls as a result. Texas was also a state where campaign visits by President Nixon and Vice President Agnew were said to be counterproductive, simply because they alerted the broad (and predominantly Democratic) populace to the fact that an election cam-paign was underway.

It should be noted that the big rural vote sometimes rears up to make decisions the monied establishment disapproves of. Preston Smith, the man who succeeded Connally as governor, was distinctly not Connally's choice. Smith's constituency is not big oil or chemicals but the trade associations and small businessmen—auto dealers, feed store operators, theatre owners—all over the state. He won election as governor by touring around to 225 counties acting as though he were running for county commissioner. Once elected, he turned out to be a routine seat-warmer, proposing few innovations in Texas government. But he did, to the surprise of many, permit some quite liberal bills to become law.

---

* Both Bush and Eggers were quite friendly to blacks and Mexicans; Bush, for instance, had voted for the 1968 open housing law. But both men were so thoroughly identified with the Nixon-Agnew Ad-ministration that minority voters instinctively chose their Democratic opponents. Shortly before the elec-tion, columnists Rowland Evans and Robert Novak reported on Bush's visits to college campuses and Negro slums (something Bentsen would never have done) and observed: "Bush—young (46), handsome, a Connecticut Yankee turned Houston oilman—is a glittering exponent of the 'modern' school of South-ern Republicans as contrasted with the 'primitives.' Like Gov. Linwood Holton of Virginia, Bush appeals to affluent suburbanites with economic conservatism while simultaneously wooing minority groups and labor. The 'primitives,' led by Sen. Strom Thurmond of South Carolina, concentrate on rural segregation-ist voters." There had even been a report that Bush, if elected, might have replaced Agnew on the 1972 Republican ballot for Vice President. But he lost by 155,334 votes (46.6 percent) and had to be content with the consolation prize of becoming U. S. Ambassador to the United Nations.

The most startling change of recent Texas politics has been the increase in voting participation. From the late 19th century until 1944 when the Supreme Court outlawed the white primary, scarcely any Negroes voted in Texas at all. The poll tax also acted as a depressant on voting. In 1920, only one in five adult Texans took the trouble to vote for President, in 1948 one in four. Then, with the Eisenhower races, interest quickened. By 1960, 41.4 percent voted. The 1960s brought two fundamental changes: the repeal of the poll tax in 1967 and, partly as a result of it, an increase in the number of voting age Negroes registered from the 1960 level of 33.7 percent to a 1968 level of 83.1 percent. But still, in the 1968 Presidential election, only 49.0 percent of voting age Texans cast ballots for President—46th rank among the states.

The continued low turnout was attributable to some of the most restrictive and regressive election laws anywhere in America. Through 1970, Texas required all voters to reregister *annually*, by January 31 of the election year. No other state required annual reregistration, a deliberate device to hold down the size of the electorate and confine it to a controlled vote. (Among the strongest proponents of annual registration was John Connally.) Finally, a federal court in 1971 declared annual registration unconstitutional and a new law was passed making registration permanent as long as a person actually votes once every three years. Yet even then, the legislature was busy trying to hold down participation in elections by decreeing that the group newly enfranchised by constitutional amendment—the 18-through-20 age group—could only register to vote in the hometowns of the parents. Two North Texas State University students quickly challenged the law as unconstitutional, and the state attorney general and secretary of state ruled in their favor. Before that, the federal courts had stepped in to invalidate Texas' sky-high filing fees for office, a percent device to keep the poor and nonestablishment types off the ballot for many offices. So it is that official Texas, resisting to the last, is propelled toward levels of participatory democracy that might just set the older order on its head in our times.

Government and Nongovernment

Texas fails to place well in any of the tests one might impose on government—breadth of services provided, innovative programming, tax effort and fairness, strong executive control, civil service, regulation of business and freedom from outside influence, and efficiency in the legislature.

In the late 1960s, Texas ranked this way in per capita government outlays for services, compared to the other states: 38th in welfare, 43rd in health and hospitals, 27th in police protection, 30th in higher education, 38th in local schools. The state's tax effort (taxes paid in relation to personal income) was 42nd among the 50 states.

With the exception of its excellent highway system, there are few areas of state legislation or programming where Texas may be considered a leader in the nation. "Nothing happens at the upper levels of our state government," a rather embittered liberal state legislator told me, "until we get sat on by the federal government." He named welfare administration, transportation control, and consumer protection as areas in which Texas government was especially weak. As an example, Texas offers splendid opportunities for rapid mass ground transit to serve its big cities; one can imagine a link connecting Dallas and Fort Worth, then a leg to Houston, spokes out to the Gulf Coast, and finally connection of San Antonio and Austin in a system serving a great megalopolitan region. But in 1970, rail transit in Texas was fast deteriorating, and the only subway in the state connected Leonard's Department store in Fort Worth with a parking lot a quarter mile away. No one in Austin was making further plans. Texans' love of the automobile seems to be second to none save Californians', and they think nothing of driving long distances, even through urban sprawl. ("Every time you drive to Houston, you get there 15 minutes earlier," goes a modern crack—referring not to improved highways, but uncontrolled growth out across the coastal plain.)

Texas' inactive state government is matched by a regressive tax structure. About 63 percent of government income is provided by sales, license, and property taxes which place the greatest burden on middle- and low-income persons. In 1970, one study showed that a Houston family in poverty at $3,500 a year paid 9.6 percent of its total income in state and local taxes. A family earning $25,000 in the same city paid 3.3 percent. At $50,000, the family paid a scarcely significant 2.5 percent. To a slightly lesser degree, the same type of discrepancies were apparent in other Texas cities. The better way to tap the growth in the state's economy would be an income tax, anathema in modern-day political debate in Texas. By 1971, no governor had ever proposed it, but its inevitability (in the face of grave budget deficiencies) was generally admitted. An ultimate establishment figure, Frank Erwin, made a speech late in 1970 saying that the legislature would have to pass either a sales tax on food (an especially regressive device) or a personal income tax. The alternative, Erwin said, would be to repeal salary increases for school teachers, turn 14,000 high school graduates away from state colleges and universities because there would be no room for them, tell the families of the mentally malfunctioning to keep them in back rooms at home, and inform the old, the blind, the fatherless children and indigent ill that the state won't help them any more. "I don't believe in this affluent society we're going to tell people we've got no way to take care of them because we don't want to pay taxes," Erwin said.

About 32 percent of Texas' tax dollar comes from various levies on business, most significantly the 4.6 percent tax placed on the value of oil at the wellhead. Congressman Bob Eckhardt of Houston served several years in the state legislature and made repeated efforts to increase taxes on oil and gas, all to no avail. He argues that Texas oil has been undertaxed because of the political power of the small producers and independents, who until recently were responsible for half the state's production. In Louisiana, by contrast, almost all the extraction is done by "majors" with headquarters outside the state, and "you can have a Huey Long fighting 'em like the devil and taxing the hell out of oil and gas." Eckhardt favors making the wellhead tax a graduated one, depending on the amount of production. This would increase the tax share of the 17 largest producers and bring the state an extra $25 million a year. He says it would relieve some competitive pressure on the small, marginal producer who is hard put to stay profitable in the face of oil imports and the monopolistic power of the international majors. There has also been pressure for some years to impose a natural gas longlines tax. Always lurking in the wings, if Texas gets really serious about new taxes, is a possible levy on corporate profits.

The regulatory bodies of Texas state government have never earned a reputation for toughness in dealing with private interests, but the illustrious Texas Railroad Commission is a special case. In the early 1930s, when the East Texas field was being depleted at a dangerous rate and the price of oil hit an all-time low, the Railroad Commission (which had been given the job of supervision since it had long regulated oil shipments by railroad tank cars) stepped in to set production "allowables." Martial law had to be imposed before the commission's quotas on production were obeyed, but ever since the commission has wisely conserved a natural resource by its orders. The simultaneous effect, of course, has been to profit the oilmen by keeping prices up through limited supply. Oddly enough, the railroad commissioners, like the members of the state board of education, are actually chosen in statewide popular elections.

Efficient government in Texas is hampered by the 1876-vintage constitution, packed with provisions to limit the executive. Most of the actual governing is done by more than 200 boards with overlapping six-year terms. The governor gets to appoint 700 or 800 men to these commissions, but as a rule they are unpaid and simply turn administration over to the staffs they hire. Agencies become semi-independent satrapies, and their heads stay in year after year. Terms are rotating, so that a governor must be in office several years before he gets any kind of control. Even then, departments often function as if others simply didn't exist. The employment commission and welfare department, for instance, should work together closely, but they don't. Institution of any modern management techniques in such a structure is virtually impossible. Texas is completely lacking in a civil service system for state employees, but the fact of one-party control—inhibiting mass firings and hirings when administrations change—has made for relative stability.

The governor's powers are also extremely limited vis-à-vis the legislature. Ben Barnes states that "the lieutenant governor's office in Texas is by far the most powerful. . . . Our chief executive definitely needs more power and our lieutenant governor's office [powers] need to be diluted." The lieutenant governor, who presides over the senate, and his counterpart, the speaker of the house, actually appoint all legislative committees and chairmen and assign all bills to them. Much important legislation ends up being written by conference committees with five members appointed by the lieutenant governor, five by the speaker. "They operate with a free hand, and it's really a very poor system," Barnes states. Interestingly, he made his observations while serving as lieutenant governor, after four years as speaker. Texas, he believes, needs a cabinet form of government.

Court-forced reapportionment brought many new urban legislators to the Texas house and senate during the 1960s, promising long-term change in those bodies. Among the early crop were some outstanding new legislators (including the first blacks in both houses). But the stand-outs tended to be the exception rather than the rule. Again to quote Barnes, "reapportionment has made the legislature more aware of city problems and progressive minded. But the city legislators have to spend so much money to get elected that it's been my experience that many of them are so indebted to special interest groups, bloc votes, and political bosses that they don't have enough time to spend on actually solving city problems." Rural legislators, he said, build up more seniority and effective leadership, and "many of them are stronger men."

One interesting phenomenon is that the senate has become more liberal since reapportionment, but the house increasingly conservative. Eckhardt explains it this way: "The visible officeholder [a senator] is likely to be a people's man. At lower levels [the house] he's less visible and more likely to be controlled by a coalition of special interest groups." To a degree, the same phenomenon operates in the U. S. Congress.

Which are the most effective pressure groups in Austin? I heard them identified as the Texas Chemical Council (which was especially powerful under Connally), the Texas Midcontinent Oil & Gas Association (the major oil front), the Texas Independent Producers & Royalty Owners, the Texas State Teachers' Association, the Texas Manufacturers' Association (important in labor legislation and pollution control), the Texas Medical Association, the Texas Motor Transport Association, and various insurance organizations. Most lobbies pick ex-legislators to represent them in Austin.

The Texas legislature has come in for some stiff criticism in recent times. A 1971 report by the Citizens Conference on State Legislatures ranked Texas only 38th among the 50 in an aggregate rating of its ability "to perform in a functional, accountable, informed, independent and representative manner." Among the major deficiencies of the legislature are lack of annual sessions, too many committees for efficient operation (45 in the house, 27 in the senate), lack of year-round staffing for major committees, and the lack of legislative independence created by the power placed in the hands of the presiding officers. All seem to be failures that a big and prospering state like Texas could easily correct.

What it might take to improve the moral tone in Austin is another question. In 1968, Mrs. Lee Clark, wife of a Dallas legislator, wrote of the legislature as "an ethical brothel" and recorded this incident:

My husband was punching his voting button against an especially odious piece of legislation when he noted on the electronic board that a colleague seated close by was recorded for it. He turned to the man and asked how on God's earth he could vote for such a thing and still keep his dinner down. The legislator, stumpy and smoke-infested, walked over, hoisted his arm around my husband's shoulders, and affirmed with a certain pride: "I'm just a political whore, boy; that's what I am, a political whore."

He is definitely not alone. The Texas Trial Lawyers Association, fighting hard against "no fault" auto insurance that would compensate victims regardless of fault—and take away a lucrative business for many attorneys—is especially active in Texas, both in elections (where it takes credit for causing nomination of several state senators) and during legislative sessions. According to a former officer of the national trial lawyers' group, "an open bar and buffet lunch" is available at the Texas Association's Austin office every day the legislature is in session; each day 25 to 30 legislators stroll over to indebt themselves a bit further.

Vast differences of quality appear at the various levels of Texas government. For the most part, the state's cities are well administered, with an exceptionally high number of professional city managers. A promising "COG" (council of governments) movement is developing in Texas, as a way to tie together smaller governments over hundreds of square miles. (The most outstanding of these, the North Central Texas COG, is discussed in the Fort Worth subchapter below). "The COGs," Rep. James H. Clark, Jr., of Dallas told me, "will end up relating to the federal government while the state government sits here complaining about its loss of prerogatives."

When it comes to rural county government in Texas, the sands of time seem to have stopped running a few decades ago. County judges or commissioners are often heavy-handed papas who run their little domains with an iron hand. Voter registration records are often kept in a haphazard way, thus inviting irregularities, and the local powers have available to them a road and bridge fund to buy people off. Population is declining in a majority of these counties, and the low income levels create a demand for old-age assistance and welfare funds that is a major economic drain on the rest of the state. Yet in the late 1960s, even while studies were revealing shocking conditions of hunger and malnutrition in rural Texas, almost half the counties were refusing to participate in federal food programs for the needy. The stated reason: the cost of administration—30 cents per person per month—was more than they could afford to pay.

Geographic Texas: From the Gulf to the Pedernales

Alaska's unmatched size notwithstanding, Texas remains a huge and multisplendored state. It covers one-twelfth the land area of the coterminous U.S.A., a territory as large as New York, New Jersey, Pennsylvania, Ohio, Illinois, plus all of New England combined. East to west, Texas extends 773 miles, north to south an intimidating 801 miles. Just one of Texas' 254 counties (of course no other state has so many) is larger than the entire state of Connecticut. There are more miles of roads and highways in Texas

(247,000 in 1967) than there are miles to the moon.

The Texan empire is so vast that Stephen F. Austin, the Virginia-born "Father of Texas" who started the first important colony in 1821, once called it "a wild, howling, interminable solitude." Even with the civilizing influence of 11 million people, getting one's bearings is still difficult. The basic division the geologists talk about is the Balcones Escarpment, a fault line that splits Texas into basic eastern and western regions. The line runs generally north to south, dropping from the Oklahoma border to a point between Dallas and Fort Worth and then by Waco, Austin, and San Antonio; there it veers westerly for 150 miles until it meets the Rio Grande and the Mexican border.

East of the escarpment lies the Gulf Coastal Plain—hot, low country (the center of Texas' oil and chemical industries) which includes big cities like Houston and Corpus Christi, the "Piney Woods" section covering the whole northeastern corner of the state (north of Houston, east of Dallas), and the fertile lower Rio Grande Valley, known for its winter gardens and citrus fruit.

Two plains regions lie west of the escarpment, actually the southernmost extension of two broad continental divisions. First come the Central Plains, which in some physiographic maps are shown to range as far northward as the Great Lakes; in Texas they vary greatly in form, but are mostly rolling prairie between 1,000 and 2,500 feet in altitude, classic cattle, sheep, and goat country that was once the southernmost range of the buffalo. Farther west lie the arid, level High Plains, which form a clear-cut belt all the way to the Canadian border along the North Dakota and Montana lines. The entire Texas Panhandle lies within the High Plains region.

Finally, there is the desert-like triangle of westernmost Texas, which actually lies south of New Mexico. This is Trans-Pecos Texas, a land of gaunt scenery, high mountains (actually the southernmost extension of the Rockies), mesquite, cacti, and lonely distances. Here one finds the Big Bend National Park on the Rio Grande and, at the state's westernmost extremity, the city of El Paso. At El Paso, the average annual rainfall is less than eight inches; a measure of the contrast of Texas places is that at Houston, a few hundred miles to the east, the figure is over 45 inches (with humidity to match).

The Gulf Coast, with its 370-mile long window to the sea, is Texas' most cosmopolitan region, heavily peopled with Mexican-Americans toward the Rio Grande and mixtures of rural white Southerners, Negroes, and Cajuns up toward the Louisiana border.

Some of Texas' most important oil fields lie in an arc just inland from the Gulf, as do the low, damp lands in which a major portion of the U. S. rice crop is produced. Not to be overlooked is the huge 118-year-old King Ranch, covering 865,000 acres, the equivalent of 1,350 square miles, traversed by more than 500 miles of paved road, the grazing land of some 45,000 head of cattle and more than 2,000 horses. Oil was discovered under King Ranch land in 1939, and by the late 1960s there were 504 oil and 138 gas wells, bringing the owning Kleberg family fantastic yearly earnings of $20 million—compared to livestock operations which *Fortune* in 1969 estimated probably did not exceed $5 million annually.*

A review of the major gulf area cities, moving northeasterly: Corpus Christi (1970 population 204,525, up from a mere 27,741 in 1930) booms with a magnificent yacht basin and marina in its downtown section, plus oil in its backlands. It refuses to be daunted by events like the 1970 hurricane which damaged 80 percent of its buildings. Up the coast, the history of Galveston (pop. 61,809) includes "The Storm" of 1900, a hurricane that demolished the city and left more than 6,000 dead. These days, Galveston is still staggering from a state crackdown in the late 1950s on its then notorious gambling, prostitution, and narcotics trade. Now the city has a cleaner sea-and-surf tourism but seems forever afflicted by environmental pollution, including raw sewage and petrochemical discharges into its bay. Beaumont (115,919) and Port Arthur (57,371), both parts of the Houston industrial triangle, were likewise plagued by gambling, prostitution, and liquor violations until a 1961 investigation. Now they are "clean" like Galveston, but honesty does not always equal prosperity, and all three cities have lost population since 1960. Politically, the Gulf Coast cities are the most liberally Democratic in Texas, a phenomenon explained by a high percentage of organized labor, a heavy black contingent, and many Catholics. Near Beaumont lies the inconspicuous mound of earth called Spindletop, where the first great oil strike of Texas history was made in January 1901.

As important as it was, Spindletop would be dwarfed in importance by the strike made 170 miles north, in the peanut and sweet potato patches of Rusk County, in 1930. A determined old "wildcatter," 71-year-old C. M. "Dad" Joiner, had sunk his last dollars into a makeshift drilling rig that finally hit oil at 3,600 feet, thus opening up the vast East Texas field—the greatest field ever located in the United States until, possibly, the North Slope Alaska strike of the 1960s.

The great oil strike never altered the character of East Texas. It remained—and remains—the "piney woods" it has always been, a touch of the Deep South, the most backward section of all Texas. In 1968, Wallace got 35 percent of the vote here, his best showing in the state. Negroes represent 40 to 55 percent of the population in some counties but can, to date, count none of their number as elected officials; the baronial system of white county bosses still holds firm. State representative Curtis Graves of Houston, a Negro, told me: "Traditionally the people who are elected in East Texas are those who can hate the most. There are still killings by local sheriffs and the establishment. One young man was shot with handcuffs on, allegedly running away from a policeman. . . . He had front entrance wounds. You know that all Negroes run backward. Everyone knows that. I call it murder."

Starting just west of the piney woods, in a broad swatch coming down from Oklahoma and reaching almost to the gulf, is a strip of dark, rich prairie

* Readers interested in the fabulous story of the Klebergs and King Ranch, a true American classic, should see Charles J. V. Murphy's article "Treasures in Oil and Cattle," in *Fortune*, August 1969.

soil some call the Blacklands. Sorghum, soybeans, and corn, supporting a flourishing cattle industry, have gradually replaced cotton here.

Five major Texas cities—Dallas, Forth Worth, Waco, Austin, and San Antonio—lie astride the Blacklands. Surely the loveliest and most livable of these is Austin, possessed of the state capitol, the University of Texas campus, and in recent times an increasingly prosperous base in "light and clean" industry which helped to balloon the population from 132,459 in 1950 to 251,808 in 1970. Now the massive $18.6 million complex of the Lyndon Baines Johnson Library and School of Public Affairs, planned on a typically Johnsonian grandiose scale that dwarfs the libraries of previous Presidents, crowds the already jam-packed campus of the University of Texas.

The most outstanding achievement of the Connally administration may have been the effort to transform the University of Texas into one of the leading state universities of the country and create an academic establishment and training capability to draw aerospace-type industries. A major point of emphasis was improving the faculty and library resources at the mother campus in Austin. By 1970, UT had become one of the nation's outstanding teaching and research institutions and rated among the top 15 universities in the American Council on Education's report on graduate education. And it had become a truly statewide institution with branch campuses at Houston, El Paso, Arlington, Odessa, Dallas, and San Antonio, including several medical schools.*

Trouble was waiting, though, in the person of Frank Erwin, Jr., Connally's close personal and political friend, whom he appointed to the board of regents in 1963. Erwin's love for UT was hardly to be doubted, but his idea of a great university turned out to be one in which teachers teach but steer clear of politics, students study and never demonstrate, and the regents govern at his direction. Erwin was enraged by any student demonstrations (of which UT had relatively few) and became upset with professors and administrators who refused to crack down hard on any student insurgence.

By 1971, there was real question whether UT could retain its newly won academic eminence. In less than a year, Erwin had forced the dismissal or resignation of Chancellor Harry Ranson (a nationally renowned scholar), the vice chancellor for academic affairs, the president (Norman Hackerman) and vice president of the Austin campus, the dean of Austin's highly regarded college of arts and sciences (John R. Silber, now president of Boston University), and three of five teachers who had held the title of "university professor." Erwin stepped down as chairman of the regents in 1971 but would remain a board member until 1975 and was replaced by a man of the same ideological stripe.

Austin's other great landmark is the 308-foot-high capitol building, set in lovely tree-filled grounds and commanding a long view down Congress Avenue, the city's major thoroughfare. Of course the capitol building is the

---

* In all, Texas has 124 institutions of higher education. Among the private universities, Rice (at Houston) and Southern Methodist University (at Dallas) are generally considered the most illustrious. UT was peaceably integrated in the mid-1950s but still has only a few hundred Negro enrollees. The major Negro universities are Texas Southern University at Houston and Prairie View A & M.

largest in any of the 50 states, and in likewise typical old-Texas style, one learns that it was paid for by deeding more than three million acres of public land to a Chicago syndicate in return for building it. But in other ways, Austin is so un-Texan. Austin is described quite accurately by Texas novelist Larry McMurtry as "a pretty, sunny town, the climate warm, the sky blue and unsmogged," where "the sun sets plangent and golden into the purple of the Austin hills at evening, and the moon, whiter than a breast, lights the Colorado River."

Our account returns later to the most metropolitan Blacklands cities (Dallas-Fort Worth, San Antonio), but a word might be said about Waco (population 95,326), midpoint between Austin and Dallas. Waco is filled with so many lavishly built Baptist churches that some have nicknamed it the Baptists' Rome. Baylor, the well known Southern Baptist university, is in town too. Waco survives off surrounding farmlands and big factories of General Tire & Rubber and Owens-Illinois Glass. Oddly enough, it is the home base of an extremely skillful and influential fund-raiser for liberal political contenders and the "peace" cause, insurance executive Bernard Rapoport.

West of Fort Worth, Austin, *et al.*, the Central Plains begin. The ride west from Austin is best known since it leads through the famed hill country to the LBJ Ranch.

Just a few miles west of the LBJ Ranch is the little city of Fredericksburg, a reminder of the strong German heritage of many counties in this part of Texas. Founded by German colonists in 1846, it has been a stronghold of German habits and customs ever since with Abendglocken (evening church bells) and Sängerfeste (song festivals).

Before we leave the Central Plains, three other cities require brief mention. Wichita Falls (pop. 97,564), near the Oklahoma border, is a dull faced North Texas oil town. It also has a hefty payroll from nearby Sheppard Air Force Base, and culture intrudes in the form of Midwestern University, where Republican John G. Tower was a professor of political science before his forensic skills and good luck catapulated him into Lyndon Johnson's old Senate seat in 1961. Some 140 miles southwesterly is the fabled old cattle town of Abilene (pop. 89,653), living off an air force base, regional oil and agricultural activity, and miscellaneous manufacturing. A few more miles south is San Angelo (pop. 63,884), heart of one of the world's greatest sheep and goat raising territories.

From the Panhandle to the Rio Grande

Now we move onto the High Plains. I still recall my first drive up from Wichita Falls toward Amarillo on the Panhandle, seeing the ground turn flat, so incredibly flat, and the fields of wheat stretching out endlessly across the prairie. We drove on for hours, and then the first structures jutted up on the horizon, and if I am not mistaken, we drove another full 20 miles until we actually came on them. They turned out to be huge grain elevators, outside

Amarillo. Here Texas gets its only taste of the "continental climate": frigid winters, hot summers, and the wind blowing and blowing and blowing. World War I stimulated such a huge wheat demand that the number of farms on the Panhandle and related plains area below it increased 48 percent in five years; then with the native buffalo grass plowed under, wind eroison took hold, production fell precipitously, and Texas took years to dig away the Dust Bowl wreckage and recultivate the earth. In the early 1950s, another cruel drought hit western Texas. And starting in late 1970, there was yet another which some feared might match the worst of the past.

Except in drought times, the High Plains now support not only wheat but a thriving cattle industry and huge cotton harvests. There is even some protection from drought, since some 6 million acres are irrigated from underground wells, enabling farmers to grow sorghum grains in vast quantities and feed hundreds of thousands of head of cattle. (The country's biggest cattle auction takes place in Amarillo each year.) Ten percent of the cotton grown in the U.S. is harvested within 50 miles of Lubbock, which has long since replaced East Texas and the Blacklands as the cotton center of Texas.

The people of the plains tend to be tough, independent, politically conservative types—in some people's eyes, the purest examples of *Tejano erectus* to be found anywhere.

Three big cities thrive on the High Plains—Amarillo, Lubbock, and Midland-Odessa. The only one of the group most non-Texans have any image of is Amarillo (1970 population 127,010), the natural capital of a huge region extending over all the Panhandle and deep into Oklahoma and Kansas. Aside from its renowned attractions of high winds, oil, cattle, and wheat, the town actually has some civic attractions you might not expect on the prairies (even a zoo and several good art galleries). In recent years the city has been a citadel of right-wingism with one of the country's most powerful John Birch Society chapters. Lubbock (population 149,101) is not well known because as recently as 1940, the Census count was only a fifth of that. I can think of no other American city that has grown so fast in modern times on the basis of agriculture. In May 1970, 600 ramshackle wood houses of Lubbock's "Little Mexico" were virtually leveled by a vicious tornado, which killed 20 people. It was Texas' worst since 1953, when a twister reeled out of a thunderstorm at Waco and killed 114 persons.

Still farther to the south, on the harsh and desolate West Texas plain about on the level of the southern border of New Mexico, are Midland and Odessa, begun 90 years ago as sidings on the line of the Texas and Pacific Railway line from Fort Worth to El Paso. In the 1940s and 1950s, they became gold dust twins of the rapid oil and gas exploitation of the 90,000-square-mile Permian Basin. Midland, which had 5,484 people in 1930, boasted 62,625 in 1960; Odessa grew from 2,407 to 80,338. Then, in the 1960s, as the oil boom began to wind down, both cities lost a small percentage of their population. Midland has been a city of millionaire owners, of white-collar workers and executives, working in big high-rise office buildings incongruously set on the plains. Odessa, by contrast, is a hard-hat town, filled with roughnecks, roustabouts, maintenance men, and engineers.

Now our focus shifts 225 miles westward, over the ravished glories of Trans-Pecos Texas, and we are at the westernmost extremity of this gargantuan state, and the city of El Paso. Together with its sister city of Ciudad Juarez, directly across the Rio Grande, El Paso forms part of the largest bilingual metropolis on an international boundary anywhere in the world. Spurred on by military installations and new industries, El Paso more than doubled its population (from 130,485 to 276,687) between 1950 and 1960, and then added another 16 percent growth in the following decade for a 1970 total of 322,261.

El Paso's ingrained attitude of indifference toward the impoverished Mexican-Americans in its midst, especially those in the festering southside ghetto, began to loosen some in the late 1960s as civic leaders took an interest in programs to alleviate severe unemployment and the problems of youth, vandalism and narcotics use.

The lowest per capita income rates in the U.S. are along the Rio Grande; conversely, the Mexican area with the highest incomes are directly across the river.

With good reason, Walter Prescott Webb classified all of Texas from San Antonio westward as "desert rim" territory. Each of the cities there has had to depend on rather precarious sources of water, often involving importation over long distances. Most of the territory was restricted to grazing or dry farming until the 1940s, when discoveries were made of enormous amounts of water in aquifers far below the bone-dry surface of the land. Thousands of artesian wells, many sunk thousands of feet, have made possible vast harvests of cotton and grain sorghum and maintenance of huge feedlots for cattle. In West Texas, where as late as the 1950s thousands of farmers fled before drought conditions, the impact has been almost beyond description. In fact, by the late 1960s it was estimated that 75 percent of the state of Texas' *total* water consumption was from underground sources.

But the underground water, built up over centuries, is not being replenished and in fact is dropping in many areas (especially the West) by two to three feet each year. By 1985, according to state officials, the huge Ogallala aquifer in West Texas will begin to decline as a source of supply. Then that area, which presently accounts for most of the irrigated farmland in Texas, will be forced to start a retrenchment to dryland farming with markedly adverse effects on Texas' farm output ($2.8 billion annually in the late 1960s, supporting a related annual $6–7 billion in commerce and industry). By the year 2020, according to state estimates, remaining water sources will supply only 50 percent of Texas' total developed irrigated acres. This grim prospect led some ambitious Texans to spawn the idea of a fantastic water diversion scheme to bring 12 to 13 million acre-feet of flood river from the Mississippi River to West Texas canals and pipelines. The cost would be about $9 billion, financed mostly by the federal government. But so far, Texas voters have refused to obligate themselves to pay what would be their share (about $3.5 billion) for a project that would benefit principally big agriculture—and cost four times as much as the entire TVA.

A big enough federal water project is already underway in Texas: the $1 billion Trinity River Waterway, involving construction of a navigation channel 370 miles long from the Gulf of Mexico to Dallas and Fort Worth.

Houston: Boom Town on the Bayou

Houston, Texas, sixth largest city in the United States, having registered an impressive 31 percent population gain in the 1960s, is expected to double its population of 1,232,802 people in the 1970s. (Counting the metropolitan area, almost 2 million people already live there.) Among the 50 largest cities of America, there is only one growing as fast—Phoenix—and its population is less than half of Houston's today. *Fortune* has identified Houston's great new growth as a management boom, based on the decision of scores of great American corporations to move major operations, or even headquarters, to the city. Brash Houston promoters point out to industrialists in the problem-plagued Northeast that they can avoid congestion and high costs—in fact, even reduce their labor costs substantially—by a move to Houston. Thus having already established itself as the greatest commercial and population center of the Southwest, Houston shows its usual ebullience and vigor as it tries to fulfill the predictions of admirers who say it will be, by the year 2000, one of the great cities of the world.

The irony of it all is the location. Beset by fantastic heat and humidity, Houston was just a mosquito-infested, muddy tract of land near the sluggish Buffalo Bayou in 1836 when two New York real estate developers, the Allen brothers, paid a dollar an acre to buy it from the widow of the great Texan settler, John Austin. Marvin Hurley, executive vice president of the present-day Houston Chamber of Commerce, cheerily observes that it was "the most inhospitable place to start a city that anyone could have found." Air conditioning takes the worst edge off that condition, and no one thinks of Houston as a sleepy bayou town anymore. Instead, Houston is spoken of as a remarkably open, young, informal, progressive city—and a place that revels in the conspicuous consumption of its new wealth. Other Gulf-area cities, like New Orleans and Galveston, might as easily have seized the place in the sun Houston has made its own, but they were encumbered by a clannishness and old-family culture.

It was old Jesse Jones, the renowned "Mr. Houston" of his time, who summed up Houston the best, shortly before he died in 1956: "I always said that someday Houston would be the Chicago of the South, and it is. Railroads built this town, the port made it big, cotton and cattle kept it rich, oil boomed it, and now we're the chemical capital of the world. Growing, growing, growing, that's Houston."

Amazingly, Houston was still growing at the start of the 1970s, and at an ever accelerating rate, precisely when most of the U.S. was cooling off from the "Soaring Sixties." *Fortune* declared in 1971 that Houston was in a great "management" boom, evidenced not by refineries or mills but rather by "curtain-wall skyscrapers, shopping arcades, and new suburban homes." Between 1959 and 1969, office space in the central business district rose from 10 million to 16.4 million square feet, but by the end of the 1970s the figure was confidently projected at 50 million. An interesting change in the type of new development was also occurring. During the 1960s, suburban office space rose from 2 to 9 million square feet and there was a great concentration on low-level shopping centers, parks, apartment complexes, and offices that gave the city a horizontal look. But around the start of the 1970s, developers and especially the big corporations decided the time had come to return to and humanize downtown with large but well proportioned developments, fountains, small shops, and living areas.

Anyone who has visited Houston in the last 20 years can appreciate the desirability of tasteful, big-scale corporate development in center city. Alone among the great cities of America, Houston has no zoning, and city planning has been at a minimum. While many great office buildings already stand there, the spaces between them are often a dreary no-man's land. For an interview with M. A. Wright, chairman of the board of Humble Oil, I went to Humble's handsomely designed white marble skyscraper, the way to Wright's office preceded by long, carpeted corridors with rich wood doorways. From his office, there was a stunning view over some distance to the south, the white Astrodome glistening in the morning sun. But directly below, all around the building, the view was of one- and two-story ramshackle retail outlets, endless parking lots, and empty spaces, the prototype of the city where the planners never had their day. (A local editor explained the lack of zoning to me this way: "Houston is populated with people from small towns and farms of the old, rural South. Their salient characteristic is fierce, don't-fence-me-in individualism—the psychology that 'If I want to have a pigpen in my backyard, by God I can!' ")

Zoning or not, a lot of impressive building had been done in Houston by the end of the 1960s. From a slight distance, where one couldn't see the blank spaces between, the vista was one of a spectacular skyline of shiny new squares and rectangles, topped by the oil company signs like those one normally sees lining the tawdry auto alley approaches to American cities. Closer examination of the city revealed some splendid embellishments, including the Houston Civic Center with a convention hall and the celebrated Alley Theater.

Houston's most grandiose construction undertaking of the 1970s is to be what the local press unabashedly calls "the boldest, biggest, and most imaginative downtown redevelopment project ever attempted"—the massive Houston Center. It will cover 75 acres immediately east of the principal Main Street thoroughfare, land which for decades has been a hodgepodge of filling stations, unsightly warehouses, parking lots, and cheap hotels. The sponsor is Texas Eastern Transmission Corp., a prosperous firm that never before ventured beyond its basic business of transporting and selling oil and gas products. The development will cost $1.5 *billion*, but it is only one of several developments in central Houston and its suburbs that rank in the several-hundred-million-dollar class, combining office buildings, apartments, enclosed shopping centers, gigantic parking facilities, and entertainment and cultural facilities.

Such are the Bayou City's incredibly ambitious plans. The question raised is—why Houston? Foremost, there is the momentum Jesse Jones began. Secondly, land, construction, and operating costs are substantially lower than in most other large cities (as an example, $30 to $35 a square foot construction costs, compared to as much as $45 in New York). State taxes are low, and commercial property in Houston, according to Ralph Nader, is being assessed "at a rate approximately one-half that used for residential property." Houston's cost of living ranks among the lowest of major U. S. cities, meaning that labor can be paid less. Between 1967 and 1970, it was estimated that 5,000 executives and middle-echelon employees of major corporations had moved to Houston, including about half of Shell Oil's New York staff.

Any view of Houston's successes must be considered in the context of the city's remarkable strides throughout this century. First came the Houston Ship Channel, opened in 1914, which snakes through some 50 miles of bayou, river, and Galveston Bay shallows to the Gulf of Mexico. Thirty-six feet deep and 400 feet wide, the channel is big enough for large oceangoing ships.

In terms of total tonnage, the port of Houston ranks third in the U.S., behind New York and New Orleans. It is seventh or eighth in foreign trade, a factor that seems to contribute to Houston's very open economic and political atmosphere (especially in contrast to other Texas cities). Thirty-nine foreign countries have consulates in Houston, and close to $400 million worth of trade is done each year with Japan alone. The deepwater port gives Houston a stake in a national free trade policy and makes it much less parochial than inland cities like Dallas.

Spindletop made Houston a big oil center, and the visitor need only glance at the names on the skyscrapers of downtown Houston to see who's there now—Gulf, Shell, Texaco, Conoco, Humble, Tenneco, Texas Gulf Sulphur, Texas Eastern, Schlumberger Limited—in several instances, world headquarters of those gigantic firms.

Oil was a huge business before World War II, but then came the great petrochemical thrust that stemmed from disruption of the hitherto-dominant German chemical industry, combined with the need for synthetic rubber after the Japanese closed off U. S. raw rubber sources in the South Pacific. Some $325 million worth of petrochemical and synthetic rubber plants were constructed along the Ship Channel during the war, and since then the dramatically increased world demand for chemicals has resulted in about $3 billion in petrochemical investment in the Houston area. The industry has been based largely on the hydrocarbon from oil and natural gas, plus two other resources abundant in the Houston area—sulphur and salt. A whole range of plastics and synthetic materials have emerged, with Houston the national center of it all.

Unfortunately, the environmental impact of the industry is immense.

The Ship Channel, with miles of refineries and almost all of Harris County's 150-odd chemical plants along its banks, is so high in bacteria counts that people are warned not to let it touch their skin. The channel has long since been devoid of any aquatic life, the bottom is lined with a pollution-bred putrid sludge, and the surface is frequently covered with floating grease, oil, debris, and colored chemicals. There is so little natural flushing action that, as one official has put it, "virtually everything that keeps the channel wet is industrial effluent." * Compounding this "ecological Armageddon," as some have called it, is the fact that the port of Houston is literally ready to explode. Seventy percent of the cargo which moves through the port is classified as dangerous, and with a lack of licensing requirements for river pilots, sometimes an inexperienced tugboat captain will be pushing three to six barges of highly explosive material around the multitudinous curves of the channel. What happens if a huge fire does erupt in the channel? Just one fireboat, 20 years old in 1970, and with a maximum speed of eight knots, would be on hand to fight it. (State legislation passed in 1971, enhancing the port authority's power in the safety area, may begin an improvement.)

The channel and its chemical plants also make Houston's air incredibly vile when the wind blows in an unfavorable direction. In 1969, one company at Houston was said to dump 48 tons of sulphur dioxide and sulphur trioxide into the air every 24 hours. Whether the stiffer new standards set by the Texas Air Pollution Control Board will correct the situation, it is still too early to say.

Despite the importance of oil and chemicals, Houston's economy is not of the single-track variety. Instead, it is what the economists call "vertically integrated." Oil and gas are at the base, topped by succeeding layers of petrochemicals, metal fabrication, and food processing. Not far from the port, U. S. Steel recently built one of the largest and most automated steel works in the nation, and total manufacturing payrolls are close to $1 billion annually. The status of the Houston area and the port as a great farm center is often forgotten; Harris County ranks second in all of Texas in its numbers of cattle, and the region provides nearly 30 percent of the national rice production. The port of Houston is the country's number one wheat exporter, and in fact more than half the port's export tonnage is in farm products.

To all of this, of course, one must add a rapidly growing service industry, a huge medical research center, a booming convention business, and the federal space program. But NASA notwithstanding, only a small fraction of the area economy is dependent on government contracts. Metropolitan Houston is relatively "depression-proof." It is no wonder that so many top managers of major U. S. corporations now live in Houston (often at New York's expense). And the economic power structure includes—and some say is

---

* A field investigation team of the federal Environmental Protection Agency found in 1971 that 315,000 tons of suspended solids were dumped into the ship channel each day, including 1,600 pounds of lead, 5,000 pounds of cadmium, 7,900 pounds of zinc, 300 pounds of chromium, 400 pounds of phenols, 1,000 pounds of cyanide, and 55,000 pounds of oil and grease—plus 215 million gallons a day of domestic waste. Congressman Eckhardt of Houston urged the federal government to limit the discharges, saying action was necessary to save Galveston Bay, and that if control were left to state officials, they would "study the problem to death."

even dominated by—the big law firms, which end up being the negotiators, arbiters, and processors of the million and one deals, from downtown building to oil leases and shipping deals, that keep Houston humming.

Few spots on the American continent have been so totally transformed as one 22 miles southeast of center Houston, on the flat, green carpet of the Coastal Plains near Clear Lake, a place where cattle roamed and bounty hunters tracked wolves until a very few years ago. This was the site of a 30,-000-acre ranch, owned by one of those fabulous, eccentric Texas millionaires, J. M. (Silver Dollar) West.* Back in 1938, West had sold his ranchland to Humble Oil & Refining, and from this ownership it passed in the early 1960s to the U. S. government. The purpose: to construct the Manned Spacecraft Center of the National Aeronautics and Space Administration, the command post for man's flight to the moon. Eventually, some $312 million was spent on a vast complex of buildings and equipment. Most Americans were keenly aware of just one activity: actual control of manned missions in space, beginning in 1965 and culminating with the successful lunar landing in 1969 and subsequent Apollo trips to the moon. A lot else happened at this huge NASA facility, however, including testing of explosives and rocket thrusters, activities like a thermonuclear test range, an antenna test range, space environment simulation and flight acceleration chamber, the testing of crew equipment, and finally the training of astronauts.

The manned space program contributed handsomely to the Houston economy. A peak of more than 4,000 personnel at Clear Lake produced an annual payroll of $100 million in the late 1960s, and some 10,000 other workers in nearby supporting industries earned $250 million a year. It was the kind of economic stimulus hundreds of American cities would have loved —and which Houston, among them, probably needed the least. But the selection was made in the days before anyone thought of population dispersal, and when rawboned, old-style Texas pressure politics were still in style in Washington. At the time Lyndon B. Johnson was Vice President and head of the National Aeronautics and Space Council. Sam Rayburn was still Speaker of the House. Houston's Congressman Albert Thomas was chairman of the House Appropriations subcommittee handling NASA's budget, and President Kennedy needed his help on several other funding bills. James E. Webb, then head of NASA, was a close friend of LBJ. Another figure seemed to play no little part: George Brown of Brown & Root, LBJ's close friend. Brown was also chairman of the board of trustees of Rice University, which was interested in seeing the center come to Houston. Brown was said to have played a central role in having Houston selected after one of the most spirited competitions for a federal installation the country had ever seen. The other contending areas perhaps never realized how strongly the odds were against them. Putting the manned spacecraft center at Houston instead of Cape Kennedy almost surely added hundreds of millions of unnecessary dollars to the nation's space budget—an egregious example of

* After West's death in 1957, eight tons of silver dollars were found in a secret cellar of his Houston home. He had loved to scatter them around town, tossing them to pedestrians out of the windows of one of his 41 Cadillacs.

Texas' private profit at the national taxpayers' expense.

Some miles northwest of Clear Lake, a ways south of central Houston, lies that most splendiferous of all modern Texan creations, Roy Mark Hofheinz's Astrodome. The Astrodome is the world's first and only all-purpose, air-conditioned domed stadium, 4½ times the diameter of Rome's Colosseum, a colossal amphitheater that cost $38 million. Within its vast cavity, rising 208 feet above the flat plains (and surrounded by a sea of 30,000 parking spaces), one finds the great field for football, baseball, soccer, boxing, motorcycle racing, polo, bloodless bullfights, curling, and Gaelic football, with 45,000 upholstered armchairs for the spectators. There is also a variety of glittering restaurants and bars (including, of course, the longest bar in Texas), the Astrodome Club with thick carpets and rich, tapestried walls for season ticket holders, and finally, in the ethereal blue upper reaches of the stadium, 53 very exclusive sky boxes that rich Texans can rent for $18,000 to $24,000 a season. Behind the sky boxes are posh and garish private salons for party giving, each equipped with closed-circuit television of the field, a Dow Jones monitor, a bar and kitchen.

Roy Hofheinz, the man who conceived, financed (through public bonds) and now directs Astrodome-Astroworld, is the prototype of the *echt*-Texan promoter, equipped with physical bulk, string ties, a huge cigar, and ego to match. His daughter was moved to write a book about him, in which she said he was "a dreamer, a big thinker, a doer, and, most of all—a finisher. He is both lovable and bold, crude and suave, profane and gentle, shy yet outspoken, flamboyant, dynamic and charming." It has also been said that Hofheinz has "a mind as quick as a cash register."

Inevitably, Astrodome has some critics, most articulate among them the novelist Larry McMurtry. After an early visit to the huge white dome poking "soothingly above the summer heat-haze like the working end of a gigantic rub-on deodorant," McMurtry suggested that "pallid though the argument may appear, it seemed a bit conscienceless for a city with leprous slums, an inadequate charity hospital, a mediocre public library, a needy symphony, and other cultural and humanitarian deficiencies," to sink tens of millions of dollars "into a ballpark."

Houston: The Human Element

Geographically, Houston is a sprawling city, covering 450 square miles, the fourth largest in area of the U.S. (after Jacksonville, Los Angeles, and Oklahoma City). Under state law, the city has extraterritorial rights that enable it to stop new incorporations over an area of some 2,000 square miles and regularly annex huge chunks of land, preventing the kind of white noose suburbia that plagues so many American cities. Heavy industry is generally confined to the area along the Ship Channel on the city's east and southeast, and most of the industrial workers live in that part of town. Huge middle-class, white-collar areas are north and south of the city, and out to the west are the poshest executive type communities like River Oaks and others around Memorial Park.

Negroes, who numbered 316,992 in 1970 (25.7 percent of the population), are scattered through many parts of Houston, much like the pattern in Atlanta, though the heaviest concentrations are in a Y-like shape with the convergence point at center city. Together with Mexican-Americans, who number about 140,000 in Houston, Negroes occupy the worst slum areas like Pear Harbor, Sunnyside, Third Ward, and Acres Homes; within such areas are found pockets of the classic Southern slum dwelling, the shotgun house.

Jobs are unquestionably the worst problem of blacks and Mexicans, a continuing problem despite an innovative annual city-sponsored Job Fair that has been quite successful in getting employment for young men just entering the job market. At 1970 hearings of the federal Equal Employment Opportunity Commission held in Houston, its chairman, William H. Brown, III, said Houston was a "very sick city" for not providing more jobs for minorities. Several major firms (with Gulf Oil and IBM singled out for special criticism) were found to have black and Latin employment far below the share of the population those groups represent.

Yet despite such discouragements, leading Houston blacks are willing to acknowledge that the job situation for blacks has indeed improved vastly over the past 10 to 15 years. There has even been a flickering of help from the kind of white business establishment least known for helping Negroes— the Rotary Club. The Houston Rotary, which claims to be the world's largest local Rotarian group, in 1969 began a tentative but promising program for its members to counsel with and assist up-and-coming black businessmen.

Houston's Mayor Louie Welch set up a human relations division in his administration that spearheaded a Job Fair (beginning in 1965) and unusually innovative police-community relations projects. The police agreed to set up an observer corps of black and Latin youngsters who were even allowed to ride around in patrol cars from time to time to see how the police function on the job.

Militant black activity in Texas is extremely limited compared to other metropolitan areas of the country. I have heard this explained on the grounds that Texas has been more "open" than other Southern states, and that blacks live better, even in the Houston and Dallas ghettos, than in the North. Houston blacks have made great political advances in recent years, sending to the legislature at Austin two spokesmen of distinction, state representative Curtis Graves and state senator Barbara Jordan. Graves, as articulate a black leader as I met anywhere in the U. S., ran in 1969 at the age of 31 for mayor of Houston against Mayor Welch, who had been criticized that year for his private land holdings. Graves defanged the right by running on a "law and order" platform, his billboards resplendent with American flags. As it turned out, the "criminals" he was after were those responsible for "social conditions closely associated with crime," and he placed a lot of emphasis on improving the quality of police work. On election day, Welch got just over 50 percent of the vote, Graves only 32 percent. In 1971, against other opposition (reformist Fred Hofheinz, son of Judge Roy Hofheinz), Welch won again.

A coalition known as the Harris County Democrats has been active in Houston for years, combining labor, Negroes, Mexican-Americans, and liberal whites; in the 1950s, it often made headlines as it sought to liberalize not only the official party organization in Houston but also the state Democratic party. (Among the celebrated leaders of that era was Mrs. Frankie Randolph, who combined the attributes of scrappy liberalism and substantial wealth. For years, she personally bankrolled the *Texas Observer.*) But internal divisions, and especially the problem of low minority group turnout, have numbed the Houston liberals in recent years. Graves in his 1969 mayoral race got a 56-percent turnout in black precincts, but that kind of participation is rarely achieved. As for the Mexican-Americans, they not only turn out in low numbers but are strangely unaware of their own political interests; in 1969, for instance, they cast a majority of their vote against Graves, even though he had championed their cause in the legislature. This disarray on the left, combined with the ever increasing numbers of middle-management conservatives moving into the Houston area, has shifted the entire political balance of Harris County toward the right, and toward Republicans, in statewide elections.

I was surprised when I went to Austin to walk into the senate chamber and see the presiding officer wearing a yellow dress and black skin. It turned out to be Houston's Barbara Jordan, temporarily lent the gavel by Lt. Gov. Barnes. Many regard Miss Jordan, a calm liberal, as the single most influential black in Texas politics. She went to Boston University Law School, came back to Houston with a law degree and no clients, and decided to get into politics. In the 1960 campaign, she began licking stamps and sweeping floors at the Kennedy-Johnson campaign headquarters but soon advanced and in 1962 and 1964 made strong though losing races for the state legislature when elections were all at large in Harris County. Then came court-forced redistricting, and she found herself in a senate district that was 46 percent black. By winning 98.6 percent of the black vote and 37 percent of the white vote, she won election in 1966, the first Negro state senator since 1883. She turned out to be an able legislator, eventually got a major committee chairmanship (Labor and Management Relations), and was an important figure in passage of landmark workmen's compensation and minimum wage bills.

As time went on, Miss Jordan began to get support from some of Houston's business establishment and was expected to win election to Congress from a new Houston House district, about 50 percent black and 15 percent Mexican-American, which emerged from redistricting after the 1970 Census. She would be the first black member of Congress from the South since 1901, but faced primary opposition from Curtis Graves.

The longest tension between the races in Houston has revolved about the school system, sixth largest in the nation and largest in the South, extending far into the suburbs. For most of 20 years up to 1969, the school board was controlled by a coterie of right-wingers who furiously fought integration, banned books that hinted of internationalism, insisted on massive doses of

Texas history, and hounded opponents on the board or in the school administration. But the right-wingers were not always conservative with the taxpayer's money. Just before they were finally voted out of office in 1969, they completed an opulent white marble administration building, complete with fountains, gardens, and ornamental staircases, that cost the taxpayers $6 million. At about the same time, the board decided to eliminate free kindergarten classes for 18,000 children, most of them poor blacks and Mexican-Americans. The reason given: lack of funds. One establishment-type figure in Houston, not normally given to strong language, described the board to me as "a dumb, backward looking, incompetent bunch of racists," which had hired "a school administration not much better."

Finally, a broad coalition formed to elect qualified board members. The group included Republicans, Democrats, liberals, conservatives, professors, priests, housewives, businessmen, real estate salesmen, college professors, Negroes, Anglos, and Mexican-Americans, united simply in the interest of better quality education. And in 1969, it elected a board majority including one local NAACP leader.

Violence has played a special part in Houston's life for many years. The most recent and publicized episodes came in 1969–70 when right-wing elements, including members of the Ku Klux Klan, began what seemed like a systematic drive to rid the city of all forms of liberal thought. Twice in a five-month period, the transmitter of KPTF-FM, the listener-supported station of the Pacifica Foundation, was ripped by explosions that forced the station off the air for months. The office of a New Left tabloid, *Space City News*, was bombed and its employees subjected to threats, their autos burned and riddled with bullets. Hippie cafes went up in smoke, and many liberal opinion leaders were subjected to ominous threats. Through it all, the Houston police seemed singularly powerless. Outside of the beleagured left and liberals, no one seemed too concerned about the violence in the city. The Houston *Post* did condemn the Pacifica bombings as "a throwback to barbarism reminiscent of the book burning of Hitler's Germany," but regular press coverage did not make of the violence the *cause célèbre* one might have expected. Finally, after much pressuring from the National Association of Broadcasters and others, the FBI agreed to move into the Pacifica station investigation and aided the local police in the arrest of a suspect well known in the city all along—Jimmy Dale Hutto, leader of the local Ku Klux Klan. He was later convicted of conspiracy to destroy the transmitters.

When Jimmy Dale Hutto was arrested, he was found to have a loaded .45-caliber revolver with him. That in itself, however, is nothing unusual in Texas, where a pistol is about as easy to purchase as a bottle of cough medicine, where it is legal to carry a loaded rifle or shotgun down Main Street, and where the law allows a man to shoot his wife's lover if he discovers them in the act of sexual intercourse. Houston for several years led the nation in per capita murders. (In 1969, the rate in Dallas and Birmingham actually edged ahead, but Houston still had a body count of 300.)

As far as Texas courts are concerned, a man is usually much better off to be convicted of murder than drug possession or child molesting. Things do not seem to have advanced far from the frontier psychology of a judge in the 1930s, who proclaimed, "In Texas the first question to be decided by a jury in a homicide case is, 'Should the deceased have departed?'" To this day, five-year suspended sentences are frequent in murder cases. But in 1968, Lee Otis Johnson, a young black Houston dissident identified with civil rights causes, was convicted of giving an undercover agent one marijuana cigarette. His sentence: 30 years in the state penitentiary.

Before we depart from Houston, we must mention its two powerful, separately owned and operated newspapers—the *Post* (A.M.) and *Chronicle* (P.M.). The *Chronicle*, as previously noted, is owned by Jesse Jones' legacy, the Houston Endowment Inc., which has substantial interests in some 100 corporations, including downtown office buildings, hotels, oil royalties, ranchland and blue chip stocks. *Chronicle* editors have learned not to buck those interests. The *Post* is the domain of that attractive and forceful woman, Oveta Culp Hobby, who served as Secretary of Health, Education and Welfare in the Eisenhower Administration and had the remarkable foresight to select that promising young multimillionaire, Nelson A. Rockefeller, as her chief deputy. Her son, William P. Hobby, Jr., second in command, has developed into an able journalist and enjoys good ties into both the liberal and conservative communities.

Dallas: Tragedy and Growth

On the 22nd of November, 1963, three shots rang out under a Texas sky— and the brightest light of our time was snuffed out by senseless evil. The voice which had always been calm even in the face of adversity was silenced. The heart which had always been kind even in the midst of emergency was stopped. And the laugh which had always been gay even in reply to abuse was heard no more in the land.

With those words, Theodore Sorensen, confidant and counselor of the fallen President, John F. Kennedy, described his death in Dallas. The trauma of the event still numbs the mind, for its unspeakable cruelty, for the dark tide of violence it set loose in our time. I sought many other ways to start this Dallas subchapter, but there was no avoiding that central event by which Dallas became known to all corners of the earth.

Yet, having said it, there is little to add to the millions and millions of words, wise and foolhardy alike, that have been written of the assassination, of the presumed murderer Lee Harvey Oswald and his murderer Jack Ruby, of troubled Marina Oswald and the exploitress Mother Marguerite, of the Secret Service, the Dallas police and the Warren Commission, and all the rest.

Today at crowded Dealey Plaza, that junction place of superhighways where it all took place, the Texas School Book Depository Building still stands, gaunt and ugly as ever, purchased in 1970 by a collector of Kennedy memorabilia from Nashville. At a site 200 yards from the assassination was dedicated a 32-foot-high cenotaph, or empty tomb, in 1970, the design of New York architect Philip Johnson. It is 50 feet square and roofless, and Kennedy's name appears in gold on a slab of black granite.

Oswald's politics, with their Cuban-Soviet tinge, were diametrically opposite to Dallas' prevailing conservatism. But it is extraordinary that the deed of violence was performed in a city where violent rhetoric had come into vogue, where Lyndon Johnson and his wife were subjected to shouting, shoving, and spitting in the 1960 campaign, and United Nations Ambassador Adlai Stevenson had to bear similar abuse in October 1963.

Why right-wing extremism in Dallas? One reason is the new money syndrome. Dallas has thousands who have come into new wealth of the kind their parents never knew. Unlike those who have been wealthy over many years, they harbor deep resentments against taxes and see the chief tax collector, the federal government, as a threat to their gains. Another factor is the strong—almost overwhelmingly—Protestant complexion of Dallas, stemming in major part from its Deep South roots. The First Baptist Church, with a membership of about 15,000 and annual budgets of about $2 million, is the biggest Southern Baptist Church in the U.S. The Highland Park Methodist Church has 9,000 members, the Lover's Lane Methodist (what a wonderful church name!) some 6,000. It is a city where sermon titles like "God's Business Is Big Business" are not considered offensive, and where the churches have steered deliberately clear of social action. In this milieu, bland Protestantism seems to give way to uninhibited superpatriotism.

The ultraconservative tide that peaked in the early 1960s was aided and abetted by the right-leaning Dallas *Morning News*, which even permitted publication of a hateful advertisement against President Kennedy the day he was to appear in Dallas (though, to its credit, the paper had been curbing its editorial page vendetta against the national administration and printed a gracious editorial of welcome that day).

After the assassination, there was a tremendous backlash against right-wingism. The Dallas *Times-Herald*, which had been quite conservative, moderated its positions; the *News* became less strident. Stanley Marcus, president of Neiman-Marcus, placed a widely read New Year's Day advertisement in the papers in which he said: "The [absolutist] is the man who thinks that he alone possesses wisdom, patriotism, and virtue, who recognizes no obligation to support community decisions with which he disagrees; who . . . views the political process as a power struggle to impose conformity rather than [as] a means of reconciling differences."

To a degree, right-wingism went underground in the mid-1960s, even though Dallas remained a closed community to outsiders, one intensely aware of its own image and resentful of much of the outside world. Then came 1968, and the Wallace movement made it somewhat "respectable" again to rail against the old, suspected Eastern liberal establishment and to take semi-racist positions. A big fund-raising lunch was held for Wallace in Dallas with reports (unconfirmed) that $2 million was raised for his campaign.

Still, there was reason to believe that Dallas would not return to the extremism of the early 1960s. At City Hall, there were signs that the ancient resistance against accepting "tainted" federal money was breaking down. The *Times-Herald*, already moved to an essentially centrist position editorially, was purchased by the Los Angeles *Times* in 1969; in time this might mean a strong infusion of new thought and direction, along progressive lines, in step with the changing impact of the Los Angeles *Times* in Southern California in the last several years.

Finally, the Dallas news-reporting scene was enlivened when the city's aggressive public television outlet, KERA-TV, inaugurated a "Newsroom" on the model of the successful experiment pioneered by San Francisco's KQED during a newspaper strike in 1968. The idea is to go beyond the crime-sports-weather syndrome of local commercial television with a format in which reporters, grouped informally before the cameras, actually discuss, analyze, and even argue the news. KERA hired an illustrious local newsman, Jim Lehrer (author of *Viva Max*, from which a successful movie was made) as its "man in the slot" for Newsroom; Lehrer in turn assembled a young, socially conscious staff that began to report on local events—education, environment, politics, county government, welfare, and poverty—in a probing way Dallas had never seen before. The objections of the Dallas conservatives were immediate and predictable, especially as some blacks and longhairs got included in Lehrer's reporter panels.

While all this was transpiring, the suffocating hold on Dallas of its highly organized establishment power structure was beginning to loosen, ever so slightly. The organization which symbolizes, and in effect *is* the ultimate power in Dallas, is the Dallas Citizens' Council. Before we discuss the Council, however, let it be said that despite the conservatism of all but two or three of its members (including Stanley Marcus), it has never been associated with the militant right-wingism of Dallas. Instead, the Council's interests have been civic and philanthropic or, to put it more precisely, to do whatever is good for business growth in Dallas.

Membership qualifications for the Dallas Citizens' Council are fairly simple. You must be the president or chief executive officer of your company. You must have the ultimate authority in your company, to commit it to civic expenditures (for hospitals, United Fund, symphony drives, or whatever). And you must be invited to join the Council. Almost inevitably, you will be a millionaire—the leading force in one of the big Dallas insurance, banking, retailing, finance, real estate, contracting, oil, or savings and loan organizations, or the media.

The Dallas Citizens' Council has some 200 members, which means a small inner coterie has to make most of the decisions. Erik Jonsson, a former head of DCC and mayor from 1964 to 1971, has long been of that group—indeed it was a decision of the DCC inner circle that made him mayor originally, with practically no one in Dallas objecting. While he served as mayor, a "Mutt and Jeff" pair of Councilites emerged as the two most powerful figures of Dallas—John M. Stemmons, a six-foot, six-inch executive in commercial investments and properties, and Robert Cullum, the diminutive chairman of the board of Tom Thumb Stores. Other powerful figures were C. A. Tatum, president of Texas Utilities and chief leader in Dallas' successful integration, and James Aston, chairman of the board of Republic National Bank. In 1967, the DCC spearheaded the successful drive for a $175 million bond issue, largest ever proposed for a Southwestern city. Stemmons and Cullum, especially, gave their time, speaking all over the city and persuading leaders of all political and racial groups to support the effort.

Under the Citizens' Council there is a larger group of aspirants known as the Dallas Assembly. The original idea was to involve younger men, presidents of companies, who were climbing the ladder to a Citizens' Council position. By 1969, the Assembly was beginning to age, and an even younger group of aspiring Dallas businessmen formed a group. All the branches, however, seem firmly committed to the same goals—expressed in words like "keeping Dallas clean," "getting good government," "avoiding ward politics." If any indiscretions in a man's personal life become known, he is immediately frozen out of the structure. Bucking the decisions of the powerful men at the top of the DCC would also be fatal. Actual political activity is taken care of by a DCC offshoot known as the Citizens Charter Association, which almost always dictates the choice of mayor of Dallas and other major city officeholders. The control of big business is further extended through its close alliance with the conservatively oriented Dallas *Morning News* and the television and radio stations.

A system which leaves so much power in the hands of so few is bound to evoke criticism. Warren Leslie noted that "in the end, government by private club is government by *junta*, whether benevolent or not." Richard Austin Smith wrote for *Fortune* in 1964 of a feeling on the part of DCC critics that the Council was doing too much for too many, that it was a "self-perpetuating oligarchy" that made major decisions molding the political, cultural, economic, and social life of the entire Dallas community despite the fact that it was "unreachable" by the majority of Dallasites. It was precisely that issue that in 1971 permitted an insurgent candidate, Wes Wise, a 42-year-old political neophyte and former television sportscaster, running on a shoestring budget of $15,000, to win election as mayor.

The wave of resentment against the CCA oligarchy would doubtless have risen earlier and stronger in Dallas if it had not been for the visionary program to involve Dallas citizens in planning for their own future which was undertaken in the mid-1960s by the Dallas establishment's own man, then-Mayor Erik Jonsson. I spent several hours with Jonsson, an engaging blue-eyed Swede, on a leisurely Saturday morning while he was still in office. I came away feeling I had met one of the most dedicated, able men to lead an American city in our times. The story is best told in his own words:

I had been mayor for three months or so when "I discovered I wasn't farming as well as I knew how," as the old Arkansas saying goes. I was reacting to emergencies rather than trying to control the events before they became events —the universal problem of cities. I said to myself, "Old boy, you're not using all the things used in a lifetime in business and industry. It's time to get back to the fundamentals of good management principles and see if they can't be applied here."

Jonsson then recalled the success of his firm, Texas Instruments, in increasing its business 30 percent a year, compounded annually, and speculated that one reason for that performance was management's insistence on setting sound goals and reevaluating them constantly in the light of experience.

But cities rarely do this. They live within one- and two-year budgets. Planning is usually limited to the expected lifetime of a few politicians in their jobs. Mayors and councilmen are often just two- and four-year people and their own career objectives are often outside city government. . . . Cities rarely look at the totality of their problems, unlike corporations which think five to 10 years ahead, the better ones 20 to 30 years ahead. In cities, the squeaky wheel gets the grease. The newspapers are full of headlines on the immediate problem; the politicians react.

So it was that in December 1965, Jonsson picked the downtown Rotary Club for a famed "Days of Decision" speech in which he asked: "Shall we deal adequately with the future or be run over by it?" Jonsson named a 27-member Goals Planning Committee for Dallas and then called on 12 local writers to draft 12 essays highlighting the city's problems. Six months later Jonsson expanded his first (and very establishment-oriented) group of 27 to 87, including 10 blacks, a number of college students, and 20 percent women. For three days, he took them to the little town of Salado, halfway to Austin, and told them to hammer out mutually agreeable goals.

I went from group to group for those three days, and slept no more than three hours a night. And at the end of the conference, several people came to me and used similar words—"You know, when I came here I looked at my opposite numbers and here were far-left Democrats and far-right Republicans and here were Negroes and Latins and whites, and here were Catholics, Protestants, and Jews, and here were well educated people and the stockroom clerk and the transcontinental truck driver, and here were preachers, and educators and heads of corporations. And I said to myself, 'Nothing will ever come of this; we can't even talk to each other. We have nothing in common.' But I found when I got talking to these people that they weren't really so far at all from what I've been thinking." And then came the payoff phrase—"This has been almost a religious experience."

The consensus of Salado, together with the 12 original study essays, was published in a 300-page paperback of which 20,000 copies were distributed in the city. Late in 1966, 33 "town hall" type meetings were held all over Dallas, attended by some 6,380 people. The Salado 87 then reconvened, heard the major modifications requested, revised some 60 percent of their recommendations (but few fundamentally), and in 1967 another book came out with 114 goals outlined. The next problem was to blueprint means for achieving the goals, a task assigned to 12 task forces manned by 293 Dallas citizens.

By late 1970, work had started on three-quarters of the goals and some had already been achieved. Public school kingergartens, which Dallas had lacked, were begun. The ambitious Dallas-Fort Worth Regional Airport was under way, financed in part by the 1967 bond issue which had borrowed from the earliest findings of the goals program. Family planning services were being expanded; the city had a new pretrial release system; a community relations commission (originally opposed by Jonsson himself) was in operation. The proposals, which would take many years to complete—far beyond Jonsson's own retirement as mayor in 1971—would have a major physical and programmatic impact on Dallas, touching the lives of virtually all its citizens. Even those who felt the "committee system" had watered down many goals acknowledged the immense benefit in involving such a broad cross-section of the people. (The only serious private grumblings were said to come from some members of the Dallas Citizens' Council, Jonsson's old alma mater.)

One of Jonsson's chief concerns, he said, was getting young and highly trained personnel for city government:

> Most cities hold down on staff in order to save taxes. There are few young people in city government. They go where the glamor is, where the stock options are, the big, quick rise to money and fame. And the dedicated ones almost always go to the federal government—at least 95 percent of them—even to the Peace Corps with no money. After all, that bunch down at city hall, who wants to rub elbows with *them?*

Dallas, it might be noted, is the largest city in the world with a city manager–city council form of government; thus it has a fairly unique capacity to maintain programs over a continuum and to hire bright young executives and promise them a real career.

But to return to Jonsson for one last thought. Why, I asked him, did a man of his age (mid-sixties) and standing (he is personally worth about $100 million) choose to undergo the pressures of city government when comfortable retirement was open to him? His reply, in part:

> The Council asked me to serve in February 1964. It was in the wake of Kennedy's assassination, and the town needed to be pulled together. We were seen falsely, all over the world, as a city of hate—which is the last thing Dallas really was or is. . . .
> I've since weathered three elections. . . . I look at myself as just as draftable for a public purpose as a kid is to go to Vietnam. Why the hell shouldn't they draft me if I'm needed? I don't think a man can lay down his kit of tools as long as they are useful. My philosophy is you're in a society, and you owe a great deal to it. What good is a man? As I think of him, he has to fulfill the requirements that come out of saying, "The value of a man to his society is the sum total of all he puts in it in a lifetime, less the cost of sustaining any negative forces he's supplied to it in his time."
> I look back on some of my early years as years when I didn't do very well for my society. I didn't do what I could do. I'm accelerating as my life goes on. I'm trying to make up for what I should have done. It's that simple.

Dallas: A Wooden Spoon Turned to Gold

Dallas, I heard it said, was the city born with a wooden spoon in its mouth. Its location was remote, it had no port or access to the sea, the farmland about it was not particularly fertile, and anyway neighboring Fort Worth soon monopolized the western cattle trade. Nor have oil or gas ever been found beneath it.

But cotton buoyed the early economy after the railroads were bribed or forced to divert their tracks through the town. When the East Texas oil field came in four decades ago, Dallas quickly cashed in as banker for the operation. Hundreds of Dallasites became millionaires, and the huge capital reserves created were then available to finance more exploration for oil and also diversification into fields like insurance and electronics manufacture. Dallas also became a great gateway for the Southwestern trade, leading the region in banks, distribution, and even fashions.

Dallas' population has been soaring upward in the postwar era at a rate just a little behind Houston's. In 1940, there were 294,734 people in Dallas, in 1970 a total of 844,401; within that period, Dallas had risen from 31st largest city in the U.S. to eighth largest, while Houston rose from 21st place to sixth.

By a dollar-and-cents measure, Dallas' wooden spoon has turned to gold. A 1969 study of the top 100 Texas-based companies showed that 38 had their headquarters in Dallas, compared to 31 in Houston. Dallas was also booming as regional headquarters for national firms, with offices of 311 of the 500 largest industrial corporations on *Fortune's* list. The city had Texas' largest bank (Republic National, with assets of more than $2 billion), the regional Federal Reserve Bank, and 200 insurance companies with assets of some $13 billion. The manufacturing economy was humming along with technologically advanced, "clean" high-growth companies. Early in the 1960s, Dallas was deliberately cut out of new federal employment through Democratic retaliation against the city's extremist right-wing Republican Congressman of the time, Bruce Alger. But Alger was beaten in 1964 and times changed; by 1970, there were 13,000 federal employees in Dallas and the number was continuing to grow as a result of President Nixon's designation of the city as the center for Southwest regional offices. The city was the nation's No. 4 cotton market and farm implement center and had more than 500 million-dollar-asset firms.

Old-fashioned entrepreneur daring had a lot to do with Dallas' postwar growth. Midas stories like that of Erik Jonsson, who built Texas Instruments from a $2 million-a-year business in 1946 to an $850 million giant, abound.

Another, even more famous story is that of James J. Ling, a one-time oil roustabout and self-taught financial wizard who succeeded in building Dallas' Ling-Temco-Vought from a small electrical contracting firm back in 1959 to the 14th largest industrial firm of the U.S., doing $3.75 billion worth of business, a decade later.* Much of that multibillion dollar volume, however, represented the business of a broad array of other firms, including Jones

---

* Aside from business acumen, politics had something to do with L-T-V's success. Seats on private company planes were regularly made available to Texas Congressmen commuting between their home state and Washington. After the 1970 election, the Associated Press reported L-T-V executives had given $100,000 in campaign gifts through a "Citizens for Good Government" front, including $2,000 to House Republican Leader Gerald R. Ford of Michigan. In violation of federal law, the committee made no public report to Congress.

& Laughlin Steel, brought in by acquisition and merger in a heady process of conglomeration. But when the stock market soured and investors decided conglomerates like L-T-V were spread too thin, Ling suddenly faced crises in carrying the huge debt incurred through acquisitions. Government trust-busters sued to force L-T-V to divest itself of its Jones & Laughlin stock. With debts mounting rapidly, the L-T-V directors, including spokesmen for Dallas banks carrying a major share of the company's indebtedness, forced Jim Ling to relinquish his executive control of the company. Short months after that crash landing, Ling was back in business again with a new conglomerate (Omega-Alpha, Inc.) that soon had annual sales of close to $400 million.

Dallas' answer to the massive Houston Center project is called Griffin Square, a $200 million project on 32 acres of old railroad and warehouse property. The land was assembled in 1970 in what the Dallas *News* termed "the largest downtown land transaction in Dallas since John Neely Bryan subdivided the prairie." The plans include a 913-foot-high cylindrical office-hotel tower to be the highest building west of the Mississippi. Dallas is also receiving a $21 million Federal Center and a daringly designed new City Hall, akin to Boston's in its unusual form and monumental size.

Writer Warren Leslie has defined five general socio-geographic areas of Dallas—"five cities in the middle of nowhere." There is, of course, downtown, packed with hundreds of thousands of busy workers in the day, left to conventioneers at night (Dallas is strictly a home entertainment, not a nightclub city). The inner city alternates between great skyscrapers and tawdry structures like a fifth-rate short-order and beer place across the street from Neiman-Marcus and a Gospel Mission that gathers up its human outcasts each night half a block down the street.

Out beyond Dealey Plaza on the west is the sprawling community of Oak Cliff with several hundred thousand people. As one goes from east to west in Oak Cliff, the houses and apartments progress from a seedy mediocrity to high quality. Some sections are enhanced by that Dallas rarity, hills and woods.

North Dallas is the fashionable part of town, where house prices rarely dip below $30,000 and frequently go well over $100,000. This is the home of the establishment and would-be establishment types. In the postwar era it has stretched farther and farther north with huge residential building projects on the flat prairie; Leslie quotes a prominent builder as saying, "I sometimes wonder how far north these nuts will go in order to be chic. I have a feeling it's St. Louis." Within North Dallas, there are two independent islands, the incorporated townships of Highland Park and University Park, surrounded entirely by city territory. The *median* value of a house in Highland Park is $49,700, in University Park $32,700.

There is also an "apartment Dallas" which grew up after the war as an exception to the old rule of single-family homes. Finally, there are the slums, clustered west and south of center city, almost in the shadow of the downtown skyscrapers.

Fort Worth: Cowtown Gone Modern

Nothing in Texas seems so immutable as the fact that Dallas and Fort Worth are different. Though a mere 33 miles divide them, John Gunther wrote, there "is a chasm practically as definitive as the Continental Divide." Dallas was forever written of as the place where the East ends, Fort Worth as the place "where the West begins." Even geologically, there is some truth to this; Dallas' climate and topography belong to the Mississippi Valley, but it is just west of Fort Worth that the land slopes into the gently rolling prairies of the Central Plains. The ancient and bitter rivalry between the two towns has been greatly ameliorated. And those 33 miles are filling so fast with factories and suburbia that it will all soon be a single metropolis. Yet somehow the fundamental difference in character remains. Dallas is still uptight, self-conscious, often intolerant. Fort Worth is relaxed, gentle, and courteous. Much of the flavor of the small town is still there, even though the population reached 393,476 in 1970. In Fort Worth, people rarely bother to lock their cars. Instead of sullen stares between people on the sidewalks, one sees nods and smiles. Political extremism is virtually unknown. The stranger is welcomed warmly.

Fort Worth, it can be reported conclusively and finally, is no longer "Cowtown, U.S.A." Swift & Co., the last big meat processor, closed down its Fort Worth plant in April 1971. Now, where a thousand carloads of livestock poured daily into 100 acres of stockyards for their last roundup, silence reigns. The great cattle industry had been born back in the 1870s, boomed through World War I and into the 1920s but then began a slow death with the great Depression. Good roads and trucks made cattle shippers less dependent on the railroads, cattle buyers began to go to cattle auctions directly in the ranchlands, and eventually local feedlot operations made it possible to fatten animals and then truck them directly to slaughter.

In place of cattle, Fort Worth turned to aerospace. Convair, bought out by General Dynamics, got in on some of the great defense contracts of the postwar era, including the highly controversial, multibillion dollar TFX (F-111) project. At one point General Dynamics hired 28,000 workers at Fort Worth, though the figure had sunk substantially by the start of the 1970s. The Bell Helicopter Company became another major aerospace manufacturer, with 85 percent of its output going to the military. Finally, the L-T-V aircraft production facilities at Arlington, east of the city, hired several thousand workers from Fort Worth. The aerospace giants had heavy parts and service needs, stimulating the growth of well over 1,000 subcontractors around Fort Worth, most specializing in electronics and tool manufacture. The aerospace business, however, was a perilous one. In 1970, the loss of the $1.8 billion B1 bomber contract to North American Rockwell stunned General Dynamics executives at Fort Worth, some of whom wept when the bad news came. The company said it would eventually have to lay off 14,000 workers. And Bell Helicopter's outlook after the end of the Vietnam war was not bright at all.

The 1960s brought a major revitalization of downtown Fort Worth, which at one point had 60 vacant stores and seemed to be dying. One major point of the revitalization is a striking convention center, its great round shape contrasting with the rectangular high-rise office buildings.

Proof that the old rivalry with Dallas has been tamed is the half-billion-dollar regional airport the two cities are building jointly at a point equidistant between them (precisely 17 miles from each city limit). It will be the largest commercial airport in the world and, in the opinion of many, will dominate air traffic in the southwestern U.S., even though Houston completed a handsome intercontinental jetport in 1969.

A landmark in cooperation between Dallas and Fort Worth was the formation in 1966 of the North Central Texas Council of Governments, the first of what were to become many "COG" organizations in Texas. Within three years, the North Central COG had 115 communities signed up, but the two big cities naturally dominated and headquarters were thoughtfully located in booming Arlington on the Dallas–Fort Worth Turnpike.* The original impetus for COGs came from federal legislation like the 1962 Highway Act, which required urban transportation studies by metropolitan-wide agencies in order to qualify for more federal highway funds, and from urban planning grant funds which financed creation of COGs. But officials like William J. Pitstick, executive director of the North Central Texas COG, see far more long-term significance. Most city managers, Pitstick points out, are burdened with "day-to-day" problems that can range from garbage collection and catching dogs to answering complaints. A COG director, by contrast, can concentrate on long-range planning and effective coordination in areas like regional water supply and pollution control, sewage, criminal justice, highways, airports, and the like.

Fort Worth is a city free of most pollution, with clean streets and clear skies; the pockets of poverty (Mexican-Americans and Negroes) are scattered and light in population. Likewise, the posh areas of Fort Worth (most notably Westover Hills) are only a fraction of the size of those in Dallas. Preeminently, this is a middle-class, middle-income city, and one of moderation. Though Negroes represent only 7 percent of the population, for instance, one sits on the city council, another on the school board. Even labor and management, which used to suffer bitter splits in the city, are talking more amicably with each other these days.

This is not to suggest a millennium in Fort Worth. As I wrote this section, a *Texas Observer* arrived with an exposé of the Joe Louis Addition, an all-black section on the Trinity River bottoms in Fort Worth, where the people pay city taxes but there are no city water lines or sewer lines, the

* The population growth along the turnpike has been sudden and huge. Arlington had 7,692 people in 1960 and 90,643 in 1970—an increase of more than 1,000 percent. Irving, on Dallas' western border, rose from 2,621 in 1950 to 97,260 in 1970—up 2,700 percent! Another major concentration in the corridor is composed of the towns of Hurst, Euless, and Bedford, prairie waystations a few years ago with 56,580 people by 1970.

streets are not paved, the garbage is not collected, and the rats are not exterminated. When the city planning commission held a zoning hearing on the Joe Louis community, an elderly black resident, Harry Smith, rose with the aid of his thick, old cane and glared at the commissioners. "We don't live in America!" he declared. "People in America don't live the way we do down there! Why do they take our tax dollar and don't do nothin' about it?" No one answered.

San Antonio: 254 Years Old and Thriving

> *San Antonio . . . is of Texas, and yet it transcends Texas in some way, as San Francisco transcends California, as New Orleans transcends Louisiana. Houston and Dallas express Texas—San Antonio speaks for itself. . . .*
>
> *We have never really captured San Antonio, we Texans—somehow the Spanish have managed to hold it. We have attacked with freeways and hotels, shopping centers, and now . . . HemisFair, but happily the victory still eludes us. San Antonio has kept an ambiance that all the rest of our cities lack.*
>
> —*Larry McMurtry*, In a Narrow Grave: Essays on Texas

Even while the French were settling New Orleans, the Spanish advanced northward from Mexico and in 1718 founded San Antonio and made it the capital of their province of Texas. Franciscan friars came and erected a series of missions. Four of these—San José, Concepción, Capistrano, and Espada—still stand, and together with the Alamo and the Spanish Governor's Palace, their wonderfully distinctive style is a reminder of empire, a tie to the past that the rest of Texas scarcely knows.

Right after the Civil War, San Antonio became the first of the cowtowns of the legendary West, a base area for the cattle trails—Chisholm, Shawnee, Western—heading up to final destination points in Missouri, Kansas, and Nebraska. The railroad came in 1877, and the lusty business of the open range made San Antonio into a veritable cattle capital, filled with picturesque saloons and gaming tables where men whose herds ranged over millions of acres played recklessly for high stakes. Eventually the cattle trade began to share the scene with pedestrian breweries, cement factories, milling, and oil. San Antonio became one of the great military cities of the United States. But still, that Spanish admixture and Latin population remained, together with a strong dose of German immigration that leavened the urban mix and created an atmosphere unduplicated anywhere in America.

Through downtown San Antonio, on a meandering course once known as "A-Drunken-Old-Man-Going-Home-At-Night," runs the San Antonio River, America's most delightful city waterfront, lined with restaurants and shops, an open-air theater, and nightclubs.

On occasion, San Antonio will do something really boosterish, like the 1968 HemisFair staged to celebrate the city's 250th birthday. On 92 acres near center city that had long been due for urban renewal, 33 world nations erected striking pavilions. The city got a new landmark in the 622-foot Tower of the Americas with its revolving restaurant. Culturally, HemisFair will long be remembered; for instance, even Russia's Bolshoi Ballet journeyed deep into the heart of Texas to perform. Financially, the results were not so happy; the 6 million people who came were 4 million less than the city had hoped for, and the final operating deficit was an immodest $7.4 million. Some of San Antonio's poor thought the fair was a wasteful boondoggle.

Razzle-dazzle, Texas-style promotions are strictly out of character for San Antonio, however. It is an essentially finished city, with a complement of old and powerful families who made their fortunes from ranching or industry generations ago. San Antonio is occasionally accused of provincialism and having a closed society, but at the same time it is an informal place in a Southwest sort of way, and not at all stodgy. As substantial wealth is gained by aggressive business leaders outside the old family circles, San Antonio may begin to show more business-civic aggressiveness.

A glance at San Antonio's skyline reveals its dowdy middle age. From the HemisFair tower, one sees scarcely any buildings of postwar vintage. The big office structures are all of the more conservative styles of the '20s and '30s. The exceptions are a new hotel and a few other more modern structures around the HemisFair site. Much of the inner city is occupied by parking lots. From the same tower vantage point, one looks west past center city to the heavily Latin areas, east to San Antonio's larger pockets of Negroes, north to the wealthier precincts of the old Anglos, and south to a mixed bag of neighborhoods, plus a lot of the military-industrial complex.

No major American city has a greater percentage of Mexican-Americans than San Antonio (about 308,000, or 37 percent on a countywide basis in 1970, for instance). The informal Jim Crow practices prevalent until the 1950s have disappeared, and now there are many Mexican-Americans of high professional standing who are silently but rapidly integrating the entire area.

Still, there is the great West Side barrio, one of the most striking slums of the continent. For block after block after block, the tiny shacks and hovels stretch on, many with outdoor privies and lacking water, the conditions not much better than those suffered by destitute blacks along the Mississippi Delta. But the Mexican-Americans add verve and color to San Antonio. Throughout the barrio, people are everywhere, on the sidewalks, in the streets, on porches, leaning out of windows, a moving, laughing, and yet sad mass of humanity.

Since the 1950s, many of San Antonio's city elections (all nonpartisan) have been won by candidates of the Good Government League, a group of private citizens who started as a reform group but later became highly conservative. The long-time mayor, elected with League support, was Walter W. McAllister, 82 when he finally retired in 1971. His relations with the Mexican-Americans were disastrous, based on remarks like these: "Welfare is like feeding the birds in the summer. You don't want to give them too much or they won't go away in the winter and will starve." Or, on a nationally televised program in 1970: Mexican-Americans are "wonderful people who love music, dancing, and flowers but who just do not have as much ambition as Anglos." Bexar County Commissioner Albert Peña said McAllister should resign and that the statement was "the same old gringo racist rhetoric."

San Antonio government gets a distinctly conservative input from the Good Government Leaguers, but enough other types are elected (including a few Mexican-American city councilmen) to keep the city, as a whole, off the extremist track.

Even without the supercharged atmosphere of a Houston or Dallas, the San Antonio population has risen smartly in the postwar years. Counting surrounding Bexar County, the figure was 338,176 in 1940, 500,460 in 1950, and 830,460 in 1970; as for the city alone, it had 654,153 people in 1970, making it 15th largest in the U.S.A.

The military is definitely the biggest business in San Antonio, a city long nicknamed the "mother-in-law of the Army." The single largest employer of the area is Kelly Air Force Base, a massive repair and maintenance facility for aircraft that hires 24,000 persons locally.

The military hospitals, along with a number of civilian facilities, including the new University of Texas Medical School, are fast making San Antonio into a leading medical center of the U.S. The military bases and hospitals, of course, are an inducement to military personnel to retire in the San Antonio area. Many of the officers retire in their forties after 20 years of service and have been able to get attractive jobs in the local economy. Another inducement may be San Antonio's salubrious climate (hot but not too humid summers, winters with morning temperatures in the mid-30s rising to the 70s by later in the day). One mystery to me, however, is how San Antonio has been able to absorb so many military, including retirees, without getting the reservoir of archconservatives apparent in a city like San Diego. To the contrary, one hears that the constant change of population created by military assignments, plus the broad experiences of the military, have actually contributed to a harmonious community and the lack of narrow views.

Mextex

As many as two and a half million Mexican-Americans—no one knows the number positively—live in Texas. One finds them still in the quiet, sun-baked towns of Rio Grande Texas and near the Gulf, in the vast San Antonio barrio, in Corpus Christi or El Paso or Brownsville, and now in ever increasing numbers in metropolitan Houston and Dallas, in Austin, and even around farming cities like Lubbock on the High Plains. Statistically, the Mexican-American is more and more an urban man, but his most vivid existence is still centered on the land or in the smaller cities of the Valley.

The life story of these people was traditionally one of cruelest poverty: their income but a fraction of Anglos, education minuscule (with substantial illiteracy), all but the most menial jobs denied, and of course the barriers of language. Outright discrimination—in schools, public places, restaurants, theaters—was often as cruel as that practiced on Negroes. Only a small, small minority managed to earn an average or better-than-average income, to keep their children in school through high school, or to send them to college. Real change did not begin until World War II, the civil rights efforts of the 1950s and 1960s, and the development of the Mexican vote into an independent, not-for-sale commodity in the 1950s and 1960s. A key development, many now think, were the Viva Kennedy Clubs of 1960, of which a San Antonio Mexican leader (and now Congressman), Henry B. González, was national cochairman. Here was a fellow Roman Catholic running for President, and one who really seemed to care.

For generations, the Valley counties were under the unshakable hold of "heavies," or *patrons*, who were sheriffs and judges, frequently tied in with the Texas power structure of oil, gas, and banks. The *patron* would look after the well-being of his Mexican charges like a northern city ward leader and obligingly pay their poll taxes for them. In return, the Mexicans would simply wait for a signal on how they should vote, and scarcely a man or woman would deviate from the *patron's* instructions.

The most famous *patrons* have been the Parrs of Duval County in the dusty oil-cattle-sagebrush territory of South Texas. Archie Parr, the original *patron*, came on the scene as a red-necked cowhand around the turn of the century, slowly built economic and political power, served 20 years in the state senate, and died rich in lands and cattle. His son George expanded the usual benevolent ways of the patron by maintaining an army of some 200 gun-toting *pistoleros*, who masqueraded as deputy sheriffs and helped keep the electorate in line. Starting in the 1920s, individual state candidates blessed by the Parrs usually received close to 100 percent of the vote.

All of this received ample national attention in 1948, when Lyndon Johnson ran against former Governor Coke Stevenson for the Democratic Senate nomination. When the final statewide returns were in, it seemed that Stevenson had won by a margin of 112 out of nearly a million cast. Then, on the sixth day, Precinct 13, a Parr stronghold in neighboring Jim Wells County, sent in an amended return with 203 more votes—201 for Johnson, 2 for Stevenson. The new totals made LBJ Senator with a plurality of 87 votes and won him the nickname "Landslide Lyndon." In that same election, Duval County itself went 4,622 for Johnson, 40 for Stevenson.

Former Senator Ralph Yarborough tells a colorful story of his attempt to campaign for governor in 1954 in Laredo, largest city in Webb County, which had been boss controlled for decades:

> No candidate for governor had spoken in Laredo for 30 years. I was warned not to come through. I said I was coming through there with all the flags flying. That night, they fired off a Chinese bomb within 10 feet of the platform where we were speaking. It let off a tremendous roar but hurt no one. The crowd was 98 percent Latino; the local powers had hoped to scare them off. But I was making a special appeal to veterans, and they are not scared by explosives. Next

thing, a huge fiery cross, doused with gasoline, was moved up and set afire right behind where I was speaking.

Webb County, Yarborough recalled, customarily went against him 10–1. The heavies of many Valley counties still supervise a controlled vote, in fact. One of the most efficient of these is still George Parr of Duval County. In 1968, Duval's 4,483 votes split 3,978 for Humphrey, 384 for Nixon, 121 for Wallace. In the 1970 Democratic Senate primary, Parr decided to back Yarborough over Lloyd Bentsen. The vote: 3,993 for Yarborough, 264 for Bentsen.

But political and economic progress, as it came, came slowly and presented new sets of problems. After the U. S. Commission on Civil Rights held open hearings in San Antonio in 1968, the findings were summarized this way:

> Outside forces predominate in the life of the Mexican-American. He is forced to migrate thousands of miles to other states for farm work; he is forced to move into hostile cities in the quest for a better life; he is forced to cut ties with the familiar way of life, in order to relocate where the opportunity is best; he is forced to send his children to schools where an alien language and tradition may abort aspiration; he is forced to accept the lowest paying jobs, menial labor, and often forsake hope for anything better.

Mexican-Americans from Texas constitute a huge proportion of America's migrant farm workers. Their preponderance is borne home if one looks at a map of the U. S. showing the travel patterns of the migrants. One flow (mostly Negroes or Puerto Ricans) goes up from Florida as far as New York

Travel Patterns of Seasonal
Migratory Agricultural Workers

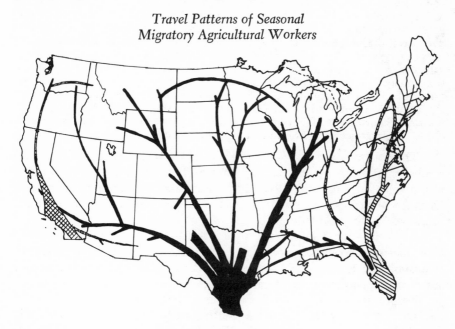

Source: U. S. Public Health Service.

State and New England in the East; then there is another Western division (largely Mexican), up from Southern California, through the Central Valley into the Pacific Northwest.

But there is one great central migrant system, and its massive roots blanket South Texas like those of a mighty tree. The great branches push up through the heart of the continent. One stops in just a few hundred miles, still within Texas, for cotton on the High Plains. Another moves across New Mexico and Arizona and then joins the stream of California Mexican migrants picking cotton and a multitude of fruits, from strawberries at Salinas to apples in Washington. One of the Texan branches heads northwesterly to Colorado, Wyoming, and Montana, chiefly for sugar beets harvesting. Another group of migrants goes straight up through the Central Plains to help with grain harvesting as far north as the Dakotas, though mechanization is cutting back on the need here. Finally, one great migrant branch heads toward the Great Lakes to help harvest vegetables, tomatoes, apples, berries, peaches, nuts, and potatoes.

Year after year, the great waves of migration originate out of Texas in early spring, rise to cover the continent by autumn, and then subside again toward the ancestral homes on the Rio Grande. Writers Michael McCrery and Sixto Gómez have painted a touching picture of the life of Mexican-Americans who feel they have no real alternative to the life of following the crops and doing stoop labor:

> Shunned by the racist prejudices of the white farming communities in which you work and inhibited by low pay, you probably live in a "labor camp," a fifth-rate ghetto officially set up by cooperation of the farmers and respective city government. These "labor camps," usually located 20–30 miles out of town, in part serve the purpose of keeping the "wetbacks" (or "those goddamn greasy Mexicans," as they are often called) from "moving in" and lowering property values, not to mention preying upon the supposed chastity of white Anglo-Saxon womanhood. "Labor camp" housing is also a profitable racket for slum landlords. A family of 12 may pay $50 to $60 a month for a cramped, one-room wooden shack that is rotting and falling down, in which rats, lice and other vermin are rampant. Sanitation is often non-existent, as are such amenities as running water, toilets, electricity or proper heating or air conditioning. . . .

There are of course migrants who live in far superior surroundings, earn a substantial income each year, and have a life style (and expectancy) akin to that of most Americans. But such cases are a tiny minority. Agriculture Department figures for migrants showed a median income level of only $1,200 a year in the mid-1960s.

An irony—one might almost say a scandal—is that no one really knows how many migrant workers there are. Low estimates are around 200,000, high estimates close to 400,000. If one adds in the families and nonworkers who accompany the migrants, the total may run close to 800,000 to 1,000,000.

Despite the vast flow of migrants out of Texas, perhaps 75,000 to 100,000 stay entirely within the state, picking early crops in the Lower Rio Grande Valley and late crops on the High Plains. And despite all the federal job training and educational programs, the Mexican-Americans in Texas face a seemingly permanent, almost fatal type of competition: the hundreds of thousands of illegal immigrants from Mexico. No one knows just how many such entries there are, though the figure must surely run into the hundreds of thousands. Since the legal flow of temporary workers under the *bracero* program terminated in 1964 (to the dismay of the big growers who had profited from the exceedingly inexpensive labor), illegal entries have soared.* Along the entire Mexican border, 43,789 illegal immigrants were seized in 1964, but 348,172 in the year ending June 30, 1971.

One major point of illegal entry is El Paso, where 43,640 were apprehended and sent back in 1970 alone. The bulk of the wetbacks at El Paso, I heard, enter the U.S. through huge underground sewage conduits that go into the river, much like the fabled sewers of Paris. The illegal immigrants simply go down to the riverbed and enter by one of the sewers, and thousands must succeed in escaping capture.

Each illegal immigrant is easy picking for unscrupulous employers who can pay disgracefully low wages, ignore all Social Security or other benefits, and in the process depress the wage scales for the great legal body of Mexican-Americans. González was the leading force in getting Congress to discontinue the *bracero* program, just a year after he entered Congress in 1962.

Even today, the U. S. Immigration Service refuses to crack down on Mexicans who hold resident alien cards but actually live in Mexico and commute over the border daily. David North, former assistant to Labor Secretary W. Willard Wirtz during dismemberment of the *bracero* program, writes: "The Immigration Service, with some justice, is regarded by its critics as the lackey of the Establishment, actively or passively greasing the way for the entry of tens of thousands of alien workers, who, poor souls, busily depress wage levels along the border, increase unemployment among U. S. residents, discourage union organization, and increase migrancy."

A movement like César Chávez's farm workers in California will never succeed in Texas, one concludes, until such conditions are corrected. Nevertheless, the effort is being made. Chávez has taken a lively interest in the Texas situation, visiting the state quite frequently to confer with farm and AFL-CIO union leaders. In 1966, during the first year of Chávez's grape strike in California, one of his lieutenants, Gene Nelson, showed up in Rio Grande City to investigate rumors of rebellion among the melon pickers of Starr County (average annual income $1,000, poorest county in Texas and 18th poorest in the U. S.). Under Nelson's leadership, some 1,300 Mexican-American farm workers soon joined the new union. Earning 65 cents an hour for a 10- to 18-hour day, it could have been argued they had little to lose. Predictably, the growers were adamant against recognizing the union, and a strike was called. Eventually, the strike was to fail. But its byproducts would long be remembered in Texas.

The first was a great march, modeled after the Delano-to-Sacramento march in California. Out of Rio Grande City on the Fourth of July, 1966,

* The *bracero* program was inaugurated by Congress in 1942 when manpower was exceedingly short, and later continued at the insistence of the growers. Congress finally abolished the program in 1962.

they began, led by a Catholic priest and a Baptist minister, the marchers including some wonderful brown- and leathery-faced old men, veterans of thousands and thousands of days working the fields of the Valley, carrying with them a dignity and purpose as Texas had perhaps never expected to see in its *Mexicanos*. Allies were soon forthcoming. The state AFL-CIO raised $17,-539 to support the costs of the march. Archbishop Robert E. Lucey of San Antonio, long interested in the plight of the poor in South Texas, held a mass for the marchers and said: "It is with a large measure of reluctance and regret that we endorse and approve your demand for an hourly wage of $1.25. No sane man would consider that a fair wage in these days. . . . $1.25 is ghastly recompense for exhausting labor under the burning sun of Texas."

As the march went along, others joined in—laborers in Corpus Christi and Houston, steelworkers from Port Lavaca, teachers, college students, even some government workers. On the final day at Austin, 40 Negroes, completing a 200-miles walk from Huntsville in East Texas, would merge with the group.

Perhaps the greatest surprise came a few days before the marchers were to enter Austin. Suddenly, autos holding Governor Connally, Attorney General Waggoner Carr (then running for the U. S. Senate), and Ben Barnes (then speaker of the Texas house) swooped down on the line of march some miles north of New Braunfels. Connally's message to the strikers was simple. He told them (1) he would not be in Austin to meet them, despite their invitation, (2) and that even if he planned to be in Austin, "I still would not have met with you . . . because I'm not unaware of the difficulties that have arisen out of marches throughout this nation [which] for various reasons have resulted in riots and bloodshed . . .", and (3) that they should be complimented on having a peaceful march—so far. (It would remain peaceful to the end. Connally, one of his critics said later, "thought he was still on the ranch; he thought he was still the Anglo foreman talking to those little Mexicans back on the ranch in Wilson County, telling the people to go on back home.") And after some minutes of talk, during which Connally refused to commit himself for a Texas minimum wage, his cavalcade of Lincolns swept away from the disappointed marchers.

Spirits soon buoyed, however, and on Labor Day, 64 days after their start, the line of marchers (now swollen to 6,500) streamed into Austin to be met by 4,000 supporters at the capitol steps and a round of brave, glad oratory. The *Texas Observer* welcomed the marchers with an editorial saying: "The Valley farm workers who are walking 490 miles from Rio Grande City to Austin have walked step by step from obscurity and exploitation into Texas history."

And so it was to be. In two and a half years, the minimum wage law indeed became law. There were reverses too—like the failure, in 1967, of the strike at Rio Grande City. Later, as we shall note, the Mexican-Americans of Texas began to divide into old-style "liberal" and new-style "militant" camps. The march and that Labor Day in Austin might be to Texas what the 1963 Civil Rights March in Washington became to America—an exultant day of unity when all seemed possible, to be followed by an ugly day of reckoning of division and violence. But still, one knew Texas could never regard its Mexican-Americans, and its farm workers, in quite the same light as before.

The Mexican-Americans' quandary is what form their Texan "revolution" ought to take, and what type of leadership they ought to turn to. As a people, they have never been able to organize into strong political units, choose able leaders, and stick with them; many are the jokes, indeed, about the surfeit of would-be Mexican leaders and their inability to lead anyone but themselves. Right after World War I, there was the League of United Latin American Citizens, which still exists, most of its members now prospering in the professions or business, a Latino country club set. After World War II, Dr. Héctor García established the American G. I. Forum, a veterans group to aid Mexican-Americans. The Viva Kennedy movement of 1960 evolved into PASO (Political Association of Spanish-Speaking Organizations), which in turn was supplanted by two or three others including MAPA (Mexican-American Political Action organization), the Southwest Council on La Raza, and MAYO (Mexican-American Youth Organization)—the latter two more radical offshoots of modern times.

In like fashion, the Mexican-Americans are confused about what manner of man they should recognize as a leader. San Antonio's Congressman Henry González should perhaps be considered first, because he was in truth the first Mexican-American to win election to the Texas legislature in 110 years (by winning a senate seat in 1956) and later the first Mexican-American Congressman in the history of Texas—or for that matter, any other state—in 1961.

González's Mexican roots are as direct as can be. In 1911, five years before his birth, his father, then mayor of a town in Mexico, had barely escaped revolutionaries' bullets and brought his family across the Rio Grande to San Antonio where for 40 years he would edit a Spanish-language newspaper, always so Mexican in his thinking that he refused to become a naturalized U. S. citizen. Young Henry started part-time work when he was 10 years old, taking the taunts leveled at "greasers" in the San Antonio streets; years later, even after election to the San Antonio City Council, he would get another taste of discrimination when he and his family were ejected from a public park reserved for "white only." "When I ran for state senator from Bexar County (San Antonio) in 1956, that was considered as unachievable and as radical as if I were to tell you I was going to seek the Vice Presidency next year," González told me in 1971. He did win—by 309 votes out of 100,000 cast, after three recounts.

Big, loquacious "Henry B." soon made his mark in the state senate, fighting with a record-long filibuster a move which was then afoot to uphold and enforce ancient patterns of racial segregation in the state. Other legislators respected him, but to run-of-the-mill Texas conservatives the González name was anathema.

In 1961, the San Antonio seat in the U. S. House opened up and González ran. Even more groups joined his coalition of Mexicans, teachers, policemen, firemen, and unionists. As González puts it, "my five years in the state senate had proven to some local oilmen, to some people who had been against me in previous elections, that I was honest, that I did work, and that I was fair." His enemies see it differently—that this may have been the moment when González "sold out" to the "Establishment." I have heard the process described as one in which the Establishment "picks off" Mexican or Negro leaders who might be dangerous to its interests, by a mortgage, or a loan, or social inducements (invitations to parties), or in the case of politicians, campaign contributions. In the case of Negroes, one then says the man "has been seen"; Mexicans call him a "coyote." Yet the charge, leveled at González, is highly dubious, because in subsequent years he voted a virtually 100 percent liberal line in the House, championed progressive legislation, and on occasion was known to rebuff efforts of special interests to compromise his position.

González insists he is a Congressman for all his constituents, not just the Mexican-Americans. "I don't want to be the Moses of the Mexican people. I don't pretend to be. I don't have that ambition," González insists. Instead, he turns out to be a superbly successful politician (reelected by overwhelming margins) who happens also to be a Mexican-American.

Good for Henry, yes—but how about the rest of Texas' Mexican-Americans? The radical and militant among them despise him, because they see him as the greatest obstacle in their road to revolution, a buffer between them and the Anglo community. And I heard only abuse for González from Bexar County Commissioner Albert Peña, a nationally prominent Mexican-American who accuses González of "never helping any Mexican trying to confront the power structure," and of being an "Establishment liberal [who] expects always to get the Mexican-liberal vote [and] thinks the other side will aid him financially." González's comments about Peña are no more flattering, in a personal dispute that covers neither side with glory and underscores the popular image of Latin leaders always being at each other's throats.

Peña is a bridge to the ultramilitant young Mexican radicals who emerged in Texas in the late 1960s, quickly ruffling the feathers of establishments, Anglo and Latin alike. The first visible step was the formation in 1967 of MAYO (Mexican-American Youth Organization), the brainchild of five young Mexican-American college students who were depressed by the slow progress of their race in civil rights and disgusted with the policies of traditional leaders. After a number of staged confrontations with the local power structures, both in San Antonio and some of the smaller villages, the young Chicanos *—as they prefer to be called—switched their attention to the lower Rio Grande Valley in 1970, formed their own political party (La Raza Unida) and actually won several elections in areas where Mexican-Americans are a clear majority of the population.

One of the most remarkable interviews I have ever had was with the brilliant and charismatic leader of MAYO, José Ángel Gutiérrez, a native of Crystal City, Zavela County, in South Texas—some 125 miles south of San An-

---

* The term has been traced to the Indians of Mexico, who pronounced *Mexicano* "Meh-chee-cano" and then shortened it to "chicano."

tonio. Crystal City has a Mexican population of approximately 80 percent and will be remembered as the place that startled Texas when it elected five Mexican-Americans to its city council in 1963, an unheard-of event up to that time. Even though the Mexicans today control the mayor's job, the council, and the school board, some say the real power lies with the exclusively Anglo large landowners and major businessmen. For years, Crystal City has had a good thing going through the prosperous farm trade of the Winter Garden area in which the town (1970 population 8,104) is located. A statue of Popeye, that belligerent spinach-eating sailor of yore, adorns the town plaza, recalling Crystal City's claim to be the "spinach capital of the world." There is a well-to-do, overwhelmingly Anglo part of Crystal City, with neatly paved roadways passing middle-class homes and some high-priced ranch houses. Then there is the other side of the track, where the Chicanos inhabit a collection of wooden shacks on unpaved, muddy streets.

José Ángel Gutiérrez was born in Crystal City in 1944, the year that John Gunther passed through Texas making interviews for *Inside U. S. A.* "Because I was a doctor's son in Crystal City," Gutiérrez explains, "I was respected by the Anglo people—I call them gringos now—and I was accepted by the Mexican people because I was Mexican, and I lived in the neighborhood." But then, when he was 12, his father died, and "all the respectability was lost, because I was just another Mexican." Everything seemed to underscore the racial issue for Gutiérrez. "I started having an interest in girls, and at that time, my concept of pretty was white—you know, a blond chick with blue eyes, etc., something I couldn't have. And when I started messing around with them, I got burned."

Gutiérrez got elected president of the student body, and saw how the faculty "balanced" the tickets to give Anglo children more than their share of school positions and honors. Then came the 1963 political movement of the local Mexican-Americans, with which Gutiérrez became involved as a teenager, and his first inflammatory oratory that led to a scuffle with the Texas Rangers, who "proceeded to beat the crap out of me." Gutiérrez's only thought was "about getting revenge," but while he would have liked to do it physically, he finally decided another way would be "to get into the [Mexican-American] movement and really raise some hell."

Gutiérrez has been raising hell ever since, using skills of political organization, infiltration, and agitation which come to only a handful of people in any generation. At each of the several colleges and universities he attended, he organized the Chicano students to force concessions from ruling "gringo" administrations that were forever, by Gutiérrez's account, discriminating against Mexican-American students in forms both subtle and gross. It was hard for Gutiérrez to forget that at Uvalde Junior College, where he started out, he was labeled as a communist and atheist when he presumed to run, as a Chicano, for student body president. He received 89 votes—the precise number of Mexican-American students enrolled in a student body of 400. His tactics thereafter were a classic of minority group agitation to control a majority: packing of meetings, carefully planned appeals to the consciences of "liberal"

Anglos, rewriting of student body constitutions through no little subterfuge, taking control of a student body newspaper by abusing the Anglo editor, illegal use of ID cards to vote several times in student elections.

By 1967, Gutiérrez and a small coterie of other like-minded young Chicanos were ready to start a full-scale movement in Texas. The trouble with the existing Mexican organizations, they decided, was that their programs "were not geared for the barrios." As Gutiérrez puts it, "we felt we were victims of cultural genocide. Everything we stood for—mariachi music, speaking Spanish, frijoles [beans] and tortillas, or being a Catholic—was wrong in the eyes of the 'system' ". So MAYO was formed, and while Gutiérrez somehow found time to get married, have a child, make a start on his Ph.D. program, and serve in the Army for four and a half months, a brilliant approach to getting money was devised. "We said, it's amazing how all of these flunkies have sat around here and not even tapped foundation life." So the MAYO organizers set up a group they called the Mexican-American Unity Council, called on some of the professors and politicians, and said "now we need to have you guys be our funding agency." At the same time, reports came of similar movements in New Mexico, Arizona, and California. And in New York, the Ford Foundation was beginning to feel that Mexican-Americans were the most disorganized and fragmented minority in American life and needed national organizations to serve their social, economic, and political needs. As a result, a New Southwest Council for La Raza was set up in Phoenix with $630,000 in Ford money, involving some of the region's most prominent Mexican-American leaders (including Albert Peña of San Antonio). The Southwest Council, in turn, channeled $110,000 to the Unity Council in San Antonio. Just as importantly, Ford gave $2.2 million to a new Mexican-American Legal Defense and Educational Fund (MALDEF), with national headquarters in San Antonio. Ford's idea was that the Southwest Council would be like the NAACP, the MALDEF like the NAACP Legal Defense and Educational Fund.

Whatever New York thought, Gutiérrez and his friends had their own plans. "Ford didn't have much choice in the matter," Gutiérrez told me. "It was one of those situations that either you come across with money and be able to plug us into the system or we just tear the hell out of everything out here." Not content with the Ford money, with which they put most of their associates on payrolls of one type or another, the MAYO group also appealed for and got major assistance from the federal "war on poverty" programs, Model Cities, and church groups.

Of all the Ford-funded activities, the legal fund (MALDEF) developed as the least controversial. By April 1970, it claimed it was involved in 155 cases affecting 100,000 Chicanos from Texas to California—an historic legal breakthrough for a chronically unrepresented and discriminated-against people. But other MAYO activities, generally directed by Gutiérrez, ran into some trouble. There was an effort, at Peña's urging, to get involved in local elections, giving clandestine support to a Republican candidate against Henry González and trying to elect some of their own number to the city council.

Both efforts failed, after arousing the predictable storm of protest.

Then, in spring 1969, Gutiérrez began to resort to some highly inflammatory oratory. The enemy of all Chicanos, he proclaimed, was the "gringo" —that brand of Anglo who "has a certain policy or program or attitude that reflects bigotry, racism, discord, prejudice, and violence." Usually Gutiérrez talked of fighting the gringo politically or economically, but he also said: "We have got to eliminate the gringo, and what I mean by that is if the worst comes to the worst, we have got to kill him."

The rough language was an invitation to counterattack, and Congressman González quickly grasped the opportunity. In a series of speeches on the House floor in Washington, González said the Ford Foundation was supporting a group of "Brown Bilbos" practicing a "new racism" in Texas.

González now claims that he blew the whistle on MAYO just in time. "The only reason you haven't read a headline—'Violent Revolution in San Antonio—Men Shot'—is that I staved them off."

Finally, in June 1969, Ford officials summoned Peña, Gutiérrez, Velázquez, and others involved in the La Raza operation to a meeting in the foundation's great glass house by the East River in New York. There was reportedly a stormy session in which Mitchell Sviridoff, Ford's national affairs director, bluntly announced no more Ford money would go to MAYO. Peña told Sviridoff what he could do with all $3 billion of the foundation's assets.

A mere reduction in foundation money, however, was not to silence José Ángel Gutiérrez, a supremely self-confident young man, reveling in his own powers of organization, leadership, oratory, agitation. (He is also an extremely pleasant person to talk with, and it seems hard to imagine him following through on his murderous threats. Despite the oratory, in fact, MAYO's activities had not led to violence up to 1971.)

Where would he like to see his whole movement in five years time, I asked Gutiérrez. "All over the Southwest," he replied. "And we're going to— that, is, if I can stay alive."

As a first step, Gutiérrez returned to Crystal City and organized a massive student boycott at the local schools against mean and petty racial policies. Then, in 1970, Gutiérrez shifted his organizing skills to his new Chicano political party—La Raza Unida. For many Chicanos, the old love affair with the Democratic party was out of date. As one labor official put it, "When President Kennedy and Bob Kennedy died, the Democrat party died for the Mexican-Americans in Texas." A new party would provide a point of racial pride for Chicanos. It would be able (they hoped) to seize power in Mexican-majority counties and exercise a bargaining power in major statewide elections. The effort started well in spring 1970, when Raza Unida candidates indeed won control of the school boards in Crystal City—Gutiérrez himself becoming school board president—and in nearby Carrizo Springs and Cotulla. But in the autumn elections, even in heavily Mexican counties, Raza Unida candidates were deserted as most Chicanos voted Democratic. Gutiérrez had appealed to Mexican-Americans outside the "majority" areas of the Valley to refrain from voting at all, because of similarity of the Republican and Democratic candidates for the U. S. Senate. Available evidence indicates his advice was largely ignored.

Thus La Raza Unida faces the same difficulties of all third parties and radical political movements—winning much publicity but few elections. Its second problem is that the number of counties which have actual Mexican-American majorities is limited. By rejecting membership in the dominant local political party (the Democratic), a Raza Unida contender forecloses his own possibility for election.

The picture may be brighter for Mexican-American politicians who appeal beyond their own ethnic group. When González ran for the Democratic nomination for governor in 1958 and the U. S. Senate in 1961, he was apparently hurt by his name and ancestry, though he insists many non-Mexicans voted for him. Now he believes the day has come when a qualified Texas Mexican-American, with a moderate image and broad backing, could be elected state-wide—especially if he ran as a team candidate with a gubernatorial candidate with the huge cash resources a contest requires.

The establishment politicians, of course, prefer a politician of González's complexion to the militants of La Raza Unida stripe. Lt. Gov. Ben Barnes told me: "Henry B. has done more for the Mexican-American than any other man in the United States. He was out on the floor of the (state) senate talking about these things 15 years ago while those kids were still in short pants. He'll come back to San Antonio . . . and he'll get 85 to 90 percent of the vote down there. [In fact, González drew no opposition at all in 1970.] A militant is never going to have any real political strength—I don't care whether he be black or white or Mexican-American."

The problem is that, down through history, the ideas and stimulation of militants have been necessary to make establishment politicians move. Without that kind of pressure, a suppressed people like the Mexican-Americans of Texas would stay down forever. And in political terms, one can now begin to foresee the issues around which Texan Chicanos will rally in the 1970s and beyond. There will be an increasingly sharp demand for an end to all forms of discrimination—in schools, in public and private employment, in contests for public office. Popular Mexican causes will also include higher minimum wage laws and stopping the flow of cheap labor from across the Rio Grande.

Significant strides are already being made in bilingual education, as more and more public schools offer Spanish from the first grade forward as a second language. A bilingual commission has been set up under the Texas Education Agency, partly funded by a federal grant and headed by a Chicano, Dr. Severo Gómez. Joe Frantz, a member of the commission, writes:

> I visited several primary grades in McAllen and Edinburg, both border towns, in which the children of migrants are being taught entirely in Spanish. A group of brighter kids you have seldom seen. An experiment was made in Brownsville of sending four kids from Anglo middle-class homes to schools on the Mexican side of the river to be instructed entirely in Spanish. These kids showed the same symptoms that have always plagued the young Latino in this country—disinterest, sullenness, trouble making, and so on.

The Mexican-Americans are likely to keep up their agitation for abolition of the 150-year-old Texas Ranger force, a group surrounded by mystique like few others in the world. The Rangers, Walter Prescott Webb once wrote, were men who "could ride straight up to death." But part of their historic work was to disperse Indians and Mexicans for the benefit of Anglo settlers, and critics maintain that the elite unit, now 80 men strong, remains in effect a private police force to protect the interest of the wealthy landholders and ranchers. San Antonio's state senator Joe Bernal calls them "the Mexican-Americans' Ku Klux Klan." In 1970, the state advisory committee to the United States Commission on Civil Rights recommended the Rangers be disbanded because they had engendered "fear and bitterness" among Mexican-Americans. Capt. Clint Peoples, director of the Rangers, scoffed at the idea: "The people of Texas could never vote to abolish the Rangers and no legislature would stand for it," he said. "Abolish the Rangers? Why, that would be like tearing down the Alamo."

In social terms, it may be that the average Mexican-American is much closer to assimilation into the white culture than the militants' angry charges and demands would lead one to believe. With a decent income and ability to speak fluent English, a Chicano is at no overwhelming disadvantage in modern U.S.A., and can certainly exist like other minority groups which conform to most American norms while retaining traces of their distinctive cultural identity. "I resent the term 'brown power,'" says Dr. García, founder of the old GI Forum. "That sounds as if we were a different race. We're not. We're white. We should be Americans. But we should eat enchiladas and be proud of our names."

In 1970, *Newsweek* interviewed Peter Torres, Jr., a 36-year-old San Antonio city councilman who is close to the militants. Torres understands the stakes exceedingly well:

Many Mexican-Americans believe you can't fight City Hall. You don't question the *patron*. You don't question police brutality. I grew up in a poor section of west San Antonio and I saw people beaten in the streets. If you were poor, you said, "*Que puede hacer uno?*"—What can one do? Well, the young people today aren't going to play patsy for the establishment. There's an awareness of something among the young people that is either going to make this country and take us onto greater glories—or destroy us.

CALIFORNIA

THE GREAT NATION STATE

I. THE STATE SCENE

> *But in California the lights went on all at once, in a blaze, and they have never been dimmed.*
>
> —Carey McWilliams, *in* California: The Great Exception

THERE HAS never been a state quite like California. None has ever had so many people—by 1971 over 20 million (up from 9 million in 1945), the new sum greater than that of 20 other states combined or six times as large as the original 13 states in 1790. Every 10th resident of the U.S. is now a Californian. (In 1964, California outstripped New York to become the country's most populous; for most of the postwar era, until a slowdown in the late 1960s, it had grown by more than 1,000 people *a day*.) John Gunther pointed out a quarter-century ago that California was the one that above all others could best exist alone, and the statement is even truer today. If California were an independent country, it would exceed 111 other nations in population and 92 in land area. Its gross national product—$112 billion in 1970—would be greater than all nations of the world save six—the United States, the Soviet Union, West Germany, Great Britain, France, and Japan. Agriculturally, it would be among the leading nations; in export trade, it would rank

19th. Its per capita income would exceed that of all other countries of the world, including the United States.

California is so huge geographically—800 miles from corner to corner—that people have sometimes despaired of running it as a single entity. Two of the largest cities, Los Angeles and San Diego, are 360 and 470 air miles, respectively, from the state capital at Sacramento, a division greater than that of any other state. The legislature actually voted in 1859 (nine years after statehood) to split into north and south states, a proposal frustrated only by the failure of Congress to approve it. The two-state idea has never died, and there was a renewed flutter of interest in it during the 1960s, when Northern California viewed with alarm its loss of voting power under one-man, one-vote in the state legislature. The suggestion then, as traditionally, was to split California along the crest of the Tehachapi Mountains, approximately 335 miles south of San Francisco and 115 miles north of Los Angeles. (Fred Tyson of the State Environmental Quality Study Council had a different idea—to split California where the smog from Los Angeles meets the smog from San Francisco, the idea being that each state would then be in a position to control its air quality.)

The state-splitting ideas are not likely to come to fruition. Reapportionment gave the vote weight to Southern California, and it is not about to release it. Water, as we shall see later, may no longer be the great bone of contention between north and south that it appeared to be just a few years ago. And there are strong bonds of unity. The expressways between Northern and Southern California are packed with traffic, and the San Francisco–Los Angeles air corridor is the most heavily traveled in the world. Even the University of California, for all its campuses, offers unity. There are almost as many students at Berkeley from Southern California as would be proportionate to the California population (11.3 million people in the south, 8.4 million in the north, according to the 1970 Census).

But what, one asks, lies at the heart of this peculiar vortex of human energy and desire called California? Theories abound—futurism, *anomie*, boosterism, sun and leisure culture in a beneficent climate, a lemming-like rush to the precipice of the next great earthquake—and we shall examine some in turn. Capturing, at any moment in time, the spirit and direction of California is an almost impossible task; what one records will surely be transmuted by the time it reaches print. As Gladwin Hill, veteran California correspondent for the New York *Times*, wrote in his book *Dancing Bear*: "The endless tide of immigration, peculiarities of geography, and the forced-draft growth of California's economy have made it a kaleidoscopic succession of states, changing from year to year, almost from day to day."

What does seem constant, as Carey McWilliams (a foremost interpreter of modern California) tells the story, is "rapid, revolutionary change":

Just as the energies released by the discovery of gold put California into orbit with one mighty blast-off, so it has been kept spinning, faster and faster, by a succession of subsequent, providentially timed discoveries and "explosions" of one kind or another: the "green gold" of lettuce and other produce crops; . . .

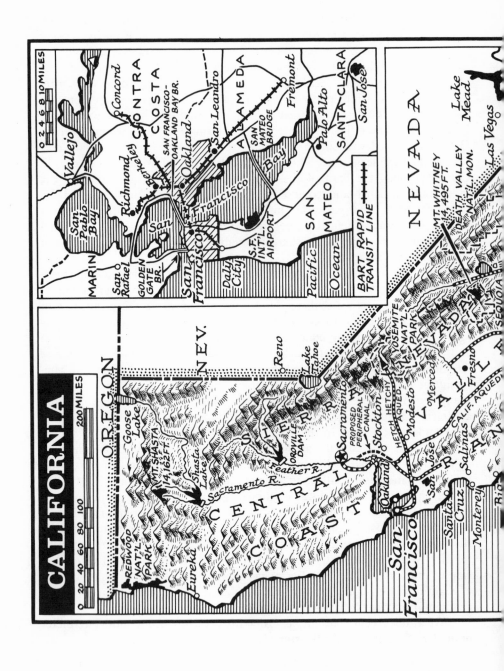

CALIFORNIA

0 20 40 60 80 100 200 MILES

OREGON

N. EV.

Goose Lake

MT. SHASTA 14,162 FT.

Shasta Lake

Sacramento R.

Feather R.

OROVILLE DAM

REDWOOD NAT'L PARK

Eureka

SIERRA

Reno

Lake Tahoe

NEVADA

CENTRAL

COAST

VALLEY

Sacramento

PROPOSED PERIPHERAL CANAL

Stockton

HETCH HETCHY AQUED.

YOSEMITE NAT'L PARK

Modesto

Merced

Fresno

CALIF. AQUEDUCT

SEQUOIA

San Francisco

Oakland

San Jose

Santa Cruz

Salinas

Monterey

MT. WHITNEY 14,495 FT.

DEATH VALLEY NAT'L MON.

Las Vegas

Lake Mead

0 2 4 6 8 10 MILES

CONTRA COSTA

Concord

Vallejo

Richmond

Berkeley

San Pablo Bay

MARIN

San Rafael

GOLDEN GATE BR.

San Francisco

Daly City

S.F. INT'L. AIRPORT

SAN FRANCISCO-OAKLAND BAY BR.

Oakland

San Leandro

ALAMEDA

San Francisco Bay

SAN MATEO BRIDGE

SAN MATEO

Palo Alto

SANTA CLARA

Fremont

San Jose

Pacific Ocean

BART RAPID TRANSIT LINE

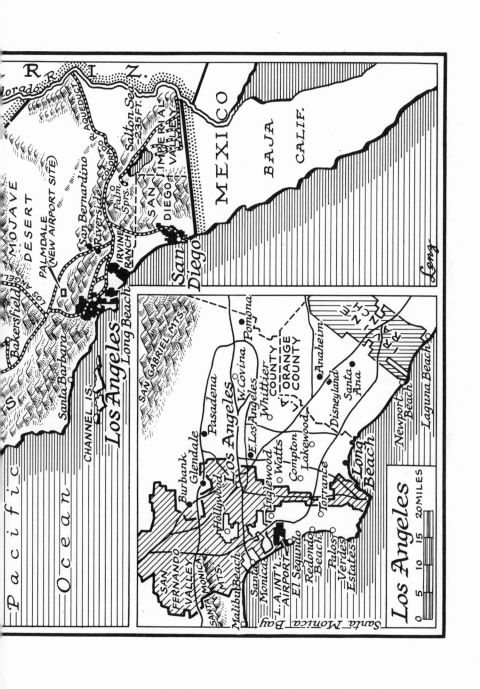

the "black gold" of oil; motion pictures, tourism, the aerospace industry. . . . California has raced through the familiar evolutionary cycle—pastoral, agricultural, industrial, post-industrial. . . .

The pace of technological change is matched by the societal. One out of every three California families moves each year (compared to one out of four in the U.S.A. as a whole); Californians change houses as other Americans change automobiles, forever searching for the better life on the other side of the freeway. Telephone and address books are forever out of date, the sense of impermanence overwhelming. California has become an unstratified society made up of communities of strangers; the sociologists speak of *anomie*, the state in which humans find themselves uprooted, drifting, and unfocused. Even the special-purpose communities by interest and age groups—retirement communities, swinging single colonies, college dormitory communities, not to mention income and racial ghettoes—fail to bring real cohesion and may in fact be symptomatic of the ills, since they accentuate the divisions in society. (There is no easier place to become a roaring John Bircher than in a golden-age community where one never has to come to grips with the young or minorities *as persons*; no better place to develop exaggerated hostilities about the whole society than in a student ghetto; no better place to become embittered about all honkies than in a black or Mexican quarter where the only whites seen are police or merchants.)

Californians, Neil Morgan observes in *California Syndrome*, have also built a civilization "quintessentially American," perhaps because they are a cross-section of Americans, or, as some insist, a selection of them. What America is, California is more so. As Wallace Stegner, an adopted Californian, wrote in 1959:

In a prosperous country, we are more prosperous than most; in an urban country, more urban than most; in a gadget-happy country, more addicted to gadgets; in a mobile country, more mobile; in a tasteless country, more tasteless; in a creative country, more energetically creative; in an optimistic society, more optimistic; in an anxious society, more anxious. Contribute regionally to the national culture? We *are* the national culture, at its most energetic end.

A few years later, Stegner was able to add to his list phenomena like air and water pollution, literary despair, increased leisure, the sexual revolution, widespread agnosticism, last-ditch religiosity, and Birchite reaction. "These are tunes that do not change when you cross the border into California," he noted. "Only the volume goes up, the tape spins faster, the tempo accelerates into a hysterical twittering." Today, the catalogue of California firsts and excesses could be broadened to include the age of student revolt and campus violence (dating from Berkeley in 1964), drugs and turned-off kids, alcoholism—850,000 afflicted by last count (the highest rate for any state except Nevada)—anti-university and anti-young politics (pioneered by Ronald Reagan), taxpayer rebellion against the welfare system, law-and-orderism and the political tug to the right, municipal radicalism (Berkeley in 1971), ghetto riots (starting with Watts in 1964) and guerilla warfare between the races, the Mexican-American awakening and organization of the nation's long-downtrodden farm workers, cybernetic politics (à la Spencer-Roberts), and the conservationists' demand to save not only the air and water but the whole natural environment (starting with the pioneer efforts of the Sierra Club).

And in a country swept by self-doubt, California seems to doubt the most. Pollster Don Muchmore told me that in his first surveys after World War II and up to the early 1960s, people were still excited about California and believed in its golden future like an article of faith. Since 1960, this has been replaced by creeping negativism, more doubt about the state's future, discontent with the taxes, and responsibilities that come with the trademarks of success (the bigger car, the lot, the house). "Instead of our state moving toward a cohesive unit, we're breaking into little pieces. There is little common belief of the people—not even in their own state," Muchmore said.

Of the millions who have poured into California in recent decades, a substantial portion has been from the Midwest. But somehow, the new Californians quickly put Iowa and American Gothic behind them for what seems an easier life in the sun—yet a life, too, of frenetic economic activity. Thus California can at once demonstrate such startlingly different characteristics. This lotus land is also America's aerospace capital. Los Angeles may be the blandest great city ever built; San Francisco, with its wonderful spirit and élan, competes with Manhattan as America's most colorful. California is number one in the U.S.A. in think tanks, psychologists, aeronautical and eletrical engineers, mathematicians, Nobel Prize winners, and, of late, unemployed intelligentsia—a surfeit of the well-educated. It is a land of incredible creative energy. But it is also first or near the top in crime, drug addiction, suicide, divorce (Californians seem to exchange mates as readily as they do houses), homosexuality, and every other form of libidinal indulgence and aberration, not to mention bizarre religious cults and offbeat political movements, Black Pantherism, and hippieism. It may be the capital of the promising "Jesus Revolution" of the 1970s. California has half the backyard swimming pools in all the U.S.A., a fifth of the mobile homes, and is the top national market for pleasure boats, garbage disposals, frozen food, automobiles foreign and domestic, portable barbecues, and king-sized beds and water beds. As if this were not revealing enough, it can also be reported that California led America in the rush to such passing or permanent diversions as surfing, bikinis, topless/bottomless bars and restaurants, wife-swapping, communal living, drive-ins, dietetic foods, triple garages, second-home communities, credit cards, dune buggies, campers, and drag strips. The comment of BBC producer John Morgan after a study of the state: Californians have "seen the future and it plays." There are some dissenters to that future; Nancy Banks-Smith wrote: "With a spot of luck, I hope to die before it happens!"

Wishing the future away won't do the trick, though, since it will come. The question is: Can California (and in turn, the rest of the U.S.A.) turn its brilliance and its playfulness to creative ends? Somehow the playfulness will have to find room for new social cohesion and human cooperation, perhaps abetted by great state leaders of a quality not seen since the days of Earl Warren. As for California's intellectual and technical brilliance, every ounce of it will be needed to cope with the perplexing problems of teeming cities, transportation, the environment. Along the Pacific reaches of the continent, the first and quite tentative steps have been taken to apply advanced systems analysis methods (pioneered in the aerospace industry) to such problems. So far, the payoff has been disappointingly small. But if such efforts fail substantially in the next few years, then not only California but all the U.S.A. could face a grim future in the quality of life it will have to lead in the closing years of this century, or the next. Old hit-and-miss U. S.-style problem solving will no longer do, for there are too many people, too many pent-up demands, and a vanished frontier.

Equally vital are the issues posed by ownership of such large swaths of California's private land by so few gigantic companies, the rapid spread of corporate farming, exorbitantly expensive water projects of principal benefit to a narrow few, ineffective pollution control, "freeway mania," corrupting campaign contributions, and the power of big landholders to compromise government at every level. Long apparent to thoughtful people in the state, these abuses were dramatized in a 1971 report of a Ralph Nader task force entitled "Land and Power in California," prepared under the direction of a 26-year-old Stanford graduate, Robert C. Fellmeth. The report was faulted by many for pejorative language, some factual errors, and lack of historic perspective. But it was filled with documentation. And as newsman Lou Cannon reported to the Ridder newspapers, the practices revealed by the task force are "the stuff of which crusades are made, or better yet, lawsuits. One doesn't have to buy Nader's moralistic view of California to believe that this report may be the best thing that's happened to the state in many years."

The Grand Tradition: Hiram Johnson to Earl Warren

California long ago got the reputation of being a land of loony schemes and political extremes, an image which has stuck and somehow refuses to come unglued. It is common to talk of California as the state with the oddest political structure among the 50, although perhaps that sobriquet should be assigned to New York instead. And Herbert L. Phillips, retired dean of California political reporters, has warned: "The quest for orderliness [in California politics] has tempted many able scholars to undertake huge, solemn and painstaking chronological recitations, in the hope that political symmetry somehow would appear out of the fog. It seldom does."

With the reader properly forewarned, we begin a cursory review of the unfathomable.

The dominant themes of California politics are weak party organizations, the dominance of personalities, wide use of referendum and initiative, and maximum feasible nonpartisanship. All this came about as a reaction to what came before—the era of heavy-handed control by the railroad barons, stretching from 1870 to 1910, a control so complete it has been called "absolute dictatorship." As the state's largest landowner (thanks to the gift of alternate sections of land along the right of way made by the government), the Southern Pacific Railroad exercised monopolistic control of the principal means of transportation. It used every means, bribery the most prevalent, to control California politics for the purpose of enriching the corporate coffers.

The agent of reform was Hiram Warren Johnson, a fiery attorney whose father had been the chief lobbyist for Southern Pacific. Twice elected governor, in 1910 and 1914, Johnson then went on to the U. S. Senate, where he lived out the remainder of his turbulent days (to 1945). "Get the Southern Pacific Railroad out of politics!" Johnson bellowed in his 1910 campaign. When he won, he quickly secured passage of an arsenal of bills intended to cripple political machines and old-style patronage politics. Initiative, referendum, and recall were enacted, as well as nonpartisan election of judges, a cross-filing system for primaries, county home rule, and civil service throughout the state government. Other bills made the railroad commission into an effective regulatory body, controlled utilities and their rates, prohibited child labor, instituted workmen's compensation, and began many flood and conservation projects. Former President Theodore Roosevelt called the work of the 1911 legislature "the most comprehensive program of constructive legislation ever passed at a single session of an American legislature." It was the golden era of Progressive reform, and determined the character of California politics up to the present day. Turbulent California, as much as it has an historic memory, will never forget Hiram Johnson.

But a pleasant or easy man to get along with he was not. A fellow Senator once described him as "a bifurcated, peripatetic volcano, in perpetual eruption, belching fire and smoke." Physically, in Gladwin Hill's words, Johnson was "stocky and jowly, with a made-in-America face and gimlet eyes peering intently through rimless glasses," a man who "compensated for inner insecurity and chronic pessimism with vitriolic belligerence toward any opposition."

Johnson was a Republican but broke with the GOP in 1912 to run for Vice President on Theodore Roosevelt's Progressive ticket, and 20 years later he supported Franklin Roosevelt for President. In 1920, he was offered the Vice Presidency on the Republican ticket with Warren Harding, but refused; had he accepted, he would have been President. As it was, he stayed on in the Senate, remaining a rabid isolationist, but never losing Californians' affection.

The not unfair criticism leveled against Johnson the reformer is that he threw out the baby of normal two-party operation with the bath water of corruption. "In its place," Hill wrote, "has evolved what might be called a politics of pragmatism—a milieu of opportunism and improvisation, in which party structures are weak, party loyalties are flimsy, 'party responsibility' is unknown, and in which continuity, in personalities and policies, is tenuous and electoral consistency is rare." The wonder is that under those conditions, a large share of able and moderate politicians, both Republican and Democratic, were able to mold in California one of the best state governments in history, remarkably honest and responsive during decades of chaotic growth.

By the 1920s, Progressivism had spent itself and a succession of regular Republican governors kept things on an even keel in Sacramento. The Depression, however, hit California especially hard, with high unemployment and severe strikes. Tens of thousands were on relief, and crops rotted in the field for lack of a market. In 1934, Upton Sinclair, the famous novelist and former Socialist nominee for governor, captured the Democratic gubernatorial nomination and shocked California with his "EPIC" platform—to End Poverty in California. Applying simple Marxist theory, Sinclair advocated turning over to workers some of the means of production—in this instance, the farms and factories of California idled by the Depression. The other elements of Sinclair's platform—graduated income taxes, state support of those unable to work, and a $50-a-month pension for the aged and widows—hardly sound revolutionary today. In desperate, Depression-time Californians, especially the aged without work or hope, they struck an instant spark. The propertied California "establishment" was horrified beyond description and poured a reported $10 million, more money than ever before or since spent on a California campaign, into the effort to stop Sinclair. Among other things, he was charged with being "an anarchist, a free-lover, an agent of Moscow, a Communist, an anti-Christ." In fact, Sinclair was a mild-mannered vegetarian with a searing belief in social justice, preaching ideas a few years ahead of his time. Eventually he was defeated by 259,000 votes, but only after giving the capitalist class the fright of its life.

Sinclair's EPIC was not the only strange idea to hit California in the mid-1930s. Another was Technocracy, a proposal to let the country be run by engineers and technicians; still another was the New England–born Utopian Society, which would have overthrown capitalism for a controlled society in which all work would be done in three hours a day by the working population 25 to 45 years of age. And soon, thousands of California oldsters were being attracted to the Townsend plan, authored by a retired Long Beach physician, Dr. Francis Townsend. He advocated $200-a-month pensions for all citizens over 60, financed by a 2-percent federal sales tax on all business. At one point, Townsend's clubs claimed 2.5 million members. After hitting their peak in 1936, they began a decline, only to be succeeded by the even more politically potent "Ham & Eggs" movement, which offered pensions somewhat lower—and thus more realistic—than Townsend's but picked up extra support by dropping the minimum pension age to 50. The cost of Ham & Eggs would have been a then-astronomical $30 million a week, but it gained wide support (including that of organized labor) and was placed on the state's 1938 general election ballot by petitions which were signed by 789,000 voters, a full quarter of the electorate. The plan was narrowly defeated, but the momentum behind it helped carry into office the first Democratic governor of the century—Culbert Olsen, a Populist, foe of the oil companies, and party chairman during the Sinclair campaign four years before. Olsen had visions of being an historic reform governor like Johnson, but while he began some worthwhile changes—the penal reform, for instance, which came to fruition under his successor—his record was largely an inept one, most of his ideas being brushed aside by the legislature. In 1942, he lost decisively to one Earl Warren.

Earl Warren is the watershed figure of modern-day California politics, the man who took the nonpartisanship of Hiram Johnson (whom he revered) and gave it its ultimate expression; in a wider sense, he is the man who prepared California to become the nation it is today. No politician of modern times has been so popular. Warren is the only man ever elected to three terms as governor of California (in 1942, 1946, and 1950), the only man to serve so long (almost 11 years), and the only gubernatorial candidate ever to win the nominations of both parties (in 1946, before cross-filing was abolished). In 1953, he resigned to accept President Eisenhower's appointment as Chief Justice of the United States.

To the world, Earl Warren offered a wholesome, pleasant exterior, a big, six-foot, 215-pound man exuding good-willed Americanism. No one ever accused him of being a deep intellectual. But somehow, the man's basic instincts—political, judicial, moral—proved superb for his times. About the only incident of a long state career for which Warren is still criticized in California is his consenting to the wartime incarceration of 110,000 Japanese-Americans—some 70,000 of them American citizens—in concentration camps.

Warren showed amazing capacity for growth. For his start in politics, he owed much to the hotly partisan Old Guard Republican faction headed by the Oakland *Tribune* Knowland family. But he not only cross-filed when he ran for state office but seemed to choose his cabinet and other chief officers on the basis of capabilities, regardless of whether they were Republicans or Democrats.

Warren's nonpartisanship drove doctrinaire Democrats and reactionary Republicans to apoplexy, but it never failed at the ballot box. It even drew the grudging admiration of President Truman, who once said of Warren: "He's a Democrat—and doesn't know it." The specific list of things Warren accomplished in California would seem to bear out Truman's assessment. Among them were major advances in state welfare programs, including increased old age pensions and workmen's compensation, mental hospital and prison reforms, a state crime commission (predating Senator Estes Kefauver's national investigation by several years), and enthusiastic backing of the Central Valley Project. Warren also showed a willingness to take on some of California's toughest lobbies, including oil and private power. Years before the idea of Medicare was raised in Washington, Warren fought for a general health insurance plan in California, to be financed by joint employer-employee contributions. It was one of the few big fights he ever lost.

One Warren program was peculiarly un-Democratic, however. It involved saving money. During the Depression days, the state treasury had been sorely strapped, and the budget was barely in the black when Warren took office. But the year was 1943, and since aircraft and other defense industries were burgeoning in California, and since the chief revenue methods, sales and income taxes, quickly reflected increases in economic activity, the state suddenly faced the pleasant miracle of tremendous annual surpluses. Herbert L. Phillips describes how Warren met the situation:

> As an alternative to haphazard disbursements, the Governor sponsored a policy of siphoning off into earmarked reserve funds every nickel of wartime treasury income in excess of the state's actual operating needs. . . . [He also] set up special wartime agencies to take inventory of California's accumulated needs, intelligently plan in advance for postwar reconstruction and indicate priorities for a multiplicity of scheduled statewide governmental building programs and public works expansions. Meantime, revenue poured into the treasury at such an unexampled pace that it was possible to authorize a temporary reduction in state tax rates. . . .
> In the middle 1940s, after Germany and Japan finally surrendered, releasing men and materials for nonmilitary use, the gigantic California melon was ripe to be cut. Hundreds of millions of dollars in reserve savings were appropriated for the rehabilitation of the state's long-neglected physical plant—the schools, colleges, prisons, hospitals and all the rest. Money was made available for district water projects. . . . Governmental retirement systems were refinanced. Local political subdivisions shared. . . .

Without Warren's hoarding of California's unexpected pot of gold in the 1940s, California might well have been unable to make the quantum jump in services indispensable to accommodating its fantastic postwar population inflow. Had the millions come anyway, one fears, they might have found chaos rather than the semblance of progress in the Golden State.

Even while Warren was scoring these accomplishments in California, some observers wrote him off as a genial extrovert. One of these was John Gunther in *Inside U.S.A.* "Earl Warren," he wrote, "is honest, likeable, and clean; he will never set the world on fire or even make it smoke; . . . he is a man who has probably never bothered with an abstract thought twice in his life . . ."

Yet in 1953, Warren went to the Supreme Court, and within less than a year had persuaded his fellow Justices to agree to a unanimous decision in the school desegregation case, doubtless the single most important decision of the court in modern times. And as the years went on, the "Warren court" assured itself a place in history by altering the basic thrust of American law in the fields of civil rights and liberties, the rights of the accused, and legislative apportionment. Thousands of Americans (including John Gunther) changed their minds about Earl Warren, dividing into camps of strong approval or bitter dissent.

Latter-Day Personalities

Now to review some of the personalities who have crowded the klieg-lit stage of California politics in recent times:

RICHARD M. NIXON. Nixon's name must lead the list, for he was the first Californian since Herbert Hoover to win the Presidency. Nixon's personality and national record will be well known to the reader. His contribution to California is more difficult to discern, for he never held a state or local office. As a successful candidate for the U. S. House (1946, 1948) and Senate (1950), he was mainly known for the skilled way that he suggested communist or other radical tendencies in his liberal Democratic opponents. After his eight years as Eisenhower's Vice President and his defeat for President in 1960, Nixon returned to his native state, ran a race for governor in which he charged incumbent Edmund G. Brown with being less than hard on communists and of bungling the administration of the state, and lost by 296,758 votes. Then ensued Nixon's famous outburst at his "last press conference," his departure for a lucrative law practice in New York City, and Ronald Reagan's eclipse of him as the controlling Republican politician of California. Following his 1968 Presidential election, Nixon shifted his voting residence back from New York (to the "Western White House" at San Clemente). But except, perhaps, in Orange County, he was about as well liked or disliked in California as in any other place in the U.S.A. His intervention in the 1970 Senate campaign, in an attempt to save GOP Senator George Murphy (including a celebrated, disputed "rock throwing" incident at San Jose, which the Republicans tried to turn to their political advantage), proved singularly unsuccessful.

RONALD REAGAN. It is hard to imagine any other state that would take a veteran movie actor, without a day's experience in public office in his life, and elect him governor—and even harder to imagine that the player chosen would turn out to be one of America's most adept politicians, elected once by a plurality of close to one million votes, a second time by more than a half-million, and to be dark horse Presidential candidate of one wing of his party. California did all this with Ronald Reagan, native of Tampico, Illinois; graduate of Eureka College; Des Moines radio announcer; actor in 40 films (mostly B grade); a president of the Screen Actors Guild; onetime liberal Democrat (a cofounder, with Melvyn Douglas, of the state ADA); host for television's "General Electric Theatre"; conservative evangelizer for GE around the U.S.A.; and California cochairman for Barry Goldwater in 1964. From there, it was only two years and a careful cram-course in state government, arranged by Spencer-Roberts & Associates of Los Angeles, for Reagan to become the preeminent citizen politician, and then governor of the nation state.

Reagan's message in his first campaign was that it was time that something be done about runaway taxes, soaring welfare costs, the escalating crime rate, and violence on the campuses. Four years later, in 1970, California was worse off, if anything, in all those areas. The incumbent should have been in trouble, but he was not. For each evil, there was an appropriate villain. Taxes and high budgets were the fault of inflation and spendthrift legislators. High welfare costs were to be blamed on welfare cheaters, permissive social workers, and federal regulations that hamstrung California's cost-cutting program. Crime was the fault of judges, cop haters, bombers and Democratic legislators who resisted Reagan's law enforcement programs. Campus unrest was the fault of undisciplined students, rascally professors, and outside agitators. All these problems remained, but the voter could count on Reagan to stand between him and the unruly ones, to stop the outrage short of the patio gate. The natural political charm and telegenic appeal of the man, an aura of modesty even while being tough, of sounding liberal even while taking terribly illiberal positions, set Reagan apart from other conservative leaders—and in tone, if not in substance, from his wealthy, right-wing backers. The engaging smile, the soft-spoken aura of "how can you question my motives?", of utter reasonableness and occasional put-upon-ness, all superbly transmitted by television, made Reagan a unique commodity among American politicians.

Reagan was fortunate, however, that his reelection to a second term preceded by several months the revelation that he paid no California state income tax for 1970. Someone in the state tax office apparently leaked the fact to the press, and Ronald Reagan, the man who had campaigned against withholding on the ground that "taxes should hurt," and who earned $76,500 in salary and perquisites in 1970, was forced to make a lame explanation that because of "business reverses," he had not paid a penny to the state. But he refused to divulge the nature of his business holdings (saying reporters should be "ashamed" of themselves for delving into personal matters). The New York *Times* reported in June 1971 that Reagan may have been spared tax paying by joining other wealthy persons in using a legal "tax shelter," based on the preferential treatment given by the tax laws to owners of cattle herds.

What actual record, behind the image, was Reagan making? He had appointed some top-drawer men to the judiciary, and his tax reform package, rejected by the legislature, at least incorporated the sound principle of taxing income more and property less. In his first year in office, he had the courage to ask for $946 million in new taxes, though the rapidly escalating budget gave him little choice. He certainly knew how to articulate the outrage that average people felt about student violence. Polls showed the percentage of Californians who considered themselves "conservative" had increased from 32 percent in 1964 to 42 percent in 1969 (compared to 27 percent middle-of-the-roaders and 24 percent liberals); whether author or reflection of the trend, Reagan seemed to match it perfectly.

In many respects, Reagan seemed like a "breather" governor, as Eisenhower was a "breather" President for the U.S.A. in the 1950s. But where Ike had been a healing influence, Reagan deliberately scorned and alienated minorities in his society—browns and blacks, the students, and the poor—to create his political majority.

A prime example of Reagan's attitude toward the unfortunate in society was his 1970 veto of the federal grant for the California Rural Legal Assistance Agency. CRLA had begun in 1966 after César Chávez and his farm workers' union focused attention on the problems of the rural poor. Tens of thousands of indigent Californians were able to turn to CRLA offices for help. But local power structures and especially the big farmers, which include key Reagan supporters, were enraged, and he exerted heavy political pressure on the Nixon administration in Washington to have the whole program killed. Despite repeated high-level reports exonerating CRLA of wrongdoing and praising its work, its long-term future remained much in doubt.

Discussing Reagan's short supply of creative solutions to California's multitudinous problems, political editor Richard Bergholz of the Los Angeles *Times* commented to me: "Reagan has not been an especially good governor, but then again he has been better than a lot of people thought he would be. What troubles me is that so little has been done specifically about the state's long-range problems. What has the state really done to come to grips with smog and water pollution, transit and parks, open space and land planning? When the Reagan image is forgotten, what will his actual record look like 20 or 30 years from now?"

EDMUND G. ("PAT") BROWN. A native of San Francisco (where he was born in 1905, a year before the great earthquake and fire), Brown knocked down two great Republican heavies to win two terms as governor—William F. Knowland in 1958, Richard M. Nixon in 1962. On a third-term try, Ronald Reagan proved his nemesis. Brown was a moderate Democrat and often shunned partisanship on the model of Earl Warren and the Republican who succeeded Warren from 1953 to 1959, Goodwin Knight. He rose to power as Warren had done—as a crime fighter and attorney general—but he lacked any measure of the glamour of his more famous opponents. But he was an honest, capable administrator, and the Republicans also obliged by helping to defeat themselves.

With the hindsight of the early 1970s, Brown emerges as the last of California's governors who could or did believe that growth in itself was a desirable end. While Brown was in office, the great (and now, it appears, possibly unnecessary) $1.7 billion California Water Plan was passed. Some 1,000 miles of freeway, now seen as mitigated blessings, were constructed. In terms of Brown's times, these were great achievements. His years in office also saw the first major overhaul of the executive branch in 30 years, abolition of the troublesome cross-filing system in primaries, and creation of California's first fair employment practices commission. The universities and schools made great strides, and the state began to invest more in aid for the needy aged and in mental care facilities.

WILLIAM F. KNOWLAND. Big Bill Knowland, once aptly called "the Lone Moose," still lives in Oakland, publishing his family newspaper, and, by latest reports, taking a conciliatory position on black-white relations in that troubled city. It is a new role for Knowland, former U. S. Senator (1945–59), the inflexible conservative who succeeded Robert Taft as Senate Republican Leader. In 1958, Knowland almost caused the ruination of the California GOP when he returned to California determined to run for governor in a thinly disguised move to position himself for the 1960 Republican Presidential nomination. Governor Knight, planning to run that year, had to be forced out of the race and persuaded to run for Knowland's Senate seat instead. The game of musical chairs offended the voters, as did Knowland's conscious, strong partisanship and his identification with the "right-to-work" proposition on the 1958 ballot. Knowland went crashing down to defeat by a margin of more than one million votes, while Knight, forced into a Senate race he had not sought, lost by 723,000.

JESS UNRUH. Jesse M. Unruh, the man whom Reagan defeated to win a second term as governor in 1970, was born the youngest of five children of an illiterate and impoverished Kansas sharecropper, grew up in Texas, hitchhiked to California at 18 with five dollars in his pocket, and became the speaker of the state assembly at 39. Unruh has appeared in three quite disparate incarnations since the late 1950s. First, he was "Big Daddy" Unruh, the heavy-drinking, cigar-smoking, 290-pound, five-foot-nine-inch speaker of the assembly, ruthlessly making and breaking bills and other politicians' careers through his absolute power over committee memberships and connections with fund-providing lobbyists. In those early years, Unruh uttered two harsh dicta still remembered: "Money is the mother's milk of politics," and, speaking of lobbyists: "If you can't take their money, drink their booze, screw their women, and look them in the eye and vote against them, you don't belong here."

Starting about 1963, Unruh entered a new stage. During that year, he had foolishly invoked a little-used parliamentary rule to have Republican assemblymen opposing him on a bill locked up in the chamber for 23 hours. "The Lockup," as it became known, generated bales of bad publicity for "Big Daddy." At the same time, Unruh was becoming concerned about his image, especially after a political cartoon that depicted him as a fat Buddha. So he cut way back on the Scotch and martinis and undertook a rigorous non-starch diet that had his weight down 100 pounds in a few months. He remained a powerful politician, but turned his attention increasingly in two directions: shaping the assembly into the most professional, best-staffed legislative house in the United States, and becoming a national authority and lecturer on state legislatures and government. He succeeded brilliantly in both pursuits, acting as a consultant for the Eagleton Institute at Rutgers and winning election in 1966 as head of the National Conference of State Legislative Leaders.

The third incarnation began in the Ambassador Hotel in Los Angeles the night that Bobby Kennedy was shot. Unruh had been an early supporter of John F. Kennedy in 1960 and was heading Robert Kennedy's slate in the 1968 California primary. Unruh was only a few feet away when Sirhan Sirhan shot the Senator, and later said: "I nearly went crazy." He said he found that Kennedy's death taught him "a sense of high-risk politics," persuading him to abandon the "cautious, close-to-the-vest" politics of his middle years in a return to the less cautious idealism of his youth. At the Chicago convention that summer, leading the Kennedy delegation chosen in the primary, Unruh eschewed all strong-arm tactics, ran the delegation in a democratic manner, and won national notice by his clear dissent from the brutal manner in which the convention was run.

That fall, Democrats lost control of the assembly, making Unruh into minority leader instead of speaker. In 1970, came the showdown in the gubernatorial contest with the highly popular—and strongly favored—Reagan. Unruh was strapped for campaign funds—a result of wealthy Democrats' deep resentments about his refusal to support Governor Brown, with whom he often feuded, for reelection in 1966, and his late endorsement of Humphrey in 1968. (Final reports indicated Unruh had contributions of $887,822 to run his campaign, compared to a Reagan total of $2,200,223.) Unruh ran a Populist-style, "give-'em-hell" campaign in the style of Harry Truman in 1948, painting Reagan as the creature of "half-hidden millionaires" who Unruh said were running the state for their own private interest. Lacking money for television, Unruh would take along a busload of TV newsmen to "events" such as an uninvited appearance before the home of Reagan-backer Henry Salvatori, charging on camera that the wealthy oilman would benefit from Reagan's tax reform package. The tactic did get attention, and there was doubtless merit in many of his charges, but may also have detracted from the dignity of Unruh the candidate.* Only time would tell whether his new Populism could really tie together the "little people" of California in a revolt against wealthy, Republican-led government. With unemployment drawing voters back to the Democratic line, Unruh did hold Reagan to half his plurality in the 1966 race against Brown. If the California press had not prematurely discounted Unruh's viability as a candidate, he might have come much closer.

MAX RAFFERTY. In Rafferty, state superintendent of public instruction from 1963 to 1971, California produced an extraordinarily contentious and publicized education chief. California in the postwar era was faced with the problem of creating virtually one school a day, accommodating growing minority group enrollments with special education problems, and cutting down on an alarmingly high school dropout rate. "War babies" reached school age before localities were equipped to deal with them, thousands of school bond issues had to be passed, and a teacher shortage had to be met. At first all the initiatives were left to an in-group of professional educationalists who had formulated state policy under a string of "prestige superintendents," working hand-in-hand with a powerful teachers' lobby, since the early 1920s. In the late 1950s and early '60s, protests began to mount about the way school districts were shortchanging students in favor of high pay for teachers (at average wages second only to Alaska). Sputnik aroused concern about the quality of education, and social tensions in the schools began to mount. So did the percentage of voter rejections of new school bond issues.

Rafferty, a bombastic, ultraconservative, no-nonsense academician, burst onto the scene in the 1962 state superintendent's race on a platform denouncing "permissive, pragmatic progressivism" in the schools. In a close election, he beat a liberal opponent and began a divisive eight years in office during which he dwelt on issues like sex education, drugs, and school busing, adding much heat but little light to solution of California's education dilemmas. Fortunately, the legislature was authorizing a number of innovative new pro-

* Lou Cannon, author of the excellent book *Ronnie and Jesse—A Political Odyssey*, wrote in his *California Journal* column during the 1970 campaign that voters were "not idiots" and couldn't be expected to buy Unruh's "half-hidden millionaires" thesis because "it requires people to distrust Reagan's motivations. . . . Unruh, of all people, should have known better. Only the really bum politicians are used by the very rich. The good politicians, and Unruh used to be a very good one, use the rich to accomplish their own ends, which is one of Unruh's best rebuttals to the criticisms of his own legislative career."

grams and the state board of education moved ahead with new approaches in math, sciences, and social sciences, plus a reform in the training of teachers that culminated with abolition of education as a major in California's colleges.

In 1968, Rafferty made a bid for higher office by challenging liberal U. S. Sen. Thomas H. Kuchel in the Republican primary. The campaign was a right-wing classic, in which Rafferty said Kuchel had failed to deal with "the four deadly sins" he saw confronting the U.S.—violence, pornography, drugs, and lawlessness. Among other things, Rafferty said it was time to "stop naming social reformers, political hacks, and child-marrying mountain climbers to the Supreme Court." He narrowly beat Kuchel, but lost the general election.

In 1970, Rafferty ran for a third term as superintendent and was a strong early favorite in a year when the voters were said to be already aroused about busing, drugs, and "permissiveness." But apparently the rhetoric had lost its appeal. Rafferty was challenged and defeated that year by Dr. Wilson C. Riles. Riles for six years headed the multimillion-dollar California compensatory education program, winning the reputation among professionals of being the best administrator of federal "Title One" moneys in the entire U.S. Riles said Rafferty had turned teachers, parents, and school boards against each other with a surfeit of inflammatory rhetoric and demagoguery. Riles's own image was that of a cool professional, who seemed to be talking sense about financing the schools, making them more accountable to the people, and pouring more money and energy into the vital area of early (preschool) education. Many thought the fact that Riles was a Negro would preclude his election. But it did not, as he defeated Rafferty with a plurality of close to a half-million votes (54.1 percent).*

At least a million voters, it appeared, had voted for Reagan and Riles on the same day. The results made one wonder about any neat ideological pigeonholing of the California voter. Even Orange and San Diego Counties —the only two heavily populated counties in the U.S. to go for Goldwater in 1964—gave Riles a respectable share of their vote (46 and 49 percent respectively). Riles carried Los Angeles County by 53 percent and then swamped Rafferty in Northern California with majorities like 63 percent in San Francisco and 65 percent in suburban Marin and Santa Clara counties. In 1968, it may be recalled, Wallace got only 6.7 percent of the California vote, less than in states like Illinois, Michigan, Ohio, and Pennsylvania.

The Rafferty sun seems finally to have set in California; after the 1970 election he went off to Alabama to teach.

The California canvas is so broad one could go on and on with a parade of personalities. In large measure because of their poor Republican opposition, two Democrats now hold the state's U. S. Senate seats—Alan Cranston, first head of the California Democratic Clubs, now in his late 50s, and John V. Tunney, former Congressman and son of the ex-heavyweight boxing champion Gene Tunney, a man in his mid-30s. Both men have served too briefly (Cranston since 1969, Tunney since 1971) to make a major mark in the Sen-

* To Rafferty's credit, it must be recorded that he promoted more members of ethnic minorities to high posts than any previous state superintendent. It was a marvelous irony that one of them beat him.

ate. California's Thomas H. Kuchel was Republican Whip in the Senate until he was upset by Max Rafferty in the 1968 primary; Cranston then seized the middle of the road and easily defeated Rafferty in the general election.

Considering its size, California's big House delegation (increased from 30 in the 1950s to 43 in the 1970s) has not made a major impact in Washington. Some of its members have stood out on occasion, however. Among Democrats, Chet Holifield, dean of the delegation, has served with distinction as chairman of the Joint Committee on Atomic Energy despite some run-ins with conservationists on the issue of hazards from atomic power generation. In 1971, he took over chairmanship of the Government Operations Committee and proceeded to rule in an arbitrary and highhanded manner by abolishing subcommittees that had taken a special interest in consumer affairs and the invasion of privacy. George Miller has been chairman of the House Science and Astronautics Committee for several years. B. F. Sisk, a powerful member of the Rules Committee, handled the 1970 Congressional Reform Bill on the floor and the next year ran for House Majority Leader; his district, including part of the Central Valley, tends to make him conservative and grower-oriented. Another Central Valley Congressman, John E. Moss, won a measure of fame for the Freedom of Information Act he authored. Phillip Burton, from San Francisco, has been a leader in welfare legislation, and, according to my friend Lou Cannon, who covers Capitol Hill for the Ridder papers, "one of the few Congressmen who'd rather have the bill than the credit." Another Bay Area Democrat, Jerome P. Waldie, is a tough, brainy man with driving ambition who dared early in the game to suggest (while his colleagues maintained discreet silence) that it was time for aging House Speaker John W. McCormack to retire. Waldie is also a major opponent of the State Water Plan because of what he says would be its disastrous ecological effects. He intends to run for governor in 1974, and it should be a colorful campaign. Finally, mention should be made of James C. Corman of Los Angeles, a key operative in passage of several of the major civil rights bills of the 1960s, and Thomas M. Rees, also of Los Angeles, who like Waldie was willing to buck the old House leadership, campaign against the Vietnam war, and take a strong role in environmental reform.

Most powerful among Republicans is H. Allen Smith of Pasadena, ranking member of his party on the Rules Committee. Smith's philosophy of government seems several degrees to the right of Herbert Hoover, but he is a key negotiator with younger members of Congress, even those he disagrees with, and he has taken an interest in some aspects of congressional reform. Charles S. Gubser of the Bay Area is a conservative who believes his party must modernize itself in many areas; he has been active in air pollution control and in parks and rules legislation, and coauthored the proposal to make public teller votes in the House. Craig Hosmer of Long Beach is a leading Republican hawk and his party's ranking member on Joint Atomic Energy; William Mailliard of San Francisco is considered a leading House authority on maritime issues. San Diego's Bob Wilson, an old Nixon intimate, wields great potential power as chairman of the National Republican Congressional

Committee, a group which hands out millions of dollars to Republican House candidates across the country in each election.

Finally, the Republican delegation includes the remarkable figure of Paul N. (Pete) McCloskey, Jr., the ex-Marine who was decorated for "extraordinary heroism" in the Korean War and broke into politics by sinking the good ship *Lollipop*, Mrs. Shirley Temple Black, in a 1967 special election for a seat from San Mateo County, south of San Francisco. McCloskey suddenly became a national figure in 1971 when he announced he might run for President unless President Nixon stopped the "demeaning and cowardly" use of air power in Indochina and "hiring" South Vietnamese "mercenaries to do our dying for us." His apostasy quickly brought the ire of standard Republicans down upon his head, but McCloskey is no ordinary politician. McCloskey believes, with utter sincerity, that "the American political process depends on people willing to lose their seats and offices to do what's right. I think we have to prove to young people that politics is an honorable profession."

Innovative Politics

Hiram Johnson invented and Earl Warren institutionalized a lot of devices to make California's politics unique among the states, but even after them California has been busy on innovations the rest of the country may pick up later. Some prime examples of the old and new:

INITIATIVE AND REFERENDUM. California has one of the nation's best legislatures, but the people trust it the least. Since 1911, when initiative and referendum were written into the state constitution, almost 500 consitutional changes and 65 new statutes have been placed on the ballot for the people to decide on, not to mention referendums on about 35 laws already passed by the legislature. Initiatives can go on the ballot by vote of the legislature, or by popular petition of a set percentage of the state's voters. In Johnson's day, it took about 30,000 signatures to put an initiative on the ballot; now close to 500,000 are required, and signature-gathering has become a big business at an average of 25¢ a head. For 500,000 signatures, that is a lot of money. "Whatever its noble origins," L. A. *Times* columnist Art Seidenbaum has written, "the initiative has lately become the most questionable single entry on an interminable ballot; instead of being responsive to the grass roots, it may now be a device for special interests, interests wealthy enough first to buy their way into an election and then to seduce the voters with come-on advertising."

The focus of initiatives on the ballot has changed over time. In the first decade, many proposals dealt with moral and economic problems such as prohibition, prize fighting, compulsory vaccination, and the eight-hour day. In the 1920s, several dealt with public education (in an attempt to get the state to shoulder a greater cost burden). The voters also forced the state to adopt an executive budget, still hailed by many as the initiative's greatest accomplishment. The 1930s saw the focus turn to the various pension plans; Ham

& Eggs alone made it to the ballot five times between 1938 and 1948. In 1948, an initiative organized by George McLain and his senior citizen followers was passed; it actually appeared to transfer control of social welfare money to McLain himself, and was undone in the next election. The biggest battle of the 1950s was over "Right to Work," on which proponents reported spending $954,389 to win its passage and organized labor countered with $2,556,037 in the successful effort to defeat it.

In 1964, the people approved two initiatives, only to have them found unconstitutional thereafter. One was the famous Proposition Fourteen to repeal the Rumford Housing Act, an open housing statute the legislature had approved. Out of fear of a black neighbor, perhaps with a dash of free-enterprise, the people approved the proposition by a 2–1 margin. But the NAACP filed suit charging the proposition constituted state action for discriminatory practices, in violation of the 14th Amendment of the U. S. Constitution; the California and U. S. Supreme Courts, in turn, upheld the NAACP. The other, Proposition Seventeen, outlawed pay television. Its supporters, notably movie theater owners who feared empty seats if people could pay to see more sports and theatrical events at home, spent $1.9 million to put it across. For no apparent reason, save their ignorance and confusion, the voters approved the move, but the courts reversed it on constitutional grounds.

A bewildering array of propositions greet the voter each election day. In 1966, there were 16 on the state ballot; in 1970, exactly 20. The subject matter in those elections ranged from regulation of chiropractors to how farmland should be taxed, regulation of boxing and wrestling, and a constitutionally dubious amendment to suppress "obscenity" which the voters, *mirabile dictu,* voted down.

RECALL. Also enacted by Johnson and his followers in 1911, recall has been used frequently in local elections. There have been aborted recall movements against governors, none ever coming to a vote.

LOCAL NONPARTISANSHIP. The state constitution requires nonpartisan elections for all county and municipal offices. The result is quite simple: no local partisan "machines" in the style known to the East and Midwest; rarely, if ever, a serious election fraud; an entrenched civil service often indifferent to elected officials and new policies they may try to effect.

CROSS-FILING. From 1913 until its repeal in 1959, California's partisan elections (Congress, governor, legislature, etc.) were held under this curious device, one that lets members of each party run in the other party's primary as well. Until 1952, party designations did not even appear beside candidates' names on the primary ballots. The most famous of all the cross-filers was Earl Warren, who thus won both parties' gubernatorial nominations in 1946 and didn't even have to compete in the general election. But Warren was not alone. Between 1914 and 1950, the offices of attorney general, secretary of state, and controller were won in the primary in seven out of 10 elections. Often the nonincumbent party despaired of winning an office and ran no candidate at all; in 1944, for instance, 12 of 20 state senate seats went by default (one candidate only), six were determined in contested primaries, and only two were decided in the general election. But after 1952, when a new law went into effect requiring a "Rep." or "Dem." beside each candidate's name, things changed rapidly. In 1952, with no party designation, 14 out of 30 congressional races were won in the primary by cross-filed or unopposed candidates; in 1954 the number fell to two.

Cross-filing was accused throughout its half-century career of crippling strong or well-organized parties and thus undermining any real party responsibility. It gave rise to auxiliary, or volunteer, party groups, for the purpose of making endorsements (of which more later); perpetuated "incumbent empires"; and, in the words of political scientist Totton J. Anderson, led to the "loss of partisan identification with issues of public policy, since candidates campaigned under a 'middle-of-the-road' banner, often refusing to identify themselves publicly with any party."

And intrinsically, cross-filing worked to the advantage of the Republicans. California has long had many more registered Democrats than Republicans, so a GOP contender always benefited from having any attention removed from the partisan issue. And since Republicans were long able to get preferential press treatment in major California newspapers, they tended to be better known to the voters.

Wisely for their self-interest, the Democrats repealed cross-filing, once and for all, when they had control of both the governorship and both houses of the legislature in 1959. The result, in almost everyone's view, has been to make California politics conform more to a national norm than at any time since Hiram Johnson arrived on the scene. Partisanship, for instance, has been growing by leaps and bounds in California, as voting patterns in recent legislative sessions show.

VOLUNTEER GROUPS. Progressive-era legislation so closely circumscribed the legal activities of the regular political parties—even forbidding them to make pre-primary endorsements—that volunteer or extralegal party groups naturally sprang into being. The first was the California Republican Assembly, formed in 1934–35 by a group including Earl Warren, to improve the party's organizational efforts and make pre-primary endorsements. Part of the goal was to revive the party and wrest control from Old Guard reactionaries, thought responsible for the party's losses. CRA became a kind of elite party organ, always with a fairly limited membership (never over 25,000). In various years it helped Warren get elected governor and gave Goodwin Knight and Richard Nixon their starts in California politics. Warren "willed" CRA to Sen. William Knowland when he left for Washington in 1953, but modern Republicans remained influential. The bitter GOP infighting of 1958 virtually immobilized CRA; in 1964, the Goldwaterites took control, hastening its decline. Gladwin Hill reported in 1968 that CRA had "deteriorated into a strident right-wing splinter claiming 12,000 adherents," competing with United Republicans of California, a right-wing spinoff with 9,000 members.

The Democrats' counterpart—the California Democratic Council (CDC), a federation of Democratic clubs—got started in 1953, 19 years later than CRA. But it made even more of a splash in state and nation. CDC's inspirer was the late Adlai E. Stevenson, its ideology left-wing with a bent for participatory politics, its main activity endorsing candidates for office. Hundreds of clubs were chartered and membership eventually rose to close to 100,000. CDC conventions were never afraid to take controversial positions on public issues, often causing no little embarrassment for Democratic officeholders. But the publicity was magnificent—in many years, CDC conventions were the biggest Democratic gatherings in the U.S., complete with delegates, emotional oratory, and maneuvering. In 1958, CDC hit its zenith when all but one of the statewide candidates it endorsed were elected. One of them was CDC's first president, Alan Cranston, former head of the United World Federalists, who got elected state controller. Now he is a U. S. Senator.

CDC has always had its problems, however. For one thing, professional Democratic politicos like Jess Unruh (until a latter-day conversion) viewed with disdain what they considered CDC's amateurism and ideological excesses. In 1964, Unruh helped fashion a bitter defeat for the CDC by backing for the U. S. Senate former White House Press Secretary Pierre Salinger in place of the CDC's Cranston. Two years later, CDC president Simon Cassady struck out at President Johnson and his war policies with such vitriol that Governor Brown felt obliged to force his removal; some believe CDC never recovered from that internal struggle. By 1970, CDC had declined to less than 10,000 members, a thin shadow of its former self. Its endorsements were scarcely taken seriously by major candidates.

What had happened? Lou Cannon (who believes the CDC "was never as powerful as it thought it was and isn't as impotent now as some critics would like to think") says the demise of cross-filing deprived CDC of its basic reason for existence. Without cross-filing, Democrats no longer needed a special mechanism to keep Republicans from gaining Democratic endorsements.

DECEPTIVE REGISTRATION FIGURES. For decades, Democrats have had a substantial majority of party registrations in California—about 60–40 in most years, in 1970 like this:

Democratic	4,154,016	54.2%
Republican	3,139,007	41.0
American Independent	72,781	0.9
Peace and Freedom	35,756	0.5
Miscellaneous, Declined to state	260,073	3.4

This does not mean that the Democrats automatically win elections. As someone cracked, California is that state where "party loyalty is about as prevalent as chastity." Many who list themselves as Democrats are Southerners registering in the party of their forefathers; many were New Deal Democrats and remain registered that way out of pure inertia. What's more, California Republicans turn out a much greater share of their registrants on election day (84 percent in the 1966 election, for instance, in comparison to 77 percent of the Democrats). And Republicans have the big business backing which makes it possible for them to outspend the Democrats consistently in state and local elections, although the unions, when aroused, can even the score to some extent.

Despite their disability in registrations, the Republicans have done very well for themselves in gubernatorial and state legislature elections over the years. Since the turn of the century, the Democrats have won only three elections for governor (Olson in 1938, Brown in 1958 and 1962). Both houses of the legislature have been under Republican control for most of this century, with three years of Democratic interregnum in the Senate in the late 1930s and then a Democratic sweep of both chambers in 1958 that kept the GOP out in the cold for a full decade. Late in the 1960s, the Republicans made a comeback in both houses, only to lose out again in 1970—a crucial loss, since the new Democratic legislature could then proceed to draw congressional and state legislative lines for the 1970s to maximize Democratic seats. (The loss was especially crushing for the Republicans, who had invested years of planning and millions of dollars in a concerted campaign to get control of the 1971–72 legislature, and thus, they hoped, California for the decade of the 1970s. The heavy population growth in conservative Southern California areas like Orange County helps their cause in any event.)

Both California parties—Republicans after the 1950 Census, Democrats after the 1960 Census—have shown themselves masters of the art of gerrymandering. In 1952, for instance, the GOP was able to win 63 percent of the state's congressional seats with 54 percent of the statewide House vote; in 1962, after they had gerrymandered, the Democrats got 66 percent of the seats with 53 percent of the vote.

No matter how carefully a party gerrymanders, however, and no matter how firmly it seems ensconced in the executive chambers of Sacramento, the voters after a while will turn it out. High intrastate mobility upsets the complexion of districts, and "safe" districts rapidly become marginal. A highly competitive, two-party system is alive and well in California today, and seems likely to remain that way.

In fact, California's political behavior is much closer to that of the entire U.S.A. than people recognize. As Richard M. Scammon and Ben J. Wattenberg point out in *The Real Majority*:

> California, viewed psephologically, is not really atypical, screwballs notwithstanding. . . . California is known as an excellent *barometric* state. Among large states, Illinois and California are the two that vote most consistently like America as a whole. Since 1948 California has never been more than two percentage points away from the final national percentage for the Presidential winner.

Will California continue to be a barometric state? The extension of the vote to 18-through-20-year-olds could move it a degree or two to the left, perhaps even more so than the rest of the country because of the state's heavy youth population. Of the 9.9 million new potential voters under 21 in the U.S.A. in 1972, 1.1 million will be in California alone. They will represent 8 percent of the entire California eligible electorate of 13,317,000. A little arithmetic applied to some not impossible assumptions indicates a potentially decisive impact. If 60 percent of the youths register to vote, and two-thirds of them vote Democratic for President, the Democrats will experience a net gain of 213,000 votes in California.* It should be remembered that Nixon carried California against Humphrey by only 223,346 votes in 1968, and against an even more youthful John F. Kennedy by only 35,623 in 1960. Thus the youth vote has the potentiality of wiping out the entire Republican plurality.

PRESIDENTIAL PRIMARIES. Popular election of national convention delegate slates was another one of Hiram Johnson's ideas and early enactments. But despite 60 years of use, the California Presidential primary—up to now, in any event—has rarely played a crucial role in a nomination fight. This is because any Presidential candidate must consent to having a slate of delegates pledged to him entered in the primary. Since California itself so often has a "favorite son," out-of-state candidates hesitate to enter the primary, with the result that the contest is meaningless.

There have been three crucial postwar primaries, however. In the 1956 Democratic primary, Adlai Stevenson's slate defeated one pledged to Estes Kefauver by a margin of better than 2–1. Stevenson's nomination up to that point had been quite uncertain; after California it was almost assured. Likewise, in the Republican primary of 1964, Goldwater got 51.6 percent of the vote, Rockefeller 48.4 percent. This was the primary that knocked Rockefeller out of the Presidential race and insured Goldwater's nomination. But in the fall election, Goldwater lost California to President Johnson by 1.3 million votes.

The 1968 Democratic primary featured a close fight between Senators Robert F. Kennedy of New York and Eugene J. McCarthy of Minnesota. Kennedy, who had lost a key race to McCarthy in Oregon just seven days before, needed a victory to restore his "winner's image" and prepare him for the decisive convention contest with Vice President Hubert H. Humphrey. Kennedy did win, by a margin of 140,000 votes out of 3.1 million cast. But just after acknowledging the cheers of his supporters in a Los Angeles hotel, Kennedy was shot to death.

The assassination of the young Senator, brother of slain President John F. Kennedy, was to be of momentous import. With his death, Hubert Humphrey's nomination was virtually decided—and with it, the possibility of any rapprochement of the Humphrey regulars with the left wing of the Democratic party that might have lessened the violence in Chicago and put the Democrats in better position for the fall election. As it was, Nixon's national lead over Humphrey slipped from 16 points in midsummer polls to practically zero by election day; his final plurality of 510,315 votes (0.7 percent) would be one of the narrowest of the century. California itself went for Nixon by a plurality of 223,346 votes—3.1 percentage points; without the state's 40 electoral votes, Nixon would have lacked the electoral vote majority required for election, thus throwing the election open to bargaining with Wallace's electors or decision by the House of Representatives.

Reagan in 1968 used the "favorite son delegation" device to freeze other

* Early reports of registration by the under-21 voters, from 14 of California's largest counties, showed 59 percent registering Democratic, 20 percent Republican, and the remaining 21 percent independent or in minor parties.

candidates out of the Republican Presidential primary. Twice in the late 1960s, bills were passed by the legislature to establish an open Presidential primary along the lines of the Oregon law, with voters permitted to express a preference among all nationally recognized Presidential candidates. Such a shift would automatically make California *the* crucial test of strength in every Presidential nomination fight. Reagan, however, vetoed the legislation each time it reached him.

But the day of "favorite sons" may fast be fading, especially in this state, which a serious candidate for a Presidential nomination simply cannot ignore if he hopes to be a strong factor in his party's convention. David Broder of the Washington *Post* suggests California is "The Political Giant" of the U.S.A. today:

> The national political news continues to be written from Washington, but more and more of it is being made in California, a continent away. The increasing dominance of American politics by the giant on the Pacific is one of the significant facts of the 1970s. . . .
>
> In part, it is the sheer size of the state that has given it its dominant role. [In 1972], for the first time, California will replace New York as the No. 1 prize in the election, with 45 electoral votes.
>
> Its wealth, too, commands respect. San Francisco, Los Angeles, Beverly Hills and Palm Springs probably pour as much money into national campaign treasuries now as do New York or Texas.
>
> And the Californians, by accident or design, have achieved a crucial role for themselves by staging their winner-take-all Presidential primary in June— making it nearly the last and by all odds the largest payoff tournament on the road to a Presidential nomination.
>
> With 271 votes in [the 1972] Democratic convention, California has the power to put its favorite candidate more than one-fifth of the way to the nomination.

It is worth noting that when the Democratic party's reform commission tried to persuade California to abandon its "winner-take-all" primary feature, the proposal was flatly rejected. "There isn't a chance of a snowball in hell that we will change this," M. Larry Lawrence, Southern California state chairman, told the *National Journal* in 1971. "We like the power and strength. . . . California is going to be the dominant force at the convention."

CAMPAIGN MANAGEMENT FIRMS. California is the state where the first professional campaign management firms appeared, and where the largest national firms are still located. Granddaddy of the profession is the San Francisco firm of Whitaker and Baxter, begun in 1933 as the professional (and later matrimonial) alliance of Clem Whitaker, a young reporter and public relations man, and Leone Baxter, manager of the Redding chamber of commerce. Their idea was simple, but revolutionary: a public relations firm specializing in politics. California provided especially fertile ground because (a) each ballot was crowded with initiatives and referenda, many so important to certain groups that they would spend up into the millions to ensure their passage or defeat, and (b) professional assistance for candidates was needed to fill the vacuum created by the lack of adequate party organizations. In all, W & B won 70 of the 75 campaigns it managed between 1933 and 1955. In classic PR firm style, a single, preferably emotional issue would be found as the central theme of a campaign, and then driven home again and again. "The average American," Whitaker once said, "doesn't want to be educated; he doesn't want to improve his mind; he doesn't even want to work, consciously, at becoming a good citizen."

Over the years, W & B coordinated the 1934 California League Against Sinclairism, helped Earl Warren warm up his fairly austere public image when he first ran for governor in 1942, helped run campaigns for William Knowland and Richard Nixon, and was retained at $100,000 a year to publicize the American Medical Association's campaign against federal-aid medical programs. Whitaker died in 1961, but his son Clem Whitaker, Jr., carried on in his place. In the mid-1960s, the firm was hired to publicize a national campaign to overturn the one-man, one-vote decisions of the U. S. Supreme Court. Some unwanted publicity accrued from the company's belated entry into the ill-starred campaign to elect former child actress Shirley Temple Black to Congress in 1967. W & B of late seems to have moved, intentionally, into the shadows, taking on low-profile bond and initiative issues and providing services for handsome retainers paid by some large corporations.

As campaign costs soared in California—to $50,000 for a close state legislature race, $100,000 or even more in a tight congressional contest, and up to several millions in a gubernatorial campaign—so did the need for professional campaign management. Firms sprouted up left and right, some fly-by-night, some formidable and permanent. Among the permanent was Baus & Ross, a Los Angeles firm, founded in 1946, that worked for Nixon (1960 Presidential primary and general election), Goldwater (1964 primary) and Brown (1968 campaign for third term as governor). The firm created a stir in 1964 when it signed off the Goldwater campaign after he won the primary; four years later owners Herbert M. Baus and William B. Ross explained that "the money was good in the primary, but it could have been better in the final had [we] been willing to give obeisance to gung-ho Goldwaterism gone rampant."

California's most publicized and effective campaign management group of recent years has been Spencer-Roberts & Associates of Los Angeles. William Roberts was a television time salesman, Stuart Spencer a recreation director in Alhambra when the two met doing volunteer Republican work in the late 1950s and decided "there must be a more scientific way to get our men elected." It was a crucial moment in American politics, with the age of the computer just dawning, traditional party organizations in decline, and campaigns becoming incredibly more complex and expensive than they had been in the past. A kind of systems approach to political campaigning was required, and S-R became a leading U.S. firm in developing the system needed.

Since the mid '60s, Spencer-Roberts has operated by providing the candidate with "all-encompassing" services, starting with counsel on the qualities he should look for in his campaign chairman, "kitchen cabinet," legal adviser, and executive committee. The firm schedules the opening of campaign headquarters, design and distribution of printed brochures, the purchases of advertising in all media, and coordination of volunteer services. (Average fee

—10 to 20 percent of the gross cost of a campaign.) S-R also orders one or more polls to show voter attitudes within any district it enters. Issue development and media use are directly related to the survey data.

An organization known as Decision Making Information (DMI), which functioned until 1971 as a subsidiary of S-R but then became independent, has concentrated on advanced computer techniques, including sophisticated analysis of the socioeconomic characteristics of each precinct or township within a district, employing Census Bureau reports down to the tract level. Such factors as education, occupation, fertility ratios, race, and ethnic status are all fed into the system. Then they are compared with party registration data and returns from one or more past elections—all weighted as the campaign managers may consider the most relevant, so that in reality an important element of human judgment is part of the "system." The final precinct priority lists should reveal those in which the candidate can anticipate the most support. A cardinal rule is to "deal from strength." Rather than concentrating on hostile areas with minimal gain opportunities for the candidate, all direct mailing, telephone campaigns, and final get-out-the-vote efforts on election day can be concentrated in the most promising precincts.

A well-fed computer, DMI men say, can also suggest names for fund-raising appeals, create walking lists for precinct workers, and suggest, down to fine geographical subdivisions, the areas for targeted mailings on set subjects and themes for appearances and campaign speeches by the candidate. Finally, whether a campaign is won or lost, S-R and DMI try to get the candidate and his manager together for post-mortems on what went right and wrong, and why.

Roberts of S-R has said his firm will direct the campaign of "any reasonable, responsible Republican, without hyphenating him," providing he had adequate campaign finances and seems to hold some affection for the free enterprise system. The S-R clientele of "reasonable, responsible" Republicans has ranged from Congressman John H. Rousselot of Los Angeles (who later became a national spokesman for the John Birch Society) to Nelson Rockefeller in the 1964 California Presidential primary. The company participated in liberal Senator Thomas H. Kuchel's 1962 campaign and ran the 1968 campaign (winning the first, losing the second in the primary). But in 1966, it agreed to take on the campaign of Ronald Reagan, a man it had listed two years before as one of the "right-wing extremists" backing Goldwater. Before accepting Reagan as a client, Roberts and Spencer subjected him to long grillings on his philosophy and approach to government; then they took the account and proceeded to do what seemed like the impossible—to make the public forget all about Ronald Reagan the movie actor and exponent of right-wing causes, and instead think of Ronald Reagan the citizen-politician, the moderate candidate.

S-R succeeded, as its competitors stood back to watch the show in awe. The New York *Times* was upset by the feat, editorializing that "the cool professionalism of [S&R's] operations in California is chilling." Many feared that through sophisticated campaign management techniques, the public mind could be manipulated virtually at will; along with this would come a new cynicism of candidates, an inclination of public leaders to read the polls instead of following their own consciences. Some people had expressed the same concerns after the 1960 campaign, when it learned that Simulmatics, a group of MIT academicians working for John F. Kennedy that year, had tried to forecast voter responses to hypothetical events or policy positions, based on the public's reaction to thousands of polling questions in the past. Simulation may be carried to new heights in the 1970s. DMI board chairman Vincent Barabba pointed out in an interview, for instance, that his company and S-R have now been involved in dozens of congressional campaigns across the U.S.A., using a fairly standardized format of in-depth voter study. Between 30,000 and 40,000 persons are interviewed in an election year, each carefully tabbed by age, race, party, and various socioeconomic factors. With such a huge universe, one is not restricted to analyzing the impact of an issue or development on the whole electorate, but can zero in to see how identifiable subgroups, by region, profession, race, or ethnic group, react specifically. A candidate can learn by simulation how the public, and specific voter groups within it, will react to any given policy position he may take.

Such techniques are on a level of sophistication unknown before. But they are also simply modern-day extrapolations, by infinitely superior tools of analysis and communication, of the seat-of-the-pants, instinctive political sensibilities that successful candidates for public office have demonstrated through history. What's more, the simulators and image-makers are only human, and can make mistakes, and frequently lose elections despite their best efforts. Spencer-Roberts' track record includes many defeats in U. S. House elections, the Rockefeller defeat in 1964, the Kuchel defeat in 1968, and Senator George Murphy's loss in 1970. In many cases of defeat, the candidate made fundamentally wrong decisions despite the campaign intelligence brought him by his managers. "My chief problem," Spencer said in an interview, "is to get clients to use the information—to accept the conclusions of the simulation model or other political intelligence." In addition, many slick television advertising campaigns end up harming more than helping a candidate. One likes to think that the public often sees through them to the true mettle of a man.

But campaign management, with polls, computers, sophisticated use of television, and all the rest, has arrived in the U.S.A., courtesy largely of the Californians, and is sure to stay. Serious candidates of the future will be simply unable or unwilling to turn down a tool that can give them the extra votes they need to win instead of losing.

John S. Saloma and Frederick H. Sontag, in a study for the Twentieth Century Fund, suggest that two prototype "conglomerates" are developing in the political management field, both dedicated to helping Republican candidates. (Working for a single party, managers insist, is easier on their nerves, fosters client trust, and avoids awkward potential conflicts of interest.) One "conglom" is the Spencer-Roberts/Decision Making Information complex, with a base in the West and South; another is the Detroit firm of Market Opinion Research, allied with Bailey, Deardourff & Bowen of Washington, D.C., and concentrating on the East and Midwest. Both groups of firms have gained access to the innermost circles of the Republican National Committee and many state headquarters. Naturally, such consulting firms reach out to create or acquire other firms with electronic data processing capacity, and then the network of new subsidiaries, subcontracting to other firms, shared facilities, and wide links of professional contacts, grows apace. DMI, for instance, has given seminars or presentations on campaign management information and techniques for dozens of organizations, including the U. S. Chamber of Commerce, the American Farm Bureau, the American Medical Political Action Committee, Republican organizations from local to national level, and university-connected groups across the continent.

Both eastern and western GOP "conglomerates," Saloma and Sontag point out, have an interest in electing a Republican President one day. MOR/ DB&D hope to see a swing to the left in Republican policy, enabling them to elect a moderate Republican President by the mid-1970s; Spencer-Roberts/ DMI since 1966 have become generally identified with the GOP-conservative wing and seem firmly committed to Reagan and his still unquenched ambitions for higher office.

Democratic-oriented professional campaign management firms have yet to advance so far. But the techniques are not secret, and it seems only a matter of time—and money—until they do.

POLITICAL MONEY. The sources of big political money in California (the kind needed to run expensive operations like Spencer-Roberts) are predictable—wealthy "Wasp" businessmen for the GOP, well-heeled Jewish business figures and organized labor for the Democrats. Big oil, big farm interests, big real estate, savings and loan, and entertainment industry money are all major factors in the political money game; aerospace interests, surprisingly, are not—perhaps because their chief wealth comes from Washington. Most of the political fat cats hail from Southern California. The Democratic sources have never reached comparability with the Republicans'. Organized labor, for instance, is strong in certain areas—Longshoremen in the big ports, UAW in the Los Angeles area, Teamsters everywhere—but with the exception of the Teamsters, the unions' contributions to the Democrats are more in the form of manpower than dollars. Despite membership rolls of about two million, California unions are still frozen out in large segments of the aerospace industry and pack none of the weight their counterparts do in Michigan, New York, or even Texas.

Thus Democrats often are obliged to look to alternative fund sources like the controversial political fund accumulated by Jess Unruh as speaker of the Assembly in the early 1960s. Unruh milked the money from lobbyists at high-priced testimonial dinners; then he doled it out to Democrats in close election races, a sure-fire way to solidify his own power.

One of the most interesting figures in Republican money-raising circles is Patrick J. Frawley, Jr., chief executive officer of companies with sales of more than $200 million annually—Eversharp, Schick, and, until a few years ago, Technicolor. Along with Salvatori, Holmes Tuttle, and the late A. C. Rubel, Frawley helped get Reagan into the 1966 governorship campaign; the group then provided the financial muscle for victory. Two years before, Frawley served as a chairman of American Businessmen for Goldwater and TV for Goldwater-Miller; in 1968 he helped Max Rafferty defeat Senator Kuchel in the GOP Senate primary. Frawley sees the Communist menace everywhere and has opened his checkbook for many causes like Fred Schwarz's Christian Anti-Communism Crusade. William L. Taylor, an ex-FBI agent specializing in investigative reporting, asserted in a 1970 article that "Frawley has no compunctions about appointing corporate dilettantes who are political kinsmen to the boards of directors" of the companies he controls; in addition his companies have footed the bills for a number of anti-Red extravaganzas on national television. Frawley also gave freely to the campaign of Senator George Murphy, the first of the California actors to break into big-time politics with his election in 1964. Before becoming a Senator, Murphy was an executive of Technicolor. Everyone assumed the relationship was ended, but in 1970 it became known that for five and a half years while serving in Washington, Murphy had been receiving $20,000 per annum "consultant's fee" from Technicolor. The company also paid the rent on Murphy's Washington apartment and provided him with credit cards. The revelations played a role in the old actor's defeat in 1970, and robbed Frawley of a friend good and true in Washington. Frawley, though, continued to shell out what writer Turner estimated was $1 million a year, personally and through his companies, for right-wing causes. Frawley's case is not altogether typical, however; some of the other Reagan moneybags, Holmes Tuttle in particular, are quite pragmatic men with a clear distaste for ideology.

Reagan and Murphy are not the only past or present members of the Hollywood film colony to take an active role in politics. On the Republican side, Bob Hope, Jimmy Stewart, Buddy Ebsen, and John Wayne are among the many celluloid personalities who have opened their checkbooks and lined up support; in 1970, Wayne headed a "Golden Circle" club that signed up supporters of the GOP campaign for state legislative races at membership fees of $1,000 to $5,000. Big celebrities and sometimes givers for the Democrats have included Shirley MacLaine, Henry Fonda, Dean Martin, and Frank Sinatra (though Sinatra deserted the reservation in 1970 to back Reagan for governor, reportedly because of a personal distaste for Unruh). But it would be a mistake to think that California politics is entirely supported by big names and big money. There is a lot of small-giver, ideological money in California, ranging from right-wing gun nuts on one side to "peace" givers on the other.

California's Aerojet-General in 1958 kicked off a promising experiment to make candidates less dependent on the fat cats. Under the A-G plan, the corporation itself launches a major bipartisan campaign to encourage employees to register, vote, and contribute to the candidate or party of their choice. Interest is stirred up by inviting big- and small-name candidates to appear at rallies on the factory grounds.

By 1970, the Aerojet idea had been adopted by a score of California corporations, had won wide acclaim, but had failed to raise more than a few hundred thousand dollars, statewide, in any single year. The company permits payroll deductions for the program, a key part of its success. In the early years of the program, there was a fairly clear line between white-collar workers giving to the Republicans, blue-collarites to the Democrats, a distinction that is now becoming blurred.

Perhaps the most impressive program of late has been the Hughes Aircraft Company's "Active Citizenship Campaign." In 1968, over 5,000 employees were registered on company premises, $101,000 was raised in contributions from a quarter of the employees (average gift $16.47), and at rallies held at Hughes plants there were appearances by one Presidential, 23 congressional, and 44 state office candidates. Another big California corporation, Pacific Gas & Electric, is into the business of encouraging interest in politics through a limited bipartisan fund-raising program for employees, big candidate rallies, and an excellent eight-week practical politics training course offered employees on company time, free of charge.

Governing Nation State

> California spends nearly $2 million a day just building and maintaining highways. It spends nearly $2 million a day operating its state university system alone. It spends more on education than 43 other states spend on all government services. Altogether, it spends more than $125 million a week. California gets close to $3 billion a year in grants from the federal government. But this is a pittance compared with its own resources. The income of its citizens runs more than $1 billion a week.
>
> —Gladwin Hill, in Dancing Bear (figures updated)

Despite the quality of California's state government, it is beset with California-size difficulties.

The weakest link may be the state constitution. Last subjected to major revision in 1879, it has been amended about 350 times and presently runs to some 83,000 words. California voters have repeatedly turned down proposals for a constitutional convention to start from scratch. The reason, in the words of Totten J. Anderson: "In no state in the Union are interest group prerogatives more thoroughly impacted in the fundamental law, to a large extent through hundreds of constitutional amendments." One of the more innocent examples: a provision that the legislature "shall have no power to prohibit wrestling and 12-round boxing contests in the State of California."

The most recent effort at constitutional reform started in the early 1960s when Assembly Speaker Unruh pushed through authorization of a blue ribbon constitutional revision committee with citizen and legislature members. The recommended reforms, covering some of the major departments of government and authorizing the legislature, for the first time, to set its own rate of pay and hold annual sessions, got strong bipartisan endorsement. Unruh and Robert T. Monagan, Republican leader of the assembly, campaigned hard for passage, and the people approved by a wide margin in 1966. But a second group of revisions, covering such areas as education, local governments, civil service, and state lands, was turned down by the people in 1968 for reasons still obscure. In net, the reforms effected through constitutional revision have been minor.

There are redeeming features. One is the power to guide and shape state government which a strong governor can exert. For 50 years, California has had the executive budget, which permits the governor, through his department of finance—a highly professional arm of state government, akin to the national Budget Bureau—to guide the operation of state government. Favored programs can be increased, others held at *status quo* levels or reduced, subject to the legislature's approval. More than a financial ledger sheet, the budget is a plan of operation. The governor's authority is enhanced by an item veto authority, permitting him to reduce the dollar amount for any item in an appropriation bill—a power U. S. Presidents would dearly love to have. A vitiating factor, however, is the fact that two-thirds of the budget is locked in by constitutional provisions or statutes, beyond gubernatorial control.

Bypassing cumbersome constitutional amendment, Governor Brown undertook the first comprehensive reorganization of the executive branch in 30 years, consolidating numerous boards and commissions into eight broad-gauged agencies through use of his executive powers. Several of the changes were made permanent by the legislature. Reagan took the process a step further by setting up four superagencies—business and transportation, resources, human relations, and agriculture and services. The creative legislative team of Unruh and Monagan contributed to the process, co-authoring, for example, legislation in the social welfare field that solidified under the secretary of human relations virtually all the agencies dealing with deprived areas—correction, youth authority, rehabilitation, health care, public health, social welfare, mental hygiene, employment, and the like.

The Unruh-Monagan legislative role brings us to the next great strength of California government: its superbly staffed, full-time, well paid legislature. The lion's share of credit for this goes to Unruh, with important help from Monagan, who succeeded him as speaker in 1969–70. Unruh gave the assembly the tools it needed to handle research and program development, largely through high-grade, professional staffs assigned to the committees—probably the best of any of the 50 states. Individual legislators were also given budgets for staff assistance—administrative assistants, secretaries, and field representatives—reminiscent of the U. S. Congress.* And they were accorded a new measure of independence by the highest legislative salaries in the U.S.—$16,-000 per annum in 1967, raised to $19,200 in 1970, with another several thousand dollars each year in such fringe benefits as a $30-a-day living allowance in Sacramento during sessions and an automobile with an oil company credit card. Assemblymen—and the state senators, who soon followed suit—became freer of lobbyists and the administration for basic information.

---

* By 1971, the legislature's staff numbered 1,500, of which 500 were professionals. Annual cost: about $15 million.

When Reagan, a budget-minded governor little interested in new programs, took office, the legislature became the programmatic, innovative branch of state government. In 1971, after his unsuccessful race for governor, Unruh retired—at least for the time being—from active participation in government. But one of his young staff men seemed justified in saying: "If Jesse never does anything else politically he will at least get a line in the history books for what he did with the legislature in California.* That judgment seemed vindicated in 1971 when a nonpartisan national study group, the Citizens Conference on State Legislatures, issued a report and ranking on the procedures and operations of the 50 state legislatures and found California number one in the U.S.A. The executive director of the Citizens Conference, ironically, is Larry Margolis, who was Unruh's right-hand man at Sacramento during the 1960s. But no one doubts that California deserves its number one position.

Have the reforms made the legislature a more honest place? The answer is probably yes, with some major reservations. Things have surely come a long way since the 1940s and the days of Arthur H. ("Artie") Samish, a six-foot, two-inch, 300-pound wheeler-dealer lobbyist who boasted to a writer for *Collier's* magazine: "I'm the governor of the legislature. To hell with the governor of the state. If you get a long enough ladder and put it up against the Capitol dome, you can take a picture of me unscrewing the gold cupola." For this indiscretion, Samish ended up being grilled by the Kefauver committee, being barred "forever" from lobbying in the California legislature, and catching the attention of the federal government, which finally sent him to jail for income tax evasion.

The "Third House" of lobbyists still flourishes in Sacramento. Those with great influence are said to include such as the Pacific Gas & Electric Co., Standard Oil of California, the Bank of America, the California Teachers Association, Lockheed Aircraft, Transamerica, the Kern County Land Co., the Bankers Association of California, the California Real Estate Association, the California Growers Association, and the University of California. Lobbyists are supposed to register, but many blandly disregard the law; among these, in 1968–69, were men lobbying on two of the most controversial bills: William Burke for the Catholic Church on abortion reform, and E. F. (Tod) Sloan of the National Rifle Association, when gun-control legislation was being considered. As a part of the 1969 package of constitutional revisions, "conflict of interest" provisions applicable to legislators were included. But the restrictions, Lou Cannon has reported, "were totally platitudinous and frankly designed to ease the qualms of newspapers reluctant to see the legislature with power over its own salary scale." Just how platitudinous they were was illustrated in 1969 when the Los Angeles *Times* reported that state senate president pro tem Hugh Burns had shared with an insurance lobbyist and another associate $500,000 in profits of an insurance company that had profited from legislation Burns sponsored. It turned out that the chairman

---

* The Unruh system has also turned out to be a great boon to legislators trying to solidify themselves for the next election. At state expense, they have a television and radio tape service, personalized mass mailings, and, of course, their permanent field staff.

of the Joint Legislative Ethics Committee created by the 1966 vote of the people was none other than Senator Burns himself. He said he had done nothing illegal, and there the matter rested. In the same year, Unruh introduced and secured passage of a bill requiring quite thorough disclosure of outside income by legislators and all other high state and local officials, but in 1970 the state supreme court struck it down as unconstitutional.

Up to the 1960s, California operated under a "federal plan" of legislative apportionment which divided the assembly by relatively equal population units but required geographic representation in the senate. The formula had been voted for by the people in 1926 and they refused on three subsequent occasions—in 1948, 1960, and 1962—to overturn it for equal population districts in both bodies. Malapportionment in the senate reached such egregious proportions that the six million people of Los Angeles County had exactly the same representation as 15,000 in the eastern Sierra district of Alpine, Inyo, and Mono counties—exactly one senator. The disparity in populations was 450 to 1. Then the courts, in the wake of *Baker v. Carr,* intervened in the California situation and reapportionment became mandatory. Overnight, L. A. County's representation shot up to 14 seats; overall Southern California went from nine to 22 seats, while Northern California slipped from 31 to 18.

The popular expectation was that the old conservative core of the senate—rural, Northern, and close to entrenched business interests like Standard Oil, PG&E, and the Southern Pacific Railroad, all of whom fought hard against reapportionment—would be immediately dislodged. It turned out not to be so. Senator Burns, the crusty old Fresno Democrat and embodiment of the *ancien régime,* was actually retained as president pro tem when the newly apportioned senate met in 1967. Committees remained tightly locked in control of the Old Guard, and the Third House seemed to be carrying on business as usual. Even in winter 1969, when the Republicans finally broke the decades-old Democratic majority in the Senate, Burns stayed on.* A few months later, however, a group of Young Turks of varied ideological stripes ousted Burns and enjoyed a month of reform; soon, however, an old-guard Republican, Jack Schrade of San Diego, got the job. Schrade quickly became the center of a nasty scandal involving a $5,000 "campaign contribution" which looked suspiciously like a direct payoff by the California Association of Thrift and Loan Companies to get one of its favorite bills approved. The Third House seemed in the saddle again.

A new generation of legislative leaders came to power after the 1970 elections, in which the Democrats took control of both houses. California journalist Mary Ellen Leary has described the new assembly leaders as part of a new political generation, just past 30, "schooled in the tough-minded political drive of the Kennedys, . . . clean-cut and incisive as a crew of aerospace engineers." Robert Moretti, 34, a protege of Jesse Unruh from the same Los Angeles community of Van Nuys, became the youngest speaker in the history of the assembly. Moretti differs somewhat from Unruh in that he is

* Burns voluntarily retired from the Senate at the end of 1970. His service totaled 34 years.

committed more to teamwork than to personality. While in college in 1960, he was drawn into politics by the Kennedy campaign.* He grew up in a Detroit immigrant ghetto, the son of an Italian father and an Armenian mother, and was an honor graduate of Notre Dame.

The Moretti leadership team in the assembly includes Walter Karabian, the son of Armenian immigrants who was elected majority leader; Henry Waxman, from a solidly Jewish Los Angeles district, who is chairman of the Elections and Reapportionment Committee; and the sharp-minded and skillful black attorney from San Francisco, Willie Brown, who helped Moretti win election as speaker and was rewarded with the powerful post of chairman of the Ways and Means Committee. The position makes Brown, 37, as influential in Sacramento as Wilbur Mills is in Washington—a breakthrough of immense importance for American blacks. He quickly showed his muscle by eliminating from the 1972 state budget all funds for the state Office of Economic Opportunity, which had been headed by a Reagan appointee, Lewis Uhler, a former John Birch Society member. Brown conducted an investigation of the state OEO office and concluded it duplicated the efforts of other local and federal agencies; he then persuaded his committee to kill a $70,000 budget request for the Uhler office. (Uhler had been accused of hiring political cronies and spying on local poverty agencies, a process even one Republican, William T. Bagley of San Rafael, called "like putting arsonists in charge of the fire department.")

In the senate, the power figure is now Democratic floor leader and caucus chairman George Moscone, an avowed 1974 gubernatorial candidate who is regarded by many as the Democrats' brightest hope in the state today. Moscone is a handsome, articulate San Francisco lawyer in his early forties who has attracted a "brain trust" of bright young men who advise him on fiscal problems, general legislation, politics, and communications. Another liberal Democrat, James R. Mills of San Diego, was elected senate president pro tem.† And in the Senate, too, one black has taken over a committee chairmanship —Los Angeles' Mervyn Dymally, who heads the Elections and Reapportionment Committee, a position of critical importance in a session which draws legislative and congressional district lines for a decade. Both Dymally and Brown on the assembly side preach the need for black involvement in the political process; as Dymally puts it, "The young bloods say the system is racist and irrelevant. True, . . . [but] if you aren't there when the man is cutting up the pie, you aren't going to get any of it." Brown, who was leading street demonstrations before he got into politics, says: "Blacks who are willing to do the homework and learn the techniques will be able through politics to

* It may be that the lasting Kennedy impact on American politics will be in the generation of the very young he attracted into politics, now moving into their thirties and forties and assuming positions of real power. The first generation of John Kennedy's closest associates (men like Pierre Salinger, Kenneth O'Donnell, and Theodore Sorensen), by contrast, has done very poorly in elective politics.

† Mills, along with Moretti, Moscone, and Congressman Waldie, is among the potential 1974 Democratic gubernatorial nominees. On the Republican side, potential names include State Controller Houston I. Flournoy (a highly regarded moderate), Lt. Gov. Ed Reinecke (a popular conservative who outpolled Reagan in 1970), Robert T. Monagan (who is now minority leader of the assembly), and Robert H. Finch (Presidential adviser, former lieutenant governor and U.S. Secretary of Health, Education, and Welfare, who has announced he will leave the White House and return to California after the 1972 elections).

make just incredible changes in the whole life style of black people in this country."

The new leadership bodes ill for the Third House, especially in view of the young Democrats' intention to redirect government benefits from those who possess to those who are dispossessed. But it would be naive to think that the lobbyists are in a hopeless position. A state Democratic party reaching for power will need money, and since business (especially savings and loan and insurance companies) is an important fund sources for the Democrats, a stridently antibusiness tone to the new legislation is unlikely.

Campaign contributions—some $5 million in 1968 and again in 1970, by official reports—are the most important conduit of special-interest money in Sacramento today. Direct bribes and similar skulduggery, by most accounts, are much less of a problem than they once were. By 1970, it was reported, Sacramento had an increasing number of "new breed" lobbyists, men with more governmental expertise who are more likely to be effective with the group of legislators increasingly in evidence after reapportionment: men and women generally younger, including many issue-oriented professionals and businessmen. According to the L. A. *Times*'s Tom Goff, the "old breed" is expert in the nuances of the legislative process, trades on old friendships, entertains more heavily, contributes heavily to fund-raising dinners, but rarely testifies before legislative hearings. Goff named Daniel J. Creedon, who was conduit for the controversial $5,000 gift to Schrade, as a typical "old breed" lobbyist. Like many of the "old breed," Creedon works for multiple clients at one time—in Creedon's case, not only the thrift companies but also beer and racetrack interests, highway patrolmen, funeral directors, consulting engineers, and certainly city governments. He operates out of a well-staffed office in the penthouse of the El Mirador Hotel, across from the Capitol. The California legislature may, as Unruh has often said, be "the finest in the nation." But if New Politics has come to town, Old Politics has apparently failed to get the message.

The California state budget, in the same pattern we have noted across the U.S.A., has shot upward at what seems like a geometric rate in recent years. In fiscal year 1945–46, its budget was $324 million; in 1971–72 the governor submitted a $6.7 billion budget. The increases just over a 12-year period, showing the overall figure and some major components, are illustrative:

	Fiscal Year 1959–60	Fiscal Year 1971–72
	(Figures in millions)	
Assistance to local school districts and community colleges	$ 635	$1,702
Higher education (University of California, state colleges)	175	675
Assistance to localities for public assistance (aid to the aged, blind, needy children, etc.)	191	563
Division of Highways	253	343
Total budget	$2,200	$6,789

Inflation, higher salaries, and expansion of activity in all departments were responsible for these fantastic increases. Despite Governor Reagan's heroic budget-cutting efforts, the figures would probably not look too different if Brown or another Democrat were still governor. In eight years in office, Brown's budget rose by $2.5 billion; in Reagan's first four years, the increase was $2.2 billion.

To pay these spiraling bills, California has been forced to periodic tax increases of massive proportions. The state has a steeply graduated personal income tax that provides about 23 cents of each dollar of income, but the system as a whole cannot be called especially progressive because much larger revenues come from sales taxes (a 4-percent rate, plus 1 percent for localities) and highway user taxes, which, between them, account for 46 cents of the tax dollar. A variety of other charges, ranging from the bank and corporation tax (nine cents) to horse racing fees (one cent) make up the rest of the revenue dollar.

The fiscal woes of California's counties and cities are just as great as the state's, and localities have the feeling that Sacramento has not gone nearly far enough to help them. Hard-pressed county governments, for instance, find 55 percent of their budgets going for welfare, an expenditure item they have great difficulty controlling. They complain that the state legislature often originates programs with costs shared on a percentage basis, but fails to give the counties money increases in proportion to the mandated expansion of services.

Like most states of the Union, California has paid for the bulk of local school costs through local property taxes, a system that has resulted in gross inequalities since the tax base within the state ranges from a low of $103 per child in the poorest communities to a high of $925,156—a ratio of almost 1 to 10,000. State aid to school districts has been only partially effective in equalizing funds, as it covers only 35 percent of local school costs. But in one fell swoop, the California supreme court in 1971 cut the ground out from under the old system. Ruling on a class action brought by Los Angeles parents, it ruled, 6–1, that raising school funds through local property taxes violates the equal protection clause of the 14th Amendment because it "invidiously discriminates against the poor because it makes the quality of a child's education a function of the wealth of his parents and neighbors." Unless reversed by the U. S. Supreme Court, the decision will force the state to adopt a new method of equalized school financing and could, in the words of M. Carl Holman, president of the National Urban Coalition, trigger "dramatic reform for an increased equal educational opportunity for poor children throughout the country." Wilson Riles pointed out that it would wipe out the existing inequalities that make it possible for the city of Beverly Hills to tax its citizens $2.60 per $100 of assessed valuation and come up with $1,500 per child, while West Covina, also in Los Angeles County, taxes $4.30 per $100 and raises less than $700.

At the end of the 1960s, California's per capita local property tax revenue was $226—highest in the nation, where the average figure was $139. Combined state and local tax collections in California were $488 (trailing only

New York); as a percentage of personal income they were 12.3 percent (trailing only Wyoming). Per capita welfare expenditures were second highest in the country. It was true that a federal input of close to $3 billion sweetened the picture somewhat, but the reasons for Californians' outraged resistance to higher taxes were not hard to see.

In the area of welfare, a well-intentioned temporary relief program of the 1930s had become a Frankenstein monster of seemingly permanent dependence for 620,000 Californians by 1961. And by 1969, 1.5 million of the United States's eight million welfare recipients lived in California. In California as in many other states, welfare had become a sizzling political issue, with many politicians (including Reagan) contributing to the false public image of the average welfare recipient as a healthy, husky 26-year-old male sitting in front of a color television set guzzling beer instead of working. But as Spencer Williams, then Reagan's secretary of human relations, pointed out in an interview, the number of cheaters was probably not great compared to the whole. California's welfare rolls carried 300,000 aged—typically, a 77-year-old widow. Then there were 12,500 blind, 150,000 disabled (mostly bedridden), 750,000 children, and 250,000 adults 21 to 65 years old. Of these, only 15,000 were male heads of households—and they tended to be seasonal workers, going on and off the rolls. There were more than 200,000 mothers on welfare who were heads of households. "If we could really reach this group and do a good job with it," Williams said, "we'd take about 350,000 off the rolls, because each head of household would take a couple of kids off with her." The problem was that neither California nor any other state, under excruciating budget shortages, was ready to invest the additional millions in employment counseling and rehabilitation care to do the job.

And as Williams acknowledged, only half the eligibles were on the rolls in 1969, many kept off by ignorance or pride. The activist welfare groups were just beginning to go out and recruit more eligibles to go on the rolls. On top of it all, the recession hit California, and by the time this book was written in 1971, the number of welfare recipients in California had burgeoned to 2.5 million. By 1971, in fact, welfare had emerged as the most controversial single issue of state government. Asserting that welfare was going to many "whose greed is greater than their need," Reagan pressed hard for a number of welfare cutbacks. After protracted negotiations, he and the Democratic legislative leadership agreed on a number of reforms that included Reagan recommendations like tighter residency and eligibility requirements, a pilot work program for welfare recipients, and stronger enforcement of child support payments by absentee fathers (one of the most serious abuses in the system). But he had to back down on a rather cold-hearted proposal to put an absolute lid in welfare spending. The compromise included cost-of-living increases, child care for working mothers, and family planning assistance for welfare mothers.

There are several areas in which California's state government has excelled. Its multibillion-dollar State Water Plan, inaugurated under Brown, was long cited as one of these, though there is now serious questioning of how necessary that full investment may have been, and how damaging the plan may be to California's ecology—a story we will look at in our section on the California Southland.

Perhaps the most brilliant success of recent times has been in the field of mental health, as California has shifted away from the big, custodial type of state hospitals to more responsive community health centers. California had pioneered in community health center development with legislation in the mid-1950s. Then, as a result of a legislative study, came landmark 1968 legislation which shifted the basic responsibility for treatment of the mentally ill from state to local government. The state continued to bear 90 percent of the costs and the counties 10 percent, but the first stop was local government. The state contracted with community agencies, medical centers and children's hospitals to operate regional centers for the retarded. The centers were required to provide comprehensive diagnosis. Where necessary, families were given guidance and financial aid to place children in privately operated, state-approved community residential facilities; others were given help, through visiting nurses, babysitters, or day-care centers, to keep their children at home. The average cost was about half that of state hospital care, with no capital outlay. Finally, the legislation took massive strides to protect mentally ill persons. Involuntary commitment to mental hospitals was made a cumbersome process, subject to mandatory court review each 90 days and continuable only if the hospital could show the person dangerous to others. Patients were guaranteed, except in the most exceptional cases, the right to wear their own clothes, send and receive uncensored letters, have daily visitors, and refuse shock treatment or lobotomy. On their release, they would be guaranteed full civil rights.

By 1969, there were only 13,363 patients in the state hospitals (just over a third of the figure 10 years before), and the number was dropping rapidly. Not only had California saved millions of dollars, but it had created a new system that would respect the rights and interests of the mentally disturbed and keep them in the mainstream of their communities, where the hope for eventual full recovery would be the greatest.

In fields of social legislation, California has moved in the last few years to liberalize its divorce laws (imperiling the divorce mill in neighboring Nevada) and to relax its restrictive, century-old abortion laws. As a result of a 1971 court decision, in fact, all abortions in California are now legal if performed by a licensed physician in a licensed hospital.

California has the dubious distinction, according to FBI statistics, of leading the United States in both the number and rate of crimes (3,764 per 100,000 inhabitants in 1968, for example). But it is also a national leader in advanced police training, and has put into operation a $5 million computerized system to link 450 state law enforcement agencies with crime files in Sacramento and Washington, D.C. It was also a pioneer state (in 1966) in putting into operation a state system of financial aid to victims of serious crimes.

In Washington, Justice Department officials say that California's prisons are the best run in the country. Governor Warren instituted the first major change, from an emphasis on punishment to one on rehabilitation, work programs, and indeterminate sentences. Several new pieces of progressive correctional legislation have come under Reagan, and he personally proposed that the department of corrections try out a system of family visitation for prisoners within 90 days of release. Unlike Mississippi's conjugal visitations, the California program provides for visits of a full family for two-day weekends at cottages outside the prison walls. Inmates within 90 days of release are also given 72-hour passes to go see their families and apply for jobs. And the state has been a leader in the nationally popular work furlough program, in which an inmate goes out to work during the day and returns to prison at night. In 1969, a shocking total of 50,000 California adults were convicted of felonies, but only 13.5 percent of them were sent to state prisons—generally the "repeaters" or those convicted of such crimes as homicide, armed robbery, or drug trafficking. The state pays $4,000 a year to any county which will keep a felon in the community, providing him with professional counseling and job training. The recidivism rate has dropped from 50 percent, an average figure in the U.S., to less than 35 percent. And under progressive parole and probation programs, the prison population dropped from an all-time high of 28,600 in January 1969 to 22,000, a 10-year low, in late 1971.

Part of California's relative success is doubtless based on its variety of prisons. Of the 14 state prisons, two are maximum security, no-nonsense types for hardened criminals—Folsom (near Sacramento) and San Quentin (in the Bay Area). Then there are prison hospitals, a number of "medium security" institutions, and some minimum security installations which are generally conservation camps run jointly with the state department of forestry.

Nevertheless, life for a California convict can be living hell. Some critics suggest that the state's prisons, rather than models of achievement for criminal justice, are merely the best of a frightening lot across the U.S.A. Sweeping reforms were recommended, in fact, in a report to the state board of corrections by a 62-member staff directed by Oakland criminologist Robert Keldgord. Among the salient proposals: that San Quentin and Folsom, which are 116 and 91 years old respectively, be closed down because they are "ugly and depressing" and "not secure or safe"; that conjugal visits be allowed at all penitentiaries; that two-man cells be eliminated to decrease homosexuality; that prisoners be allowed to wear civilian clothes; that mail censorship be abandoned; and that the maximum time allowable for sentences to isolation be reduced from 30 to 10 days. But the acceptance of many of these proposals by the Reagan administration was much in doubt. "How high on the priority list," one Reagan aide asked me, "can you put improvements in penology, when dollars are scarce for schools, medical care, and social welfare? After all, you're talking about people who have committed a crime against society."

As racial tensions mounted in the country during the 1960s, the effects were felt in California's prisons, first through organization by the Black Muslims behind the prison walls, then by other black prisoners with a political-revolutionary awareness. In 1969, at the correctional training facility of Soledad, a white guard killed three black prisoners during a disturbance in the exercise yard; the guard was quickly exonerated, and soon afterward a white guard was found beaten to death. Three black convicts were charged with the murder; these were the famed "Soledad Brothers" of whom one, George Jackson, would gain national fame through his book, *Soledad Brother*. His brother, Jonathan Jackson, was killed in a 1970 shoot-out at the Marin County courthouse, part of an audacious kidnap plot to force George's release, which ended in the death of four persons, including a judge. (This was the incident for which Angela Davis, the ex-UCLA instructor and Communist party member, was accused of procuring the weapons.) A bloody encore came in August 1971 when George Jackson smuggled a gun into his cellblock at San Quentin and touched off a mutiny in which three white guards and two white inmates were killed. In his book, Jackson had repeatedly prophesied that he would not leave the California prison system alive. The prophecy came true as, in a run for freedom across a yard toward the wall, the hardened and embittered young revolutionary was cut down by gunfire from the guards.

University of California: Pain and Progress of "Multiversity"

Many things Californian evoke superlatives; no institution merits them more than the University of California. Despite its many tribulations, UC remains the most successful institution of higher education that the United States, and perhaps the world, has ever known. From humble beginnings as an academy in an Oakland dance hall in 1853, it has developed into a "multiversity" of more than 100,000 students and a staff of 50,000, working and studying in nine distinct campuses. The university has an annual budget of well over $1 billion,* offers in excess of 10,000 courses, operates two nuclear laboratories and close to 100 research and experimental stations. It leads the nation in the number of Nobel laureates on its faculty (14 at last count) and in the number of National Merit Scholars who choose to enroll.

The benefit that has accrued to California's people through their fantastic investment in UC is almost beyond estimation. Without the university's distinction in agricultural research, the physical sciences, technology, and water conservation, California would be, as an economic entity, a weak shadow of what it is today.

And preeminently among the American states, California has given its young people an opportunity to take advantage of higher public education. Under the master plan for higher education, adopted in 1960, every California youngster interested in continuing his education beyond high school has an opportunity to do so under a three-tiered program, which, by latest count, accommodated about 1.2 million students:

COMMUNITY COLLEGES (or junior colleges, as they used to be called). The community college is basically a California model, pioneered by Pasa-

---

* Of the $1 billion, about three-quarters is paid for by the state of California, the remainder from federal grants and research contracts.

dena City College over 60 years ago. There are now 93 such campuses, located throughout the state, guaranteeing a place to any California high school graduate, or, in fact, anyone over 18 "who can profit from the instruction." Enrollment in 1970–71 totaled 800,000.

STATE COLLEGES. There are presently 19 such colleges, with an enrollment of 227,000 students. Their four-year program, leading to a bachelor's degree, is open to any California high school graduate who placed in the upper 33⅓ percent of his class, plus successful community college graduates. The emphasis is on undergraduate instruction, and some of the state colleges —notably San Jose State, San Diego State, and Long Beach State—compare well in program and teaching to the best state universities of the country.

THE UNIVERSITY. UC, at the top of the pyramid, accepts only the top 12.5 percent of California high school graduates, plus a limited number of out-of-state students who placed in the top 6 percent of their class. Academically, the university is intended to be, and is, an elitist institution. It also has three exclusive and jealously guarded functions within California public higher education: to act as the state's primary agency for research; to grant doctorates; to train students for certain professions such as medicine, dentistry, pharmacy, law, and architecture. The master plan assigned these functions to the university campuses to avoid the cost and chaos many feared if the state colleges tried to duplicate them.

UC's tight admission requirements came under increasing criticism in the late 1960s because of the minuscule numbers of blacks and Mexican-Americans who could qualify under them. (The percentage of these minorities enrolled at the eight campuses was less than 2 percent in the late 1960s —even while they represented 19 percent of California high school enrollment.) Thus a special quota of 2 percent, with an option of up to 4 percent, was set for culturally and economically deprived applicants who, admissions officers believe, could, with proper motivation and counseling, perform satisfactorily at the university level. Early experience showed this 4 percent segment earning grades about comparable with the rest of the university's students.

The nine UC campuses provided a fascinating study in diversity. UCLA, in a posh Los Angeles suburb, did not grant a doctorate before 1938 but now ranks among the nation's top 15 universities; it is strong in community involvement, athletics, and several academic disciplines. San Diego, with four Nobel laureates, has one of the best natural science faculties of the U.S. (Scripps Institution of Oceanography, etc.), plus a unique system of "cluster colleges"—science-oriented Revelle, academically and socially freer John Muir, and a controversial Third College especially for blacks, Mexican-Americans, and independently minded whites. Santa Barbara has been a poor sister on the academic scale, seen by many as a surfboard-and-bikini haven; in 1970 it became a center of the most violent campus discord. San Francisco has no undergraduates, just the prestigious UC Medical Center. Santa Cruz, opened in 1965, tries to conquer academic impersonality by division into physically separated colleges of 650 students each. Davis, in the Central Valley between

San Francisco and Sacramento, has outstanding liberal arts and physical science programs but is most famous for its agricultural research. Riverside, outside Los Angeles, a pioneer in citrus research and now smog research, has been referred to as "the most tranquil and conservative outpost in the UC system." Irvine, on land donated by the ranch of the same name in booming Orange County, stresses interdisciplinary courses and individual counseling.

But Berkeley, mother of all the others, is still the brightest light of the UC system. Academically, it may be the most famous for its work in physics (the Lawrence Radiation Laboratory), biochemistry, and English, but scores of its faculty, in widely divergent disciplines, stand at the top of their fields. In 1966, the respected American Council on Education found that Berkeley's graduate departments made it "the best balanced, distinguished university in the country." The conclusion came as a rude shock to Harvard, hitherto considered the finest. In a 1971 sequel, the Council found Berkeley had actually widened its lead. In comparison to Berkeley's 32 top-ranked departments, Harvard had 27, Stanford 16, the University of Chicago 14, Yale 13, Michigan, MIT and Princeton 12 each, Caltech 11, and Wisconsin 8.

Berkeley can also offer a magnificent 3.5-million-volume library, a $4.8 million University Art Museum in which visitors move from level to level in a flow of curving space, and now historic Sproul Plaza (made famous by the inauguration of the Free Speech Movement in what now seems a very long ago 1964). As *Newsweek* summarized this turbulent heartland of UC, "Whatever any campus has, Berkeley can usually match, whether the measure be distinguished faculty, student radicals, lab facilities, 'street people,' or beauty —in its girls and its setting."

At times in the late 1960s, it appeared that the chain of violent events that afflicted Berkeley would begin to drive away some of the university's outstanding faculty. Isolated cases of prestigious scholars packing up to go back East were publicized in the press. But in fact, Berkeley averaged only 24 annual resignations out of a tenured faculty of 1,000 in the years following 1964. In 1969, only 17 resigned. One reason was the immense power and independence still enjoyed by the UC faculty; in 1964, for instance, the American Association of University Professors called UC's academic senate the strongest such organization in the country. Another reason was UC's reserve capital of high prestige, accumulated during the regimes of presidents like Robert Gordon Sproul (1929–58), who brought many Nobel Prize winners to the university and is credited by many with making it into a great world institution, and Clark Kerr (1958–67), who helped formulate the master plan for higher education, guided development of the innovative new campuses like those at Irvine and Santa Cruz, and sought more independence for students and faculty.

Finally, Berkeley in particular offers an intellectual excitement and sense of currency with its times hard to duplicate elsewhere. As sociologist Robert N. Bellah wrote in his book *Beyond Belief*, explaining why he chose to leave Harvard for Berkeley in 1967:

As against the magisterial certainty of Harvard, Berkeley stands in sharp antithesis; not the calm order of Protestant tradition but the wide-open chaos of the post-Protestant, post-modern era. For all its inner problems, for all of its tensions with an increasingly unsympathetic environment, Berkeley evinces the intensity, the immediacy, the openness of an emergent social order. For one trying to grapple with and define what that order is, it is a good place to be.

Even scholars less attracted to the societal cutting edge were realizing by the late 1960s that they might as well remain at or seek out UC for its many advantages, since the pattern of campus revolt and discord invented at Berkeley had apparently become a national phenomenon. There were few if any safe islands left.

Heaven for a UC professor, it is said, is to have six or seven graduate students interested in his field of concentration, so that he can do his research using their imagination and talents, even while he is training them. The result is that UC does more research and turns out more doctorates than any other institution of higher learning in America. Much of the work is vital, economically, to the state of California. Even through the years that "liberal" Edmund G. Brown was governor, the all-powerful UC board of regents remained a highly business- and establishment-oriented body. Neither Brown, nor any of his predecessors, nor Reagan, have ever appointed a black, Chicano, Indian, or Oriental to the board of regents. Instead, corporate interests like the Hearst Corporation and Bank of America (both with economic interests ranging far beyond their immediate fields of publishing and banking) have held seats over long periods of years. The age of the average regent has hovered around 60. And through the Brown administration, the board remained essentially noncontroversial; in fact the governor himself rarely attended meetings. (All this changed under Reagan, a forceful and regular participant.) Beneath the lofty, distant regents is the huge bureaucracy needed to administer the gigantic UC empire. And then there is the faculty, preoccupied with prestige- and award-winning research, often oblivious to the interests and intellectual development of all save the brightest and most aggressive students. A UC official told me it was perfectly true that the quiet, nonaggressive, A-average high school student who goes to the University of California will get a worse education than he would at a mediocre college where the faculty have time and interest to work with students.

All these factors played a role in the ill-defined but powerful Free Speech Movement of 1964–65, and remain important today. The students were protesting what seemed to them the impersonality and dehumanization of the university through its bureaucracy, the premium placed on research over teaching, the factory-like approach to producing people for industry, and, above all else, the lack of any real student role in shaping the goals and values of the university. By today's standards, the protests of the Free Speech Movement—entirely student-based, completely nonviolent—seem innocent indeed. Clark Kerr recognized the demands for a greater student voice as having some currency. If he had been permitted to deal in a forthright manner with the grievances of that time, as he sought to do, the university might well have been spared most if not all of the extreme militancy and violent turmoil it has since experienced. By responding with some positiveness to student demands, and beginning some democratization of its own structure, UC could have made an invaluable contribution to constructive university change all over America. Other universities, recognizing UC's preeminent position, would have moved voluntarily to make the same reforms.

But it was not to be so. The broad California public was angered and frustrated by the seeming uprising in the university that public tax dollars supported. The faculty, with its own entrenched privileges to defend, was reluctant to accommodate. The board of regents was not anxious to see fundamental reforms, and was concerned about the public reaction. Kerr found himself almost isolated as an apologist for student unrest, refusing to pander to public opinion. Then came 1966 and Reagan's first gubernatorial campaign, in which he called for an investigation of UC Berkeley, a campus he said was dominated by "a minority of malcontents, beatniks, and filthy-speech advocates." Students must "obey the rules or get out," Reagan said repeatedly.

Once in office, Reagan tried to keep his campaign promises. He announced that the fiscal policy of his administration would be to "squeeze, cut, and trim." And he suggested both a 25 percent budget cut and charging of tuition for the first time in UC's history. Kerr warned that UC would be forced, as it never had before, to turn away qualified applicants. Alarmed over the budget cuts, he suspended all new fall admissions and unwisely sought a vote of confidence from the board of regents. And on January 20, 1967, at the first meeting attended by Reagan, the regents voted 14–8 to dismiss him. The reaction to Kerr's firing—across state and nation—was one of shock. Flags flew at half mast at all UC campuses. The lead editorial in the New York *Times* was entitled "Twilight of a Great University."

Subsequently, it took nine months to find a successor to Kerr. The man picked was Dr. Charles J. Hitch. He has performed creditably if not brilliantly in his terribly difficult job; at one point he told the Los Angeles *Times* that his greatest accomplishment as president was survival.

Even with Reagan in office, working assiduously (through persuasion and appointments) to build a permanent majority of regents favorable to his position on university affairs, it is possible that accommodations between students and administration would eventually have been made, letting the Free Speech Movement fade into history as a fairly isolated phenomenon. But in the same years, the Vietnam war boiled to the surface as a national issue, inflaming campuses everywhere. The plight of the nation's black and Mexican-American minorities was dramatized by the civil rights movement, urban riots, and the war on poverty. Hard-core radicalism took root on the campuses with organizations like Students for a Democratic Society. More importantly, a whole generation of American students became "radicalized" —the vast majority opposed to violence in demonstrations, but still committed to a general restructuring of American society to make it less war-oriented, more responsive to human needs. "The students here," I heard from one UC official, "believe that the last 25 years devoted to physical sciences must be followed by 25 years of advance in social sciences. They see we've developed great technological skills but few social skills to deal with the multiple social injustices of our system. And the students say, if society can't see that, perhaps a little demonstration and rioting will get its attention."

At least in the short term, of course, the rioting can be highly unproductive—and dangerous to the university. Every public opinion poll shows large majorities of the people in favor of "cracking down" on campus dissent. The image is typically one of wild destruction of university property that the taxpayers financed, flying of Vietcong flags, use of the vilest obscenities. What the disillusioned "middle American" taxpayer does not know is that only a small minority of students engage in the most violent forms of demonstrations. In California of late, the most frenzied demonstrators have often turned out to be nonstudents. Nor is it well known that one in 10 UC students puts idealism into very practical volunteer help in disadvantaged areas throughout California, helping in schools, tutoring, building clinics, and staffing summer camps for needy youngsters. Through 1969, UC-Berkeley accounted for 10 percent of the entire membership of the Peace Corps.

The Reagan years have predictably plunged the university into political turmoil on a scale hitherto unknown in America. At one point Reagan suggested—he later said "figuratively"—that a "bloodbath" might be needed to quell violent campus demonstrations. Students and like-thinking faculty responded in kind, accusing Reagan of trying to "repeal the Renaissance," of replacing "the creative society with an illiterate society."

What the rhetoric sometimes obscures is what has actually happened to the university in the Reagan years. It has not, as Reagan's enemies predicted, plunged into fiscal chaos, with massive faculty departures and thousands of rejected students. But the budget has been subjected to intense scrutiny by the regents and the legislature. UC is no longer, as Jay Michael, its chief legislative lobbyist puts it, the "sacred cow" it once was. Hitch cannot do what Clark Kerr did—plead emotionally for any and all projects desired by his administration and faculty, practically breaking into tears when any program, however mediocre, was suggested for cutting. The UC operating budget has increased by about 50 percent since the mid-1960s, but most of the increase has been eaten up by inflation, merit pay raises, and the costs of a 28-percent increase in enrollment. Capital construction has been cut back drastically, both by the regents and even more by the legislature. Funding shortages are equally if not more serious within the state colleges. As a temporary expedient, budget cuts for the universities and colleges may not prove to be fatal; were they to continue for several years, however, the situation could become desperate, both in research and teaching.

The omens for California higher education were not bright as the decade of the 1970s began. Still fresh in memory was the 1968–69 uprising at San Francisco State College, in which a black instructor, associated with the Black Panthers, urged students to bring guns on campus and a long strike ensued, with the support of radical factions both among students and faculty. Campus bombings occurred and as many as 700 San Francisco policemen were on duty; the college president resigned, to be replaced by the controversial semanticist-turned-administrator, Dr. S. I. Hayakawa. The pitched battle of 1969 at Berkeley over the "People's Park," marked by one death and helicopter gassing of the main campus, was followed by the 1970 demonstrations against the U.S. invasion of Cambodia, during which some radical faculty members made the inflammatory suggestion that the university be "reconstituted" into a political force. Level-headed moderates on campus faculties had their hands full in restoring and keeping order, trying to keep communications open with students, and at the same time diverting attention from Reagan's continued suggestion of the use of raw force to repress demonstrations. By damning students, faculty, and administrators in a blanket fashion, and resorting quickly to force, Reagan was driving many peaceful and nonviolent students into the camp of the hard-core militants.

There was danger of public higher education falling into general disrepute in the very state where it had made its greatest achievements in America. Granting a 5-percent pay increase for state employees in 1970, the legislature took a gratuitous slap at the universities by specifically exempting their employees. Despite a desperate need for more medical personnel, voters rejected a $246 million health sciences bond issue endorsed by most major officials (including Reagan) and newspapers in the state—the rejection coming, many thought, because that now-so-controversial name "University of California" was attached. (More doctors die in California each year than are trained there, the medical manpower deficit made up by what amounts to parasitizing of other states and foreign countries—most of them poorer than California—which have spent heavily to train physicians, dentists, and nurses.)

The students had reason to bemoan the regents' decision, in 1970, to go along with Reagan on imposing the first tuition fees in the university's history. There were no signs that faculty were giving more time to teaching; quite the reverse, the average UC faculty member's weekly time devoted to teaching of undergraduates fell from 13.5 hours in 1960 to 9.7 hours in 1970.

By 1970 there were signs that the political assault on the universities might have reached the point of overkill. Reagan himself saw his winning election margin cut in half, and Senator George Murphy, who had campaigned fiercely against students, was defeated. Rafferty, the rabid right-winger who had once called Berkeley "a four-year course in sex, drugs, and treason," was defeated for reelection by Wilson Riles. By virtue of his position, Riles became a member of the university board of regents—the first black man ever to serve there.

In 1971, Reagan seemed to be shifting his fire to a new target of opportunity, the welfare mess, and he missed regents meetings, including the one at which a successor to retiring Roger W. Heyns as chancellor at Berkeley was chosen. The regents picked Albert H. Bowker, who in eight years as chancellor of the City University of New York had shown remarkable talent in getting public funds for rapid expansion. Before that, he had upgraded the faculty as dean of the Stanford graduate school. Bowker looked like just the man Berkeley needed to maintain its preeminence in the face of Reagan's budget cuts.

The Environment: Desecration and Hope

Californians rank among the most determined exploiters, desecraters, and protectors of the natural environment that the world has ever seen. Like its citizens, the state government has a spotty record that began in despoliation, turned in recent years to the possibilities of conservation, and may yet—if there is time—save for future generations much of the magnificent heritage of natural California.

Smog, now a severe national problem, came first to the Los Angeles Basin, later to appear in alarming measure in cities like San Jose, Oakland, and Fresno. For almost two decades, air pollution bills have been winning approval in Sacramento, the most famous being the nation's first serious efforts to control automobile emissions. California's emission standards remain the toughest in the nation, and beginning with 1973 models, carmakers will be fined up to $5,000 for each vehicle that fails to meet the state's standards. In 1969, the state senate surprised the world by passing a bill to prohibit the sale of motor vehicles powered by internal combustion engines. The assembly killed the measure, but it was reintroduced in 1970 and might just be passed one day.

California has been less innovative in water pollution control. In 1969, it passed a water quality control act setting up nine regional boards with clear-cut regulatory powers. But the 1971 Nader task force report included a charge that the act was "written by polluters and for polluters, weakened further by nonenforcement." State authorities, of course, denied the charge. In autumn 1970, voters by a 3–1 margin approved a $250 million bond issue for sewage treatment facilities.

Of California's 100 million acres, the federal government owns about half—largely as national forests, parks, and military bases. Private holdings total 50 million acres, with about 38 million in farming and 6.5 million in commercial forestry. Little more than 3 percent of the land area, in fact, is occupied by cities. But those cities often occupy the choicest locations, and their environs have been in peril ever since the great postwar housing push began. Obviously, there was a need for a state plan to show where open space should be preserved (and purchased by the state, if necessary), where transportation corridors might go, where the cities of the future should be located. Beaches are another critical problem; along the whole coastline from Oregon to Mexico, only 90 miles are open to the public, and real estate billboards march up the coastline in tasteless profusion.

The state planning office spent five years and $4 million on a state plan in the 1960s, but the result was a fiasco, hopelessly unspecific and wrapped up in bureaucratise. Disgusted with the state agency's performance, the San

Francisco-based conservation group California Tomorrow announced in 1970 it would go to work on a state plan with private financing, and issue it early in the decade.

The legislature did take a forward step in 1965–66 with passage of its "Open Space Land Program," which seeks to create "green belts" of prime agricultural land near urban areas. When the suburban housing tracts started their hedgehop growth across the orchards and open fields, taxes on nearby farms soared under the "highest and best use" formula of assessment, forcing many farmers to sell out. The new legislation permitted farmers to enter into contracts with county governments to keep their taxes based on agricultural use of the land. But according to the Nader task force, the result has been "the twisting of a legitimate concern over the plight of prime crop land into an unjustifiable boondoggle for rich landowning corporations."

Some notable conservation victories have included bond issues for purchase of new and development of old parklands, defeat of a freeway through virgin redwood forests in the north, and the halt called to filling-in of San Francisco Bay. A scenic roads program got its start in the early 1960s when conservationists became upset by the state highway department's plan to "improve" the twisty, picturesque old Route 1 along the Big Sur coastline into a four- or eight-lane highway, a step which would have taken much of the magnificence away. At the urging of then state senator Fred Farr of nearby Carmel, the legislature agreed to a cooperative effort by state and local governments to select and then protect scenic corridors. This initiative later led to the federal scenic roads program as well. California is also creating what will eventually be a 4,000-mile system of parkways—low-speed, scenic roadways through elongated parks—the antithesis of freeways.

Aesthetics, however, have not been the main point of California's gargantuan postwar freeway development. More than 4,000 miles of freeways have been built since the Pasadena Freeway, California's first, in 1940. In 1959, the state started a 20-year plan to build 12,400 *more* miles of controlled access highway at a cost of more than $10 billion. By 1980, California will have 17 million motor vehicles; in 1970, it already had 12 million, 75 percent more than any other state. Builder and advocate of the great freeway system is the state division of highways and its ruling commission, a combine Wallace Stegner of Stanford has referred to as "having nobody to control it, too much money, too much power, and an engineering mentality."

The highway division has extraordinary powers of eminent domain; even more important, some billion dollars a year are assured it, without the possibility of gubernatorial or legislative review. This stems from a provision of the California constitution, actually an amendment added by popular vote in 1937, which states that highway user taxes (gasoline, oil, vehicle registrations) must be used directly for highway building or improvement. Proposals that any of these huge revenues might be diverted to alternate transportation systems, or air pollution control, are assailed as unconscionable "raids on the highway fund." In 1970, for instance, a modest proposal for diversion of up to 25 percent of locally generated gas taxes for smog prevention and mass transit was overwhelmingly voted down in statewide referendum after a scare campaign (warning of new taxes) launched by the highway lobby with heavy oil contributions. In addition to petroleum interests, according to *Cry California*, the "Freeway Establishment" includes the trucking industry, automobile clubs (AAA), heavy-equipment manufacturers and dealers, concrete producers, general contractors, the lumber industry, rock and aggregate producers, and, of course, the state division of highways. There is no mightier lobby in California.

Many of the new freeways, like Interstate 5, which cuts north to south through the Central Valley and runs clear from Oregon to San Diego, generate scant opposition and are welcomed by communities along their route. Coastal and urban California have begun to react differently, starting with the now famous revolt of San Franciscans against the unsightly Embarcadero Freeway in the late 1950s. Subsequent revolts against the freeway builders' plans have been noted in such places as Beverly Hills, Laguna Beach, the Monterey Peninsula, and Santa Barbara, with varying results.

California has spawned more conservation groups than any other state, the most famous of all being the Sierra Club, founded by the famed naturalist John Muir in 1892 to "explore, enjoy, and preserve the Sierra Nevada and other scenic resources of the U.S." The club still has a lot of hikers, but its principal visibility has come through the great fights to preserve the natural environment. Examples: fighting for a Redwoods National Park, lobbying Congress to prohibit dams that would encroach on the Grand Canyon of the Colorado, trying to halt a six-lane expressway along the banks of the Hudson in New York state, opposing the supersonic transport and the Alaskan oil pipeline. In addition to lobbying (which caused Internal Revenue Service cancellation of the club's tax-exempt status), the club has increasingly resorted to lawsuits to protect the public's right to a clean environment. Naturally, big industries have become highly irate; one criticism is that "the club has gone overboard, mounting irresponsible drives to preserve everything in sight." But the Sierra Club has thrived on controversy, growing from 14,500 members in 1960 to almost 100,000 in 1970—a quarter of whom live east of the Mississippi. Offices are as widespread as San Francisco and Washington, New York and Alaska. The growth has continued, even since the forced resignation in 1969 of David Brower, the club's longtime executive director, in a dispute over financing and publication of lavish books depicting the glories of the natural environment. Brower went off to form a new group known as Friends of the Earth, another of the plethora of conservation groups crowding the California (and now national) stage.

The lobbying efforts of California's multiple conservation groups, once poorly organized and coordinated, are now served collectively by the Planning and Conservation League, set up in 1966 with a full-time staff in Sacramento. (The Sierra Club also has a full-time lobbying operation in the capital.) PCL programs, reflecting the interests of its 87 affiliated organizations, range over such fields as auto emissions, state planning, low-cost housing, mass transit, scenic highways, billboard controls, underground power lines, and open-space protection. In 1971, PCL was in the forefront of a fight to pass legislation to provide orderly planning and growth along the California coastline—an idea vigorously fought by oil companies, utilities concerned about their power plant sites, and owners of major seashore land developments.

The fight to save the Golden State will doubtless be a difficult one, against entrenched and well-funded interests, inertia, and the continuing effects of damage already done to the natural landscape. But now, at least, the conservationists have become strong in number and more sophisticated in technique, and their efforts will be supplemented in the next years by various activities designed to follow up on the Nader task force report. These include a "public interest corporation" set up by Keith Roberts (author of the Nader study on the State Water Project), and a contemplated new Sacramento lobby, probably to be headed by Richard Fellmeth, to press for reforms on land ownership, water projects and pollution control, using the weapons of legislative persuasion, class action litigation and new investigations. Such efforts to redress the lobbying imbalance in favor of the special interests were scarcely dreamed of a few years past. In the years to come, they may play a vital role in reordering Californian priorities—and values.

Geographic California

"Of the states subsequent to the original thirteen, California is the only one with a genuine natural boundary," James Bryce observed in *The American Commonwealth*. Westward lies the iridescent Pacific; to the south the Colorado River and the Mexican desert; to the east the high, snowy peaks of the Sierra Nevadas; to the north more mountains and forests of Oregon. Superimposed on the east coast, the outline of California would run from New York City on the north to within a few miles of Jacksonville, Florida, on the south. It is a land of startling contrasts—dense forests, sun-scorched deserts, alpine mountains, fruitful valleys. The most cited contrast is between 14,494-foot Mt. Whitney, highest peak south of Alaska, and Death Valley, just 60 miles to the southeast, dipping 282 feet below sea level, the lowest point of the Western Hemisphere and the hottest and driest in the United States. Rainfall along the moist northern coast averages 35 inches a year and has gone to a record 190 inches at Honeydew; at Bagdad, a weather station in the Mojave Desert, two years have been known to pass without a drop of precipitation.

Most of coastal California is sunny and balmy, the kind of lotus land that has drawn millions. But nature can play cruel tricks. Californians live in uneasy knowledge, and some in intense terror, of the San Andreas fault, which runs practically the entire length of the state, the longest and most exposed fracture anywhere in the world's crust. It has been in motion 65 million years, with slippage between the two sides of 300 miles. West of the fault, which is 20 miles deep, the land is moving northward about two centimeters a year faster than the land to the east. What concerns geologists is that the two abutting edges of the fault near San Francisco and Los Angeles are presently frozen together. Incredible amounts of restrained energy are thus built up. Eventually, they demand release. More than 20 severe earthquakes have struck California in the past century. In 1857, an earthquake in the Techachapis, north of Los Angeles, caused a 30-foot jump in the western edge. The great 1906 earthquake in San Francisco caused a 30-foot movement. Buildings collapsed, streets sank, fires ravaged the heart of the city, and close to 700 were killed. In February 1971, Californians got another grim reminder that they live atop one of the most active earthquake zones in the world. A tremor officially described as "moderate" occurred near Los Angeles' San Fernando Valley on the line of the San Gabriel fault, which is part of the San Andreas network.* The quake took 64 lives, caused damage that may cost $1 billion to restore, triggered more than 1,000 landslides, and released methane gas from the ocean floor near Malibu Point. This is mere child's play in comparison to the potential destruction of a really serious quake, like that of 1906. Respected seismologists estimate the damage might be $10 billion and cost hundreds of thousands of lives. It is "reasonable" to expect, according to a state legislative committee report, that a great earthquake—7.75 or higher on the Richter scale—may occur "once in every 60 to 100 years." The time frame thus suggested: 1966 to 2006.

Scientists discount the suggestion that all of California west of the San Andreas might slip into the ocean in a great Superquake. But Curt Gentry, in his book *The Late, Great State of California,* makes just that suggestion and calls his book "nonfiction."

Earthquake is not the only threat to naturally pleasant California. The Southern coastal region is caught in a cycle of wind, fire, floods, and mudslides. Over the low hills near the ocean grows a low, dry undergrowth known as chaparral, along with pine forests a few miles further inland. At the end of a long, dry summer, the prevailing wind patterns from the ocean may change and the Santa Ana winds, crackling dry and powerful, come sweeping in from the desert. The slightest spark on the chaparral and a conflagration ensues.

In autumn 1970, after Southern California had gone without significant rain for 200 days, humidity had dropped to 5 percent and temperatures were over 100°. The hot Santa Anas swept in again, often at velocities of as much as 70 mph., starting 10 simultaneous timber and brush fires. In the most extensive fires of California's history, a half-million acres were burned over, eight lives lost, more than 1,000 homes and other buildings burnt, with damage of $170 million.

Fire is not alone in the cycle. In winter, especially after bad fires which have destroyed the ground cover, torrential downpours on the desert-like land may cause mudslides that come down the canyons to envelop houses and cost incalculable damage. In 1969, the worst rains, mudslides, landslides, and damage of modern times hit Southern California. Hundreds of homes built precariously on cliffs or flood-prone areas were destroyed.

* The 1971 quake shocked scientists because the precise area struck had been seismically inactive since about the end of the last Ice Age—about 10,000 years ago.

For all of California's sweetness and artificiality, the primordial cycles of fire and rain and earthquake continue, nature keeping man in his place.

Befitting California's nation size, its geography may be reviewed in three distinct parts.

First, there is the California which remains fairly close to its original condition. Here one speaks of the mountain and big timber country of the North Coast and lordly Sierra Nevada, the forbidding southern desert, and the great Central Valley. This discussion follows in the next several pages.

Second, there is the man-made civilization around the shores of San Francisco Bay. This section begins on page 628.

Finally, there is the California Southland, a megalopolis stretching from San Diego to Santa Barbara, with Los Angeles its linchpin. See page 650.

A review of natural California could well dwell on its grandeurs and the perils to them. There is the rugged, lonely coastline stretching north from San Francisco, a still sparsely populated land of rolling fog, breakers smashing against high bluffs, and moist, deep forests. The Redwood National Park, created in 1968, will save some 58,000 acres of the most handsome virgin redwood stands that remain, but such compromises were made with the lumber industry that the park is truncated and scarcely viable in its present form.

The redwoods fight, some believe, is just the first chapter of a battle to preserve Northern California's treasures, including wilderness areas, the state's few wild rivers, the lush Napa Valley vineyards, and some of the best open land in California. Conservationists are also fighting the logging plans of the lumber industry in Northern and Sierra California. Counting not only redwoods but other tree species—pine and Douglas fir, incense cedar, mountain birch and white oak—the area still has the greatest virgin forest of the contiguous U.S., some 10 million acres in all.

Then there is the great granite spine of the Sierra Nevada Mountains, separating California from the rest of the continent. As Neil Morgan has written, "the Sierra Nevada tend to unite Californians in some sense of community. In its alpine fastness, one cannot escape the feel of history. Here lies an unyielding, unchanging California in contrast to the one below." But the jewel of the Sierras, Yosemite National Park, is imperiled by the tens of thousands of tourists who rush in on summer weekends, all in their private fume-spewing vehicles that add to the smog problem created by the thousands of campfires they build. (Eventually, most auto traffic will be banned from the valley floor.) The next most popular spot in the Sierra Nevada is cold, radiant Lake Tahoe, now pollution-threatened and afflicted by incredibly cheap gambling casinos just over the Nevada border. Now, man-made pollution is even threatening the trails and summit of lordly Mount Whitney. As recently as 1963, only 2,000 people reached the summit; I can remember reaching the top in 1955, gasping for breath in the thin air, but exalted to stand alone, without another human in sight, on the highest spot in the then 48 states. Now the National Park Service is considering a heliport on the summit to facilitate trash removal!

The Great Central Valley: Cornucopia of Fruit and Vegetables

The topographic map of the western U.S.A., honeycombed with mountains and outthrusts, reveals no level area to compare with California's Great Central Valley. The dimensions of the valley, covering a sixth of California's land area, are hard to grasp; as Neil Morgan points out, the Appalachian mountain range of the east could easily fit into the valley, and its land area is greater than all of Denmark. Within the valley, the fields are flat and monotonous; the dusty little farm towns click off every few miles with scarcely a distinguishing mark. Great irrigation canals flow soundlessly through the fields, adding mugginess to the hot air. Only occasionally do tall windbreaks of cottonwoods or eucalyptus break the dull infinity of straight crop lines. For Californian and visitor alike, there seems little reason to tarry.

But this great mechanized farm plant is a wonder all in itself. Chiefly because of it, California leads the U.S.A. in the value of farm products—more than $4 billion each year, the heart of an overall state "agribusiness" of some $15 billion. No other California business—not even aerospace—is of comparable magnitude. Within the valley grows every species of temperate-zone or subtropical fruit, vegetable, or field crop known to man, tobacco alone excepted. The valley is also a major producer of beef and dairy cattle, concentrated in its dry borders. The state is second only to Iowa in livestock, second to Florida in citrus, second to Texas in cotton, and the preeminent or exclusive producer of a wide variety of exotic fruits and nuts.

California's great vineyards—in the Napa and Sonoma Valleys, and now more and more in the Salinas Valley near Monterey—produce 85 percent of the U.S.A.'s wine output, a $700-million-a-year business for the state. Wine consumption in America has increased 60 percent just since 1960, five times as fast as the population growth. (The quality is improving through advanced technology. A visiting British wine expert, Hugh Johnson, reported after a 1970 trip that "California is making wine as good as the wine of France. At the peaks not quite so good, but on the average maybe better.")

Technically, the Central Valley is two—the valley of the Sacramento River to the north, of the San Joaquin to the south. Both valleys are served by waters flowing down from the Sierras through the most intricate and extensive irrigation system ever built by man. A major portion of the labyrinth of dams, pumping stations, and canals has been financed by federal dollars through the Central Valley Project, which was first approved as a state project in the 1930s. Among other things, the CVP transfers water from the mountainous upper reach of the Sacramento River Valley to the drier San Joaquin Valley, where the combination of water and high temperatures makes possible a phenomenal growing season of nine to ten months.* Already, farm produc-

---

* The Central Valley Project should not be confused with the subsequently developed California Water Plan to transfer water from the north as far as Los Angeles and San Diego, which will be dis-

tion in the San Joaquin Valley exceeds that of 44 other states, and three of its counties—Fresno, Kern, and Tulare—lead all counties in America. Something over $1 billion has already been invested in CVP, with projected expenditures as high as $4 billion to bring another three million acres of irrigable but still unexploited Central Valley land into production by later in this century. The land will be needed, for freeways and the cannibalization of prime producing farmland for suburban sprawl have taken well over a million acres out of production since World War II, a process that is continuing.

Without the massive technical assistance it has received from the University of California—in development of hybrid strains, fertilizers, mechanical harvesters, pesticides, scientific irrigation, and feeding and extension courses—the state's farm industry would never have attained the heights it now occupies.

Since the days of the gigantic Spanish and Mexican landholdings, most of which fell into Anglo hands after 1848, California has been preeminently a state of big farms. The number of farms has fallen by more than half since 1950 and is expected to drop to 30,000 by 1980; already two-thirds of the production comes from 15 percent of the farms. Big "factory" farm operations are obviously more practical in an economy dependent on massive and expensive irrigation practices, airborne pest control and seeding, and the huge expense of sophisticated mechanical plowing and harvesting equipment. Today millionaire big-city entrepreneurs and giants like the Kern County Land Company, the Di Giorgio Corporation, and Schenley Industries own an ever increasing portion of Central Valley farmland. The trend is toward more and more bigness, and some of the nation's biggest corporations—like Standard Oil, Tenneco, Kaiser Aluminum, and Southern Pacific—have diversified into agriculture. According to writer Nick Kotz, just three corporations—United Brands, Purex, and Bud Antle, a company partly owned by Dow Chemical—already dominate California lettuce production. Tenneco, which had 1970 sales of $2.5 billion, has told its stockholders: "Tenneco's goal in argiculture is integration from the seedling to supermarket." The economic muscle and competitive advantages of such corporations, aided and abetted by favorable tax laws and a U.S. Department of Agriculture friendly to their interests, may spell extinction for most small farms in California and other parts of the nation.

California's big farm landholding interests have for decades been favored by subsidization by state and federal governments alike. A principal reason that the state of California moved so rapidly into vast water projects for irrigation was that the big Central Valley landholders would be ineligible to receive water under federally sponsored irrigation projects, which have a 160-acre limitation for a single owner. (The average farm unit in the Central Valley is close to 1,000 acres.) The landowners made sure that California enacts no such restriction on its own projects. Former U.S. Budget Director Charles L. Schultze wrote in 1968:

---

five acre feet of water; even with California's huge population, nine-tenths of the water use in the state is still for agriculture.
cussed later. It should be borne in mind that producing an average acre of crops on desert land requires

In many parts of Southern California, irrigators pay $2.80 per acre foot for water from federal projects. The value of water for other uses is about $35 per acre foot. A typical 320-acre cotton farm will use about 1,300 acre feet per year. The opportunity cost of the subsidy to such a farm is, therefore, about $42,-000 *per year*. The same farm may grow 450 bales of cotton per year, receiving an average subsidy of $28,000 on its cotton production. The two subsidies combined are worth $70,000 per year. The subsidy cost of placing one low-income family in decent housing averages about $800 per year.

One celebrated California case is that of the San Luis dam and water distribution system in the San Joaquin Valley, authorized by Congress in 1959 at a cost of $480 million. The Nader California report charges that the project was set up to "benefit" only 130 large landowners and corporations that own 83 percent of the land in the area. Land values in the parched territory served by the system rose by $300 an acre, bringing just one company, Southern Pacific, a reported "windfall" of more than $23 million.

Critics in California delight in calling J. G. Boswell of Fresno "the number one welfare recipient." In truth, his farm received in 1969 the largest subsidy of any in the United States—precisely $4,370,657. Of the 25 U.S. farms getting the largest farm payments under cotton, wheat, and feed-grain programs, 14 (including the top eight) were from California.* By contrast, a farm worker in California is ineligible under state law to collect unemployment compensation for those months of the year when he can't get work.

Farm Labor, César Chávez, La Huelga!

Thus we come to the seamy, often shameful underside of Central Valley life: the condition of those who till the fields. Today mechanization is cutting back sharply on the number of field workers required, and a modicum of laws are being enacted to protect them. Fewer are migrants: more are permanent residents of the valley towns. There is a marked difference between the east side of the Central Valley, where family farms predominate (due to cheap water), and the west side where the big farms dominate. But a huge farm labor pool is still required. In 1967, the last year for which full statistics are available, there were 700,000 laborers in California's fields and vineyards, the vast majority working in the Central Valley. Their average annual income for *all* work (both farm and nonfarm) was only $1,709; their living conditions in many places were still reminiscent of what John Steinbeck described in *Grapes of Wrath*.

To offset the farm labor shortage as the Okies drifted off to more lucrative wartime jobs in shipyards and aircraft factories, Congress in 1942 approved the *bracero* program to import temporary Mexican laborers, who came

---

* Profits of the biggest California growers were sure to decline under the 1970 farm bill, which limited individual growers to a subsidy of $55,000 for each of the major crop programs (cotton, wheat, and feed grains). Before the bill, 265 California cotton farmers were making more than the new limit. These big growers have now been forced to lease out their cotton land (with reduced profits) or switch to other crops. But the big landholders have many ways to turn government programs to their benefit. They have been principal beneficiaries of the state's "Open-Space Land Program," which saved Boswell, according to a report of the Public Interest Research Group, $298,300 in taxes in 1970 alone.

by the hundreds of thousands. Many Mexicans, who found low California farm wages opulent by standards in their own country, also stole across the border illegally—the so-called "wetbacks," in honor of the practice of some in swimming or wading across the Rio Grande out of sight of border guards. After the war, the growers' lobbies fought fiercely to retain the *bracero* program while organized labor, frustrated in its earlier attempts to recruit the farm workers into unions, strove to end the program on the grounds that it provided cheap and unfair competition for American workers. Finally, in 1964, Congress killed the *bracero* program; an interim "green card" program to let in smaller numbers of Mexican workers continued for some years.

Even with the *braceros* gone, though, the Mexican-Americans and Filipinos working the Californian fields were earning an average of less than $1,-400 a year, far below the federal poverty level. Wages were often advertised at $1.40 an hour, then reduced to $1.10 when the workers arrived. Work was unavailable several months of the year, and such amenities as overtime pay, paid holidays, vacation, sick leaves, and pensions were virtually unknown. Indiscriminate grower use of highly toxic pesticides led to illness among many farm workers and their children, whom they were often obliged to bring to the fields to work with them. Workers also found themselves at the mercy of the labor contractors, the middlemen between them, and the growers. Less of them than in the past were living in the growers' sterile compounds, but the housing available was often in the category of dirt-floored, tin and tarpaper shanties. No people ever more clearly needed a savior, a Moses to lead them from the wilderness. In 1965, such a man appeared. His name was César Estrada Chávez.

Chávez had been born in 1927 in Yuma, Arizona, but the stability of his early childhood was shattered in 1937 when his father's farm failed and the family took to the road as migrant laborers, following the crops in Arizona and California. The only home César and his four brothers and sisters often knew was a tent or the back seat of the family automobile; education was sporadic, and César made it only through the seventh grade. Later he married, acquired a taste for biography and history, especially of the Mexican people, and began to emerge as a spokesman for his fellow migrant workers in the field.

In 1961, after several years of work with the Los Angeles-based Community Service Organization, Chávez returned to Delano with his wife and eight children to work in the vineyards at $1.25 an hour and to start the long process of community organization that would lead to unionization of farm workers. At that time, he recalled in an interview, he thought it would be "at least 10 years before we had our first contract. But we had one four days short of four years. It was beyond all my wildest expectations." No such prospects for early success were apparent in 1962, however, when he formally organized the National Farm Workers Association. In a battered old station wagon, Chávez drove hundreds of miles through the Central Valley, talking with farm workers. Years later, one of his fervent followers recalled Chávez at that time: "Here was César, burning with a patient fire, poor like us, dark like us, talking quietly, moving people to talk about their problems, attacking the little problems first, and suggesting, always suggesting—never more than that—so-lutions that seemed attainable. We didn't know it until we met him, but he was the leader we had been waiting for." Chávez has been compared with Martin Luther King, a man whom he corresponded with but never met. "Some of the press," he told me, "say our movement is almost like a religion. And we say, well, it's the religion of fair play and justice." The model, of course, is a truly remarkable one in a day when so many, including young militants among Chávez's fellow Chicanos, are prone to often vengeful and spiteful paths of separatism and self-proclaimed radicalism. Chávez comments:

> We consider ourselves, in our own quiet way, to be very radical. It takes a lot of radicalism to be willing to work without a paycheck and it takes quite a bit more to be willing to give up food for 10 days or so and it takes quite a bit to be able to struggle for five years when a lot of people are in doubt whether you're going to win or not. That's the radicalism I think pays off. The desire to get things done is very deep among us, and we're willing to sacrifice and pay the price. We feel the problem is not only a Chicano problem, but a problem of everyone. We're committed to human beings and we don't care what color they are.

Having witnessed the failure of many farm strikes for lack of proper orga-nization, Chávez thought his NFWA should wait several years for a strike or run the risk of being crushed. But in 1965, the previously ineffectual AFL-CIO Agricultural Workers' Organizing Committee made demands of a $1.40-an-hour year-round wage and piece-rate bonuses of the grape growers around Delano, and, when the growers refused to even discuss the matter, called a strike. Some 1,000 workers, mostly Filipino, walked out of the fields. The growers started evicting families, and Chávez immediately offered the strikers the unconditional help of the NFWA. It was a different kind of a strike, and a different kind of a battle, than the growers had ever faced before. At Chávez's insistence, it remained nonviolent (or almost totally so), even when the growers brought in strikebreakers from other localities. And drawing on his contacts from earlier years, Chávez organized broad outside support from mi-nority and antipoverty organizations, clergymen of various faiths (especially the Migrant Ministry of the Northern California Council of Churches), la-bor unions, students, and liberal political leaders. They gathered contribu-tions, sent food, joined picket lines at the vineyards and at the metropolitan headquarters of the big growers.

That the strike would be a long, difficult one could have been predicted from the first, because the growers are closely associated with the long-domi-nant power structure of California, ranging from the big banks and oil com-panies to the Santa Fe Railroad and the ever helpful University of California. In Delano, the local powers were adamantly opposed; Chávez was accused of importing troublemakers, of forcing a union on workers who didn't want one, of having Communist backing.

But Chávez had the right touch of charisma and drama to transform *La Huelga* into *La Causa*. Just six months after the strike had begun, he called a great pilgrimage march, 300 miles from Delano to the steps of the State Cap-itol at Sacramento, every inch by foot. Down the flat, long black ribbon of

Highway 99 marched the farm workers, Chávez's 82-year-old father among them. Chávez decreed it would be a nonsectarian march, and at the forefront went the banner depicting Our Lady of Guadalupe together with a large cross and the Star of David. There were Mexican and American flags, and behind, a dozen brilliant red pennants with the black eagle, symbol of the National Farm Workers Association. Twenty-five days later, on Easter Sunday, the footsore marchers arrived in Sacramento. As they had marched, there had been two great capitulations: Schenley and Di Giorgio. But at Sacramento, Governor Brown was not present. He was spending the weekend at Frank Sinatra's home in Palm Springs.

Support, great and small, poured in—winning for Chávez and the movement press coverage and television exposure worth millions. Once convinced they should visit the valley and view the action first hand at Delano, the most hardened newsmen found themselves turned on and strangely drawn to the movement. United Auto Workers president Walter Reuther came and marched with the strikers through the streets of Delano; later, after Chávez undertook a 25-day fast "as an act of penance, recalling workers to the nonviolent roots of their movement," Senator Robert F. Kennedy came to kneel beside Chávez at the Communion at which he broke his fast. In 1967, the AFL-CIO—which had long been dubious about the wisdom of sinking serious resources into the difficult farm organization field—nevertheless chartered Chávez's group as the United Farm Workers Organizing Committee, merged its own group into it, and dispatched William Kircher, a top organizer, to help Chávez with a $10,000-a-month budget.

At no point was the strike in the fields particularly effective; the labor pool of impoverished migrants the growers could draw on was simply too great. Thus came the boycott of the grapes produced by Joseph Guimarra's 5,000-acre vineyards, which would spread to a general national boycott of all California table grapes after Guimarra started shipping its grapes in the cartons of its competitors. (Guimarra, who came to the U.S. from Southern Europe in the 1920s, built his holdings from scratch and by the late 1960s was California's top grape producer, producing 52 million to 65 million tons of grapes a year. His corporation grossed $5.5 million to $7.5 million. In a 1968 article, labor editor Dick Meister of the San Francisco *Chronicle* reported that "Strikers like to picture Joe Guimarra and his fellow growers as devils. They are not, but they do seem quaintly out of touch with what has been going on beyond the vineyards since they moved into the valley beside the Mexican-Americans three decades ago.")

The national grape boycott eventually became the most effective boycott in American labor history, with all Americans, in effect, taking a stand for or against La Huelga. The boycott was not without its enemies. Governor Reagan called the strike and boycott "immoral" and "attempted blackmail." During the 1968 Presidential campaign, Richard Nixon publicly condemned it and gleefully ate grapes at a public rally in California. Nixon declared that "we have laws on the books to protect workers who wish to organize, a National Labor Relations Board to impartially supervise the election of collective-bargaining agents"—disingenuously failing to mention that federal law specifically exempts farm workers from protection under the National Labor Relations Act. (Ironically, the grape boycott would have been illegal if agricultural interests had not managed to have their industry exempted in the basic labor law of the 1930s.) Now many growers would like to be under NLRA coverage, since it would deprive Chávez of the right to use his favorite and most effective weapon, the secondary boycott, which was made illegal by the 1947 Taft-Hartley Act. Chávez argues that the industrial unions, from the Wagner Act in 1934, developed without the antiboycott restriction until passage of Taft-Hartley. They had real protection from the NLRB in those years, and were thus able to organize their industries, build large memberships, and "stand the unfairness of Taft-Hartley when it came," he maintains. "I want those 12 years too. If you give us Taft-Hartley now, you'll kill us."

The boycott was supported by millions, and in 1970, having lost millions of dollars in income, Guimarra and the other great growers capitulated. In an agreement arranged by a high-level committee of Catholic bishops, the growers agreed to recognize Chávez's union and to a sign a three-year contract, with wages going up to $2.05 an hour by 1972—with a 20¢ bonus for each box of grapes at harvest time. Signing the agreement with Guimarra, Chávez said simply: "This is the beginning of a new day."

The new day promised to have many dimensions. On the union front, it suggested that Chávez's union would be the catalytic force in organizing the farm workers of California, and quite possibly in achieving what had seemed forever impossible in the annals of American unionism—organizing the great army of farm workers across the U.S.A. But it would be a long, difficult struggle. By late 1971, the UFWOC had only 80,000 members in California, and of them, only 30,000 under contract. The organization was also signing up members in other great farm labor states, especially Texas, Florida, Michigan, Oregon, and Washington—but a minuscule percentage, to date, of the 1.5 million farm labor pool. Chávez told me the organization struggle would be "a lifetime process," successful first with the large ranches, much later with the smaller farm operations. Even in the Central Valley, opposition to him remained bitter and obdurate among the growers. Salinas Valley lettuce growers rushed to make labor agreements with the Teamsters lest the detested Chávez organize their fieldhands; Chávez responded by calling a successful strike of the lettuce workers and then ordering a national boycott against all non-UFWOC lettuce from California and Arizona. Then he was jailed for pressing the boycott, and again seemed the martyr as famous people like Coretta King and Ethel Kennedy came to Salinas in his support. In spring 1971, an uneasy truce was reached with the Teamsters which would leave the field workers to Chávez's union and the processing workers to the Teamsters.

Chávez's success had immense implications for the traditionally disjointed, seemingly indifferent Mexican-Americans of the Southwest. *La Causa* could be for them what the garment unions were for the Jews of New York or the railway porters' union for the black bourgeoisie—a solid economic institution representing and fighting for their interests, a point of pride. The Chávez union, related directly to the strong family structure of the Mexican-American and cooperative in its spirit and approach, quickly provided a model too for the Mexicans in the urban Los Angeles setting through their East Los Angeles Community Union. Chávez found a way to make Mexican-Americans proud of their heritage, and he could be called the real father of the Mexican-American civil rights movement. There was doubt whether this soulful, almost mystical man, forever clothed in the simple garb of a field worker, would want to bid for status as a leader of all Mexican-Americans. But of them all, he alone seemed to have the promise and the power.

*   *   *

Before we leave the Central Valley, some concluding notes on its cities. The largest, of course, is Sacramento, the state capital, which started in the Gold Rush days around Sutter's Fort. Now, with government, agribusiness, an inland port, and a vigorous injection of defense-space industries, Sacramento has reached a quarter of a million people (metro area 800,592). Palms, verdant lawns, and colorful flowerbeds surround the glistening wedding-cake-like capitol building, but the city has more than its share of dreary, boxlike government buildings packed with civil servants and computers to manage a complex nation state.

Sacramento's leading newspaper, the McClatchy-owned *Bee*, provides excellent coverage but is liberal-Democratic to a fault; in 1966, for instance, writers were instructed to refer to Reagan in every story as "the Goldwater Republican." The Copley-owned *Union* provides an opposite ideology, but is read by only half as many people.

Miles to the south, approximately halfway between San Francisco and Los Angeles, lies the city of Fresno (pop. 165,972 metro area 413,053), one of the most important centers of agribusiness in the nation. What Fresno has become famed for of late, though, is something altogether different—its handsome downtown mall, stretching six blocks through the center business district, with fountains, cascades, brooks and pools, statuary, a softly ebbing and flowing pavement, islands of trees, light fixtures, small playgrounds, sidewalk cafes, trees, flowers, and shrubs. Architectural critic Wolf Von Eckhardt credits it with being the "most exciting" pedestrian city center this side of the Atlantic.

At the midpoint of the valley lies Stockton (pop. 107,644), which suffers from excessive unemployment, especially in the winter, when the canneries are out of operation, but can boast a bustling port.

Far to the south, not far from Los Angeles, is Bakersfield (pop. 69,515, metro 329,162), center of about a third of California's $1.1 billion annual oil and gas production and hub of a prosperous farm area. The city has a population that ranges from millionaires who support one of California's most prosperous Cadillac agencies to destitute out-of-work Chicanos and blacks living in ramshackle houses on the fringes of the city. The scene is repeated in many towns, large and small, up and down the Central Valley, where the strong Southern roots of the population still influence behavior.

Life and Water in Desert California

A great swath of the Southland, covering practically a quarter of the entire Californian land surface, is harsh, unredeemed desert, a land of stark, treeless mountains, baked flatlands, and an infinity of rock and sand. The geographers define two principal California deserts, though the casual traveler will notice little difference between them—the northern, or higher, desert, called the Mojave, and the southern, lower, and even hotter desert, which is named Colorado after the river on its eastern side. Some half-million visitors a year now make their way to the otherwordly wasteland of Death Valley, renowned for its great wind-riffled sand flows, the dried lake bottom of lacerated salt crystal, brilliantly hued canyons and mountains, and below-sea-level depths.

Since 1939, a principal source of water for Los Angeles and San Diego has been the Colorado River Aqueduct, coursing over the parched Colorado Desert, its passage facilitated by 42 tunnels through the mountains and five great pumping stations. But in 1901, long before the aqueduct to Los Angeles was thought of, the waters of the Colorado were siphoned off into the Imperial Valley, along the Mexican border. The desert began to bloom, but that first effort ended in disaster four years later when spring floods broke out of the canals and poured the entire flow of the Colorado into the valley—thus creating the body of water now known as the Salton Sea. Three decades later, the All-American Canal was built to link, safely, the Colorado with the Imperial Valley. Now one of the most productive farm areas of the country, the hot, sun-baked Imperial Valley—sometimes called the Algiers of the U.S.A.—produces rich crops of melons, tomatoes, carrots, cotton, tangerines, asparagus, lettuce, and sugar beets, some even in the dead of winter, and virtually the total U.S. date corp. Feed crops are growing in importance, providing fodder for a growing number of feed lots. Yet every one of the half-million acres would quickly return to desert dust without irrigation.

The true power in the Imperial Valley is in the hands of the prosperous growers who sit on the board of and control the Imperial Immigration District (IID). There is no more poignant case in America of government subsidy designed to help the "little man"—in this case, the small farmer—being siphoned off to the advantage of the quite rich and very rich. The federal intent in subsidizing the irrigation systems in the Imperial Valley was to encourage small farming; in fact, a key provision of the Reclamation Act of 1902, which has never been repealed, says that no person owning more than 160 acres may receive federally supplied water, and that the owner must reside on or near the land to qualify. But in practice, the IID simply ignored the 160-acre provision; the Interior Department, in a questionable 1933 ruling of the lame duck Hoover Administration, countenanced the violation, and it was not until Stuart Udall was Secretary of the Interior in the 1960s that enforcement was ordered. But the IID stalled, and a federal court case seeking compliance languished in district court for several years and was then decided in favor of the big landowners (whose friends include some of the mighty in both parties, including Governor Reagan, President Nixon, and Senator Tunney, whose old congressional district included the Imperial Valley). The Nixon Administration inexplicably decided not to appeal the case beyond the federal district court level, despite the fundamental issues of law compliance, agrarian democracy, and the use of millions of dollars of taxpayers' money.

Today owners of more than 160 acres control in excess of 50 percent of the irrigated acreage in the Imperial Valley. Two-thirds of the land is owned by absentees, and some holdings are as large as 10,000 acres. Some of the big corporate owners include United Fruit, Purex, Dow Chemical, Tenneco, and the Irvine Land Company. With a pliable local press, the politicians safely in their corner, and the economic muscle on their side, this established order seems, and probably is, totally impregnable. (Not even the Los Angeles *Times* reports fairly or adequately on the land and water issue in the valley, some say because the Chandlers personally own large tracts that benefit from the federal doles.) But there is a gadfly—a valiant, almost pathetic figure who has been fighting the big landowners almost singlehandedly over several years. He is Dr. Ben Yellen, now in his early sixties, a Jewish doctor from Brooklyn who moved to California and runs a small clinic in Brawley where he treats 50 or 60 patients a day, most of them poor Mexican-Americans whom other doctors won't handle. Writer Michael E. Kinsley, who visited Yellen, reports that he sleeps on a cot in his clinic and uses virtually all of his money filing lawsuits against the establishment and issuing periodic mimeographed newsletters clobbering the existing order in Tom Paine-like fashion.

As Yellen sees it, the big owners have perpetrated a massive fraud on the United States and the poorer people of the valley. To their argument that farms as small as 160 acres simply aren't practical because of massive farm machinery investments required, Yellen replies that the irrigated acreage will grow five times as much food as land elsewhere in the U.S., and that a husband and wife, each with 160 acres (which the law permits) "can farm here 320 acres, which is equivalent to 1,600 acres in the rest of the United States." The rich growers, he argues, are being paid huge government subsidies in cheap water * in violation of the law, to farm land on which they don't pay enough taxes, so that they can cultivate crops harvested by Mexican workers imported fraudulently across the border, so that they can be paid huge sums of money by the government not to grow anything at all.

In perennial California style, bright new possibilities for the Imperial Valley always seem to be right around the corner. In 1970, scientists of the University of California at Riverside announced they had discovered seven exploitable geothermal fields in the Imperial Valley, estimated to have the potential to produce 20,000 megawatts of power and up to seven million acre-feet of distilled water annually for up to three centuries. The implications for the Southwest are immense. The electric power generation, involving no

* The IID uses 2.8 million acre feet of water each year, 70 percent of the Colorado River water allotted to California. The amount is almost twice the water consumption of the city of New York, sold at but a fraction of cost.

air pollution, would be 15 times that of the Hoover Dam, or by another estimate, enough to provide electrical power to run 33 cities the size of San Francisco for a century. The water flow might make the Imperial Valley virtually self-sufficient in irrigating its 400,000 acres of farmland, thus freeing vast quantities of Colorado River water for Southern California or parched Arizona. Yet despite these immense stakes, the U.S. is far behind Mexico in building of pilot power generation stations to exploit the geothermal fields, despite one PG & E station north of San Francisco. And the state of California has refused to invest any of its own funds in a program which might provide the power and the water to make Southern California a viable place to live in future times.

A final note before we leave the never-never world of the Imperial Valley. Its largest city, El Centro (19,272), claims to be the biggest settlement below sea level in this hemisphere; the lowest city of all in the valley, Calipatria (1,824), runs colored lights up a 184-foot flagpole at Christmastime. The top is precisely at sea level.

Miles to the northwest lies the resort of Palm Springs (20,936), set on the desert floor in the lee of Mt. San Jacinto, the steepest mountain escarpment (10,831 feet) in the U.S.A. Conspicuous consumption reaches rare heights in this town. Famous movie stars and big business moguls, a generation of the proudful self-made, congregate here in half-million-dollar houses, patronize the expensive golf clubs, and drive the most luxurious autos. Former President Eisenhower, drawn by the fabulous winter golfing rather than the rest of the glitter, was probably the most modest resident of recent times.

Nowhere is the swimming pool more rampant; there are some 4,000 in Palm Springs, some even designed, Stephen Birmingham notes in *The Right People*, in the monogram form of the owner with whirlpools. Bikini-clad dowagers bask in the sun like fat lizards with no more serious concern than the caloric count; the intellectual interests of the males are said to be truncated at the level of the dollar.

Like its Los Angeles parent, Palm Springs is low and slung-out; a shadow law prohibits any building in the shadow of another. By day, the city can scarcely be distinguished from the palmier shopping centers of the Los Angeles area; by night, amber floodlights playing on the palms create an atmosphere of warmth and opulence contrasted with the backdrop of gaunt mountains etched against the dark purple desert sky.

But this is not exclusively a town of the very rich, gathered in their own gentile and Jewish ghettos. The well-to-do must share the scene with Mexicans and blacks, crowded into an appalling slum called Section 14, and with the remarkably fortunate Agua Caliente Indians. Less than 100 in number, the Indians own huge sections of land throughout the city which they lease out to palefaces for about $860,000 a year. Some of America's wealthiest Indians live here, but others, unfortunate enough to hold undesirable tracts of land, are virtually penniless. The Riverside *Press-Enterprise* won a Pulitzer Prize for its exposé on the misuse of some of the lands supposedly reserved for the Indians at Palm Springs.

II. THE BAY AREA

San Francisco: City and Skyline

San Francisco put on a show for me. I saw her across the bay, from the great road that bypasses Sausalito and enters the Golden Gate Bridge. The afternoon sun painted her white and gold—rising on her hills like a noble city in a happy dream. A city on hills has it over flat-land places. New York makes its own hills with craning buildings, but this gold and white acropolis rising wave on wave against the blue of the Pacific sky was a stunning thing, a painted thing like a picture of a medieval Italian city which can never have existed. . . .

Over the green higher hills to the south, the evening fog rolled like herds of sheep coming to cote in the golden city. I've never seen her more lovely. When I was a child and we were going to the City, I couldn't sleep for several nights before, out of bursting excitement. She leaves a mark.

—John Steinbeck, in Travels With Charley

WHEN THE GALLUP POLL IN 1969 asked Americans what city they would most like to live in, San Francisco won hands down, by a 2–1 margin over its closest rival.* "I like the hills, the ocean and the people," said a 28-year-old technician from Akron, Ohio. "San Francisco's got something all its own."

Clearly, it has. I saw it for the first time myself from the Golden Gate on a summer afternoon some 25 years ago, and in my own unformed, boyish way had many of the same feelings John Steinbeck recorded. The red-orange lines of that high, daring bridge, the sparkling bay to one side, the fog-banked ocean to the other, the rows of chalk-white buildings running uphill and down— who can forget them? Walk through San Francisco today, and you find streets filled with life at almost every hour of the day, from center city to the neigh-

---

* The runners-up in the 1969 survey were Los Angeles, Miami, Denver, New York City, Phoenix, San Diego, Chicago, Honolulu, and Portland, Oregon—in that order. Interesting omissions, in this writer's opinion: Boston, Seattle, New Orleans, Atlanta.

borhoods. Most colorful of all is Union Square, faced by the regal old St. Francis Hotel, jammed with secretaries and shoppers, demonstrators and businessmen, walking, sunning, sprawling on the grass, singing songs, playing music, a microcosm of San Francisco. If there is an urban glory in America, here it is.

Much of San Francisco's charm lies in its geographic compactness (46.6 square miles), the water on three sides, the 40-odd hills, the constantly shifting panoramas of hillcrest, blue ocean and bridge, spots of fog, gargoyled houses and towers—a city fashioned to a human scale. In a single morning or afternoon, the walker can stroll from the downtown financial district to Union Square to Chinatown, check the North Beach, swing onto a cable car and wind up at Fisherman's Wharf for a seafood delicacy, and then browse about new Ghiradelli Square (a pleasing complex of ships, restaurants, fountains, and lights fashioned out of the buildings of an old chocolate and spice factory). Many remember San Francisco as the city where you could sit in the lounge at the Top of the Mark at day's end and see the city spread before you, the Bay Bridge arching gracefully across to the East Bay, ships to and from the Orient steaming under the Golden Gate, twilight azure giving way to a million night lights.

Such a city, certainly, needs no massive urban facelifting to make it livable. Its people love it as it is. Sometimes they have risen up to save what gives it character. In the 1940s, a single person, one Mrs. Klussmann, organized a great petition drive to save those dangerous, silly, delightful cable cars—and won. In 1958, a great "freeway revolt" erupted against the ugly double-decked superhighway being built along the Embarcadero. The road was cutting across the face of the venerable Ferry Building and blocking the view to the bay; in an historic bow to people interests, the freeway builders had to stop in midcourse, and today the road ends like a knife-cut where they stopped. Several years later, a freeway route that would have cut through part of Golden Gate Park was successfully blocked.

But inexorable physical change is pressing in on San Francisco, threatening what some call "Manhattanization"—the brutalization of its uniquely delicate skyline with sterile, forbidding monuments of glass and steel twice as high as anything that preceded them and totally out of scale with the existing hills and city setting. The most alarming of these was what Nicholas Van Hoffman calls "the Bank of America's sinister black and brown tower which rises up like an emblem of corporate insensitivity, giving the finger to the city's people." The 52-story building was the highest West of the Mississippi, and its darkness contrasted unpleasantly with San Francisco's traditional pattern of white, slim structures. In 1960, the last obstacles were cleared for the Transamerica Corporation to build an 835-foot, spire-surmounted, pyramidal office building on Montgomery Street, the "Wall Street of the West." Such monsters may be welcomed in a flat, plains city like Chicago, fulfilling that city's historic role as an architectural experiment station; in a delicate, hilly city like San Francisco, the result can be disastrous.

During the 1960s, 21 high-rise buildings sprouted in the heart of the city, and 23 more are scheduled for completion by 1975. From the Top of the Mark and other promontories of the city, much of the Bay view is already irremediably blanked out. But San Franciscans are unwilling to accept the theory that they have passed the fail-safe point on the road to Manhattanization. In 1970, public protest thwarted the proposal of U.S. Steel to build a 550-foot office building and commercial structure on public land at the waterfront, a project critics said would be a crass exploitation of a precious community resource—the view of their bay, the Ferry Building, and the Bay Bridge Tower.

Most of the startling new high-rises have gone up in the Montgomery Street–Market Street financial district. Market Street itself, an old commercial thoroughfare, is being made into more of a promenade than a boulevard, with broad walks, sycamore trees, benches, and flowers.

In a classic case of urban renewal equaling Negro removal, large swaths of the Western Addition—a bay-windowed, gingerbread-trimmed area of Victorian homes miraculously saved from the fire that came with the 1906 earthquake—have been levelled for new apartment houses, most occupied by middle- and upper-class whites. One of the positive results was the new Japanese Cultural and Trade Center, a complex of restaurants, shops, and a hotel which has grown as a tourist attraction. But community groups in the still-standing sections of the Western Addition are fighting further encroachment by the developers' bulldozers. One of San Francisco's most severe problems is the flight of young people with children from the city. This is more acute in San Francisco than some other towns because the city is so small that no one has to live there to work there. In a part of America where rapid population growth has been the norm, San Francisco has slipped in population by 59,683 people in the last two decades (to 715,674 in 1970). It is now 13th largest in population among U.S. cities.

San Francisco: Mood and Life Style

The diversity of this city of light and color has attracted, from others, words like these: Mediterranean, Renaissance, Athens of America, a place of *joie de vivre*, elegant, witty. San Francisco has a lovely sense of the absurd, preserved in the artful foolishness of old Victorian houses and the ding-dong cable cars, sure cures for depression. It is also like an elegant woman, with an indefinable mystique all its own. As Herbert Gold wrote, it "is still the great city of America where a walker can experience nostalgia for the place while he is still there—a little, even a lot, like the *nostalgie de Paris*."

Among other things, San Francisco also has the best little restaurants, in every ethnic variety imaginable, of any American city except, of course, New York. Its stores, both big and small, are often a joy and delight. It also has the highest suicide rate in the country—two and a half times the national average.

These days, the Golden Gate Bridge is the most celebrated place in the city to commit suicide; every pedestrian is watched by closed circuit television, and a suicide patrol car is on hand to question those who act suspiciously. At least 370 men and women have taken the leap from the Golden Gate, not counting those whose bodies were swept out to sea and never found. But the fact is that less than 5 percent of San Francisco's suicides are from the bridge; most are by swallowing pills, and there is a suspicion that the especially alert city coroner's office, which conducts frequent autopsies in suspicious cases, may identify suicides that would be certified as deaths from natural causes in other cities. The suicide rate is particularly high among the elderly, the homosexual, and the otherwise lonely. Two-thirds of the city's people are single, divorced, or widowed. And the city is also number one in the U.S.A. in per capita consumption of alcohol.

But what is bane may also be blessing. Where else on the North American continent, one may ask, can one find such a fantastic mix of people—singles and oldsters, Caucasian and Oriental, Negro and Mexican, Wasp and old-line Catholic ethnic, and every deviant life style imaginable—*all living together in relative peace?* In what other city could one imagine candidates for public office making an open pitch for the homosexual vote, estimated at 90,000? Where else could I have found a police chief who, with an amused wave of his hand, said: "Sure, we've got our problems with homosexuals, transsexuals, and bisexuals, and all the rest of 'em. You name it and we have it in San Francisco. But it's still one of the great, storied cities of the world."

"The culture of civility," Howard Becker and Irving Horowitz suggested in a 1970 article in *Trans-action*, sets San Francisco apart from its sister cities of the continent. The mix of undigested ethnic minorities, colonies, and societies, they say, creates "a mosaic of life styles, the very difference of whose sight and smell give pleasure." Natives of San Francisco "enjoy the presence of hippies and take tourists to see their areas, just as they take them to see the gay area of Polk Street. Deviance, like difference, is a civic resource, enjoyed by tourist and resident alike." Admittedly, this flies in the face of conventional reasoning that when one sees normally proscribed behavior, there is worse to come. But in the free atmosphere of San Francisco, "we see more clearly and believe more deeply that hippies or homosexuals are not dangerous when we confront them on the street day after day or live alongside them and realize that beard plus long hair does not equal a drug-crazed maniac." And the deviants, when they discover via the culture of civility that they are not regarded as an unfortunate excrescence to be suppressed by police and other authorities, "sink roots like more conventional citizens: find jobs, buy houses, make friends, vote and take part in political activities and all the other things that solid citizens do."

What gives rise to a culture of civility? Authors Becker and Horowitz name these possibilities: San Francisco has a Latin heritage and has always been a seaport that tolerates the vice sailors seek out. Explosive growth at the time of the Gold Rush inhibited conventional social controls. Ethnic minorities, especially the Chinese, were ceded the right to engage in activities like prostitution and gambling. An image of wickedness and high living helps draw tourists, and some minor downtown streets are even named for famous madames of the Gold Rush era. And "a major potential source of repressive action—the working class—is in San Francisco more libertarian and politically sophisticated than one might expect. Harry Bridges' Longshoremen act as bellwethers." * San Francisco is one of the few large American cities ever to experience a general strike; the memory lingers, and workingmen remember the policeman may not be their friend. There is a left-wing, honest cast to trade unionism. And finally, San Francisco's high complement of single people worry a lot less than married ones about what public deviance may do to children.

All of this is not to suggest that the square community in San Francisco does not, on occasion, move to stamp out certain vices or to limit others. When the flower children's dream community of Haight-Ashbury turned into a crashpad ghetto of LSD and speed use (as opposed to mere marijuana) in 1967, the city moved in with the police tactical squad and the city health department orders. Later, there was a crackdown on the users and purveyors of methedrine and other narcotics thought to result in violence and crime. When the "Third World Liberation Front" at San Francisco State College tried in 1968–69 to shut the university down unless it yielded to their 15 "nonnegotiable demands," the police intervened and were kept on campus by the new president, S. I. Hayakawa, until permanent order was restored.

San Francisco police, in their heart of hearts, differ little from their compatriots in cities across the U.S.A. I spent an evening cruising the city streets with two of their inspectors, hearing opinions such as this: "A police officer's duty has always been to enforce the law and keep the peace. Now they're trying to turn us into social workers, counseling and tutoring—a misuse." Or about the suggestion that police should be more educated and professional: "Look at some of the morons going to the universities; is that what education means? They should learn to obey the law first."

And all the glamour notwithstanding, San Francisco's police have a lot to worry about. Six of their number were gunned down in the streets between 1967 and 1971. Counting the suburban area, San Francisco has the highest crime rate of any city—bar none—in the U.S.A. FBI figures for 1969, for instance, showed a crime index of 5,441 incidents per 100,000 population in San Francisco. New York City had 4,731, Washington 4,019, and Chicago 2,680. (In large measure, high crime rates correlate with high population mobility. Where less of the population lives in close-knit neighborhoods, there may be an open, free, tolerant city atmosphere. But with everyone an island unto himself, it is easier for crime to flourish.)

The story of San Francisco's pioneering in the new and open life style of our times began, some think, with the arrival on the North Beach of Jack Kerouac and his unbarbered street saints in the 1950s. The bohemian-beatniks first encamped on the North Beach, but, eventually, rising rents, throngs of tourists, and some degree of police harassment triggered a move to the Haight-

---

* The West Coast Longshoremen, economically vigorous, intellectually strong, long past their days of alleged Communist involvement, are San Francisco's most influential union now.

Ashbury district. The colony at first went largely unnoticed because its members preferred to sedate themselves on nothing more unconventional than alcohol and marijuana, their preoccupation was with art, and most lived as couples or alone. The life style was free, joyous, and, in its own way, talking sensitively to America. But all this changed drastically in 1964 "with the popular acceptance of mescaline, LSD and other hallucinogens and the advent of the Ginsberg-Leary-Kesey nomadic, passive, communal electric and acid-oriented life style," according to a *Trans-action* study. Rock groups began to prepare what would soon be known as the "San Francisco sound."

In 1966, a Trips Festival was hosted at Longshoreman's Hall by Ken Kesey. The attendance figure was 15,000, and the word "hippie" was born. A year later, the new community staged a Human Be-In for 20,000 on the polo fields of Golden Gate Park; the movement of the hippie flower people was now a familiar one in the national media. The publicity may have been its undoing, for thousands of young people from California and across the country poured in, and soon the Haight was so crowded that a new living unit—the crash pad—emerged. Hundreds suffered frightening hallucinogenic drug reactions, and in the unsanitary, crowded environment, infectious diseases abounded—influenza, streptococcal pharyngitis, hepatitis, genitourinary-tract infections, and venereal disease. A free medical center, set up with volunteer doctors and helpers, opened up in Haight-Asbury and fought valiantly to help kids coming off bad trips and to stem the disease rate. But with the city health department's refusal of serious help—and even harassment, in contrast to the customary tolerance of the city government—the problem proved beyond manageable proportions. Gradually all but the most unredeemed hard drug users fled the Haight, its days of flowers and love long past.

The way of life born in the halcyon days of Haight-Ashbury lives on, reflected in virtually every corner of America, the expression still most intense in Northern California. Its components are radical political action (descending from what happened at Berkeley in 1964), continued free drug use, principally of marijuana; sexual freedom and experimentation; and a modern-day revival of what some religious groups had experimented with in the past century —the expanded family and commune. Enlarging on this theme, young Richard Atcheson writes:

Although Ken Kesey's Merry Pranksters exist today only in Tom Wolfe's brilliant evocation of them, *The Electric Kool-aid Test,* the sort of tribal life they evolved has fired the imagination of many Californians, young and old, drug users and not. Most of the famous San Francisco rock groups are communal, and tribalization has come to the Bay area in an amazing number of forms. In many cases, the tribe may consist only of three people or two couples, and their children, bound together in loose economic ties or in thoroughgoing, total communality. There are tribes of single people, all straight, all gay, and even cross-sexual. . . .

Basically, the dropout economy—or the tribal society, as insiders call it— runs on a combination of odd-jobbing, crafts, marijuana dealing, sharing, trading, scrounging, welfare and unemployment checks and contributions from parents.

San Francisco: Society, Culture, Counterculture, Press, and TV

San Francisco has its Social Establishment, a modern gentility descended in large measure from the rough-hewn capitalists of the Gold Rush and railroad-building eras; there are even a select few whose families came *before* 1849. Social arbiter Stephen Birmingham lists eight of the 19th-century names as the core of the present-day San Francisco *Social Register*—Crocker, Huntington, Stanford, Hopkins, Flood, Fair, Mackay, O'Brien; then he adds a group whose money comes from only more slightly recent mercantile, banking, and shipping fortunes, and a number of wealthy Jewish families, well accepted in their cosmopolitan city. High-society life revolves around institutions and events like the "Monday lunch" in the St. Francis Hotel's Mural Room; the opening of the San Francisco Opera; traditional old clubs like the Pacific Union, the Burlingame, and the Bohemian; and the still-by-invitation-only Debutante Cotillion. The disdain with which the San Francisco blue-bloods regard the upstart Society of the California Southland has, of course, no bounds. In fact, there is a marked provincialism to San Francisco and a closed character to its old society and highest business positions which explains why many Californians are much less enthusiastic about the city than eastern and foreign visitors. An ambitious young man can "make it" much faster in the go-go world of Southern California, which may be one reason that so many more of them have chosen to live there.

In almost narcissistic measure, San Francisco prides itself on the brilliance of its arts. "I'm a nut on culture," Mayor Joseph Alioto effuses: "I think cities have souls. There's a special uniqueness to San Francisco. We spend public money on our Opera, and it's second only to the Met. We have a great Symphony Orchestra and Ballet and American Conservatory Theatre . . ." But the base of support may not be as wide as it seems; much of the city's cultural life has been sustained by a relatively narrow group of brilliant Jews plus Italians interested in music. Los Angeles has certainly done much more in recent times. Even some of San Francisco's own accuse it of being too self-contented, of having only passable opera and symphony. Writes San Franciscan author Herbert Gold: "The theater is as bad as New York's, but there is less of it. The three scattered major museums add up to less than Cleveland's magnificent art institute, nor does the music equal Cleveland's."

Of the city that fostered Mark Twain, Ambrose Bierce, and Bret Harte, Gold says: "Maybe the major arts are literature, painting, sculpture, and music. Maybe some minor knockoffs of the major arts are posters, street and improvisational theater, happenings and the sound of rock. Maybe San Francisco majors in the minors."

The literary flames have never been extinguished in the Bay Area, a tradition carried on today by countless starving young poets and by writers of substance including the likes of Herbert Gold and Wallace Stegner, Barnaby

Conrad, Paul Jacobs, and Jessica Mitford. North Beach is a gaudy carnival for tourists by night but still a light-hearted bohemia with film-makers, Hare Krishna beggars, poets, runaway kids, and local Italians and Chinese thronging the street by day; here, at the flowery bower of the Minimum Daily Requirement Cafe, the artists and literati gather with regularity, finding comfort in their numbers. Bookstores abound, as do small presses like City Lights, the Four Seasons Foundation, and the Grabhorn Press. America's greatest poster-makers—Satty and Mouse and Wes Wilson—work around the Bay; so do underground figures making films that range from the political to the pornographic. Dance troupes and little theaters keep emerging and dying. There is even guerrilla park theater under R. G. Davis' San Francisco Mime Troupe, which adapts classical comedies to local themes and goes on, usually free, with masks and rock improvisations to audiences of enraptured children and adults—by Gold's account—"grooving in the open air." The amplified joyrock of the San Francisco sound offers such as the Jefferson Airplane, the Grateful Dead, the Quicksilver Messenger Service, and, until her early death by drugs in 1970, Janis Joplin.

As for the press, it goes without saying that the Bay Area has more than its share of underground papers—the San Francisco *Oracle, Good Times*, the Berkeley *Barb* and its competitive offspring, the *Tribe* (published, literally, by a tribe of one-time *Barb* reporters who objected when publisher Max Sherr refused to share the wealth), and *Dock of the Bay*.

But for several years, San Francisans have not needed to look to the underground press for counsel about the world of counterculture and sympathy for new life styles. They have found it right there on the front page of the once rather staid and responsible San Francisco *Chronicle*. One young *Chronicle* reporter is said to have boasted: "If there was a wholesale pot bust in San Francisco tomorrow, 80 percent of the city-side reporters and copy-desk would be in jail." One of its editors called the paper's formula one of "fact, truth and fun"; executive editor Scott Newhall, who managed the transformation of the *Chronicle* between 1962 and 1971, once likened the front page to a circus barker saying, "Hurry, hurry, hurry, the girls are just about to take off their clothes." Once lured inside, the reader, in theory, gets serious coverage. But as the *Columbia Journalism Review* reported in 1969, what one got "often seemed to add up to little more than a ton of feathers"—even if spiced with the writings of two of America's cleverest newspaper columnists, Herb Caen and political satirist Art Hoppe. The political tone is superficially liberal, but two-minute stories, breezy headlines, and lots of sex are (after Caen and Hoppe) what most readers remember.

The evening *Examiner*, part of the Hearst chain, has a totally different editorial face, condemning almost everything associated with youth culture, hippies, drugs, and deviance. Its quality is not outstanding. In fact, the truth is that urbane, cosmopolitan San Francisco, this great world city, has no newspaper of stature.

San Francisco also has a peppery independent monthly, the *Bay Guardian*, edited by Bruce Brugmann, one of America's most skillful muckrakers.

One San Francisco television station gets practically all kudos, no brick bats. It is KQED, a public broadcaster supported in major part by 42,000 audience-members who annually pay from $14.50 to $100. Reaching a maximum audience of 400,000, the station pioneered in such new approaches to television news as its "Newsroom" program, in which expert journalists sit around a U-shaped table to report on and discuss the day's events—a device later copied widely by other noncommercial stations. KQED has received several broadcasting industry awards and was praised in the Columbia University *Survey of Broadcast Journalism* for having done the most extensive job of local coverage in the 1968 election of any station in the U.S.

San Francisco: Economics, Government, Minorities

San Francisco, it has been said, has two establishments—a Big Establishment peopled by industrialists and financiers whose interests run beyond the Bay Area to the nation and the world, and a Small Establishment of those whose activities are almost exclusively city or at most Bay Area–oriented. Among the latter are the multitudinous ethnic group leaders, and, of course, the politicians.

First a word on the Big Establishment. Trading off the initial advantages of its port and the Gold Rush, San Francisco for more than a century has been a great commercial, banking and managerial center. "We're the shipping, financial, and great headquarters city of the West—the place where the boards of directors, the chairmen, the underwriters, the big money are to be found, the place where the big decisions are made," an official of Pacific Gas & Electric, itself headquartered in San Francisco, told me. The statement ignores the strong shift of headquarters cities to Los Angeles, noted throughout the 1960s. By 1970, metropolitan Los Angeles had 120 headquarters offices of California's largest businesses, San Francisco and nearby Bay Area cities only 61.

Nevertheless, San Francisco—by the standards of any other American city —must be considered a financial giant. Its annual bank clearings rank sixth among all cities of the nation. Here is the home office of the Bank of America, the world's largest nongovernmental bank, with assets of $25 billion and almost 1,000 branches in the state of California, plus many overseas.

Except for the huge corporate complexes and its port, the city of San Francisco has little industry-related activity; one good reason is that its land area is simply too limited. Together with other Bay Area cities, the port leads the West Coast in general cargo shipping; oil cargoes make Los Angeles–Long Beach greater in overall tonnage. The suburbs are the locale of the Bay Area's manufacturing growth; just in the peninsular suburbs south of the city, for instance, 200 electronics firms have set up plants, including national leaders like IBM, ITT, Ampex, Western Electric, Raytheon, Remington Rand, Sylvania, Sperry-Rand, Zenith, Motorola, Philco, and General Electric.

The visible involvement in city politics of San Francisco's corporate giants, their interests focused out into the state and nation, is not great. There is, however, a fairly active chamber of commerce which works behind the scenes in city elections, reflecting big business interests. The real estate operators, benefiting from the great construction boom, are also very powerful beneath the surface, and the thriving tourist industry plays an important role. Such interests share influence (in differing coalitions, dependent on the issue) with the old propertied class and Brahmin Jews (Zellerbachs, Magnins, and Swigs), the unions, and the assorted ethnics who sturdily resist amalgamation. There are the Chinese in their own great Chinatown; Japanese in the Western Addition; Italians in North Beach, Russians and Poles along Clement Street; German, Irish, and Mexicans in the Mission; and blacks in the Fillmore and Hunters Point districts—the most polyglot, unassimilated assortment of nationalities and races in California. The Italians and Orientals have made perhaps the deepest imprint on San Francisco's style and cultural life, but the Irish have traditionally been more successful politicians. Mayor Alioto, an Italian elected in 1967, won office—like every other successful San Francisco politician—by assiduous courting of the whole panoply of ethnic groups.

In state and national politics, San Francisco is a liberal bastion and strongly Democratic. The two Burton brothers—Congressman Phillip Burton and state Assemblyman John L. Burton—have long been the acknowledged leaders of the Democratic left wing, one of the few radical city political families in the nation. (A third brother, Robert, teaches English to the convicts at San Quentin.) San Francisco's powerful labor unions, traditionally in the same mold, have been swinging some to the right in recent years in a fit of enthusiasm over the jobs generated by all the new downtown construction. Municipal politics are officially nonpartisan and hard for an outsider to follow; in 1967, for instance, Alioto incurred the disafavor of the Burtons but won election by coalescing the conservative and usually more affluent Irish, the labor unions, upper-middle-class intellectuals, and many blacks whom he was able to lure away from his more liberal opponent. George Christopher, the energetic mayor of the late '50s and early '60s, was a Republican, but of such liberal-to-moderate image that he could peel away thousands of normally Democratic votes.

Met privately or seen in public, San Francisco's Alioto almost overwhelms the beholder with his rapid-talking eloquence, enthusiasm, and imagination. The son of an immigrant Sicilian fisherman, he made his fortune as an aggressive attorney, building the country's largest civil antitrust practice. He was also active in business and banking. By the late 1960s, by Alioto's own acknowledgement, he was "bored with making money." When the man whose mayoralty campaign he was managing suddenly died of a heart attack, Alioto jumped in and won in a whirlwind 56-day campaign. At his inaugural, he played the violin and quoted Jeremy Bentham, Heraclitus, Edmund Burke, Matthew Arnold, Will Irwin, and Gertrude Atherton in an address which called for a pulling together of San Francisco's disparate ethnic groups and an effort to correct the sad living conditions of the Negro ghetto.

Early in his mayoralty term, Alioto helped settle newspaper and symphony strikes, and tried to alleviate the financial pinch on City Hall through new business levies and a commuters' tax. He took a stiff line with the Black Panthers—whom he calls "a bunch of cons, ex-cons, narcotics and gun pushers who not only practice violence but exhort children to violence." But Alioto also met frequently with other young black militants, trying to foster programs that would give them, as he described it to me, "some status, credentials, position in their own community. We couldn't have taken on the Panthers if we didn't work with the young, nonviolent militants."

With his persuasive style and successful mixture of rapping with minorities while suppressing violence, Alioto soon drew national attention and was actually given serious consideration as Hubert Humphrey's Vice Presidential running mate on the 1968 Democratic ticket. He was considered a strong early contender for the 1970 Democratic gubernatorial nomination. And he might well have been nominated, and conceivably have been elected, if it had not been for a September 1969 article in *Look* accusing him of being "enmeshed in a web of alliances with at least six leaders of La Cosa Nostra." Alioto responded with a $12.5 million libel suit, and a first trial, in which careful observers believe *Look* failed to substantiate its charges well, ended in a hung jury. In 1971 an even more serious blow fell. A federal grand jury in Seattle indicted Alioto on nine counts of bribery, conspiracy, and mail fraud. The indictment was based on the way Alioto, as a private attorney in early 1960s, had shared with John O'Connell (then the Democratic attorney general of Washington state) some $925,000 of a $2.3 million fee Alioto received for successfully suing, on Washington's behalf, electrical equipment manufacturers who had overcharged the state. Alioto charged the indictment was "a 14-karat fake" initiated by a Republican-run Justice Department to harass a popular Democratic mayor up for reelection. The scandals did not, as many expected, mark Alioto with a political death certificate; in fact he charged to a clear-cut victory in November 1971, carrying 37.7 percent of the vote in a field of 11 candidates. In the same election, a ballot proposition to ban all new buildings over six stories was overwhelmingly rejected.

San Francisco now seems to be shifting from a Wasp-Catholic citadel into a heavy minority city, particularly yellow, black, and brown (Mexican and Central American).* And as more and more middle-class whites depart for the suburbs, the city's societal mix is more and more one of the very rich and the welfare poor. Ethnic conflicts seem to escalate, with militants gaining more and more powerful voices. The housing shortage (in a city with less than a 1-percent vacancy rate) gets worse and the tax load heavier—the typical ailments of almost every great American city today.

Conditions remain deplorable among the two minority groups now strongest and fastest-growing in San Francisco—Negroes and Chinese. The blacks are crowded into the shabby inner-city Fillmore district and into Hunters Point, a depressed and isolated shantytown of "temporary" World War II housing on the southeastern edge of the city. In 1940, there were 4,000 Ne-

* In 1970, Orientals were 13.5 percent of the city population, blacks 13.4 percent. California, of course, has more people of oriental ancestry than any other state: 170,131 Chinese, 213,280 Japanese, and 138,859 Filipinos in the latest Census.

groes in San Francisco; in 1970, 96,078. The familiar litany of black ghettos, ranging from broken families and menial jobs to police harassment, are evident. (A hard-working police community relations unit has had only moderate success. In 1969, blacks still numbered only 4.5 percent of the police force. But the newly-formed "Officers for Justice" was developing into probably the most militant and political of the nascent black police officer associations around the U.S.) In 1966, San Francisco had its own black riot at Hunters Point; the damage and bloodshed were minor compared to Watts, but the pervasive despair of ghetto residents which caused it was just the same.

Chinatown—America's greatest Oriental population concentration and oldest ghetto—lies squeezed into 42 square blocks of land between elegant Nob Hill and Montgomery Street.* Tourists throng Grant Avenue, the main drag, packed with colorful curio shops, banks, and savings and loan associations, tile fronts, bright signs and colors of gold and turquoise, yellow and red. There are some 80 restaurants and numerous food import stores selling everything from quail eggs, squid and shark fins to bamboo shoots, dry fungus, rice, and tea. Daily Chinese newspapers flourish, along with Chinese movies, Chinese radio stations, and Chinatown's own telephone exchange (in a pagoda on Washington Street). Chinatown also has its own unofficial government—the Chinese Consolidated Benevolent Association. Better known as the Six Companies, this is an institution complex, obscure, and still powerful, though not as powerful as it once was, since Chinese youth now seeks its own way and rejects a feudalistic structure that leaves all decisions to an aged elite. The Six Companies still seek to represent the Chinese to the white world and to function as a court in disputes between district or family groups.

The old-time image of the coolie, the shuffling Chinese houseboy, and the corrupt opium den having dissipated, most Americans in modern times have regarded the Chinese in their midst as hard-working, frugal, and the most uncomplaining ingredient of the melting pot. For the thousands of Chinese who have moved out into the greater society, landing good jobs and living in comfortable communities, the middle-class stereotype is true. For most of Chinatown's people, it is highly misleading. By any normal standards, Chinatown is a slum—perhaps the most or only glamorous slum in America, but still a slum:

▪ Three-quarters of the families earn less than $6,000 a year, one-third are below the federal poverty level.

▪ The 1969 unemployment rate was 12.8 percent, versus 6.7 percent for San Francisco and 3.9 percent for the country as a whole. Workers are often so desperate for work that they will stay on the job 10 hours a day, seven days a week, and not complain for fear of being blackballed.

▪ The population density ranges up to 231 people per acre, several times the city average. (In all, the city has 58,696 Chinese people.)

▪ Of the housing, 51 percent is substandard; 60 percent of the families share a bathroom with another or have none at all.

* Many of the specifics of this account are from an article, "San Francisco's Chinatown," by Mary Ellen Leary, *Atlantic Monthly,* March 1970, as well as other sources cited in the bibliography to this book.

- In the Chinatown "core" area, median schooling is 1.7 years; in surrounding "greater" Chinatown, the level is 8 years—versus 12 years for the city as a whole. (Yet in 1971, when citywide school busing was ordered, Chinese parents were strongly opposed, fearing a disruption in community life if their children no longer received a unique education in Chinese culture.)
- The number of people needing medical care—but unable to afford it— is 16,000. The tuberculosis rate is three times that of Caucasians in the city. The suicide rate is far above the already-spectacular city rate.
- In crowded sewing-factory sweatshops, 3,000 seamstresses produce garments for major American firms on a piece-rate basis, sometimes earning only half California's $1.65 minimum wage. They lack all medical, health, vacation, overtime, or sick-pay benefits.

All of these problems are being aggravated by a heavy influx of new Chinese immigrants, the great bulk of whom speak no English, feel frightened and insecure in their new country, and almost inevitably head for the seeming protection of the Chinatown ghetto. The Chinese exclusion laws, enacted in 1882 on a wave of fear about the "yellow peril," were first modified in 1943, further liberalized under the terms of the 1952 McCarran-Walter Act, and substantially removed by abolition of the old national origin quota system in 1965. Now up to 20,000 Chinese may enter the U.S., and the city of San Francisco estimates it is getting as many as 8,000 a year.*

Many of the immigrants are teenagers whose language problem makes them high-school dropouts and unemployables. At the same time, many of the more intelligent young Chinese have begun to challenge the family-based, hierarchical authority imposed on them by the old Chinatown power structure. Petty criminal gangs and a rise in individual acts of delinquency began to appear by the early 1960s; by the latter part of the decade, the hostility of youth to the system was coalescing into a movement of ideological proportions. Militant young "Red Guards" adopted a platform and tactics almost identical to those of the Black Panthers—whom they frankly copied. San Francisco could hardly believe that traditionally docile Chinese youth would resort to such tactics, but the first sporadic acts of social violence were there for all to see. Without concentrated city- and federally-supported programs for employment, language training, housing, and health, the outlook was for a new and bitter chapter in Chinatown's history.

San Francisco: Saving the Bay and Building BART

The city of San Francisco itself accounts for only 15 percent of the 4.6 million people scattered through the nine counties surrounding San Francisco Bay, living in countless suburban towns plus big cities like Oakland and San

---

* The 1965 immigration law also resulted in a five-year doubling of San Francisco's Filipino population, to a total of 24,694 in the 1970 Census. In the city's predominantly Mexican-American Mission District, theaters showing films in Tagalog, the Filipino language, are proliferating. A majority of the new Filipino immigrants are professionals looking for better income opportunities.

Jose. In terms of votes and thus power, San Francisco's weight has been declining steadily since 1940, when it had 37 percent of the Bay Area population.

The great population spurts have come in sprawling suburban counties like Santa Clara (up 500 percent since 1946), a pattern all too reminiscent of Southern California. With the unremitting and inadequately guided growth have come the inevitable problems. The air over San Francisco itself is constantly cleansed by strong offshore winds, but around the interior bay perimeter, smog now builds up to alarming levels many days of each year; in Oakland and San Jose, air pollution has reached L.A. proportions. Massive traffic congestion is noted in San Francisco and other heavily built-up areas. Subdivisions and highways gobble up thousands of acres of farmland and green space each year. No sound regional development plan has been enacted; in fact the dedication to local self-government is so strong that almost 575 local governments have sprung up in the Bay Area. Without strong regional (as opposed to local) government, the area is often at a loss to deal with regional-scale problems like waste disposal, air- and water-pollution control, mass transit, and open space.*

Perhaps the region's greatest problem is the protection and preservation of San Francisco Bay, a priceless asset well described by writer Judson Gooding as "an immense, extraordinarily lovely series of inland seas stretching 50 miles from north to south, and extending inland to the great Sacramento delta where the waters from 16 rivers flow down from the Sierras." Over a century, diking and filling by developers has reduced the water area of the entire bay by a third, from 680 to 400 square miles. By the 1960s, conservationists became highly alarmed by the rapidity with which landfill operations were proceeding; one of them predicted that unless a halt were called, the bay within 50 years would be nothing more than a filthy river surrounded by housing tracts and freeways. Conservationists also pointed to the uncontrolled way the 276-mile shoreline was being gobbled up by industry, from docks and shipyards to oil tank farms and salt-manufacturing lagoons, not to mention the dumping of garbage into diked-off areas. Dire peril was seen for the chain of life dependent on the bay—its fringe of estuarine marshland, with fish, plants, and shorebirds—and for every recreational and aesthetic enjoyment of the bay waters.

Added to this, there were run-of-the-mill problems of raw or inadquately treated sewage pouring into the bay from the cities around its rim. San Francisco itself was the prime offender, discharging about 487,000 gallons a day into the bay from a rudimentary treatment plant near the famed Fishermen's Wharf restaurant complex. In the background, there were two proposed government projects which could inflict even greater damage. One was the San Luis Drain to bring in agricultural waste waters—heavy in nutrients from fertilizers, pesticides, and boron that leaks from the soil—from the Central Valley. The other was the Peripheral Canal, a suggested $480 million, 43-mile-

* An eight-county Association of Bay Governments was created in 1966 and produced a preliminary area plan; to date, however, its powers are not great and it acts primarily as a conveyor of federal sewer grants.

long conduit to divert Sacramento River water that normally flows into the delta and carry it on down to Central Valley farms and Los Angeles as part of the California Water Plan. Ecologists argued that lowering the water in the delta would allow salt water to flow "upstream" into the verdant delta region, threatening its ecological balance, and that disruption of the normal westerly water flow would disrupt the natural flushing action which cleanses the bay of industrial and agricultural wastes.

The conservationists scored one spectacular victory when the "Save Our Bay" campaigners, spearheaded by some determined women who had worked in Paul McCloskey's congressional campaigns, got the legislature to pass and Reagan to sign a 1969 bill establishing permanent controls over landfill and dredging in the bay. "Save Our Bay" was not only a conservationist victory but perhaps the most determined and effective demonstration of woman-power in California history. And it helped to transform San Mateo County (just to the south of San Francisco) from one dominated by on-the-take, reactionary politicians into one of California's most progressive political seedbeds. For the change, McCloskey can take a lot of the credit.

The outlook for the bay's future has been brightening up in other ways, too. In 1970, both San Francisco and Oakland passed large bond issues for high-grade sewage treatment plants. Limping after fervent attacks by Bay Area Congressman Jerome R. Waldie and others, both the San Luis Drain and Peripheral Canal projects were in deep trouble in Congress, which would have had to bear a major share of the expense of each. With the moratorium on landfill operations, San Francisco had to find a new place to dump its 1,800 tons of garbage each day. The final solution: to haul the waste 375 miles in 30-car freight trains to a remote desert location in Lassen County in northeastern California, where it is dumped in a cut-and-cover operation.* Hardly anyone can mourn for that particular location, so heavily alkaline that sagebrush scarcely survives there. And the site is big enough to accommodate refuse for several hundred years.

Except for the saving of its bay, no modern development has been so important to the Bay Area as a whole as the authorization and construction of BART—short for the San Francisco Bay Area Rapid Transit District, the first major subway system to be built in the United States since 1906. Construction of the 75-mile system, linking San Francisco with the East Bay counties of Alameda and Contra Costa, began on a June day in 1964 when President Johnson touched off a small charge of dynamite in an onion field in far-out suburban Concord. After many delays, the system was finally scheduled to go into operation in 1972; it is the United States' most advanced modern transit system, both in its technological and aesthetic aspects. The sleek aluminum cars are fully automated, their start-up, speed, and braking controlled by a central computer bank, so that the attendant on board has little to do except attend to the psychological well-being of the passengers and make station announcements. From zero, the cars can accelerate to a top speed of 80 miles

* Lassen County, strapped for funds, welcomes the garbage because it gets paid about 21 cents for every ton dumped. For hauling and dumping, San Francisco pays the railroad $6.50 a ton.

per hour in 45 seconds; average speed is 45 to 50 miles per hour, including stops. With seats like those of a commercial airliner, air conditioning, carpeted floors, big windows, and good lighting, the cars are a world away from the screeching underground horrors of the New York system.* The stations are designed with a careful eye to aesthetics, well lighted and attractively decorated at underground locations, landscaped at above-ground stops. About the only old-fashioned element of the system is that it still rides on rails.

BART had a host of engineering problems to overcome. One was laying down the world's largest underwater tube—3.6 miles long, as deep as 130 feet below the bay surface, sitting in the soft bay muds and away from rock so that in case of an earthquake, the double-barrelled tube can just move about like a rubber hose. But in the words of B. R. Stokes, the former Oakland *Tribune* urban affairs reporter who went aboard as BART's first employee in 1958 and remained as general manager throughout the construction of the system, "all our engineering problems, however great, were simpler than getting adequate financing, and then dealing with the officials of 27 cities, three counties and at least 50 other governmental agencies, ranging down from the federal to local districts." A quarter-century, Stokes points out, elapsed between the first germ of the idea of a Bay Area rapid transit system in 1947 and completion in the early 1970s—perhaps a harbinger of what the country's other cities will face in improving their public transportation.

The first impetus for BART came not from a single person, but rather from a group of prestigious businessmen and civic leaders who were concerned about the city's congestion and the need to knit the Bay Area together. San Francisco's obstacle-ridden topography—water, hills, and narrow connecting points—provided a greater feeling of crisis in the Bay Area about continued reliance on the automobile; Los Angeles, by contrast, is like Kansas, where there are (or were) seemingly unlimited amounts of ground, from a highway engineer's point of view, to lay out concrete. While the first pressures for mass transit were local, the state legislature took the initiative in 1951 to set up and finance a study commission on the problem, to which the nine Bay counties —in an unusual demonstration of regional cooperation—then lent their cooperation and more financial support. In 1957, the legislature created BART as a political subdivision of the state.

Two of the biggest counties—San Mateo and Marin—withdrew from BART before a specific plan could be put to a popular vote in 1962. San Mateo opted out under pressure from its local merchants, who were afraid BART would siphon shopping traffic to San Francisco. Marin withdrew after a petulant Golden Gate Bridge authority refused to allow tracks to run across the bridge's span. Finally, only three major counties—San Francisco, Contra Costa, and Alameda—voted on the $792 million bond issue. The affirmative vote was 61.2 percent—just over the 60 percent required. BART thus became

---

* BART's cars were manufactured by the Rohr Corporation of San Diego, which outbid two veteran car builders—Pullman and the St. Louis Car Division of General Steel industries—to get the job. Rohr used aerospace techniques and a systems approach to construction, but nevertheless (or perhaps one should say appropriately) the first test cars presented a myriad of problems, especially in their automated control functions.

the largest locally or regionally financed public works project in U.S. history. And local approval triggered operation of a state law authorizing $180 million in bridge toll funds to finance BART's bay tube (the theory being that the tube would eliminate the need for at least one additional future bridge).

By 1967, runaway inflation and increased costs in aesthetic design had put BART $150 million beyond its budget. Jealous automobile and highway lobbies in the state legislature were not anxious to help, but eventually a one-half-percent sales tax increase in the three counties was authorized. By then, BART was well along with its urgent program of real estate acquisition (some 3,600 pieces of property, with thousands of condemnations), and construction could move ahead to scheduled completion. Final cost: about $1.4 billion.

Now BART's lines throw out three great spokes on the East Bay Side— south to Fremont near the foot of the bay, east to Concord, north past Berkeley to Richmond. In San Francisco proper, the first station is at the Embarcadero; then the line moves southwest, one spur going down to Daly City (site of the Cow Palace), two others out toward the Pacific. Some critics have suggested BART will further the "Manhattanization" of San Francisco as more and more commuters come in just for working hours in the downtown, leaving few tax dollars or other benefits for the city behind. (The proven fact is that BART stimulates office construction. Some $1 billion worth has gone in during the past decade in locations within five minutes' walking time of BART stations.) But the line will have other functions. It passes through or close to ghetto areas of Negroes, Mexican-Americans and others in San Francisco and Oakland, giving the people of those areas new mobility and a chance to get to better-paid jobs in the thriving suburban factories. It provides rapid access to major universities, including San Francisco State and the University of California at Berkeley. And what's more (as if San Francisco needed another), it's sure to be a grand tourist attraction.

In San Francisco's Orbit

What San Francisco represents among cities, Marin County—just to the north over the Golden Gate—represents among suburbs. Still fairly light on people (206,038 in 1970), its geography is varied and a pleasure to the eye—a place where mountains, ocean, and bay meet, known for its canyons, loamy farmland, lagoons, and streams. Primarily, Marin is a commuter county for San Francisco's well-heeled, a place that has changed suddenly from rural backwardness like most of the North Coast to a sophisticated and urbane community. San Rafael (population 38,977) is the closest thing to a city in Marin County and also has a newspaper—the *Independent-Journal*, superior to any San Francisco paper.

The two counties of "the Peninsula"—directly south of San Francisco— are San Mateo and Santa Clara, living in major degree off the heavy modern-day concentration of aerospace industries. San Mateo (pop. 556,234), has boomed from the population flow of San Francisco to the north, the employment at San Francisco International Airport on the bayside, and the research overflow from Stanford University, just beyond its borders on the south.

Santa Clara County, at the foot of the bay, is an area of explosive growth in which the population has risen from 290,547 in 1950 to 1,064,714 in 1970. Once a placid farm territory, the county by the late 1960s was suffering from monotonous tract development, arteries clogged with gas stations and taco stands, glaring lights and gaudy signs, traffic congestion, noise problems, and air pollution.

The fulcrum of Santa Clara's growth has been the city of San Jose, a quiet farm capital of 95,280 souls in 1950, today a sprawling boom town of 445,779 (fourth largest in California). After years of rapacious annexation and new development at any price, the city switched to an approach of controlled growth in the late 1960s, selecting as city manager the capable former city manager of San Diego and deputy mayor of Washington, D.C., Thomas Fletcher. Residents of a big barrio are said to live in the most miserable conditions, but San Jose can boast one of California's most progressive school administrations and best newspapers, the *Mercury News*. In 1971 it elected as mayor Norman Y. Mineta, who had spent two years of his boyhood interned with other Japanese in a World War II relocation camp.

Further north, close to the San Mateo line, is Palo Alto (55,966), where Stanford University has risen to a position of prominence, along with Cal-Tech, in a state where public higher education is so preeminent. Stanford has also become the centerpiece of a scientific and military-industrial complex spreading across the Southern Peninsula, ranking with Route 128–Cambridge and Los Angeles as one of the most important in America.

In contrast to the beehive of activity along the bay side, the ocean side of the San Francisco Peninsula is quiet and low-keyed, a place where gentle mountainsides go down to beaches and the settlement is still remarkably light. Here one finds massive Fort Ord and the weathered beach-resort community of Santa Cruz (32,076), which combines one of the highest percentages of retired oldsters in the country with a new life-style campus of the University of California. Just below Santa Cruz is the famed town of Monterey (26,302), steeped in ancient Spanish and Mexican history; a few miles inland lies Salinas, a great vegetable capital made famous (along with Monterey) by John Steinbeck's writing. Finally, south of Monterey is Big Sur country, where the land drops precipitously from towering cliffs down to the raging sea, one of the continent's most awesome and exhilarating sights.

Across the bay from San Francisco lies Alameda County, dominated by Oakland (pop. 361,561) and Berkeley (116,716), both old and established cities now afflicted by thorny problems of race, poverty, and student revolt. The East Bay also has a boom county, Contra Costa, whose population rose from 100,450 in 1940 to 558,389 by the 1970 Census count. William Bronson charges that Contra Costa "has undergone perhaps the worst-planned growth in the state," relinquishing its shoreline and most of its land with a view over water to industry and permitting half its rich agricultural land to be taken over by crowded and undistinguished tract housing.

The city of Oakland suffers from two hang-ups, each serious enough in itself but fatal in combination: self-identity and race.

There is still a lot of truth to the comment of Gertrude Stein, who was raised in the city but left for good at 18. "The trouble with Oakland," she said, "is that there's no *there* there." Oakland labors under what observers of such things call the "second-city syndrome," much like Newark or East St. Louis. Across a body of water, easily reached, there is the glittering core of the metropolitan area, offering good restaurants, theater, the business center, and a vibrant street scene. Thus the second city becomes increasingly dreary and commonplace and suffers from an acute feeling of communal inferiority. One young Oaklander put it to me this way: "I can go to San Francisco and stand on the corner and know something's going to happen; I can stand on a street corner in Oakland and know nothing will." On first impression, downtown Oakland has a clean, antiseptic look with its wide streets, brutalizing freeways, and a scattering of modern buildings—a bit reminiscent, shall we say, of Tulsa, Oklahoma. On closer examination, one notes how many empty lots there are, where decayed and unoccupied buildings were bulldozed. Only one central park—occupied by beautiful Lake Merritt—relieves the monotony.* There are few quality stores—mostly discount houses, tattoo stores, and the like. The antithesis to San Francisco's warmth, variety, and color could scarcely be greater.

Completion of the BART system may, if anything, make the situation worse. "Why should anyone get off in Oakland if Rome is only nine minutes away?" the question goes. In the long run, however, this might reverse, especially as the overcrowding in downtown San Francisco becomes less tolerable. The same BART trains that will take passengers from Oakland to San Francisco in nine minutes will do the reverse, too. Big corporations may opt for Oakland, with its lower real estate costs, as a place for runover office space, computer installations, and the like, since they can all be a few minutes from Montgomery Street. Or at least some people in Oakland hope so. Already there are claims that $50 million or more of construction in Oakland is due to the BART stimulus.

Oakland has had a substantial number of Negroes ever since the first came a century ago as railroad construction men or porters. Then, with World War II, came a major influx of blacks to work in the shipyards and in defense industries like Kaiser Steel. Since then the black percentage has risen steadily, with the familiar flight of whites to the suburbs. Negroes now account for 34.5 percent of the population. By 1980, blacks are expected to be in the majority.

Oakland has an oligarchic, historically unresponsive establishment, led by the person and family of Oakland *Tribune* publisher (and former U. S. Senator) William Knowland, together with Edgar Kaiser of Kaiser Industries, and unusually powerful real estate interests. The powers-that-be have traditionally treated Oakland's blacks like invisible people. Nevertheless, Oak-

* The Kaiser Building, which overlooks the lake, is architecturally outstanding and perhaps the most eye-catching building of the Bay Area.

land's black community has become nationally famous as the original spawning ground of the Black Panthers—founded, as the story goes, over expresso coffee one day in early October 1966 by Bobby G. Seale (who became chairman) and Huey P. Newton (minister of defense). The brief but complex history of the Panthers—Newton's conviction and imprisonment for the shooting of an Oakland policeman, and his subsequent retrial, ending in a hung jury; the role of the brilliant and later self-exiled Eldridge Cleaver; the phenomenon of black-bereted street bloods risen up against the established order; the bloody shootouts with often repressive police, Maoism, and flagrant racism ("Off the pigs!"); breakfasts for little black children with an admixture of hostile racial propaganda; the effort to write a new constitution for America after the inevitable revolution; the Panthers' amazing success in avoiding conviction on federal charges—is too long to be told here, and may change fundamentally at any time.

It does seem proper to ask why Oakland, of all places, gave birth to the Black Panther movement, which has succeeded Malcolm X and Stokley Carmichael and H. Rap Brown at the hard edge of black militancy in America. The conscious and unconscious racism of Oakland's white leadership may be considered part of the answer, but it is certainly not unique. A second, though only partial answer, may be the fact that the Oakland Negro community has long had a segment of especially intelligent and imaginative leaders, sensitive to the city's indifference and aware of the abject poverty and hopelessness of many black youths living close at hand. Many of the black leaders, I heard in the city, come from Louisiana, where they had received more basic education than most Alabama or Mississippi blacks. Huey Newton, for instance, was named after Huey Long, and many French names are noted among Oakland Negro leaders.

The Panthers have been at the forefront of those trying to keep the Oakland situation cool, on the simple grounds that they lack the firepower to win if a real riot breaks out. Another factor may be the gradually softening attitudes on race matters of the Oakland *Tribune,* which used to take stands almost deliberately designed to exacerbate tensions. By 1970, publisher Knowland seemed to have had at least a partial change of heart. His paper began to give more coverage to black demands, and Knowland moved quietly to form a coalition between white businessmen and black leaders. (Knowland, remembered as a stony and forbidding figure in earlier years, also sprouted a very with-it mustache; the resultant image was almost grandfatherly.)

Next door Berkeley, once known as "the Athens of the West," differs from Oakland as day from night. Knowledgeable Californians insist that Berkeley's government is the most responsive in the state, with high-grade political leadership and a well trained civil service open to creative solutions of problems. Because the level of services has been consistently high, so have the city taxes, among California's highest. But there is a big, wealthy outfit in town with a payroll of $11 million a month. Its name is the University of California, providing jobs for a third of the city's people.

The prime example of Berkeley's creativity is its school integration scheme. What the city has done since the mid-1960s is to institute citywide busing to achieve racial integration. Thousands of children are transported daily from the wooded, hillside suburbs of white affluence to the once heavily Negro schools in the flatlands near the bay. Thousands of Negro children are transported in the other direction. After several years of trial, the system seems to be a clear success. Part of the reason is small classrooms, guidance counselors for troubled students, and sophisticated audio-visual aids—in short, quality education at the end of the bus ride. The long-term benefits may be immense. Unlike other cities with a strong black population (23.5 percent in 1970), Berkeley is not experiencing further white flight from its schools. And it is one of the few cities of the U.S. with a large minority population where student scores on achievement tests rank above national averages. The Berkeley plan was put through by a liberal board of education, which survived a recall attempt in 1964, and Dr. Neil V. Sullivan, a powerful innovator as school superintendent. Sullivan later went on to become commissioner of education in Massachusetts.

Since the Free Speech Movement erupted in 1964, Berkeley has been a city in turmoil, the scene in the first six years of 67 major rallies, riots, bombings, and demonstrations. Sproul Plaza, the crossroads of the university, and Telegraph Avenue, once a quiet half-mile of quaint shops adjoining the campus, have become the scene of as weird a collection of youthful counterculturites as the continent has ever seen. The "street people" are in large part not students but a wild collection of youthful dropouts and runaways, pot smokers, and tear-down-everything political theorists drawn from all over America—and abroad as well.

The unlucky Berkeley police, some 275 men strong (150 of them patrolmen), members of a department long regarded as one of California's best, have shown skill and restraint in dealing with the street people. Occasionally some members of the force will rough up a protestor, and some of the street people's charges of misconduct probably have good basis. But the fact is that in all the violence since 1964, no Berkeley policeman has drawn his revolver.

Despite its concerns about street rioting and destruction, Berkeley's politics make it perhaps the most liberal, leftward-oriented community in America. In 1970, it helped elect one of its city councilmen, Ronald V. Dellums, to Congress. Dellums, a black who refuses to shun the description of "radical," sided with the youths involved in the People's Park incident and the San Francisco State strike, and often defended the Black Panthers. Putting together a coalition of blacks from Oakland and Berkeley, students, university intellectuals, and war opponents, he unseated six-term Congressman Jeffrey Cohelan, a staunch—but not extreme—liberal in the Democratic primary. Perfectly in character, Dellums greeted his supporters at a victory celebration with the black radicals' familiar clenched-fist salute. Then he went on to win the general election with 25,021 votes to spare. Not in decades—perhaps not since the late Vito Marcantonio (American Labor Party, 1939–51)—had a man regarded as so far to the left of the American political mainstream gone to Congress. There Dellums began to speak for a black–New Left constituency often voiceless in the past.

Building in part on the organization that sent Dellums to Congress, a group of acknowledged radicals (three blacks and a white) took control of the Berkeley City Council in April 1971 elections. What they meant by "radical," at least in terms of municipal politics, has a very non-revolutionary aura. For instance, they suggested new city services for the poor and minority group members, including rent control on apartments and free child-care centers, and replacing the property tax with a city tax on income over $12,000 a year. The voters seemed willing to accept that, but they overwhelmingly defeated one of the radicals' pet ideas: a ballot proposal to end the existing structure of the city police force and replace it with three separate units to operate in "the black community, the campus community, and the predominantly white community."

Two prominent radical groups—a Black Coalition and a gathering of liberal-leftists called the April Coalition—unified to elect the new Berkeley office-holders. Groups of poor people, antiwar organizers, students (some 10,000 new voters were registered, mostly in the university community), feminists, ecologists, and skilled young professionals all took part in the drive. It is a combination unlikely to reach a majority in many American communities, but it could be the model—especially with the advent of the 18-year-old vote—for contained university communities across America. "Haven't you heard?", Mrs. Ilona Hancock, one of the newly elected council members, asked the New York *Times*'s Steven V. Roberts, "Berkeley is at least five years ahead of the rest of the country."

III. THE SOUTHLAND

Growth for Growth's Sake

RICHARD G. LILLARD * tells the story of Earl G. Gilmore, who died in 1964 in the adobe ranch house at Third and Fairfax in Los Angeles where he had been born in 1887. In Gilmore's lifetime, he had seen the land around his home change from dairy ranch to oil field to Gilmore Stadium and Pan-Pacific Auditorium and Television Studio and the million-dollar Farmer's Market, where one finds everything but farmers. "Anyone who has lived his whole life in metropolitan Southern California," Lillard notes, "has seen some such series of transformations, as if the history of civilization were passing in quick review." I recall a 1955 drive along Wilshire Boulevard with a Los Angelan great-uncle already in his eighties, he pointing ruefully to pieces of property now worth millions that he could have snapped up for a song short decades before. Here is the legendary city of the Angels, the city of palms and mountains and the ranch house and the easy life and the benign climate, the city of movie stars and aerospace, the largest heavy-industrialized, semitropical area in the world, beckoning so many new settlers in a generation that its population has more than doubled.

And so it is in Los Angeles (1970 population 2,816,061) a city variously described as "40 suburbs in search of a city," or conversely, "The Ultimate City" (title of a delightful little book by Christopher Rand, based on articles he wrote for *The New Yorker*). The story is much the same throughout megalopolitan Southern California, where some 11 million people lead their lives within a narrow coastal strip some 210 miles in length, from San Diego in the

* In his book *Eden in Jeopardy* (New York: Knopf, 1966).

south to Santa Barbara in the north. In Los Angeles County alone, there are now 24 cities of more than 50,000 population—any one of which, set alone, would qualify as a metropolitan area. (Have you ever heard of Norwalk or Torrance? Each has more than 90,000 people and would be big news indeed set in the midst of most American states. In L. A. County, they are just part of never-ending suburbia.) On a population map of the U.S.A., the big black blotch for the Los Angeles urban conglomerate is sharply set off from the relative nothingness between it and metropolitan Texas, 1,200 miles to the east. The westward tilt is amply illustrated by the growth figures of Southern California in the past three decades:

County	1940	1950	1960	1970	% Change 1940–1970
Los Angeles	2,785,643	4,151,687	6,038,771	7,032,075	+152%
Orange	130,760	216,224	703,925	1,420,386	+986
San Diego	289,348	556,808	1,033,011	1,357,854	+369
San Bernardino*	161,108	281,642	503,591	684,072	+325
Riverside*	105,524	170,046	306,191	459,074	+335
Ventura	69,685	114,647	199,138	376,430	+340
Santa Barbara	70,555	98,220	168,962	264,324	+275
Regional total	3,612,623	5,589,274	8,953,589	11,594,215	+221
Percentage of U.S. population	2.7	3.7	5.0	5.7	

* San Bernardino and Riverside counties actually stretch across the desert to the Nevada and Arizona lines, but all save an infinitesimal part of their population is concentrated in the territory just over the mountains from the Los Angeles Basin.

To general astonishment, the Southern California population boom began to level off in the mid-1960s, and in the year ending June 30, 1971, Los Angeles County actually *declined* in population by 91,600. As California headed into the 1970s, in fact, the state's great population boom had suddenly halted; whether it was simply the aerospace and general economic recession that began in 1969, or a permanent shift because California finally was "filled up," no one was quite sure. But the figures were there to see: from a net immigration rate that was close to or over 300,000 annually in the early 1960s, the rate was almost zero in 1970 and projected to stay there for at least two or three years.

A slowdown in development may discourage the chambers of commerce but be just the medicine Southern California, in particular, now needs. One looks at what the bulldozers have done to accommodate new population in the quarter-century since World War II and shudders at the prospect of more. There are of course thousands of new homes and larger developments, mostly for the privileged classes, that have been creative and earth-respecting. (Some excellent samples are Rancho Santa Fe near San Diego and the Hope Ranch at Santa Barbara.) But this is not the mass market. In most instances the land developers, unguided by any master plan, have snapped up land parcels of opportunity (especially near freeways), staked out rectangular blocks because they are the easiest to plot, and then built tight-pressed little houses, superficially smart but often of flimsy construction, each with just enough space for their inevitable California backyard "patio." "The only saving grace of these houses is their expendability," according to one local architect; indeed, at such locations as Santa Monica and the southern end of the San Fernando Valley, whole housing tracts of the 1940s and 50s are being torn down for higher density and (hopefully) higher quality construction.

What has been done to the natural landscape in many of the Southern California housing tracts is probably beyond repair, however. As Lillard points out, "Everywhere [the rectangular block] has ignored the natural varied lines of hills and beach fronts, ignored watercourses and barrancas, rocky landmarks and noble old trees. Its monotonous, unalluring pattern has encouraged expansive, ugly grading and filling, and a disdain for the ancestral landscape." A thousand transplanted palms cannot correct such damage, as the visitor will quickly see when he speeds through the Southern California "slurbs" *—endless rows of pastel-colored boxlike homes, occasional industrial parks, low-lying shopping centers filled with stereotyped branches of the big chains, and strips of neon-beckoning honky-tonk gas stations, hot dog stands, and pizza parlors. Often the very land where all this stands was occupied until a few years ago by lovely orange and lemon groves, the very symbol of the semitropical good life that lured so many to California in the first place.

Auto Culture Extraordinary

A few years ago, columnist Art Hoppe of the San Francisco *Chronicle* ventured south of the Tehachapis in search of the typical Los Angeles resident. He found him to be "a well-preserved, middle-aged, middle-class, two-door Chevrolet sedan." Nowhere in the motorized U.S.A., and indeed nowhere in the world, is there a civilization so shaped to automobile culture as Southern California. In Los Angeles County, a motor vehicle is registered every eight seconds. If all the vehicles in the county were lined up bumper-to-bumper on a four-lane freeway they would stretch from downtown L.A. to Fairbanks, Alaska. Of the workers in the Los Angeles area, 80 percent drive their cars to work, averaging an hour and 36 minutes each day in their private little transportation systems, which are also handy if not absolutely necessary tools in reaching the far-flung centers of their metropolitan area, the beaches and the mountains.†

Virtually all Southern Californians own automobiles; the ratio of people to vehicles in the region is 1.5. (In 1967, for instance, the region had 11.2 million people, 5.9 million autos, three-quarter-million trucks, a quarter-mil-

---

* "Slurb" is a word coined by California Tomorrow, an environmental protection group, to describe "sloppy, sleazy, slovenly, slipshod demi-cities." The slurb is becoming as common to Northern as Southern California.

† There are several thousand Southern Californians who live in the San Diego area but commute daily to jobs in Los Angeles—a round trip of more than 200 miles.

lion house trailers, and a like number of motorcycles.) The automobile is also the prime killer of California, at least for everyone up to age 36 (when cancer and heart disease take over). More than 4,000 Californians die on the highways annually, with several times that number maimed and wounded. The pedestrian is strictly *persona non grata* in Southern California; in fact several areas have dispensed with sidewalks altogether. Pedestrians or bicyclists will be ticketed if they venture onto a freeway.

The motorist, by contrast, can engage in a dazzling variety of activities without even emerging from his car. California pioneered in, and still leads the U.S., in drive-in movies, drive-in restaurants, drive-in banks, and yes, drive-in churches. People have been seen necking or getting dressed at 60-plus miles per hour, not to mention shaving, telephoning, and dictating letters; there is even the story of a two-girl whorehouse on wheels, with the girls taking turns at driving and servicing their customers in the back of their camper. Of course there is no place in the world where so many people live in mobile homes, some of which qualify as the ultraluxurious, semipermanent type, others less formal and ready at a moment's notice to head back onto the freeway. Californians delight in apocryphal stories like that of the Los Angeles family that decided to skip all the discomforts of credit-installment debt by abandoning its house and living in a mobile home forever in movement on the freeways, always a ramp ahead of the bill collectors.

At ground level, the millions of automobiles, by their sheer numbers, provide any visitor's first and overwhelming image of Southern California. But only from the air can one fully grasp the auto's full land-devouring impact. In downtown Los Angeles, for instance, a concrete and asphalt jungle of freeways, feeder streets, gas stations, and interminable parking lots covers 55 percent of the land area; as one moves toward the suburbs the arresting sights are the football-field sized parking lots of black asphalt encompassing the shopping centers. Thus the automobile, heralded as a device to conquer space, has come to fill it. At the start of World War II, there were eight miles of controlled access highway in all of California; since then, in Los Angeles County alone, 325 miles of freeway have been built, at a cost of $1.5 billion. The freeway juggernaut is scheduled to expand within this single county by an incredible 1,127 additional miles, covering 55 more square miles, at a cost of $5 billion, by 1985. Slicing cruelly across mountains, elevated for mile after mile across the basin areas like a labyrinth of Chinese walls, the freeways represent the points of reference in a far-flung region. A given spot, one is told, is just west of the Harbor Freeway where it meets the Santa Monica Freeway, or two exits east of the Long Beach Freeway interchange on the San Bernardino—and suddenly a hard-to-grasp location has meaning, and one knows how to get there.

A few bright spots should be reported. Los Angeles has installed the country's best advance warning street signs (halfway down the block before the intersection), an innovation most American cities would do well to emulate. (The country's worst street signs happen to be found at opposite poles from Los Angeles—in Portland, Maine, and Honolulu, Hawaii.) Under pressure, the freeway builders are showing more concern than they did for many decades over the siting of freeways. And here and there, as businessmen learn how self-defeating the garish, sign-clogged, traffic-clogged, county-long streets of stores and restaurants and gas stations can be, they have turned to well-designed pedestrian malls where the autos are out-of-sight on the periphery. Some fine examples are to be found in Pomona, Riverside, San Diego, Anaheim, and the San Fernando Valley.

The inevitable question raised by Los Angeles' auto and freeway snarl is: why not mass transit? The irony is that the region once had an extensive, successful interurban rail system, the Pacific Electric. The big red cars of the PE ran outward from downtown Los Angeles to reach the mountains and the ocean, doing much to develop such far-flung communities as Pasadena, Hollywood, Long Beach, Santa Ana, and San Bernardino. By 1930, with 1,200 miles of track, it was the longest city rail system in the U.S., and in 1945, it was still carrying 109 million passengers in a year. But then competition from the automobile, and PE's own failure to improve its equipment and lines, led to rapid decline. The last big red car ran in 1963.

Now the only public transit Los Angeles has left is a quite minimal and universally scorned bus system. And Los Angeles is toying with the idea of investing billions in a replacement for the PE system it so blithely neglected. More than $2 million has been invested in transit studies in recent years. In 1968, a proposed 89-mile network of electric-powered, air-conditioned trains, to cost $2.5 billion, was put on the ballot, but only 47 percent of Los Angeles voters approved (with 60 percent needed for approval). High- and low-income voters approved, but the proposition lost in an avalanche of negative votes from tax-conscious middle-income taxpayers. Thus Los Angeles, with the worst public transportation system of any major U.S. metropolis, and most in need of rapid transit because of its huge distances, is left with none. Many believe that what Los Angeles will eventually try, as a partial or complete substitute for mass transit, will be such devices as freeway lanes reserved for exclusive bus use or some form of electronic control of vehicles on the freeways. The early success or failure of San Francisco's BART system will doubtless have a major influence on what Los Angeles finally decides to do about mass transit; so may an experimental federally funded 19-mile air-cushioned passenger train line between the L. A. Airport and the San Fernando Valley, scheduled to be built in the early 1970s on guideways elevated 20 to 60 feet above the San Diego Freeway.

Air to Breathe . . .

There are still days when the wind flows in briskly from the Pacific, across the Los Angeles basin, and up into the surrounding hills. And if, on such a day, there has also been a rain to cleanse the air, the ring of the hills stands out with startling clarity, the city takes on a scrubbed luminescence, and suddenly the "city of the angels" seems worthy of its name.

Unfortunately, the occurrence is rare. Air-traffic controller John Roger, who works up in the tower at the International Airport, describes a typical summer morning this way: *

When I come to work at 6 A.M.., visibility is often 15 miles or better; you can see the mountains rimming the basin. But when the commuting hour starts, a wave of grey smoke fans out from the freeways. It's like watching a science-fiction movie. The stuff billows thicker and thicker, starts turning yellow, then brown. By 9 A.M., visibility is down to two miles, and then we have to start landing planes on instruments, just to get them down through the smog. A lot of times we can't even see from the tower to the end of the runway, so we have to watch touchdown on our closed-circuit television monitors.

The scientific explanation for the bane of Los Angeles, its smog, is now well known. Set in a poorly ventilated saucer-like basin, the city has the lowest average wind velocity of any major U.S. city. Cool Pacific air, moving in low over the city, becomes trapped in the basin by higher, warm air, creating a classic "air inversion" that can last for days. On the basin floor, some four million automobiles each day burn eight million gallons of gasoline and spew forth 12,000 tons of noxious chemical compounds—hydrocarbons (unburned gasoline) and nitrogen oxides (created by high-temperature combustion). The hydrocarbons and oxides react to the ultraviolet radiation of the sun to produce ozone, a photochemical smog which irritates eyes, disturbs respiratory systems, and casts its hazy pall across the basin—the workings of a veritable chemical factory in the sky.

Up through the 1950s, automobile-loving Angelenos could assume that the smoke pall over their city came from the thousands of factories scattered across the city. But in that decade, a phenomenal effort was made to control industrial pollution, one without precedent in the U.S. Enforcing its own tight rules, the Los Angeles County Air Pollution Control District took tens of thousands of cases of pollution violation to court, and won some 95 percent. By the early 1960s, virtually every type of industrial polluter—from oil refineries, incinerators, chemical plants, open-hearth furnaces, and auto assembly plants to restaurants, crematories, and housing developers who cleared acreage with open fires—were under tight control. But still the pollution increased each year, and it became all too obvious that the automobile was the chief culprit. (Today the internal combustion engine is blamed for 90 percent of Los Angeles' pollution problem.)

Starting in 1961, the state of California, followed later by the federal government, began to impose standards for motor vehicle emissions and requirements for devices to reduce pollution. The effectiveness of the control devices, however, was questionable from the start. Los Angeles really achieved nothing more than a precarious status quo in its air pollution problem (marginal control effectiveness balanced out by vehicle population increases). Future hope must lie in radical alterations or a replacement of the internal combustion engine. In the meantime, reports emerge of smog attacking San Diego or Santa Barbara, slipping over the mountains to Riverside or even to Palm

---

* Quoted in "Los Angeles Has a Cough," by Roger Rapoport, *Esquire,* July 1970.

Springs in the once inviolate desert far to the east. A thousand acres of towering ponderosa pines in the San Bernardino Mountains are fatally afflicted with smog and must be cut down. California agriculture reports losses exceeding $100 million a year from smog: citrus trees producing only half their normal yield; growers of crops like spinach, celery, and beets forced to flee the L. A. area; the production of such cut flowers as orchids, roses, snapdragons all but impossible in polluted territory. Effects of smog on humans are less well known, but throat and chest irritation is well proven, the death rate from emphysema doubles every four years, and Los Angeles physicians, according to their own medical association, counsel at least 10,000 people a year to leave the area for their own health. Several days each year children up to high school age are not allowed to exercise at all, for fear their lungs might be harmed by the high ozone level in the air. And occasionally, doomsday warnings begin to surface. In 1970, a study council of the state legislature, citing the urban sprawl and air pollution of the Los Angeles basin, suggested it may already have more population than it can properly sustain.

Each great public interest fight has its heroes, and Los Angeles, first with the smog problem, was also the first to try to do something about it. For this, major credit goes to Dr. A. J. Haagen-Smit, a CalTech biochemist now in his early seventies who was the first man to prove just how smog is chemically created in the atmosphere; later, as chairman of the California Air Resources Board, he did royal battle with the auto companies over the effectiveness of their antipollution devices—and won. The tough, uncompromising chief air pollution control officers of Los Angeles County—Smith Griswold and later Louis J. Fuller—provided examples of law enforcement against polluters so straightforward and fearless that they were a class to themselves.

But the problem outpaces the solutions, and the U. S. Environmental Protection Agency has set air quality standards so stringent that the EPA's administrator, William P. Ruckelshaus, says they will make "drastic changes" in urban California life styles. Under present laws and policies, Los Angeles would not meet the new standards until the mid-1980s. But now the federal government requires compliance, including a reduction of 50 to 66 percent in carbon monoxide levels, by 1975. To reach the goal, Los Angeles may have to make a quick transition to rapid transit, stagger its work hours, and resort to extensive car pooling. Ruckelshaus even suggested the necessity of closing sections of Los Angeles and similar affected cities to all motor vehicle traffic.

The situation is not to be taken lightly. Without rapid, effective countermeasures, according to Kenneth Watt, a respected University of California ecologist, smog in the Los Angeles basin may be bad enough to cause mass deaths by the winter of 1975–76.

. . . and Water to Drink

With an annual average rainfall of about 15 inches—and virtually all of that in the winter months—Southern California is technically a desert and has no natural way to support the water needs of its millions. The region has 60 percent of California's people but only 2 percent of its water; by contrast, almost 40 percent of the state's water originates in the high mountains of northwestern California, where a meager 2 percent of the state's people live. Only through massive amounts of water importation has Southern California been able to grow into the formidable megalopolis it is today.

In its early years, Los Angeles depended for water on the unpredictable Los Angeles River (a torrent in winter, a trickle in summer, and still a major flood problem), plus hundreds of artesian wells. Capitalizing on a drought in 1904, a young Irish immigrant named William Mulholland, who had worked his way up to the position of chief engineer of the L. A. Water Department, set out to find new water sources. Traveling by buckboard through the desert and mountains, he finally discovered what he was looking for some 240 miles northeast of the city, in the fertile Owens Valley, irrigated by runoff from the Sierra Nevada. Secretly, Los Angeles interests bought up Owens Valley land to which control of its water was attached, and a great aqueduct to Los Angeles was begun—but not until some of the Owens Valley farmers, furious over the loss of water that turned their own fields into parched wastelands, had tried to dynamite the dams.

Owens Valley water is still an important source for Southern California, but the region's burgeoning population has made necessary the creation of vast new supplements. In the 1930s, as the first shortages loomed into view, the region's aggressive Metropolitan Water District proved itself willing and eager to undertake the complex negotiations with other western states and federal departments to get a share of Colorado River water. The point of origin would be the new Parker Dam, some 150 miles below the new Hoover Dam along the Arizona border. Those great dams and the amazing Colorado River Aqueduct (of which we have spoken before) completed, Colorado River water began to flow into the Los Angeles basin in 1941.

Soon it appeared that even this would not be enough, especially as Californians read and began to believe the demographers' extravagant projections of tens of millions of additional people by the end of the century, and projections of a water shortage by the early 1970s. For close to a century, some had dreamed of a massive water diversion program from watery Northern California to its arid south. Now the plan began to take shape. Along the Sierra-fed Feather River above Sacramento, it would be possible to build one of the continent's largest dams—the Oroville, a mile wide and 730 feet high, impounding more than a trillion gallons of water for hydroelectric production, flood control, and especially storage of the water for thirsty Southern California and agricultural irrigation along the way. Numerous other dams and storage reservoirs would also be included. To transfer the huge water load (4¼ million acre-feet), a new California Aqueduct was planned to run 444 miles down the heart of the Central Valley and over the Tehachapis into the south. Under Governor Brown's leadership, most disputes over the California Water Plan (except for hard-core Northern California resistance to theft of its water) were ironed out. The issue was sent to the voters of the state, who in 1960 obligingly authorized $1.75 billion in bonds to get the construction underway. The whole episode was typical of California: the largest bond issue ever voted (up to then) by the voters of any state; a guarantee of delivery of a phenomenal 1.8 billion gallons a day, over hundreds of miles, to Southern California's Metropolitan Water District; a scope to the project which simply dwarfed all earlier water-transfer agreements in American history. "By the time our astronauts reach the moon," the state water resources director grandly proclaimed, "the California Aqueduct of the State Water Project will take its place with the Great Wall of China and become one of only two man-made things on earth the moon visitors are expected to be able to see with the naked eye." (California reporter Lou Cannon appropriately calls this the "monument complex.") Yet even this stupendous project, Californians were told, would only provide enough water to last until the year 2020; by then it would be necessary to develop economical ways of desalinating sea water or to import water from afar (perhaps the Columbia River basin).

Inauguration of the California Water Plan seemed to be all the more far-sighted when the U.S. Supreme Court in 1963 ruled against California in the long litigation with Arizona over the allotment of Colorado River Water. The decision, in effect, meant less Colorado River water for Los Angeles.

But as the 1960s wore on, the crucial question became not whether Southern California might run dry, but whether the State Water Plan was not an ill-advised extravagance to provide more water than the Los Angeles area really needed. Several factors contributed to the change in attitude. One was the dropoff in California's phenomenal population growth, thus lessening water demand. The second was the rapidly developing technology of waste-water recycling and reclamation, which some experts suggested would provide a source great enough to satisfy Southern California water needs for another half-century with use of ground water. It was pointed out that Southern California coastal areas were dumping a billion gallons of waste water into the Pacific each day, water of better chemical quality than that being imported across the desert from the Colorado River. Finally, angry voices were raised about the ecological damage that full implementation of the State Water Plan might inflict. The wild rivers of California's North Coast (the Eel, Klamath, and Trinity) would be damned up, diverted, and in effect ruined. It was charged that diversion to the south of water from the Sacramento–San Joaquin delta, just east of San Francisco, would permit encroachment of seawater and incalculable damage to aquatic life in the delta.

In 1971, just as the State Water Plan was delivering its first water south of the Tehachapis, new controversy broke out as a result of the Nader report charges that the project was "the largest special interest boondoggle in history." It was alleged that state water officials had misrepresented the actual cost of the project, using a $2.8 billion figure when the actual cost (including finance costs on bonds) will be close to $10 billion. And while Southern California property owners will pay from 48 to 65 percent of the costs through taxation, the report said, the heaviest users of the water—corporate farms and industries—would receive water far below its actual cost. To these charges, the general manager of the Metropolitan Water District of Southern California, Henry J. Mills, replied that "the Nader report can only be termed a highly irresponsible and slapdash compilation of inaccuracies, untruths, malicious rumors, unsupported charges, distortions, and headline-hunting generalizations."

Even when one discounted the rhetoric on both sides, it was clear that the Metropolitan Water District, largely through property taxes, would be obliged to spend $6 billion by the year 2050 in paying its obligated share of aqueduct construction costs and necessary additions to its own system to use the water. Southern Californians, once thought to have scored a great victory over Northern California in approval of the plan, would be bearing a heavy tax burden to finance the growth they themselves demanded—the same growth that pollutes their air, crowds their beaches, clogs their freeways, and defiles their natural landscape. And the argument was strong, if not conclusive, that they might have gotten along well enough without any California Water Plan at all.

Suddenly, a Downtown Los Angeles

Downtown Los Angeles, 1,000 acres of real estate wedged in between four freeways, is perhaps the least "swinging" center city of any large American metropolis. Except for the start and end of the commuting day and the lunch hour, its streets tend to be deserted; at nighttime, when a city with soul would pulse with life, downtown L.A. is positively moribund. Until a few years ago, all that motorists whizzing by on the elevated freeways could see were a few civic center buildings, including the City Hall (then L.A.'s only claim to a skyline), rows of down-at-the-heels stores, a handful of oil company offices and banks, newspaper offices, cheap bars, and dowdy hotels. Fashionable Los Angeles had long since passed downtown by in a westward rush along the elegant Wilshire Corridor, and the old core was populated principally by low-income Mexican-Americans, blacks, and old people. The ultimate sprawl city seemed to have neither interest in nor need for a downtown.

But starting in the early 1960s, and gathering increased momentum in recent years, a great building boom has hit downtown L.A. An essential prerequisite was the 1959 repeal of a 34-year-old limitation of 13 stories on building heights, which had ostensibly been enforced to protect against earthquake damage. (Many believed its true reason was the influence of fringe landowners who wanted to keep down density to insure horizontal rather than vertical growth of the city.) No sooner had the height limitation been lifted than the United California Bank put up a new 18-story building downtown. Since then, the momentum has never stopped. The long-discussed 136-acre Bunker Hill Redevelopment Project moved forward between the old business district and the Music Center site, with skyscraper apartment and office buildings; despite warnings of skeptics that suburban-minded Angelenos would never forsake their ranch houses to live in urban rabbit warrens, former residents of distant suburban communities began to move in to be close to work. One huge new steel-and-glass tower after another rose in the city, and early in 1970, the United California Bank announced it would build a 62-story downtown office tower, the tallest building west of Chicago. By that time, more than $1 billion of construction was underway in downtown L.A. It was enough to assure that this core area would be not only western GHQ for many of America's largest corporations, but the financial, legal, governmental, and cultural center of the far-flung Los Angeles metropolitan region. At last, Los Angeles would have a real downtown—and, by 1971, its first office-space glut.

Unfortunately, there has been precious little planning for the new downtown, despite a belated start under joint business-city funding. No one yet knows how to funnel the hundreds of thousands of additional automobiles off the freeways and into L.A. each day without traffic jams of historic proportions. And the skeptics wonder if the final result will include the kind of things that make cities a delight for people—coffee shops and good restaurants and bookstores and theaters, a relief from sterile suburbia. What many fear is that downtown L.A., when completed, may be gray, a chrome-and-steel wonder of modern construction but a city without a soul.

There are some elements that could be built on to humanize a new downtown. Olvera Street, for instance, is a colorful block-long slice of Old Mexico in downtown, selling foods and giftwares of the native country. Logically this could be expanded to provide not only a tourist attraction, but a cultural and handwork center for the thousands of Mexicans in the city.

The downtown section includes Little Tokyo, where many Japanese found themselves restricted in ghetto-like fashion before World War II. It remains the daytime center of life for many of Los Angeles County's 104,078 Japanese, but less of the housing center it once was. Recovering from the humiliation of the forced evacuations from the West Coast to inland relocation camps after Pearl Harbor, the Japanese, by dint of hard labor and through the respect they won through their wartime loyalty, have been able to move into almost any L..A. area neighborhood they choose, and to branch out professionally. A significant number, for instance, hold highly skilled positions with aerospace firms; many of the less highly educated are expert freelance landscape gardeners, a lucrative profession in garden-conscious Southern California. With succeeding generations, the Japanese become more culturally attuned to American life, less bound to ancestral ways, less obedient to familial authority, and less willing to accept discrimination.

Among other things, Los Angeles has a substantial Indian population, growing by leaps and bounds to about 25,000 in 1970. The lot of the urban Indian, often living in poverty, drifting from place to place, frequently afflicted by alcoholism, is not a happy one. But it is in the cities, rather than on the reservations, that one today finds the cutting edge of new Indian nationalism.

All Around L.A.

Once one has accounted for the limited area of "downtown," the geographic ordering of Los Angeles becomes a nightmarish puzzle. The city itself, 469 square miles of territory in a county of 4,068 square miles, is laid out in a crazy-quilt pattern that starts high in the San Fernando Valley, jumps over the Santa Monica Mountains, goes through downtown, and then plunges down an 18-mile-long corridor, just a half-mile wide, so that the city limits can reach the harbor at San Pedro without interruption (much like the corridor that linked ancient Athens and Piraeus.) Enclaves are carved into every edge of the city, and in fact independent cities like San Fernando (254,413) and Beverly Hills City (33,416) are completely surrounded by it.

Los Angeles County, on the other hand, is shaped normally enough, with the ocean on its western and southwestern flanks (offering miles of still magnificent beaches), the desert over the hills to the east (in the direction of San Bernardino and Riverside), an unobstructed opening to Orange County on the southern flank, and the massive San Gabriel Mountains rising to the north. Some 700 square miles are urbanized and built up, but forests and federal lands comprise more than 1,000 acres, and in the late 1960s there were still more than 600 acres devoted to agriculture.

Perhaps Los Angeles' ultimate urban sprawl can be visualized by imagining downtown L.A. as the center of a great clock and the great hunks of land as hour segments, with 12 o'clock due north, 6 o'clock south, etc. We can start clockwise at 9 o'clock:

9 TO 10 O'CLOCK. The most dominant feature as we start out from downtown is Wilshire Boulevard, frightfully stretched out (15 miles in all) but still the most elegant street in the California Southland and one of the U.S.A.'s most sumptuous. Sleek high-rise apartment and office buildings line mile after mile of Wilshire where beanfields still abounded in the 1920s; the Wilshire Corridor also has Los Angeles' finest stores, the excellent County Museum of Art, and such adornments as Beverly Hills and the new Century City (six million square feet of floor space in elegant office buildings, apartments and hotels) along its way or nearby.

Further out on Wilshire one can get a view of one of the world's great Mormon Temples—a reminder that the Latter-Day Saints have one of their most powerful outposts in Southern California. And at well-to-do Westwood Village is the 50-year-old campus of the University of California at Los Angeles, fast rivaling Berkeley to the north (of which it was once just the "Southern campus") in prestige and weight in California affairs. The UCLA commitment to solving race and class problems has been strong, and in the 1960s it was becoming increasingly involved in Los Angeles affairs with institutes or study programs in every area from local smog and transit problems to urban planning and architecture.

The whole outer flank of our 9-to-10-o'clock belt is dominated by the

Santa Monica Mountains, 92 square miles of extremely rugged territory (as big as Pittsburgh and San Francisco put together), intruded into the heart of a heavily urbanized area. Where they meet the sea, one finds famous Malibu Beach.

10 TO 11 O'CLOCK. Close-in, there's Hollywood; out further, the San Fernando Valley; in between, more of the Santa Monica Mountains. Physical Hollywood (as opposed to the broader celluloid center) has been declining as a shopping center for some time, has mixed housing and commercial neighborhoods, and harbors some 15,000 sexual deviates, according to one local official with whom I spoke. Unlike Beverly Hills, Hollywood itself is not a separate city, but just a neighborhood of the city of Los Angeles.

Out beyond the Santa Monicas is the San Fernando Valley, which was mostly farmland in the 1930s, accommodated only 112,000 people in 1940, and today has a population exceeding a million—a vast slurb which covers 235 square miles (the size of the city of Chicago). Its center is deadly flat; around it are mountains which seal it off from the ocean and the rest of Los Angeles like an immense football stadium. The worst damage of the 1971 earthquake was felt here; more than 40 people died when a Veterans Administration hospital collapsed, and tens of thousands of homes would have been obliterated if the Van Norman Dam, holding back a 100-foot-high wall of water, had not barely held together. The valley is no longer so much a bedroom for L.A. as its own commercial and industrial base, providing jobs for 85 percent of its workers within its own confines. Many San Fernando Valleyans never see downtown Los Angeles.

11 TO 12 O'CLOCK. Close-in, there is the Los Angeles Dodgers' Stadium; then, with the Golden State Freeway the connector, the cities of Glendale (population 132,752, site of gaudy Forest Lawn Memorial Park) and Burbank (88,871), both filled with middle-to-upper-middle-income families.

12 TO 1 O'CLOCK. This segment starts with a jumble of freeways, then encompasses the eastern portion of Glendale and moves on out into the mountains until 35 miles from downtown (as the crow flies), one comes on the dusty town of Palmdale (pop. 8,511) in the Antelope Valley. Here, in flat, high-desert country studded with spiky Joshua trees, one of the world's great airports will be built during the 1970s. According to William Pereira, the L.A. architect-planner for the project, Palmdale will be one of the world's major metropolitan centers, "grand in dimension as well as population," with 2.5 million or more people living in a metropolis centered on the idea of fast and efficient air and ground travel. The environmentalists, however, are now fighting the Palmdale plan.

1 TO 2 O'CLOCK. Here the dominant feature is the smog-plagued city of Pasadena (1970 population 113,327—down 2.6 percent from 1960), long a household word in the U.S.A. for its dazzling New Year's Day Tournament of Roses, the outgrowth of a village flower fete and sports tourney of 1890. Pasadena embellishments also include the CalTech campus and close to 200 plants in the fields of scientific, pharmaceutical, and cosmetic products; Pasadena's chief problems revolve about race, specifically the influx of blacks,

Mexican-Americans, and other minorities, who now represent about a quarter of the city population—and more than 40 percent of the public school enrollment. Amid intense controversy, a radical school busing plan went into effect in 1970—and seemed to be working.

2 TO 3 O'CLOCK. Now our orientation moves to the east of downtown L.A., and for the next 180 degrees, we must deal mostly with characterless suburbia. First in this segment is the San Gabriel Valley. One town there polled its citizens and discovered, to its horror, that fully one-third of the population moved each year. (One writer's comment: "That isn't a town—it's a gypsy encampment.")

If one sticks it out far enough on the San Bernardino Freeway, the way leads up over the hills, out of the L.A. Basin, and into the desert and the city of San Bernardino (pop. 104,251). Impelled by heavy military and aerospace employment, healthy agriculture (it is host city to the National Orange Show), and aggressive local leadership, San Bernardino has advanced by leaps and bounds since 1940, when it had less than half as many people.

3 TO 5 O'CLOCK. Now we come to East Los Angeles and the Mexican-Americans—so many of them, in fact, that only Mexico City has more. But first a quick review of what lies beyond them, starting with Whittier (pop. 72,863), a spot of dullsville suburbia where Richard M. Nixon spent his boyhood. After Whittier come the Puente Hills, a barrier of no mean proportions, and beyond them, the city of Pomona (pop. 87,384), site of the Los Angeles County Fair (largest in the U.S.A.) and a distinguished modern shopping mall. And several miles further in the desert comes the city of Riverside (population 140,089), a citrus center of long standing, the site of an agriculturally inclined University of California campus, and a town expanding with aggressive industrial development programs.

The sprawling Mexican barrio (or ghetto) of East Los Angeles, some 40 percent of its territory in the city of L.A. and the remainder in unincorporated area of the adjoining county, is the biggest single concentration of L.A. County's 1.1 million Mexican-Americans. The classic conditions to fill a people with clotted rage are to be seen in East L.A.—insensitive schools, abhorrent housing, inadequate health care, few decent job opportunities, constant police harassment. Fearful of rising militancy in the barrio (which they attributed to "known dissidents"), the police by 1970 appeared to have adopted a policy of "preemptive strike"—to smash independence before it could take hold. Predictably, the Brown Power movement of young militants, led by the Brown Berets (a sort of Mexican-American equivalent of the Black Panthers), began to sway increasing numbers of the normally quiescent Latins.

Writing in the spring of 1970, Los Angeles *Times* columnist Rubén Salazar, a native Mexican and one of the foremost interpreters of his people, warned that the truculent mood in the barrio was "not being helped by our leaders who are trying to discredit militants in the barrios as subversive or criminal." Just a few months later, 20,000 young militants engaged in a Chicano Moratorium to protest the disproportionate loss of Mexican-American lives in Vietnam. Rioting broke out, and newsman Salazar, covering the scene, was suddenly struck dead by a tear gas projectile designed to pierce barricades but fired by the police into a bar. It would not be the last violent conflict between Chicanos and the police, a problem which drew in U.S. Senator Cranston and other respected figures in an effort to sooth tensions and get the police to adopt a less truculent attitude.

By developing stronger leadership and more political finesse, the Mexican-Americans might get many more concessions from local and state governments in California. Numbering some two million statewide, they could be the balance of power in a close election. Yet through the 1960s, the Mexicans' ostensible political friends, the Democrats, saw to it that the areas of Chicano population concentration were gerrymandered to bolster Anglo Democrats in nearby districts, not to elect Mexicans. Thus there was no Mexican-American state senator, city councilman, or county supervisor, and only one member of the state assembly and one Congressman (Edward R. Roybal, a Democrat).

5 TO 7 O'CLOCK. This "two-hour" segment, defining a broad arc of land running south from downtown, encompasses L.A.'s black ghettos, big bland suburban cities, and then, at the ocean's edge, the thriving submetropolis of Long Beach and posh Palos Verdes Estates.

Close to 700,000 Negroes now live in Los Angeles, almost ten times the figure at the eve of World War II. What L.A.'s Negroes call "Watts" is actually a fairly small area of some 65,000 people; whites sometimes substitute the term "curfew area" (in honor of 1965) and mean a sprawling south L.A. area, larger than all of Manhattan, including both Watts and other heavily black communities like Huntington Park and now areas further and further west, in the process of white-to-black transition. Just a few miles south is the city of Compton (78,611), heavily middle class and the so-called "Beverly Hills of the Black Belt." It has an outstanding black mayor.

Watts' spread-out, palm-lined streets are in such vivid contrast to the stark tenements of South Side Chicago, Harlem, and Bedford-Stuyvesant that no one would ever have imagined this area as the one where the spark of black riots, later to spread to Newark, Detroit, and across scores of American cities, would be ignited. But what looked good in comparison to other ghettos was hardly adequate in comparison to the "good life" of Southern California —and especially the opulent, flashy world of Hollywood and the Miracle Mile reported regularly to Watts by television. Employment, the commission appointed by Governor Brown would later report, was a key factor; only 14 percent of the people in Watts had automobiles; the closest employment agency was an hour and a half away on three separate bus lines. Added to this were strained relations between the black community and the police, high welfare dependency, and a crazyquilt net of county and local welfare agencies, substandard schools where 40 percent of the girls dropped out because of pregnancy, and the highest disease rates in Los Angeles County. The area had no hospital—the nearest public hospital was two hours away by bus.

For the four days of the 1965 riot, the Los Angeles ghetto was convulsed by a sickening orgy of destruction and death, interspersed with carnival-like looting. The toll: 34 killed (mostly Negroes), 1,034 injured, close to $40 million in damage, some 4,000 arrested in a one-square-mile burned-over area. On the worst hit street, 103rd, so many of the businesses burned out that it would be called Charcoal Alley thereafter. Of the blacks arrested, many charged they had been treated with brutality at the hands of the Los Angeles Police. As the riots tapered off, the late William H. Parker, then L.A. police chief, went on television to announce, with typical tact: "Now we're on top and they're on the bottom." One observer's comment: "Many Negroes felt this represented no change."

What has happened to Watts since the '65 riots? In some respects, it has deteriorated. Many shops and restaurants were frightened away, leaving a surfeit of pawnshops and bail-bond offices. Joblessness, by 1970, had soared 61 percent over the 1965 rate, and little was done to correct the woeful transportation situation. Housing remains poor, most of the schools abysmal, and welfare is a way of life. Racial antagonism still simmers below the surface.

Still, there is a residue of progress that has come to Watts to stay. An especially bright development is the Watts Labor Community Action Committee (WLCAC), a true effort at a locally run and controlled community union. WLCAC's chief sponsor is the United Auto Workers, that union again demonstrating its advanced social creativity.* In running WLCAC, major help comes from other unions, foundations, and federal grants and loans. WLCAC has a dazzling variety of activities—comparable probably only to Operation Breadbasket in Chicago and OIC in Philadelphia. It has acquired a chain of supermarkets operating within Watts, operated a string of highly profitable local gas stations, offered vocational training in several fields (especially the skills required at a new community hospital) and built a score of vest-pocket parks, and planted several thousand trees to help beautify the area. The man chiefly responsible for WLCAC's success is a husky, barrel-chested ex-Mississippi farm boy, Ted Watkins, who took the program over in 1966 and soon distinguished himself as a master orchestrator and bargainer. Watkins' salary is paid by the UAW, for which he had previously been an international representative.

Private enterprise deserves high marks for a serious effort in Watts. The first big firm to move into the area after the riots was Aerojet-General, which set up a subsidiary, the Watts Manufacturing Company, with a staff of all black executives in control. Watts Manufacturing went to work making tents for the military and survived principally on federal contracts for crates, post office equipment, and electronic assembly items.

The plant of Watts Manufacturing is in a series of low-slung structures strung out along El Segundo Boulevard; as one moves through the shops, the *esprit de corps* of the workers—mostly black, with a scattering of Mexican-Americans and whites—is clear to see. From the outset, Aerojet-General in-

* With 60,000 to 70,000 workers in California auto assembly plants and aircraft factories, the UAW is a significant liberal voice in the state's labor and politics. The regional UAW chief is Paul Schrade, a bearded, highly articulate man who was once a personal aide to Walter Reuther. He is an advocate of aligning the labor movement with student groups, and under his leadership the UAW went all-out to help Robert Kennedy in the 1968 Presidential primary. Schrade was with Kennedy at the Ambassador Hotel and was grievously wounded by Sirhan Sirhan's bullets, though he did recover. More recently, he has incurred criticism from UAW dissidents who say he should devote more time to union business and less to politics.

tended to turn over Watts Manufacturing to the subsidiary's employees when the operation became profitable. The subsidiary moved into the black in 1969, and a year later 80 percent of the company's stock was placed in a trust fund for purchase by employees (then numbering about 200) over seven years.

Nartrans, a subsidiary of North American Rockwell set up in central L.A. to draw workers both from Watts and heavily Mexican-American East Los Angeles, scored a success in machining, wood and plastic products, drafting, and keypunch operations. A very tangible sign of new hope in Watts is the 470-bed Martin Luther King Jr. Hospital, the largest of several medical facilities that have come into a section of the city that had virtually none at the time of the riots.

The bulk of southern Los Angeles County, divided by the rather ludicrous commercial strip of L.A. city territory that goes south to the harbor, is filled with instant cities of the 1940s and '50s, many now turning into practically instant slums or close to it—Gardena (1970 population 41,021), Torrance (134,584), Carson (71,150), and Lakewood (82,973). The scene is overwhelmingly one of little frame houses, set on monotonous straight-line streets, mile after mile after mile.

Moving still further south in the 5-to-6-o'clock segment, we finally reach Long Beach and the oceanside. With 358,633 people in the 1970 Census, Long Beach is California's sixth largest city. The booming port, and especially the great oozy oil field underlying its city, port, and harbor, make Long Beach one of the U.S.A.'s richest cities. With the tidelands oil royalties, which it shares with the state, Long Beach has spent millions on recreational development in the harbor area and begun to bill itself as a major convention center —a little Miami Beach.

Oil also brings its problems, which Long Beach has been trying to meet. Oil rigs still mar the landscape and contribute to depressing stretches of waterfront, but in the harbor they have been camouflaged to look like highrise buildings, surrounded by waterfalls and trees. As for Long Beach's people, they are a fair prototype of Middle America. The Iowa picnic each year draws tens of thousands from the heartland. Blacks are less than 10 percent of the population. The vote each election is overwhelmingly Republican. For employment, Long Beachers look first to Douglas Aircraft, then to the harbor facilities. California State College, Long Beach, has a phenomenal enrollment of 28,000 students, the largest of any state college in the United States.

Moving westward from Long Beach, one passes the Los Angeles Harbor area and settlements like Wilmington and Harbor City—an ugly hodgepodge of workers' houses, stores, warehouses, oil wells, and storage tanks. Then there is the fishing village of San Pedro, and suddenly one has left the flatlands and come again to ragged mountain and canyon country on the Palos Verdes Peninsula, a quiet and beautiful spot inhabited by the rich and the very rich.

7 TO 8 O'CLOCK. Here we pass through the western extremities of the black ghetto, encounter another one of those bland, sprawling suburban cities —Inglewood (population 89,985)—the Los Angeles International Airport, and finally the ocean and a string of middle-class beach communities.

The L. A. International Airport has developed into a very unwelcome neighbor on its site between Inglewood and the sea. The jet roar, vibrations, air pollution, and congestion of local roads by airline passengers and workers have surrounding communities up in arms—so far that they and their citizens have sued the city of Los Angeles for more than $1.5 billion in damages. Local protests are only one reason, however, that the Los Angeles airport planners are starting the huge new facility at Palmdale.

8 TO 9 O'CLOCK. In this final segment, we move westerly through nondescript commercial and residential sections of the city and the University of Southern California campus, through Culver City (31,035), of M-G-M fame, and finally to the coastal region, rich in aerospace firms, the art community of Venice, and proud, successful Santa Monica (88,289).

And now we are back to 9 o'clock and the Santa Monica-Wilshire axis, from which we started; our long day's swing around the spokes of Los Angeles is finished.

The Multicultures of Los Angeles

"With all our tough problems," Los Angeles *Times* publisher Otis Chandler said in an interview, "it is easy to forget that Southern California still offers the good life for most people, and they are enjoying it in their immediate environs." The problems of smog, transportation, education, or taxes, he said, will all have to get a lot worse before people are forced to look for solutions. In the meantime, life offers the warm climate, informal style, nearby beaches and mountains, the backyard swimming pool, the tennis court, the camper or boat for the weekend—the world glorified in *Sunset* magazine (a journal that so scorns the East that it charges two dollars extra a year for any subscription addressed to the other side of the Mississippi).

The greatest asset of this way of life, as many have testified, is the sense of freedom it gives the individual. A typical newcomer, the New York *Times*'s Steven V. Roberts, has described that asset as "the lack of community structure, or hoary institutions looming over you psychologically as well as physically, of rules and traditions and expectations." No more fluid society has ever existed, nor one in which impermanence, rootlessness, lack of belonging seems so strong. Many fight loneliness through the "singles only" apartment complexes (described as "a sort of perpetual freshman mixer"), or through senior citizens' retirement villages with their multiple activities to keep the aged active and in contact.

The same culture seems to breed materialism and hedonism faster, or at least more obviously, than the rest of the U.S.A. In large measure, materialism is what Hollywood "culture" has always stood for. Sexual permissiveness—the body-conscious society—flourished first and foremost in Southern California, first in Hollywood's purveyance of the single female sex symbol (and God rest the soul of poor, troubled Marilyn Monroe), then in the beach-and-auto society of unfettered, bronzed young bodies, the golden California girls and their swains. The universality of sexual tastes and opportunities is amply illustrated in the remarkable classified section of the Los Angeles *Free Press*. For instance:

> SEXUAL FREEDOM PARTY—This Sat. nite 8 pm—Limit 15
> couples. Call for res. 660-0500.
>
> SWINGERS—Dial-A-Soulmate: Guys—Low Fee—655-5377;
> Chicks-Free—752-3711.
>
> INTERRACIAL LOVE—Meets Wed., Fri. & Sun. 9112 S. Western.
> 957-1808.
>
> BLONDE GIRL WANTED to share cabin in canyon with generous
> young man. Must be between 21 and 30 for romantic & steady
> relationship. Preferably European. Please write Dennis,
> Rte. 2, Box 110, Saugus, Calif. 91350.

For all such aberrations, the Southern Californian tells a visitor, there are hundreds of examples of normal families of children who grow and date and marry and carry on their lives in very normal ways—an assertion doubtless true. Yet the journalist's attention is seized again by the bizarre, which flourishes here so openly. For example, the gangsterish young motorcycle gang, Hell's Angels, sprang to life first in Fontana, in the L.A. hinterland, the cyclists spreading across California on their big Harleys, sowing terror as they went, fast men with weapons and drugs.

Within this same Southern California flourishes every type of cult, religion, life style imaginable. Part of the disparity, as *Los Angeles* magazine has suggested, is that while Los Angeles by all outward appearances is an overwhelmingly middle-class community, there are in fact two very different kinds of middle-class communities. There is one which is older (not so much chronologically as culturally), whose members work at jobs they mainly dislike, watch television, take their kids to Disneyland, and worry about being correct. There is another which is younger (especially in its culture), which feels both free and alienated and attempts to resolve its paradox by creative acts, uncommon thoughts, and a strange variety of innovative life styles.

Among the "straights," for instance, one could classify most members of Los Angeles' Protestant churches and certainly all but a few of the flock of 1.6 million built up over 21 years (until his 1970 retirement) by James Francis Cardinal McIntyre of the Roman Catholic Archdiocese, the first Prince of the Church to be elevated from a see west of St. Louis.

Yet it is Protestantism, not Catholicism, that sets the tone of Los Angeles; as Christopher Rand has remarked, the city "is the last station . . . of the Protestant outburst that left northern Europe three centuries ago and moved across America." In Los Angeles, the Protestant component covered not only every standard denomination—a sampling from low Baptist to high Episcopalian, accurately reflecting the population mix—but an assortment of kooky cults such as the world has rarely seen. From Thomas Lake Harris (California's first self-proclaimed Messiah) to Sister Aimee Semple McPherson, from the leaders of Theocracy to the fascistic Christian Nationalist Crusade of Gerald L. K. Smith and the modern Sky Pilot Radio Church, where a reader can pursue truth in the I Am Accredited White Temple Reading Room, Los Angeles has had a bit of everything. Some say the cultism is more sedate than it once was, but it is still there. Today there are fervid evangelistic faith healers from the South, and an absolute first in the U.S.A., a church (the nondenominational Metropolitan Community Church) which openly identifies itself as a church for male and female homosexuals. It has several hundred members and, according to reports, probably a truer Christian spirit than thousands of the world's "straight" churches.

To Los Angeles, too, one must travel to find the greatest American flowering of fad and the phenomenon of astrology, enthusiastically practiced witchcraft, and such occult arts as palmistry, numerology, and fortunetelling. And somewhere far out beyond these, at the demonic edge of a troubled and rootless society, stood a figure like Charles Manson, Rasputin-like leader of a band of hippies convicted of having murdered actress Sharon Tate and four others in an orgy of hacking, stabbing, and shooting at the end of the 1960s. Sex, drugs, hypnotism, communal living, hallucinatory thinking—all seemed to have played a role in the events leading up to this murder, perhaps the bloodiest and most senseless of our century. Yet it was not an isolated instance of violent crime in Los Angeles; the area crime rate vies with New York City's as the highest in the U.S.A., with alarmingly high levels of murder, forcible rape, and aggravated assault, in addition to the various forms of property crime. Not all of this is amateur stuff: the Mafia has thrived in Los Angeles since early in the century, prospering today on drugs and a variety of other sidelines as it did on illegal booze about a half-century ago.

A huge nonestablishment, underground community does thrive in the Los Angeles area, but like everything else it is so spread out—from artist communes in the canyons to hippies' beach pads or semiresort hideaways—that it fails to make an impact like the action along Telegraph Avenue in Berkeley.

A major unifying force in the underground world is the Los Angeles *Free Press*, written distinctly for the young, uncommitted, and turned off. Editor Art Kunkin tells how he started the *Free Press*, up to 90,000 circulation at the time of this writing, with a total initial investment of $15 in 1964. Journalistically, it is somewhere between the advocacy papers of the standard underground press (the 200-odd papers in the U.S. which cater mostly to young people of hippie or radical leanings) and more sedate but leftish organs like New York's *Village Voice*.

A discussion of the L.A. multicultures, and especially the drug scene, must include mention of the remarkable Synanon movement, begun at Santa Monica in the late 1950s by Charles E. Dederich. Synanon began, almost spontaneously, as a self-help organization for alcoholics, then expanded to take in heroin and other drug addicts, and finally became a haven for almost anyone in trouble or looking for a new order in his life. Founder Dederich, a lusty iconoclast and former alcoholic, has been variously described as a latter-day Socrates, a madman, a perpetrator of self-glorification, and a herd of one elephant. His movement has now spread to centers at Oakland and Tomales

Bay north of San Francisco, to San Diego, and even as far east as Detroit and New York, and has provided a temporary home for more than 10,000 narcotics addicts and other "misfits." Synanon officials, however, insist they are not in the rehabilitation business but are a social movement, "a small model for a better world."

L.A. Arts and the Press

Until a very few years ago, Southern California seemed to all the world to be a brash and shallow place, preoccupied with its roads, bridges, hotels, and dams.

Two developments of the past generation, however, have elevated Los Angeles into a first-rate cultural center. First, in the immediate pre–World War II era, there was the arrival of talented European refugees, some but not all of them Jews fleeing the Hitlerian onslaught, a group that included figures like Bertolt Brecht, Igor Stravinsky, Arnold Schoenberg, Artur Rubinstein, and Jascha Heifetz. As Christopher Rand points out, they were attracted by the climate, the movies, and eventually, each other's presence; almost without exception they chose to settle in the Santa Monica mountains, between Hollywood and the sea. The exiles made Los Angeles into a music center second only to New York in this hemisphere, and stimulated the growth of bookshops, art dealers, and the like. Los Angeles is now the nation's second largest painting and sculpture market, the galleries along La Cienega Boulevard inferior only to Madison Avenue's. The exiles also helped inspire UCLA to inaugurate the best extension courses in the U.S.A. and broadened the professions in Southern California, especially psychoanalysis.

The 1950s and especially the 1960s brought, for the first time, a determination on the part of Los Angeles' old and leading families to make their city a High Culture leader of the country. Rising like an acropolis on a hill in the center of downtown Los Angeles is the massive Los Angeles Music Center, opened in 1964, the home of the Los Angeles Philharmonic (considered one of the country's greatest symphonies), the Center Theatre Group (an ambitious regional theatre), and the Civic Light Opera and Choral Society. Designed by California architect Welton Beckett, the Music Center adds the one touch of true elegance and style to downtown L.A. Some seven miles to the west, on Wilshire Boulevard, is the strikingly designed County Art Museum, opened in 1965. Neither of these projects would have been possible without the extraordinary fund-raising activities of Dorothy (Mrs. Norman) Chandler, mother of the L. A. *Times* publisher and wife of his predecessor.

Yet it would be unfair to say that Los Angeles is preoccupied with top-level culture to be enjoyed principally by the upper classes. Los Angeles teems with amateur musicians and artists, community orchestras (there are 60 symphony orchestras in the area), and chamber-music societies. San Diego and Santa Barbara offer much more of the same; in San Diego, for instance, four to six playhouses are busy at a time, including Coronado Playhouse, California Western University, the Old Globe Theater, and the Art Center in La Jolla. And if anyone tires of the standard fare, he can always make a trip to see the intriguing Watts Towers built by Italian immigrant Simon Rodia, a set of three spires almost 100 feet high and composed of everything from pipes, broken bottles, and cement to iron rods, tiles, and seashells, the fruit of 33 years of labor by the lonely man who died in 1965.

Culture is not the only area in which Los Angeles has grown up. Today its dominant newspaper, the Los Angeles *Times*, competes closely with other great dailies like the New York *Times* and Washington *Post* for the honor of being considered the finest in the U.S.A. Until 1960, when Otis Chandler succeeded his father Norman as publisher, the paper was a fat mediocrity—highly provincial (a Washington bureau of three, a foreign staff of exactly one), slanted in coverage, uncrusading, the safe and sound voice of the Republican party in California and the Wasp community of Los Angeles. Otis Chandler and his editor until 1971, Nick B. Williams (an intellectual Southerner considered one of the best U.S. postwar editors) decided to go first class, with spectacular results in content, style, and editorial direction.

The *Times* has protected its vital flank in Middle America by building or developing excellent sports and financial, entertainment, and women's features. Even black and Mexican-American community news is now covered with care. But the paper has also been able to appeal to Southern California's highly literate leadership community—university and aerospace and think tank people—with a strong diet of national and foreign news and carefully developed interpretive stories. Williams hired many expert reporters—not a few of them from the defunct but still warmly remembered New York *Herald Tribune*. The *Times* correspondent network was widened to 18 in Washington, 16 abroad (from Mexico City to Moscow), and a half-dozen in major U.S. cities (including some of the very best regional reporters in the business). Some of the most important national news breaks of the late 1960s and early 1970s emerged from the *Times;* locally the paper unearthed such corruption in the Board of Zoning Adjustment and the Los Angeles Harbor Commission (including influence peddling and personal profiteering) that Mayor Sam Yorty became a mortal enemy.

Slowly at first, then more rapidly, the *Times* broke loose from its old conservative editorial moorings. Formerly, it had called itself a Republican newspaper; now this was changed to "independent Republican," and finally just to "independent." In 1964, the paper supported Goldwater for President (after backing Rockefeller in the California GOP primary and promising to support the winner in the fall), but in 1970, Chandler told me that under similar circumstances the *Times* would *not* again support a candidate like Goldwater, and that in fact its endorsement in any future electoral race should be considered doubtful.

Part of the wonder of the *Times*'s modern-day success has been that Otis Chandler, who came upon his position by sheer rank of family succession,*

---

* Otis is the son of Norman Chandler, who had followed his father, Harry Chandler, who had stepped into the publisher's slot to succeed his father-in-law, Harrison Gray Otis, a Civil War veteran who acquired a quarter-interest in the paper 90 years ago.

should have turned out to be such a skilled publisher. To the casual visitor, Chandler looks like a typical young California businessman—tall, blond, svelte, athletic, genial. But as *New York* magazine summed him up: "California, yes. Beach boy, no." The record shows that Chandler has proven no one's fool in coping with the built-in obstacles to a successful newspaper business in Los Angeles—readers who commute in autos, not trains where there's time to read; the soft outdoor life, competing for attention; fiercely competitive sub-urban dailies; disparate, farflung and often indifferent communities; and top-drawer local news programming by NBC and CBS outlets, which operate on budgets way over even New York locals and go in heavily for original news and editorials. Between 1960 and 1970, the *Times* increased its daily circula-tion from 500,000 to almost a million, its Sunday circulation from 900,000 to 1,400,000. In daily circulation, it is now second only to the New York *Daily News*, on Sunday behind only the *News* and the New York *Times*. Its adver-tising linage *and* its line count of editorial content is by far and away the greatest of any U.S. newspaper.

The horizons of the *Times* and its parent Times Mirror Corporation (1968 gross $352 million) are not limited to the California Southland. Early in the 1960s, the *Times* began to "go national" through its successful joint news service with the Washington *Post* (a service now subscribed to by many other papers). As the decade progressed, several moderate-sized book and magazine operations were purchased. Then, in 1969, came acquisition of the Dallas *Times Herald* (a paper that needed a lot of improving) and CBS affili-ate KRLD-TV in Dallas–Fort Worth. And in 1970, it was announced that the *Times* had purchased perhaps the finest afternoon paper of the U.S. to-day, Long Island's *Newsday*. What was Chandler aiming at? He himself said: "We looked at growth and population figures and concluded that there are four states we should be in—California, Texas, New York, and Florida. . . ." Commented Edward Diamond in *New York* magazine: "The evidence sug-gests that he is out to create nothing less than the biggest, best communica-tions complex in the nation."

Searching for motivation to explain the expansionist and perfectionist drive from the Chandler empire in Los Angeles, as it now begins to take con-trol of parts of the nation that once treated L.A. as a colony, multiple motives are suggested. One is simply the drive to excel of Otis Chandler, born of two highly ambitious parents. A second is "the Eastern thing"—the Westerner's desire to prove himself equal or superior on the very home grounds, by the very rules, of the Eastern Establishment.

L.A. Power and Politics

There is scarcely any American city where the question "Who holds the power in this town?" evokes such unsatisfactory answers as Los Angeles. Offi-cials at the Rand Corporation told me that when they wanted to identify the major business and other leaders with influence on city and state governments, they found the task almost impossible. Their net impression: Los Angeles is so diffuse that no one knows what's going on, let alone controls it. There is simply no "establishment" comparable to New York, Chicago, or even San Francisco. Scarcely any "old families" qualify. Otis Chandler's own name automatically goes on any tentative list of Los Angeles leaders, but he told me: "There is no power structure here—only people who think they are."

Even when one looks to the holders of great wealth as natural holders of power, no strong "establishment" comes into focus. Aerospace, big oil, and what's left of Hollywood play little role in local affairs. Fortunes are rarely more than a generation old, and at least until recently, their holders were distinctly disinclined toward politics. The business establishment, such as it is, includes bankers, real estate men, merchandizers, some oilmen, and not a few wealthy owners of savings and loan associations who saw their investments balloon into billion-dollar enterprises during the postwar housing booms.

In recent years, Los Angeles has begun to register a growing number of major contributors to political and civic causes, representing at least an embryonic power structure. The L. A. *Times'* Bill Boyarsky, in a 1970 magazine article written jointly with his wife, Nancy, reported that a careful observer could notice the same names appearing as major donors to big L.A. cultural, charitable, and medical projects. Among the major names the Boyarskys reported were these:

▪ Asa Call, in his late seventies, conservative and successful businessman, ex-president of the state chamber of commerce and the Southern California Auto Club (largest in the world), a position in which he successfully lobbied the state legislature to adopt California's huge freeway system.

▪ Leonard Firestone, chief of Firestone Tire and Rubber Co., a moderate Republican who initially opposed Ronald Reagan and was cochairman of the 1964 Rockefeller for President campaign in California. In 1969, Firestone raised money for black City Councilman Thomas Bradley's unsuccessful campaign. He gives freely to such projects as the Boy Scouts.

▪ Taft Schreiber, a moderate Republican, Jewish, big in the philanthropies, who was Ronald Reagan's old movie agent and helped launch Reagan's political career. Schreiber is an executive of Music Corporation of America, the giant show business combine that controls Universal Studios.

▪ Mark Boyar, chairman of the board of Metropolitan Development Corporation, a land development firm. He is a big Democratic contributor who, along with oilman Ed Pauley, raced up to San Francisco in 1948 to rescue Harry Truman's campaign train, which had been stalled by railroad officials who demanded cash to pay for it. Boyar was also a big Humphrey contributor in 1968. He says: "The hacks like myself have just about had it. The younger men coming up, Democrats and Republicans, worry about social problems and the environment."

▪ Eugene Wyman, former Democratic National Committeeman and state chairman and big fund-raiser for his party, head of the prestigious law firm of Wyman, Bautzer, Finell, Rothman and Kuchel. A "regular" Democrat, Wyman is one of many important Jewish contributors to the Democratic party.

• Martin Stone, president of Monogram Industries (a manufacturing combine that grosses $150 million a year). In his early forties, Stone is a big money-raiser for the liberal wing of the Democratic party, as opposed to what he calls "traditionalists" like Wyman and Boyar. He has served as president of the Los Angeles Urban Coalition and is candid about his interest in running for governor in 1974.

• Holmes Tuttle, in his late sixties, a successful owner of five Ford-Lincoln-Mercury dealerships; he is described by the Boyarskys as "the single most influential Republican contributor and money-raiser in the state." Tuttle has been a Reagan friend since 1945, helped launch Reagan's political career, and directed fund-raising in the Reagan gubernatorial campaigns.

A name many would place close to the top of the L.A.-California money-power structure is that of Henry Salvatori, son of Italian immigrant parents, self-made multimillionaire in oil geology, confidant and major fund-raiser for President Nixon, Mayor Sam Yorty, and especially Governor Reagan. (Salvatori is one of a group of businessmen who bought the house Reagan lives in in Sacramento, leasing it to Reagan at a reasonable fee.) Salvatori's big interest is in fighting Communism, and he has given heavily to groups like the Christian Anti-Communism Crusade and to conservative politicians who make opposition to Communism a chief talking point.

Los Angeles politics have a turbulent and sometimes violent history. There were many Confederate sympathizers in town at the time of the Civil War who dealt harshly with Negroes and in turn were subdued by Union troops. Public hangings of criminals used to be commonplace near where the Federal Building now stands. Afflicted by a political boss system and the machinations of power-hungry corporations, Angelenos some 70 years ago rose up in a great municipal reform movement that resulted in the recall of the mayor, who was involved in sugar company stock speculation; it was the first use of the recall method in U.S. history. Los Angeles politics turned non-partisan, but up to the 1930s it was known as an open town, with gambling, prostitution, and other diversions. But in January 1938, a couple of police officers planted a bomb in a private investigator's car. The explosion blew the mayor of the moment out of office (again via the recall route). The captain of police went to San Quentin. The new mayor, Fletcher Bowron, closed up the town, reorganized the police and other public boards, and proved so popular he was reelected for three terms. The 1950s brought Mayor Norris Poulson, a pleasant spokesman for GOP business interests running under a nonpartisan banner. During these years the L. A. *Times* came close to dictating the exact course of municipal government. Then, in 1961, Sam Yorty became mayor.

Sam Yorty had come to California from Nebraska when he was 17, first dabbled in politics as a local secretary of the Technocracy movement, and in 1936 went to the state assembly, where he was considered a "flaming liberal" in his first term but then turned sharply to the right. Remaining a Democrat, he alternated the practice of law and occasional runs of public office (winning two terms in Congress). In 1960, he bolted his own party to endorse Nixon for President, authoring a pamphlet, "Why I Cannot Take Kennedy," a tract that did not leave the issue of Kennedy's Catholicism unmentioned. The next year, Yorty got elected mayor, capitalizing on his neopopulist image as a gutsy politician for the little guy against the "bosses" and the politicians.

Came the 1969 election and the *Times*, previously friendly to Yorty, refused to support him (largely because of the scandals its reporters had unearthed). In a first primary, with 14 candidates on the ballot, Yorty picked up only 26 percent of the vote. But the man he was forced to face in the runoff election, Thomas Bradley, a quiet, bright, moderate city councilman who had served 21 years on the L.A. police force, was a Negro. Yorty took the issue and exploited it to the hilt, suggesting that Bradley was linked to radicals, that he would ruin the police (a patently absurd charge in view of Bradley's own police background), and that somehow Reds and blacks and long-haired students and criminals would all "take over" Los Angeles if Bradley were elected. The tactic worked, and Yorty won with 53 percent of the vote. (Of equal significance, however, was the fact that Bradley, a Negro, almost did win in a city where the Negro population is only 17 percent, and that most of the downtown white establishment backed Bradley.)

It may be argued that the identity of the mayor of Los Angeles is of little importance—a position which Mayor Yorty took indirectly a few years ago when he was testifying on the problems of U.S. cities before the Senate Subcommittee on Executive Reorganization:

> *Senator Abraham Ribicoff*: This morning you have really waived authority and responsibility in the following areas of Los Angeles: schools, welfare, transportation, employment, health and housing, which leaves you as the head of the city basically with a ceremonial function, police and recreation.
> *Yorty*: That is right, and fire.
> *Ribicoff*: Collecting of sewage?
> *Yorty*: Sanitation, that is right.
> *Ribicoff*: In other words, basically you lack jurisdiction, authority, responsibility for what makes a city move?
> *Yorty*: That is exactly it.

The obvious alternative to weak city government would be a strong metropolitan government—a not novel idea which has been justified by Councilman Ernani Bernardi in these words:

> We ought to face the fact that we simply can't solve the really big problems —race relations, smog, rapid transit, crime—within the present structure of city government. Urbanization has made city governments obsolete. None of these problems can be contained within municipal boundary lines. Before we can even begin to solve them we will have to have one, integrated countywide government.

There is a chance that county government may fill the void. In California, the counties handle "people problems" like health, welfare, criminal justice, pollution, and housing—the very functions that have grown so rapidly in recent years. The cities are left with fire protection, street sanitation, municipal planning, and zoning. An evolution to stronger county power—fighting the inevitable opposition of cities anxious to preserve prerogatives—may be in the making. Already, L.A. County government has multipurpose citizen service centers spread all around the county. In the area of federal grants, L.A. County has an extremely effective lobbyist, James M. Pollard, in Washington. The county's weaknesses are its multiheaded leadership (five supervisors instead of a single executive) and the fact that so many California government functions (education, rapid transit, etc.) are fulfilled by special-purpose districts.

L.A. Economy: Overview and Hollywood

It seems difficult to believe today, but not many decades ago Los Angeles was just emerging from its drowsy, Arcadian era of citrus groves, exotic shrubbery, and resort life. As a harbinger of things to come, oil was discovered in 1890 and the first movies filmed soon after the turn of the century. But serious growth began only after World War I, as the movies made Hollywood a fashion and scandal center of the world, the aircraft business grew toward major-industry status, and the first large residential subdivisions appeared. In World War II, the big aircraft plants (Douglas, North American, Northrup, Hughes, and others) manufactured a hefty chunk of the planes that fought the war. Millions of dollars also poured into California's new steel mills and into her shipyards as Southern California, for the first time, became really important to the entire U.S. economy.

The postwar story is one of superlatives. Just in manufacturing, for instance, the value of goods produced went up from $2 billion in 1940 to $9 billion in 1963. Personal income soared from $3 billion in 1940 to $48 billion in 1970. Los Angeles County is not only the economic center of the Southwestern U.S.A., but one of the world's largest industrial, financial, and commercial complexes. With the exception of agriculture, every major industry has participated in the area's growth since World War II. In 1965, L.A. surpassed San Francisco as the financial center of the West by forging ahead in three critical measures—total loans, deposits, and savings. Tourism, with only a shadow of the relative importance it had a half-century ago, nevertheless adds more than $1 billion to the Southland's economy each year.

A normally perspicacious San Francisco businessman tells a visitor, "I for one can't see how L.A. can be so damned affluent. There are so many people down there they must just take in each other's laundry." The comment may not be too far from the mark. Jane Jacobs, in her *Economy of Cities*, shows how Los Angeles defied the normal laws of export and import by growing immediately after World War II, even while her exports (wartime ships and planes) fell catastrophically. With Hollywood about to begin its decline and oil eliminated as an export because of local need, many people predicted severe economic distress and depression for Los Angeles. Instead, employment grew. What was happening was that Los Angeles was beginning to replace the goods it used to import with local manufactures, and accommodating the pent-up consumer demands of the war years. It was a period of immense entrepeneureal enterprise, as Jacobs explains:

The new enterprises started in corners of old loft buildings, in Quonset huts and in backyard garages. But they multiplied swiftly, mostly by the break-away method. And many grew rapidly. They poured forth furnaces, sliding doors, mechanical saws, bathing suits, underwear, china, furniture, cameras, hand tools, hospital equipment, scientific instruments, engineering services and hundreds of other things. One-eighth of all the new businesses started in the United States during the latter half of the 1940s were started in Los Angeles.

Many of the new companies themselves became successful exporters, and many national firms that used to export to Los Angeles opened branch plants there to produce the goods close to the burgeoning Southern California market. The national auto makers expanded their assembly plants in the city and soon made it the leading exporter of autos in the territory west of the Rockies. L.A. the exporting center might have boomed even more if Japan had not cut into its Pacific basin sales in steel and autos.

A revived and expanded aircraft and general aerospace business was to provide the vigorous export base on which much of L.A.'s modern day prosperity is based, starting with important production during the Korean war. In addition to its new banking power, the city and region forged continuously ahead as corporate headquarters locations, widening a lead over San Francisco and the Bay region.

Los Angeles trade not only dominates western U.S. markets, but is internationally important as well. Both Los Angeles and Long Beach have magnificent, side-by-side, and highly competitive sea harbors behind nine miles of breakwater (actually the world's largest man-made harbor). Scores of freighters can be handled at a time, and the tonnage handled (36.6 million tons in 1967) ranks eighth among U.S. ports if one counts the two rivals as one. Famed San Francisco Harbor handles only a ninth as much tonnage. By some estimates, one worker out of four in Los Angeles is substantially dependent on foreign trade for his livelihood. Out of the ports move oranges, cotton, potash, coke, iron-ore pellets, and thousands of other commodities; in come everything from bananas and Mexican salt to Scotch whiskey, petroleum (which Los Angeles must now import to satisfy its fantastic demand), crude rubber, and foreign autos. One of the most astounding port sights is the acres of Volkswagens awaiting delivery to the auto-hungry Southland market.

The saddest Los Angeles story is the decline and fall of Hollywood movie-making, the city's great seminal industry and its most unique contribution to American culture. Writing some 25 years ago in *Inside U.S.A.*, Gunther began a few pages on the movie industry with these words:

> I would like nothing better than to describe Hollywood at length—that fabulous world of profit, hunger, agents, ulcers, all the power and vitality and talent and craftsmanship with so little genius, options, dynastic confusions, the vulgarization of most personal relationships, and 8,000 man hours spent on a sequence that takes three minutes to see. . . . Or its preoccupation with gossip, personality, dramatic nuances, "entrances." . . . Or on the quasi-theological aspects of the star system. . . .

Today the temptation to write of such things is less, or nonexistent. So much of what was called "Hollywood" (always a euphemism for the studios and lots scattered from Burbank to Culver City) has faded away; in fact the decline has been rather steady since the mid-1940s, when the industry was grossing $1.5 billion and making almost 400 movies each year. The villains in the decline have been, most obviously, television; secondly, foreign competition; third, rising costs (up 50 percent in the 1960s); fourth, the industry's own antediluvian economic practices (overpaid stars, huge lots, overinvestment in individual films, an archaic distribution system); fifth, the unions and "runaway" film production; and, finally, American youth, who are simply turned off by the old ballyhoo, extravaganzaitis, and superficiality.

No one questions that movie-making will continue to be a vital industry in the 1970s and beyond; the question is whether the big Hollywood studios will show enough flexibility to hold a major piece of the action. While the big producers boast they possess the ultimate in technical movie-making skills, some of their most successful ventures are simply to bankroll young, independent producers who know how to turn out the almost psychedelic imagery —split screens, images flashing on and off, images that remain on the screen like stills—popular in the McLuhanesque generation. By 1969, a majority of the big Hollywood studios were losing money, including the once-titanic Metro-Goldwyn-Mayer, Paramount, and 20th Century Fox. (Exceptions to the losing rule: Columbia Pictures and the hard-headed successors of Walt Disney.) Inevitably, the conglomerates and proxy challengers moved in: Gulf & Western Industries bought Paramount; Kinney National Service acquired Warner Brothers–Seven Arts; Distillers Corp.–Seagrams and Time, Inc., bought control of Metro-Goldwyn-Mayer. M-G-M in 1969 was obliged to hold a monstrous $5 million auction of properties ranging from famous stars' costumes to an 1878 train; also sold were three warehouses packed with tapestries, chandeliers, and furniture of past centuries, picked up during the 1930s when the studios followed authenticity; the auction was a kind of farewell to an era.

Aerospace, Think Tanks, and Systems Analysis

The 60-year-old aviation industry and its lively offspring, aerospace, have represented the most dynamic element in Southern California's postwar economy. Through aerospace, California became the leading defense contracting state.

Earnest aircraft production got underway in California soon after World War I, led by Lockheed and Douglas, and later, Northrup, Hughes, North American, and Ryan Aeronautical Corporation. By 1937, California led the U.S. in aircraft production. When airplane factories expanded spectacularly during World War II, California made fighters and bombers (20,000 by Lockheed alone) which were a cornerstone of American air power.

Immediately after the war, defense contracts sagged, depressing aircraft employment. But strong ties had been formed between government, the California aircraft plants and the state's scientifically oriented university communities. When the Korean War arrived, escalating aircraft demands, and the important shift to missiles and spacecraft occurred, California was ready to seize the business. Complementary defense installations (the Air Force's Space Technology Laboratory, the Pacific Missile Range, Vandenberg Air Force Base with its rocket-launching capabilities) also gravitated to California. By the 1960s, people were talking of Los Angeles as a "federal city" because of the close relationship between its economy and that of Washington. Some 40 percent of the area's manufacturing employment was tied directly or indirectly to defense and space spending. In 1962, about 24 percent of all U.S. government military contracts (close to $6 billion worth) went to California, and for several years about 40 percent of contracts for military R & D work were let to Golden State firms. The state's advantage in space agency contracts was almost as great. Congressmen from other regions complained hotly about alleged preference shown California, but the fact was that a huge proportion of the firms and personnel with appropriate R & D and aerospace manufacturing backgrounds were on the coast, plus universities turning out a disproportionately large share of the country's new scientists and engineers. The multiplier effect of research, development, academic, and manufacturing facilities, all in California, would prove hard to break. By 1970, federal military prime contract awards to California were down to 19.6 percent of the U.S. total, but the dollar amount—$5.8 billion—was still close to twice the amount in second- and third-ranking New York and Texas.

While San Diego, Sacramento, and the San Francisco Bay Area have a share of aerospace factories, the great concentration is in Los Angeles County. Here they are dotted about, Christopher Rand points out, in a discernible pattern. Some are grouped around Pasadena, northeast of center L.A., near CalTech and its spinoffs. Others are in the San Fernando Valley, miles to the north and northwest of central L.A.; here, for instance, is the long-time home of Lockheed, the biggest of them all. But the major concentration is down along a 20-mile stretch of L.A.'s West Side, close to the ocean. The coastal strip is home for Douglas, North American, TRW, and Hughes, as well as the nonprofit Aerospace and Rand corporations, and innumerable electronics suppliers and computer firms.

At the end of the '60s and the start of the '70s, events took a menacing turn for the long-prosperous aerospace industry and the hundreds of thousands of Californians employed by it or related defense industries. A deescalation of the arms race with the Soviets became a distinct possibility. The once-sacred defense budget came under close congressional scrutiny and there was mounting criticism of the huge cost overruns that had led the government to pay two or three times first estimates for several weapons systems. Then came a sharp tapering-off in NASA orders for rockets and space equipment as the Apollo moon-landing program reached its completion. Finally, it became clear that there were simply too many airframe manufacturers for the available volume of business, either military or domestic. As the missile age advanced, many legislators viewed the military plane as an anachronism—and an intolerably expensive one. The airlines, already well stocked with jets and facing a dollar pinch themselves, cut back on their orders.

Between 1967 and 1971, California slipped from 616,000 aerospace jobs to about 450,000. By autumn 1971, the state had an unemployment rate of 7.1 percent—compared to 6.0 percent in the country as a whole. San Francisco and Oakland, the least dependent on aerospace, were the best off (5.9 percent); Los Angeles and Orange County were among the worst off (7.7 and 8.0 percent respectively). "This is now the worst period of unemployment in this state in the last 20 years," the *California Journal* reported.

Even Lockheed—the General Motors of aerospace—found itself in serious trouble at the start of the 1970s. Threatened by inflation and public doubt about its capacity to deliver on promises, the company was in a severe dollar-delivery-performance crisis on four big programs—the Air Force C5A cargo jet, the Army's Cheyenne helicopter, the rocket engine for the Air Force's short-range attack missile, and 22 Navy ships. It was obliged to take a loss of $480 million in a negotiated settlement over four of these disputed government contracts. And its first entry into the field of commercial jet aviation, the L-1011 TriStar, was dealt a staggering blow when England's Rolls Royce, the company that made the engine, went bankrupt in February 1971. Threatening, as it were, to die, Lockheed went hat-in-hand to the government and appealed for a federal loan guarantee of $250 million to stave off bankruptcy. Congress reluctantly approved. Another firm with less than a guaranteed future was North American Rockwell, which had 106,000 workers and yearly sales exceeding $2 billion in the mid-1960s. By spring 1970, it was down to 50,000 workers and faced with near disaster when McDonnell Douglas took away the contract for the F-15 fighter plane in which NAR had invested years of engineers' time, at a cost of millions. Finally, North American did land the Pentagon contract for the proposed B-1 bomber, causing cheers and open joyous weeping at its El Segundo headquarters. But there was a danger that Congress might scuttle the whole B-1 program long before the projected $12 billion was spent on it.

How can aerospace avoid the disarmament blues and survive? Its brightest future would logically lie in fields like mass transit design, environmental control, or information systems—those areas which require systems analysis and a high technological component. Several firms in the industry have ventured into these fields in recent years. Overall, the success has not been great. The basic problem has been aerospace's unfamiliarity with building inexpensive systems. The industry has been accustomed to rapid work in a high-cost environment where it could afford tremendous redundancies, all on rather generous federal patronage. The social fields, performing for tight-budgeted state and local governments, permit no such luxuries. And most aerospace companies are deficient in personnel trained in the social sciences.

Of all the aerospace firms, the most active in the social field has been TRW, Inc., a far-flung, diversified manufacturer of spacecraft, electronics, automotive parts, jet engine components, and defense systems. TRW has its headquarters in Cleveland but its heart and spirit in California. The scientific-social genius of the firm (his name corresponding to the R in TRW) is Dr.

Simon Ramo, a Utah-born electrical engineer who picked California as the land of golden opportunity after the war—figuring, quite simply, that the atomic age would require a greater electronic than aerodynamic component in its weapons, and that a great technological industry could be built on the coast. As head of electronics for Hughes Aircraft, and later in his own firm (Ramo Wooldridge), Ramo became the foremost expert in the guidance and control system of airborne weapons and then the chief scientist of the United States' ICBM program. In 1958, Ramo Wooldridge merged with Thompson Products, an auto-and-aviation firm from Cleveland, to make TRW; in the succeeding 12 years, sales of the new firm increased 337 percent to $1.5 billion and it became the 57th largest industrial corporation of the U.S., with more than 80,000 employees and 300 plants. At one time TRW depended on the federal government for 70 percent of its sales; by the late 1960s, that figure had dropped to 36 percent.*

Ramo, now in his late fifties, is a charming, voluble, self-confident and farsighted man, adept not only in science but also in business, sociology, urban problems, and music (he is an accomplished concert violinist)—about as close to the "universal man" as the confused and complex latter 20th century will permit. Speaking of TRW, Ramo explains: "Our life's work is that part of technology which requires interdisciplinary science. We concentrate on putting together the social and the economic with the technological —combining software or systems analysis or analytic thinking, creative and mathematical work, with hardware." Despite the "spacecraft" image of TRW, Ramo insists, "we're involved in information handling more than spacecraft —the sensing, accumulation, storage, deliberation by automatic techniques. Those same techniques can be used to run an airline or a hospital or manufacturing operation, or to examine the resources of an area."

As examples, TRW has in recent years developed integrated, cost-effective operational systems for hospitals in the U.S. and Canada; explored a systems analysis of national and regional air pollution as a basis for a national air pollution control information system; led in developing major-city police command and control systems designed to get more efficient control with less forces; employed automatic data processing techniques to show how the multiplicity of data available about local land use can be correlated for intelligent evaluation of governments in land use planning; established the country's only computerized nationwide credit information system; performed detailed engineering studies and systems analysis of transportation requirements in the northeast (Washington to Boston) corridor; and worked on plans for complete "new cities" set far apart from existing urban areas. Ramo sees the systems analysis method as one of great promise in every field from housing and education to transportation and urban development.

Like a Renaissance man, Ramo takes an optimistic view of the world, believing that sufficient information and analysis will eventually lead to right decisions and the better society. He acknowledges that application of the sys-

* Even in the recession year of 1970, TRW held its total sales virtually steady and increased its earnings slightly.

tems approach in the social arena is still at an embryonic stage, and that no example can yet be cited of a completed systems approach application to a problem primarily social in character. He also confesses that any complete systems approach will raise questions many would like to ignore—to wit, in an urban rapid transit system, which city communities should prosper and which wither by the selection of transit right-of-way. But he insists that crises in U.S. life, especially the inner city, are too explosive to permit long delays.

Set close by the glistening Pacific at Santa Monica are the buildings of the Rand Corporation—the name stands for R(esearch) AN(d) D(evelopment)—foremost think tank of Los Angeles and perhaps the world. Rand was born at the end of World War II when high Air Force officials wanted to maintain and develop a civilian brain trust well removed from Washington. Air Force contracts, originally close to 100 percent of Rand's project load, declined over the years to about 50 percent, with another 10 percent for other defense agencies and 40 percent of the nonprofit corporation's work devoted to domestic programs. Some 1,000 mathematicians, chemists, physicists, social scientists, computer experts, and other scholars work for Rand at Santa Monica, another 100 in a Washington office, and a like number in New York.

Rand's specialty since its first days has been to take a clear-eyed look into the future. A 1946 paper clearly outlined the possibilities of satellites circling the earth and returning human passengers through the atmospheric shield. (The worst mistake of the paper was its estimate of the cost of orbiting a man: a paltry $150 million.) Rand studies revealed possible obliteration of the Strategic Air Command's planes in the late 1950s under then-programmed strategic basing, predicted the Soviet's Sputnik launch, encouraged the start of the country's ICBM program, and influenced almost all Air Force strategic weapons over a quarter century.

War gaming has been popular at Rand since its early years, leading some critics to call Santa Monica "the most famous casino of fun-in-death games in the country." Rand, however, insists that war gaming makes up a small portion of its work, although a vital one in analyzing and synthesizing information for broad strategic or tactical studies.

A semimilitary aura hangs over the Rand buildings at Santa Monica, with guards, security passes, and big signs on files indicating whether they hold classified material—all underscoring the secret and sensitive nature of Rand's work for the defense establishment over the years. But a talk with officials of Rand's domestic component—on my visit, Anthony Pascal, director of human resource studies, and John Pincus, chief of Rand's California program—quickly dispels the weighty military-industrial complex feel. The ebullient Pascal, in his late thirties and possessed of what must be the handsomest handlebar moustache west of Milwaukee, quickly launched into a description of a Rand project to aid a large school district like Los Angeles' in meeting court requirements that it reassign pupils to end de facto school segregation. A solution would require a fantastically complex balancing of factors like busing, boundary changes, costs, population forecasting, and other devices to prevent resegregation.

The first stage of Rand's California program was directed at education, intergovernmental relations, and air pollution. Within elementary and secondary schools in several California locations, for instance, Rand experimented with methods to develop a new education information system as a tool for economies in scarce tax dollars, better management, and accountability in terms of just what quality of education is delivered. In 1971, Rand's California program broadened with the opening of a Sacramento office to perform broader research and analysis tasks for the state in cooperation with state universities. Some specific state contracts were granted and Rand began to move into new policy areas like health, manpower, and energy problems in relation to the environment.

By 1970–71, the recession had hit major think tanks in California and other spots across the country. Like the aerospace companies, the think tanks found themselves victims of government spending cutbacks, public disenchantment with technology (a trend that upsets aerospace and think tank officials more than anything else, as they look to the 1970s), and their general isolation from political and economic realities. Some companies lost so much business they had to pare their staffs by as much as 50 percent. Rand's cutbacks were much less (around 10 percent) but the firm in 1971 faced an uncertain future in the wake of the disclosure that its copy of the top-secret Pentagon study of the Vietnam war, released to the press by Daniel Ellsberg in 1971, was obtained by him during the time that he was a Rand researcher.

Setting Records in Orange County

To reach Orange County, they say in Los Angeles, "You go down the freeway and turn right." In all America, there is no greater bastion of conservative voting strength. Goldwater got 56 percent of its vote in 1964, Nixon 63 percent in 1968, Reagan 72 percent in 1966 and 67 percent in 1970. The last time Orange voted Democratic for President was 1936. For 16 years, the county sent to Congress James B. Utt, a man who once said: "Government is like a child molester who offers candy before his evil act." When Utt died in 1969, he was replaced by John Schmitz, an avowed member of the John Birch Society. And for 35 years prior to his demise in 1970, Orange County was home for Raymond Cyrus Hoiles, publisher of the Santa Ana *Register*, who spurned the Presidential candidacy of Robert A. Taft because he considered him not conservative enough and wanted to abolish the public schools because he thought their financing a form of compulsory taxation.

There is a lot more to Orange County than its ultraconservatism, of course. It has Mission San Juan Capistrano, where the swallows unfailingly depart every St. John's Day (October 23) to return on St. Joseph's Day (March 19); 40 miles of magnificent beach and choice surfside communities like Newport Beach and Laguna Beach; world-famed Disneyland; oil wells; mountains; remnants of the orange groves which gave the county its name; the birthplace of Richard M. Nixon at Yorba Linda and his western White

House at San Clemente; the Irvine Ranch, six times as big as Manhattan; hundreds of aerospace-defense firms, which account for half the employment rolls; pockets of affluence and wretched slums; but above all, endless suburbia and the great middle-class society.

Orange has also been the fastest-growing big county in the United States, up almost 1,000 percent from a 1940 Census count of 130,760 to 1,420,386 in 1970. Just in the 1960s, the population went up by 716,461. And while this vast suburb lacks a metropolitan heart, it has four cities with more than 100,-000 souls—Anaheim (1970 population of 166,701), Santa Ana (156,601), Garden Grove (122,524) and Huntingdon Beach (115,960). The population is 92 percent Caucasion, 7 percent Mexican-American (mostly old field hands and their descendants), and less than 1 percent Negro.

The homogeneity of Orange County is about the best explanation I have ever seen for its conservatism. Engineers, technicians, aircraft workers account for a large share of Orange County's population, a class with a high technological but low humanistic education. It is an eminently middle-society, with middle-class fears: Will taxes take away one's hard-earned prosperity? Will a black move in next door and spoil property values? The flame of resistance to taxes and big government burns bright, even though the county has exceptionally low property taxes and federal spending accounts for so much of the income. Big government outlays for social welfare are bad, but for weapons systems, they are good. Yet even in the ordered world of Orange County, there are now major intrusions of the drug traffic, hippies, campus disorders, smog. All are distinct threats to a people who want to be left alone to coast along.

A word about the world that lies behind the 20-foot-high wall of the late Walt Disney's Magic Kingdom at Anaheim. It is all in the furtherance of fun, of course, but overwhelmingly the image of Disneyland is cleanliness and well-scrubbed Americanism. Horse dung disappears in a whisk, mules are sprayed to make them odorless and insect-repellant. Any disreputable types of visitors are turned away at the gate. There is an electronically operated figure of Abraham Lincoln that seems almost human on the Disneyland Opera House stage. The figure speaks selected passages, such as defending the spirit of liberty, but it is a bleached-out history in which nothing is said about the Civil War or slavery. It was here at Disneyland that Ronald Ziegler, later to become President Nixon's youthful press secretary, got his start as a tour guide. ("Welcome aboard, folks, my name is Ron and I'll be your skipper and guide down the rivers of adventure. . . . Note the alligators. Please keep your hands inside the boat. They're always looking for a hand-out.") Not until 1968 did Disneyland hire its first Negroes in such "people contact" jobs.

Whatever its social implications, Disneyland has been a fantastic financial success, easily overshadowing the once-dominant Disney film operations, which have prospered ever since the founder introduced Mickey Mouse to the world in 1928. The investment at Disneyland has grown from $17 million to $126 million, and the parent company moved from $11.6 million gross in

1954 to $143.3 million in 1969.

Disneyland could scarcely be anything but the event of the century for the host city of Anaheim. In 1950, the city had 14,556 people; by 1970 166,-701. In the first decade of Disneyland, it generated some $560 million in local business, not to mention millions paid in taxes. Local writers described Anaheim as Orange County's "Cinderella City" and speculated on what could ever make the bubble burst.

While Anaheim boomed, the county's long-time leading city, Santa Ana, increased a mere 239 percent in population. By the late '60s, it was suffering from severe growing pains. Despite studies showing Santa Ana would need more than $100 million to meet sewer, park, and other capital improvement needs through 1980, its voters (egged on by Hoiles's newspaper) rejected $25 million in bond issues to finance the first five years' improvements. With a great wrench of their conservative consciences, civic leaders were just beginning in 1970 to accept their first aid funds from the federal government.

The great city in Orange County's future scarcely exists yet. It is Irvine, a projected metropolis of 430,000 people on the vast expanses of the greatest piece of undeveloped urban land in America, the Irvine Ranch. The story of the Irish immigrant James Irvine, I, and the four generations that followed him, the last in open rebellion against a foundation that now controls the ranch, is quintessentially American—of the self-made founder and the first great acquisitions (once totaling 110,000 acres), sheep-herding, fighting off the Southern Pacific Railroad crews at gunpoint, irrigated farming over great swaths of land, commercial reversals, the unhappy and morose later years of James Irvine, II, before his death in 1947, the takeover by the charitable foundation he created (headed by his former accountant), and the spunky, headstrong fight of young Joan Irvine Smith, last of the famous line, to take control of the ranch away from the foundation.

As in so many stories Californian, the University of California plays a key role in the modern Irvine story. Master planner-architect William Pereira of Los Angeles, commissioned by the UC board of regents to find a new campus site in the South L.A. County–Orange County area, settled on Irvine as the best possibility. With what must have been masterful tact, he won over the members of the board of the Irvine Company to the idea of donating 1,000 acres to the University of California. As Pereira planned UC Irvine, it would be the focal point for a European-style university community of 100,-000 people living on 10,000 acres of that part of the ranch. University and town government would be closely tied together.

In time, the Irvine Company officials took over more and more of their own planning and decided they ought to have not just another city of some 100,000, but a great metropolis that would dominate Orange County. It would stretch across 82 square miles, the full 53,000-acre central valley of the ranch. Within the city, there would be 40 residential villages, 33 miles of aesthetically landscaped "environmental corridors," recreation facilities, and carefully planned commercial and industrial centers.

Not everyone was delighted by the shape of the new plan. Writing in the Los Angeles *Times* in 1970, writer David Shaw said there was a question whether Irvine would become a true "new town" free of congestion and socially integrated, or whether it might "be just a mammoth subdivision"—or, in the words of one USC critic, "a white, upper-middle-class, sterile, suburban ghetto." *

The compromise in values is already appearing. While many of the first housing developments at Irvine allowed a felicitous treatment of the land, with wide-open spaces, more recent developments have a density pattern reminiscent of the worst slurbs. It is not only the profit motive, but fear of the market, that may hold the Irvine planners back from a socially imaginative community. In short, as writer Shaw himself asked, is there a large enough "liberal" market in conservative California? The cosmopolitan, liberal atmosphere of new cities like Reston (Virginia) and Columbia (Maryland) is almost tangible. A similar "liberal" market, only four or five times larger, might be hard to find in Southern California—or at least so the planners of Irvine say. One looks at the temper of the California university generation of today and wonders whether the planners are not planning for an already mature generation, not the one that will be occupying their new community as it is completed over 50 years. But one thing is sure: Irvine, as it is now being planned, will fit right in with the rest of Orange County.

San Diego: City of Promise

Gunther wrote well of San Diego as "a shining plaque of a city, built around a great park with glorious views of hill and harbor." Here, at the southwestern extremity of the continental U.S.A., we come on one of the world's great natural harbors, set off by shining hills and mesas, and, in winter, snow-capped mountains. Seaward lies the steep-sided, wind-swept promontory of Point Loma, that last point of land for the hundreds of thousands of sailors who have ridden out and back with the fleets for more than a century now.

San Diego's role in California history was vital, for it was on a parched, sun-bleached hill overlooking her harbor that Father Junípero Serra stood in 1769 to proclaim the founding of the first permanent Christian settlement of California. Through the mission years, Mexican rule and the American ascendancy, little changed; the city's age-old rival, Los Angeles, started ahead and remained ahead in population and wealth and power.

The pace quickened with World War I, the coming of the early aviation companies (Convair and Ryan Aeronautical) in the '20s and '30s, and finally, with the onset of World War II, America's first great Pacific conflict. The Navy-dominated "Dago" of the war years was prosperous but incredibly crowded; suddenly San Diego found itself in a boom-and-bust cycle not yet broken. A postwar dip was followed by salad days for the big aircraft and missile build-

* Santa Ana is already developing its own shabby and forlorn racial ghettos with 66 percent of Orange County's 10,000 Negroes and many of its Mexican-Americans. City Manager Carl Thornton fears that unless Irvine developers can be persuaded to include substantial amounts of low-income housing in their plans, "our city will look like downtown Kansas City, downtown Detroit."

ers (Convair, Rohr, Ryan Aeronautical) in the 1950s, then a cruel recession in the early '60s, strong recovery in mid-decade, and finally, around 1970, a new but not so serious recession. The experience has made San Diego determined to break free of its stepchild relationship to the Navy and Pentagon contractors, and in fact its widened economic base—in tourism, research, and educational complexes—has carried it far beyond its old dependency status. Once San Diego was literally the end of the line; now it is a gateway, seeking direct air connections to Hawaii and beyond, pressing into new areas of scientific exploration. On America's Pacific coast, only two cities are larger—Los Angeles and San Francisco. In 1970, the Census takers found 1,357,854 people in San Diego County, 696,769 in the city itself. The area total was more than four times what it had been just before Pearl Harbor.

Headquarters of the Eleventh Naval District, San Diego ranks with Norfolk as one of the two biggest Navy cities in the U.S.A. One out of four San Diegoans works for the Navy or Marines as serviceman or civilian employee, or is a military dependent. When not working in aerospace factories or tending the military, San Diegoans have three basic sources of income—agriculture, science, and tourism. The least of these is agriculture, but there is still major activity in the growing of citrus trees, avocados, and even flowers not too far from the city.

Science is everywhere, from Scripps Pier to Palomar Mountain, the fulfillment of a prophecy made by a city official about a decade ago: "Rosie the Riveter is leaving town but Sammy the Scientist is coming in." San Diego is becoming a national center in oceanography, a development perhaps preordained by the founding, in 1912, of the Scripps Institution of Oceanography at La Jolla. Now more than 80 companies, military units and universities in the area are in oceanographic research ranging from potential fishery sources and developing underwater instruments to sea-floor topography and possible exploitation of its natural resources. The Scripps Institution has been involved with the National Science Foundation's Deep Sea Drilling Project. Also in the area are the Salk Institute (headed by Dr. Jonas E. Salk, who developed the vaccine for poliomyelitis), Lockheed's oceanographic facility, Gulf General Atomic and Western Behavioral Sciences Institute. Not to be overlooked is the big business of higher education—perhaps worth $100 million annually to the San Diego economy. More than 70,000 students are enrolled at local colleges and universities.

San Diego was the surprise last-minute choice as the site of the 1972 Republican National Convention—apparently because President Nixon found it so convenient to his digs at San Clemente. But San Diego is an old hand at accommodating visitors; in fact it welcomes tens of thousands of visitors each day, who spend some $400 million a year. The tourist tradition goes back to highly successful expositions in 1915–16 and 1935–36, and one can see their physical legacy in 1,400-acre Balboa Park, which houses theaters, galleries, and museums. Neil Morgan, the Western writer who makes his home in La Jolla and writes for the San Diego *Evening Tribune*, notes that while competitive San Diegoans of past decades "glowered while Los Angeles became a runaway megalopolis," it is now apparent that San Diego's failure to burgeon like L.A. was a blessing. "Lacking crowding and smog and the other badges of industrial triumph, San Diego has become the playground for Los Angeles' millions, a kind of weekend patio for the Southwest."

San Diego Bay is a sparkling crescent some 15 miles long and a quarter to two and a half miles wide. On a weekend the bay waters flash a thousand white sails and the white wakes of countless powerboats; on the beaches opposite the Naval Station there are swimmers and water-skiers, and fishermen line the sea-walls of the harbor. All this might not be, however, if San Diego's people had not voted in 1960 to indebt themselves for $42.5 million to build a sewage treatment and offshore dispersal system to save the bay from encroaching pollution. Each day, some 60 million gallons of inadequately treated sewage from San Diego and its suburbs were flowing into the bay, plus millions more from Coronado, the Naval Amphibious Base, and local canneries and commercial ships. From its primeval blue, the bay had turned to a brownish-reddish cast, imparted by the proliferation and death of phytoplankton. Along one harbor stretch in the central city, solids had formed a sludge mat along the bay floor 900 yards long. Threatening health, high densities of coliform bacteria were noted. Several beaches were quarantined.

An earlier bond issue for treatment and dispersal of sewage had been rejected by the San Diego voters in 1953, but by 1960 the problem was so egregious that overwhelming approval went to the proposal for a monstrous set of interceptors, carrying the sewage to a plant on the seaward side of Point Loma. There it would be treated and then conveyed more than two miles out under the ocean by two Y-shaped diffuser legs. Construction started in 1961, and was finished in 1965 at a final cost of about $60 million. And then, as if there had been a series of great tidal flushings, the bay quickly cleared, and what had been brown and red became blue and sparkling. Back into the bay swarmed the sea-life it had once known—sculpin, sole, sand bass, steelhead trout, silver salmon, bonefish, baracuda, octopus, shark, seal, and porpoise. The sludge beds began to shrink and the coliform density dropped, permitting reopening of the beaches. With the possible exception of Seattle's Lake Washington, it is difficult to think of a more dramatic victory of an American city in the battle against water pollution.

Another new thing in San Diego Bay is the blue arc thrown against the sky by the superstructure of the Coronado Bridge, completed in 1969 to make a linkage (previously possible only by ferry) between San Diego and the sleepy little city of Coronado. A town long famous for its great, lumbering, white Victorian wonder, the Hotel del Coronado, Coronado is populated by many of the retired Navy brass who give San Diego County its distinctively conservative political coloration.

Lack of early and sound planning, in fact, has been San Diego's greatest failure and poses the gravest threat to its future. The city's central growth has turned its back on the magnificent harbor; once-beautiful Harbor Drive has become a heavily traveled airport service road (the airport is set down squarely in an anachronistic center-city location with jets swooping past the high-rises); haphazard commercial development was permitted in Mission Valley; the community of Lemon Grove was allowed to cut down *all* its lemon trees and to put up a huge and atrocious looking concrete lemon at its entrance. The metropolitan concentrate now sprawls 15 miles south of Broadway to the Mexican border and 20 miles north, past wealthy La Jolla on its lovely hill beside the sea, towards Orange County. San Diego's closer-in suburbia, architect Richard Neutra wrote, "is blighted by a kind of elephantiasis." Blacks and Mexican-Americans generally fail to share the middle-class affluence, and the Mexican-American ghetto community of San Ysidro is a forgotten pocket of misery that relates about as well to greater San Diego as Anacostia does to metropolitan Washington, D.C.

Yet there is so much positive—the harbor, parks, and fine colleges and universities; the wonderful climate; the canyons that separate the metropolis into relatively distinct communities on a very human scale. In contrast to most American metropolises, San Diego is less hurried, angry, or intense; though part of Southern California, it blessedly lacks Los Angeles' bedlam and the igloo-shaped ice cream palace culture. The city is still young and malleable, and may well mature into one of America's finest in times to come.

Virtually every researcher into the city's power structure has concluded that influence is exerted primarily through the business-financial community, not through the politicians. (The development of powerful political machines nourished by patronage is stymied because of the nonpartisan nature of local politics.) The two businessmen long considered most powerful in San Diego have been C. Arnholt Smith, who controls the U.S. National Bank of San Diego, and John Alessio, a big race-track developer and sometimes associate of Smith. Smith's holdings, many through his own mini-conglomerate (Westgate-California Corp.) include insurance companies, two small airlines, taxicab, bus and limousine services, ranches, food processors, a luxury hotel and the Padres baseball team. He gives generously to GOP campaigns and in 1964 was one of a select, small group of men who urged Goldwater to enter the state's Presidential primary. One of his employees is chairman of the county Republican committee, and the *Wall Street Journal* has estimated his wealth from multitudinous business undertakings at more than $20 million. Alessio, likewise a big GOP contributor (to the Nixon-Agnew 1968 campaign in the tens of thousands, for instance), has race-track interests in Mexico, with an inevitable gambling tie-in through his Mexican operations. Early in 1970, the federal government indicted him for evading income tax payments over several years. He entered a plea of guilty and began a three-year prison sentence in 1971.

In 1970, San Diego was shaken by a series of indictments against eight local officials—including Mayor Frank Curran—on bribery and conspiracy charges surrounding a fare increase for the Yellow Cab Company, which enjoys a near-monopoly position in the city. All but one of the men were exonerated, but the trials left lingering public suspicions about political corruption. Curran was decisively defeated when he ran again for mayor in 1971; his successor is Pete Wilson, an able young Republican state assemblyman.

Except for Dallas, San Diego is the largest city of the U.S.A. which retains the city manager form of government; some believe that power brokers like Smith and Alessio prefer having a single powerful city official to deal with. But there has never been a suggestion of impropriety in the manager's office, as there has been with the mayor, the council, and the police. An especially outstanding manager was Thomas Fletcher (1961–66), who pioneered in the creation of neighborhood planning councils to give citizens a maximum voice in their government. Fletcher also helped San Diego avoid the hang-ups of neighboring Orange County cities about accepting federal urban assistance grants.

Well-to-do Republicanism, aided and abetted by the predictably military orientation of those who sup at the Navy-aerospace table, makes San Diego County a disaster area for most Democratic candidates. The prevailing Republican conservatism and militarism of San Diego is reflected and relentlessly reinforced by the San Diego *Union*, the "flagship" of James S. Copley's string of 29 California and Illinois newspapers (including the Sacramento *Union* and the evening San Diego *Tribune*). The loyalties of the San Diego *Union* are amply illustrated by some of its chief executives. Editor Herb Klein regularly took time off from his job in San Diego to handle Richard Nixon's press relations in various campaigns of the 1950s and '60s, finally getting his reward as communications director in the Nixon Presidential Administration. In 1968, the *Union* chose as its editorial and news director retired Lt. Gen. Victor Krulak, a peppery ex-Marine officer (nickname: Brute) who quit the service after heading the corps in Vietnam and being passed over for commandant; it was Krulak's first newspaper job. James Copley himself is a former Navy captain; and the head of his Washington bureau is a retired admiral. "Hawkish" in the extreme, the *Union* is also strong for fiscal conservatism, hostile to students and dissent, and predictably Republican. But its election coverage is now fairer than it was in 1960, when it ran heads like this: "Election of Sen. Kennedy Would Please Russians."

In 1970, the *Union* found itself under fire within its own journalistic profession. *Newsweek* ran a bitterly critical (though not wholly accurate) attack, followed up by a full-scale critique by the liberal, muckraking *San Diego Magazine*. The *Union-Tribune* zapped back with a full-scale defense of its policies and professionalism, but the critics' message about the paper's distorted coverage and tedious moralizing was likely to be remembered.

Neither television nor outside newspaper competition provide any real alternative or counterforce to the *Union* in its home town; an underground newspaper, the *Street Journal*, has mounted blistering attacks on the ethics of the power machinations of Copley, Arnholt Smith, and the entire San Diego establishment, but its readership is not wide and its journalistic standards open to question. San Diego moderates dream of the day the *Union* may go centrist, just as the Los Angeles *Times*—not dissimilar from the *Union* until the late 1950s—has done. And in fact, the "new" L. A. *Times* has been besieged with requests to set up a satellite edition in San Diego.

Santa Barbara: Trouble in Eden

Our tour of Southern California now ends with gardened Santa Barbara, 100 miles up the coast from Los Angeles, a city set in a crescent-shaped valley between the honey-colored Santa Ynez Mountains and the Pacific. Santa Barbara is so imbued with quiet gentility and tradition that its real soul sister is San Francisco, not the flashy new urban creations of the Southland. No California city is so close, in architecture and life style, to the ancient Spanish. Here is the Queen of the Missions, where the altar candle flame the Padres lighted in 1786 has never been snuffed out.

Nor is there any California city so Eastern; as the social historian Cleveland Amory noted, Santa Barbara is the Western front of the Eastern establishment. The Los Angeles *Times* commented in a review not long ago: "Color it Boston, little Back Bay West with blooming begonias, a New England style blueblood community with two social registers, a court house which looks like a Moorish palace and the third oldest polo playing club in America."

Mr. Santa Barbara of the 20th century was Thomas M. Storke, who became editor and publisher of the Santa Barbara *News-Press* in 1901; prior to his death at the age of 94 in 1971, he was the oldest native among Santa Barbara's 70,215 people * and still the city's guiding spirit. Wearer of a vest and a Dakota sombrero, Storke was a direct descendant of José Francisco Ortego, the Spaniard who founded Santa Barbara. Over a long and illustrious lifetime, he was a college classmate of Herbert Hoover at Stanford, a U.S. Senator, a delegate to five national political conventions, a winner of the Pulitzer Prize, and a major benefactor of the University of California at Santa Barbara. A staunch Democrat and liberal in a wealthy and Republican town, Storke helped it advance in the arts and also become a place for the free exchange of ideas—symbolized by the Center for the Study of Democratic Institutions, which he helped attract to the city. I well remember a 1961 interview with Storke in which he brought to my attention, for the first time, the inanities in Birch Society founder Robert Welch's *Blue Book*.

The most cataclysmic event in Santa Barbara's modern-day history occurred on January 28, 1969. Workmen on Union Oil's "Platform A," drilling for oil six miles off the Santa Barbara shore, cut a hole into a high-pressure deposit of oil and gas. The huge oil bubble boiled up to the surface of the channel at the rate of almost 1,000 gallons an hour, spreading across the blue water for 11 days. Finally, 400 square miles of the ocean were affected and 40 miles of beach front covered with acrid, tarlike slime. Birds diving through the oily swells for fish failed to surface alive. Along the mucky shoreline, thousands more birds lay dying, unable to raise their oil-soaked wings. Oil which had been emulsified by the surf sank to the bottom to kill lobsters, mussels, clams, and some fish.

* 1970 Census figure for the city alone; including all of Santa Barbara County, the figure was 264,324.

For Santa Barbara, it was like a horrible dream come true. There had been strong local resistance in 1968 when the U. S. Interior Department auctioned off nearly 600 square miles of channel leases for $603 million—a decision then-Interior Secretary Stewart Udall would later call his own "Bay of Pigs." The city had every reason to be unenthusiastic. Drilling activity brings little money into a community, and even without accidents, Santa Barbara's azure channel view is marred by the unsightly drilling platforms and the attendant bustle of oil activities along the waterfront. For most cities, a nearby oil spill would be a scandal; for Santa Barbara, living basically off tourism, it can be a near disaster. Within a year of the 1969 spill, the city's tourist business fell off seriously. Smaller leaks followed, and the channel remained geologically unstable. As drilling continued, the danger of newer and possibly even worse oil spills remained.

The oil industry considers the risks well worth taking. The Santa Barbara Channel happens to cover one of the world's richest oil fields, right beside the world's biggest market for oil—auto-happy Southern California. The loss of some birds and sealife, oilmen maintain, is a small price to pay for the oil that human "progress" demands; anyway, there have been small normal oil "leaks" in the strata near Santa Barbara for as long as the white man can remember. One study of the 1969 blowout showed remarkably little long-term damage.

Santa Barbara citizens see it differently; in fact they are almost unanimous in wanting all oil drilling stopped (a step the federal government refuses to take). Immediately after the big blowout, a community organization called "GOO"—standing for Get Oil Out!—sprang into being. The issue, in fact, "radicalized" a wealthy and conservative community with amazing rapidity. But two years after the big blowout at Santa Barbara, despite temporary suspensions of drilling and restrictions of new sites, despite heated protests by California in Congress, the oil activity at Santa Barbara was going ahead.

An account of the Santa Barbara scene written before 1970 could easily have brushed off the University of California branch there. The school's image, in the words of one writer, was "that of the fun-loving school where blond, sun-tanned youths romped on surfboards and at fraternity parties." Yet suddenly, California and the nation were hearing that these "golden" California youth were engaged in massive rioting and had actually *burned a bank*. These were not the offspring of liberal, intellectual families like those at Berkeley or Madison or Columbia; they were predominately products of conservative, business-oriented homes. How could disorders happen *here?* *

The physical setting and a diabolically unfortunate chain of events appeared to be responsible. The UCSB branch is outside the city of Santa Barbara, separated by 10 miles of airport, swamp, and freeway. And where the students mostly live is not the campus, but the adjoining, unincorporated area of Isla Vista, a mile-square community built for the sole purpose of housing students. Isla Vista, in fact, is a ghetto, set in total isolation, suffering

* Many details of this account are drawn from excellent accounts by UCSB sociologists Richard Flacks and Milton Mankoff in *The Nation* and Leroy F. Aarons in the Washington *Post*.

from constant harassment by the police, afflicted by minimal municipal services, crowded and cheap housing, high rents, and the like. With students thus isolated from the outside world, the conditions were perfect for creation of an alien youth culture—of rock music, widely available drugs (marijuana usage estimated at well over 50 percent), extravagant hippie dress and hairdos, and sex both free and frequent.

Alienation alone, though, does not lead to bank-burning. Within a very few months, these other things happened: the oil spill in the channel, imperiling the students' beaches, followed by much rhetoric but no corrective action from Sacramento or Washington; formation of a radical union which briefly took over the university center; the continuing Vietnam war and President Nixon's disdain for moratorium demonstrations; the draft lottery, highly advertised, but turning out not to be "safe" for anyone anyway; new movies like *Easy Rider* and *Alice's Restaurant,* which reinforced the basic lessons of insecurity and impotence; and finally the early 1970 dismissal by UCSB of Professor William Allen, an unorthodox but popular anthropology teacher. A protest against Allen's firing was signed by 7,776 students (well over a majority), but totally ignored by the university. Then came massive but peaceful student demonstrations over the issue; they likewise were ignored by the university. Instead, university officials called in the police, questionable raids were staged, and the groundwork was set for violence. Police harassment got increasingly worse, students one night beat up a policeman, Chicago Seven lawyer William Kunstler came to speak, police unjustifiably attacked a youth carrying a bottle of wine—and a night of rampage had begun, during which the Isla Vista branch of the Bank of America was burned to the ground.

Even the bank-burning failed to burn out the passions; in the next weeks came more riots, constant clashes with the police, the accidental killing of a student by a stray bullet from a policeman's gun, and then, in June 1970, one of the most frightening police rampages of modern times, in which officers kicked down apartment doors, dragged students out of bedrooms and bathrooms, menacing, gassing, and clubbing, and arresting hundreds. It was the police's way to "teach the kids a lesson." Perhaps they remembered what Governor Reagan had said earlier in the spring about campus violence: "If it takes a bloodbath, let's get it over with. No more appeasement."

Incredibly, this was happening in progressive and tolerant California, land of golden opportunity, and within the greatest state university of America.

But violence was not to have the last word at Isla Vista. The bank-burning, as Norman Cousins reported in the *Saturday Review* in June 1971, had the effect of undermining the influence of extremist student factions and bringing to the fore a new type of student activist—"intellectually sophisticated, politically adroit, less concerned with ideological sloganeering than with the dynamics of change." Out of regular student fees, these new activists were able to launch a food cooperative where students can buy meat and groceries (some organically grown); a credit union; a legal assistance office for students; a unit providing psychiatric, drug, and contraceptive services; and a facility akin to the Travelers Aid Society, to assist itinerant, homeless young "floaters." Most of these activities were run out of a Service Center made possible in part by a $25,000 contribution from none other than Louis B. Lundborg, chairman of the board of the Bank of America. Lundborg decided after the Santa Barbara bombing that even while violence was to be condemned, it mirrored wells of deep-lying discontent with the Vietnam war and other practices of society, and that "a new value system" was coming to the country, starting with its youth, which the older generation would ignore at its peril. Lundborg's leadership and the emergence of a more mature and self-confident group of student leaders helped open new avenues of communication between the community and campus at Isla Vista. As a result of a special commission's report, the university itself was working to improve student conditions and effect local police reforms.

The 1970–71 academic year witnessed another amazing event: a decision by the Student Body Residents Council to hire a lobbyist to represent student views in Sacramento—on issues of students' rights, but also low-cost housing, equal opportunity for women, minority rights, and environmental protection. After a spirited debate, the regents approved the new lobbying—in large part because several members (including Norton Simon and Lt. Gov. Reinecke) had visited Isla Vista and held personal meetings with the students.

A throwback to the times of violence remains a distinct possibility in California, and probably will for years to come. But out of the valley of discord, new forms of social organization, and responsive forms of intergenerational dialogue, begin to emerge. California, where America gets the signals of what is about to happen to it, may be in trouble. But it is not dead or frozen. It yearns and grows and changes, and it may yet be our best hope.

BIBLIOGRAPHY

Despite the extensive interviews for this book, it would have taken several additional years in the field to compile, personally, all the data which appears within it. By the time the process were completed, of course, many of the original interviews would have been hopelessly out of date. For that reason, I made extensive reference to books and articles on these United States, their history, and present-day condition. To the authors whose work I have drawn upon, my sincerest thanks.

The first list below includes books on national themes, or which cover several states at once. They are followed by an individual bibliography for each of the megastates.

Automobile Facts and Figures, 1971. Automobile Manufacturers Assn., Detroit, 1971.

Barrett, Marvin, ed. *Survey of Broadcast Journalism, 1968–69 and 1969–70* (sponsored by Alfred I. duPont and Columbia University). New York: Grosset & Dunlap, 1969, 1970.

Birmingham, Stephen. *The Right People—A Portrait of the American Social Establishment.* Boston: Little Brown, 1968.

Book of the States, 1968–69. The Council of State Governments, Chicago, 1968.

Brownson, Charles B. *Congressional Staff Directory.* Published annually, Washington, D.C.

The Capitol and the Campus—State Responsibility for Postsecondary Education. Report and Recommendation by the Carnegie Commission on Higher Education. New York: McGraw-Hill, 1971.

1970 Census of Population. Bureau of the Census, Washington, D.C.

Citizens Conference on State Legislatures. Various studies including "Recommendations for the States," by Larry Margolis, Kansas City, Mo., 1971, 1972.

Congress and the Nation, 1945–64, and Vol. II, *1965–68.* Congressional Quarterly Service, Washington, D.C., 1967 and 1969.

Dixon, Robert G., Jr. *Democratic Representation—Reapportionment in Law and Politics.* New York: Oxford University Press, 1968.

Editor and Publisher International Year Book—1971. Editor and Publisher, New York, 1971.

Employment and Earnings—States and Areas, 1939–69. U. S. Department of Labor, Bureau of Labor Statistics, Washington, D.C., 1970.

Encyclopedia Americana, 1969 Edition. New York: Americana Corporation. (Includes excellent state and city review articles.)

Farb, Peter. *Face of North America—The Natural History of a Continent.* New York: Harper & Row, 1963.

Fodor-Shell Travel Guides U.S.A. Fodor's Modern Guides, Inc., Litchfield, Conn., 1966, 1967. (In several regional editions, the best of the travel guides.)

From Sea to Shining Sea—A Report on the American Environment—Our Natural Heritage. President's Council on Recreation and Natural Beauty, Washington, D.C., 1968.

Gunther, John. *Inside U.S.A.* New York: Harper & Row, 1947 and 1951.

Hess, Stephen. *American Political Dynasties—From Adams to Kennedy.* Garden City, N.Y.: Doubleday, 1966.

Hess, Stephen, and Broder, David S. *The Republican Establishment—The Present and Future of the G.O.P.* New York: Harper & Row, 1967.

Jacobs, Jane. *The Economy of Cities.* New York: Random House, 1969.

Life Pictorial Atlas of the World. Editors of *Life* and Rand McNally. New York: Time, Inc., 1961.

Lundberg, Ferdinand. *The Rich and the Super-Rich.* New York: Lyle Stuart, 1968.

Man . . . An Endangered Species? U. S. Department of the Interior Conservation Yearbook, Washington, D.C., 1968.

Marine, Gene. *America the Raped—The Engineering Mentality and Devastation of a Continent.* New York: Simon & Schuster, 1969.

The National Atlas of the United States of America. Geological Survey, U. S. Department of the Interior, Washington, D.C., 1970.

New York Times Encyclopedic Almanac. New York Times Book & Educational Division, New York, 1970.

Pearson, Drew, and Anderson, Jack. *The Case Against Congress.* New York: Simon & Schuster, 1968.

Phillips, Kevin H. *The Emerging Republican Majority.* New Rochelle, N.Y.: Arlington House, 1969.

Presidential Nominating Conventions—1968. Congressional Quarterly Service, Washington, D.C., 1968.

Rankings of the States, 1971. Research Division,

National Education Assn., Washington, D.C., 1971.

Reichley, James, and others. *States in Crisis—Politics in Ten American States, 1950–62.* Chapel Hill: University of North Carolina Press, 1964.

Reid, Ed. *The Grim Reapers—The Anatomy of Organized Crime in America.* Chicago: Henry Regnery, 1969.

Report of the National Advisory Commission on Civil Disorders, Washington, D.C., 1968.

Ridgeway, James. *The Closed Corporation—American Universities In Crisis.* New York: Random House, 1968.

Ruchelman, Leonard I., ed. *The Big City Mayors—The Crisis In Urban Politics.* Bloomington: Indiana University Press, 1969.

Sanford, Terry. *Storm Over the States.* New York: McGraw-Hill, 1967.

Scammon, Richard M., ed. *America Votes—A Handbook of Contemporary American Election Statistics.* Published biennially by the Governmental Affairs Institute, through Congressional Quarterly, Washington, D.C.

Scammon, Richard M., and Wattenberg, Ben J. *The Real Majority—An Extraordinary Examination of the American Electorate.* New York: Coward-McCann, 1970.

State and Local Finances—Significant Features, 1967 to 1970. Advisory Commission on Intergovernmental Relations, Washington, D.C., November 1969.

State Government Finances in 1969. U. S. Department of Commerce, Bureau of the Census, Washington, D.C., June 1970.

Statistical Abstract of the United States, 1970. U. S. Department of Commerce, Bureau of the Census, Washington, D.C., 1970.

Steinbeck, John. *Travels With Charley—In Search of America.* New York: Viking, 1961.

Steiner, Stan. *La Raza—The Mexican-Americans.*

New York: Harper & Row, 1969.

Survey of Current Business. U. S. Department of Commerce, Office of Business Economics, Washington, D.C., monthly. August editions contain full reports on geographic trends in personal income and per capita income.

Thayer, George. *The Father Shores of Politics.* New York: Simon & Schuster, 1967.

These United States—Our Nation's Geography, History and People. Reader's Digest Assn., Pleasantville, N.Y., 1968.

Time-Life Library of America. New York: Time, Inc., 1967, 1968. (In several excellent regional volumes, cited individually under the separate states.)

Tour Books, 1970–71. American Automobile Assn., Washington, D.C., 1970.

Trippett, Frank. *The States: United They Fell.* New York: World, 1967.

Uniform Crime Reports for the United States, 1969. U. S. Department of Justice, Federal Bureau of Investigation, Washington, D.C., 1970.

Von Eckardt, Wolf. *A Place To Live—The Crisis of the Cities.* New York: Delacorte, 1967.

Wattenberg, Ben J., in collaboration with Richard M. Scammon. *This U.S.A.—An Unexpected Family Portrait of 194,067,296 Americans Drawn from the Census.* Garden City, N.Y.: Doubleday, 1965.

White, Theodore H. *The Making of the President, 1960, 1964, 1968.* New York: Atheneum, 1961, 1965, 1969.

Whyte, William H. *The Last Landscape.* Garden City, N.Y.: Doubleday, 1968.

Williams, Joe B. *U. S. Statistical Atlas.* Elmwood, Neb., 1969.

The World Almanac and Book of Facts. Published annually by Newspaper Enterprise Assn., Inc., New York and Cleveland.

NEW YORK

For an overview of New York's development, no book is finer than *A History of New York State,* by David M. Ellis, James A. Frost, Harold C. Syrett, and Harry J. Carman (Ithaca, New York: Cornell University Press, 1967). Other books that provided valuable background: *The Gateway States,* by Seymour Freedgood (New York: Time-Life Library of America, 1967); *New York State Statistical Yearbook,* by Theresa M. Speciale (Albany, New York: New York State Division of the Budget, Office of Statistical Coordination, 1970); *New York: A Guide to the Empire State,* compiled by writers of the Writers' Project Administration of the WPA, American Guide Series (New York: Oxford University Press, 1940); *Politics in the Empire State,* by Warren Moscow (New York: Knopf, 1948).

Other sources: Regular coverage of the New York *Times,* New York *Daily News,* New York magazine, *Newsday,* the Gannett newspapers, and the following articles:

STATE GOVERNMENT "Requiem in Albany," New York *Times* editorial, Jan. 7, 1971; "Governor Sees 'Disaster' Unless U. S. Aid Grows," by Richard L. Madden, New York *Times,* Nov. 24, 1970.

"Anti-Racial Bill Signed by Dewey," by Leo Egan, New York *Times,* March 13, 1945; "1948 Revisited: A Political Lesson," by Henry Owen, Washington *Post,* April 7, 1971; "Elder Statesman:

Thomas E. Dewey," *Newsweek,* March 29, 1971. The Public Record of Nelson A. Rockefeller, *Congressional Quarterly Weekly Report,* July 21, 1967; "The Case against Nelson Rockefeller," by Jack Newfield, *New York,* March 9, 1970.

"New York's Mr. Urban Renewal," by Richard Schickel, New York *Times Magazine,* March 1, 1970; *The New York State Urban Development Corporation Annual Report,* 1970; "Notes from the Underground," by John Fischer, *Harper's Magazine,* February 1970; "The Wholly Ronan Empire," by Fred C. Shapiro, New York *Times Magazine,* May 17, 1970; *New Priorities for Urban Transportation* and *Regional Transportation,* addresses by William J. Ronan, chairman, New York State Metropolitan Transportation Authority, Feb. 23 and March 8, 1971; "State Clean-Water Aides Cheered by U. S. Promises," by David Bird, New York *Times,* March 23, 1971; "Born to Judge," *Time,* May 10, 1971.

"Rising Protests and Lawsuits Shake Routine in State Prisons," by Michael T. Kaufman, New York *Times,* Nov. 15, 1970; "Troubles Persist in Prison at Auburn," by Michael T. Kaufman, New York *Times,* May 17, 1971; "Once a Community Blight, Sing Sing Prison Now Mourned by Neighbors," by Owen Moritz, *National Observer,* April 6, 1970; "Governor Defends Order to Quell Attica Uprising," by William E. Farrell, New York *Times,* Sept. 16, 1971; " 'New Breed' Sparked Attica Uprising," by Philip D. Carter and Stephen

Isaacs, Washington *Post*, Sept. 15, 1971; "Prison Paradox: Life for Many Inmates Improves, but Chances of More Atticas Rise," *Wall Street Journal*, Sept. 16, 1971.

"State U. Expects 195,000 to Enroll," by M. S. Handler, New York *Times*, Sept. 8, 1970; "Abortion Reform after Long Fight," by Bill Kovach, New York *Times*, April 12, 1970; "N.Y. Studies Abortion-Law Repeal," by Jo Ann Levine, *Christian Science Monitor*, June 3, 1971; "State Finds Drug Abuse Is Rising," by Richard Severo, New York *Times*, June 24, 1971; "What New York Has Discovered by Running the Nation's Biggest Anti-Drug Program," by Milton Luger, *State Government*, Spring 1971.

LEGISLATURE "Duryea Is Emerging as New State Power," by Frank Lynn, New York *Times*, June 10, 1971; "Albany's Power Twins: Know Your Enemy," by Paul Hoffman, *New York*, June 28, 1971; "Lobbyists Play Big Role in Albany Lawmaking," by David K. Shipler, New York *Times*, Feb. 1, 1970; "Banking 'Conflict' in Legislature Charged," by Charles Grutzner, New York *Times*, March 12, 1971; "Brown, Mayor's Man in Albany, Serves Legislators in Serving City," by Martin Tolchin, New York *Times*, May 26, 1971; "Legislative Swing to Right Clips Governor's Power," by Frank Lynn, New York *Times*, June 9, 1971.

POLITICS "This Rockefeller Campaign Is the Biggest, Maybe Best," by James M. Perry, *National Observer*, Oct. 26, 1970; "The Marketing of Nelson Rockefeller," by Fred Powledge, *New York*, Nov. 30, 1970; "Rockefeller Funds Key Factor in Race," by Richard Phalon, New York *Times*, Oct. 25, 1970; "Well-Oiled Political Organization," by Richard Reeves, New York *Times*, Oct. 12, 1970; "Teamsters Break Custom and Back Rockefeller," by Emanuel Perlmutter, New York *Times*, June 2, 1970; "State Politicians' 1970 Forecast: GOP United, Democrats Not," by Richard Reeves, New York *Times*, Dec. 11, 1969; "The End of Liberalism," by Paul Hoffman, *The Nation*, April 12, 1971.

"The New York Primary: Return of Pre-Primary Designating Conferences," by Robert L. Tienken, *Harvard Journal on Legislation*, January 1969; "Many Democrats Assail State Nominating System," by Thomas P. Ronan, New York *Times*, April 3, 1970; "The Pressure to Run," and "Something Is Missing in the Primary System," by Richard Reeves, New York *Times*, Feb. 23 and June 21, 1970.

"These Two Parties Could Make All the Difference," by Richard Reeves, New York *Times*, April 12, 1970; "Liberal Party Swings Weight in New York Despite Its Small Size," by Richard Stone, *Wall Street Journal*, Oct. 5, 1970; "Right Wing Irks G.O.P." by Leo Egan, New York *Times*, March 12, 1962; "Conservatives Eye '73 Mayoral Race," by Maurice Carroll, New York *Times*, Nov. 6, 1970; "The Beginning of the End of the State's Minor Parties?" by Gus Tyler, *New York*, May 3, 1971.

"New York's Congressmen: The House Is Not a Home," by Martin Nolan, *New York*, March 22, 1971; "The Public Record of Jacob K. Javits." *Congressional Quarterly Weekly Report*, Aug. 18, 1967; "Ham' Fish the Third," by Alan Emory, Washington *Star*, Dec. 13, 1970.

UPSTATE CITIES "Buffalo, N.Y.," article by Millard C. Browne in *Encyclopedia Americana;* "Searching for the Perfect University President," by Warren G. Bennis, *Atlantic*, April 1971.

"Xerox No Dropout," by William D. Smith, New York *Times*, Dec. 27, 1970; "Living Up to Kodak Past Is Part of Picture," by Robert A. Wright, New York *Times*, Feb. 2, 1969.

"Snow Doesn't Bother Syracuse," by Clarence

D. Bassett, Washington *Post*, March 8, 1970; "Syracuse Split by Racial Views," by Thomas A. Johnson, New York *Times*, Aug. 11, 1971.

"What Price Glory on the Albany Mall?" by Eleanore Carruth, *Fortune*, June 1971; "Rocky's Monumental Error, or the Billion-Dollar Misunderstanding," by Wolf Von Eckardt, *New York*, April 20, 1970; "Rockefeller, 'Edifice Rex,' Builds a Monument in Albany," by James M. Perry, *National Observer*, Sept. 28, 1970; "Last Old-Time Political Boss Never Loses," by Richard Dougherty, Los Angeles *Times*, Feb. 22, 1970; "Albany 'Resolutely Backward'," by Sydney H. Schanberg, New York *Times*, March 19, 1969; "The O'Connell Machine in Albany," by Charles Van Devander, *American Mercury*, Oct. 1, 1944.

REGIONS "New Policy Urged for Adirondacks," by Bayard Webster, New York *Times*, Jan. 3, 1971; "'Taming' of Adirondacks Feared," by Bayard Webster, New York *Times*, Dec. 21, 1970; "Beauty of Upstate County Hides Poverty of Its Residents," New York *Times*, March 24, 1971.

"The Hudson River Lives," by Robert H. Boyle, *Audubon*, March 1971; "F.P.C. Authorizes Con Ed to Build Storm King Plant," by Richard L. Madden, New York *Times*, Aug. 20, 1970; "Hudson River Cleanup Turns Out to Be Slow and Frustrating Task," by John Barnett, *Wall Street Journal*, Dec. 18, 1969.

"U. S. Military Academy Struggles to Maintain Traditional Prestige," by Neil Ulman, *Wall Street Journal*, June 18, 1969; "The Tainted Image of West Point," by Robert B. Johnson, Jr., *The Progressive*, February 1971; "The Roar of Bulldozers Echoes through Once-Rural Rockland County as Rapid Growth Continues," by Ralph Blumenthal, New York *Times*, March 25, 1968; "Rockland: The Longer View," by Lesley Oelsner, New York *Times*, Jan. 1, 1971.

WESTCHESTER "Westchester Disproves Suburban Myth," New York *Times*, May 31, 1971; "Blacks Take Pride in New Rochelle Role," by C. Gerald Fraser, New York *Times*, Dec. 6, 1970; "Westchester Government Needs Modernization, Ottinger and Reid Agree," by Linda Greenhouse, New York *Times*, Feb. 22, 1970.

LONG ISLAND "Politics in the Suburbs," by Stanley J. Hinden, chapter in *Practical Politics in the United States*, ed. Cornelius P. Cotter (Boston: Allyn & Bacon, 1969); "Silver Anniversary Edition," *Newsday*, Sept. 10, 1965; "Levittown: 25 Years Later," *Newsday*, July 9, 1971; "Plan for Development by 1985 Studied by Politicians on L.I.," New York *Times*, Sept. 20, 1970.

"Nickerson Sets Nassau Goals," by Roy R. Silver, New York *Times*, Jan. 5, 1970; "Zoning Suit Threatens Oyster Bay," by Peter Braestrup, Washington *Post*, May 9, 1971; "NAACP Sues to Tear Down Oyster Bay Zoning Barrier," by Owen Moritz, New York *Daily News*, March 26, 1971; "Can Anyone around Here Beat Arthur Goldberg?" by Harvey Aronson, *New York*, April 6, 1970.

NEW YORK CITY—GENERAL *The Epic of New York City*, by Edward Robb Ellis (New York: Coward-McCann, 1966); *To the Victor . . . Political Patronage from the Clubhouse to the White House*, by Martin and Susan Tolchin (New York: Random House, 1971); *Governing New York City*, by Wallace S. Sayre and Herbert Kaufman (New York: W. W. Norton and Co., 1965); *New York, N.Y.* by David G. Lowe (New York: American Heritage, 1968); *AIA Guide to New York City*, by Norval White and Elliot Willensky (New York: Macmillan, 1967); *When the Cathedrals Were White*, by Le Corbusier (West Caldwell, N.J.: William Morrow, 1947); *What Have*

You Done for Me Lately?—The Ins and Outs of New York City Politics, by Warren Moscow (Englewood Cliffs, N.J.: Prentice-Hall, 1967); *The Great American Motion Sickness—Or Why You Can't Get There from Here,* by John Burby (Boston: Little, Brown & Co., 1971).

NEW YORK CITY—GOVERNMENT Series of articles in the New York *Daily News* entitled "Spend City," 1971; "The Changing City: Power Is Limited," by Richard Reeves, New York *Times,* June 8, 1969; "Who Runs the City Government," by Edward N. Costikyan, *New York,* May 26, 1969; "New York City Goes Out in a Rowboat," *Time,* June 21, 1971; "Lindsay Proposes National Cities," by John Herbers, New York *Times,* May 28, 1971; "Governor Says State Helps City Meet Responsibilities," by Frank Lynn, New York *Times,* June 24, 1971; "A Nightmare for Urban Management," by A. James Reichley, *Fortune,* March 1969; "The Ten Most Powerful Men in New York," by Edward Costikyan, *New York,* Jan. 5, 1970, and *ibid.,* by Dick Schaap, Jan. 4, 1971.

NEW YORK CITY—POLITICS "Image over Performance," by Amitai Etzioni, *Wall Street Journal,* Jan. 21, 1971; "City Hall's Public Relations Costs Have Trebled Since Mayor Lindsay Took Office," by Martin Tolchin, New York *Times,* March 22, 1971; "Rockefeller Leads Attack on Mayor; Calls Him Inept," by Frank Lynn, New York *Times,* June 4, 1971; "Lindsay vs. Rocky," by William Chapman, Washington *Post,* June 12, 1971; "Feud," by Richard Reeves, *Life,* June 25, 1971; "The Two John Lindsays," by David K. Shipler, *New Republic,* May 1, 1971; "But Is Statehood for New York City Really the Answer?" by Michael Harrington, *New York,* Aug. 23, 1971; "Both Parties Ready to Scrap Grant Programs in Favor of 'City Strategy' Package of Aid," by William Lilley, III, *National Journal,* July 3, 1971.

"57% of City's Public School Enrollment Is Black and Puerto Rican," by Gene I. Maeroff, New York *Times,* June 18, 1971; "Up the Down Campus—Notes from a Teacher on Open Admissions," by M. Ann Petrie, *New York,* May 17, 1971.

NEW YORK CITY—HOUSING "Housing Woes Dim Hopes of City," by Robert Alden, New York *Times,* Nov. 1, 1970; "Shortage of Housing in New York Gets Worse with Every Day," by Richard Stone, *Wall Street Journal,* Dec. 2, 1970; "The Changing City: Housing Paralysis," by David K. Shipler, New York *Times,* June 5, 1969; "Desperate All Over," *Time,* Aug. 30, 1968; "City Said to Need Billion a Year to End Spiral of Housing Decay," New York *Times,* Nov. 7, 1969; "Co-op City, Home to 40,000, Is Given Tempered Praise," by James F. Clarity, New York *Times,* May 27, 1971; "Vast Co-op City Is Dedicated in Bronx," by William E. Farrell, New York *Times,* Nov. 25, 1968.

NEW YORK CITY—THE ECONOMY "Why Companies Are Fleeing the Cities," *Time,* April 26, 1971; "Far from the Madding Crowd," *Forbes,* Jan. 15, 1971; "The Future of Corporate Geography," *Corporate Financing,* November/December 1970; "New Protection for Investors When Brokers Go Under," *U. S. News & World Report,* Jan. 4, 1971; "Wall Street: The Martin Report," *Newsweek,* Aug. 16, 1971; "ILGWU: The Old Age of a Union," by David Gumpert, *The Nation,* June 7, 1971; "AT&T Says It Will Not Leave New York, Plans City Expansion, Nonwhite Recruiting," *Wall Street Journal,* Oct. 20, 1971.

NEW YORK CITY—COMMUNICATIONS AND CULTURE "TV: Is the Bloom Off the Old Rose?" *Forbes,* Oct. 15, 1970; "Making It,"

Newsweek, July 27, 1970. "New Life in New Places for the American Theater," *U. S. News & World Report,* May 4, 1970; "Off-Broadway: Economic Tragedy in Rehearsal?" by Clive Barnes, New York *Times,* Jan. 10, 1971; "Hoving of the Metropolitan," *Newsweek,* April 1, 1968; "Sounds in the Streets," *Newsweek,* Aug. 16, 1971.

NEW YORK CITY—CRIME AND JUSTICE "Graft Paid to Police Here Said to Run into Millions," by David Burnham, New York *Times,* April 25, 1970; "New York's Rotten Apples," *Newsweek,* July 12, 1971; "A Cop Quits," *Newsweek,* Sept. 21, 1970; "NYPD: Nightmare for a 'Dream Cop'," by Karl E. Meyer, Washington *Post,* Sept. 28, 1970; "Leary Assails Articles in *Times* on Police Corruption as Unfair," by William E. Farrell, New York *Times,* April 29, 1970; "Gamblers' Links to Police Lead to Virtual 'Licensing'," by David Burnham, New York *Times,* April 26, 1970; "Organized Crime in City Bleeds Slums of Millions," by Nicholas Gage, New York *Times,* Sept. 27, 1970; "Why They Had to Shoot Colombo," by Nicholas Pileggi, *New York,* July 12, 1971; "The Mafia: Portrait of an Empire in Trouble," by Fred J. Cook, New York *Times,* March 29, 1970; "Crime: Taking Dirty Money," *Time,* Sept. 13, 1971.

"Logjam in Our Courts," by Dale Wittner, *Life,* Aug. 7, 1970; "Crisis in Prisons Termed Worst Mayor Has Faced," by Paul L. Montgomery, New York *Times,* Oct. 15, 1970; "Tombs: An Ideal Breeding Ground for Riots," by Martin Arnold, New York *Times,* Aug. 16, 1970.

"Memorandum" by Robert Sullivan, New York City Off-Track Betting Corp., regarding operation of the numbers game and its relationship to drug traffic (dated Jan. 28, 1971); "Memorandum" by Rich Tapia, New York City Off-Track Betting Corp., regarding forms of numbers-game operations in the city (dated Oct. 12, 1970); "Big Gamble on Gambling," by Fred J. Cook, *The Nation,* July 6, 1970; "Offtrack Betting Attracting Nationwide Interest," by Charles Grutzner, New York *Times,* April 17, 1971.

NEW YORK CITY—GEOGRAPHY One of the most fascinating public planning documents ever published is the profusely illustrated *Plan for New York City—A Proposal,* with separate volumes: *Critical Issues, The Bronx, Brooklyn, Manhattan, Queens, Staten Island* (New York: New York City Planning Commission, 1969).

NEW YORK CITY—MANHATTAN "Notes on the New York Skyline . . . ," by Anthony Lewis, *Atlantic,* June 1971; "Violence Common in Nether World of Lower East Side," by Sylvan Fox, New York *Times,* March 20, 1959; "Law and Order Gains Where Least Likely—Greenwich Village," by Roger Ricklefs, *Wall Street Journal,* July 9, 1971; "Passive Protesters," *Time,* Feb. 28, 1969.

"Slaughter on Sixth Avenue," by Peter Blake, *New York,* April 12, 1971; "Touches of Sidewalk Splendor Planned for Midtown," by Murray Schumach, New York *Times,* Aug. 6, 1971; "The West Side: A Polyglot of Races, Creeds and Cultures," by Richard F. Shepard, New York *Times,* Oct. 25, 1968; "A Day in Harlem," by David Butwin, *Saturday Review,* July 25, 1970; "Neighborhoods: The Home of Harlem's Affluent," by C. Gerald Fraser, New York *Times,* June 29, 1970; "Homage to Adam Clayton Powell," *The Black Politician,* July 1971 (reprinted from the New York *Times*).

NEW YORK CITY—THE BRONX *The Block,* by Herb Goro (New York: Random House, 1970); "Neighborhoods: A Bit of Italy in Bronx," by Murray Schumach, New York *Times,* March 27, 1970; "Neighborhoods: Baychester Racially Tense beneath a Calm Veneer," by Joseph Lelyveld, New York *Times,* Aug. 15, 1969; "Uptight in Riverdale," by Fred Ferretti, *New York,* Oct. 6, 1969; "The Puerto Ricans," *Newsweek,* June 15, 1970.

NEW YORK CITY—QUEENS "Queens Striving to Keep Balance," by Murray Schumach, *New York Times,* March 1, 1970.

NEW YORK CITY—BROOKLYN "Let's Break Up the City . . . Starting with Brooklyn," by Pete Hamill, *New York,* June 21, 1971; "Robert Kennedy's Bedford-Stuyvesant Legacy," by Jack Newfield, *New York,* Dec. 16. 1968; "A 90-Cent Riot," *Newsweek,* May 17, 1971; "Neighbor-

hoods: West Indies Flavor Bedford-Stuyvesant," by C. Gerald Fraser, New York *Times,* Oct. 28, 1970; "Good News from Bed-Stuy," by John J. Goldman, *New York,* Sept. 7, 1970; "Superblock in Bed-Stuy: Just a Million Dollar Slum," by Mark Zussman, *Village Voice,* Dec. 11, 1969.

NEW YORK CITY—STATEN ISLAND June 15, 1970; "Neighborhoods: Staten Island Continues to Be Isolated," by Linda Greenhouse, *New York Times,* Jan. 8, 1970; "The Urbanization of Staten Island," by Fred Powledge, *New York,* May 24, 1971.

MASSACHUSETTS

Two recent books offer excellent insights into Massachusetts politics: *The Political Cultures of Massachusetts,* by Edgar Litt (Cambridge: MIT Press, 1965), and *The Compleat Politician: Political Strategy in Massachusetts,* by Murry B. Levin with George Blackwood (New York: Bobbs Merrill, 1962). The state's culture and geography are well covered in *New England,* by Joe McCarthy (New York: Time-Life Library of America, 1967), and *Massachusetts: A Guide to the Pilgrim State,* ed. Ray Bearse, a second edition of the American Guide Series volume (Boston: Houghton Mifflin, 1971). For information on the Boston suburbs, I am indebted to John C. Burke, suburban editor of the Boston *Globe,* who prepared a special review used as background in the chapter.

The chapter draws on regular coverage of Massachusetts newspapers, especially the Boston *Globe* and *Christian Science Monitor,* and the following articles in particular:

GENERAL "Massachusetts Builds for Tomorrow," by Robert De Roos, *National Geographic,* December 1966; *Some Facts About Massachusetts* (Boston: Massachusetts Department of Commerce and Development, 1969); and other publications of state government.

POLITICS "Bay State GOP Missed a Comeback Chance," by George B. Merry, *Christian Science Monitor,* Aug. 7, 1970; "Mass. Legislature . . . Imbalance by Default," by Kenneth D. Campbell, Boston *Globe,* Oct. 20, 1970; "Figures Prove Democrats' Advantage in State," by Cornelius Dalton, Boston *Herald Traveler,* Nov. 17, 1968; "New Party Confronts State GOP," by David Mutch, *Christian Science Monitor,* March 11, 1971.

"Bay Staters Shun Ceremony—Even the Political Variety," by David S. Broder, *Washington Post,* June 16, 1970; "Chaos Wins as Massachusetts Democrats Stage a Donnybrook," by R. W. Apple, Jr., New York *Times,* June 14, 1970; "How to Run & Win," by James Higgins, *The Nation,* Dec. 21, 1970; "Citizens Caucus . . . a Political Innovation," by John S. Saloma, Boston *Globe,* Feb. 28, 1970; "Work Is Cut out for Fr. Drinan in Cross-Section Constituency," by George B. Merry, *Christian Science Monitor,* Dec. 9, 1970.

STATE GOVERNMENT "Governor's Council: Going—or More Pay?" by George B. Merry, *Christian Science Monitor,* Dec. 22, 1970; "Massachusetts Passes Cabinet Bill," by Victoria Schuck, *National Civic Review,* July 1969.

"Bay State's Moral Crisis," by Edgar M. Mills, *Christian Science Monitor,* April 9, 1962; "Era May Be at End in Massachusetts," by John H. Fenton, New York *Times,* Nov. 16, 1969; "Massachusetts Is Aroused by Corruption Scandals," by Anthony Lewis, New York *Times,* June 19, 1961; "Poisoned Politics," by Elliot L. Richard-

son, *Atlantic,* October 1961.

"Sargent Sees 'No-Fault' Success," by Monty Hoyt, *Christian Science Monitor,* April 24, 1971; "Bay State Sales-Tax Boost May Fund Towns— a Little," by George B. Merry, *Christian Science Monitor,* June 25, 1971; "Will Reform Slash Bay State Property Tax?" by George B. Merry, *Christian Science Monitor,* Nov. 11, 1970; "Bay State Taxes 6th Highest in Land," by Robert L. Turner, Boston *Globe,* Jan. 19, 1969; "$2 Billion Budget?" by George B. Merry, *Christian Science Monitor,* Jan. 15, 1971; "Bay State Foes Rap Racial-Imbalance Law," by George B. Merry, *Christian Science Monitor,* Feb. 23, 1971; "Apartheid in Urban Schools," by Peter Milius, *Washington Post,* April 4, 1971.

LEGISLATURE "Legislators Apply Polish to Their Image," by George B. Merry, *Christian Science Monitor,* Dec. 12, 1970; "David Michael Bartley: The Speaker," by David Ellis, Boston *Globe,* June 27, 1971; "Higoodtaseeyahowsitgoin? or What I Do All Day," by Rep. Martin F. Linsky, *Ripon Forum,* August 1969; "Lobbyists Bend Sargent Tax Bill," by Joanne Leedom, *Christian Science Monitor,* March 12, 1971; "Youth Wins More Votes," by George B. Merry, *Christian Science Monitor,* Nov. 16, 1970; "Women in the Legislature," by Scott Pecker, *Christian Science Monitor,* Aug. 21, 1970; "I Wish to Change My Vote—Story of House Cut Defeat," by David Nyhan, Boston *Globe,* March 22, 1970; "Membership in the Club: Denizens of the Massachusetts House of Representatives," by Barry M. Portnoy, *Harvard Journal on Legislation,* January 1969.

EDUCATION "Conditions Favoring Major Advances in Social Science," by Karl W. Deutsch, John Platt, and Dieter Senghaas, *Science,* Feb. 5, 1971.

"Harvard Clings to Shaky Peace," by Jim Mann, *Washington Post,* May 3, 1970; "A Farewell to Fair Harvard—Healing but Still Threatened," by David S. Broder, *Washington Post,* June 23, 1970; "My Several Lives," book review by Harold Taylor, New York *Times Book Review,* March 22, 1970; "Harvard Picks a Young Face for the '70s," *Life,* Jan. 22, 1971

"MIT's Main Problem: Determining Its Role," by Eric Wentworth, *Washington Post,* Nov. 10, 1969; "Wiesner Named President at MIT," by Victor F. McElheny, *Washington Post,* March 6, 1971.

"Gathering Storms Over Once Quiet Campuses," by Michael Dorfsman, *Boston Magazine,* May 1970; "The First Hurrah," *Newsweek,* Jan. 4, 1971; "Quest for a Silver Unicorn," by Edward Kern, *Life,* June 4, 1971; "Bitterness at Brandeis," *Newsweek,* Nov. 9, 1970; "Brandeis U.: What Are They Doing out There?" by Lynn Sherr, *AP Dispatch,* Dec. 6, 1970; "A Jewel in the Rough," *Newsweek,* Sept. 28, 1970; "Broader Scope for Higher Ed Urged," by Muriel L. Cohen, Boston

Herald Traveler, June 27, 1971.

ECONOMY *Massachusetts Trends in Employment and Unemployment,* Division of Employment Security, Herman V. Lamark, Director, May 1971; "Slowdown on Route 128," by Gene Smith, New York *Times,* Oct. 11, 1970; "Raytheon Co. Prospers Despite Big Slowdown in the Defense Industry," by David Gumpert, *Wall Street Journal,* March 5, 1971; "State May Gain 34,000 Jobs by 1975," by Ken O. Botwright, Boston *Globe,* Nov. 11, 1970; "Down and Out Along Route 128," by Berkeley Rice, New York *Times Magazine,* Nov. 1, 1970; "Polaroid: Make It Unique—and Wanted," *Forbes,* June 1970; "Unemployment Picture in Mass. Grim for Next Year," by Ken O. Botwright, Boston *Globe,* Oct. 11, 1970; "Ex-NASA Lab Gets Down to Earth," by John Lannan, Washington *Star,* Oct. 26, 1970; "Will New Container Crane Revitalize Boston's Port?" by Richard W. McManus, *Christian Science Monitor,* June 21, 1971; "Boston Shipyard Reprieved," by Monty Hoyt, *Christian Science Monitor,* Jan. 21, 1971; "Plymouth Mass. Gets With It," by John H. Fenton, New York *Times,* May 3, 1970.

FARM AND FISH "Record Cranberry Harvest?" by Dorothea Kahn Jaffee, *Christian Science Monitor,* Sept. 23, 1970; "Depression, Despair Mark Fishing Industry," by Frank Donovan, Boston *Globe,* June 27, 1970; "Business Is Good, but Fishing Isn't," by Frank Donovan, Boston *Globe,* June 28, 1970.

RELIGION "The Many Mansions of Cardinal Cushing," by John Fenton, Boston *Magazine,* August 1970; "Big Man in a Long Red Robe," *Time,* Nov. 16, 1970; "Cardinal Cushing Dies in Boston at 75," New York *Times,* Nov. 3, 1970; "Medeiros Installed Before 2,500 as Boston Archbishop, Succeeding Cushing," by Robert Reinhold, New York *Times,* Oct. 8, 1970; "Clergymen Reply in Boston Dispute," New York *Times,* Jan. 3, 1971; "Negro Is Installed as Bishop of Mass. Episcopal Diocese," UPI Dispatch, Washington *Post,* Jan. 18, 1970; "Court Overturns Birth Control Law: Baird Is Freed," by Diane White, Boston *Globe,* July 7, 1970.

BOSTON—GENERAL "The Two Most Exciting Cities in the Nation?" by Ian Menzies, Boston *Globe,* Sept. 27, 1970; "Boston," by George Sessions Perry, *Saturday Evening Post,* Sept. 1945; "Boston's Marvelous Marathon," *Reader's Digest,* April 1971; "Boston Campaign Uses Computers," by Bill Kovach, New York *Times,* Oct. 24, 1971; "Who Is John Marttila and Why Is He Saying All Those Nice Things About Kevin White?" by James

Higgins, *Boston Magazine,* October 1971.

BOSTON—GOVERNMENT "Regional Government Proposed for Mass.," *National Civic Review,* February 1971; "White Corrals Few Tax Votes," by George B. Merry, *Christian Science Monitor,* March 23, 1971; "Hub-Vote Analysis Bodes Ill for White," by George B. Merry, *Christian Science Monitor,* Nov. 25, 1970; "The Beggars' War," *Newsweek,* Sept. 7, 1970; "Rerun of Hicks vs. White?" by Richard C. Halverson, *Christian Science Monitor,* June 8, 1971; "Mrs. Hicks Tosses Bonnet into Mayor Ring," by Richard Halverson, *Christian Science Monitor,* June 15, 1971.

The Economics of Air Pollution, a symposium by Harold Wolozin (New York: Norton, 1966); "When 'Go It Alone' Breaks Down," by George B. Merry, *Christian Science Monitor,* April 29, 1970; "Boston Tests Public Transit," by William Raspberry, Washington *Post,* Feb. 25, 1971; "Bay State Transit Agency Hit by Revolt," New York *Times,* March 14, 1971; "Drive in Boston May Bring a New Urban Transit Mix," by Bill Kovach, New York *Times,* July 25, 1971.

BOSTON—URBAN RENEWAL "A Boston Interview with I. M. Pei," *Boston Magazine,* June 1970; "Construction at Full Speed," by Richard W. McManus, *Christian Science Monitor,* Aug. 22, 1970; "Tall Stories About Boston," by Arthur Monks, *Boston Magazine,* November 1970; "Boston's New City Hall: A Public Building of Quality," by Ada Louise Huxtable, New York *Times,* Feb. 8, 1969; "A New City Hall: Boston's Boost for Urban Renewal," by John Conti, *Wall Street Journal,* Feb. 12, 1969; "A Noble Sequence," by Brigitte Weeks, *Boston Magazine,* February 1969; "Housing and Renewal," by John D. Warner, *Boston Magazine,* January 1970.

BOSTON—CULTURE, COMMUNICATIONS "Fiscal Performance," by Bernard Taper, *Boston Magazine,* March 1970; "Accounting for the Arts," by Bernard Taper, *Boston Magazine,* November 1969; "Spiraling Look into the Sea," *Time,* March 1970; "Herald Traveler TV Split Would Hurt," by Richard W. McManus, *Christian Science Monitor,* Dec. 2, 1970; "Who Really Runs the Globe," by George V. Higgins, *Boston Magazine,* May 1971.

BOSTON—ETHNIC, GEOGRAPHIC "Only 22 Percent of Hub Is Irish," by Bruce McCabe, Boston *Globe,* July 8, 1970; "Jet-Age Rivals: Can Boston Steal JFK's Thunder," by Arthur S. Harris, Jr., New York *Times,* April 11, 1971; "The Little People of East Boston Fight Back," by Arnold R. Isaacs, Baltimore *Sun,* Nov. 3, 1969.

NEW JERSEY

The best general history of New Jersey is John T. Cunningham's *New Jersey—America's Main Road* (Garden City, N.Y.: Doubleday, 1966); the same author has also written an interesting account, *Newark* (Newark: New Jersey Historical Society, 1966). The New Jersey League of Women Voters published in 1969 an excellent examination of state policy and programs, *New Jersey—Spotlight on Government,* ed. Elizabeth Brody with an introduction by Richard P. McCormick (League of Women Voters, Montclair). Other helpful sources included: *The Gateway States,* by Seymour Freedgood (New York: Time-Life Library of America, 1967); "New Jersey," by Carl L. Biemiller, chapter in *American Panorama* (Garden City, N.Y.: Doubleday, 1960); and *Six Cities Forward,* by John T. Cunningham (a promotional folder published by Public Service Electric and

Gas Co., Newark, about 1970).

Other sources: Regular coverage of New Jersey events in the Newark *Evening News,* the New York *Times* and Philadelphia *Evening Bulletin,* and the following articles:

POLITICS "Vote Gain: Vote Drain," by Angelo Baglivo, Newark *Sunday News,* Sept. 28, 1969; "State Politics Facing 1970s," by Angelo Baglivo, Newark *News,* Dec. 28, 1969; "I Am The Law," by Thomas J. Fleming, *American Heritage,* June 1969; "State Democrats Call for Reapportioning of Party Committees," by Angelo Baglivo, Newark *News,* Dec. 9, 1970; "Ten From New Jersey—A Report on the State's Ten Most Influential People," by John T. McGowan, Newark *Sunday News,* May 31, 1970; "G.O.P. Looks to Jersey to Help Shift Senate Control," by R. W.

Apple, Jr., New York *Times*, March 1, 1970; "Hits 'Lily-Whiteness' Of Democratic Talks," by Angelo Baglivo, Newark *News*, Feb. 8, 1970; *Financing Campaigns for Governor: New Jersey, 1965*, by Herbert E. Alexander and Kevin L. Mc-Keough (Princeton: Citizens Research Foundation, 1969); "Unpredictable New Jersey," by Angelo Baglivo, Newark *Sunday News*, Nov. 3, 1968; "Nixon Feared in Trouble," by John J. Farmer, Newark *News*, Nov. 29, 1970; "Old Order Changeth for N.J. Democrats," Angelo Baglivo, Newark *News*, Nov. 10, 1968.

STATE GOVERNMENT "Now Cahill Inherits a Few Disasters," by Ronald Sullivan, New York *Times*, Jan. 18, 1970; "Praise for N.J. a Welcome Rarity," by William May, Newark *News*, Sept. 27, 1970; "Jersey Justice Has Prestige, but Problems, Too," by Lesley Oelsner, New York *Times*, Sept. 17, 1970; "Jersey Bars Jail for First Arrest in Marijuana Use," by Ronald Sullivan, New York *Times*, Oct. 27, 1970; "Youth's Death Changed N.J. Drug Laws," by Leon Zimmerman, Atlanta *Journal and Constitution*, Jan. 17, 1971; "Cahill's Plan to Reduce Drug Penalties Enacted," by Ronald Sullivan, New York *Times*, Oct. 9, 1970; "New Jersey Master-Zoning Fight Looms," by Peter Bridge, *Christian Science Monitor*, Aug. 15, 1970; "N.J.'s Lottery: Hope Sells for 50 Cents," by Rose De Wolf, Philadelphia *Bulletin*, Dec. 18, 1970; *Direction for Urban Progress* (interim report of the New Jersey Select Legislative Committee on Civil Disorders in Urban Affairs), State Senator James H. Wallwork, chairman, January 1969.

"Cahill Planning Major Toll Road," by Ronald Sullivan, New York *Times*, Dec. 25, 1970; "Cahill Drafts Plan On Transportation," by Ronald Sullivan, New York *Times*, Oct. 2, 1970; "Jersey Turnpike Soon to Be Billion-Dollar Borrower," by Robert D. Hershey, Jr., New York *Times*, Nov. 23, 1969; "New Jersey Acts on Transportation," by David J. Goldberg, *State Government*, Autumn 1968; "The New Jersey Department of Community Affairs," by Paul N. Ylvisaker, *The Urban Lawyer*, Winter 1971; "The Workings of Urban Politics, Problems, and Alleged Payoffs Within Paul Ylvisaker's New Jersey," by Louise Campbell, *City*, April–August 1969.

ENVIRONMENT "Jersey Cites Shore Area Water Pollution Crisis," and "Jersey Extends Ban on Dumping," by Ronald Sullivan, New York *Times*, May 9 and June 2, 1971; "Pollution Tour Runs Aground on Muck," by David Bird, New York *Times*, Dec. 6, 1969; "The Pine Barrens," *Princeton Alumni Weekly*, April 20, 1971.

MIGRANT LABOR "Cahill Proposes Farm Workers Aid," by Ronald Sullivan, New York *Times*, March 16, 1971; "Jersey's Migrants: A Hardly Human Existence," by Ronald Sullivan, New York *Times*, Aug. 23, 1970; "New Jersey Court Rules Farmers Can't Prohibit Visits to Migrants," by Ronald Sullivan, New York *Times*, May 12, 1971; "What Ever Happened to Merry Maria," *New South*, Winter 1968.

UNIVERSITIES "Experimental Program For Ghetto Students Stirs Hope at Rutgers," by Thomas J. Bray, *Wall Street Journal*, May 13, 1970; "Experiment in Relevance," *Time*, April 20, 1970; "A Rating of Graduate Schools," by John M. Fenton, *Princeton Alumni Weekly*, Jan. 26, 1971; "The Hard Mechanics of Peacemaking," by Colman McCarthy, Washington *Post*, June 20, 1970; "Last Hurrah for the MNC?" by Robert L. Taylor, *Princeton Alumni Weekly*, Dec. 1, 1970; "Changing Times Beset Princeton Clubs," New York *Times*, May 18, 1970; "The Institute Advances," *Newsweek*, April 6, 1970.

ECONOMY "A Pill-Giving Maverick," by Judy Gurovitz, *Life*, February 1969; "N. J. Laws Now Lure Industry," AP Dispatch, New York *Times*, May 25, 1969.

CRIME "The People v. the Mob; Or, Who Rules New Jersey?" by Fred J. Cook, New York *Times Magazine*, Feb. 1, 1970; "The Mob's Grip on New Jersey," by William Schulz, *Reader's Digest*, February 1971; "Jersey Legislature Approves Stiff Anticrime Bills," by Ronald Sullivan, New York *Times*, May 8, 1970; "The Mafia in Jersey: Nervous and No Longer Above the Law," by Ronald Sullivan, New York *Times*, March 16, 1970; "How 'Mama' and 'Andy' Helped to Break up a Mafia Organization," by Monroe W. Karmin, *Wall Street Journal*, April 27, 1971; "Why New Jersey?" by Richard Reeves, New York *Times*, Dec. 16, 1969; "The Cosa Nostra Finally Is Put on the Defensive," by Patrick Young, *National Observer*, Dec. 22, 1969; "Jersey I.R.S. Men Backed, But New Indictments Loom," by Ronald Sullivan, New York *Times*, Dec. 17, 1969; "A Jersey Legislator Cited on Bar Ethics; 2nd Guilty in U.S. Suit," by Ronald Sullivan, New York *Times*, Feb. 24, 1971; "Bartels of New Jersey," *Time*, Jan. 11, 1971; "Jersey Mafia Guided from Prison by Genovese," by Charles Grutzner, New York *Times*, Dec. 25, 1968; "An Overseer of Mafia," by Charles Grutzner, New York *Times*, Dec. 19, 1968; "FBI Tapes Underworld Talk," UPI Dispatch, Washington *Star*, Jan. 7, 1970; "Jersey Leaders Deny Mafia Ties Implied on Tapes," by Douglas Robinson, New York *Times*, Jan. 7, 1970; "In Jersey They Are Calling It a 'Pogrom'," by Sidney E. Zion, New York *Times*, Dec. 21, 1969; "Jersey Investigation," New York *Times*, Dec. 18, 1968; "Corruption by Consent," *Time*, Dec. 26, 1969; "The Mob: New Jersey's Second Government," by William Federici and David Hardy, New York *Daily News*, Jan. 23, 1969; "Can the Garden State Weed Out Organized Crime?," by William Federici and David Hardy, New York *Daily News*, Jan. 24, 1969; "Knowlton, Burkhardt Indicted in Building Firm Shakedowns," by Robert Rudolph, Newark *Star-Ledger*, Aug. 12, 1971; "N. J. Politico Indicted in 2.4M Fraud," by Alex Michelini, New York *Daily News*, Aug. 26, 1971.

HUDSON COUNTY "Where the Ward Politicians Still Call the Shots," by Martin Arnold, New York *Times*, Nov. 22, 1970; "Crime Gaze Hits New Jersey County," by Peter J. Bridge, *Christian Science Monitor*, Aug. 3, 1970; "Jersey Mayor Indicted with 3 Alleged Mafiosi," by Ronald Sullivan, New York *Times*, May 7, 1970; "John J. Kenny, Ousted Hudson County Leader, Is Indicted for Extortion," by Ronald Sullivan, New York *Times*, Sept. 16, 1970; "Jersey City Mayor, Aides Are Indicted," Washington *Post*, Nov. 17, 1970; "Reversal of Kenny Organization's Mayoral Strategy Beclouds Race in Jersey City," by Ronald Sullivan, New York *Times*, Oct. 7, 1971; "Dr. Jordan Breaks Grip of Jersey City Machine," by Roger Harris and Lawrence H. Hall, Newark *Star-Ledger*, Nov. 3, 1971.

PHILADELPHIA ORBIT "Fasten Your Seatbelts. You Are Now Entering Camden," by Barry Rosenberg, *Philadelphia Magazine*, October 1968; "The Trouble Maker," by Barry Rosenberg, *Philadelphia Magazine*, September 1970; "Forgotten Camden Faces Uncertain Future," by Leroy F. Aarons, Washington *Post*, April 6, 1969; "Most of 1976 Bicentennial Fair to Be Held in New Jersey," by Ronald Sullivan, New York *Times*, Sept. 19, 1971.

ATLANTIC CITY "A Dowager's Decline," *Newsweek*, June 8, 1970; "No Tears for Atlantic City," by Anthony M. Rey (letters to the editor), *Newsweek*, June 22, 1970; "Bust-Out Town," by Gaeton Fonzi and Bernard McCormick, *Philadel-*

phia Magazine, August 1970; "Atlantic County Under Scrutiny," by Joseph Carragher, Newark *Star-Ledger*, Aug. 14, 1971.

NEWARK—GENERAL "Newark Held an Angry and Anguished City," by Fox Butterfield, New York *Times*, April 12, 1971; "The City: Problems of a Prototype," *Time*, March 21, 1969; "Heirs to Disaster," *Newsweek*, May 25, 1970; "The First Nine Months," by Peter J. Bridge, Newark *Sunday News*, March 21, 1971; "Gibson Finds Graft Worse than Expected," by David K. Shipler, New York *Times*, Sept. 20, 1970; "The City Politic," by Frank Borsky, *New York*, Feb. 9, 1970; "Is Newark Where the Death Throes of Cities are Starting?" by Theo Lippman, Jr., Baltimore *Sun*, June 8, 1969; *Testimony before the Joint Economic Committee of the 92nd Congress*, by Mayor Kenneth A. Gibson, January 22, 1971; "Gain in Power by LeRoi Jones Shown in Newark Poverty Vote," by Ronald Sullivan, New York *Times*, June 19, 1971; "Gibson Is Widely Regarded As Successful in Restoring Integrity to City Hall," by Fox Butterworth, New York *Times*, Oct. 3, 1971.

NEWARK—RACE "Police Brutality Seen Rising under Gibson in Newark," by Larry Jackson, Washington *Post*, May 8, 1971; *Report of the National Advisory Committee on Civil Disorders* (Washington, 1968); "Autopsy in Newark," *Newsweek*, Feb. 19, 1968; "What Are the Problems of Health Care Delivery in Newark?" by Paul N. Ylvisaker, reprint from *Medicine in the Ghetto* (New York: Meredith, 1969).

NEWARK—POLITICS AND GOVERNMENT "For Newark's Future, It Matters Not Who Wins or Loses Runoff," by Ronald Sullivan, New York *Times*, June 15, 1970; "Gibson Drives in Newark to Get Blacks to Polls," by Walter H. Waggoner, New York *Times*, May 31, 1970; "Let Us Enjoy Our Victory," *Newsweek*, June 29, 1970; "Hugh Joseph Addonizio," by Robert D. McFadden, New York *Times*, June 16, 1970; "Riches Cited as Motive of Addonizio," by George Lardner, Jr., Washington *Post*, June 6, 1970; "Addonizio, 4 Others Are Found Guilty," AP Dispatch, Washington *Star*, July 23, 1970; "Savage Strike in Newark," *Time*, April 19, 1971; "Newark at the Brink," *Newsweek*, April 26, 1971; "Newark Negroes Fight School Pact," by Fox Butterfield, New York *Times*, April 7, 1971.

PENNSYLVANIA

Considering its size and importance, Pennsylvania has been the subject of remarkably few modern-day books. Among the works to which primary reference was made on the statewide scene were: *The Middle Atlantic States*, by Ezra Bowen (New York: Time-Life Library of America, 1968); *Pennsylvania Politics*, revised edition, by Edward F. Cooke and Edward G. Janosik (New York: Holt, Rinehart & Winston, 1965); *Discover the New Pennsylvania* (Harrisburg: Pennsylvania Department of Commerce, 1967); *Poverty in Pennsylvania* (Harrisburg: Community Services of Pennsylvania, 1968); "Pennsylvania," by Conrad Richter, chapter in *American Panorama* (Garden City, N.Y.: Doubleday, 1960); *Pennsylvania—A Guide to the Keystone State*, compiled by the Writers' Program of the WPA (New York: Oxford, 1940); *New Growth . . . New Jobs for Pennsylvania*, by Milton J. Shapp and Ernest H. Jurkat (Philadelphia: Shapp Foundation, 1962); "Pennsylvania: Business As Usual," chapter in *States in Crisis*, by James Reichley (Chapel Hill: University of North Carolina Press, 1964).

Other Sources: Regular coverage of the Philadelphia *Evening Bulletin*, Philadelphia *Inquirer*, Pittsburgh *Press*, and *Philadelphia Magazine*, as well as the following articles:

STATE GOVERNMENT "It's Twilight in Pennsylvania and the Bills Are Coming Due," by James M. Perry, *National Observer*, Dec. 14, 1970; "Income Tax Voted in Pennsylvania," New York *Times*, March 5, 1971; "Shafer Signs Public Employee Strike Bill," by Sanford R. Starobin, Washington *Post*, July 26, 1970; "Pennsylvania Cultivates the Capacity to Manage," by William R. Monat, Arthur C. Eckerman, and Robert D. Lee, Jr., *State Government*, Autumn, 1969; "Pennsylvania Is Pressing Blue Cross to Curb Costs," by Donald Janson, New York *Times*, March 28, 1971; "Some Health Care Industry Reform," by Judith Randal, Washington *Star*, March 22, 1971; "In Pennsylvania, a Man Can Be a Lawbreaker for Selling Milk Cheap," by James P. Gannon, *Wall Street Journal*, May 24, 1971; "Has Constitutional Reform Ruined Ray Shafer?" *Ripon Forum*, June 1968.

LEGISLATURE "The House of Ill Repute," by Bernard McCormick, *Philadelphia Magazine*, November 1969; "Pennsylvania Legislature Not in the Top 20," by Rem Rieder, Philadelphia *Bulletin*, Feb. 3, 1971; "New Lawmakers?" by Robert Heath and Joseph H. Melrose, Jr., *National Civic Review*, October 1969; "The Electronic Age and the Pennsylvania Legislature," by R. D. Steighner, *State Government*, Spring 1968; "A State Legislature Is Not Always a Model of Ideal Government," by Jack H. Morris, *Wall Street Journal*, July 28, 1971.

EDUCATION "Students Lobby in Pennsylvania," by Donald Janson, New York *Times*, Feb. 16, 1970; "Saving Parochial Schools," *Time*, Dec. 19, 1969.

ENVIRONMENT "Our Stinking Schuylkill," series of articles by Gary Brooten, Philadelphia *Bulletin*, Sept. 29, 30, Oct. 1, 1970; "Waste Lagoons in State Likened to 'Time Bomb,' " by Gary Brooten, Philadelphia *Bulletin*, Nov. 17, 1970; "The Battle to Save the Susquehanna," by Fred Jones, *Pittsburgh Press*, Oct. 1, 1970; "Donora, Pennsylvania," by Croswell Bowen, *Atlantic Monthly*, November 1970; "Legal Watchdogs Fight Pollution," *Saturday Review*, April 3, 1971.

POLITICS "Shapp Is Sworn in Pennsylvania," by Donald Janson, New York *Times*, Jan. 20, 1971; "Agnewism Befouls a State Campaign," by David S. Broder, Washington *Post*, Oct. 15, 1970; "Jim Duff Died As He Lived—Making His Own Way," Pittsburgh *Press*, Dec. 21, 1969; "Taxes Key in Pennsylvania," by James Doyle, Washington *Star*, Oct. 22, 1970; "Pennsylvania Primary Now Binds Delegates," by Jules Witcover, Los Angeles *Times*, Sept. 26, 1971.

CONGRESS "The Politician Starring Hugh Scott," by Julius Duscha, *Washingtonian Magazine*, October 1970; "Whips in the Senate," by Roy Reed, New York *Times*, Jan. 4, 1969; "Pepper Pot—Recessional," *Philadelphia Magazine*, December 1968; "Pennsylvania—Case History of Decay," *Time*, Oct. 18, 1968.

STEEL, THE STEELWORKERS "Trying to Avoid an Unwanted Strike," *Time*, May 24, 1971; "A New U.S. Campaign," *Newsweek*, May 31, 1971; "Foreign Threats to a Basic Industry—

Interview with Edwin H. Gott, Chairman of U.S. Steel Corporation," *U.S. News and World Report,* Oct. 26, 1970; "Young Workers Raising Voices for Factory and Union Changes," by Agis Salpukas, New York *Times,* June 1, 1970; "The Steelworkers' Militant Mood Deepens," *Business Week,* April 3, 1971; "Abel of Steelworkers," by Robert Walker, New York *Times,* Oct. 25, 1970.

COAL, THE UMW "Anarchy Threatens the Kingdom of Coal," by Thomas O'Hanlon, *Fortune,* January 1971; "Coal Mining," by A. Britton Hume, *Atlantic Monthly,* November 1969; "UMW Money Maze," by George Lardner, Jr., Washington *Post,* Feb. 28, 1971; "Rough, Tough Yablonski Accepted Death Risk," by Fred Barnes, Washington *Star,* Jan. 6, 1970.

RAILROADS "The Penn Central," by Rush Loving, Jr., *Fortune,* August 1970; "Penn Central Officials in Investment Club Used Insider Information, Patman Charges," *Wall Street Journal,* Feb. 16, 1971; "How Decaying Service, Bickering Officials Led to Penn Central Crisis," *Wall Street Journal,* June 12, 1970; "Pennsy Officials Bought 'Wrongdoing' Insurance," by H. L. Schwartz III, *Associated Press Dispatch,* Jan. 25, 1971.

PHILADELPHIA—GENERAL *The Perennial Philadelphians,* by Nathaniel Burt (Boston: Little, Brown, 1963); *Philadelphia Gentlemen,* by E. Digby Baltzell (Glencoe, Ill.: The Free Press, 1968); "Survival Through Planning—Philadelphia's Style," chapter in *Cities in a Race with Time,* by Jeanne R. Lowe, (New York: Vintage Books, Random House, 1958); *Philadelphia Magazine Guide,* by Nancy Love, (Philadelphia: Philadelphia Magazine, 1965); "Philadelphia, a Triumph over Time," by John Keats, *Holiday,* April 1971; "Philadelphia," by George Sessions Perry, *Saturday Evening Post,* Sept. 14, 1946; "The Champ's Town," by David Butwin, *Saturday Review,* April 3, 1971.

PHILADELPHIA—GOVERNMENT AND POLITICS "City, Schools May Face Total $1.3 Billion Deficit by 1975, Bank Study Says," by James B. Steele, Philadelphia *Inquirer,* March 26, 1971; "The Financial Future of City and School Government in Philadelphia," by David W. Lyon, *Business Review,* March 1971; "Urban Renewal Beset by Delay and Scandal in Fourth Biggest City," by Stephen J. Sansweet, *Wall Street Journal,* March 17, 1970; "Richardson Dilworth: My Dream for Philadelphia," Philadelphia *Bulletin Magazine,* Oct. 3, 1965.

"Camiel and Meehan: Politics and Power," by Sandy Grady, Philadelphia *Bulletin,* Nov. 29, 1970; "Why the Democrats Sing Chorus of Big-City Blues," by James R. Dickenson, *National Observer,* Dec. 22, 1969; "Plumber's Friend," by Gaeton Fonzi and Greg Walter, *Philadelphia Magazine,* October 1967; "Jim Does the Job but Civic Types Leave Him Cold," by Joseph R. Daughen, Philadelphia *Bulletin,* July 29, 1968; "Rizzo's Primary Victory Seems to Be Narrowly Based," by Bernard D. Nossiter, Washington *Post,* May 20, 1971; "Supercop," *Newsweek,* March 15, 1971; "Philadelphia Nominee," by Donald Janson, New York *Times,* May 20, 1971; "Philadelphia's Law-and-Order Candidate," by Stephen J. Sansweet, *Wall Street Journal,* April 21, 1971; "Philadelphia Boomerang," by James Higgins, *The Nation,* Oct. 12, 1970; "It's Hard to Be Neutral about Super Cop," by Fred Hamilton and Jon Katz, Philadephia *Daily News,* Feb. 3, 1971; "The Toughest Cop in America Campaigns for Mayor of Philadelphia," by Lenora E. Berson, New York *Times Magazine,* May 16, 1971; "Boss Cop Takes Philadelphia," by Stephen Isaacs, Washington *Post,* Nov. 3, 1971; "The Union League Club of Philadelphia Clings to Conservative

Ways," by Glynn Mapes, *Wall Street Journal,* Sept. 23, 1968; "The Pews of Philadelphia," by Michael C. Jensen, New York *Times,* Oct. 10, 1971.

PHILADELPHIA—ECONOMY "Headquarters Have Human Problems," by Elizabeth P. Deutermann, *Business Review,* February 1970; "Penn Central Debacle Creates Repercussions in Much of Philadelphia," by Jack H. Morris, *Wall Street Journal,* Aug. 10, 1970; "Jack Bunting, the All-American Boy Banker," by Willard S. Randall, *Philadelphia Magazine,* February 1971; "Bunting's Bet," *Time,* June 28, 1971; "Suburban Shift Problem to Philadelphia's Blacks" New York *Times,* Nov. 16, 1969; "Easy Ride on a Philadelphia Transit Line," by Robert Lindsey, New York *Times,* Feb. 16, 1970.

PHILADELPHIA—RELIGION "Bishop De-Witt Awakens Diocese to Issues Long Kept under Wraps," by Willard S. Randall, Philadelphia *Bulletin,* Sept. 2, 1969; "The Changing Catholic Church," by Willard S. Randall, series in Philadelphia *Bulletin,* May 24–31, 1970.

PHILADELPHIA—PUBLISHING "The Saturday Evening Post's Resurrection Is Planned by Curtis," *Wall Street Journal,* Nov. 6, 1970; "Post Mortem," by Charles MacNamara, *Philadelphia Magazine,* September 1970; *Decline and Fall,* by Otto Friedrich (New York: Harper & Row, 1970); *The Curtis Affair,* by Martin S. Ackerman (Los Angeles: Nash Publishing, 1970); "Return of the Post," *Time,* June 14, 1971; "Moe's Boy Walter at the Court of St. James's," by A. James Reichley, *Fortune,* June 1970; "Review of *Annenberg,*" by Edward W. Barrett, *Columbia Journalism Review,* Spring 1970; "The Knights Invade Philadelphia," by Eugene L. Meyer, *Columbia Journalism Review,* May/June 1971; "Newspapers Vie in Philadelphia," by Donald Janson, New York *Times,* Dec. 6, 1970; "Getting the Old Lady off Her Duff," by Bernard McCormick, *Philadelphia Magazine,* October 1969; "The Name of This Game Is *Philadelphia Magazine,*" by Robert W. Ankerson, *Pennsylvania Gazette,* March 1970.

PHILADELPHIA—GEOGRAPHY *Man Made Philadelphia,* by Richard S. Wurman and John Andrew Gallery (Cambridge Mass.: Philadelphia Magazine–MIT Press, 1971).

PHILADELPHIA—NEGROES *The Philadelphia Negro*—A Social Study, by W. E. B. Du Bois, with an introduction by E. Digby Baltzell (New York: Schocken Books, 1967); "The Blacks of Philadelphia," by Joseph R. Daughen, Philadelphia *Bulletin,* Dec. 6, 1970; "Right On!" by Maury Levy, *Philadelphia Magazine,* June 1970; "Black Mayor for Philadelphia in the '70s?" by Sandy Grady, Philadelphia *Bulletin,* June 21, 1970; "Hiring Plan: An Exercise in Frustration," by Nick Kotz, Washington *Post,* Dec. 13, 1970; *Housing in Philadelphia* and *Criminal Justice in Philadelphia* (Information Papers issued by the Greater Philadelphia Movement, March 1971); *Build Brother Build,* by Leon H. Sullivan (Philadelphia: Macrae Smith, 1969); "A Black Director Pushes Reforms at GM," *Business Week,* April 10, 1971.

PITTSBURGH "The New Coalition—Pittsburgh's Action Formula Saves a City," chapter of *Cities in a Race with Time,* by Jeanne Lowe (New York: Vintage Books, Random House, 1968); *Pittsburgh—The Story of an American City,* by Stefan Lorant (Garden City, N.Y.: Doubleday, 1964); *Reports of the Allegheny Conference on Community Development* for 1968, 1969, 1970; *Social Planning in Pittsburgh—A Preliminary Appraisal* (Kansas City, Mo.: Institute for Community Studies, 1969—Homer C. Wadsworth, project director); "Pittsburgh—Is It Pennsylvania's Second City . . . or Its First?" by Jack Markowitz,

Philadelphia Magazine, September 1969; "See How Pittsburgh Got Itself Cleaned Up," by John Koenig, Jr., Washington *Post,* Nov. 15, 1970; "Pittsburgh: A Brawny City Puts on a Silk Shirt," by Douglas E. Kneeland, New York *Times,* Oct. 3, 1970; "Nobody's Boy in Pittsburgh," by Donald Janson, *The Progressive,* June 1970; "Pittsburgh Renewal Plan Completes Major Phase," by Donald Janson, New York *Times,* Nov. 29, 1969; "An Old Fortune Moves On," by Michael C. Jensen, New York *Times,* May 2, 1971; "Rehabilitation of Slums Gaining in Pittsburgh After Failing Elsewhere," by James P. Gannon, *Wall Street Journal,* Sept. 3, 1970; "Pittsburgh's Much-heralded Educational Superplan Is Beset by Rising Costs and Raging Public Dissent," *City,* August 1969; "Pittsburgh Cracks Down on Polluters," *Business Week,* Dec. 27, 1969.

"The Mayor Is Nobody's Boy," by Ralph Z. Hallow, *The Nation,* April 19, 1971; "Pittsburgh Council Debate and Political Reform—Mark Flaherty's First 100 Days as Mayor," by Donald Janson, New York *Times,* April 19, 1970; "Lochinvar of the West," by Stuart Brown, *Philadelphia Magazine,* January 1971; "Pittsburgh's Flaherty: Nobody's Boy," by James P. Gannon, *Wall Street Journal,* Jan. 22, 1971.

OHIO

In addition to personal interviews and observations, major reliance was placed on the outstanding analysis of the state's politics in the Ohio chapter of John H. Fenton's *Midwest Politics* (New York: Holt, Rinehart & Winston, 1966). For local color, I turned to *Ohio—A Personal Portrait of the 17th State,* by Dick Perry (Garden City, N.Y.: Doubleday, 1969). Interesting background appears in *The Heartland,* by Robert McLaughlin (New York: Time-Life Library of America, 1967). Among the sources used for miscellaneous facts and figures was the *Ohio Almanac,* published by the Lorain *Journal,* as well as various publications of the Ohio state government.

Reference was made to ongoing news coverage of the Cleveland *Plain-Dealer,* Cleveland *Press,* Cincinnati *Enquirer,* Columbus *Dispatch,* Akron *Beacon-Journal,* and other newspapers and magazines, including the *Ohio Republican News* and *AFL-CIO Focus.* Articles of special use included:

STATE POLITICS AND GOVERNMENT "The Decline of Ohio," by David Hess, *The Nation,* April 13, 1970; "The Governor and the Mobster," by Denny Walsk, *Life,* May 2, 1969; "Rhodes Exonerated in Licavoli Probe," *Ohio Republican News,* Oct. 31, 1969; "How the Ohio Legislature Really Works," by Richard Zimmerman and Robert Burdock, a series in the Cleveland *Plain-Dealer* between Dec. 29, 1968, and Jan. 3, 1969; "'Better Men' Running?" by Louis H. Masotti and Kathleen Barber, *National Civic Review,* October 1967; "Ohio's Election Laws Still in the Horse-and-Buggy Days," *Focus,* November 1969; *Expenditures and Revenues of the State of Ohio 1950–1967, A Comparative Analysis,* by John F. Burke, Jr., and Edric A. Weld, Jr. (Institute of Urban Studies, Cleveland State University, 1969); "Fund Scandal Perils Ohio's GOP Ticket," by Abe Zaidan, Washington *Post,* May 27, 1970; "Ohio State Loans Affect the GOP," New York *Times,* May 17, 1970; "Ohio Study Upholds Reports of Illegal Loans from State Treasury," by Donald Hanson, New York *Times,* June 17, 1970; "Ohio: Law and Order Vies with Scandal," *Ripon Forum,* November 1970; "Scandalous Doings Rock Ohio Politics, but Who Can Profit," by Mark R. Arnold, *National Observer,* Sept. 14, 1970; "Ohio Income Taxes Urged by Governor," by Abe Zaidan, Washington *Post,* March 16, 1971; "Ohio Governor Outlines High-Tax, High-Service Plan," by R. W. Apple, Jr., New York *Times,* March 17, 1971; "Deferred Tuition Sought for Ohio Public Colleges," by Andrew H. Malcolm, New York *Times,* March 21, 1971.

ECONOMY "Ohio Labor Market Sets a Dozen New Records in 1968," by William Papier, Columbus *Dispatch,* Jan. 5, 1969; "Ohio Agriculture Led to Rapid Advancement," reprinted from the *Ohio Farmer* in the *Ohio Republican News,* Nov. 28, 1969.

CONGRESSIONAL DELEGATION "Senator Saxbe's Surprising Behavior," by Alan L. Otten, *Wall Street Journal,* July 30, 1969; "Unionists Vote Saxbe a Hit," by Robert J. Havel, Cleveland *Plain-Dealer,* May 2, 1969; "How You Gonna Keep Him Back in the Woods After He's Seen D.C.?", by Terry A. Barnett, *Ripon Forum,* October 1969; "The Senate's Oldest Youngster" (Senator Young), by Margaret Kilgore (UPI), Boston *Globe,* May 4, 1969; "U.S. Reps. Vanik, Stokes Earning Points," by James M. Naughton, Cleveland *Plain-Dealer,* March 9, 1969; "Wayne Hays: a Petulant and Plucky Congressman," by Aldo Beckman, Chicago *Tribune,* Nov. 23, 1969; "Ohio Congressman (William M. McCulloch) Girds to Fight for Civil Rights," by Robert J. Havel, Cleveland *Plain-Dealer,* Aug. 10, 1969. Also, subchapter entitled "Let's Build This Ditch for Mike!" in *The Case Against Congress,* by Drew Pearson and Jack Anderson (New York: Simon & Schuster, 1968).

CLEVELAND "Cleveland: The Flicker of Fear," by John Skow, *Saturday Evening Post,* Sept. 7, 1968; "Cleveland's Carl Stokes: Making It," *Newsweek,* May 26, 1969; "She Urged Sons 'To Be Somebody'," by David Hess, *Christian Science Monitor,* Dec. 16, 1968; "Fire Fight in Cleveland," *Newsweek,* Aug. 5, 1968; "My First Year," by Carl B. Stokes, *Ebony,* January 1969; "Business Helps Showman Mayor," by Bernard D. Nossiter, Washington *Post,* March 23, 1969; "Despite Some Woes, Black Mayor Stokes Is Likely to Win Again," by Kenneth G. Slocum, *Wall Street Journal,* Sept. 26, 1969; "Cleveland: Now! One Year Later," by Robert T. Stock, Cleveland *Plain-Dealer,* April 6, 1969; "Oh, That Ahmed. Poor, Poor Ahmed. They're Going to Fry His Black, Skinny Ass," by Donn Pearce, *Esquire,* March 1970; "The Making of the Negro Mayors 1967," by Jeffrey K. Hadden, Louis H. Masotti, and Victor Thiessen, *Trans-action,* January 1968; "$3.5 Million Fund Set Up to Solve Area's Problems," Cleveland *Plain-Dealer,* Dec. 19, 1961; "Dolph Norton Leads Urban-Problem Fight," by James M. Naughton, Cleveland *Plain-Dealer,* March 31, 1969; "Foundation Keeps Funds 'in the Family'," by William C. Barnard, Cleveland *Plain-Dealer,* June 17, 1969; "Cleveland Opens First Airport Rapid Transit," *Newsletter of the Institute for Rapid Transit,* December 1968; "Cleveland: The Black Machine Bid," by George Lardner, Jr., Washington *Post,* Oct. 31, 1971; "Republican Wins Cleveland Race," by James M. Naughton, New York *Times,* Nov. 3, 1971.

Reference was also made to several issues of a

biweekly anti-establishment newsletter, *Point of View*, prepared by Roldo Bartimole, especially the edition of April 21–27, 1969, "Many Roads Lead to Jack Reavis," from which I drew the specific facts cited in the chapter regarding Reavis, his law firm and corporate directorships.

COLUMBUS "Columbus, Ohio: A Contented City," by Charlotte Curtis, New York *Times*, Dec. 30, 1969; "Charges of Graft Sadden Columbus," by John Kifner, New York *Times*, June 6, 1969; "In Darkest Ohio," by James Ridgeway, *The New Republic*, Feb. 5, 1966; "Outerbelt Industry: New Highway Attracting Ring of Industry and Commerce," by Mardo Williams, Columbus *Dispatch*, March 1, 1970; "The Big Football Weekend Is Still Big in Columbus," by George Vecsey, New York *Times*, Nov. 23, 1970.

OTHER CITIES "The Reform That Reformed Itself," by William H. Hessler, *The Reporter*, June 13, 1957; "Toledo Clerics Easing Tensions," New York *Times*, April 12, 1970; Dayton section of booklet, *The Model Cities Program* (Department of Housing and Urban Development, Washington, D.C., 1968); "Akron Giving Democratic Ticket Little to Cheer About," New York *Times*, Oct. 26, 1968; "Getting the Point" (regarding Youngstown school closings), *Newsweek*, May 19, 1969; "Youngstown Gets New Image," Cleveland *Plain-Dealer*, Jan. 29, 1971; "Troubled Dayton Has a New Mayor, and He's the Frst Negro in the Job," by Richard L. Brown, *National Observer*, July 20, 1970; "The 'Grimiest Town' in the Nation Certainly Lives up to Its Title," by James MacGregor, *Wall Street Journal*, Aug. 7, 1970.

ILLINOIS

Excellent though slightly dated accounts of the Illinois political scene appear in the Illinois chapter of John H. Fenton's *Midwest Politics* (New York: Holt, Rinehart & Winston, 1966) and Austin Ranney's *Illinois Politics* (New York: New York University Press, 1960). A number of excellent essays on Illinois' past and present appear in *Prairie State*, Paul M. Angle, ed., University of Chicago Press, 1968. Ovid Demaris' *Captive City* (New York: Lyle Stuart, 1969) is a frightening but well documented account of organized crime and corrupt politics in Chicago. Other books used as background for this chapter, or quoted in the text, include: Arthur M. Brazier, *Black Determination: Story of the Woodlawn Organization* (Grand Rapids, Mich.: William B. Eerdmans Publishing Co., 1969); Baker Brownell, *The Other Illinois* (New York: Duell, Sloan & Pearce, 1958); *Boss: Richard J. Daley of Chicago*, by Mike Royko (New York: E. P. Dutton, 1971); *The Heartland*, by Robert McLaughlin (New York: Time-Life Library of America, 1967).

Other Sources—Regular coverage of the *Chicago Tribune*, *Chicago Daily News* (including Mike Royko columns), Chicago *Sun-Times*, *Chicago Today*.

CHICAGO "Portrait of a Lusty City," by Russell Owen, New York *Times Magazine*, April 6, 1947; "The Cities of America: Chicago," by George Sessions Perry, *Saturday Evening Post*, Nov. 3, 1945; "The Chicago the Delegates Won't See," by Leon M. Despres, *The Progressive*, August 1968; "Chicago Stretching Its Seams," by Donald Janson, New York *Times*, Jan. 6, 1969.

DALEY "Daley of Chicago," by David Halberstam, *Harper's Magazine*, August 1968; "New Life in Old Politics," by R. W. Apple Jr., New York *Times*, March 19, 1970; "Voting in Chicago West Side Ghetto Is Mockery of Democratic Process," by Rowland Evans and Robert Novak, Washington *Post*, Nov. 11, 1968; "Suburbia's New Politics," by Milton Rakove, Chicago *Sun-Times*, May 21, 1967; "Chicago Dumps Kelly," by Milburn P. Akers, *The Nation*, Jan. 4, 1947; *Quotations from Mayor Daley*, compiled by Peter Yessne (New York: G. P. Putnam's Sons, 1969); "Mayor Daley Battles a New Chicago Fire," by Dan Cordtz, *Fortune*, July 1968; "Challenge to Daley Machine," by Rowland Evans and Robert Novak, Washington *Post*, May 24, 1971; "Dick Daley: The Business Candidate," *Business Week*, April 10, 1971; "The World's Greatest," by Joseph Kraft, Washington *Post*, March 7, 1971; "A Mobilized Feast for Mayor Daley," *Time*, March 15, 1971; "Politics of

Clout Serves Daley Well," by David S. Broder, Washington *Post*, April 8, 1971; "Daley Wins Fifth Term by a Landslide Vote," Washington *Post*, April 7, 1971; "Daley's Followers Take Victory Seriously," by John Kifner, New York *Times*, April 8, 1971; "Daley Agrees to End Patronage if Illinois GOP Reciprocates," New York *Times*, Oct. 24, 1971.

POLICE AND CRIME "Daley Loosed a Terror That Won't Die," by D. J. R. Bruckner, Washington *Post*, April 21, 1968; *Life* magazine report on the Walker Report (Dec. 6, 1968), including article, "You Can't Expect Police on the Take to Take Orders," by Sandy Smith; "The Battle of Chicago," *Newsweek*, Sept. 9, 1968; "Miami Beach and Chicago," by Norman Mailer, *Harper's Magazine*, November 1968; "Keeper of the Peace," *Newsweek*, March 31, 1969; "The BGA Is Coming!," *Newsweek*, Sept. 22, 1969; "Private Inquiry Group Stirs Both Parties in Illinois," by Seth S. King, New York *Times*, Jan. 4, 1970; 1967, 1968 and 1969 *Reports of the Better Government Association*, Chicago.

BLACKS "Black Powerlessness in Chicago," by Harold M. Baron, *Trans-Action*, November 1968; "Jesse Jackson: Heir to Dr. King?," by Richard Levine, *Harper's Magazine*, March 1969; "Jackson Resourceful Black Militant," by Charles Bartlett, Washington *Evening Star*, Nov. 1, 1969; "Black Hope—White Hope," by John Pekkanen, *Life*, Nov. 3, 1969; "Chicago's Operation Breadbasket is Seeking Racial Solutions in Economic Problems," by John Herbers, New York *Times*, June 2, 1969; "Interview: Jesse Jackson," *Playboy*, November 1969; "Black Expo," *Ebony*, December 1969; "Chicago: Jackson's Expo," *Newsweek*, Oct. 4, 1971; "Chicago's Blackstone Rangers," by James Alan McPherson, *Atlantic Monthly*, May, June 1969; "Chicago Drifts Deeper into Polarization," by Ralph Whitehead, Jr., *National Catholic Reporter*, Dec. 24, 1969; "Black Panther Killings Leave Chicago a City on Edge," by Edward Shanahan, Detroit *Free Press*, Dec. 21, 1969; "Desegregating Public Housing," by Mark R. Killingsworth, *The New Leader*, Oct. 7, 1968; "Chicago Guilty of Housing Bias," by Fred Failey, Washington *Post*, Feb. 11, 1969; "The Professional Radical, 1970," by Marion K. Sanders, *Harper's Magazine*, January 1970; section on William Dawson in Chuck Stone, *Black Political Power in America* (New York: The Bobbs-Merrill Co., 1968); "Daley Favorite Survives Panther Furor," by William Chapman, Washington *Post*, May 1, 1971; "A Professional Radical Reproaches the Far Left," by Nan Robertson, New York *Times*, Nov.

20, 1970; "Alinsky: Lessons in Social Change," by Michael Kernan, Washington *Post*, Nov. 20, 1970.

ARCHITECTURE *The One Book Story of Chicago Architecture* (First National Bank of Chicago, 1969); "Chicago's Giantism: Monumental Curse or Towering Blessing?" by W. W. Newman, Chicago *Daily News*, April 5, 1969; "X Marks Skyline of Windy City," by Wolf Von Eckardt, Washington *Post*, Dec. 8, 1968; "View from the 92nd Floor," *Newsweek*, Feb. 2, 1970; "New Sears Building In Chicago Planned As World's Tallest," New York *Times*, July 28, 1970; ". . . but They Keep Getting Bigger!" by D. J. R. Bruckner, Los Angeles *Times*, July 31, 1970; "The Disposable Sullivans," *Time*, Nov. 1, 1971.

RELIGION "Negro Pastor in Chicago Says Cody Is 'Unconsciously Racist'," New York *Times*, Jan. 11, 1969; "Urban Training Center: Helping the Church to Know the City," by Paige Carlin, *Together*, March 1967; "Clergy: School for a New Creation," *Time*, 1965; "The Plunge," *Newsweek*, Feb. 15, 1965; "The Church Rediscovers the City," *Nation's Cities*, December 1965; "The Priests Take on the Bishops," by Better Medsger, Washington *Post*, June 20, 1971; "Chicago Priests Urge Censure of Cardinal Cody," by Better Medsger, Washington *Post*, June 6, 1971; "Huge Roman Catholic School System Readies Itself for Independence," by Art Gorlick, *National Observer*, Oct. 2, 1971.

UNIVERSITY "Leads Columbia Could Have Followed," by George and Patricia Nash, *New York*, June 3, 1968; "University of Chicago Free of Student Unrest," by Barnard L. Collier, New York *Times*, April 25, 1969; "Chicago Campus Is Like a Paradise, with Confident, No-Nonsense Faculty," by Rowland Evans and Robert Novak, Washington *Post*, March 4, 1970; "Conditions Favoring Major Advances in Social Science," by Karl W. Deutsch, John Platt, and Dieter Senghaas, *Science*, Feb. 5, 1971.

ENVIRONMENT AND TRANSPORTATION "Prosecuting Pollution," *Time*, Jan. 5, 1970; "How Our Community is Fighting Air Pollution" and "Housewives for Cleaner Air," by Laura Fermi, *New City*, January 1963 and February 1966; "O'Hare Airport to Be Expanded," New York *Times*, Nov. 23, 1969; "Urban Expansion Takes to the Water," by Walter McQuade, *Fortune*, September 1969; "What the Pennsy Doesn't Know about Commuting Chicago Does," *Philadelphia Magazine*, 1968; "Study Finds Private Mass Transit in a Cost Squeeze," by Seth S. King, New York *Times*, Jan. 10, 1971; "U. S. Steel Accepts '75 Deadline for Halting Pollution," Chicago *Sun-Times*, Jan. 19, 1971; "U.S. To Heed Law On Lake Michigan," New York *Times*, June 6, 1971; "Illinois Establishes Major Antipollution Agencies," *State Government News*, December 1970; "95% of Sewage Plants in State Called Polluters," by Bruce Ingersoll, Chicago *Sun-Times*, Oct. 6, 1970; "1973 Deadline Likely on Illinois Sewage Plan," by Taylor Pensoneau, St. Louis *Post-Dispatch*, Dec. 23, 1970.

OTHER CHICAGO COVERAGE "The Early Bird" (re nuclear power), *Forbes*, Sept. 15, 1969; "Slave Shops" (re Uptown day-labor market), *Newsweek*, March 9, 1970; "A Basis for the Selection of the Chicago (Weston) Site for Location of the 200-BEV Accelerator Laboratory," release of Atomic Energy Commission, Jan. 20, 1967; "The Italians," by Jory Graham, *Chicago Magazine*, Winter 1969; "Uncovered News" (re suburban press), by David L. Beal, *Columbia Journalism Review*, Fall 1968; "Chicago Paper Changes, but Too Slow for Some, Too Fast for Others," by A. Kent MacDougall, *Wall Street Journal*, Feb. 25, 1971; "Chicago Tribune Shows New Face," by Seth S. King, New York *Times*, Oct. 10, 1971; "Chicago and New York: Contrasts," by John Kifner, New York *Times*, May 16, 1971; "Hog Butcher for the World Is No More," by Seth S. King, New York *Times*, May 13, 1970; "Farewell to Hog Alley," *Newsweek*, July 20, 1970; "The Second Sex in the Second City," by Jean Komaiko, *Chicago Magazine*, May–June 1971.

STATEWIDE ILLINOIS The City and the Plain," by Robert Paul Jordan, *National Geographic*, June 1967; "Illinois—Mid-American Empire," *Fortune*, January 1968; "The Prairie State —Illinois," New York *Times*, Oct. 2, 1956.

POLITICAL "State Statistical Outlook: Democrats Face Disaster," by John Dreiske, Chicago *Sun-Times*, April 23, 1967; "The Illinois Legislature—A Study in Comparison," by Paul Simon, *Harper's*, September 1964; *Bipartisan Coalition in Illinois*, by Thomas B. Littlewood (The Eagleton Institute—McGraw-Hill Book Co., 1960); "Illinois: Chaos at the Polls," by James L. McDowell, *The Reporter*, March 26, 1964; "Illinois Auditor Quits in Inquiry" and "Hodge Sentenced to 20-Year Term," New York *Times*, July 16 and Aug. 15, 1956; "Expense-Account Gouging by State Payrollers Bared," Chicago *Sun-Times*, Dec. 19, 1968; "Charges of State Fair Corruption Investigated by Illinois and U.S.," by John Kifner, New York *Times*, Aug. 19, 1969; "Mystery in Illinois: Millionaire Aide," by John Kifner, New York *Times*, Jan. 15, 1971; "How One Legislator Linked With Lobbyists Made a Tidy Fortune," by Jonathan R. Laing, *Wall Street Journal*, Jan. 14, 1971; "Powell Bogey Confronts Legislature," by Charles N. Wheeler, III, Chicago *Sun-Times*, Jan. 17, 1971.

"Gov. Ogilvie: Taking a Calculated Risk," by Dan Rottenberg, *Wall Street Journal*, May 19, 1969; "Ogilvie Showing Lively Leadership," by Charles Bartlett, Washington *Evening Star*, Dec. 2, 1969; "Ogilvie Tells It Like It Is," editorial in Chicago *Sun-Times*, April 2, 1969; "Ogilvie Star Rises," by Guy Halverson, *Christian Science Monitor*, Feb. 27, 1970; "Illinois: Ogilvie's Offensive," *Time*, April 18, 1969; "Illinois Demonstrates State Responsibility," remarks of Sen. Charles H. Percy, *Congressional Record*, July 10, 1969, p. S7857; "Ogilvie Learns From Rocky," by Rowland Evans and Robert Novak, Washington *Post*, May 27, 1971.

"Illinois: Money Isn't Everything," and "For Top Giver, Obscure Rewards," by Bernard D. Nossiter, Washington *Post*, Nov. 22, 1970 and Jan. 3, 1971; "Stone's Millions: High Finance in Illinois," *National Journal*, Oct. 10, 1970; "Sen. Smith's Ad Barrage Seems Failure in Illinois," by R. W. Apple Jr., New York *Times*, Oct. 25, 1970; "Daley Is Called Key To Illinois Campaign," by George Lardner, Jr., Washington *Post*, Oct. 12, 1970; "Stevenson Defeats Smith for Illinois Senate Seat," by E. W. Kenworthy, New York *Times*, Nov. 5, 1971; "Senate Race: The Men, the Issues," by James W. Singer and Charles N. Wheeler, III, Chicago *Sun-Times*, Oct. 4, 1970; "He Hopes to Win Illinois Race in a Walk" (re Daniel Walker), by R. W. Apple, Jr., New York *Times*, Oct. 21, 1971.

OTHER LEADERS "The Other Ev Dirksen," by Charles Roberts, *Newsweek*, June 16, 1969; "Everett McKinley Dirksen," *Congressional Quarterly*, July 26, 1968, p. 1904; *Dirksen: Portrait of a Public Man*, by Neil MacNeil (New York: World Publishing Co., 1970); "Ev Dirksen: The Compleat Senator," by Robert Novak, *Book Week*, Nov. 22, 1970; "Dirksen Worth Put at $302,235," UPI dispatch in Washington *Post*, March 6, 1971; "The Adlai III Brand of Politics," by William Barry Furlong, New York *Times Magazine*, Feb. 22, 1970; "Adlai Hits 'Feudal' Party," by John Dreiske, Chicago *Sun-Times*, Sept. 18, 1968; "Illinois' Adlai Stevenson," *Time*, Nov. 16, 1970; "Charles H. Percy: The Middle Man," a chapter

of *The Republican Establishment,"* by Stephen Hess and David S. Broder (New York: Harper & Row, 1967); "Paul H. Douglas," *Congressional Quarterly,* July 22, 1966, p. 1532.
EAST ST. LOUIS "The City: The East St. Louis Blues," *Time,* April 11, 1969; "East St. Louis' Financial Blues," by Philip Sutin, *CITY Chronicle,* February 1969; "East St. Louis Begins

to Live Down Its Past," *Business Week,* Oct. 26, 1968; "City on the Ropes," by James W. Singer, Chicago *Sun-Times,* May 4, 1969.
OTHER "The Census: Middle America," *Newsweek,* May 10, 1971; "Ecstasy in Rockford," *Newsweek,* Nov. 30, 1970; "Peoria, Ill.: Job Oasis in a Period of Recession," by Philip Shabecoff, New York *Times,* May 8, 1971.

MICHIGAN

An excellent review of the state's political trends appears in the Michigan chapter of John H. Fenton's *Midwest Politics* (New York: Holt, Rinehart & Winston, 1966); valuable background material may also be found in *Political Party Patterns in Michigan,* by Stephen B. and Vera H. Sarasohn (Detroit: Wayne State University Press, 1957). I am indebted to both books for insights and a number of quotations used in the chapter. Also of use were several publications of the Citizens Research Council of Michigan (a nonprofit group, supported by state businesses, that furnishes excellent research material on the state's tax structure), as well as material from the state chamber of commerce. Reference was made to several reports of the Detroit Regional Transportation and Land Use Study and *The Heartland,* by Robert McLaughlin (New York: Time-Life Library of America, 1967).

The chapter draws on ongoing coverage of Michigan newspapers, especially the Detroit *Free Press* and Detroit *News,* as well as the following articles in particular:

POLITICS "Soapy, the Boy Wonder," by Beverly Smith, Jr., *Saturday Evening Post,* Nov. 9, 1957; "27,000 Go Unpaid in Michigan Crisis" and "Michigan's Crisis Worries Leaders," by Damon Stetson, New York *Times,* May 7 and June 6, 1959; "GOP Aides Gloomy on State Party Setup," Detroit *News,* Oct. 2, 1957; "The Public Record of George W. Romney," *Congressional Quarterly Weekly Report,* June 16, 1967; "Romney: A Tough Act to Follow," by Glenn Engle, Detroit *News,* Jan. 19, 1969; "Bill Milliken May Look Like a Boy, but He's a Man," by Will Muller, Detroit *News Magazine,* Jan. 5, 1969; "Michigan Seeking State Take-over of School Costs," by Jerry M. Flint, New York *Times,* Sept. 30, 1969; "A New Governor Finds Civility Pays," by Anthony Ripley, New York *Times,* Feb. 2, 1969; "Tax Panel Studies State School Financing," by Angelo Baglivo, Newark *Sunday News,* May 9, 1971; "Unicameral proposal—Reforms demanded in Michigan," by David A. Hanson, *Christian Science Monitor,* Sept. 9, 1971.
UNIVERSITIES "University Presidents—Exit Methuselah," *Time,* March 21, 1969; "MSU 'Army' Growing," *The State Journal* (Lansing), Sept. 25, 1969; "Strike Ends at University of Michigan," New York *Times,* April 3, 1970. Also *The Commuting Student,* report of the Commuter Centers Project, Wayne State University, Detroit, 1969, by Richard F. Wald and Theodore E. Kurz; and *Wayne and the Inner City,* survey published by Wayne State University, 1968.
CONGRESSIONAL DELEGATION "Michigan's Hart Emerges as Ball-Carrier for Liberals," by Spencer Rich, Washington *Post,* Feb. 15, 1970; "Establishment Rebel: Michigan's Senator Philip Hart," by Saul Friedman, Detroit *Free Press,* March 1969; "Griffin's Election as Senate Whip Caps Quiet Rise in GOP Politics," by Saul Friedman, Detroit *Free Press,* Sept. 27, 1969; "Our

Freshman Senator: Apple Pie and Ambition," by Saul Friedman, Detroit *Free Press,* March 23, 1969; "Michigan Congressman Aims High—Donald Riegle Wants to Be President in About 15 Years," by Richard L. Lyons, Washington *Post,* June 1, 1969; "Equal Rights Champion—Martha Wright Griffiths," New York *Times,* Aug. 11, 1970; "Rights Advocates Retreat in Michigan Busing Furor," by Peter Milius, Washington *Post,* Oct. 24, 1971.
AUTOS "A Beleaguered Detroit Fights Back," *Newsweek,* April 6, 1970; "General Motors Gears for the Seventies," *Fortune,* April 1970; "Henry Ford Shows Who's Boss," *Fortune,* October 1969; "Where Auto Defects Come from," *Time,* March 28, 1969; "Autos Seen Changing Radically," by Thomas O'Toole, Washington *Post,* Feb. 11, 1970; "America-Car Honeymoon Nearly Over," by Wolf Von Eckardt, Washington *Post,* Jan. 23, 1970; "Henry Ford Vows 'Intensified Effort' to Curb Pollution," by Jerry M. Flint, New York *Times,* Dec. 11, 1969; "The Way Detroit 'Wages War' on Pollution," by Colman McCarthy, Washington *Post,* Jan. 26, 1970; "Government Assumes Major Planning Role," by William H. Jones, Washington *Post,* Jan. 23, 1970; "Detroit Pushes Search for Answer to Problem of Pollution by Autos," by Charles B. Camp, *Wall Street Journal,* March 31, 1970; "Detroit and Pollution," by Jerry M. Flint, New York *Times,* Jan. 16, 1970; "Ford Has Some Winners—but Big Losers, Too," by William Serrin, Milwaukee *Journal,* October 1969; "Detroit Car Makers Adding Negro Dealers," New York *Times,* May 11, 1969; "Detroit's New Models: Black Auto Dealers," *Ebony,* February 1970; "The Fords of Dearborn," subchapter in *The Rich and the Super-Rich,* by Ferdinand Lundberg (New York: Lyle Stuart, 1968).
"U. S. Love for Auto Wanes as More Demand Cheap Transportation," by Walter Mossberg and Laurence G. O'Donnell, *Wall Street Journal,* March 30, 1971; "Transportation Report —New Approach to Auto Safety Stresses Performance—Not Hardware," by Vera Hirschberg, *National Journal,* April 17, 1971; "Autos: A Hazardous Stretch Ahead," by Dan Cordtz, *Fortune,* April 1971; "Mister Ford: They Never Call Him Henry," *Time,* July 20, 1970; "Settlement at G. M. Revives 'Progress Sharing'," by A. H. Raskin, New York *Times,* Nov. 15, 1970; "The GM Strike—What Happened?," by Laurence G. O'Donnell, *Wall Street Journal,* Nov. 20, 1970; "Auto Industry Struggling to Stop Lag in Productivity," by Jerry M. Flint, New York *Times,* Aug. 8, 1970.
"GM Responds to Charges of Job Discrimination," by Morton Mintz, Washington *Post,* May 2, 1971; "Black Car Dealers Struggle to Exist," *Business Week,* April 10, 1971.
LABOR "Detroit's Armed Camps," by Earl Brown, *Harper's Magazine,* July 1945; Black Rage on the Auto Lines," *Time,* April 11, 1969; "Alliance of Teamsters, UAW Maps Bold Plans in Labor, Social Fields," by James P. Gannon and Laurence G. O'Donnell, *Wall Street Journal,* May 14, 1969.

"Young Workers Raising Voices for Factory and Union Changes," by Agis Salpukas, New York *Times*, June 1, 1970; "UAW Mourns Walter Reuther," by Ken W. Clawson, Washington *Post*, May 11, 1970; "Reuther: Authentic American Radical," by William J. Eaton, Los Angeles *Times*, May 17, 1970; "Walter Reuther," Washington *Post* editorial, May 12, 1970; "Reuther's Life, Goals Offer Democrats a Useful Lesson," by David Broder, Washington *Post*, May 19, 1970; "End to Violence Urged by Reuther," by Jerry M. Flint, New York *Times*, April 21, 1970; "Reuther's Legacy," *Newsweek*, May 25, 1970; "Violence in the Factories," *Newsweek*, June 29, 1970; "The Unknown Who Leads the Walter P. Reuther Memorial Strike," by William Serrin, New York *Times Magazine*, Sept. 27, 1970; "Firm Support for a Shaky Alliance," *Business Week*, March 6, 1971; "Blue-Collar Blues on the Assembly Line," by Judson Gooding, *Fortune*, July 1970; "UAW General Fund Scraping the Bottom," *Christian Science Monitor*, July 30, 1970; "UAW narrows lobbying focus, stresses issues vital to members," by Charles Culhane, *National Journal*, July 3, 1971; "UAW Owes $43 Million, Sells Realty to Teamsters," by Frank C. Porter, Washington *Post*, July 6, 1971.

DETROIT   "The Cities of America—Detroit," by George Sessions Perry, *Saturday Evening Post*, June 22, 1946; "Detroit: A City in Pain," by Jerry M. Flint, New York *Times*, May 1, 1969; "The Changes the City Has Felt, the Problems That Change Has Brought," Detroit *Free Press*, March 9, 1969; "Is Detroit Dying Because No One Cares?" by Robert A. Popa, Detroit *News*, Sept. 21, 1969; "God Help Our City," by William Serrin, *Atlantic Monthly*, March 1969; "Detroit Club's Members Help Change the World but Keep the Club Unchanged," New York *Times*, Oct. 12, 1969; "How One Big City Defeated Its Mayor," by William Serrin, New York *Times Magazine*, Oct. 27, 1968;

"City That Made Jerry Also Tarnished Image," by Barbara Stanton, Detroit *Free Press*, June 25, 1969; "Sullen Settlement in Detroit," *Newsweek*, Sept. 8, 1969; "If We Can't Solve the Problems of the Ghetto Here, God Help Our Country," by Bill Davidson, *Saturday Evening Post*, Oct. 5, 1968; "The Trouble with Uplift," *Newsweek*, June 2, 1969; "Analyzing Detroit's Riot: The Causes and Responses," by Irving J. Rubin, *The Reporter*, Feb. 22, 1968; "Detroit Poles, Blacks Form Coalition," by William Greider, Washington *Post*, Oct. 11, 1969; "Poles in Detroit Ally with Blacks," by Frye Gaillard, *Race Relations Reporter*, April 5, 1971; "Was Justice Done in the Algiers Motel Incident?" by Yale Kamisar, New York *Times*, March 1, 1970; "Mystery Lingers in Detroit Shootout," by Robert C. Maynard, Washington *Post*, April 7, 1969; "Judge in a City of Fear," *Time*, April 6, 1970; "U. S. Funds Pour into Town of Black Republican Mayor," by Larry Green, Washington *Post*, June 29, 1969.

THE SUBURBS   *Data on Cities of Michigan* (Jackson, Mich.: Consumers Power Company, 1969); "One Man's Fortune," by Patrick J. Owens, Detroit *Free Press*, Jan. 19, 1969; "Pontiac Brothers Spearhead Drive for a Black Republic," by Gary Blonston, Detroit *Free Press*, Jan. 4, 1969; "HUD Tests Integration Drive in Michigan," by Hugh McDonald, Washington *Post*, July 27, 1970; "Blue Collar Workers of Warren, a Detroit Suburb, Fight to Keep Negroes Out," by Jerry M. Flint, New York *Times*, Aug. 17, 1970; "A Blue-Collar Town Fears Urban Renewal Perils Its Way of Life," by Walter S. Mossberg, *Wall Street Journal*, Nov. 2, 1970; "Don't Laugh at Hamtramck," *Newsweek*, May 17, 1971; "Detroit School Segregation Deliberate, U.S. Judge Rules," and "School Plan Ordered for Detroit, Suburbs," by Robert Popa, Washington *Post*, Sept. 28 and Oct. 5, 1971; "Busing Is Michigan's Biggest Political Issue," by Jerry M. Flint, New York *Times*, Oct. 18, 1971.

FLORIDA

Books offering valuable background on Florida include: *Florida: The Long Frontier*, by Marjory Stoneman Douglas (New York: Harper & Row, 1967); "Florida: The Different State," by Manning J. Dauer, chapter in *Politics of the Contemporary South*, ed. William C. Havard (Baton Rouge: Louisiana State University Press, 1972); *Florida: A Guide to the Southernmost State*, compiled by the Federal Writers' Project of the WPA, American Guide Series (New York: Oxford University Press, 1939); *Gothic Politics in the Deep South*, by Robert Sherrill (New York: Grossman, 1968); *The Old South*, by John Osborne (New York: Time-Life Library of America, 1968); "Florida: Every Man for Himself," chapter in *Southern Politics in State and Nation*, by V. O. Key (New York: Random House, 1949); "Florida Republicanism: A House Divided," chapter in *Southern Republicanism and the New South*, by John C. Topping, Jr., John R. Lazarek, and William H. Linder (Cambridge, Mass.: Ripon Society, 1966); "Florida," by Budd Schulberg, chapter in *American Panorama* (Garden City, N.Y.: Doubleday, 1960); *Bean Soup—Or Florida with a Spanish Accent*, by M. Lisle Reese (Crawford, Jacksonville, Fla.: 1964).

Other Sources: Regular coverage of state and local events by the Miami *Herald* and St. Petersburg *Times*, and the following articles and reports:

GENERAL   "Many Older Adults Moved

Southward," by Jack Rosenthal, New York *Times*, March 29, 1971; "Industry, More Citizens? Some in Florida Veto Them," by Charles F. Hesser, Atlanta *Journal-Constitution*, Feb. 14, 1971; It's Back: Divide Florida," by John Pennekamp, Miami *Herald*, July 21, 1970; "Florida Rides a Space-Age Boom," by Benedict Thielen, *National Geographic*, December 1963; "Having Fun With Florida," by Roger M. Williams, *The Nation*, Aug. 17, 1970; "Kirk Against the World," by Michael Lottman, *Ripon Forum*, August 1970; "Florida: The State with the Two-Way Stretch," by William L. Rivers, *Harper's Magazine*, February 1955; "Growth Plan Reversal Studied," by Charles F. Hesser, Atlanta *Journal-Constitution*, Oct. 10, 1971.

ENVIRONMENT   "Park Rich Florida is Getting Even Richer," by C. E. Wright, New York *Times*, March 8, 1970; "Indifference Builds a Gravestone for a Lake," Tampa *Tribune*, Jan. 31, 1969; "Keep Out People to Save the Glades?," by Richard Pothier, Miami *Herald*, Feb. 28, 1970; "Florida to Drain a Polluted Lake," by Martin Waldron, New York *Times*, Jan. 4, 1970; "Pensacola Is Paying for 20 Years' Abuse," by Mike Toner, Miami *Herald*, Dec. 6, 1970; "Biscayne Bay," *Audubon*, September 1970; "Miami River's Filth Blamed on Airport," by Don Bedwell, Miami *Herald*, Jan. 22, 1971.

"President Blocks Canal in Florida," by Robert B. Semple, Jr., New York *Times*, Jan. 20, 1971;

"Blocking Florida's Ditch," *Newsweek,* Feb. 1, 1971; "What Can Be Done with Part of Canal?" by Charles F. Hesser, Atlanta *Journal-Constitution,* Jan. 31, 1971.

"Everglades Jetport Barred by a U. S.-Florida Accord," by Robert B. Semple, Jr., New York *Times,* Jan. 16, 1970; "Florida," *Life,* July 4, 1970; "Everglades Jetport," by Luna B. Leopold, *National Parks Magazine,* November 1969; "Oil Exploration a Peril to Everglades," by Jon Nordheimer, New York *Times,* July 8, 1970; "Fiery Ordeal of the Everglades," *Life,* May 7, 1971; "Water Rationing, Raging Fires Plague Florida," *National Observer,* May 10, 1971; "Florida May Be Next Big Oil State," by Roberta Hornig, Washington *Star,* June 16, 1971.

MIGRANTS "Rate of Disease among Migrants' Children 'Startling'," by Samuel Adams, St. Petersburg *Times,* April 4, 1968; "Migrants to Get Help in Florida," New York *Times,* Nov. 9, 1969; "OMICA: A Nonviolent Way to Equality," by Bruce Galphin, Washington *Post,* April 26, 1970; "Hunger in America: Stark Poverty Leaves Florida Migrants Vulnerable to Disease," by Homer Bigart, New York *Times,* Feb. 20, 1969; "Coca-Cola Says Migrant Reforms Planned," Washington *Star,* July 23, 1970; "Corporation: The Candor that Refreshes," *Time,* Aug. 10, 1970; "Migrants: Florida's Shame," *South Today,* September 1970; *Migrant: An NBC White Paper* (NBC broadcast of July 16, 1970); "President Orders Relief for Migrant Workers after Florida Crop Failure," Robert H. Phelps, New York *Times,* March 16, 1971; "Jobless Migrant Workers 'Ambush' President Nixon and the Press," by William Tucker, *National Observer,* March 22, 1971; "New Moves May End State's 'Harvest of Shame'," by John McDermott, Miami *Herald,* Feb. 2, 1969.

POLITICS "Piney Woods, Urban Dade Went for Askew," by Juanita Greene, Miami *Herald,* Nov. 5, 1970; "Carswell Hits Liberals Who Killed Court Bid as He Runs for Senate," by Arlen J. Large, *Wall Street Journal,* July 30, 1970; "Carswell: Defeat from the Jaw of Victory," New York *Times,* April 12, 1970; "Florida's GOP Primary Tests Kirk and Carswell," by Bruce Galphin, Washington *Post,* Aug. 2, 1970; "Carswell's Campaign," *Newsweek,* June 29, 1970; "Chiles Walks to Prominence on Only a Shoestring Budget," by Hunter George, Miami *Herald,* Sept. 10, 1970; "Florida: A Battle of Styles," by Rowland Evans and Robert Novak, Washington *Post,* Oct. 19, 1970; "Carswell's Loss Blocks Kirk's Bid for Party Control," by Jon Nordheimer, New York *Times,* Sept. 10, 1970; "Governor's Office Returns to Demos as Kirk Leaves," by Charles F. Hesser, Atlanta *Journal-Constitution,* Jan. 10, 1971; "NAACP Chief: Black Voters 'Strike Out'," Miami *Herald,* Aug. 23, 1970; "A Presidential Primary at the Beach," by Charles F. Hesser, Atlanta *Journal-Constitution,* April 4, 1971; "Florida Becomes a Primary Factor," by Stanley J. Hinden, *Newsday,* June 11, 1971; "Election Report: Florida's Changing Political Climate Makes Its Primary Crucial to '72 Campaign," by Gene Baro, *National Journal,* Sept. 4, 1971; "Paper Links Smathers to Deal With Contractor He Promoted," New York *Times,* Oct. 12, 1971.

STATE GOVERNMENT "Cabinet, PSC Indebted to Those They Control," St. Petersburg *Times* and Miami *Herald,* Feb. 9, 1969; "Reorganization Bill Is Passed," by Martin Dyckman, Miami *Herald,* June 4, 1969; "Legislative Modernization—The Florida Experiment," by Fred Schultz, *State Government,* Autumn 1969; "Florida Prison Shootings Called Effort 'to Protect the Inmates'," by Jon Nordheimer, New York *Times,* Feb. 28, 1971; "Judges, Goode Seek Better Jail," by James

Buchanan, Miami *Herald,* Jan. 28, 1971; "Prison Reforms Coming?" by Charles F. Hesser, Atlanta *Journal-Constitution,* Feb. 21, 1971; "Florida Ban on Closed Meetings Merges Candor and Confusion," New York *Times,* Feb. 28, 1971; "All Secret Meetings Illegal, Florida's High Court Rules," by Susan Burnside, Miami *Herald,* Jan. 28, 1971.

"Florida: The Limits of Public Disclosure," chapter in *Development of Campaign Finance Regulation, Electing Congress: The Financial Dilemma,* by The Twentieth Century Fund Task Force (New York: The Twentieth Century Fund, 1970); *Representation and Apportionment* (Washington: Congressional Quarterly Service, 1966); "Campaign Fund Cap Clears Legislature," by William Mansfield, Miami *Herald,* June 5, 1970; "2-Party System to Add to Dixie Campaign Cost," by Bruce Galphin, Washington *Post,* Oct. 3, 1969; "Florida: Reporting Law Helps," by Philip D. Carter, Washington *Post,* Nov. 22, 1970; "Election Law Reform," by Elston Roady, *National Civic Review,* April 1970.

"The Public Record of Claude R. Kirk, Jr.," *Congressional Quarterly Weekly Report,* Aug. 18, 1967, p. 1607; "Florida's Defiant Governor," New York *Times,* April 7, 1970; "Governor Kirk Fails to Stifle Controversy over Donations," Washington *Post,* March 19, 1970; "Florida Sunshine," by Ernest B. Furgurson, Baltimore *Sun,* Dec. 14, 1969; "War-Like Kirk Attacked Legislators' Integrity," by Bill Mansfield and Jim Minter, Miami *Herald,* April 25, 1969; "A Governor on the Go Carries a High Price," Miami *Herald,* Dec. 14, 1969; "Kirk Had Chance to 'Beat System'," by Clarence Jones, Miami *Herald,* Dec. 18, 1969; "2nd County May Go to GOP," Associated Press dispatch in Miami *Herald,* Aug. 7, 1970.

"Ed Ball's Grip Is Felt by All," by Juanita Greene, Miami *Herald,* Sept. 22, 1969; "Florida Makes News by Not Passing a Bill," by Bruce Galphin, Washington *Post,* June 11, 1970; "Congress May Bounce Ed Ball from Grip on Florida Banking," by Charles Stafford, Miami *Herald* and St. Petersburg *Times,* March 23, 1969; "Mr. Ball," by Nixon Smiley, *Floridian,* May 5, 1968.

MIAMI *Psycho-Social Dynamics in Miami,* Report of a Summer Study Conducted under the Auspices of the University of Miami, Prepared for the Department of Housing and Urban Development, January 1969; "The Gleaming Shores of Miami," by Dick Schaap, *Holiday,* June 1968.

MIAMI—CUBANS "Havana, Florida: Cubans Thrive in Miami Area and So Does the City," by Yvonne Thayer, *Wall Street Journal,* Dec. 12, 1969; "Success Story: U. S. Cubans," by Haynes Johnson, Washington *Post,* March 28, 1971; *Cubans in Miami: A Third Dimension in Racial and Cultural Relations,* by John Egerton (Nashville, Tenn.: Race Relations Information Center, November 1969); "Cuban Refugee Aid Cost Spirals," by Charles F. Hesser, Atlanta *Journal-Constitution,* June 20, 1971.

MIAMI—MIAMI BEACH "Miami Beach, the All-Too-American City," by Robert Sherrill, New York *Times Magazine,* Aug. 4, 1968; "Wish You Were Here," by E. M. Michel, Miami *Herald Tropic,* Nov. 15, 1970; "Miami Beach Oceanfront," by Morris David Rosenberg, Washington *Post,* Nov. 8, 1970; "The Sands of Time Are Running Out for Miami Beach," by Jay Clarke, New York *Times,* May 10, 1970; "Miami Beach: A Steel and Concrete Shore," by Susan Miller and Joseph P. Averill, Miami *Herald,* May 24, 1970; "Gambling Defeat in Poll Is Hailed," New York *Times,* April 26, 1970; "South Beach: Ripe Area for New Face," by Bill Amlong, Miami *Herald,* Feb. 22, 1969;

"Face to Face with the G.O.P.," by Elia Kazan, *New York,* Aug. 26, 1968; "Miami Beach and Chicago," Norman Mailer, *Harper's Magazine,* November 1968.

MIAMI—CRIME "The Little Big Man Who Laughs at the Law," by Nicholas Gage, *Atlantic,* July, 1970; *The Grim Reapers,* by Ed Reid (Chicago: Henry Regnery, 1969); "Lansky Is Indicted again in Miami," *Washington Post,* March 26, 1971; "Illicit Traffic of Cocaine 'Growing by Leaps and Bounds' in Miami," by George Volsky, New York *Times,* Feb. 1, 1970; "Faircloth's Law: A New Way to Nail Elusive Mobsters?" by Denny Walsh, *Life,* Oct. 24, 1969.

OTHER CITIES AND PLACES "Jacksonville: Emerging from Morass of Mediocrity," by Jeff Nesmith, Atlanta *Journal-Constitution,* Sept. 21, 1969; "Jacksonville Area Highlights Activity," *National Civic Review,* June, 1970; "Metro Aided Jacksonville as Ship Nearly Swamped," by Les Seago, Chattanooga *Times,* April 12, 1970; "Newcomer to City Gave Impetus to Consolidation in Jacksonville," by Les Seago, Chattanooga *Times,* April 13, 1970; "Mayor Hails Merger in Jacksonville," by Ralph D. Olive, Milwaukee *Journal,* April 19, 1970; "The Jacksonville Story," by L. A. Hester, *National Civic Review,* February 1970; "Racial Unrest Hits Jacksonville Despite Efforts

to Ease Tensions," by Martin Waldron, New York *Times,* June 21, 1971; "Jacksonville: So Different You Can Hardly Believe It," by John Fischer, *Harper's Magazine,* July 1971.

"Disney World Wakes Sleepy Orlando, *Business Week,* Nov. 14, 1970; "Florida's Manmade Magic," by Brad Byers, *Southern Living,* June 1966; "The Man Who Can't Stop Running," by Nixon Smiley, Miami *Herald Sunday Magazine,* Feb. 5, 1967.

CAPE KENNEDY "Blues at the Cape," by Thomas O'Toole, *Washington Post,* Jan. 31, 1971; "Cape Kennedy: Eclipse on the Ground," *Newsweek,* June 2, 1969; "Cape May Lose Out on Space Shuttle Shots," by Chuck Hoyt, Miami *Herald,* Jan. 24, 1971; "The Heron and the Astronaut," by Anne Morrow Lindberg, *Life,* Feb. 28, 1969; *Summary Report: NASA Impact on Brevard County,* by Annie Mary Hartsfield, Mary Alice Griffin, and Charles M. Grigg (Tallahassee: Institute for Social Research, Florida State University, 1966); *The Kennedy Space Center Story* (Kennedy Space Center, Fla.: National Aeronautics and Space Administration, 1968); " 'Space Coast' Tightens Belt," by James Russell, Miami *Herald,* Oct. 11, 1970; "Floridians Ask Hill to Restore Name of Cape Canaveral," by William Greider, *Washington Post,* Nov. 25, 1969.

TEXAS

These books provided generally helpful background and, on occasion, some good quotes: *In A Narrow Grave—Essays on Texas,* by Larry McMurtry (Austin: Encino Press, 1968); *Texas After Spindletop,* by Seth S. McKay and Odie B. Faulk (Austin: Steck-Vaughn Co., 1965); "Texas, A Politics of Economics," chapter of *Southern Politics In State and Nation,* by V. O. Key (New York: Random House, 1949); "Texas Politics," by O. Douglas Weeks, chapter of *Politics of the Contemporary South,* ed. William C. Havard (Baton Rouge: Louisiana State University Press, 1972); *The South Central States,* by Lawrence Goodwyn (New York: Time-Life Library of America, 1967); *Texas: A Guide to the Lone Star State,* compiled by writers of the Writers' Project Administration of the WPA (Hastings House, New York: American Guide Series, 1940); *Metropolitan Texas: A Workable Approach to its Problems,* report of the Texas Research League (Austin, 1967); *Texas Almanac* (Dallas *Morning News,* annual).

Other sources: The most probing coverage of the Texas statewide scene has for years been provided by the *Texas Observer,* a liberal biweekly published in Austin, and materials from its past issues were widely drawn on in preparing the chapter. Also consulted was ongoing coverage of major Texas dailies including the Dallas *Morning News,* Houston *Chronicle,* Houston *Post,* as well as the specific articles cited:

GENERAL "The Fabulous State of Texas," by Stanley Walker, *National Geographic,* February 1961; "The Tin Star State," by Gary Cartwright, *Esquire,* February 1971; "The Texan Myth and Tradition," by Joe B. Frantz, *Texas Observer,* May 1, 1964; "The Guns of Texas," by Eric Morgenthaler, *Wall Street Journal,* Nov. 20, 1969; "The Phenomenal Custom," by Gary Cartwright, *Texas Observer,* Dec. 19, 1969; " 'Pot' Giver Gets 30-Yr. Taste of Texas Justice," by Molly Ivins, Washington *Post,* Nov. 29, 1970; "Texas: Land of Wealth and Fear," by Theodore H. White, *The Reporter,*

May 25, 1954.

"ESTABLISHMENT," CONNALLY, BARNES "Texas Establishment Is Alive and Well—Somewhere," by Lee Jones, *Houston Chronicle,* May 1, 1969; "Everyone Eager to Help in the Texas Campaign," by Morton Mintz, *Washington Post,* Nov. 22, 1970; "Texas Records Show Businessmen Are Biggest Political Givers," by Morton Mintz, Washington *Post,* Dec. 6, 1970; "Can a Rich Guy Lose in Texas?," by William W. Hamilton, Jr., *The Nation,* Sept. 28, 1970; "John Connally and SMIC," by Stephen D. Berkowitz, *Ripon Forum,* February 1971; "The Connally Years," *Texas Observer,* Oct. 4, 1968; "Connally and the Issue," *Texas Observer,* Aug. 9, 1963; "Connally and the Richardson Estate," *Texas Observer,* May 1, 1964; "Juan John's Fortune," *Texas Observer,* Jan. 8, 1971; "A Matter of Sides," *Time,* July 27, 1970; "New Texan on the Potomac," *Time,* Dec. 28, 1970; "John Connally's Other Careers," *Newsweek,* Dec. 28, 1970; "Connally Selection Seen As Bid for Texas in 1972," by Don Oberdorfer, Washington *Post,* Dec. 15, 1970; "Foundation Paid Connally $225,000 While Governor," by Martin Waldron, New York *Times,* Feb. 1, 1971; "Connally Says He Did Not Violate Texas Law," by John W. Finney, New York *Times,* Feb. 2, 1971; "Connally Backed By Senate Panel," by Don Oberdorfer, Washington *Post,* Feb. 3, 1971; "Connally: Nixon Is on the Right Track," by David S. Broder, Washington *Post,* Feb. 19, 1971; "Connally Revitalizes Treasury, Assumes Stewardship of Nixon's New Economic Policy," by Frank V. Fowlkes, *National Journal,* Oct. 2, 1971.

"The Heir Apparent," by Dennis Farney, *Wall Street Journal,* May 14, 1969; "Ben Barnes: Young, Smart and Possibly Another LBJ," by Bo Byers, Houston *Chronicle,* Jan. 5, 1969; "The Barnes Dinner," *Texas Observer,* Sept. 4, 1970; "Barnes and the Senate Liberals," *Texas Observer,* May 9, 1969; "How Good Ol' Boys Seek Glory in Texas," by Wesley Pruden, Jr., *National Observer,* Feb. 15, 1971.

POLITICS "Results Show Texas Still One-Party State," by Felton West, Houston *Post*, Nov. 5, 1970; "Texas Primary Candidate Fee Ruled Illegal," Washington *Evening Star*, Dec. 20, 1970; "Election Law Changes Needed," Houston *Chronicle*, Jan. 21, 1969; "Committee Calls for Permanent Voter Registration," by Mary Rice Brogan, Houston *Chronicle*, Jan. 16, 1969; "GOP in Texas Shattered by Loss at Polls," Los Angeles *Times*, Nov. 22, 1970; "The GOP's Southern Star," by Rowland Evans and Robert Novak, Washington *Post*, Nov. 1, 1970; "How Texas Became a No-Party State," by Paul B. Holcomb, *State Observer*, Oct. 19, 1953; "A Texas Size Political Battle," by David S. Broder, Washington *Post*, March 8, 1971; "The Winnahs," *Texas Observer*, Nov. 13, 1970; "Opportunity Without Parallel," by Michael S. Lottman, *Ripon Forum*, July-August 1970; "Texas Democrats Seek to Avoid 1970 Primary Fights for Top Offices," by Neal R. Peirce, *National Journal*, Dec. 6, 1969; "Oil, Defense Firm Political Funds Didn't Report Gifts," Associated Press dispatch in Washington *Post*, April 11, 1971; "Young Voter Residency Killed," *Texas AFL-CIO News*, September 1971; "Labor Witty-Gritty," *Texas Observer*, Aug. 22, 1971; "Microcosm in Texas: An Achilles Heel for a Liberal Coalition," by E. Larry Dickens, *New South*, Summer 1971.

"Yarborough's Record," by Ronnie Dugger, *Texas Observer*, April 3, 1970; "Yarborough's Safety Bill Becomes Law," *Texas AFL-CIO News*, January 1971; "Yarborough Named Panel Chairman," by Sam Kinch, Jr., Dallas *Morning News*, Jan. 11, 1969; "Yarborough's Final Record," by Pete and Elizabeth Gunter, *Texas Observer*, Dec. 25, 1970; "Hot Time In Texas for a Flaming Liberal," by R. W. Apple, Jr., New York *Times*, April 26, 1970.

STATE GOVERNMENT "Texas Taxes Texas Taxes," by Ronnie Dugger, *Texas Observer*, Jan. 29, 1971; "May the Lobby Hold You in the Palm of Its Hand," by Lee Clark, *Texas Observer*, May 24, 1968; "Lawyers' Plan to Beat No-Fault Aired on Hill," by Morton Mintz, Washington *Post*, May 7, 1971; "The Emperor of U.T.," *Time*, Aug. 10, 1970; "Hooking Horns at U.T.," *Newsweek*, Feb. 1, 1971; "Higher Education in Texas," *Texas Observer*, Dec. 13, 1968.

ECONOMY "Cattle: Marketing Improves," by James J. Nagle, New York *Times*, Nov. 15, 1970; "Texas Now Rates No. 1 in the Fattening of Cattle," by Martin Waldron, New York *Times*, Sept. 21, 1971; "The Oil Lobby Is Not Depleted," by Erwin Knoll, New York *Times Magazine*, March 8, 1970; "Oil and Politics," by Ronnie Dugger, *Atlantic Monthly*, September 1969; "Flashy Texas Millionaires a Dying Breed," by Nicholas C. Chriss, Los Angeles *Times*, Nov. 29, 1970; "Super-Rich Texan Fights Social Ills," by Jon Nordheimer, New York *Times*, Nov. 28, 1969; "H. Ross Perot Pays His Dues," by Fred Powledge, New York *Times Magazine*, Feb. 28, 1971; "Texas Facts" (compiled and published by the Texas Highway Department); "Wildcatting for Oil Becomes a Game of Percentage," by B. Drummond Ayres, Jr., New York *Times*, March 26, 1971.

HOUSTON—ECONOMY *Decisive Years for Houston*, by Marvin Hurley (Houston Magazine, 1966); *Houston, The Bayou City*, by David G. McComb (Austin: University of Texas Press, 1969); "Houston: Oil at Bottom of Texas-Sized Boom," by Nicholas C. Chriss, Los Angeles *Times*, June 21, 1970; " 'Don't-Zone-Me-In' Houston Is Fastest-Growing U.S. City," by George H. Favre, *Christian Science Monitor*, Jan. 3, 1969; "Houston May Be No. 2 by 1972," by Tommy Thompson, Houston *Chronicle*, Jan. 18, 1970;

"This Is Houston," supplement to Houston *Chronicle*, March 9, 1969; "Greater Houston: Its First Million People—And Why," *Newsweek*, July 5, 1954; "Houston Is Where They're Moving," *Fortune*, February 1971; "Houston: Boom in the Heart of Texas," *Business Week*, May 23, 1970; "City of Tomorrow Planned Here," by Charlie Evans, Houston *Chronicle*, Oct. 11, 1970; "Forward-Thinking Texans Have Their City Booming," by Frank Schneider, New Orleans *Times-Picayune*, May 11, 1969; "Shell Oil Plans Real Estate Development on 526 Acres in Houston Near Astrodome," *Wall Street Journal*, June 10, 1970; "Houston Seeks the Refugees," *Time*, June 8, 1970; "Midtown Building Boom Will Add More Skyscrapers on Houston Skyline," by Charlie Evans, Houston *Chronicle*, Sept. 5, 1970.

"Space Age Transformed Ranch Into Megalopolis," by Nicholas C. Chriss, Los Angeles *Times*, July 23, 1969; "An Ecological Armageddon," by Kaye Northcott, *Texas Observer*, Feb. 6, 1970; "Pollution Checks Grow," by Harold Scarlett, Houston *Post*, Nov. 2, 1970; "Houston Port Volatile," by Jim Barlow, Dallas *News*, Feb. 22, 1970; "Channel a Cesspool," by Susan Kent Caudill, Houston *Post*, Oct. 11, 1970; "Water Pollution in Texas Studied," by Martin Waldron, New York *Times*, June 8, 1971.

HOUSTON—RACES "Boom in Houston No Boom to Blacks," by Paul Delaney, New York *Times*, June 8, 1970; "Rights Aide Criticizes Houston as Federal Job Hearing Opens," by Paul Delaney, New York *Times*, June 3, 1970; "Rights' Aide in Houston Charges Threats to Victims of Job Bias," by Paul Delaney, New York *Times*, June 4, 1970; "Houston Companies and Unions Face Charges of Discrimination," by Paul Delaney, New York *Times*, June 5, 1970; "Putting Together a Coalition in Houston," by Harold A. Nelson, *New South*, Fall 1970; "Psychotherapy for Houston Police," by L. Deckle McLean, *Ebony*, October 1968; "Black Capitalism: A Rotary Takes the Plunge," by Paul Bernish, *Wall Street Journal*, Aug. 27, 1969; "Houston School Board—an Ideological Camp," by Nicholas C. Chriss, Los Angeles *Times*, Dec. 25, 1969; "Desegregation Moves in Houston Made Amidst Clamor of Protest," by Martin Waldron, New York *Times*, March 1, 1970; " 'Huelga' Schools Open in Houston," by Martin Waldron, New York *Times*, Sept. 6, 1970.

HOUSTON—POLITICS "Liberal Demos Ask New Blood Reorganization," by Fred Bonavita, Houston *Post*, Dec. 9, 1968; "Houston Postmortem," by Tony Proffitt and Hawkins Menefee, *Texas Observer*, Dec. 19, 1969; "A Black Candidate Tries 'Law and Order,' " by David Brand, *Wall Street Journal*, Nov. 12, 1969.

DALLAS—GENERAL *Dallas Public and Private*, by Warren Leslie (New York: Grossman Publishers, 1964); "Dallas-Fort Worth," chapter of *Cities of America*, by George Sessions Perry (Freeport, N.Y.: Books for Libraries Press, 1970); "Dallas in City-Planning Forefront," and "Dallas Spells Out Goals in Paperback Series," by Jack Waugh, *Christian Science Monitor*, Nov. 24, 1970; "Dallas Code No Cure-All, But It Helps," by Dave Beckwith, Houston *Chronicle*, March 3, 1969; "How Business Failed Dallas," by Richard Austin Smith, *Fortune*, July 1964; "Up the Establishment," *Newsweek*, May 3, 1971.

"Dallas Memorial Dedicated to Kennedy 200 Yards From Site of Slaying," by Martin Waldron, New York *Times*, June 25, 1970; "Dealey Plaza," by Liz Smith, *Holiday*, November 1969.

"Where God's Business Is Big Business," *Time*, Nov. 8, 1968; "Los Angeles Times Seeks Dallas Paper for $91.5-Million Stock," by Henry Raymont, New York *Times*, Sept. 15, 1969;

"KERA's Newsroom," by Jack Canson, *Texas Observer*, Sept. 18, 1970; "Why Dallas' Public Television Station Is Emerging as a Major Communications Force," by Carolyn Barta, *Dallas*, August 1970.

DALLAS—ECONOMY "Dallas Boasts Big Share of Texas Top 100 Firms," by Al Altwegg, Dallas *News*, July 13, 1969; "Dallas First as Texas Business Hub," New York *Times*, July 20, 1969; "Federal Employee Growth Continues in Dallas," by Earl Golz, Dallas *News*, Oct. 4, 1970; "Dallas Boom Adds 228,380 Jobs," by Al Altwegg, Dallas *News*, Jan. 26, 1969; "Room For Rent," by John Davis, *Dallas*, November 1969; "Going Up: Some Major Structures," by Doug Domeier, Dallas *News*, May 11, 1969; "In Dallas: A Skyline in Change," New York *Times*, August 9, 1970; "Big Griffin Square Deal Closed," by Dorothie Erwin, Dallas *News*, Feb. 3, 1970; "Wesley Goyer Jr. And His Golden Acres," by John Davis, *Dallas*, June 1970; "How a Good Idea Can Be Turned Into Riches," *U.S. News and World Report*, Dec. 15, 1969; "Loss Leader," *Newsweek*, June 1, 1970; "Ling Tries Old Tricks at a New Stand," *Business Week*, Oct. 30, 1971.

FORT WORTH—"Happy Triumph of a City That Once Seemed a Place to Run Away From," by Thomas Thompson, *Life*, Oct. 2, 1970; "Vast Effect Seen From Dallas Airport," New York *Times*, Feb. 15, 1970; "Air Power Propels Fort Worth's Upward Economic Spiral," by Guy Halverson, *Christian Science Monitor*, March 28, 1969; "Hitting the Skids," by W. Stewart Pinkerton, Jr., *Wall Street Journal*, Aug. 24, 1970; "The Joe Louis Addition," *Texas Observer*, Dec. 25, 1970; "Fort Worth: Cowtown May Become Nowtown," New York *Times*, Jan. 3, 1971.

SAN ANTONIO "The Part of San Antonio Tourists Do Not See Is Mexican-American and Poor," by Weldon Wallace, Baltimore *Sun*, Nov. 15, 1970; "Checking HemisFair's Figures," *Texas Observer*, March 28, 1969; "Fair Enough," *Newsweek*, Sept. 30, 1968; "Booked for Travel," by Horace Sutton, *Saturday Review*, May 9, 1970; "Western Hemisfair," by Richard Spong, *Editorial Research Reports*, March 29, 1968; "The Priests' Rebellion," *Newsweek*, Nov. 11, 1968.

OTHER CITIES AND PLACES "Austin Is Bustling as Johnson Labors to Set the Record Straight," by Henry Raymont, New York *Times*, Nov. 9, 1969; "Austin's New Politics," by Dean Rindy, *Texas Observer*, May 21, 1971; "Austin Snares U.S. Jobs," Dallas *News*, Aug. 20, 1969; "Amarillo: The Show Goes On," by Buck Ramsey, *Texas Observer*, May 23, 1969; "Lubbock Left a Dead City by Tornado," Washington *Post*, May 13, 1970; "Rio Grande: Odyssey from a Wintry Birth," by Paul Horgan, Washington *Post*, Aug. 9, 1970; "El Paso: Profile of a City," *Monitor* (magazine of Mountain States Telephone Co., No. 2, 1968).

MEXICAN-AMERICANS "Tío Taco is Dead," *Newsweek*, June 29, 1970; "Latins in U.S. Trail in Income," by William Chapman, Washington *Post*, March 3, 1971; "The Mexican American," *Civil Rights Digest*, Winter 1969; "The Misery of Our Mexican Americans," by Michael McCrery and Sixto Gómez, *Ripon Forum*, April 1969; "The Chicanos Want In," by Leroy F. Aarons, Washington *Post*, Jan. 11, 1970; "Chicanos Troubled," by John Geddie, Dallas *News*, Sept. 20 1970; "Chicanos in Texas Bid for Key Political Role," by Martin Waldron, New York *Times*, Aug. 2, 1970; "Tyranny in Texas," by Harold H. Martin, *Saturday Evening Post*, June 26, 1954; "Mexican-American Drive Makes Gringos the Target," by Carlos Conde, Houston *Chronicle*, April 6, 1969; "Labor Day in Austin," by Greg Olds, *Texas Observer*, Nov. 13, 1966; "Texas Unionists Win School Bias Lawsuit," *Texas AFL-CIO News*, June 6, 1970; "Schools in Texas Face Rights Fight," by Martin Waldron, New York *Times*, Aug. 30, 1970; "Chicano Power," by Stan Steiner, *New Republic*, June 20, 1970; "MAYO Members Most Active of Activist Chicanos," by Leo Cardenas, San Antonio *Express*, April 16, 1969; "Brown Power Victories May Spur a New Push," by Richard Beene, Houston *Chronicle*, April 19, 1970; "Walkout in Crystal City," *Texas Observer*, Jan. 2, 1970; "'Brown Bilbos' Scored," by Kemper Diehl, San Antonio *News*, April 15, 1969.

"Ford Foundation: Its Works Spark a Backlash," by Laurence Stern and Richard Harwood, Washington *Post*, Nov. 2, 1969; "Liberal Hits Ford Foundation," by Victor Lasky, *Human Events*, May 10, 1969; "Texas Rangers Dodge Critics as Ranks Swell," Atlanta *Journal and Constitution*, Sept. 21, 1969; "Texas Rangers Not a Hero to All," by John Kifner, New York *York Times*, March 23, 1970; "The Texas Ranger . . . His Heritage, His Modern Role and His Critics," by Stan Redding, Houston *Chronicle*, Feb. 9, 1969.

CALIFORNIA

California, as state and culture, has been the subject of more books, and many of them excellent, than any other state. Those which provided the most helpful background for this book included: *The California Syndrome*, by Neil Morgan (Englewood Cliffs, N.J.: Prentice-Hall, 1969); *The Pacific States*, by Neil Morgan (New York: Time-Life Library of America, 1967); *The Last Days of the Late, Great State of California*, by Curt Gentry (New York: Putnam's, 1968); *Dancing Bear—An Inside Look at California Politics*, by Gladwin Hill (New York: World, 1968); *Ronnie and Jesse—A Political Odyssey*, by Lou Cannon (Garden City, N.Y.: Doubleday, 1969); *Big Wayward Girl—An Informal Political History of California* by Herbert L. Phillips (Garden City, N.Y.: Doubleday, 1968); *The California Revolution*, ed. Carey McWilliams (New York: Grossman, 1968); *California—A History*, second edition, by Andrew F. Rolle (New York: Crowell, 1969); *Beautiful California*, by the editorial staffs of Sunset Books and Sunset Magazine (Menlo Park, Calif.: Lane Books, 1963); *How to Kill a Golden State*, by William Bronson (Garden City, N.Y.: Doubleday, 1968); *California Government—One Among Fifty*, second edition, by C. E. Jacobs and A. S. Sokolow (London: Macmillan, 1970); *The Challenge of California*, ed. Eugene C. Lee and Willis D. Hawley (Boston: Little Brown, 1970); *California Government and Politics*, fourth edition, by Winston W. Crouch, John C. Bollens, Stanley Scott, and Dean E. McHenry (Englewood Cliffs, N.J.: Prentice-Hall, 1967); *California: The Great Exception*, by Carey McWilliams (New York: Wyn, 1949).

Eden in Jeopardy—Man's Prodigal Meddling With His Environment: the Southern California Experience, by Richard G. Lillard (New York: Knopf, 1966); *North from Mexico—The Spanish-Speaking People of the United States*, by Carey

McWilliams (New York: Greenwood, 1968); *Politics Battle Plan,* by Herbert M. Baus and William B. Ross (New York: Macmillan, 1968); *The Politics and Economics of Public Spending,* by Charles L. Schultze (Washington, D.C.: Brookings Institution, 1968); "California: Enigmatic Eldorado of National Politics," by Totten J. Anderson, in *Politics in the American West,* ed. Frank J. Jonas (Salt Lake City: University of Utah Press, 1969); "California," by Irving Stone, in *American Panorama* (Garden City, N.Y.: Doubleday, 1960); *California: People—Problems—Potential* (San Francisco: Bank of America, 1970); *Western Market Almanac 1969–70* (Menlo Park, Calif.: Sunset Magazine, 1969); *Wells Fargo Country Factbook—California Business Statistics by Counties* (San Francisco: Wells Fargo Bank, Winter 1968–69).

Other sources: Regular news coverage of the *Los Angeles Times,* San Francisco *Chronicle,* Sacramento *Bee, Los Angeles* (city magazine), *San Diego* (city magazine), *Cry California* (publication of California Tomorrow), and the *California Journal,* an excellent monthly digest of California government and politics which began publication in 1970. Listed below, by subject matter and geographic area, are articles from which material was drawn for the chapter.

GENERAL "California: A State of Excitement," *Time,* Nov. 7, 1969; "California: The Rending of the Veil," by Marshall Frady, *Harper's Magazine,* December 1969; "Legally California May Be a Single State, Actually It is Cruelly Fragmented," by Alan Cranston, Sacramento *Bee,* Aug. 15, 1965; "Theoretical Look at Proposals for Two Californias," by John Pastier, Los Angeles *Times,* July 26, 1970; "California's Top Court Rules System of School Financing Unconstitutional," *Wall Street Journal,* Aug. 31, 1971; "The Welfare Compromise," editorial in Los Angeles *Times,* Aug. 8, 1971; "Nader Task Force Blasts State Officials, Land Use Practices," and "Background on the Report: How It Was Done, What Happens Next," *California Journal,* September 1971, "Water, Land Plundered, Nader Team Says," by Linda Mathews, and "Officials Assail Nader Report as Malicious," by Paul Houston, Los Angeles *Times,* Aug. 22, 1971; "Nader Has Wrong Gun, Right Target," by Lou Cannon, Long Beach *Press-Telegram,* Sept. 1, 1971.

POLITICS "Comparing Political Regions: The Case of California," and "The Repeal of Fair Housing in California: An Analysis of Referendum Voting," both articles by Raymond E. Wolfsinger and Fred I. Greenstein, *American Political Science Review,* March 1969 and September 1968 respectively; "California Shift Will Help Voter," by Gladwin Hill, New York *Times,* April 26, 1959; "California GOP Faces Task of Reforming Image," by Curtis J. Sitomer, *Christian Science Monitor,* March 5, 1970; "The Palsy of the CDC," by Francis Carney, *The Nation,* May 4, 1970; "Meeting May Determine CDC 'Life or Death'," by Richard Bergholz, Los Angeles *Times,* May 5, 1970; "Pat Frawley: Right-wing Money Bag," by William W. Turner, *The Progressive,* September 1970; "The Bloodiest Ballot in the United States," by Art Seidenbaum, chapter of *The California Revolution* (previously cited); "The Democratic New Guard," by Mary Ellen Leary, *The Nation,* March 8, 1971; "The Political Giant," by David S. Broder, Washington *Post,* May 11, 1971; "Moscone Is Preparing to Run for Calif. Governorship in '74," by Syd Kossen, Washington *Post,* Dec. 26, 1970; "Reagan Spent $2.1 Million on Campaign, Unruh $873,552," by Jerry Gillam, Los Angeles *Times,* Dec. 6, 1970; "Politicians and the Poor," by Steven V. Roberts, New York *Times,* Dec. 30, 1970; "The Legal Battle in California," by John

V. Tunney, New York *Times,* May 28, 1971.

PERSONALITIES, LEADERS "The Hottest Candidate in Either Party" (Reagan), by Paul O'Neil, *Life,* Oct. 30, 1970; "The Public Record of Ronald Reagan," *Congressional Quarterly Weekly Report,* July 28, 1967; "Ronald Reagan: The Man of Parts," chapter of *The Republican Establishment,* by Stephen Hess and David S. Broder (New York: Harper & Row, 1967); "California's Governor Finds Old Issues Work in Bid for a New Term," by Norman C. Miller, *Wall Street Journal,* Oct. 9, 1970; "Senator Murphy Defends Fee He Receives from Technicolor," by Warren Weaver, Jr., New York *Times,* March 13, 1970; "Reagan May Have Found a Tax Shelter in Cattle Breeding Herds," by Wallace Turner, New York *Times,* June 13, 1971; "Taxing Reagan," *Newsweek,* May 17, 1971.

"The New Jesse Unruh," *Time,* Sept. 14, 1970; "Unruh: Campaigning on a Shoestring," by Leroy F. Aarons, Washington *Post,* Aug. 24, 1970; *Californians in Congress, 1967, 1968* and *1970* (Reports of the California Congressional Recognition Plan, Claremont, Calif.); " 'Pete' McCloskey vs. Richard Nixon," by James M. Perry, *National Observer,* March 22, 1971; "Is McCloskey the McCarthy of '72?," by R. W. Apple, Jr., New York *Times Magazine,* April 18, 1971; "Challenging Rafferty," *Time,* Nov. 2, 1970; "California School Race Touchy," by Curtis J. Sitomer, *Christian Science Monitor,* Oct. 17, 1970; "Cool, Tough and Black" (Wilson Riles), by Tom Wicker, New York *Times,* Oct. 13, 1970.

LEGISLATURE "California Legislature Goes 'Revolutionary'," by John C. Waugh, *Christian Science Monitor,* Aug. 2, 1968; "Unruh Departs, Leaving List of Achievements," by Robert S. Fairbanks, Los Angeles *Times,* Jan. 7, 1969; "Conflict of Interest Law Dying," by Sydney Kossen, San Francisco *Examiner & Chronicle,* April 19, 1970; "Capitol Lobbyists: How They Operate Behind the Scenes," by Tom Goff, Los Angeles *Times,* Feb. 22, 1970; "California Lobbying Undergoes Change," by Robert Fairbanks, Washington *Post,* April 27, 1969; "Why Burns Lost Out in Senate Fight," by Jack S. McDowell, San Francisco *Examiner & Chronicle,* May 18, 1969; "Burns' Long Reign Over Senate Ends," by Tom Goff, Los Angeles *Times,* May 14, 1969; "Sacramento: A Capital Offense," by Myron Roberts, *Los Angeles,* March 1970; "The Secret Boss of California," by Lester Velie, *Collier's,* Aug. 13 and 30, 1949; "Black Power: A Political Surge," by Robert C. Maynard, Washington *Post,* May 2, 1971.

MENTAL HEALTH, PENOLOGY "Legislative Initiative in the Mental Health Field," by Arthur Bolton, *State Government,* Summer 1968; *When Governors Change: The Case of Mental Hygiene* (Institute of Government, University of California, Davis, 1968); California's Soledad Prison: A 'Pressure Cooker' for Rage Among Inmates," by Steven V. Roberts, New York *Times,* Feb. 7, 1971; "The California Plan—How One State Is Salvaging Its Convicts," *U. S. News & World Report,* Aug. 24, 1970; "Prisons in Turmoil," *Newsweek,* Sept. 14, 1970; "Do California Prisons Lag?" by David Holmstrom, *Christian Science Monitor,* Nov. 4, 1970; "Reforms and Violence in California's Prisons," by Barry Kalb, Washington *Star,* Aug. 29, 1971; "San Quentin Massacre," *Newsweek,* Aug. 30, 1971.

UNIVERSITY "California: University on Trial," *Newsweek,* Nov. 23, 1970; "California Facing Campus Crisis," by John Berthelsen, Washington *Post,* Nov. 9, 1969; "The Governor v. The University," *Time,* March 30, 1970; "Berkeley's Meddlesome Regents," by Bettina Aptheker, *The Nation,* Sept. 7, 1970; "Full Impact of Budget Cut Jolts State Colleges," by Noel Greenwood, Los

Angeles *Times*, July 29, 1970; *Confrontation*, NBC White Paper on "The Ordeal of the American City," broadcast April 22, 1969; "Still No. 1," *Newsweek*, Jan. 11, 1971; "Bowker for Berkeley," *Time*, April 26, 1971.

CONSERVATION "A Wink at the Environment," by Robert A. Jones, *The Nation*, April 27, 1970; "Conservation Comes of Age," by Scott Thurber, chapter of *The California Revolution* (previously cited); "Sierra Club Mounts a New Crusade," *Business Week*, May 23, 1970; "Private Group Maps Plan for State Growth," by Daryl Lembke, Los Angeles *Times*, Nov. 9, 1970; "Scenic Roads," chapter of *The Last Landscape*, by William H. Whyte (Garden City, N.Y.: Doubleday, 1968); "Lobbying: The Case of the Freeway Establishment," by Bob Simmons, *Cry California*, Spring 1968.

GEOGRAPHY "In California, the Earthquake Threat Is Real," by Walter Sullivan, New York *Times*, March 23, 1969; "Waiting for the Big Bump," *Newsweek*, Sept. 28, 1970; "Hopeful Scientists Run a Hard Race to Control Earthquakes," by John Peterson, *National Observer*, Oct. 12, 1970; "A Shock to Seismologists," *Time*, Feb. 22, 1971; "Millions on Coast Ignore Peril of a Cataclysmic Quake," by Sandra Blakeslee, New York *Times*, April 29, 1971; "California: Ordeal by Fire Storm," *Time*, Oct. 12, 1970; "Southern California: Rain . . . Rain . . . and More Rain," by Leroy F. Aarons, Washington *Post*, March 1, 1969; "Southern California's Trial by Mud and Water," by Nathaniel T. Kenney, *National Geographic*, October 1969; "Fires Strip 500,000 Acres —California Studies Flood Problem," by Kimmis Hendrick, *Christian Science Monitor*, Oct. 13, 1970.

DESERT "Death Valley, the Land and the Legend," by Rowe Findley, *National Geographic*, January 1970; "New Signs of Life in Death Valley," New York *Times*, Feb. 22, 1970; "The Palmy Springs (All that Money Can Buy)," chapter of *The Right People*, by Stephen Birmingham (New York: Dell, 1968); "Ben Yellen's Fine Madness," by Michael E. Kinsley, *Washington Monthly*, January 1971; "The Crooks' Dilemma," *Newsletter from Dr. Ben Yellen*, Brawley, California, April 5, 1971; "Water, Water For the Wealthy," by Peter Barnes, *New Republic*, May 8, 1971; "Geothermal Power—Virtually Pollutionless," by Eric Burgess, *Christian Science Monitor*, Nov. 4, 1970; "The Steam Inside," *Newsweek*, June 7, 1971.

CENTRAL VALLEY, CÉSAR CHÁVEZ "New Drive to Cut Subsidies for Giant Farms," *U. S. News & World Report*, July 27, 1970; "Movements: A New Breed of Lawyer, with the Poor as His Client, Is Forcing Basic Reform of the System," by Lisa Hirsh, *City*, October 1969; "Nerve Gas in the Orchards," by Ronald B. Taylor, *The Nation*, June 22, 1970; "The Little Strike that Grew to La Causa," *Time*, July 4, 1969; "Sal Si Puedes," by Steven V. Roberts, New York *Times Book Review*, Feb. 1, 1970; " 'La Huelga' Becomes 'La Causa'," by Dick Meister, New York *Times Magazine*, Nov. 17, 1968; "La Raza in Revolt," by Roy Bongartz, *The Nation*, June 1, 1970; "California Grape Boycott," *Trans-action*, February 1969; "Vineyards Giving in to Once-Hated Union," by Leroy F. Aarons, Washington *Post*, July 6, 1970; "Pacts Bring Labor Peace to Vineyards at Delano," by Bill Boyarsky, Los Angeles *Times*, July 30, 1970; "With the Grape Pacts Signed, César Chávez Looks to Other Crops," by Henry Elliot Weinstein, *Wall Street Journal*, July 31, 1970; "The California Wine Rush," *Time*, March 3, 1971; "Chávez Union Sees Salinas Strawberries Ripe for Boycott," by Curtis J. Sitomer, *Christian Science Monitor*, May 29, 1971; "To Die

Standing," by John Gregory Dunne, *Atlantic Monthly*, June 1971; "Subsidy Cuts Hit Big Cotton Farmers," by Herbert Koshtez, New York *Times*, Jan. 10, 1971; "Dancing on the Street," chapter of *A Place to Live*, by Wolf Von Eckardt (New York: Delacorte Press, 1967); "Conglomerates Reshape Food Supply" and "U.S. Policy Handcuffs Small Farmer," by Nick Kotz, Washington *Post*, Oct. 3 and 5, 1971; "Nader Brands San Luis Dam 'Boondoggle'," by David Holmstrom, *Christian Science Monitor*, Sept. 24, 1971.

SAN FRANCISCO—GENERAL Articles in *Holiday*, special issue on San Francisco, March 1970: "In San Francisco, You Can (Still Just Barely) See Forever," by the editors; "The Light and Color of a Lovely City," by Bruce Davidson; "Who's in Charge Here?" by Nicholas von Hoffman; "God, Gurus and Gay Guerrillas," by Richard Atcheson; "Culture, Counter-culture, or 'Barbaric Intrusion,' There's Something Going on in San Francisco," by Herbert Gold; "The Overheated Campuses of the Bay Area," by Herbert Wilner.

Articles in *Trans-action*, special issue on "Deviance and Democracy in San Francisco," April 1970; "The Culture of Civility," by Howard S. Becker and Irving Lou Horowitz; "The Health of Haight-Ashbury," by David E. Smith, John Luce, and Ernest A. Dernburg; "Alioto and the Politics of Hyperpluralism," by Frederick M. Wirt; "Red Guard on Grant Avenue," by Stanford M. Lyman, "The Game of Black & White at Hunters Point," by Arthur E. Hippler; "San Francisco's Mystique," by Fred Davis.

"San Francisco Wins, 2–1, As America's Favorite City," by George Gallup, Des Moines *Register*, Sept. 8, 1969; "San Francisco—Plenty of Avant Left in the Garde," by Herbert Gold, New York *Times Book Review*, Jan. 11, 1970; "San Francisco: the City that Enjoys," by George Barmann, Cleveland *Plain-Dealer*, March 11, 1969; "San Francisco Suicides," segment of *60 Minutes*, CBS News, Dec. 16, 1969; "In San Francisco's North Beach, the Many Different Worlds and Generations Never Meet," by Steven V. Roberts, New York *Times*, Nov. 4, 1969; *San Francisco— City on Golden Hills*, by Herb Caen and Dong Kingman (Garden City, N.Y.: Doubleday, 1967).

PRESS "The Chronicle: Schizophrenia by the Bay," by David M. Rubin and William L. Rivers, *Columbia Journalism Review*, Fall 1969; "The Golden Gate's TV," *U. S. News & World Report*, Sept. 7, 1970.

GOVERNMENT, POLITICS "Mayor with a Flair," by John C. Waugh, *Christian Science Monitor*, June 11, 1968; "Alioto One Year Later," by Russ Cone, San Francisco *Examiner and Chronicle* magazine, *California Living*, Jan. 26, 1969; "San Francisco's Mayor Alioto and the Mafia," by Richard Carlson and Lance Brisson, *Look*, Sept. 23, 1969; "Alioto: A Politician Lands in Hot Water," by Wallace Turner, New York *Times*, Dec. 28, 1969; "Alioto's Woes," *Newsweek*, April 5, 1971.

BUILDING "Skyscraper Plan Debated on Coast," by Lawrence E. Davies, and "High Skyline Opposed on Coast," by Robert A. Wright, New York *Times*, Aug. 24, 1969 and Oct. 26, 1970; "A Love Affair With S. F. Has Its Ups, Downs," by Jerry Hulse, Los Angeles *Times*, May 3, 1970; "Bay Waterfront High-Rises Draw San Franciscans' Ire," by Rasa Gustaitis, Washington *Post*, Nov. 11, 1970; "Slum Clearance Makes Agonizing Gains in S. F.," by Daryl Lembke, Los Angeles *Times*, March 2, 1969; "The Two Most Exciting Cities in the Nation?—Boston and San Francisco, Some Say . . . ," by Ian Menzies, Boston *Globe*, Sept. 27, 1970.

ECONOMY "The *Times*' Roster of California's 100 Top Industrials," "Top Financial Institutions," etc., Los Angeles *Times*, May 10, 1970; "Sibley of Pacific Gas & Electric," *Fortune*, September 1969; "From Dustbowl to Saigon: The 'People's Bank' Builds an Empire," by Michael Sweeney, *Ramparts*, November 1970; various reports of Pacific Gas & Electric Co.

MINORITIES "Chinatown in Crisis," by Min Yee, *Newsweek*, Feb. 23, 1970; "San Francisco's Chinatown," by Mary Ellen Leary, *Atlantic Monthly*, March 1970; "Filipinos: A Fast-Growing U. S. Minority," by Earl Caldwell, New York *Times*, March 5, 1971.

SAN FRANCISCO BAY "Victory on San Francisco Bay," by Judson Gooding, *Fortune*, February 1970; "That Grass May Grow by San Francisco Bay," *Life*, July 4, 1970; " 'Save' San Francisco Bay Hearings On," and " 'Save Bay' Drive Wins Long Fight," by Gladwin Hill, New York *Times*, March 23 and Aug. 9, 1969; "Powerful Twosome Leads Ecology Campaign," by Evelyn Radcliffe, *Christian Science Monitor*, June 29, 1970; "Canal Plan Stirs Calif. Environmental Fight," by John Berthelsen, Washington *Post*, Feb. 22, 1970; "Quenching California's Thirst," *Time*, July 6, 1970; "The Battle of the Bay," *Newsweek*, Dec. 28, 1970.

BART "The City: A Different Kind of Trip," *Time*, May 16, 1969; "Space Age Commuting," *Newsweek*, June 16, 1969; "BART: Years of Decision," advertisement in *Fortune*, September 1970; "BART—Catalyst for Bay Area Planning," *Going Places* (publication of General Electric), Third Quarter, 1968; various releases and publications of the San Francisco Bay Area Rapid Transit District; "San Francisco's New Transit Era Leaves Driving to Computers," by David Holmstrom, *Christian Science Monitor*, June 11, 1971.

WEST BAY "Marin County: San Francisco's Connecticut," *Holiday*, March 1970; "The End of a California Dream?" by Philip Hager, Los Angeles *Times*, July 31, 1970; "Santa Clara Goes Urban at Expense of Farming," by Daryl E. Lembke, Los Angeles *Times*, Jan. 1, 1964; "Idyllic Valley Now Urban Anthill, Planner Charges," by Wallace Turner, New York *Times*, Sept. 7, 1970; "The Making of Slurban America," by Karl Belser, *Cry California*, Fall 1970.

EAST BAY, OAKLAND, BERKELEY "Is Oakland There?" *Newsweek*, May 18, 1970; "Oakland: That Troubled Town Across the Bay," by Sol Stern, *Holiday*, March 1970; "Leader of Panthers—Bobby George Seale," by Lawrence Van Gelder, New York *Times*, Aug. 22, 1970; "The Ordeal of a City," series by Charles Howe and Charles Raudebaugh in San Francisco *Chronicle*, Sept. 14-18, 1970; "Berkeley, 5 Years Later, Is Radicalized, Reaganized, Mesmerized," by A. H. Raskin, New York *Times Magazine*, Jan. 11, 1970; "Occupied Berkeley," *Time*, May 30, 1969; "Public Schools—Buses Can Travel Both Ways," *Time*, Nov. 8, 1968; "How School Busing Works in One Town," by Gertrude Samuels, New York *Times Magazine*, Sept. 27, 1970; "Berkeley Vote Lesson," by Steven Roberts, New York *Times*, April 9, 1971.

LOS ANGELES—GENERAL *Los Angeles: The Ultimate City*, by Christopher Rand (New York: Oxford, 1967); *Los Angeles—Portrait of an Extraordinary City*, by the editors of Sunset Books and Sunset Magazine (Menlo Park, Calif.: Lane Magazine & Book Co., 1968); "Los Angeles," by Steven V. Roberts, *Atlantic Monthly*, September 1969; "The Forces At Work on Our Next Five Years," by Myron Roberts, John Pastier, and John Haase, *Los Angeles* (magazine), January 1970; "Los Angeles," by Robert De Roos, *National Geographic*, October 1962; "Take

Me to Your Power Structure," by Bill and Nancy Boyarsky, Los Angeles *Times West Magazine*, Oct. 4, 1970; "Friendly Administration, Growth of Suburbs Boost Counties' Influence," by William Lilley III, *National Journal*, May 29, 1971; "This Is the Valley," by Michael Fessier, Jr., Los Angeles *Times West Magazine*, Nov. 1, 1970.

CRIME AND CULTURE "Los Angeles Area Is Shaken Over a Series of Violent Acts," by Steven V. Roberts, New York *Times*, May 3, 1960; "Hell's Angels Have Changed a Bit, but the 'People Haters' Are Still There," by Jim Stingley of the Los Angeles *Times* in the Boston *Globe*, July 12, 1970; "For Squares: Open House at Synanon," by Gertrude Samuels, New York *Times*, Sept. 6, 1970; "Synanon City: A New Community Designed for People who Have Been Damaged by Old Ones," by Gail Miller, *City*, August 1969; "Homosexuals in Los Angeles, Like Many Elsewhere, Want Religion and Establish Their Church," by Edward B. Fiske, New York *Times*, Feb. 15, 1970.

AIR POLLUTION "Los Angeles Has a Cough," by Roger Rapoport, *Esquire*, July 1970; "L. A. Area Called Free of Power Plant Smoke," by George Getze, Los Angeles *Times*, July 23, 1969; "Pollution Dims Los Angeles' Lofty Dreams," by Haynes Johnson, Washington *Post*, Feb. 12, 1970.

PRESS "The Los Angeles Times," by John Corry, *Harper's Magazine*, December 1969; "Will Big Otis Try to Cross the East River?" by Edwin Diamond, *New York*, Aug. 24, 1970.

ECONOMY "L.A. in 1970s: Much More of Everything," by Ray Hebert, Los Angeles *Times*, Dec. 29, 1969; "State's Top Companies Grow Larger—Times Roster Shows L. A. Widens Lead as Headquarters City," Los Angeles *Times*, May 10, 1970; "Aerospace Companies, Workers Hurt by Cuts in Government Outlays," by Earl C. Gottschalk, Jr., *Wall Street Journal*, May 15, 1970; "The Withering Aircraft Industry," by Dan Cordtz, *Fortune*, September 1970; "The Aerospace Industry Hits Some Bumpy Air," *Newsweek*, March 2, 1970; "Lockheed's Illness Is Contagious," by Robert A. Wright, New York *Times*, April 12, 1970; "Coming Up Unk-Unks," by Harold B. Meyers, *Fortune*, Aug. 1, 1969; "The 'One More Chance' Bomber," *Fortune*, July 1970; "Cheers and Tears," *The Nation*, June 22, 1970; "A Quartet for the Seventies," *Fortune*, January 1970; "Head of Lockheed Offers to Resign," by Robert J. Samuelson, Washington *Post*, June 12, 1971; "Troubled Think Tanks," *Newsweek*, Jan. 25, 1971.

HOLLYWOOD "Hollywood: The Year You Almost Couldn't Find It," by Jack Hamilton, and "Hollywood: Broke—And Getting Rich," by Fletcher Knebel, *Look*, Nov. 3, 1970; "The Last Days of Babylon?" *Forbes*, Nov. 1, 1969; "Hollywood: Will There Ever Be a 21st-Century Fox?" *Time*, Feb. 9, 1970; "The Old Hollywood: They Lost It at the Movies," *Newsweek*, Feb. 2, 1970; "Holywood's 'Dream' Turns to Nightmare," by Michael Kernan, Washington *Post*, March 23, 1970.

ETHNIC GROUPS "The Old Order Passes for L. A. Japanese," by Stanley O. Williford, Los Angeles *Times*, Aug. 24, 1969; "Chicanos Stirring with New Ethnic Pride," by Steven V. Roberts, New York *Times*, Sept. 20, 1970; "Mexican-American Hostility Deepens in Tense East Los Angeles," by Steven V. Roberts, New York *Times*, Sept. 4, 1970; "The Gentle Revolutionaries: Brown Power," by Ralph Guzman, *Black Politician*, July 1969; "Urban Indians, Driven to Cities by Poverty, Find Harsh Existence," by Barbara Isenberg, *Wall Street Journal*, March 9, 1970.

NEGROES "Thomas Bradley—Rising Political Star in the West," *Ebony*, June 1969; "Watts: Everything Has Changed—And Nothing," *Newsweek*, Aug. 24, 1970; "Watts Is Being Reborn," by Leroy F. Aarons, Washington *Post*, April 16, 1970; "Watts 1970: Despite Changes, Much Remains the Same Five Years After Riots," by Robert A. Wright, New York *Times*, Sept. 13, 1970; "Labor-Aided Enterprise Applies Union Expertise to Ghetto's Problems," by Mitchell Gordon, *Wall Street Journal*, July 7, 1969; "Watts Company, Established After 1965 Riot, Sold," by Jack Jones, Los Angeles *Times*, May 8, 1970.

GEOGRAPHIC "Sprawling Los Angeles Gets a New Skyline," *Business Week*, Dec. 13, 1969; "Folks in Pasadena Say Running a Huge Parade Is No Bed of Roses," by Earl C. Gottschalk, Jr., *Wall Street Journal*, Dec. 30, 1969; "Broad Busing Plan in Pasadena Is Implemented With Harmony," and "Pasadena Voters Support School Board Members Who Back Integration Plan," by Steven V. Roberts, New York *Times*, Sept. 20, and Oct. 15, 1970.

ORANGE COUNTY "Nixon Birthplace Safe for G.O.P.," by Gladwin Hill, New York *Times*, Nov. 2, 1969; "Nixon's Native County Viewed as Sample of Wave of Future," by Don Oberdorfer, Washington *Post*, Jan. 8, 1970; "Nixon Among the Oranges," by Ernest B. Furgurson, Baltimore *Sun*, June 9, 1969; "Disneyland: Can It Top 15 Years of Success?" by Herman Wong, Los Angeles *Times*, July 12, 1970; "Anaheim—Cinderella City of the Southland," by Jack Boettner and Don Smith, Los Angeles *Times*, March 20, 1966, and successive articles in same series; "Irvine—City or Super Subdivision?" by David Shaw, Los Angeles *Times*, June 14, 1970; "Irvine Heiress—Two Sides of an Enigma," by Howard Seelye, Los Angeles *Times*, Feb. 23, 1970.

SAN DIEGO "San Diego: 200 but Still a Mover," by Ellen Shulte, Los Angeles *Times*, March 9, 1969; "San Diego: California's Plymouth Rock," by Allan C. Fisher, Jr., *National Geographic*, July 1969; "San Diego Cleans up Once-Dirty Bay as Model for U.S.," by E. W. Kenworthy, New York *Times*, Sept. 25, 1970; "Richard Neutra Looks at San Diego," by George Waldo, *San Diego Magazine*, May 1970; "A Vision of San Diego," by Harry Antoniades Anthony, *San Diego Magazine*, June 1970; "Who's In Charge Here?" by Harold Keen, *San Diego Magazine*, February 1970; "San Diego—City on the Verge of Controlled Growth," by James Bassett, Los Angeles *Times*, Feb. 14, 1971; "California Goes After a Transportation Octopus" (about activities of C. Arnholt Smith), *Business Week*, Sept. 25, 1971.

"Herb Klein's Old Paper," *Newsweek*, Jan. 5, 1970; "*Union-Tribune*, The Mute Town Crier," by Ed Self, *San Diego Magazine*, June 1970; "*Union-Tribune* Zaps Back," letter from *Union-Tribune* news director Milford Chipp, and "The Editor Replies," by Ed Self, *San Diego Magazine*, August 1970; "Commissar of Credibility," by Dom Bonafede, *The Nation*, April 6, 1970; "Censorship by Harassment," by Kingsley Widmer, *The Nation*, March 30, 1970.

SANTA BARBARA "Santa Barbara: Old Guard and New Life-Style," by Kelly Tunney, Los Angeles *Times*, Dec. 28, 1969; "Environment: Tragedy in Oil," *Time*, Feb. 14, 1969; "One Year Later, Impact of Great Oil Slick Is Still Felt," by Gladwin Hill, New York *Times*, Jan. 25, 1970; "Santa Barbarans Cite an 11th Commandment: 'Thou Shalt Not Abuse the Earth'," by Ross MacDonald and Robert Easton, New York *Times Magazine*, Oct. 12, 1969; "Oil in Santa Barbara and Power in America," by Harvery Molotch, *Ramparts*, November 1969; "Bank Burning Shows New Side of Youth Revolt," by Leroy F. Aarons, Washington *Post*, May 3, 1970; "Why They Burned the Bank," by Richard Flacks and Milton Mankoff, *The Nation*, March 23, 1970; "The Isla Vista War —Campus Violence in a Class by Itself," by Winthrop Griffith, New York *Times Magazine*, Aug. 30, 1970; "California's Isla Vista: 'From Anathema to Dialogue'," by Norman Cousins, *Saturday Review*, June 5, 1971.

ACKNOWLEDGMENTS

THIS BOOK had to be, by its very character, a personal odyssey and personal task. But it would never have been possible without the kind assistance of hundreds of people. First there were those who encouraged me to go forward when the idea was first conceived: my wife Barbara (little imagining the long curtailments of family life that would ensue, and whose encouragement was vital throughout); my parents and other relatives; my editor, Evan W. Thomas, vice president and editor of W. W. Norton & Co.; John Gunther; my agent, Sterling Lord, and his assistant at that time, Jonathan Walton; Richard Kluger, editor of my first book, *The People's President;* writer Roan Conrad; editor Joseph Foote (who would later help with many other aspects of the book); William B. Dickinson, editor of *Editorial Research Reports;* Thomas Schroth, then the editor, and Nelson Poynter, publisher of *Congressional Quarterly;* author Michael Amrine and his wife Rene; Richard M. Scammon, director of the Elections Research Center and coauthor of *The Real Majority;* and D. B. Hardeman, professor of political science and biographer of the late House Speaker Sam Rayburn. Later on, those who encouraged or helped me to keep the project moving included F. Randall Smith and Anthony C. Stout of the Center for Political Research; author David Wise; columnist-reporters Bruce Biossat and David S. Broder; and Bernard Haldane. A year's fellowship at the Woodrow Wilson International Center for Scholars provided intellectual and physical sustenance toward the end of the project.

My very warmest thanks go to those who read the draft manuscript in its entirety: Evan W. Thomas; Russell L. Bradley; Jean Allaway; Frederick H. Sontag, public relations consultant of Montclair, N.J.; Kay Gauss Jackson, former critic for *Harper's Magazine;* Donald Kummerfeld of the Center for Political Research; and copy editors Nelda Freeman, Calvin Towle, and their colleagues at W. W. Norton & Co. In addition, each of the state chapters was submitted to several persons living in, and having extensive knowledge of, the state in question. The returning corrections and amendments were immensely helpful. The names of those readers appear in the longer list of names below; I choose not to list them here lest someone hold them responsible for something said or unsaid in one of the chapters, and of course the full responsibility for that lies with me.

Various friends and associates helped with many of the details of research, and for that I am especially indebted to Prentice and Alice Bowsher, Oliver Cromwell, Martha Gottron, Monica and Jason Benderly, Barbara Hurlbutt, Barbara Gaw, Richard Baker, Nancy Nelson, Sibylle Wehner, James Allaway, William Brobst, David B. H. Martin, Ann Just, Maria Sturm, Jane Denison, Alan McElroy, John Gibson, James Mulligan, DeMar and Claudia Teuscher, John Nicholson, Charles Dennis McCamey, Timothy B. Clark, Hildegard Ibing, Ronald Henry, Mary Joanna Perkins, Stuart Pregnall, and Gillian Rudd. And without the cheery and efficient services of my typist, Merciel Dixon, and her occasional back-up, Marjorie Lash, the manuscript would never have seen the light of day at all. Rose Franco of W. W. Norton helped in innumerable ways; I am indebted to designer Marjorie Flock of the Norton organization; and credit goes to Russell Lenz, chief cartographer of the *Christian Science Monitor,* for what I feel is the superb job he did on the state and city maps for this book.

Across the country, people gave generously of their time to brief me on the developments of the past several years in their states and cities. I am listing those from the 10 megastates below, together with many people who helped with national and interstate themes. The names of some officials are included whom I had interviewed in the year or two prior to beginning work on this project, when the background from those interviews proved to be helpful with the book. To all, my sincerest thanks.

PERSONS INTERVIEWED

Affiliations of interviewees are as of time of author's interview with them

ABEL, I. W., President, United Steelworkers of America, Pittsburgh, Pa.

ABRAMS, Herbert W., Director of Public Affairs, Chase Manhattan Bank, New York City

ALCADE, Hector, Administrative Assistant to U. S. Rep. Sam M. Gibbons (Fla.)

ALEXANDER, Herbert, Director, Citizens Research Foundation, Princeton, N.J.

ALIOTO, Joseph L., Mayor of San Francisco, Calif.

ANDERSON, Gerald, Urban Redevelopment Consultant and Member, Cleveland Transit System Board, Cleveland, Ohio

ANDERSON, John, Former Governor of Kansas and Chairman, Citizens Conference on State Legislatures, Kansas City, Mo.

ANDREWS, John S., Chairman, Republican State Committee, Columbus, Ohio

ARONOFF, Stanley J., State Senator, Cincinnati, Ohio

ASHDOWN, Sam, Special Assistant to Lt. Gov. Tom Adams (Fla.)

AURELIO, Richard, Deputy Mayor, New York City

BACHELDER, Glen, Policies & Program Division, Executive Office of the Governor, Lansing, Mich.

BACON, Edmund N., Former Executive Director, Philadelphia Planning Commission, Philadelphia, Pa.

BADILLO, Herman, U. S. Representative from New York

BAGLIVO, Angelo, Political Writer, Newark *News,* Newark, N.J.

BAIRD, William, Lansing *State Journal,* Lansing, Mich.

BALDWIN, David G., Director of Communications, Washington Office, American Medical Association, Washington, D.C.

BALLERINO, John, Farm Labor Representative, Florida Industrial Commission, Orlando, Fla.

BALTZELL, E. Digby, Professor of Sociology, University of Pennsylvania, Philadelphia, Pa.

BARABBA, Vincent, Chairman of the Board, Decision Making Information, Los Angeles, Calif.

BARKDULL, Walter, California Human Relations Agency, Sacramento, Calif.

BARNARD, William C., Political Writer, Cleveland *Plain-Dealer,* Cleveland, Ohio

BARNES, Alan, Senior Research Associate, Texas Research League, Austin, Texas

BARNES, Ben, Lieutenant Governor of Texas, Austin, Texas

BARO, Gene, Associate Editor, *National Journal,* Washington, D.C.

BASS, Andrew, Director, Bureau of the Budget, Cleveland City Council, Cleveland, Ohio

BASSETT, James, Director, Editorial Pages, Los Angeles *Times,* Los Angeles, Calif.

BATEMAN, Raymond H., State Senate President, Trenton, N.J.

BEHRENS, Earl C., Correspondent, San Francisco *Chronicle,* Sacramento, Calif.

BENEDICT, Howard, Correspondent, Associated Press, Cocoa Beach, Fla.

BENNETT, Charles E., U. S. Representative from Florida

BENNETT, Robert L., Director, American Indian Law Center, University of New Mexico, Albuquerque, N.M.

BERGHOLZ, Richard, Political Editor, Los Angeles *Times,* Los Angeles, Calif.

BERRISFORD, Christopher, Headmaster, St. Mark's School, Dallas, Texas

BIOSSAT, Bruce, National Correspondent, Newspaper Enterprise Association, Washington, D.C.

BIXBY, R. Burdell, Attorney and Republican Campaign Manager, New York City

BLISS, George W., Director of Investigations, Better Government Association, Chicago, Ill.

BLISS, Ray C., Former Chairman, Republican Ohio State & National Committees, Akron, Ohio

BOHNING, Don, Correspondent, Miami *Herald,* Miami, Fla.

BOND, Richard C., President of the Board of Trustees, John Wanamaker Department Store, Philadelphia, Pa.

BOOKER, James E., James E. Booker Associates, Inc., New York City

BORELLA, Victor, Special Adviser to Governor Rockefeller on Labor Affairs, New York City

BOWMAN, Joseph M., Assistant to the Secretary of the Treasury for Congressional Relations, Washington, D.C.

BOWSER, Charles, Executive Director, Urban Coalition of Philadelphia, Philadelphia, Pa.

BOYD, William J. D., Assistant Director, National Municipal League, New York City

BRAUN, Rex, State Representative, Houston, Texas

BRIDGE, Peter, Correspondent, Newark *Evening News,* Newark, N.J.

BRODER, David S., Correspondent and Columnist, Washington *Post,* Washington, D.C.

BROWN, Richard, Texas Municipal League, Austin, Texas

BROWN, Ted W., Secretary of State of Ohio, Columbus, Ohio

BROWNE, James, Community Relations Officer, Bay Area Rapid Transit District, San Francisco, Calif.

BROWNE, Millard C., Editorial Page Editor, Buffalo *Evening News,* Buffalo, N.Y.

BROWNE, Stanhope S., Attorney and Civic Leader, Philadelphia, Pa.

BUCCI, John, Public Opinion Analyst, Swarthmore, Pa.

BULGER, William M., State Representative, Boston, Mass.

BUNDY, McGeorge, President, The Ford Foundation, New York City

BURBY, John F., Editor, *National Journal,* Washington, D.C.

BURGER, Alvin A., Executive Director, Texas Research League, Austin, Texas

BURKE, John, Suburban Editor, Boston *Globe,*

Boston, Mass.

BURKHARDT, Robert J., Former Secretary of State and Democratic State Chairman, Trenton, N.J.

BURNS, James MacGregor, Professor of History, Williams College, Williamstown, Mass.

BURNS, John, Chairman, Democratic State Committee, New York City

BURT, Nathaniel, Author, Princeton, N.J.

BURTON, Phillip, U. S. Representative from California

BUSBY, Horace, Former Presidential Assistant, Washington, D.C.

BUSHNELL, David, Director, Division of Comprehensive and Vocational Education Research, Office of Education, Department of Health, Education and Welfare, Washington, D.C.

BUTTON, H. Warren, Professor, State University of Buffalo, Buffalo, N.Y.

BYERS, Bo, Bureau Chief, Houston *Chronicle,* Austin, Texas

BYRNE, Michael, Former Deputy Mayor, Philadelphia, Pa.

CAHILL, Thomas J., Chief of Police, San Francisco, Calif.

CALKINS, Judson W., Correspondent, St. Louis *Post-Dispatch,* East St. Louis, Ill.

CALLAHAN, Eugene, Administrative Assistant to Lt. Gov. Paul Simon, Springfield, Ill.

CAMPBELL, Allen, B., Dean, Maxwell Graduate School of Citizenship and Public Affairs, Syracuse University, New York

CANNON, Lou, Correspondent, Ridder Newspapers, Washington, D.C.

CANTY, Donald, Editor, *City* magazine, Washington, D.C.

CARPENTER, Richard, Executive Director, League of California Cities, Sacramento, Calif.

CARTER, Chester C., Former Deputy Chief of Protocol, Department of State, Washington, D.C.

CARTER, Peter, Bureau Chief, Newark *News,* Trenton, N.J.

CASSELLA, William N., Jr., Executive Director, National Municipal League, New York City

CHANCE, Mrs. Ruth, The Rosenberg Foundation, San Francisco, Calif.

CHANDLER, Otis, Publisher, Los Angeles *Times,* Los Angeles, Calif.

CHÁVEZ, César, Director, United Farm Workers Organizing Committee, Delano, Calif.

CHILES, Lawton, U. S. Senator from Florida

CHOATE, Robert, National Institute of Public Affairs, Washington, D.C.

CITRINO, Robert, Vice-Chairman, N. J. Turnpike Authority, Nutley, N.J.

CLARK, James H., Jr., State Representative, Dallas, Texas

CLARK, Joseph S., Former U.S. Senator from Pennsylvania and Mayor of Philadelphia

CLARK, Judson, California Research Associates, Sacramento, Calif.

CLARK, Ramsey, Attorney General of the U.S., Washington, D.C.

COLEMAN, William, Executive Director, Advisory Committee on Intergovernmental Relations, Washington, D.C.

COLLIER, Howard L., Director of Finance, State of Ohio, Columbus, Ohio

COLLINS, John F., Former Mayor of Boston; Professor, Department of Urban Studies, Massachusetts Institute of Technology, Cambridge, Mass.

CONMY, Jack, Press Secretary, Office of Sen. Richard Schweiker (Pa.)

CONTE, Silvio O., U. S. Representative from Massachusetts

CONWAY, Jack, Director, Center for Community Change, Washington, D.C.

COSTON, Dean, Executive Assistant to the Secretary, Department of Health, Education and Welfare, Washington, D.C.

COUSINEAU, Stanley, Rouge Plant, Ford Motor Co., Dearborn, Mich.

COWAN, Eugene, Assistant to the President, Washington, D.C.

CRELLIN, Jack, Labor Reporter, Detroit *News,* Detroit, Mich.

CROSS, Edward, M.D., Department of Health, Education and Welfare, Washington, D.C.

CROSS, Travis, Vice President, University Relations, University of California, Berkeley, Calif.

CULHANE, Charles, Correspondent, *National Journal,* Washington, D.C.

CURRIER, Fred, President, Market Opinion Research, Detroit, Mich.

DALY, Robert, Appointments Secretary, Office of Gov. John Gilligan (Ohio)

DANIEL, John A., Attorney, San Antonio, Texas

DARLING, Charles, Research Director, National Industrial Conference Board, New York City

DAUER, Manning J., Professor of Political Science, University of Florida, Gainesville, Fla.

DAY, Anthony, Editorial Page Editor, Los Angeles *Times,* Los Angeles, Calif.

DEDMON, Emmett, Vice President & Editorial Director, Chicago *Sun-Times & Daily News,* Chicago, Ill.

DE GRANDIS, Paul, Deputy Director, Cleveland Board of Elections, Cleveland, Ohio

deGRAZIA, Victor, Director, The Kate Maremount Foundation, Chicago, Ill.

DEINEMA, J. W., Regional Forester, U. S. Forestry Service, USDA, San Francisco, Calif.

DE MENT, George, Chairman, Transit Board, Chicago Transit Authority, Chicago, Ill.

DEMORO, Harre, Urban Affairs Editor, Oakland *Tribune,* Oakland, Calif.

DEVLIN, Dan, Inspector, San Francisco Police Department, San Francisco, Calif.

DEWITT, The Right Reverend Robert L., Episcopal Bishop of Pennsylvania, Philadelphia, Pa.

deZUTTER, Henry, Education Writer, Chicago *Daily News,* Chicago, Ill.

DISTEFANO, Robert, Correspondent, Oakland *Tribune,* Oakland, Calif.

DIXON, John, Director, Center for a Voluntary Society, Washington, D.C.

DIXON, Robert G., Jr., Professor of Law, George Washington University Law School, Washington, D.C.

DODDS, William, Political Director, United Auto Workers, Washington, D.C.

DOERR, David, Committee Coordinator, Assembly Committee on Revenue & Taxation, Sacramento, Calif.

DOUGHERTY, Richard, New York Correspondent, Los Angeles *Times,* New York City

DOWNS, Anthony, Senior Vice President & Treasurer, Real Estate Research Corporation, Chicago, Ill.

DREISKE, John, Political Editor, Chicago *Sun-Times,* Chicago, Ill.

DROUGHT, James, Administrator for Staff Service, Boston Redevelopment Authority, Boston, Mass.

DYMALLY, Mervyn, State Senator, Los Angeles, Calif.

EAMES, William, News Director, KNXT–TV, Los Angeles, Calif.

EASTBURN, David, President, Federal Reserve Bank, Philadelphia, Pa.

ECKHARDT, Bob, U. S. Representative from Texas

EDDY, Dr. Edward D., President, Chatham College, Pittsburgh, Pa.

EGAN, Very Rev. Msgr. John, Presentation Church, Chicago, Ill.

ELLIOTT, Lee Ann, Assistant Director American Medical Political Action Committee, Chicago, Ill.

EMMERICH, John, Editorial Page Editor, Houston *Chronicle,* Houston, Texas

ENGLE, Glenn, Bureau Chief, Detroit *News,* Lansing, Mich.

EPPS, Richard, Economist, The Federal Reserve Bank, Philadelphia, Pa.

ETHRIDGE, Mark, Jr., Editor, Detroit *Free Press,* Detroit, Mich.

EVANS, Roy, Secretary-Treasurer, Texas State AFL-CIO, Austin, Texas

FAY, Albert, Former Republican National Committeeman, Houston, Texas

FELTON, David, Correspondent, Los Angeles *Times,* Los Angeles, Calif.

FERMI, Mrs. Laura, Author and Civic Leader, Chicago, Ill.

FISHER, Francis B., Regional Administrator, Department of Housing & Urban Development, Chicago, Ill.

FISHMAN, Sam, Director, Community Action Program, United Auto Workers, Detroit, Mich.

FLANIGAN, Jack, Republican State Committee, Columbus, Ohio

FOOTE, Joseph, Author, Washington, D.C.

FOX, Francis, Director of Aviation, Hughes Nevada Operations, Las Vegas, Nev.

FRALEY, Frederick W., III, Attorney, Dallas, Texas

FRANKLIN, Ben, Correspondent, New York *Times,* Washington, D.C.

FRANTZ, Joe B., Director, Oral History Project, University of Texas, Austin, Texas

FRASER, Douglas, Vice President, United Auto Workers, Detroit, Mich.

FREE, Lloyd, Public Opinion Analyst for Gov. Nelson Rockefeller (New York), Chevy Chase, Md.

FREEDMAN, Marvin, County of Los Angeles, Dept. of Public Social Services, Commerce, Calif.

FREELAND, Wendell G., Attorney and Republican Leader, Pittsburgh, Pa.

FREEMAN, David, Executive Director, Council on Foundations, New York City

FREEMAN, Orville, Secretary of Agriculture, Washington, D.C.

FRIEDMAN, Eugene, Reading *Times,* Reading, Pa.

FRY, Rev. John, First Presbyterian Church, Chicago, Ill.

GALLEGOS, Herman E., Executive Director, Southwest Council of La Raza, San Francisco, Calif.

GALLERY, John Andrew, Acting Director, Philadelphia 1976 Bicentennial Commission, Philadelphia, Pa.

GARDINER, John A., Law Enforcement Assistance Administration, Washington, D.C.

GARDNER, Bill, Bureau Chief, Houston *Post,* Austin, Texas

GERMOND, Jack W., Correspondent, Gannett News Services, Washington, D.C.

GIBBONS, Harold, President, Missouri-Kansas Council of Teamsters, St. Louis, Mo.

GIBBONS, Sam M., U. S. Representative from Florida

GIBSON, Kenneth, Mayor of Newark, N.J.

GILLIGAN, John J., Governor of Ohio

GIRARD, Karen, Economic Consultant on Urban Affairs, Chase Manhattan Bank, New York City

GLASS, Andrew J., Congressional Correspondent, *National Journal,* Washington, D.C.

GOLDFIELD, Edwin D., Assistant Director for Program Development, Bureau of the Census, Washington, D.C.

GONZÁLEZ, Henry B., U. S. Representative from Texas

GONZMART, César, Proprietor, The Columbia Restaurant, Tampa, Fla.

GRAHAM, Robert E., Jr., Director, Office of Business Economics, Department of Commerce, Washington, D.C.

GRAVES, Curtis, State Representative, Houston, Texas

GREENBERG, Carl, Political Editor, Los Angeles *Times,* Los Angeles, Calif.

GREENLEAF, Charles, Policies & Program Division, Executive Office of the Governor, Lansing, Mich.

GUNTHER, John, Author, New York City (deceased)

GUNTHER, John, U. S. Conference of Mayors, Washington, D.C.

GUTIÉRREZ, José Angel, Mexican-American Youth Organization, San Antonio, Texas

HAAR, Charles M., Assistant Secretary for Metropolitan Development, Department of Housing and Urban Development, Washington, D.C.

HAGA, Thomas H., Chairman, Genesee County Planning Commission, Flint, Mich.

HAGUE, Howard, Former Vice President, United Steelworkers of America, Pittsburgh, Pa.

HALEY, James A., U. S. Representative from Florida

HALL, John H., Assistant Executive Secretary —Governmental Services, Ohio Education Association, Columbus, Ohio

HALLGREN, Art, First Vice President, Florida AFL-CIO, Miami, Fla.

HALPERN, Alan, Editor, *Philadelphia Magazine,* Philadelphia, Pa.

HAMILTON, Calvin S., Director, Department of City Planning, Los Angeles, Calif.

HARDING, Kenneth, Executive Director, House Democratic Congressional Committee, Washington, D.C.

HARRIS, Gordon, Director of Public Affairs, John F. Kennedy Space Center, Fla.

HARRIS, Louis, Louis Harris & Associates, New York City

HARRIS, Roger, Correspondent, Newark *Star-Ledger,* Newark, N.J.

HARRISON, David E., Chairman, State Democratic Committee, Boston, Mass.

HAVARD, William C., Dean, Virginia Polytechnic Institute and State University, Blacksburg, Va.

HAYDEN, Martin, Editor, Detroit *News,* Detroit, Mich.

HAZARD, Leland, Civic Leader and Author, Pittsburgh, Pa.

HEALY, Robert, Executive Editor, Boston *Globe,* Boston, Mass.

HENKIN, Daniel Z., Assistant Secretary for Public Affairs, Department of Defense, Washington, D.C.

HEREFORD, Peggy G., Public Relations Director, Los Angeles Department of Airports, Los Angeles, Calif.

HERMANN, Ray, Correspondent, Buffalo *Courier-Express,* Buffalo, N.Y.

HESSER, Charles, Correspondent, Miami *News,* Miami, Fla.

HINDEN, Stan, Washington Correspondent, *Newsday,* Washington, D.C.

HOBBY, William P., Jr., Executive Editor,

Houston *Post*, Houston, Texas

HOFFMAN, Hattie Belle, Van Cronkhite & Maloy, Inc., Dallas, Texas

HOGE, James F., Jr., Editor, Chicago *Sun-Times*, Chicago, Ill.

HOLMES, The Rev. Zan W., State Representative, Dallas, Texas

HORN, Stephen, President, California State College, Long Beach, Calif.

HURD, T. Norman, Director of State Operations, State of New York, Albany, N.Y.

HURLEY, Marvin, Executive Vice President, Houston (Texas) Chamber of Commerce.

IKARD, Frank, President, American Petroleum Institute, Washington, D.C.

IRWIN, William P., Professor, Department of Political Science, Case Western Reserve University, Cleveland, Ohio

IVORY, Marcellius, Director, Region IA, United Auto Workers, Detroit, Mich.

JACOBSON, Joel, Director, Community Relations, Region 9, United Auto Workers, Cranford, N.J.

JAFFY, Stewart R., Attorney, Columbus, Ohio

JANOWITZ, Morris, Professor, Department of Sociology, University of Chicago, Chicago, Ill.

JAVITS, Jacob K., U. S. Senator from New York

JOHNSON, Nicholas, Commissioner, Federal Communications Commission, Washington, D.C.

JOHNSON, Roland H., Staff Associate, The Cleveland Foundation, Cleveland, Ohio

JONES, Carlisle, Director of Public Affairs, Aerospace Industries Association, Washington, D.C.

JONSSON, Erik, Mayor of Dallas, Texas

JORDAN, Barbara, State Senator, Houston, Texas

JORDAN, Richard D., Selvage, Lee & Howard, Inc., Washington, D.C.

JOSEPH, Stephen, M.D., Department of Health, Education and Welfare, Washington, D.C.

JUSTICE, Blair, Head, Human Relations Division, Office of the Mayor, Houston, Texas

KALODNER, Philip, Attorney and Civic Leader, Philadelphia, Pa.

KAMINSKI, Duke, Bureau Chief, Philadelphia *Evening Bulletin*, Harrisburg, Pa.

KANTOR, MacKinlay, Author, Sarasota, Fla.

KARAYN, James, President, National Public Affairs Center for Television, Washington, D.C.

KAY, Norton, "Chicago Today," Chicago, Ill.

KAYE, Peter, News & Public Affairs, KEBS-TV, San Diego, Calif.

KEAST, William R., President, Wayne State University, Detroit, Mich.

KEENAN, Francis, Administrative Assistant, Office of Rep. Florence Dwyer (N.J.)

KELLOGG, James, Director, Policies & Program Division, Executive Office of the Governor, Lansing, Mich.

KENDALL, William, Administrative Assistant, Office of Rep. Peter Frelinghuysen (N.J.)

KENNEDY, Robert E., Associate Editor, Chicago *Sun-Times*, Chicago, Ill.

KEY, Jack, Florida Bureau of Law Enforcement, Miami, Fla.

KIMBALL, The Hon. Dan A., Aerojet-General Corporation, El Monte, Calif. (deceased)

KIRKLAND, Lane, Secretary-Treasurer, AFL-CIO, Washington, D.C.

KLEIN, Bernie, Controller, City of Detroit, Detroit, Mich.

KLEIN, Howard B., Chairman, Cleveland Planning Commission and President, Burrows Booksellers, Cleveland, Ohio

KNEALLY, Don, Inspector, San Francisco Police Department, San Francisco, Calif.

KNOWLES, Robert P., Wisconsin State Senator

and Arrangements Director, 1964 and 1968 Republican National Conventions, New Richmond, Wis.

KOST, Blair, Executive Assistant to the Director, Citizens League of Ohio, Cleveland, Ohio

KOTZBAUER, Robert, Editorial Writer, Akron *Beacon-Journal*, Akron, Ohio

KRAFT, Mr. and Mrs. John, Public Opinion Analysts, Washington, D.C.

KRAVITZ, Walter, Legislative Reference Service, Library of Congress, Washington, D.C.

KULSEA, William, Correspondent, Booth Newspapers, Lansing, Mich.

KUMMERFELD, Donald D., Director of Research, Center for Political Research, Washington, D.C.

KUNKIN, Art, Publisher & Editor, Los Angeles *Free Press*, Los Angeles, Calif.

KURZMAN, Peter, Public Relations, New York City

KUSSEROW, Hank, San Francisco *Examiner*, San Francisco, Calif.

LANG, Raymond, Miami Metro Publicity Bureau, Miami, Fla.

LAVIN, Allen S., Attorney for The Metropolitan Sanitary District of Greater Chicago, Ill.

LEE, J. Bracken, Mayor of Salt Lake City, Utah

LEE, Philip R., M.D., Assistant Secretary for Health and Scientific Affairs, Department of Health, Education and Welfare, Washington, D.C.

LEFKOWITZ, Stephen, New York State Urban Development Corporation, New York City

LEHRER, Jim, City Editor, Dallas *Times-Herald*, Dallas, Texas

LEO, John, Press Relations, Environmental Protection Administration, New York City

LESSINGER, Dr. Leon, Office of Education, Department of HEW, Washington, D.C.

LEVIN, Sander M., State Senator, Berkley, Mich.

LEVITT, Arthur, Comptroller, State of New York

LEWIS, David L., Professor, Graduate School of Business, Univ. of Michigan, Ann Arbor, Mich.

LIBASSI, F. Peter, The Urban Coalition, Washington, D.C.

LINDSAY, John V., Mayor of New York City

LINDSAY, Mrs. Mary Anne, New York, N.Y.

LINSKY, Martin A., State Representative, Brookline, Mass.

LIPPER, J. J., Corporate Director, Public Communications, Aerojet-General Corporation, El Monte, Calif.

LITTLEWOOD, Tom, Washington Correspondent, Chicago *Sun-Times*

LONG, Stuart, Long News Service, Austin, Texas

LOVENHEIM, David, Administrative Assistant, Office of Rep. Frank Horton (N.Y.)

LYNN, Frank, Albany Correspondent, New York *Times*, Albany, N.Y.

MACKEY, Morris Cecil, Jr., Former Assistant Secretary for Policy and Planning, Department of Transportation, Washington, D.C.

MAHAN, James F., Attorney, Boston, Mass.

MARGOLIS, Larry, Executive Director, Citizens Conference on State Legislatures, Kansas City, Mo.

MARTIN, David B. H., Assistant to the Secretary, Department of Health, Education and Welfare, Washington, D.C.

MARTIN, Louis, *The Defender*, Chicago, Ill., (Former Deputy Director for Minority Affairs, Democratic National Committee)

MATHEWSON, Ken, President, The Metropolitan Fund, Inc., Detroit, Mich.

MATTHEWS, D. R. Billie, Administrator, Rural Community Development Service, Department of Agriculture, Washington, D.C.

MATTHEWS, Steve, Executive Director, Texas Municipal League, Austin, Texas

MAVERICK, Maury, Jr., Attorney, San Antonio, Texas

McALLISTER, Robert L., Director, Realtors' Ohio Committee, Columbus, Ohio

McCOLLUM, A. James, Manager, Advertising and Publicity Dept., Pacific Gas & Electric Company, San Francisco, Calif.

McCREE, Floyd, Former Mayor of Flint, Mich.

McCULLOUGH, John, Editorial Page Editor, Philadelphia *Evening Bulletin,* Philadelphia, Pa.

McDERMOTT, John, Correspondent, Miami *Herald,* Miami, Fla.

McELROY, John M., Assistant to Governor James Rhodes (Ohio)

McGANNITY, Dr. William, University of Texas Medical Branch, Galveston, Texas

McGONIGLE, George, Model Cities Director, Houston, Texas

McGRATH, Thomas H., Assistant Executive Vice Chancellor, The California State Colleges, Los Angeles, Calif.

McGREW, James W., Research Director, Texas Research League, Austin, Texas

McGWIRE, John, National Instiute of Public Affairs, Washington, D.C.

McLAREN, John, Legislative Assistant, Office of Rep. Lionel Van Deerlin (Calif.)

McPHERSON, Harry C., Jr., Special Counsel to the President (Lyndon B. Johnson), Washington, D.C.

MEDSGER, Betty, Religion Reporter, Washington *Post,* Washington, D.C.

MEEGAN, Joseph B., Executive Secretary, Back of the Yards Neighborhood Council, Chicago, Ill.

MEEHAN, William A., General Counsel, Republican City Committee, Philadelphia, Pa.

MEYER, Hank, Hank Meyer Associates, Miami Beach, Fla.

MICHAEL, Jay, Special Assistant to the President, University of California, Sacramento, Calif.

MIKVA, Abner, U. S. Representative from Illinois

MILLER, Arthur S., Professor of Law, George Washington University, Washington, D.C.

MILLIKEN, William, Governor of Michigan

MINOW, Newton, Attorney, Former Chairman, Federal Communications Commission, Chicago, Ill.

MOCCIA, Thomas J., Director, Public Affairs, Greater Boston Chamber of Commerce, Boston, Mass.

MOLITOR, Graham, Washington Representative, General Mills Inc., Washington, D.C.

MOORE, Joe G., Jr., Commissioner, Federal Water Pollution Control Administration, Department of the Interior, Washington, D.C.

MOREHEAD, Richard, Austin Correspondent, Dallas *Morning News,* Austin, Texas

MORGAN, Neil, Author and Columnist for the San Diego *Evening Tribune,* San Diego, Calif.

MORGAN, Thomas B., Press Secretary for Mayor John V. Lindsay, New York City

MORROW, Hugh, Director of Communications, Staff of Governor Nelson A. Rockefeller, New York

MORTON, The Rev. James P., Director, Urban Training Institute, Chicago, Ill.

MOTT, Charles Stewart, Mott Foundation, Flint, Mich.

MOTT, Harding, Mott Foundation, Flint, Mich.

MUCHMORE, Don, Opinion Research of California, Long Beach, Calif.

MULLER, Will, Columnist, Detroit *News,* Detroit, Mich.

NAUGHTON, James, Washington Correspondent,

New York *Times;* Former Political Editor, Cleveland *Plain-Dealer*

NEUMAN, Robert, Legislative Assistant, Office of Rep. Jerome R. Waldie (Calif.)

NEWMAN, William, Architecture Writer, Chicago *Daily News,* Chicago, Ill.

NEWMYER, James M., Newmyer Associates, Washington, D.C.

NOLAN, Martin, Washington Correspondent, Boston *Globe,* Washington, D.C.

NORRIS, William, Attorney, Los Angeles, Calif.

NORTON, James A., President & Director, The Cleveland Foundation, Cleveland, Ohio

NOVAK, Robert, Columnist, Washington, D.C.

O'BRIEN, Emmet N., Bureau Chief, Gannett News Service, Albany, N.Y.

O'CONNOR, Ralston, Manager, Harlem Heights Station Farm Labor Camp, Winter Garden, Fla.

O'DONNELL, Harry, Deputy Commissioner, N.Y. State Department of Commerce, Albany, N.Y.

OGLIVIE, Richard B., Governor of Illinois

O'GRADY, Eugene P., Chairman, Democratic State Committee, Columbus, Ohio

O'HARA, Richard, Correspondent, Dayton *Daily News,* Dayton, Ohio

O'HARE, Robert J. M., Director, Bureau of Public Affairs, Boston College, Chestnut Hill, Mass.

OLIVER, Jack L., Chief, Bureau of Information, Cleveland City Council, Cleveland, Ohio

PACKARD, George, Managing Editor, Philadelphia *Evening Bulletin,* Philadelphia, Pa.

PALMER, Bruce, President, National Industrial Conference Board, New York City

PARADISO, Louis, Associate Director, Office of Business Economics, Department of Commerce, Washington, D.C.

PARR, Rex, Manager, Old Top Labor Camp, Tildenville, Fla.

PASCAL, Anthony, Director of Human Resource Studies, RAND Corp., Santa Monica, Calif.

PASNICK, Raymond W., Director of Public Relations, United Steelworkers of America, Pittsburgh, Pa.

PATTON, D. Kenneth, Economic Development Administrator, New York City

PEACE, John, Attorney, Houston, Texas

PEASE, Robert B., Executive Director, Allegheny Conference on Community Development, Pittsburgh, Pa.

PEÑA, Albert A., Jr., Bexar County Commissioner, San Antonio, Texas

PEPPER, Claude, U. S. Representative from Florida

PERRY, John, Jr., President, Perry Publications, Inc., West Palm Beach, Fla.

PFAUTCH, Roy, Civic Services Inc., St. Louis, Mo.

PICKUP, Robert, Executive Director, Citizens Research Councill of Michigan, Detroit, Mich.

PIKE, Otis, U.S. Representative from New York

PINCUS, John, Director, California Program, RAND Corp., Santa Monica, Calif.

PISOR, Robert, Correspondent, Detroit *News,* Detroit, Mich.

PITSTICK, William J., Executive Director, North Central Texas Council of Governments, Arlington, Texas

PLISSNER, Martin, CBS News, New York City

POPA, Robert, Correspondent, Detroit *News,* Detroit, Mich.

POPE, Richard, Owner, Cypress Gardens, Winter Haven, Fla.

POTTER, Todd, Director, Bureau of Employment Security, Department of Labor, Washington, D.C.

QUELLER, Robert, Citizens Research Council of Michigan, Detroit, Mich.

QUINN, Donald, Director of Communications, Citizens Conference on State Legislatures, Kansas City, Mo.

QUINN, Louis, Louis Quinn & Associates, Los Angeles, Calif.

RAFSKY, William, Executive Director, Greater Philadelphia Movement, Philadelphia, Pa.

RAMO, Dr. Simon, Vice Chairman of the Board, TRW, Inc., Beverly Hills, Calif.

RAWSON, Mrs. Barbara, Assistant Director, The Cleveland Foundation, Cleveland, Ohio

RAYNER, A. A. Sammy, Alderman, 6th Ward, Chicago, Ill.

RECKTENWALD, William A., Investigator, Better Government Association, Chicago, Ill.

REES, Ed, Regional Director, Corporate Communications, TRW, Inc., Los Angeles, Calif.

REES, Thomas, U.S. Representative from California

REEVES, Richard, Correspondent, New York *Times*, New York City

REICHLEY, James, Writer, *Fortune*, New York City

RESTLE, Roland, Investigator, Better Government Association, Chicago, Ill.

RICHARDS, Mr. and Mrs. Lawrence, Los Angeles, Calif.

RICHARDS, Peter, Director of Administration, New York City Planning Commission

RICHARDSON, Elliot L., Secretary of Health, Education and Welfare, Washington, D.C.

ROBB, Rick, Administrative Assistant, Office of Rep. Albert Johnson (Pa.).

ROBERTS, Dr. Ernest R., Aerojet-General Corporation, El Monte, Calif.

ROCKEFELLER, Nelson A., Governor of New York

RODDA, Richard, Correspondent, Sacramento *Bee*, Sacramento, Calif.

RUBIN, Irving J., Director, Detroit Regional Transportation & Land Use Study, Detroit, Mich.

RUMSFELD, Donald, Assistant to the President, Washington, D.C.

RUSSO, Louis J., Director of the Budget, Erie County, New York

RUTTENBERG, Stanley H., Assistant Secretary for Manpower, Department of Labor, Washington, D.C.

SALOMA, John S., III, Associate Professor of Political Science, Massachusetts Institute of Technology, Cambridge, Mass.

SAMPSON, Arthur, Commissioner of Public Building Service, General Services Administration, Washington, D.C.

SAMUELS, Howard, President, New York City Off-Track Betting Corporation

SANCHEZ, Felix, Migrant Farm Worker, Winter Garden, Fla.

SCAMMON, Richard M., Director, Elections Research Center, and former Director of the Census, Washington, D.C.

SCARIANO, Anthony, State Representative, Park Forest, Ill.

SCHILDHOUSE, Burt, Public Relations, Columbus, Ohio

SCHOLLE, August, President, Michigan State AFL-CIO, Lansing, Mich.

SCHRADE, Paul, Director, Region 6, United Auto Workers, Los Angeles, Calif.

SCHRADER, George R., Assistant City Manager, Dallas, Texas

SCHROTH, Thomas N., Assistant Director for Information Services, Environmental Protection Agency, Washington, D.C.

SCOTT, Dwight, Director of Public Affairs, National Biscuit Co., New York City

SCOTT, Fred, Legislative Reference Service, Library of Congress, Washington, D.C.

SCOTT, Robert, Peirce-Phelps, Inc., Philadelphia, Pa.

SCRANTON, William W., Former Governor of Pennsylvania

SCRIVEN, D. E., Ford Motor Company, Dearborn, Mich.

SEID, Marvin, Editorial Writer, Los Angeles *Times*, Los Angeles, Calif.

SENNETT, William, Former Attorney General of Pennsylvania, Erie, Pa.

SENSENING, Jack, Director, Washington Office, Commonwealth of Pennsylvania

SHANDS, The Rev. Alfred R., III, Washington, D.C.

SHAPP, Milton, Governor of Pennsylvania

SHEA, John, Chairman, Reform Caucus, N. Y. State Democratic Committee, New York City

SHEA, Nancy, Office of Governor Nelson A. Rockefeller, New York City

SHELTON, Donn, The Metropolitan Fund, Inc., Detroit, Mich.

SICKLES, Trent, Assistant to Management, Lazarus Department Store, Columbus, Ohio

SIMON, Ed, Assistant to Governor Milton Shapp of Pennsylvania

SIMON, Paul, Lieutenant Governor of Illinois

SKLOOT, Ed, Office of Mayor John V. Lindsay, New York City

SLAYTON, William L., Executive Vice President, Urban America, Washington, D.C.

SMITH, Henry, Public Information Office, Bureau of the Census, Washington, D.C.

SOLER, Frank, Correspondent, Miami *Herald*, Miami, Fla.

SONTAG, Frederick H., Public Relations Consultant, Montclair, N.J.

SPENCER, Stuart, Spencer-Roberts Associates, Los Angeles, Calif.

SPOFFORD, William, Attorney, Trustee of Temple University, Philadelphia, Pa.

SULLIVAN, The Rev. Dr. Leon H., Chairman of the Board, Opportunities Industrialization Center, Inc., Philadelphia, Pa.

SULLIVAN, Richard J., Commissioner, Department of Environmental Protection, Trenton, N.J.

SULLIVAN, Robert J., Director of Research, New York City Off-Track Betting Corporation

SUTIN, Philip, St. Louis *Post-Dispatch* Bureau, East St. Louis, Ill.

STAFFORD, Charles, Washington Bureau Chief, St. Petersburg *Times*

STANTON, James V., President, Cleveland City Council, Cleveland, Ohio

STEVENSON, Adlai, III, State Treasurer of Illinois (now U.S. Senator from Illinois)

STEWART, R. Jaffy, Attorney, Columbus, Ohio

STOCKTON, Dr. John, Texas Research League, Austin, Texas

STOKES, B. R., General Manager, Bay Area Rapid Transit District, San Francisco, Calif.

STOVER, Carl, President, National Institute of Public Affairs, Washington, D.C.

STRAUSS, Robert, Democratic National Committeeman, Dallas, Texas

TAGGE, George, Correspondent, Chicago *Tribune*, Springfield, Illinois

TAYLOR, H. Ralph, Assistant Secretary for Demonstrations and Intergovernmental Relations, Department of Housing and Urban Development, Washington, D.C.

TEER, Fred L., Director, Model Cities Agency, East St. Louis, Ill.

TEETER, Robert M., Market Opinion Research, Detroit, Mich.

TER HORST, Jerry, Washington Correspondent, Detroit *News*

THAYER, George, Author, Washington, D.C.

THEIS, Paul, Public Relations Director, National Republican Congressional Campaign Committee, Washington, D.C.

THIES, Stanton W., Deputy Director of Information, Bay Area Rapid Transit District, San Francisco, Calif.

THOMAS, Mr. and Mrs. Evan W., New York City

THOMPSON, Mrs. Edna, Migrant Farm Worker, Winter Garden, Fla.

THORNBURG, Richard, U. S. Attorney, Pittsburgh, Pa.

TODD, A. Ruric, Manager, Governmental and Political Affairs, Pacific Gas & Electric Co., San Francisco, Calif.

TOWNSEND, Leonard, Attorney-at-Law, Detroit, Mich.

TRENT, Peter, of CBWL-Hayden Stone Inc., New York City

TROVILLION, Frank, Florida Citrus Mutual, Lakeland, Fla.

TURCO, Louis, President, Newark City Council, Newark, N.J.

TURNER, Robert L., Correspondent, Boston *Globe,* Boston, Mass.

UHL, Sherley, Correspondent, Pittsburgh *Press,* Pittsburgh, Pa.

UNRUH, Jesse, Former Speaker, California Assembly, Inglewood, Calif.

VAN BUSKIRK, Arthur B., Former Attorney for T. Mellon Sons, Pittsburgh, Pa.

VAN CRONKHITE, John, Van Cronkhite, & Maloy, Inc., Dallas, Texas

VAN DEERLIN, Lionel, U.S. Representative from California

VAUGHAN, Mr. & Mrs. Samuel, Atherton, Calif.

VINSON, Fred, Jr., Assistant Attorney General, Criminal Division, Department of Justice, Washington, D.C.

VISSER, Paul, Administrative Assistant to Rep. Donald Riegle, Flint, Mich.

WADSWORTH, Homer C., President, Kansas City Association of Trusts and Foundations, Kansas City, Mo.

WAGNER, Thomas J., Administrative Assistant to Sen. Adlai Stevenson (Ill.)

WALLWORK, James H., State Senator, Essex County, N.J.

WALTERS, Robert G., Assistant to the Secretary, California Human Relations Agency, Sacramento, Calif.

WARNER, John, Director, Boston Redevelopment Authority, Boston, Mass.

WASHBURN, Dr. C. L., Higher Education Specialist, California Council for Higher Education, Sacramento, Calif.

WASHINGTON, Lawrence, Ford Motor Company, Dearborn, Mich.

WASHINGTON, The Rev. Paul, Rector, Church of the Advocate, Philadelphia, Pa.

WASHNIS, George, Administrative Assistant to the Mayor, East St. Louis, Ill.

WEINBERG, Edward, Attorney and former Deputy Solicitor, Department of the Interior, Washington, D.C.

WEINGARTEN, Victor, Director, Institute for Public Affairs, New York City

WHITE, F. Clifton, Public Affairs Consultant, New York City

WIECK, Paul R., Correspondent, Washington, D.C.

WILCOX, William, Secretary of Community Affairs, Commonwealth of Pennsylvania

WILHELM, Al, Flint *Journal,* Flint, Mich.

WILLIAMS, James D., Public Information Officer, U.S. Commission on Civil Rights, Washington, D.C.

WILLIAMS, Spencer, Secretary, California Human Relations Agency, Sacramento, Calif.

WILLIE, Charles V., Professor of Sociology, Maxwell Graduate School of Citizenship and Public Affairs, Syracuse University, N.Y.

WILSON, Malcolm, Lieutenant Governor of New York State

WINSHIP, Thomas, Editor, Boston *Globe,* Boston, Mass.

WINSLETT, Merrill, Administrative Assistant, Office of Sen. Spessard Holland (Fla.)

WIRTHLIN, Richard, Decision Making Information, Los Angeles, Calif.

WISHART, Alfred W., Jr., Director, The Pittsburgh Foundation, Pittsburgh, Pa.

WOOD, Dr. Robert, President, University of Massachusetts

WOODMAN, D. K., Editor, Mansfield *News-Journal,* Mansfield, Ohio

WOODS, Leon, Vice President & General Manager, Watts Manufacturing Co., Compton, Calif.

WRICE, Herman, The Young Great Society, Philadelphia, Pa.

WRIGHT, M. A., Chairman of the Board, Humble Oil & Refining Company, Houston, Texas

WRIGHT, Jim, U. S. Representative from Texas.

WYATT, George E., Budget Division, City of Buffalo, Buffalo, N.Y.

YARBOROUGH, Ralph, U. S. Senator from Texas

YELLEN, Ben, M.D., Brawley (Imperial Valley), Calif.

YLVISAKER, Paul, Professor, Princeton University; Former Director, New Jersey Department of Community Affairs

YOUNG, W. W., President, Retail Clerks Union Local 1357, Philadelphia, Pa.

ZIMMERMAN, Richard, Columbus Bureau Chief, Cleveland *Plain-Dealer,* Columbus, Ohio

ZUCKERT, Eugene, Former Secretary of the Air Force, Washington, D.C.

INDEX

Page references in **boldface** type indicate inclusive or major entries.

THE AUTHOR

NEAL R. PEIRCE began political writing in Washington in 1959 and is author of the definitive work on the electoral college system, *The People's President*, published in 1968. He was political editor of *Congressional Quarterly* for nine years and became a consultant on network election coverage, initially for NBC News and after 1966 for CBS News. In 1969 he became a founding partner of the Center for Political Research and subsequently politics consultant for its weekly publication, the *National Journal*. In 1971, he became a Fellow of the Woodrow Wilson International Center for Scholars.

A native of Philadelphia, Mr. Peirce graduated from Princeton University, Phi Beta Kappa, in 1954. He lives in Washington with his wife and their two daughters and a son.

DATE DUE

GAYLORD			PRINTED IN U.S.A.